a RIGHT to be HOSTILE

ALSO BY AARON McGRUDER

THE BOONDOCKS: BECAUSE I KNOW YOU DON'T READ THE NEWSPAPER

FRESH FOR '01 . . . YOU SUCKAS! A BOONDOCKS COLLECTION

a RIGHT to be HOSTILE

THE BOONDOCKS TREASURY

AARON McGRUDER

FOREWORD BY MICHAEL MOORE

 THREE RIVERS PRESS • NEW YORK

FOR DEDRIC AND ALICE, MOM AND BILL, ANTHONY, COLE, ARIELLE,
AND, OF COURSE, MY GRANDPARENTS . . .
LOVE YOU ALL.

Copyright © 2003 by Aaron McGruder

Published by Three Rivers Press, New York, New York.
Member of the Crown Publishing Group, a division of Random House, Inc.
www.randomhouse.com

THREE RIVERS PRESS and the Tugboat design are registered trademarks of
Random House, Inc.

Some of the comic strips in this work have previously appeared in
The Boondocks and *Fresh for '01 . . . You Suckas!*

Printed in the United States of America

Design by Max Werner

Library of Congress Cataloging-in-Publication Data
is available upon request.

ISBN 1-4000-4857-5

10 9 8 7 6 5

First Edition

ACKNOWLEDGMENTS

I hate this part because when you stop to thank people it's inevitable that you'll leave somebody out. But I have been fortunate to have so many people around me who have gone out of their way to help me elevate my career, elevate my intellect, and elevate my life. Some of those people are (in no particular order):

Chrisette and Reginald Hudlin
Byron Hord
Michelle Veluz
Julian Bond
Stephen Barnes
Norman Aladjem
The Reverend Eugene Rivers
Byron Phillips
Greg Melvin
Robert Hightower
Quincy Jones
Rashon Khan
John McMeel and Cathy Andrews
Congresswoman Barbara Lee
Lee Salem
Jeff Orridge
Bob Duffy
John Vivona
Ken Abrams
Lonnae O'Neal Parker
Garry Trudeau

Although we occasionally have our disagreements, I would like to express my deep gratitude to the hundreds of newspaper editors who have bravely stood by the strip year after year.

Last, I owe a very special thanks to Michael Moore for his tremendous generosity.

FOREWORD
BY MICHAEL MOORE

I can't remember what those kids were doing in the first *Boondocks* comic I saw, but I do remember exactly what passed through my mind when I read it: "How the hell did this get into a daily newspaper?"

I stopped reading the comics page a long time ago. It seems that whoever is in charge of what to put on that page is given an edict that states: "For God's sake, try to be as bland as possible and by no means offend anyone!" Thus, whenever something like *Doonesbury* would come along, it would be continually censored and, if lucky, eventually banished to the editorial pages. The message was clear: Keep it simple, keep it cute, and don't be challenging, outrageous, or political.

And keep it white!

It's odd, considering all the black ink that goes into making up the comics section (and color on Sundays) that you rarely see any black faces on that page. Well, maybe it's not so odd after all, considering the makeup of most newsrooms in our country. It is even more stunning when you consider that in many of our large cities like New York, Los Angeles, or Chicago, where the white population is barely a third of the overall citizenry, the comics pages seem to be one of the last vestiges of the belief that white faces are just . . . well, you know . . . so much more happy and friendly and funny!

Of course, the real funnies are on the front pages of most papers these days. That's where you can see a lot of black faces. The media loves to cover black people on the front page. After all, when you live in a society that will lock up 30 percent of all black men at some time in their lives and send more of them to prison than to college, chances are a fair number of those black faces will end up in the newspaper.

But, to be honest, the newspapers don't just show bad black. They have "good" black people they cover too! Like Clarence Thomas. And Condoleezza Rice. See, they care.

Oops. There I go playing the race card. You see, in America these days, we aren't supposed to talk about race. We have been told to pretend that things have gotten better, that the old days of segregation and cross-burnings are long gone, and that no one needs to talk about race again because, hey, we fixed that problem.

Of course, nothing could be further from the truth. Sure, the "whites only" signs are down, but they have just been replaced by invisible ones that, if you are black, you see hanging in front of the home loan department of the local bank, across the entrance of the ritzy suburban mall, or on the doors of the U.S. Senate (100 percent Caucasian and going strong!).

Except for the occasional op-ed, where is the discussion of any of this in our daily newspapers? Fortunately, and hilariously, it is on the comics page in the form of Aaron McGruder's *The Boondocks*. With bodacious wit, in just a few panels, each day Aaron serves up—and sends up—life in America through the eyes of two African-American kids who are full of attitude, intelligence, and rebellion. Each time I read the strip, I laugh, and I wonder how long McGruder is going to keep this gig going. How long can *The Boondocks* get away with the things it says? How far will he take it tomorrow? How on earth can the most truthful thing in the newspaper be the comics?

Of course, *The Boondocks* has had a rough road to travel. It has seen its share of censorship. Papers have been deluged with angry letters. Some have moved it to the editorial pages. A few have dropped it. But, fortunately for all of us, more newspapers than ever now carry *The Boondocks*. And these papers are not just in urban (read: black) areas but in places like Albuquerque, New Mexico, and Dubuque, Iowa. The strip has crossed over into the vast American mainstream, proving once again that the best art finds its way to all people regardless of their background. And when you have a society where 50 million people work for a living but have no health insurance, where millions have lost their savings and pensions due to the Wall Street scandals, where no one feels secure that his job will be his job a year from now—well, those aren't race issues (although African-Americans are the ones hit the hardest), those are bread-and-butter nightmares facing *all* Americans who are not privileged to be in the upper 10 percent. They are issues of class, and once the discussion turns to class, those in charge seek to shut it down as quickly as possible. Why? Because class is what will unite white and black and brown in this country and, God forbid, if that day ever comes . . . well, let's just say the powers that be will be wringing their hands over much more than some smart-ass comic strip.

So, until that day, let *The Boondocks* go on its merry, subversive way ("Hey, it's just a cartoon") and hope that, somewhere down the road, when we all live in a more just America, we will look back and say that, in the beginning, the revolution wasn't televised, it was on the comics page.

INTRODUCTION

The Boondocks has seen its fourth anniversary come and go—and now the publication of its third book. Four years is not a long time in the life span of comic strips, which are now, incidentally, outliving their creators. But it has felt like a long time to me. A very long time. The days may pass quickly when you're having fun, but they have a way of slowing down dramatically when you have to create a comic strip for each and every twenty-four-hour period that passes.

I have changed considerably in the past four years, and the strip has changed as a result. Some changes, I believe, have been for the better; some have not. The first year or two of the strip was a story about characters and conflicts, with little story arcs and short narratives and all that good stuff that my heroes (Breathed, Watterson, and Trudeau) had done. Everyone seemed to really love that stuff—from the fans to the newspaper editors to the syndicate—and wanted more of the same.

Everyone but me.

It's not that I somehow lost interest in the characters as much as I lost interest in trying to tell narrative stories in such an impossibly small space. My sense of comic claustrophobia only grew as I expanded my endeavors into the realm of screenwriting. It's extremely difficult to tell stories from joke to joke as opposed to doing it from plot point to plot point. Not impossible . . . just difficult.

Last, the world changed dramatically in the past four years, in ways that I'm sure are not lost on anyone reading this, so I don't have to repeat the details. One night a couple of years ago we all went to bed in one era of history and woke up in another. Suddenly, a lot of what I had been thinking about and writing about felt . . . dated. And I was also very aware of how valuable that little piece of real estate in the newspapers had become when the so-called free press lost their minds and started censoring themselves. I knew on that tragic day that many more tragic days were to follow, and I made the decision that I would use my little space to scream out louder against the great injustices the United States government was about to unleash upon the planet.

That mission gave me a new sense of purpose with regard to my work. A part of me believes that without September 11, *The Boondocks* would have ended sometime in 2002—a victim of early burnout and creative frustration. It is no secret within the industry that I have always had enormous difficulty in meeting the deadlines this job demands. For years I heard the threats from newspapers almost weekly (delivered to me in loving fashion by my faithful and underappreciated editor, Greg Melvin): Get the strips in earlier or we cancel. After two years the situation seemed as though it would never improve. I don't remember the name of that guy in mythology who constantly had to push the boulder up the hill, but that's what I felt like. September 11, and the shift of focus in *The Boondocks* from the characters to the weekly politics of the country, didn't *exactly* put me ahead of schedule, but my passion about politics did make the job of daily gags a much easier task. That, combined with simplifying the artwork (accomplished in part by avoiding some of the characters), did make the deadline situation bearable. Incidentally, I've always been horrified at the artwork of the strip in those early years—when the deadlines were consistently kicking my ass and my beautiful little characters whom I had painstakingly been designing for years now looked like grotesque versions of themselves.

But with that renewed sense of purpose came the tunnel vision of a satirist who cares way too much about what he's satirizing. Yes, it's sometimes more than a little soapboxy. I have heard whispers of complaints here and there from readers—and much louder and more forceful gripes from certain newspaper editors—that the strip has gotten "too political." I recently got a two-page letter from one editor at the *Washington Post* who was bemoaning the disappearance of the other cast members. After a great deal of hesitation (I have a strict "no fan mail/no hate mail" rule, which does extend to newspaper editors), I read (most of) her letter. After some complaining about a strip where Caesar (jokingly) said the secret to happiness was white women, she got to the crux of the matter. "What happened to Brandy and her family?" this editor asked.

I tried to look past the fact that there never *was* a character named Brandy in the strip, because that's beside the point. Point is, this editor felt as though the strip had changed for the worse over the last year or so. She missed the other cast members who brought a sense of balance and diversity to the humor. Of course, she couldn't have missed them *that* much since she couldn't remember their names, but the point is still well taken, and one that I have been aware of. But the way I look at it, the shift of focus in the strip from several characters to two or three—from life and love and teachers and lawnmowers to Bush and Bush and, well, Bush—was a way to keep the strip in the newspaper and still have it be relevant and (at least occasionally) funny. To me, it was a better alternative than doing a bunch of insincere family humor, or blowing deadlines week after week, or just walking away from it altogether.

Ironically, it is that strict focus on politics that has brought the strip, and me personally, the amazing success we've enjoyed in the past two years. I get big awards, I get to do lectures, I get to go on TV, I get to write movies and books and develop shows—all because of the post–September 11 *Boondocks.* As a comic strip, it is not as good as *Calvin and Hobbes,* it's not as good as *Doonesbury,* it's not as good as *Bloom County* or *Peanuts.* Eventually I realized it doesn't have to be. It does what I want it to do. It's better, more honest, and more truthful than a lot of what's in the newspapers today. And (sometimes) it's funny. That's enough. When the time is right, the other characters will come back more often, and it will be a better comic strip. For right now, it's a daily foot in the ass of The Man, and I think that's what Huey would want.

Thank you, all of you, for reading.

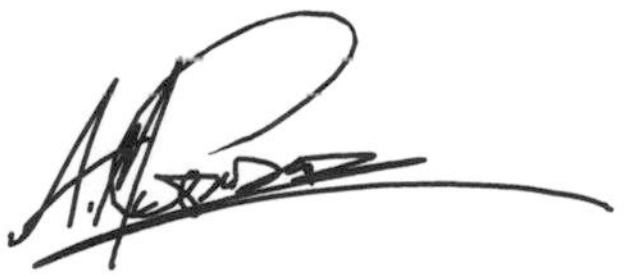

Part 1: The Classics

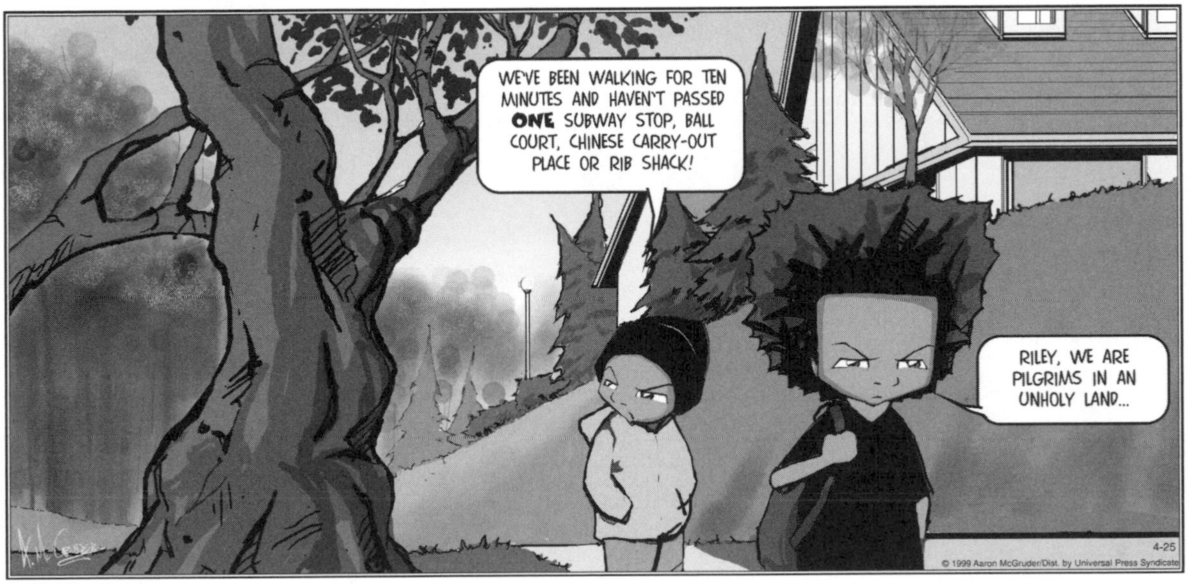

WE'VE BEEN WALKING FOR TEN MINUTES AND HAVEN'T PASSED ONE SUBWAY STOP, BALL COURT, CHINESE CARRY-OUT PLACE OR RIB SHACK!
RILEY, WE ARE PILGRIMS IN AN UNHOLY LAND...
4-25
© 1999 Aaron McGruder/Dist. by Universal Press Syndicate

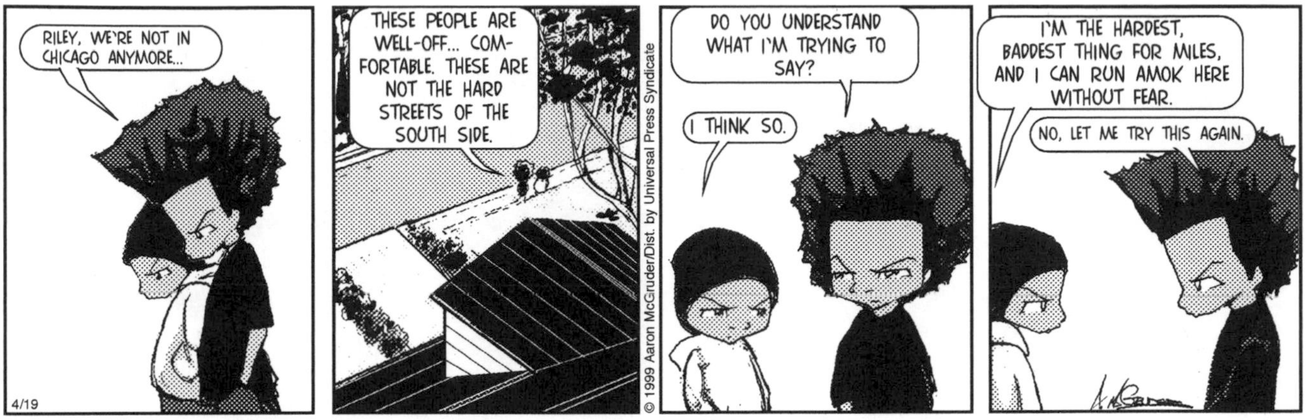
RILEY, WE'RE NOT IN CHICAGO ANYMORE...
THESE PEOPLE ARE WELL-OFF... COMFORTABLE. THESE ARE NOT THE HARD STREETS OF THE SOUTH SIDE.
DO YOU UNDERSTAND WHAT I'M TRYING TO SAY?
I THINK SO.
I'M THE HARDEST, BADDEST THING FOR MILES, AND I CAN RUN AMOK HERE WITHOUT FEAR.
NO, LET ME TRY THIS AGAIN.
4/19
© 1999 Aaron McGruder/Dist. by Universal Press Syndicate

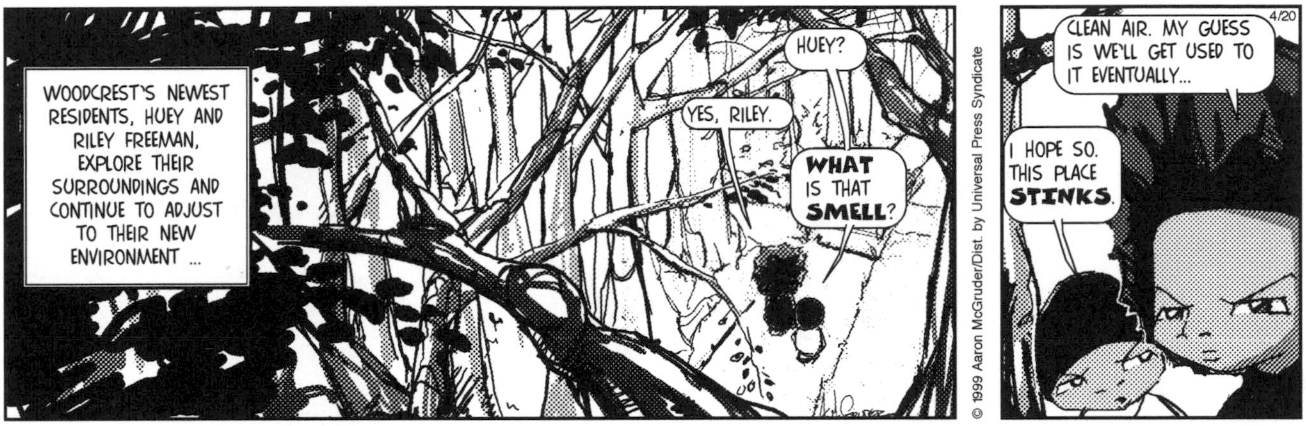
WOODCREST'S NEWEST RESIDENTS, HUEY AND RILEY FREEMAN, EXPLORE THEIR SURROUNDINGS AND CONTINUE TO ADJUST TO THEIR NEW ENVIRONMENT ...
HUEY?
YES, RILEY.
WHAT IS THAT SMELL?
CLEAN AIR. MY GUESS IS WE'LL GET USED TO IT EVENTUALLY...
I HOPE SO. THIS PLACE STINKS.
4/20
© 1999 Aaron McGruder/Dist. by Universal Press Syndicate

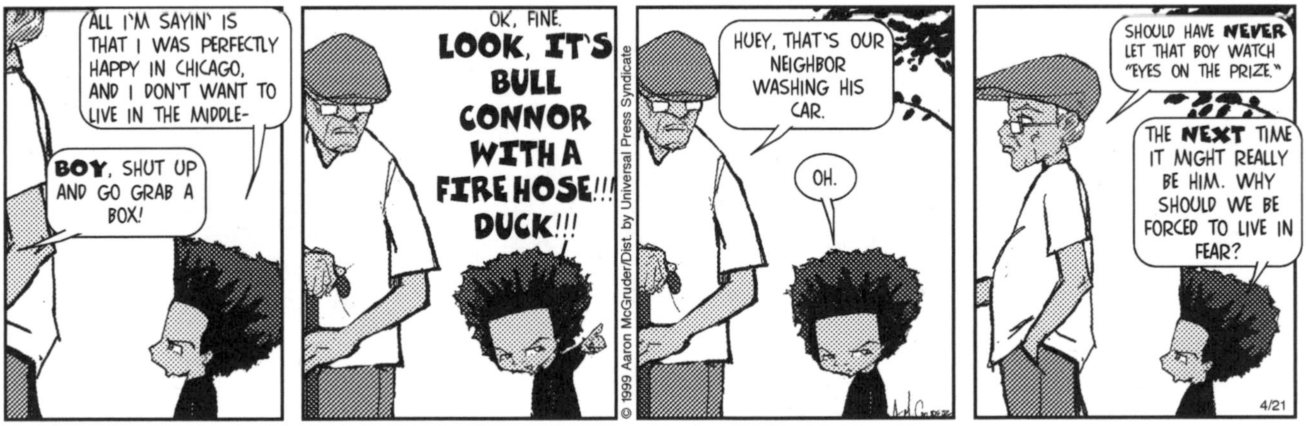
ALL I'M SAYIN' IS THAT I WAS PERFECTLY HAPPY IN CHICAGO, AND I DON'T WANT TO LIVE IN THE MIDDLE-
BOY, SHUT UP AND GO GRAB A BOX!
OK, FINE.
LOOK, IT'S BULL CONNOR WITH A FIRE HOSE!!! DUCK!!!
HUEY, THAT'S OUR NEIGHBOR WASHING HIS CAR.
OH.
SHOULD HAVE NEVER LET THAT BOY WATCH "EYES ON THE PRIZE."
THE NEXT TIME IT MIGHT REALLY BE HIM. WHY SHOULD WE BE FORCED TO LIVE IN FEAR?
4/21
© 1999 Aaron McGruder/Dist. by Universal Press Syndicate

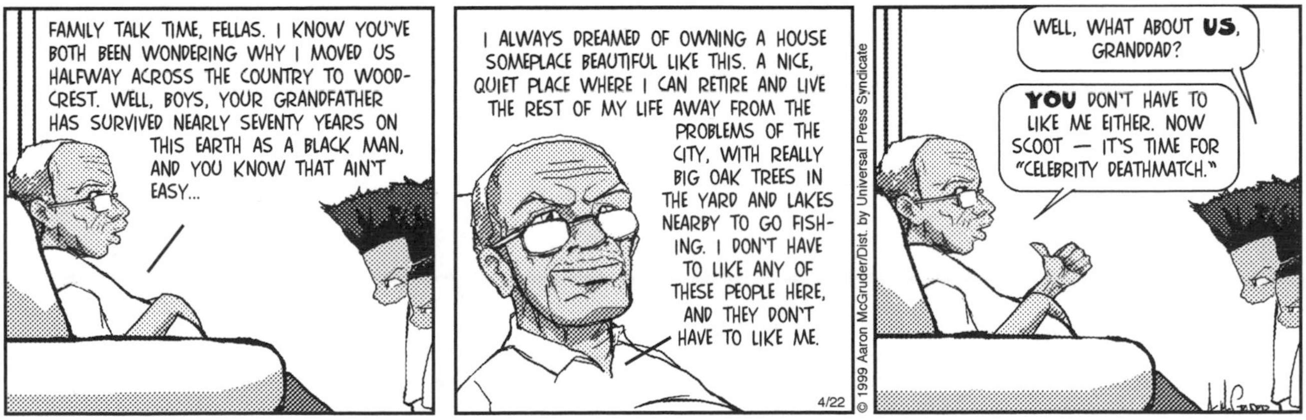
FAMILY TALK TIME, FELLAS. I KNOW YOU'VE BOTH BEEN WONDERING WHY I MOVED US HALFWAY ACROSS THE COUNTRY TO WOODCREST. WELL, BOYS, YOUR GRANDFATHER HAS SURVIVED NEARLY SEVENTY YEARS ON THIS EARTH AS A BLACK MAN, AND YOU KNOW THAT AIN'T EASY...
I ALWAYS DREAMED OF OWNING A HOUSE SOMEPLACE BEAUTIFUL LIKE THIS. A NICE, QUIET PLACE WHERE I CAN RETIRE AND LIVE THE REST OF MY LIFE AWAY FROM THE PROBLEMS OF THE CITY, WITH REALLY BIG OAK TREES IN THE YARD AND LAKES NEARBY TO GO FISHING. I DON'T HAVE TO LIKE ANY OF THESE PEOPLE HERE, AND THEY DON'T HAVE TO LIKE ME.
WELL, WHAT ABOUT US, GRANDDAD?
YOU DON'T HAVE TO LIKE ME EITHER. NOW SCOOT — IT'S TIME FOR "CELEBRITY DEATHMATCH."
4/22
© 1999 Aaron McGruder/Dist. by Universal Press Syndicate

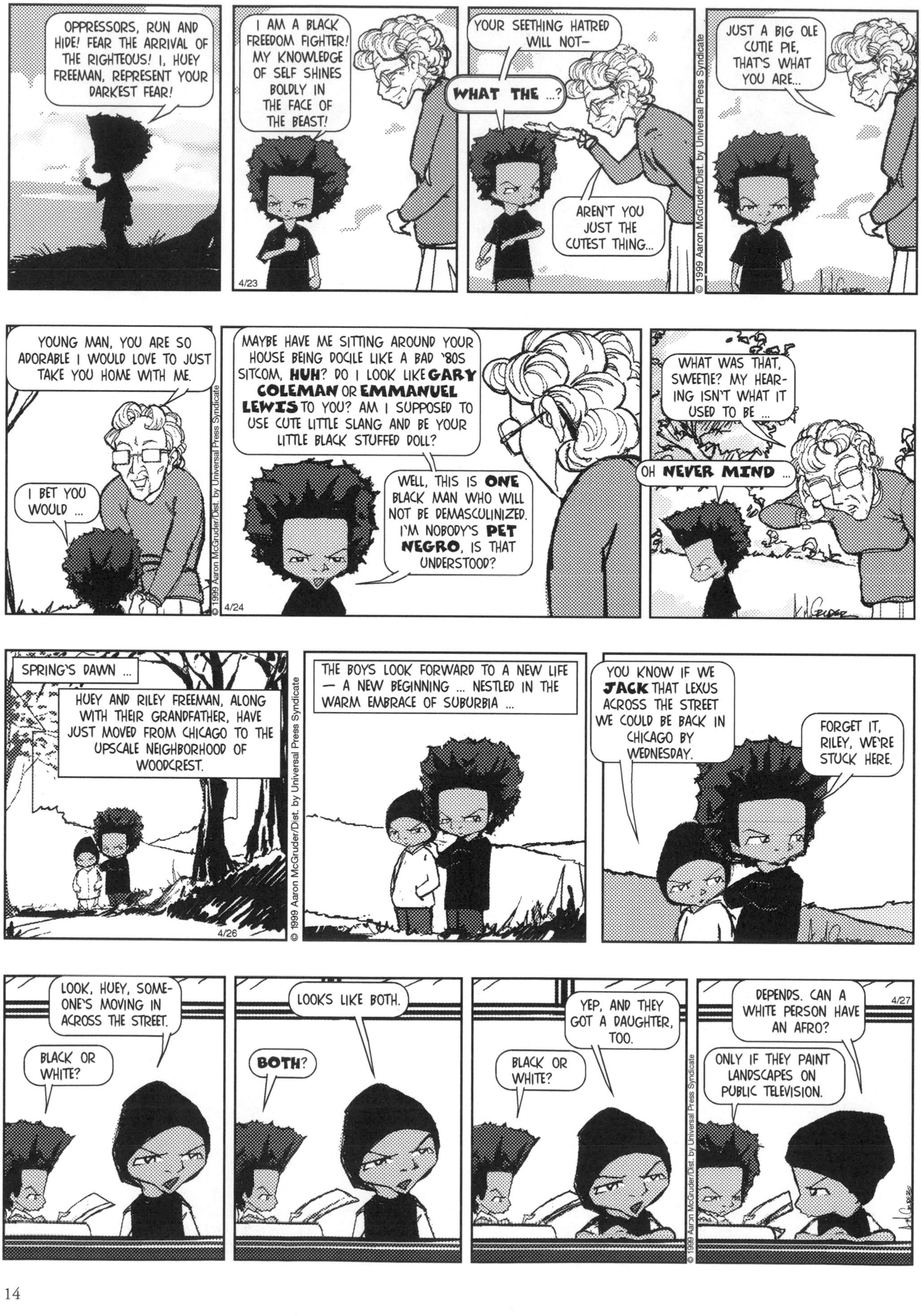

OPPRESSORS, RUN AND HIDE! FEAR THE ARRIVAL OF THE RIGHTEOUS! I, HUEY FREEMAN, REPRESENT YOUR DARKEST FEAR!
I AM A BLACK FREEDOM FIGHTER! MY KNOWLEDGE OF SELF SHINES BOLDLY IN THE FACE OF THE BEAST!
4/23
YOUR SEETHING HATRED WILL NOT–
WHAT THE ...?
AREN'T YOU JUST THE CUTEST THING...
JUST A BIG OLE CUTIE PIE, THAT'S WHAT YOU ARE...
© 1999 Aaron McGruder/Dist. by Universal Press Syndicate
YOUNG MAN, YOU ARE SO ADORABLE I WOULD LOVE TO JUST TAKE YOU HOME WITH ME.
I BET YOU WOULD ...
© 1999 Aaron McGruder/Dist. by Universal Press Syndicate
4/24
MAYBE HAVE ME SITTING AROUND YOUR HOUSE BEING DOCILE LIKE A BAD '80S SITCOM, HUH? DO I LOOK LIKE GARY COLEMAN OR EMMANUEL LEWIS TO YOU? AM I SUPPOSED TO USE CUTE LITTLE SLANG AND BE YOUR LITTLE BLACK STUFFED DOLL?
WELL, THIS IS ONE BLACK MAN WHO WILL NOT BE DEMASCULINIZED. I'M NOBODY'S PET NEGRO, IS THAT UNDERSTOOD?
WHAT WAS THAT, SWEETIE? MY HEARING ISN'T WHAT IT USED TO BE ...
OH NEVER MIND ...
SPRING'S DAWN ...
HUEY AND RILEY FREEMAN, ALONG WITH THEIR GRANDFATHER, HAVE JUST MOVED FROM CHICAGO TO THE UPSCALE NEIGHBORHOOD OF WOODCREST.
4/26
© 1999 Aaron McGruder/Dist. by Universal Press Syndicate
THE BOYS LOOK FORWARD TO A NEW LIFE — A NEW BEGINNING ... NESTLED IN THE WARM EMBRACE OF SUBURBIA ...
YOU KNOW IF WE JACK THAT LEXUS ACROSS THE STREET WE COULD BE BACK IN CHICAGO BY WEDNESDAY.
FORGET IT, RILEY, WE'RE STUCK HERE.
LOOK, HUEY, SOMEONE'S MOVING IN ACROSS THE STREET.
BLACK OR WHITE?
LOOKS LIKE BOTH.
BOTH?
YEP, AND THEY GOT A DAUGHTER, TOO.
BLACK OR WHITE?
© 1999 Aaron McGruder/Dist. by Universal Press Syndicate
4/27
DEPENDS. CAN A WHITE PERSON HAVE AN AFRO?
ONLY IF THEY PAINT LANDSCAPES ON PUBLIC TELEVISION.

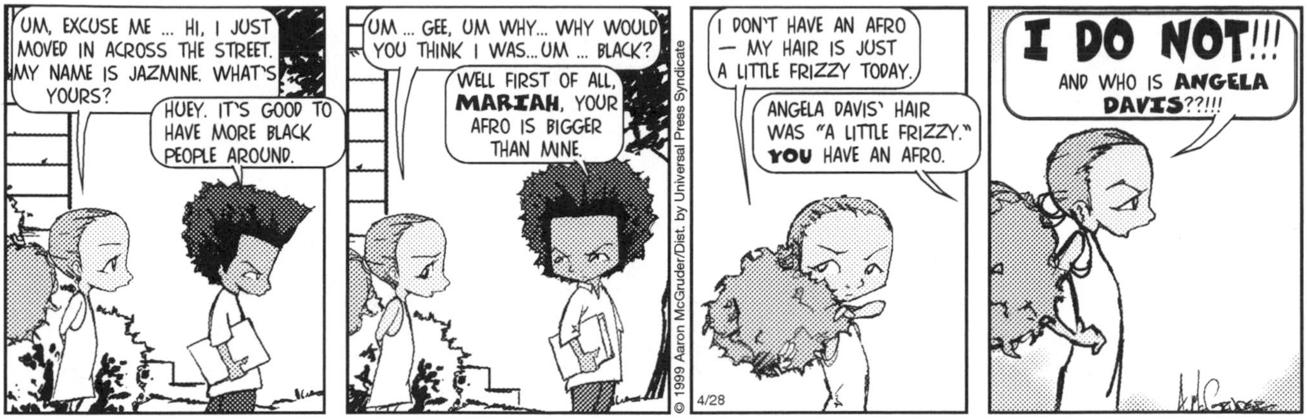
UM, EXCUSE ME ... HI, I JUST MOVED IN ACROSS THE STREET. MY NAME IS JAZMINE. WHAT'S YOURS?
HUEY. IT'S GOOD TO HAVE MORE BLACK PEOPLE AROUND.
UM ... GEE, UM WHY... WHY WOULD YOU THINK I WAS...UM ... BLACK?
WELL FIRST OF ALL, MARIAH, YOUR AFRO IS BIGGER THAN MINE.
© 1999 Aaron McGruder/Dist. by Universal Press Syndicate
I DON'T HAVE AN AFRO — MY HAIR IS JUST A LITTLE FRIZZY TODAY.
ANGELA DAVIS' HAIR WAS "A LITTLE FRIZZY." YOU HAVE AN AFRO.
4/28
I DO NOT!!!
AND WHO IS ANGELA DAVIS??!!!

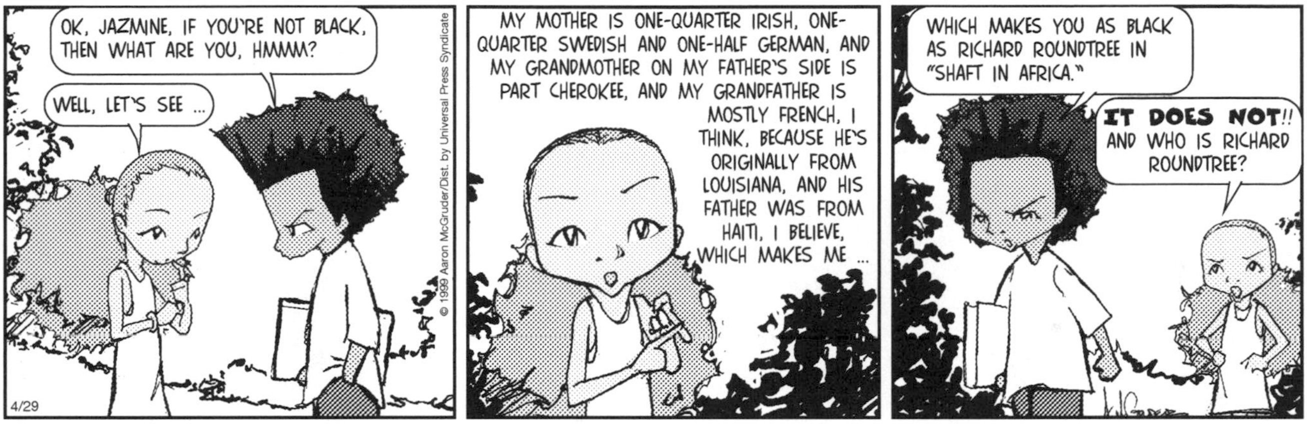
OK, JAZMINE, IF YOU'RE NOT BLACK, THEN WHAT ARE YOU, HMMM?
WELL, LET'S SEE ...
4/29
© 1999 Aaron McGruder/Dist. by Universal Press Syndicate
MY MOTHER IS ONE-QUARTER IRISH, ONE-QUARTER SWEDISH AND ONE-HALF GERMAN, AND MY GRANDMOTHER ON MY FATHER'S SIDE IS PART CHEROKEE, AND MY GRANDFATHER IS MOSTLY FRENCH, I THINK, BECAUSE HE'S ORIGINALLY FROM LOUISIANA, AND HIS FATHER WAS FROM HAITI, I BELIEVE, WHICH MAKES ME ...
WHICH MAKES YOU AS BLACK AS RICHARD ROUNDTREE IN "SHAFT IN AFRICA."
IT DOES NOT!! AND WHO IS RICHARD ROUNDTREE?

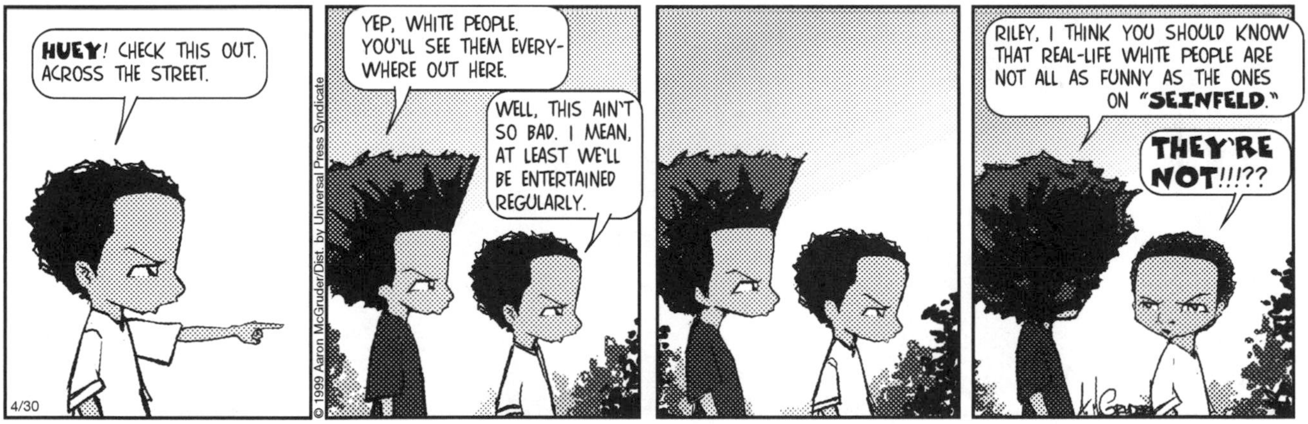
HUEY! CHECK THIS OUT. ACROSS THE STREET.
4/30
© 1999 Aaron McGruder/Dist. by Universal Press Syndicate
YEP, WHITE PEOPLE. YOU'LL SEE THEM EVERYWHERE OUT HERE.
WELL, THIS AIN'T SO BAD. I MEAN, AT LEAST WE'LL BE ENTERTAINED REGULARLY.
RILEY, I THINK YOU SHOULD KNOW THAT REAL-LIFE WHITE PEOPLE ARE NOT ALL AS FUNNY AS THE ONES ON "SEINFELD."
THEY'RE NOT!!!??

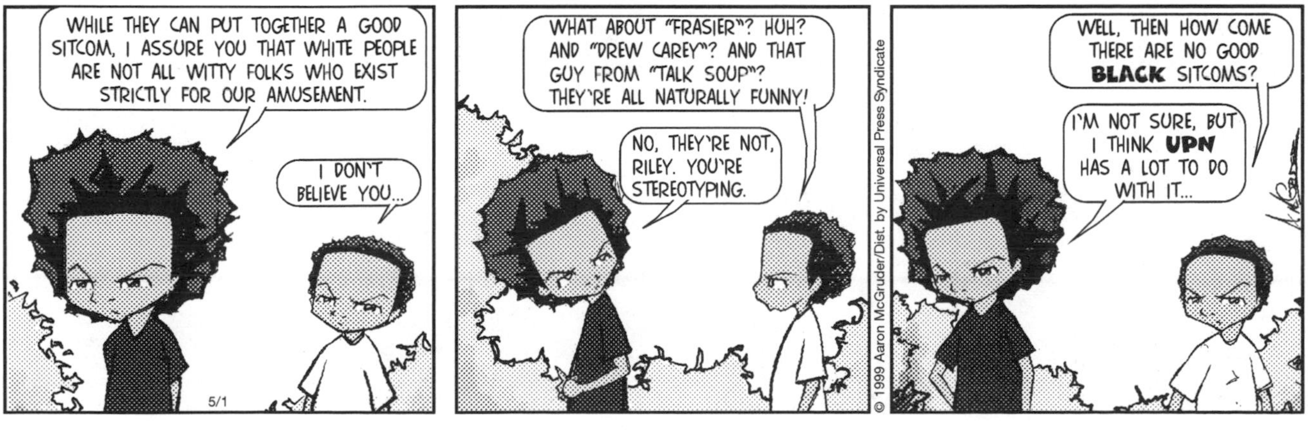
WHILE THEY CAN PUT TOGETHER A GOOD SITCOM, I ASSURE YOU THAT WHITE PEOPLE ARE NOT ALL WITTY FOLKS WHO EXIST STRICTLY FOR OUR AMUSEMENT.
I DON'T BELIEVE YOU...
5/1
WHAT ABOUT "FRASIER"? HUH? AND "DREW CAREY"? AND THAT GUY FROM "TALK SOUP"? THEY'RE ALL NATURALLY FUNNY!
NO, THEY'RE NOT, RILEY. YOU'RE STEREOTYPING.
© 1999 Aaron McGruder/Dist. by Universal Press Syndicate
WELL, THEN HOW COME THERE ARE NO GOOD BLACK SITCOMS?
I'M NOT SURE, BUT I THINK UPN HAS A LOT TO DO WITH IT...

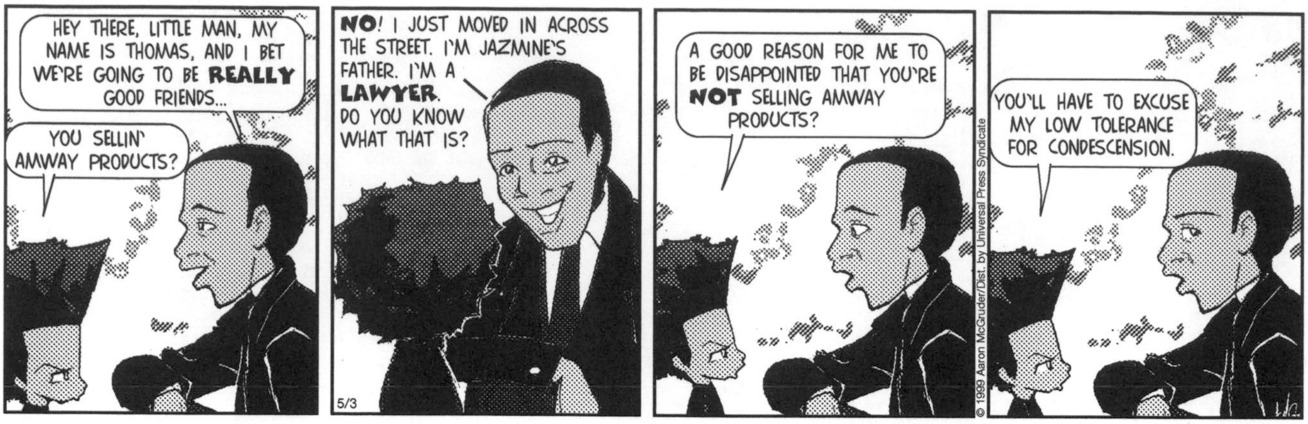
HEY THERE, LITTLE MAN, MY NAME IS THOMAS, AND I BET WE'RE GOING TO BE **REALLY** GOOD FRIENDS...
YOU SELLIN' AMWAY PRODUCTS?
NO! I JUST MOVED IN ACROSS THE STREET. I'M JAZMINE'S FATHER. I'M A **LAWYER**. DO YOU KNOW WHAT THAT IS?
5/3
A GOOD REASON FOR ME TO BE DISAPPOINTED THAT YOU'RE **NOT** SELLING AMWAY PRODUCTS?
© 1999 Aaron McGruder/Dist. by Universal Press Syndicate
YOU'LL HAVE TO EXCUSE MY LOW TOLERANCE FOR CONDESCENSION.

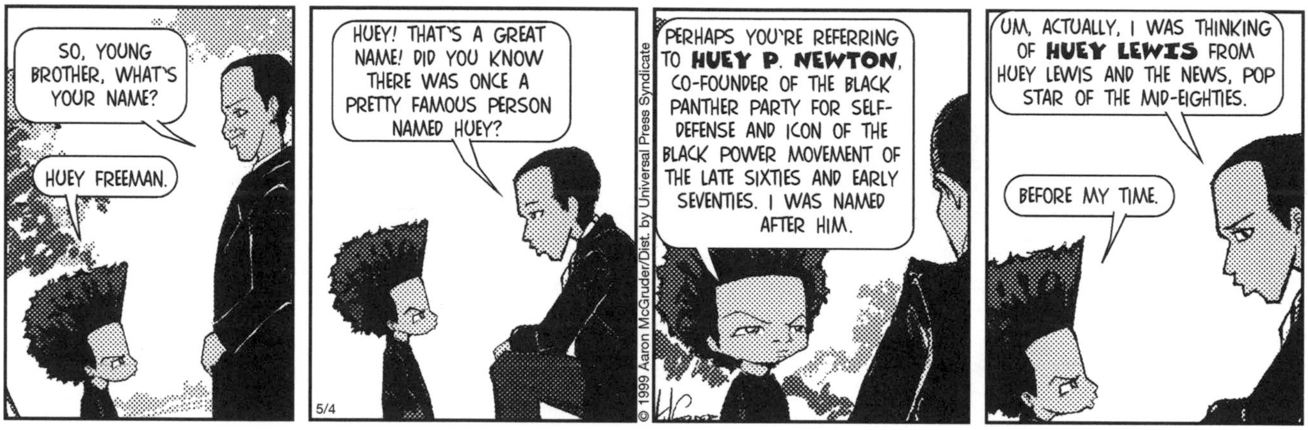
SO, YOUNG BROTHER, WHAT'S YOUR NAME?
HUEY FREEMAN.
HUEY! THAT'S A GREAT NAME! DID YOU KNOW THERE WAS ONCE A PRETTY FAMOUS PERSON NAMED HUEY?
5/4
© 1999 Aaron McGruder/Dist. by Universal Press Syndicate
PERHAPS YOU'RE REFERRING TO **HUEY P. NEWTON**, CO-FOUNDER OF THE BLACK PANTHER PARTY FOR SELF-DEFENSE AND ICON OF THE BLACK POWER MOVEMENT OF THE LATE SIXTIES AND EARLY SEVENTIES. I WAS NAMED AFTER HIM.
UM, ACTUALLY, I WAS THINKING OF **HUEY LEWIS** FROM HUEY LEWIS AND THE NEWS, POP STAR OF THE MID-EIGHTIES.
BEFORE MY TIME.

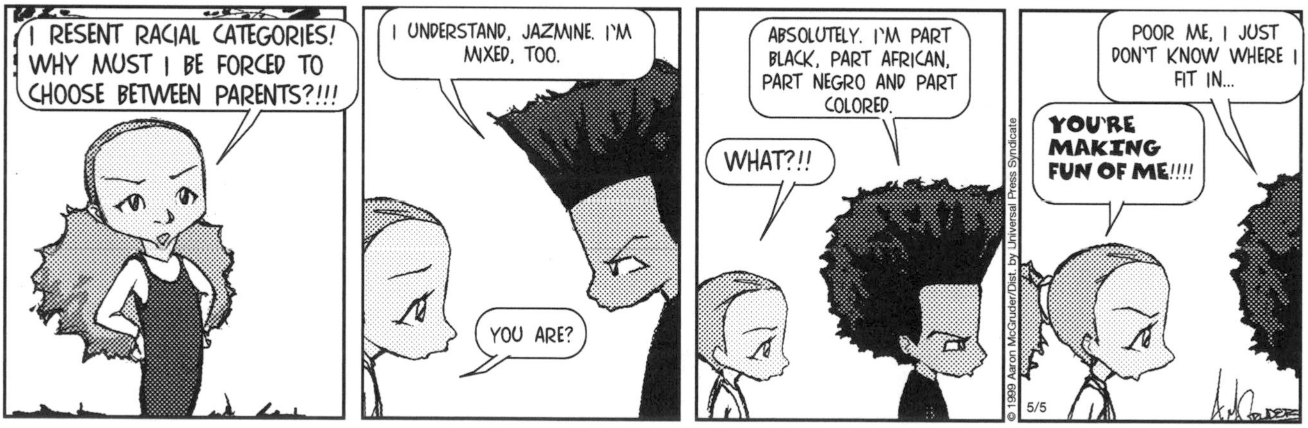
I RESENT RACIAL CATEGORIES! WHY MUST I BE FORCED TO CHOOSE BETWEEN PARENTS?!!!
I UNDERSTAND, JAZMINE. I'M MIXED, TOO.
YOU ARE?
ABSOLUTELY. I'M PART BLACK, PART AFRICAN, PART NEGRO AND PART COLORED.
WHAT?!!
© 1999 Aaron McGruder/Dist. by Universal Press Syndicate
POOR ME, I JUST DON'T KNOW WHERE I FIT IN...
YOU'RE MAKING FUN OF ME!!!!
5/5

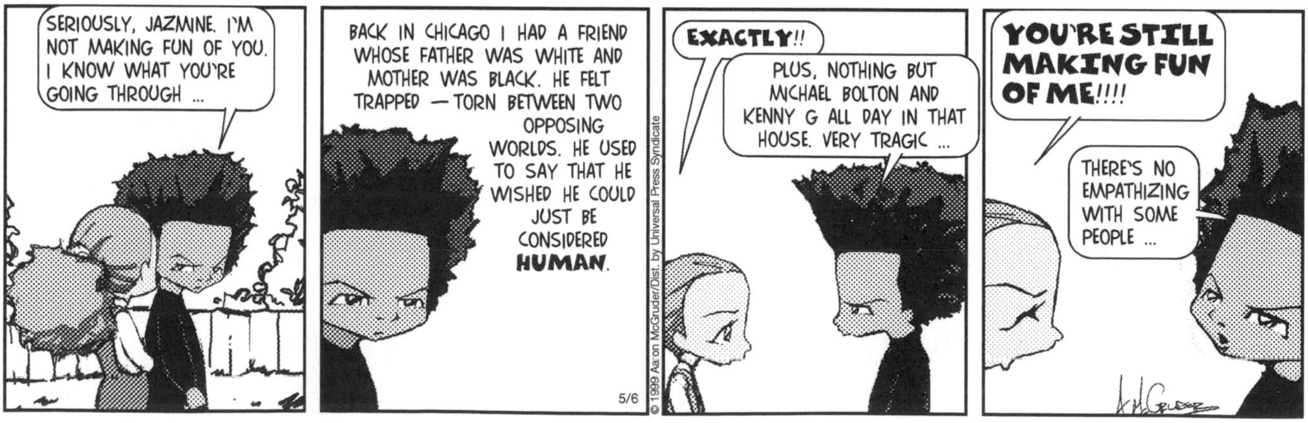
SERIOUSLY, JAZMINE. I'M NOT MAKING FUN OF YOU. I KNOW WHAT YOU'RE GOING THROUGH ...
BACK IN CHICAGO I HAD A FRIEND WHOSE FATHER WAS WHITE AND MOTHER WAS BLACK. HE FELT TRAPPED — TORN BETWEEN TWO OPPOSING WORLDS. HE USED TO SAY THAT HE WISHED HE COULD JUST BE CONSIDERED **HUMAN**.
5/6
© 1999 Aaron McGruder/Dist. by Universal Press Syndicate
EXACTLY!!
PLUS, NOTHING BUT MICHAEL BOLTON AND KENNY G ALL DAY IN THAT HOUSE. VERY TRAGIC ...
YOU'RE STILL MAKING FUN OF ME!!!!
THERE'S NO EMPATHIZING WITH SOME PEOPLE ...

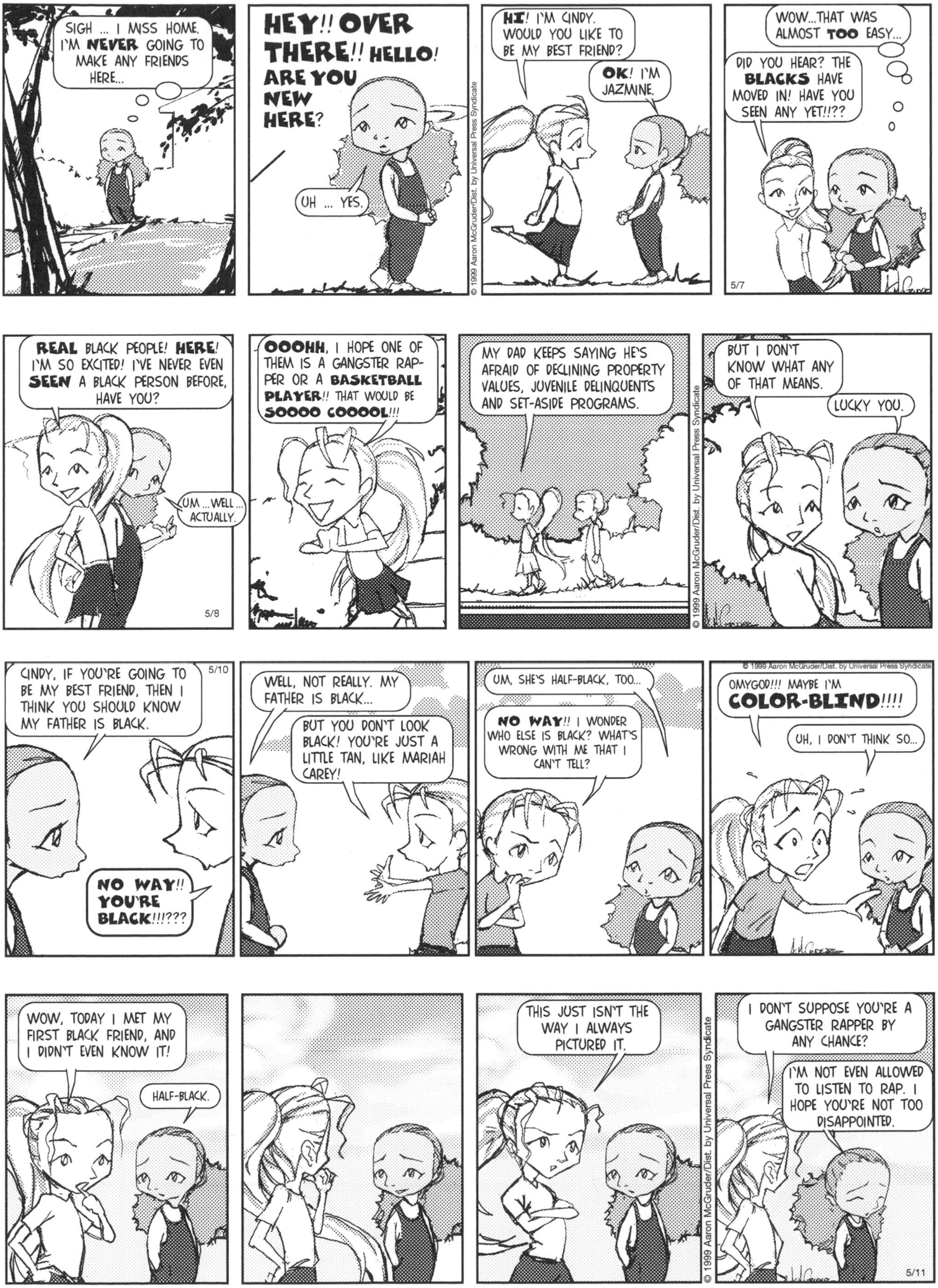
SIGH ... I MISS HOME. I'M NEVER GOING TO MAKE ANY FRIENDS HERE...
HEY!! OVER THERE!! HELLO! ARE YOU NEW HERE?
UH ... YES.
© 1999 Aaron McGruder/Dist. by Universal Press Syndicate
HI! I'M CINDY. WOULD YOU LIKE TO BE MY BEST FRIEND?
OK! I'M JAZMINE.
WOW...THAT WAS ALMOST TOO EASY...
DID YOU HEAR? THE BLACKS HAVE MOVED IN! HAVE YOU SEEN ANY YET!!??
5/7
REAL BLACK PEOPLE! HERE! I'M SO EXCITED! I'VE NEVER EVEN SEEN A BLACK PERSON BEFORE, HAVE YOU?
UM ...WELL ... ACTUALLY.
5/8
OOOHH, I HOPE ONE OF THEM IS A GANGSTER RAPPER OR A BASKETBALL PLAYER!! THAT WOULD BE SOOOO COOOOL!!!
MY DAD KEEPS SAYING HE'S AFRAID OF DECLINING PROPERTY VALUES, JUVENILE DELINQUENTS AND SET-ASIDE PROGRAMS.
© 1999 Aaron McGruder/Dist. by Universal Press Syndicate
BUT I DON'T KNOW WHAT ANY OF THAT MEANS.
LUCKY YOU.
CINDY, IF YOU'RE GOING TO BE MY BEST FRIEND, THEN I THINK YOU SHOULD KNOW MY FATHER IS BLACK.
5/10
NO WAY!! YOU'RE BLACK!!!???
WELL, NOT REALLY. MY FATHER IS BLACK...
BUT YOU DON'T LOOK BLACK! YOU'RE JUST A LITTLE TAN, LIKE MARIAH CAREY!
UM, SHE'S HALF-BLACK, TOO...
NO WAY!! I WONDER WHO ELSE IS BLACK? WHAT'S WRONG WITH ME THAT I CAN'T TELL?
© 1999 Aaron McGruder/Dist. by Universal Press Syndicate
OMYGOD!!! MAYBE I'M COLOR-BLIND!!!!
UH, I DON'T THINK SO...
WOW, TODAY I MET MY FIRST BLACK FRIEND, AND I DIDN'T EVEN KNOW IT!
HALF-BLACK.
THIS JUST ISN'T THE WAY I ALWAYS PICTURED IT.
© 1999 Aaron McGruder/Dist. by Universal Press Syndicate
I DON'T SUPPOSE YOU'RE A GANGSTER RAPPER BY ANY CHANCE?
I'M NOT EVEN ALLOWED TO LISTEN TO RAP. I HOPE YOU'RE NOT TOO DISAPPOINTED.
5/11

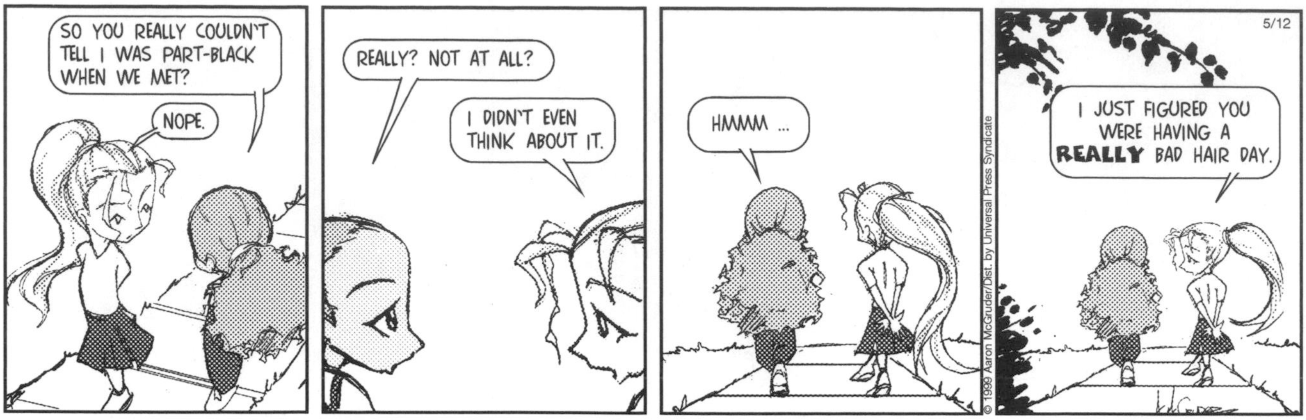
SO YOU REALLY COULDN'T TELL I WAS PART-BLACK WHEN WE MET?
NOPE.
REALLY? NOT AT ALL?
I DIDN'T EVEN THINK ABOUT IT.
HMMM ...
5/12
I JUST FIGURED YOU WERE HAVING A **REALLY** BAD HAIR DAY.
© 1999 Aaron McGruder/Dist. by Universal Press Syndicate

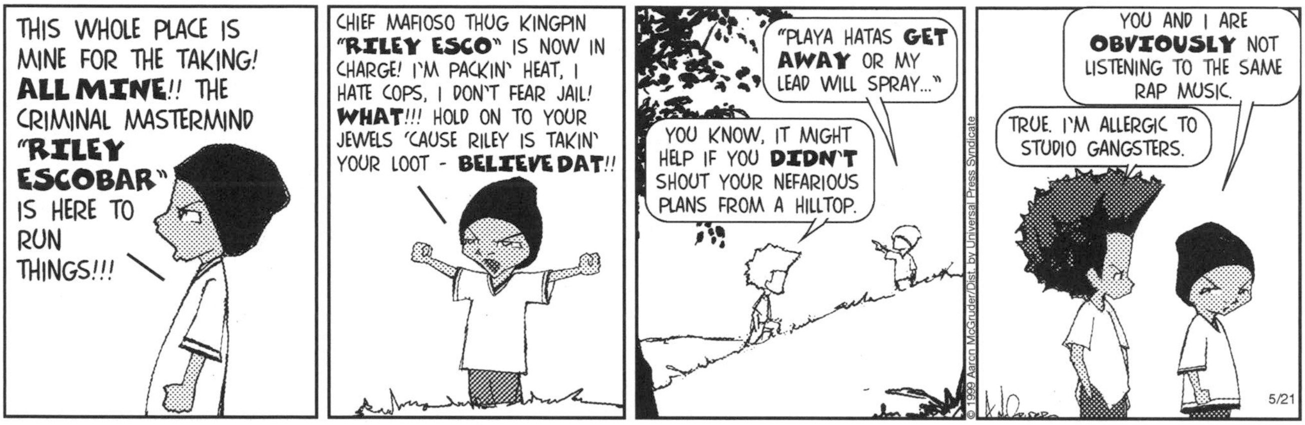
THIS WHOLE PLACE IS MINE FOR THE TAKING! **ALL MINE**!! THE CRIMINAL MASTERMIND "**RILEY ESCOBAR**" IS HERE TO RUN THINGS!!!
CHIEF MAFIOSO THUG KINGPIN "**RILEY ESCO**" IS NOW IN CHARGE! I'M PACKIN' HEAT, I HATE COPS, I DON'T FEAR JAIL! **WHAT**!!! HOLD ON TO YOUR JEWELS 'CAUSE RILEY IS TAKIN' YOUR LOOT - **BELIEVE DAT**!!
"PLAYA HATAS **GET AWAY** OR MY LEAD WILL SPRAY..."
YOU KNOW, IT MIGHT HELP IF YOU **DIDN'T** SHOUT YOUR NEFARIOUS PLANS FROM A HILLTOP.
YOU AND I ARE **OBVIOUSLY** NOT LISTENING TO THE SAME RAP MUSIC.
TRUE. I'M ALLERGIC TO STUDIO GANGSTERS.
5/21
© 1999 Aaron McGruder/Dist. by Universal Press Syndicate

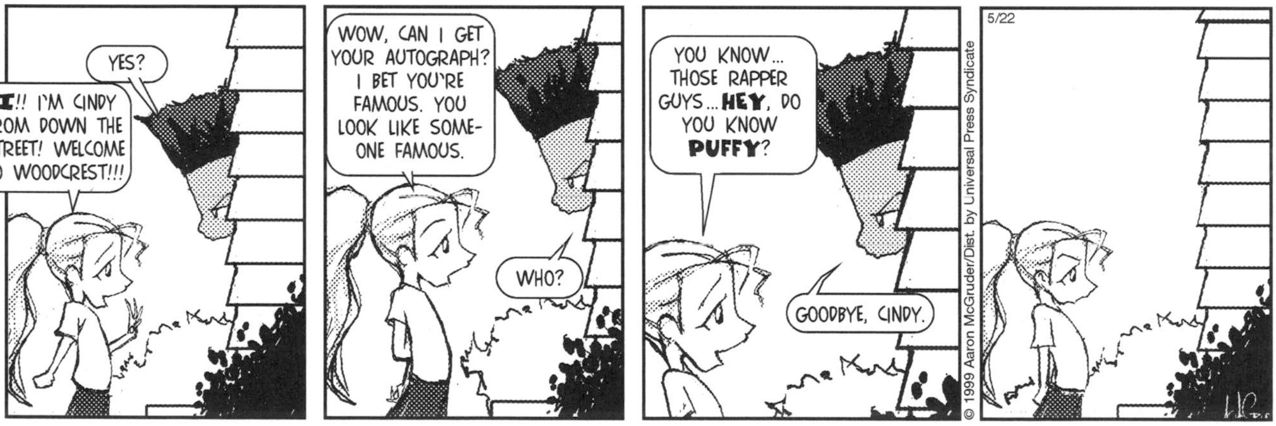
HI!! I'M CINDY FROM DOWN THE STREET! WELCOME TO WOODCREST!!!
YES?
WOW, CAN I GET YOUR AUTOGRAPH? I BET YOU'RE FAMOUS. YOU LOOK LIKE SOME-ONE FAMOUS.
WHO?
YOU KNOW... THOSE RAPPER GUYS... **HEY**, DO YOU KNOW **PUFFY**?
GOODBYE, CINDY.
5/22
© 1999 Aaron McGruder/Dist. by Universal Press Syndicate

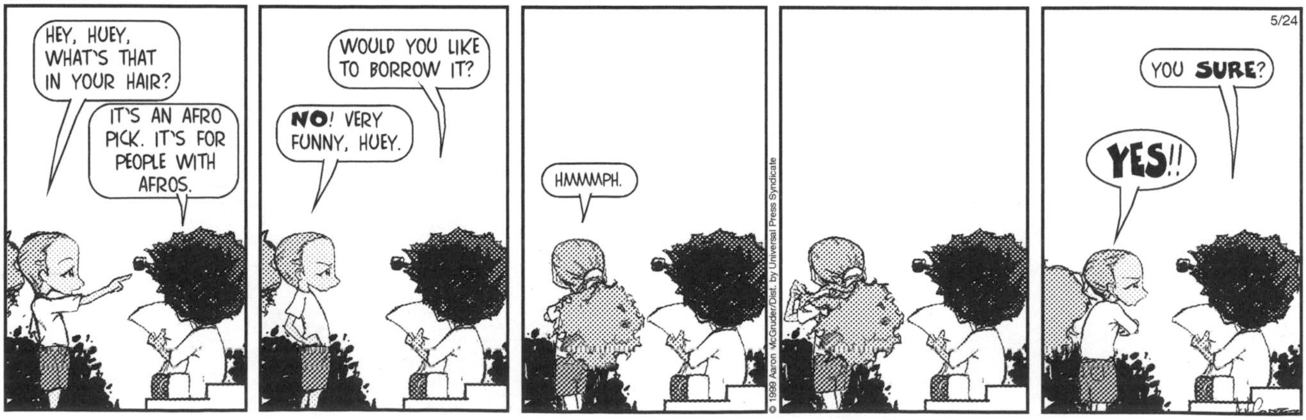
HEY, HUEY, WHAT'S THAT IN YOUR HAIR?
IT'S AN AFRO PICK. IT'S FOR PEOPLE WITH AFROS.
WOULD YOU LIKE TO BORROW IT?
NO! VERY FUNNY, HUEY.
HMMMPH.
5/24
YOU **SURE**?
YES!!
© 1999 Aaron McGruder/Dist. by Universal Press Syndicate

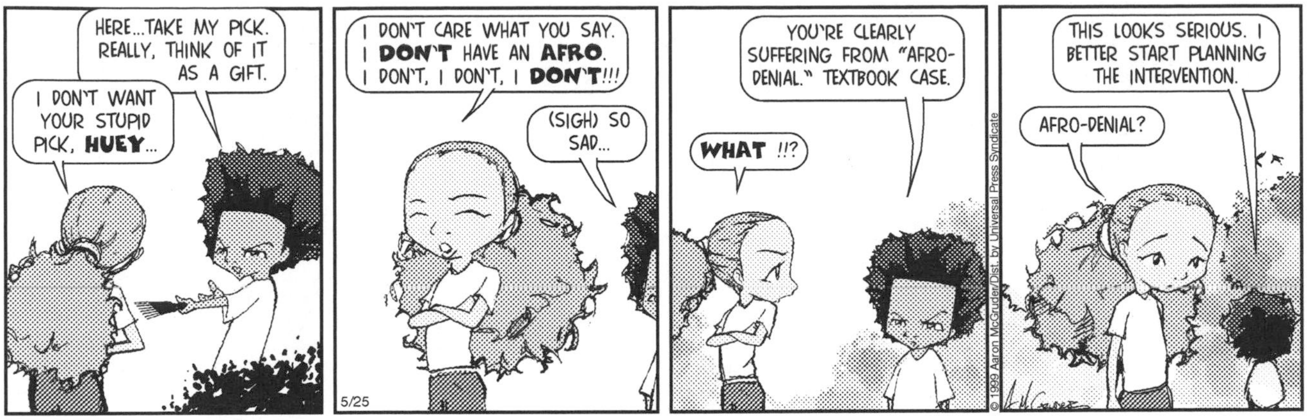
I DON'T WANT YOUR STUPID PICK, HUEY...
HERE...TAKE MY PICK. REALLY, THINK OF IT AS A GIFT.
5/25
I DON'T CARE WHAT YOU SAY. I DON'T HAVE AN AFRO. I DON'T, I DON'T, I DON'T!!!
(SIGH) SO SAD...
WHAT !!?
YOU'RE CLEARLY SUFFERING FROM "AFRO-DENIAL." TEXTBOOK CASE.
AFRO-DENIAL?
THIS LOOKS SERIOUS. I BETTER START PLANNING THE INTERVENTION.
© 1999 Aaron McGruder/Dist. by Universal Press Syndicate

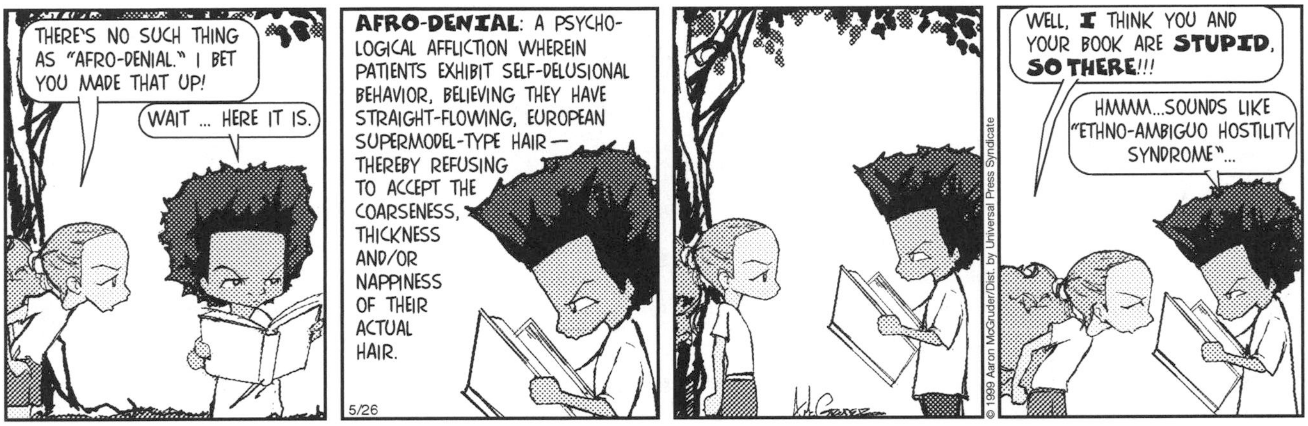
THERE'S NO SUCH THING AS "AFRO-DENIAL." I BET YOU MADE THAT UP!
WAIT ... HERE IT IS.
AFRO-DENIAL: A PSYCHOLOGICAL AFFLICTION WHEREIN PATIENTS EXHIBIT SELF-DELUSIONAL BEHAVIOR, BELIEVING THEY HAVE STRAIGHT-FLOWING, EUROPEAN SUPERMODEL-TYPE HAIR — THEREBY REFUSING TO ACCEPT THE COARSENESS, THICKNESS AND/OR NAPPINESS OF THEIR ACTUAL HAIR.
5/26
WELL, I THINK YOU AND YOUR BOOK ARE STUPID, SO THERE!!!
HMMM...SOUNDS LIKE "ETHNO-AMBIGUO HOSTILITY SYNDROME"...
© 1999 Aaron McGruder/Dist. by Universal Press Syndicate

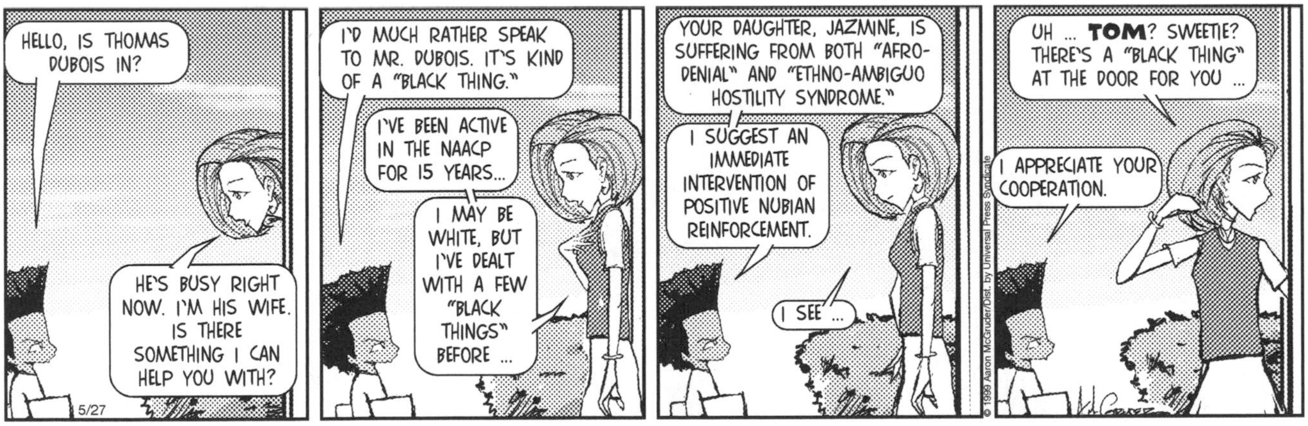
HELLO, IS THOMAS DUBOIS IN?
HE'S BUSY RIGHT NOW. I'M HIS WIFE. IS THERE SOMETHING I CAN HELP YOU WITH?
5/27
I'D MUCH RATHER SPEAK TO MR. DUBOIS. IT'S KIND OF A "BLACK THING."
I'VE BEEN ACTIVE IN THE NAACP FOR 15 YEARS...
I MAY BE WHITE, BUT I'VE DEALT WITH A FEW "BLACK THINGS" BEFORE ...
YOUR DAUGHTER, JAZMINE, IS SUFFERING FROM BOTH "AFRO-DENIAL" AND "ETHNO-AMBIGUO HOSTILITY SYNDROME."
I SUGGEST AN IMMEDIATE INTERVENTION OF POSITIVE NUBIAN REINFORCEMENT.
I SEE ...
UH ... TOM? SWEETIE? THERE'S A "BLACK THING" AT THE DOOR FOR YOU ...
I APPRECIATE YOUR COOPERATION.
© 1999 Aaron McGruder/Dist. by Universal Press Syndicate

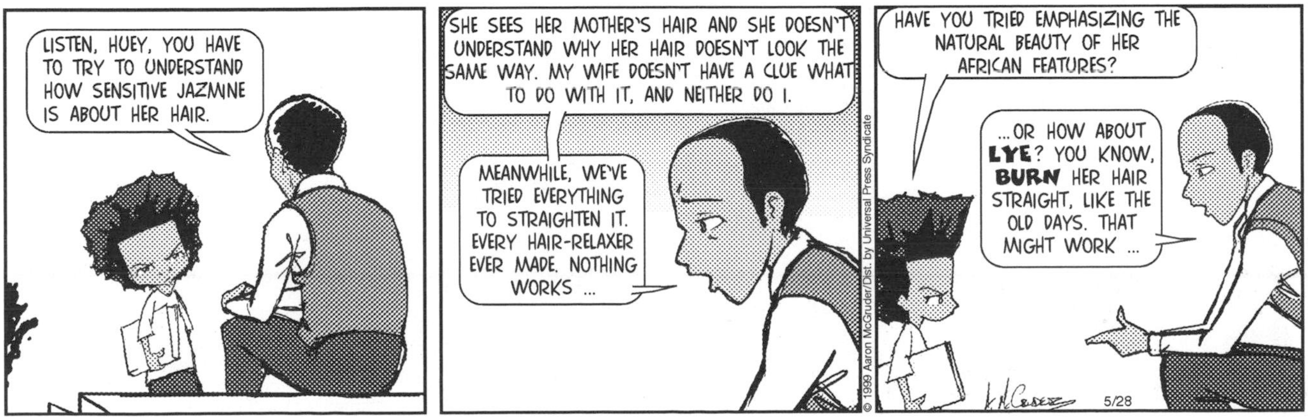
LISTEN, HUEY, YOU HAVE TO TRY TO UNDERSTAND HOW SENSITIVE JAZMINE IS ABOUT HER HAIR.
SHE SEES HER MOTHER'S HAIR AND SHE DOESN'T UNDERSTAND WHY HER HAIR DOESN'T LOOK THE SAME WAY. MY WIFE DOESN'T HAVE A CLUE WHAT TO DO WITH IT, AND NEITHER DO I.
MEANWHILE, WE'VE TRIED EVERYTHING TO STRAIGHTEN IT. EVERY HAIR-RELAXER EVER MADE. NOTHING WORKS ...
© 1999 Aaron McGruder/Dist. by Universal Press Syndicate
HAVE YOU TRIED EMPHASIZING THE NATURAL BEAUTY OF HER AFRICAN FEATURES?
...OR HOW ABOUT LYE? YOU KNOW, BURN HER HAIR STRAIGHT, LIKE THE OLD DAYS. THAT MIGHT WORK ...
5/28

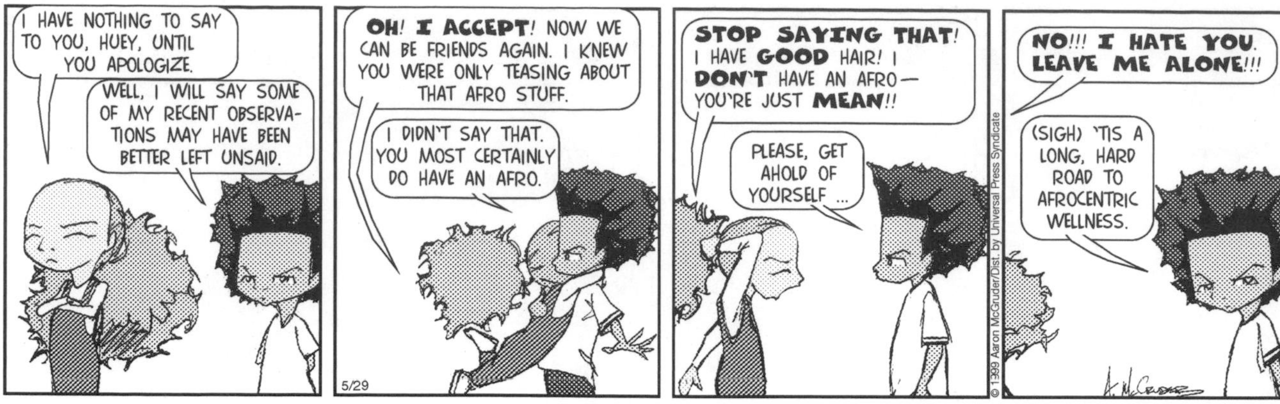
I HAVE NOTHING TO SAY TO YOU, HUEY, UNTIL YOU APOLOGIZE.
WELL, I WILL SAY SOME OF MY RECENT OBSERVATIONS MAY HAVE BEEN BETTER LEFT UNSAID.
OH! I ACCEPT! NOW WE CAN BE FRIENDS AGAIN. I KNEW YOU WERE ONLY TEASING ABOUT THAT AFRO STUFF.
I DIDN'T SAY THAT. YOU MOST CERTAINLY DO HAVE AN AFRO.
5/29
STOP SAYING THAT! I HAVE GOOD HAIR! I DON'T HAVE AN AFRO— YOU'RE JUST MEAN!!
PLEASE, GET AHOLD OF YOURSELF ...
NO!!! I HATE YOU. LEAVE ME ALONE!!!
(SIGH) 'TIS A LONG, HARD ROAD TO AFROCENTRIC WELLNESS.
© 1999 Aaron McGruder/Dist. by Universal Press Syndicate

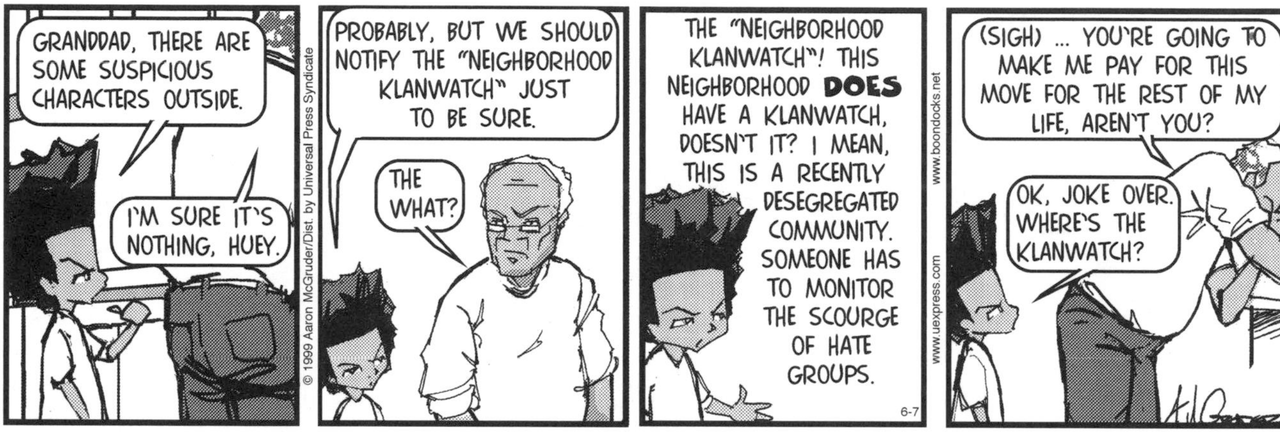
GRANDDAD, THERE ARE SOME SUSPICIOUS CHARACTERS OUTSIDE.
I'M SURE IT'S NOTHING, HUEY.
© 1999 Aaron McGruder/Dist. by Universal Press Syndicate
PROBABLY, BUT WE SHOULD NOTIFY THE "NEIGHBORHOOD KLANWATCH" JUST TO BE SURE.
THE WHAT?
THE "NEIGHBORHOOD KLANWATCH"! THIS NEIGHBORHOOD DOES HAVE A KLANWATCH, DOESN'T IT? I MEAN, THIS IS A RECENTLY DESEGREGATED COMMUNITY. SOMEONE HAS TO MONITOR THE SCOURGE OF HATE GROUPS.
6-7
www.boondocks.net
www.uexpress.com
(SIGH) ... YOU'RE GOING TO MAKE ME PAY FOR THIS MOVE FOR THE REST OF MY LIFE, AREN'T YOU?
OK, JOKE OVER. WHERE'S THE KLANWATCH?

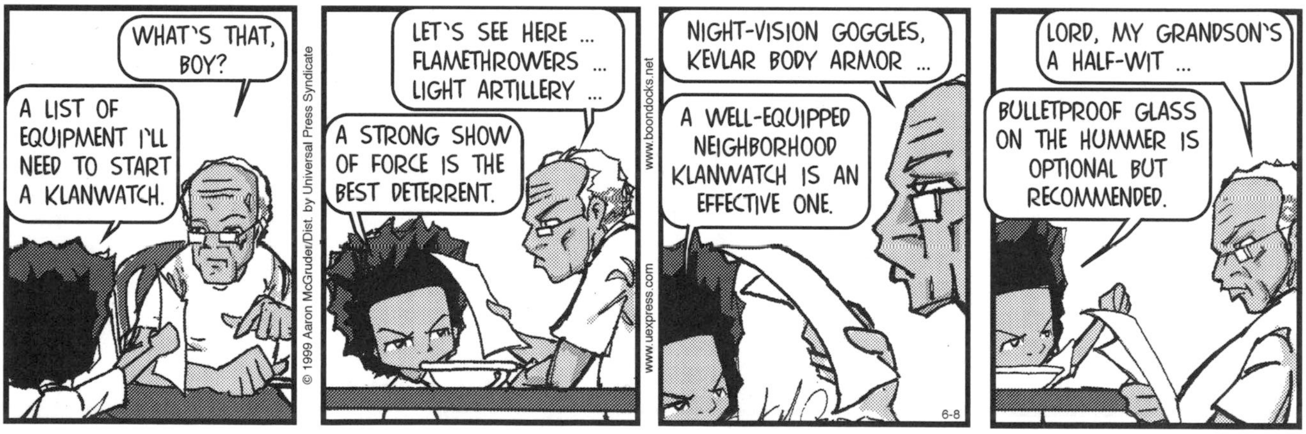
WHAT'S THAT, BOY?
A LIST OF EQUIPMENT I'LL NEED TO START A KLANWATCH.
© 1999 Aaron McGruder/Dist. by Universal Press Syndicate
LET'S SEE HERE ... FLAMETHROWERS ... LIGHT ARTILLERY ...
A STRONG SHOW OF FORCE IS THE BEST DETERRENT.
www.boondocks.net
www.uexpress.com
NIGHT-VISION GOGGLES, KEVLAR BODY ARMOR ...
A WELL-EQUIPPED NEIGHBORHOOD KLANWATCH IS AN EFFECTIVE ONE.
6-8
LORD, MY GRANDSON'S A HALF-WIT ...
BULLETPROOF GLASS ON THE HUMMER IS OPTIONAL BUT RECOMMENDED.

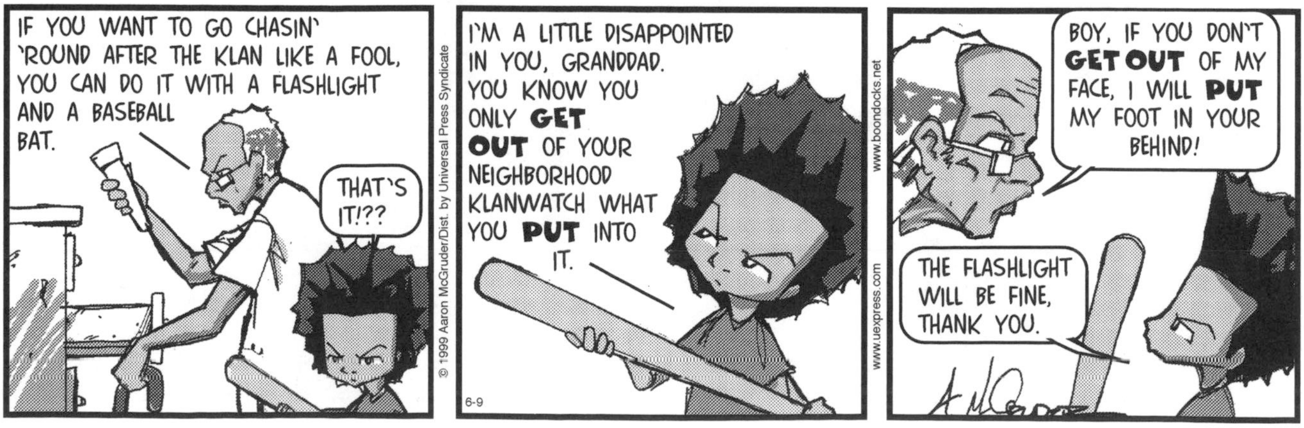
IF YOU WANT TO GO CHASIN' 'ROUND AFTER THE KLAN LIKE A FOOL, YOU CAN DO IT WITH A FLASHLIGHT AND A BASEBALL BAT.
THAT'S IT!??
© 1999 Aaron McGruder/Dist. by Universal Press Syndicate
I'M A LITTLE DISAPPOINTED IN YOU, GRANDDAD. YOU KNOW YOU ONLY GET OUT OF YOUR NEIGHBORHOOD KLANWATCH WHAT YOU PUT INTO IT.
6-9
www.boondocks.net
www.uexpress.com
BOY, IF YOU DON'T GET OUT OF MY FACE, I WILL PUT MY FOOT IN YOUR BEHIND!
THE FLASHLIGHT WILL BE FINE, THANK YOU.

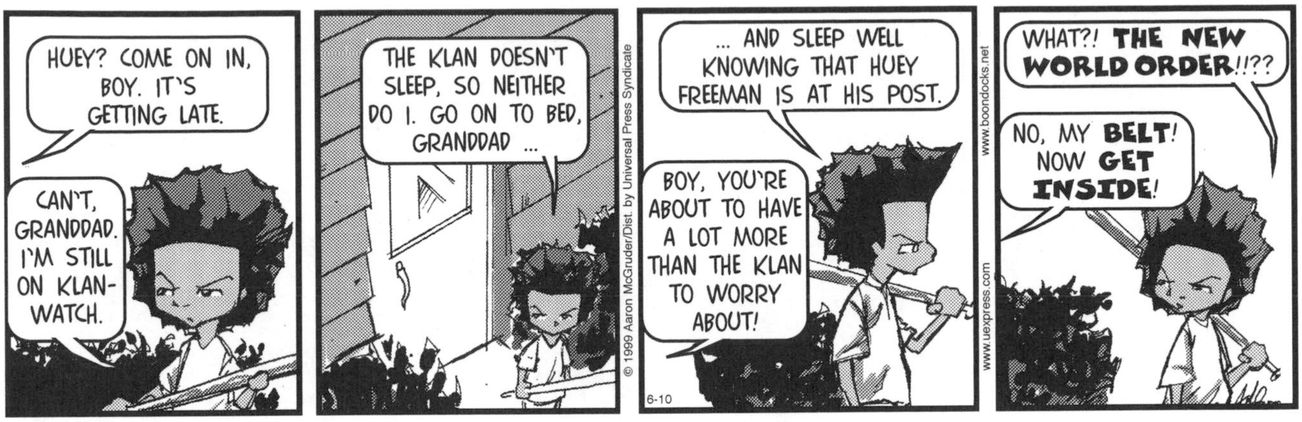
HUEY? COME ON IN, BOY. IT'S GETTING LATE.
CAN'T, GRANDDAD. I'M STILL ON KLAN-WATCH.
THE KLAN DOESN'T SLEEP, SO NEITHER DO I. GO ON TO BED, GRANDDAD ...
© 1999 Aaron McGruder/Dist. by Universal Press Syndicate
6-10
... AND SLEEP WELL KNOWING THAT HUEY FREEMAN IS AT HIS POST.
BOY, YOU'RE ABOUT TO HAVE A LOT MORE THAN THE KLAN TO WORRY ABOUT!
www.boondocks.net
www.uexpress.com
WHAT?! **THE NEW WORLD ORDER**!!??
NO, MY **BELT**! NOW **GET INSIDE**!

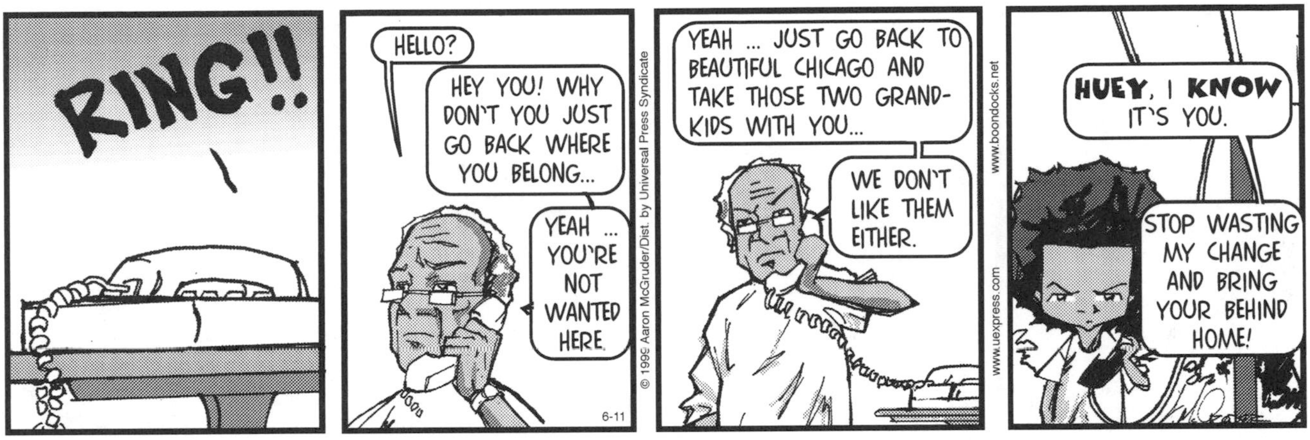
RING!!
HELLO?
HEY YOU! WHY DON'T YOU JUST GO BACK WHERE YOU BELONG...
YEAH ... YOU'RE NOT WANTED HERE.
6-11
© 1999 Aaron McGruder/Dist. by Universal Press Syndicate
YEAH ... JUST GO BACK TO BEAUTIFUL CHICAGO AND TAKE THOSE TWO GRAND-KIDS WITH YOU...
WE DON'T LIKE THEM EITHER.
www.boondocks.net
www.uexpress.com
HUEY, I **KNOW** IT'S YOU.
STOP WASTING MY CHANGE AND BRING YOUR BEHIND HOME!

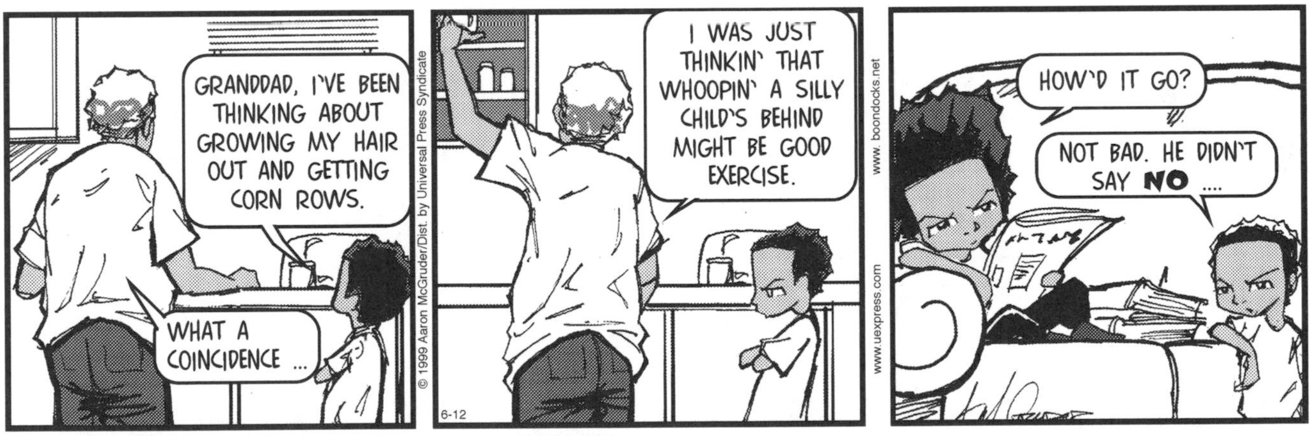
GRANDDAD, I'VE BEEN THINKING ABOUT GROWING MY HAIR OUT AND GETTING CORN ROWS.
WHAT A COINCIDENCE ...
© 1999 Aaron McGruder/Dist. by Universal Press Syndicate
6-12
I WAS JUST THINKIN' THAT WHOOPIN' A SILLY CHILD'S BEHIND MIGHT BE GOOD EXERCISE.
www. boondocks.net
www.uexpress.com
HOW'D IT GO?
NOT BAD. HE DIDN'T SAY **NO** ....

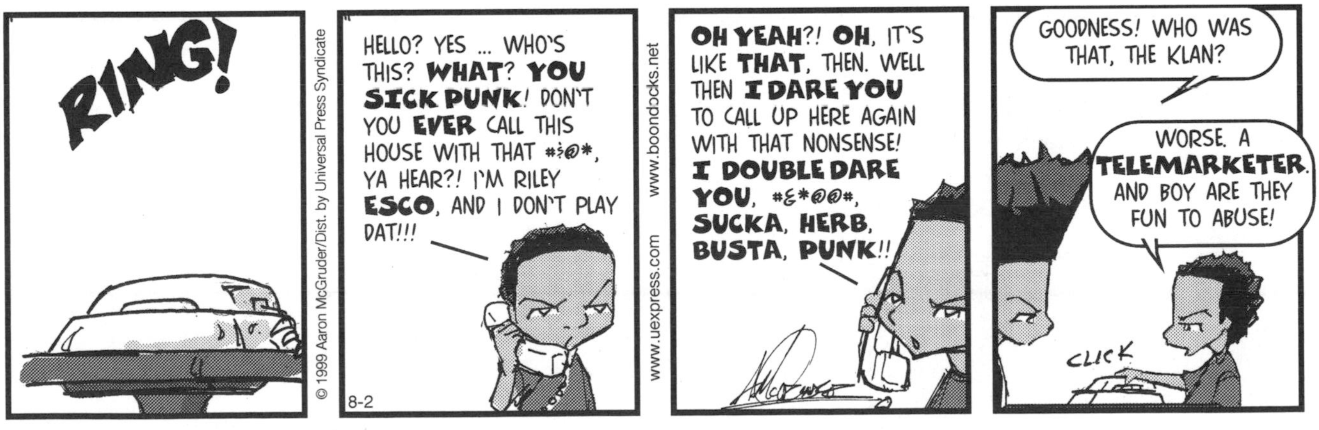
RING!
© 1999 Aaron McGruder/Dist. by Universal Press Syndicate
HELLO? YES ... WHO'S THIS? **WHAT**? **YOU SICK PUNK**! DON'T YOU **EVER** CALL THIS HOUSE WITH THAT #$@*, YA HEAR?! I'M RILEY **ESCO**, AND I DON'T PLAY DAT!!!
8-2
www.boondocks.net
www.uexpress.com
OH YEAH?! **OH**, IT'S LIKE **THAT**, THEN. WELL THEN **I DARE YOU** TO CALL UP HERE AGAIN WITH THAT NONSENSE! **I DOUBLE DARE YOU**, #&*@@#, **SUCKA**, **HERB**, **BUSTA**, **PUNK**!!
GOODNESS! WHO WAS THAT, THE KLAN?
WORSE. A **TELEMARKETER**. AND BOY ARE THEY FUN TO ABUSE!
CLICK

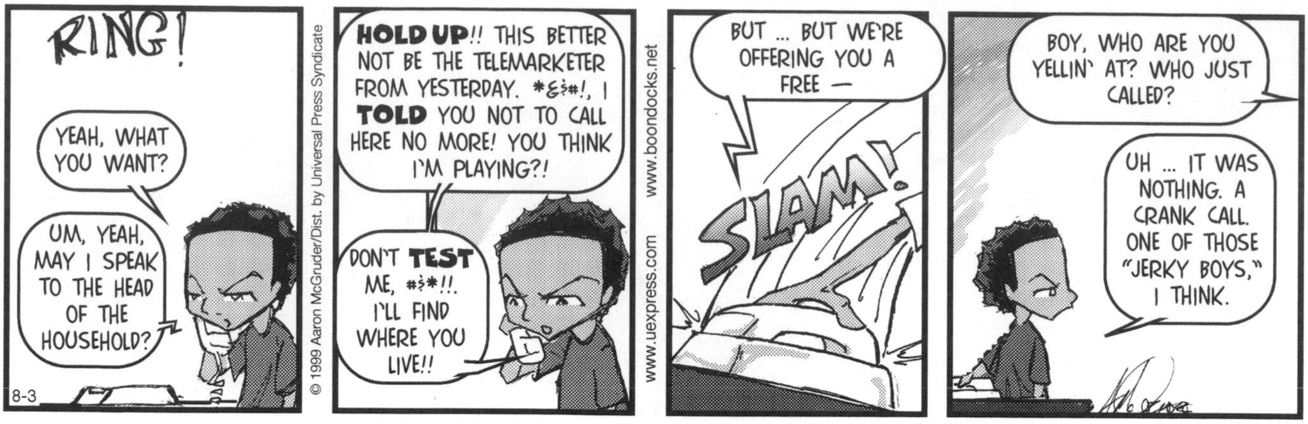
RING!
YEAH, WHAT YOU WANT?
UM, YEAH, MAY I SPEAK TO THE HEAD OF THE HOUSEHOLD?
8-3
HOLD UP!! THIS BETTER NOT BE THE TELEMARKETER FROM YESTERDAY. *&$#!, I TOLD YOU NOT TO CALL HERE NO MORE! YOU THINK I'M PLAYING?!
DON'T TEST ME, #$*!!. I'LL FIND WHERE YOU LIVE!!
BUT ... BUT WE'RE OFFERING YOU A FREE —
SLAM!
BOY, WHO ARE YOU YELLIN' AT? WHO JUST CALLED?
UH ... IT WAS NOTHING. A CRANK CALL. ONE OF THOSE "JERKY BOYS," I THINK.

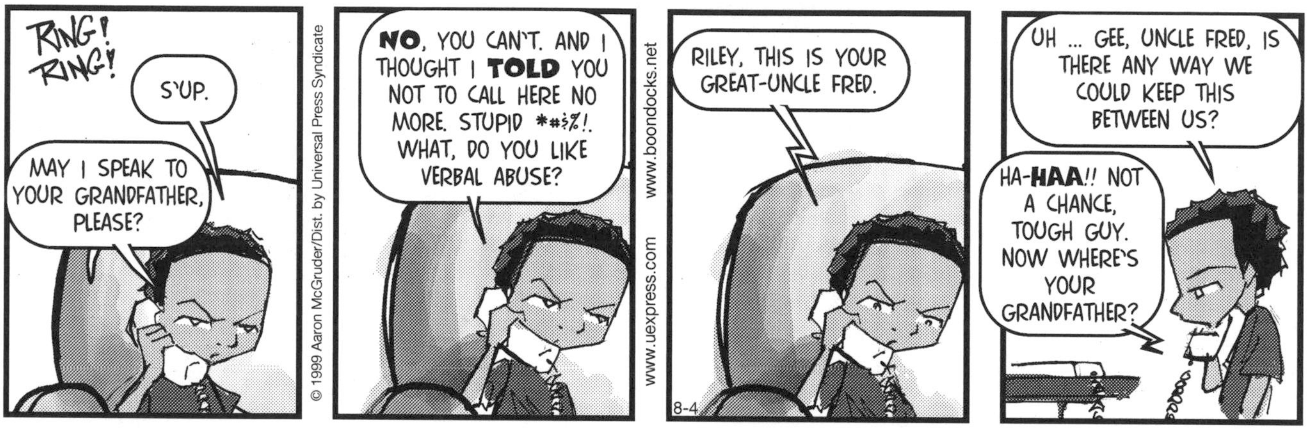
RING! RING!
S'UP.
MAY I SPEAK TO YOUR GRANDFATHER, PLEASE?
NO, YOU CAN'T. AND I THOUGHT I TOLD YOU NOT TO CALL HERE NO MORE. STUPID *#$%!. WHAT, DO YOU LIKE VERBAL ABUSE?
RILEY, THIS IS YOUR GREAT-UNCLE FRED.
8-4
UH ... GEE, UNCLE FRED, IS THERE ANY WAY WE COULD KEEP THIS BETWEEN US?
HA-HAA!! NOT A CHANCE, TOUGH GUY. NOW WHERE'S YOUR GRANDFATHER?

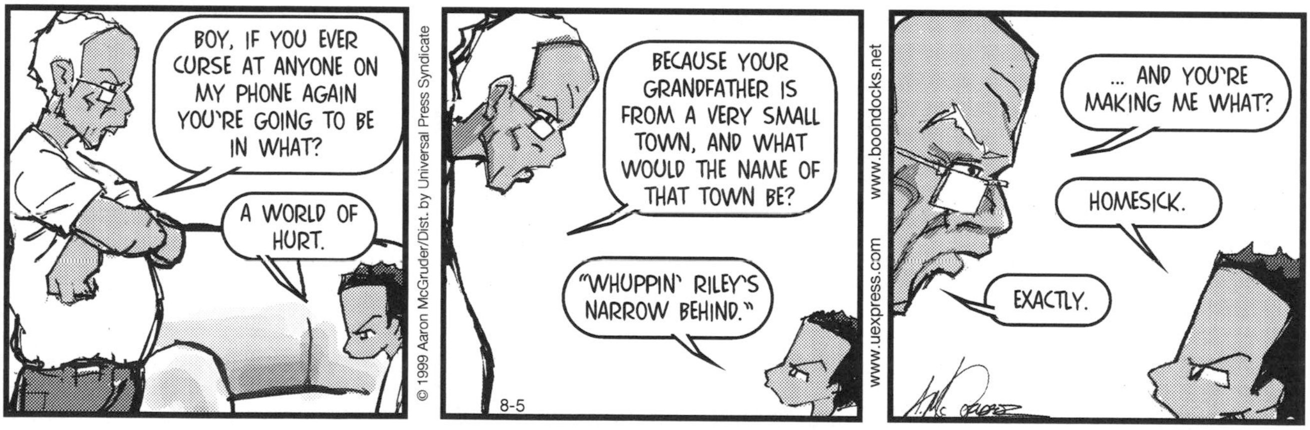
BOY, IF YOU EVER CURSE AT ANYONE ON MY PHONE AGAIN YOU'RE GOING TO BE IN WHAT?
A WORLD OF HURT.
BECAUSE YOUR GRANDFATHER IS FROM A VERY SMALL TOWN, AND WHAT WOULD THE NAME OF THAT TOWN BE?
"WHUPPIN' RILEY'S NARROW BEHIND."
8-5
... AND YOU'RE MAKING ME WHAT?
HOMESICK.
EXACTLY.

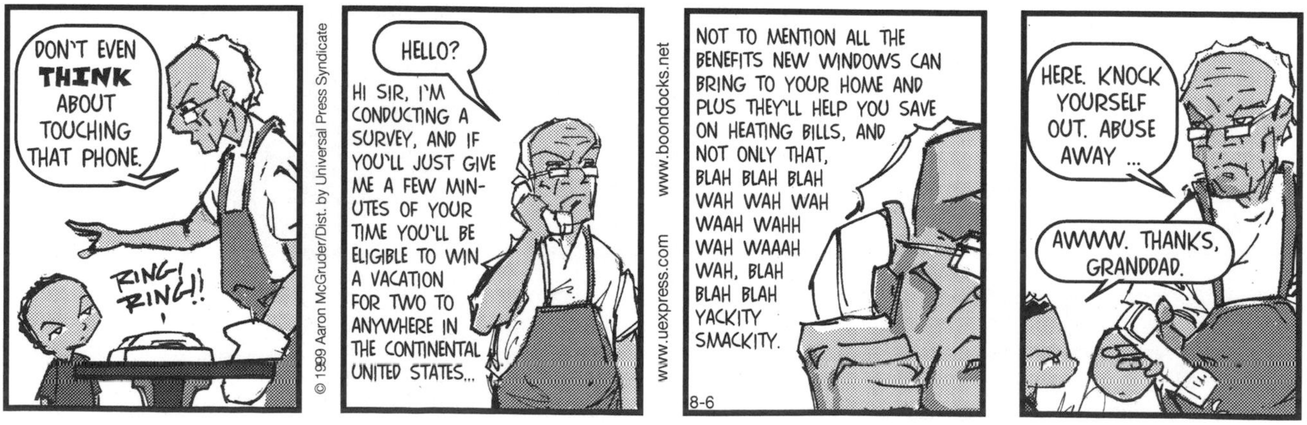
DON'T EVEN THINK ABOUT TOUCHING THAT PHONE.
RING! RING!!
HELLO?
HI SIR, I'M CONDUCTING A SURVEY, AND IF YOU'LL JUST GIVE ME A FEW MIN-UTES OF YOUR TIME YOU'LL BE ELIGIBLE TO WIN A VACATION FOR TWO TO ANYWHERE IN THE CONTINENTAL UNITED STATES...
NOT TO MENTION ALL THE BENEFITS NEW WINDOWS CAN BRING TO YOUR HOME AND PLUS THEY'LL HELP YOU SAVE ON HEATING BILLS, AND NOT ONLY THAT, BLAH BLAH BLAH WAH WAH WAH WAAH WAHH WAH WAAAH WAH, BLAH BLAH BLAH YACKITY SMACKITY.
8-6
HERE. KNOCK YOURSELF OUT. ABUSE AWAY ...
AWWW. THANKS, GRANDDAD.

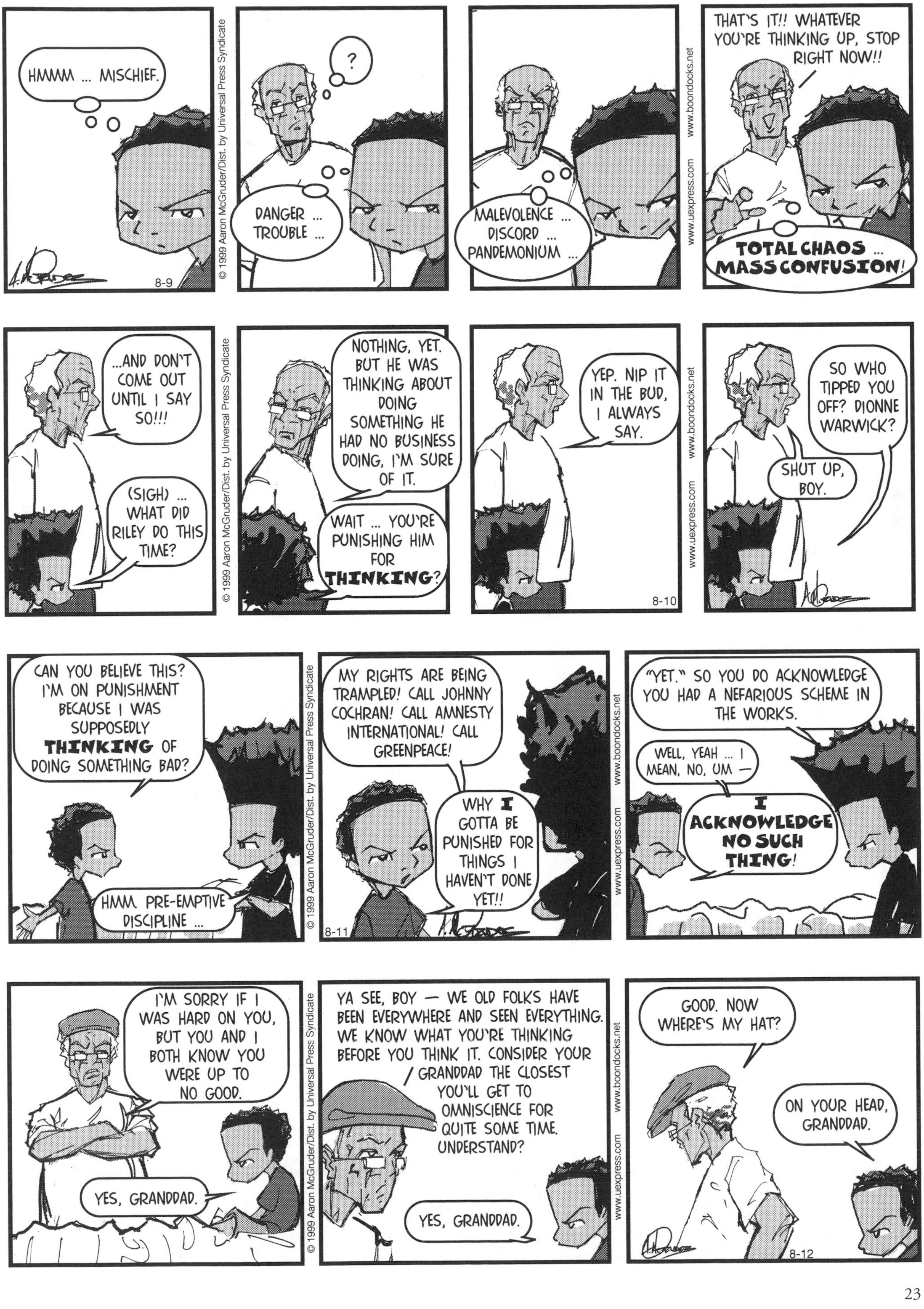
HMMM ... MISCHIEF.
8-9
© 1999 Aaron McGruder/Dist. by Universal Press Syndicate
?
DANGER ... TROUBLE ...
MALEVOLENCE ... DISCORD ... PANDEMONIUM ...
www.boondocks.net
www.uexpress.com
THAT'S IT!! WHATEVER YOU'RE THINKING UP, STOP RIGHT NOW!!
TOTAL CHAOS ... MASS CONFUSION!
...AND DON'T COME OUT UNTIL I SAY SO!!!
(SIGH) ... WHAT DID RILEY DO THIS TIME?
© 1999 Aaron McGruder/Dist. by Universal Press Syndicate
NOTHING, YET. BUT HE WAS THINKING ABOUT DOING SOMETHING HE HAD NO BUSINESS DOING, I'M SURE OF IT.
WAIT ... YOU'RE PUNISHING HIM FOR THINKING?
YEP. NIP IT IN THE BUD, I ALWAYS SAY.
8-10
www.boondocks.net
www.uexpress.com
SO WHO TIPPED YOU OFF? DIONNE WARWICK?
SHUT UP, BOY.
CAN YOU BELIEVE THIS? I'M ON PUNISHMENT BECAUSE I WAS SUPPOSEDLY THINKING OF DOING SOMETHING BAD?
HMM. PRE-EMPTIVE DISCIPLINE ...
© 1999 Aaron McGruder/Dist. by Universal Press Syndicate
8-11
MY RIGHTS ARE BEING TRAMPLED! CALL JOHNNY COCHRAN! CALL AMNESTY INTERNATIONAL! CALL GREENPEACE!
WHY I GOTTA BE PUNISHED FOR THINGS I HAVEN'T DONE YET!!
www.boondocks.net
www.uexpress.com
"YET." SO YOU DO ACKNOWLEDGE YOU HAD A NEFARIOUS SCHEME IN THE WORKS.
WELL, YEAH ... I MEAN, NO, UM —
I ACKNOWLEDGE NO SUCH THING!
I'M SORRY IF I WAS HARD ON YOU, BUT YOU AND I BOTH KNOW YOU WERE UP TO NO GOOD.
YES, GRANDDAD.
© 1999 Aaron McGruder/Dist. by Universal Press Syndicate
YA SEE, BOY — WE OLD FOLKS HAVE BEEN EVERYWHERE AND SEEN EVERYTHING. WE KNOW WHAT YOU'RE THINKING BEFORE YOU THINK IT. CONSIDER YOUR GRANDDAD THE CLOSEST YOU'LL GET TO OMNISCIENCE FOR QUITE SOME TIME. UNDERSTAND?
YES, GRANDDAD.
www.boondocks.net
www.uexpress.com
GOOD. NOW WHERE'S MY HAT?
ON YOUR HEAD, GRANDDAD.
8-12

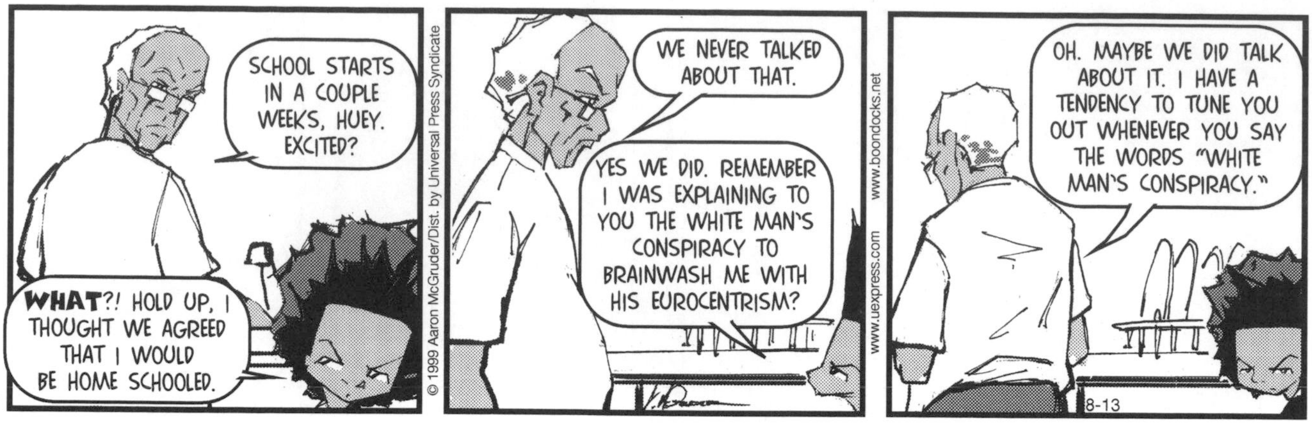
SCHOOL STARTS IN A COUPLE WEEKS, HUEY. EXCITED?
WHAT?! HOLD UP, I THOUGHT WE AGREED THAT I WOULD BE HOME SCHOOLED.
© 1999 Aaron McGruder/Dist. by Universal Press Syndicate
WE NEVER TALKED ABOUT THAT.
YES WE DID. REMEMBER I WAS EXPLAINING TO YOU THE WHITE MAN'S CONSPIRACY TO BRAINWASH ME WITH HIS EUROCENTRISM?
www.uexpress.com
www.boondocks.net
OH. MAYBE WE DID TALK ABOUT IT. I HAVE A TENDENCY TO TUNE YOU OUT WHENEVER YOU SAY THE WORDS "WHITE MAN'S CONSPIRACY."
8-13

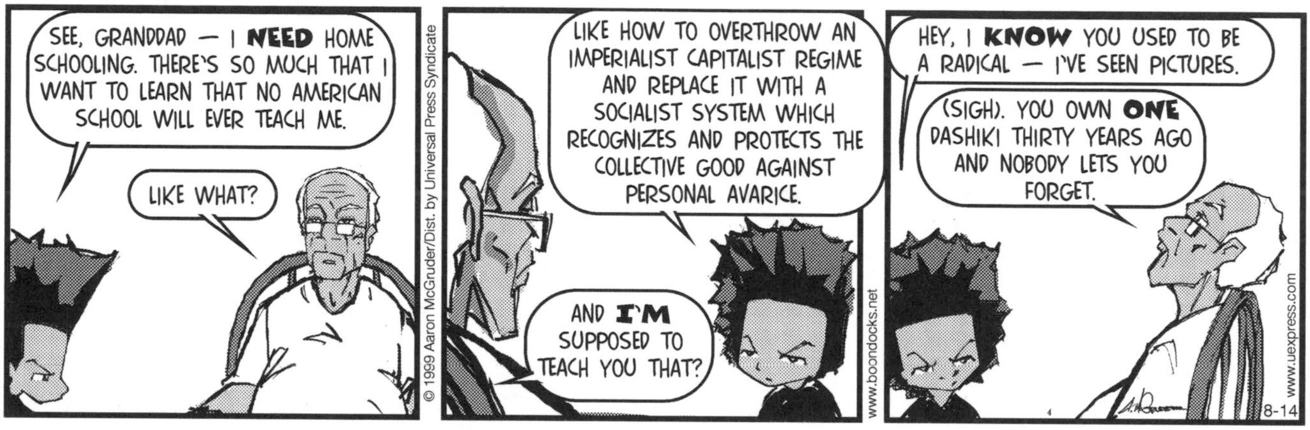
SEE, GRANDDAD — I NEED HOME SCHOOLING. THERE'S SO MUCH THAT I WANT TO LEARN THAT NO AMERICAN SCHOOL WILL EVER TEACH ME.
LIKE WHAT?
© 1999 Aaron McGruder/Dist. by Universal Press Syndicate
LIKE HOW TO OVERTHROW AN IMPERIALIST CAPITALIST REGIME AND REPLACE IT WITH A SOCIALIST SYSTEM WHICH RECOGNIZES AND PROTECTS THE COLLECTIVE GOOD AGAINST PERSONAL AVARICE.
AND I'M SUPPOSED TO TEACH YOU THAT?
www.boondocks.net
HEY, I KNOW YOU USED TO BE A RADICAL — I'VE SEEN PICTURES.
(SIGH). YOU OWN ONE DASHIKI THIRTY YEARS AGO AND NOBODY LETS YOU FORGET.
www.uexpress.com
8-14

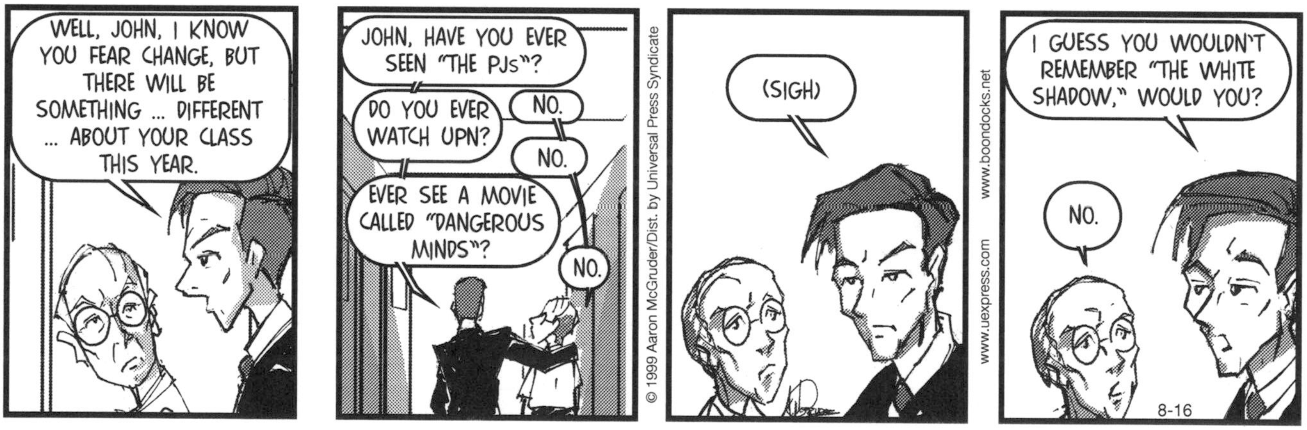
WELL, JOHN, I KNOW YOU FEAR CHANGE, BUT THERE WILL BE SOMETHING ... DIFFERENT ... ABOUT YOUR CLASS THIS YEAR.
JOHN, HAVE YOU EVER SEEN "THE PJs"?
NO.
DO YOU EVER WATCH UPN?
NO.
EVER SEE A MOVIE CALLED "DANGEROUS MINDS"?
NO.
© 1999 Aaron McGruder/Dist. by Universal Press Syndicate
(SIGH)
www.uexpress.com
www.boondocks.net
I GUESS YOU WOULDN'T REMEMBER "THE WHITE SHADOW," WOULD YOU?
NO.
8-16

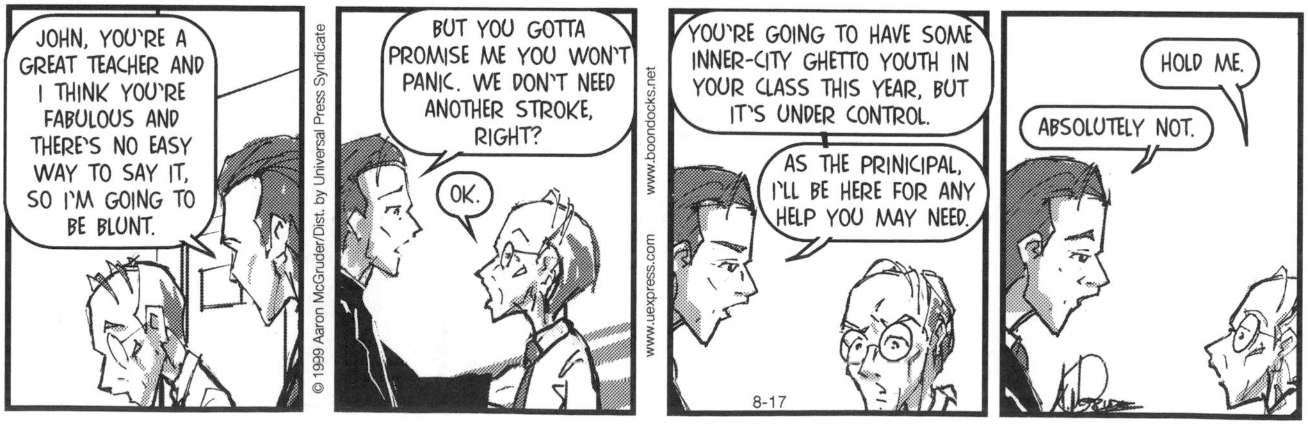
JOHN, YOU'RE A GREAT TEACHER AND I THINK YOU'RE FABULOUS AND THERE'S NO EASY WAY TO SAY IT, SO I'M GOING TO BE BLUNT.
© 1999 Aaron McGruder/Dist. by Universal Press Syndicate
BUT YOU GOTTA PROMISE ME YOU WON'T PANIC. WE DON'T NEED ANOTHER STROKE, RIGHT?
OK.
www.boondocks.net
www.uexpress.com
YOU'RE GOING TO HAVE SOME INNER-CITY GHETTO YOUTH IN YOUR CLASS THIS YEAR, BUT IT'S UNDER CONTROL.
AS THE PRINCIPAL, I'LL BE HERE FOR ANY HELP YOU MAY NEED.
8-17
HOLD ME.
ABSOLUTELY NOT.

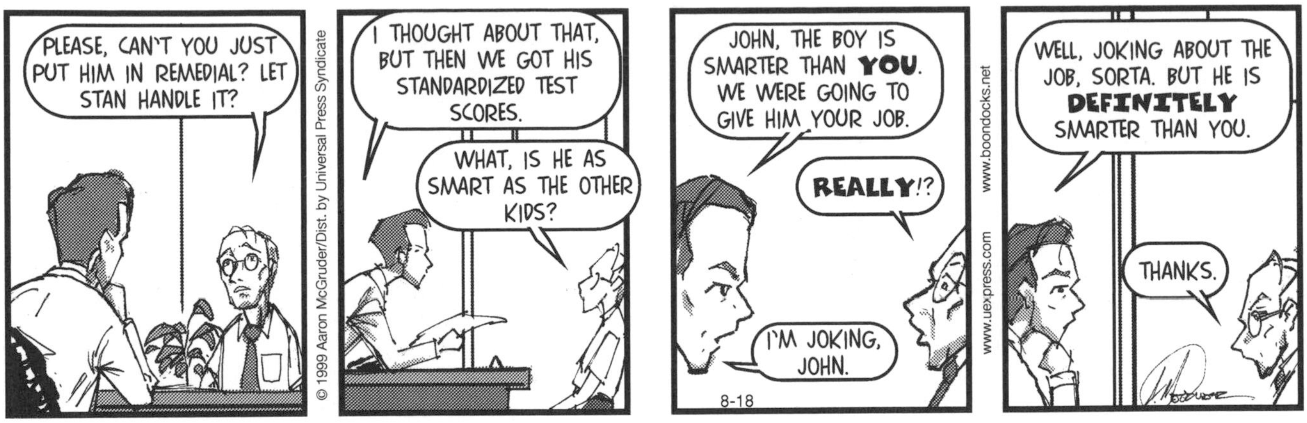

PLEASE, CAN'T YOU JUST PUT HIM IN REMEDIAL? LET STAN HANDLE IT?
© 1999 Aaron McGruder/Dist. by Universal Press Syndicate
I THOUGHT ABOUT THAT, BUT THEN WE GOT HIS STANDARDIZED TEST SCORES.
WHAT, IS HE AS SMART AS THE OTHER KIDS?
JOHN, THE BOY IS SMARTER THAN YOU. WE WERE GOING TO GIVE HIM YOUR JOB.
REALLY!?
I'M JOKING, JOHN.
8-18
www.uexpress.com www.boondocks.net
WELL, JOKING ABOUT THE JOB, SORTA. BUT HE IS DEFINITELY SMARTER THAN YOU.
THANKS.

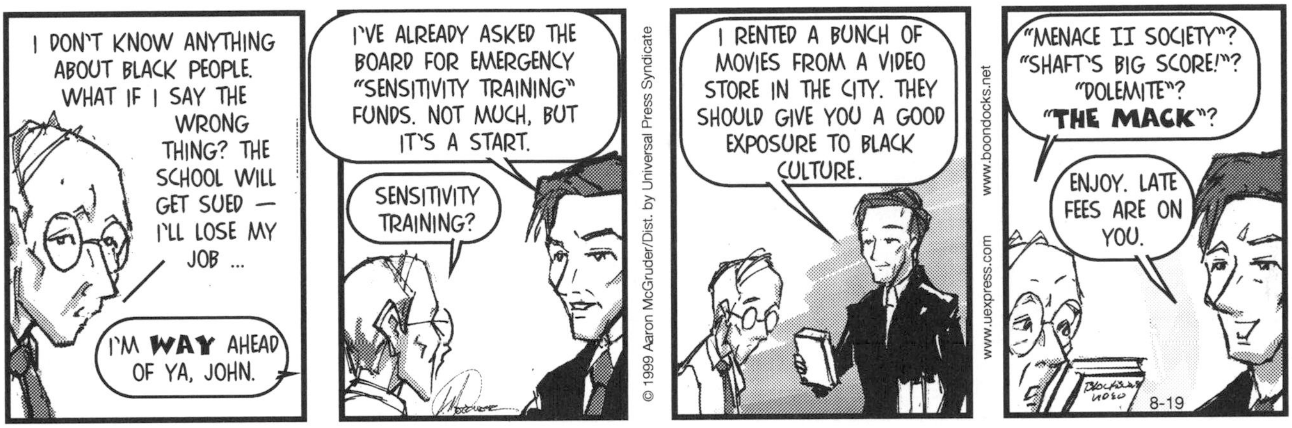

I DON'T KNOW ANYTHING ABOUT BLACK PEOPLE. WHAT IF I SAY THE WRONG THING? THE SCHOOL WILL GET SUED — I'LL LOSE MY JOB ...
I'M WAY AHEAD OF YA, JOHN.
I'VE ALREADY ASKED THE BOARD FOR EMERGENCY "SENSITIVITY TRAINING" FUNDS. NOT MUCH, BUT IT'S A START.
SENSITIVITY TRAINING?
© 1999 Aaron McGruder/Dist. by Universal Press Syndicate
I RENTED A BUNCH OF MOVIES FROM A VIDEO STORE IN THE CITY. THEY SHOULD GIVE YOU A GOOD EXPOSURE TO BLACK CULTURE.
www.uexpress.com www.boondocks.net
"MENACE II SOCIETY"? "SHAFT'S BIG SCORE!"? "DOLEMITE"? "THE MACK"?
ENJOY. LATE FEES ARE ON YOU.
8-19

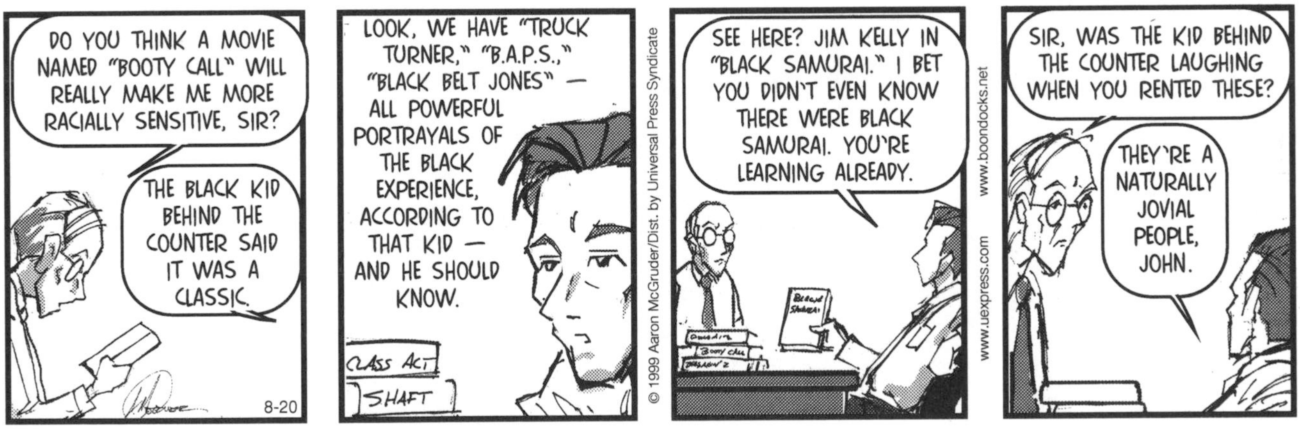

DO YOU THINK A MOVIE NAMED "BOOTY CALL" WILL REALLY MAKE ME MORE RACIALLY SENSITIVE, SIR?
THE BLACK KID BEHIND THE COUNTER SAID IT WAS A CLASSIC.
8-20
LOOK, WE HAVE "TRUCK TURNER," "B.A.P.S.," "BLACK BELT JONES" — ALL POWERFUL PORTRAYALS OF THE BLACK EXPERIENCE, ACCORDING TO THAT KID — AND HE SHOULD KNOW.
CLASS ACT
SHAFT
© 1999 Aaron McGruder/Dist. by Universal Press Syndicate
SEE HERE? JIM KELLY IN "BLACK SAMURAI." I BET YOU DIDN'T EVEN KNOW THERE WERE BLACK SAMURAI. YOU'RE LEARNING ALREADY.
www.uexpress.com www.boondocks.net
SIR, WAS THE KID BEHIND THE COUNTER LAUGHING WHEN YOU RENTED THESE?
THEY'RE A NATURALLY JOVIAL PEOPLE, JOHN.

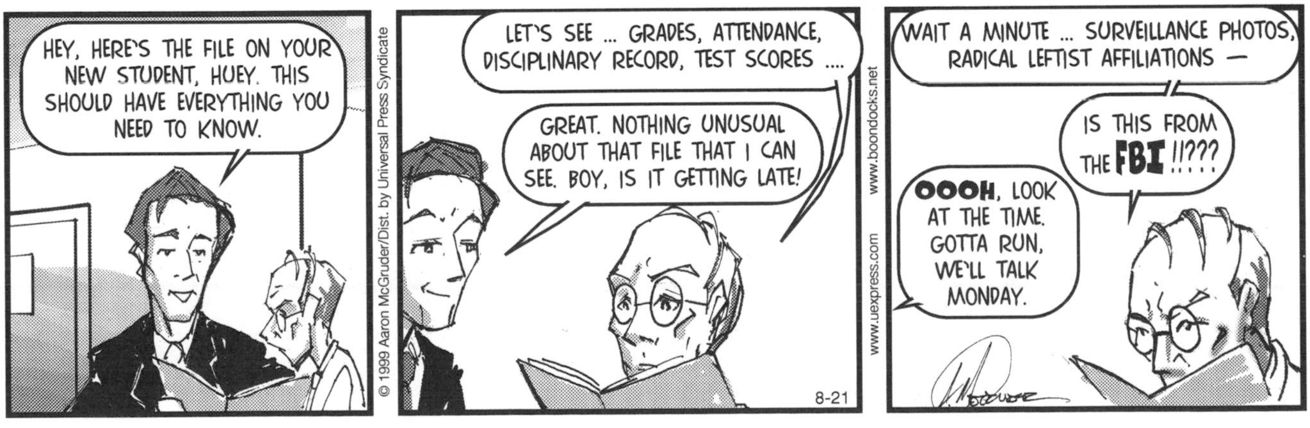

HEY, HERE'S THE FILE ON YOUR NEW STUDENT, HUEY. THIS SHOULD HAVE EVERYTHING YOU NEED TO KNOW.
© 1999 Aaron McGruder/Dist. by Universal Press Syndicate
LET'S SEE ... GRADES, ATTENDANCE, DISCIPLINARY RECORD, TEST SCORES ....
GREAT. NOTHING UNUSUAL ABOUT THAT FILE THAT I CAN SEE. BOY, IS IT GETTING LATE!
8-21
www.uexpress.com www.boondocks.net
WAIT A MINUTE ... SURVEILLANCE PHOTOS, RADICAL LEFTIST AFFILIATIONS —
IS THIS FROM THE FBI !!???
OOOH, LOOK AT THE TIME. GOTTA RUN, WE'LL TALK MONDAY.

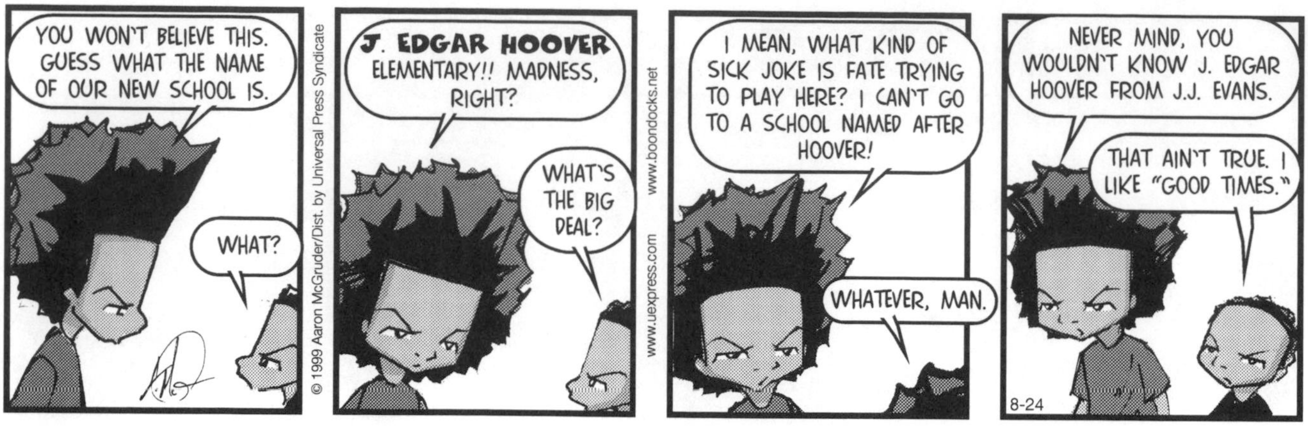
YOU WON'T BELIEVE THIS. GUESS WHAT THE NAME OF OUR NEW SCHOOL IS.
WHAT?
© 1999 Aaron McGruder/Dist. by Universal Press Syndicate
J. EDGAR HOOVER ELEMENTARY!! MADNESS, RIGHT?
WHAT'S THE BIG DEAL?
www.boondocks.net
www.uexpress.com
I MEAN, WHAT KIND OF SICK JOKE IS FATE TRYING TO PLAY HERE? I CAN'T GO TO A SCHOOL NAMED AFTER HOOVER!
WHATEVER, MAN.
NEVER MIND, YOU WOULDN'T KNOW J. EDGAR HOOVER FROM J.J. EVANS.
THAT AIN'T TRUE. I LIKE "GOOD TIMES."
8-24

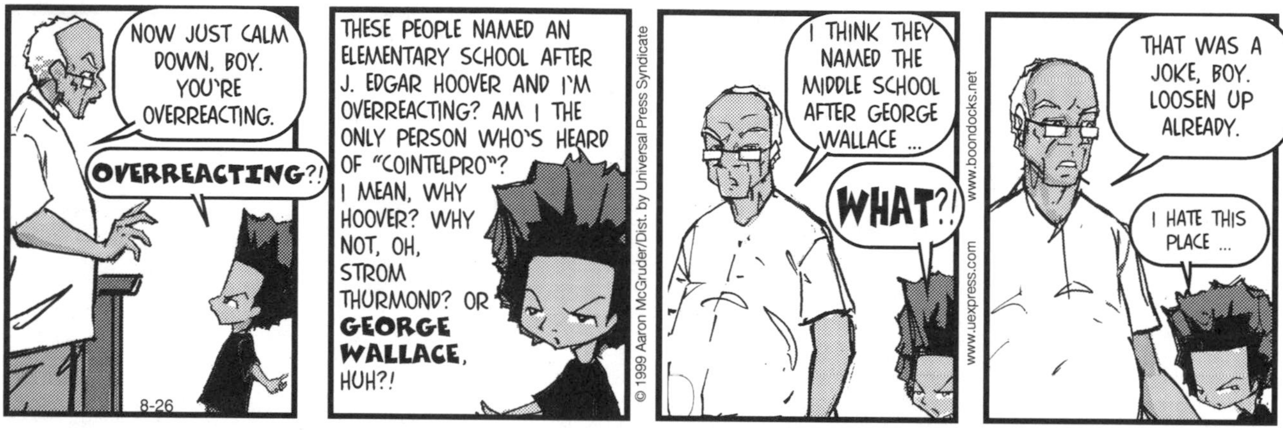
NOW JUST CALM DOWN, BOY. YOU'RE OVERREACTING.
OVERREACTING?!
8-26
THESE PEOPLE NAMED AN ELEMENTARY SCHOOL AFTER J. EDGAR HOOVER AND I'M OVERREACTING? AM I THE ONLY PERSON WHO'S HEARD OF "COINTELPRO"? I MEAN, WHY HOOVER? WHY NOT, OH, STROM THURMOND? OR GEORGE WALLACE, HUH?!
© 1999 Aaron McGruder/Dist. by Universal Press Syndicate
I THINK THEY NAMED THE MIDDLE SCHOOL AFTER GEORGE WALLACE ...
WHAT?!
www.boondocks.net
www.uexpress.com
THAT WAS A JOKE, BOY. LOOSEN UP ALREADY.
I HATE THIS PLACE ...

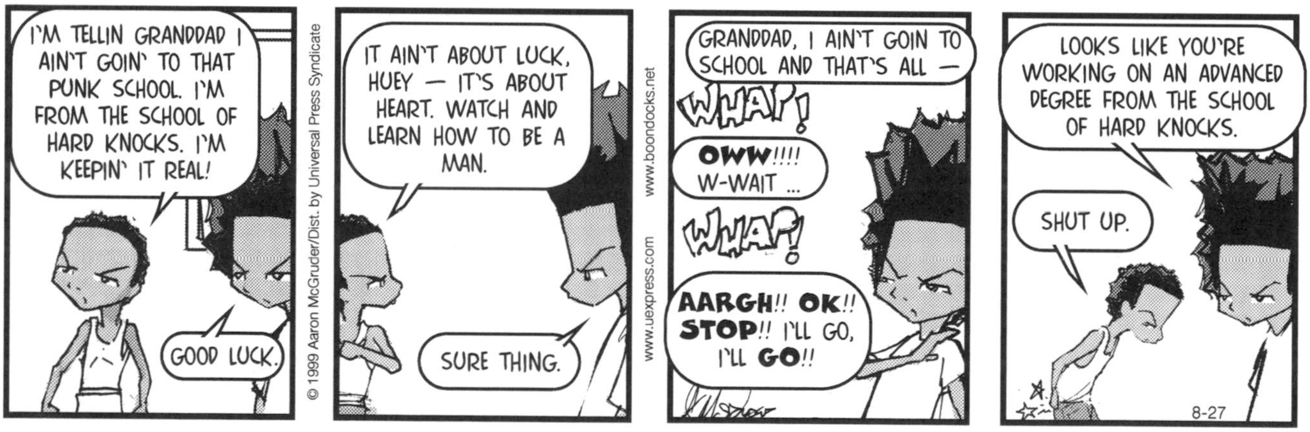
I'M TELLIN GRANDDAD I AIN'T GOIN' TO THAT PUNK SCHOOL. I'M FROM THE SCHOOL OF HARD KNOCKS. I'M KEEPIN' IT REAL!
GOOD LUCK.
© 1999 Aaron McGruder/Dist. by Universal Press Syndicate
IT AIN'T ABOUT LUCK, HUEY — IT'S ABOUT HEART. WATCH AND LEARN HOW TO BE A MAN.
SURE THING.
www.boondocks.net
www.uexpress.com
GRANDDAD, I AIN'T GOIN TO SCHOOL AND THAT'S ALL —
WHAP!
OWW!!!! W-WAIT ...
WHAP!
AARGH!! OK!! STOP!! I'LL GO, I'LL GO!!
LOOKS LIKE YOU'RE WORKING ON AN ADVANCED DEGREE FROM THE SCHOOL OF HARD KNOCKS.
SHUT UP.
8-27

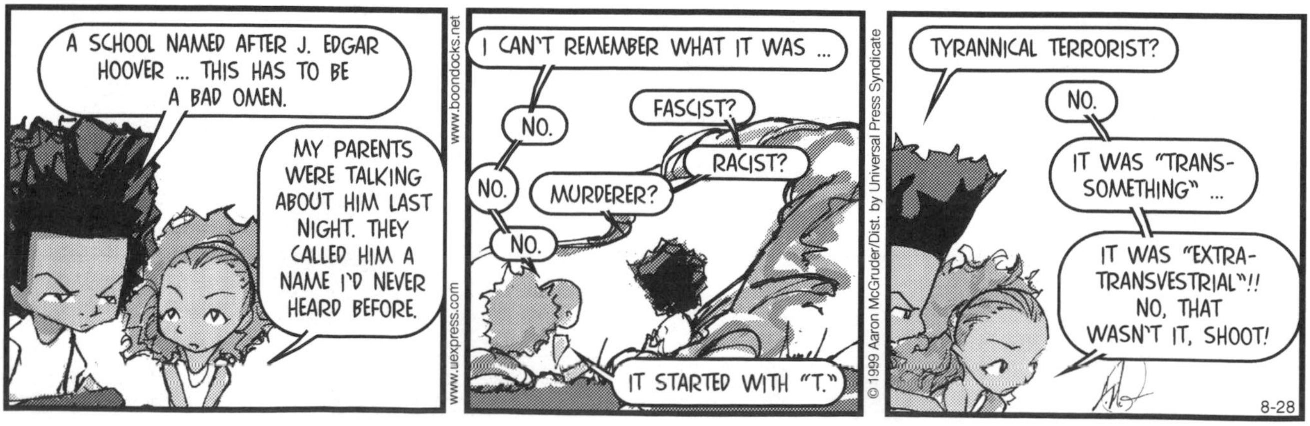
A SCHOOL NAMED AFTER J. EDGAR HOOVER ... THIS HAS TO BE A BAD OMEN.
MY PARENTS WERE TALKING ABOUT HIM LAST NIGHT. THEY CALLED HIM A NAME I'D NEVER HEARD BEFORE.
www.boondocks.net
www.uexpress.com
I CAN'T REMEMBER WHAT IT WAS ...
NO.
FASCIST?
RACIST?
NO.
MURDERER?
NO.
IT STARTED WITH "T."
© 1999 Aaron McGruder/Dist. by Universal Press Syndicate
TYRANNICAL TERRORIST?
NO.
IT WAS "TRANS-SOMETHING" ...
IT WAS "EXTRA-TRANSVESTRIAL"!! NO, THAT WASN'T IT, SHOOT!
8-28

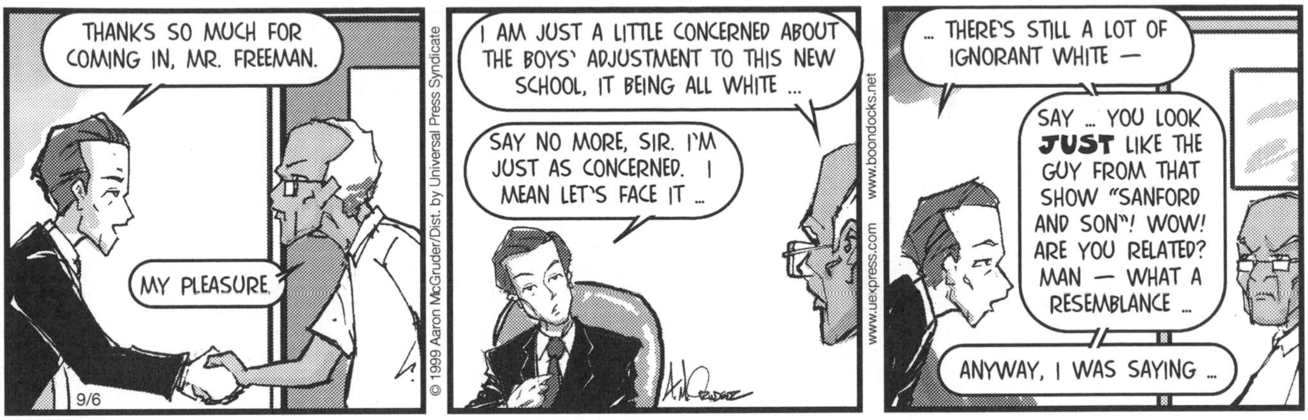
THANKS SO MUCH FOR COMING IN, MR. FREEMAN.
MY PLEASURE.
9/6
© 1999 Aaron McGruder/Dist. by Universal Press Syndicate
I AM JUST A LITTLE CONCERNED ABOUT THE BOYS' ADJUSTMENT TO THIS NEW SCHOOL, IT BEING ALL WHITE ...
SAY NO MORE, SIR. I'M JUST AS CONCERNED. I MEAN LET'S FACE IT ...
www.boondocks.net www.uexpress.com
... THERE'S STILL A LOT OF IGNORANT WHITE —
SAY ... YOU LOOK **JUST** LIKE THE GUY FROM THAT SHOW "SANFORD AND SON"! WOW! ARE YOU RELATED? MAN — WHAT A RESEMBLANCE ...
ANYWAY, I WAS SAYING ...

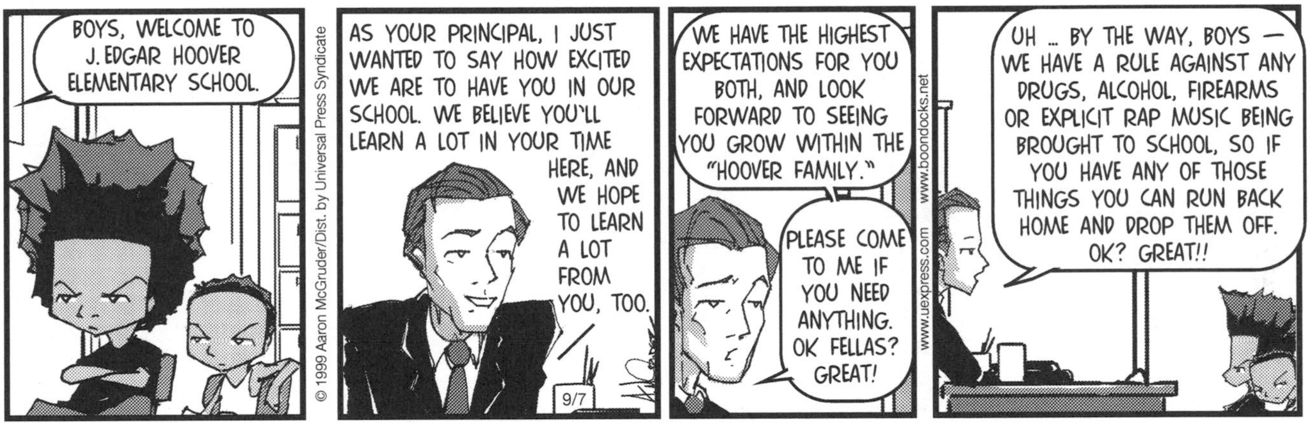
BOYS, WELCOME TO J. EDGAR HOOVER ELEMENTARY SCHOOL.
© 1999 Aaron McGruder/Dist. by Universal Press Syndicate
AS YOUR PRINCIPAL, I JUST WANTED TO SAY HOW EXCITED WE ARE TO HAVE YOU IN OUR SCHOOL. WE BELIEVE YOU'LL LEARN A LOT IN YOUR TIME HERE, AND WE HOPE TO LEARN A LOT FROM YOU, TOO.
9/7
WE HAVE THE HIGHEST EXPECTATIONS FOR YOU BOTH, AND LOOK FORWARD TO SEEING YOU GROW WITHIN THE "HOOVER FAMILY."
PLEASE COME TO ME IF YOU NEED ANYTHING. OK FELLAS? GREAT!
www.boondocks.net www.uexpress.com
UH ... BY THE WAY, BOYS — WE HAVE A RULE AGAINST ANY DRUGS, ALCOHOL, FIREARMS OR EXPLICIT RAP MUSIC BEING BROUGHT TO SCHOOL, SO IF YOU HAVE ANY OF THOSE THINGS YOU CAN RUN BACK HOME AND DROP THEM OFF. OK? GREAT!!

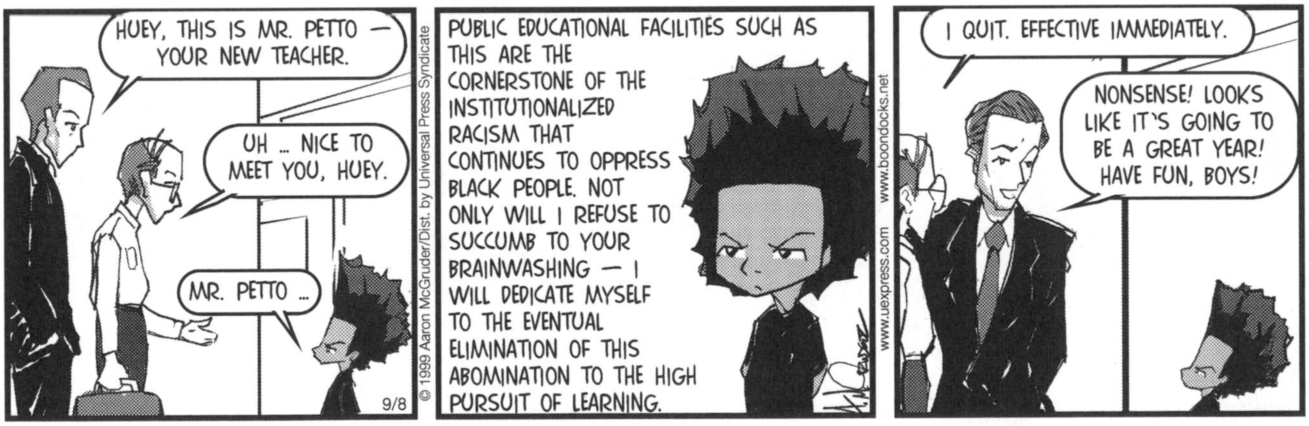
HUEY, THIS IS MR. PETTO — YOUR NEW TEACHER.
UH ... NICE TO MEET YOU, HUEY.
MR. PETTO ...
9/8
© 1999 Aaron McGruder/Dist. by Universal Press Syndicate
PUBLIC EDUCATIONAL FACILITIES SUCH AS THIS ARE THE CORNERSTONE OF THE INSTITUTIONALIZED RACISM THAT CONTINUES TO OPPRESS BLACK PEOPLE. NOT ONLY WILL I REFUSE TO SUCCUMB TO YOUR BRAINWASHING — I WILL DEDICATE MYSELF TO THE EVENTUAL ELIMINATION OF THIS ABOMINATION TO THE HIGH PURSUIT OF LEARNING.
www.boondocks.net www.uexpress.com
I QUIT. EFFECTIVE IMMEDIATELY.
NONSENSE! LOOKS LIKE IT'S GOING TO BE A GREAT YEAR! HAVE FUN, BOYS!

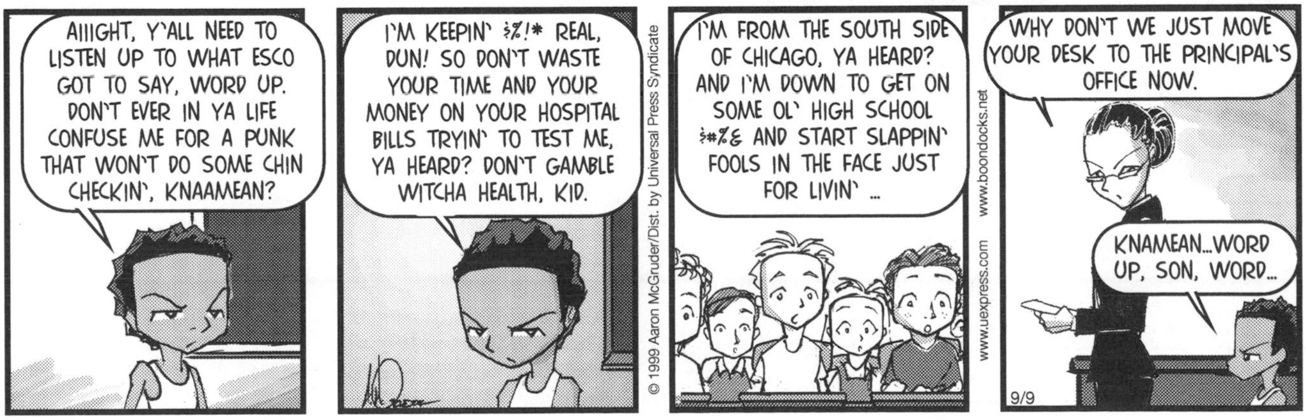
AIIIGHT, Y'ALL NEED TO LISTEN UP TO WHAT ESCO GOT TO SAY, WORD UP. DON'T EVER IN YA LIFE CONFUSE ME FOR A PUNK THAT WON'T DO SOME CHIN CHECKIN', KNAAMEAN?
I'M KEEPIN' $%!* REAL, DUN! SO DON'T WASTE YOUR TIME AND YOUR MONEY ON YOUR HOSPITAL BILLS TRYIN' TO TEST ME, YA HEARD? DON'T GAMBLE WITCHA HEALTH, KID.
© 1999 Aaron McGruder/Dist. by Universal Press Syndicate
I'M FROM THE SOUTH SIDE OF CHICAGO, YA HEARD? AND I'M DOWN TO GET ON SOME OL' HIGH SCHOOL $#%& AND START SLAPPIN' FOOLS IN THE FACE JUST FOR LIVIN' ...
www.boondocks.net www.uexpress.com
WHY DON'T WE JUST MOVE YOUR DESK TO THE PRINCIPAL'S OFFICE NOW.
KNAMEAN...WORD UP, SON, WORD...
9/9

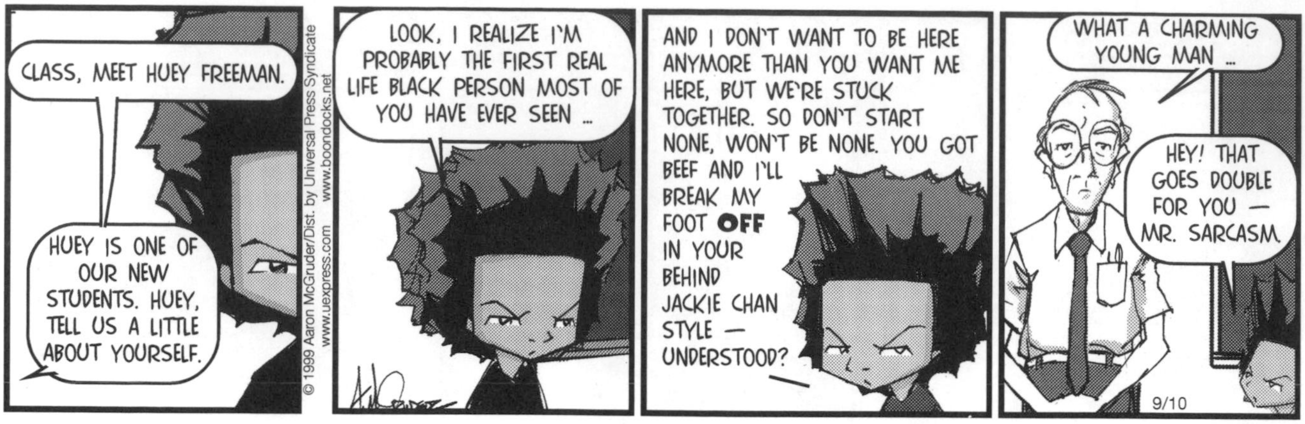
CLASS, MEET HUEY FREEMAN.
HUEY IS ONE OF OUR NEW STUDENTS. HUEY, TELL US A LITTLE ABOUT YOURSELF.
© 1999 Aaron McGruder/Dist. by Universal Press Syndicate www.uexpress.com www.boondocks.net
LOOK, I REALIZE I'M PROBABLY THE FIRST REAL LIFE BLACK PERSON MOST OF YOU HAVE EVER SEEN ...
AND I DON'T WANT TO BE HERE ANYMORE THAN YOU WANT ME HERE, BUT WE'RE STUCK TOGETHER. SO DON'T START NONE, WON'T BE NONE. YOU GOT BEEF AND I'LL BREAK MY FOOT OFF IN YOUR BEHIND JACKIE CHAN STYLE — UNDERSTOOD?
WHAT A CHARMING YOUNG MAN ...
HEY! THAT GOES DOUBLE FOR YOU — MR. SARCASM.
9/10

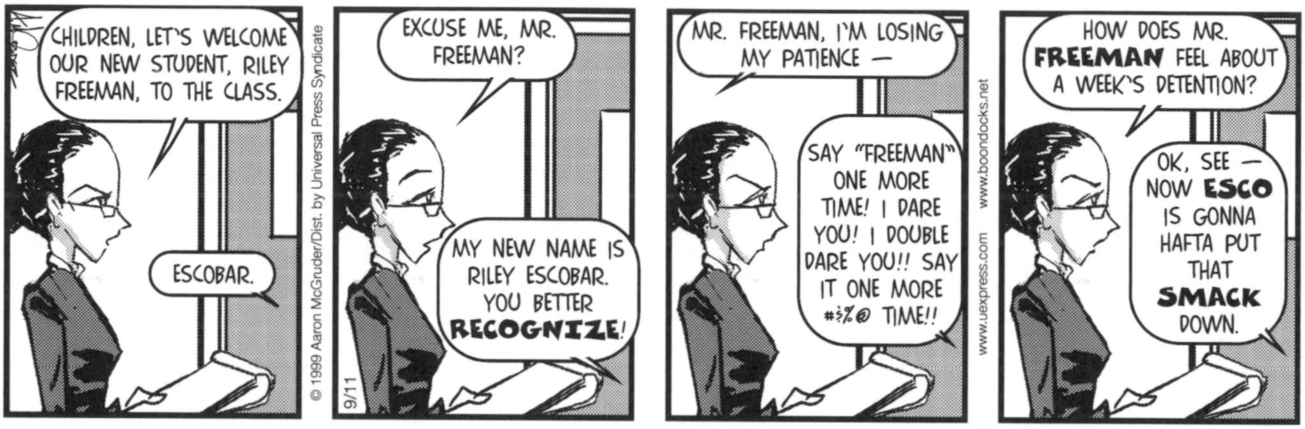
CHILDREN, LET'S WELCOME OUR NEW STUDENT, RILEY FREEMAN, TO THE CLASS.
ESCOBAR.
© 1999 Aaron McGruder/Dist. by Universal Press Syndicate
9/11
EXCUSE ME, MR. FREEMAN?
MY NEW NAME IS RILEY ESCOBAR. YOU BETTER RECOGNIZE!
MR. FREEMAN, I'M LOSING MY PATIENCE —
SAY "FREEMAN" ONE MORE TIME! I DARE YOU! I DOUBLE DARE YOU!! SAY IT ONE MORE #$%@ TIME!!
www.uexpress.com www.boondocks.net
HOW DOES MR. FREEMAN FEEL ABOUT A WEEK'S DETENTION?
OK, SEE — NOW ESCO IS GONNA HAFTA PUT THAT SMACK DOWN.

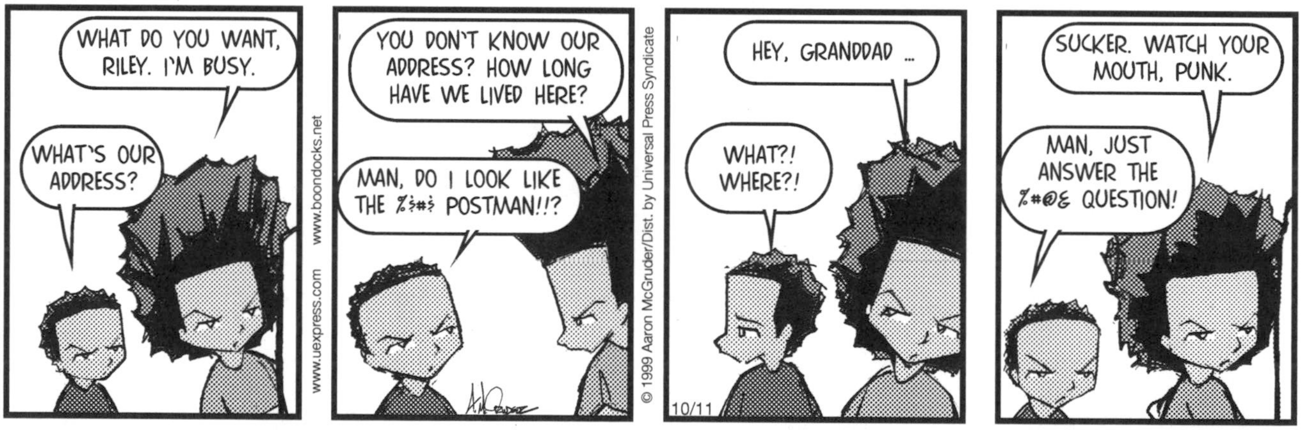
WHAT DO YOU WANT, RILEY. I'M BUSY.
WHAT'S OUR ADDRESS?
www.uexpress.com www.boondocks.net
YOU DON'T KNOW OUR ADDRESS? HOW LONG HAVE WE LIVED HERE?
MAN, DO I LOOK LIKE THE %$#$ POSTMAN!!?
© 1999 Aaron McGruder/Dist. by Universal Press Syndicate
10/11
HEY, GRANDDAD ...
WHAT?! WHERE?!
SUCKER. WATCH YOUR MOUTH, PUNK.
MAN, JUST ANSWER THE %#@& QUESTION!

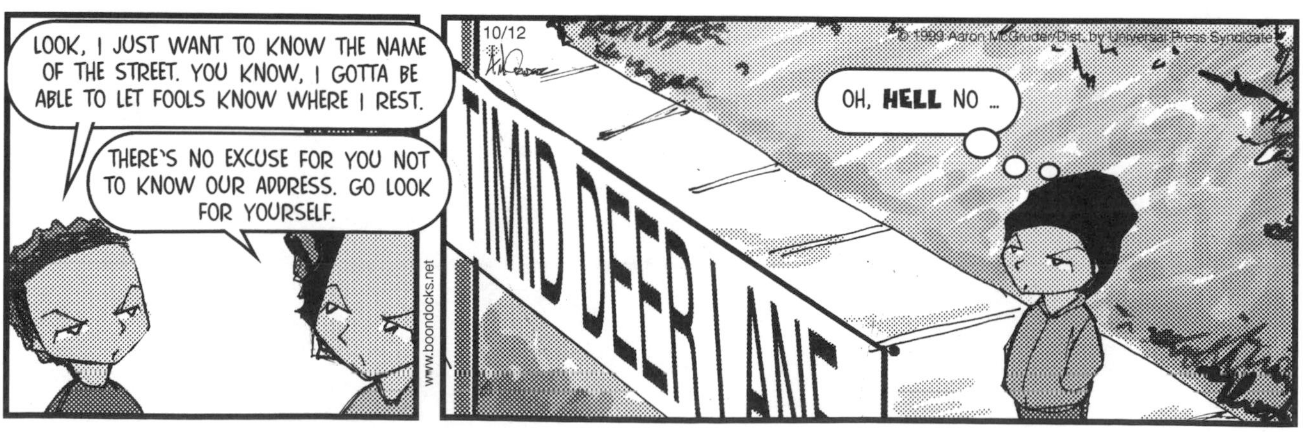
LOOK, I JUST WANT TO KNOW THE NAME OF THE STREET. YOU KNOW, I GOTTA BE ABLE TO LET FOOLS KNOW WHERE I REST.
THERE'S NO EXCUSE FOR YOU NOT TO KNOW OUR ADDRESS. GO LOOK FOR YOURSELF.
www.boondocks.net
10/12
© 1999 Aaron McGruder/Dist. by Universal Press Syndicate
TIMID DEER LANE
OH, HELL NO ...

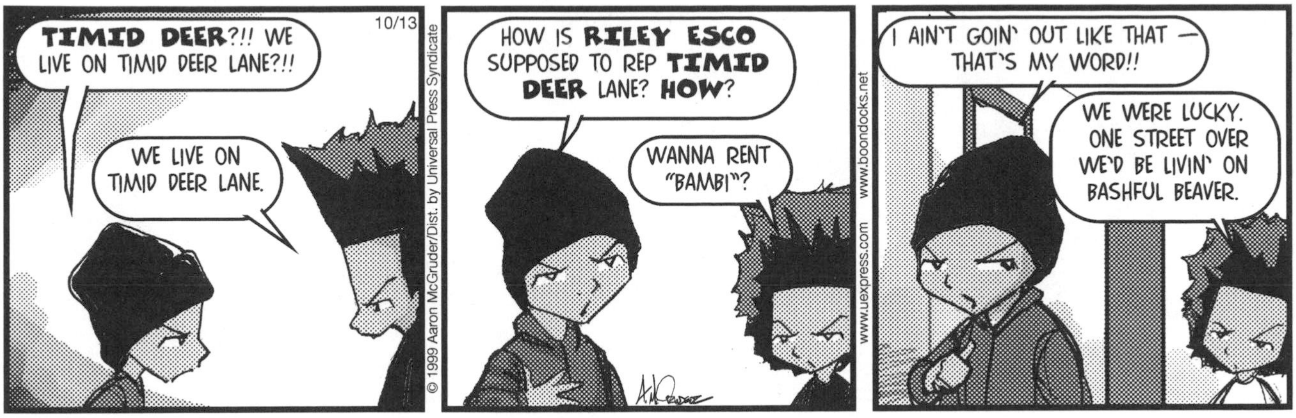
10/13
TIMID DEER?!! WE LIVE ON TIMID DEER LANE?!!
WE LIVE ON TIMID DEER LANE.
© 1999 Aaron McGruder/Dist. by Universal Press Syndicate
HOW IS RILEY ESCO SUPPOSED TO REP TIMID DEER LANE? HOW?
WANNA RENT "BAMBI"?
www.uexpress.com www.boondocks.net
I AIN'T GOIN' OUT LIKE THAT — THAT'S MY WORD!!
WE WERE LUCKY. ONE STREET OVER WE'D BE LIVIN' ON BASHFUL BEAVER.

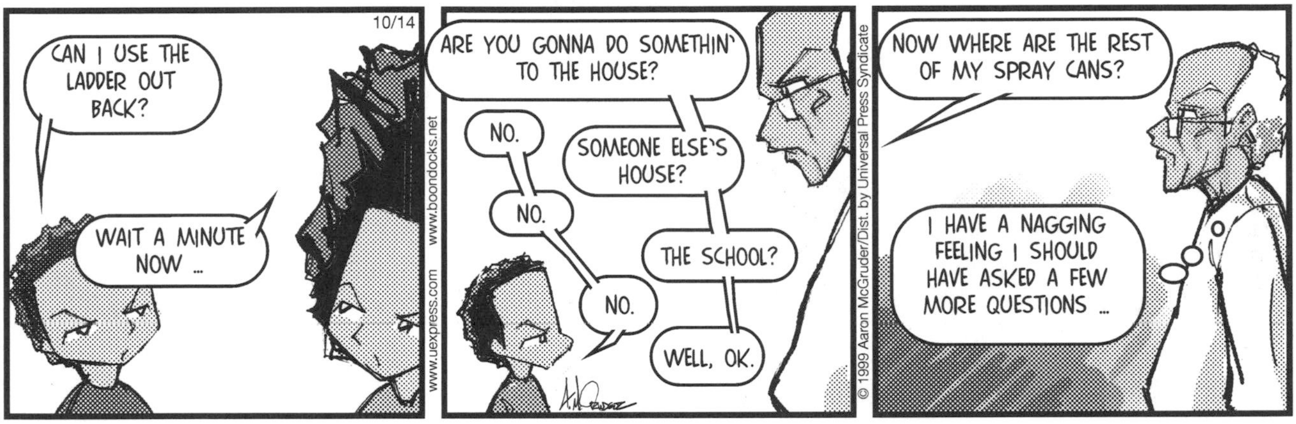
10/14
CAN I USE THE LADDER OUT BACK?
WAIT A MINUTE NOW ...
www.uexpress.com www.boondocks.net
ARE YOU GONNA DO SOMETHIN' TO THE HOUSE?
NO.
SOMEONE ELSE'S HOUSE?
NO.
THE SCHOOL?
NO.
WELL, OK.
© 1999 Aaron McGruder/Dist. by Universal Press Syndicate
NOW WHERE ARE THE REST OF MY SPRAY CANS?
I HAVE A NAGGING FEELING I SHOULD HAVE ASKED A FEW MORE QUESTIONS ...

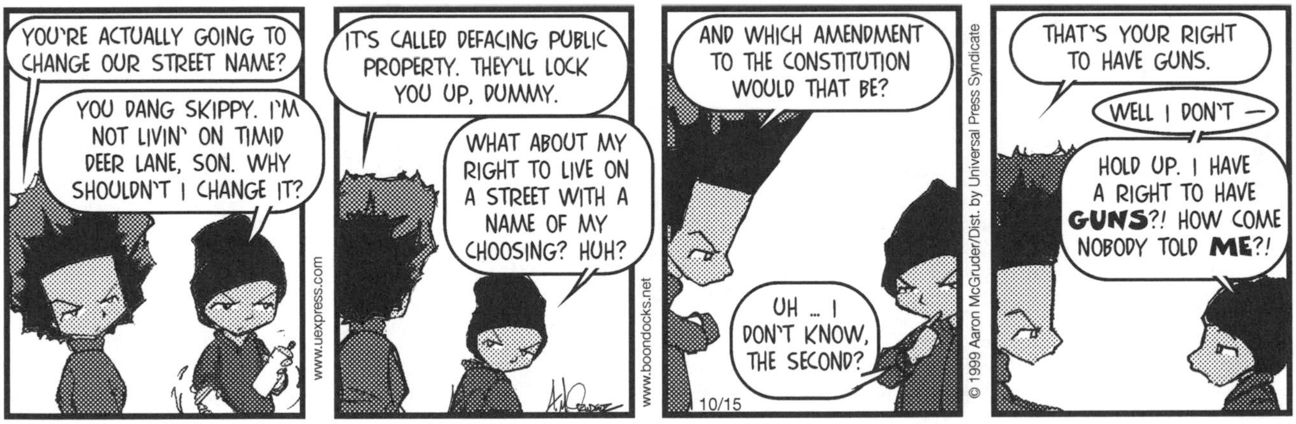
YOU'RE ACTUALLY GOING TO CHANGE OUR STREET NAME?
YOU DANG SKIPPY. I'M NOT LIVIN' ON TIMID DEER LANE, SON. WHY SHOULDN'T I CHANGE IT?
www.uexpress.com
IT'S CALLED DEFACING PUBLIC PROPERTY. THEY'LL LOCK YOU UP, DUMMY.
WHAT ABOUT MY RIGHT TO LIVE ON A STREET WITH A NAME OF MY CHOOSING? HUH?
www.boondocks.net
AND WHICH AMENDMENT TO THE CONSTITUTION WOULD THAT BE?
UH ... I DON'T KNOW, THE SECOND?
10/15
© 1999 Aaron McGruder/Dist. by Universal Press Syndicate
THAT'S YOUR RIGHT TO HAVE GUNS.
WELL I DON'T —
HOLD UP. I HAVE A RIGHT TO HAVE GUNS?! HOW COME NOBODY TOLD ME?!

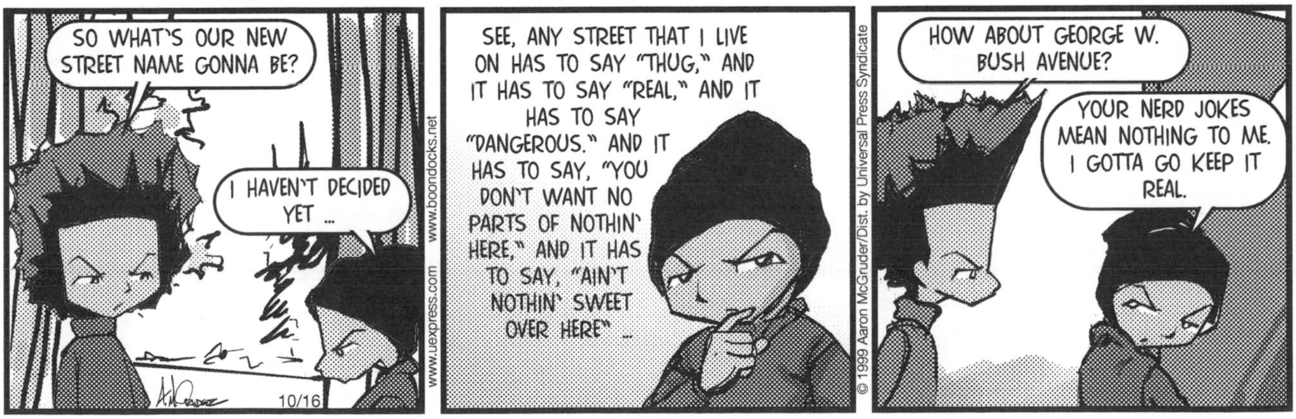
SO WHAT'S OUR NEW STREET NAME GONNA BE?
I HAVEN'T DECIDED YET ...
10/16
www.uexpress.com www.boondocks.net
SEE, ANY STREET THAT I LIVE ON HAS TO SAY "THUG," AND IT HAS TO SAY "REAL," AND IT HAS TO SAY "DANGEROUS." AND IT HAS TO SAY, "YOU DON'T WANT NO PARTS OF NOTHIN' HERE," AND IT HAS TO SAY, "AIN'T NOTHIN' SWEET OVER HERE" ...
© 1999 Aaron McGruder/Dist. by Universal Press Syndicate
HOW ABOUT GEORGE W. BUSH AVENUE?
YOUR NERD JOKES MEAN NOTHING TO ME. I GOTTA GO KEEP IT REAL.

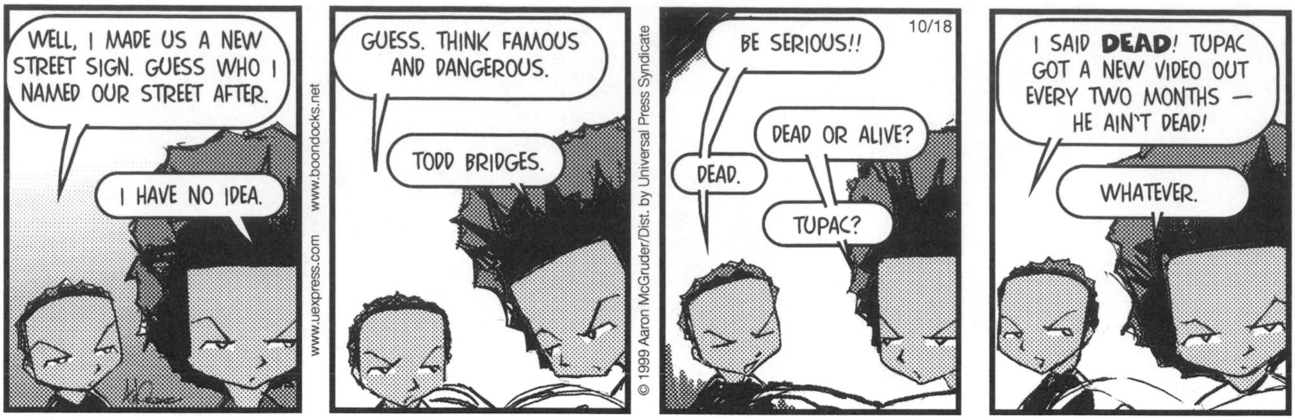
WELL, I MADE US A NEW STREET SIGN. GUESS WHO I NAMED OUR STREET AFTER.
I HAVE NO IDEA.
www.uexpress.com www.boondocks.net
GUESS. THINK FAMOUS AND DANGEROUS.
TODD BRIDGES.
© 1999 Aaron McGruder/Dist. by Universal Press Syndicate
10/18
BE SERIOUS!!
DEAD OR ALIVE?
DEAD.
TUPAC?
I SAID DEAD! TUPAC GOT A NEW VIDEO OUT EVERY TWO MONTHS — HE AIN'T DEAD!
WHATEVER.

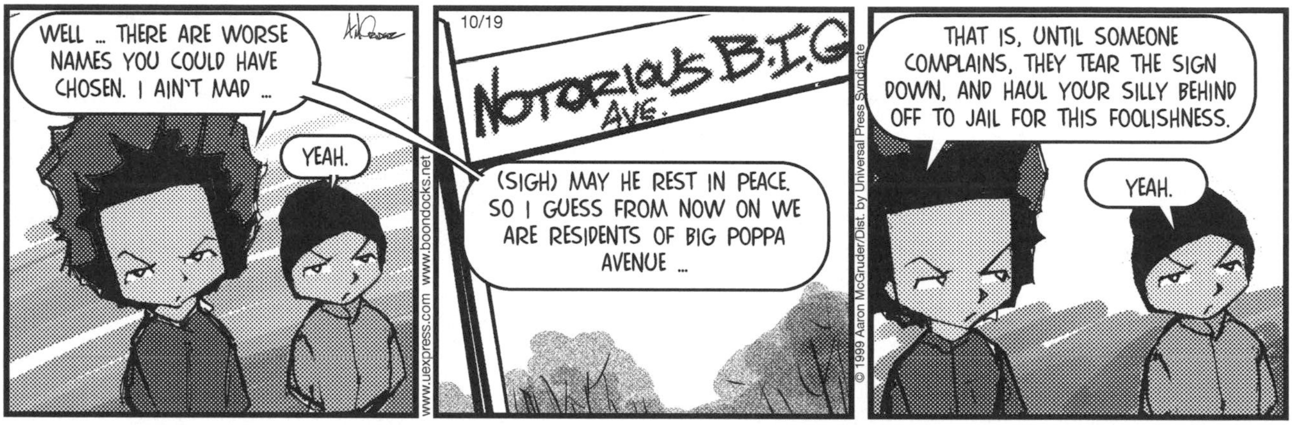
WELL ... THERE ARE WORSE NAMES YOU COULD HAVE CHOSEN. I AIN'T MAD ...
YEAH.
www.uexpress.com www.boondocks.net
10/19
NOTORIOUS B.I.G AVE.
(SIGH) MAY HE REST IN PEACE. SO I GUESS FROM NOW ON WE ARE RESIDENTS OF BIG POPPA AVENUE ...
© 1999 Aaron McGruder/Dist. by Universal Press Syndicate
THAT IS, UNTIL SOMEONE COMPLAINS, THEY TEAR THE SIGN DOWN, AND HAUL YOUR SILLY BEHIND OFF TO JAIL FOR THIS FOOLISHNESS.
YEAH.

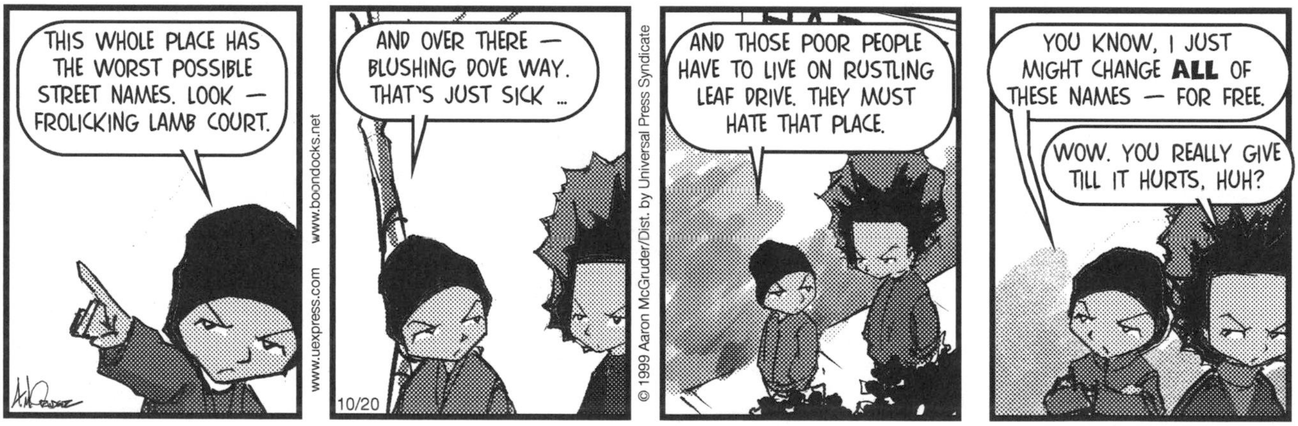
THIS WHOLE PLACE HAS THE WORST POSSIBLE STREET NAMES. LOOK — FROLICKING LAMB COURT.
www.uexpress.com www.boondocks.net
AND OVER THERE — BLUSHING DOVE WAY. THAT'S JUST SICK ...
10/20
© 1999 Aaron McGruder/Dist. by Universal Press Syndicate
AND THOSE POOR PEOPLE HAVE TO LIVE ON RUSTLING LEAF DRIVE. THEY MUST HATE THAT PLACE.
YOU KNOW, I JUST MIGHT CHANGE ALL OF THESE NAMES — FOR FREE.
WOW. YOU REALLY GIVE TILL IT HURTS, HUH?

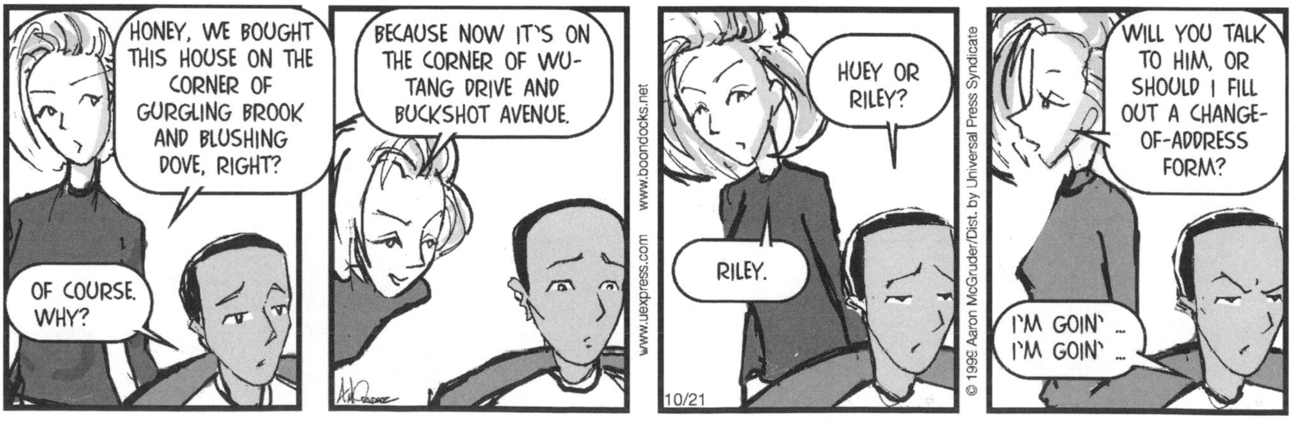
HONEY, WE BOUGHT THIS HOUSE ON THE CORNER OF GURGLING BROOK AND BLUSHING DOVE, RIGHT?
OF COURSE. WHY?
BECAUSE NOW IT'S ON THE CORNER OF WU-TANG DRIVE AND BUCKSHOT AVENUE.
www.uexpress.com www.boondocks.net
HUEY OR RILEY?
RILEY.
10/21
© 1999 Aaron McGruder/Dist. by Universal Press Syndicate
WILL YOU TALK TO HIM, OR SHOULD I FILL OUT A CHANGE-OF-ADDRESS FORM?
I'M GOIN' ... I'M GOIN' ...

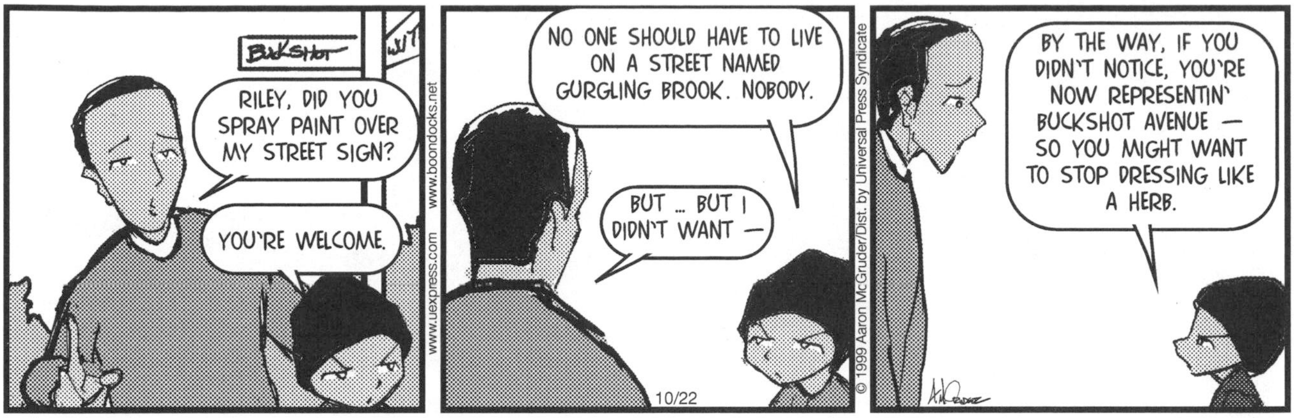
BUCKSHOT
RILEY, DID YOU SPRAY PAINT OVER MY STREET SIGN?
YOU'RE WELCOME.
www.uexpress.com www.boondocks.net
NO ONE SHOULD HAVE TO LIVE ON A STREET NAMED GURGLING BROOK. NOBODY.
BUT ... BUT I DIDN'T WANT —
10/22
© 1999 Aaron McGruder/Dist. by Universal Press Syndicate
BY THE WAY, IF YOU DIDN'T NOTICE, YOU'RE NOW REPRESENTIN' BUCKSHOT AVENUE — SO YOU MIGHT WANT TO STOP DRESSING LIKE A HERB.

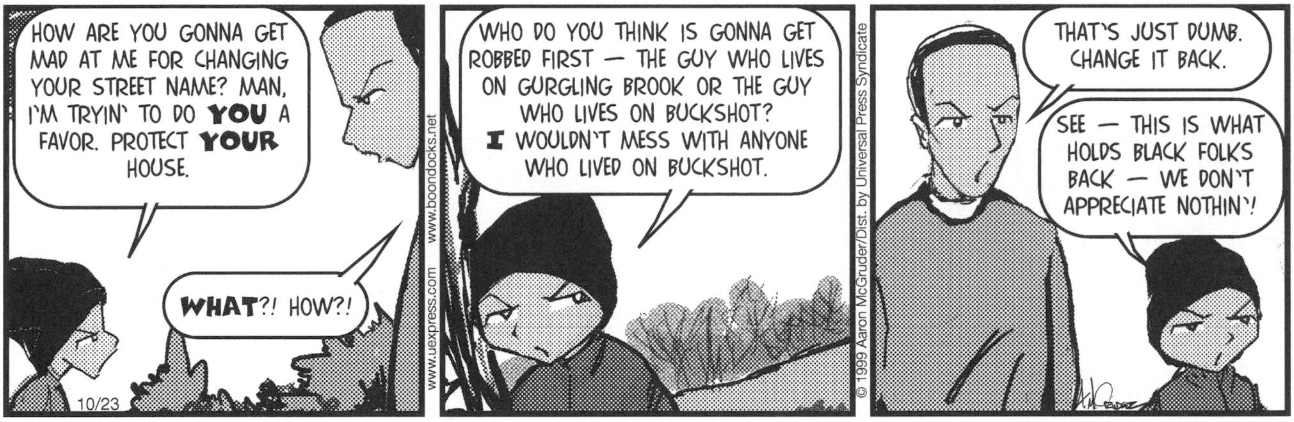
HOW ARE YOU GONNA GET MAD AT ME FOR CHANGING YOUR STREET NAME? MAN, I'M TRYIN' TO DO YOU A FAVOR. PROTECT YOUR HOUSE.
WHAT?! HOW?!
10/23
www.uexpress.com www.boondocks.net
WHO DO YOU THINK IS GONNA GET ROBBED FIRST — THE GUY WHO LIVES ON GURGLING BROOK OR THE GUY WHO LIVES ON BUCKSHOT? I WOULDN'T MESS WITH ANYONE WHO LIVED ON BUCKSHOT.
© 1999 Aaron McGruder/Dist. by Universal Press Syndicate
THAT'S JUST DUMB. CHANGE IT BACK.
SEE — THIS IS WHAT HOLDS BLACK FOLKS BACK — WE DON'T APPRECIATE NOTHIN'!

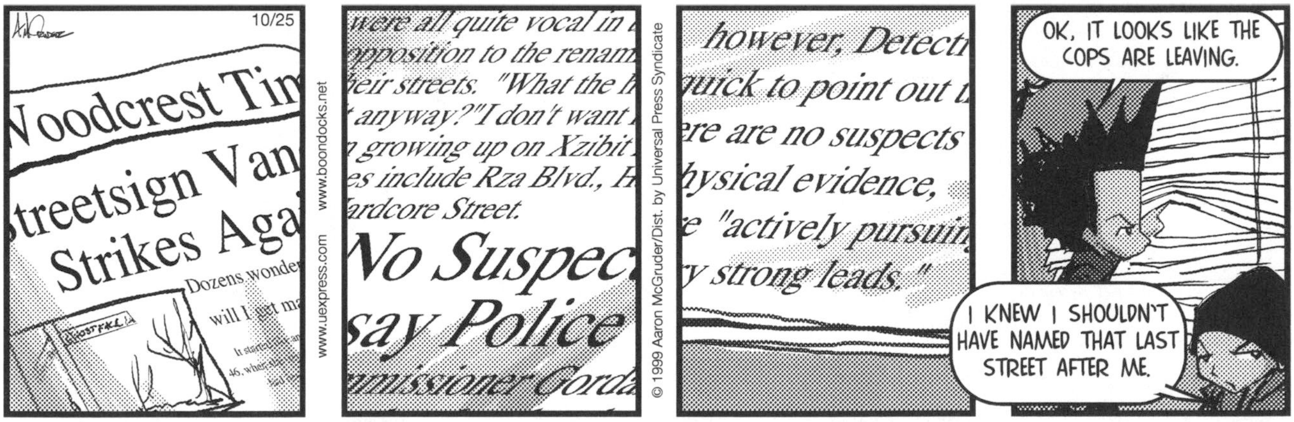
10/25
Woodcrest Tim
Streetsign Van
Strikes Aga
Dozens wonder
will I get ma
www.uexpress.com www.boondocks.net
were all quite vocal in
opposition to the renam
heir streets. "What the h
t anyway?" I don't want
n growing up on Xzibit
es include Rza Blvd., H
Hardcore Street.
No Suspec
say Police
mmissioner Gorda
© 1999 Aaron McGruder/Dist. by Universal Press Syndicate
however, Detect
quick to point out t
ere are no suspects
physical evidence,
e "actively pursuin
y strong leads."
OK, IT LOOKS LIKE THE COPS ARE LEAVING.
I KNEW I SHOULDN'T HAVE NAMED THAT LAST STREET AFTER ME.

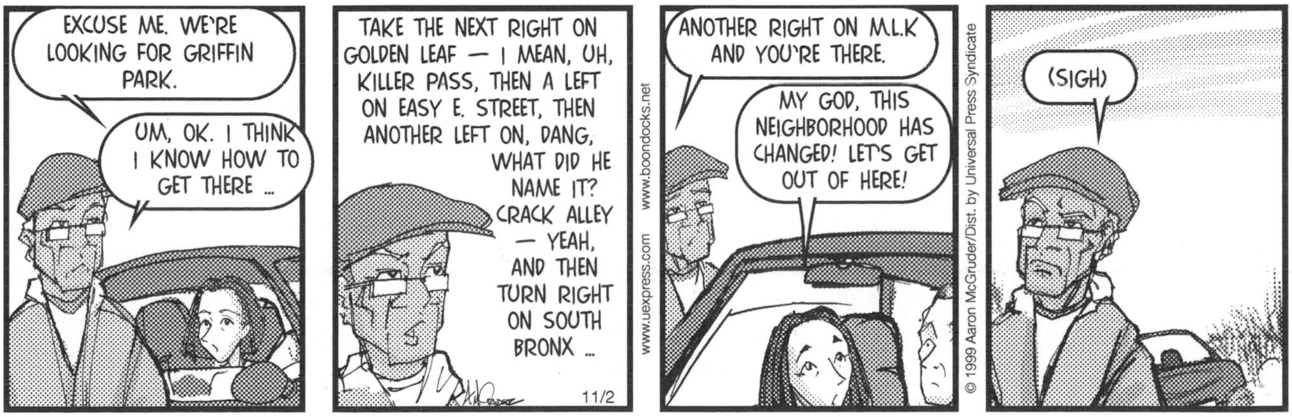
EXCUSE ME. WE'RE LOOKING FOR GRIFFIN PARK.
UM, OK. I THINK I KNOW HOW TO GET THERE ...
TAKE THE NEXT RIGHT ON GOLDEN LEAF — I MEAN, UH, KILLER PASS, THEN A LEFT ON EASY E. STREET, THEN ANOTHER LEFT ON, DANG, WHAT DID HE NAME IT? CRACK ALLEY — YEAH, AND THEN TURN RIGHT ON SOUTH BRONX ...
11/2
www.uexpress.com www.boondocks.net
ANOTHER RIGHT ON M.L.K AND YOU'RE THERE.
MY GOD, THIS NEIGHBORHOOD HAS CHANGED! LET'S GET OUT OF HERE!
© 1999 Aaron McGruder/Dist. by Universal Press Syndicate
(SIGH)

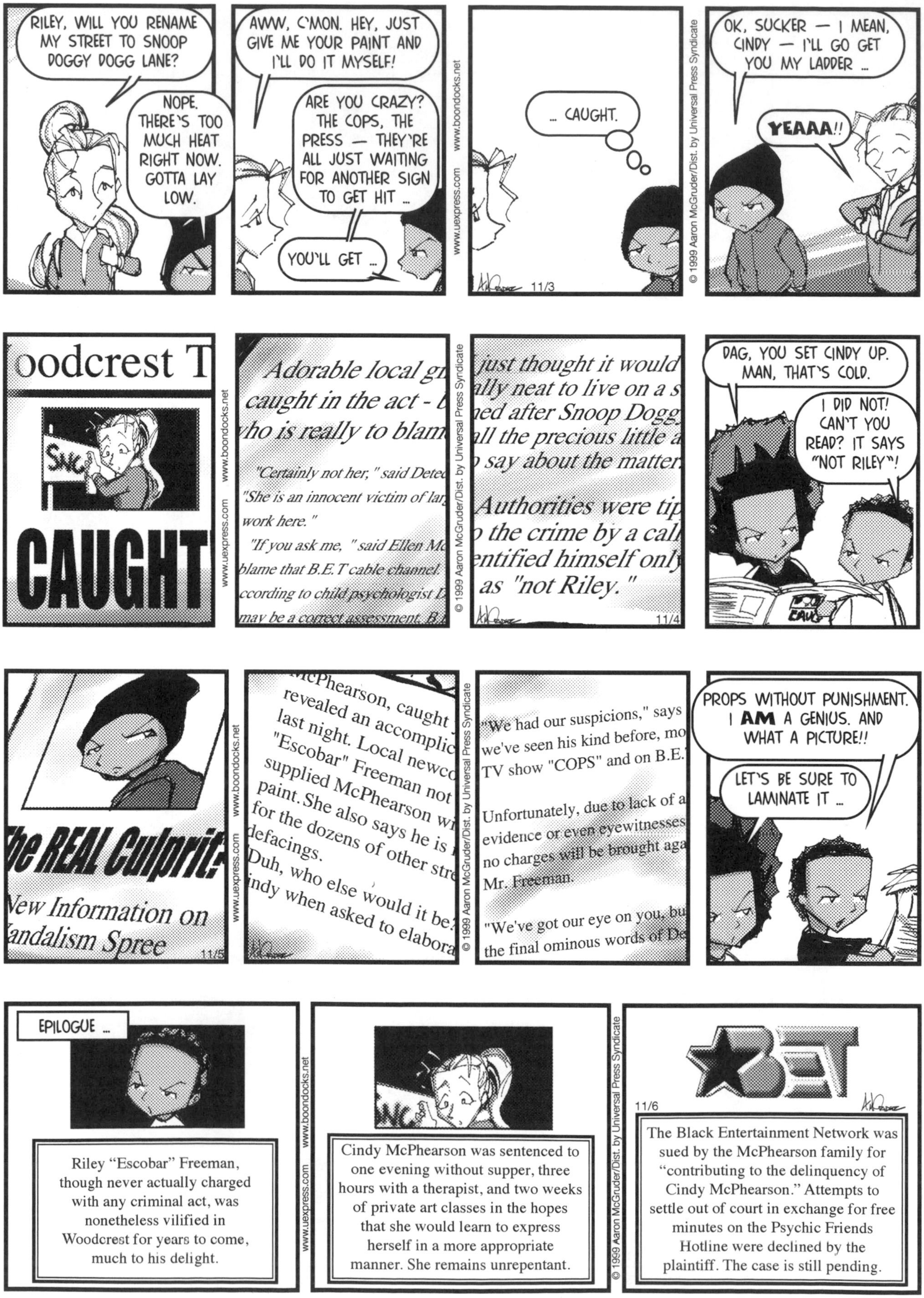

RILEY, WILL YOU RENAME MY STREET TO SNOOP DOGGY DOGG LANE?
NOPE. THERE'S TOO MUCH HEAT RIGHT NOW. GOTTA LAY LOW.
AWW, C'MON. HEY, JUST GIVE ME YOUR PAINT AND I'LL DO IT MYSELF!
ARE YOU CRAZY? THE COPS, THE PRESS — THEY'RE ALL JUST WAITING FOR ANOTHER SIGN TO GET HIT ...
YOU'LL GET ...
... CAUGHT.
OK, SUCKER — I MEAN, CINDY — I'LL GO GET YOU MY LADDER ...
YEAAA!!
www.uexpress.com www.boondocks.net
© 1999 Aaron McGruder/Dist. by Universal Press Syndicate
11/3
oodcrest T
CAUGHT
Adorable local gi
caught in the act -
who is really to blam
"Certainly not her," said Detec
"She is an innocent victim of lar
work here."
"If you ask me," said Ellen Mc
blame that B.E.T cable channel.
ccording to child psychologist D
may be a correct assessment. B.
just thought it would
ally neat to live on a s
ned after Snoop Dogg
all the precious little a
o say about the matter
Authorities were tip
o the crime by a call
entified himself only
as "not Riley."
11/4
DAG, YOU SET CINDY UP. MAN, THAT'S COLD.
I DID NOT! CAN'T YOU READ? IT SAYS "NOT RILEY"!
The REAL Culprit?
New Information on
Vandalism Spree
11/5
McPhearson, caught
revealed an accomplic
last night. Local newco
"Escobar" Freeman not
supplied McPhearson wi
paint. She also says he is
for the dozens of other str
defacings.
Duh, who else would it be?
indy when asked to elabora
"We had our suspicions," says
we've seen his kind before, mo
TV show "COPS" and on B.E.
Unfortunately, due to lack of a
evidence or even eyewitnesses
no charges will be brought aga
Mr. Freeman.
"We've got our eye on you, bu
the final ominous words of De
PROPS WITHOUT PUNISHMENT. I **AM** A GENIUS. AND WHAT A PICTURE!!
LET'S BE SURE TO LAMINATE IT ...
EPILOGUE ...
Riley "Escobar" Freeman, though never actually charged with any criminal act, was nonetheless vilified in Woodcrest for years to come, much to his delight.
Cindy McPhearson was sentenced to one evening without supper, three hours with a therapist, and two weeks of private art classes in the hopes that she would learn to express herself in a more appropriate manner. She remains unrepentant.
11/6
The Black Entertainment Network was sued by the McPhearson family for "contributing to the delinquency of Cindy McPhearson." Attempts to settle out of court in exchange for free minutes on the Psychic Friends Hotline were declined by the plaintiff. The case is still pending.

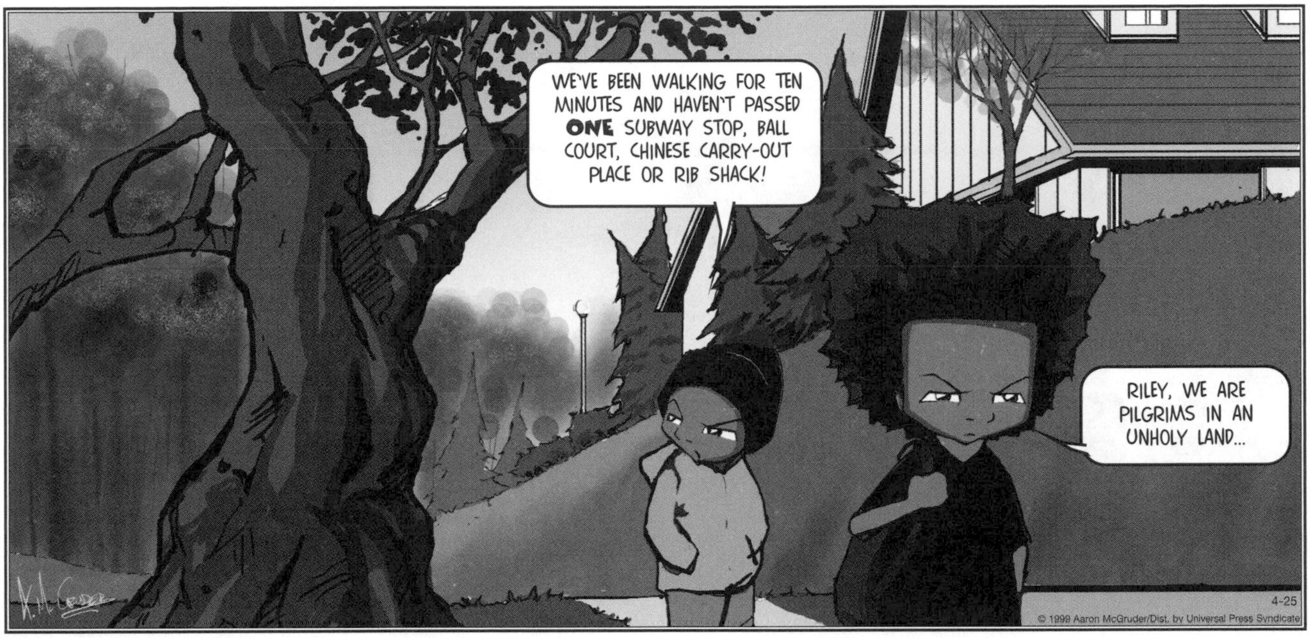
WE'VE BEEN WALKING FOR TEN MINUTES AND HAVEN'T PASSED ONE SUBWAY STOP, BALL COURT, CHINESE CARRY-OUT PLACE OR RIB SHACK!
RILEY, WE ARE PILGRIMS IN AN UNHOLY LAND...
4-25
© 1999 Aaron McGruder/Dist. by Universal Press Syndicate

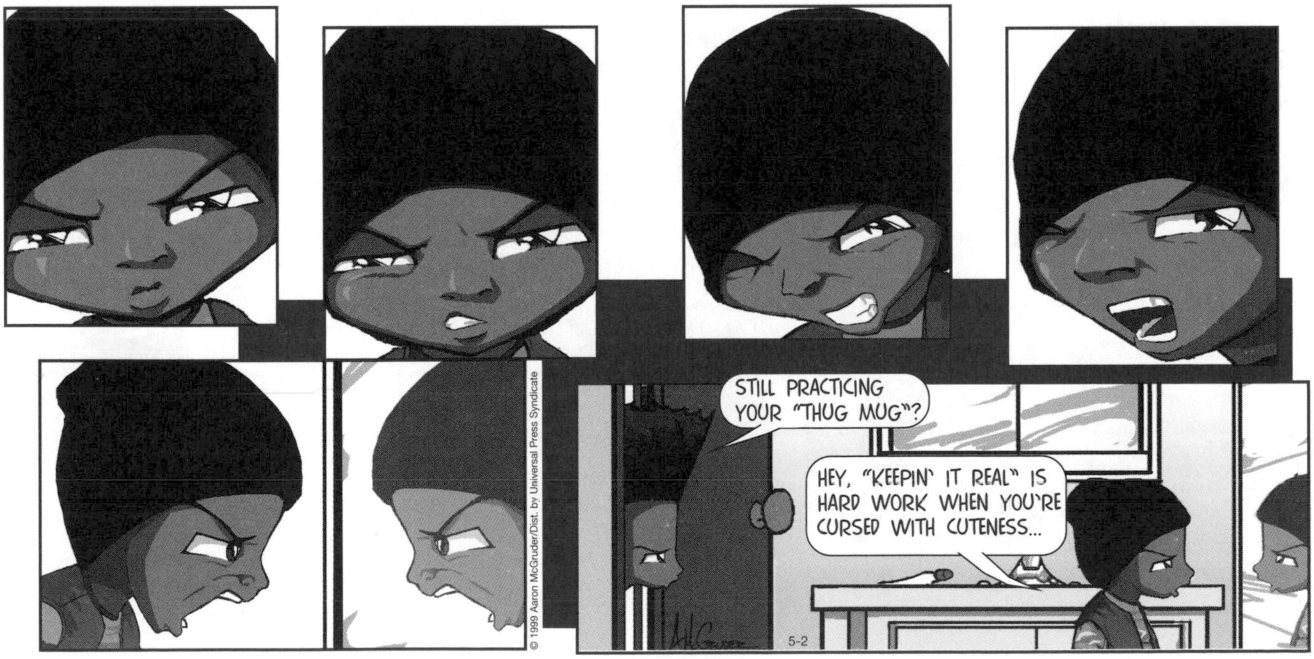
© 1999 Aaron McGruder/Dist. by Universal Press Syndicate
STILL PRACTICING YOUR "THUG MUG"?
HEY, "KEEPIN' IT REAL" IS HARD WORK WHEN YOU'RE CURSED WITH CUTENESS...
5-2

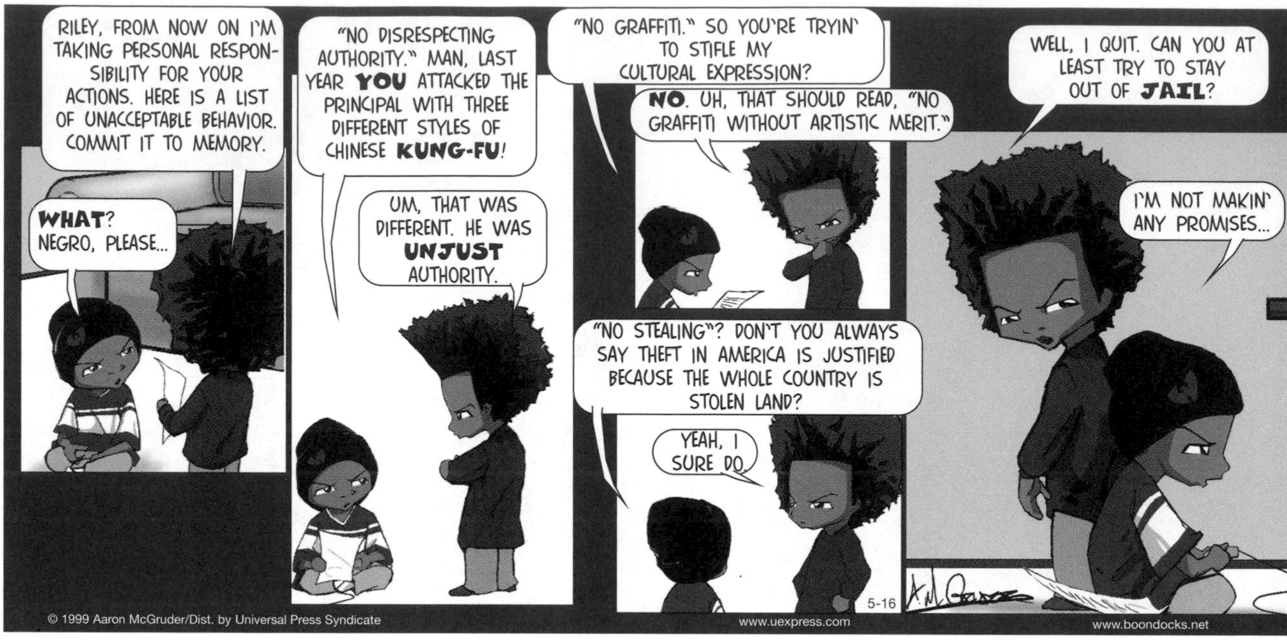
RILEY, FROM NOW ON I'M TAKING PERSONAL RESPONSIBILITY FOR YOUR ACTIONS. HERE IS A LIST OF UNACCEPTABLE BEHAVIOR. COMMIT IT TO MEMORY.
WHAT? NEGRO, PLEASE...
"NO DISRESPECTING AUTHORITY." MAN, LAST YEAR YOU ATTACKED THE PRINCIPAL WITH THREE DIFFERENT STYLES OF CHINESE KUNG-FU!
UM, THAT WAS DIFFERENT. HE WAS UNJUST AUTHORITY.
"NO GRAFFITI." SO YOU'RE TRYIN' TO STIFLE MY CULTURAL EXPRESSION?
NO. UH, THAT SHOULD READ, "NO GRAFFITI WITHOUT ARTISTIC MERIT."
"NO STEALING"? DON'T YOU ALWAYS SAY THEFT IN AMERICA IS JUSTIFIED BECAUSE THE WHOLE COUNTRY IS STOLEN LAND?
YEAH, I SURE DO.
WELL, I QUIT. CAN YOU AT LEAST TRY TO STAY OUT OF JAIL?
I'M NOT MAKIN' ANY PROMISES...
© 1999 Aaron McGruder/Dist. by Universal Press Syndicate
5-16
www.uexpress.com
www.boondocks.net

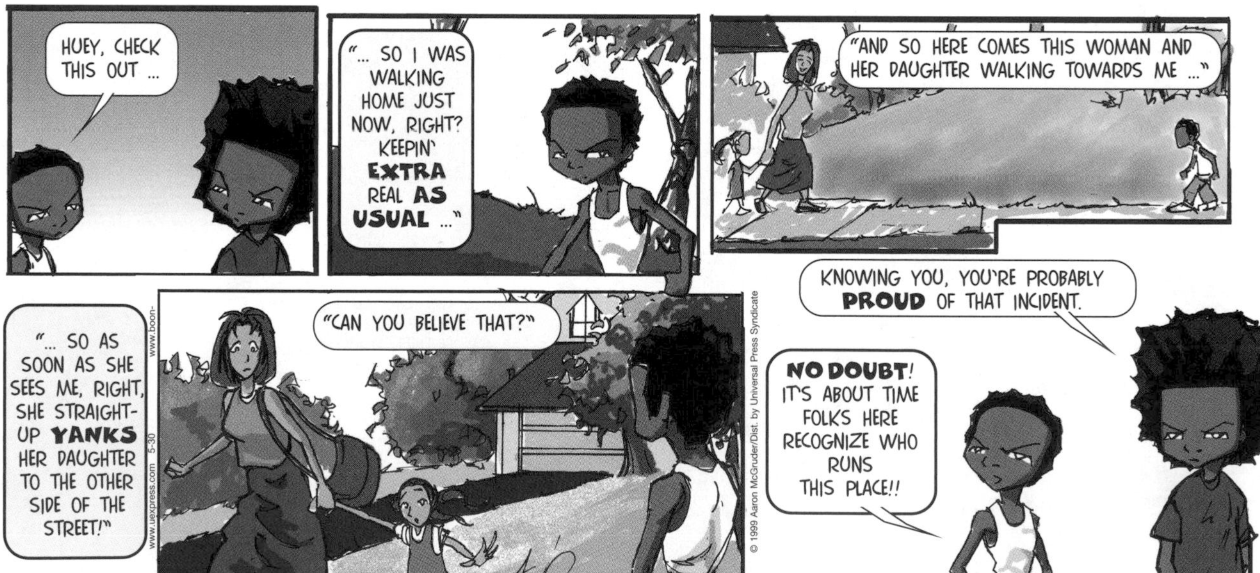
HUEY, CHECK THIS OUT ...
"... SO I WAS WALKING HOME JUST NOW, RIGHT? KEEPIN' EXTRA REAL AS USUAL ..."
"AND SO HERE COMES THIS WOMAN AND HER DAUGHTER WALKING TOWARDS ME ..."
"... SO AS SOON AS SHE SEES ME, RIGHT, SHE STRAIGHT-UP YANKS HER DAUGHTER TO THE OTHER SIDE OF THE STREET!"
"CAN YOU BELIEVE THAT?"
KNOWING YOU, YOU'RE PROBABLY PROUD OF THAT INCIDENT.
NO DOUBT! IT'S ABOUT TIME FOLKS HERE RECOGNIZE WHO RUNS THIS PLACE!!
www.uexpress.com www.boon-
5-30
© 1999 Aaron McGruder/Dist. by Universal Press Syndicate

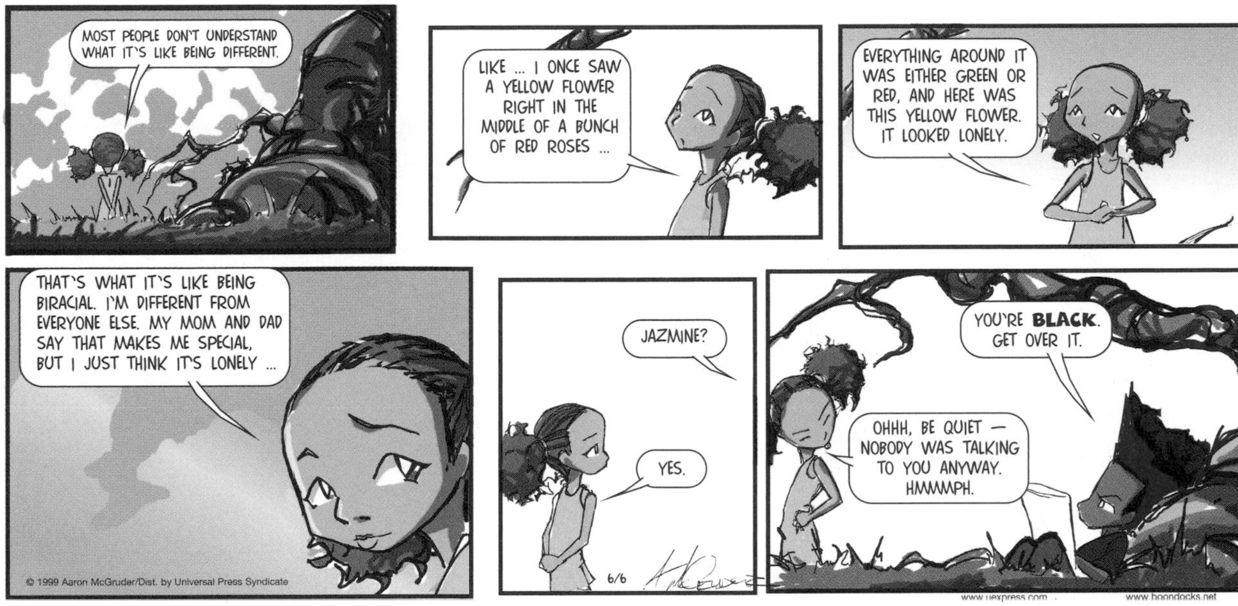
MOST PEOPLE DON'T UNDERSTAND WHAT IT'S LIKE BEING DIFFERENT.
LIKE ... I ONCE SAW A YELLOW FLOWER RIGHT IN THE MIDDLE OF A BUNCH OF RED ROSES ...
EVERYTHING AROUND IT WAS EITHER GREEN OR RED, AND HERE WAS THIS YELLOW FLOWER. IT LOOKED LONELY.
THAT'S WHAT IT'S LIKE BEING BIRACIAL. I'M DIFFERENT FROM EVERYONE ELSE. MY MOM AND DAD SAY THAT MAKES ME SPECIAL, BUT I JUST THINK IT'S LONELY ...
© 1999 Aaron McGruder/Dist. by Universal Press Syndicate
JAZMINE?
YES.
6/6
YOU'RE **BLACK**. GET OVER IT.
OHHH, BE QUIET — NOBODY WAS TALKING TO YOU ANYWAY. HMMMPH.
www.uexpress.com
www.boondocks.net

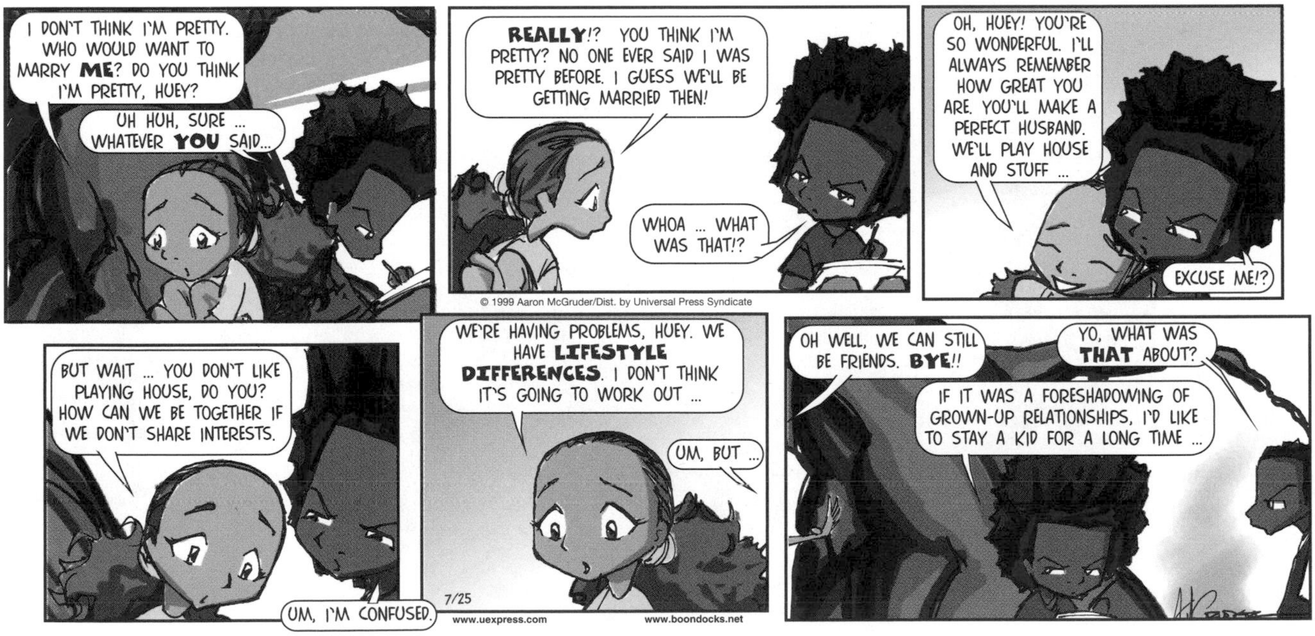
I DON'T THINK I'M PRETTY. WHO WOULD WANT TO MARRY **ME**? DO YOU THINK I'M PRETTY, HUEY?
UH HUH, SURE ... WHATEVER **YOU** SAID...
REALLY!? YOU THINK I'M PRETTY? NO ONE EVER SAID I WAS PRETTY BEFORE. I GUESS WE'LL BE GETTING MARRIED THEN!
WHOA ... WHAT WAS THAT!?
© 1999 Aaron McGruder/Dist. by Universal Press Syndicate
OH, HUEY! YOU'RE SO WONDERFUL. I'LL ALWAYS REMEMBER HOW GREAT YOU ARE. YOU'LL MAKE A PERFECT HUSBAND. WE'LL PLAY HOUSE AND STUFF ...
EXCUSE ME!?
BUT WAIT ... YOU DON'T LIKE PLAYING HOUSE, DO YOU? HOW CAN WE BE TOGETHER IF WE DON'T SHARE INTERESTS.
UM, I'M CONFUSED.
WE'RE HAVING PROBLEMS, HUEY. WE HAVE **LIFESTYLE DIFFERENCES**. I DON'T THINK IT'S GOING TO WORK OUT ...
UM, BUT ...
7/25
www.uexpress.com
www.boondocks.net
OH WELL, WE CAN STILL BE FRIENDS. **BYE**!!
YO, WHAT WAS **THAT** ABOUT?
IF IT WAS A FORESHADOWING OF GROWN-UP RELATIONSHIPS, I'D LIKE TO STAY A KID FOR A LONG TIME ...

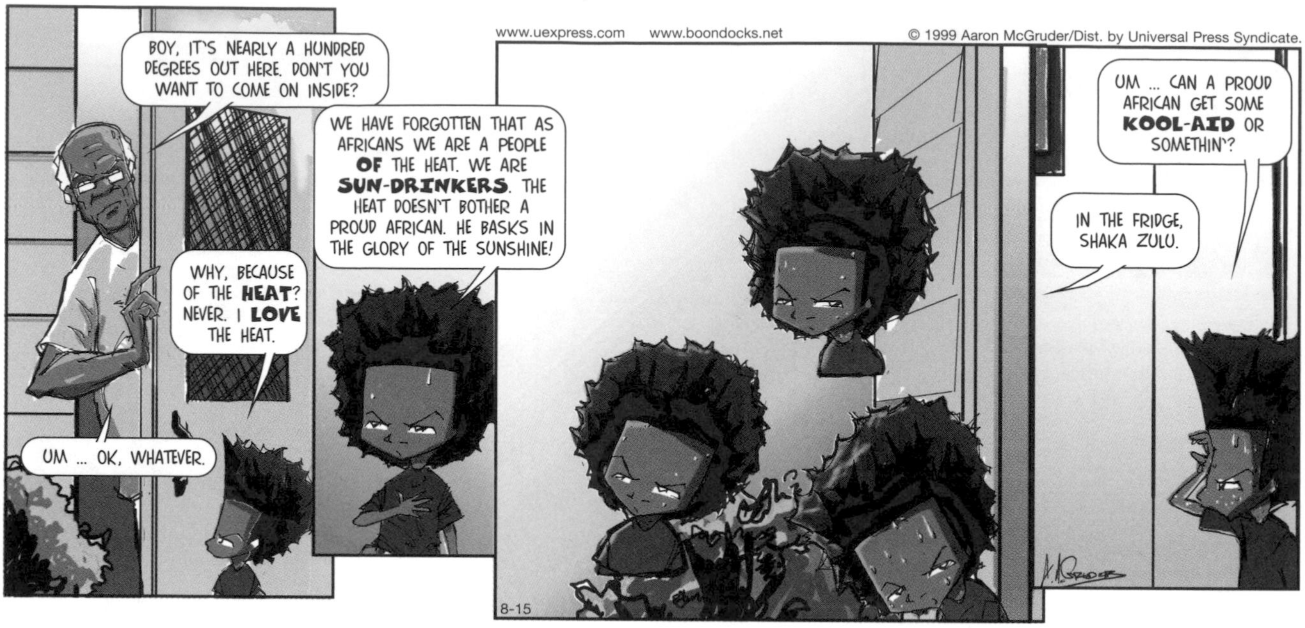

www.uexpress.com www.boondocks.net © 1999 Aaron McGruder/Dist. by Universal Press Syndicate.
BOY, IT'S NEARLY A HUNDRED DEGREES OUT HERE. DON'T YOU WANT TO COME ON INSIDE?
WHY, BECAUSE OF THE HEAT? NEVER. I LOVE THE HEAT.
UM ... OK, WHATEVER.
WE HAVE FORGOTTEN THAT AS AFRICANS WE ARE A PEOPLE OF THE HEAT. WE ARE SUN-DRINKERS. THE HEAT DOESN'T BOTHER A PROUD AFRICAN. HE BASKS IN THE GLORY OF THE SUNSHINE!
UM ... CAN A PROUD AFRICAN GET SOME KOOL-AID OR SOMETHIN'?
IN THE FRIDGE, SHAKA ZULU.
8-15

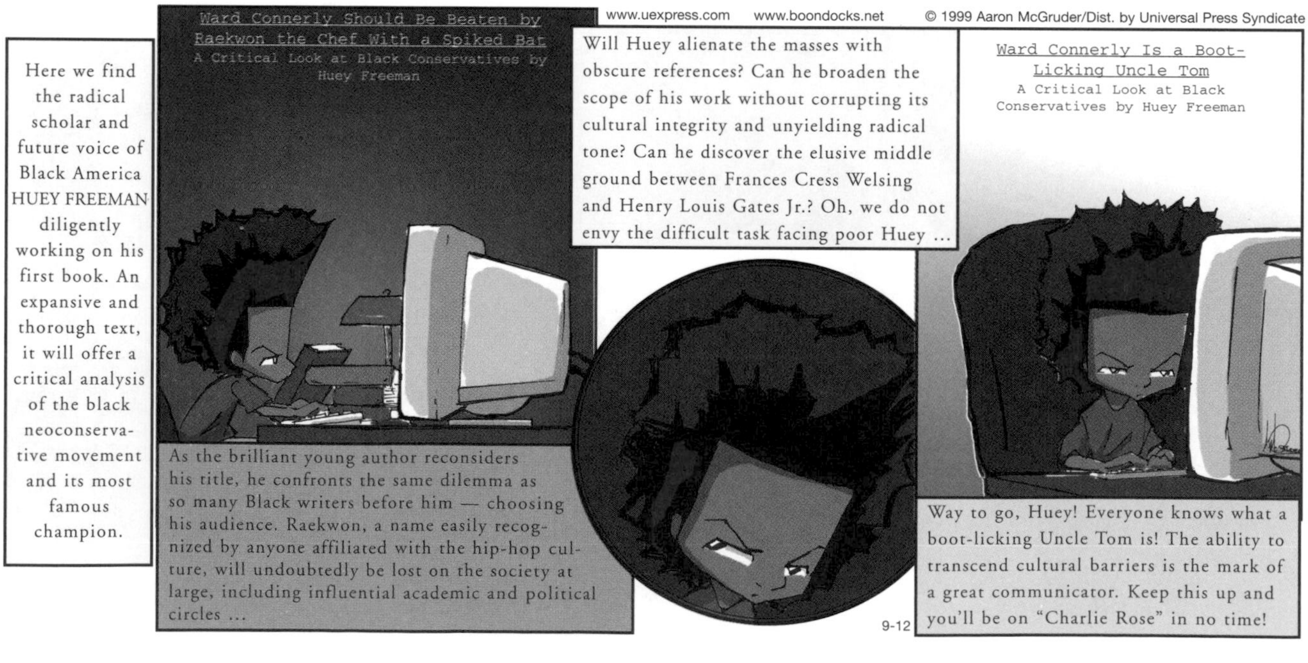

www.uexpress.com www.boondocks.net © 1999 Aaron McGruder/Dist. by Universal Press Syndicate
Here we find the radical scholar and future voice of Black America HUEY FREEMAN diligently working on his first book. An expansive and thorough text, it will offer a critical analysis of the black neoconservative movement and its most famous champion.
Ward Connerly Should Be Beaten by Raekwon the Chef With a Spiked Bat
A Critical Look at Black Conservatives by Huey Freeman
As the brilliant young author reconsiders his title, he confronts the same dilemma as so many Black writers before him — choosing his audience. Raekwon, a name easily recognized by anyone affiliated with the hip-hop culture, will undoubtedly be lost on the society at large, including influential academic and political circles ...
Will Huey alienate the masses with obscure references? Can he broaden the scope of his work without corrupting its cultural integrity and unyielding radical tone? Can he discover the elusive middle ground between Frances Cress Welsing and Henry Louis Gates Jr.? Oh, we do not envy the difficult task facing poor Huey ...
Ward Connerly Is a Boot-Licking Uncle Tom
A Critical Look at Black Conservatives by Huey Freeman
Way to go, Huey! Everyone knows what a boot-licking Uncle Tom is! The ability to transcend cultural barriers is the mark of a great communicator. Keep this up and you'll be on "Charlie Rose" in no time!
9-12

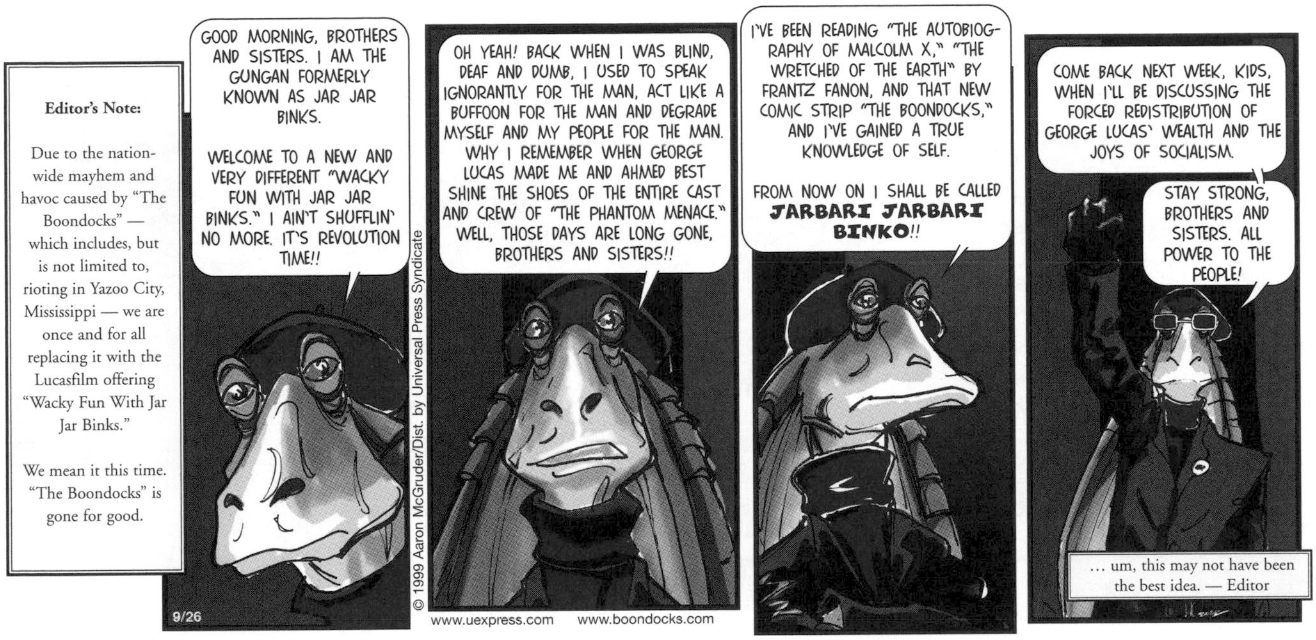
Editor's Note:
Due to the nationwide mayhem and havoc caused by "The Boondocks" — which includes, but is not limited to, rioting in Yazoo City, Mississippi — we are once and for all replacing it with the Lucasfilm offering "Wacky Fun With Jar Jar Binks."
We mean it this time. "The Boondocks" is gone for good.
GOOD MORNING, BROTHERS AND SISTERS. I AM THE GUNGAN FORMERLY KNOWN AS JAR JAR BINKS.
WELCOME TO A NEW AND VERY DIFFERENT "WACKY FUN WITH JAR JAR BINKS." I AIN'T SHUFFLIN' NO MORE. IT'S REVOLUTION TIME!!
9/26
OH YEAH! BACK WHEN I WAS BLIND, DEAF AND DUMB, I USED TO SPEAK IGNORANTLY FOR THE MAN, ACT LIKE A BUFFOON FOR THE MAN AND DEGRADE MYSELF AND MY PEOPLE FOR THE MAN. WHY I REMEMBER WHEN GEORGE LUCAS MADE ME AND AHMED BEST SHINE THE SHOES OF THE ENTIRE CAST AND CREW OF "THE PHANTOM MENACE." WELL, THOSE DAYS ARE LONG GONE, BROTHERS AND SISTERS!!
© 1999 Aaron McGruder/Dist. by Universal Press Syndicate
I'VE BEEN READING "THE AUTOBIOGRAPHY OF MALCOLM X," "THE WRETCHED OF THE EARTH" BY FRANTZ FANON, AND THAT NEW COMIC STRIP "THE BOONDOCKS," AND I'VE GAINED A TRUE KNOWLEDGE OF SELF.
FROM NOW ON I SHALL BE CALLED JARBARI JARBARI BINKO!!
COME BACK NEXT WEEK, KIDS, WHEN I'LL BE DISCUSSING THE FORCED REDISTRIBUTION OF GEORGE LUCAS' WEALTH AND THE JOYS OF SOCIALISM.
STAY STRONG, BROTHERS AND SISTERS. ALL POWER TO THE PEOPLE!
... um, this may not have been the best idea. — Editor
www.uexpress.com www.boondocks.com

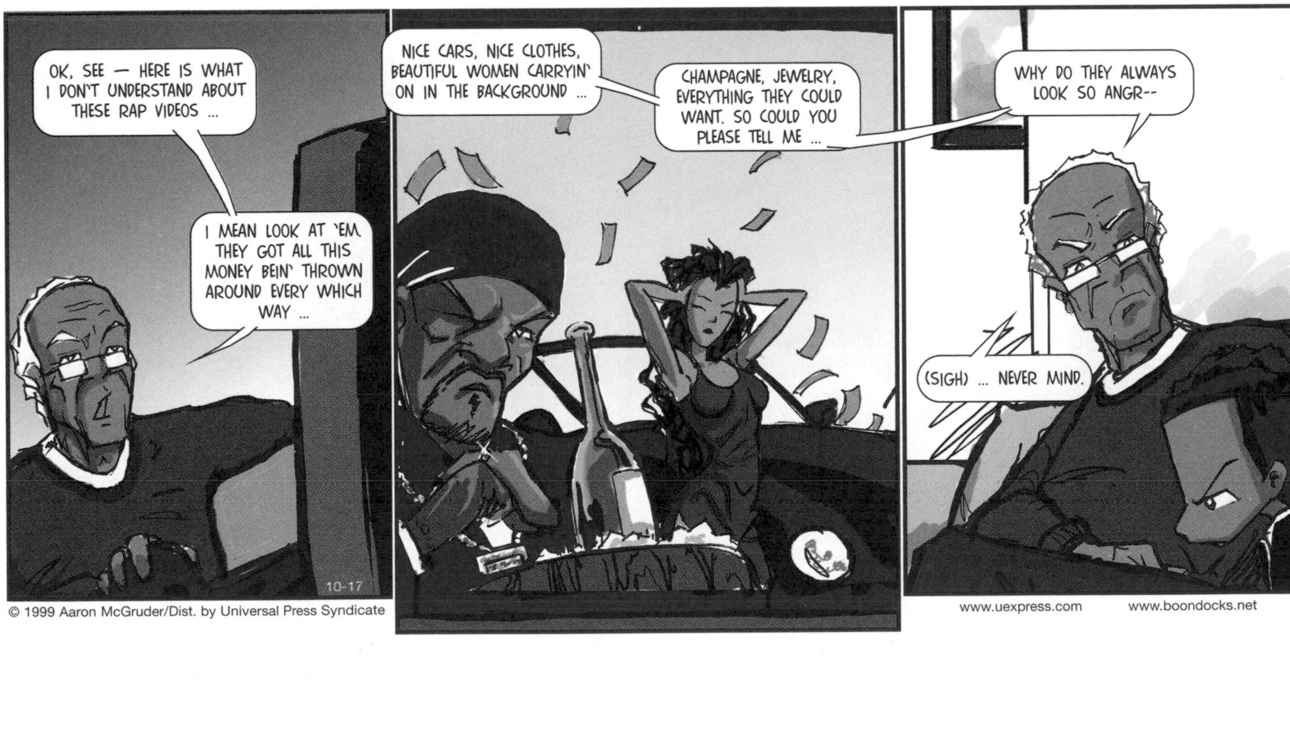
OK, SEE — HERE IS WHAT I DON'T UNDERSTAND ABOUT THESE RAP VIDEOS ...
I MEAN LOOK AT 'EM. THEY GOT ALL THIS MONEY BEIN' THROWN AROUND EVERY WHICH WAY ...
10-17
NICE CARS, NICE CLOTHES, BEAUTIFUL WOMEN CARRYIN' ON IN THE BACKGROUND ...
CHAMPAGNE, JEWELRY, EVERYTHING THEY COULD WANT. SO COULD YOU PLEASE TELL ME ...
WHY DO THEY ALWAYS LOOK SO ANGR--
(SIGH) ... NEVER MIND.
© 1999 Aaron McGruder/Dist. by Universal Press Syndicate
www.uexpress.com www.boondocks.net

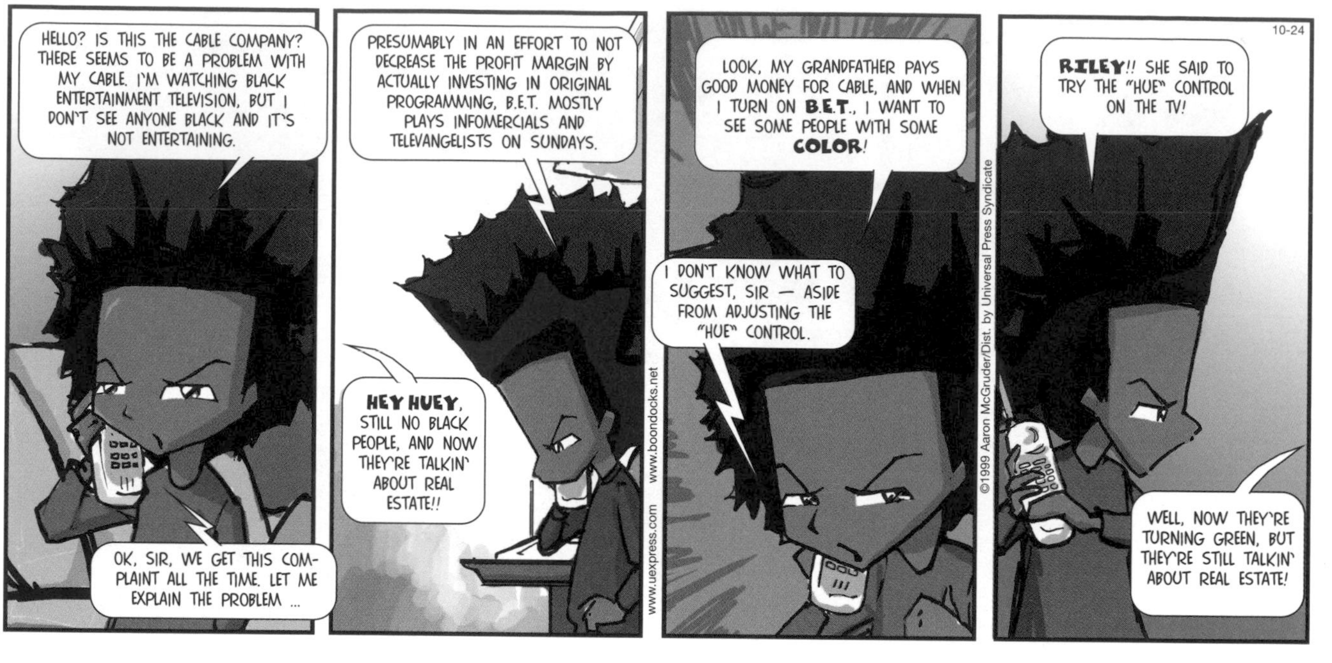
HELLO? IS THIS THE CABLE COMPANY? THERE SEEMS TO BE A PROBLEM WITH MY CABLE. I'M WATCHING BLACK ENTERTAINMENT TELEVISION, BUT I DON'T SEE ANYONE BLACK AND IT'S NOT ENTERTAINING.
OK, SIR, WE GET THIS COMPLAINT ALL THE TIME. LET ME EXPLAIN THE PROBLEM ...
PRESUMABLY IN AN EFFORT TO NOT DECREASE THE PROFIT MARGIN BY ACTUALLY INVESTING IN ORIGINAL PROGRAMMING, B.E.T. MOSTLY PLAYS INFOMERCIALS AND TELEVANGELISTS ON SUNDAYS.
HEY HUEY, STILL NO BLACK PEOPLE, AND NOW THEY'RE TALKIN' ABOUT REAL ESTATE!!
www.uexpress.com www.boondocks.net
LOOK, MY GRANDFATHER PAYS GOOD MONEY FOR CABLE, AND WHEN I TURN ON B.E.T., I WANT TO SEE SOME PEOPLE WITH SOME COLOR!
I DON'T KNOW WHAT TO SUGGEST, SIR — ASIDE FROM ADJUSTING THE "HUE" CONTROL.
©1999 Aaron McGruder/Dist. by Universal Press Syndicate
10-24
RILEY!! SHE SAID TO TRY THE "HUE" CONTROL ON THE TV!
WELL, NOW THEY'RE TURNING GREEN, BUT THEY'RE STILL TALKIN' ABOUT REAL ESTATE!

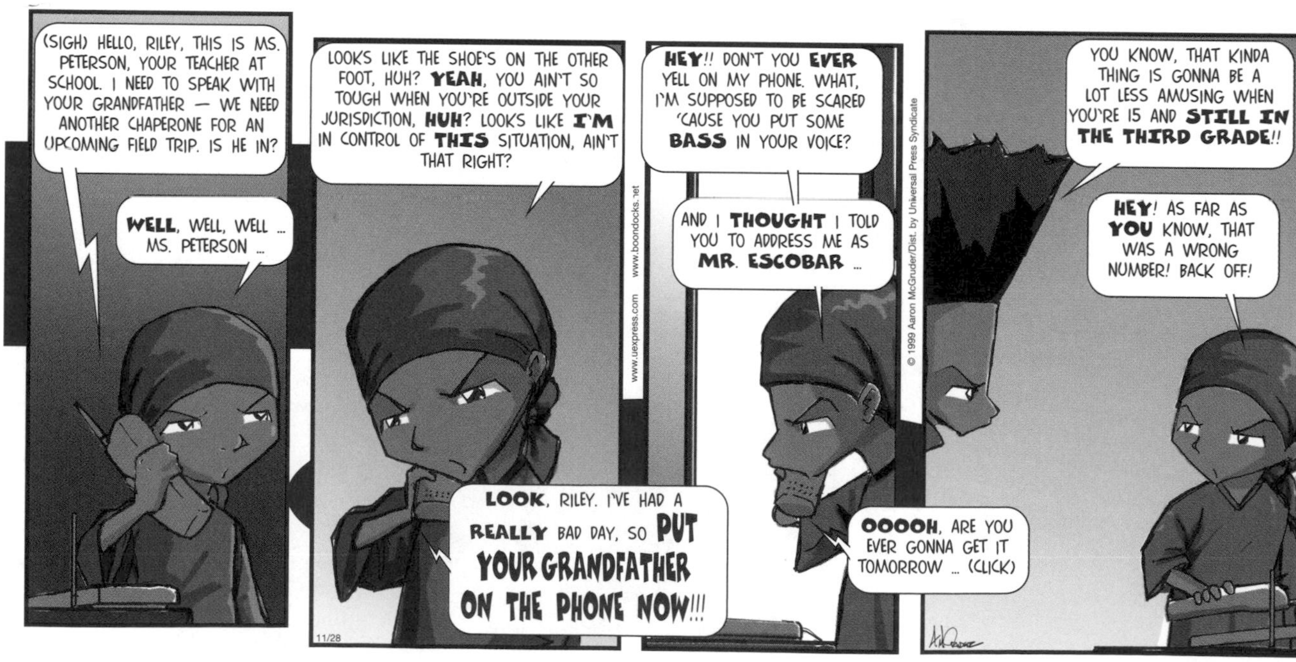
(SIGH) HELLO, RILEY, THIS IS MS. PETERSON, YOUR TEACHER AT SCHOOL. I NEED TO SPEAK WITH YOUR GRANDFATHER — WE NEED ANOTHER CHAPERONE FOR AN UPCOMING FIELD TRIP. IS HE IN?
WELL, WELL, WELL ... MS. PETERSON ...
LOOKS LIKE THE SHOE'S ON THE OTHER FOOT, HUH? YEAH, YOU AIN'T SO TOUGH WHEN YOU'RE OUTSIDE YOUR JURISDICTION, HUH? LOOKS LIKE I'M IN CONTROL OF THIS SITUATION, AIN'T THAT RIGHT?
LOOK, RILEY. I'VE HAD A REALLY BAD DAY, SO PUT YOUR GRANDFATHER ON THE PHONE NOW!!!
11/28
www.uexpress.com www.boondocks.net
HEY!! DON'T YOU EVER YELL ON MY PHONE. WHAT, I'M SUPPOSED TO BE SCARED 'CAUSE YOU PUT SOME BASS IN YOUR VOICE?
AND I THOUGHT I TOLD YOU TO ADDRESS ME AS MR. ESCOBAR ...
OOOOH, ARE YOU EVER GONNA GET IT TOMORROW ... (CLICK)
© 1999 Aaron McGruder/Dist. by Universal Press Syndicate
YOU KNOW, THAT KINDA THING IS GONNA BE A LOT LESS AMUSING WHEN YOU'RE 15 AND STILL IN THE THIRD GRADE!!
HEY! AS FAR AS YOU KNOW, THAT WAS A WRONG NUMBER! BACK OFF!

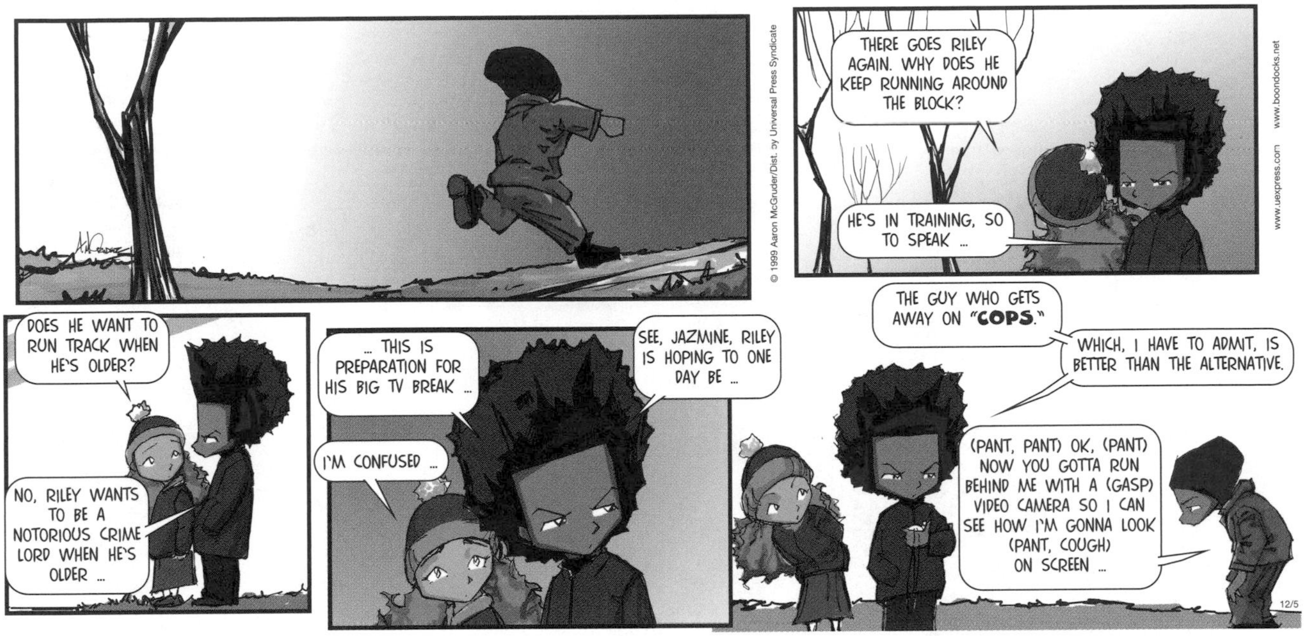
THERE GOES RILEY AGAIN. WHY DOES HE KEEP RUNNING AROUND THE BLOCK?
HE'S IN TRAINING, SO TO SPEAK ...
DOES HE WANT TO RUN TRACK WHEN HE'S OLDER?
NO, RILEY WANTS TO BE A NOTORIOUS CRIME LORD WHEN HE'S OLDER ...
... THIS IS PREPARATION FOR HIS BIG TV BREAK ...
I'M CONFUSED ...
SEE, JAZMINE, RILEY IS HOPING TO ONE DAY BE ...
THE GUY WHO GETS AWAY ON "COPS."
WHICH, I HAVE TO ADMIT, IS BETTER THAN THE ALTERNATIVE.
(PANT, PANT) OK, (PANT) NOW YOU GOTTA RUN BEHIND ME WITH A (GASP) VIDEO CAMERA SO I CAN SEE HOW I'M GONNA LOOK (PANT, COUGH) ON SCREEN ...
© 1999 Aaron McGruder/Dist. by Universal Press Syndicate
www.uexpress.com www.boondocks.net
12/5

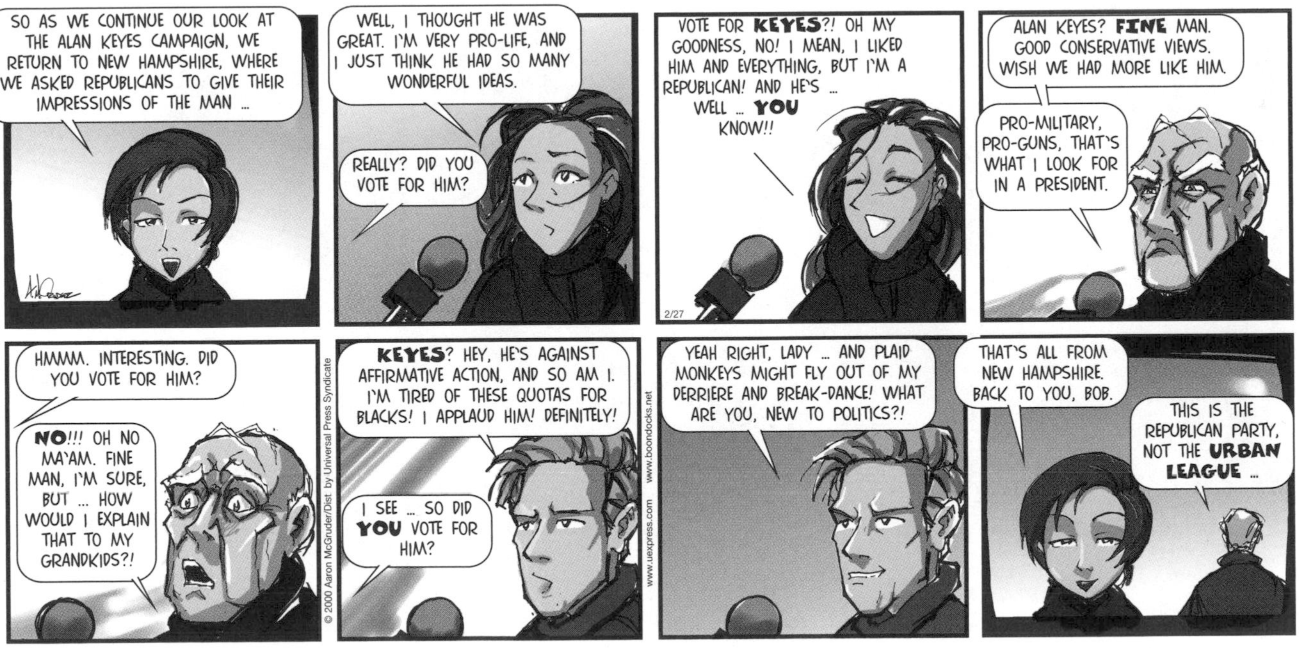
SO AS WE CONTINUE OUR LOOK AT THE ALAN KEYES CAMPAIGN, WE RETURN TO NEW HAMPSHIRE, WHERE WE ASKED REPUBLICANS TO GIVE THEIR IMPRESSIONS OF THE MAN ...
WELL, I THOUGHT HE WAS GREAT. I'M VERY PRO-LIFE, AND I JUST THINK HE HAD SO MANY WONDERFUL IDEAS.
REALLY? DID YOU VOTE FOR HIM?
VOTE FOR KEYES?! OH MY GOODNESS, NO! I MEAN, I LIKED HIM AND EVERYTHING, BUT I'M A REPUBLICAN! AND HE'S ... WELL ... YOU KNOW!!
2/27
ALAN KEYES? FINE MAN. GOOD CONSERVATIVE VIEWS. WISH WE HAD MORE LIKE HIM.
PRO-MILITARY, PRO-GUNS, THAT'S WHAT I LOOK FOR IN A PRESIDENT.
HMMM. INTERESTING. DID YOU VOTE FOR HIM?
NO!!! OH NO MA'AM. FINE MAN, I'M SURE, BUT ... HOW WOULD I EXPLAIN THAT TO MY GRANDKIDS?!
© 2000 Aaron McGruder/Dist. by Universal Press Syndicate
KEYES? HEY, HE'S AGAINST AFFIRMATIVE ACTION, AND SO AM I. I'M TIRED OF THESE QUOTAS FOR BLACKS! I APPLAUD HIM! DEFINITELY!
I SEE ... SO DID YOU VOTE FOR HIM?
www.uexpress.com www.boondocks.net
YEAH RIGHT, LADY ... AND PLAID MONKEYS MIGHT FLY OUT OF MY DERRIERE AND BREAK-DANCE! WHAT ARE YOU, NEW TO POLITICS?!
THAT'S ALL FROM NEW HAMPSHIRE. BACK TO YOU, BOB.
THIS IS THE REPUBLICAN PARTY, NOT THE URBAN LEAGUE ...

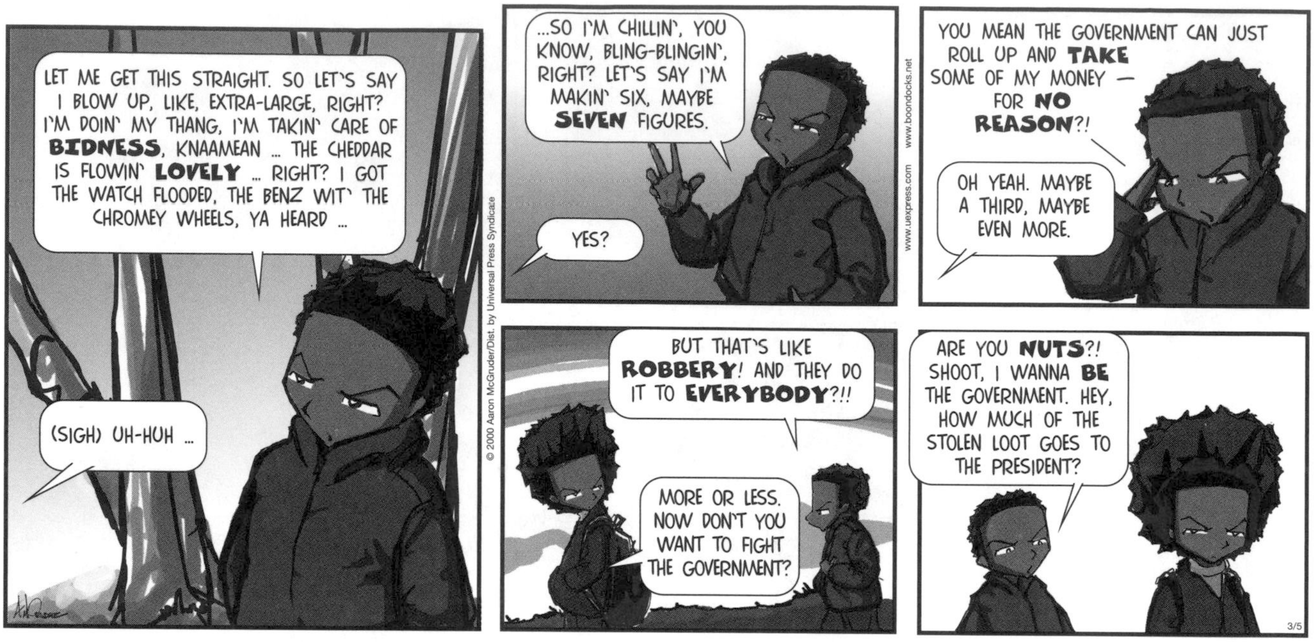
LET ME GET THIS STRAIGHT. SO LET'S SAY I BLOW UP, LIKE, EXTRA-LARGE, RIGHT? I'M DOIN' MY THANG, I'M TAKIN' CARE OF BIDNESS, KNAAMEAN ... THE CHEDDAR IS FLOWIN' LOVELY ... RIGHT? I GOT THE WATCH FLOODED, THE BENZ WIT' THE CHROMEY WHEELS, YA HEARD ...
(SIGH) UH-HUH ...
© 2000 Aaron McGruder/Dist. by Universal Press Syndicate
...SO I'M CHILLIN', YOU KNOW, BLING-BLINGIN', RIGHT? LET'S SAY I'M MAKIN' SIX, MAYBE SEVEN FIGURES.
YES?
www.uexpress.com www.boondocks.net
YOU MEAN THE GOVERNMENT CAN JUST ROLL UP AND TAKE SOME OF MY MONEY — FOR NO REASON?!
OH YEAH. MAYBE A THIRD, MAYBE EVEN MORE.
BUT THAT'S LIKE ROBBERY! AND THEY DO IT TO EVERYBODY?!!
MORE OR LESS. NOW DON'T YOU WANT TO FIGHT THE GOVERNMENT?
ARE YOU NUTS?! SHOOT, I WANNA BE THE GOVERNMENT. HEY, HOW MUCH OF THE STOLEN LOOT GOES TO THE PRESIDENT?
3/5

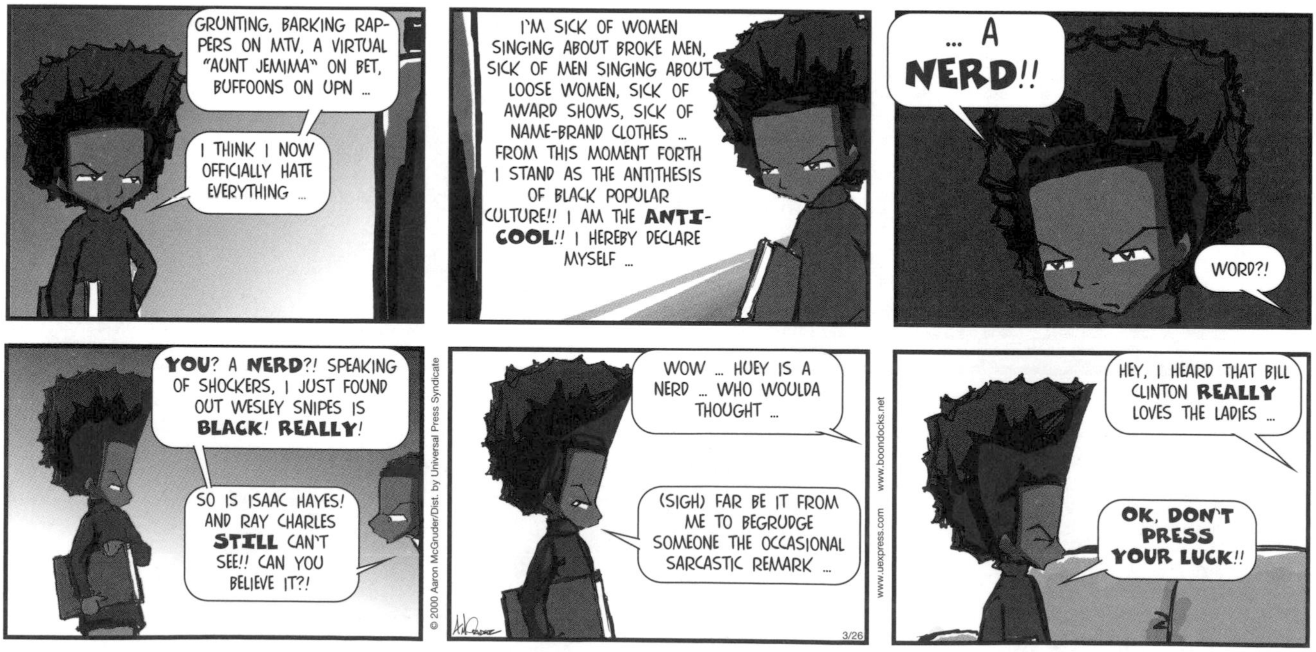
GRUNTING, BARKING RAPPERS ON MTV, A VIRTUAL "AUNT JEMIMA" ON BET, BUFFOONS ON UPN ...
I THINK I NOW OFFICIALLY HATE EVERYTHING ...
I'M SICK OF WOMEN SINGING ABOUT BROKE MEN, SICK OF MEN SINGING ABOUT LOOSE WOMEN, SICK OF AWARD SHOWS, SICK OF NAME-BRAND CLOTHES ... FROM THIS MOMENT FORTH I STAND AS THE ANTITHESIS OF BLACK POPULAR CULTURE!! I AM THE ANTI-COOL!! I HEREBY DECLARE MYSELF ...
... A NERD!!
WORD?!
YOU? A NERD?! SPEAKING OF SHOCKERS, I JUST FOUND OUT WESLEY SNIPES IS BLACK! REALLY!
SO IS ISAAC HAYES! AND RAY CHARLES STILL CAN'T SEE!! CAN YOU BELIEVE IT?!
© 2000 Aaron McGruder/Dist. by Universal Press Syndicate
WOW ... HUEY IS A NERD ... WHO WOULDA THOUGHT ...
(SIGH) FAR BE IT FROM ME TO BEGRUDGE SOMEONE THE OCCASIONAL SARCASTIC REMARK ...
3/26
www.uexpress.com www.boondocks.net
HEY, I HEARD THAT BILL CLINTON REALLY LOVES THE LADIES ...
OK, DON'T PRESS YOUR LUCK!!

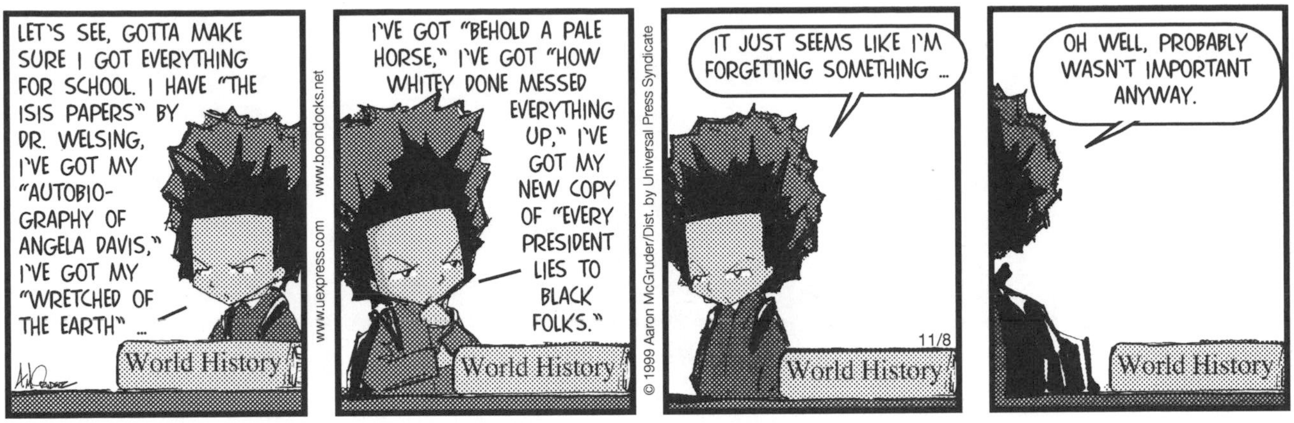
LET'S SEE, GOTTA MAKE SURE I GOT EVERYTHING FOR SCHOOL. I HAVE "THE ISIS PAPERS" BY DR. WELSING, I'VE GOT MY "AUTOBIOGRAPHY OF ANGELA DAVIS," I'VE GOT MY "WRETCHED OF THE EARTH" ...
World History
www.uexpress.com www.boondocks.net
I'VE GOT "BEHOLD A PALE HORSE," I'VE GOT "HOW WHITEY DONE MESSED EVERYTHING UP," I'VE GOT MY NEW COPY OF "EVERY PRESIDENT LIES TO BLACK FOLKS."
World History
© 1999 Aaron McGruder/Dist. by Universal Press Syndicate
IT JUST SEEMS LIKE I'M FORGETTING SOMETHING ...
11/8
World History
OH WELL, PROBABLY WASN'T IMPORTANT ANYWAY.
World History

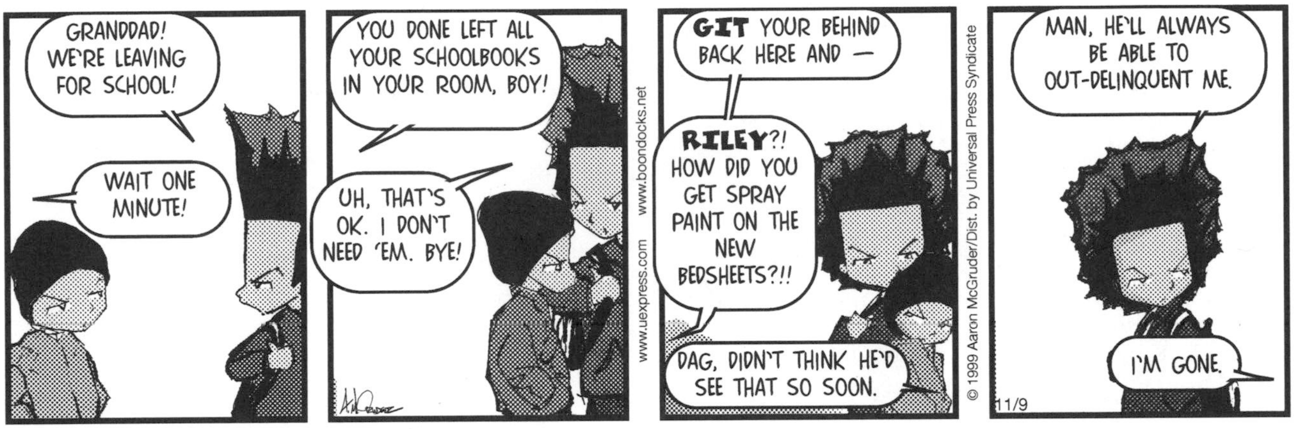
GRANDDAD! WE'RE LEAVING FOR SCHOOL!
WAIT ONE MINUTE!
YOU DONE LEFT ALL YOUR SCHOOLBOOKS IN YOUR ROOM, BOY!
UH, THAT'S OK. I DON'T NEED 'EM. BYE!
www.uexpress.com www.boondocks.net
GIT YOUR BEHIND BACK HERE AND —
RILEY?! HOW DID YOU GET SPRAY PAINT ON THE NEW BEDSHEETS?!!
DAG, DIDN'T THINK HE'D SEE THAT SO SOON.
© 1999 Aaron McGruder/Dist. by Universal Press Syndicate
MAN, HE'LL ALWAYS BE ABLE TO OUT-DELINQUENT ME.
I'M GONE.
11/9

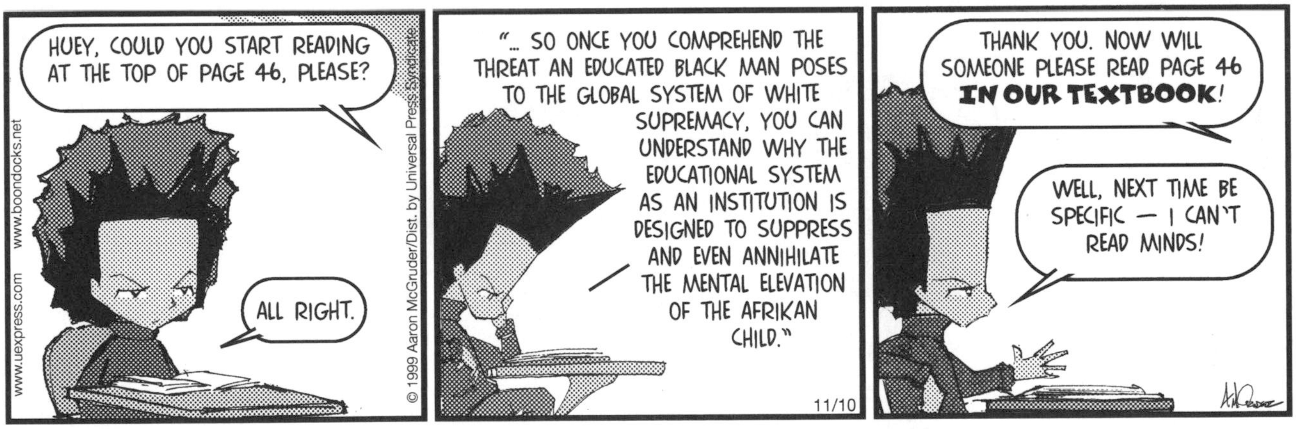
HUEY, COULD YOU START READING AT THE TOP OF PAGE 46, PLEASE?
ALL RIGHT.
www.uexpress.com www.boondocks.net
© 1999 Aaron McGruder/Dist. by Universal Press Syndicate
"... SO ONCE YOU COMPREHEND THE THREAT AN EDUCATED BLACK MAN POSES TO THE GLOBAL SYSTEM OF WHITE SUPREMACY, YOU CAN UNDERSTAND WHY THE EDUCATIONAL SYSTEM AS AN INSTITUTION IS DESIGNED TO SUPPRESS AND EVEN ANNIHILATE THE MENTAL ELEVATION OF THE AFRIKAN CHILD."
11/10
THANK YOU. NOW WILL SOMEONE PLEASE READ PAGE 46 IN OUR TEXTBOOK!
WELL, NEXT TIME BE SPECIFIC — I CAN'T READ MINDS!

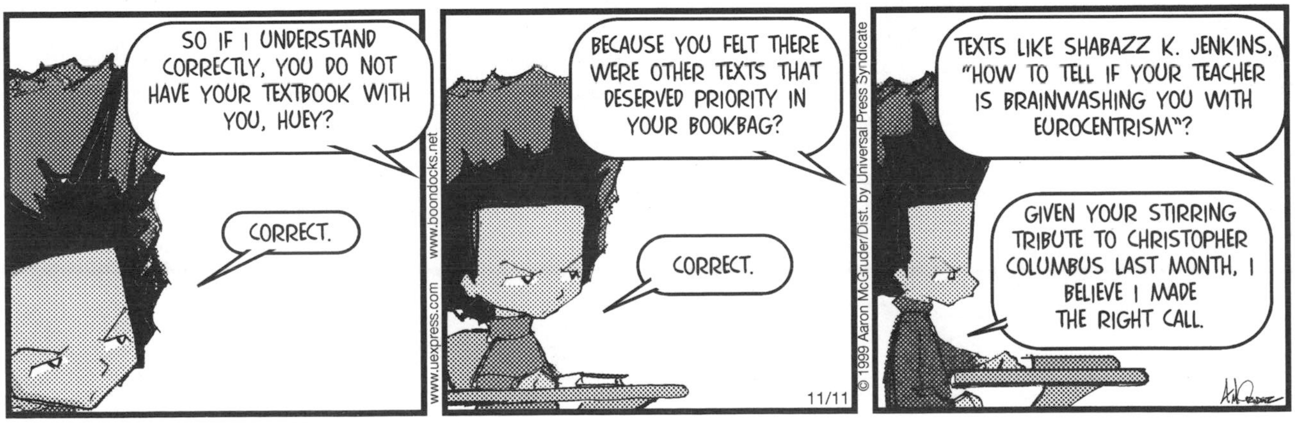
SO IF I UNDERSTAND CORRECTLY, YOU DO NOT HAVE YOUR TEXTBOOK WITH YOU, HUEY?
CORRECT.
www.uexpress.com www.boondocks.net
BECAUSE YOU FELT THERE WERE OTHER TEXTS THAT DESERVED PRIORITY IN YOUR BOOKBAG?
CORRECT.
11/11
© 1999 Aaron McGruder/Dist. by Universal Press Syndicate
TEXTS LIKE SHABAZZ K. JENKINS, "HOW TO TELL IF YOUR TEACHER IS BRAINWASHING YOU WITH EUROCENTRISM"?
GIVEN YOUR STIRRING TRIBUTE TO CHRISTOPHER COLUMBUS LAST MONTH, I BELIEVE I MADE THE RIGHT CALL.

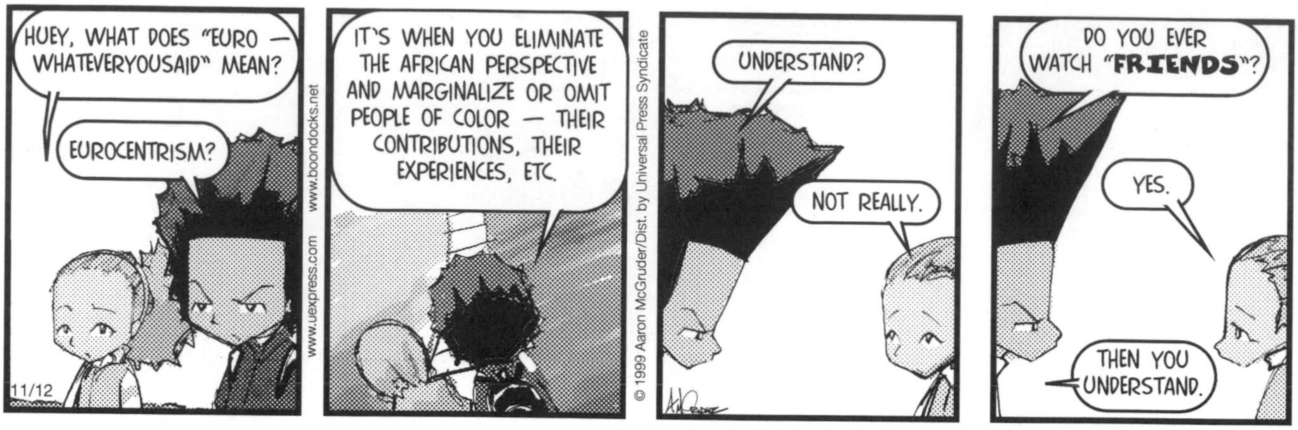
HUEY, WHAT DOES "EURO — WHATEVERYOUSAID" MEAN?
EUROCENTRISM?
11/12
www.uexpress.com www.boondocks.net
IT'S WHEN YOU ELIMINATE THE AFRICAN PERSPECTIVE AND MARGINALIZE OR OMIT PEOPLE OF COLOR — THEIR CONTRIBUTIONS, THEIR EXPERIENCES, ETC.
© 1999 Aaron McGruder/Dist. by Universal Press Syndicate
UNDERSTAND?
NOT REALLY.
DO YOU EVER WATCH "**FRIENDS**"?
YES.
THEN YOU UNDERSTAND.

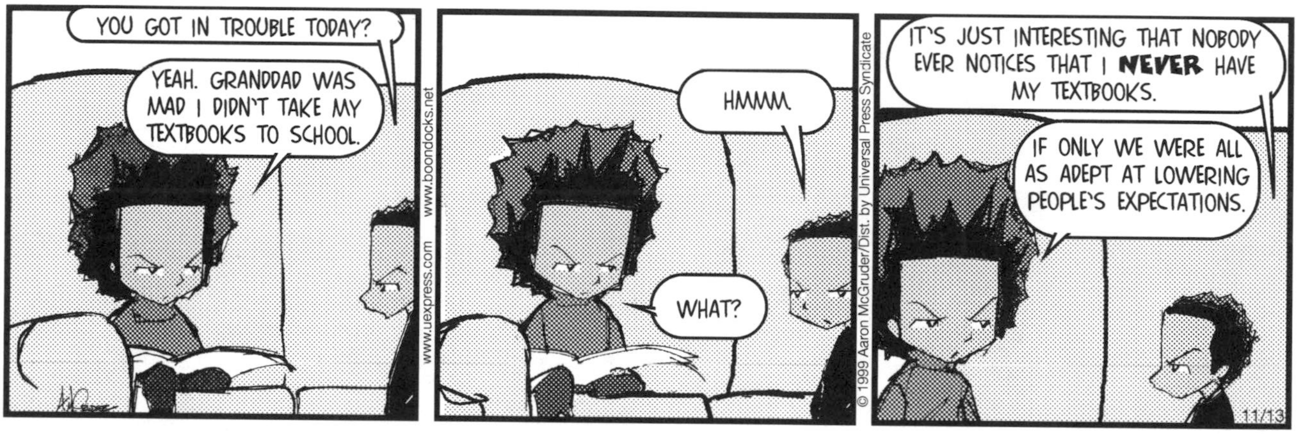
YOU GOT IN TROUBLE TODAY?
YEAH. GRANDDAD WAS MAD I DIDN'T TAKE MY TEXTBOOKS TO SCHOOL.
www.uexpress.com www.boondocks.net
HMMM.
WHAT?
© 1999 Aaron McGruder/Dist. by Universal Press Syndicate
IT'S JUST INTERESTING THAT NOBODY EVER NOTICES THAT I **NEVER** HAVE MY TEXTBOOKS.
IF ONLY WE WERE ALL AS ADEPT AT LOWERING PEOPLE'S EXPECTATIONS.
11/13

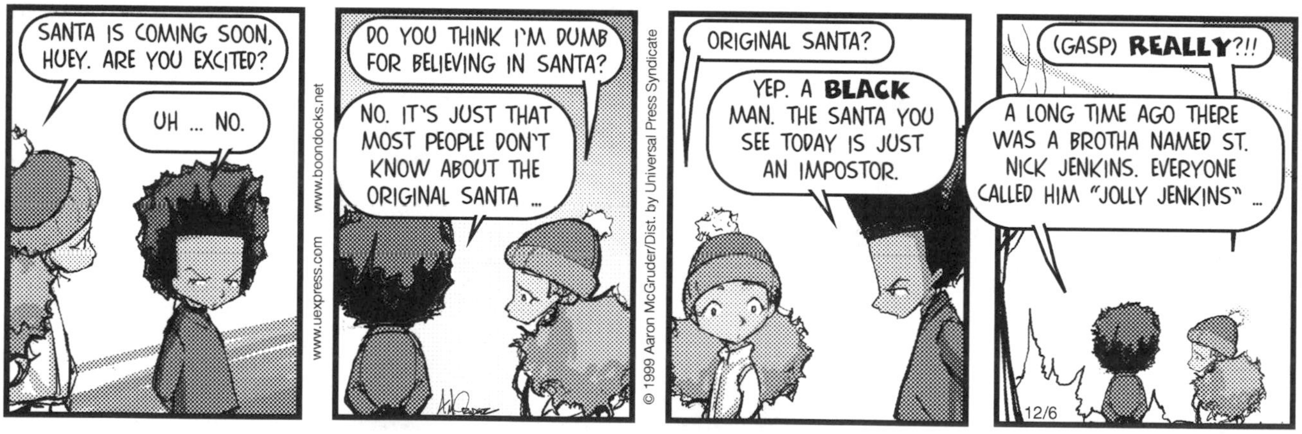
SANTA IS COMING SOON, HUEY. ARE YOU EXCITED?
UH ... NO.
www.uexpress.com www.boondocks.net
DO YOU THINK I'M DUMB FOR BELIEVING IN SANTA?
NO. IT'S JUST THAT MOST PEOPLE DON'T KNOW ABOUT THE ORIGINAL SANTA ...
© 1999 Aaron McGruder/Dist. by Universal Press Syndicate
ORIGINAL SANTA?
YEP. A **BLACK** MAN. THE SANTA YOU SEE TODAY IS JUST AN IMPOSTOR.
(GASP) **REALLY**?!!
A LONG TIME AGO THERE WAS A BROTHA NAMED ST. NICK JENKINS. EVERYONE CALLED HIM "JOLLY JENKINS" ...
12/6

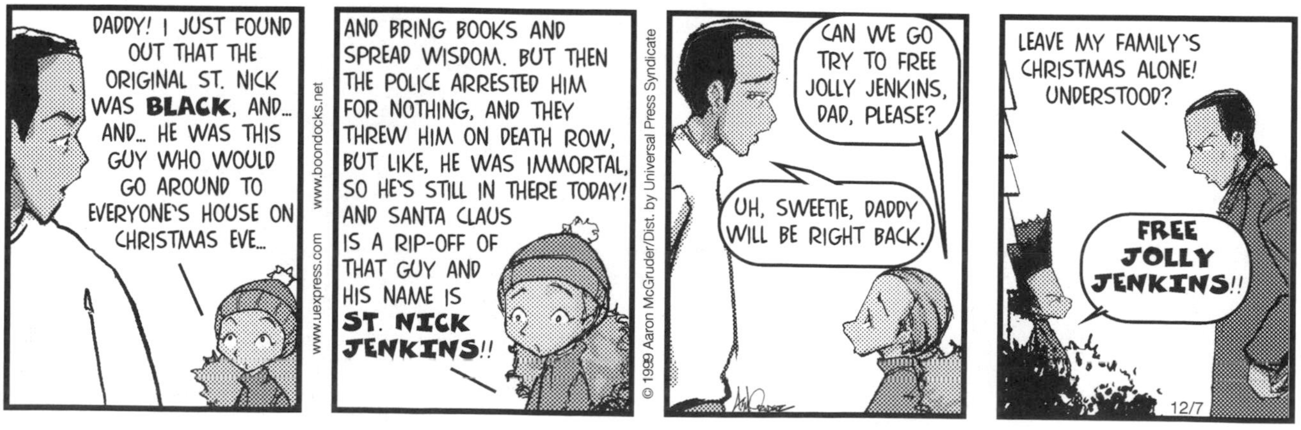
DADDY! I JUST FOUND OUT THAT THE ORIGINAL ST. NICK WAS **BLACK**, AND... AND... HE WAS THIS GUY WHO WOULD GO AROUND TO EVERYONE'S HOUSE ON CHRISTMAS EVE...
www.uexpress.com www.boondocks.net
AND BRING BOOKS AND SPREAD WISDOM. BUT THEN THE POLICE ARRESTED HIM FOR NOTHING, AND THEY THREW HIM ON DEATH ROW, BUT LIKE, HE WAS IMMORTAL, SO HE'S STILL IN THERE TODAY! AND SANTA CLAUS IS A RIP-OFF OF THAT GUY AND HIS NAME IS **ST. NICK JENKINS**!!
© 1999 Aaron McGruder/Dist. by Universal Press Syndicate
CAN WE GO TRY TO FREE JOLLY JENKINS, DAD, PLEASE?
UH, SWEETIE, DADDY WILL BE RIGHT BACK.
LEAVE MY FAMILY'S CHRISTMAS ALONE! UNDERSTOOD?
FREE JOLLY JENKINS!!
12/7

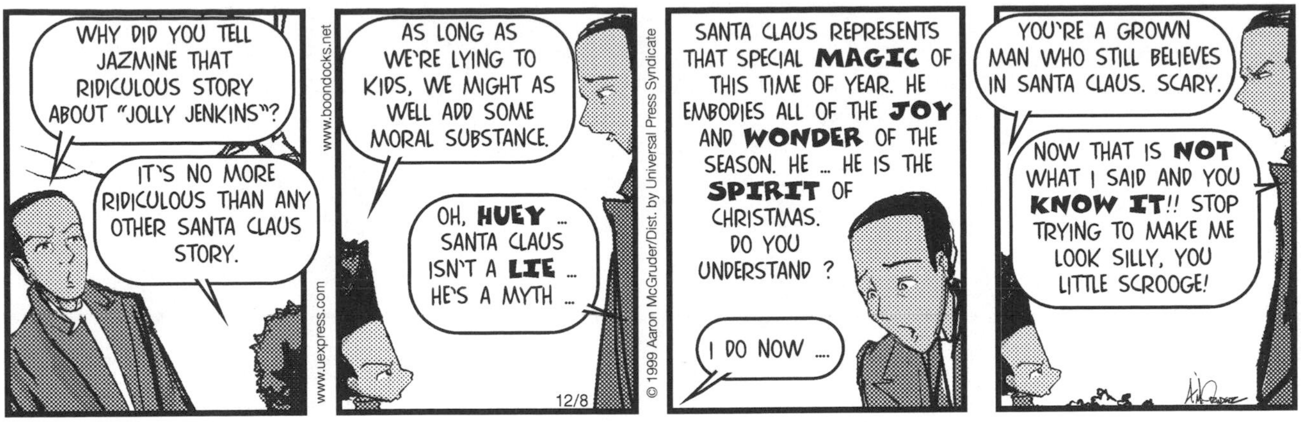
WHY DID YOU TELL JAZMINE THAT RIDICULOUS STORY ABOUT "JOLLY JENKINS"?
IT'S NO MORE RIDICULOUS THAN ANY OTHER SANTA CLAUS STORY.
www.boondocks.net
www.uexpress.com
AS LONG AS WE'RE LYING TO KIDS, WE MIGHT AS WELL ADD SOME MORAL SUBSTANCE.
OH, **HUEY** ... SANTA CLAUS ISN'T A **LIE** ... HE'S A MYTH ...
12/8
© 1999 Aaron McGruder/Dist. by Universal Press Syndicate
SANTA CLAUS REPRESENTS THAT SPECIAL **MAGIC** OF THIS TIME OF YEAR. HE EMBODIES ALL OF THE **JOY** AND **WONDER** OF THE SEASON. HE ... HE IS THE **SPIRIT** OF CHRISTMAS. DO YOU UNDERSTAND ?
I DO NOW ....
YOU'RE A GROWN MAN WHO STILL BELIEVES IN SANTA CLAUS. SCARY.
NOW THAT IS **NOT** WHAT I SAID AND YOU **KNOW IT**!! STOP TRYING TO MAKE ME LOOK SILLY, YOU LITTLE SCROOGE!

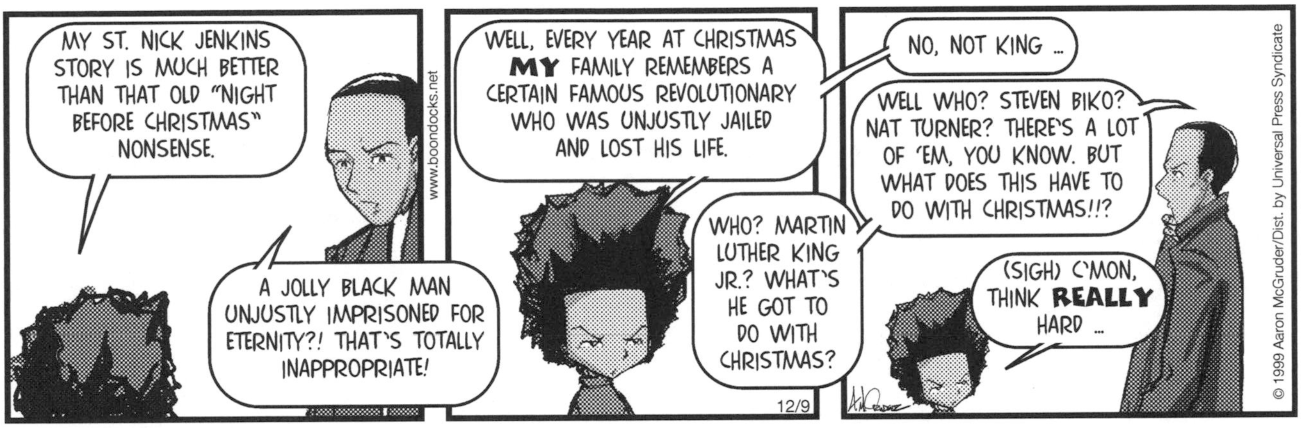
MY ST. NICK JENKINS STORY IS MUCH BETTER THAN THAT OLD "NIGHT BEFORE CHRISTMAS" NONSENSE.
A JOLLY BLACK MAN UNJUSTLY IMPRISONED FOR ETERNITY?! THAT'S TOTALLY INAPPROPRIATE!
www.boondocks.net
WELL, EVERY YEAR AT CHRISTMAS **MY** FAMILY REMEMBERS A CERTAIN FAMOUS REVOLUTIONARY WHO WAS UNJUSTLY JAILED AND LOST HIS LIFE.
WHO? MARTIN LUTHER KING JR.? WHAT'S HE GOT TO DO WITH CHRISTMAS?
12/9
NO, NOT KING ...
WELL WHO? STEVEN BIKO? NAT TURNER? THERE'S A LOT OF 'EM, YOU KNOW. BUT WHAT DOES THIS HAVE TO DO WITH CHRISTMAS!!?
(SIGH) C'MON, THINK **REALLY** HARD ...
© 1999 Aaron McGruder/Dist. by Universal Press Syndicate

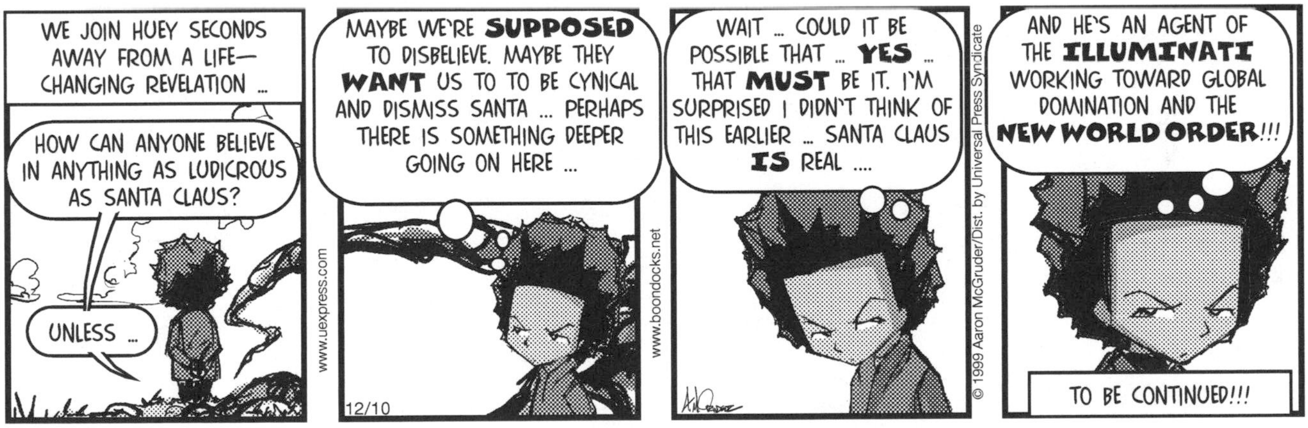
WE JOIN HUEY SECONDS AWAY FROM A LIFE—CHANGING REVELATION ...
HOW CAN ANYONE BELIEVE IN ANYTHING AS LUDICROUS AS SANTA CLAUS?
UNLESS ...
www.uexpress.com
12/10
MAYBE WE'RE **SUPPOSED** TO DISBELIEVE. MAYBE THEY **WANT** US TO TO BE CYNICAL AND DISMISS SANTA ... PERHAPS THERE IS SOMETHING DEEPER GOING ON HERE ...
www.boondocks.net
WAIT ... COULD IT BE POSSIBLE THAT ... **YES** ... THAT **MUST** BE IT. I'M SURPRISED I DIDN'T THINK OF THIS EARLIER ... SANTA CLAUS **IS** REAL ....
© 1999 Aaron McGruder/Dist. by Universal Press Syndicate
AND HE'S AN AGENT OF THE **ILLUMINATI** WORKING TOWARD GLOBAL DOMINATION AND THE **NEW WORLD ORDER**!!!
TO BE CONTINUED!!!

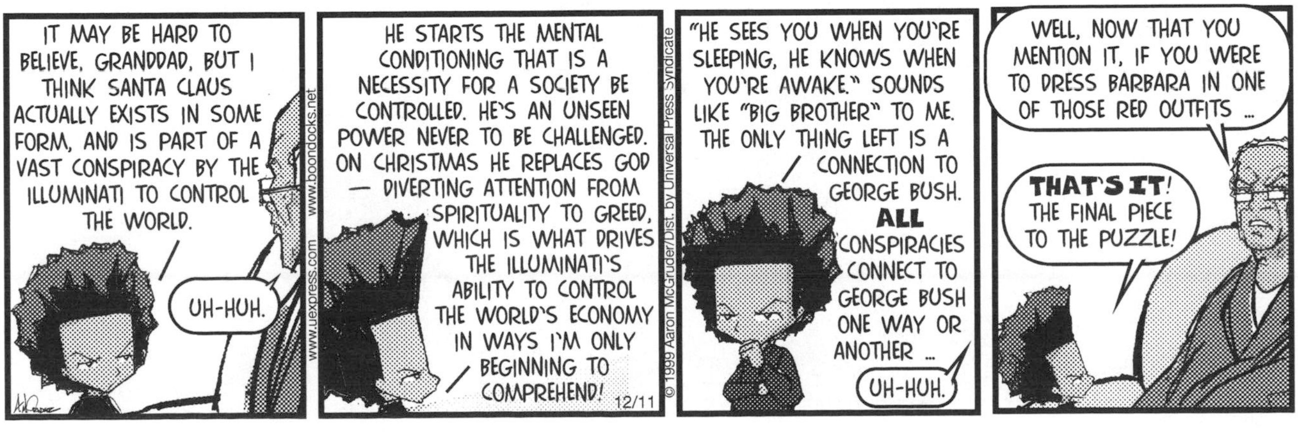
IT MAY BE HARD TO BELIEVE, GRANDDAD, BUT I THINK SANTA CLAUS ACTUALLY EXISTS IN SOME FORM, AND IS PART OF A VAST CONSPIRACY BY THE ILLUMINATI TO CONTROL THE WORLD.
UH-HUH.
www.boondocks.net
www.uexpress.com
HE STARTS THE MENTAL CONDITIONING THAT IS A NECESSITY FOR A SOCIETY BE CONTROLLED. HE'S AN UNSEEN POWER NEVER TO BE CHALLENGED. ON CHRISTMAS HE REPLACES GOD — DIVERTING ATTENTION FROM SPIRITUALITY TO GREED, WHICH IS WHAT DRIVES THE ILLUMINATI'S ABILITY TO CONTROL THE WORLD'S ECONOMY IN WAYS I'M ONLY BEGINNING TO COMPREHEND!
12/11
© 1999 Aaron McGruder/Dist. by Universal Press Syndicate
"HE SEES YOU WHEN YOU'RE SLEEPING, HE KNOWS WHEN YOU'RE AWAKE." SOUNDS LIKE "BIG BROTHER" TO ME. THE ONLY THING LEFT IS A CONNECTION TO GEORGE BUSH. **ALL** CONSPIRACIES CONNECT TO GEORGE BUSH ONE WAY OR ANOTHER ...
UH-HUH.
WELL, NOW THAT YOU MENTION IT, IF YOU WERE TO DRESS BARBARA IN ONE OF THOSE RED OUTFITS ...
THAT'S IT! THE FINAL PIECE TO THE PUZZLE!

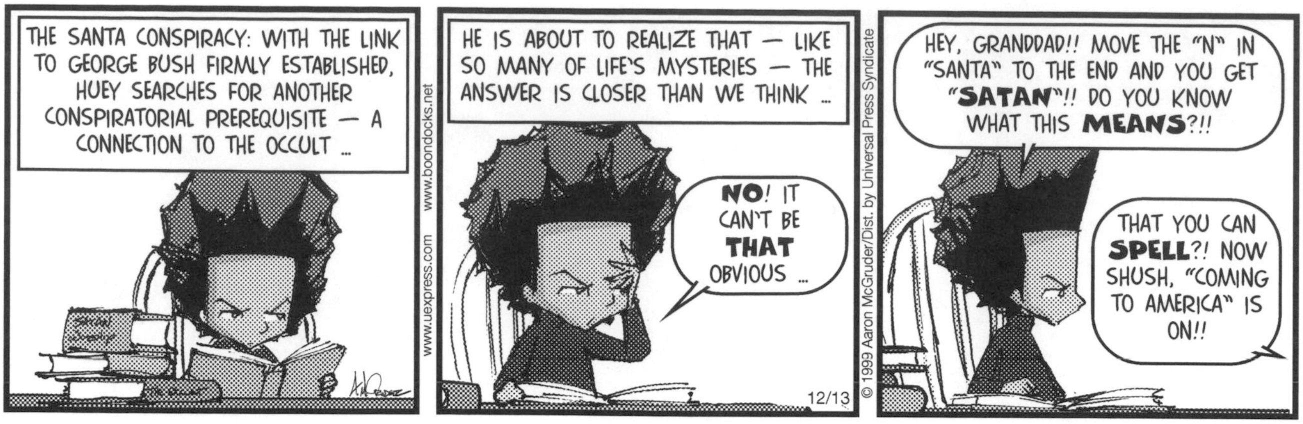

THE SANTA CONSPIRACY: WITH THE LINK TO GEORGE BUSH FIRMLY ESTABLISHED, HUEY SEARCHES FOR ANOTHER CONSPIRATORIAL PREREQUISITE — A CONNECTION TO THE OCCULT ...
www.uexpress.com www.boondocks.net
HE IS ABOUT TO REALIZE THAT — LIKE SO MANY OF LIFE'S MYSTERIES — THE ANSWER IS CLOSER THAN WE THINK ...
NO! IT CAN'T BE THAT OBVIOUS ...
12/13
© 1999 Aaron McGruder/Dist. by Universal Press Syndicate
HEY, GRANDDAD!! MOVE THE "N" IN "SANTA" TO THE END AND YOU GET "SATAN"!! DO YOU KNOW WHAT THIS MEANS?!!
THAT YOU CAN SPELL?! NOW SHUSH, "COMING TO AMERICA" IS ON!!

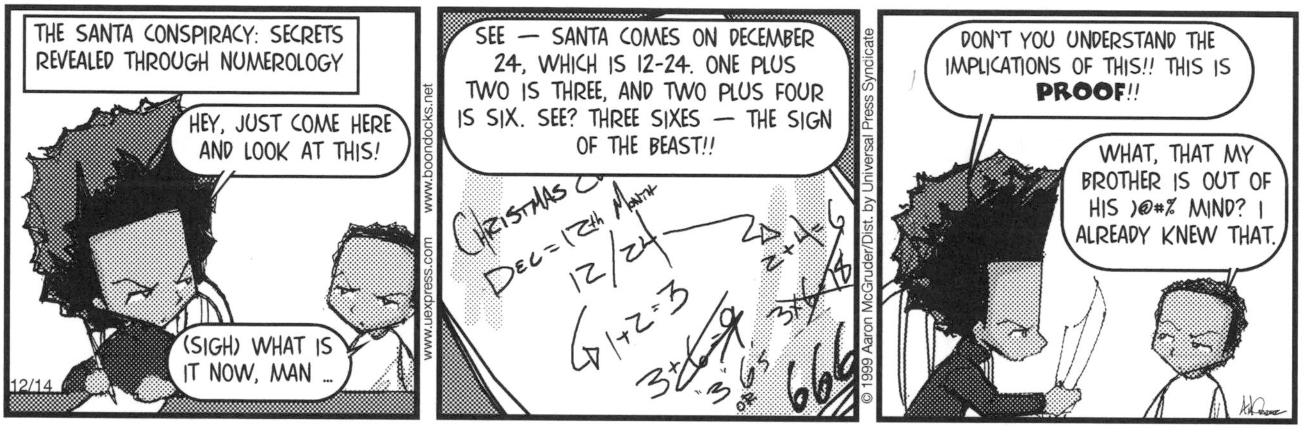

THE SANTA CONSPIRACY: SECRETS REVEALED THROUGH NUMEROLOGY
HEY, JUST COME HERE AND LOOK AT THIS!
(SIGH) WHAT IS IT NOW, MAN ...
12/14
www.uexpress.com www.boondocks.net
SEE — SANTA COMES ON DECEMBER 24, WHICH IS 12-24. ONE PLUS TWO IS THREE, AND TWO PLUS FOUR IS SIX. SEE? THREE SIXES — THE SIGN OF THE BEAST!!
666
© 1999 Aaron McGruder/Dist. by Universal Press Syndicate
DON'T YOU UNDERSTAND THE IMPLICATIONS OF THIS!! THIS IS PROOF!!
WHAT, THAT MY BROTHER IS OUT OF HIS)@#% MIND? I ALREADY KNEW THAT.

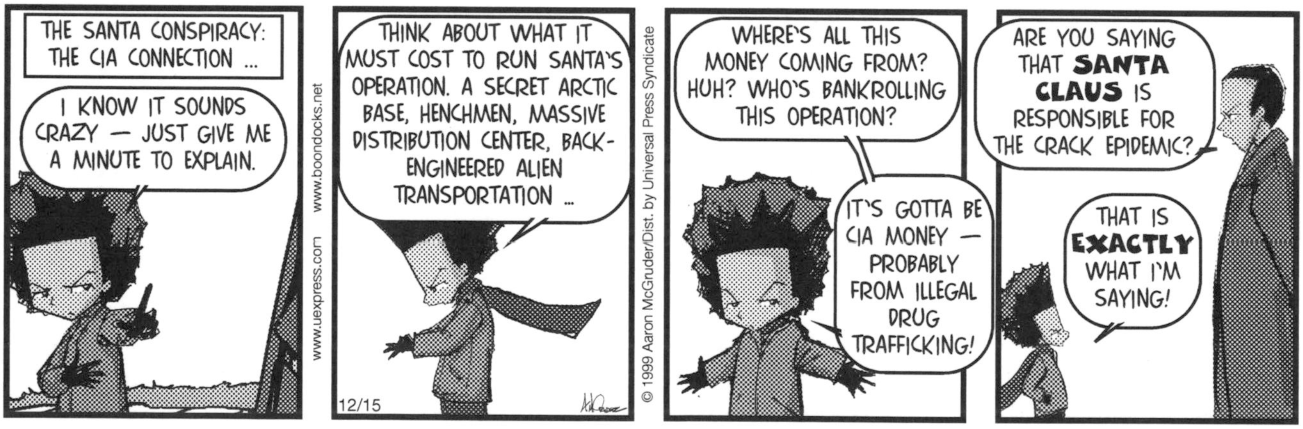

THE SANTA CONSPIRACY: THE CIA CONNECTION ...
I KNOW IT SOUNDS CRAZY — JUST GIVE ME A MINUTE TO EXPLAIN.
www.uexpress.com www.boondocks.net
THINK ABOUT WHAT IT MUST COST TO RUN SANTA'S OPERATION. A SECRET ARCTIC BASE, HENCHMEN, MASSIVE DISTRIBUTION CENTER, BACK-ENGINEERED ALIEN TRANSPORTATION ...
12/15
© 1999 Aaron McGruder/Dist. by Universal Press Syndicate
WHERE'S ALL THIS MONEY COMING FROM? HUH? WHO'S BANKROLLING THIS OPERATION?
IT'S GOTTA BE CIA MONEY — PROBABLY FROM ILLEGAL DRUG TRAFFICKING!
ARE YOU SAYING THAT SANTA CLAUS IS RESPONSIBLE FOR THE CRACK EPIDEMIC?
THAT IS EXACTLY WHAT I'M SAYING!

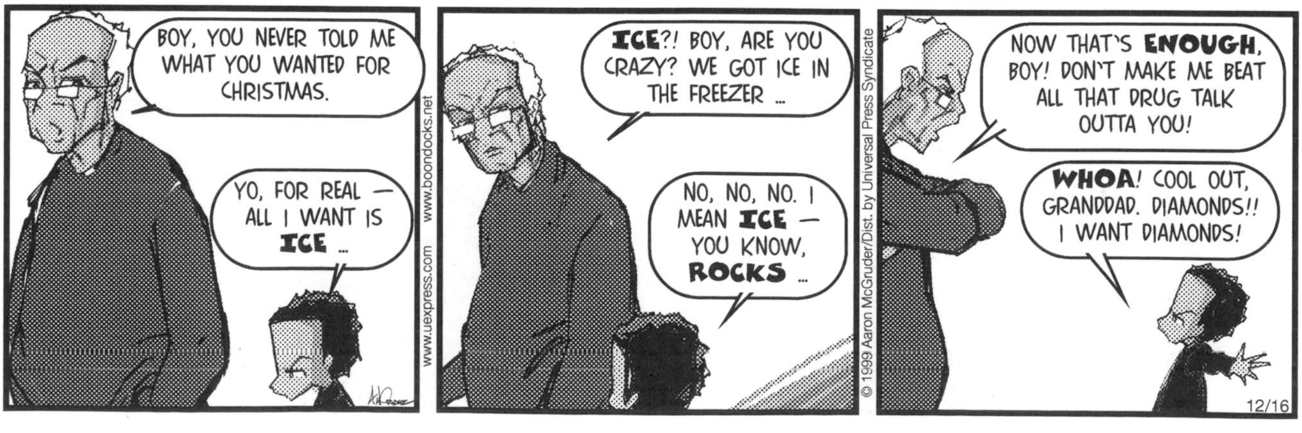

BOY, YOU NEVER TOLD ME WHAT YOU WANTED FOR CHRISTMAS.
YO, FOR REAL — ALL I WANT IS ICE ...
www.uexpress.com www.boondocks.net
ICE?! BOY, ARE YOU CRAZY? WE GOT ICE IN THE FREEZER ...
NO, NO, NO. I MEAN ICE — YOU KNOW, ROCKS ...
© 1999 Aaron McGruder/Dist. by Universal Press Syndicate
NOW THAT'S ENOUGH, BOY! DON'T MAKE ME BEAT ALL THAT DRUG TALK OUTTA YOU!
WHOA! COOL OUT, GRANDDAD. DIAMONDS!! I WANT DIAMONDS!
12/16

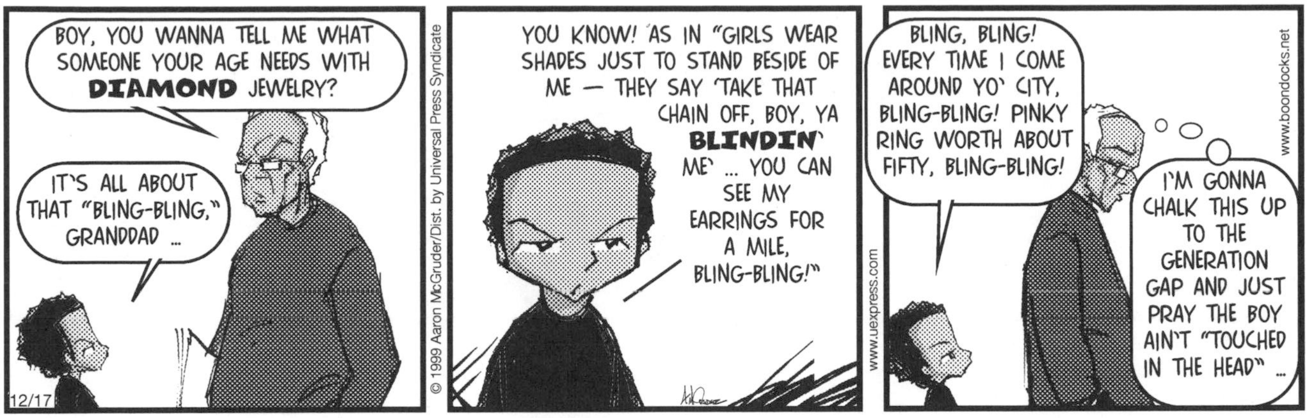
BOY, YOU WANNA TELL ME WHAT SOMEONE YOUR AGE NEEDS WITH **DIAMOND** JEWELRY?
IT'S ALL ABOUT THAT "BLING-BLING," GRANDDAD ...
12/17
© 1999 Aaron McGruder/Dist. by Universal Press Syndicate
YOU KNOW! AS IN "GIRLS WEAR SHADES JUST TO STAND BESIDE OF ME — THEY SAY 'TAKE THAT CHAIN OFF, BOY, YA **BLINDIN'** ME' ... YOU CAN SEE MY EARRINGS FOR A MILE, BLING-BLING!"
www.uexpress.com
BLING, BLING! EVERY TIME I COME AROUND YO' CITY, BLING-BLING! PINKY RING WORTH ABOUT FIFTY, BLING-BLING!
I'M GONNA CHALK THIS UP TO THE GENERATION GAP AND JUST PRAY THE BOY AIN'T "TOUCHED IN THE HEAD" ...
www.boondocks.net

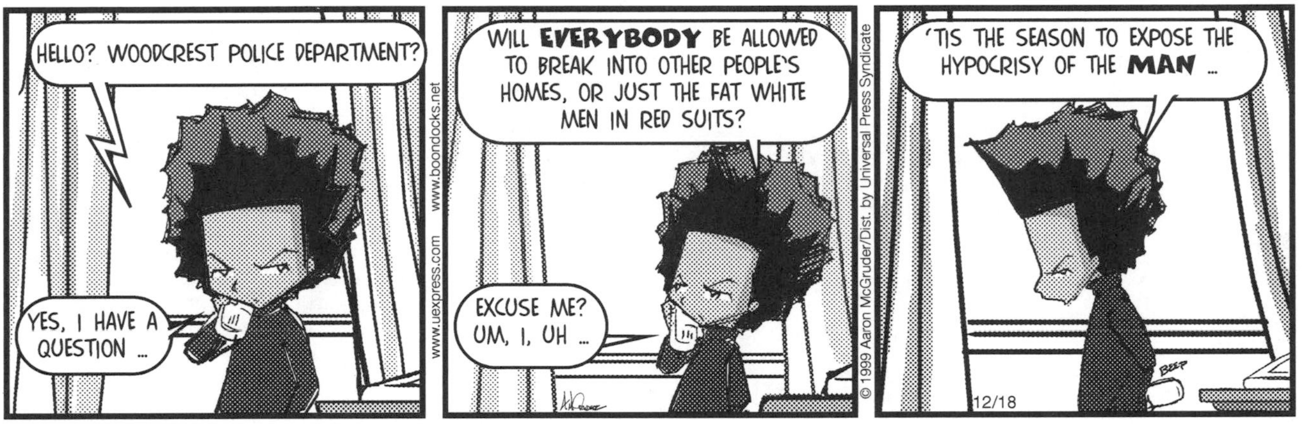
HELLO? WOODCREST POLICE DEPARTMENT?
YES, I HAVE A QUESTION ...
www.uexpress.com
www.boondocks.net
WILL **EVERYBODY** BE ALLOWED TO BREAK INTO OTHER PEOPLE'S HOMES, OR JUST THE FAT WHITE MEN IN RED SUITS?
EXCUSE ME? UM, I, UH ...
© 1999 Aaron McGruder/Dist. by Universal Press Syndicate
'TIS THE SEASON TO EXPOSE THE HYPOCRISY OF THE **MAN** ...
BEEP
12/18

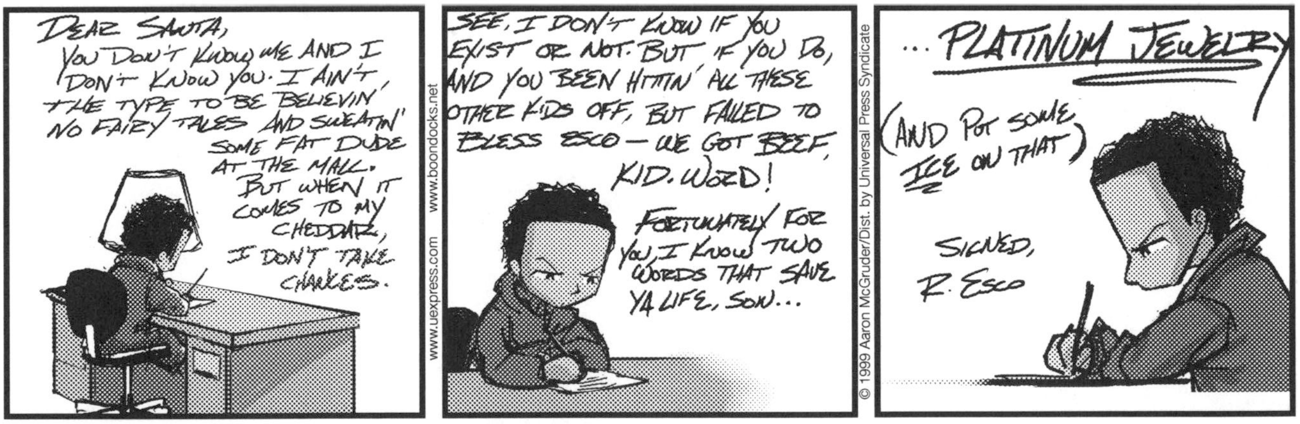
DEAR SANTA,
YOU DON'T KNOW ME AND I DON'T KNOW YOU. I AIN'T THE TYPE TO BE BELIEVIN' NO FAIRY TALES AND SWEATIN' SOME FAT DUDE AT THE MALL. BUT WHEN IT COMES TO MY CHEDDAR, I DON'T TAKE CHANCES.
www.uexpress.com
www.boondocks.net
SEE, I DON'T KNOW IF YOU EXIST OR NOT. BUT IF YOU DO, AND YOU BEEN HITTIN' ALL THESE OTHER KIDS OFF, BUT FAILED TO BLESS ESCO — WE GOT BEEF, KID. WORD!
FORTUNATELY FOR YOU, I KNOW TWO WORDS THAT SAVE YA LIFE, SON...
© 1999 Aaron McGruder/Dist. by Universal Press Syndicate
... PLATINUM JEWELRY
(AND PUT SOME ICE ON THAT)
SIGNED,
R. ESCO

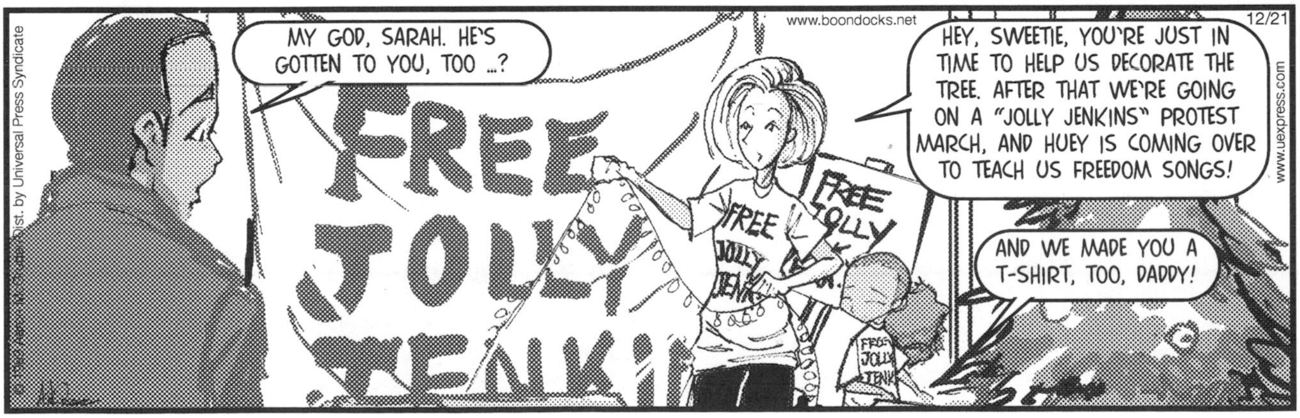
MY GOD, SARAH. HE'S GOTTEN TO YOU, TOO ...?
www.boondocks.net
FREE JOLLY JENKI
HEY, SWEETIE, YOU'RE JUST IN TIME TO HELP US DECORATE THE TREE. AFTER THAT WE'RE GOING ON A "JOLLY JENKINS" PROTEST MARCH, AND HUEY IS COMING OVER TO TEACH US FREEDOM SONGS!
AND WE MADE YOU A T-SHIRT, TOO, DADDY!
12/21
www.uexpress.com

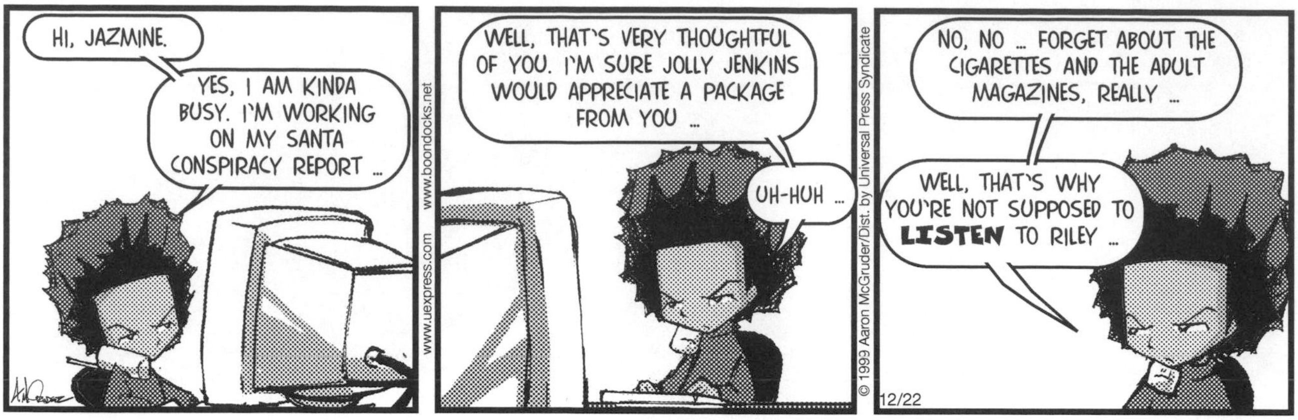
HI, JAZMINE.
YES, I AM KINDA BUSY. I'M WORKING ON MY SANTA CONSPIRACY REPORT ...
WELL, THAT'S VERY THOUGHTFUL OF YOU. I'M SURE JOLLY JENKINS WOULD APPRECIATE A PACKAGE FROM YOU ...
UH-HUH ...
NO, NO ... FORGET ABOUT THE CIGARETTES AND THE ADULT MAGAZINES, REALLY ...
WELL, THAT'S WHY YOU'RE NOT SUPPOSED TO **LISTEN** TO RILEY ...
www.uexpress.com www.boondocks.net
© 1999 Aaron McGruder/Dist. by Universal Press Syndicate
12/22

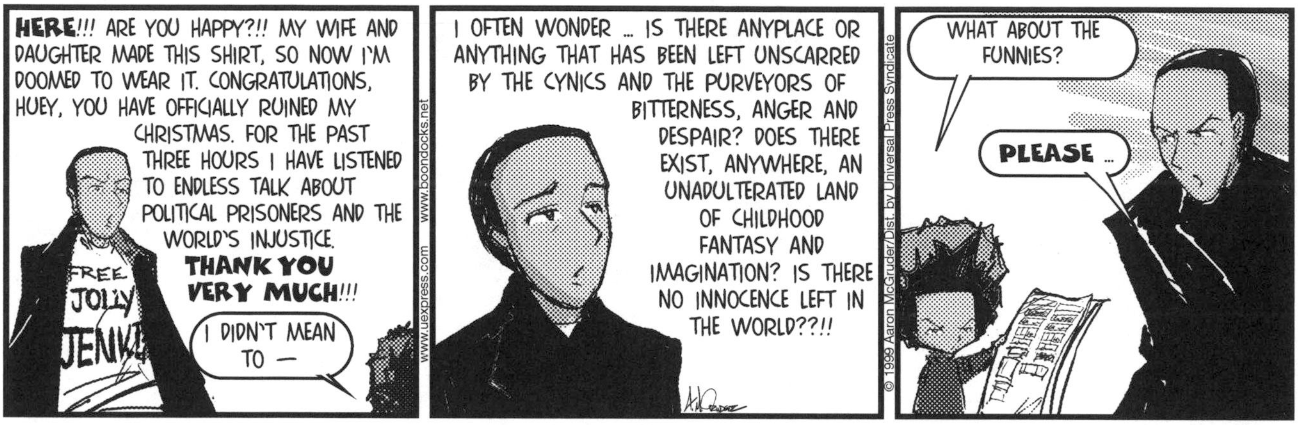
HERE!!! ARE YOU HAPPY?!! MY WIFE AND DAUGHTER MADE THIS SHIRT, SO NOW I'M DOOMED TO WEAR IT. CONGRATULATIONS, HUEY, YOU HAVE OFFICIALLY RUINED MY CHRISTMAS. FOR THE PAST THREE HOURS I HAVE LISTENED TO ENDLESS TALK ABOUT POLITICAL PRISONERS AND THE WORLD'S INJUSTICE. **THANK YOU VERY MUCH**!!!
FREE JOLLY JENKI
I DIDN'T MEAN TO —
www.uexpress.com www.boondocks.net
I OFTEN WONDER ... IS THERE ANYPLACE OR ANYTHING THAT HAS BEEN LEFT UNSCARRED BY THE CYNICS AND THE PURVEYORS OF BITTERNESS, ANGER AND DESPAIR? DOES THERE EXIST, ANYWHERE, AN UNADULTERATED LAND OF CHILDHOOD FANTASY AND IMAGINATION? IS THERE NO INNOCENCE LEFT IN THE WORLD??!!
© 1999 Aaron McGruder/Dist. by Universal Press Syndicate
WHAT ABOUT THE FUNNIES?
PLEASE ...

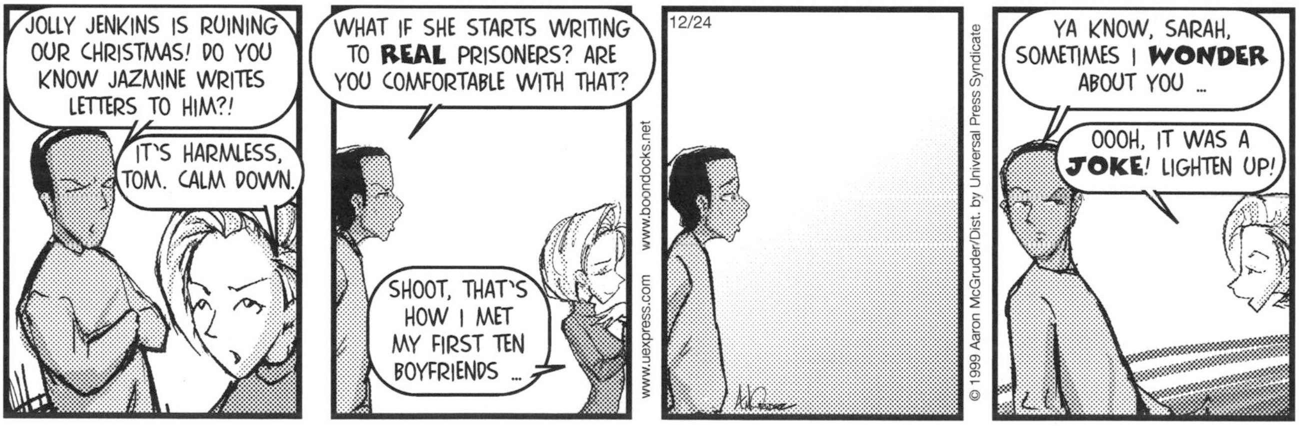
JOLLY JENKINS IS RUINING OUR CHRISTMAS! DO YOU KNOW JAZMINE WRITES LETTERS TO HIM?!
IT'S HARMLESS, TOM. CALM DOWN.
WHAT IF SHE STARTS WRITING TO **REAL** PRISONERS? ARE YOU COMFORTABLE WITH THAT?
SHOOT, THAT'S HOW I MET MY FIRST TEN BOYFRIENDS ...
www.uexpress.com www.boondocks.net
12/24
© 1999 Aaron McGruder/Dist. by Universal Press Syndicate
YA KNOW, SARAH, SOMETIMES I **WONDER** ABOUT YOU ...
OOOH, IT WAS A **JOKE**! LIGHTEN UP!

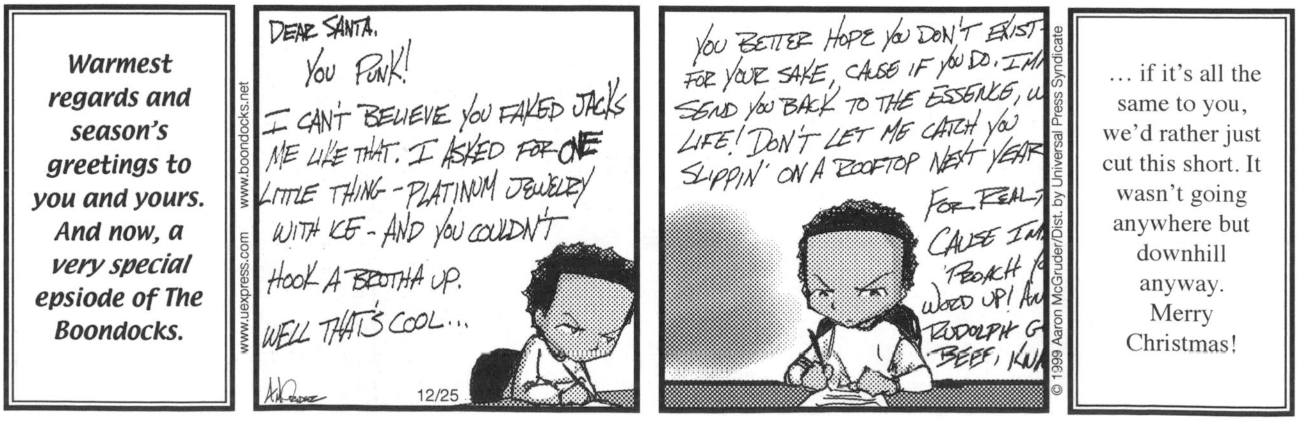
Warmest regards and season's greetings to you and yours. And now, a very special epsiode of The Boondocks.
www.uexpress.com www.boondocks.net
DEAR SANTA,
YOU PUNK!
I CAN'T BELIEVE YOU FAKED JACKS ME LIKE THAT. I ASKED FOR ONE LITTLE THING - PLATINUM JEWELRY WITH ICE - AND YOU COULDN'T HOOK A BROTHA UP.
WELL THAT'S COOL...
12/25
YOU BETTER HOPE YOU DON'T EXIST-
FOR YOUR SAKE, CAUSE IF YOU DO, I'M
SEND YOU BACK TO THE ESSENCE, W
LIFE! DON'T LET ME CATCH YOU
SLIPPIN' ON A ROOFTOP NEXT YEAR
FOR REAL
CAUSE I'M
'PROACH
WORD UP! AN
RUDOLPH G
BEEF, KN
© 1999 Aaron McGruder/Dist. by Universal Press Syndicate
... if it's all the same to you, we'd rather just cut this short. It wasn't going anywhere but downhill anyway. Merry Christmas!

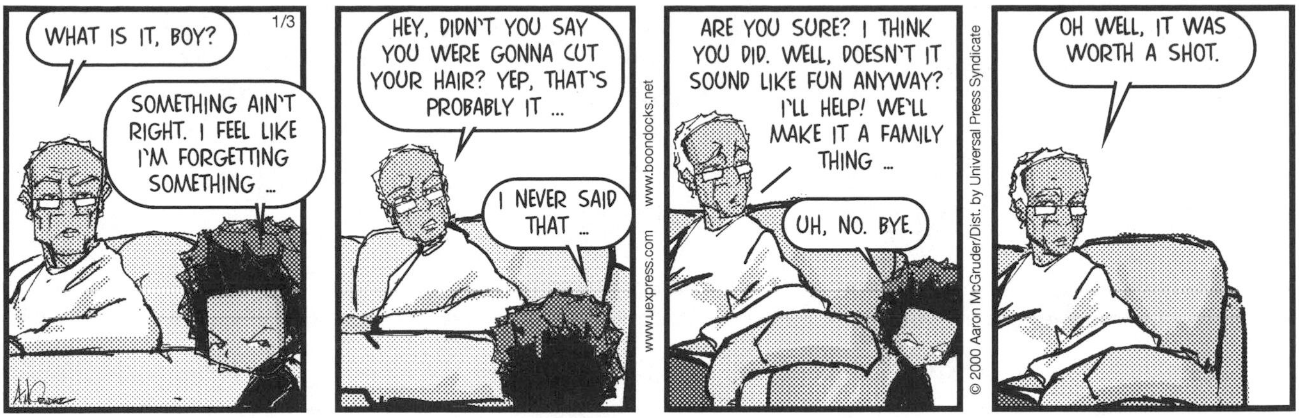
1/3
WHAT IS IT, BOY?
SOMETHING AIN'T RIGHT. I FEEL LIKE I'M FORGETTING SOMETHING ...
HEY, DIDN'T YOU SAY YOU WERE GONNA CUT YOUR HAIR? YEP, THAT'S PROBABLY IT ...
I NEVER SAID THAT ...
www.uexpress.com www.boondocks.net
ARE YOU SURE? I THINK YOU DID. WELL, DOESN'T IT SOUND LIKE FUN ANYWAY? I'LL HELP! WE'LL MAKE IT A FAMILY THING ...
UH, NO. BYE.
© 2000 Aaron McGruder/Dist. by Universal Press Syndicate
OH WELL, IT WAS WORTH A SHOT.

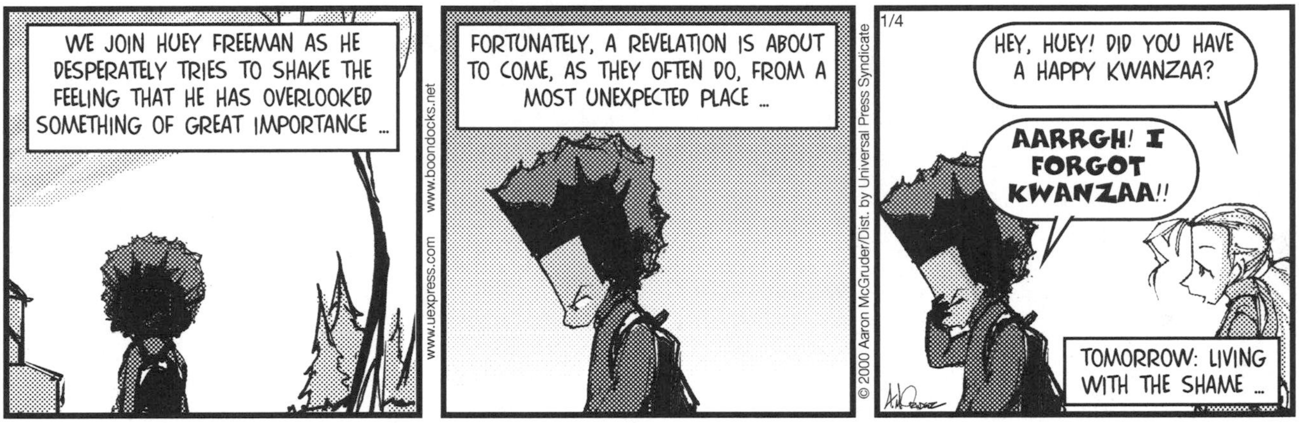
WE JOIN HUEY FREEMAN AS HE DESPERATELY TRIES TO SHAKE THE FEELING THAT HE HAS OVERLOOKED SOMETHING OF GREAT IMPORTANCE ...
www.uexpress.com www.boondocks.net
FORTUNATELY, A REVELATION IS ABOUT TO COME, AS THEY OFTEN DO, FROM A MOST UNEXPECTED PLACE ...
© 2000 Aaron McGruder/Dist. by Universal Press Syndicate
1/4
HEY, HUEY! DID YOU HAVE A HAPPY KWANZAA?
AARRGH! I FORGOT KWANZAA!!
TOMORROW: LIVING WITH THE SHAME ...

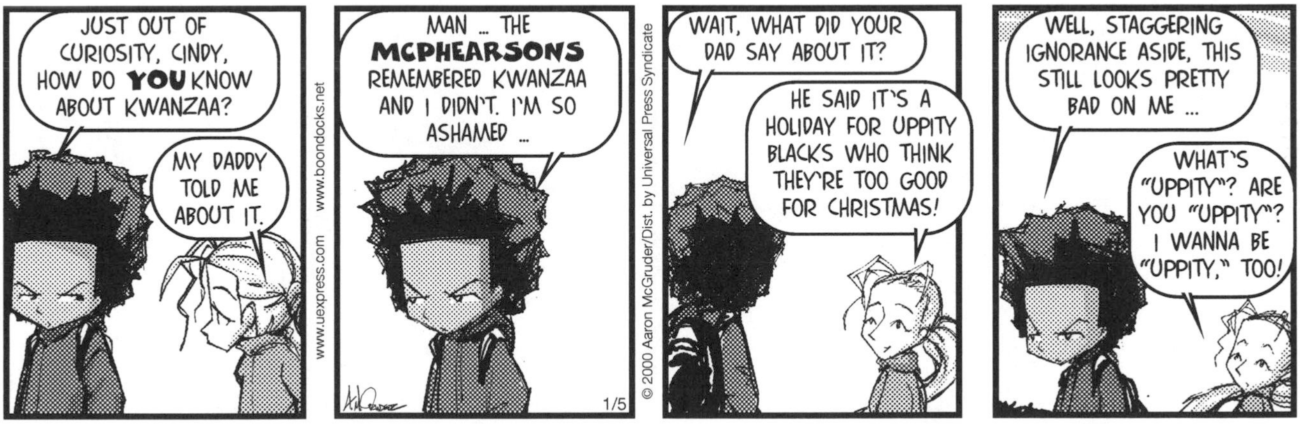
JUST OUT OF CURIOSITY, CINDY, HOW DO YOU KNOW ABOUT KWANZAA?
MY DADDY TOLD ME ABOUT IT.
www.uexpress.com www.boondocks.net
MAN ... THE MCPHEARSONS REMEMBERED KWANZAA AND I DIDN'T. I'M SO ASHAMED ...
1/5
© 2000 Aaron McGruder/Dist. by Universal Press Syndicate
WAIT, WHAT DID YOUR DAD SAY ABOUT IT?
HE SAID IT'S A HOLIDAY FOR UPPITY BLACKS WHO THINK THEY'RE TOO GOOD FOR CHRISTMAS!
WELL, STAGGERING IGNORANCE ASIDE, THIS STILL LOOKS PRETTY BAD ON ME ...
WHAT'S "UPPITY"? ARE YOU "UPPITY"? I WANNA BE "UPPITY," TOO!

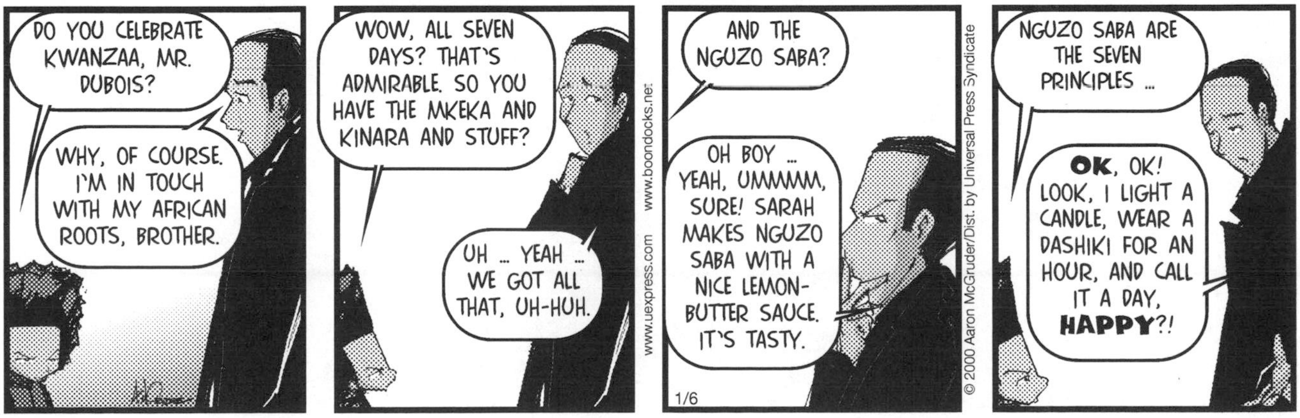
DO YOU CELEBRATE KWANZAA, MR. DUBOIS?
WHY, OF COURSE. I'M IN TOUCH WITH MY AFRICAN ROOTS, BROTHER.
WOW, ALL SEVEN DAYS? THAT'S ADMIRABLE. SO YOU HAVE THE MKEKA AND KINARA AND STUFF?
UH ... YEAH ... WE GOT ALL THAT, UH-HUH.
www.uexpress.com www.boondocks.net
AND THE NGUZO SABA?
OH BOY ... YEAH, UMMMM, SURE! SARAH MAKES NGUZO SABA WITH A NICE LEMON-BUTTER SAUCE. IT'S TASTY.
1/6
© 2000 Aaron McGruder/Dist. by Universal Press Syndicate
NGUZO SABA ARE THE SEVEN PRINCIPLES ...
OK, OK! LOOK, I LIGHT A CANDLE, WEAR A DASHIKI FOR AN HOUR, AND CALL IT A DAY, HAPPY?!

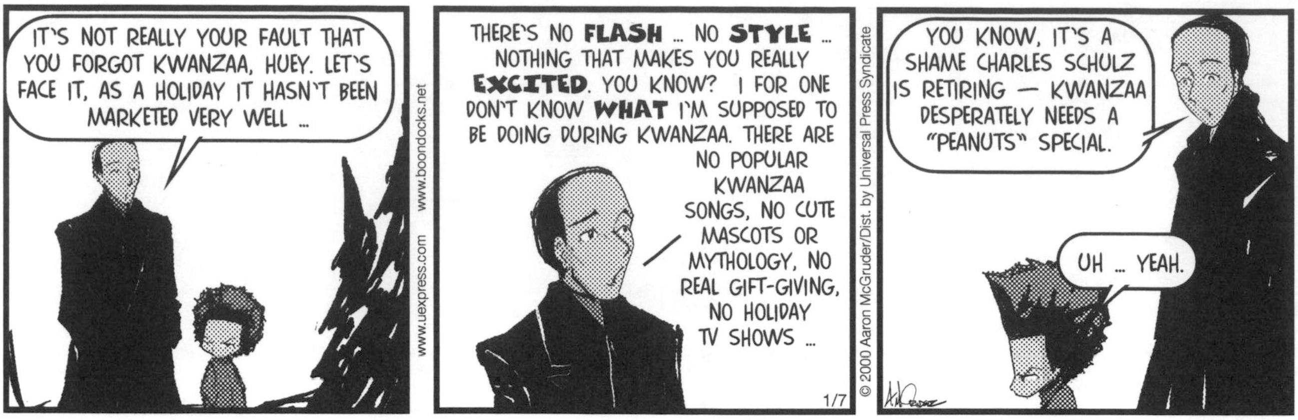
IT'S NOT REALLY YOUR FAULT THAT YOU FORGOT KWANZAA, HUEY. LET'S FACE IT, AS A HOLIDAY IT HASN'T BEEN MARKETED VERY WELL ...
www.boondocks.net
www.uexpress.com
THERE'S NO FLASH ... NO STYLE ... NOTHING THAT MAKES YOU REALLY EXCITED. YOU KNOW? I FOR ONE DON'T KNOW WHAT I'M SUPPOSED TO BE DOING DURING KWANZAA. THERE ARE NO POPULAR KWANZAA SONGS, NO CUTE MASCOTS OR MYTHOLOGY, NO REAL GIFT-GIVING, NO HOLIDAY TV SHOWS ...
1/7
© 2000 Aaron McGruder/Dist. by Universal Press Syndicate
YOU KNOW, IT'S A SHAME CHARLES SCHULZ IS RETIRING — KWANZAA DESPERATELY NEEDS A "PEANUTS" SPECIAL.
UH ... YEAH.

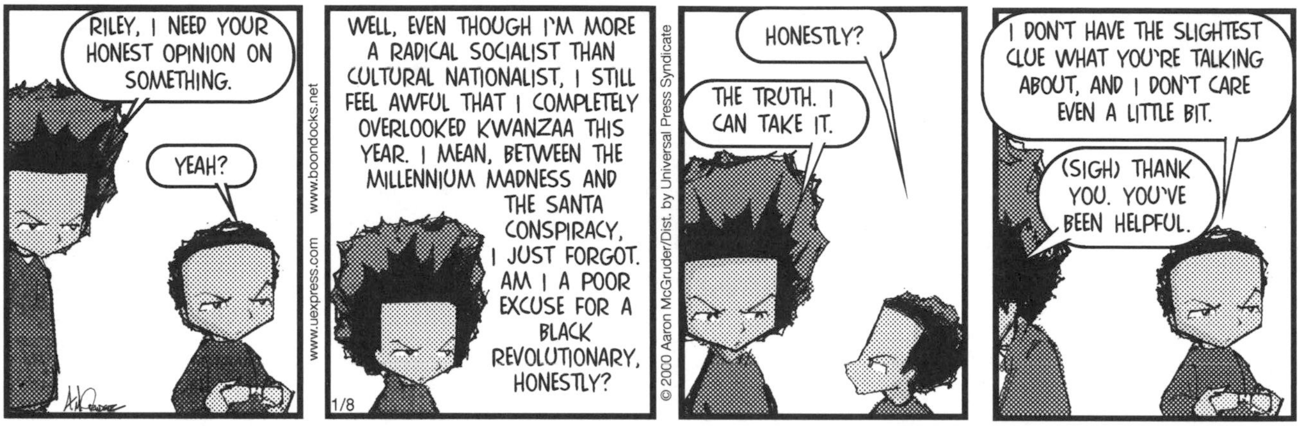
RILEY, I NEED YOUR HONEST OPINION ON SOMETHING.
YEAH?
www.boondocks.net
www.uexpress.com
WELL, EVEN THOUGH I'M MORE A RADICAL SOCIALIST THAN CULTURAL NATIONALIST, I STILL FEEL AWFUL THAT I COMPLETELY OVERLOOKED KWANZAA THIS YEAR. I MEAN, BETWEEN THE MILLENNIUM MADNESS AND THE SANTA CONSPIRACY, I JUST FORGOT. AM I A POOR EXCUSE FOR A BLACK REVOLUTIONARY, HONESTLY?
1/8
© 2000 Aaron McGruder/Dist. by Universal Press Syndicate
HONESTLY?
THE TRUTH. I CAN TAKE IT.
I DON'T HAVE THE SLIGHTEST CLUE WHAT YOU'RE TALKING ABOUT, AND I DON'T CARE EVEN A LITTLE BIT.
(SIGH) THANK YOU. YOU'VE BEEN HELPFUL.

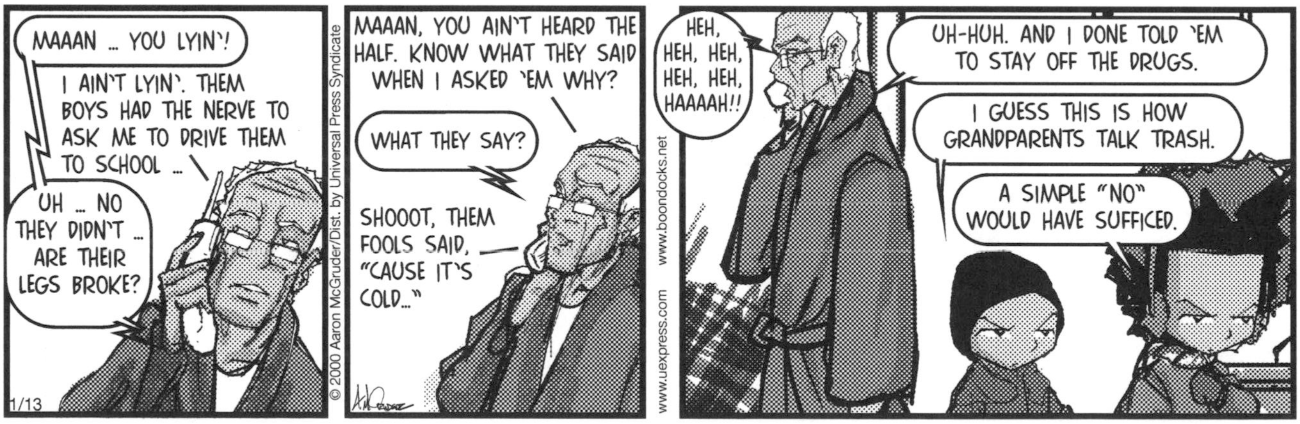
MAAAN ... YOU LYIN'!
I AIN'T LYIN'. THEM BOYS HAD THE NERVE TO ASK ME TO DRIVE THEM TO SCHOOL ...
UH ... NO THEY DIDN'T ... ARE THEIR LEGS BROKE?
1/13
© 2000 Aaron McGruder/Dist. by Universal Press Syndicate
MAAAN, YOU AIN'T HEARD THE HALF. KNOW WHAT THEY SAID WHEN I ASKED 'EM WHY?
WHAT THEY SAY?
SHOOOT, THEM FOOLS SAID, "CAUSE IT'S COLD..."
www.boondocks.net
www.uexpress.com
HEH, HEH, HEH, HEH, HEH, HAAAAH!!
UH-HUH. AND I DONE TOLD 'EM TO STAY OFF THE DRUGS.
I GUESS THIS IS HOW GRANDPARENTS TALK TRASH.
A SIMPLE "NO" WOULD HAVE SUFFICED.

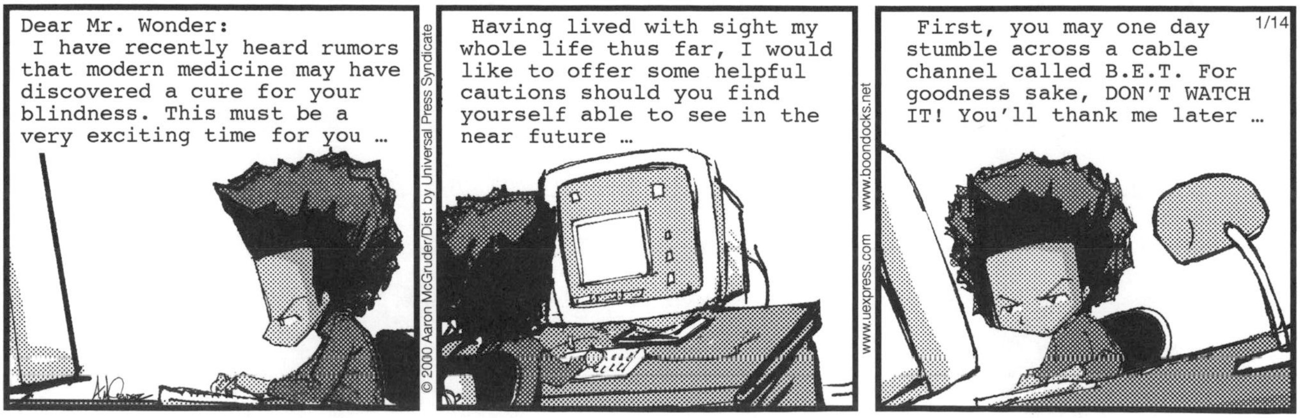
Dear Mr. Wonder:
I have recently heard rumors that modern medicine may have discovered a cure for your blindness. This must be a very exciting time for you ...
© 2000 Aaron McGruder/Dist. by Universal Press Syndicate
Having lived with sight my whole life thus far, I would like to offer some helpful cautions should you find yourself able to see in the near future ...
www.boondocks.net
www.uexpress.com
1/14
First, you may one day stumble across a cable channel called B.E.T. For goodness sake, DON'T WATCH IT! You'll thank me later ...

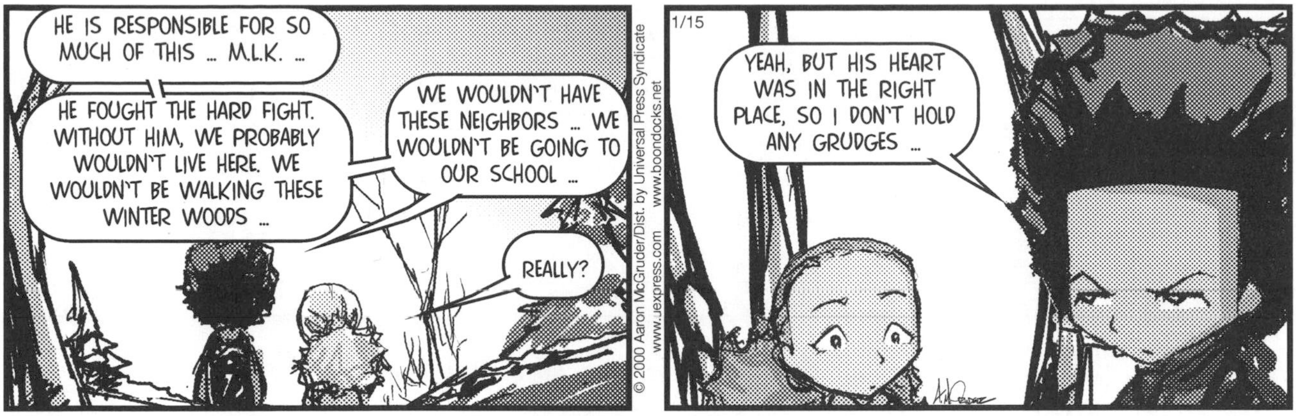
HE IS RESPONSIBLE FOR SO MUCH OF THIS ... M.L.K. ...
HE FOUGHT THE HARD FIGHT. WITHOUT HIM, WE PROBABLY WOULDN'T LIVE HERE. WE WOULDN'T BE WALKING THESE WINTER WOODS ...
WE WOULDN'T HAVE THESE NEIGHBORS ... WE WOULDN'T BE GOING TO OUR SCHOOL ...
REALLY?
© 2000 Aaron McGruder/Dist. by Universal Press Syndicate www.boondocks.net www.uexpress.com
1/15
YEAH, BUT HIS HEART WAS IN THE RIGHT PLACE, SO I DON'T HOLD ANY GRUDGES ...

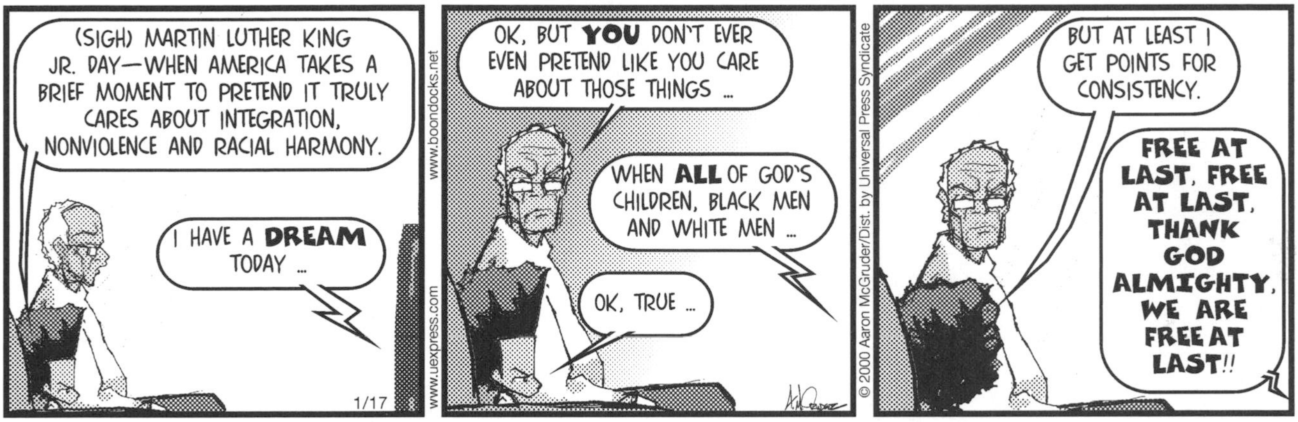
(SIGH) MARTIN LUTHER KING JR. DAY—WHEN AMERICA TAKES A BRIEF MOMENT TO PRETEND IT TRULY CARES ABOUT INTEGRATION, NONVIOLENCE AND RACIAL HARMONY.
I HAVE A DREAM TODAY ...
1/17
OK, BUT YOU DON'T EVER EVEN PRETEND LIKE YOU CARE ABOUT THOSE THINGS ...
WHEN ALL OF GOD'S CHILDREN, BLACK MEN AND WHITE MEN ...
OK, TRUE ...
BUT AT LEAST I GET POINTS FOR CONSISTENCY.
FREE AT LAST, FREE AT LAST, THANK GOD ALMIGHTY, WE ARE FREE AT LAST!!
www.boondocks.net www.uexpress.com © 2000 Aaron McGruder/Dist. by Universal Press Syndicate

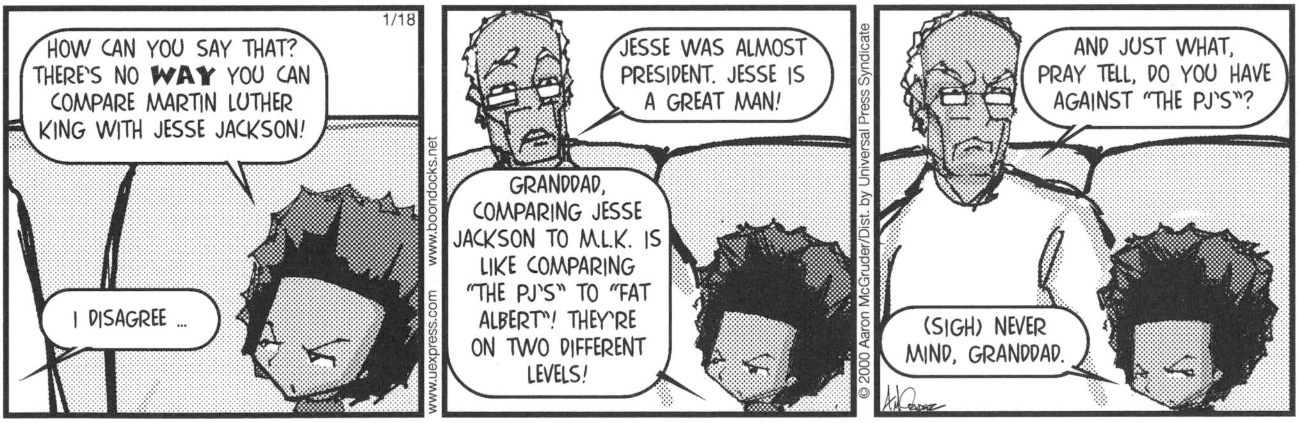
1/18
HOW CAN YOU SAY THAT? THERE'S NO WAY YOU CAN COMPARE MARTIN LUTHER KING WITH JESSE JACKSON!
I DISAGREE ...
JESSE WAS ALMOST PRESIDENT. JESSE IS A GREAT MAN!
GRANDDAD, COMPARING JESSE JACKSON TO M.L.K. IS LIKE COMPARING "THE PJ'S" TO "FAT ALBERT"! THEY'RE ON TWO DIFFERENT LEVELS!
AND JUST WHAT, PRAY TELL, DO YOU HAVE AGAINST "THE PJ'S"?
(SIGH) NEVER MIND, GRANDDAD.
www.boondocks.net www.uexpress.com © 2000 Aaron McGruder/Dist. by Universal Press Syndicate

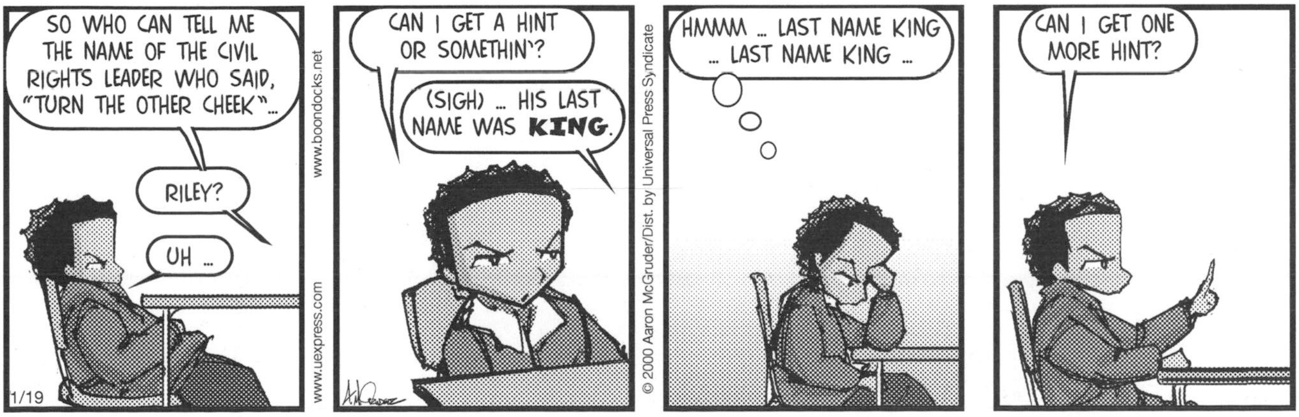
SO WHO CAN TELL ME THE NAME OF THE CIVIL RIGHTS LEADER WHO SAID, "TURN THE OTHER CHEEK"...
RILEY?
UH ...
1/19
CAN I GET A HINT OR SOMETHIN'?
(SIGH) ... HIS LAST NAME WAS KING.
HMMM ... LAST NAME KING ... LAST NAME KING ...
CAN I GET ONE MORE HINT?
www.boondocks.net www.uexpress.com © 2000 Aaron McGruder/Dist. by Universal Press Syndicate

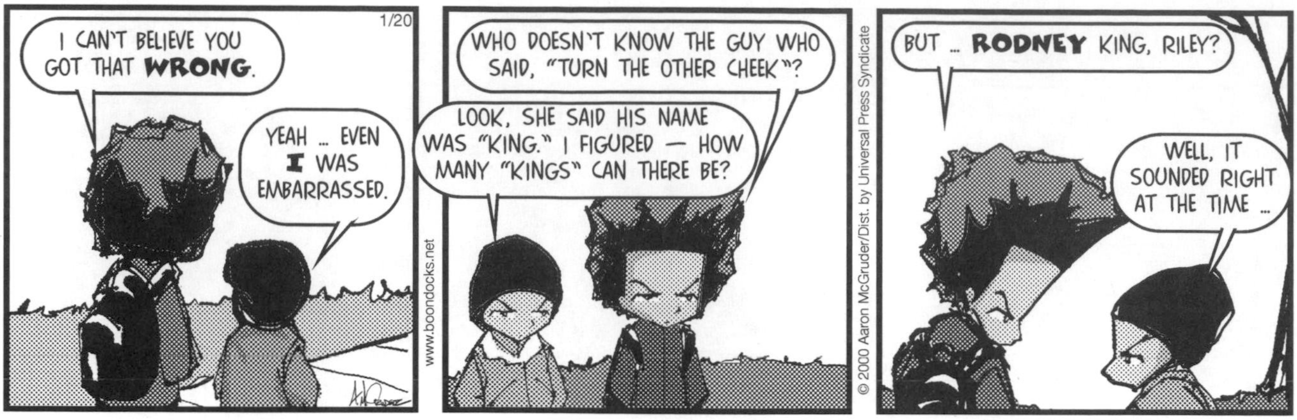
1/20
I CAN'T BELIEVE YOU GOT THAT **WRONG**.
YEAH ... EVEN **I** WAS EMBARRASSED.
www.boondocks.net
WHO DOESN'T KNOW THE GUY WHO SAID, "TURN THE OTHER CHEEK"?
LOOK, SHE SAID HIS NAME WAS "KING." I FIGURED — HOW MANY "KINGS" CAN THERE BE?
© 2000 Aaron McGruder/Dist. by Universal Press Syndicate
BUT ... **RODNEY** KING, RILEY?
WELL, IT SOUNDED RIGHT AT THE TIME ...

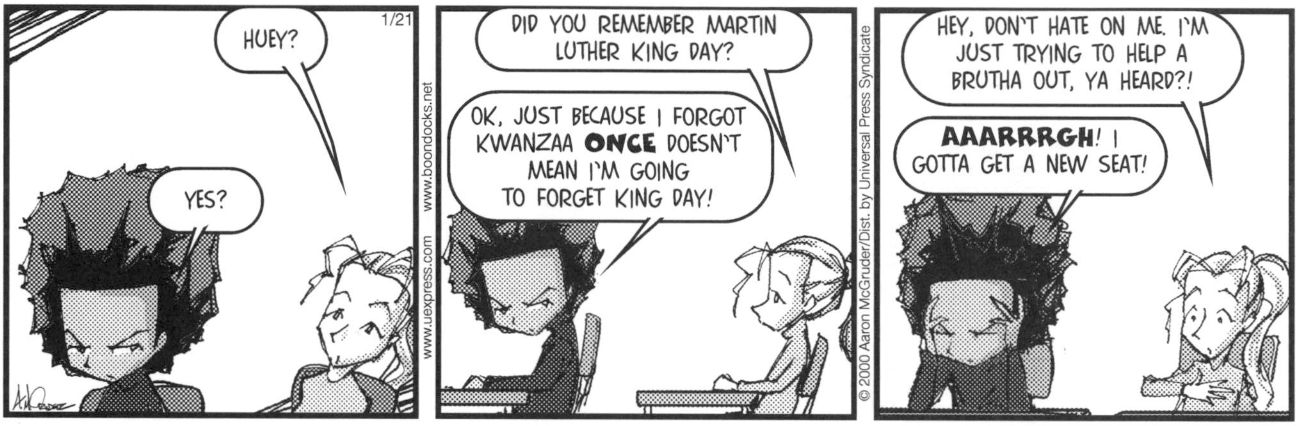
1/21
HUEY?
YES?
www.uexpress.com www.boondocks.net
DID YOU REMEMBER MARTIN LUTHER KING DAY?
OK, JUST BECAUSE I FORGOT KWANZAA **ONCE** DOESN'T MEAN I'M GOING TO FORGET KING DAY!
© 2000 Aaron McGruder/Dist. by Universal Press Syndicate
HEY, DON'T HATE ON ME. I'M JUST TRYING TO HELP A BRUTHA OUT, YA HEARD?!
AAARRRGH! I GOTTA GET A NEW SEAT!

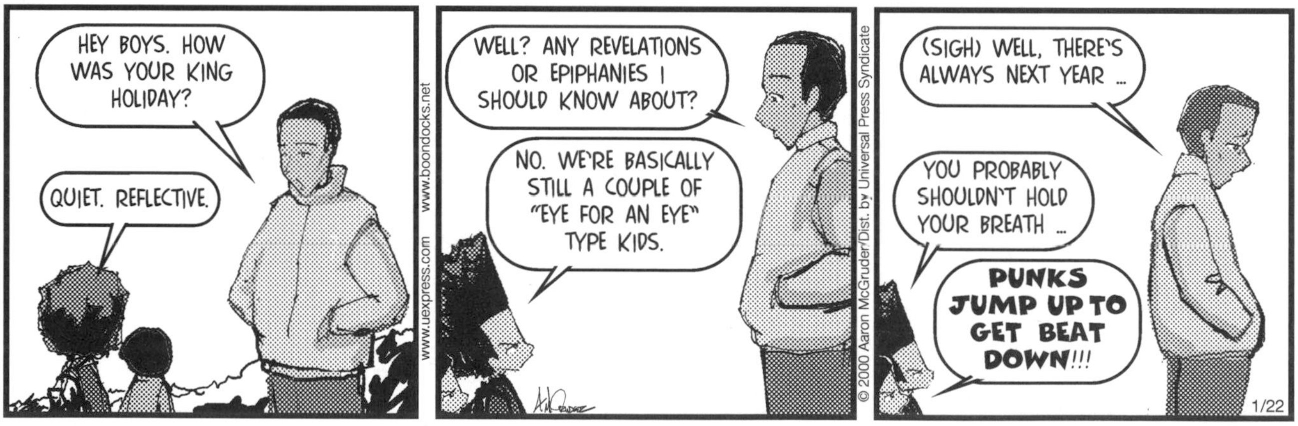
HEY BOYS. HOW WAS YOUR KING HOLIDAY?
QUIET. REFLECTIVE.
www.uexpress.com www.boondocks.net
WELL? ANY REVELATIONS OR EPIPHANIES I SHOULD KNOW ABOUT?
NO. WE'RE BASICALLY STILL A COUPLE OF "EYE FOR AN EYE" TYPE KIDS.
© 2000 Aaron McGruder/Dist. by Universal Press Syndicate
(SIGH) WELL, THERE'S ALWAYS NEXT YEAR ...
YOU PROBABLY SHOULDN'T HOLD YOUR BREATH ...
PUNKS JUMP UP TO GET BEAT DOWN!!!
1/22

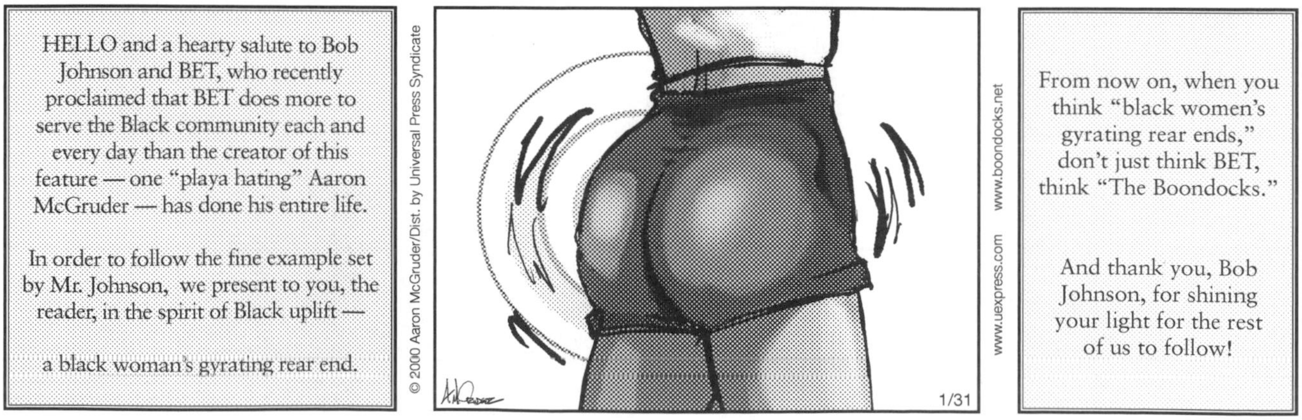
HELLO and a hearty salute to Bob Johnson and BET, who recently proclaimed that BET does more to serve the Black community each and every day than the creator of this feature — one "playa hating" Aaron McGruder — has done his entire life.
In order to follow the fine example set by Mr. Johnson, we present to you, the reader, in the spirit of Black uplift —
a black woman's gyrating rear end.
© 2000 Aaron McGruder/Dist. by Universal Press Syndicate
1/31
www.uexpress.com www.boondocks.net
From now on, when you think "black women's gyrating rear ends," don't just think BET, think "The Boondocks."
And thank you, Bob Johnson, for shining your light for the rest of us to follow!

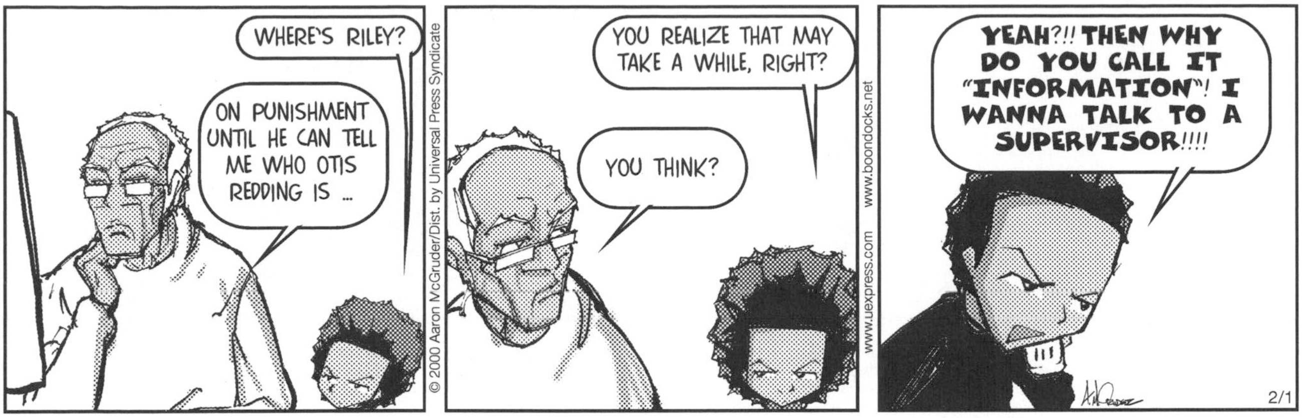

WHERE'S RILEY?
ON PUNISHMENT UNTIL HE CAN TELL ME WHO OTIS REDDING IS ...
© 2000 Aaron McGruder/Dist. by Universal Press Syndicate
YOU REALIZE THAT MAY TAKE A WHILE, RIGHT?
YOU THINK?
www.uexpress.com www.boondocks.net
YEAH?!! THEN WHY DO YOU CALL IT "INFORMATION"! I WANNA TALK TO A SUPERVISOR!!!!
2/1

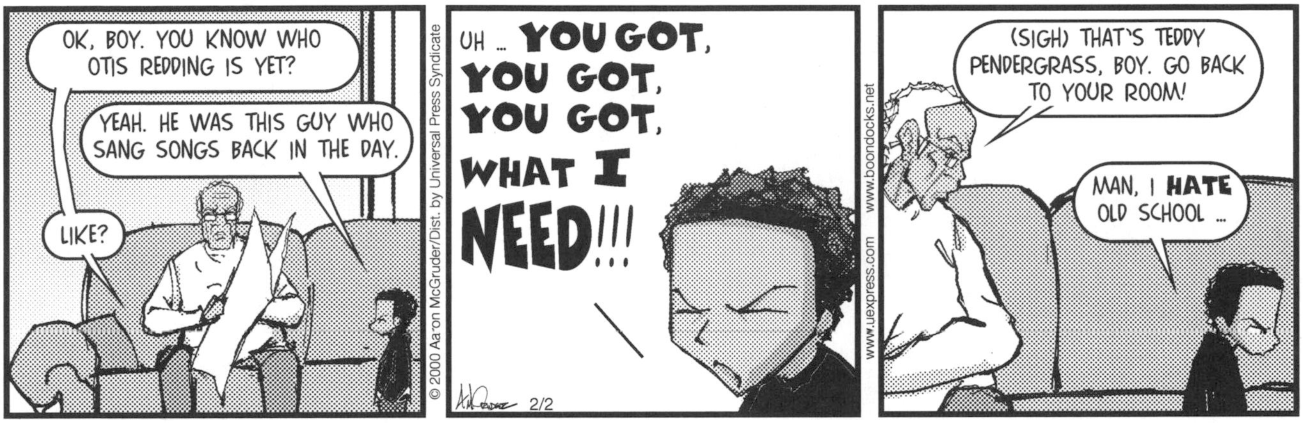

OK, BOY. YOU KNOW WHO OTIS REDDING IS YET?
YEAH. HE WAS THIS GUY WHO SANG SONGS BACK IN THE DAY.
LIKE?
© 2000 Aaron McGruder/Dist. by Universal Press Syndicate
UH ... YOU GOT, YOU GOT, YOU GOT, WHAT I NEED!!!
2/2
www.uexpress.com www.boondocks.net
(SIGH) THAT'S TEDDY PENDERGRASS, BOY. GO BACK TO YOUR ROOM!
MAN, I HATE OLD SCHOOL ...

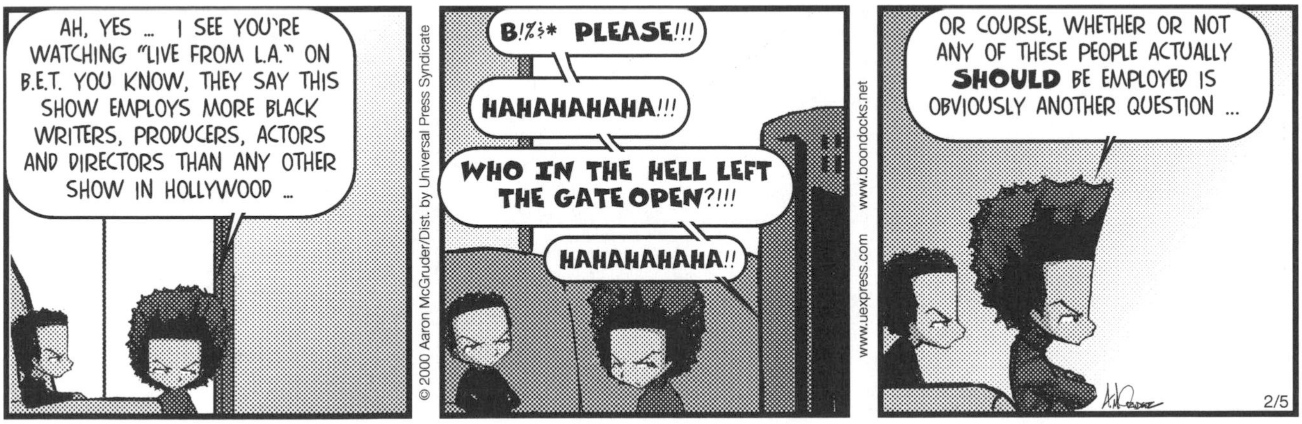

AH, YES ... I SEE YOU'RE WATCHING "LIVE FROM L.A." ON B.E.T. YOU KNOW, THEY SAY THIS SHOW EMPLOYS MORE BLACK WRITERS, PRODUCERS, ACTORS AND DIRECTORS THAN ANY OTHER SHOW IN HOLLYWOOD ...
© 2000 Aaron McGruder/Dist. by Universal Press Syndicate
B!%$* PLEASE!!!
HAHAHAHAHA!!!
WHO IN THE HELL LEFT THE GATE OPEN?!!!
HAHAHAHAHA!!
www.uexpress.com www.boondocks.net
OR COURSE, WHETHER OR NOT ANY OF THESE PEOPLE ACTUALLY SHOULD BE EMPLOYED IS OBVIOUSLY ANOTHER QUESTION ...
2/5

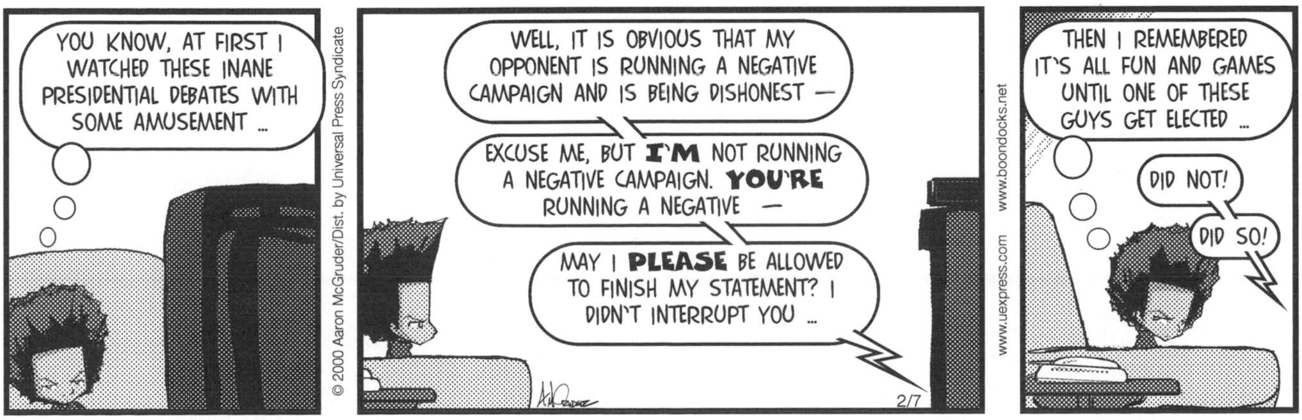

YOU KNOW, AT FIRST I WATCHED THESE INANE PRESIDENTIAL DEBATES WITH SOME AMUSEMENT ...
© 2000 Aaron McGruder/Dist. by Universal Press Syndicate
WELL, IT IS OBVIOUS THAT MY OPPONENT IS RUNNING A NEGATIVE CAMPAIGN AND IS BEING DISHONEST —
EXCUSE ME, BUT I'M NOT RUNNING A NEGATIVE CAMPAIGN. YOU'RE RUNNING A NEGATIVE —
MAY I PLEASE BE ALLOWED TO FINISH MY STATEMENT? I DIDN'T INTERRUPT YOU ...
2/7
www.uexpress.com www.boondocks.net
THEN I REMEMBERED IT'S ALL FUN AND GAMES UNTIL ONE OF THESE GUYS GET ELECTED ...
DID NOT!
DID SO!

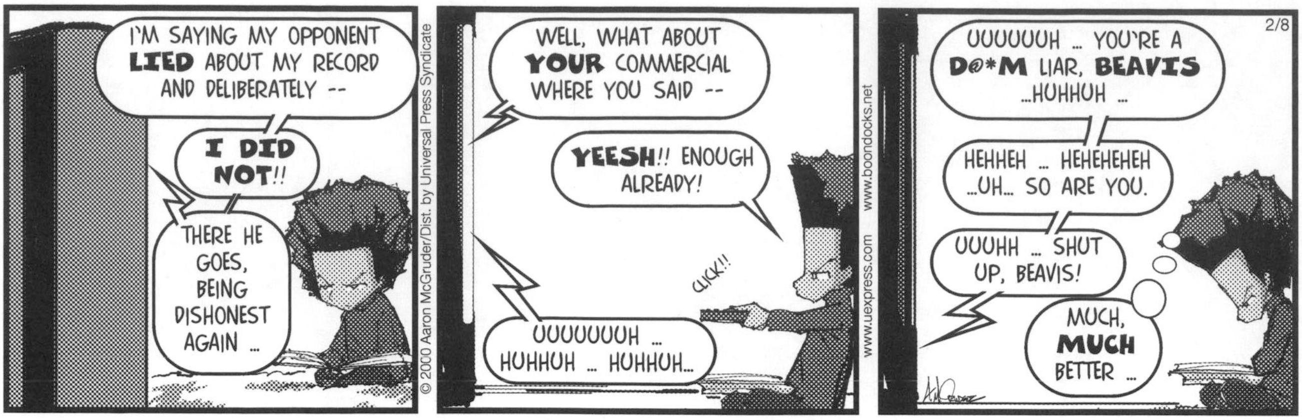
I'M SAYING MY OPPONENT **LIED** ABOUT MY RECORD AND DELIBERATELY --
I DID NOT!!
THERE HE GOES, BEING DISHONEST AGAIN ...
© 2000 Aaron McGruder/Dist. by Universal Press Syndicate
WELL, WHAT ABOUT **YOUR** COMMERCIAL WHERE YOU SAID --
YEESH!! ENOUGH ALREADY!
CLICK!!
UUUUUUUH ... HUHHUH ... HUHHUH...
www.uexpress.com www.boondocks.net
2/8
UUUUUUH ... YOU'RE A **D@*M** LIAR, **BEAVIS** ...HUHHUH ...
HEHHEH ... HEHEHEHEH ...UH... SO ARE YOU.
UUUHH ... SHUT UP, BEAVIS!
MUCH, **MUCH** BETTER ...

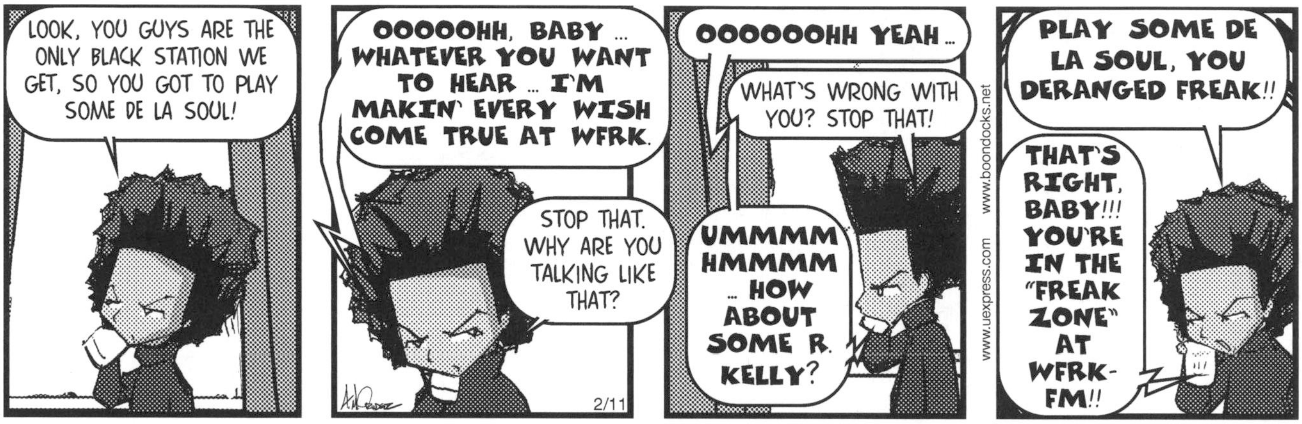
LOOK, YOU GUYS ARE THE ONLY BLACK STATION WE GET, SO YOU GOT TO PLAY SOME DE LA SOUL!
OOOOOHH, BABY ... WHATEVER YOU WANT TO HEAR ... I'M MAKIN' EVERY WISH COME TRUE AT WFRK.
STOP THAT. WHY ARE YOU TALKING LIKE THAT?
2/11
OOOOOOHH YEAH ...
WHAT'S WRONG WITH YOU? STOP THAT!
UMMMM HMMMM ... HOW ABOUT SOME R. KELLY?
www.uexpress.com www.boondocks.net
PLAY SOME DE LA SOUL, YOU DERANGED FREAK!!
THAT'S RIGHT, BABY!!! **YOU'RE IN THE "FREAK ZONE" AT WFRK-FM**!!

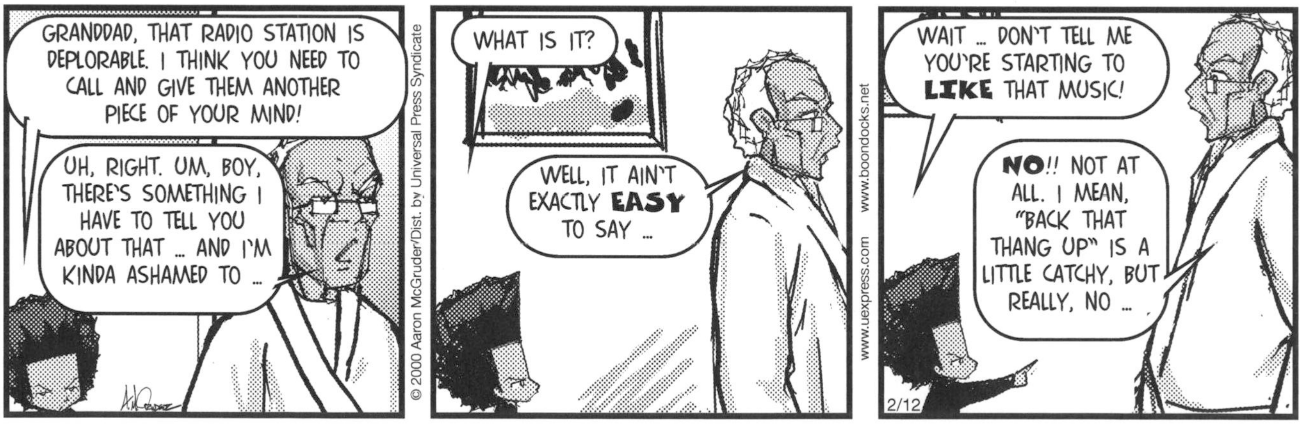
GRANDDAD, THAT RADIO STATION IS DEPLORABLE. I THINK YOU NEED TO CALL AND GIVE THEM ANOTHER PIECE OF YOUR MIND!
UH, RIGHT. UM, BOY, THERE'S SOMETHING I HAVE TO TELL YOU ABOUT THAT ... AND I'M KINDA ASHAMED TO ...
© 2000 Aaron McGruder/Dist. by Universal Press Syndicate
WHAT IS IT?
WELL, IT AIN'T EXACTLY **EASY** TO SAY ...
www.uexpress.com www.boondocks.net
WAIT ... DON'T TELL ME YOU'RE STARTING TO **LIKE** THAT MUSIC!
NO!! NOT AT ALL. I MEAN, "BACK THAT THANG UP" IS A LITTLE CATCHY, BUT REALLY, NO ...
2/12

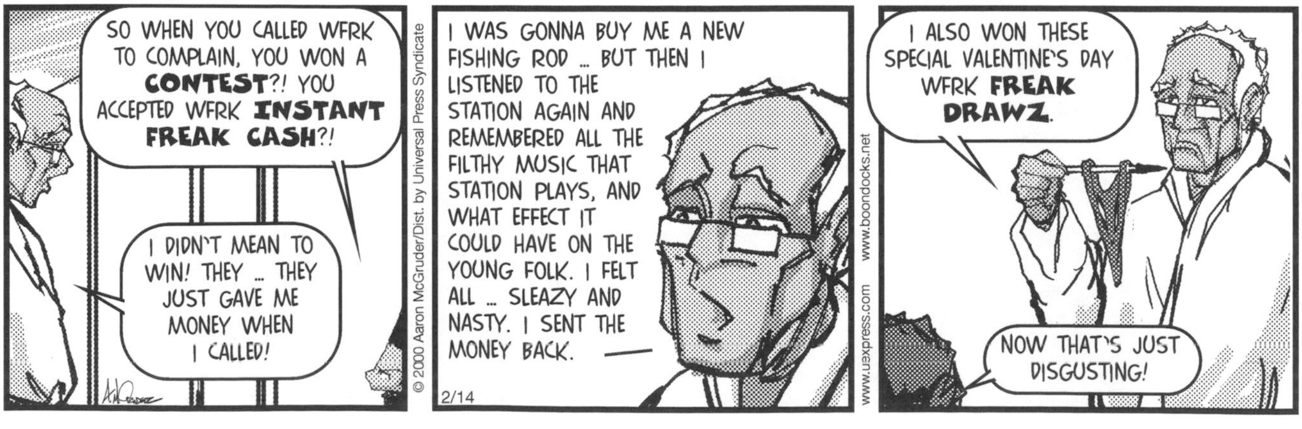
SO WHEN YOU CALLED WFRK TO COMPLAIN, YOU WON A **CONTEST**?! YOU ACCEPTED WFRK **INSTANT FREAK CASH**?!
I DIDN'T MEAN TO WIN! THEY ... THEY JUST GAVE ME MONEY WHEN I CALLED!
© 2000 Aaron McGruder/Dist. by Universal Press Syndicate
I WAS GONNA BUY ME A NEW FISHING ROD ... BUT THEN I LISTENED TO THE STATION AGAIN AND REMEMBERED ALL THE FILTHY MUSIC THAT STATION PLAYS, AND WHAT EFFECT IT COULD HAVE ON THE YOUNG FOLK. I FELT ALL ... SLEAZY AND NASTY. I SENT THE MONEY BACK.
2/14
www.uexpress.com www.boondocks.net
I ALSO WON THESE SPECIAL VALENTINE'S DAY WFRK **FREAK DRAWZ**.
NOW THAT'S JUST DISGUSTING!

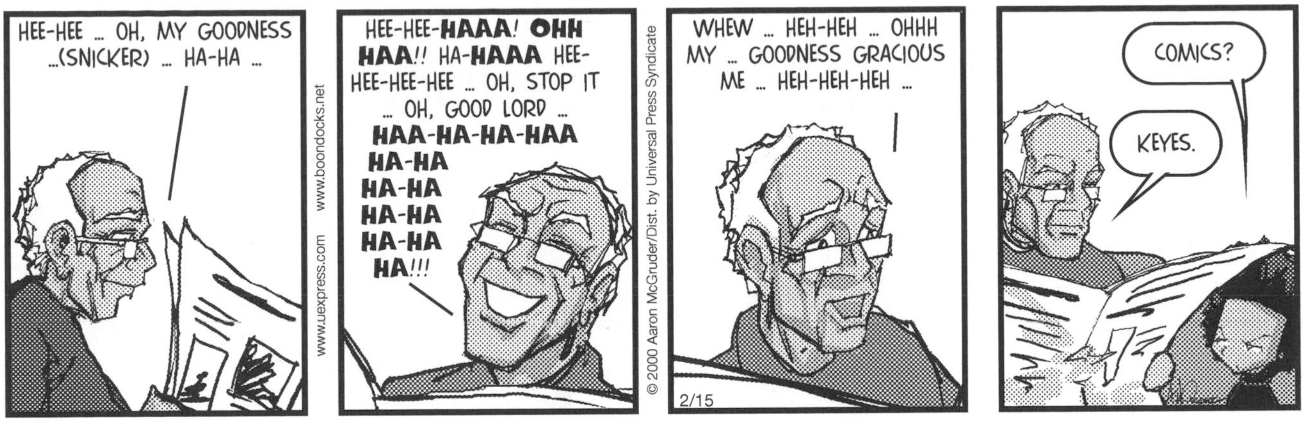
HEE-HEE ... OH, MY GOODNESS ...(SNICKER) ... HA-HA ...
www.uexpress.com www.boondocks.net
HEE-HEE-HAAA! OHH HAA!! HA-HAAA HEE-HEE-HEE-HEE ... OH, STOP IT ... OH, GOOD LORD ... HAA-HA-HA-HAA HA-HA HA-HA HA-HA HA-HA HA!!!
© 2000 Aaron McGruder/Dist. by Universal Press Syndicate
WHEW ... HEH-HEH ... OHHH MY ... GOODNESS GRACIOUS ME ... HEH-HEH-HEH ...
2/15
COMICS?
KEYES.

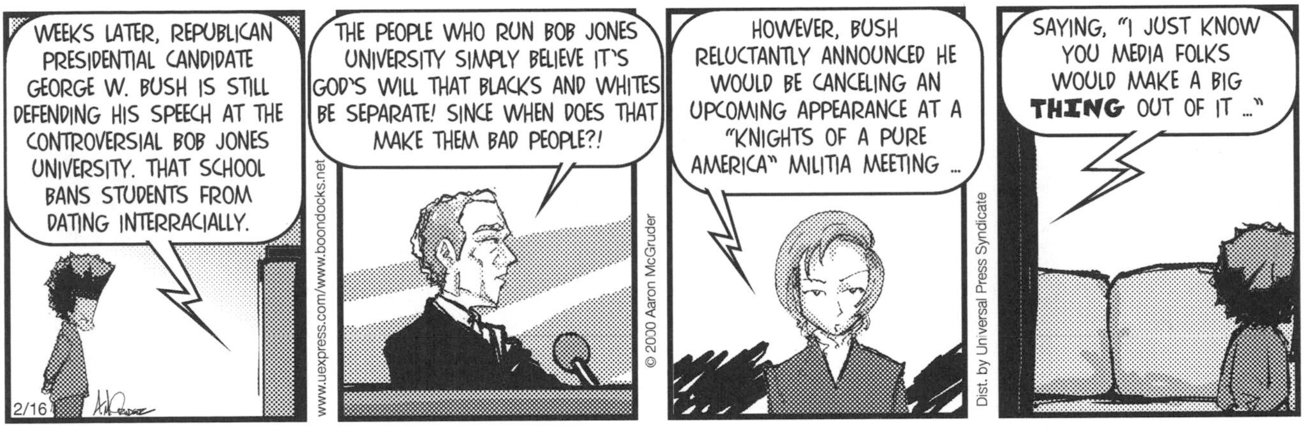
WEEKS LATER, REPUBLICAN PRESIDENTIAL CANDIDATE GEORGE W. BUSH IS STILL DEFENDING HIS SPEECH AT THE CONTROVERSIAL BOB JONES UNIVERSITY. THAT SCHOOL BANS STUDENTS FROM DATING INTERRACIALLY.
2/16
www.uexpress.com/www.boondocks.net
THE PEOPLE WHO RUN BOB JONES UNIVERSITY SIMPLY BELIEVE IT'S GOD'S WILL THAT BLACKS AND WHITES BE SEPARATE! SINCE WHEN DOES THAT MAKE THEM BAD PEOPLE?!
© 2000 Aaron McGruder
HOWEVER, BUSH RELUCTANTLY ANNOUNCED HE WOULD BE CANCELING AN UPCOMING APPEARANCE AT A "KNIGHTS OF A PURE AMERICA" MILITIA MEETING ...
Dist. by Universal Press Syndicate
SAYING, "I JUST KNOW YOU MEDIA FOLKS WOULD MAKE A BIG THING OUT OF IT ..."

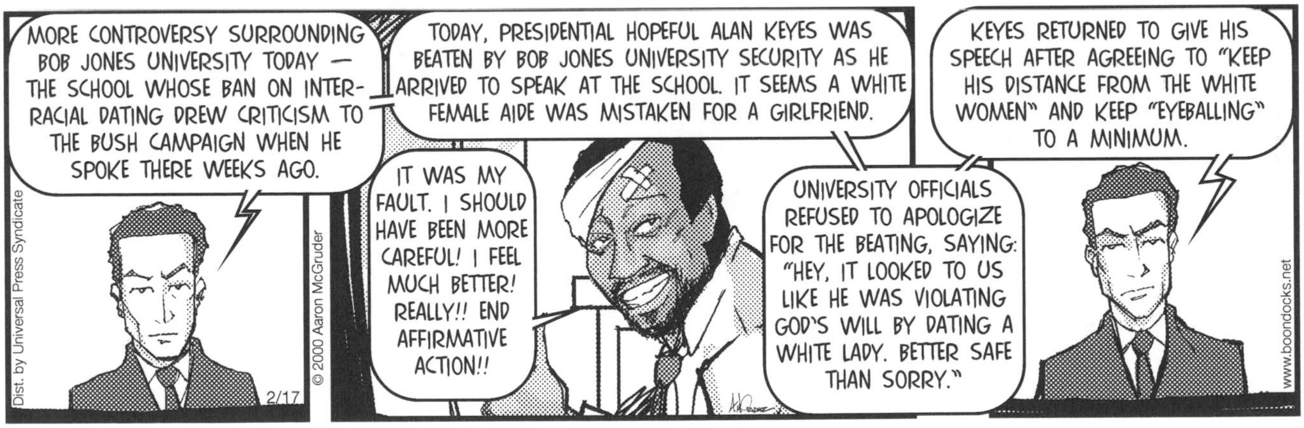
MORE CONTROVERSY SURROUNDING BOB JONES UNIVERSITY TODAY — THE SCHOOL WHOSE BAN ON INTER-RACIAL DATING DREW CRITICISM TO THE BUSH CAMPAIGN WHEN HE SPOKE THERE WEEKS AGO.
Dist. by Universal Press Syndicate
2/17
© 2000 Aaron McGruder
TODAY, PRESIDENTIAL HOPEFUL ALAN KEYES WAS BEATEN BY BOB JONES UNIVERSITY SECURITY AS HE ARRIVED TO SPEAK AT THE SCHOOL. IT SEEMS A WHITE FEMALE AIDE WAS MISTAKEN FOR A GIRLFRIEND.
IT WAS MY FAULT. I SHOULD HAVE BEEN MORE CAREFUL! I FEEL MUCH BETTER! REALLY!! END AFFIRMATIVE ACTION!!
UNIVERSITY OFFICIALS REFUSED TO APOLOGIZE FOR THE BEATING, SAYING: "HEY, IT LOOKED TO US LIKE HE WAS VIOLATING GOD'S WILL BY DATING A WHITE LADY. BETTER SAFE THAN SORRY."
KEYES RETURNED TO GIVE HIS SPEECH AFTER AGREEING TO "KEEP HIS DISTANCE FROM THE WHITE WOMEN" AND KEEP "EYEBALLING" TO A MINIMUM.
www.boondocks.net

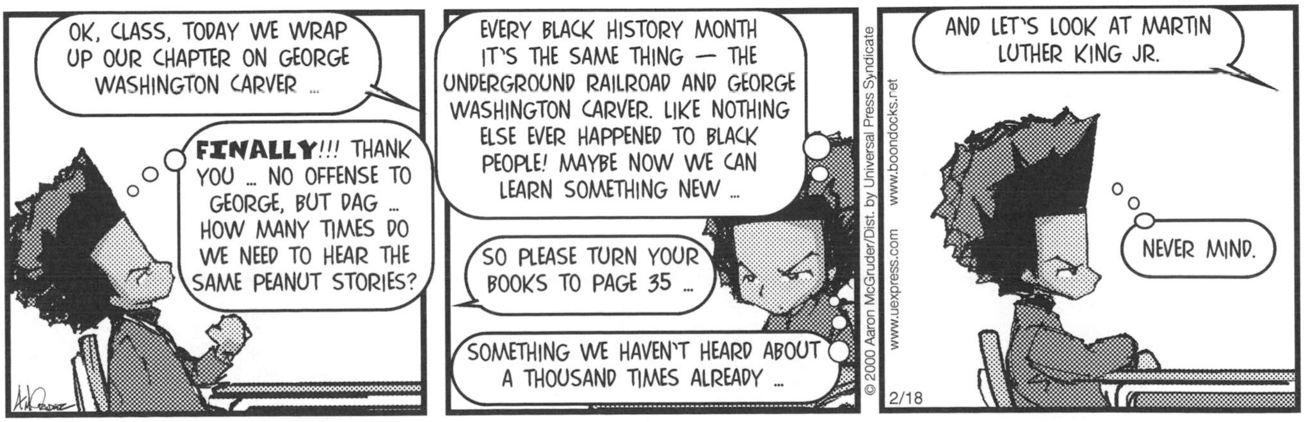
OK, CLASS, TODAY WE WRAP UP OUR CHAPTER ON GEORGE WASHINGTON CARVER ...
FINALLY!!! THANK YOU ... NO OFFENSE TO GEORGE, BUT DAG ... HOW MANY TIMES DO WE NEED TO HEAR THE SAME PEANUT STORIES?
EVERY BLACK HISTORY MONTH IT'S THE SAME THING — THE UNDERGROUND RAILROAD AND GEORGE WASHINGTON CARVER. LIKE NOTHING ELSE EVER HAPPENED TO BLACK PEOPLE! MAYBE NOW WE CAN LEARN SOMETHING NEW ...
SO PLEASE TURN YOUR BOOKS TO PAGE 35 ...
SOMETHING WE HAVEN'T HEARD ABOUT A THOUSAND TIMES ALREADY ...
© 2000 Aaron McGruder/Dist. by Universal Press Syndicate www.uexpress.com www.boondocks.net
2/18
AND LET'S LOOK AT MARTIN LUTHER KING JR.
NEVER MIND.

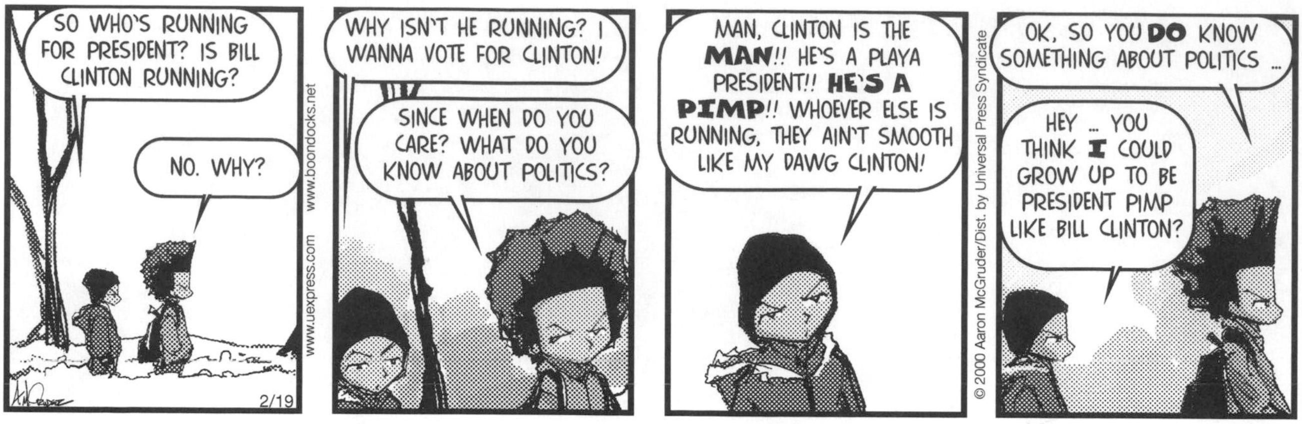
SO WHO'S RUNNING FOR PRESIDENT? IS BILL CLINTON RUNNING?
NO. WHY?
2/19
www.boondocks.net www.uexpress.com
WHY ISN'T HE RUNNING? I WANNA VOTE FOR CLINTON!
SINCE WHEN DO YOU CARE? WHAT DO YOU KNOW ABOUT POLITICS?
MAN, CLINTON IS THE MAN!! HE'S A PLAYA PRESIDENT!! HE'S A PIMP!! WHOEVER ELSE IS RUNNING, THEY AIN'T SMOOTH LIKE MY DAWG CLINTON!
© 2000 Aaron McGruder/Dist. by Universal Press Syndicate
OK, SO YOU DO KNOW SOMETHING ABOUT POLITICS ...
HEY ... YOU THINK I COULD GROW UP TO BE PRESIDENT PIMP LIKE BILL CLINTON?

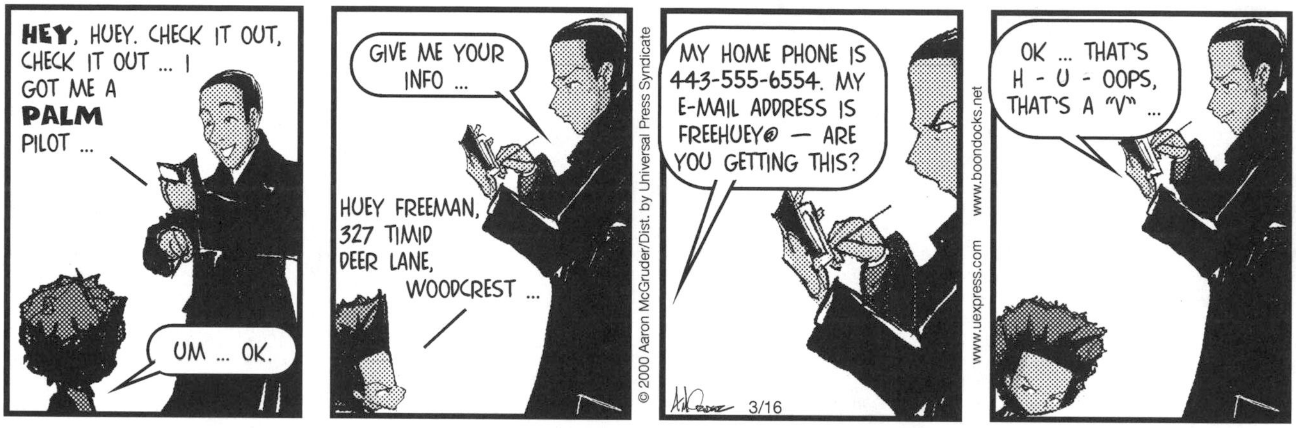
HEY, HUEY. CHECK IT OUT, CHECK IT OUT ... I GOT ME A PALM PILOT ...
UM ... OK.
GIVE ME YOUR INFO ...
HUEY FREEMAN, 327 TIMID DEER LANE, WOODCREST ...
© 2000 Aaron McGruder/Dist. by Universal Press Syndicate
MY HOME PHONE IS 443-555-6554. MY E-MAIL ADDRESS IS FREEHUEY@ — ARE YOU GETTING THIS?
3/16
www.uexpress.com www.boondocks.net
OK ... THAT'S H - U - OOPS, THAT'S A "V" ...

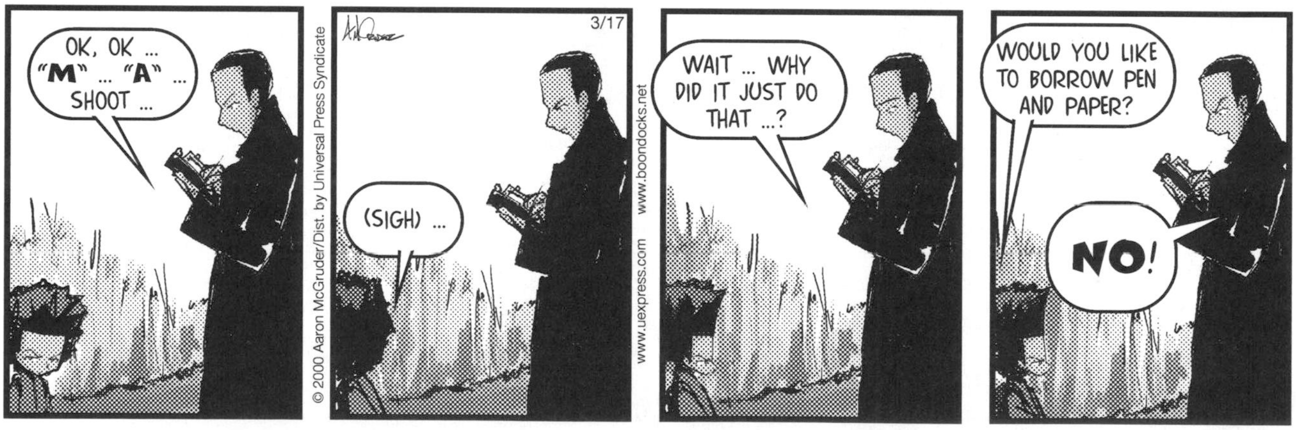
OK, OK ... "M" ... "A" ... SHOOT ...
© 2000 Aaron McGruder/Dist. by Universal Press Syndicate
3/17
(SIGH) ...
www.uexpress.com www.boondocks.net
WAIT ... WHY DID IT JUST DO THAT ...?
WOULD YOU LIKE TO BORROW PEN AND PAPER?
NO!

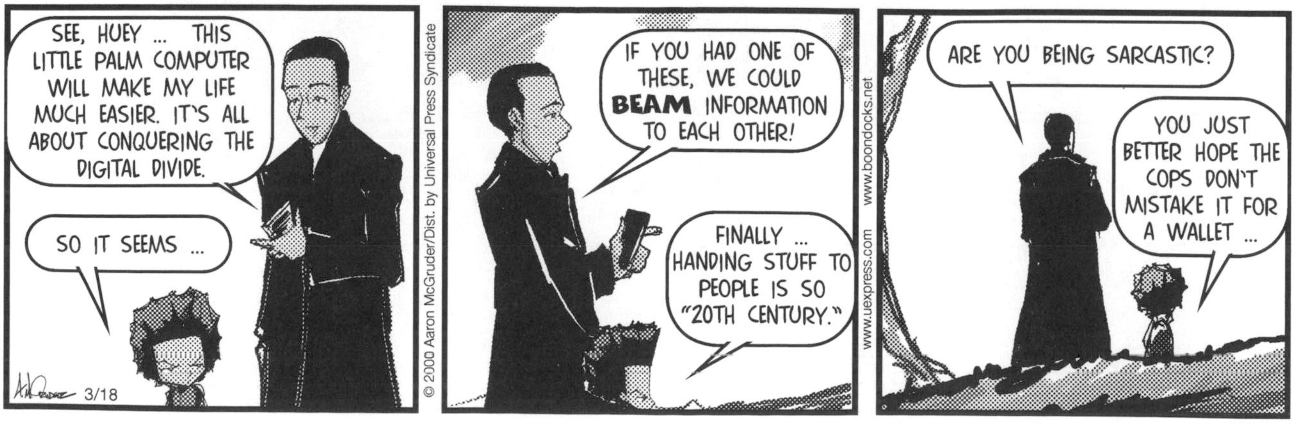
SEE, HUEY ... THIS LITTLE PALM COMPUTER WILL MAKE MY LIFE MUCH EASIER. IT'S ALL ABOUT CONQUERING THE DIGITAL DIVIDE.
SO IT SEEMS ...
3/18
© 2000 Aaron McGruder/Dist. by Universal Press Syndicate
IF YOU HAD ONE OF THESE, WE COULD BEAM INFORMATION TO EACH OTHER!
FINALLY ... HANDING STUFF TO PEOPLE IS SO "20TH CENTURY."
www.uexpress.com www.boondocks.net
ARE YOU BEING SARCASTIC?
YOU JUST BETTER HOPE THE COPS DON'T MISTAKE IT FOR A WALLET ...

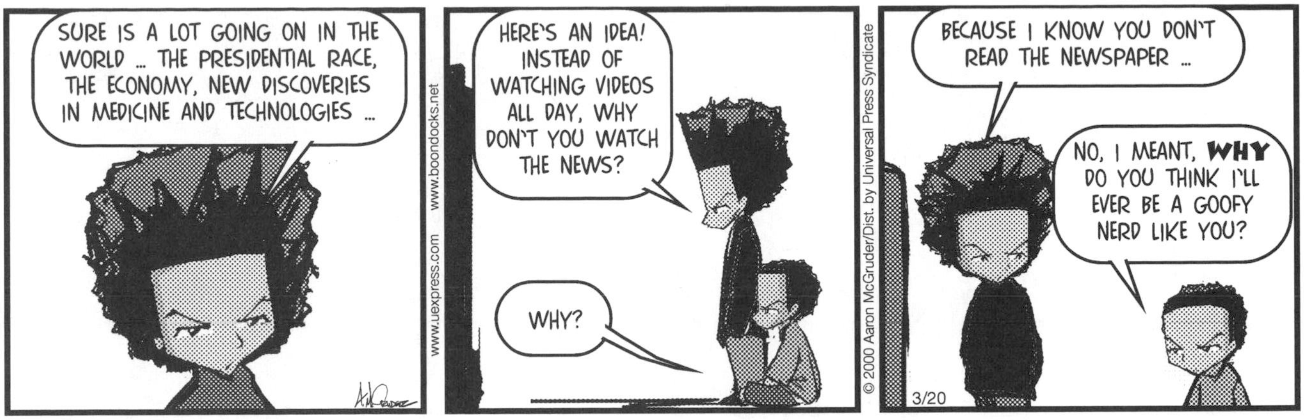
SURE IS A LOT GOING ON IN THE WORLD ... THE PRESIDENTIAL RACE, THE ECONOMY, NEW DISCOVERIES IN MEDICINE AND TECHNOLOGIES ...
www.uexpress.com www.boondocks.net
HERE'S AN IDEA! INSTEAD OF WATCHING VIDEOS ALL DAY, WHY DON'T YOU WATCH THE NEWS?
WHY?
© 2000 Aaron McGruder/Dist. by Universal Press Syndicate
BECAUSE I KNOW YOU DON'T READ THE NEWSPAPER ...
NO, I MEANT, **WHY** DO YOU THINK I'LL EVER BE A GOOFY NERD LIKE YOU?
3/20

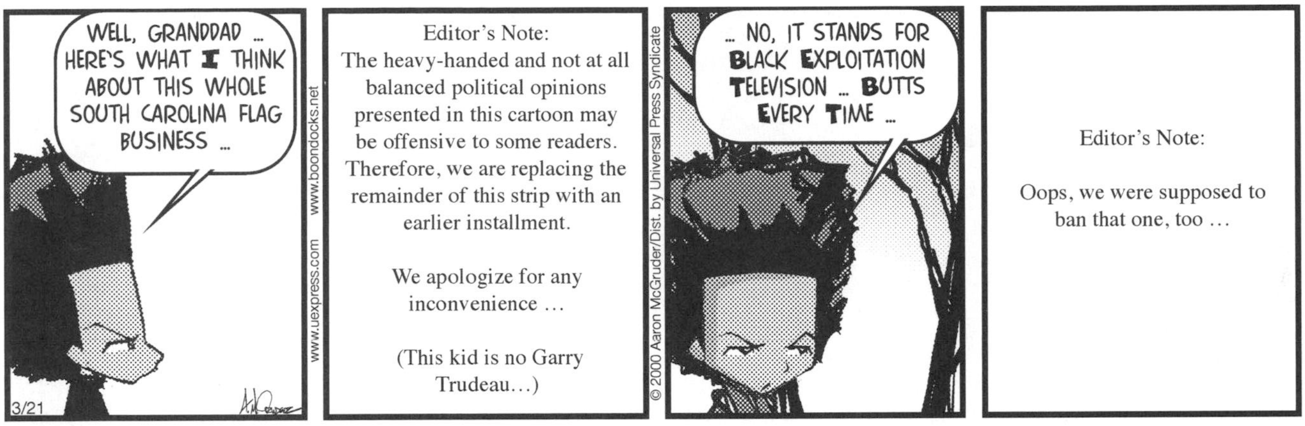
WELL, GRANDDAD ... HERE'S WHAT **I** THINK ABOUT THIS WHOLE SOUTH CAROLINA FLAG BUSINESS ...
3/21
www.uexpress.com www.boondocks.net
Editor's Note:
The heavy-handed and not at all balanced political opinions presented in this cartoon may be offensive to some readers. Therefore, we are replacing the remainder of this strip with an earlier installment.
We apologize for any inconvenience ...
(This kid is no Garry Trudeau...)
© 2000 Aaron McGruder/Dist. by Universal Press Syndicate
... NO, IT STANDS FOR **B**LACK **E**XPLOITATION **T**ELEVISION ... **B**UTTS **E**VERY **T**IME ...
Editor's Note:
Oops, we were supposed to ban that one, too ...

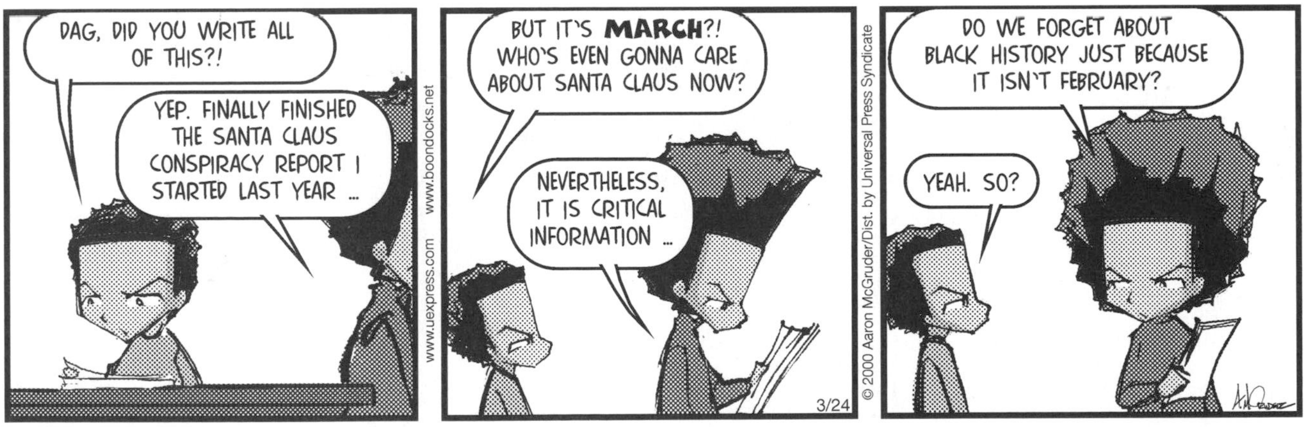
DAG, DID YOU WRITE ALL OF THIS?!
YEP. FINALLY FINISHED THE SANTA CLAUS CONSPIRACY REPORT I STARTED LAST YEAR ...
www.uexpress.com www.boondocks.net
BUT IT'S **MARCH**?! WHO'S EVEN GONNA CARE ABOUT SANTA CLAUS NOW?
NEVERTHELESS, IT IS CRITICAL INFORMATION ...
3/24
© 2000 Aaron McGruder/Dist. by Universal Press Syndicate
DO WE FORGET ABOUT BLACK HISTORY JUST BECAUSE IT ISN'T FEBRUARY?
YEAH. SO?

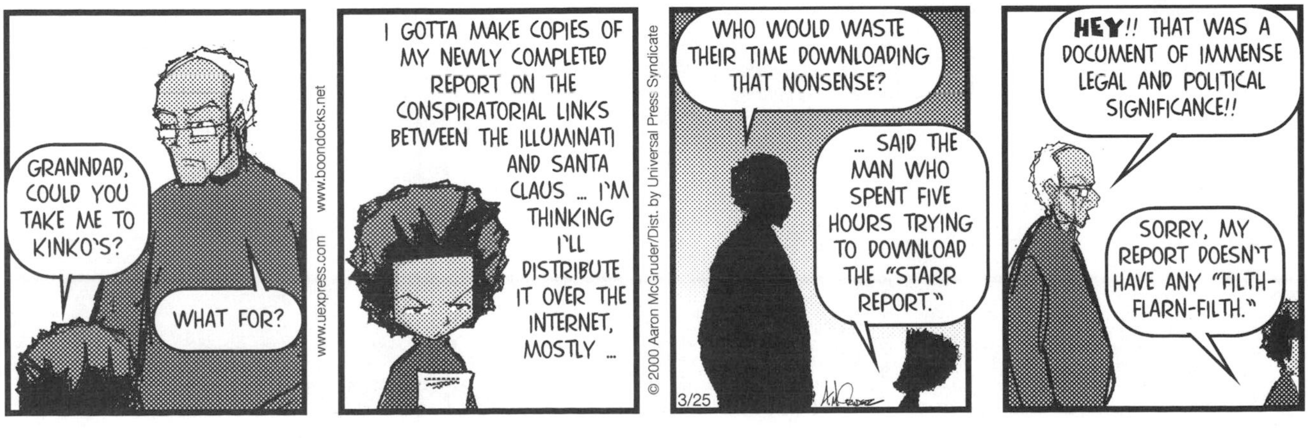
GRANNDAD, COULD YOU TAKE ME TO KINKO'S?
WHAT FOR?
www.uexpress.com www.boondocks.net
I GOTTA MAKE COPIES OF MY NEWLY COMPLETED REPORT ON THE CONSPIRATORIAL LINKS BETWEEN THE ILLUMINATI AND SANTA CLAUS ... I'M THINKING I'LL DISTRIBUTE IT OVER THE INTERNET, MOSTLY ...
© 2000 Aaron McGruder/Dist. by Universal Press Syndicate
WHO WOULD WASTE THEIR TIME DOWNLOADING THAT NONSENSE?
... SAID THE MAN WHO SPENT FIVE HOURS TRYING TO DOWNLOAD THE "STARR REPORT."
3/25
HEY!! THAT WAS A DOCUMENT OF IMMENSE LEGAL AND POLITICAL SIGNIFICANCE!!
SORRY, MY REPORT DOESN'T HAVE ANY "FILTH-FLARN-FILTH."

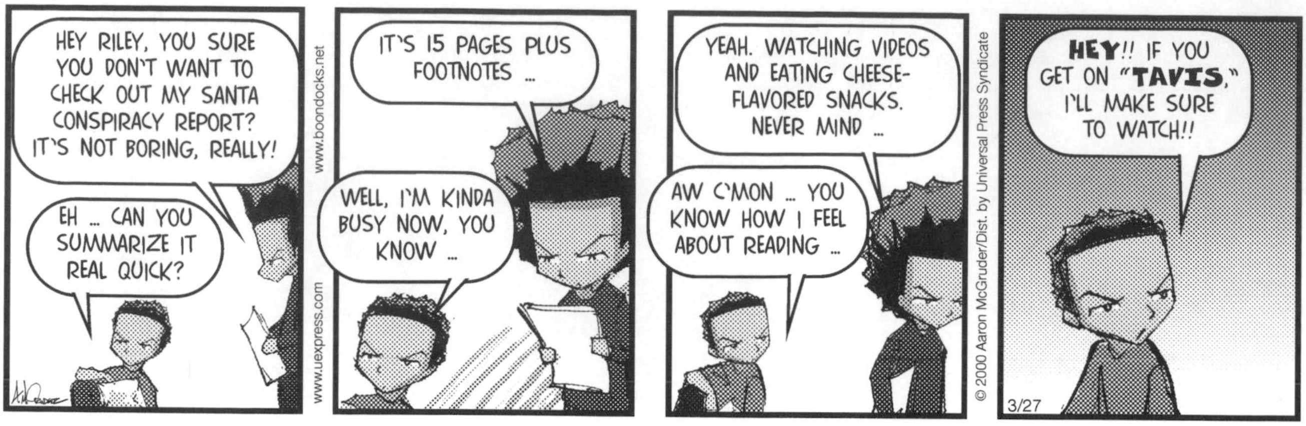
HEY RILEY, YOU SURE YOU DON'T WANT TO CHECK OUT MY SANTA CONSPIRACY REPORT? IT'S NOT BORING, REALLY!
EH ... CAN YOU SUMMARIZE IT REAL QUICK?
IT'S 15 PAGES PLUS FOOTNOTES ...
WELL, I'M KINDA BUSY NOW, YOU KNOW ...
YEAH. WATCHING VIDEOS AND EATING CHEESE-FLAVORED SNACKS. NEVER MIND ...
AW C'MON ... YOU KNOW HOW I FEEL ABOUT READING ...
HEY!! IF YOU GET ON "TAVIS," I'LL MAKE SURE TO WATCH!!
3/27
www.uexpress.com www.boondocks.net
© 2000 Aaron McGruder/Dist. by Universal Press Syndicate

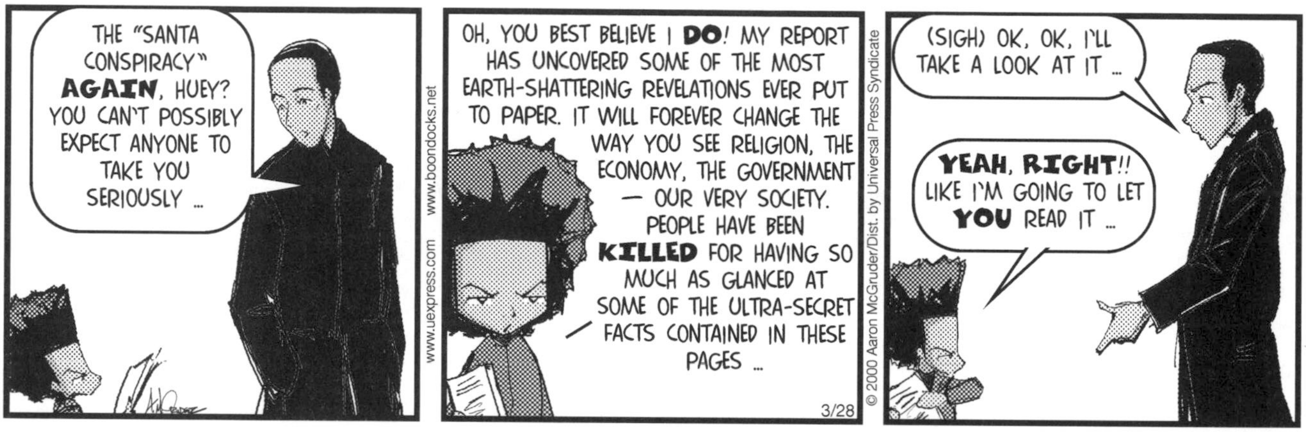
THE "SANTA CONSPIRACY" AGAIN, HUEY? YOU CAN'T POSSIBLY EXPECT ANYONE TO TAKE YOU SERIOUSLY ...
OH, YOU BEST BELIEVE I DO! MY REPORT HAS UNCOVERED SOME OF THE MOST EARTH-SHATTERING REVELATIONS EVER PUT TO PAPER. IT WILL FOREVER CHANGE THE WAY YOU SEE RELIGION, THE ECONOMY, THE GOVERNMENT — OUR VERY SOCIETY. PEOPLE HAVE BEEN KILLED FOR HAVING SO MUCH AS GLANCED AT SOME OF THE ULTRA-SECRET FACTS CONTAINED IN THESE PAGES ...
(SIGH) OK, OK, I'LL TAKE A LOOK AT IT ...
YEAH, RIGHT!! LIKE I'M GOING TO LET YOU READ IT ...
3/28
www.uexpress.com www.boondocks.net
© 2000 Aaron McGruder/Dist. by Universal Press Syndicate

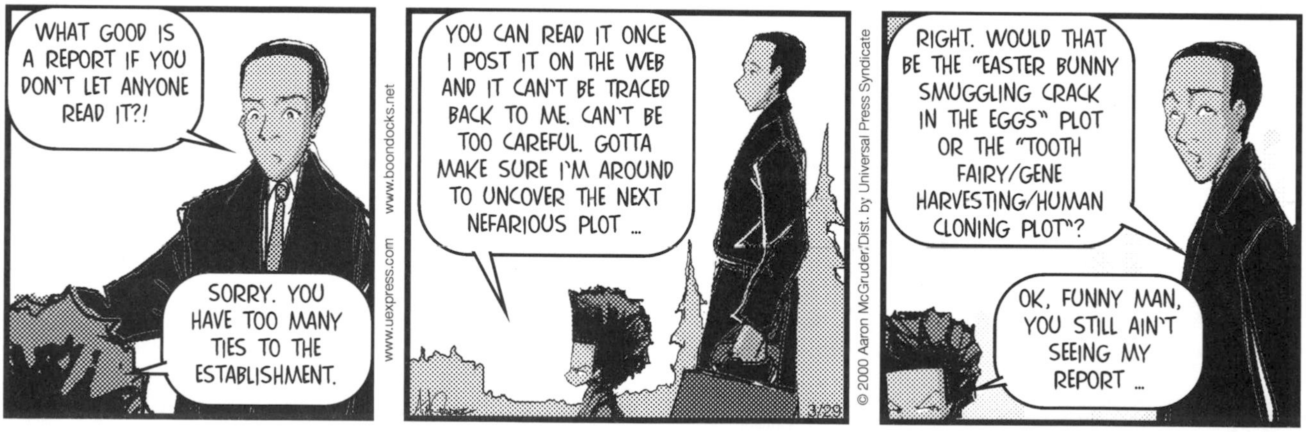
WHAT GOOD IS A REPORT IF YOU DON'T LET ANYONE READ IT?!
SORRY. YOU HAVE TOO MANY TIES TO THE ESTABLISHMENT.
YOU CAN READ IT ONCE I POST IT ON THE WEB AND IT CAN'T BE TRACED BACK TO ME. CAN'T BE TOO CAREFUL. GOTTA MAKE SURE I'M AROUND TO UNCOVER THE NEXT NEFARIOUS PLOT ...
RIGHT. WOULD THAT BE THE "EASTER BUNNY SMUGGLING CRACK IN THE EGGS" PLOT OR THE "TOOTH FAIRY/GENE HARVESTING/HUMAN CLONING PLOT"?
OK, FUNNY MAN, YOU STILL AIN'T SEEING MY REPORT ...
www.uexpress.com www.boondocks.net
© 2000 Aaron McGruder/Dist. by Universal Press Syndicate

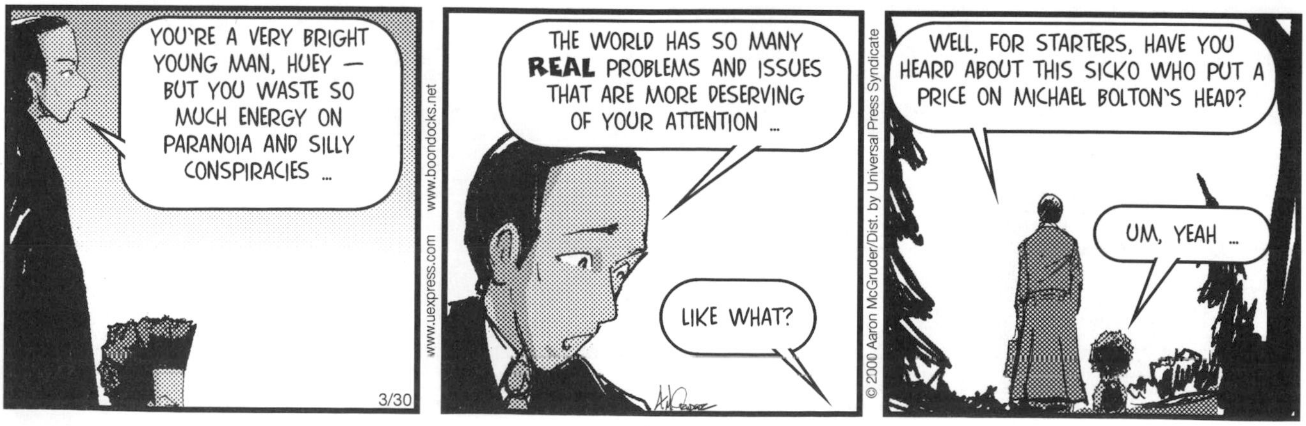
YOU'RE A VERY BRIGHT YOUNG MAN, HUEY — BUT YOU WASTE SO MUCH ENERGY ON PARANOIA AND SILLY CONSPIRACIES ...
3/30
THE WORLD HAS SO MANY REAL PROBLEMS AND ISSUES THAT ARE MORE DESERVING OF YOUR ATTENTION ...
LIKE WHAT?
WELL, FOR STARTERS, HAVE YOU HEARD ABOUT THIS SICKO WHO PUT A PRICE ON MICHAEL BOLTON'S HEAD?
UM, YEAH ...
www.uexpress.com www.boondocks.net
© 2000 Aaron McGruder/Dist. by Universal Press Syndicate

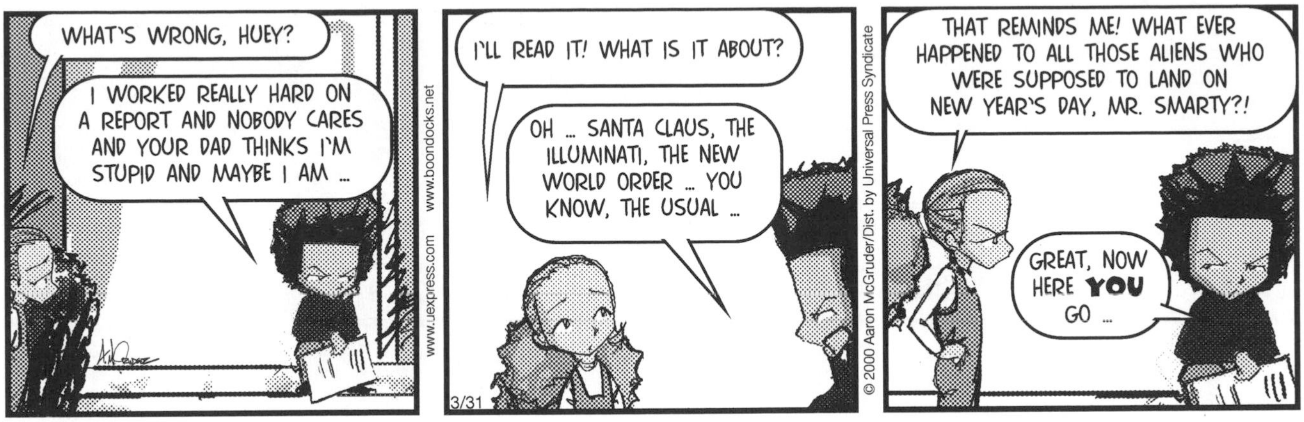
WHAT'S WRONG, HUEY?
I WORKED REALLY HARD ON A REPORT AND NOBODY CARES AND YOUR DAD THINKS I'M STUPID AND MAYBE I AM ...
www.uexpress.com www.boondocks.net
I'LL READ IT! WHAT IS IT ABOUT?
OH ... SANTA CLAUS, THE ILLUMINATI, THE NEW WORLD ORDER ... YOU KNOW, THE USUAL ...
3/31
© 2000 Aaron McGruder/Dist. by Universal Press Syndicate
THAT REMINDS ME! WHAT EVER HAPPENED TO ALL THOSE ALIENS WHO WERE SUPPOSED TO LAND ON NEW YEAR'S DAY, MR. SMARTY?!
GREAT, NOW HERE **YOU** GO ...

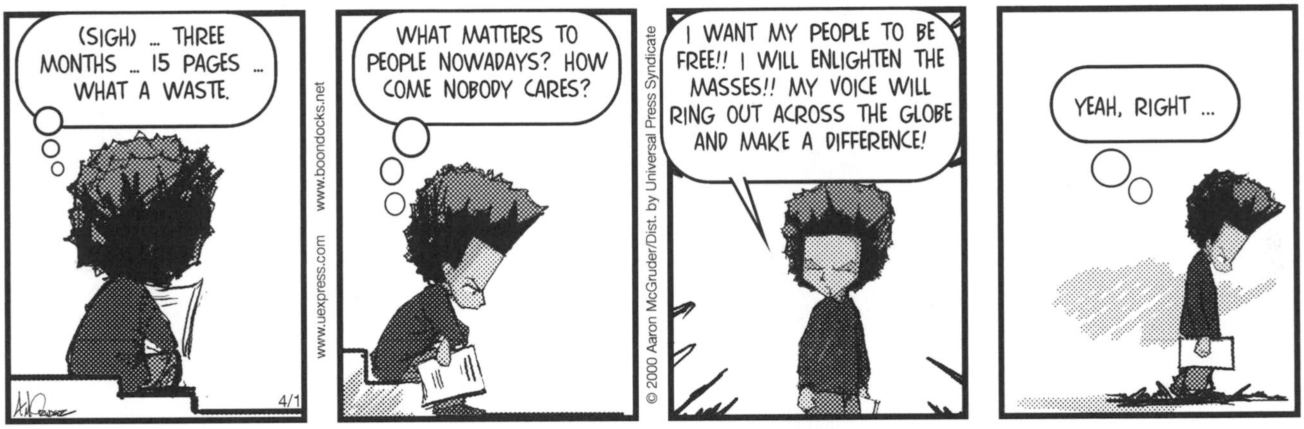
(SIGH) ... THREE MONTHS ... 15 PAGES ... WHAT A WASTE.
4/1
www.uexpress.com www.boondocks.net
WHAT MATTERS TO PEOPLE NOWADAYS? HOW COME NOBODY CARES?
© 2000 Aaron McGruder/Dist. by Universal Press Syndicate
I WANT MY PEOPLE TO BE FREE!! I WILL ENLIGHTEN THE MASSES!! MY VOICE WILL RING OUT ACROSS THE GLOBE AND MAKE A DIFFERENCE!
YEAH, RIGHT ...

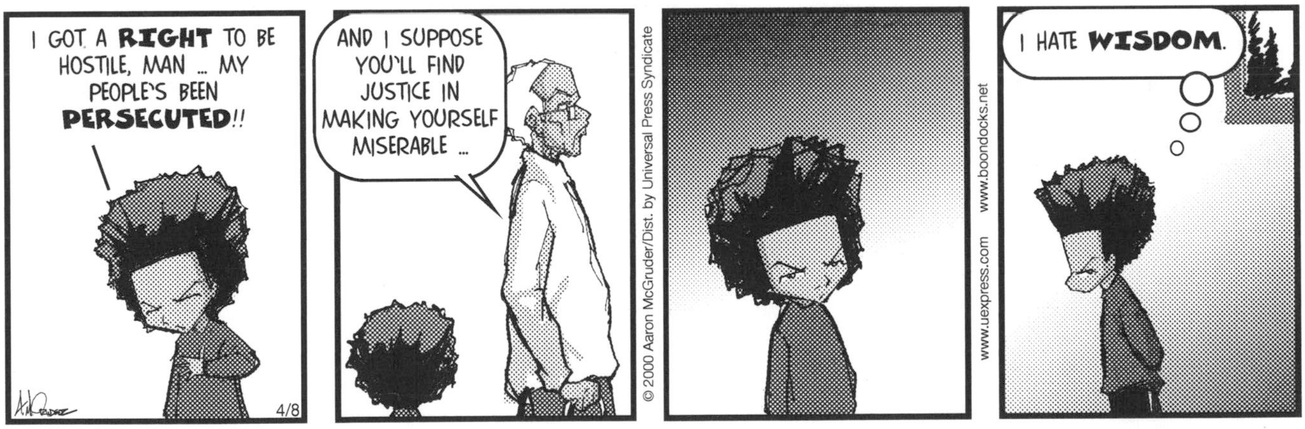
I GOT A **RIGHT** TO BE HOSTILE, MAN ... MY PEOPLE'S BEEN **PERSECUTED**!!
4/8
AND I SUPPOSE YOU'LL FIND JUSTICE IN MAKING YOURSELF MISERABLE ...
© 2000 Aaron McGruder/Dist. by Universal Press Syndicate
www.uexpress.com www.boondocks.net
I HATE **WISDOM**.

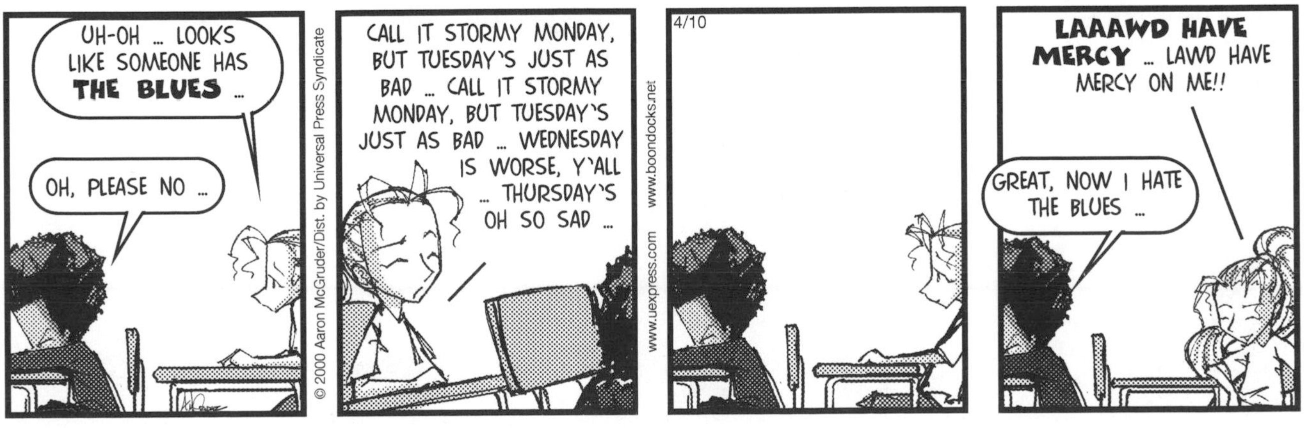
UH-OH ... LOOKS LIKE SOMEONE HAS **THE BLUES** ...
OH, PLEASE NO ...
© 2000 Aaron McGruder/Dist. by Universal Press Syndicate
CALL IT STORMY MONDAY, BUT TUESDAY'S JUST AS BAD ... CALL IT STORMY MONDAY, BUT TUESDAY'S JUST AS BAD ... WEDNESDAY IS WORSE, Y'ALL ... THURSDAY'S OH SO SAD ...
www.uexpress.com www.boondocks.net
4/10
LAAAWD HAVE MERCY ... LAWD HAVE MERCY ON ME!!
GREAT, NOW I HATE THE BLUES ...

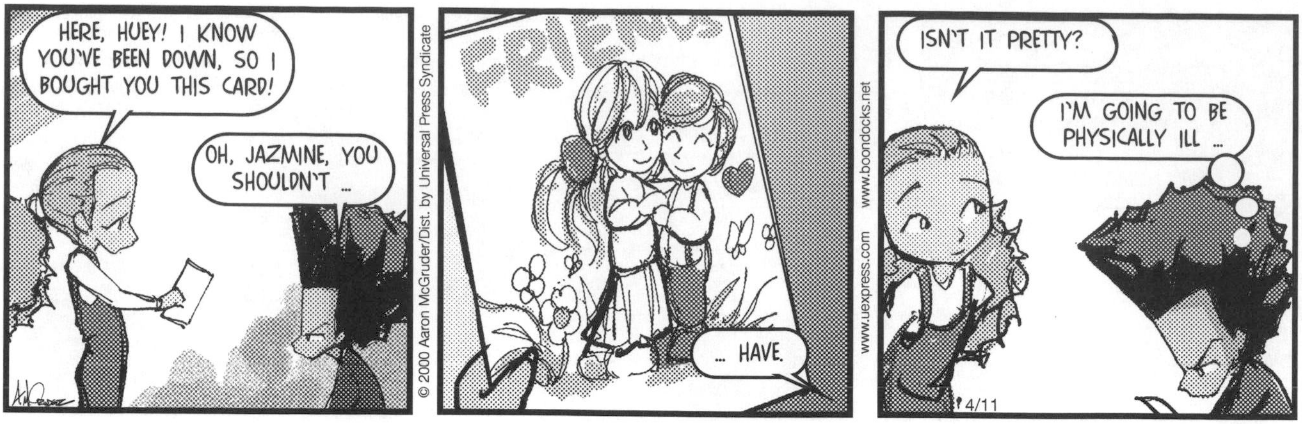
HERE, HUEY! I KNOW YOU'VE BEEN DOWN, SO I BOUGHT YOU THIS CARD!
OH, JAZMINE, YOU SHOULDN'T ...
FRIENDS
... HAVE.
ISN'T IT PRETTY?
I'M GOING TO BE PHYSICALLY ILL ...
© 2000 Aaron McGruder/Dist. by Universal Press Syndicate
www.uexpress.com www.boondocks.net
4/11

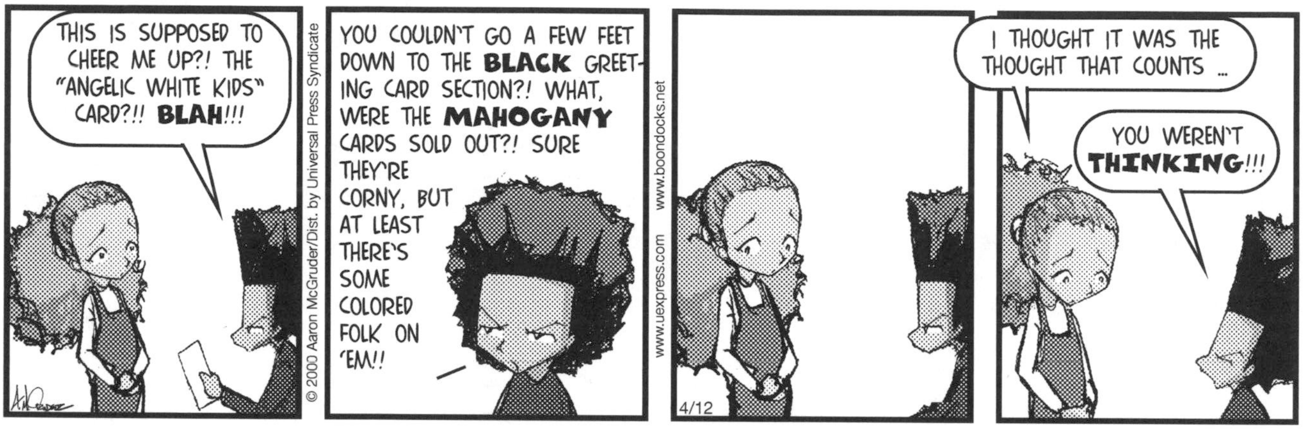
THIS IS SUPPOSED TO CHEER ME UP?! THE "ANGELIC WHITE KIDS" CARD?!! BLAH!!!
YOU COULDN'T GO A FEW FEET DOWN TO THE BLACK GREETING CARD SECTION?! WHAT, WERE THE MAHOGANY CARDS SOLD OUT?! SURE THEY'RE CORNY, BUT AT LEAST THERE'S SOME COLORED FOLK ON 'EM!!
I THOUGHT IT WAS THE THOUGHT THAT COUNTS ...
YOU WEREN'T THINKING!!!
© 2000 Aaron McGruder/Dist. by Universal Press Syndicate
www.uexpress.com www.boondocks.net
4/12

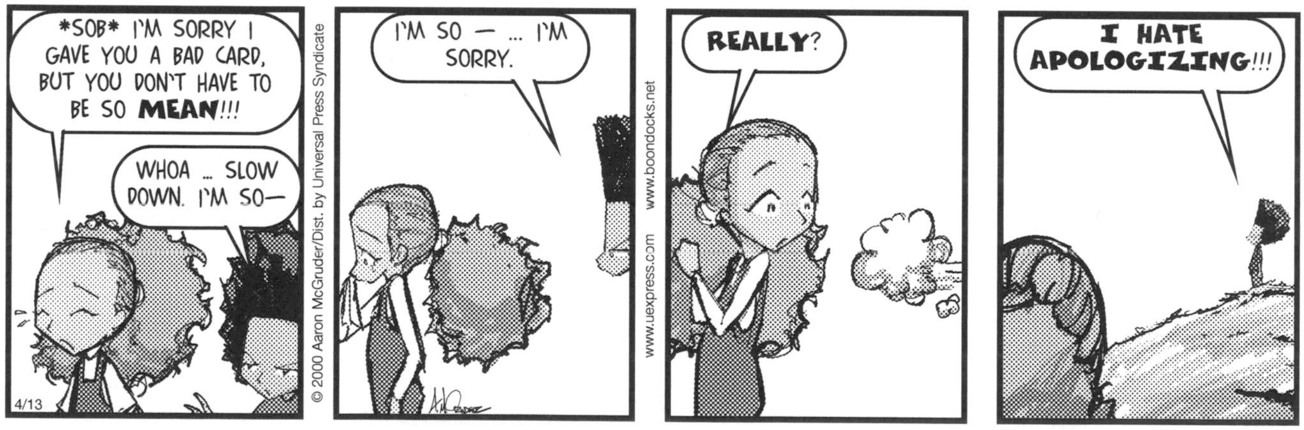
SOB I'M SORRY I GAVE YOU A BAD CARD, BUT YOU DON'T HAVE TO BE SO MEAN!!!
WHOA ... SLOW DOWN. I'M SO—
I'M SO — ... I'M SORRY.
REALLY?
I HATE APOLOGIZING!!!
© 2000 Aaron McGruder/Dist. by Universal Press Syndicate
www.uexpress.com www.boondocks.net
4/13

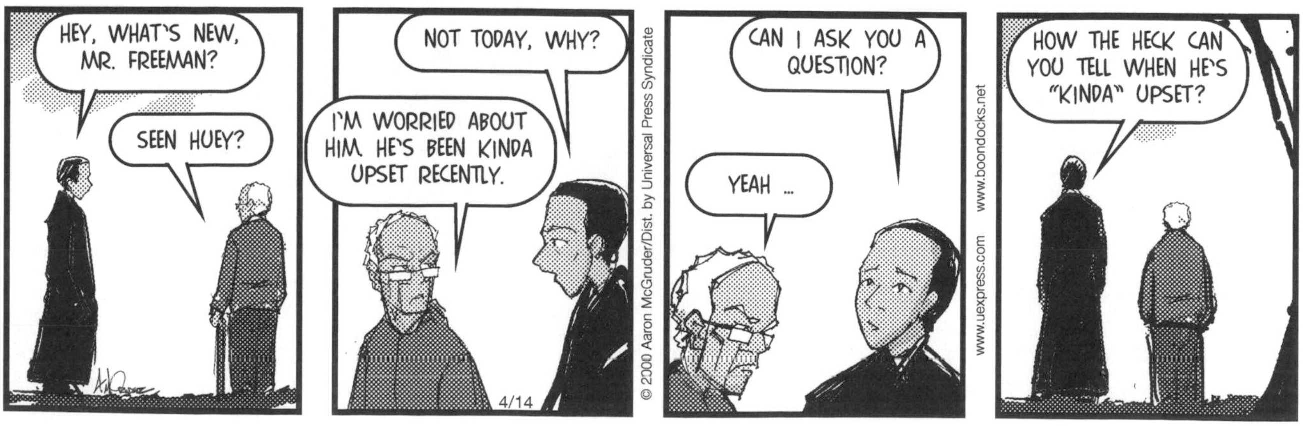
HEY, WHAT'S NEW, MR. FREEMAN?
SEEN HUEY?
NOT TODAY, WHY?
I'M WORRIED ABOUT HIM. HE'S BEEN KINDA UPSET RECENTLY.
CAN I ASK YOU A QUESTION?
YEAH ...
HOW THE HECK CAN YOU TELL WHEN HE'S "KINDA" UPSET?
© 2000 Aaron McGruder/Dist. by Universal Press Syndicate
www.uexpress.com www.boondocks.net
4/14

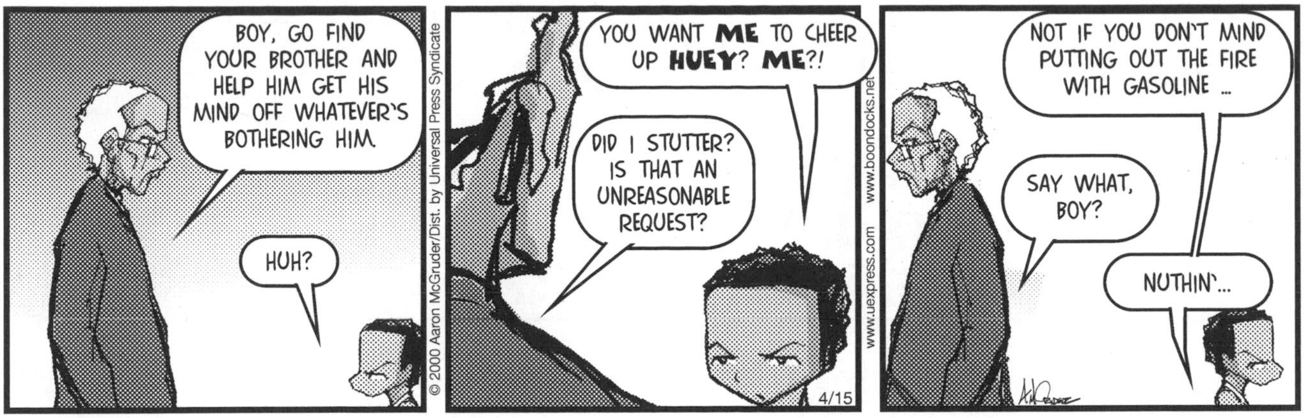
BOY, GO FIND YOUR BROTHER AND HELP HIM GET HIS MIND OFF WHATEVER'S BOTHERING HIM.
HUH?
© 2000 Aaron McGruder/Dist. by Universal Press Syndicate
YOU WANT **ME** TO CHEER UP **HUEY**? **ME**?!
DID I STUTTER? IS THAT AN UNREASONABLE REQUEST?
4/15
www.uexpress.com www.boondocks.net
NOT IF YOU DON'T MIND PUTTING OUT THE FIRE WITH GASOLINE ...
SAY WHAT, BOY?
NUTHIN'...

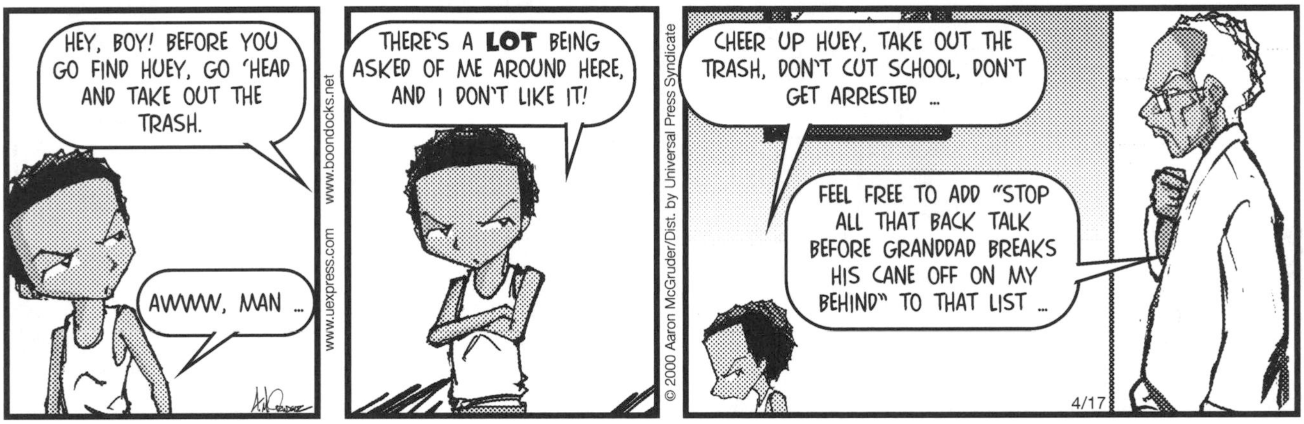
HEY, BOY! BEFORE YOU GO FIND HUEY, GO 'HEAD AND TAKE OUT THE TRASH.
AWWW, MAN ...
www.uexpress.com www.boondocks.net
THERE'S A **LOT** BEING ASKED OF ME AROUND HERE, AND I DON'T LIKE IT!
© 2000 Aaron McGruder/Dist. by Universal Press Syndicate
CHEER UP HUEY, TAKE OUT THE TRASH, DON'T CUT SCHOOL, DON'T GET ARRESTED ...
FEEL FREE TO ADD "STOP ALL THAT BACK TALK BEFORE GRANDDAD BREAKS HIS CANE OFF ON MY BEHIND" TO THAT LIST ...
4/17

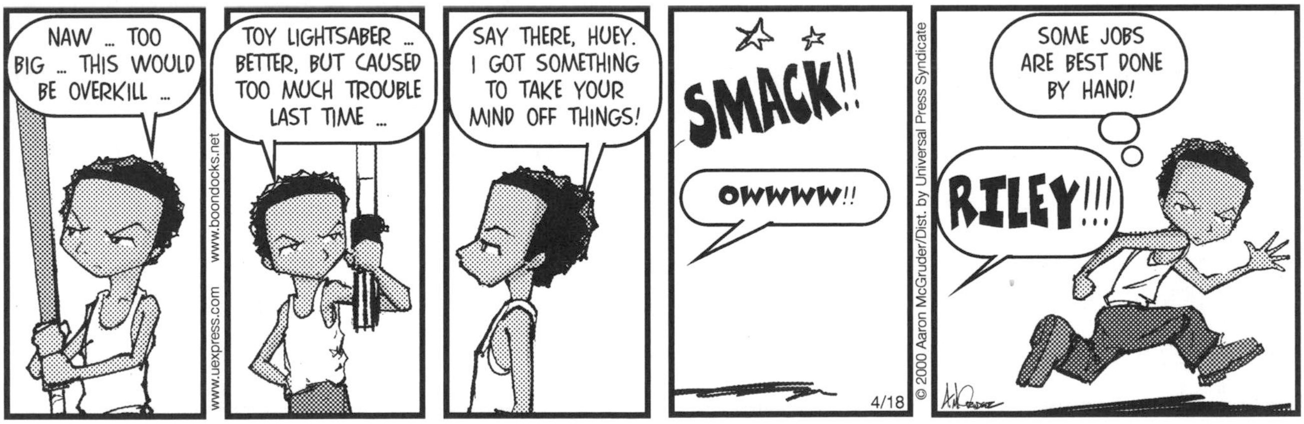
NAW ... TOO BIG ... THIS WOULD BE OVERKILL ...
www.uexpress.com www.boondocks.net
TOY LIGHTSABER ... BETTER, BUT CAUSED TOO MUCH TROUBLE LAST TIME ...
SAY THERE, HUEY. I GOT SOMETHING TO TAKE YOUR MIND OFF THINGS!
SMACK!!
OWWWW!!
4/18
© 2000 Aaron McGruder/Dist. by Universal Press Syndicate
SOME JOBS ARE BEST DONE BY HAND!
RILEY!!!

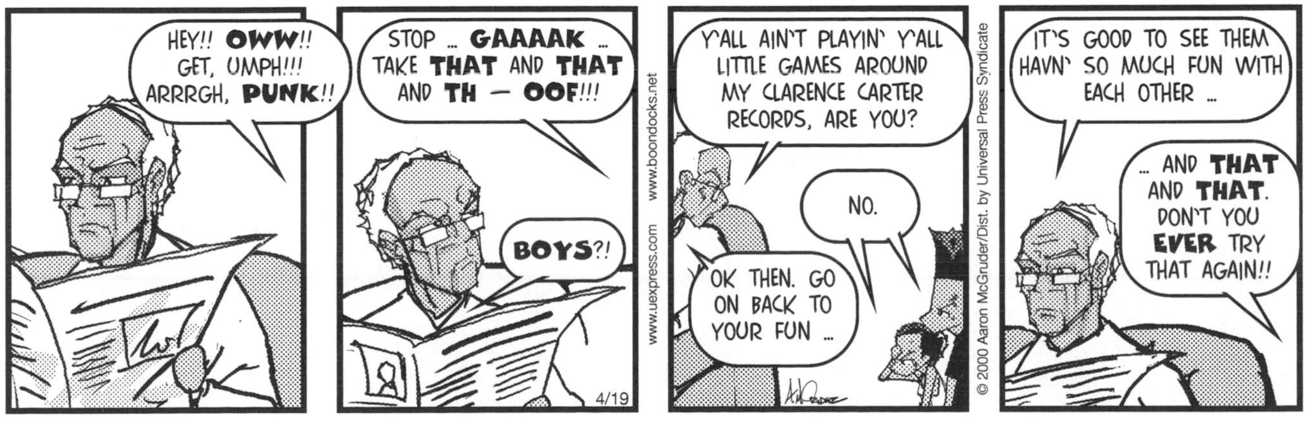
HEY!! **OWW**!! GET, UMPH!!! ARRRGH, **PUNK**!!
STOP ... **GAAAAK** ... TAKE **THAT** AND **THAT** AND **TH — OOF**!!!
BOYS?!
4/19
www.uexpress.com www.boondocks.net
Y'ALL AIN'T PLAYIN' Y'ALL LITTLE GAMES AROUND MY CLARENCE CARTER RECORDS, ARE YOU?
NO.
OK THEN. GO ON BACK TO YOUR FUN ...
© 2000 Aaron McGruder/Dist. by Universal Press Syndicate
IT'S GOOD TO SEE THEM HAVN' SO MUCH FUN WITH EACH OTHER ...
... AND **THAT** AND **THAT**. DON'T YOU **EVER** TRY THAT AGAIN!!

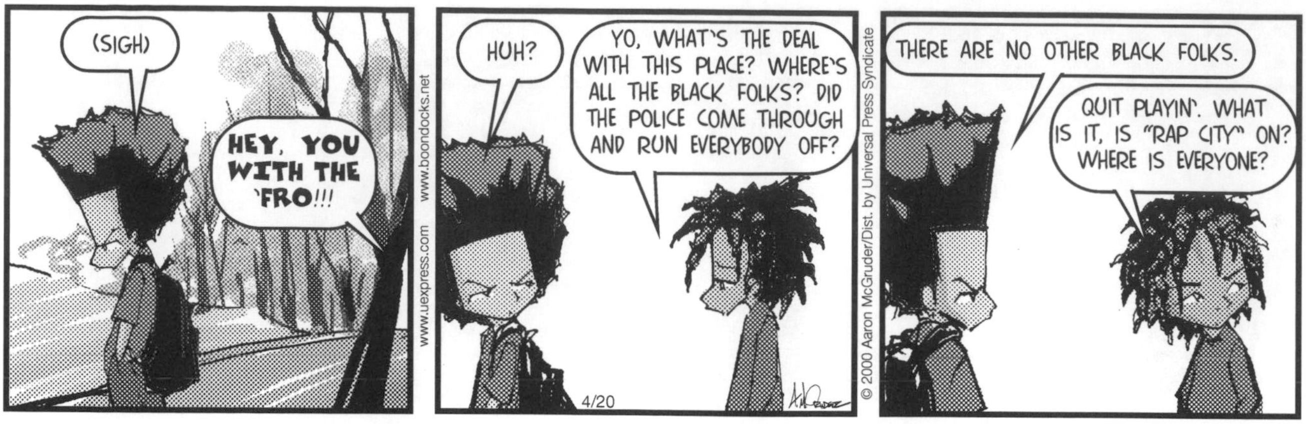
(SIGH)
HEY, YOU WITH THE 'FRO!!!
www.uexpress.com www.boondocks.net
HUH?
YO, WHAT'S THE DEAL WITH THIS PLACE? WHERE'S ALL THE BLACK FOLKS? DID THE POLICE COME THROUGH AND RUN EVERYBODY OFF?
4/20
© 2000 Aaron McGruder/Dist. by Universal Press Syndicate
THERE ARE NO OTHER BLACK FOLKS.
QUIT PLAYIN'. WHAT IS IT, IS "RAP CITY" ON? WHERE IS EVERYONE?

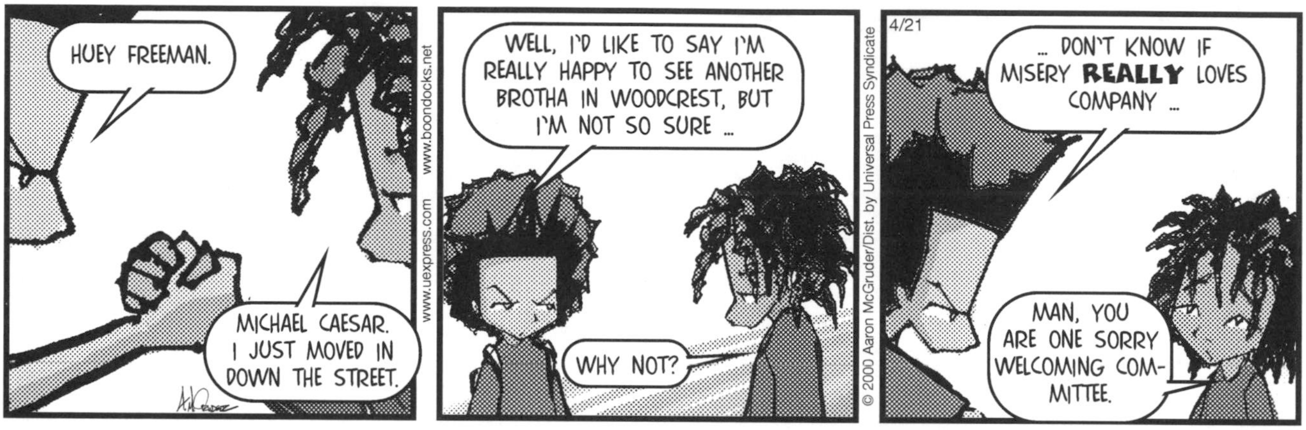
HUEY FREEMAN.
MICHAEL CAESAR. I JUST MOVED IN DOWN THE STREET.
www.uexpress.com www.boondocks.net
WELL, I'D LIKE TO SAY I'M REALLY HAPPY TO SEE ANOTHER BROTHA IN WOODCREST, BUT I'M NOT SO SURE ...
WHY NOT?
© 2000 Aaron McGruder/Dist. by Universal Press Syndicate
4/21
... DON'T KNOW IF MISERY REALLY LOVES COMPANY ...
MAN, YOU ARE ONE SORRY WELCOMING COM-MITTEE.

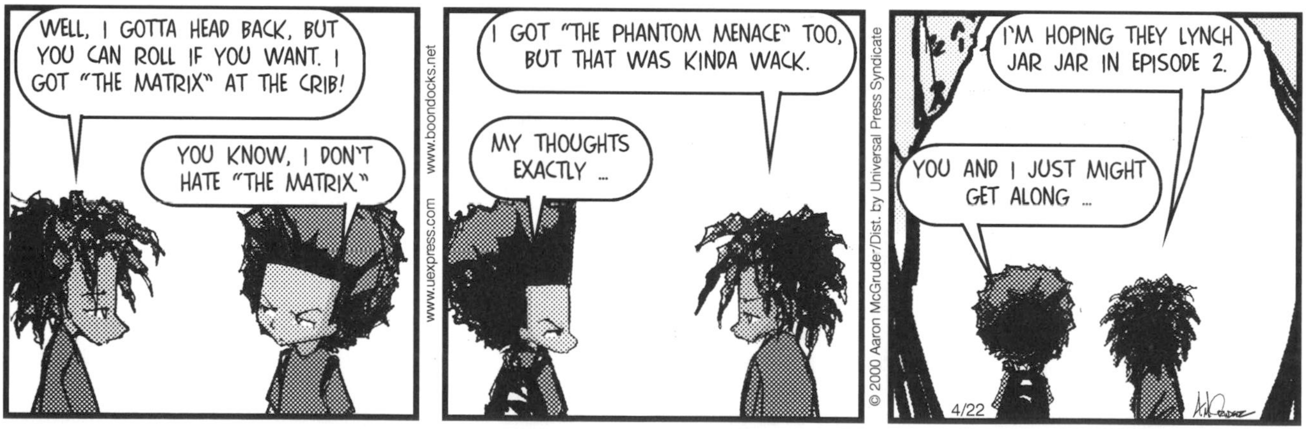
WELL, I GOTTA HEAD BACK, BUT YOU CAN ROLL IF YOU WANT. I GOT "THE MATRIX" AT THE CRIB!
YOU KNOW, I DON'T HATE "THE MATRIX."
www.uexpress.com www.boondocks.net
I GOT "THE PHANTOM MENACE" TOO, BUT THAT WAS KINDA WACK.
MY THOUGHTS EXACTLY ...
© 2000 Aaron McGruder/Dist. by Universal Press Syndicate
I'M HOPING THEY LYNCH JAR JAR IN EPISODE 2.
YOU AND I JUST MIGHT GET ALONG ...
4/22

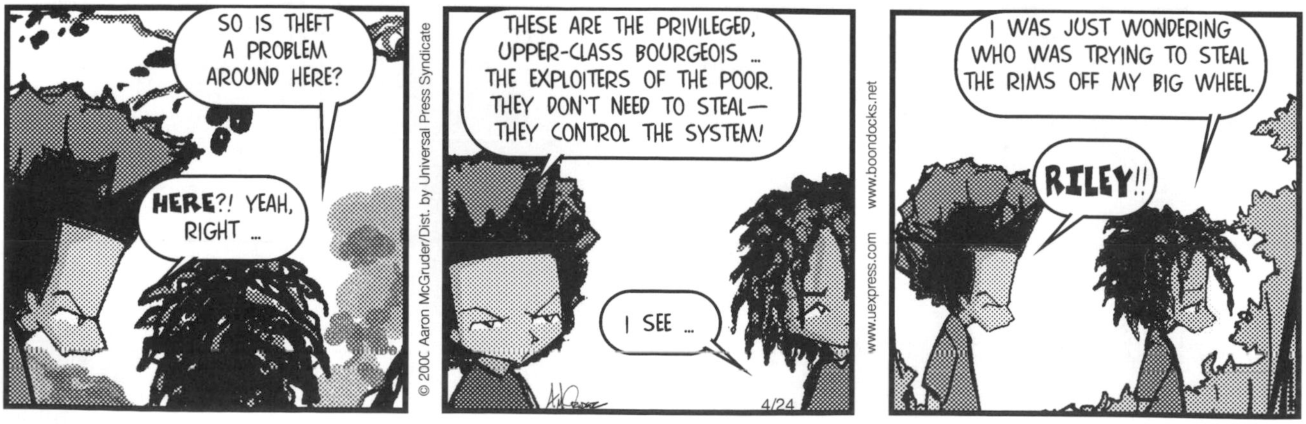
SO IS THEFT A PROBLEM AROUND HERE?
HERE?! YEAH, RIGHT ...
© 2000 Aaron McGruder/Dist. by Universal Press Syndicate
THESE ARE THE PRIVILEGED, UPPER-CLASS BOURGEOIS ... THE EXPLOITERS OF THE POOR. THEY DON'T NEED TO STEAL— THEY CONTROL THE SYSTEM!
I SEE ...
4/24
www.uexpress.com www.boondocks.net
I WAS JUST WONDERING WHO WAS TRYING TO STEAL THE RIMS OFF MY BIG WHEEL.
RILEY!!

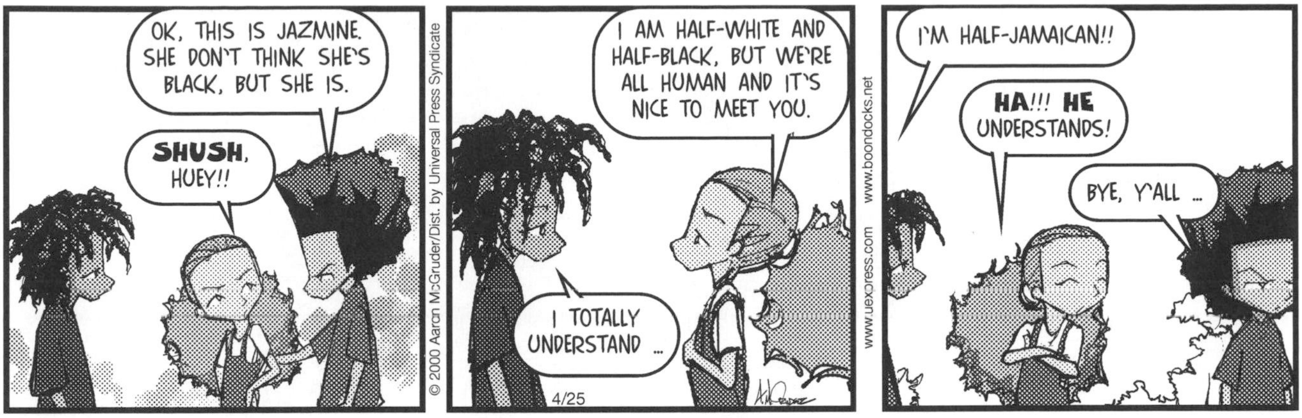
OK, THIS IS JAZMINE. SHE DON'T THINK SHE'S BLACK, BUT SHE IS.
SHUSH, HUEY!!
© 2000 Aaron McGruder/Dist. by Universal Press Syndicate
I AM HALF-WHITE AND HALF-BLACK, BUT WE'RE ALL HUMAN AND IT'S NICE TO MEET YOU.
I TOTALLY UNDERSTAND ...
4/25
www.uexpress.com www.boondocks.net
I'M HALF-JAMAICAN!!
HA!!! HE UNDERSTANDS!
BYE, Y'ALL ...

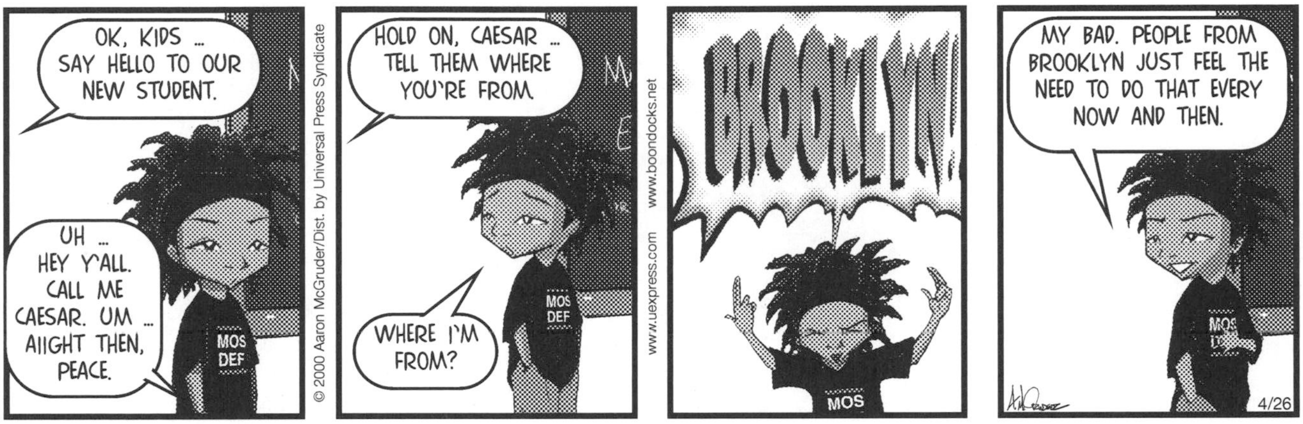
OK, KIDS ... SAY HELLO TO OUR NEW STUDENT.
UH ... HEY Y'ALL. CALL ME CAESAR. UM ... AIIGHT THEN, PEACE.
MOS DEF
© 2000 Aaron McGruder/Dist. by Universal Press Syndicate
HOLD ON, CAESAR ... TELL THEM WHERE YOU'RE FROM.
WHERE I'M FROM?
MOS DEF
www.uexpress.com www.boondocks.net
BROOKLYN!
MOS
MY BAD. PEOPLE FROM BROOKLYN JUST FEEL THE NEED TO DO THAT EVERY NOW AND THEN.
4/26

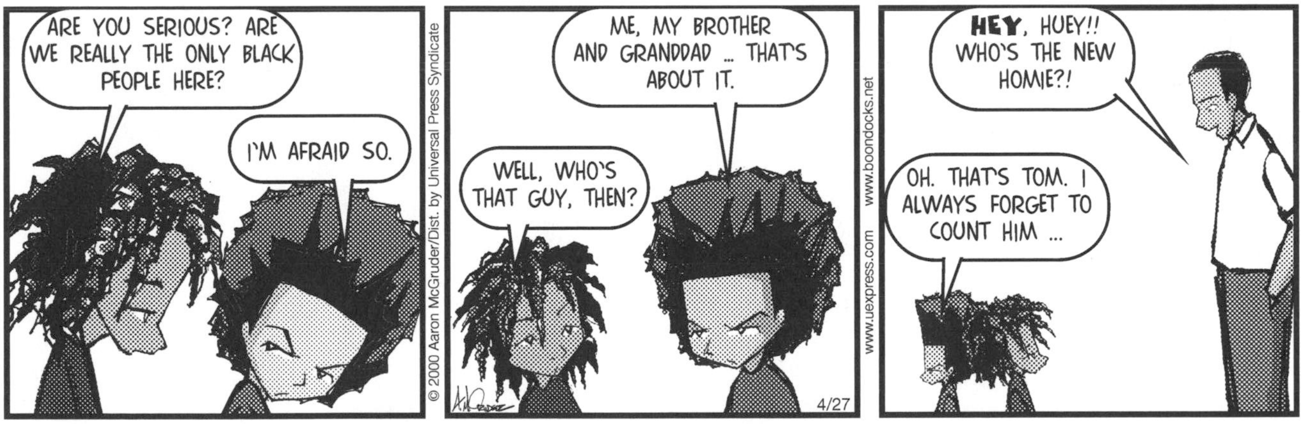
ARE YOU SERIOUS? ARE WE REALLY THE ONLY BLACK PEOPLE HERE?
I'M AFRAID SO.
© 2000 Aaron McGruder/Dist. by Universal Press Syndicate
ME, MY BROTHER AND GRANDDAD ... THAT'S ABOUT IT.
WELL, WHO'S THAT GUY, THEN?
4/27
www.uexpress.com www.boondocks.net
HEY, HUEY!! WHO'S THE NEW HOMIE?!
OH. THAT'S TOM. I ALWAYS FORGET TO COUNT HIM ...

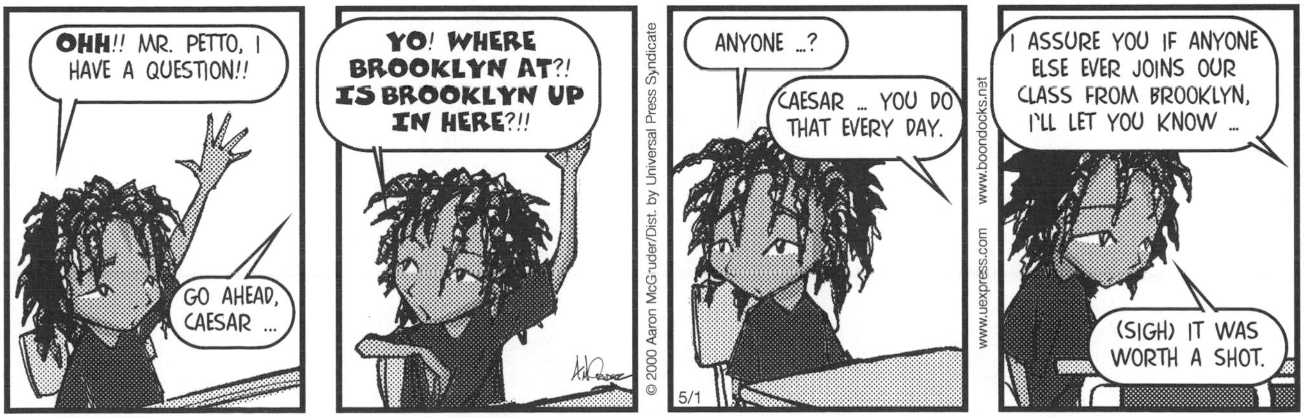
OHH!! MR. PETTO, I HAVE A QUESTION!!
GO AHEAD, CAESAR ...
YO! WHERE BROOKLYN AT?! IS BROOKLYN UP IN HERE?!!
© 2000 Aaron McGruder/Dist. by Universal Press Syndicate
ANYONE ...?
CAESAR ... YOU DO THAT EVERY DAY.
5/1
www.uexpress.com www.boondocks.net
I ASSURE YOU IF ANYONE ELSE EVER JOINS OUR CLASS FROM BROOKLYN, I'LL LET YOU KNOW ...
(SIGH) IT WAS WORTH A SHOT.

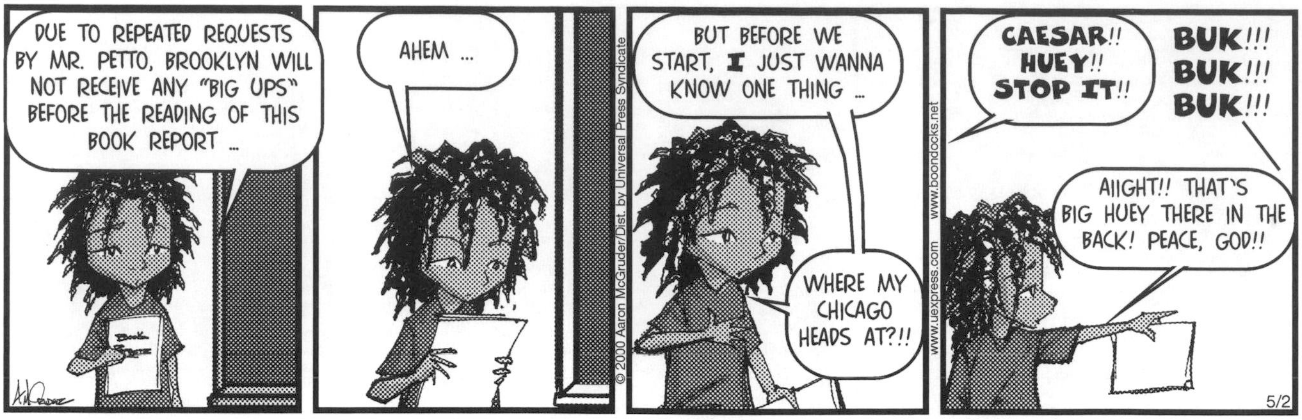
DUE TO REPEATED REQUESTS BY MR. PETTO, BROOKLYN WILL NOT RECEIVE ANY "BIG UPS" BEFORE THE READING OF THIS BOOK REPORT ...
AHEM ...
© 2000 Aaron McGruder/Dist. by Universal Press Syndicate
BUT BEFORE WE START, I JUST WANNA KNOW ONE THING ...
WHERE MY CHICAGO HEADS AT?!!
www.uexpress.com www.boondocks.net
CAESAR!! HUEY!! STOP IT!!
BUK!!! BUK!!! BUK!!!
AIIGHT!! THAT'S BIG HUEY THERE IN THE BACK! PEACE, GOD!!
5/2

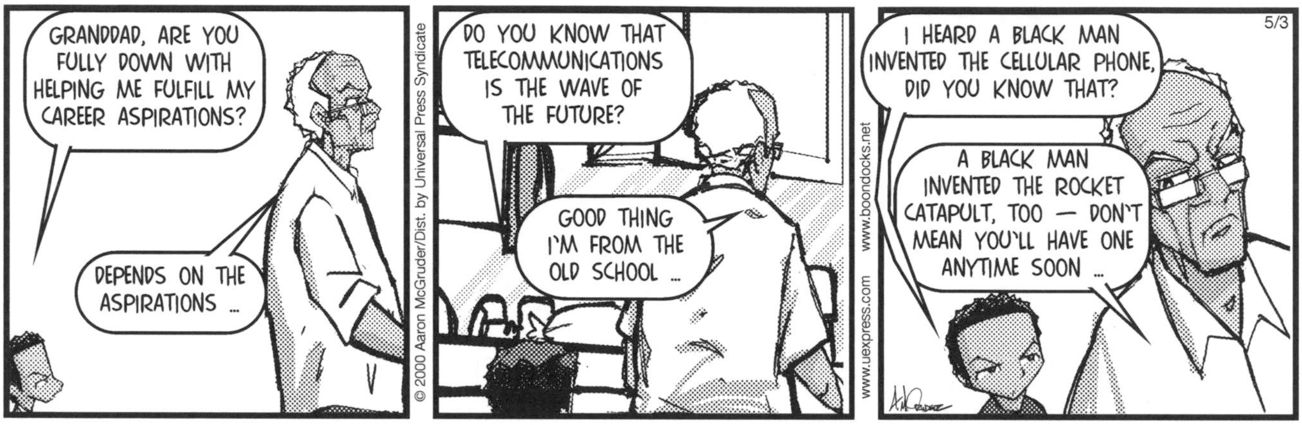
GRANDDAD, ARE YOU FULLY DOWN WITH HELPING ME FULFILL MY CAREER ASPIRATIONS?
DEPENDS ON THE ASPIRATIONS ...
© 2000 Aaron McGruder/Dist. by Universal Press Syndicate
DO YOU KNOW THAT TELECOMMUNICATIONS IS THE WAVE OF THE FUTURE?
GOOD THING I'M FROM THE OLD SCHOOL ...
www.uexpress.com www.boondocks.net
5/3
I HEARD A BLACK MAN INVENTED THE CELLULAR PHONE, DID YOU KNOW THAT?
A BLACK MAN INVENTED THE ROCKET CATAPULT, TOO — DON'T MEAN YOU'LL HAVE ONE ANYTIME SOON ...

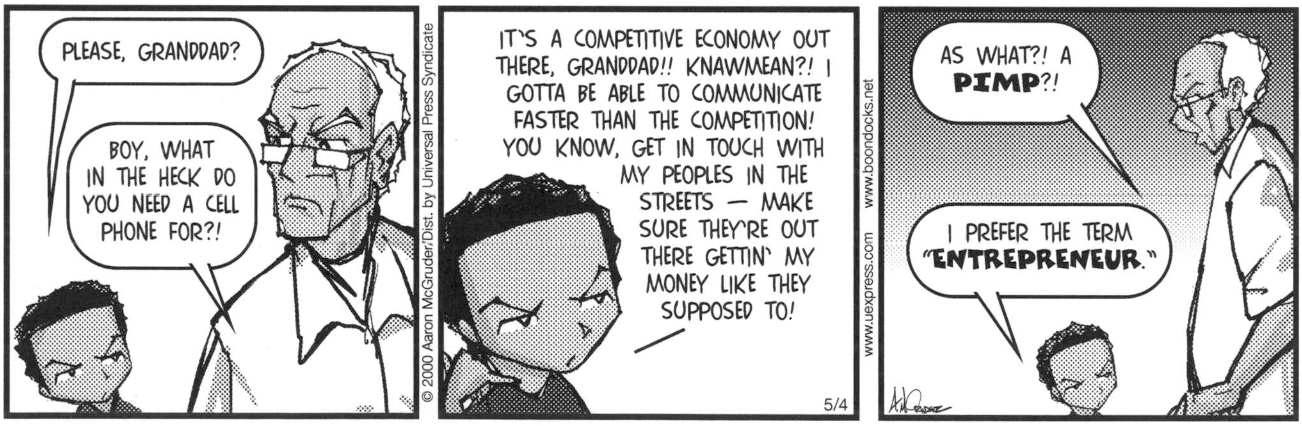
PLEASE, GRANDDAD?
BOY, WHAT IN THE HECK DO YOU NEED A CELL PHONE FOR?!
© 2000 Aaron McGruder/Dist. by Universal Press Syndicate
IT'S A COMPETITIVE ECONOMY OUT THERE, GRANDDAD!! KNAWMEAN?! I GOTTA BE ABLE TO COMMUNICATE FASTER THAN THE COMPETITION! YOU KNOW, GET IN TOUCH WITH MY PEOPLES IN THE STREETS — MAKE SURE THEY'RE OUT THERE GETTIN' MY MONEY LIKE THEY SUPPOSED TO!
5/4
www.uexpress.com www.boondocks.net
AS WHAT?! A PIMP?!
I PREFER THE TERM "ENTREPRENEUR."

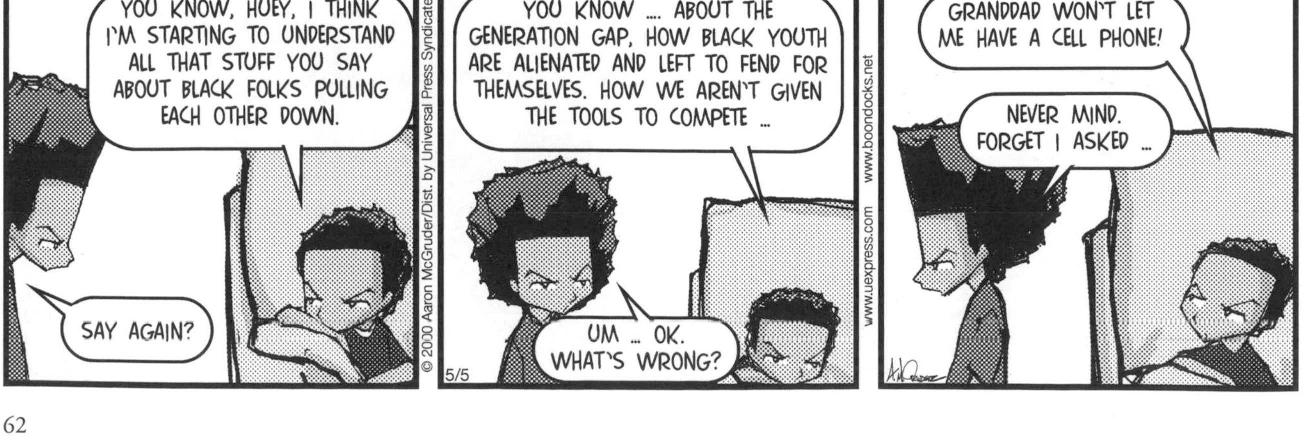
YOU KNOW, HUEY, I THINK I'M STARTING TO UNDERSTAND ALL THAT STUFF YOU SAY ABOUT BLACK FOLKS PULLING EACH OTHER DOWN.
SAY AGAIN?
© 2000 Aaron McGruder/Dist. by Universal Press Syndicate
5/5
YOU KNOW .... ABOUT THE GENERATION GAP, HOW BLACK YOUTH ARE ALIENATED AND LEFT TO FEND FOR THEMSELVES. HOW WE AREN'T GIVEN THE TOOLS TO COMPETE ...
UM ... OK. WHAT'S WRONG?
www.uexpress.com www.boondocks.net
GRANDDAD WON'T LET ME HAVE A CELL PHONE!
NEVER MIND. FORGET I ASKED ...

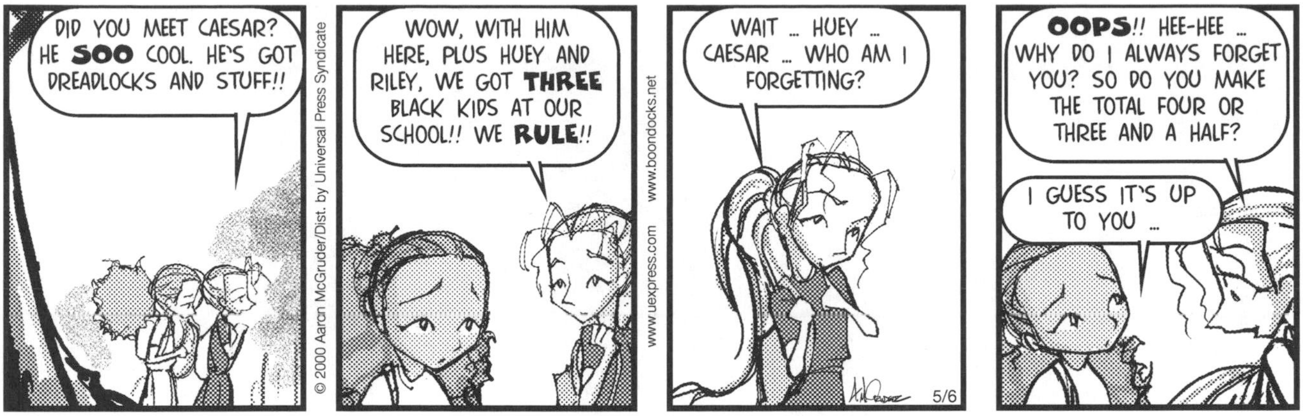
DID YOU MEET CAESAR? HE **SOO** COOL. HE'S GOT DREADLOCKS AND STUFF!!
© 2000 Aaron McGruder/Dist. by Universal Press Syndicate
WOW, WITH HIM HERE, PLUS HUEY AND RILEY, WE GOT **THREE** BLACK KIDS AT OUR SCHOOL!! WE **RULE**!!
www.uexpress.com www.boondocks.net
WAIT ... HUEY ... CAESAR ... WHO AM I FORGETTING?
5/6
OOPS!! HEE-HEE ... WHY DO I ALWAYS FORGET YOU? SO DO YOU MAKE THE TOTAL FOUR OR THREE AND A HALF?
I GUESS IT'S UP TO YOU ...

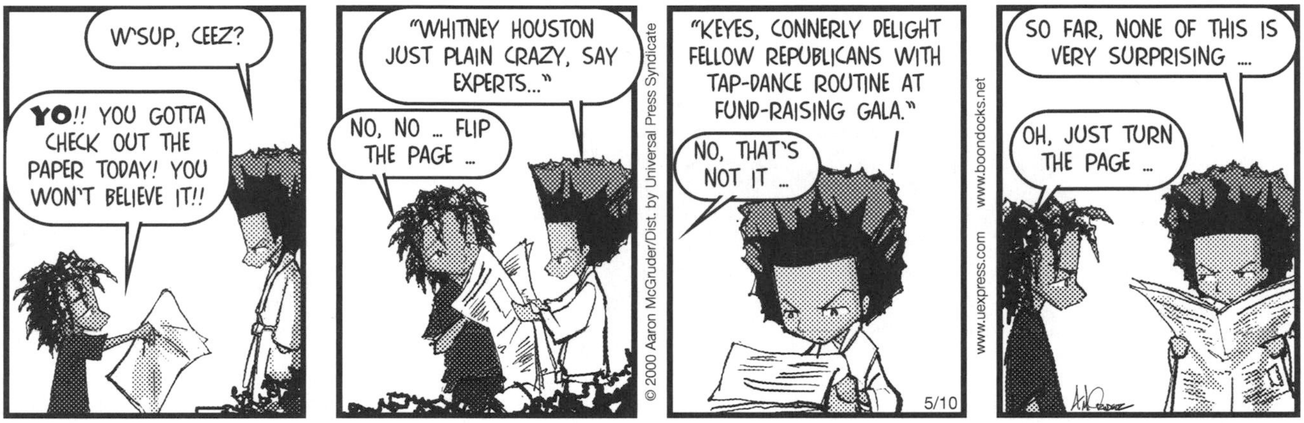
W'SUP, CEEZ?
YO!! YOU GOTTA CHECK OUT THE PAPER TODAY! YOU WON'T BELIEVE IT!!
"WHITNEY HOUSTON JUST PLAIN CRAZY, SAY EXPERTS..."
NO, NO ... FLIP THE PAGE ...
© 2000 Aaron McGruder/Dist. by Universal Press Syndicate
"KEYES, CONNERLY DELIGHT FELLOW REPUBLICANS WITH TAP-DANCE ROUTINE AT FUND-RAISING GALA."
NO, THAT'S NOT IT ...
5/10
www.uexpress.com www.boondocks.net
SO FAR, NONE OF THIS IS VERY SURPRISING ....
OH, JUST TURN THE PAGE ...

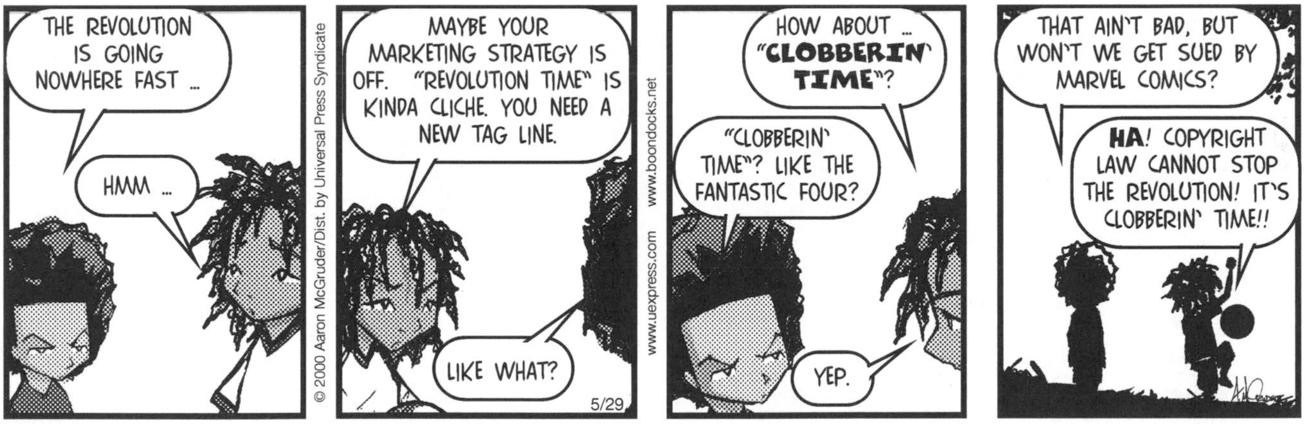
THE REVOLUTION IS GOING NOWHERE FAST ...
HMM ...
© 2000 Aaron McGruder/Dist. by Universal Press Syndicate
MAYBE YOUR MARKETING STRATEGY IS OFF. "REVOLUTION TIME" IS KINDA CLICHE. YOU NEED A NEW TAG LINE.
LIKE WHAT?
5/29
www.uexpress.com www.boondocks.net
HOW ABOUT ... **"CLOBBERIN' TIME"**?
"CLOBBERIN' TIME"? LIKE THE FANTASTIC FOUR?
YEP.
THAT AIN'T BAD, BUT WON'T WE GET SUED BY MARVEL COMICS?
HA! COPYRIGHT LAW CANNOT STOP THE REVOLUTION! IT'S CLOBBERIN' TIME!!

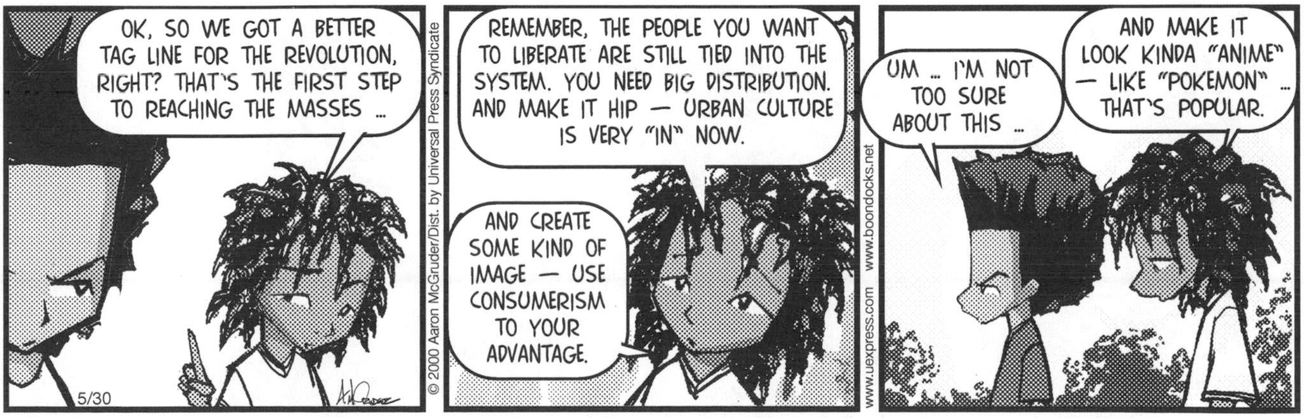
OK, SO WE GOT A BETTER TAG LINE FOR THE REVOLUTION, RIGHT? THAT'S THE FIRST STEP TO REACHING THE MASSES ...
5/30
© 2000 Aaron McGruder/Dist. by Universal Press Syndicate
REMEMBER, THE PEOPLE YOU WANT TO LIBERATE ARE STILL TIED INTO THE SYSTEM. YOU NEED BIG DISTRIBUTION. AND MAKE IT HIP — URBAN CULTURE IS VERY "IN" NOW.
AND CREATE SOME KIND OF IMAGE — USE CONSUMERISM TO YOUR ADVANTAGE.
www.uexpress.com www.boondocks.net
UM ... I'M NOT TOO SURE ABOUT THIS ...
AND MAKE IT LOOK KINDA "ANIME" — LIKE "POKEMON" ... THAT'S POPULAR.

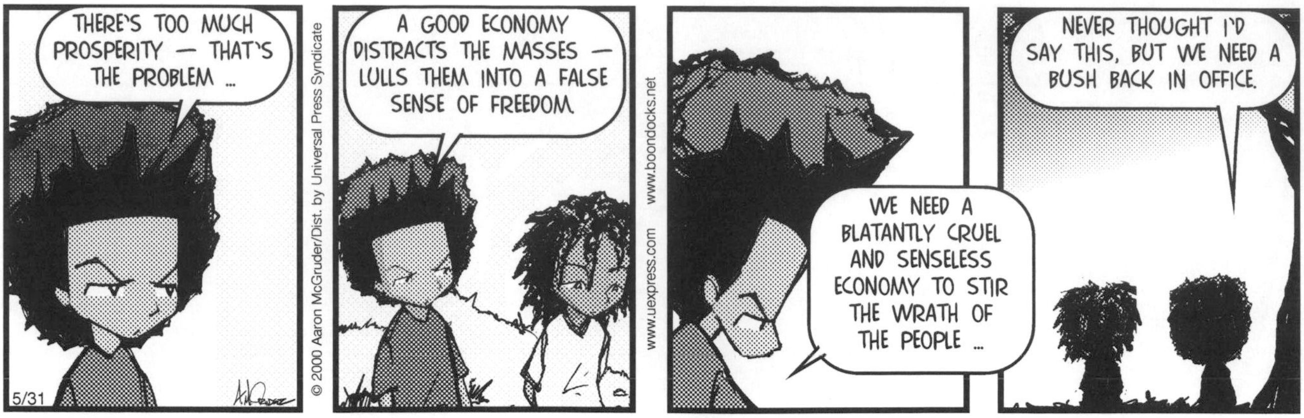
THERE'S TOO MUCH PROSPERITY — THAT'S THE PROBLEM ...
5/31
© 2000 Aaron McGruder/Dist. by Universal Press Syndicate
A GOOD ECONOMY DISTRACTS THE MASSES — LULLS THEM INTO A FALSE SENSE OF FREEDOM.
www.uexpress.com www.boondocks.net
WE NEED A BLATANTLY CRUEL AND SENSELESS ECONOMY TO STIR THE WRATH OF THE PEOPLE ...
NEVER THOUGHT I'D SAY THIS, BUT WE NEED A BUSH BACK IN OFFICE.

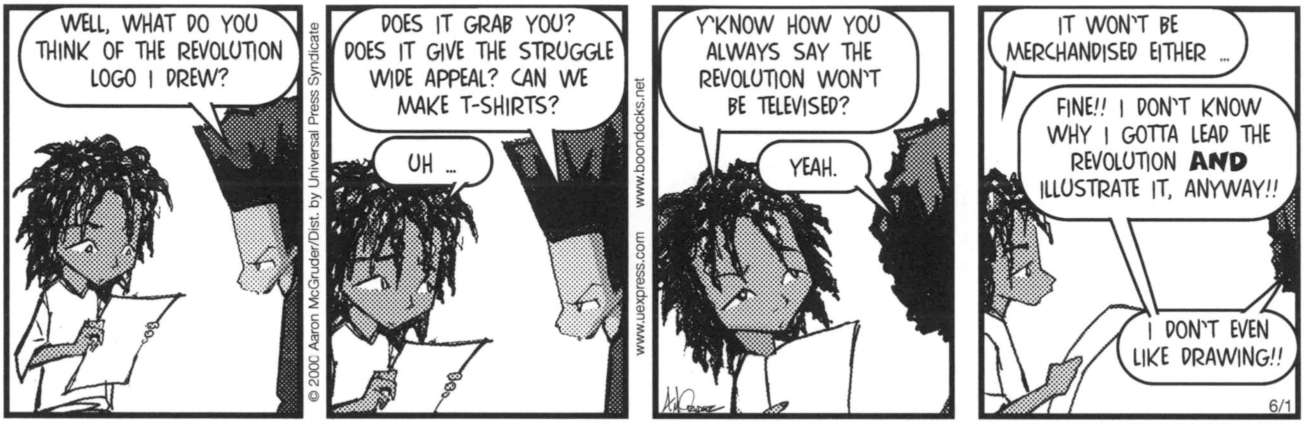
WELL, WHAT DO YOU THINK OF THE REVOLUTION LOGO I DREW?
© 2000 Aaron McGruder/Dist. by Universal Press Syndicate
DOES IT GRAB YOU? DOES IT GIVE THE STRUGGLE WIDE APPEAL? CAN WE MAKE T-SHIRTS?
UH ...
www.uexpress.com www.boondocks.net
Y'KNOW HOW YOU ALWAYS SAY THE REVOLUTION WON'T BE TELEVISED?
YEAH.
IT WON'T BE MERCHANDISED EITHER ...
FINE!! I DON'T KNOW WHY I GOTTA LEAD THE REVOLUTION AND ILLUSTRATE IT, ANYWAY!!
I DON'T EVEN LIKE DRAWING!!
6/1

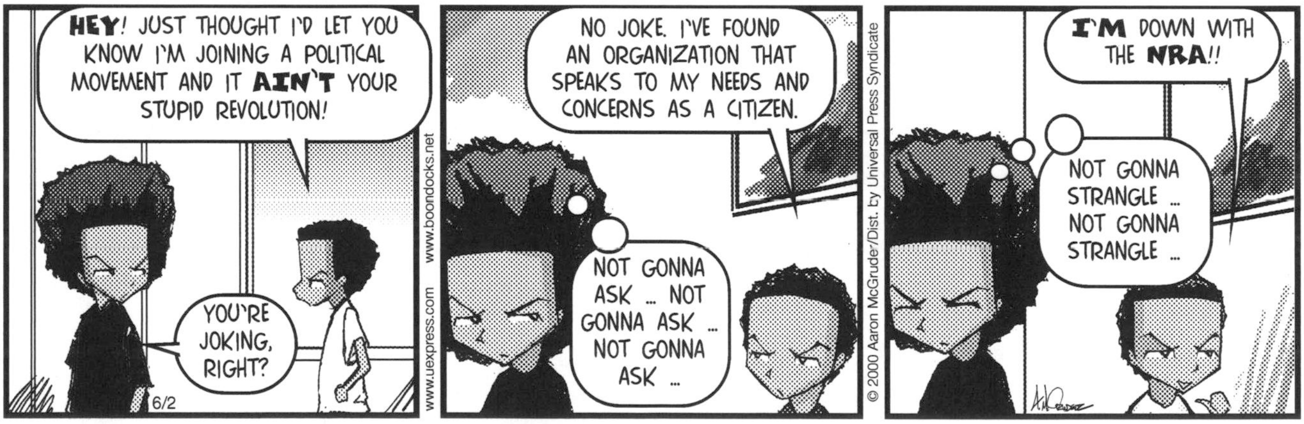
HEY! JUST THOUGHT I'D LET YOU KNOW I'M JOINING A POLITICAL MOVEMENT AND IT AIN'T YOUR STUPID REVOLUTION!
YOU'RE JOKING, RIGHT?
6/2
www.uexpress.com www.boondocks.net
NO JOKE. I'VE FOUND AN ORGANIZATION THAT SPEAKS TO MY NEEDS AND CONCERNS AS A CITIZEN.
NOT GONNA ASK ... NOT GONNA ASK ... NOT GONNA ASK ...
© 2000 Aaron McGruder/Dist. by Universal Press Syndicate
I'M DOWN WITH THE NRA!!
NOT GONNA STRANGLE ... NOT GONNA STRANGLE ...

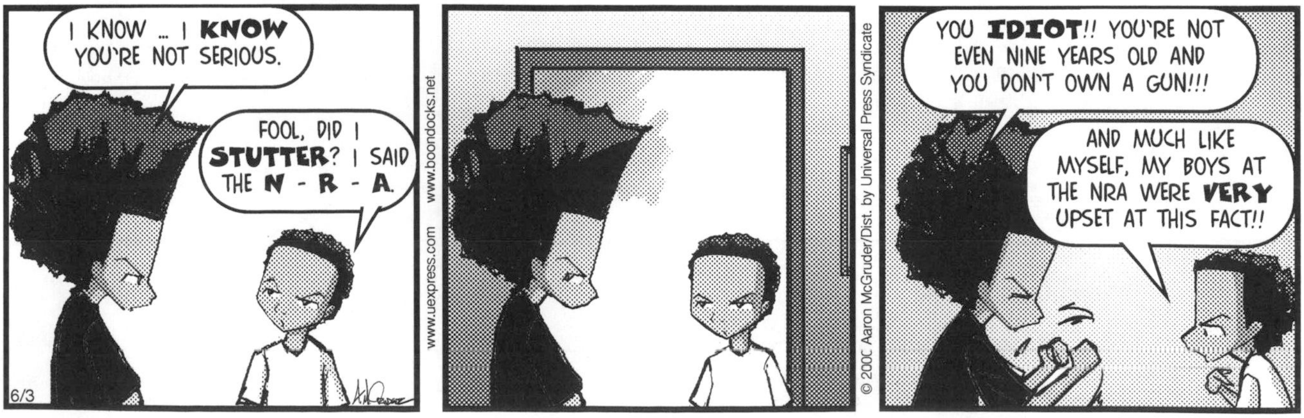
I KNOW ... I KNOW YOU'RE NOT SERIOUS.
FOOL, DID I STUTTER? I SAID THE N - R - A.
6/3
www.uexpress.com www.boondocks.net
© 2000 Aaron McGruder/Dist. by Universal Press Syndicate
YOU IDIOT!! YOU'RE NOT EVEN NINE YEARS OLD AND YOU DON'T OWN A GUN!!!
AND MUCH LIKE MYSELF, MY BOYS AT THE NRA WERE VERY UPSET AT THIS FACT!!

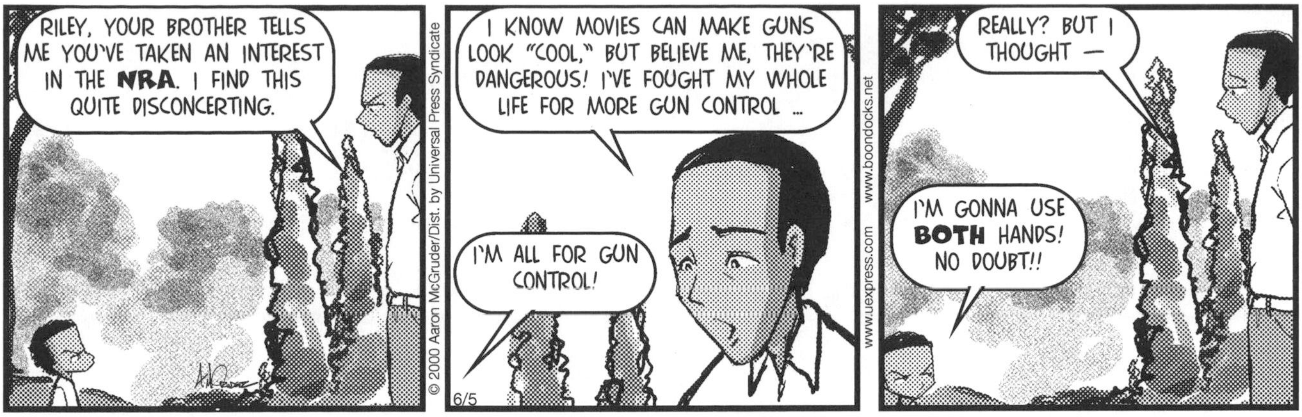
RILEY, YOUR BROTHER TELLS ME YOU'VE TAKEN AN INTEREST IN THE NRA. I FIND THIS QUITE DISCONCERTING.
© 2000 Aaron McGruder/Dist. by Universal Press Syndicate
I KNOW MOVIES CAN MAKE GUNS LOOK "COOL," BUT BELIEVE ME, THEY'RE DANGEROUS! I'VE FOUGHT MY WHOLE LIFE FOR MORE GUN CONTROL ...
I'M ALL FOR GUN CONTROL!
6/5
www.uexpress.com www.boondocks.net
REALLY? BUT I THOUGHT —
I'M GONNA USE BOTH HANDS! NO DOUBT!!

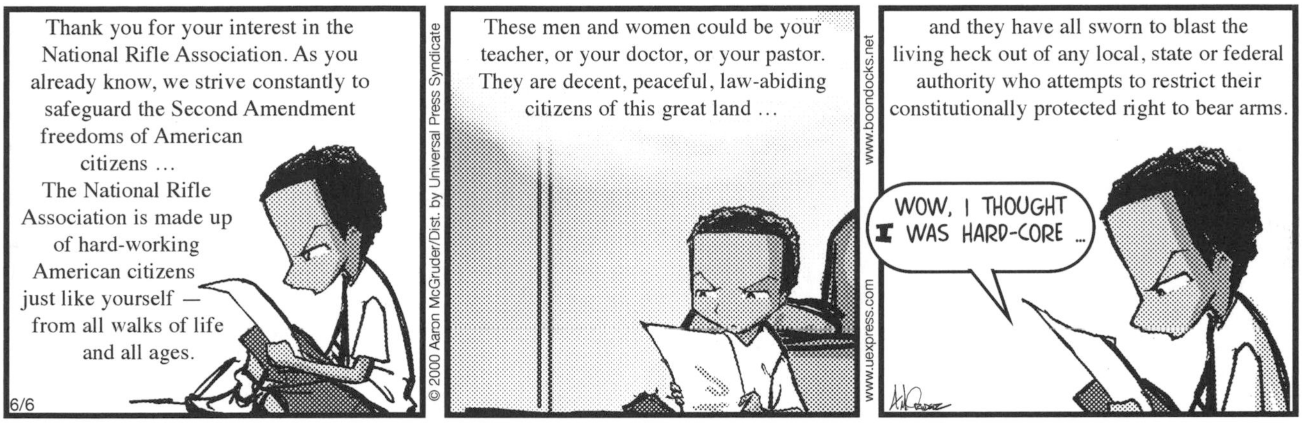
Thank you for your interest in the National Rifle Association. As you already know, we strive constantly to safeguard the Second Amendment freedoms of American citizens … The National Rifle Association is made up of hard-working American citizens just like yourself — from all walks of life and all ages.
6/6
© 2000 Aaron McGruder/Dist. by Universal Press Syndicate
These men and women could be your teacher, or your doctor, or your pastor. They are decent, peaceful, law-abiding citizens of this great land …
www.uexpress.com www.boondocks.net
and they have all sworn to blast the living heck out of any local, state or federal authority who attempts to restrict their constitutionally protected right to bear arms.
WOW, I THOUGHT I WAS HARD-CORE ...

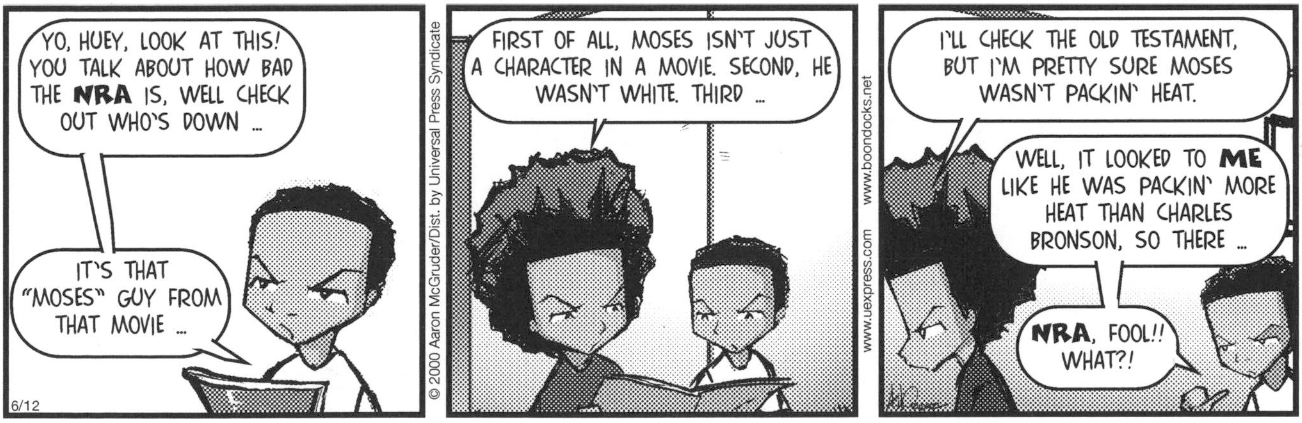
YO, HUEY, LOOK AT THIS! YOU TALK ABOUT HOW BAD THE NRA IS, WELL CHECK OUT WHO'S DOWN ...
IT'S THAT "MOSES" GUY FROM THAT MOVIE ...
6/12
© 2000 Aaron McGruder/Dist. by Universal Press Syndicate
FIRST OF ALL, MOSES ISN'T JUST A CHARACTER IN A MOVIE. SECOND, HE WASN'T WHITE. THIRD ...
www.uexpress.com www.boondocks.net
I'LL CHECK THE OLD TESTAMENT, BUT I'M PRETTY SURE MOSES WASN'T PACKIN' HEAT.
WELL, IT LOOKED TO ME LIKE HE WAS PACKIN' MORE HEAT THAN CHARLES BRONSON, SO THERE ...
NRA, FOOL!!
WHAT?!

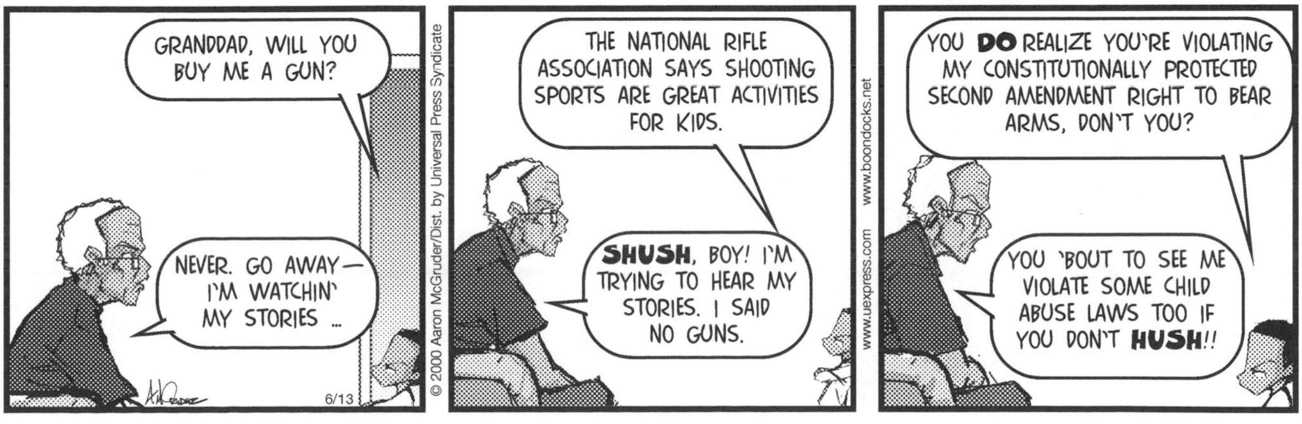
GRANDDAD, WILL YOU BUY ME A GUN?
NEVER. GO AWAY— I'M WATCHIN' MY STORIES ...
6/13
© 2000 Aaron McGruder/Dist. by Universal Press Syndicate
THE NATIONAL RIFLE ASSOCIATION SAYS SHOOTING SPORTS ARE GREAT ACTIVITIES FOR KIDS.
SHUSH, BOY! I'M TRYING TO HEAR MY STORIES. I SAID NO GUNS.
www.uexpress.com www.boondocks.net
YOU DO REALIZE YOU'RE VIOLATING MY CONSTITUTIONALLY PROTECTED SECOND AMENDMENT RIGHT TO BEAR ARMS, DON'T YOU?
YOU 'BOUT TO SEE ME VIOLATE SOME CHILD ABUSE LAWS TOO IF YOU DON'T HUSH!!

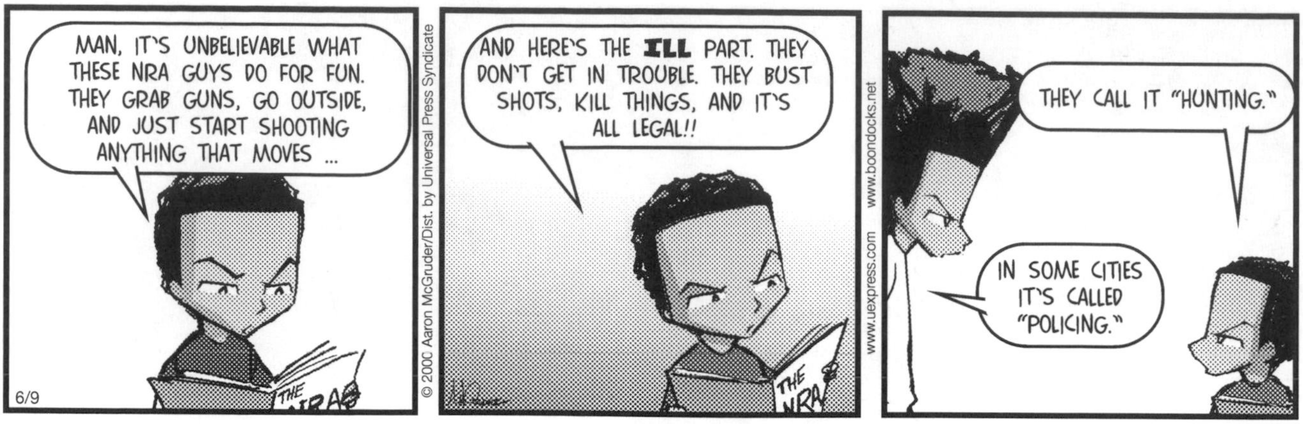
MAN, IT'S UNBELIEVABLE WHAT THESE NRA GUYS DO FOR FUN. THEY GRAB GUNS, GO OUTSIDE, AND JUST START SHOOTING ANYTHING THAT MOVES ...
THE NRA
6/9
AND HERE'S THE ILL PART. THEY DON'T GET IN TROUBLE. THEY BUST SHOTS, KILL THINGS, AND IT'S ALL LEGAL!!
THE NRA
© 2000 Aaron McGruder/Dist. by Universal Press Syndicate
THEY CALL IT "HUNTING."
IN SOME CITIES IT'S CALLED "POLICING."
www.uexpress.com www.boondocks.net

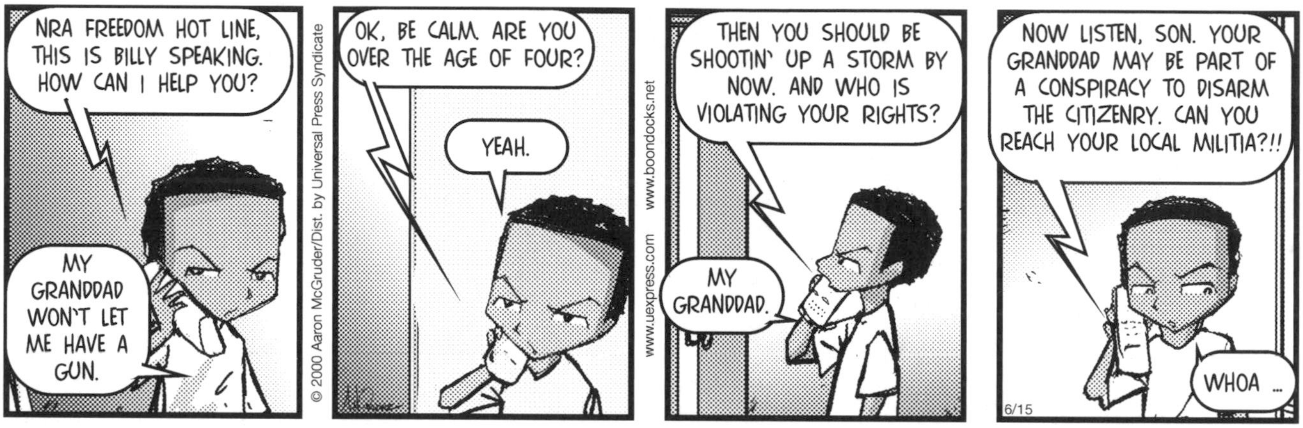
NRA FREEDOM HOT LINE, THIS IS BILLY SPEAKING. HOW CAN I HELP YOU?
MY GRANDDAD WON'T LET ME HAVE A GUN.
© 2000 Aaron McGruder/Dist. by Universal Press Syndicate
OK, BE CALM. ARE YOU OVER THE AGE OF FOUR?
YEAH.
www.uexpress.com www.boondocks.net
THEN YOU SHOULD BE SHOOTIN' UP A STORM BY NOW. AND WHO IS VIOLATING YOUR RIGHTS?
MY GRANDDAD.
NOW LISTEN, SON. YOUR GRANDDAD MAY BE PART OF A CONSPIRACY TO DISARM THE CITIZENRY. CAN YOU REACH YOUR LOCAL MILITIA?!!
WHOA ...
6/15

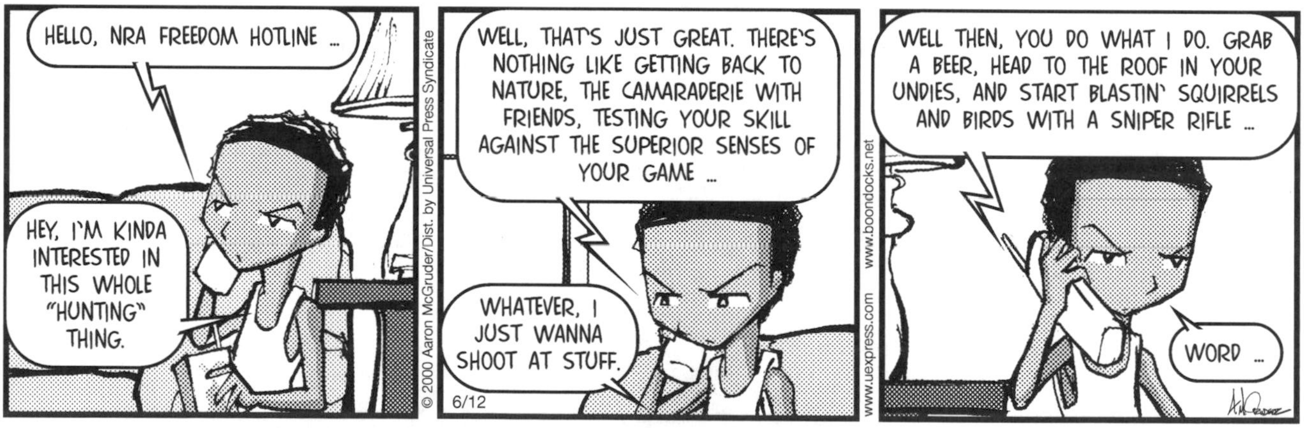
HELLO, NRA FREEDOM HOTLINE ...
HEY, I'M KINDA INTERESTED IN THIS WHOLE "HUNTING" THING.
© 2000 Aaron McGruder/Dist. by Universal Press Syndicate
WELL, THAT'S JUST GREAT. THERE'S NOTHING LIKE GETTING BACK TO NATURE, THE CAMARADERIE WITH FRIENDS, TESTING YOUR SKILL AGAINST THE SUPERIOR SENSES OF YOUR GAME ...
WHATEVER, I JUST WANNA SHOOT AT STUFF.
6/12
www.uexpress.com www.boondocks.net
WELL THEN, YOU DO WHAT I DO. GRAB A BEER, HEAD TO THE ROOF IN YOUR UNDIES, AND START BLASTIN' SQUIRRELS AND BIRDS WITH A SNIPER RIFLE ...
WORD ...

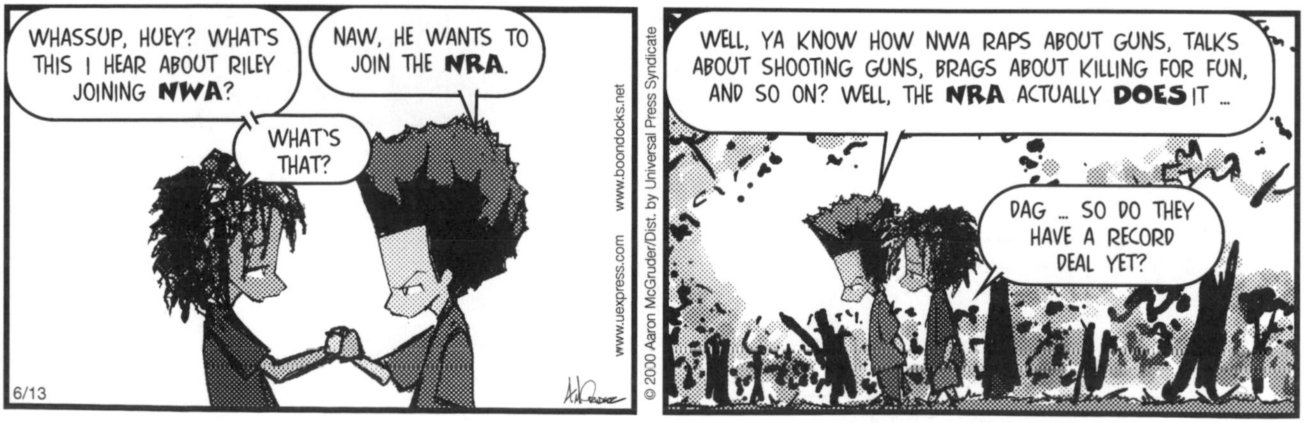
WHASSUP, HUEY? WHAT'S THIS I HEAR ABOUT RILEY JOINING NWA?
NAW, HE WANTS TO JOIN THE NRA.
WHAT'S THAT?
6/13
www.uexpress.com www.boondocks.net
© 2000 Aaron McGruder/Dist. by Universal Press Syndicate
WELL, YA KNOW HOW NWA RAPS ABOUT GUNS, TALKS ABOUT SHOOTING GUNS, BRAGS ABOUT KILLING FOR FUN, AND SO ON? WELL, THE NRA ACTUALLY DOES IT ...
DAG ... SO DO THEY HAVE A RECORD DEAL YET?

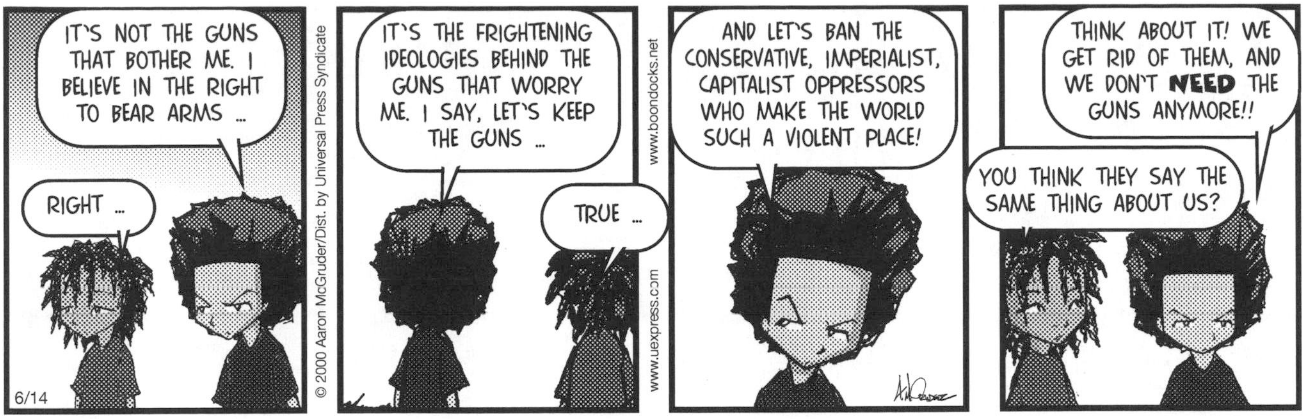
IT'S NOT THE GUNS THAT BOTHER ME. I BELIEVE IN THE RIGHT TO BEAR ARMS ...
RIGHT ...
6/14
© 2000 Aaron McGruder/Dist. by Universal Press Syndicate
IT'S THE FRIGHTENING IDEOLOGIES BEHIND THE GUNS THAT WORRY ME. I SAY, LET'S KEEP THE GUNS ...
TRUE ...
www.boondocks.net
www.uexpress.com
AND LET'S BAN THE CONSERVATIVE, IMPERIALIST, CAPITALIST OPPRESSORS WHO MAKE THE WORLD SUCH A VIOLENT PLACE!
THINK ABOUT IT! WE GET RID OF THEM, AND WE DON'T **NEED** THE GUNS ANYMORE!!
YOU THINK THEY SAY THE SAME THING ABOUT US?

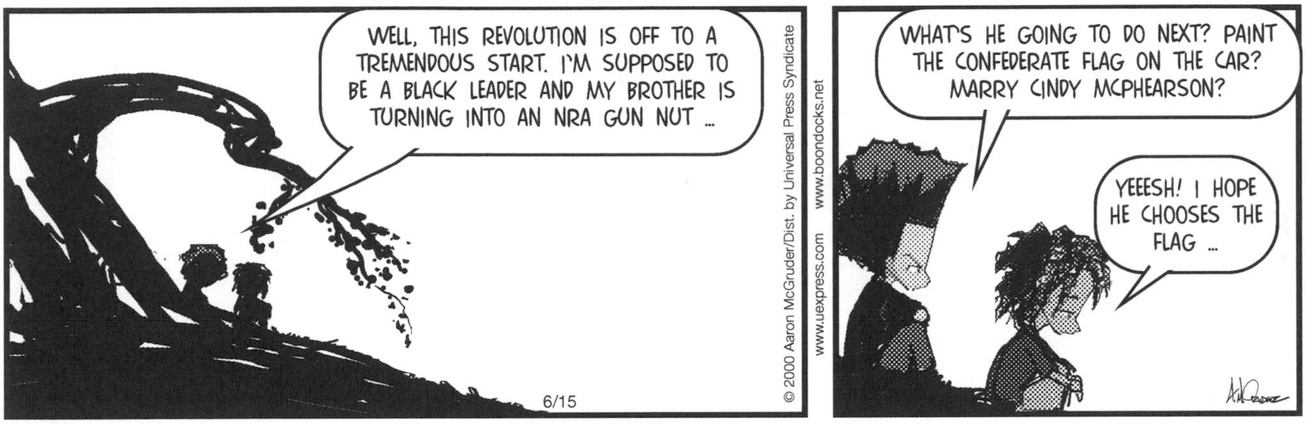
WELL, THIS REVOLUTION IS OFF TO A TREMENDOUS START. I'M SUPPOSED TO BE A BLACK LEADER AND MY BROTHER IS TURNING INTO AN NRA GUN NUT ...
6/15
© 2000 Aaron McGruder/Dist. by Universal Press Syndicate
www.uexpress.com
www.boondocks.net
WHAT'S HE GOING TO DO NEXT? PAINT THE CONFEDERATE FLAG ON THE CAR? MARRY CINDY MCPHEARSON?
YEEESH! I HOPE HE CHOOSES THE FLAG ...

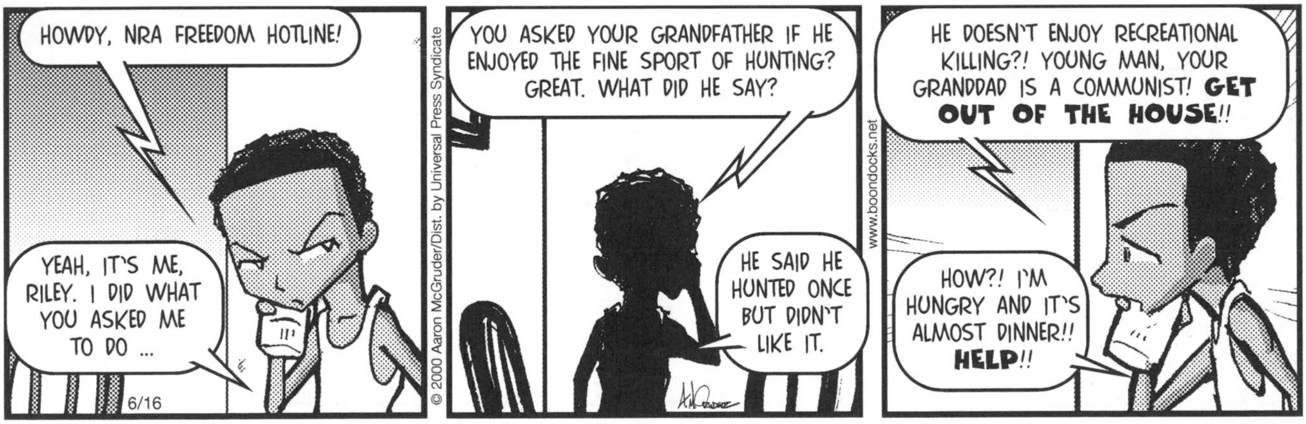
HOWDY, NRA FREEDOM HOTLINE!
YEAH, IT'S ME, RILEY. I DID WHAT YOU ASKED ME TO DO ...
6/16
© 2000 Aaron McGruder/Dist. by Universal Press Syndicate
YOU ASKED YOUR GRANDFATHER IF HE ENJOYED THE FINE SPORT OF HUNTING? GREAT. WHAT DID HE SAY?
HE SAID HE HUNTED ONCE BUT DIDN'T LIKE IT.
www.boondocks.net
HE DOESN'T ENJOY RECREATIONAL KILLING?! YOUNG MAN, YOUR GRANDDAD IS A COMMUNIST! **GET OUT OF THE HOUSE**!!
HOW?! I'M HUNGRY AND IT'S ALMOST DINNER!! **HELP**!!

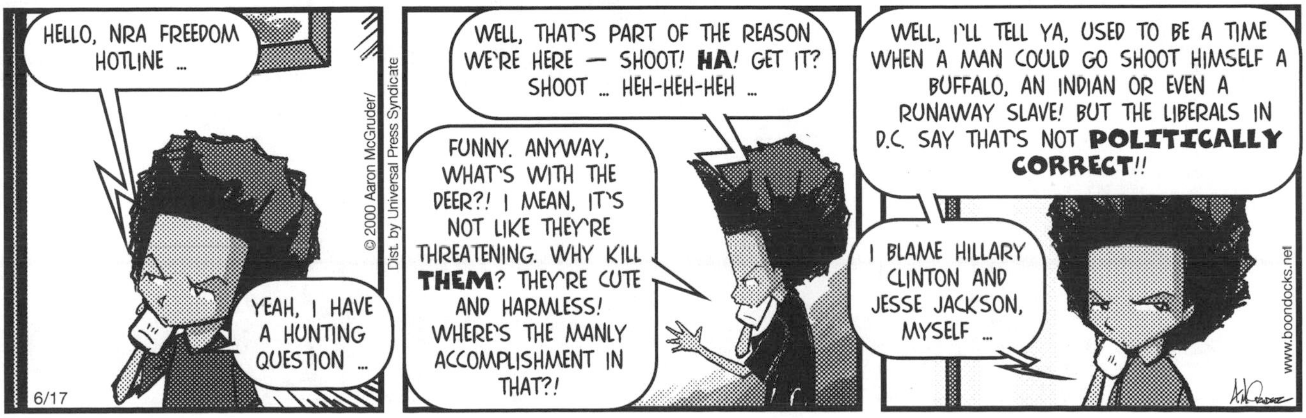
HELLO, NRA FREEDOM HOTLINE ...
YEAH, I HAVE A HUNTING QUESTION ...
6/17
© 2000 Aaron McGruder/ Dist. by Universal Press Syndicate
WELL, THAT'S PART OF THE REASON WE'RE HERE — SHOOT! **HA**! GET IT? SHOOT ... HEH-HEH-HEH ...
FUNNY. ANYWAY, WHAT'S WITH THE DEER?! I MEAN, IT'S NOT LIKE THEY'RE THREATENING. WHY KILL **THEM**? THEY'RE CUTE AND HARMLESS! WHERE'S THE MANLY ACCOMPLISHMENT IN THAT?!
WELL, I'LL TELL YA, USED TO BE A TIME WHEN A MAN COULD GO SHOOT HIMSELF A BUFFALO, AN INDIAN OR EVEN A RUNAWAY SLAVE! BUT THE LIBERALS IN D.C. SAY THAT'S NOT **POLITICALLY CORRECT**!!
I BLAME HILLARY CLINTON AND JESSE JACKSON, MYSELF ...
www.boondocks.net

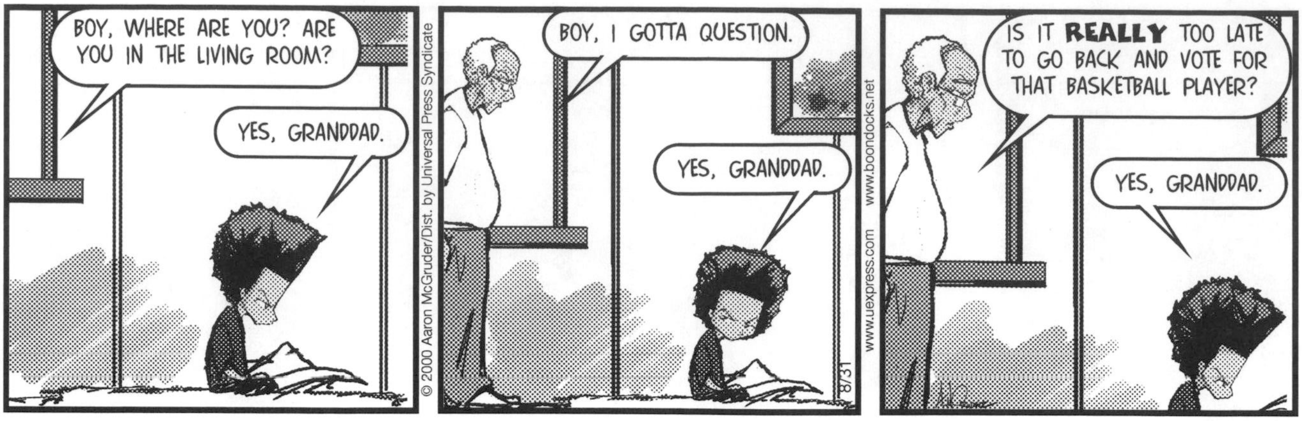
BOY, WHERE ARE YOU? ARE YOU IN THE LIVING ROOM?
YES, GRANDDAD.
BOY, I GOTTA QUESTION.
YES, GRANDDAD.
IS IT **REALLY** TOO LATE TO GO BACK AND VOTE FOR THAT BASKETBALL PLAYER?
YES, GRANDDAD.
© 2000 Aaron McGruder/Dist. by Universal Press Syndicate
8/31
www.uexpress.com www.boondocks.net

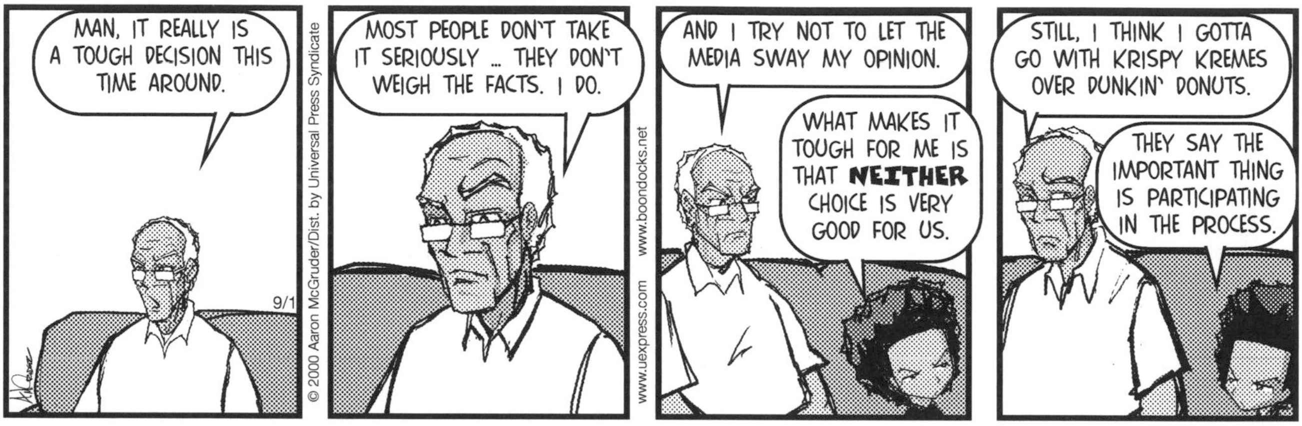
MAN, IT REALLY IS A TOUGH DECISION THIS TIME AROUND.
9/1
© 2000 Aaron McGruder/Dist. by Universal Press Syndicate
MOST PEOPLE DON'T TAKE IT SERIOUSLY ... THEY DON'T WEIGH THE FACTS. I DO.
www.uexpress.com www.boondocks.net
AND I TRY NOT TO LET THE MEDIA SWAY MY OPINION.
WHAT MAKES IT TOUGH FOR ME IS THAT **NEITHER** CHOICE IS VERY GOOD FOR US.
STILL, I THINK I GOTTA GO WITH KRISPY KREMES OVER DUNKIN' DONUTS.
THEY SAY THE IMPORTANT THING IS PARTICIPATING IN THE PROCESS.

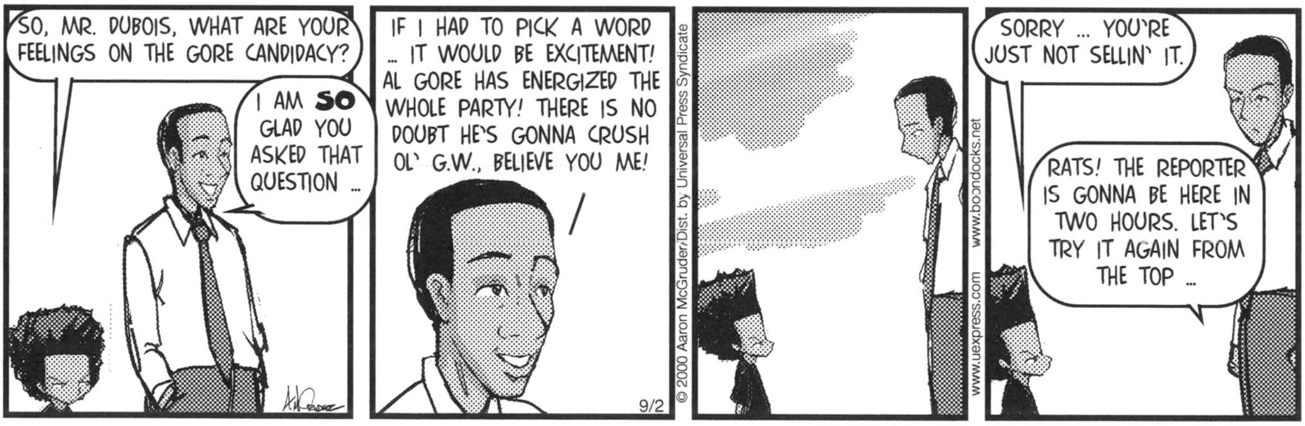
SO, MR. DUBOIS, WHAT ARE YOUR FEELINGS ON THE GORE CANDIDACY?
I AM **SO** GLAD YOU ASKED THAT QUESTION ...
IF I HAD TO PICK A WORD ... IT WOULD BE EXCITEMENT! AL GORE HAS ENERGIZED THE WHOLE PARTY! THERE IS NO DOUBT HE'S GONNA CRUSH OL' G.W., BELIEVE YOU ME!
9/2
© 2000 Aaron McGruder/Dist. by Universal Press Syndicate
SORRY ... YOU'RE JUST NOT SELLIN' IT.
RATS! THE REPORTER IS GONNA BE HERE IN TWO HOURS. LET'S TRY IT AGAIN FROM THE TOP ...
www.uexpress.com www.boondocks.net

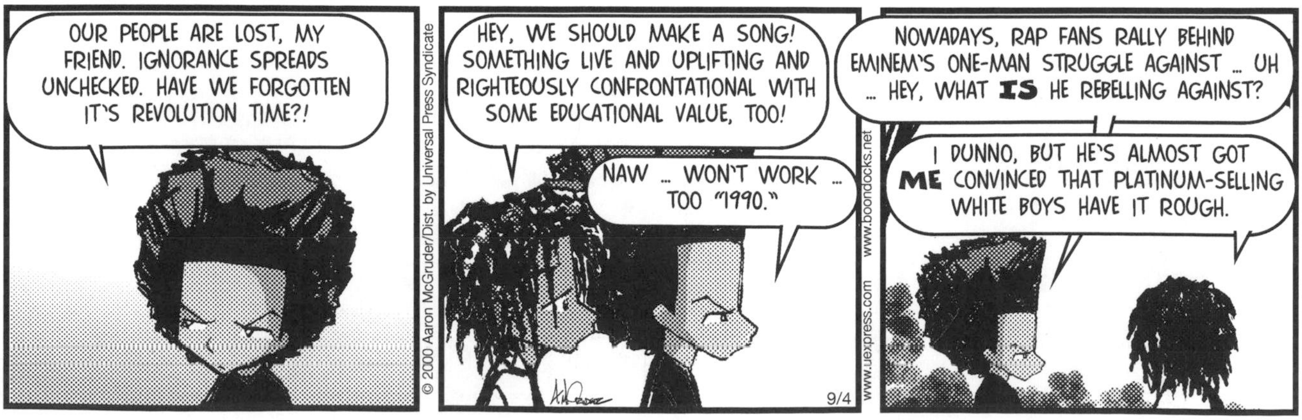
OUR PEOPLE ARE LOST, MY FRIEND. IGNORANCE SPREADS UNCHECKED. HAVE WE FORGOTTEN IT'S REVOLUTION TIME?!
© 2000 Aaron McGruder/Dist. by Universal Press Syndicate
HEY, WE SHOULD MAKE A SONG! SOMETHING LIVE AND UPLIFTING AND RIGHTEOUSLY CONFRONTATIONAL WITH SOME EDUCATIONAL VALUE, TOO!
NAW ... WON'T WORK ... TOO "1990."
9/4
www.uexpress.com www.boondocks.net
NOWADAYS, RAP FANS RALLY BEHIND EMINEM'S ONE-MAN STRUGGLE AGAINST ... UH ... HEY, WHAT **IS** HE REBELLING AGAINST?
I DUNNO, BUT HE'S ALMOST GOT **ME** CONVINCED THAT PLATINUM-SELLING WHITE BOYS HAVE IT ROUGH.

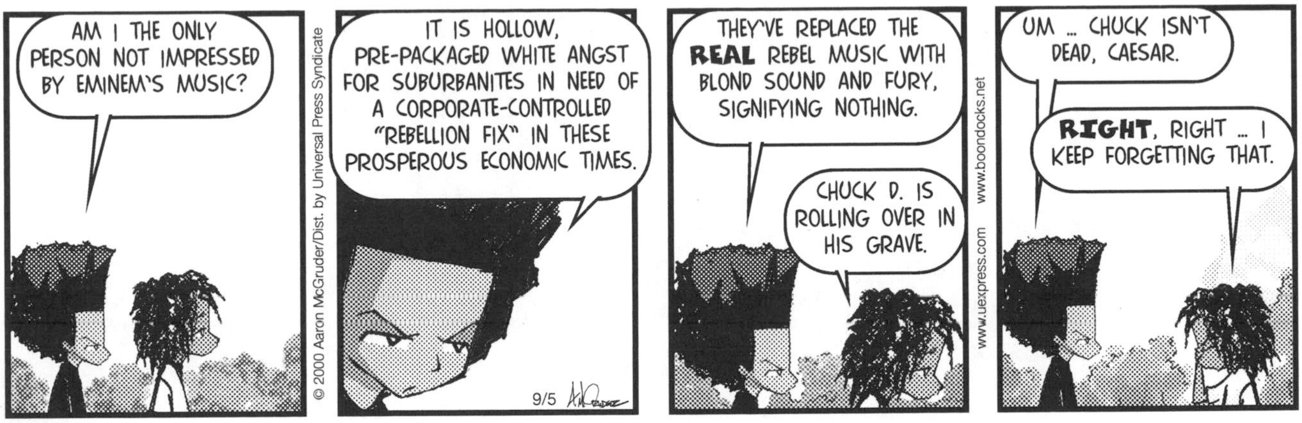
AM I THE ONLY PERSON NOT IMPRESSED BY EMINEM'S MUSIC?
IT IS HOLLOW, PRE-PACKAGED WHITE ANGST FOR SUBURBANITES IN NEED OF A CORPORATE-CONTROLLED "REBELLION FIX" IN THESE PROSPEROUS ECONOMIC TIMES.
THEY'VE REPLACED THE **REAL** REBEL MUSIC WITH BLOND SOUND AND FURY, SIGNIFYING NOTHING.
CHUCK D. IS ROLLING OVER IN HIS GRAVE.
UM ... CHUCK ISN'T DEAD, CAESAR.
RIGHT, RIGHT ... I KEEP FORGETTING THAT.
© 2000 Aaron McGruder/Dist. by Universal Press Syndicate
www.uexpress.com www.boondocks.net
9/5

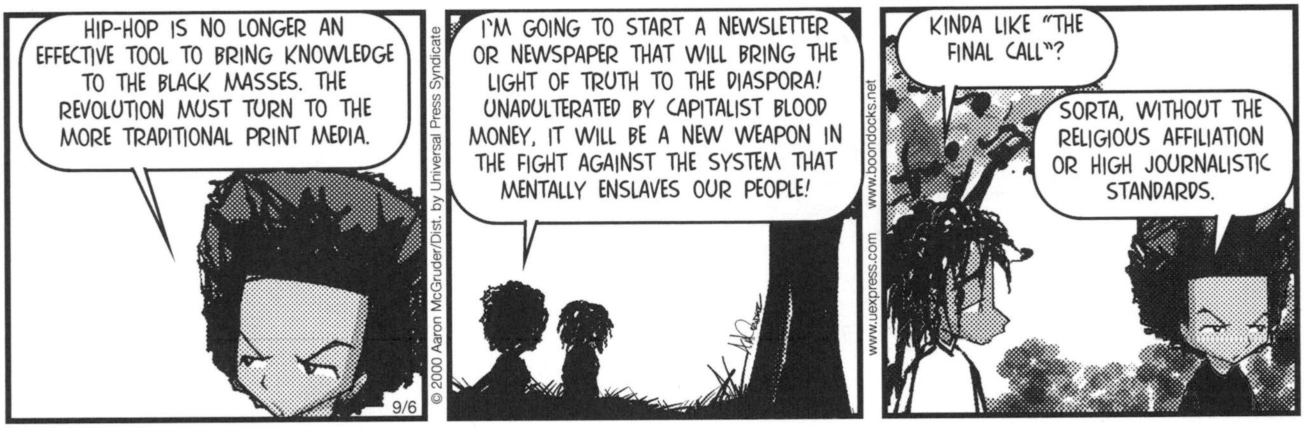
HIP-HOP IS NO LONGER AN EFFECTIVE TOOL TO BRING KNOWLEDGE TO THE BLACK MASSES. THE REVOLUTION MUST TURN TO THE MORE TRADITIONAL PRINT MEDIA.
I'M GOING TO START A NEWSLETTER OR NEWSPAPER THAT WILL BRING THE LIGHT OF TRUTH TO THE DIASPORA! UNADULTERATED BY CAPITALIST BLOOD MONEY, IT WILL BE A NEW WEAPON IN THE FIGHT AGAINST THE SYSTEM THAT MENTALLY ENSLAVES OUR PEOPLE!
KINDA LIKE "THE FINAL CALL"?
SORTA, WITHOUT THE RELIGIOUS AFFILIATION OR HIGH JOURNALISTIC STANDARDS.
© 2000 Aaron McGruder/Dist. by Universal Press Syndicate
www.uexpress.com www.boondocks.net
9/6

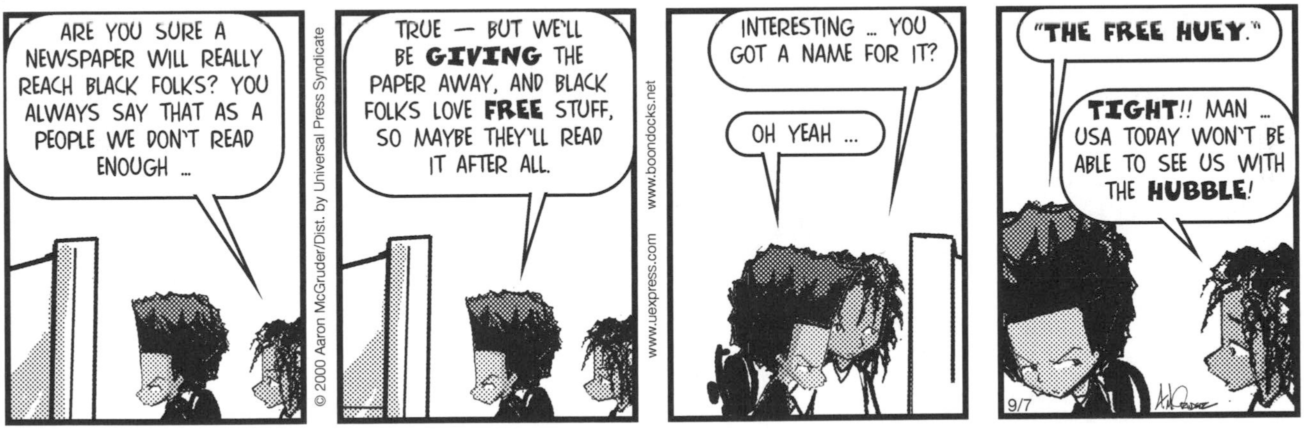
ARE YOU SURE A NEWSPAPER WILL REALLY REACH BLACK FOLKS? YOU ALWAYS SAY THAT AS A PEOPLE WE DON'T READ ENOUGH ...
TRUE — BUT WE'LL BE **GIVING** THE PAPER AWAY, AND BLACK FOLKS LOVE **FREE** STUFF, SO MAYBE THEY'LL READ IT AFTER ALL.
INTERESTING ... YOU GOT A NAME FOR IT?
OH YEAH ...
"**THE FREE HUEY**."
TIGHT!! MAN ... USA TODAY WON'T BE ABLE TO SEE US WITH THE **HUBBLE**!
© 2000 Aaron McGruder/Dist. by Universal Press Syndicate
www.uexpress.com www.boondocks.net
9/7

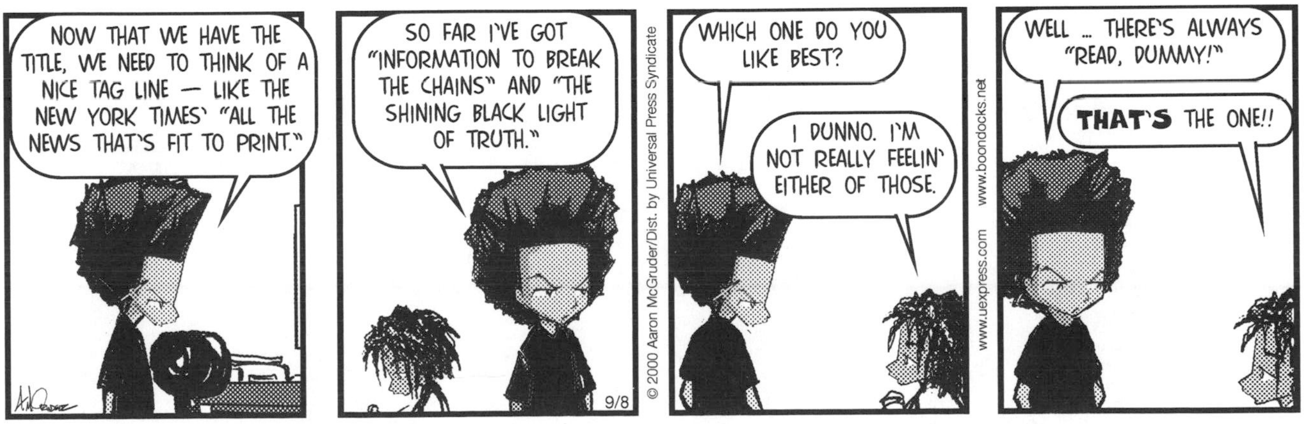
NOW THAT WE HAVE THE TITLE, WE NEED TO THINK OF A NICE TAG LINE — LIKE THE NEW YORK TIMES' "ALL THE NEWS THAT'S FIT TO PRINT."
SO FAR I'VE GOT "INFORMATION TO BREAK THE CHAINS" AND "THE SHINING BLACK LIGHT OF TRUTH."
WHICH ONE DO YOU LIKE BEST?
I DUNNO. I'M NOT REALLY FEELIN' EITHER OF THOSE.
WELL ... THERE'S ALWAYS "READ, DUMMY!"
THAT'S THE ONE!!
© 2000 Aaron McGruder/Dist. by Universal Press Syndicate
www.uexpress.com www.boondocks.net
9/8

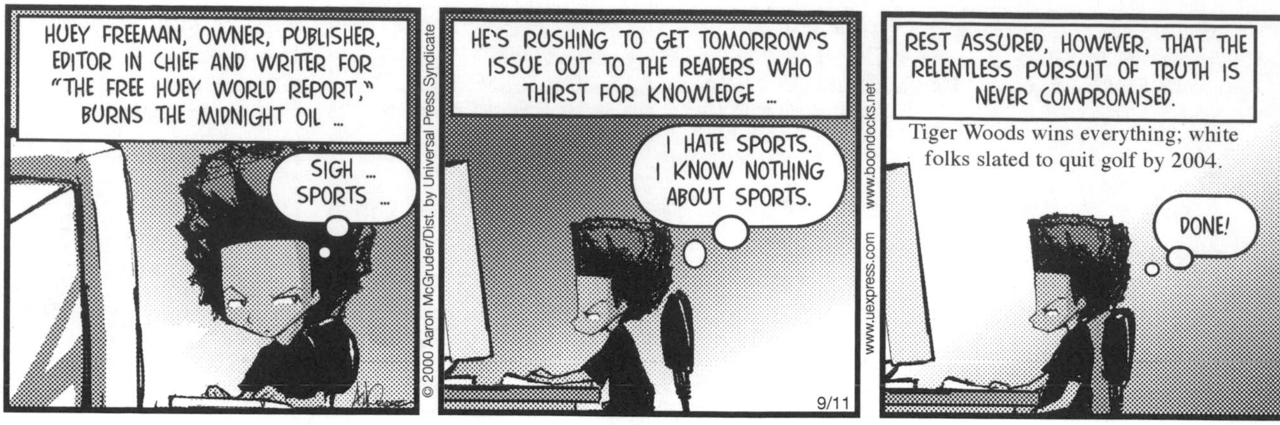
HUEY FREEMAN, OWNER, PUBLISHER, EDITOR IN CHIEF AND WRITER FOR "THE FREE HUEY WORLD REPORT," BURNS THE MIDNIGHT OIL ...
SIGH ... SPORTS ...
HE'S RUSHING TO GET TOMORROW'S ISSUE OUT TO THE READERS WHO THIRST FOR KNOWLEDGE ...
I HATE SPORTS. I KNOW NOTHING ABOUT SPORTS.
REST ASSURED, HOWEVER, THAT THE RELENTLESS PURSUIT OF TRUTH IS NEVER COMPROMISED.
Tiger Woods wins everything; white folks slated to quit golf by 2004.
DONE!
© 2000 Aaron McGruder/Dist. by Universal Press Syndicate
www.uexpress.com www.boondocks.net
9/11

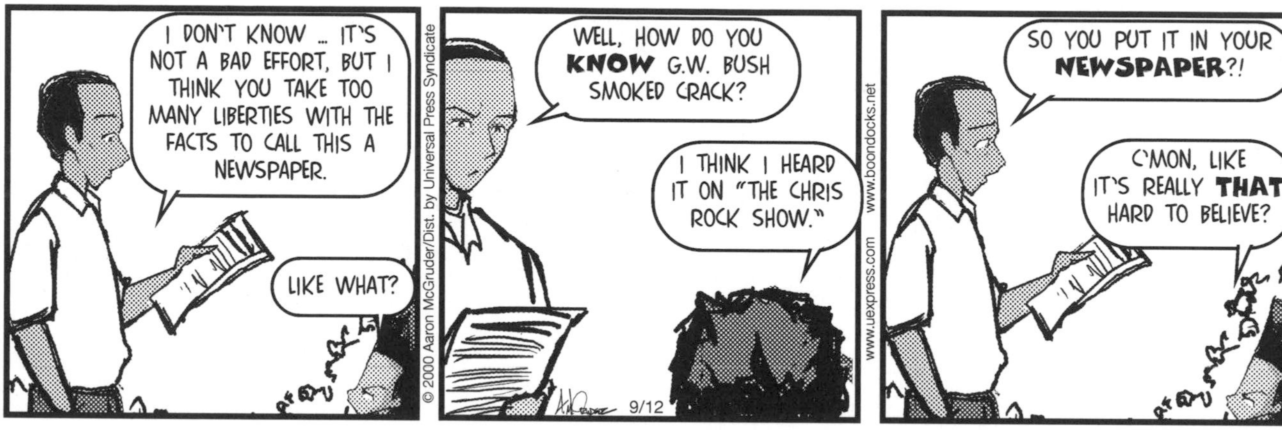
I DON'T KNOW ... IT'S NOT A BAD EFFORT, BUT I THINK YOU TAKE TOO MANY LIBERTIES WITH THE FACTS TO CALL THIS A NEWSPAPER.
LIKE WHAT?
WELL, HOW DO YOU **KNOW** G.W. BUSH SMOKED CRACK?
I THINK I HEARD IT ON "THE CHRIS ROCK SHOW."
SO YOU PUT IT IN YOUR **NEWSPAPER**?!
C'MON, LIKE IT'S REALLY **THAT** HARD TO BELIEVE?
© 2000 Aaron McGruder/Dist. by Universal Press Syndicate
www.uexpress.com www.boondocks.net
9/12

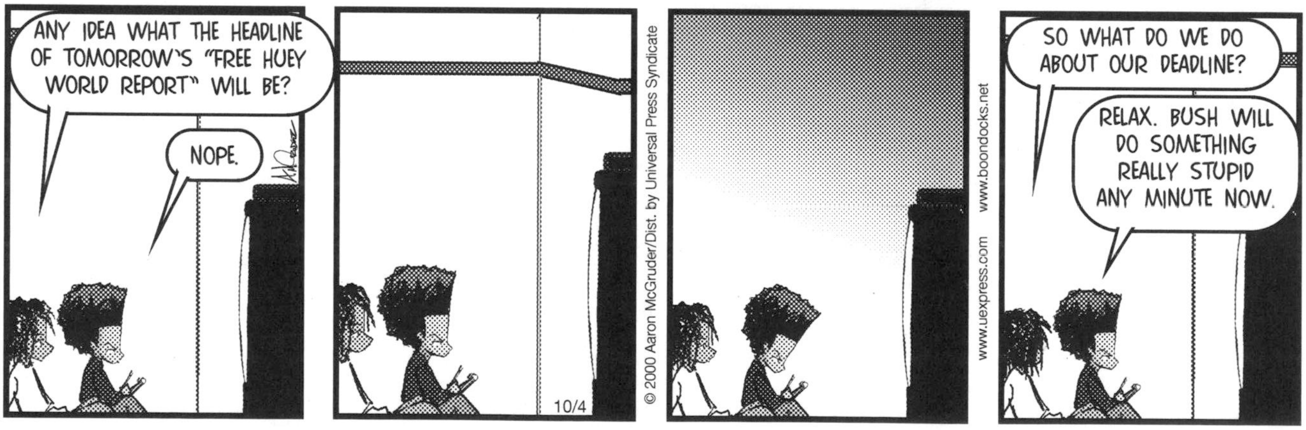
ANY IDEA WHAT THE HEADLINE OF TOMORROW'S "FREE HUEY WORLD REPORT" WILL BE?
NOPE.
SO WHAT DO WE DO ABOUT OUR DEADLINE?
RELAX. BUSH WILL DO SOMETHING REALLY STUPID ANY MINUTE NOW.
© 2000 Aaron McGruder/Dist. by Universal Press Syndicate
www.uexpress.com www.boondocks.net
10/4

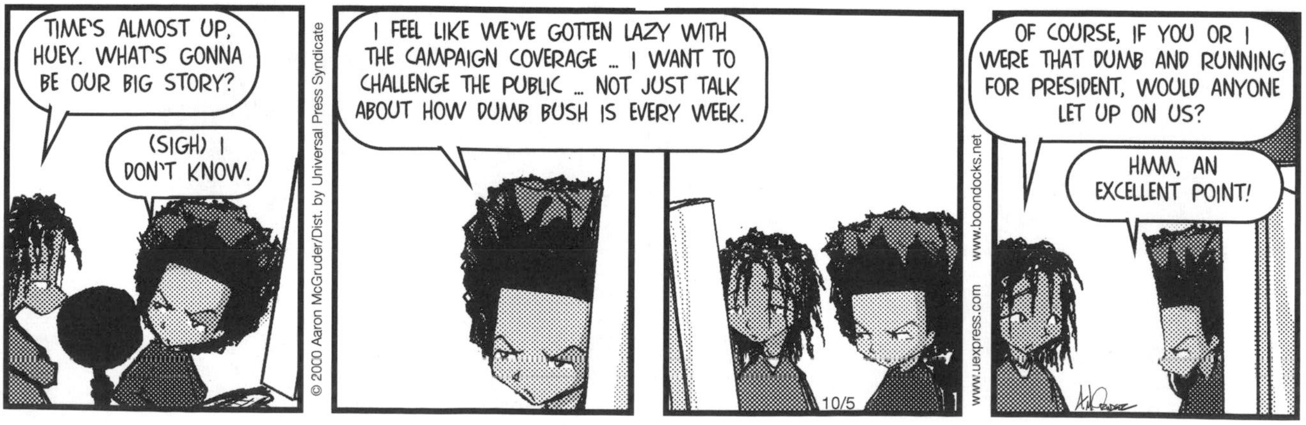
TIME'S ALMOST UP, HUEY. WHAT'S GONNA BE OUR BIG STORY?
(SIGH) I DON'T KNOW.
I FEEL LIKE WE'VE GOTTEN LAZY WITH THE CAMPAIGN COVERAGE ... I WANT TO CHALLENGE THE PUBLIC ... NOT JUST TALK ABOUT HOW DUMB BUSH IS EVERY WEEK.
OF COURSE, IF YOU OR I WERE THAT DUMB AND RUNNING FOR PRESIDENT, WOULD ANYONE LET UP ON US?
HMM, AN EXCELLENT POINT!
© 2000 Aaron McGruder/Dist. by Universal Press Syndicate
www.uexpress.com www.boondocks.net
10/5

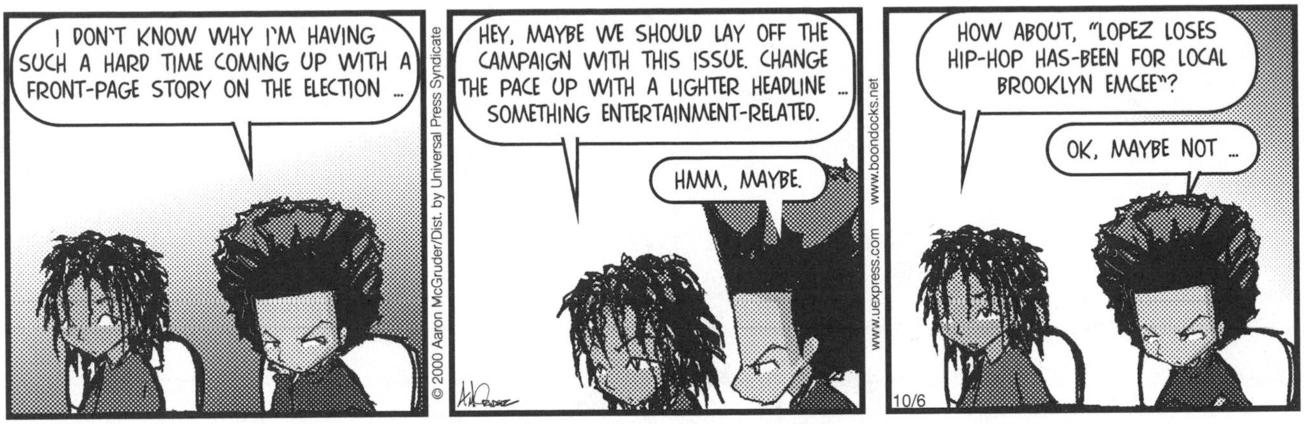
I DON'T KNOW WHY I'M HAVING SUCH A HARD TIME COMING UP WITH A FRONT-PAGE STORY ON THE ELECTION ...
© 2000 Aaron McGruder/Dist. by Universal Press Syndicate
HEY, MAYBE WE SHOULD LAY OFF THE CAMPAIGN WITH THIS ISSUE. CHANGE THE PACE UP WITH A LIGHTER HEADLINE ... SOMETHING ENTERTAINMENT-RELATED.
HMM, MAYBE.
www.uexpress.com www.boondocks.net
HOW ABOUT, "LOPEZ LOSES HIP-HOP HAS-BEEN FOR LOCAL BROOKLYN EMCEE"?
OK, MAYBE NOT ...
10/6

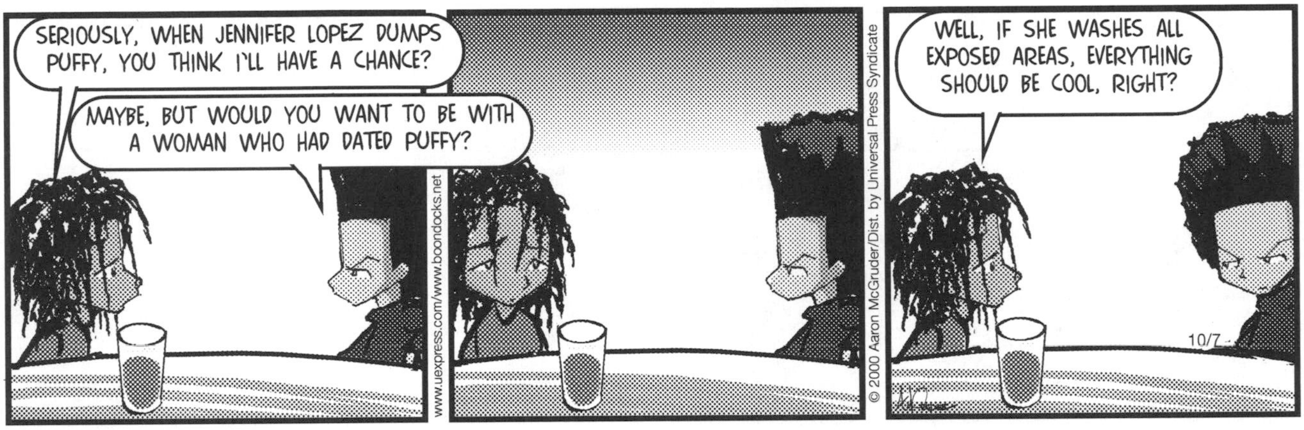
SERIOUSLY, WHEN JENNIFER LOPEZ DUMPS PUFFY, YOU THINK I'LL HAVE A CHANCE?
MAYBE, BUT WOULD YOU WANT TO BE WITH A WOMAN WHO HAD DATED PUFFY?
www.uexpress.com/www.boondocks.net
© 2000 Aaron McGruder/Dist. by Universal Press Syndicate
WELL, IF SHE WASHES ALL EXPOSED AREAS, EVERYTHING SHOULD BE COOL, RIGHT?
10/7

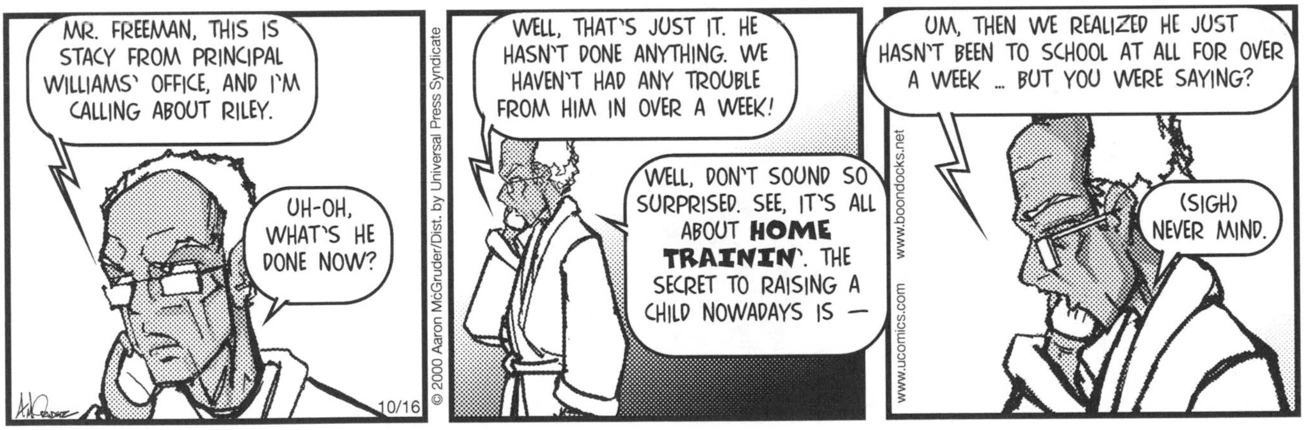
MR. FREEMAN, THIS IS STACY FROM PRINCIPAL WILLIAMS' OFFICE, AND I'M CALLING ABOUT RILEY.
UH-OH, WHAT'S HE DONE NOW?
10/16
© 2000 Aaron McGruder/Dist. by Universal Press Syndicate
WELL, THAT'S JUST IT. HE HASN'T DONE ANYTHING. WE HAVEN'T HAD ANY TROUBLE FROM HIM IN OVER A WEEK!
WELL, DON'T SOUND SO SURPRISED. SEE, IT'S ALL ABOUT HOME TRAININ'. THE SECRET TO RAISING A CHILD NOWADAYS IS —
www.ucomics.com www.boondocks.net
UM, THEN WE REALIZED HE JUST HASN'T BEEN TO SCHOOL AT ALL FOR OVER A WEEK ... BUT YOU WERE SAYING?
(SIGH) NEVER MIND.

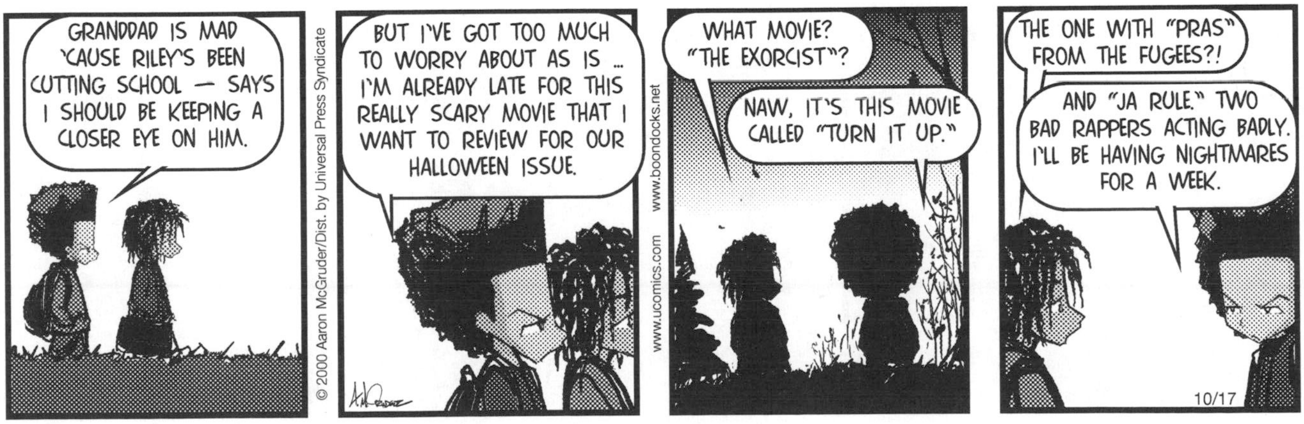
GRANDDAD IS MAD 'CAUSE RILEY'S BEEN CUTTING SCHOOL — SAYS I SHOULD BE KEEPING A CLOSER EYE ON HIM.
© 2000 Aaron McGruder/Dist. by Universal Press Syndicate
BUT I'VE GOT TOO MUCH TO WORRY ABOUT AS IS ... I'M ALREADY LATE FOR THIS REALLY SCARY MOVIE THAT I WANT TO REVIEW FOR OUR HALLOWEEN ISSUE.
www.ucomics.com www.boondocks.net
WHAT MOVIE? "THE EXORCIST"?
NAW, IT'S THIS MOVIE CALLED "TURN IT UP."
THE ONE WITH "PRAS" FROM THE FUGEES?!
AND "JA RULE." TWO BAD RAPPERS ACTING BADLY. I'LL BE HAVING NIGHTMARES FOR A WEEK.
10/17

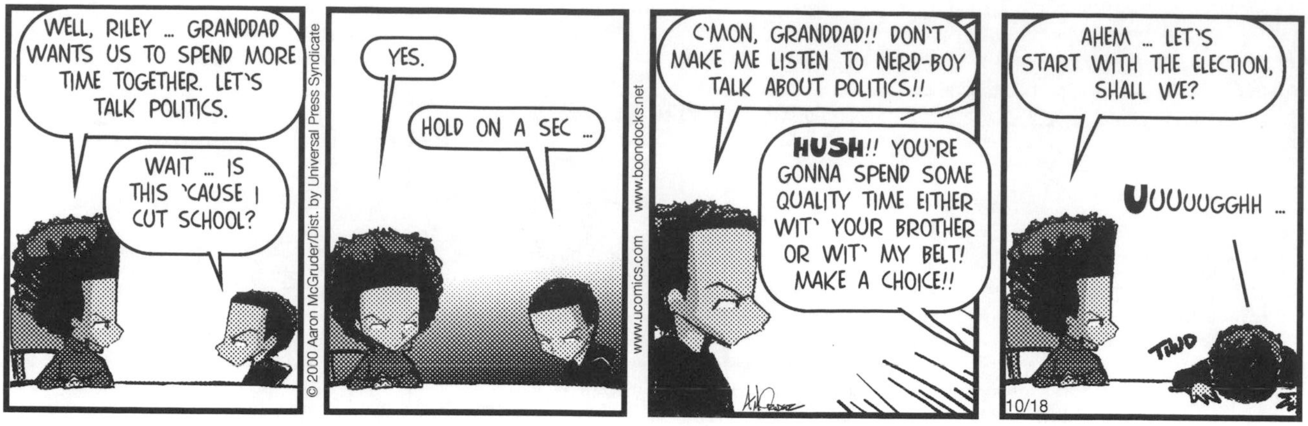
WELL, RILEY ... GRANDDAD WANTS US TO SPEND MORE TIME TOGETHER. LET'S TALK POLITICS.
WAIT ... IS THIS 'CAUSE I CUT SCHOOL?
YES.
HOLD ON A SEC ...
C'MON, GRANDDAD!! DON'T MAKE ME LISTEN TO NERD-BOY TALK ABOUT POLITICS!!
HUSH!! YOU'RE GONNA SPEND SOME QUALITY TIME EITHER WIT' YOUR BROTHER OR WIT' MY BELT! MAKE A CHOICE!!
AHEM ... LET'S START WITH THE ELECTION, SHALL WE?
UUUUUGGHH ...
THUD
10/18
© 2000 Aaron McGruder/Dist. by Universal Press Syndicate
www.ucomics.com www.boondocks.net

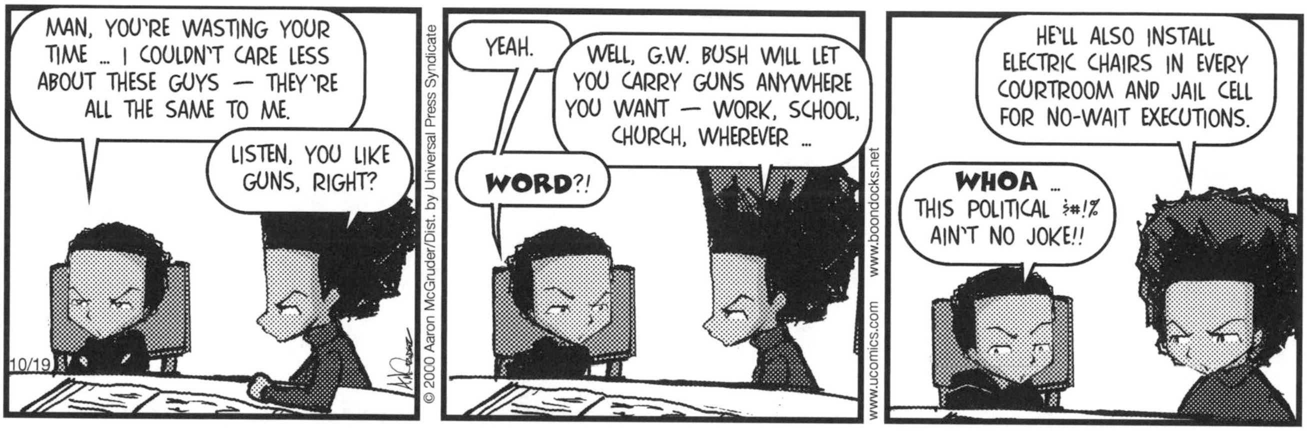
MAN, YOU'RE WASTING YOUR TIME ... I COULDN'T CARE LESS ABOUT THESE GUYS — THEY'RE ALL THE SAME TO ME.
LISTEN, YOU LIKE GUNS, RIGHT?
YEAH.
WELL, G.W. BUSH WILL LET YOU CARRY GUNS ANYWHERE YOU WANT — WORK, SCHOOL, CHURCH, WHEREVER ...
WORD?!
HE'LL ALSO INSTALL ELECTRIC CHAIRS IN EVERY COURTROOM AND JAIL CELL FOR NO-WAIT EXECUTIONS.
WHOA ... THIS POLITICAL $#!% AIN'T NO JOKE!!
10/19
© 2000 Aaron McGruder/Dist. by Universal Press Syndicate
www.ucomics.com www.boondocks.net

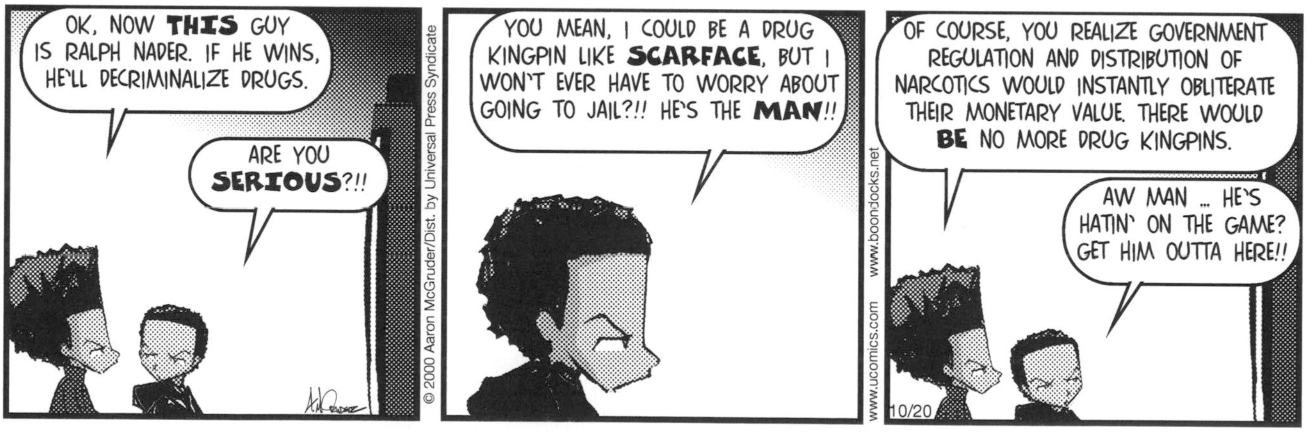
OK, NOW THIS GUY IS RALPH NADER. IF HE WINS, HE'LL DECRIMINALIZE DRUGS.
ARE YOU SERIOUS?!!
YOU MEAN, I COULD BE A DRUG KINGPIN LIKE SCARFACE, BUT I WON'T EVER HAVE TO WORRY ABOUT GOING TO JAIL?!! HE'S THE MAN!!
OF COURSE, YOU REALIZE GOVERNMENT REGULATION AND DISTRIBUTION OF NARCOTICS WOULD INSTANTLY OBLITERATE THEIR MONETARY VALUE. THERE WOULD BE NO MORE DRUG KINGPINS.
AW MAN ... HE'S HATIN' ON THE GAME? GET HIM OUTTA HERE!!
10/20
© 2000 Aaron McGruder/Dist. by Universal Press Syndicate
www.ucomics.com www.boondocks.net

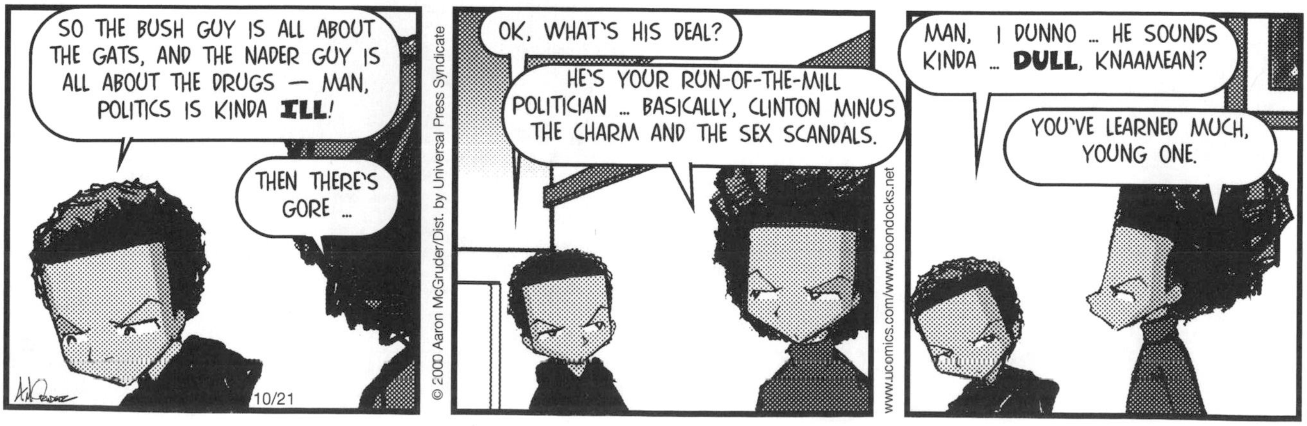
SO THE BUSH GUY IS ALL ABOUT THE GATS, AND THE NADER GUY IS ALL ABOUT THE DRUGS — MAN, POLITICS IS KINDA ILL!
THEN THERE'S GORE ...
OK, WHAT'S HIS DEAL?
HE'S YOUR RUN-OF-THE-MILL POLITICIAN ... BASICALLY, CLINTON MINUS THE CHARM AND THE SEX SCANDALS.
MAN, I DUNNO ... HE SOUNDS KINDA ... DULL, KNAAMEAN?
YOU'VE LEARNED MUCH, YOUNG ONE.
10/21
© 2000 Aaron McGruder/Dist. by Universal Press Syndicate
www.ucomics.com/www.boondocks.net

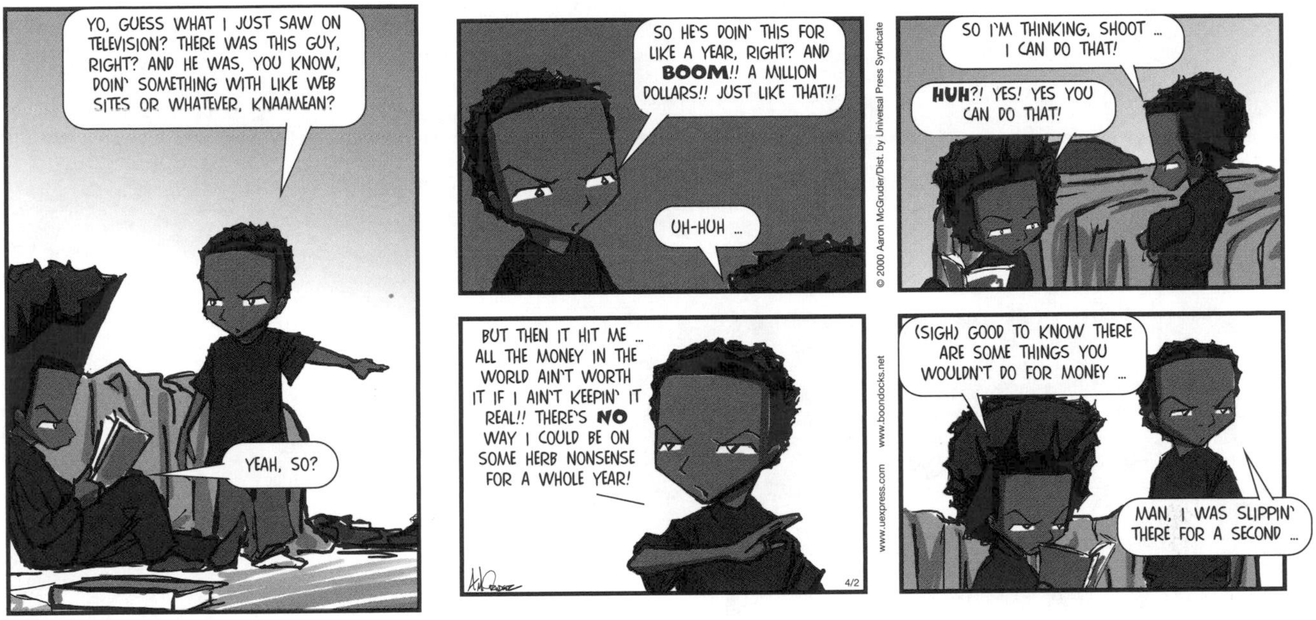
YO, GUESS WHAT I JUST SAW ON TELEVISION? THERE WAS THIS GUY, RIGHT? AND HE WAS, YOU KNOW, DOIN' SOMETHING WITH LIKE WEB SITES OR WHATEVER, KNAAMEAN?
YEAH, SO?
SO HE'S DOIN' THIS FOR LIKE A YEAR, RIGHT? AND **BOOM**!! A MILLION DOLLARS!! JUST LIKE THAT!!
UH-HUH ...
SO I'M THINKING, SHOOT ... I CAN DO THAT!
HUH?! YES! YES YOU CAN DO THAT!
BUT THEN IT HIT ME ... ALL THE MONEY IN THE WORLD AIN'T WORTH IT IF I AIN'T KEEPIN' IT REAL!! THERE'S **NO** WAY I COULD BE ON SOME HERB NONSENSE FOR A WHOLE YEAR!
(SIGH) GOOD TO KNOW THERE ARE SOME THINGS YOU WOULDN'T DO FOR MONEY ...
MAN, I WAS SLIPPIN' THERE FOR A SECOND ...
© 2000 Aaron McGruder/Dist. by Universal Press Syndicate
www.uexpress.com www.boondocks.net
4/2

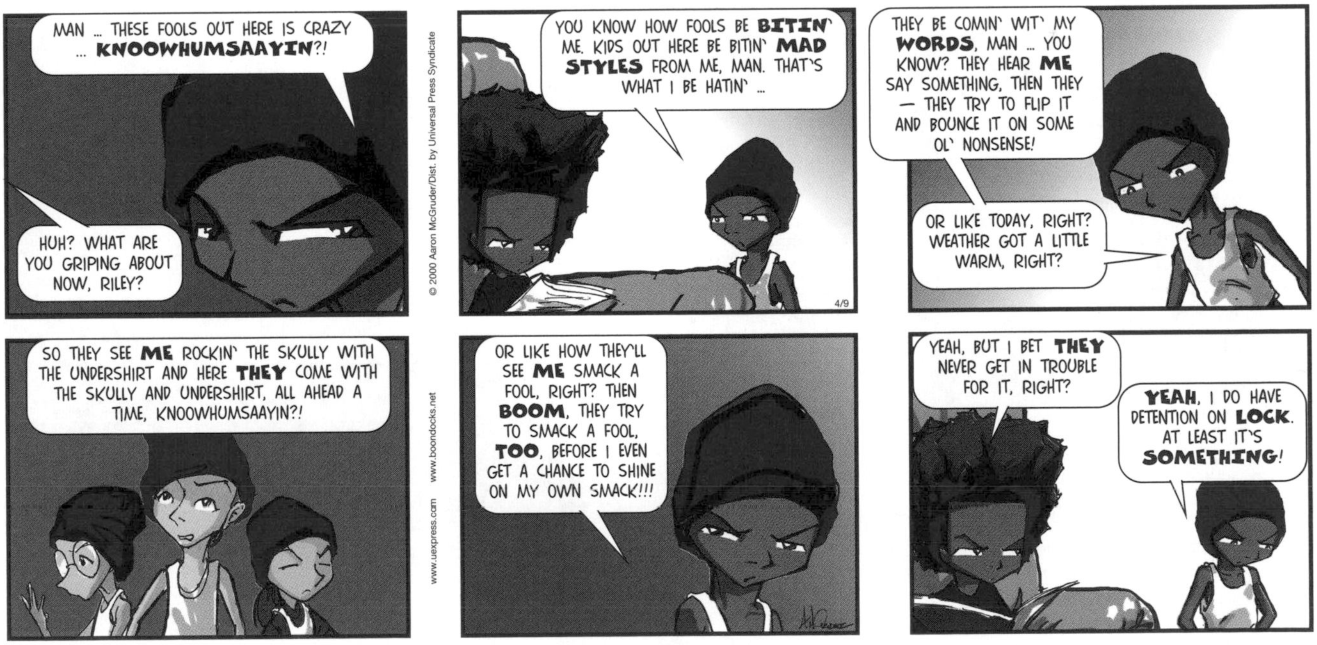
MAN ... THESE FOOLS OUT HERE IS CRAZY ... **KNOOWHUMSAAYIN**?!
HUH? WHAT ARE YOU GRIPING ABOUT NOW, RILEY?
YOU KNOW HOW FOOLS BE **BITIN'** ME. KIDS OUT HERE BE BITIN' **MAD STYLES** FROM ME, MAN. THAT'S WHAT I BE HATIN' ...
THEY BE COMIN' WIT' MY **WORDS**, MAN ... YOU KNOW? THEY HEAR **ME** SAY SOMETHING, THEN THEY — THEY TRY TO FLIP IT AND BOUNCE IT ON SOME OL' NONSENSE!
OR LIKE TODAY, RIGHT? WEATHER GOT A LITTLE WARM, RIGHT?
SO THEY SEE **ME** ROCKIN' THE SKULLY WITH THE UNDERSHIRT AND HERE **THEY** COME WITH THE SKULLY AND UNDERSHIRT, ALL AHEAD A TIME, KNOOWHUMSAAYIN?!
OR LIKE HOW THEY'LL SEE **ME** SMACK A FOOL, RIGHT? THEN **BOOM**, THEY TRY TO SMACK A FOOL, **TOO**, BEFORE I EVEN GET A CHANCE TO SHINE ON MY OWN SMACK!!!
YEAH, BUT I BET **THEY** NEVER GET IN TROUBLE FOR IT, RIGHT?
YEAH, I DO HAVE DETENTION ON **LOCK**. AT LEAST IT'S **SOMETHING**!
© 2000 Aaron McGruder/Dist. by Universal Press Syndicate
www.uexpress.com www.boondocks.net
4/9

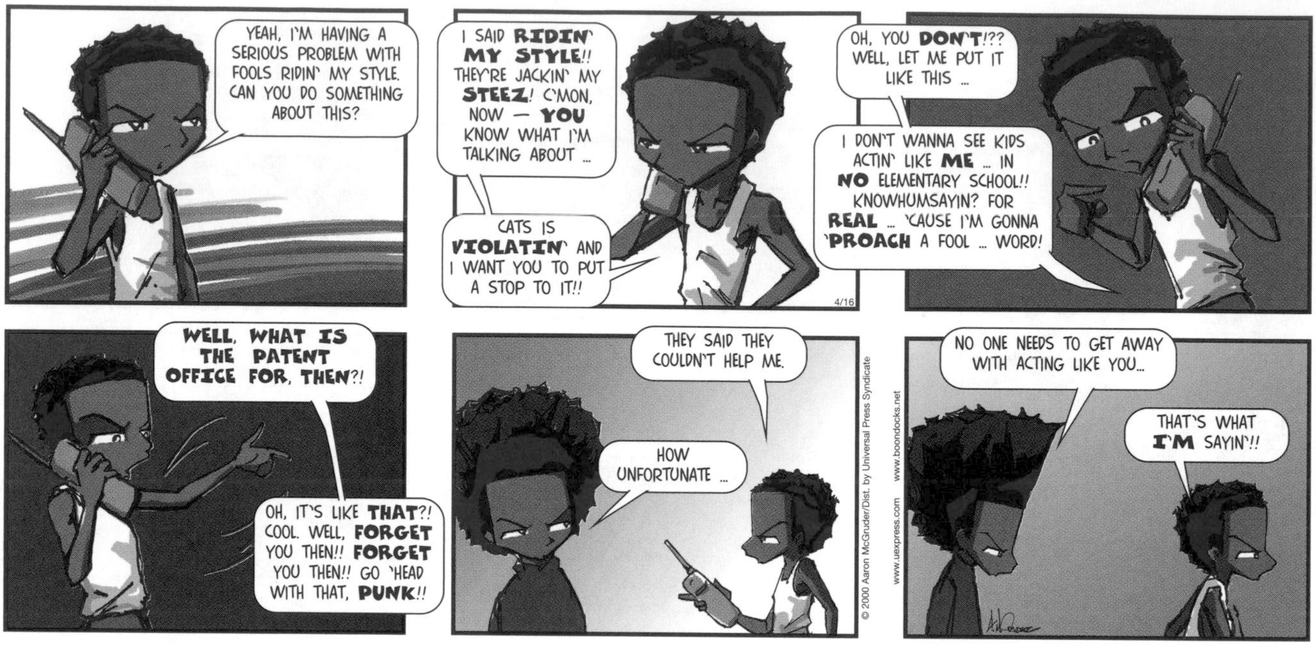
YEAH, I'M HAVING A SERIOUS PROBLEM WITH FOOLS RIDIN' MY STYLE. CAN YOU DO SOMETHING ABOUT THIS?
I SAID RIDIN' MY STYLE!! THEY'RE JACKIN' MY STEEZ! C'MON, NOW — YOU KNOW WHAT I'M TALKING ABOUT ...
CATS IS VIOLATIN' AND I WANT YOU TO PUT A STOP TO IT!!
OH, YOU DON'T!?? WELL, LET ME PUT IT LIKE THIS ...
I DON'T WANNA SEE KIDS ACTIN' LIKE ME ... IN NO ELEMENTARY SCHOOL!! KNOWHUMSAYIN? FOR REAL ... 'CAUSE I'M GONNA 'PROACH A FOOL ... WORD!
4/16
WELL, WHAT IS THE PATENT OFFICE FOR, THEN?!
OH, IT'S LIKE THAT?! COOL. WELL, FORGET YOU THEN!! FORGET YOU THEN!! GO 'HEAD WITH THAT, PUNK!!
THEY SAID THEY COULDN'T HELP ME.
HOW UNFORTUNATE ...
© 2000 Aaron McGruder/Dist. by Universal Press Syndicate
www.uexpress.com
www.boondocks.net
NO ONE NEEDS TO GET AWAY WITH ACTING LIKE YOU...
THAT'S WHAT I'M SAYIN'!!

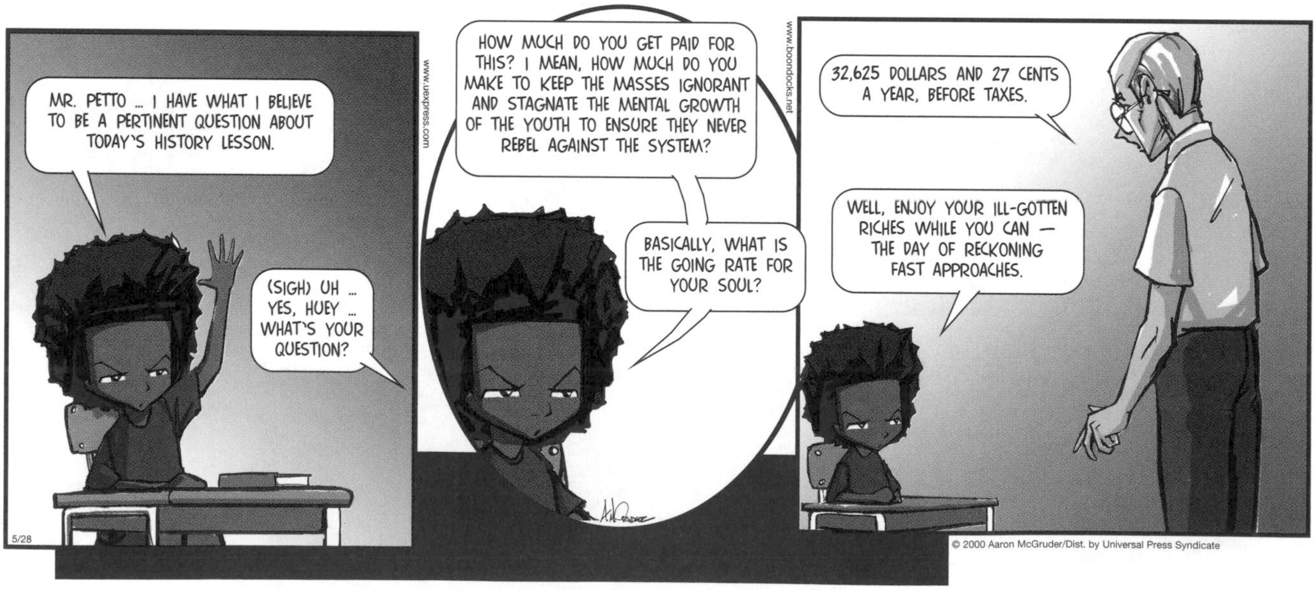
MR. PETTO ... I HAVE WHAT I BELIEVE TO BE A PERTINENT QUESTION ABOUT TODAY'S HISTORY LESSON.
(SIGH) UH ... YES, HUEY ... WHAT'S YOUR QUESTION?
5/28
www.uexpress.com
HOW MUCH DO YOU GET PAID FOR THIS? I MEAN, HOW MUCH DO YOU MAKE TO KEEP THE MASSES IGNORANT AND STAGNATE THE MENTAL GROWTH OF THE YOUTH TO ENSURE THEY NEVER REBEL AGAINST THE SYSTEM?
BASICALLY, WHAT IS THE GOING RATE FOR YOUR SOUL?
www.boondocks.net
32,625 DOLLARS AND 27 CENTS A YEAR, BEFORE TAXES.
WELL, ENJOY YOUR ILL-GOTTEN RICHES WHILE YOU CAN — THE DAY OF RECKONING FAST APPROACHES.

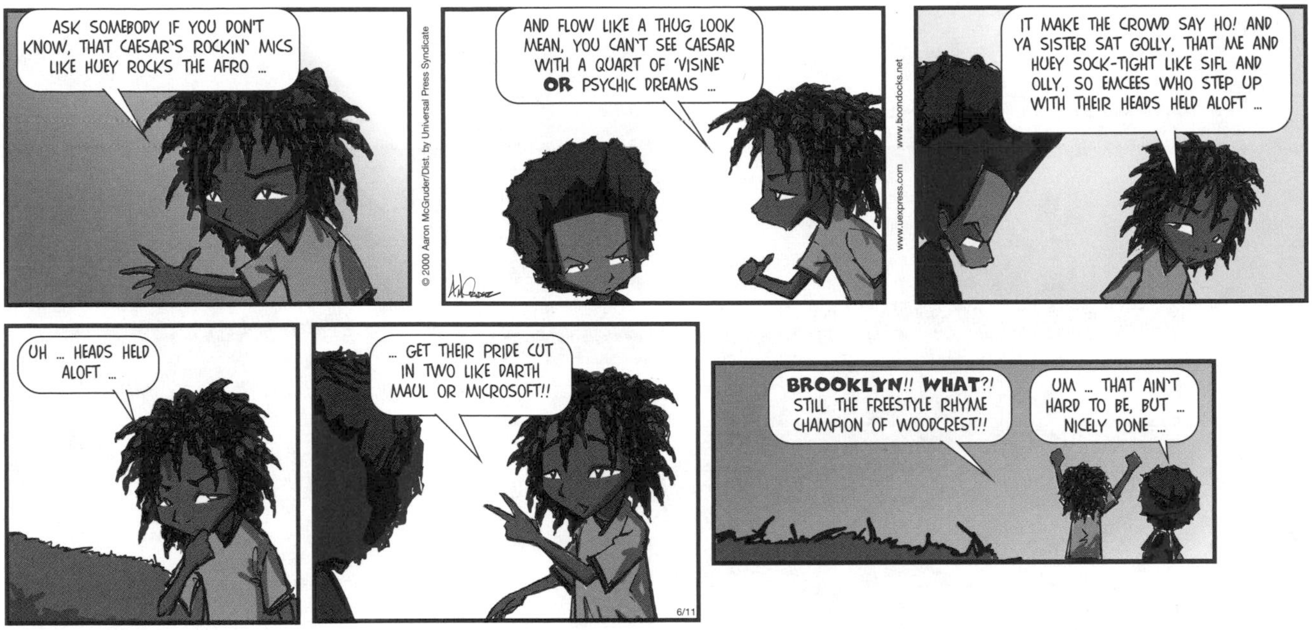
ASK SOMEBODY IF YOU DON'T KNOW, THAT CAESAR'S ROCKIN' MICS LIKE HUEY ROCKS THE AFRO ...
© 2000 Aaron McGruder/Dist. by Universal Press Syndicate
AND FLOW LIKE A THUG LOOK MEAN, YOU CAN'T SEE CAESAR WITH A QUART OF 'VISINE' OR PSYCHIC DREAMS ...
www.uexpress.com www.boondocks.net
IT MAKE THE CROWD SAY HO! AND YA SISTER SAT GOLLY, THAT ME AND HUEY SOCK-TIGHT LIKE SIFL AND OLLY, SO EMCEES WHO STEP UP WITH THEIR HEADS HELD ALOFT ...
UH ... HEADS HELD ALOFT ...
... GET THEIR PRIDE CUT IN TWO LIKE DARTH MAUL OR MICROSOFT!!
6/11
BROOKLYN!! WHAT?! STILL THE FREESTYLE RHYME CHAMPION OF WOODCREST!!
UM ... THAT AIN'T HARD TO BE, BUT ... NICELY DONE ...

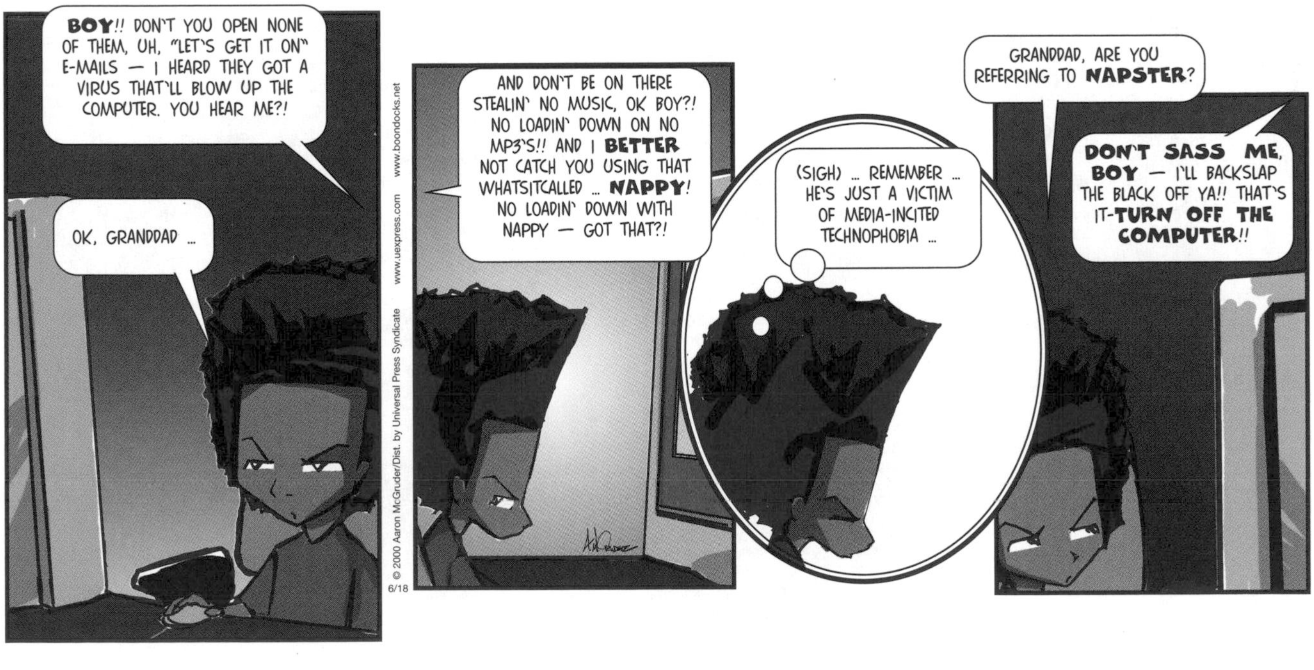
BOY!! DON'T YOU OPEN NONE OF THEM, UH, "LET'S GET IT ON" E-MAILS — I HEARD THEY GOT A VIRUS THAT'LL BLOW UP THE COMPUTER. YOU HEAR ME?!
OK, GRANDDAD ...
© 2000 Aaron McGruder/Dist. by Universal Press Syndicate www.uexpress.com www.boondocks.net
6/18
AND DON'T BE ON THERE STEALIN' NO MUSIC, OK BOY?! NO LOADIN' DOWN ON NO MP3'S!! AND I BETTER NOT CATCH YOU USING THAT WHATSITCALLED ... NAPPY! NO LOADIN' DOWN WITH NAPPY — GOT THAT?!
(SIGH) ... REMEMBER ... HE'S JUST A VICTIM OF MEDIA-INCITED TECHNOPHOBIA ...
GRANDDAD, ARE YOU REFERRING TO NAPSTER?
DON'T SASS ME, BOY — I'LL BACKSLAP THE BLACK OFF YA!! THAT'S IT-TURN OFF THE COMPUTER!!

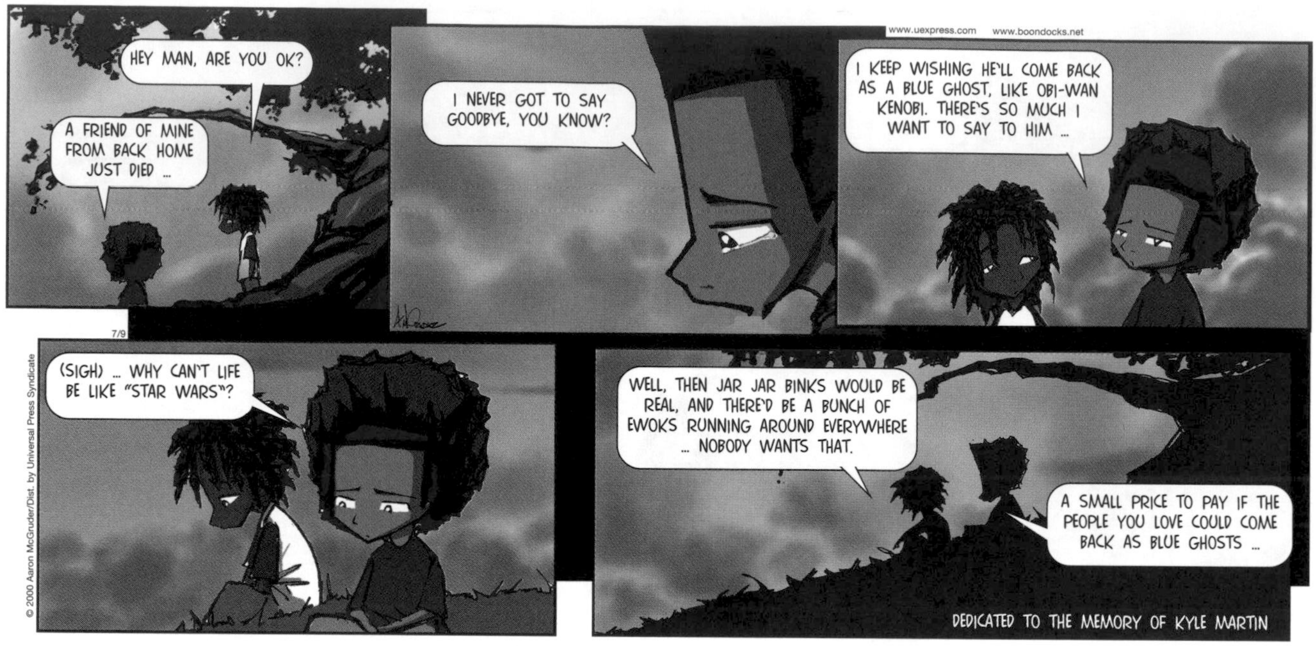

www.uexpress.com www.boondocks.net
HEY MAN, ARE YOU OK?
A FRIEND OF MINE FROM BACK HOME JUST DIED ...
I NEVER GOT TO SAY GOODBYE, YOU KNOW?
I KEEP WISHING HE'LL COME BACK AS A BLUE GHOST, LIKE OBI-WAN KENOBI. THERE'S SO MUCH I WANT TO SAY TO HIM ...
7/9
© 2000 Aaron McGruder/Dist. by Universal Press Syndicate
(SIGH) ... WHY CAN'T LIFE BE LIKE "STAR WARS"?
WELL, THEN JAR JAR BINKS WOULD BE REAL, AND THERE'D BE A BUNCH OF EWOKS RUNNING AROUND EVERYWHERE ... NOBODY WANTS THAT.
A SMALL PRICE TO PAY IF THE PEOPLE YOU LOVE COULD COME BACK AS BLUE GHOSTS ...
DEDICATED TO THE MEMORY OF KYLE MARTIN

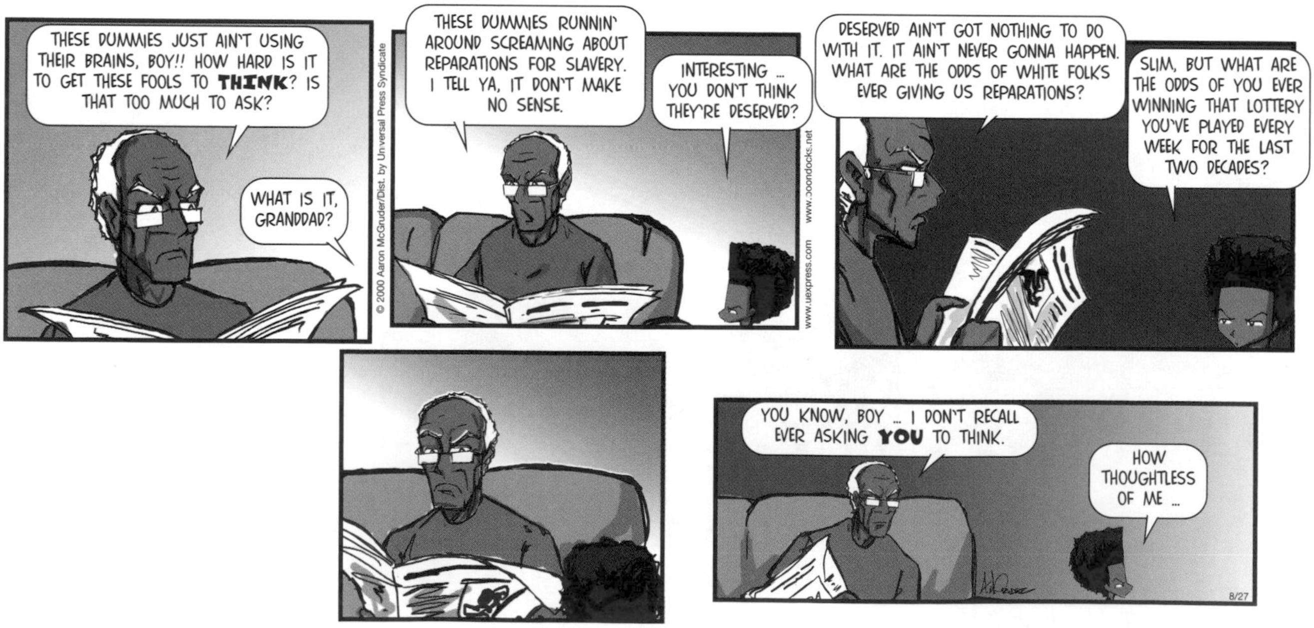

THESE DUMMIES JUST AIN'T USING THEIR BRAINS, BOY!! HOW HARD IS IT TO GET THESE FOOLS TO THINK? IS THAT TOO MUCH TO ASK?
WHAT IS IT, GRANDDAD?
© 2000 Aaron McGruder/Dist. by Universal Press Syndicate
THESE DUMMIES RUNNIN' AROUND SCREAMING ABOUT REPARATIONS FOR SLAVERY. I TELL YA, IT DON'T MAKE NO SENSE.
INTERESTING ... YOU DON'T THINK THEY'RE DESERVED?
www.uexpress.com www.boondocks.net
DESERVED AIN'T GOT NOTHING TO DO WITH IT. IT AIN'T NEVER GONNA HAPPEN. WHAT ARE THE ODDS OF WHITE FOLKS EVER GIVING US REPARATIONS?
SLIM, BUT WHAT ARE THE ODDS OF YOU EVER WINNING THAT LOTTERY YOU'VE PLAYED EVERY WEEK FOR THE LAST TWO DECADES?
YOU KNOW, BOY ... I DON'T RECALL EVER ASKING YOU TO THINK.
HOW THOUGHTLESS OF ME ...
8/27

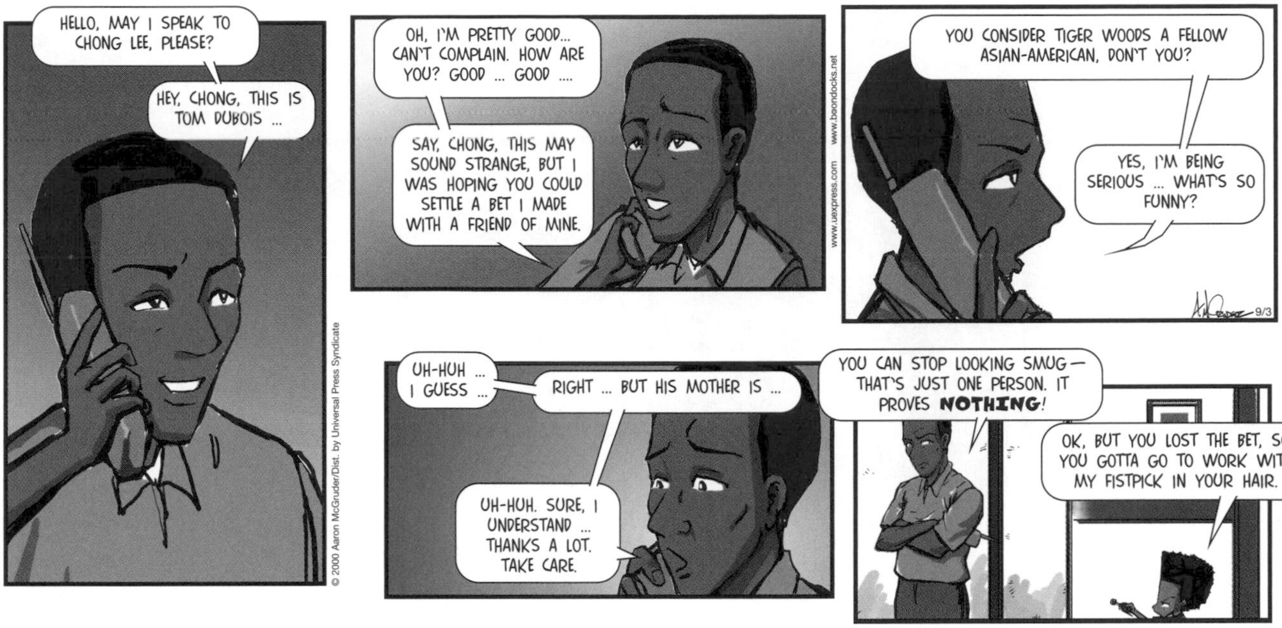
HELLO, MAY I SPEAK TO CHONG LEE, PLEASE?
HEY, CHONG, THIS IS TOM DUBOIS ...
OH, I'M PRETTY GOOD... CAN'T COMPLAIN. HOW ARE YOU? GOOD ... GOOD ....
SAY, CHONG, THIS MAY SOUND STRANGE, BUT I WAS HOPING YOU COULD SETTLE A BET I MADE WITH A FRIEND OF MINE.
YOU CONSIDER TIGER WOODS A FELLOW ASIAN-AMERICAN, DON'T YOU?
YES, I'M BEING SERIOUS ... WHAT'S SO FUNNY?
UH-HUH ... I GUESS ...
RIGHT ... BUT HIS MOTHER IS ...
UH-HUH. SURE, I UNDERSTAND ... THANKS A LOT. TAKE CARE.
YOU CAN STOP LOOKING SMUG— THAT'S JUST ONE PERSON. IT PROVES **NOTHING**!
OK, BUT YOU LOST THE BET, SO YOU GOTTA GO TO WORK WITH MY FISTPICK IN YOUR HAIR.
© 2000 Aaron McGruder/Dist. by Universal Press Syndicate
www.uexpress.com www.boondocks.net
9/3

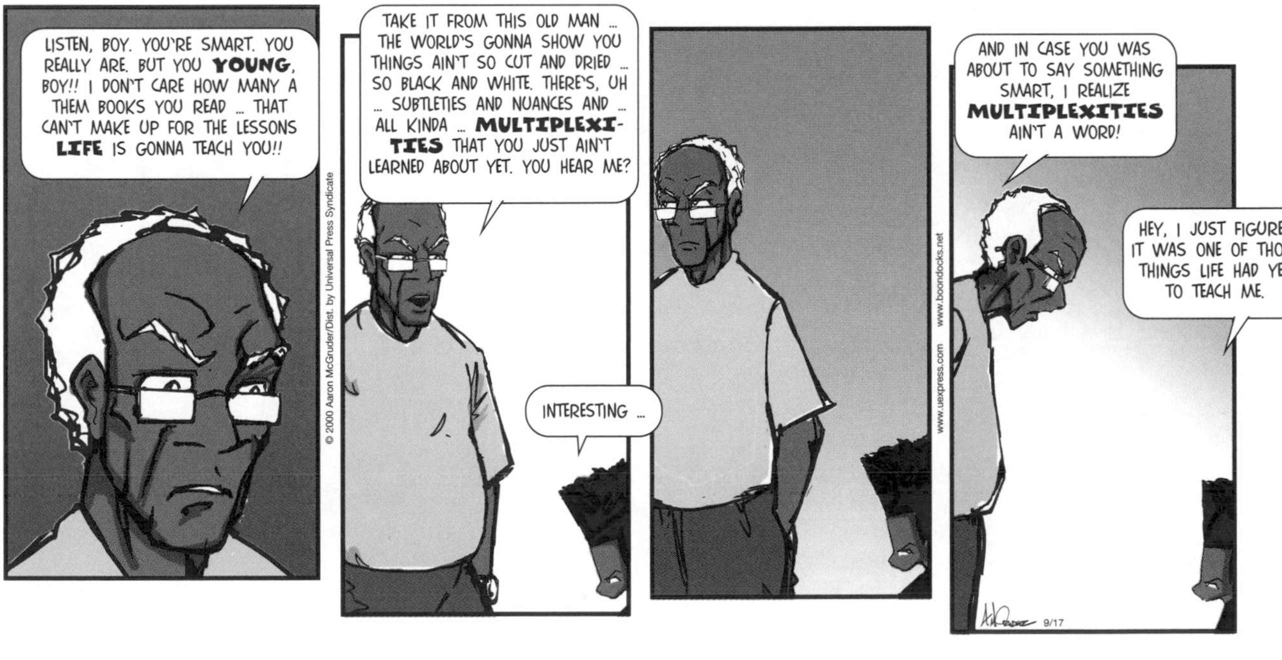
LISTEN, BOY. YOU'RE SMART. YOU REALLY ARE. BUT YOU **YOUNG**, BOY!! I DON'T CARE HOW MANY A THEM BOOKS YOU READ ... THAT CAN'T MAKE UP FOR THE LESSONS **LIFE** IS GONNA TEACH YOU!!
TAKE IT FROM THIS OLD MAN ... THE WORLD'S GONNA SHOW YOU THINGS AIN'T SO CUT AND DRIED ... SO BLACK AND WHITE. THERE'S, UH ... SUBTLETIES AND NUANCES AND ... ALL KINDA ... **MULTIPLEXI-TIES** THAT YOU JUST AIN'T LEARNED ABOUT YET. YOU HEAR ME?
INTERESTING ...
AND IN CASE YOU WAS ABOUT TO SAY SOMETHING SMART, I REALIZE **MULTIPLEXITIES** AIN'T A WORD!
HEY, I JUST FIGURED IT WAS ONE OF THOSE THINGS LIFE HAD YET TO TEACH ME.
© 2000 Aaron McGruder/Dist. by Universal Press Syndicate
www.uexpress.com www.boondocks.net
9/17

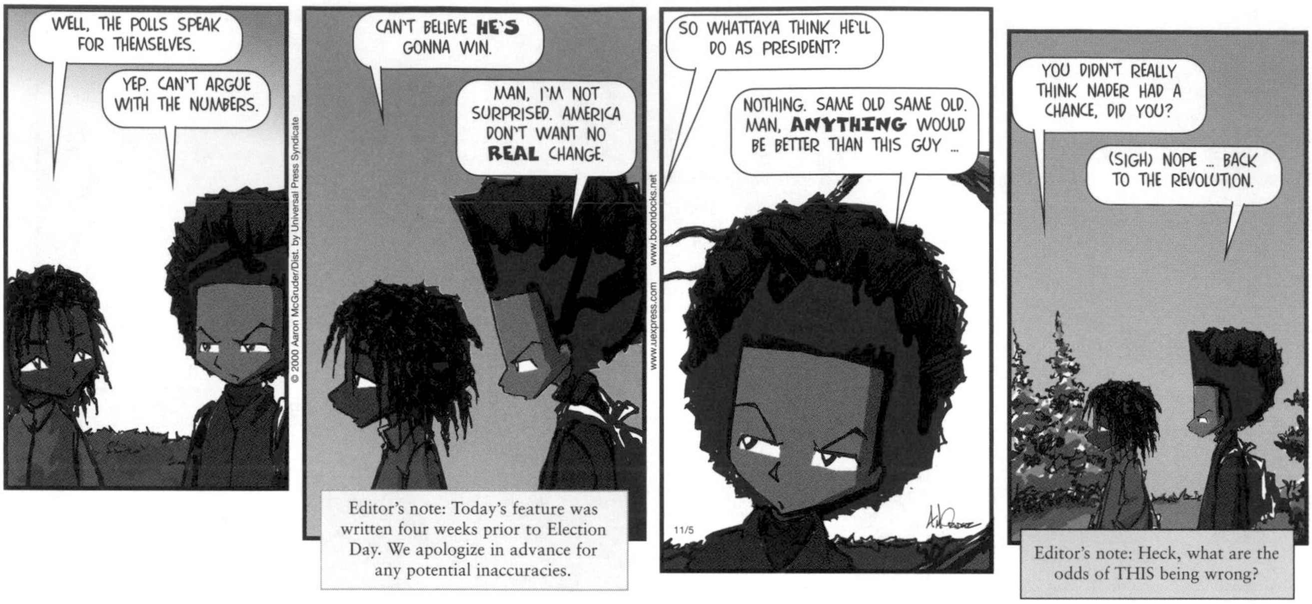
WELL, THE POLLS SPEAK FOR THEMSELVES.
YEP. CAN'T ARGUE WITH THE NUMBERS.
© 2000 Aaron McGruder/Dist. by Universal Press Syndicate
CAN'T BELIEVE HE'S GONNA WIN.
MAN, I'M NOT SURPRISED. AMERICA DON'T WANT NO REAL CHANGE.
Editor's note: Today's feature was written four weeks prior to Election Day. We apologize in advance for any potential inaccuracies.
www.uexpress.com www.boondocks.net
SO WHATTAYA THINK HE'LL DO AS PRESIDENT?
NOTHING. SAME OLD SAME OLD. MAN, ANYTHING WOULD BE BETTER THAN THIS GUY ...
11/5
YOU DIDN'T REALLY THINK NADER HAD A CHANCE, DID YOU?
(SIGH) NOPE ... BACK TO THE REVOLUTION.
Editor's note: Heck, what are the odds of THIS being wrong?

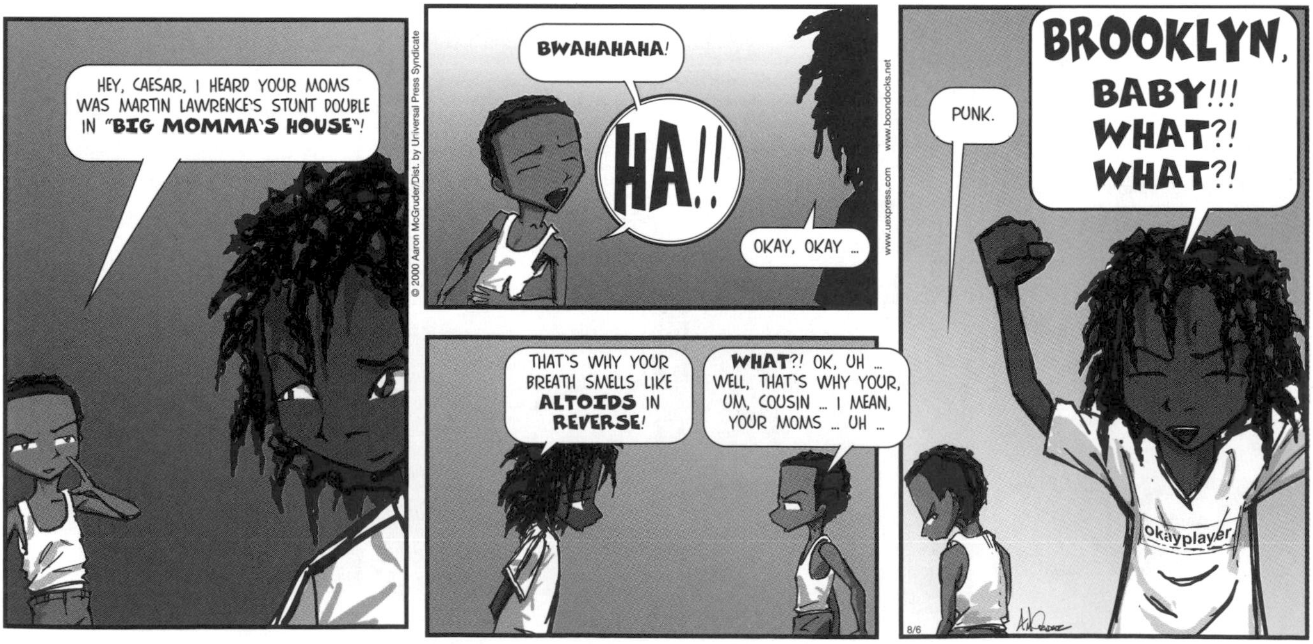
HEY, CAESAR, I HEARD YOUR MOMS WAS MARTIN LAWRENCE'S STUNT DOUBLE IN "BIG MOMMA'S HOUSE"!
© 2000 Aaron McGruder/Dist. by Universal Press Syndicate
BWAHAHAHA!
HA!!
OKAY, OKAY ...
www.uexpress.com www.boondocks.net
THAT'S WHY YOUR BREATH SMELLS LIKE ALTOIDS IN REVERSE!
WHAT?! OK, UH ... WELL, THAT'S WHY YOUR, UM, COUSIN ... I MEAN, YOUR MOMS ... UH ...
PUNK.
BROOKLYN, BABY!!! WHAT?! WHAT?!
okayplayer
8/6

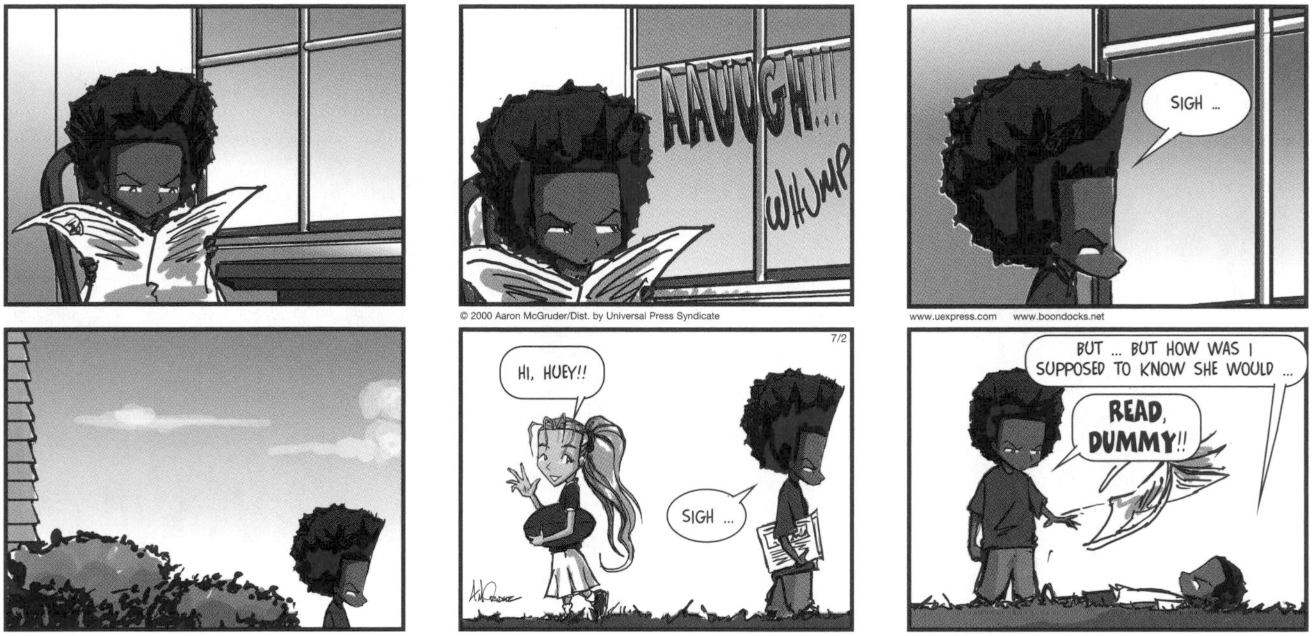
AAUUGH!!!
WHUMP
© 2000 Aaron McGruder/Dist. by Universal Press Syndicate
SIGH ...
www.uexpress.com www.boondocks.net
7/2
HI, HUEY!!
SIGH ...
BUT ... BUT HOW WAS I SUPPOSED TO KNOW SHE WOULD ...
READ, DUMMY!!

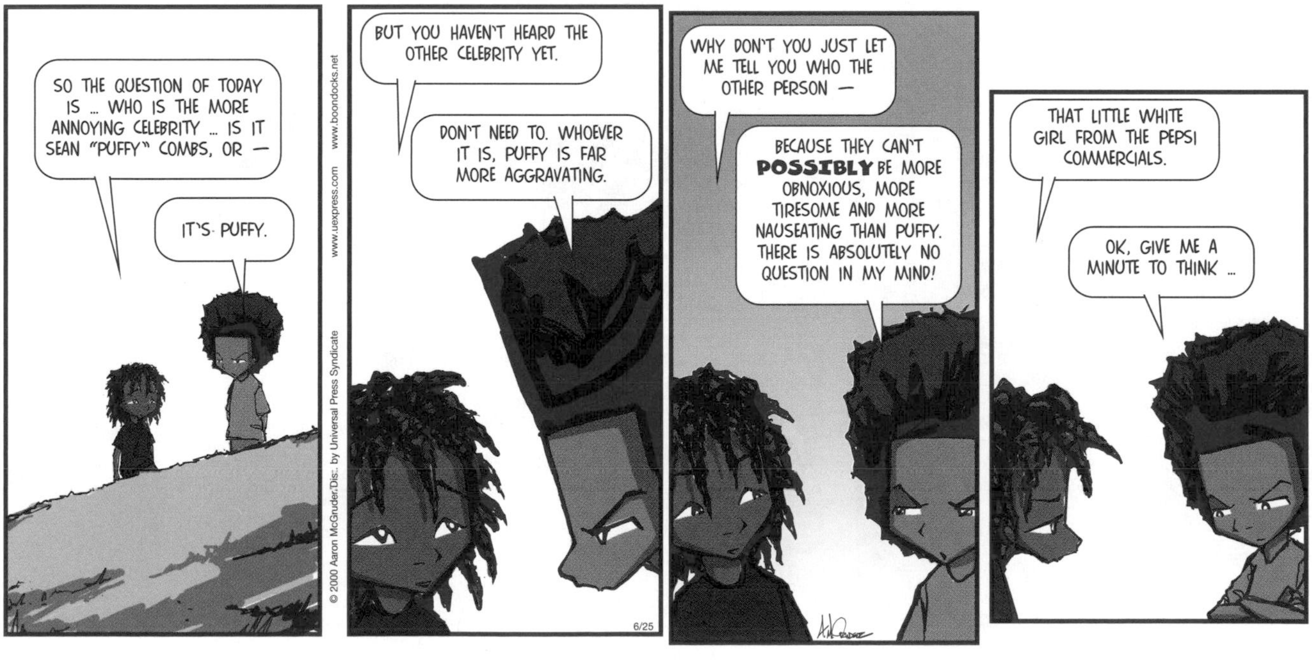
SO THE QUESTION OF TODAY IS ... WHO IS THE MORE ANNOYING CELEBRITY ... IS IT SEAN "PUFFY" COMBS, OR —
IT'S PUFFY.
© 2000 Aaron McGruder/Dist. by Universal Press Syndicate www.uexpress.com www.boondocks.net
BUT YOU HAVEN'T HEARD THE OTHER CELEBRITY YET.
DON'T NEED TO. WHOEVER IT IS, PUFFY IS FAR MORE AGGRAVATING.
6/25
WHY DON'T YOU JUST LET ME TELL YOU WHO THE OTHER PERSON —
BECAUSE THEY CAN'T POSSIBLY BE MORE OBNOXIOUS, MORE TIRESOME AND MORE NAUSEATING THAN PUFFY. THERE IS ABSOLUTELY NO QUESTION IN MY MIND!
THAT LITTLE WHITE GIRL FROM THE PEPSI COMMERCIALS.
OK, GIVE ME A MINUTE TO THINK ...

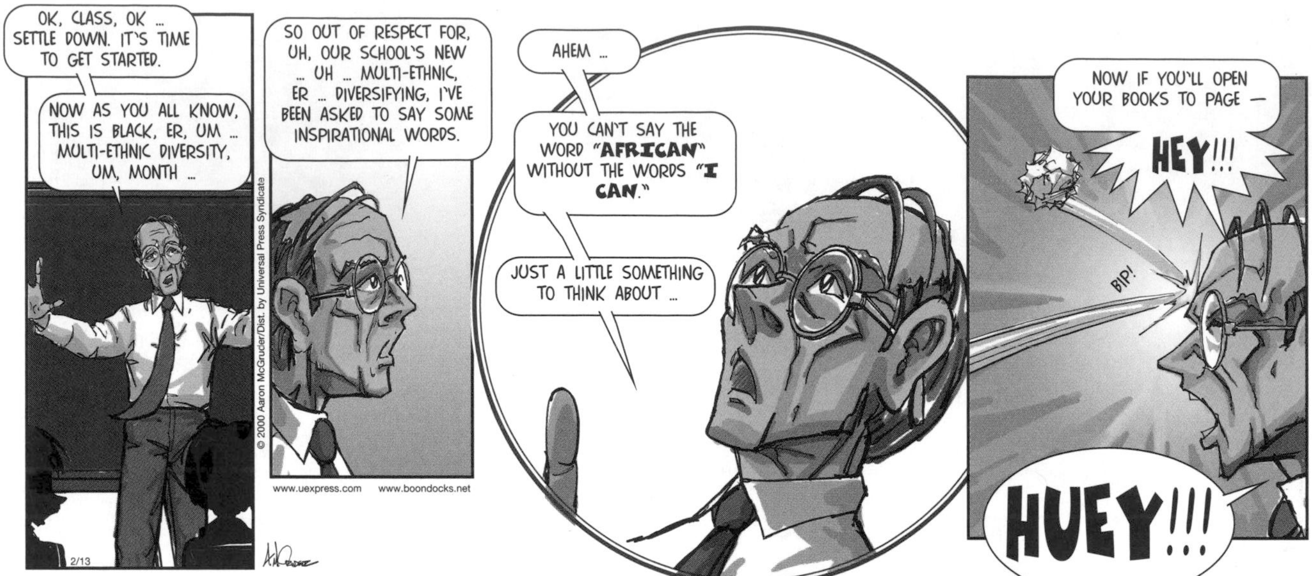
OK, CLASS, OK ... SETTLE DOWN. IT'S TIME TO GET STARTED.
NOW AS YOU ALL KNOW, THIS IS BLACK, ER, UM ... MULTI-ETHNIC DIVERSITY, UM, MONTH ...
SO OUT OF RESPECT FOR, UH, OUR SCHOOL'S NEW ... UH ... MULTI-ETHNIC, ER ... DIVERSIFYING, I'VE BEEN ASKED TO SAY SOME INSPIRATIONAL WORDS.
AHEM ...
YOU CAN'T SAY THE WORD "AFRICAN" WITHOUT THE WORDS "I CAN."
JUST A LITTLE SOMETHING TO THINK ABOUT ...
NOW IF YOU'LL OPEN YOUR BOOKS TO PAGE —
HEY!!!
BIP!
HUEY!!!
© 2000 Aaron McGruder/Dist. by Universal Press Syndicate
www.uexpress.com www.boondocks.net
2/13

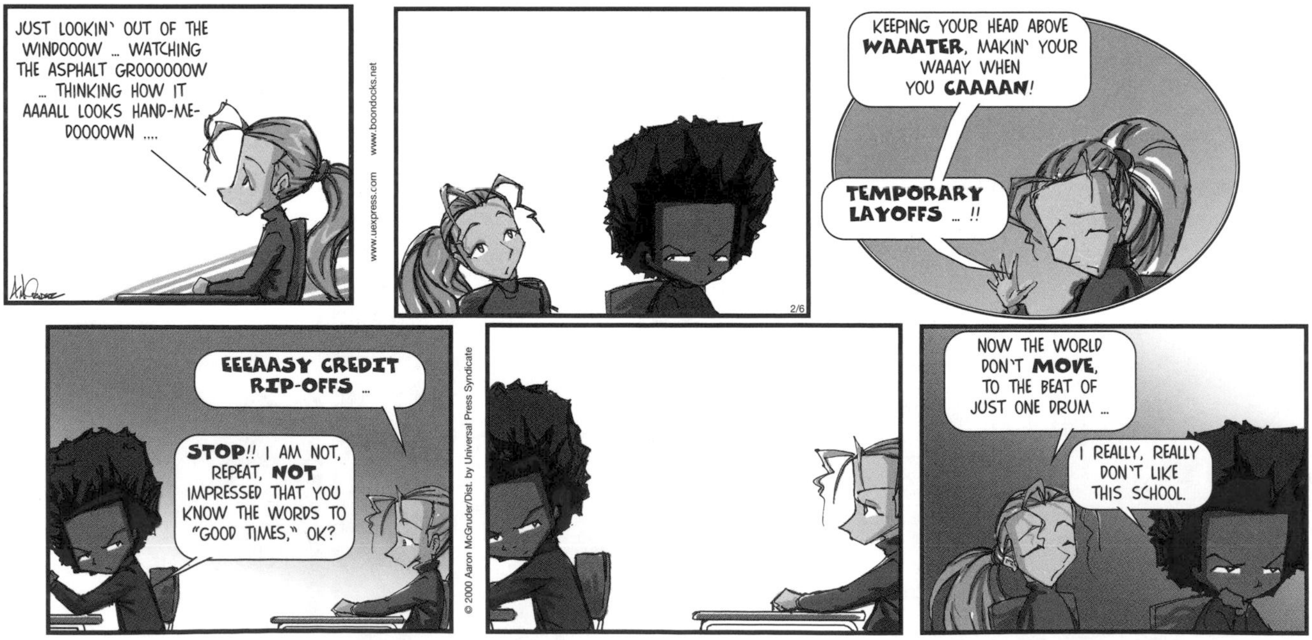
JUST LOOKIN' OUT OF THE WINDOOOW ... WATCHING THE ASPHALT GROOOOOOW ... THINKING HOW IT AAAALL LOOKS HAND-ME-DOOOOWN ....
www.uexpress.com www.boondocks.net
2/6
KEEPING YOUR HEAD ABOVE WAAATER, MAKIN' YOUR WAAAY WHEN YOU CAAAAN!
TEMPORARY LAYOFFS ... !!
EEEAASY CREDIT RIP-OFFS ...
STOP!! I AM NOT, REPEAT, NOT IMPRESSED THAT YOU KNOW THE WORDS TO "GOOD TIMES," OK?
© 2000 Aaron McGruder/Dist. by Universal Press Syndicate
NOW THE WORLD DON'T MOVE, TO THE BEAT OF JUST ONE DRUM ...
I REALLY, REALLY DON'T LIKE THIS SCHOOL.

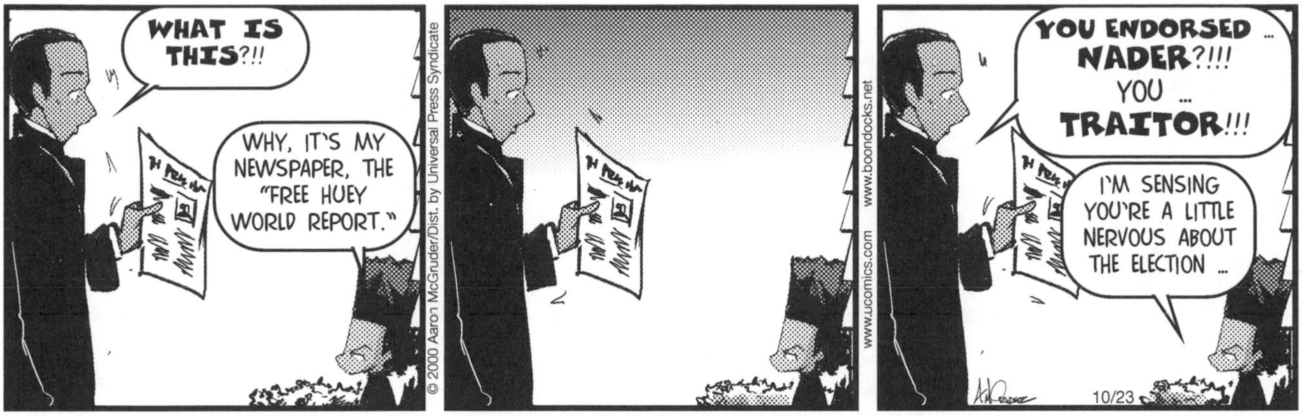
WHAT IS THIS?!!
WHY, IT'S MY NEWSPAPER, THE "FREE HUEY WORLD REPORT."
© 2000 Aaron McGruder/Dist. by Universal Press Syndicate
www.ucomics.com www.boondocks.net
YOU ENDORSED ... NADER?!!! YOU ... TRAITOR!!!
I'M SENSING YOU'RE A LITTLE NERVOUS ABOUT THE ELECTION ...
10/23

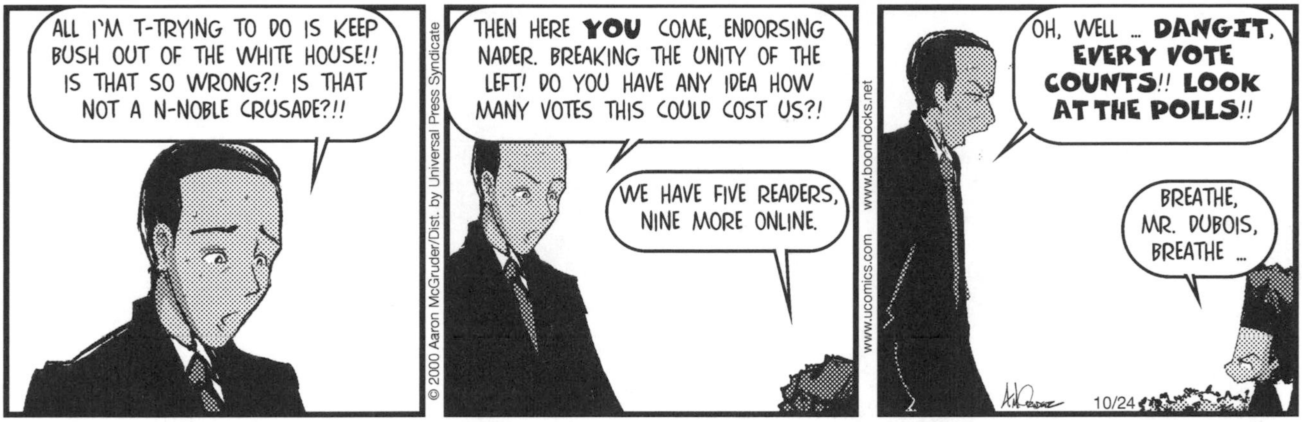
ALL I'M T-TRYING TO DO IS KEEP BUSH OUT OF THE WHITE HOUSE!! IS THAT SO WRONG?! IS THAT NOT A N-NOBLE CRUSADE?!!
© 2000 Aaron McGruder/Dist. by Universal Press Syndicate
THEN HERE YOU COME, ENDORSING NADER. BREAKING THE UNITY OF THE LEFT! DO YOU HAVE ANY IDEA HOW MANY VOTES THIS COULD COST US?!
WE HAVE FIVE READERS, NINE MORE ONLINE.
www.ucomics.com www.boondocks.net
OH, WELL ... DANGIT, EVERY VOTE COUNTS!! LOOK AT THE POLLS!!
BREATHE, MR. DUBOIS, BREATHE ...
10/24

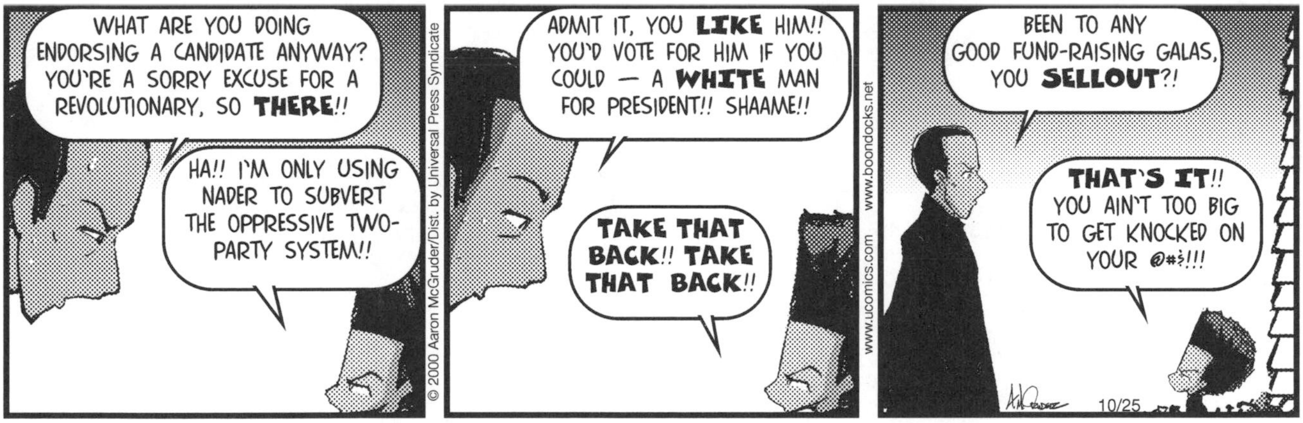
WHAT ARE YOU DOING ENDORSING A CANDIDATE ANYWAY? YOU'RE A SORRY EXCUSE FOR A REVOLUTIONARY, SO THERE!!
HA!! I'M ONLY USING NADER TO SUBVERT THE OPPRESSIVE TWO-PARTY SYSTEM!!
© 2000 Aaron McGruder/Dist. by Universal Press Syndicate
ADMIT IT, YOU LIKE HIM!! YOU'D VOTE FOR HIM IF YOU COULD — A WHITE MAN FOR PRESIDENT!! SHAAME!!
TAKE THAT BACK!! TAKE THAT BACK!!
www.ucomics.com www.boondocks.net
BEEN TO ANY GOOD FUND-RAISING GALAS, YOU SELLOUT?!
THAT'S IT!! YOU AIN'T TOO BIG TO GET KNOCKED ON YOUR @#$!!!
10/25

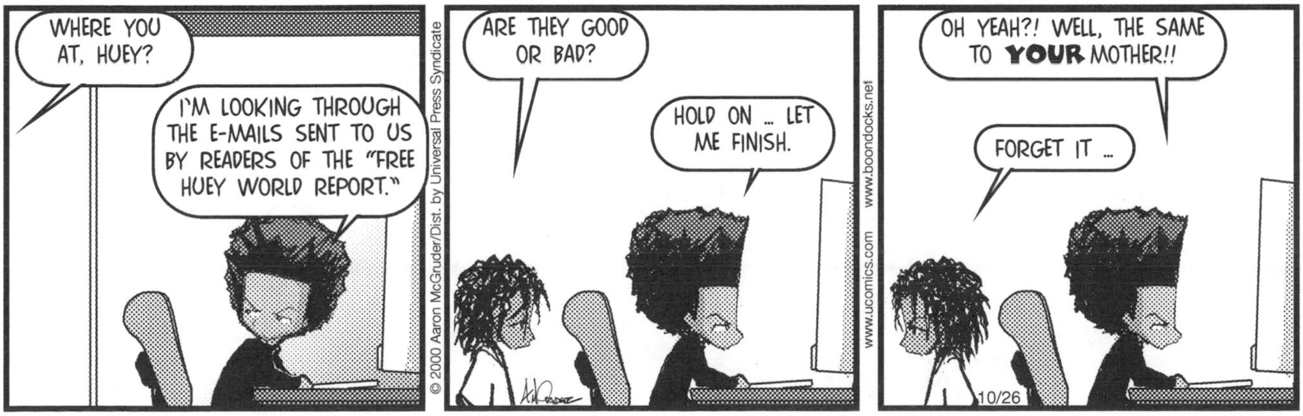
WHERE YOU AT, HUEY?
I'M LOOKING THROUGH THE E-MAILS SENT TO US BY READERS OF THE "FREE HUEY WORLD REPORT."
© 2000 Aaron McGruder/Dist. by Universal Press Syndicate
ARE THEY GOOD OR BAD?
HOLD ON ... LET ME FINISH.
www.ucomics.com www.boondocks.net
OH YEAH?! WELL, THE SAME TO YOUR MOTHER!!
FORGET IT ...
10/26

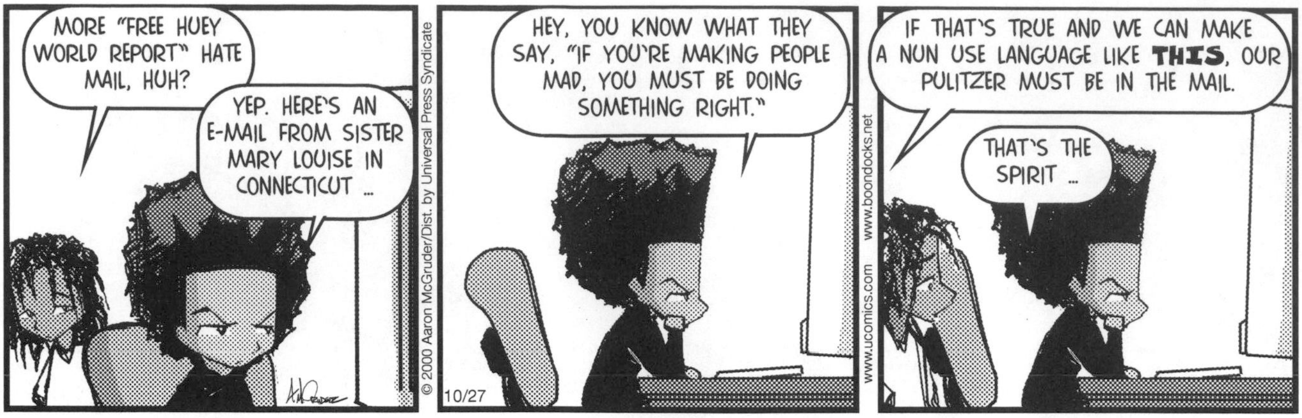
MORE "FREE HUEY WORLD REPORT" HATE MAIL, HUH?
YEP. HERE'S AN E-MAIL FROM SISTER MARY LOUISE IN CONNECTICUT ...
© 2000 Aaron McGruder/Dist. by Universal Press Syndicate
10/27
HEY, YOU KNOW WHAT THEY SAY, "IF YOU'RE MAKING PEOPLE MAD, YOU MUST BE DOING SOMETHING RIGHT."
www.ucomics.com www.boondocks.net
IF THAT'S TRUE AND WE CAN MAKE A NUN USE LANGUAGE LIKE **THIS**, OUR PULITZER MUST BE IN THE MAIL.
THAT'S THE SPIRIT ...

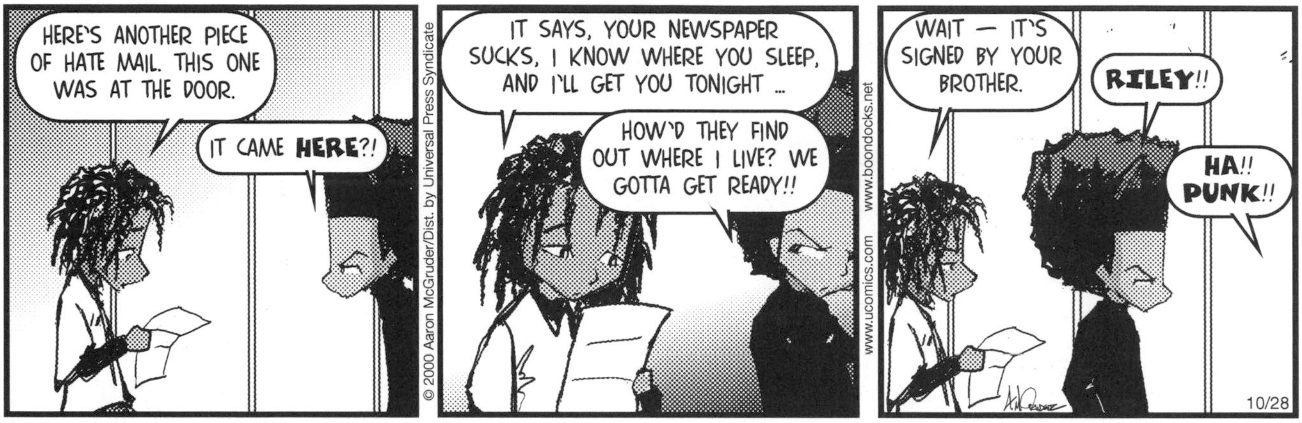
HERE'S ANOTHER PIECE OF HATE MAIL. THIS ONE WAS AT THE DOOR.
IT CAME **HERE**?!
© 2000 Aaron McGruder/Dist. by Universal Press Syndicate
IT SAYS, YOUR NEWSPAPER SUCKS, I KNOW WHERE YOU SLEEP, AND I'LL GET YOU TONIGHT ...
HOW'D THEY FIND OUT WHERE I LIVE? WE GOTTA GET READY!!
www.ucomics.com www.boondocks.net
WAIT — IT'S SIGNED BY YOUR BROTHER.
RILEY!!
HA!! PUNK!!
10/28

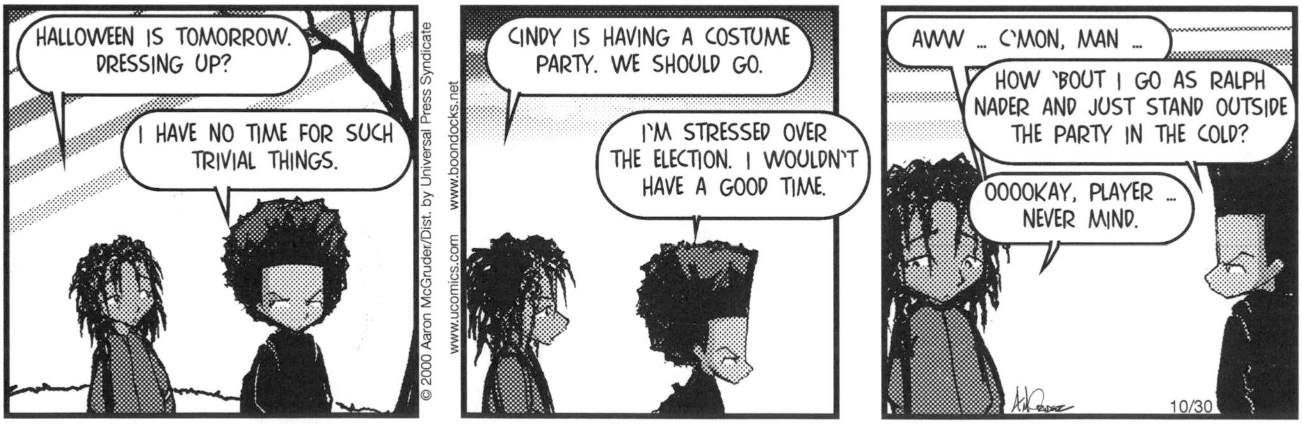
HALLOWEEN IS TOMORROW. DRESSING UP?
I HAVE NO TIME FOR SUCH TRIVIAL THINGS.
© 2000 Aaron McGruder/Dist. by Universal Press Syndicate
www.ucomics.com www.boondocks.net
CINDY IS HAVING A COSTUME PARTY. WE SHOULD GO.
I'M STRESSED OVER THE ELECTION. I WOULDN'T HAVE A GOOD TIME.
AWW ... C'MON, MAN ...
HOW 'BOUT I GO AS RALPH NADER AND JUST STAND OUTSIDE THE PARTY IN THE COLD?
OOOOKAY, PLAYER ... NEVER MIND.
10/30

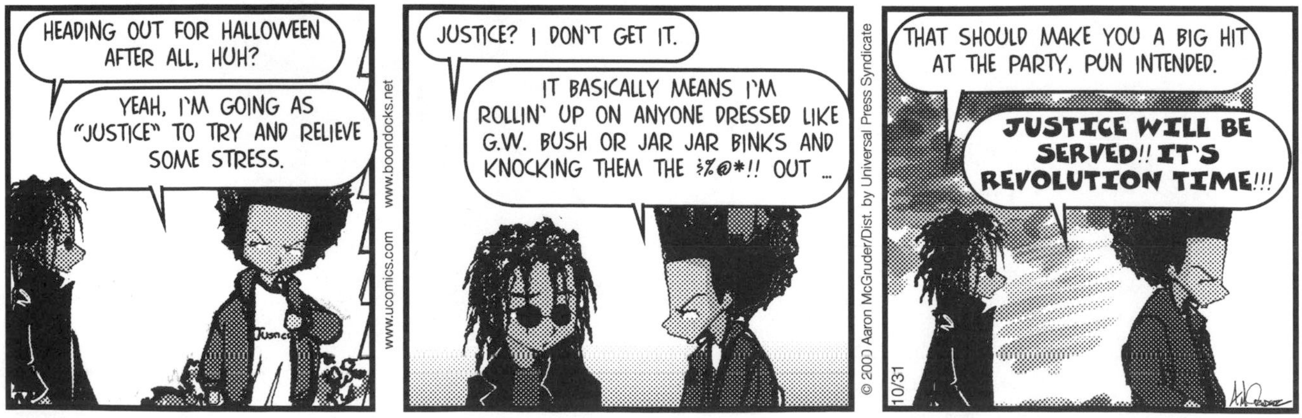
HEADING OUT FOR HALLOWEEN AFTER ALL, HUH?
YEAH, I'M GOING AS "JUSTICE" TO TRY AND RELIEVE SOME STRESS.
www.ucomics.com www.boondocks.net
JUSTICE? I DON'T GET IT.
IT BASICALLY MEANS I'M ROLLIN' UP ON ANYONE DRESSED LIKE G.W. BUSH OR JAR JAR BINKS AND KNOCKING THEM THE $%@*!! OUT ...
© 2000 Aaron McGruder/Dist. by Universal Press Syndicate
10/31
THAT SHOULD MAKE YOU A BIG HIT AT THE PARTY, PUN INTENDED.
JUSTICE WILL BE SERVED!! IT'S REVOLUTION TIME!!!

Part 2: The Story Continues . . .

WHAT'RE YOU DRAWING?
I'M TRYING MY HAND AT THE SOPHISTICATED ART OF POLITICAL CARTOONING. I JUST FINISHED A CARTOON ABOUT THE BALANCE OF POWER IN WASHINGTON AFTER THE MIDTERM ELECTIONS.
PUNK DEMOCRAT REAR END
DEMOCRATS
G.O.P.
RIGHT-WING FOOT
12/8
© 2002 Aaron McGruder/Dist. by Universal Press Syndicate
www.ucomics.com
www.boondocks.net
I LIKE THAT. IT'S SUBTLE ...
WELL, THAT'S THE KEY — NOT BEATING THE READER OVER THE HEAD WITH YOUR POINT.

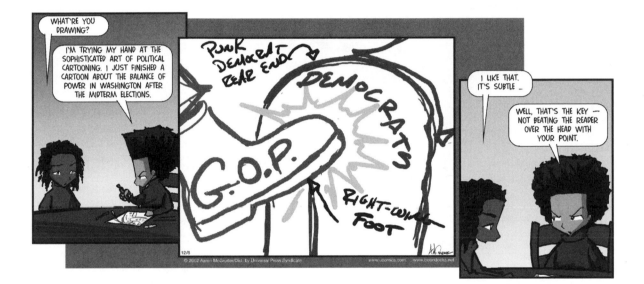

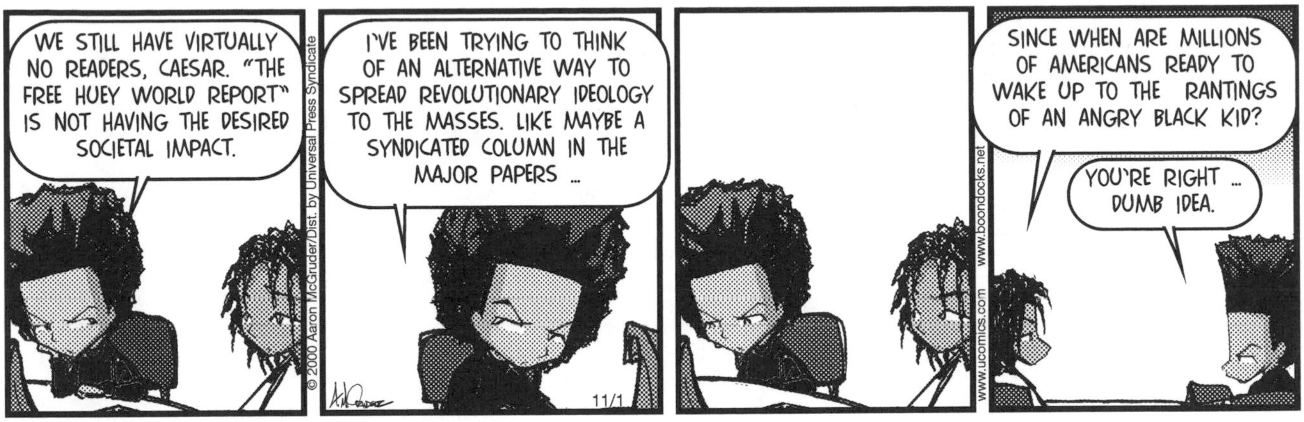
WE STILL HAVE VIRTUALLY NO READERS, CAESAR. "THE FREE HUEY WORLD REPORT" IS NOT HAVING THE DESIRED SOCIETAL IMPACT.
I'VE BEEN TRYING TO THINK OF AN ALTERNATIVE WAY TO SPREAD REVOLUTIONARY IDEOLOGY TO THE MASSES. LIKE MAYBE A SYNDICATED COLUMN IN THE MAJOR PAPERS ...
SINCE WHEN ARE MILLIONS OF AMERICANS READY TO WAKE UP TO THE RANTINGS OF AN ANGRY BLACK KID?
YOU'RE RIGHT ... DUMB IDEA.
© 2000 Aaron McGruder/Dist. by Universal Press Syndicate
www.ucomics.com www.boondocks.net
11/1

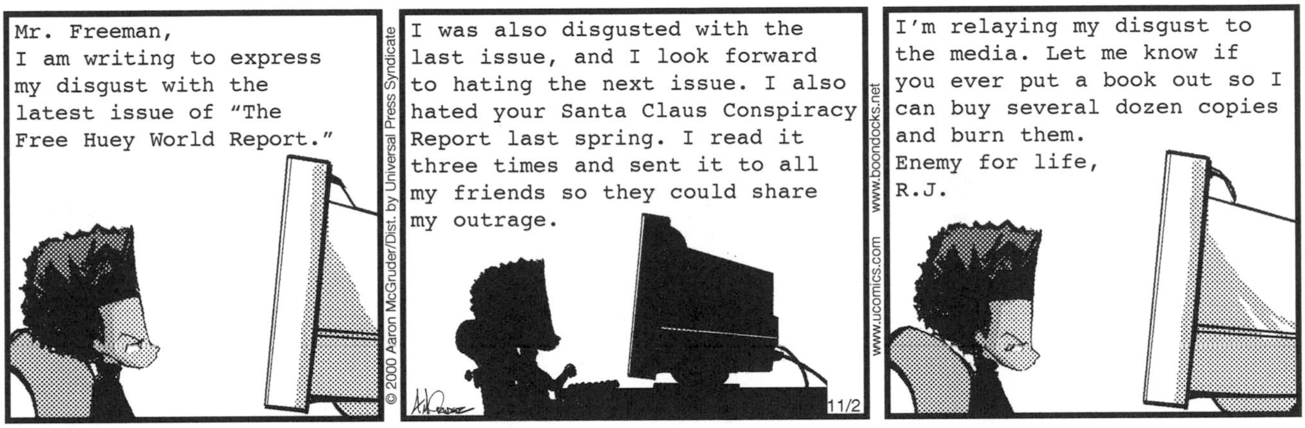
Mr. Freeman,
I am writing to express my disgust with the latest issue of "The Free Huey World Report."
I was also disgusted with the last issue, and I look forward to hating the next issue. I also hated your Santa Claus Conspiracy Report last spring. I read it three times and sent it to all my friends so they could share my outrage.
I'm relaying my disgust to the media. Let me know if you ever put a book out so I can buy several dozen copies and burn them.
Enemy for life,
R.J.
© 2000 Aaron McGruder/Dist. by Universal Press Syndicate
www.ucomics.com www.boondocks.net
11/2

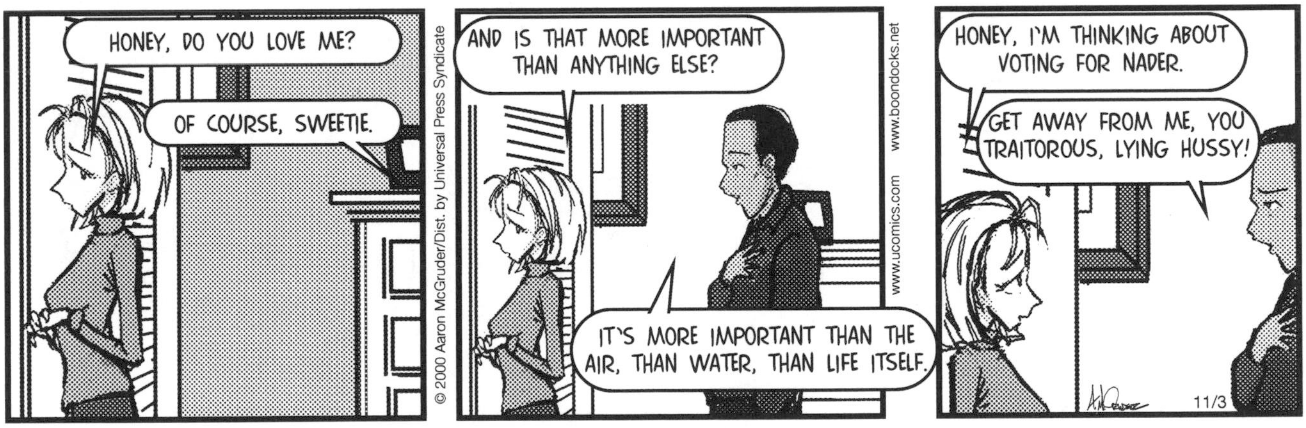
HONEY, DO YOU LOVE ME?
OF COURSE, SWEETIE.
AND IS THAT MORE IMPORTANT THAN ANYTHING ELSE?
IT'S MORE IMPORTANT THAN THE AIR, THAN WATER, THAN LIFE ITSELF.
HONEY, I'M THINKING ABOUT VOTING FOR NADER.
GET AWAY FROM ME, YOU TRAITOROUS, LYING HUSSY!
© 2000 Aaron McGruder/Dist. by Universal Press Syndicate
www.ucomics.com www.boondocks.net
11/3

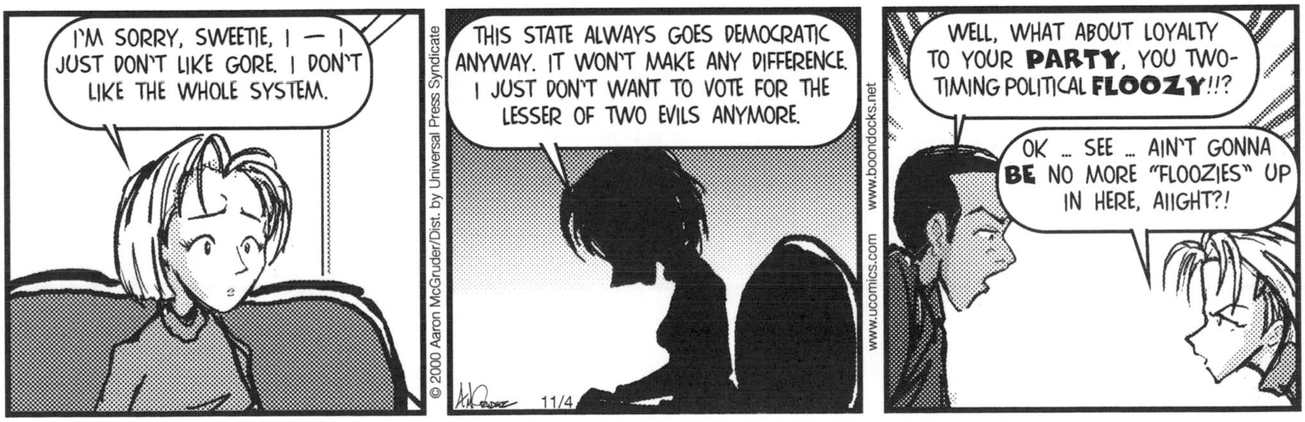
I'M SORRY, SWEETIE, I — I JUST DON'T LIKE GORE. I DON'T LIKE THE WHOLE SYSTEM.
THIS STATE ALWAYS GOES DEMOCRATIC ANYWAY. IT WON'T MAKE ANY DIFFERENCE. I JUST DON'T WANT TO VOTE FOR THE LESSER OF TWO EVILS ANYMORE.
WELL, WHAT ABOUT LOYALTY TO YOUR PARTY, YOU TWO-TIMING POLITICAL FLOOZY!!?
OK ... SEE ... AIN'T GONNA BE NO MORE "FLOOZIES" UP IN HERE, AIIGHT?!
© 2000 Aaron McGruder/Dist. by Universal Press Syndicate
www.ucomics.com www.boondocks.net
11/4

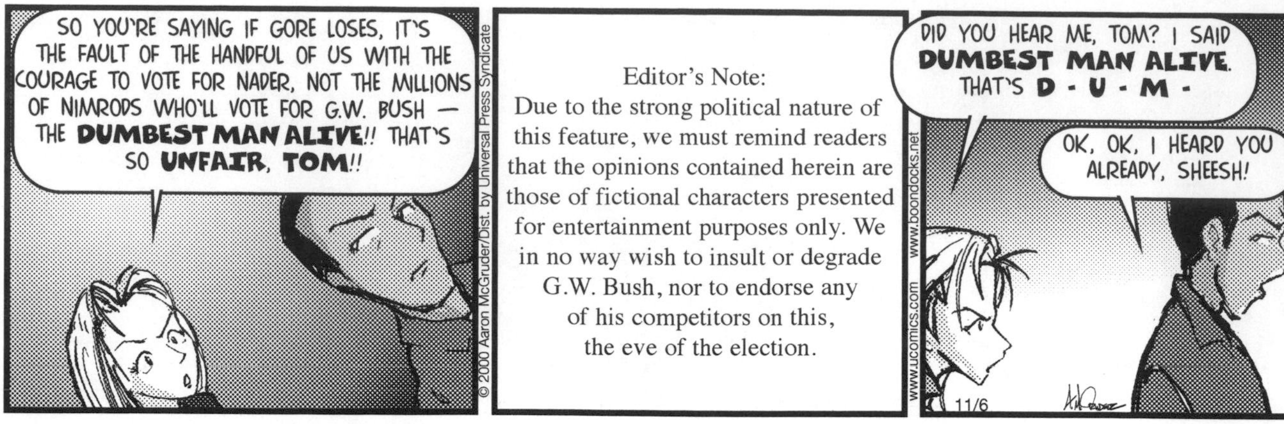
SO YOU'RE SAYING IF GORE LOSES, IT'S THE FAULT OF THE HANDFUL OF US WITH THE COURAGE TO VOTE FOR NADER, NOT THE MILLIONS OF NIMRODS WHO'LL VOTE FOR G.W. BUSH — THE DUMBEST MAN ALIVE!! THAT'S SO UNFAIR, TOM!!
© 2000 Aaron McGruder/Dist. by Universal Press Syndicate
Editor's Note:
Due to the strong political nature of this feature, we must remind readers that the opinions contained herein are those of fictional characters presented for entertainment purposes only. We in no way wish to insult or degrade G.W. Bush, nor to endorse any of his competitors on this, the eve of the election.
www.ucomics.com www.boondocks.net
DID YOU HEAR ME, TOM? I SAID DUMBEST MAN ALIVE. THAT'S D - U - M -
OK, OK, I HEARD YOU ALREADY, SHEESH!
11/6

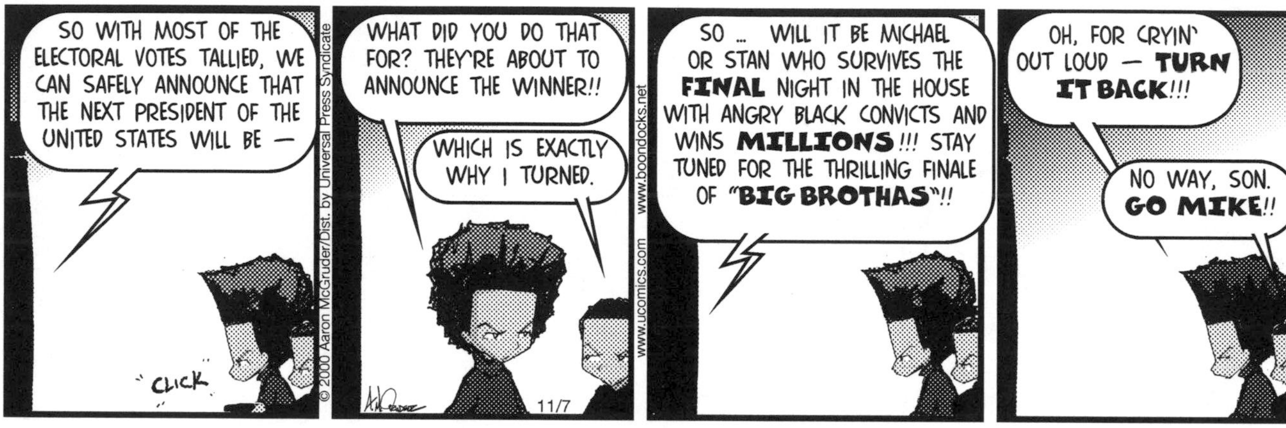
SO WITH MOST OF THE ELECTORAL VOTES TALLIED, WE CAN SAFELY ANNOUNCE THAT THE NEXT PRESIDENT OF THE UNITED STATES WILL BE —
"CLICK"
© 2000 Aaron McGruder/Dist. by Universal Press Syndicate
WHAT DID YOU DO THAT FOR? THEY'RE ABOUT TO ANNOUNCE THE WINNER!!
WHICH IS EXACTLY WHY I TURNED.
11/7
www.ucomics.com www.boondocks.net
SO ... WILL IT BE MICHAEL OR STAN WHO SURVIVES THE FINAL NIGHT IN THE HOUSE WITH ANGRY BLACK CONVICTS AND WINS MILLIONS!!! STAY TUNED FOR THE THRILLING FINALE OF "BIG BROTHAS"!!
OH, FOR CRYIN' OUT LOUD — TURN IT BACK!!!
NO WAY, SON. GO MIKE!!

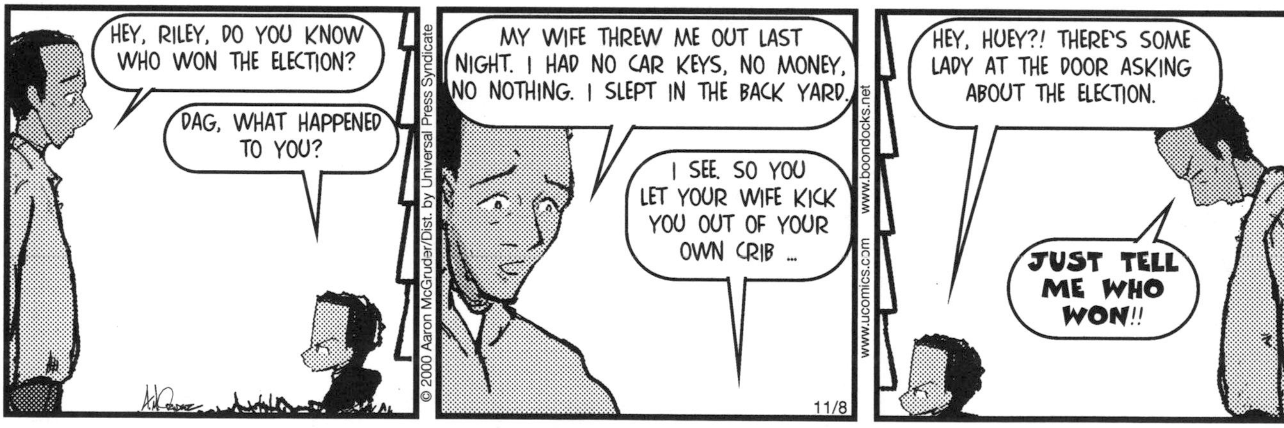
HEY, RILEY, DO YOU KNOW WHO WON THE ELECTION?
DAG, WHAT HAPPENED TO YOU?
© 2000 Aaron McGruder/Dist. by Universal Press Syndicate
MY WIFE THREW ME OUT LAST NIGHT. I HAD NO CAR KEYS, NO MONEY, NO NOTHING. I SLEPT IN THE BACK YARD.
I SEE. SO YOU LET YOUR WIFE KICK YOU OUT OF YOUR OWN CRIB ...
11/8
www.ucomics.com www.boondocks.net
HEY, HUEY?! THERE'S SOME LADY AT THE DOOR ASKING ABOUT THE ELECTION.
JUST TELL ME WHO WON!!

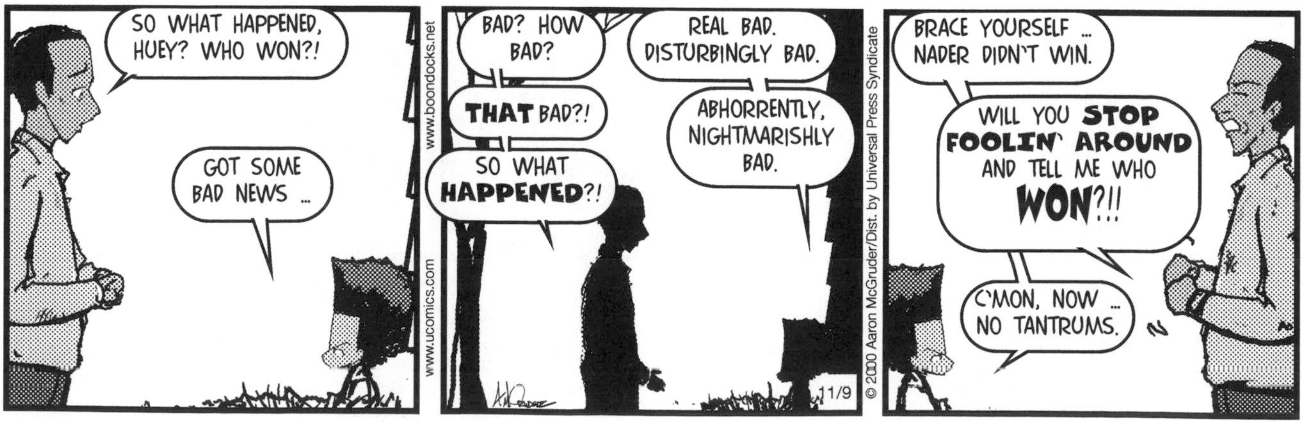
SO WHAT HAPPENED, HUEY? WHO WON?!
GOT SOME BAD NEWS ...
www.ucomics.com www.boondocks.net
BAD? HOW BAD?
REAL BAD. DISTURBINGLY BAD.
THAT BAD?!
ABHORRENTLY, NIGHTMARISHLY BAD.
SO WHAT HAPPENED?!
11/9
© 2000 Aaron McGruder/Dist. by Universal Press Syndicate
BRACE YOURSELF ... NADER DIDN'T WIN.
WILL YOU STOP FOOLIN' AROUND AND TELL ME WHO WON?!!
C'MON, NOW ... NO TANTRUMS.

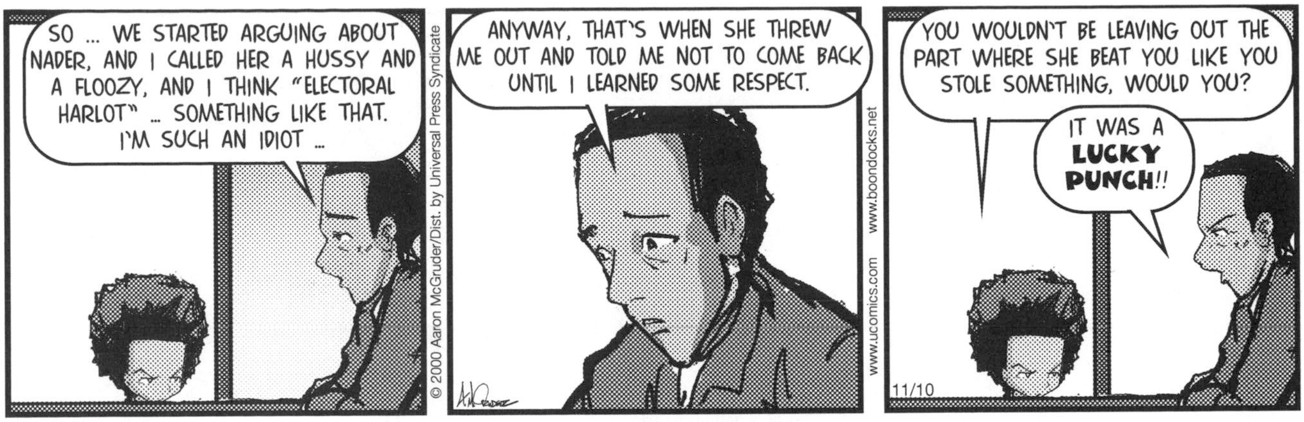
SO ... WE STARTED ARGUING ABOUT NADER, AND I CALLED HER A HUSSY AND A FLOOZY, AND I THINK "ELECTORAL HARLOT" ... SOMETHING LIKE THAT. I'M SUCH AN IDIOT ...
© 2000 Aaron McGruder/Dist. by Universal Press Syndicate
ANYWAY, THAT'S WHEN SHE THREW ME OUT AND TOLD ME NOT TO COME BACK UNTIL I LEARNED SOME RESPECT.
www.ucomics.com www.boondocks.net
YOU WOULDN'T BE LEAVING OUT THE PART WHERE SHE BEAT YOU LIKE YOU STOLE SOMETHING, WOULD YOU?
IT WAS A LUCKY PUNCH!!
11/10

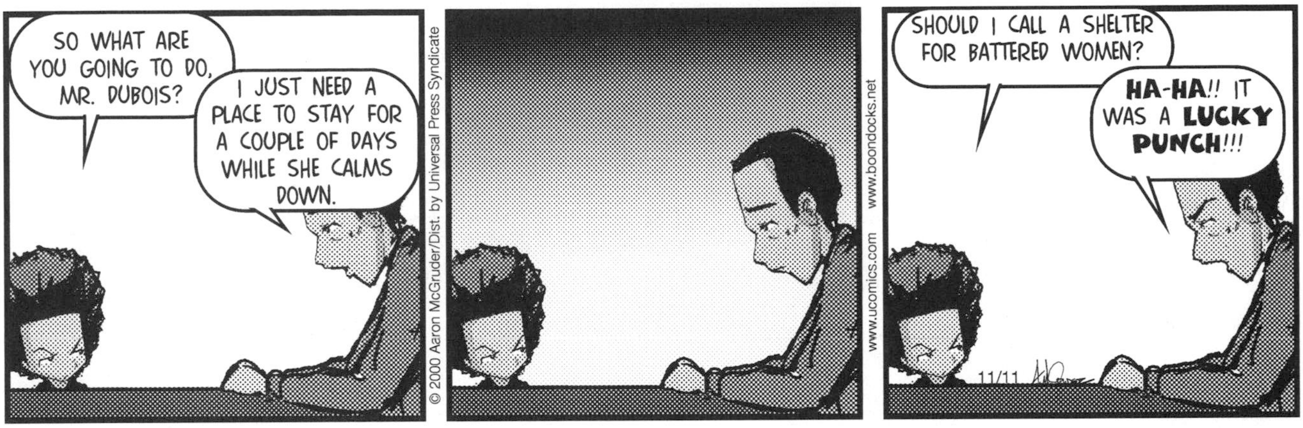
SO WHAT ARE YOU GOING TO DO, MR. DUBOIS?
I JUST NEED A PLACE TO STAY FOR A COUPLE OF DAYS WHILE SHE CALMS DOWN.
© 2000 Aaron McGruder/Dist. by Universal Press Syndicate
www.ucomics.com www.boondocks.net
SHOULD I CALL A SHELTER FOR BATTERED WOMEN?
HA-HA!! IT WAS A LUCKY PUNCH!!!
11/11

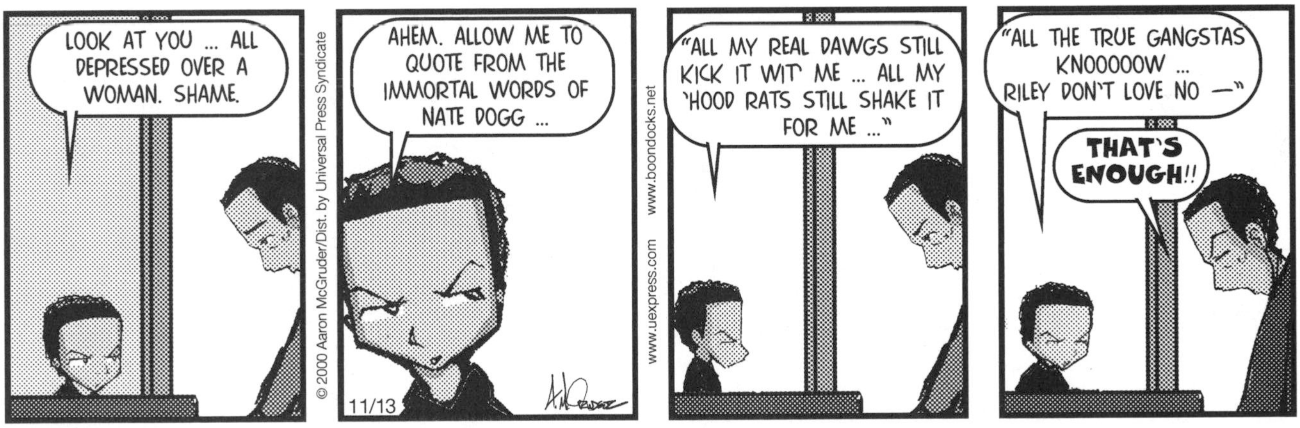
LOOK AT YOU ... ALL DEPRESSED OVER A WOMAN. SHAME.
© 2000 Aaron McGruder/Dist. by Universal Press Syndicate
AHEM. ALLOW ME TO QUOTE FROM THE IMMORTAL WORDS OF NATE DOGG ...
11/13
www.uexpress.com www.boondocks.net
"ALL MY REAL DAWGS STILL KICK IT WIT' ME ... ALL MY 'HOOD RATS STILL SHAKE IT FOR ME ..."
"ALL THE TRUE GANGSTAS KNOOOOOW ... RILEY DON'T LOVE NO —"
THAT'S ENOUGH!!

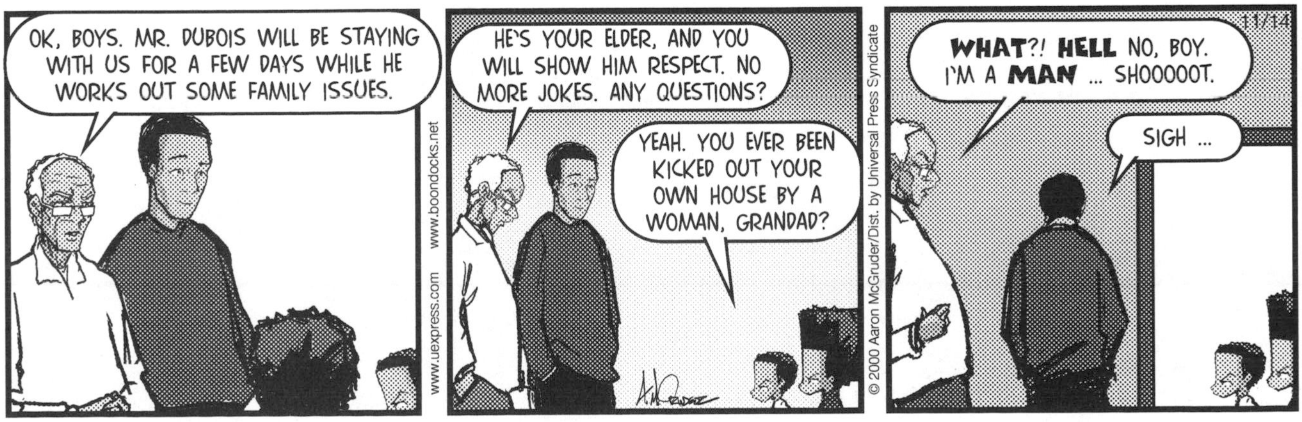
OK, BOYS. MR. DUBOIS WILL BE STAYING WITH US FOR A FEW DAYS WHILE HE WORKS OUT SOME FAMILY ISSUES.
www.uexpress.com www.boondocks.net
HE'S YOUR ELDER, AND YOU WILL SHOW HIM RESPECT. NO MORE JOKES. ANY QUESTIONS?
YEAH. YOU EVER BEEN KICKED OUT YOUR OWN HOUSE BY A WOMAN, GRANDAD?
© 2000 Aaron McGruder/Dist. by Universal Press Syndicate
11/14
WHAT?! HELL NO, BOY. I'M A MAN ... SHOOOOOT.
SIGH ...

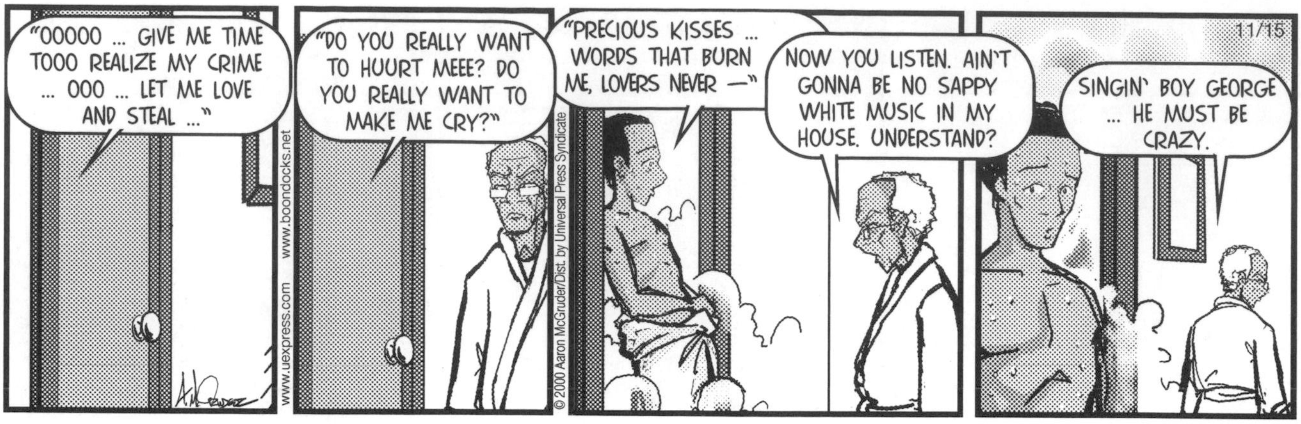
"OOOOO ... GIVE ME TIME TOOO REALIZE MY CRIME ... OOO ... LET ME LOVE AND STEAL ..."
www.uexpress.com www.boondocks.net
"DO YOU REALLY WANT TO HUURT MEEE? DO YOU REALLY WANT TO MAKE ME CRY?"
© 2000 Aaron McGruder/Dist. by Universal Press Syndicate
"PRECIOUS KISSES ... WORDS THAT BURN ME, LOVERS NEVER —"
NOW YOU LISTEN. AIN'T GONNA BE NO SAPPY WHITE MUSIC IN MY HOUSE. UNDERSTAND?
11/15
SINGIN' BOY GEORGE ... HE MUST BE CRAZY.

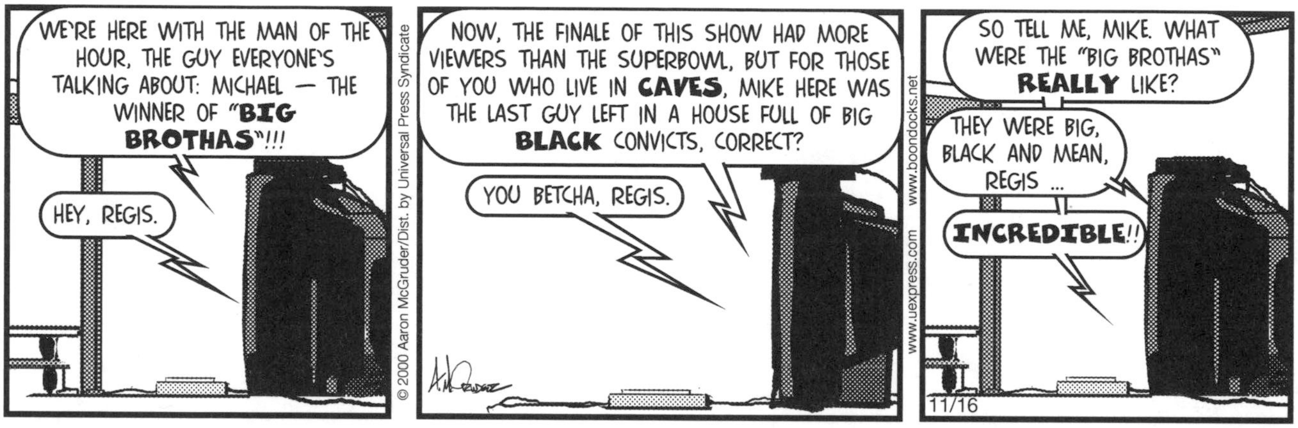
WE'RE HERE WITH THE MAN OF THE HOUR, THE GUY EVERYONE'S TALKING ABOUT: MICHAEL — THE WINNER OF "BIG BROTHAS"!!!
HEY, REGIS.
© 2000 Aaron McGruder/Dist. by Universal Press Syndicate
NOW, THE FINALE OF THIS SHOW HAD MORE VIEWERS THAN THE SUPERBOWL, BUT FOR THOSE OF YOU WHO LIVE IN CAVES, MIKE HERE WAS THE LAST GUY LEFT IN A HOUSE FULL OF BIG BLACK CONVICTS, CORRECT?
YOU BETCHA, REGIS.
www.uexpress.com www.boondocks.net
SO TELL ME, MIKE. WHAT WERE THE "BIG BROTHAS" REALLY LIKE?
THEY WERE BIG, BLACK AND MEAN, REGIS ...
INCREDIBLE!!
11/16

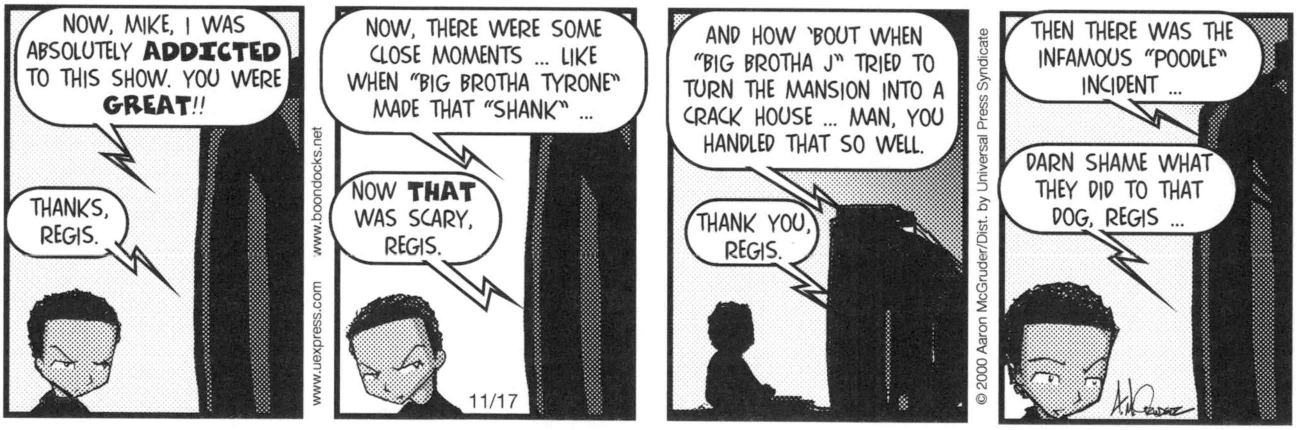
NOW, MIKE, I WAS ABSOLUTELY ADDICTED TO THIS SHOW. YOU WERE GREAT!!
THANKS, REGIS.
www.uexpress.com www.boondocks.net
NOW, THERE WERE SOME CLOSE MOMENTS ... LIKE WHEN "BIG BROTHA TYRONE" MADE THAT "SHANK" ...
NOW THAT WAS SCARY, REGIS.
11/17
AND HOW 'BOUT WHEN "BIG BROTHA J" TRIED TO TURN THE MANSION INTO A CRACK HOUSE ... MAN, YOU HANDLED THAT SO WELL.
THANK YOU, REGIS.
© 2000 Aaron McGruder/Dist. by Universal Press Syndicate
THEN THERE WAS THE INFAMOUS "POODLE" INCIDENT ...
DARN SHAME WHAT THEY DID TO THAT DOG, REGIS ...

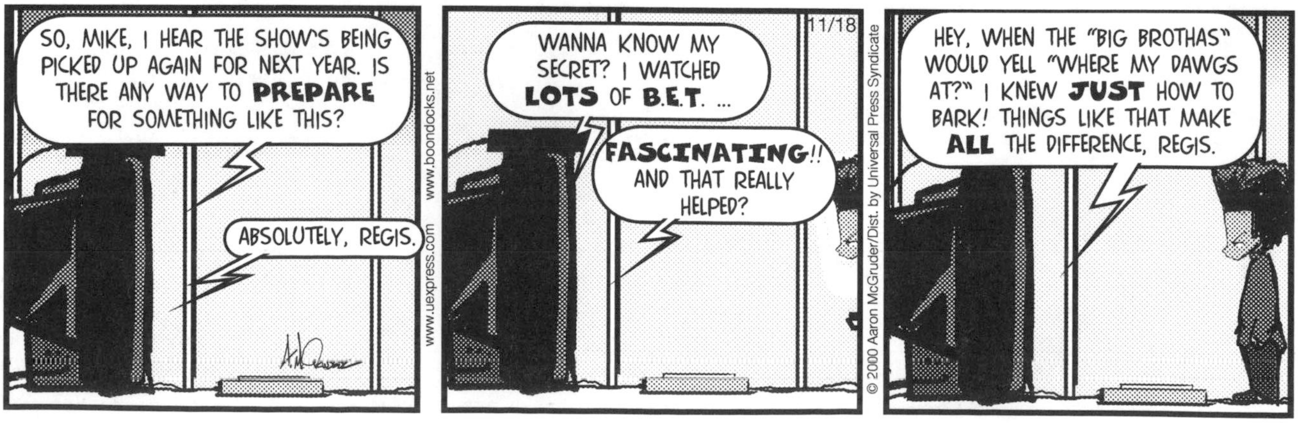
SO, MIKE, I HEAR THE SHOW'S BEING PICKED UP AGAIN FOR NEXT YEAR. IS THERE ANY WAY TO PREPARE FOR SOMETHING LIKE THIS?
ABSOLUTELY, REGIS.
www.uexpress.com www.boondocks.net
11/18
WANNA KNOW MY SECRET? I WATCHED LOTS OF B.E.T. ...
FASCINATING!! AND THAT REALLY HELPED?
© 2000 Aaron McGruder/Dist. by Universal Press Syndicate
HEY, WHEN THE "BIG BROTHAS" WOULD YELL "WHERE MY DAWGS AT?" I KNEW JUST HOW TO BARK! THINGS LIKE THAT MAKE ALL THE DIFFERENCE, REGIS.

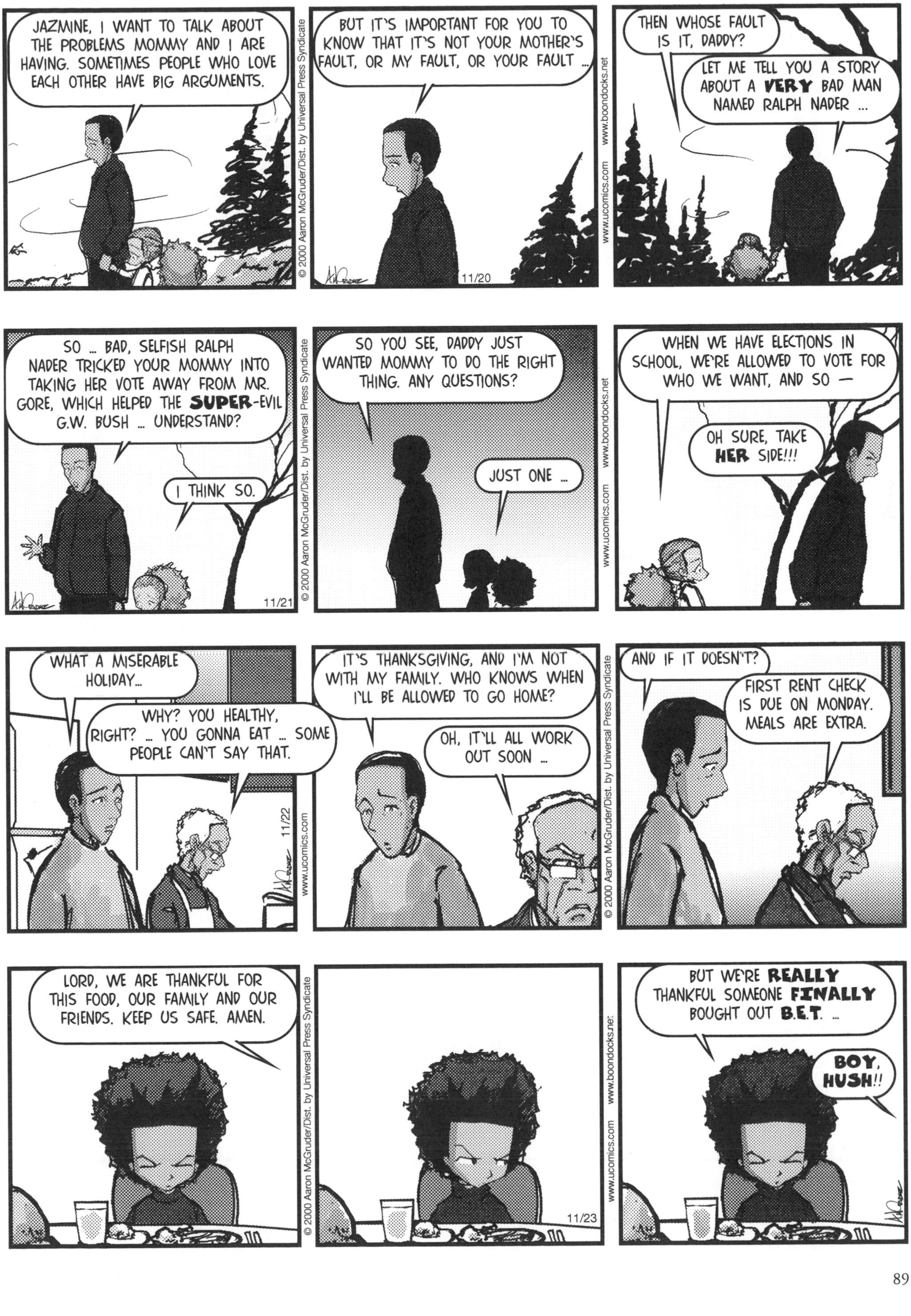
JAZMINE, I WANT TO TALK ABOUT THE PROBLEMS MOMMY AND I ARE HAVING. SOMETIMES PEOPLE WHO LOVE EACH OTHER HAVE BIG ARGUMENTS.
BUT IT'S IMPORTANT FOR YOU TO KNOW THAT IT'S NOT YOUR MOTHER'S FAULT, OR MY FAULT, OR YOUR FAULT ...
THEN WHOSE FAULT IS IT, DADDY?
LET ME TELL YOU A STORY ABOUT A VERY BAD MAN NAMED RALPH NADER ...
11/20
© 2000 Aaron McGruder/Dist. by Universal Press Syndicate
www.ucomics.com www.boondocks.net
SO ... BAD, SELFISH RALPH NADER TRICKED YOUR MOMMY INTO TAKING HER VOTE AWAY FROM MR. GORE, WHICH HELPED THE SUPER-EVIL G.W. BUSH ... UNDERSTAND?
I THINK SO.
SO YOU SEE, DADDY JUST WANTED MOMMY TO DO THE RIGHT THING. ANY QUESTIONS?
JUST ONE ...
WHEN WE HAVE ELECTIONS IN SCHOOL, WE'RE ALLOWED TO VOTE FOR WHO WE WANT, AND SO —
OH SURE, TAKE HER SIDE!!!
11/21
© 2000 Aaron McGruder/Dist. by Universal Press Syndicate
www.ucomics.com www.boondocks.net
WHAT A MISERABLE HOLIDAY...
WHY? YOU HEALTHY, RIGHT? ... YOU GONNA EAT ... SOME PEOPLE CAN'T SAY THAT.
IT'S THANKSGIVING, AND I'M NOT WITH MY FAMILY. WHO KNOWS WHEN I'LL BE ALLOWED TO GO HOME?
OH, IT'LL ALL WORK OUT SOON ...
AND IF IT DOESN'T?
FIRST RENT CHECK IS DUE ON MONDAY. MEALS ARE EXTRA.
11/22
www.ucomics.com
© 2000 Aaron McGruder/Dist. by Universal Press Syndicate
LORD, WE ARE THANKFUL FOR THIS FOOD, OUR FAMILY AND OUR FRIENDS. KEEP US SAFE. AMEN.
BUT WE'RE REALLY THANKFUL SOMEONE FINALLY BOUGHT OUT B.E.T. ...
BOY, HUSH!!
11/23
© 2000 Aaron McGruder/Dist. by Universal Press Syndicate
www.ucomics.com www.boondocks.net

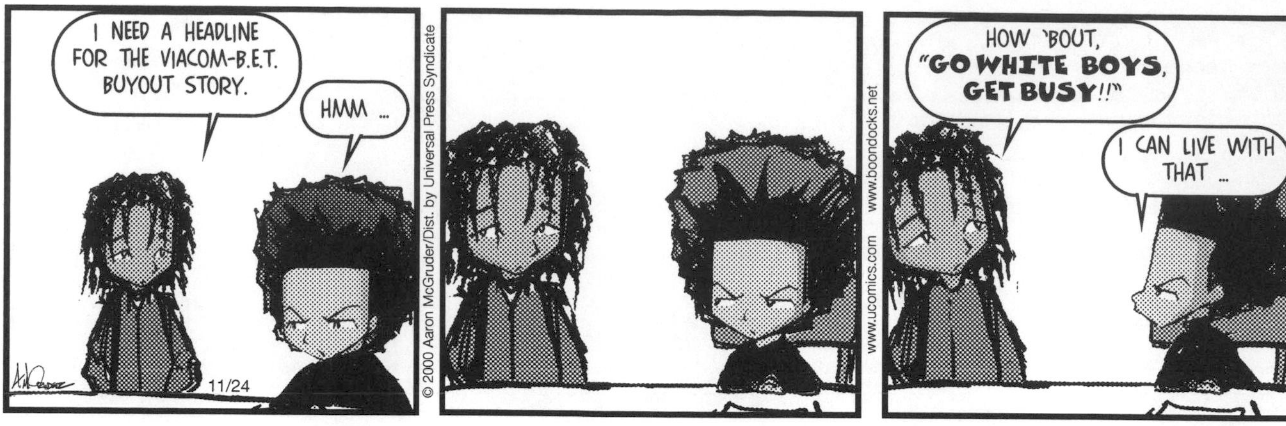
I NEED A HEADLINE FOR THE VIACOM-B.E.T. BUYOUT STORY.
HMM ...
HOW 'BOUT, "GO WHITE BOYS, GET BUSY!!"
I CAN LIVE WITH THAT ...
11/24
© 2000 Aaron McGruder/Dist. by Universal Press Syndicate
www.ucomics.com www.boondocks.net

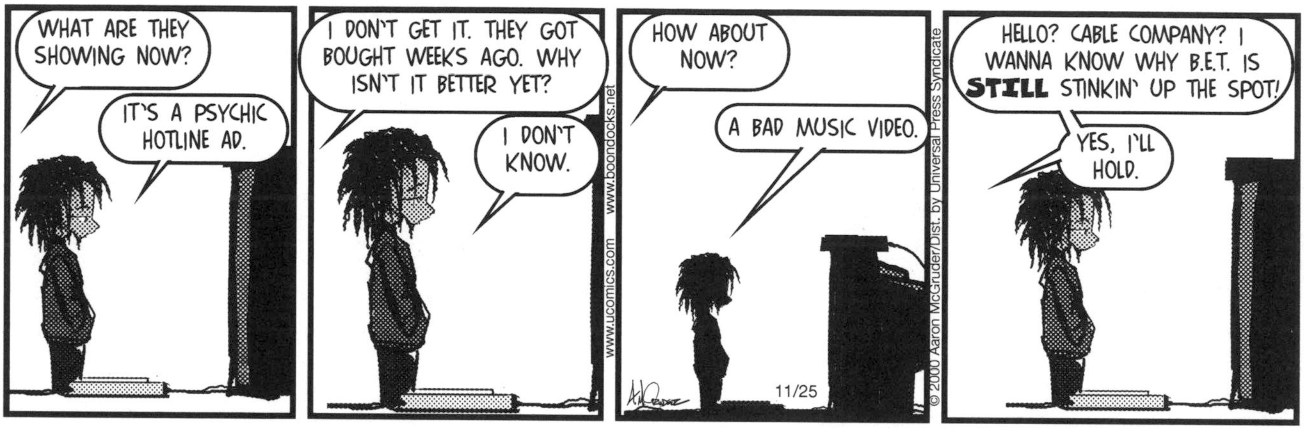
WHAT ARE THEY SHOWING NOW?
IT'S A PSYCHIC HOTLINE AD.
I DON'T GET IT. THEY GOT BOUGHT WEEKS AGO. WHY ISN'T IT BETTER YET?
I DON'T KNOW.
HOW ABOUT NOW?
A BAD MUSIC VIDEO.
HELLO? CABLE COMPANY? I WANNA KNOW WHY B.E.T. IS STILL STINKIN' UP THE SPOT!
YES, I'LL HOLD.
11/25
www.ucomics.com www.boondocks.net
© 2000 Aaron McGruder/Dist. by Universal Press Syndicate

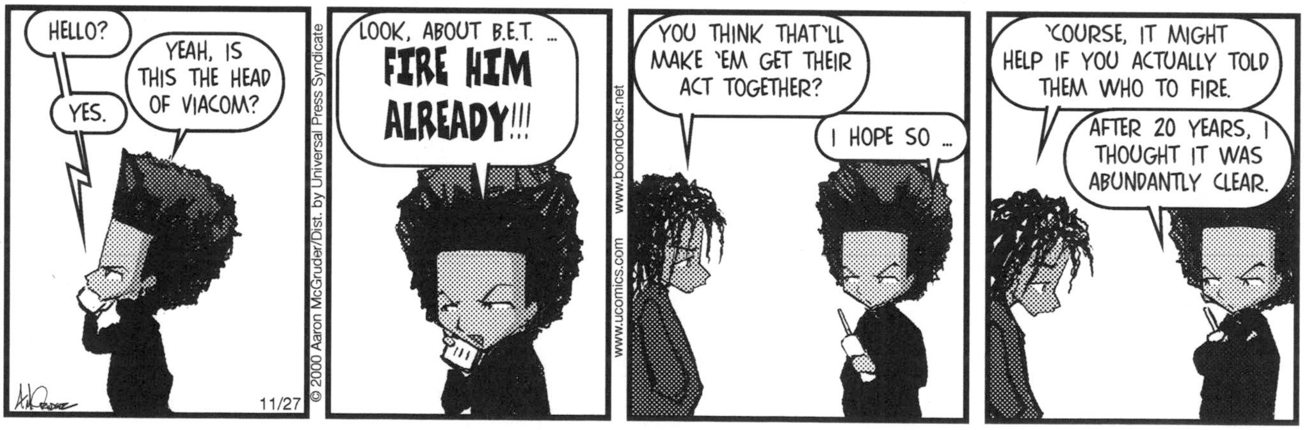
HELLO?
YES.
YEAH, IS THIS THE HEAD OF VIACOM?
LOOK, ABOUT B.E.T. ... FIRE HIM ALREADY!!!
YOU THINK THAT'LL MAKE 'EM GET THEIR ACT TOGETHER?
I HOPE SO ...
'COURSE, IT MIGHT HELP IF YOU ACTUALLY TOLD THEM WHO TO FIRE.
AFTER 20 YEARS, I THOUGHT IT WAS ABUNDANTLY CLEAR.
11/27
© 2000 Aaron McGruder/Dist. by Universal Press Syndicate
www.ucomics.com www.boondocks.net

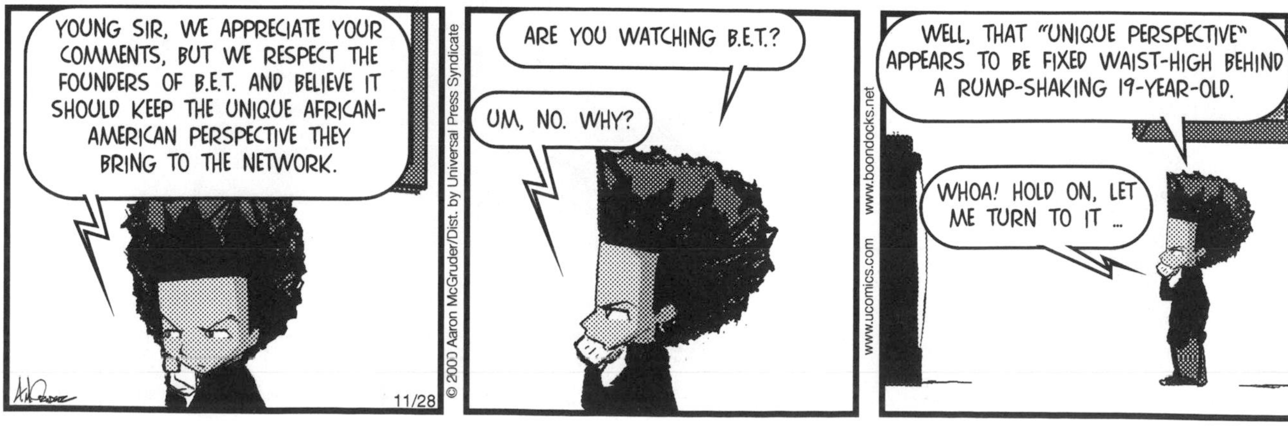
YOUNG SIR, WE APPRECIATE YOUR COMMENTS, BUT WE RESPECT THE FOUNDERS OF B.E.T. AND BELIEVE IT SHOULD KEEP THE UNIQUE AFRICAN-AMERICAN PERSPECTIVE THEY BRING TO THE NETWORK.
ARE YOU WATCHING B.E.T.?
UM, NO. WHY?
WELL, THAT "UNIQUE PERSPECTIVE" APPEARS TO BE FIXED WAIST-HIGH BEHIND A RUMP-SHAKING 19-YEAR-OLD.
WHOA! HOLD ON, LET ME TURN TO IT ...
11/28
© 2000 Aaron McGruder/Dist. by Universal Press Syndicate
www.ucomics.com www.boondocks.net

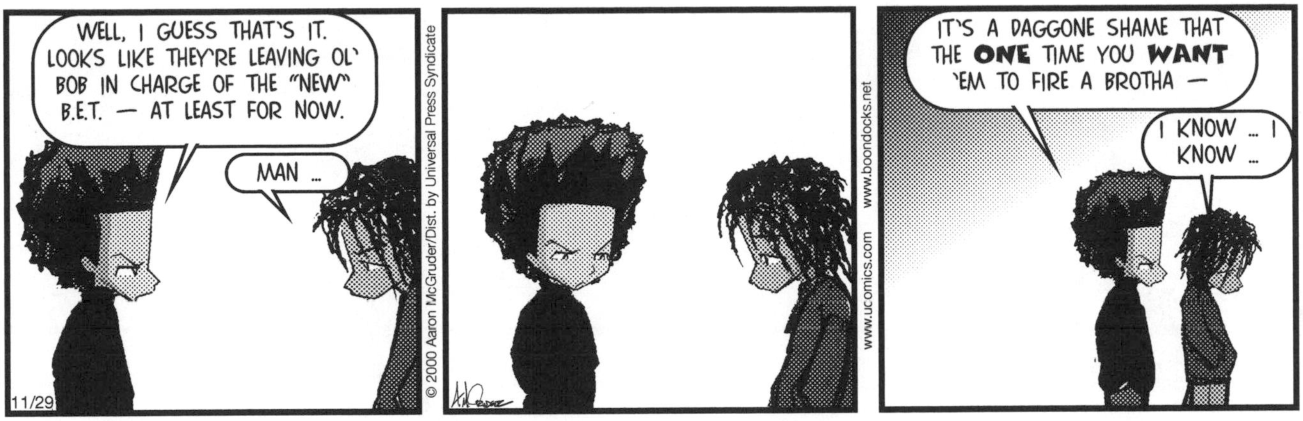
WELL, I GUESS THAT'S IT. LOOKS LIKE THEY'RE LEAVING OL' BOB IN CHARGE OF THE "NEW" B.E.T. — AT LEAST FOR NOW.
MAN ...
IT'S A DAGGONE SHAME THAT THE ONE TIME YOU WANT 'EM TO FIRE A BROTHA —
I KNOW ... I KNOW ...
11/29
© 2000 Aaron McGruder/Dist. by Universal Press Syndicate
www.ucomics.com www.boondocks.net

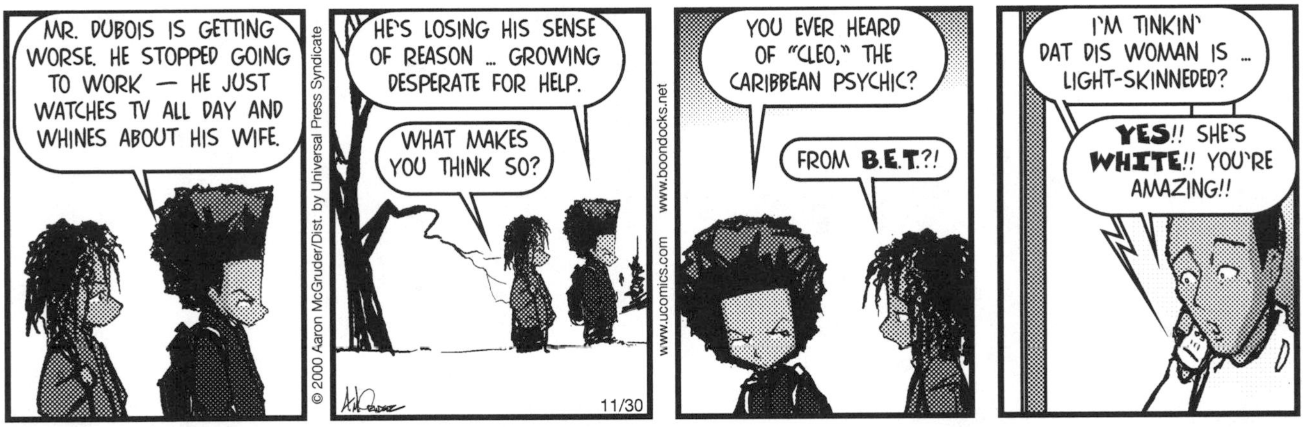
MR. DUBOIS IS GETTING WORSE. HE STOPPED GOING TO WORK — HE JUST WATCHES TV ALL DAY AND WHINES ABOUT HIS WIFE.
HE'S LOSING HIS SENSE OF REASON ... GROWING DESPERATE FOR HELP.
WHAT MAKES YOU THINK SO?
YOU EVER HEARD OF "CLEO," THE CARIBBEAN PSYCHIC?
FROM B.E.T.?!
I'M TINKIN' DAT DIS WOMAN IS ... LIGHT-SKINNEDED?
YES!! SHE'S WHITE!! YOU'RE AMAZING!!
11/30
© 2000 Aaron McGruder/Dist. by Universal Press Syndicate
www.ucomics.com www.boondocks.net

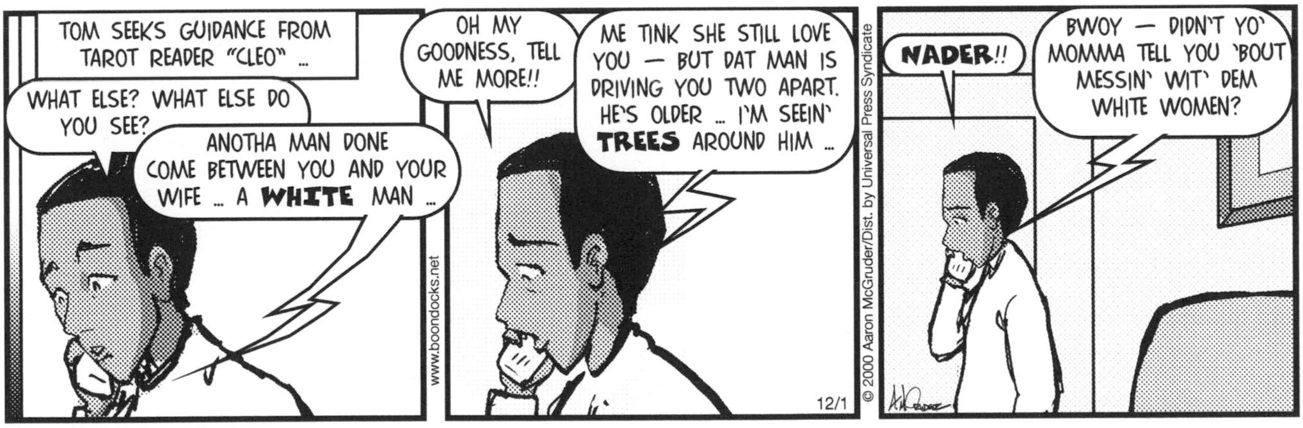
TOM SEEKS GUIDANCE FROM TAROT READER "CLEO" ...
WHAT ELSE? WHAT ELSE DO YOU SEE?
ANOTHA MAN DONE COME BETWEEN YOU AND YOUR WIFE ... A WHITE MAN ...
OH MY GOODNESS, TELL ME MORE!!
ME TINK SHE STILL LOVE YOU — BUT DAT MAN IS DRIVING YOU TWO APART. HE'S OLDER ... I'M SEEIN' TREES AROUND HIM ...
NADER!!
BWOY — DIDN'T YO' MOMMA TELL YOU 'BOUT MESSIN' WIT' DEM WHITE WOMEN?
12/1
www.boondocks.net
© 2000 Aaron McGruder/Dist. by Universal Press Syndicate

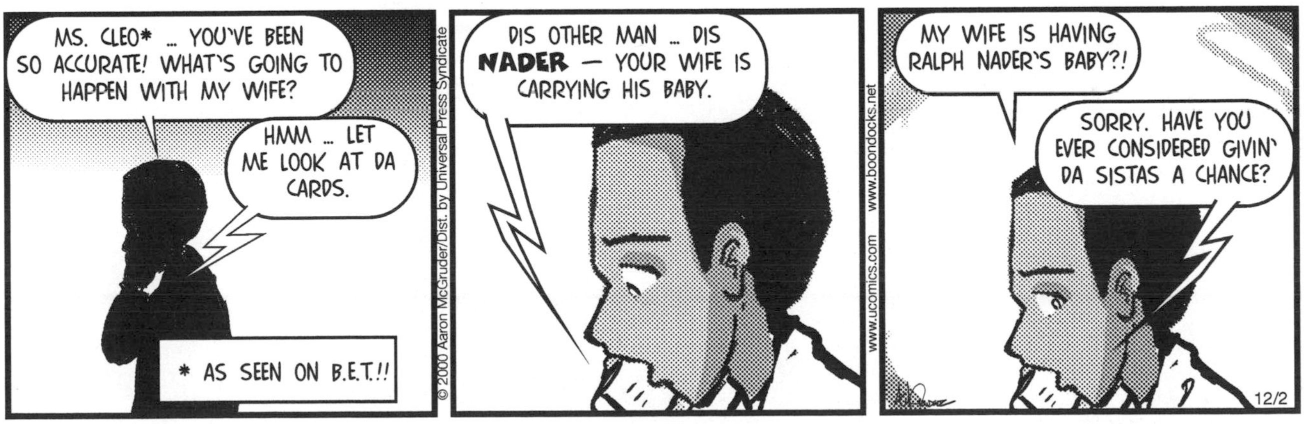
MS. CLEO* ... YOU'VE BEEN SO ACCURATE! WHAT'S GOING TO HAPPEN WITH MY WIFE?
HMM ... LET ME LOOK AT DA CARDS.
* AS SEEN ON B.E.T.!!
DIS OTHER MAN ... DIS NADER — YOUR WIFE IS CARRYING HIS BABY.
MY WIFE IS HAVING RALPH NADER'S BABY?!
SORRY. HAVE YOU EVER CONSIDERED GIVIN' DA SISTAS A CHANCE?
12/2
© 2000 Aaron McGruder/Dist. by Universal Press Syndicate
www.ucomics.com www.boondocks.net

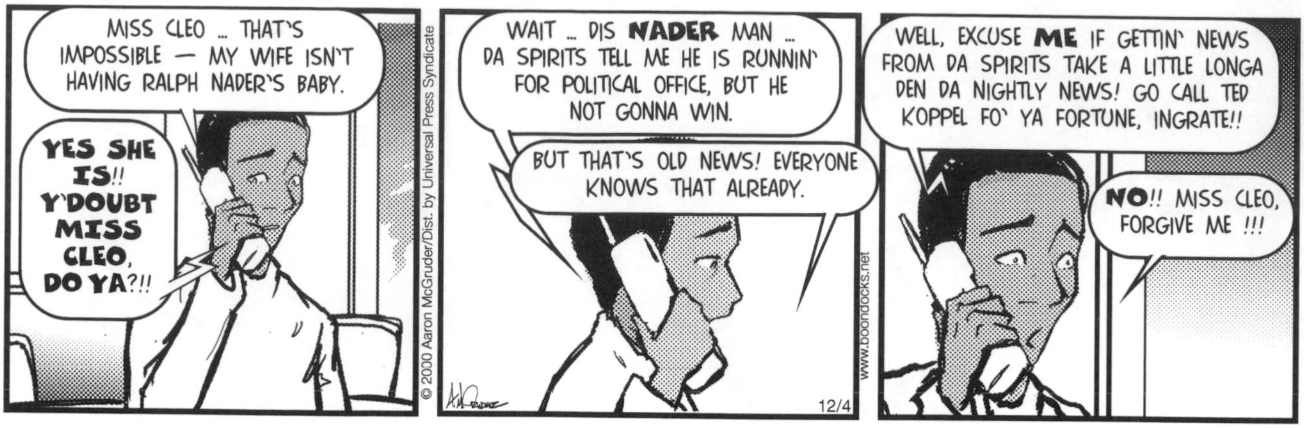
MISS CLEO ... THAT'S IMPOSSIBLE — MY WIFE ISN'T HAVING RALPH NADER'S BABY.
YES SHE IS!! Y'DOUBT MISS CLEO, DO YA?!!
WAIT ... DIS NADER MAN ... DA SPIRITS TELL ME HE IS RUNNIN' FOR POLITICAL OFFICE, BUT HE NOT GONNA WIN.
BUT THAT'S OLD NEWS! EVERYONE KNOWS THAT ALREADY.
WELL, EXCUSE ME IF GETTIN' NEWS FROM DA SPIRITS TAKE A LITTLE LONGA DEN DA NIGHTLY NEWS! GO CALL TED KOPPEL FO' YA FORTUNE, INGRATE!!
NO!! MISS CLEO, FORGIVE ME !!!
© 2000 Aaron McGruder/Dist. by Universal Press Syndicate
www.boondocks.net
12/4

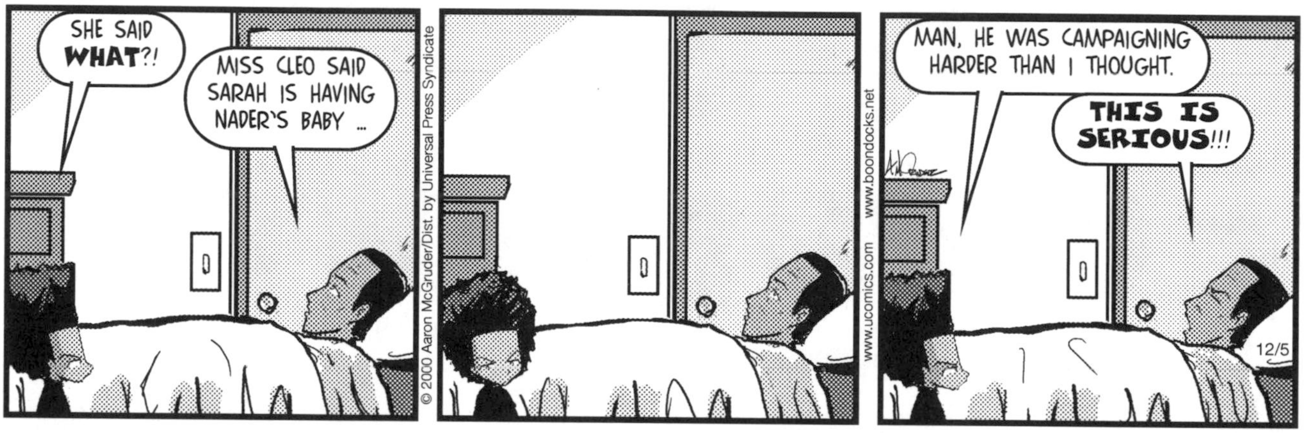
SHE SAID WHAT?!
MISS CLEO SAID SARAH IS HAVING NADER'S BABY ...
MAN, HE WAS CAMPAIGNING HARDER THAN I THOUGHT.
THIS IS SERIOUS!!!
© 2000 Aaron McGruder/Dist. by Universal Press Syndicate
www.ucomics.com www.boondocks.net
12/5

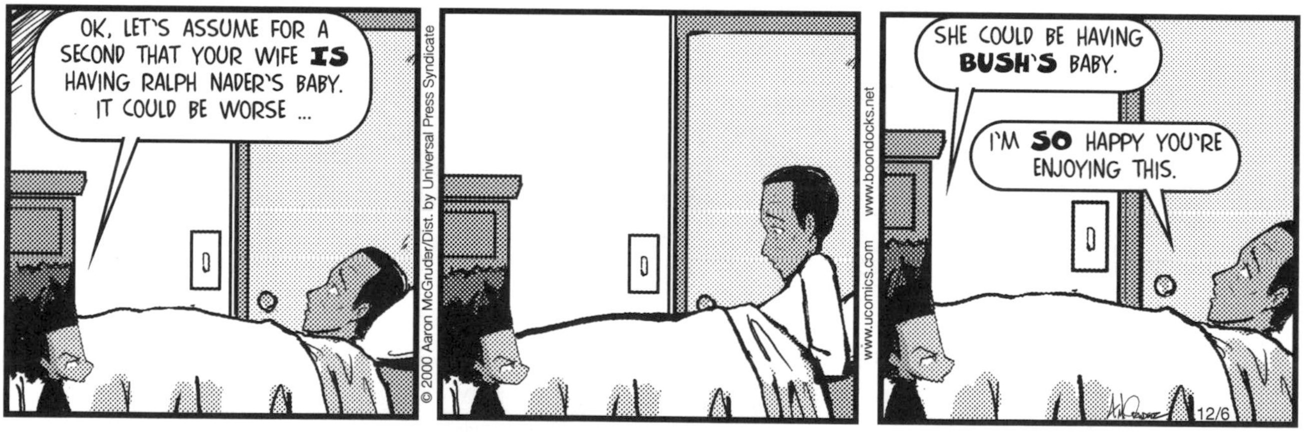
OK, LET'S ASSUME FOR A SECOND THAT YOUR WIFE IS HAVING RALPH NADER'S BABY. IT COULD BE WORSE ...
SHE COULD BE HAVING BUSH'S BABY.
I'M SO HAPPY YOU'RE ENJOYING THIS.
© 2000 Aaron McGruder/Dist. by Universal Press Syndicate
www.ucomics.com www.boondocks.net
12/6

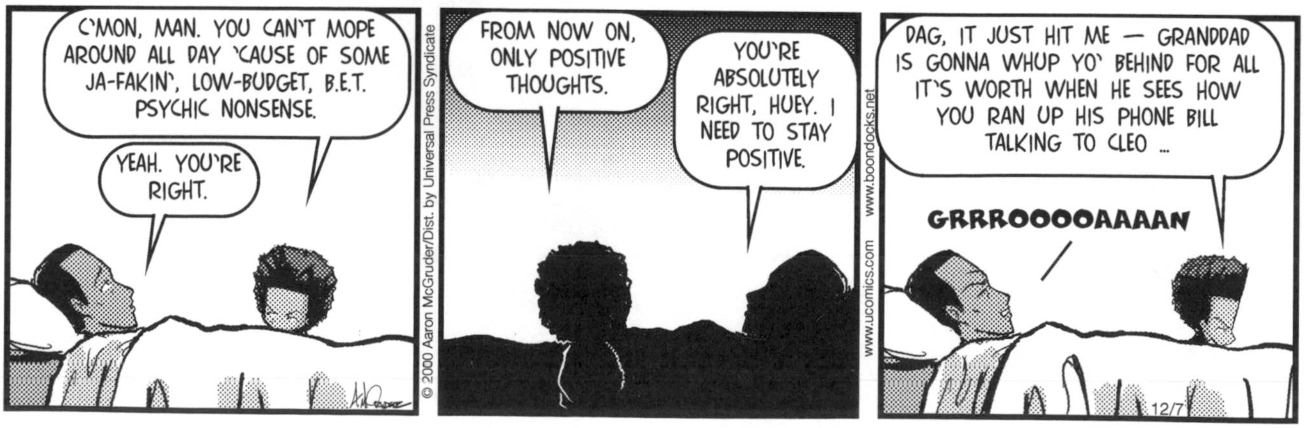
C'MON, MAN. YOU CAN'T MOPE AROUND ALL DAY 'CAUSE OF SOME JA-FAKIN', LOW-BUDGET, B.E.T. PSYCHIC NONSENSE.
YEAH. YOU'RE RIGHT.
FROM NOW ON, ONLY POSITIVE THOUGHTS.
YOU'RE ABSOLUTELY RIGHT, HUEY. I NEED TO STAY POSITIVE.
DAG, IT JUST HIT ME — GRANDDAD IS GONNA WHUP YO' BEHIND FOR ALL IT'S WORTH WHEN HE SEES HOW YOU RAN UP HIS PHONE BILL TALKING TO CLEO ...
GRRROOOOAAAAN
© 2000 Aaron McGruder/Dist. by Universal Press Syndicate
www.ucomics.com www.boondocks.net
12/7

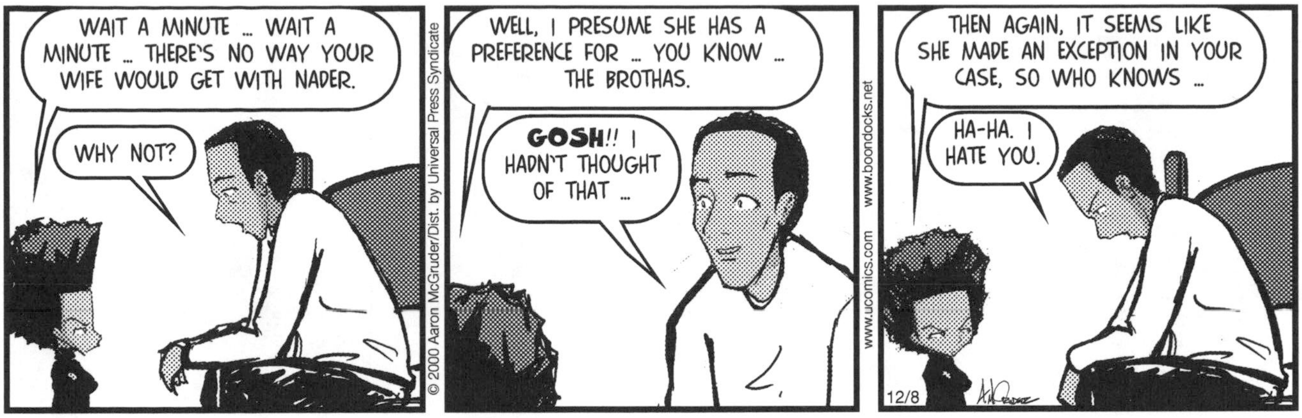
WAIT A MINUTE ... WAIT A MINUTE ... THERE'S NO WAY YOUR WIFE WOULD GET WITH NADER.
WHY NOT?
© 2000 Aaron McGruder/Dist. by Universal Press Syndicate
WELL, I PRESUME SHE HAS A PREFERENCE FOR ... YOU KNOW ... THE BROTHAS.
GOSH!! I HADN'T THOUGHT OF THAT ...
www.ucomics.com www.boondocks.net
THEN AGAIN, IT SEEMS LIKE SHE MADE AN EXCEPTION IN YOUR CASE, SO WHO KNOWS ...
HA-HA. I HATE YOU.
12/8

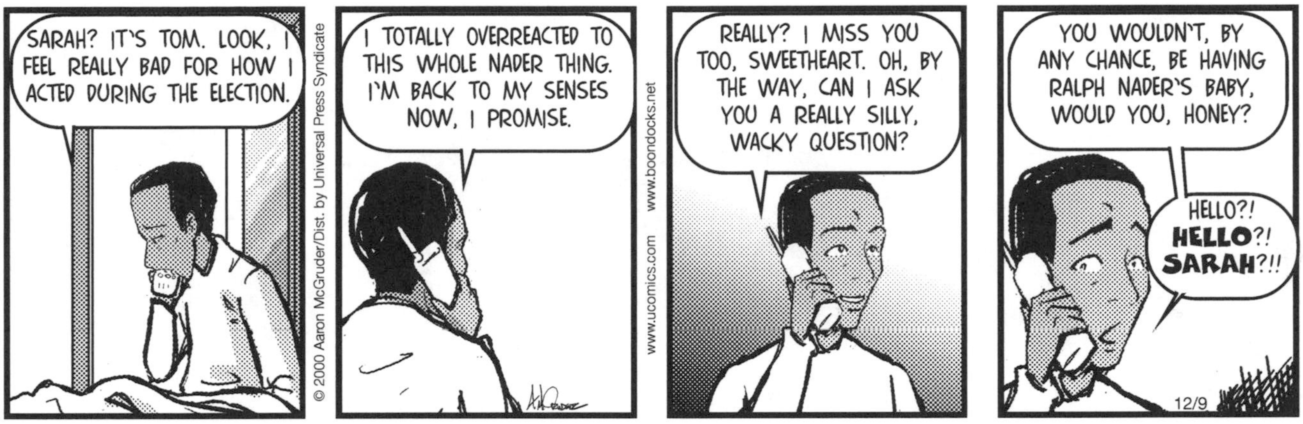
SARAH? IT'S TOM. LOOK, I FEEL REALLY BAD FOR HOW I ACTED DURING THE ELECTION.
© 2000 Aaron McGruder/Dist. by Universal Press Syndicate
I TOTALLY OVERREACTED TO THIS WHOLE NADER THING. I'M BACK TO MY SENSES NOW, I PROMISE.
www.ucomics.com www.boondocks.net
REALLY? I MISS YOU TOO, SWEETHEART. OH, BY THE WAY, CAN I ASK YOU A REALLY SILLY, WACKY QUESTION?
YOU WOULDN'T, BY ANY CHANCE, BE HAVING RALPH NADER'S BABY, WOULD YOU, HONEY?
HELLO?! HELLO?! SARAH?!!
12/9

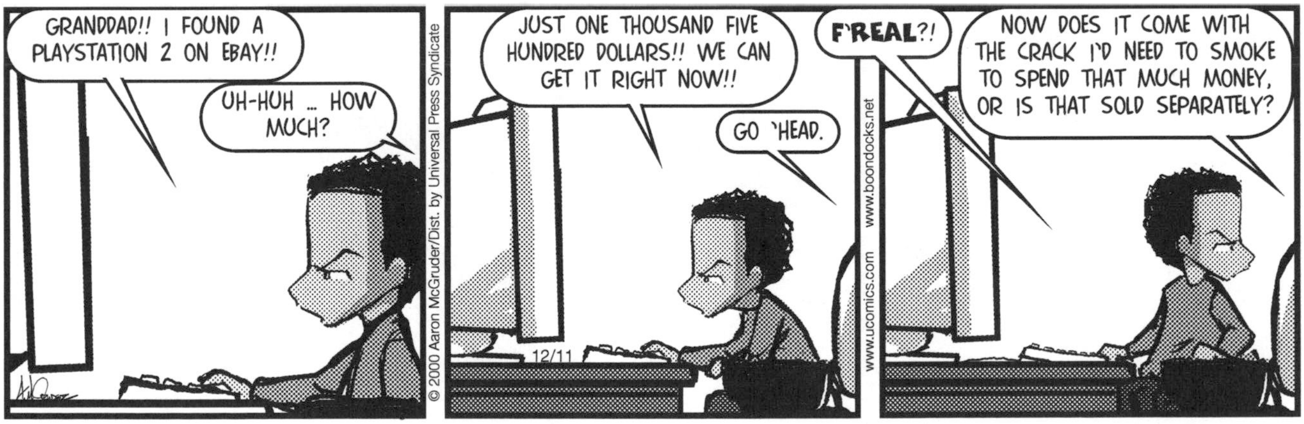
GRANDDAD!! I FOUND A PLAYSTATION 2 ON EBAY!!
UH-HUH ... HOW MUCH?
© 2000 Aaron McGruder/Dist. by Universal Press Syndicate
JUST ONE THOUSAND FIVE HUNDRED DOLLARS!! WE CAN GET IT RIGHT NOW!!
GO 'HEAD.
12/11
www.ucomics.com www.boondocks.net
F'REAL?!
NOW DOES IT COME WITH THE CRACK I'D NEED TO SMOKE TO SPEND THAT MUCH MONEY, OR IS THAT SOLD SEPARATELY?

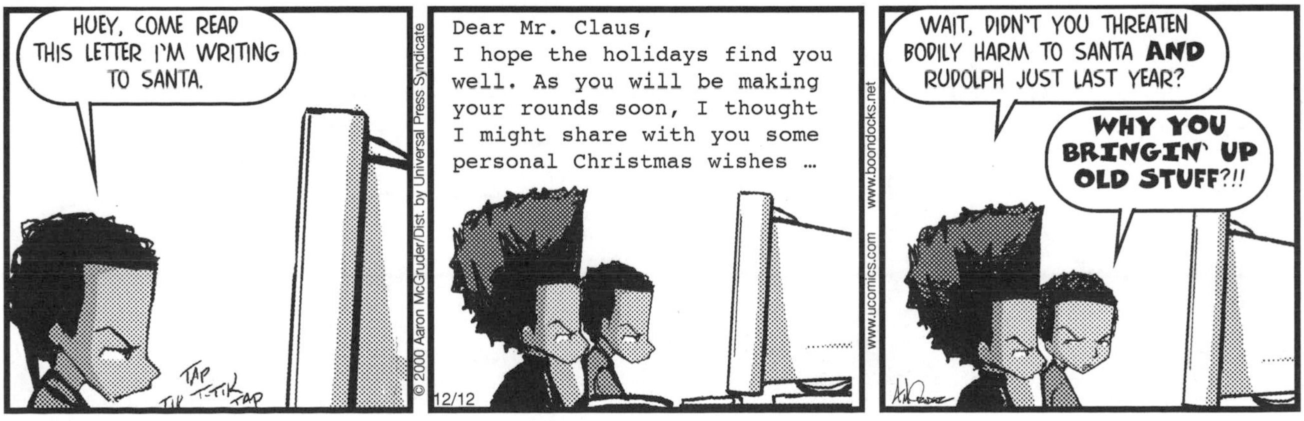
HUEY, COME READ THIS LETTER I'M WRITING TO SANTA.
TAP TIK T-TIK TAP
© 2000 Aaron McGruder/Dist. by Universal Press Syndicate
Dear Mr. Claus,
I hope the holidays find you well. As you will be making your rounds soon, I thought I might share with you some personal Christmas wishes ...
12/12
www.ucomics.com www.boondocks.net
WAIT, DIDN'T YOU THREATEN BODILY HARM TO SANTA AND RUDOLPH JUST LAST YEAR?
WHY YOU BRINGIN' UP OLD STUFF?!!

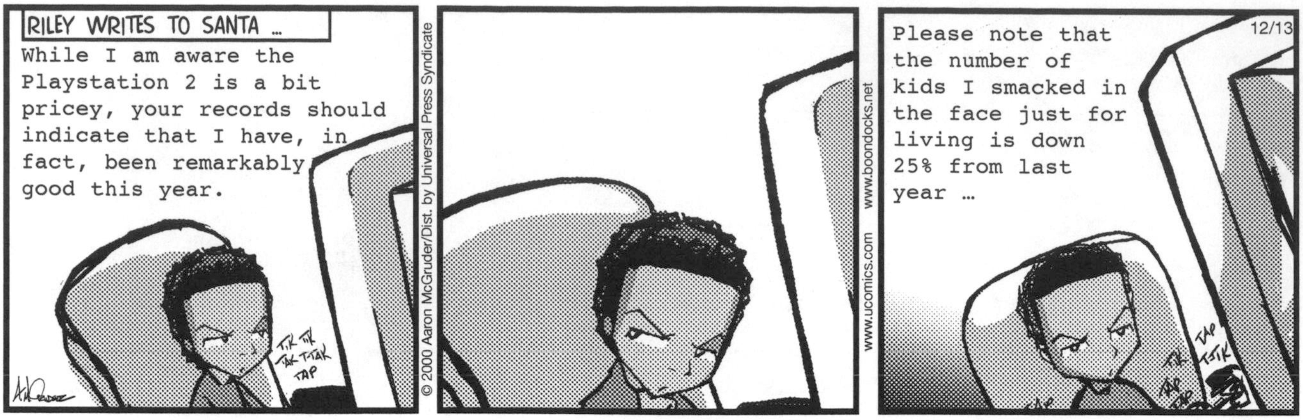
RILEY WRITES TO SANTA ...
While I am aware the Playstation 2 is a bit pricey, your records should indicate that I have, in fact, been remarkably good this year.
© 2000 Aaron McGruder/Dist. by Universal Press Syndicate
www.ucomics.com www.boondocks.net
Please note that the number of kids I smacked in the face just for living is down 25% from last year ...
12/13

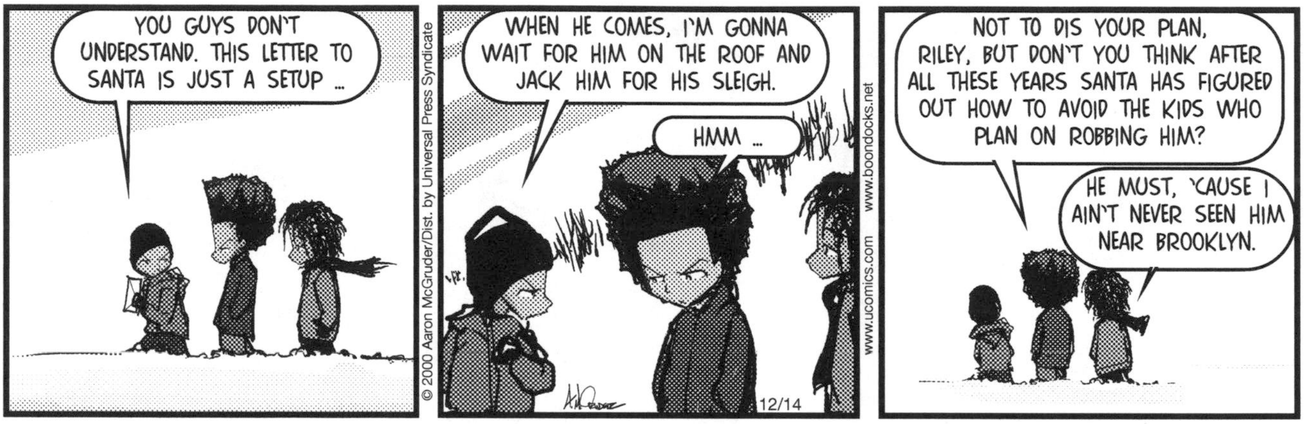
YOU GUYS DON'T UNDERSTAND. THIS LETTER TO SANTA IS JUST A SETUP ...
© 2000 Aaron McGruder/Dist. by Universal Press Syndicate
WHEN HE COMES, I'M GONNA WAIT FOR HIM ON THE ROOF AND JACK HIM FOR HIS SLEIGH.
HMM ...
12/14
www.ucomics.com www.boondocks.net
NOT TO DIS YOUR PLAN, RILEY, BUT DON'T YOU THINK AFTER ALL THESE YEARS SANTA HAS FIGURED OUT HOW TO AVOID THE KIDS WHO PLAN ON ROBBING HIM?
HE MUST, 'CAUSE I AIN'T NEVER SEEN HIM NEAR BROOKLYN.

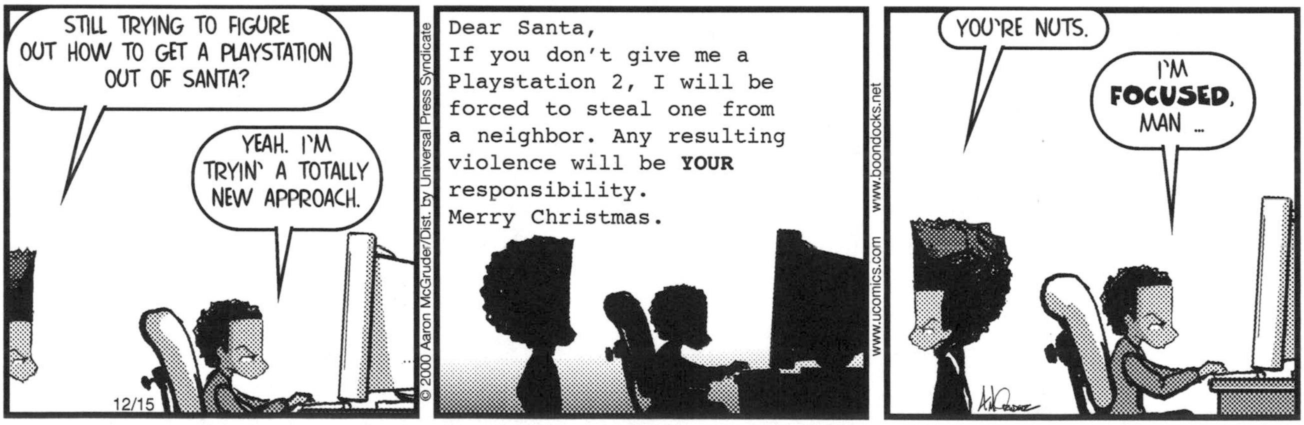
STILL TRYING TO FIGURE OUT HOW TO GET A PLAYSTATION OUT OF SANTA?
YEAH. I'M TRYIN' A TOTALLY NEW APPROACH.
12/15
© 2000 Aaron McGruder/Dist. by Universal Press Syndicate
Dear Santa,
If you don't give me a Playstation 2, I will be forced to steal one from a neighbor. Any resulting violence will be **YOUR** responsibility.
Merry Christmas.
www.ucomics.com www.boondocks.net
YOU'RE NUTS.
I'M **FOCUSED**, MAN ...

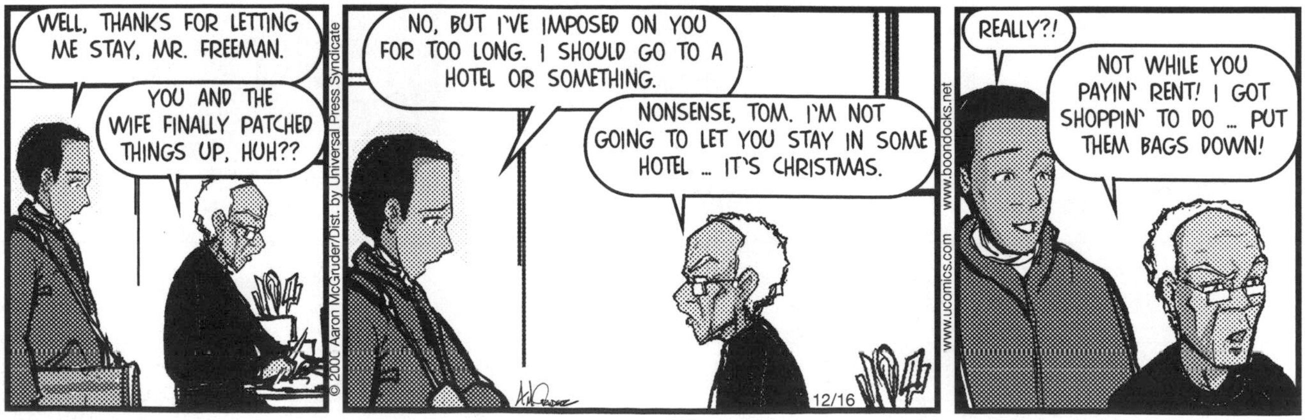
WELL, THANKS FOR LETTING ME STAY, MR. FREEMAN.
YOU AND THE WIFE FINALLY PATCHED THINGS UP, HUH??
© 2000 Aaron McGruder/Dist. by Universal Press Syndicate
NO, BUT I'VE IMPOSED ON YOU FOR TOO LONG. I SHOULD GO TO A HOTEL OR SOMETHING.
NONSENSE, TOM. I'M NOT GOING TO LET YOU STAY IN SOME HOTEL ... IT'S CHRISTMAS.
12/16
www.ucomics.com www.boondocks.net
REALLY?!
NOT WHILE YOU PAYIN' RENT! I GOT SHOPPIN' TO DO ... PUT THEM BAGS DOWN!

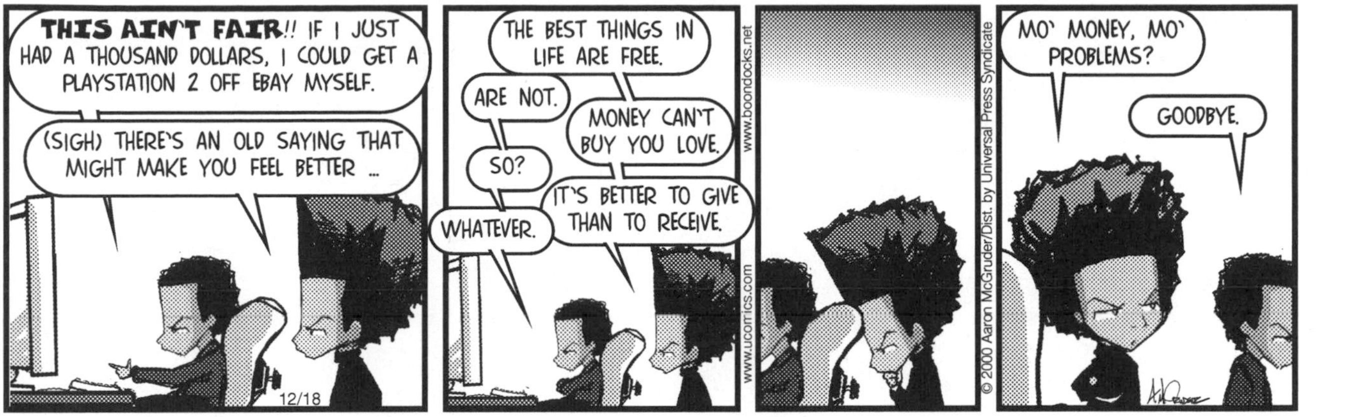
THIS AIN'T FAIR!! IF I JUST HAD A THOUSAND DOLLARS, I COULD GET A PLAYSTATION 2 OFF EBAY MYSELF.
(SIGH) THERE'S AN OLD SAYING THAT MIGHT MAKE YOU FEEL BETTER ...
12/18
THE BEST THINGS IN LIFE ARE FREE.
ARE NOT.
MONEY CAN'T BUY YOU LOVE.
SO?
IT'S BETTER TO GIVE THAN TO RECEIVE.
WHATEVER.
www.boondocks.net
www.ucomics.com
© 2000 Aaron McGruder/Dist. by Universal Press Syndicate
MO' MONEY, MO' PROBLEMS?
GOODBYE.

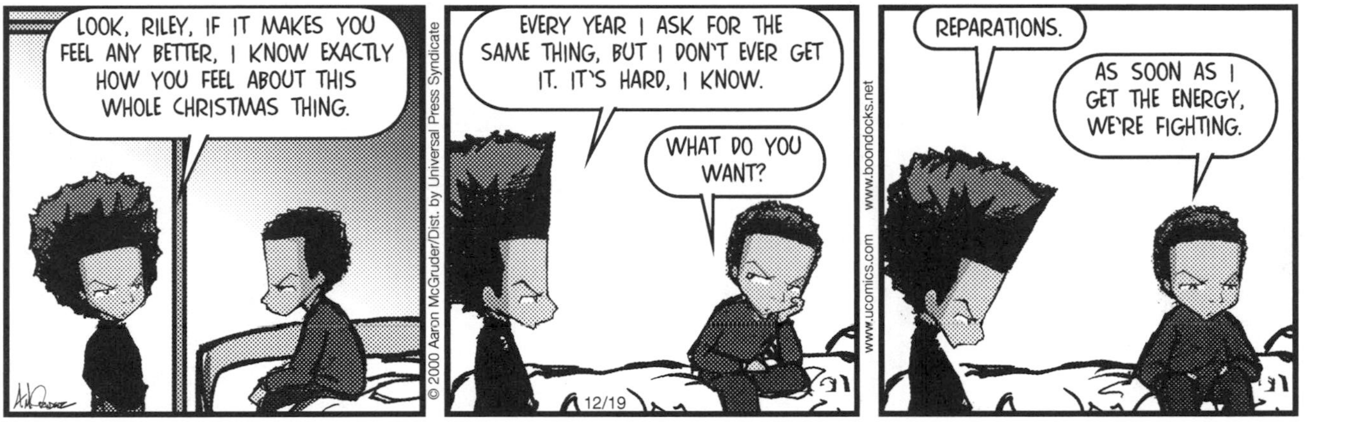
LOOK, RILEY, IF IT MAKES YOU FEEL ANY BETTER, I KNOW EXACTLY HOW YOU FEEL ABOUT THIS WHOLE CHRISTMAS THING.
© 2000 Aaron McGruder/Dist. by Universal Press Syndicate
EVERY YEAR I ASK FOR THE SAME THING, BUT I DON'T EVER GET IT. IT'S HARD, I KNOW.
WHAT DO YOU WANT?
12/19
www.boondocks.net
www.ucomics.com
REPARATIONS.
AS SOON AS I GET THE ENERGY, WE'RE FIGHTING.

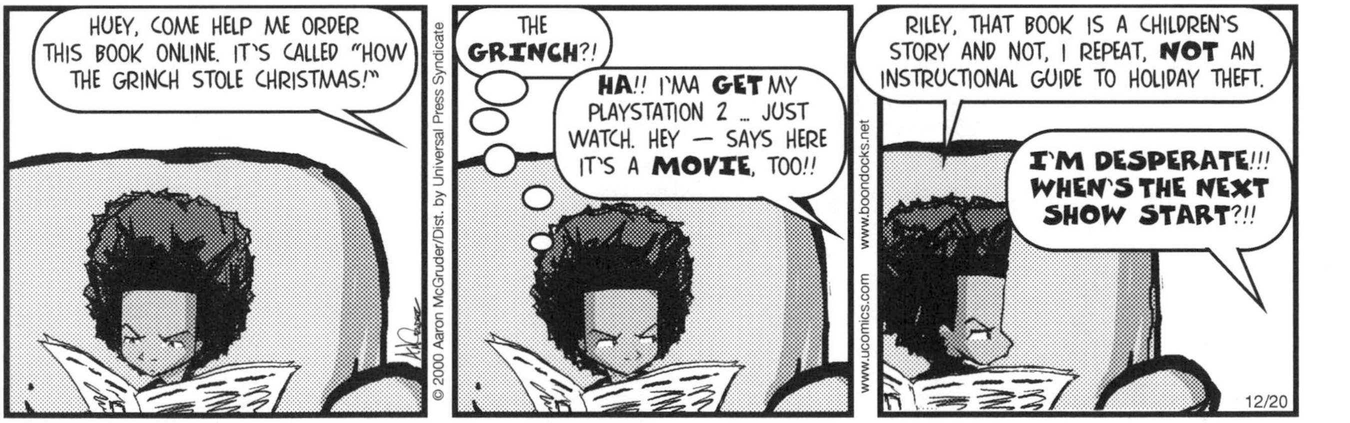
HUEY, COME HELP ME ORDER THIS BOOK ONLINE. IT'S CALLED "HOW THE GRINCH STOLE CHRISTMAS!"
© 2000 Aaron McGruder/Dist. by Universal Press Syndicate
THE GRINCH?!
HA!! I'MA GET MY PLAYSTATION 2 ... JUST WATCH. HEY — SAYS HERE IT'S A MOVIE, TOO!!
www.boondocks.net
www.ucomics.com
RILEY, THAT BOOK IS A CHILDREN'S STORY AND NOT, I REPEAT, NOT AN INSTRUCTIONAL GUIDE TO HOLIDAY THEFT.
I'M DESPERATE!!! WHEN'S THE NEXT SHOW START?!!
12/20

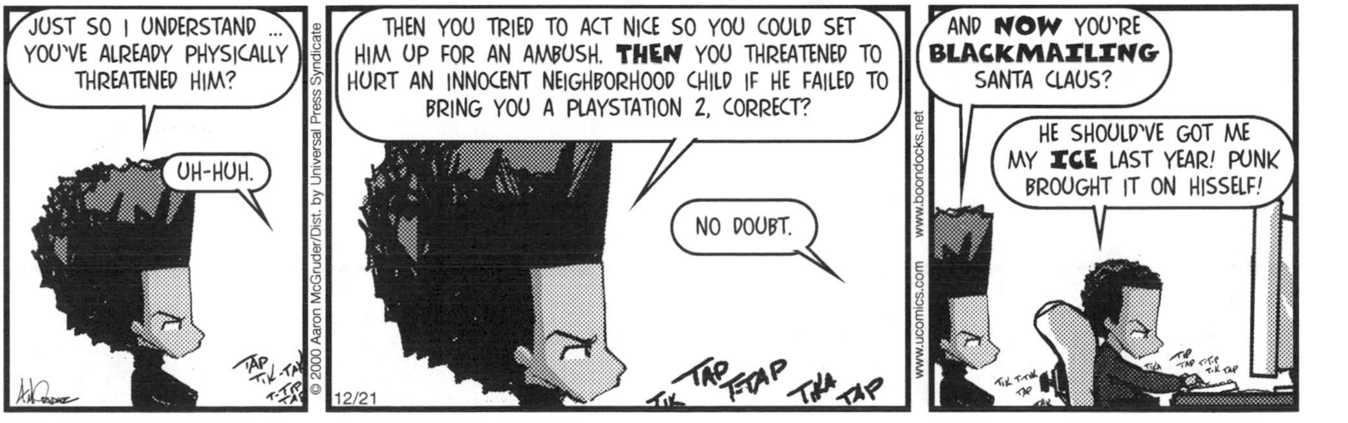
JUST SO I UNDERSTAND ... YOU'VE ALREADY PHYSICALLY THREATENED HIM?
UH-HUH.
© 2000 Aaron McGruder/Dist. by Universal Press Syndicate
THEN YOU TRIED TO ACT NICE SO YOU COULD SET HIM UP FOR AN AMBUSH. THEN YOU THREATENED TO HURT AN INNOCENT NEIGHBORHOOD CHILD IF HE FAILED TO BRING YOU A PLAYSTATION 2, CORRECT?
NO DOUBT.
12/21
TIK TAP T-TAP TIKA TAP
www.boondocks.net
www.ucomics.com
AND NOW YOU'RE BLACKMAILING SANTA CLAUS?
HE SHOULD'VE GOT ME MY ICE LAST YEAR! PUNK BROUGHT IT ON HISSELF!

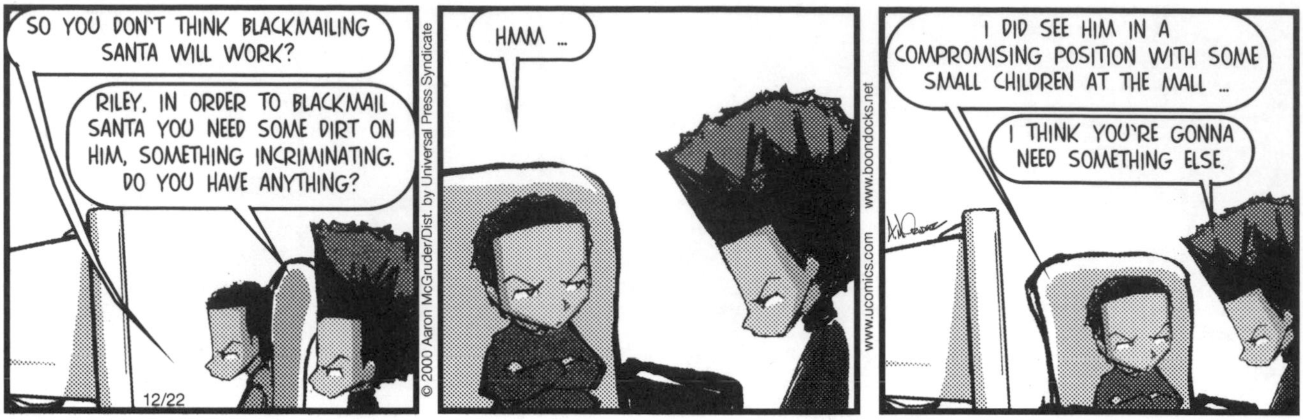
SO YOU DON'T THINK BLACKMAILING SANTA WILL WORK?
RILEY, IN ORDER TO BLACKMAIL SANTA YOU NEED SOME DIRT ON HIM, SOMETHING INCRIMINATING. DO YOU HAVE ANYTHING?
12/22
© 2000 Aaron McGruder/Dist. by Universal Press Syndicate
HMM ...
www.ucomics.com www.boondocks.net
I DID SEE HIM IN A COMPROMISING POSITION WITH SOME SMALL CHILDREN AT THE MALL ...
I THINK YOU'RE GONNA NEED SOMETHING ELSE.

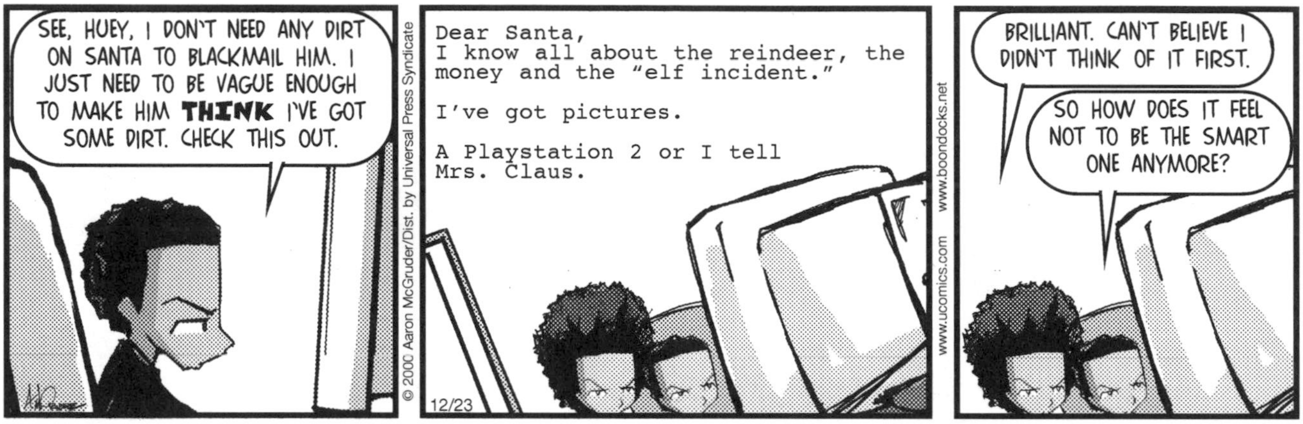
SEE, HUEY, I DON'T NEED ANY DIRT ON SANTA TO BLACKMAIL HIM. I JUST NEED TO BE VAGUE ENOUGH TO MAKE HIM **THINK** I'VE GOT SOME DIRT. CHECK THIS OUT.
© 2000 Aaron McGruder/Dist. by Universal Press Syndicate
Dear Santa,
I know all about the reindeer, the money and the "elf incident."
I've got pictures.
A Playstation 2 or I tell Mrs. Claus.
12/23
www.ucomics.com www.boondocks.net
BRILLIANT. CAN'T BELIEVE I DIDN'T THINK OF IT FIRST.
SO HOW DOES IT FEEL NOT TO BE THE SMART ONE ANYMORE?

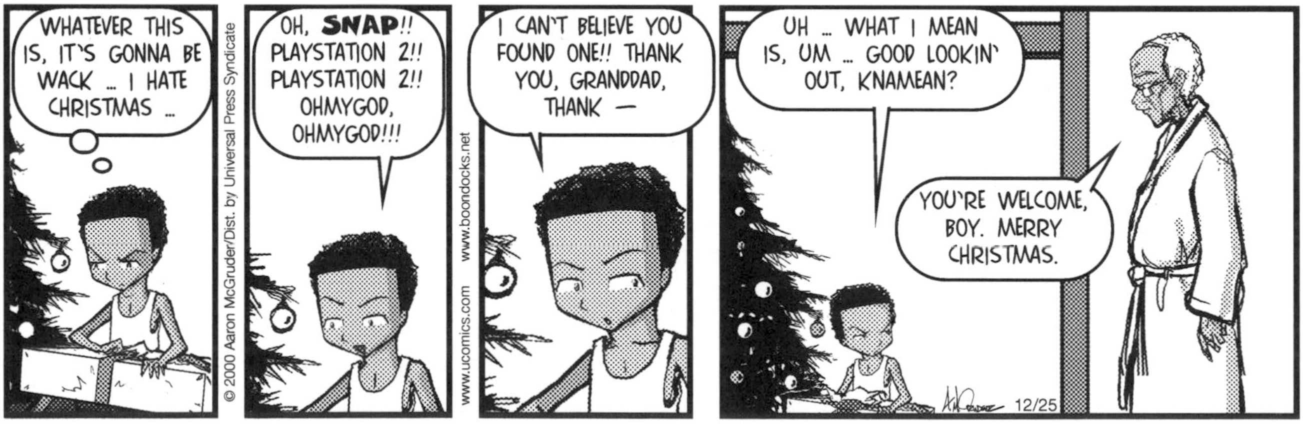
WHATEVER THIS IS, IT'S GONNA BE WACK ... I HATE CHRISTMAS ...
© 2000 Aaron McGruder/Dist. by Universal Press Syndicate
OH, **SNAP**!! PLAYSTATION 2!! PLAYSTATION 2!! OHMYGOD, OHMYGOD!!!
www.ucomics.com www.boondocks.net
I CAN'T BELIEVE YOU FOUND ONE!! THANK YOU, GRANDDAD, THANK —
UH ... WHAT I MEAN IS, UM ... GOOD LOOKIN' OUT, KNAMEAN?
YOU'RE WELCOME, BOY. MERRY CHRISTMAS.
12/25

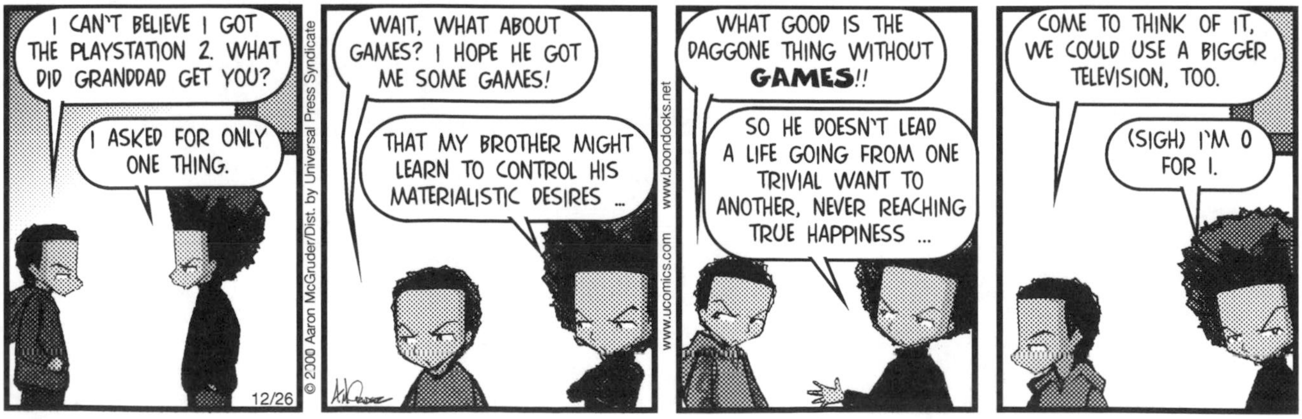
I CAN'T BELIEVE I GOT THE PLAYSTATION 2. WHAT DID GRANDDAD GET YOU?
I ASKED FOR ONLY ONE THING.
12/26
© 2000 Aaron McGruder/Dist. by Universal Press Syndicate
WAIT, WHAT ABOUT GAMES? I HOPE HE GOT ME SOME GAMES!
THAT MY BROTHER MIGHT LEARN TO CONTROL HIS MATERIALISTIC DESIRES ...
www.ucomics.com www.boondocks.net
WHAT GOOD IS THE DAGGONE THING WITHOUT **GAMES**!!
SO HE DOESN'T LEAD A LIFE GOING FROM ONE TRIVIAL WANT TO ANOTHER, NEVER REACHING TRUE HAPPINESS ...
COME TO THINK OF IT, WE COULD USE A BIGGER TELEVISION, TOO.
(SIGH) I'M 0 FOR 1.

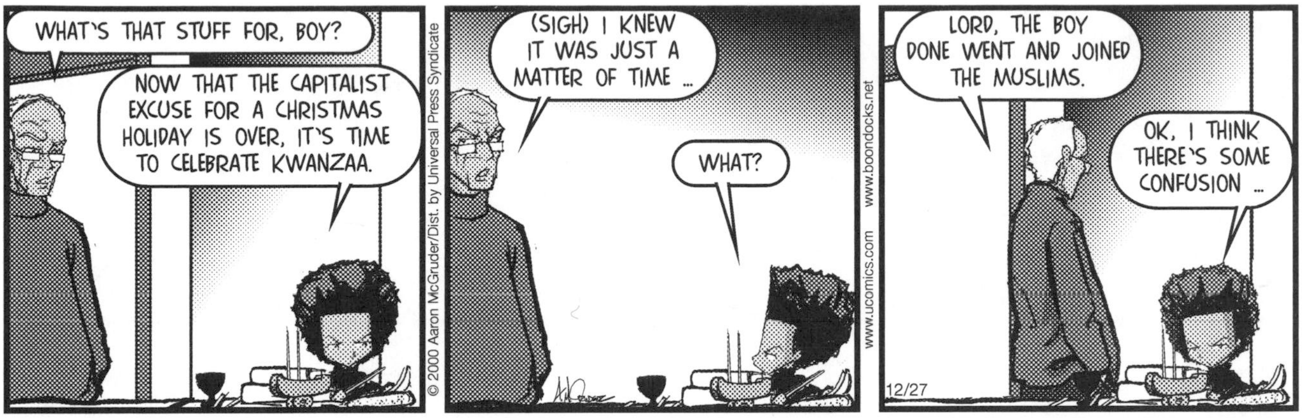
WHAT'S THAT STUFF FOR, BOY?
NOW THAT THE CAPITALIST EXCUSE FOR A CHRISTMAS HOLIDAY IS OVER, IT'S TIME TO CELEBRATE KWANZAA.
(SIGH) I KNEW IT WAS JUST A MATTER OF TIME ...
WHAT?
LORD, THE BOY DONE WENT AND JOINED THE MUSLIMS.
OK, I THINK THERE'S SOME CONFUSION ...
© 2000 Aaron McGruder/Dist. by Universal Press Syndicate
www.ucomics.com www.boondocks.net
12/27

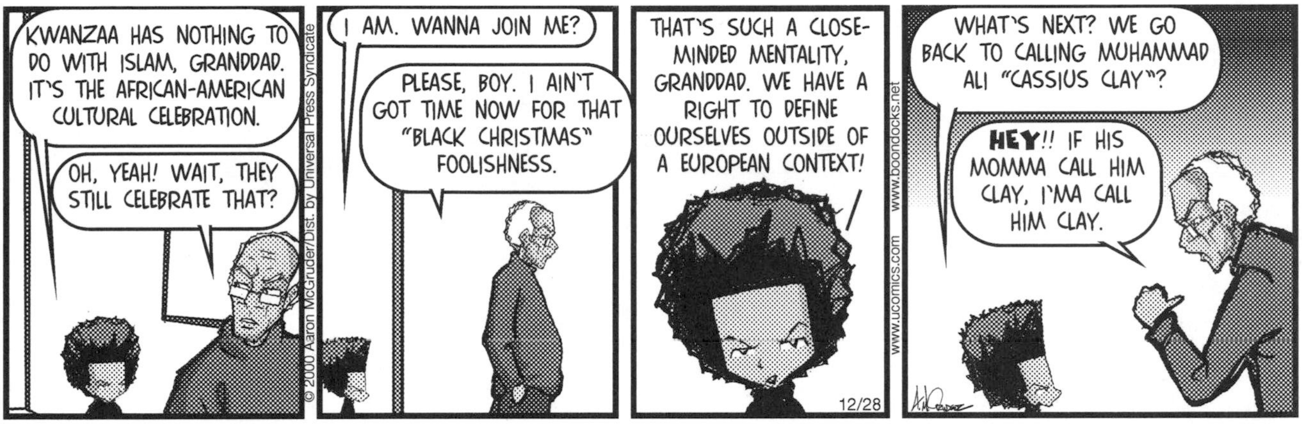
KWANZAA HAS NOTHING TO DO WITH ISLAM, GRANDDAD. IT'S THE AFRICAN-AMERICAN CULTURAL CELEBRATION.
OH, YEAH! WAIT, THEY STILL CELEBRATE THAT?
I AM. WANNA JOIN ME?
PLEASE, BOY. I AIN'T GOT TIME NOW FOR THAT "BLACK CHRISTMAS" FOOLISHNESS.
THAT'S SUCH A CLOSE-MINDED MENTALITY, GRANDDAD. WE HAVE A RIGHT TO DEFINE OURSELVES OUTSIDE OF A EUROPEAN CONTEXT!
WHAT'S NEXT? WE GO BACK TO CALLING MUHAMMAD ALI "CASSIUS CLAY"?
HEY!! IF HIS MOMMA CALL HIM CLAY, I'MA CALL HIM CLAY.
© 2000 Aaron McGruder/Dist. by Universal Press Syndicate
www.ucomics.com www.boondocks.net
12/28

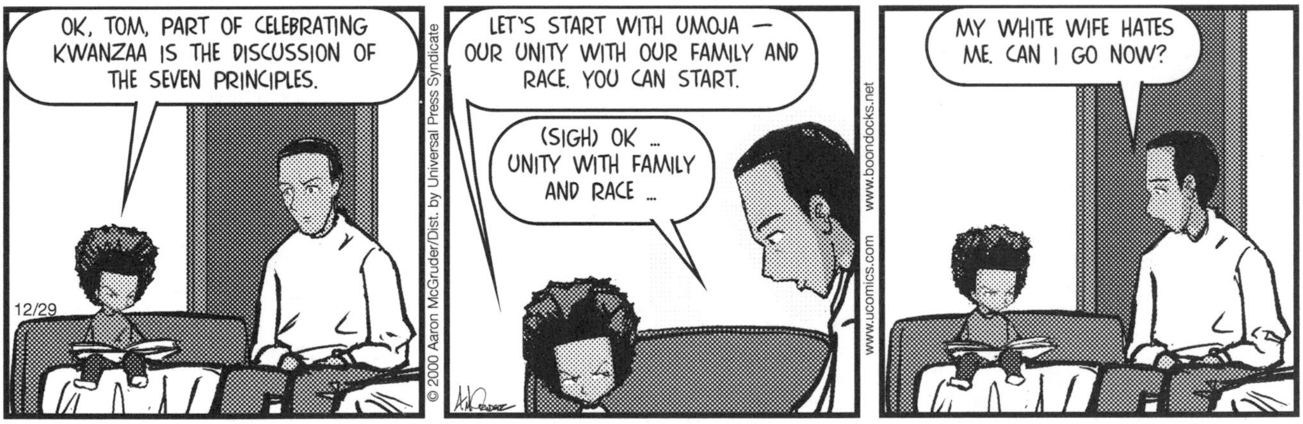
OK, TOM, PART OF CELEBRATING KWANZAA IS THE DISCUSSION OF THE SEVEN PRINCIPLES.
LET'S START WITH UMOJA — OUR UNITY WITH OUR FAMILY AND RACE. YOU CAN START.
(SIGH) OK ... UNITY WITH FAMILY AND RACE ...
MY WHITE WIFE HATES ME. CAN I GO NOW?
© 2000 Aaron McGruder/Dist. by Universal Press Syndicate
www.ucomics.com www.boondocks.net
12/29

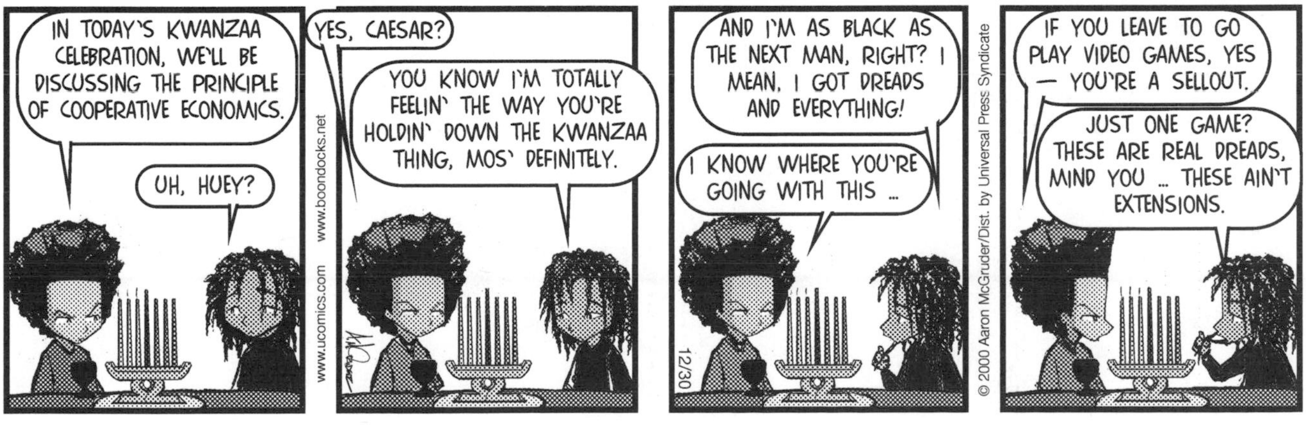
IN TODAY'S KWANZAA CELEBRATION, WE'LL BE DISCUSSING THE PRINCIPLE OF COOPERATIVE ECONOMICS.
UH, HUEY?
YES, CAESAR?
YOU KNOW I'M TOTALLY FEELIN' THE WAY YOU'RE HOLDIN' DOWN THE KWANZAA THING, MOS' DEFINITELY.
AND I'M AS BLACK AS THE NEXT MAN, RIGHT? I MEAN, I GOT DREADS AND EVERYTHING!
I KNOW WHERE YOU'RE GOING WITH THIS ...
IF YOU LEAVE TO GO PLAY VIDEO GAMES, YES — YOU'RE A SELLOUT.
JUST ONE GAME? THESE ARE REAL DREADS, MIND YOU ... THESE AIN'T EXTENSIONS.
www.ucomics.com www.boondocks.net
© 2000 Aaron McGruder/Dist. by Universal Press Syndicate
12/30

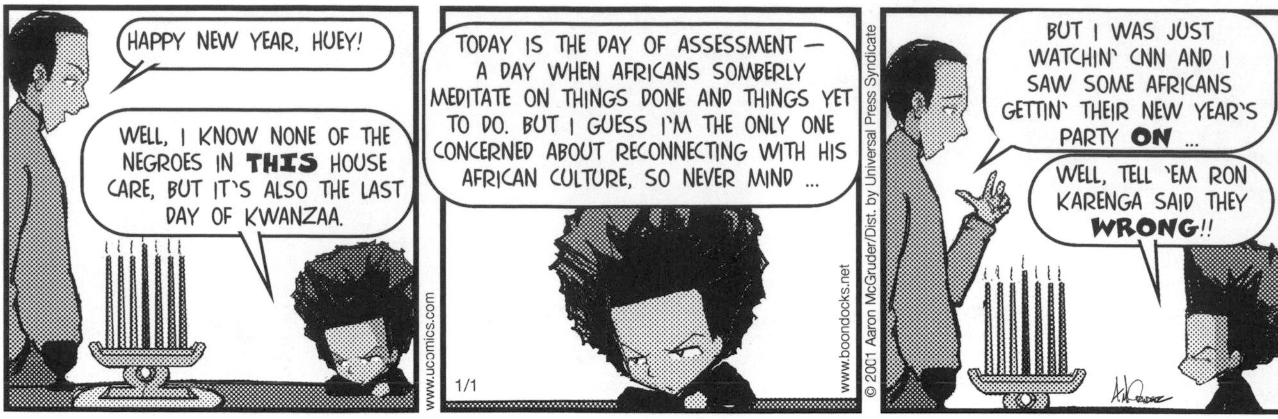
HAPPY NEW YEAR, HUEY!
WELL, I KNOW NONE OF THE NEGROES IN **THIS** HOUSE CARE, BUT IT'S ALSO THE LAST DAY OF KWANZAA.
www.ucomics.com
TODAY IS THE DAY OF ASSESSMENT — A DAY WHEN AFRICANS SOMBERLY MEDITATE ON THINGS DONE AND THINGS YET TO DO. BUT I GUESS I'M THE ONLY ONE CONCERNED ABOUT RECONNECTING WITH HIS AFRICAN CULTURE, SO NEVER MIND ...
1/1
www.boondocks.net
© 2001 Aaron McGruder/Dist. by Universal Press Syndicate
BUT I WAS JUST WATCHIN' CNN AND I SAW SOME AFRICANS GETTIN' THEIR NEW YEAR'S PARTY **ON** ...
WELL, TELL 'EM RON KARENGA SAID THEY **WRONG**!!

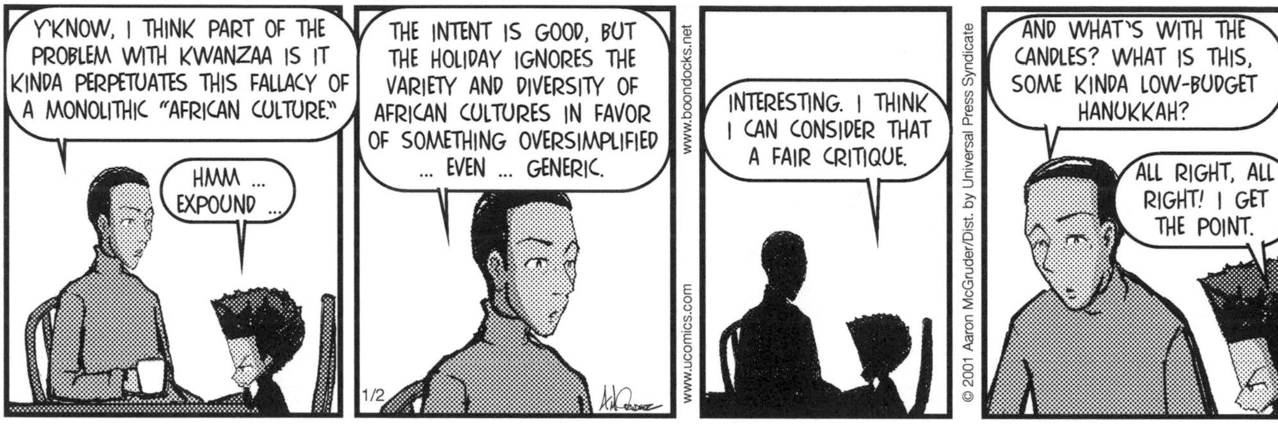
Y'KNOW, I THINK PART OF THE PROBLEM WITH KWANZAA IS IT KINDA PERPETUATES THIS FALLACY OF A MONOLITHIC "AFRICAN CULTURE."
HMM ... EXPOUND ...
THE INTENT IS GOOD, BUT THE HOLIDAY IGNORES THE VARIETY AND DIVERSITY OF AFRICAN CULTURES IN FAVOR OF SOMETHING OVERSIMPLIFIED ... EVEN ... GENERIC.
1/2
www.boondocks.net
www.ucomics.com
INTERESTING. I THINK I CAN CONSIDER THAT A FAIR CRITIQUE.
© 2001 Aaron McGruder/Dist. by Universal Press Syndicate
AND WHAT'S WITH THE CANDLES? WHAT IS THIS, SOME KINDA LOW-BUDGET HANUKKAH?
ALL RIGHT, ALL RIGHT! I GET THE POINT.

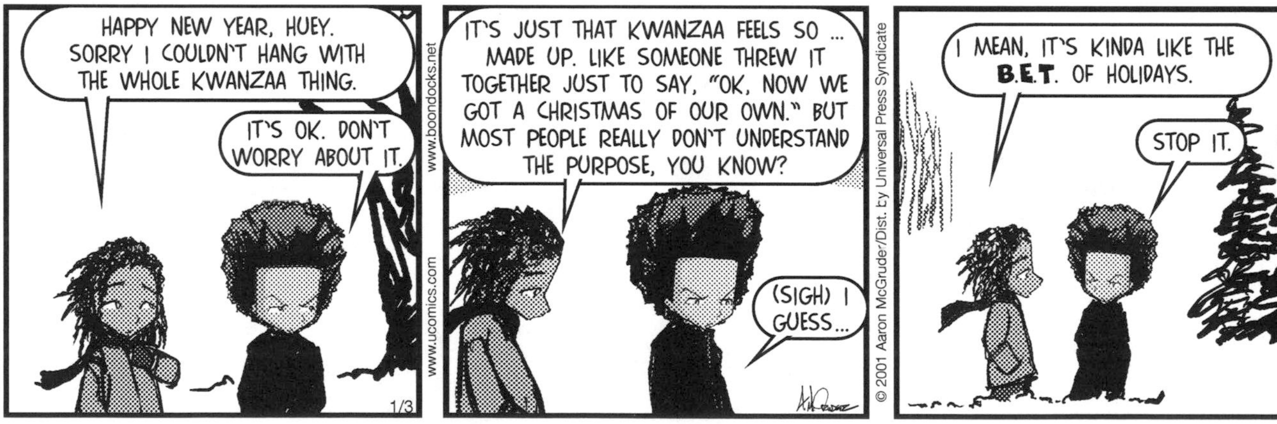
HAPPY NEW YEAR, HUEY. SORRY I COULDN'T HANG WITH THE WHOLE KWANZAA THING.
IT'S OK. DON'T WORRY ABOUT IT.
1/3
www.boondocks.net
www.ucomics.com
IT'S JUST THAT KWANZAA FEELS SO ... MADE UP. LIKE SOMEONE THREW IT TOGETHER JUST TO SAY, "OK, NOW WE GOT A CHRISTMAS OF OUR OWN." BUT MOST PEOPLE REALLY DON'T UNDERSTAND THE PURPOSE, YOU KNOW?
(SIGH) I GUESS...
© 2001 Aaron McGruder/Dist. by Universal Press Syndicate
I MEAN, IT'S KINDA LIKE THE **B.E.T.** OF HOLIDAYS.
STOP IT.

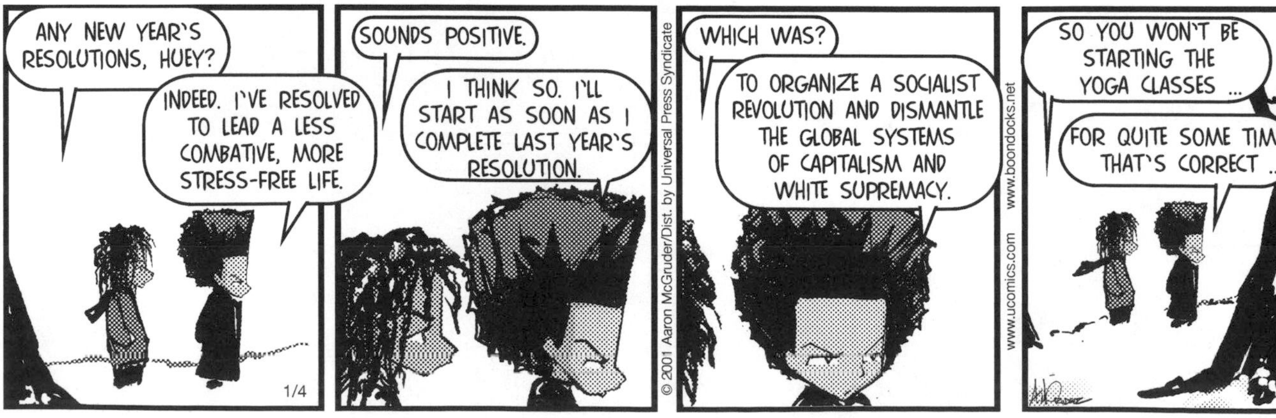
ANY NEW YEAR'S RESOLUTIONS, HUEY?
INDEED. I'VE RESOLVED TO LEAD A LESS COMBATIVE, MORE STRESS-FREE LIFE.
1/4
SOUNDS POSITIVE.
I THINK SO. I'LL START AS SOON AS I COMPLETE LAST YEAR'S RESOLUTION.
© 2001 Aaron McGruder/Dist. by Universal Press Syndicate
WHICH WAS?
TO ORGANIZE A SOCIALIST REVOLUTION AND DISMANTLE THE GLOBAL SYSTEMS OF CAPITALISM AND WHITE SUPREMACY.
www.boondocks.net
www.ucomics.com
SO YOU WON'T BE STARTING THE YOGA CLASSES ...
FOR QUITE SOME TIME, THAT'S CORRECT ...

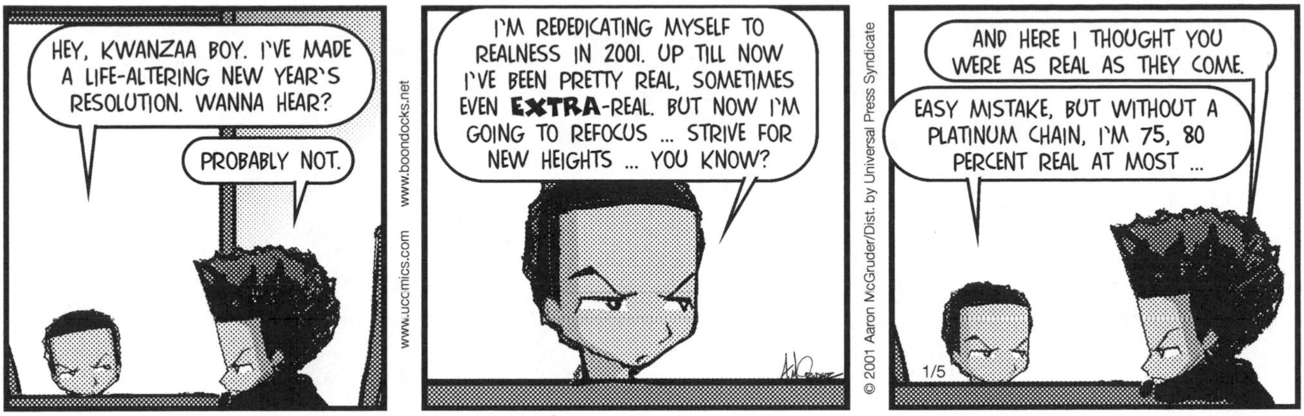
HEY, KWANZAA BOY. I'VE MADE A LIFE-ALTERING NEW YEAR'S RESOLUTION. WANNA HEAR?
PROBABLY NOT.
www.ucomics.com www.boondocks.net
I'M REDEDICATING MYSELF TO REALNESS IN 2001. UP TILL NOW I'VE BEEN PRETTY REAL, SOMETIMES EVEN **EXTRA**-REAL. BUT NOW I'M GOING TO REFOCUS ... STRIVE FOR NEW HEIGHTS ... YOU KNOW?
© 2001 Aaron McGruder/Dist. by Universal Press Syndicate
AND HERE I THOUGHT YOU WERE AS REAL AS THEY COME.
EASY MISTAKE, BUT WITHOUT A PLATINUM CHAIN, I'M 75, 80 PERCENT REAL AT MOST ...
1/5

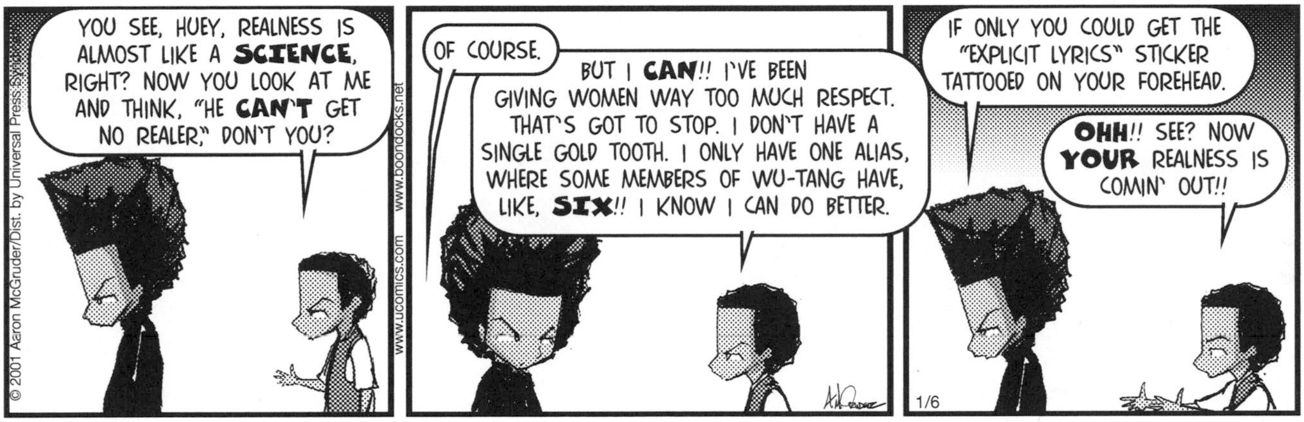
© 2001 Aaron McGruder/Dist. by Universal Press Syndicate
YOU SEE, HUEY, REALNESS IS ALMOST LIKE A **SCIENCE**, RIGHT? NOW YOU LOOK AT ME AND THINK, "HE **CAN'T** GET NO REALER," DON'T YOU?
www.ucomics.com www.boondocks.net
OF COURSE.
BUT I **CAN**!! I'VE BEEN GIVING WOMEN WAY TOO MUCH RESPECT. THAT'S GOT TO STOP. I DON'T HAVE A SINGLE GOLD TOOTH. I ONLY HAVE ONE ALIAS, WHERE SOME MEMBERS OF WU-TANG HAVE, LIKE, **SIX**!! I KNOW I CAN DO BETTER.
IF ONLY YOU COULD GET THE "EXPLICIT LYRICS" STICKER TATTOOED ON YOUR FOREHEAD.
OHH!! SEE? NOW **YOUR** REALNESS IS COMIN' OUT!!
1/6

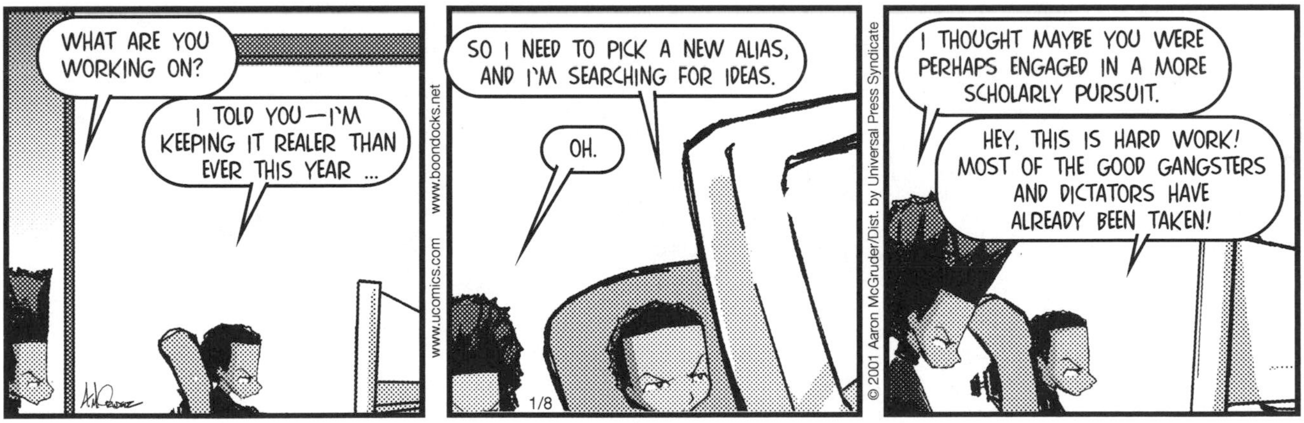
WHAT ARE YOU WORKING ON?
I TOLD YOU—I'M KEEPING IT REALER THAN EVER THIS YEAR ...
www.ucomics.com www.boondocks.net
SO I NEED TO PICK A NEW ALIAS, AND I'M SEARCHING FOR IDEAS.
OH.
1/8
© 2001 Aaron McGruder/Dist. by Universal Press Syndicate
I THOUGHT MAYBE YOU WERE PERHAPS ENGAGED IN A MORE SCHOLARLY PURSUIT.
HEY, THIS IS HARD WORK! MOST OF THE GOOD GANGSTERS AND DICTATORS HAVE ALREADY BEEN TAKEN!

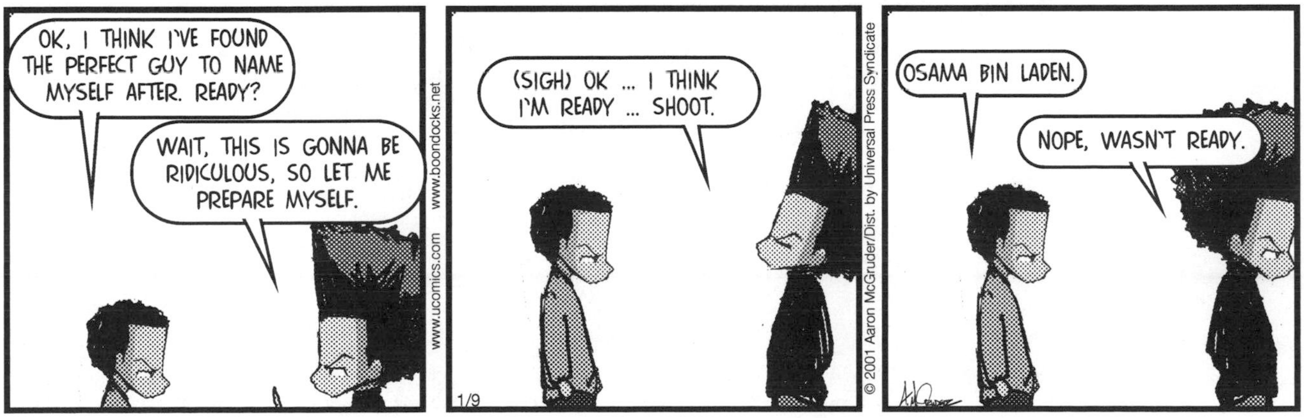
OK, I THINK I'VE FOUND THE PERFECT GUY TO NAME MYSELF AFTER. READY?
WAIT, THIS IS GONNA BE RIDICULOUS, SO LET ME PREPARE MYSELF.
www.ucomics.com www.boondocks.net
(SIGH) OK ... I THINK I'M READY ... SHOOT.
1/9
© 2001 Aaron McGruder/Dist. by Universal Press Syndicate
OSAMA BIN LADEN.
NOPE, WASN'T READY.

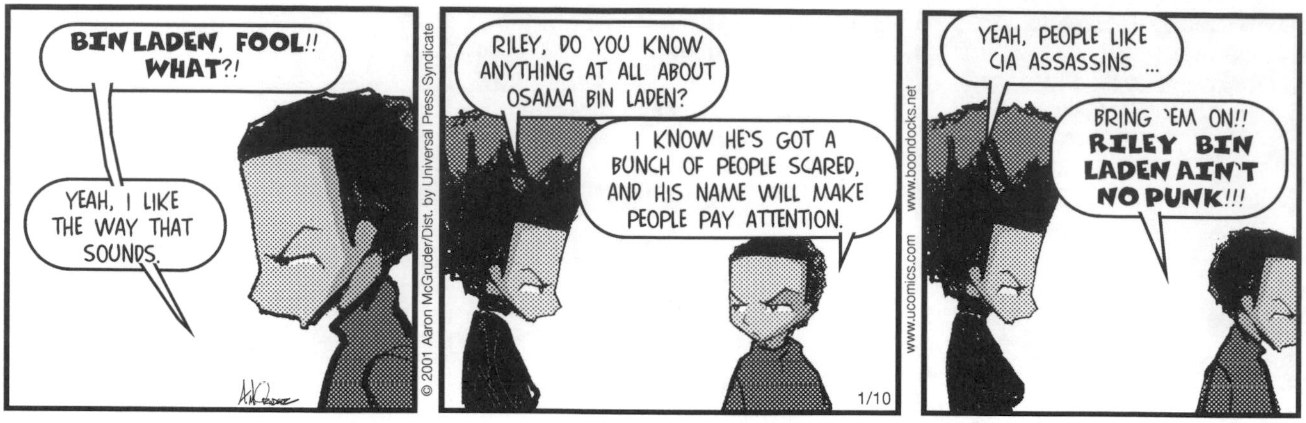
BIN LADEN, FOOL!! WHAT?!
YEAH, I LIKE THE WAY THAT SOUNDS.
RILEY, DO YOU KNOW ANYTHING AT ALL ABOUT OSAMA BIN LADEN?
I KNOW HE'S GOT A BUNCH OF PEOPLE SCARED, AND HIS NAME WILL MAKE PEOPLE PAY ATTENTION.
YEAH, PEOPLE LIKE CIA ASSASSINS ...
BRING 'EM ON!! RILEY BIN LADEN AIN'T NO PUNK!!!
© 2001 Aaron McGruder/Dist. by Universal Press Syndicate
www.ucomics.com www.boondocks.net
1/10

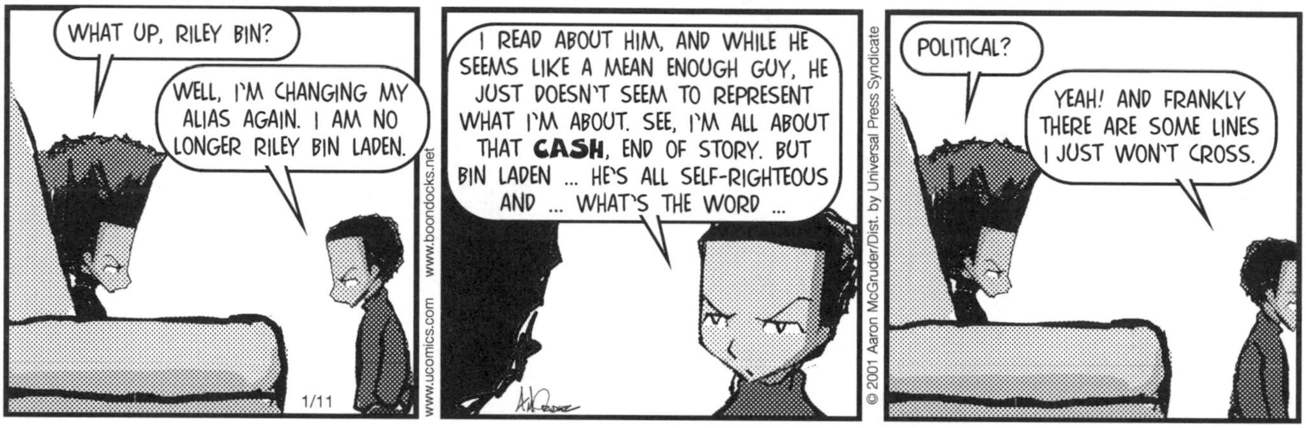
WHAT UP, RILEY BIN?
WELL, I'M CHANGING MY ALIAS AGAIN. I AM NO LONGER RILEY BIN LADEN.
I READ ABOUT HIM, AND WHILE HE SEEMS LIKE A MEAN ENOUGH GUY, HE JUST DOESN'T SEEM TO REPRESENT WHAT I'M ABOUT. SEE, I'M ALL ABOUT THAT CASH, END OF STORY. BUT BIN LADEN ... HE'S ALL SELF-RIGHTEOUS AND ... WHAT'S THE WORD ...
POLITICAL?
YEAH! AND FRANKLY THERE ARE SOME LINES I JUST WON'T CROSS.
1/11
www.ucomics.com www.boondocks.net
© 2001 Aaron McGruder/Dist. by Universal Press Syndicate

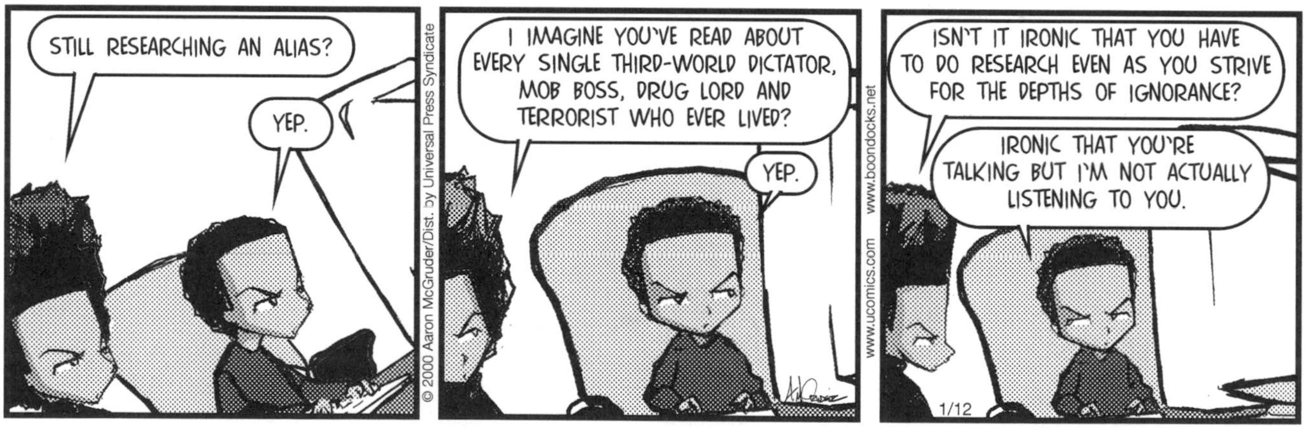
STILL RESEARCHING AN ALIAS?
YEP.
I IMAGINE YOU'VE READ ABOUT EVERY SINGLE THIRD-WORLD DICTATOR, MOB BOSS, DRUG LORD AND TERRORIST WHO EVER LIVED?
YEP.
ISN'T IT IRONIC THAT YOU HAVE TO DO RESEARCH EVEN AS YOU STRIVE FOR THE DEPTHS OF IGNORANCE?
IRONIC THAT YOU'RE TALKING BUT I'M NOT ACTUALLY LISTENING TO YOU.
© 2000 Aaron McGruder/Dist. by Universal Press Syndicate
www.ucomics.com www.boondocks.net
1/12

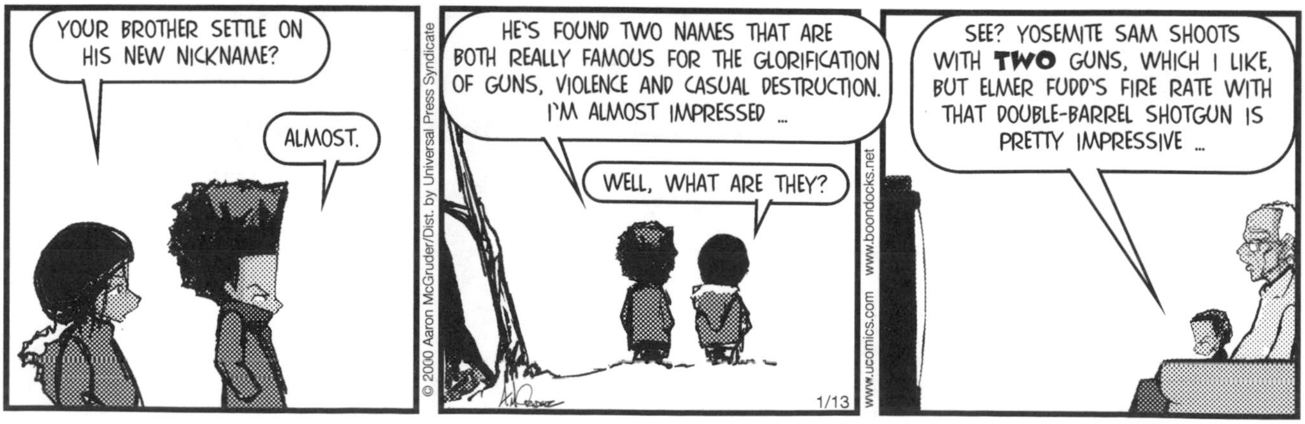
YOUR BROTHER SETTLE ON HIS NEW NICKNAME?
ALMOST.
HE'S FOUND TWO NAMES THAT ARE BOTH REALLY FAMOUS FOR THE GLORIFICATION OF GUNS, VIOLENCE AND CASUAL DESTRUCTION. I'M ALMOST IMPRESSED ...
WELL, WHAT ARE THEY?
SEE? YOSEMITE SAM SHOOTS WITH TWO GUNS, WHICH I LIKE, BUT ELMER FUDD'S FIRE RATE WITH THAT DOUBLE-BARREL SHOTGUN IS PRETTY IMPRESSIVE ...
© 2000 Aaron McGruder/Dist. by Universal Press Syndicate
1/13
www.ucomics.com www.boondocks.net

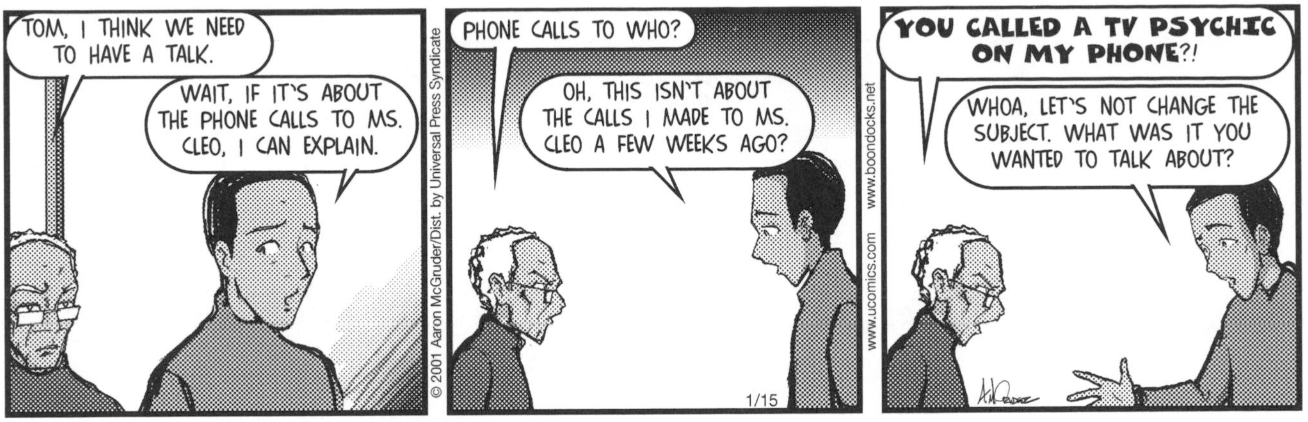
TOM, I THINK WE NEED TO HAVE A TALK.
WAIT, IF IT'S ABOUT THE PHONE CALLS TO MS. CLEO, I CAN EXPLAIN.
© 2001 Aaron McGruder/Dist. by Universal Press Syndicate
PHONE CALLS TO WHO?
OH, THIS ISN'T ABOUT THE CALLS I MADE TO MS. CLEO A FEW WEEKS AGO?
1/15
www.ucomics.com www.boondocks.net
YOU CALLED A TV PSYCHIC ON MY PHONE?!
WHOA, LET'S NOT CHANGE THE SUBJECT. WHAT WAS IT YOU WANTED TO TALK ABOUT?

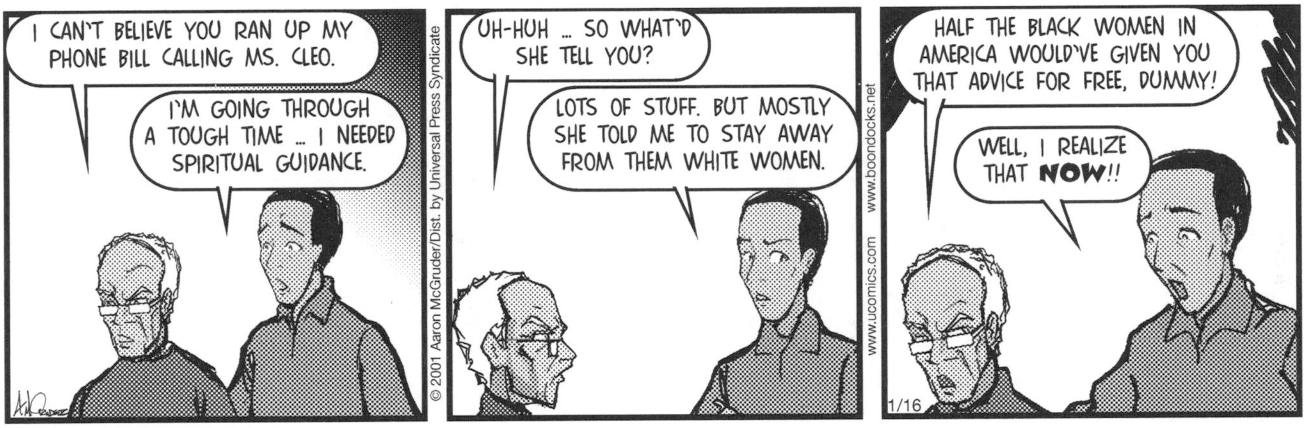
I CAN'T BELIEVE YOU RAN UP MY PHONE BILL CALLING MS. CLEO.
I'M GOING THROUGH A TOUGH TIME ... I NEEDED SPIRITUAL GUIDANCE.
© 2001 Aaron McGruder/Dist. by Universal Press Syndicate
UH-HUH ... SO WHAT'D SHE TELL YOU?
LOTS OF STUFF. BUT MOSTLY SHE TOLD ME TO STAY AWAY FROM THEM WHITE WOMEN.
www.ucomics.com www.boondocks.net
HALF THE BLACK WOMEN IN AMERICA WOULD'VE GIVEN YOU THAT ADVICE FOR FREE, DUMMY!
WELL, I REALIZE THAT NOW!!
1/16

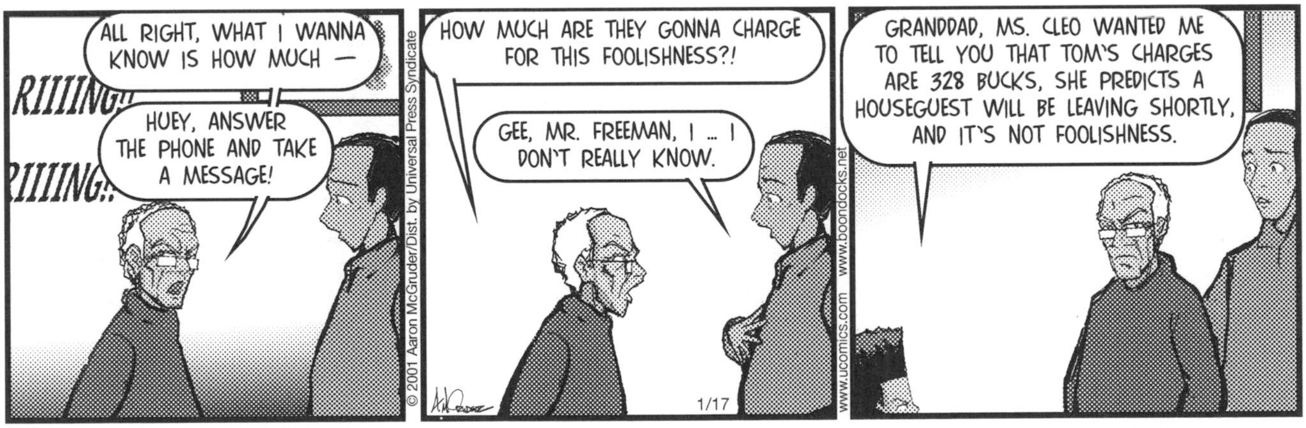
ALL RIGHT, WHAT I WANNA KNOW IS HOW MUCH —
RIIIING!!
RIIIING!!
HUEY, ANSWER THE PHONE AND TAKE A MESSAGE!
© 2001 Aaron McGruder/Dist. by Universal Press Syndicate
HOW MUCH ARE THEY GONNA CHARGE FOR THIS FOOLISHNESS?!
GEE, MR. FREEMAN, I ... I DON'T REALLY KNOW.
1/17
www.ucomics.com www.boondocks.net
GRANDDAD, MS. CLEO WANTED ME TO TELL YOU THAT TOM'S CHARGES ARE 328 BUCKS, SHE PREDICTS A HOUSEGUEST WILL BE LEAVING SHORTLY, AND IT'S NOT FOOLISHNESS.

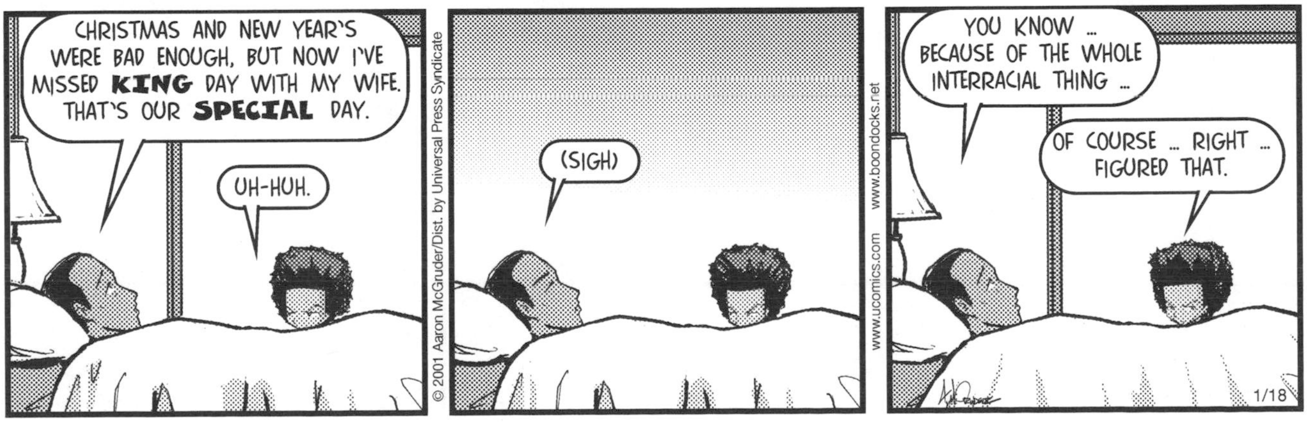
CHRISTMAS AND NEW YEAR'S WERE BAD ENOUGH, BUT NOW I'VE MISSED KING DAY WITH MY WIFE. THAT'S OUR SPECIAL DAY.
UH-HUH.
© 2001 Aaron McGruder/Dist. by Universal Press Syndicate
(SIGH)
www.ucomics.com www.boondocks.net
YOU KNOW ... BECAUSE OF THE WHOLE INTERRACIAL THING ...
OF COURSE ... RIGHT ... FIGURED THAT.
1/18

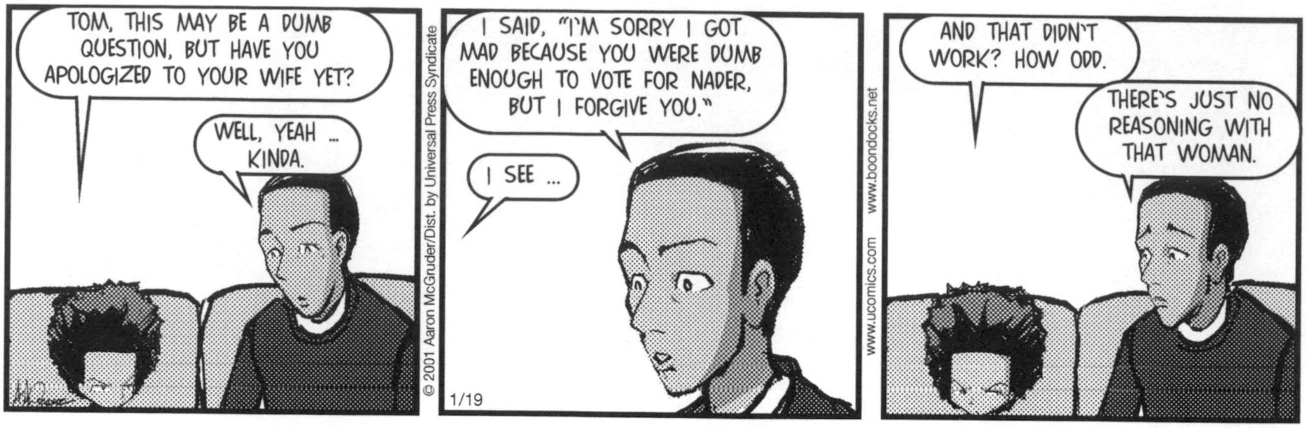
TOM, THIS MAY BE A DUMB QUESTION, BUT HAVE YOU APOLOGIZED TO YOUR WIFE YET?
WELL, YEAH ... KINDA.
© 2001 Aaron McGruder/Dist. by Universal Press Syndicate
I SAID, "I'M SORRY I GOT MAD BECAUSE YOU WERE DUMB ENOUGH TO VOTE FOR NADER, BUT I FORGIVE YOU."
I SEE ...
1/19
www.ucomics.com www.boondocks.net
AND THAT DIDN'T WORK? HOW ODD.
THERE'S JUST NO REASONING WITH THAT WOMAN.

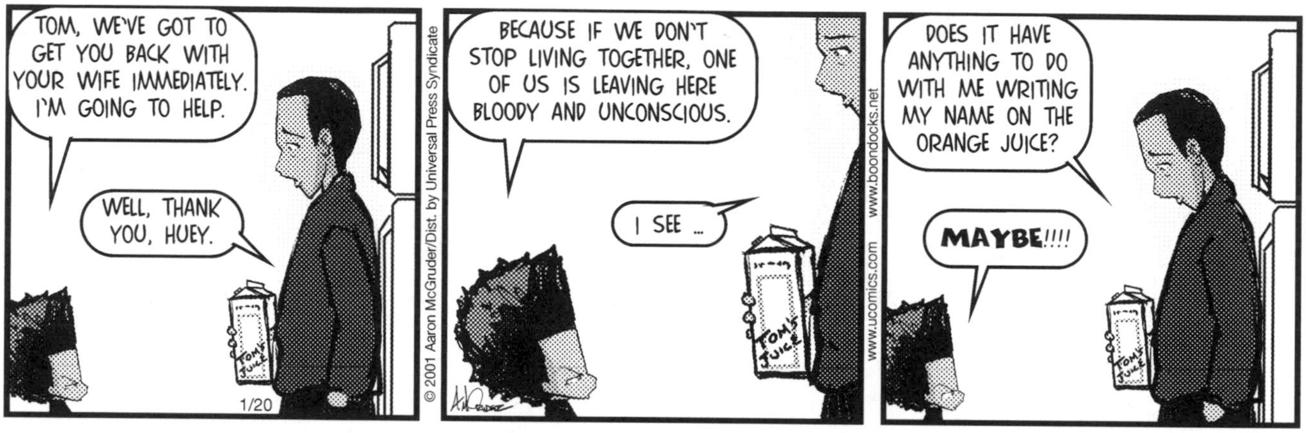
TOM, WE'VE GOT TO GET YOU BACK WITH YOUR WIFE IMMEDIATELY. I'M GOING TO HELP.
WELL, THANK YOU, HUEY.
TOM'S JUICE
1/20
© 2001 Aaron McGruder/Dist. by Universal Press Syndicate
BECAUSE IF WE DON'T STOP LIVING TOGETHER, ONE OF US IS LEAVING HERE BLOODY AND UNCONSCIOUS.
I SEE ...
TOM'S JUICE
www.ucomics.com www.boondocks.net
DOES IT HAVE ANYTHING TO DO WITH ME WRITING MY NAME ON THE ORANGE JUICE?
MAYBE!!!!
TOM'S JUICE

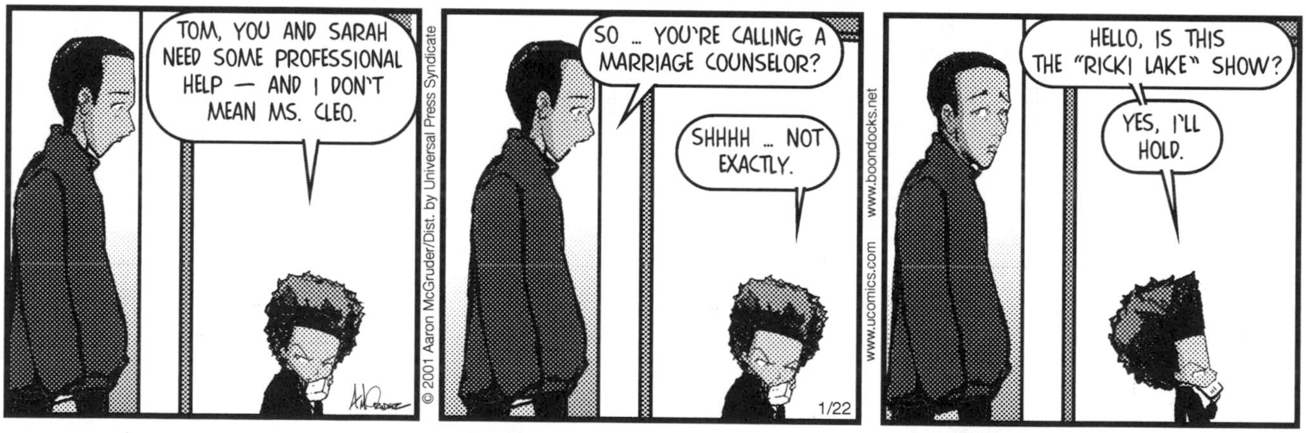
TOM, YOU AND SARAH NEED SOME PROFESSIONAL HELP — AND I DON'T MEAN MS. CLEO.
© 2001 Aaron McGruder/Dist. by Universal Press Syndicate
SO ... YOU'RE CALLING A MARRIAGE COUNSELOR?
SHHHH ... NOT EXACTLY.
1/22
www.ucomics.com www.boondocks.net
HELLO, IS THIS THE "RICKI LAKE" SHOW?
YES, I'LL HOLD.

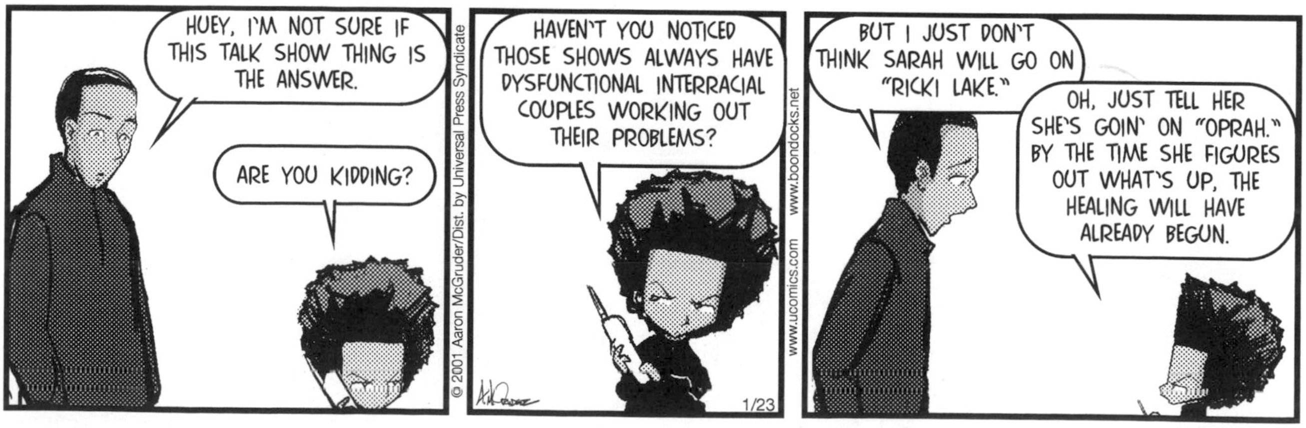
HUEY, I'M NOT SURE IF THIS TALK SHOW THING IS THE ANSWER.
ARE YOU KIDDING?
© 2001 Aaron McGruder/Dist. by Universal Press Syndicate
HAVEN'T YOU NOTICED THOSE SHOWS ALWAYS HAVE DYSFUNCTIONAL INTERRACIAL COUPLES WORKING OUT THEIR PROBLEMS?
1/23
www.ucomics.com www.boondocks.net
BUT I JUST DON'T THINK SARAH WILL GO ON "RICKI LAKE."
OH, JUST TELL HER SHE'S GOIN' ON "OPRAH." BY THE TIME SHE FIGURES OUT WHAT'S UP, THE HEALING WILL HAVE ALREADY BEGUN.

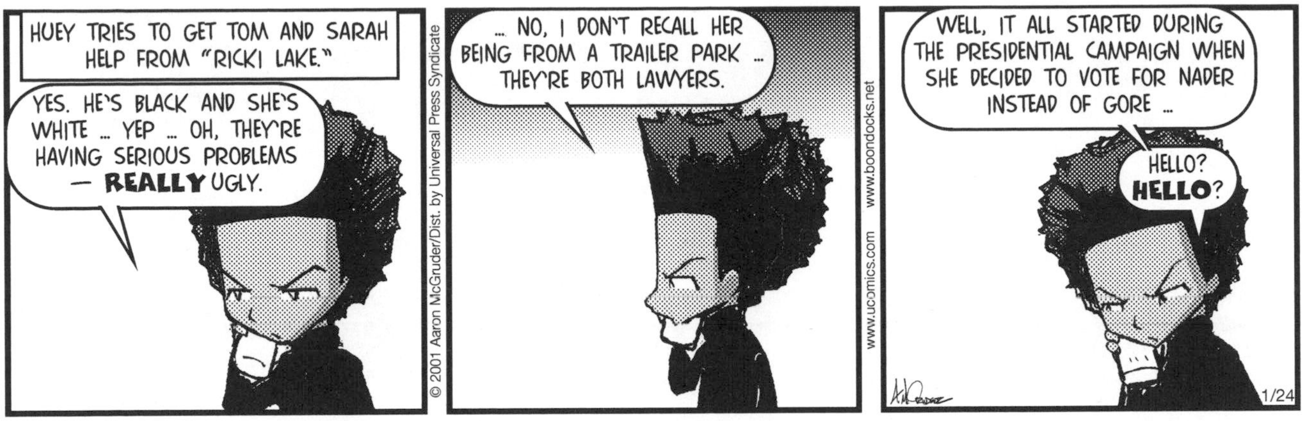
HUEY TRIES TO GET TOM AND SARAH HELP FROM "RICKI LAKE."
YES. HE'S BLACK AND SHE'S WHITE ... YEP ... OH, THEY'RE HAVING SERIOUS PROBLEMS — **REALLY** UGLY.
© 2001 Aaron McGruder/Dist. by Universal Press Syndicate
... NO, I DON'T RECALL HER BEING FROM A TRAILER PARK ... THEY'RE BOTH LAWYERS.
www.ucomics.com www.boondocks.net
WELL, IT ALL STARTED DURING THE PRESIDENTIAL CAMPAIGN WHEN SHE DECIDED TO VOTE FOR NADER INSTEAD OF GORE ...
HELLO? **HELLO**?
1/24

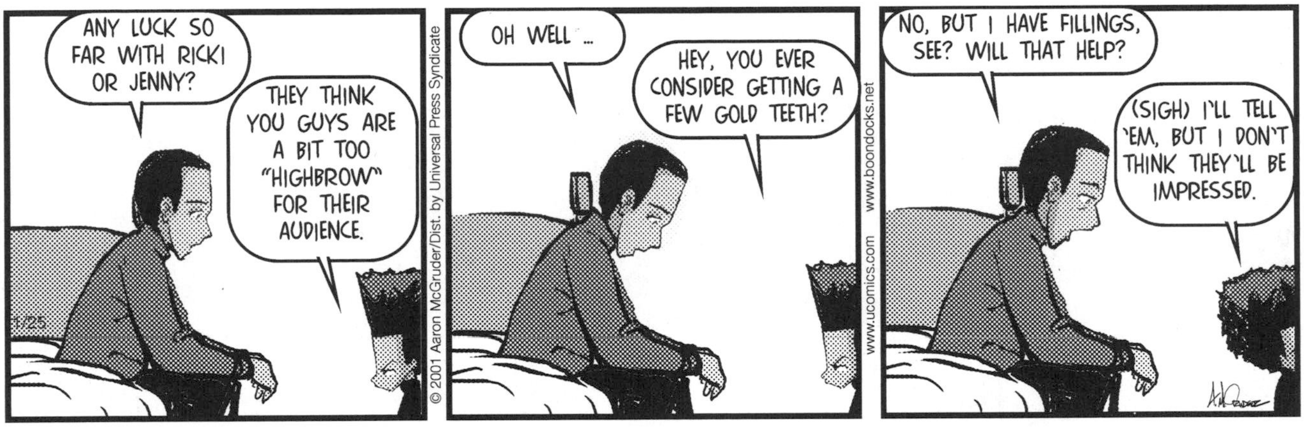
ANY LUCK SO FAR WITH RICKI OR JENNY?
THEY THINK YOU GUYS ARE A BIT TOO "HIGHBROW" FOR THEIR AUDIENCE.
1/25
© 2001 Aaron McGruder/Dist. by Universal Press Syndicate
OH WELL ...
HEY, YOU EVER CONSIDER GETTING A FEW GOLD TEETH?
www.ucomics.com www.boondocks.net
NO, BUT I HAVE FILLINGS, SEE? WILL THAT HELP?
(SIGH) I'LL TELL 'EM, BUT I DON'T THINK THEY'LL BE IMPRESSED.

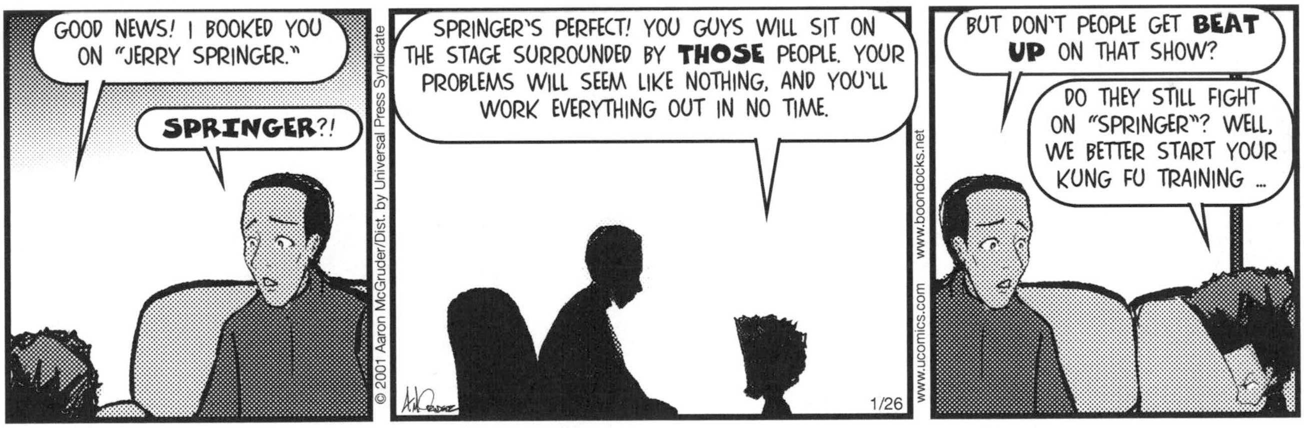
GOOD NEWS! I BOOKED YOU ON "JERRY SPRINGER."
SPRINGER?!
© 2001 Aaron McGruder/Dist. by Universal Press Syndicate
SPRINGER'S PERFECT! YOU GUYS WILL SIT ON THE STAGE SURROUNDED BY **THOSE** PEOPLE. YOUR PROBLEMS WILL SEEM LIKE NOTHING, AND YOU'LL WORK EVERYTHING OUT IN NO TIME.
1/26
www.ucomics.com www.boondocks.net
BUT DON'T PEOPLE GET **BEAT UP** ON THAT SHOW?
DO THEY STILL FIGHT ON "SPRINGER"? WELL, WE BETTER START YOUR KUNG FU TRAINING ...

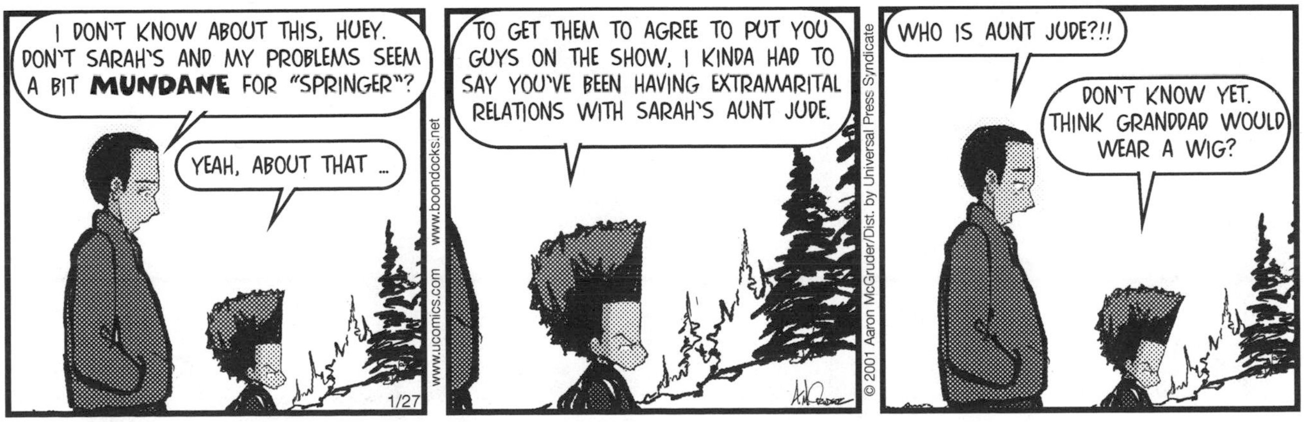
I DON'T KNOW ABOUT THIS, HUEY. DON'T SARAH'S AND MY PROBLEMS SEEM A BIT **MUNDANE** FOR "SPRINGER"?
YEAH, ABOUT THAT ...
1/27
www.ucomics.com www.boondocks.net
TO GET THEM TO AGREE TO PUT YOU GUYS ON THE SHOW, I KINDA HAD TO SAY YOU'VE BEEN HAVING EXTRAMARITAL RELATIONS WITH SARAH'S AUNT JUDE.
© 2001 Aaron McGruder/Dist. by Universal Press Syndicate
WHO IS AUNT JUDE?!!
DON'T KNOW YET. THINK GRANDDAD WOULD WEAR A WIG?

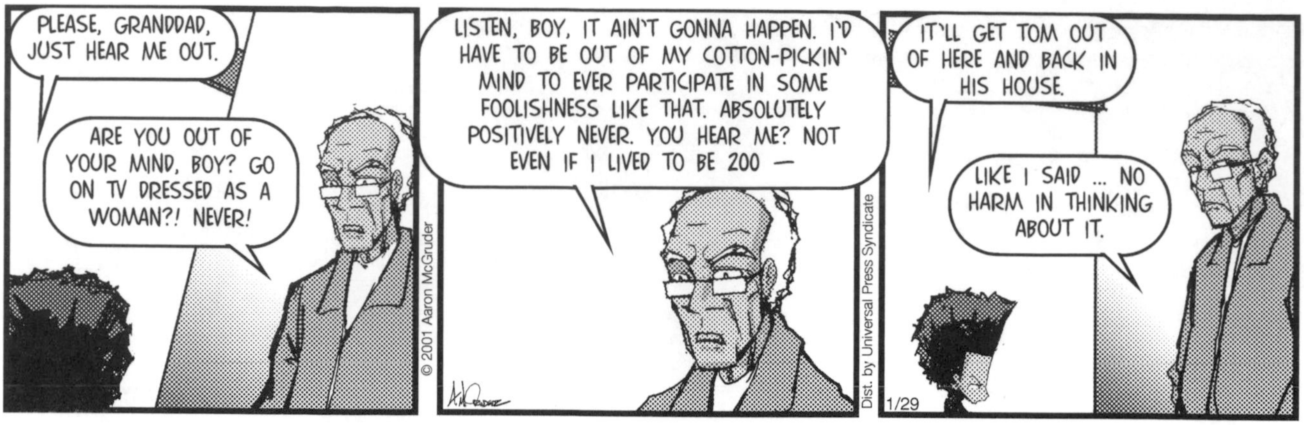
PLEASE, GRANDDAD, JUST HEAR ME OUT.
ARE YOU OUT OF YOUR MIND, BOY? GO ON TV DRESSED AS A WOMAN?! NEVER!
© 2001 Aaron McGruder
LISTEN, BOY, IT AIN'T GONNA HAPPEN. I'D HAVE TO BE OUT OF MY COTTON-PICKIN' MIND TO EVER PARTICIPATE IN SOME FOOLISHNESS LIKE THAT. ABSOLUTELY POSITIVELY NEVER. YOU HEAR ME? NOT EVEN IF I LIVED TO BE 200 —
Dist. by Universal Press Syndicate
IT'LL GET TOM OUT OF HERE AND BACK IN HIS HOUSE.
LIKE I SAID ... NO HARM IN THINKING ABOUT IT.
1/29

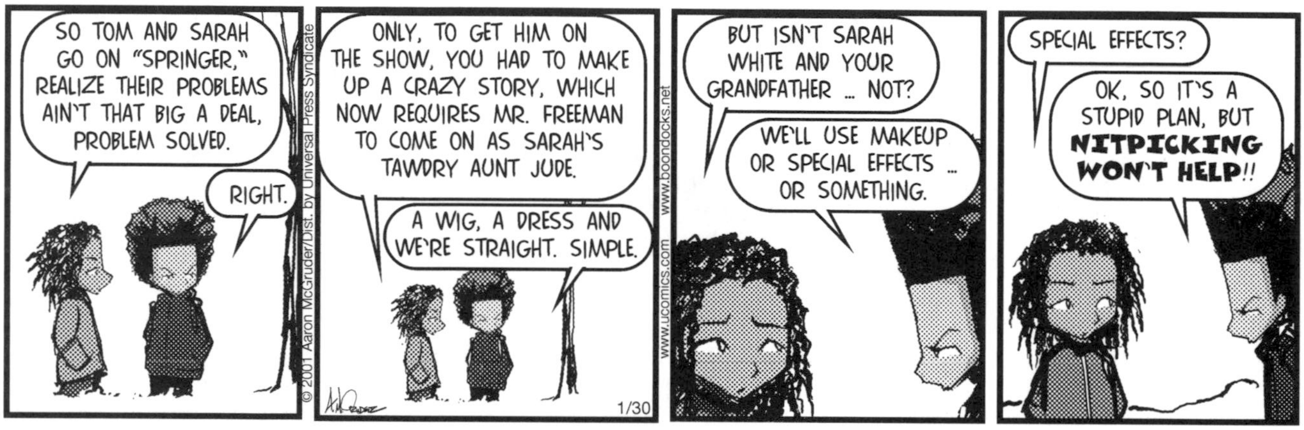
SO TOM AND SARAH GO ON "SPRINGER," REALIZE THEIR PROBLEMS AIN'T THAT BIG A DEAL, PROBLEM SOLVED.
RIGHT.
© 2001 Aaron McGruder/Dist. by Universal Press Syndicate
ONLY, TO GET HIM ON THE SHOW, YOU HAD TO MAKE UP A CRAZY STORY, WHICH NOW REQUIRES MR. FREEMAN TO COME ON AS SARAH'S TAWDRY AUNT JUDE.
A WIG, A DRESS AND WE'RE STRAIGHT. SIMPLE.
1/30
www.ucomics.com www.boondocks.net
BUT ISN'T SARAH WHITE AND YOUR GRANDFATHER ... NOT?
WE'LL USE MAKEUP OR SPECIAL EFFECTS ... OR SOMETHING.
SPECIAL EFFECTS?
OK, SO IT'S A STUPID PLAN, BUT **NITPICKING WON'T HELP**!!

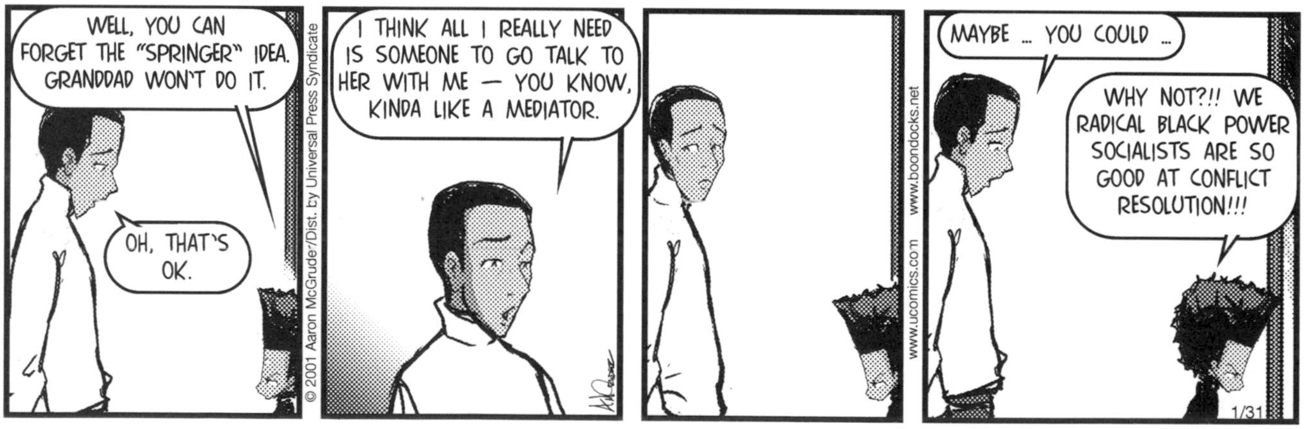
WELL, YOU CAN FORGET THE "SPRINGER" IDEA. GRANDDAD WON'T DO IT.
OH, THAT'S OK.
© 2001 Aaron McGruder/Dist. by Universal Press Syndicate
I THINK ALL I REALLY NEED IS SOMEONE TO GO TALK TO HER WITH ME — YOU KNOW, KINDA LIKE A MEDIATOR.
www.ucomics.com www.boondocks.net
MAYBE ... YOU COULD ...
WHY NOT?!! WE RADICAL BLACK POWER SOCIALISTS ARE SO GOOD AT CONFLICT RESOLUTION!!!
1/31

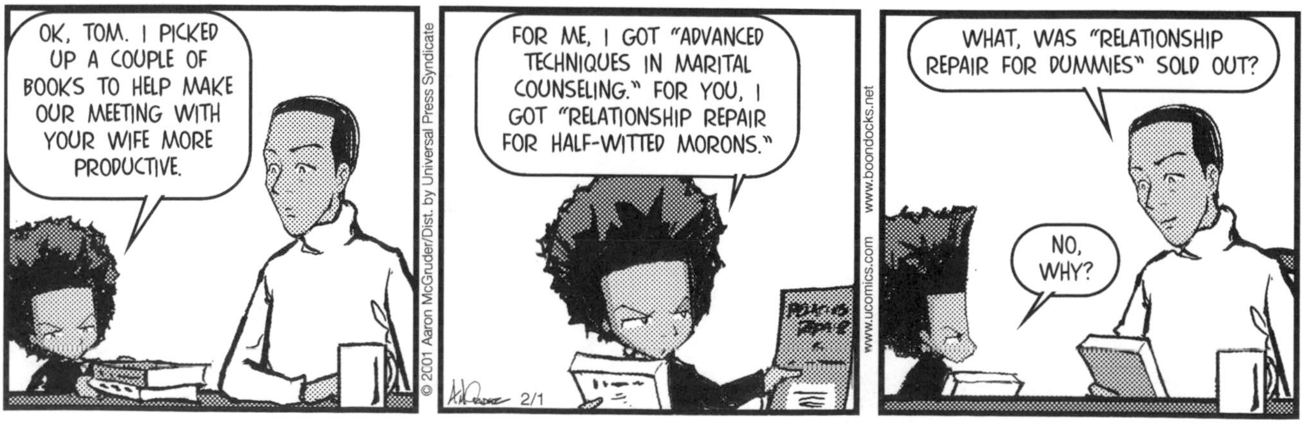
OK, TOM. I PICKED UP A COUPLE OF BOOKS TO HELP MAKE OUR MEETING WITH YOUR WIFE MORE PRODUCTIVE.
© 2001 Aaron McGruder/Dist. by Universal Press Syndicate
FOR ME, I GOT "ADVANCED TECHNIQUES IN MARITAL COUNSELING." FOR YOU, I GOT "RELATIONSHIP REPAIR FOR HALF-WITTED MORONS."
2/1
www.ucomics.com www.boondocks.net
WHAT, WAS "RELATIONSHIP REPAIR FOR DUMMIES" SOLD OUT?
NO, WHY?

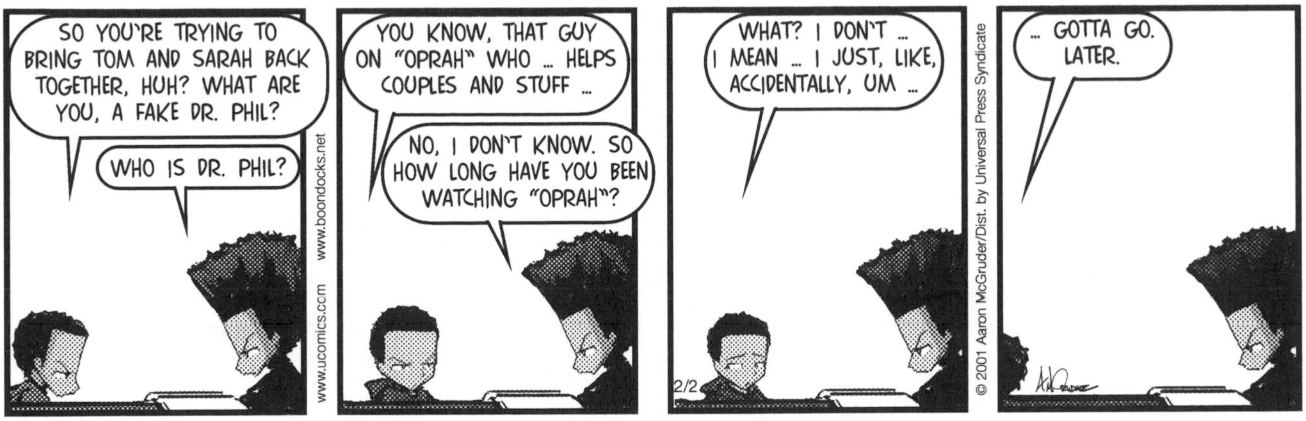
SO YOU'RE TRYING TO BRING TOM AND SARAH BACK TOGETHER, HUH? WHAT ARE YOU, A FAKE DR. PHIL?
WHO IS DR. PHIL?
YOU KNOW, THAT GUY ON "OPRAH" WHO ... HELPS COUPLES AND STUFF ...
NO, I DON'T KNOW. SO HOW LONG HAVE YOU BEEN WATCHING "OPRAH"?
WHAT? I DON'T ... I MEAN ... I JUST, LIKE, ACCIDENTALLY, UM ...
... GOTTA GO. LATER.
www.ucomics.com www.boondocks.net
© 2001 Aaron McGruder/Dist. by Universal Press Syndicate
2/2

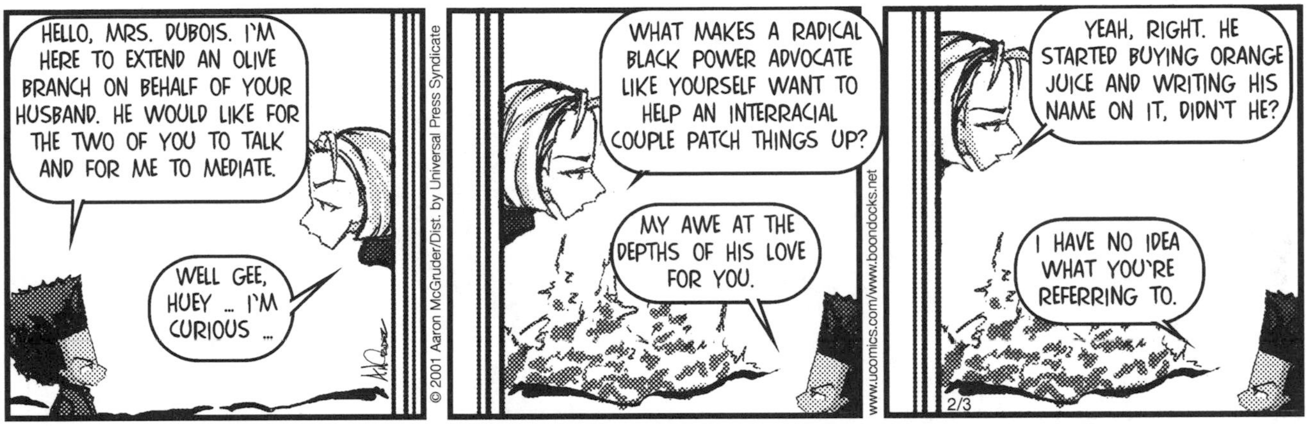
HELLO, MRS. DUBOIS. I'M HERE TO EXTEND AN OLIVE BRANCH ON BEHALF OF YOUR HUSBAND. HE WOULD LIKE FOR THE TWO OF YOU TO TALK AND FOR ME TO MEDIATE.
WELL GEE, HUEY ... I'M CURIOUS ...
WHAT MAKES A RADICAL BLACK POWER ADVOCATE LIKE YOURSELF WANT TO HELP AN INTERRACIAL COUPLE PATCH THINGS UP?
MY AWE AT THE DEPTHS OF HIS LOVE FOR YOU.
YEAH, RIGHT. HE STARTED BUYING ORANGE JUICE AND WRITING HIS NAME ON IT, DIDN'T HE?
I HAVE NO IDEA WHAT YOU'RE REFERRING TO.
© 2001 Aaron McGruder/Dist. by Universal Press Syndicate
www.ucomics.com/www.boondocks.net
2/3

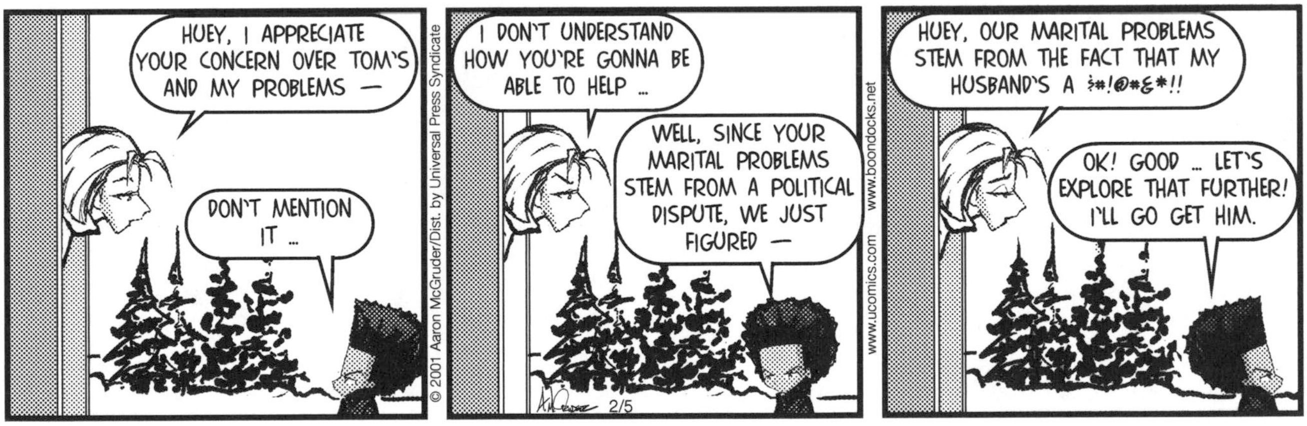
HUEY, I APPRECIATE YOUR CONCERN OVER TOM'S AND MY PROBLEMS —
DON'T MENTION IT ...
I DON'T UNDERSTAND HOW YOU'RE GONNA BE ABLE TO HELP ...
WELL, SINCE YOUR MARITAL PROBLEMS STEM FROM A POLITICAL DISPUTE, WE JUST FIGURED —
HUEY, OUR MARITAL PROBLEMS STEM FROM THE FACT THAT MY HUSBAND'S A $#!@#&*!!
OK! GOOD ... LET'S EXPLORE THAT FURTHER! I'LL GO GET HIM.
© 2001 Aaron McGruder/Dist. by Universal Press Syndicate
www.ucomics.com www.boondocks.net
2/5

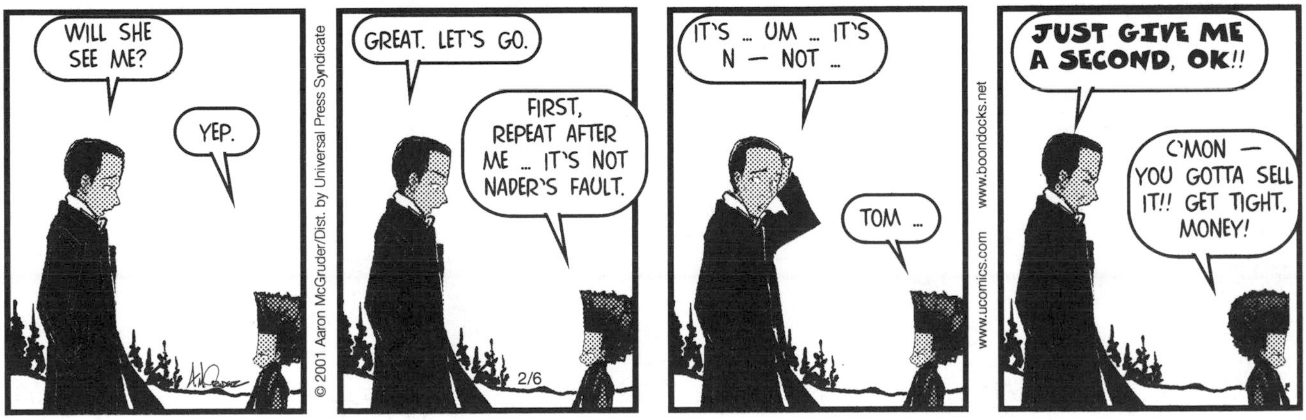
WILL SHE SEE ME?
YEP.
GREAT. LET'S GO.
FIRST, REPEAT AFTER ME ... IT'S NOT NADER'S FAULT.
IT'S ... UM ... IT'S N — NOT ...
TOM ...
JUST GIVE ME A SECOND, OK!!
C'MON — YOU GOTTA SELL IT!! GET TIGHT, MONEY!
© 2001 Aaron McGruder/Dist. by Universal Press Syndicate
www.ucomics.com www.boondocks.net
2/6

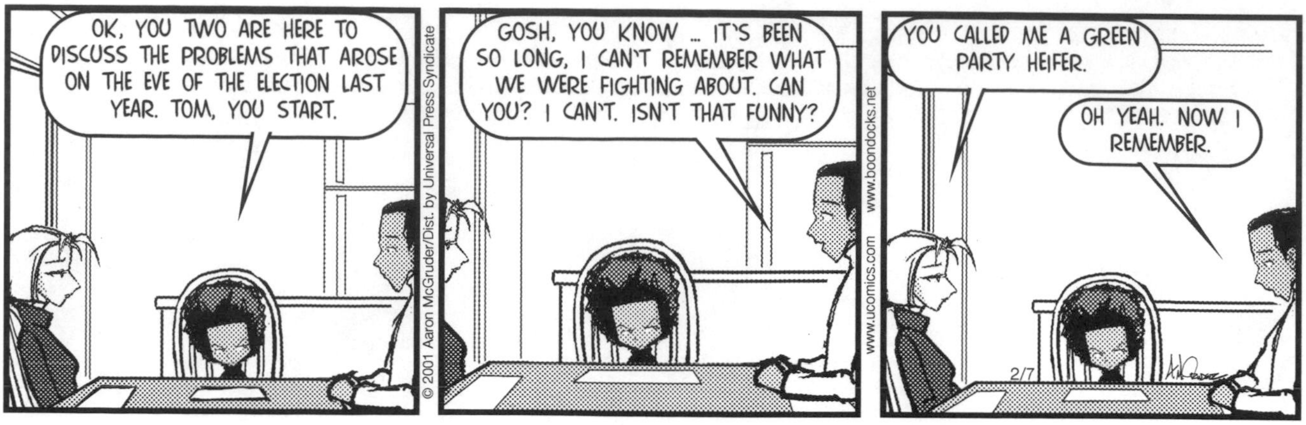
OK, YOU TWO ARE HERE TO DISCUSS THE PROBLEMS THAT AROSE ON THE EVE OF THE ELECTION LAST YEAR. TOM, YOU START.
GOSH, YOU KNOW ... IT'S BEEN SO LONG, I CAN'T REMEMBER WHAT WE WERE FIGHTING ABOUT. CAN YOU? I CAN'T. ISN'T THAT FUNNY?
YOU CALLED ME A GREEN PARTY HEIFER.
OH YEAH. NOW I REMEMBER.
© 2001 Aaron McGruder/Dist. by Universal Press Syndicate
www.ucomics.com www.boondocks.net
2/7

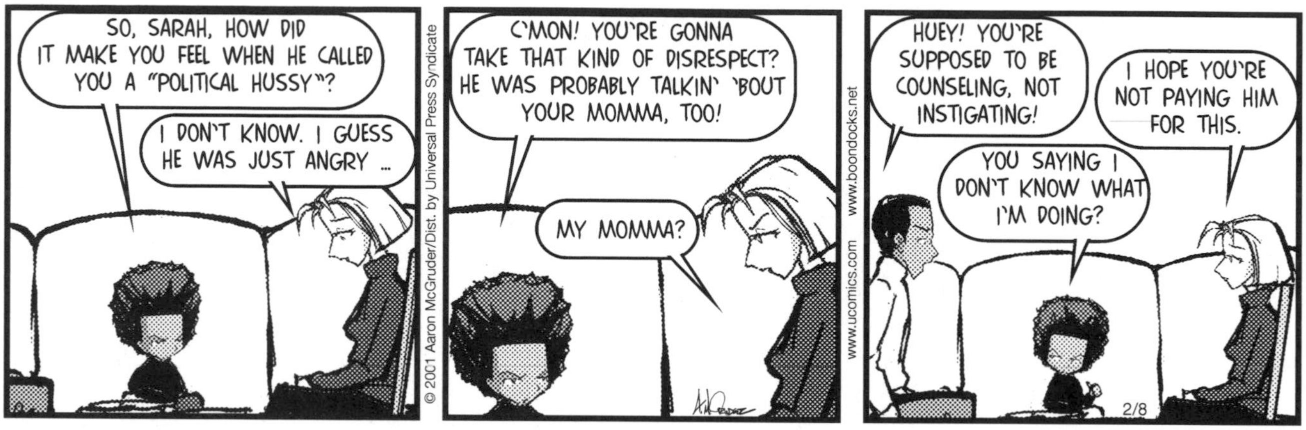
SO, SARAH, HOW DID IT MAKE YOU FEEL WHEN HE CALLED YOU A "POLITICAL HUSSY"?
I DON'T KNOW. I GUESS HE WAS JUST ANGRY ...
C'MON! YOU'RE GONNA TAKE THAT KIND OF DISRESPECT? HE WAS PROBABLY TALKIN' 'BOUT YOUR MOMMA, TOO!
MY MOMMA?
HUEY! YOU'RE SUPPOSED TO BE COUNSELING, NOT INSTIGATING!
I HOPE YOU'RE NOT PAYING HIM FOR THIS.
YOU SAYING I DON'T KNOW WHAT I'M DOING?
© 2001 Aaron McGruder/Dist. by Universal Press Syndicate
www.ucomics.com www.boondocks.net
2/8

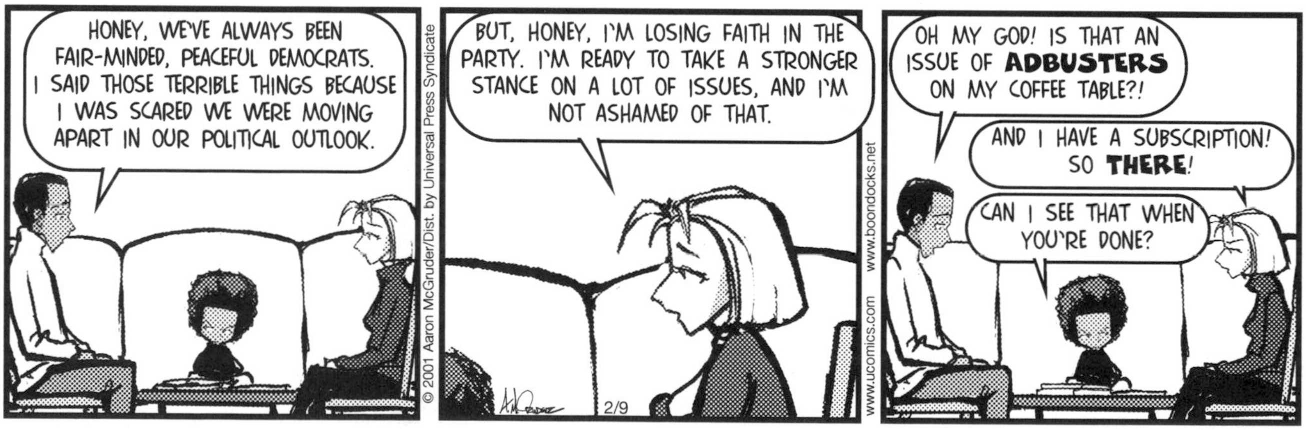
HONEY, WE'VE ALWAYS BEEN FAIR-MINDED, PEACEFUL DEMOCRATS. I SAID THOSE TERRIBLE THINGS BECAUSE I WAS SCARED WE WERE MOVING APART IN OUR POLITICAL OUTLOOK.
BUT, HONEY, I'M LOSING FAITH IN THE PARTY. I'M READY TO TAKE A STRONGER STANCE ON A LOT OF ISSUES, AND I'M NOT ASHAMED OF THAT.
OH MY GOD! IS THAT AN ISSUE OF ADBUSTERS ON MY COFFEE TABLE?!
AND I HAVE A SUBSCRIPTION! SO THERE!
CAN I SEE THAT WHEN YOU'RE DONE?
© 2001 Aaron McGruder/Dist. by Universal Press Syndicate
www.ucomics.com www.boondocks.net
2/9

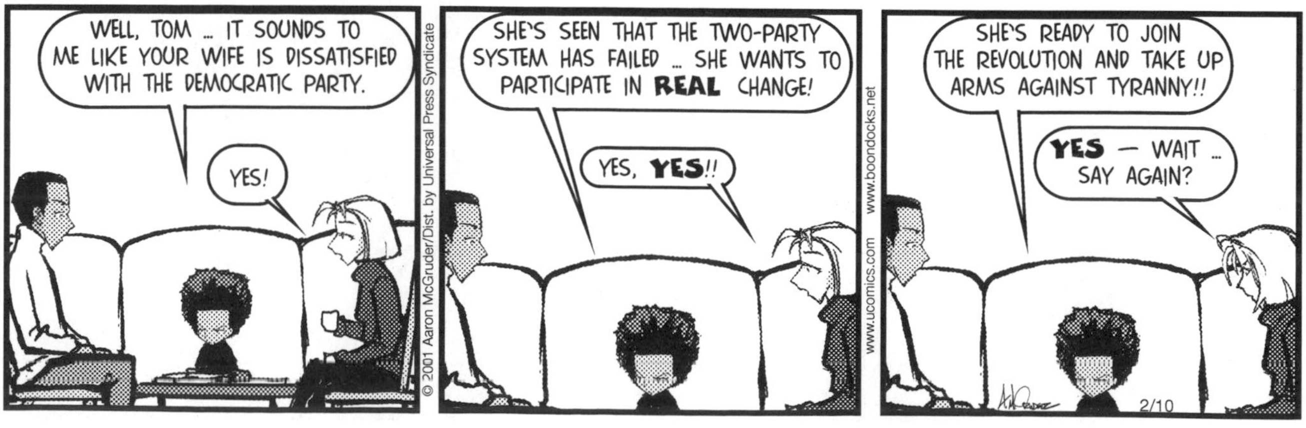
WELL, TOM ... IT SOUNDS TO ME LIKE YOUR WIFE IS DISSATISFIED WITH THE DEMOCRATIC PARTY.
YES!
SHE'S SEEN THAT THE TWO-PARTY SYSTEM HAS FAILED ... SHE WANTS TO PARTICIPATE IN REAL CHANGE!
YES, YES!!
SHE'S READY TO JOIN THE REVOLUTION AND TAKE UP ARMS AGAINST TYRANNY!!
YES — WAIT ... SAY AGAIN?
© 2001 Aaron McGruder/Dist. by Universal Press Syndicate
www.ucomics.com www.boondocks.net
2/10

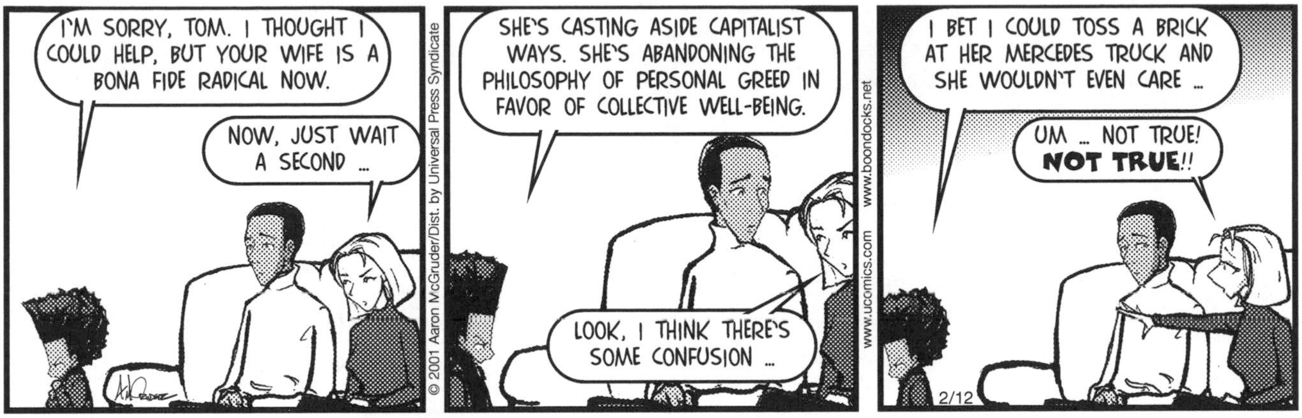
I'M SORRY, TOM. I THOUGHT I COULD HELP, BUT YOUR WIFE IS A BONA FIDE RADICAL NOW.
NOW, JUST WAIT A SECOND ...
© 2001 Aaron McGruder/Dist. by Universal Press Syndicate
SHE'S CASTING ASIDE CAPITALIST WAYS. SHE'S ABANDONING THE PHILOSOPHY OF PERSONAL GREED IN FAVOR OF COLLECTIVE WELL-BEING.
LOOK, I THINK THERE'S SOME CONFUSION ...
www.ucomics.com www.boondocks.net
I BET I COULD TOSS A BRICK AT HER MERCEDES TRUCK AND SHE WOULDN'T EVEN CARE ...
UM ... NOT TRUE! NOT TRUE!!
2/12

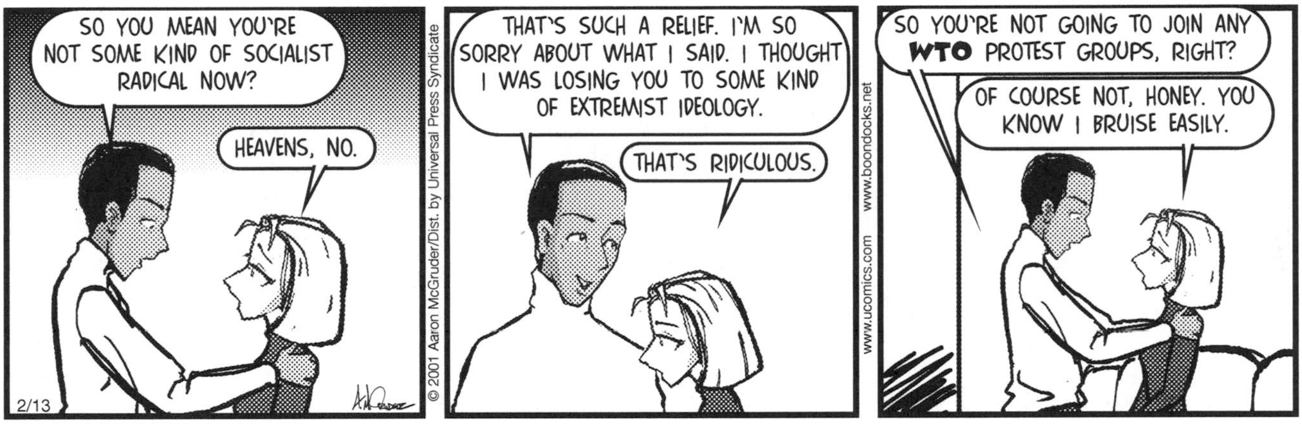
SO YOU MEAN YOU'RE NOT SOME KIND OF SOCIALIST RADICAL NOW?
HEAVENS, NO.
2/13
© 2001 Aaron McGruder/Dist. by Universal Press Syndicate
THAT'S SUCH A RELIEF. I'M SO SORRY ABOUT WHAT I SAID. I THOUGHT I WAS LOSING YOU TO SOME KIND OF EXTREMIST IDEOLOGY.
THAT'S RIDICULOUS.
www.ucomics.com www.boondocks.net
SO YOU'RE NOT GOING TO JOIN ANY WTO PROTEST GROUPS, RIGHT?
OF COURSE NOT, HONEY. YOU KNOW I BRUISE EASILY.

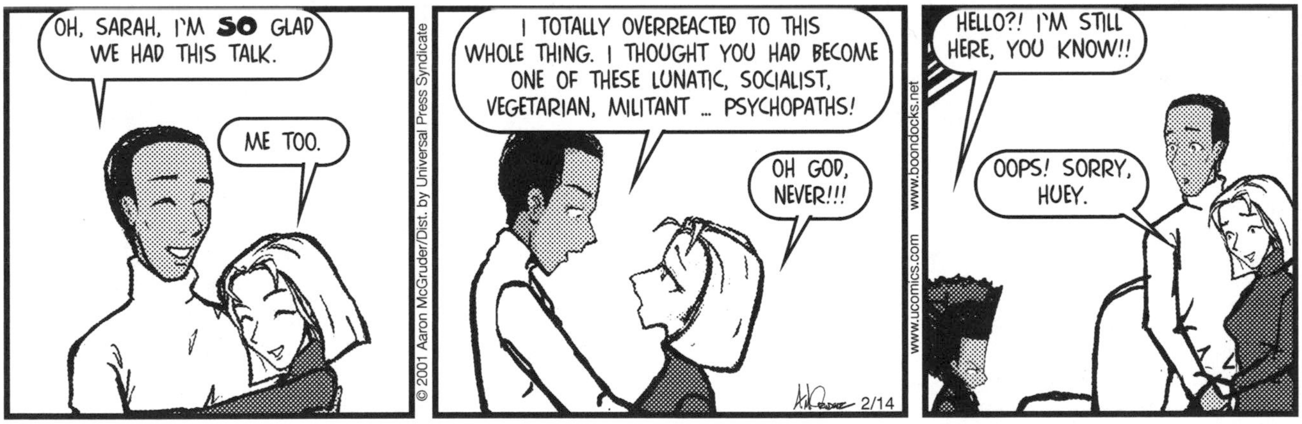
OH, SARAH, I'M SO GLAD WE HAD THIS TALK.
ME TOO.
© 2001 Aaron McGruder/Dist. by Universal Press Syndicate
I TOTALLY OVERREACTED TO THIS WHOLE THING. I THOUGHT YOU HAD BECOME ONE OF THESE LUNATIC, SOCIALIST, VEGETARIAN, MILITANT ... PSYCHOPATHS!
OH GOD, NEVER!!!
2/14
www.ucomics.com www.boondocks.net
HELLO?! I'M STILL HERE, YOU KNOW!!
OOPS! SORRY, HUEY.

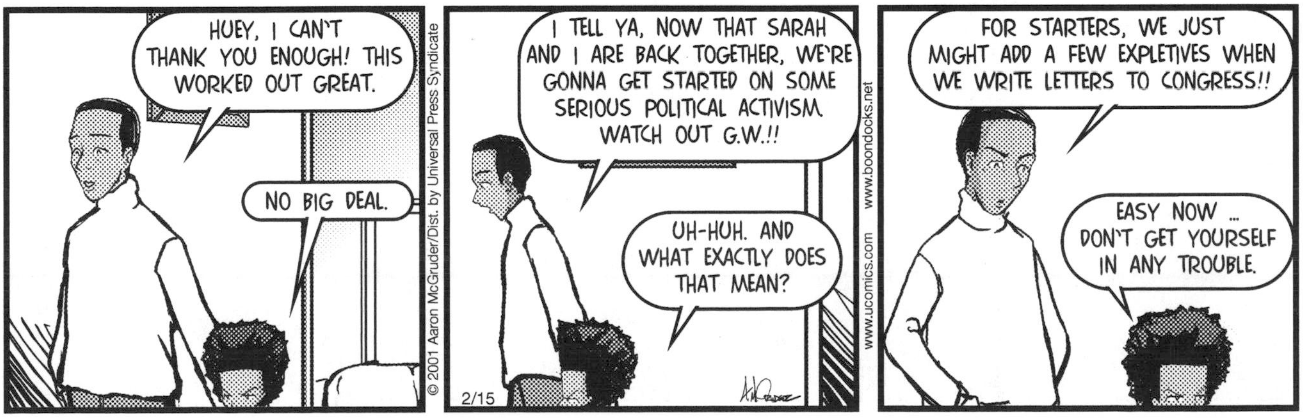
HUEY, I CAN'T THANK YOU ENOUGH! THIS WORKED OUT GREAT.
NO BIG DEAL.
© 2001 Aaron McGruder/Dist. by Universal Press Syndicate
I TELL YA, NOW THAT SARAH AND I ARE BACK TOGETHER, WE'RE GONNA GET STARTED ON SOME SERIOUS POLITICAL ACTIVISM. WATCH OUT G.W.!!
UH-HUH. AND WHAT EXACTLY DOES THAT MEAN?
2/15
www.ucomics.com www.boondocks.net
FOR STARTERS, WE JUST MIGHT ADD A FEW EXPLETIVES WHEN WE WRITE LETTERS TO CONGRESS!!
EASY NOW ... DON'T GET YOURSELF IN ANY TROUBLE.

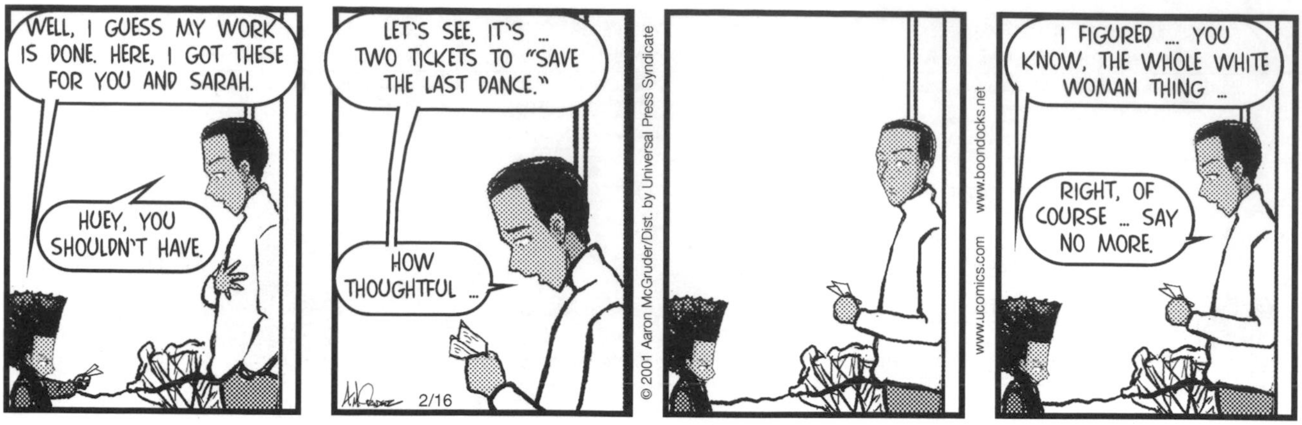
WELL, I GUESS MY WORK IS DONE. HERE, I GOT THESE FOR YOU AND SARAH.
HUEY, YOU SHOULDN'T HAVE.
2/16
LET'S SEE, IT'S ... TWO TICKETS TO "SAVE THE LAST DANCE."
HOW THOUGHTFUL ...
© 2001 Aaron McGruder/Dist. by Universal Press Syndicate
I FIGURED .... YOU KNOW, THE WHOLE WHITE WOMAN THING ...
RIGHT, OF COURSE ... SAY NO MORE.
www.ucomics.com www.boondocks.net

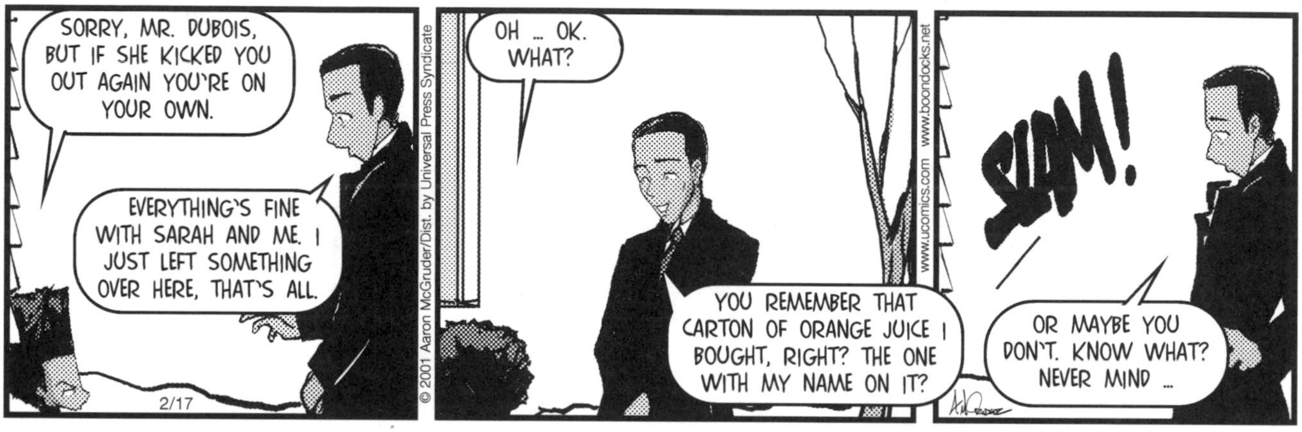
SORRY, MR. DUBOIS, BUT IF SHE KICKED YOU OUT AGAIN YOU'RE ON YOUR OWN.
EVERYTHING'S FINE WITH SARAH AND ME. I JUST LEFT SOMETHING OVER HERE, THAT'S ALL.
2/17
© 2001 Aaron McGruder/Dist. by Universal Press Syndicate
OH ... OK. WHAT?
YOU REMEMBER THAT CARTON OF ORANGE JUICE I BOUGHT, RIGHT? THE ONE WITH MY NAME ON IT?
www.ucomics.com www.boondocks.net
SLAM!
OR MAYBE YOU DON'T. KNOW WHAT? NEVER MIND ...

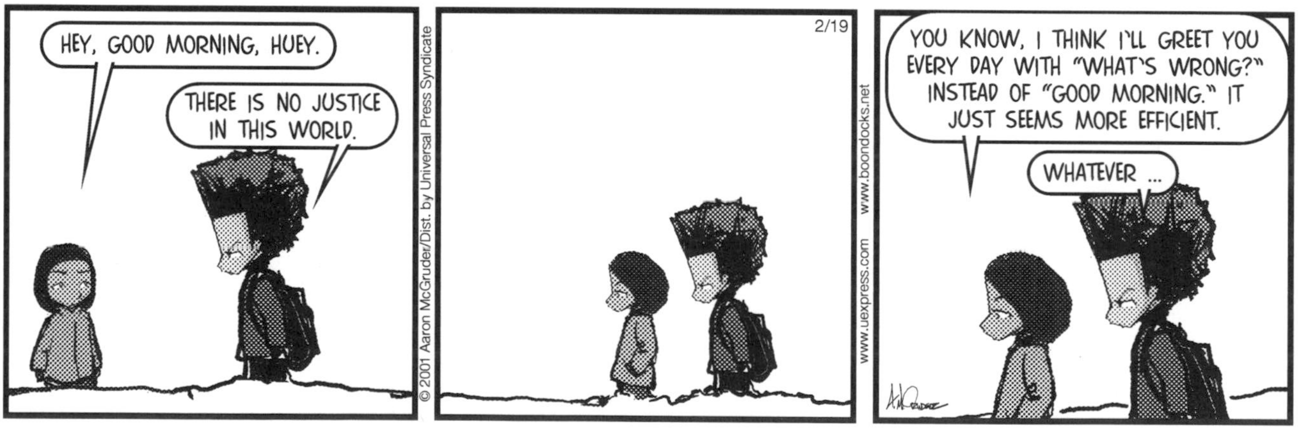
HEY, GOOD MORNING, HUEY.
THERE IS NO JUSTICE IN THIS WORLD.
© 2001 Aaron McGruder/Dist. by Universal Press Syndicate
2/19
www.uexpress.com www.boondocks.net
YOU KNOW, I THINK I'LL GREET YOU EVERY DAY WITH "WHAT'S WRONG?" INSTEAD OF "GOOD MORNING." IT JUST SEEMS MORE EFFICIENT.
WHATEVER ...

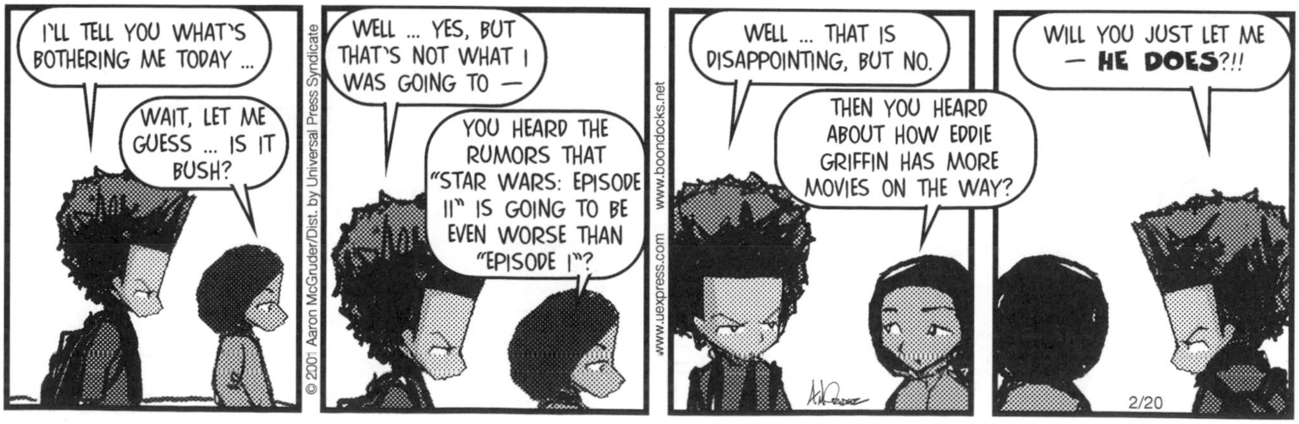
I'LL TELL YOU WHAT'S BOTHERING ME TODAY ...
WAIT, LET ME GUESS ... IS IT BUSH?
© 2001 Aaron McGruder/Dist. by Universal Press Syndicate
WELL ... YES, BUT THAT'S NOT WHAT I WAS GOING TO —
YOU HEARD THE RUMORS THAT "STAR WARS: EPISODE II" IS GOING TO BE EVEN WORSE THAN "EPISODE I"?
www.uexpress.com www.boondocks.net
WELL ... THAT IS DISAPPOINTING, BUT NO.
THEN YOU HEARD ABOUT HOW EDDIE GRIFFIN HAS MORE MOVIES ON THE WAY?
WILL YOU JUST LET ME — HE DOES?!!
2/20

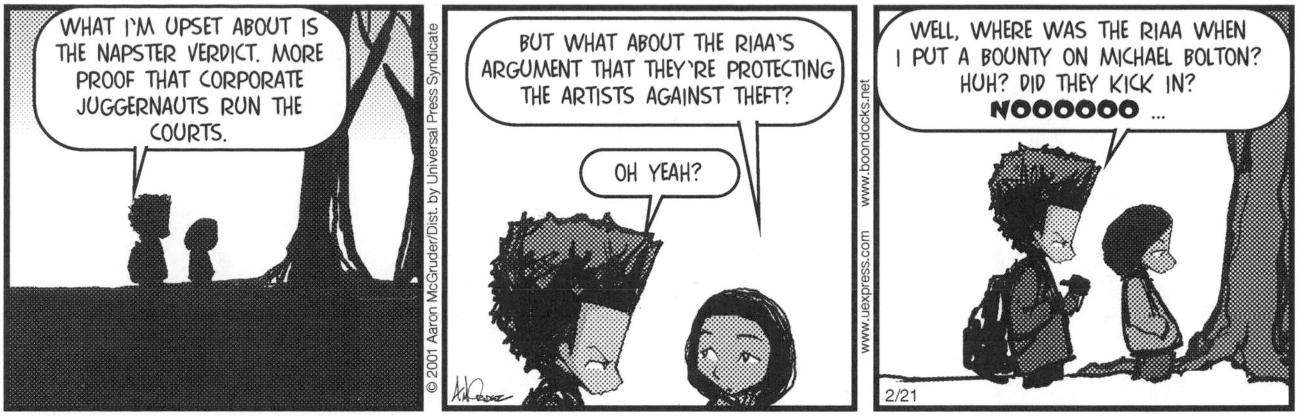
WHAT I'M UPSET ABOUT IS THE NAPSTER VERDICT. MORE PROOF THAT CORPORATE JUGGERNAUTS RUN THE COURTS.
BUT WHAT ABOUT THE RIAA'S ARGUMENT THAT THEY'RE PROTECTING THE ARTISTS AGAINST THEFT?
OH YEAH?
WELL, WHERE WAS THE RIAA WHEN I PUT A BOUNTY ON MICHAEL BOLTON? HUH? DID THEY KICK IN? NOOOOOO ...
© 2001 Aaron McGruder/Dist. by Universal Press Syndicate
www.uexpress.com
www.boondocks.net
2/21

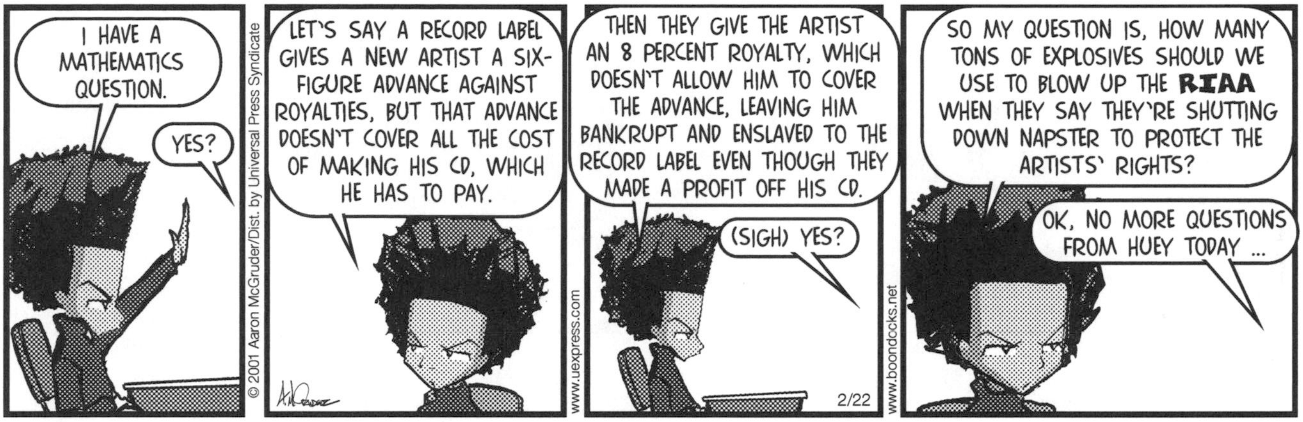
I HAVE A MATHEMATICS QUESTION.
YES?
LET'S SAY A RECORD LABEL GIVES A NEW ARTIST A SIX-FIGURE ADVANCE AGAINST ROYALTIES, BUT THAT ADVANCE DOESN'T COVER ALL THE COST OF MAKING HIS CD, WHICH HE HAS TO PAY.
THEN THEY GIVE THE ARTIST AN 8 PERCENT ROYALTY, WHICH DOESN'T ALLOW HIM TO COVER THE ADVANCE, LEAVING HIM BANKRUPT AND ENSLAVED TO THE RECORD LABEL EVEN THOUGH THEY MADE A PROFIT OFF HIS CD.
(SIGH) YES?
SO MY QUESTION IS, HOW MANY TONS OF EXPLOSIVES SHOULD WE USE TO BLOW UP THE RIAA WHEN THEY SAY THEY'RE SHUTTING DOWN NAPSTER TO PROTECT THE ARTISTS' RIGHTS?
OK, NO MORE QUESTIONS FROM HUEY TODAY ...
© 2001 Aaron McGruder/Dist. by Universal Press Syndicate
www.uexpress.com
www.boondocks.net
2/22

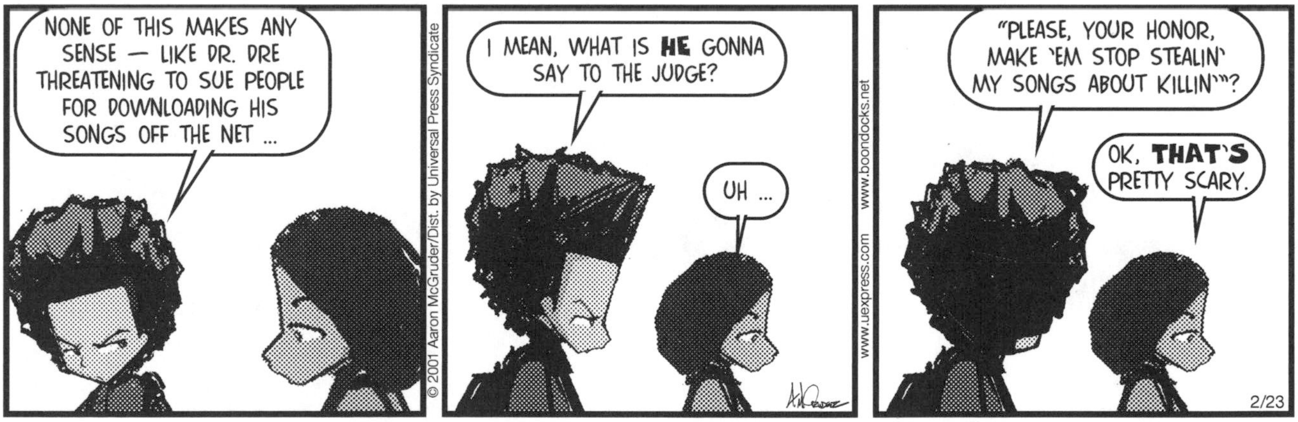
NONE OF THIS MAKES ANY SENSE — LIKE DR. DRE THREATENING TO SUE PEOPLE FOR DOWNLOADING HIS SONGS OFF THE NET ...
I MEAN, WHAT IS HE GONNA SAY TO THE JUDGE?
UH ...
"PLEASE, YOUR HONOR, MAKE 'EM STOP STEALIN' MY SONGS ABOUT KILLIN'"?
OK, THAT'S PRETTY SCARY.
© 2001 Aaron McGruder/Dist. by Universal Press Syndicate
www.uexpress.com
www.boondocks.net
2/23

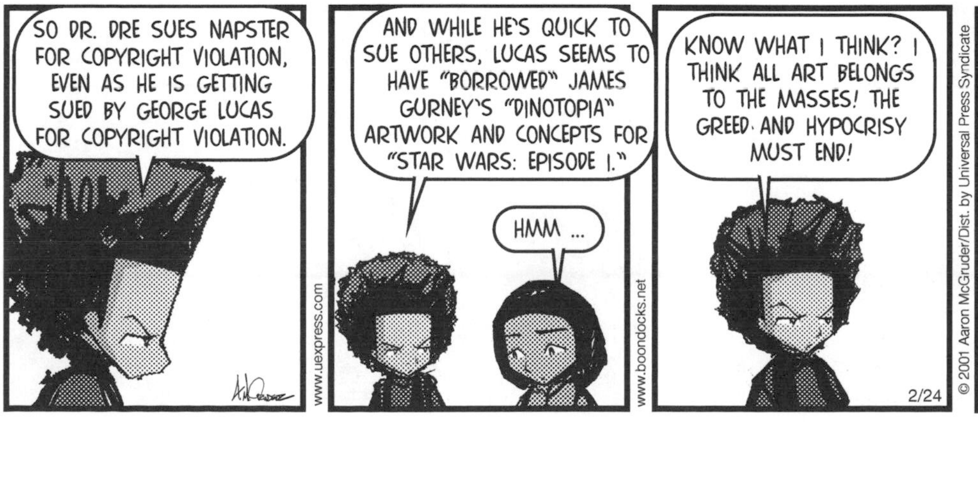
SO DR. DRE SUES NAPSTER FOR COPYRIGHT VIOLATION, EVEN AS HE IS GETTING SUED BY GEORGE LUCAS FOR COPYRIGHT VIOLATION.
AND WHILE HE'S QUICK TO SUE OTHERS, LUCAS SEEMS TO HAVE "BORROWED" JAMES GURNEY'S "DINOTOPIA" ARTWORK AND CONCEPTS FOR "STAR WARS: EPISODE I."
HMM ...
KNOW WHAT I THINK? I THINK ALL ART BELONGS TO THE MASSES! THE GREED AND HYPOCRISY MUST END!
www.uexpress.com
www.boondocks.net
© 2001 Aaron McGruder/Dist. by Universal Press Syndicate
2/24

The opinions expressed by Aaron McGruder are not necessarily those of Aaron McGruder. All images are

©

Aaron McGruder, 2001. Any unauthorized reproduction will be prosecuted to the fullest extent of the law.

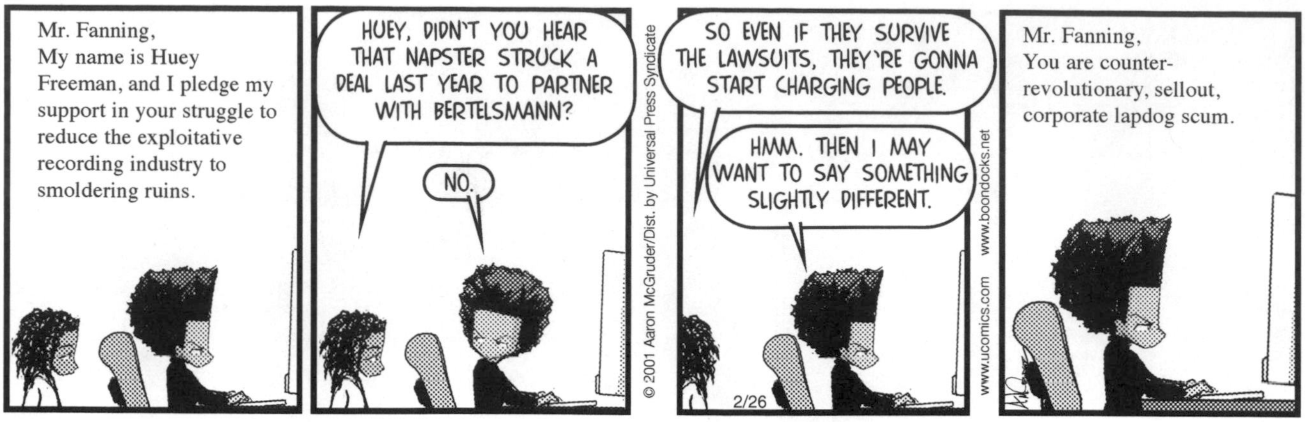
Mr. Fanning,
My name is Huey Freeman, and I pledge my support in your struggle to reduce the exploitative recording industry to smoldering ruins.
HUEY, DIDN'T YOU HEAR THAT NAPSTER STRUCK A DEAL LAST YEAR TO PARTNER WITH BERTELSMANN?
NO.
© 2001 Aaron McGruder/Dist. by Universal Press Syndicate
SO EVEN IF THEY SURVIVE THE LAWSUITS, THEY'RE GONNA START CHARGING PEOPLE.
HMM. THEN I MAY WANT TO SAY SOMETHING SLIGHTLY DIFFERENT.
2/26
www.ucomics.com www.boondocks.net
Mr. Fanning,
You are counter-revolutionary, sellout, corporate lapdog scum.

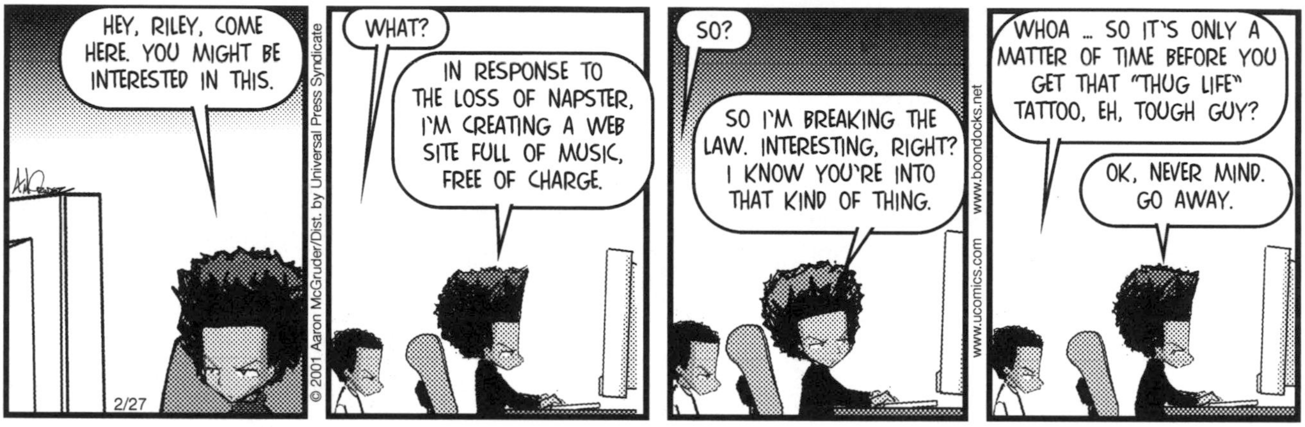
HEY, RILEY, COME HERE. YOU MIGHT BE INTERESTED IN THIS.
2/27
© 2001 Aaron McGruder/Dist. by Universal Press Syndicate
WHAT?
IN RESPONSE TO THE LOSS OF NAPSTER, I'M CREATING A WEB SITE FULL OF MUSIC, FREE OF CHARGE.
SO?
SO I'M BREAKING THE LAW. INTERESTING, RIGHT? I KNOW YOU'RE INTO THAT KIND OF THING.
www.ucomics.com www.boondocks.net
WHOA ... SO IT'S ONLY A MATTER OF TIME BEFORE YOU GET THAT "THUG LIFE" TATTOO, EH, TOUGH GUY?
OK, NEVER MIND. GO AWAY.

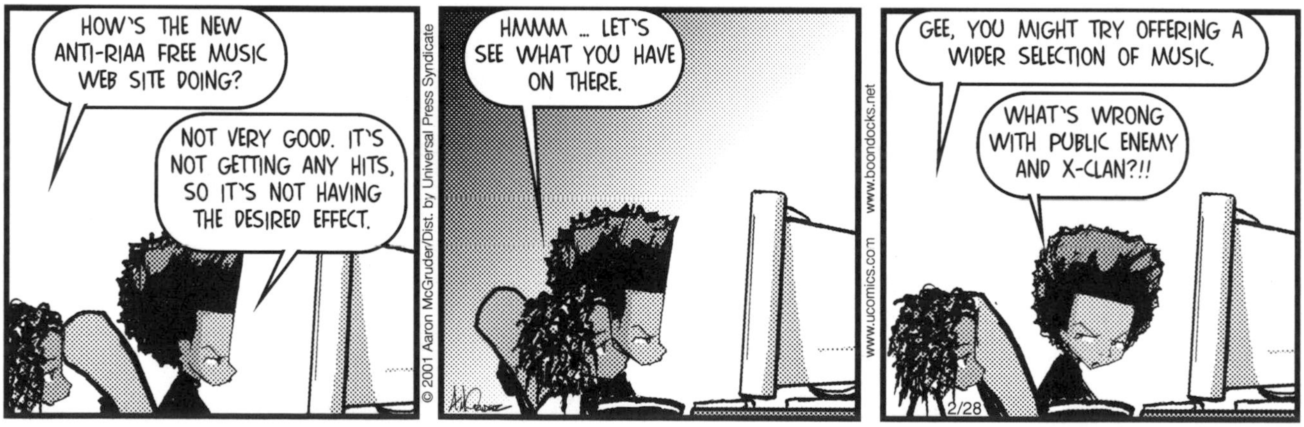
HOW'S THE NEW ANTI-RIAA FREE MUSIC WEB SITE DOING?
NOT VERY GOOD. IT'S NOT GETTING ANY HITS, SO IT'S NOT HAVING THE DESIRED EFFECT.
© 2001 Aaron McGruder/Dist. by Universal Press Syndicate
HMMM ... LET'S SEE WHAT YOU HAVE ON THERE.
www.ucomics.com www.boondocks.net
GEE, YOU MIGHT TRY OFFERING A WIDER SELECTION OF MUSIC.
WHAT'S WRONG WITH PUBLIC ENEMY AND X-CLAN?!!
2/28

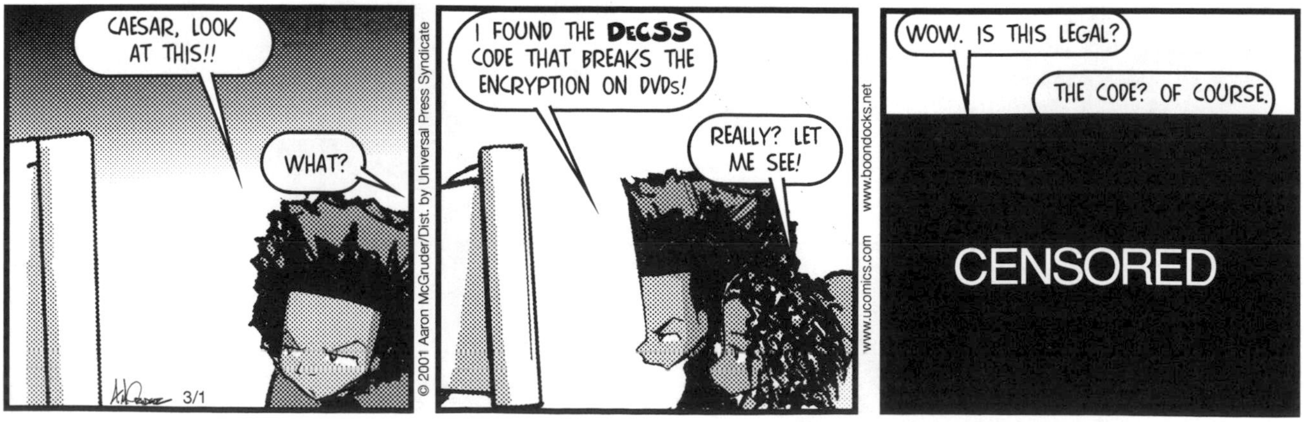
CAESAR, LOOK AT THIS!!
WHAT?
3/1
© 2001 Aaron McGruder/Dist. by Universal Press Syndicate
I FOUND THE DeCSS CODE THAT BREAKS THE ENCRYPTION ON DVDs!
REALLY? LET ME SEE!
www.ucomics.com www.boondocks.net
WOW. IS THIS LEGAL?
THE CODE? OF COURSE.
CENSORED

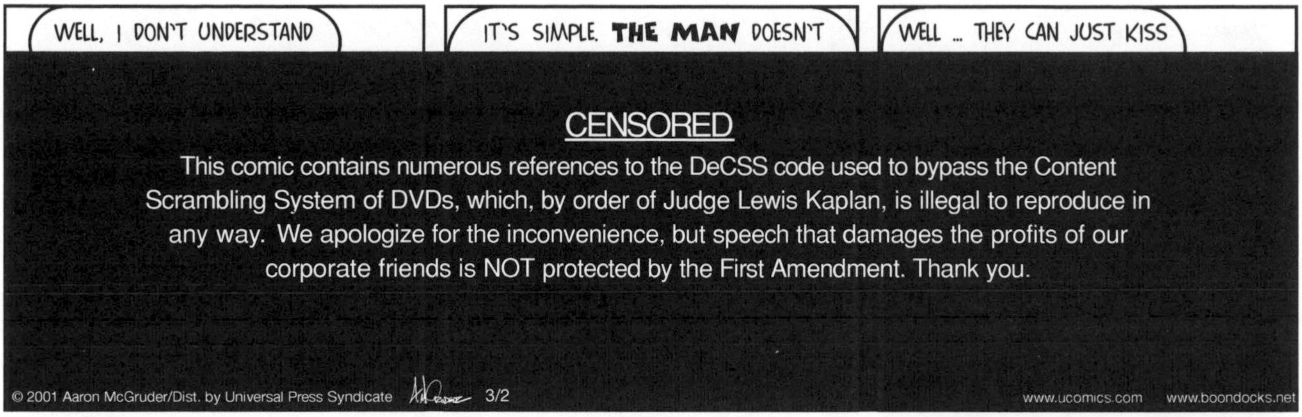
WELL, I DON'T UNDERSTAND
IT'S SIMPLE. THE MAN DOESN'T
WELL ... THEY CAN JUST KISS
CENSORED
This comic contains numerous references to the DeCSS code used to bypass the Content Scrambling System of DVDs, which, by order of Judge Lewis Kaplan, is illegal to reproduce in any way. We apologize for the inconvenience, but speech that damages the profits of our corporate friends is NOT protected by the First Amendment. Thank you.
© 2001 Aaron McGruder/Dist. by Universal Press Syndicate 3/2
www.ucomics.com www.boondocks.net

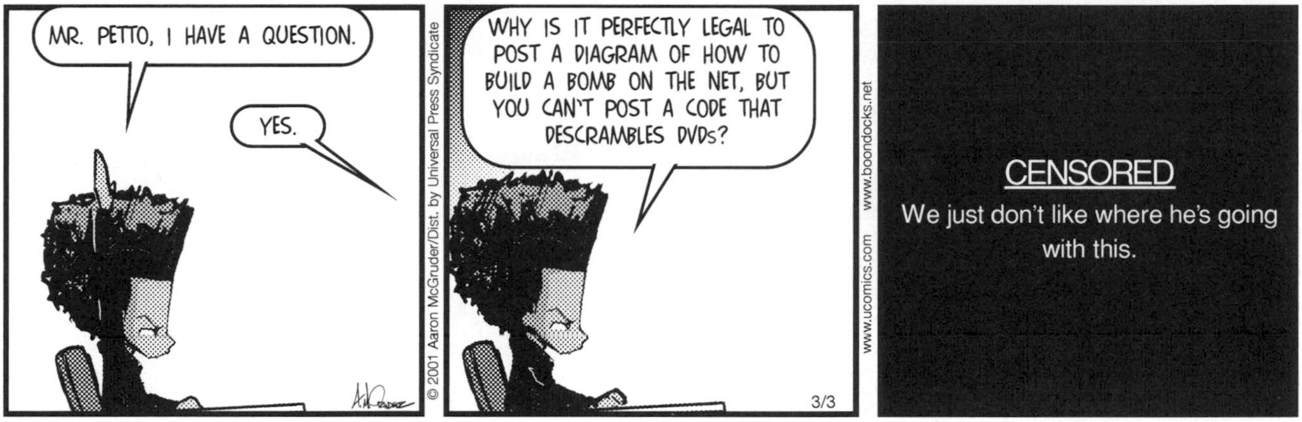
MR. PETTO, I HAVE A QUESTION.
YES.
WHY IS IT PERFECTLY LEGAL TO POST A DIAGRAM OF HOW TO BUILD A BOMB ON THE NET, BUT YOU CAN'T POST A CODE THAT DESCRAMBLES DVDs?
CENSORED
We just don't like where he's going with this.
© 2001 Aaron McGruder/Dist. by Universal Press Syndicate
www.ucomics.com www.boondocks.net
3/3

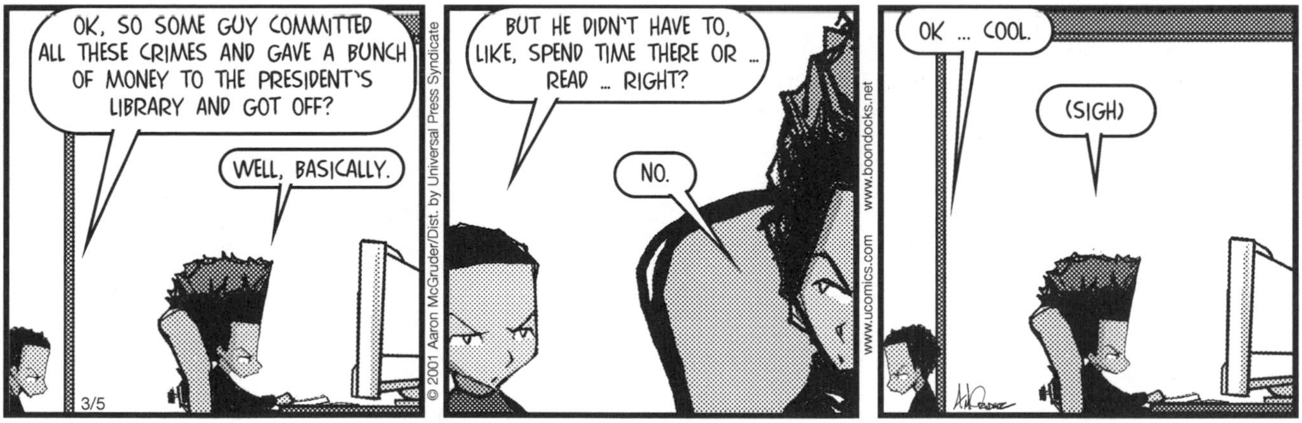
OK, SO SOME GUY COMMITTED ALL THESE CRIMES AND GAVE A BUNCH OF MONEY TO THE PRESIDENT'S LIBRARY AND GOT OFF?
WELL, BASICALLY.
BUT HE DIDN'T HAVE TO, LIKE, SPEND TIME THERE OR ... READ ... RIGHT?
NO.
OK ... COOL.
(SIGH)
3/5
© 2001 Aaron McGruder/Dist. by Universal Press Syndicate
www.ucomics.com www.boondocks.net

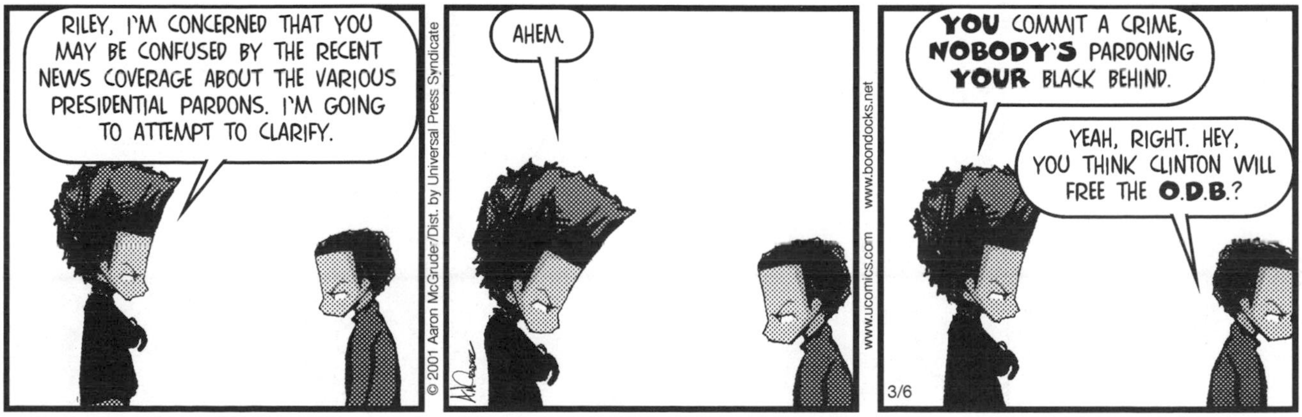
RILEY, I'M CONCERNED THAT YOU MAY BE CONFUSED BY THE RECENT NEWS COVERAGE ABOUT THE VARIOUS PRESIDENTIAL PARDONS. I'M GOING TO ATTEMPT TO CLARIFY.
AHEM.
YOU COMMIT A CRIME, NOBODY'S PARDONING YOUR BLACK BEHIND.
YEAH, RIGHT. HEY, YOU THINK CLINTON WILL FREE THE O.D.B.?
© 2001 Aaron McGruder/Dist. by Universal Press Syndicate
www.ucomics.com www.boondocks.net
3/6

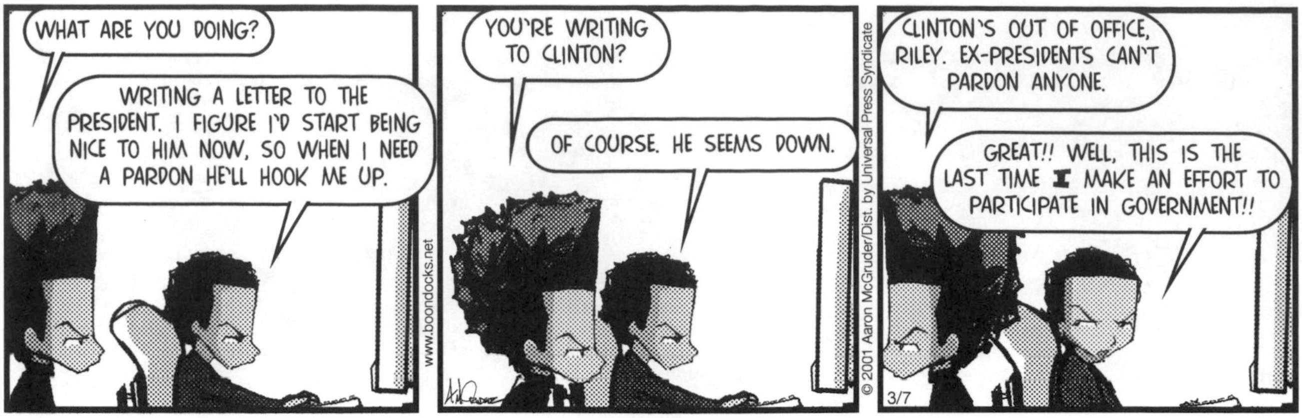
WHAT ARE YOU DOING?
WRITING A LETTER TO THE PRESIDENT. I FIGURE I'D START BEING NICE TO HIM NOW, SO WHEN I NEED A PARDON HE'LL HOOK ME UP.
www.boondocks.net
YOU'RE WRITING TO CLINTON?
OF COURSE. HE SEEMS DOWN.
© 2001 Aaron McGruder/Dist. by Universal Press Syndicate
CLINTON'S OUT OF OFFICE, RILEY. EX-PRESIDENTS CAN'T PARDON ANYONE.
GREAT!! WELL, THIS IS THE LAST TIME **I** MAKE AN EFFORT TO PARTICIPATE IN GOVERNMENT!!
3/7

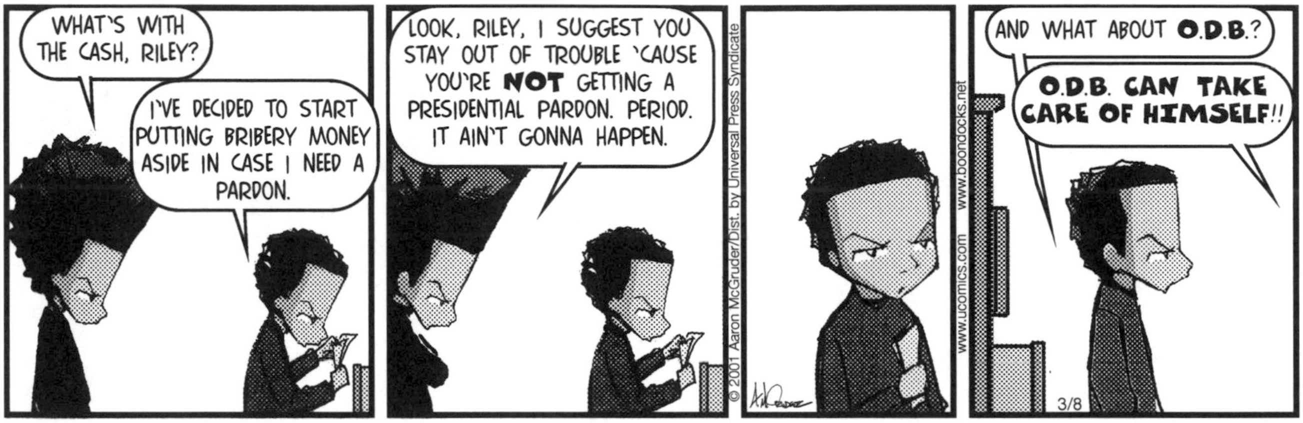
WHAT'S WITH THE CASH, RILEY?
I'VE DECIDED TO START PUTTING BRIBERY MONEY ASIDE IN CASE I NEED A PARDON.
LOOK, RILEY, I SUGGEST YOU STAY OUT OF TROUBLE 'CAUSE YOU'RE **NOT** GETTING A PRESIDENTIAL PARDON. PERIOD. IT AIN'T GONNA HAPPEN.
© 2001 Aaron McGruder/Dist. by Universal Press Syndicate
www.ucomics.com www.boondocks.net
AND WHAT ABOUT **O.D.B.**?
O.D.B. CAN TAKE CARE OF HIMSELF!!
3/8

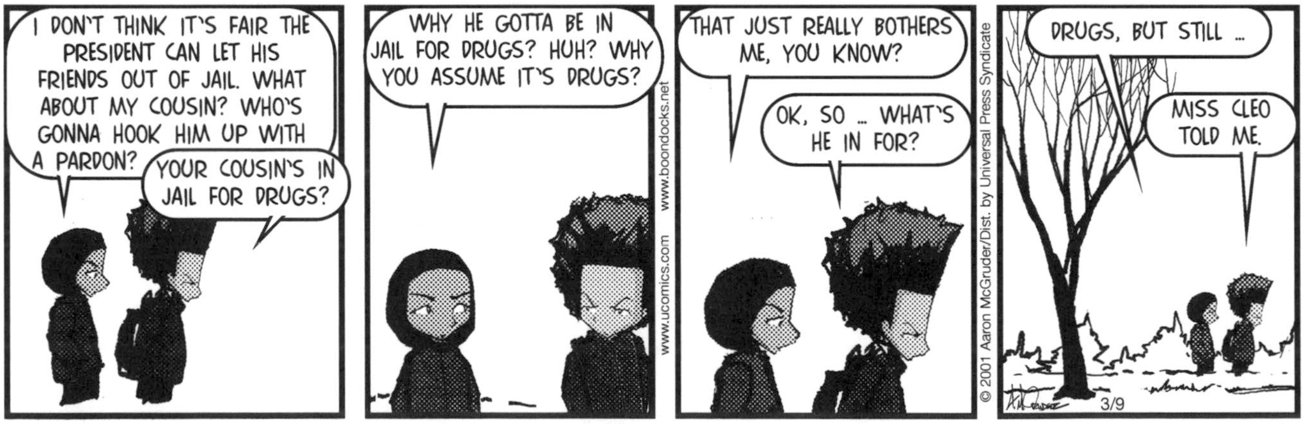
I DON'T THINK IT'S FAIR THE PRESIDENT CAN LET HIS FRIENDS OUT OF JAIL. WHAT ABOUT MY COUSIN? WHO'S GONNA HOOK HIM UP WITH A PARDON?
YOUR COUSIN'S IN JAIL FOR DRUGS?
WHY HE GOTTA BE IN JAIL FOR DRUGS? HUH? WHY YOU ASSUME IT'S DRUGS?
www.ucomics.com www.boondocks.net
THAT JUST REALLY BOTHERS ME, YOU KNOW?
OK, SO ... WHAT'S HE IN FOR?
© 2001 Aaron McGruder/Dist. by Universal Press Syndicate
DRUGS, BUT STILL ...
MISS CLEO TOLD ME.
3/9

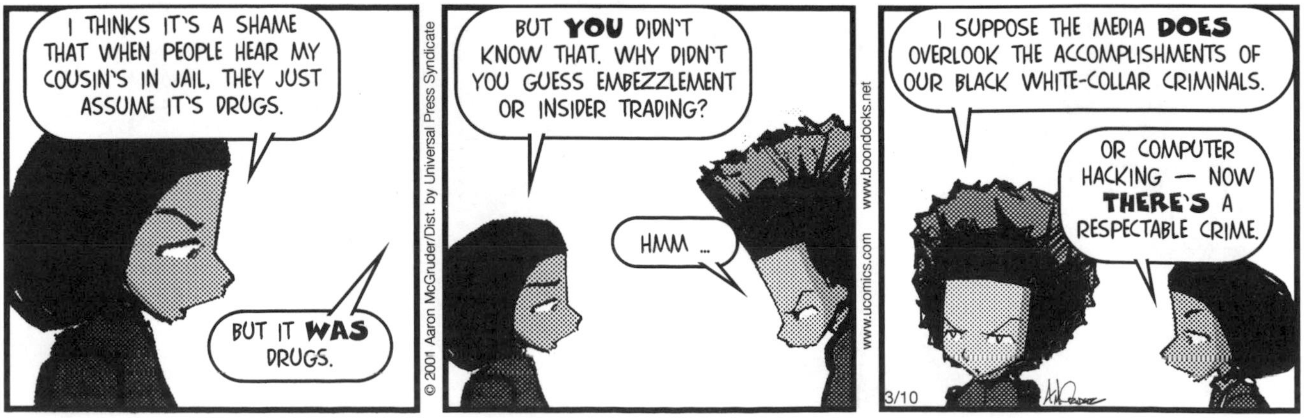
I THINKS IT'S A SHAME THAT WHEN PEOPLE HEAR MY COUSIN'S IN JAIL, THEY JUST ASSUME IT'S DRUGS.
BUT IT **WAS** DRUGS.
© 2001 Aaron McGruder/Dist. by Universal Press Syndicate
BUT **YOU** DIDN'T KNOW THAT. WHY DIDN'T YOU GUESS EMBEZZLEMENT OR INSIDER TRADING?
HMM ...
www.ucomics.com www.boondocks.net
I SUPPOSE THE MEDIA **DOES** OVERLOOK THE ACCOMPLISHMENTS OF OUR BLACK WHITE-COLLAR CRIMINALS.
OR COMPUTER HACKING — NOW **THERE'S** A RESPECTABLE CRIME.
3/10

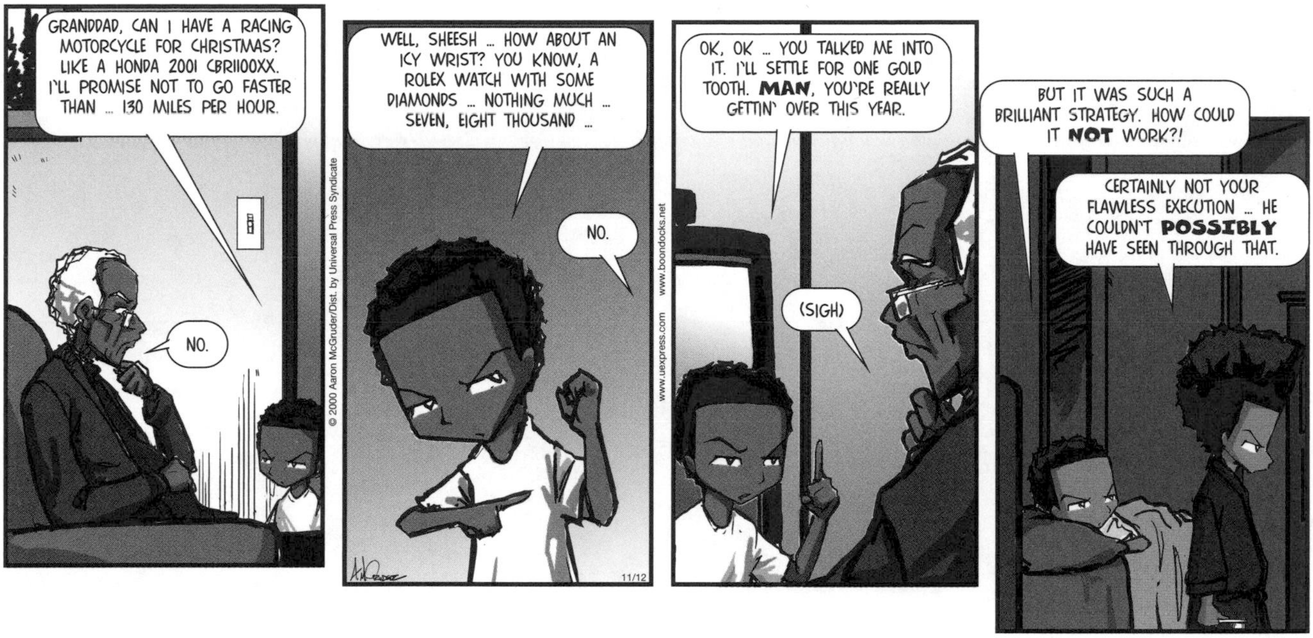
GRANDDAD, CAN I HAVE A RACING MOTORCYCLE FOR CHRISTMAS? LIKE A HONDA 2001 CBR1100XX. I'LL PROMISE NOT TO GO FASTER THAN ... 130 MILES PER HOUR.
NO.
© 2000 Aaron McGruder/Dist. by Universal Press Syndicate
WELL, SHEESH ... HOW ABOUT AN ICY WRIST? YOU KNOW, A ROLEX WATCH WITH SOME DIAMONDS ... NOTHING MUCH ... SEVEN, EIGHT THOUSAND ...
NO.
www.uexpress.com www.boondocks.net
11/12
OK, OK ... YOU TALKED ME INTO IT. I'LL SETTLE FOR ONE GOLD TOOTH. MAN, YOU'RE REALLY GETTIN' OVER THIS YEAR.
(SIGH)
BUT IT WAS SUCH A BRILLIANT STRATEGY. HOW COULD IT NOT WORK?!
CERTAINLY NOT YOUR FLAWLESS EXECUTION ... HE COULDN'T POSSIBLY HAVE SEEN THROUGH THAT.

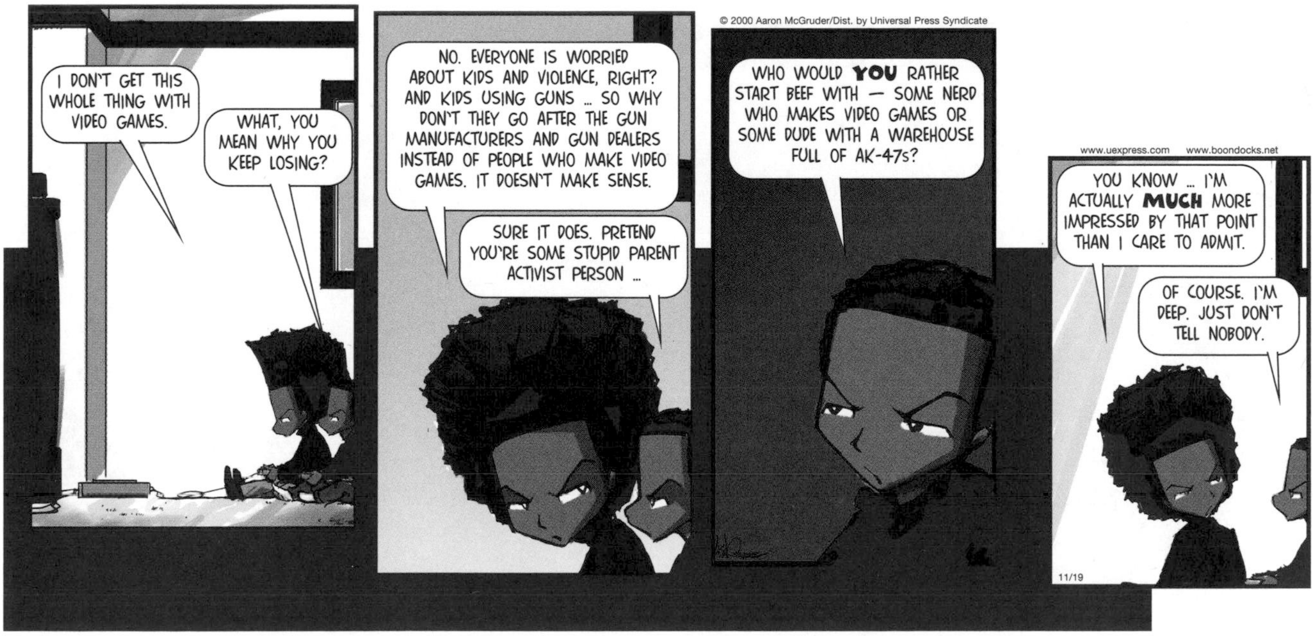
I DON'T GET THIS WHOLE THING WITH VIDEO GAMES.
WHAT, YOU MEAN WHY YOU KEEP LOSING?
NO. EVERYONE IS WORRIED ABOUT KIDS AND VIOLENCE, RIGHT? AND KIDS USING GUNS ... SO WHY DON'T THEY GO AFTER THE GUN MANUFACTURERS AND GUN DEALERS INSTEAD OF PEOPLE WHO MAKE VIDEO GAMES. IT DOESN'T MAKE SENSE.
SURE IT DOES. PRETEND YOU'RE SOME STUPID PARENT ACTIVIST PERSON ...
© 2000 Aaron McGruder/Dist. by Universal Press Syndicate
WHO WOULD YOU RATHER START BEEF WITH — SOME NERD WHO MAKES VIDEO GAMES OR SOME DUDE WITH A WAREHOUSE FULL OF AK-47s?
www.uexpress.com www.boondocks.net
YOU KNOW ... I'M ACTUALLY MUCH MORE IMPRESSED BY THAT POINT THAN I CARE TO ADMIT.
OF COURSE. I'M DEEP. JUST DON'T TELL NOBODY.
11/19

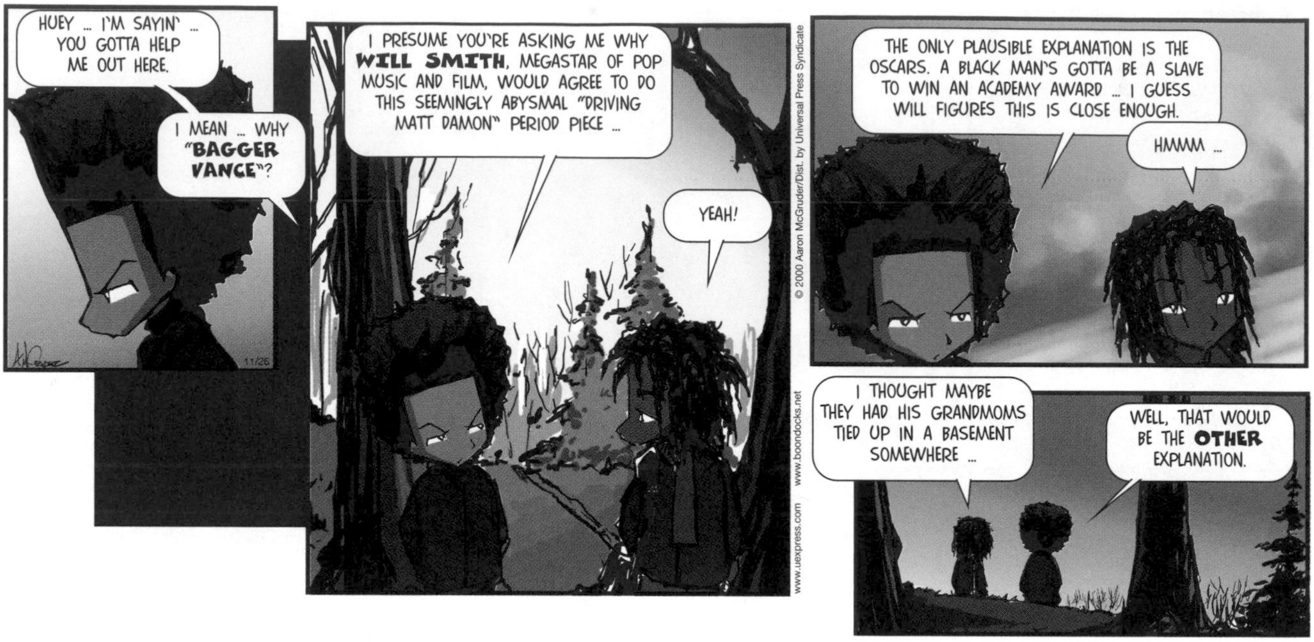

HUEY ... I'M SAYIN' ... YOU GOTTA HELP ME OUT HERE.
I MEAN ... WHY "BAGGER VANCE"?
I PRESUME YOU'RE ASKING ME WHY WILL SMITH, MEGASTAR OF POP MUSIC AND FILM, WOULD AGREE TO DO THIS SEEMINGLY ABYSMAL "DRIVING MATT DAMON" PERIOD PIECE ...
YEAH!
THE ONLY PLAUSIBLE EXPLANATION IS THE OSCARS. A BLACK MAN'S GOTTA BE A SLAVE TO WIN AN ACADEMY AWARD ... I GUESS WILL FIGURES THIS IS CLOSE ENOUGH.
HMMM ...
I THOUGHT MAYBE THEY HAD HIS GRANDMOMS TIED UP IN A BASEMENT SOMEWHERE ...
WELL, THAT WOULD BE THE OTHER EXPLANATION.
11/26
© 2000 Aaron McGruder/Dist. by Universal Press Syndicate
www.uexpress.com www.boondocks.net

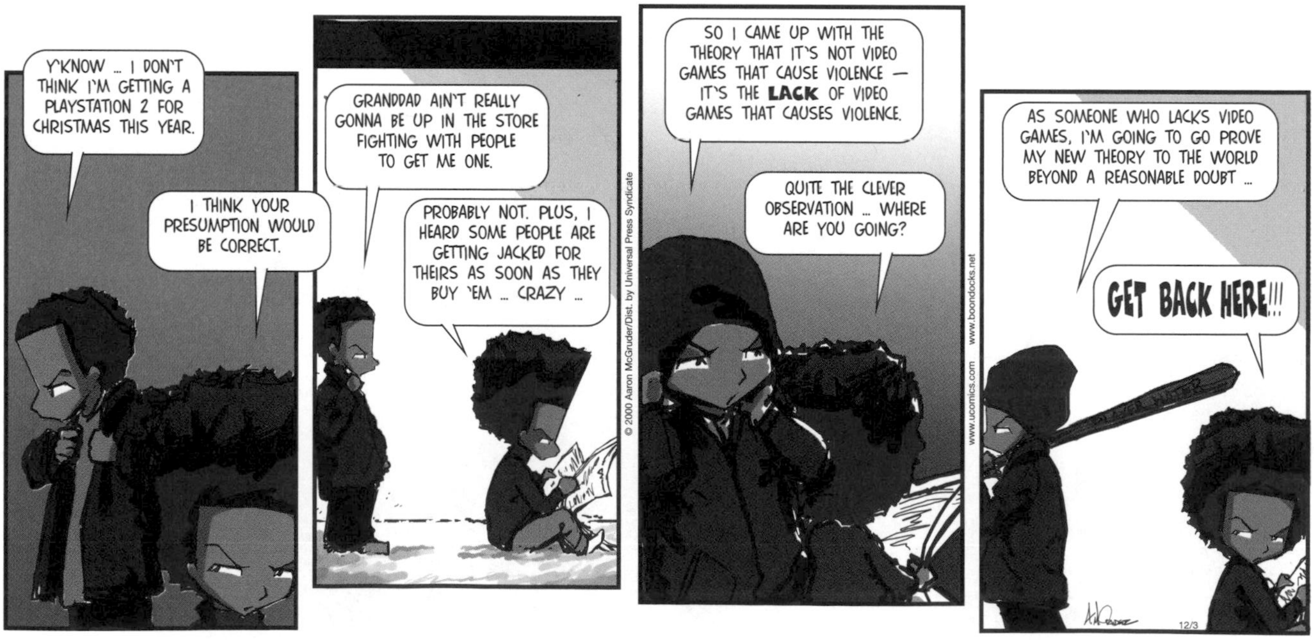

Y'KNOW ... I DON'T THINK I'M GETTING A PLAYSTATION 2 FOR CHRISTMAS THIS YEAR.
I THINK YOUR PRESUMPTION WOULD BE CORRECT.
GRANDDAD AIN'T REALLY GONNA BE UP IN THE STORE FIGHTING WITH PEOPLE TO GET ME ONE.
PROBABLY NOT. PLUS, I HEARD SOME PEOPLE ARE GETTING JACKED FOR THEIRS AS SOON AS THEY BUY 'EM ... CRAZY ...
SO I CAME UP WITH THE THEORY THAT IT'S NOT VIDEO GAMES THAT CAUSE VIOLENCE — IT'S THE LACK OF VIDEO GAMES THAT CAUSES VIOLENCE.
QUITE THE CLEVER OBSERVATION ... WHERE ARE YOU GOING?
AS SOMEONE WHO LACKS VIDEO GAMES, I'M GOING TO GO PROVE MY NEW THEORY TO THE WORLD BEYOND A REASONABLE DOUBT ...
GET BACK HERE!!!
12/3
© 2000 Aaron McGruder/Dist. by Universal Press Syndicate
www.ucomics.com www.boondocks.net

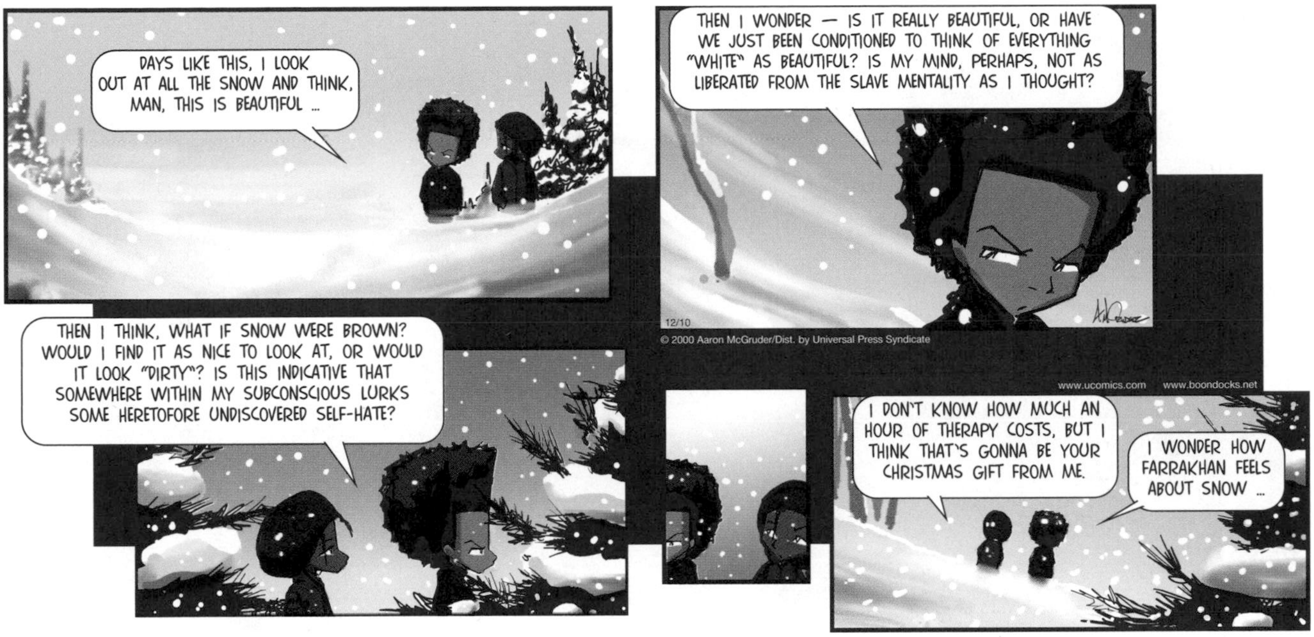
DAYS LIKE THIS, I LOOK OUT AT ALL THE SNOW AND THINK, MAN, THIS IS BEAUTIFUL ...
THEN I WONDER — IS IT REALLY BEAUTIFUL, OR HAVE WE JUST BEEN CONDITIONED TO THINK OF EVERYTHING "WHITE" AS BEAUTIFUL? IS MY MIND, PERHAPS, NOT AS LIBERATED FROM THE SLAVE MENTALITY AS I THOUGHT?
12/10
© 2000 Aaron McGruder/Dist. by Universal Press Syndicate
www.ucomics.com www.boondocks.net
THEN I THINK, WHAT IF SNOW WERE BROWN? WOULD I FIND IT AS NICE TO LOOK AT, OR WOULD IT LOOK "DIRTY"? IS THIS INDICATIVE THAT SOMEWHERE WITHIN MY SUBCONSCIOUS LURKS SOME HERETOFORE UNDISCOVERED SELF-HATE?
I DON'T KNOW HOW MUCH AN HOUR OF THERAPY COSTS, BUT I THINK THAT'S GONNA BE YOUR CHRISTMAS GIFT FROM ME.
I WONDER HOW FARRAKHAN FEELS ABOUT SNOW ...

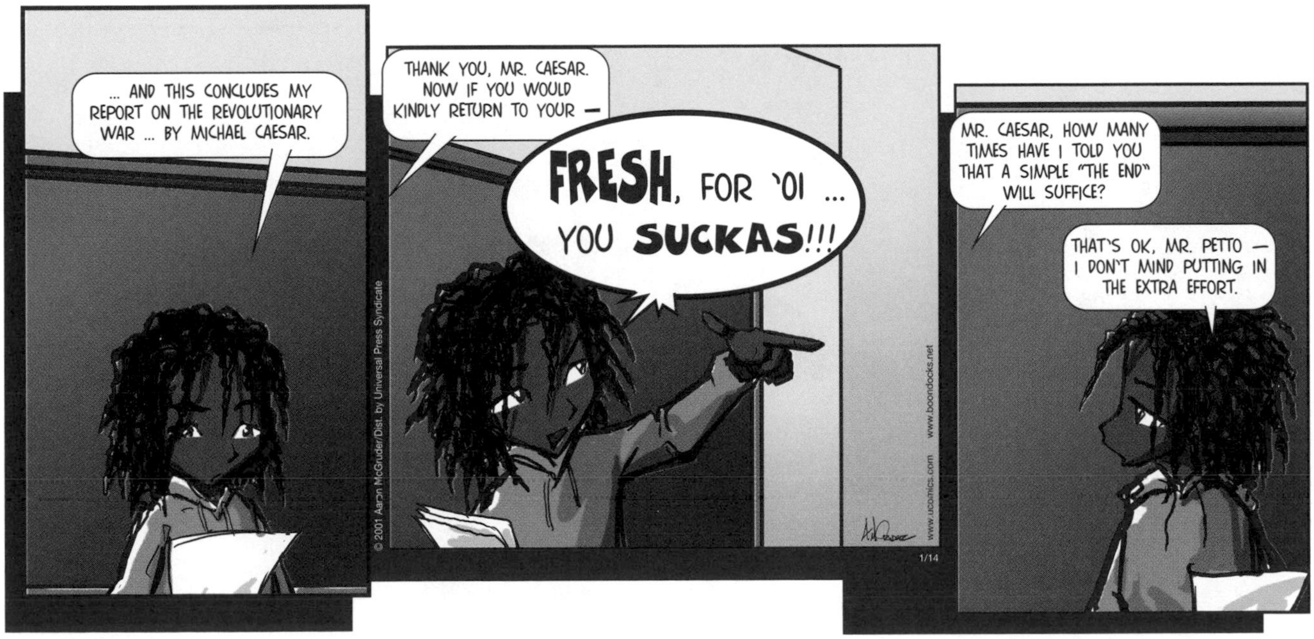
... AND THIS CONCLUDES MY REPORT ON THE REVOLUTIONARY WAR ... BY MICHAEL CAESAR.
THANK YOU, MR. CAESAR. NOW IF YOU WOULD KINDLY RETURN TO YOUR —
FRESH, FOR '01 ... YOU SUCKAS!!!
© 2001 Aaron McGruder/Dist. by Universal Press Syndicate
www.ucomics.com www.boondocks.net
1/14
MR. CAESAR, HOW MANY TIMES HAVE I TOLD YOU THAT A SIMPLE "THE END" WILL SUFFICE?
THAT'S OK, MR. PETTO — I DON'T MIND PUTTING IN THE EXTRA EFFORT.

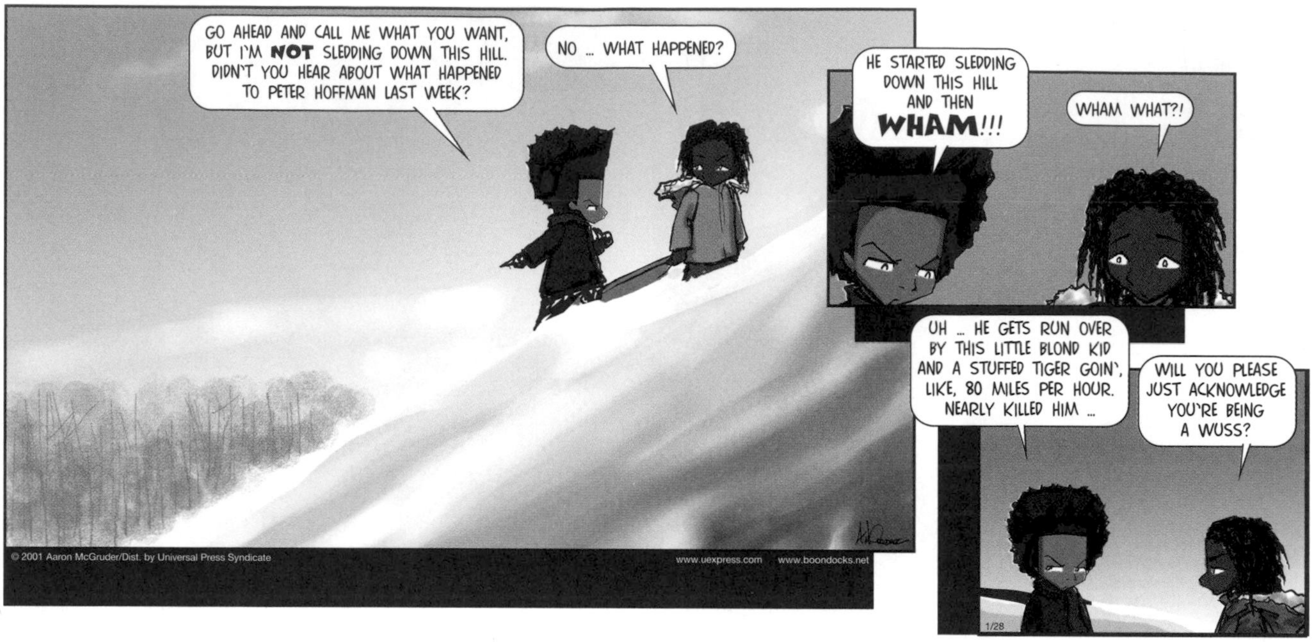
GO AHEAD AND CALL ME WHAT YOU WANT, BUT I'M NOT SLEDDING DOWN THIS HILL. DIDN'T YOU HEAR ABOUT WHAT HAPPENED TO PETER HOFFMAN LAST WEEK?
NO ... WHAT HAPPENED?
HE STARTED SLEDDING DOWN THIS HILL AND THEN WHAM!!!
WHAM WHAT?!
UH ... HE GETS RUN OVER BY THIS LITTLE BLOND KID AND A STUFFED TIGER GOIN', LIKE, 80 MILES PER HOUR. NEARLY KILLED HIM ...
WILL YOU PLEASE JUST ACKNOWLEDGE YOU'RE BEING A WUSS?
© 2001 Aaron McGruder/Dist. by Universal Press Syndicate
www.uexpress.com www.boondocks.net
1/28

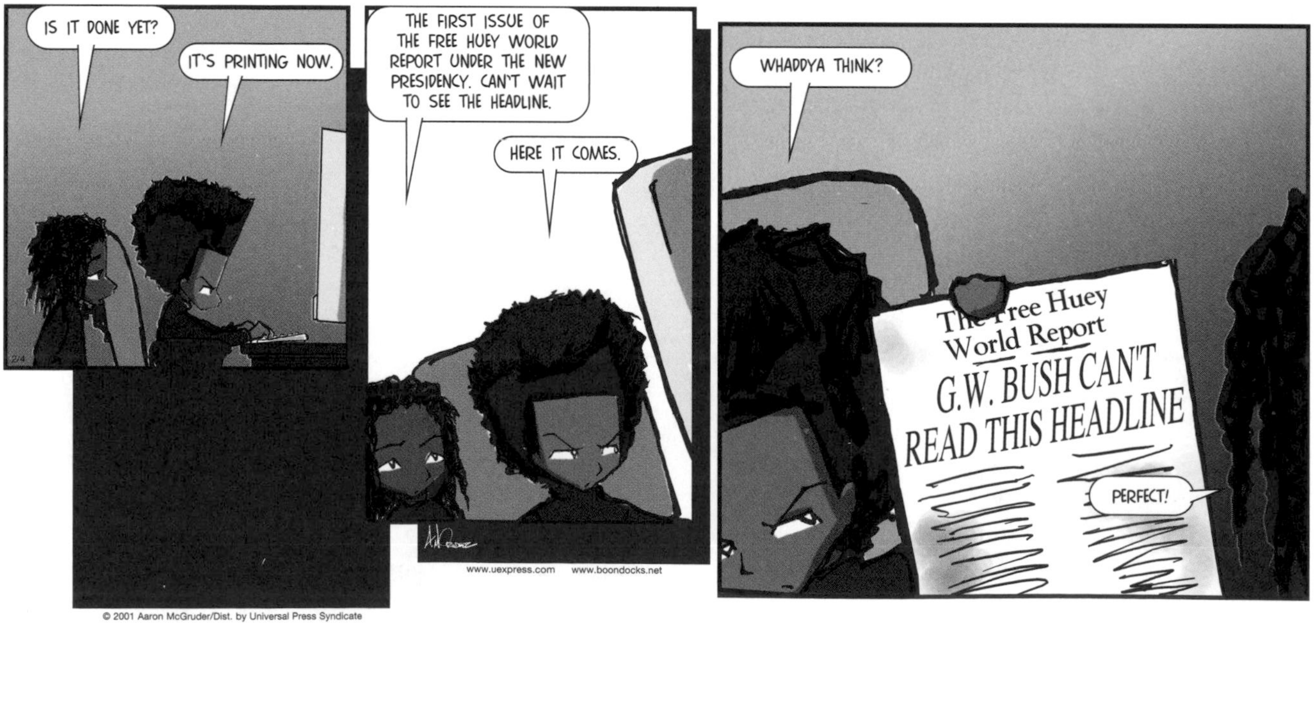
IS IT DONE YET?
IT'S PRINTING NOW.
2/4
THE FIRST ISSUE OF THE FREE HUEY WORLD REPORT UNDER THE NEW PRESIDENCY. CAN'T WAIT TO SEE THE HEADLINE.
HERE IT COMES.
WHADDYA THINK?
The Free Huey World Report
G.W. BUSH CAN'T READ THIS HEADLINE
PERFECT!
www.uexpress.com www.boondocks.net
© 2001 Aaron McGruder/Dist. by Universal Press Syndicate

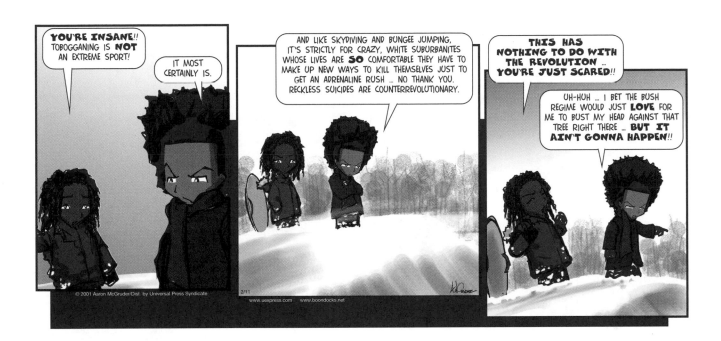

YOU'RE INSANE!! TOBOGGANING IS NOT AN EXTREME SPORT!
IT MOST CERTAINLY IS.
AND LIKE SKYDIVING AND BUNGEE JUMPING, IT'S STRICTLY FOR CRAZY, WHITE SUBURBANITES WHOSE LIVES ARE SO COMFORTABLE THEY HAVE TO MAKE UP NEW WAYS TO KILL THEMSELVES JUST TO GET AN ADRENALINE RUSH ... NO THANK YOU. RECKLESS SUICIDES ARE COUNTERREVOLUTIONARY.
THIS HAS NOTHING TO DO WITH THE REVOLUTION ... YOU'RE JUST SCARED!!
UH-HUH ... I BET THE BUSH REGIME WOULD JUST LOVE FOR ME TO BUST MY HEAD AGAINST THAT TREE RIGHT THERE ... BUT IT AIN'T GONNA HAPPEN!!
© 2001 Aaron McGruder/Dist. by Universal Press Syndicate
2/11
www.uexpress.com www.boondocks.net

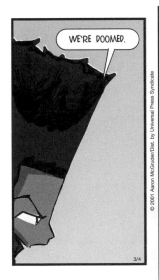

WE'RE DOOMED.
IF YOU THINK ABOUT IT, IT'S JUST NONSTOP STRUGGLE ... DISAPPOINTMENT ... SADNESS ... AND THEN IT'S OVER.
IT'S KINDA LIKE LIFE IS ITS OWN TERMINAL ILLNESS ...
HMM ... SO IT'S SAFE TO SAY WE'RE IN A "GLASS IS HALF EMPTY" MOOD TODAY ... ISN'T THAT RIGHT, MR. SUNSHINE?
3/4
© 2001 Aaron McGruder/Dist. by Universal Press Syndicate
www.uexpress.com www.boondocks.net

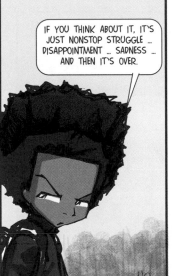

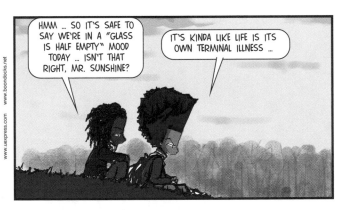

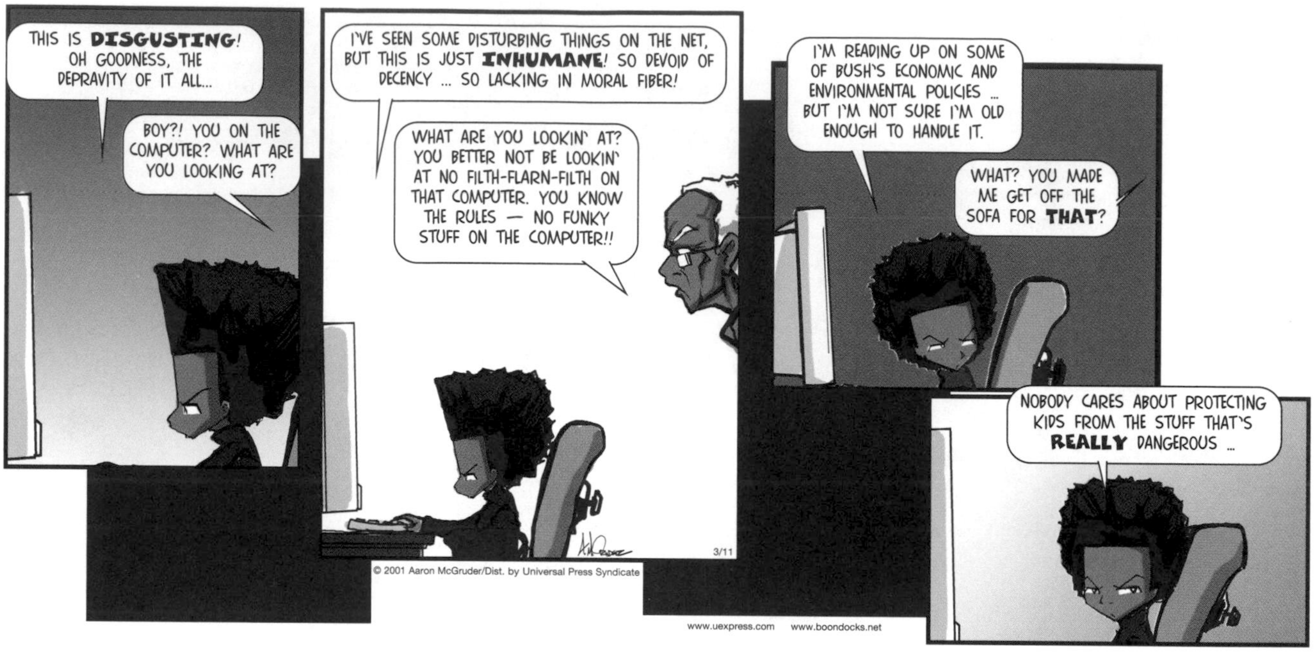

THIS IS DISGUSTING! OH GOODNESS, THE DEPRAVITY OF IT ALL...
BOY?! YOU ON THE COMPUTER? WHAT ARE YOU LOOKING AT?
I'VE SEEN SOME DISTURBING THINGS ON THE NET, BUT THIS IS JUST INHUMANE! SO DEVOID OF DECENCY ... SO LACKING IN MORAL FIBER!
WHAT ARE YOU LOOKIN' AT? YOU BETTER NOT BE LOOKIN' AT NO FILTH-FLARN-FILTH ON THAT COMPUTER. YOU KNOW THE RULES — NO FUNKY STUFF ON THE COMPUTER!!
I'M READING UP ON SOME OF BUSH'S ECONOMIC AND ENVIRONMENTAL POLICIES ... BUT I'M NOT SURE I'M OLD ENOUGH TO HANDLE IT.
WHAT? YOU MADE ME GET OFF THE SOFA FOR THAT?
NOBODY CARES ABOUT PROTECTING KIDS FROM THE STUFF THAT'S REALLY DANGEROUS ...
3/11
© 2001 Aaron McGruder/Dist. by Universal Press Syndicate
www.uexpress.com www.boondocks.net

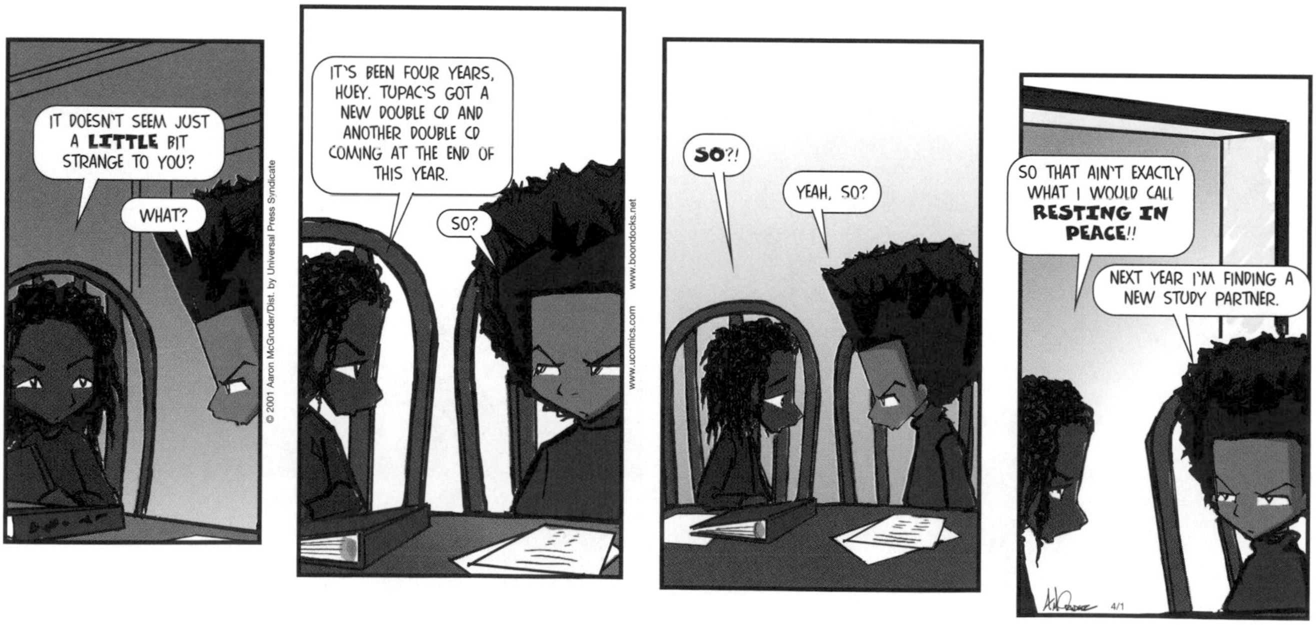

IT DOESN'T SEEM JUST A LITTLE BIT STRANGE TO YOU?
WHAT?
© 2001 Aaron McGruder/Dist. by Universal Press Syndicate
IT'S BEEN FOUR YEARS, HUEY. TUPAC'S GOT A NEW DOUBLE CD AND ANOTHER DOUBLE CD COMING AT THE END OF THIS YEAR.
SO?
www.ucomics.com www.boondocks.net
SO?!
YEAH, SO?
SO THAT AIN'T EXACTLY WHAT I WOULD CALL RESTING IN PEACE!!
NEXT YEAR I'M FINDING A NEW STUDY PARTNER.
4/1

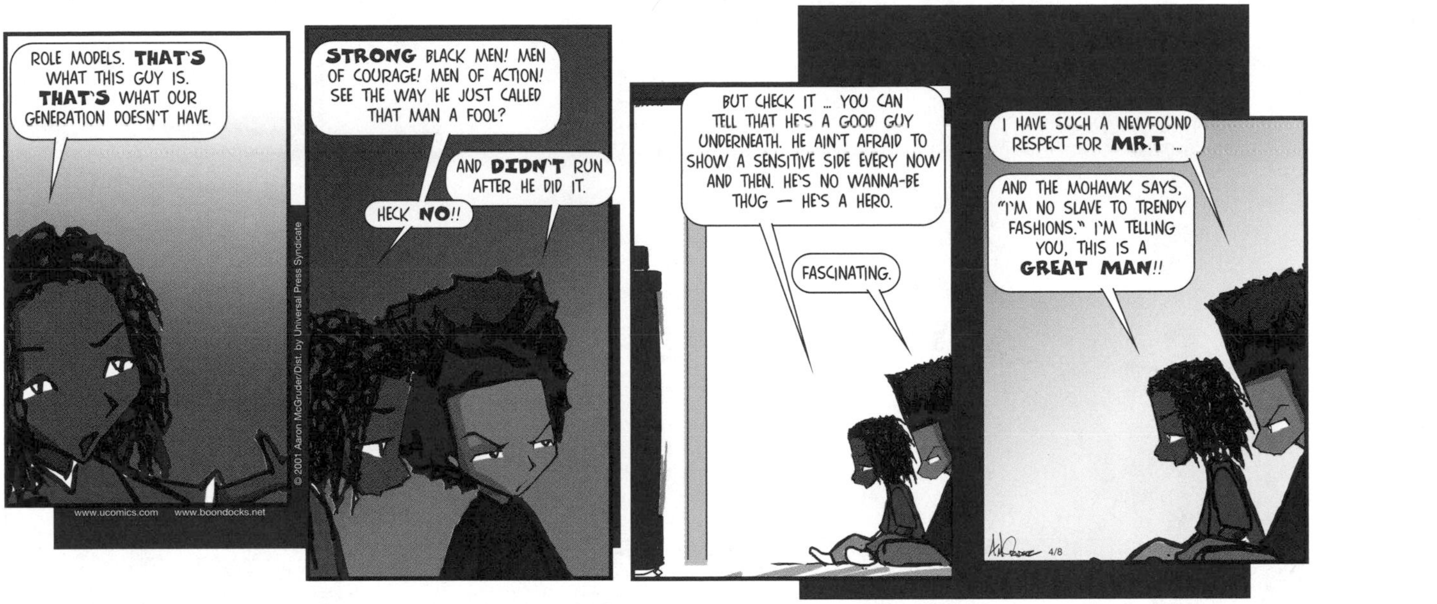
ROLE MODELS. THAT'S WHAT THIS GUY IS. THAT'S WHAT OUR GENERATION DOESN'T HAVE.
© 2001 Aaron McGruder/Dist. by Universal Press Syndicate
www.ucomics.com www.boondocks.net
STRONG BLACK MEN! MEN OF COURAGE! MEN OF ACTION! SEE THE WAY HE JUST CALLED THAT MAN A FOOL?
HECK NO!!
AND DIDN'T RUN AFTER HE DID IT.
BUT CHECK IT ... YOU CAN TELL THAT HE'S A GOOD GUY UNDERNEATH. HE AIN'T AFRAID TO SHOW A SENSITIVE SIDE EVERY NOW AND THEN. HE'S NO WANNA-BE THUG — HE'S A HERO.
FASCINATING.
I HAVE SUCH A NEWFOUND RESPECT FOR MR.T ...
AND THE MOHAWK SAYS, "I'M NO SLAVE TO TRENDY FASHIONS." I'M TELLING YOU, THIS IS A GREAT MAN!!
4/8

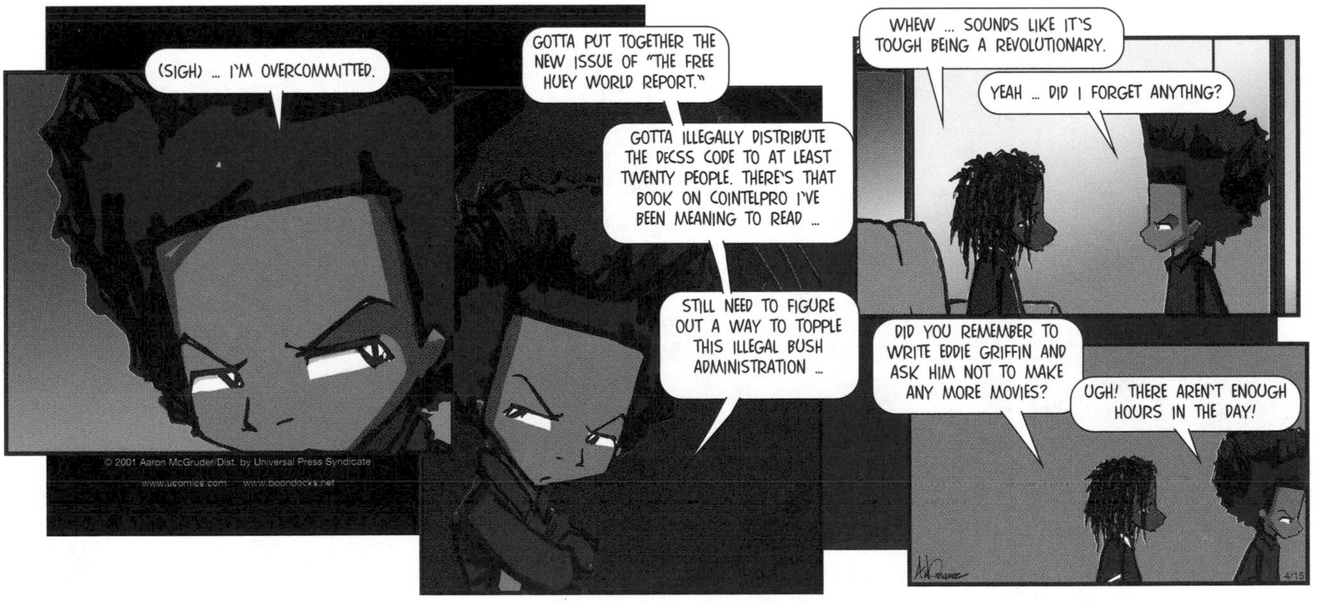
(SIGH) ... I'M OVERCOMMITTED.
© 2001 Aaron McGruder/Dist. by Universal Press Syndicate
www.ucomics.com www.boondocks.net
GOTTA PUT TOGETHER THE NEW ISSUE OF "THE FREE HUEY WORLD REPORT."
GOTTA ILLEGALLY DISTRIBUTE THE DeCSS CODE TO AT LEAST TWENTY PEOPLE. THERE'S THAT BOOK ON COINTELPRO I'VE BEEN MEANING TO READ ...
STILL NEED TO FIGURE OUT A WAY TO TOPPLE THIS ILLEGAL BUSH ADMINISTRATION ...
WHEW ... SOUNDS LIKE IT'S TOUGH BEING A REVOLUTIONARY.
YEAH ... DID I FORGET ANYTHNG?
DID YOU REMEMBER TO WRITE EDDIE GRIFFIN AND ASK HIM NOT TO MAKE ANY MORE MOVIES?
UGH! THERE AREN'T ENOUGH HOURS IN THE DAY!
4/15

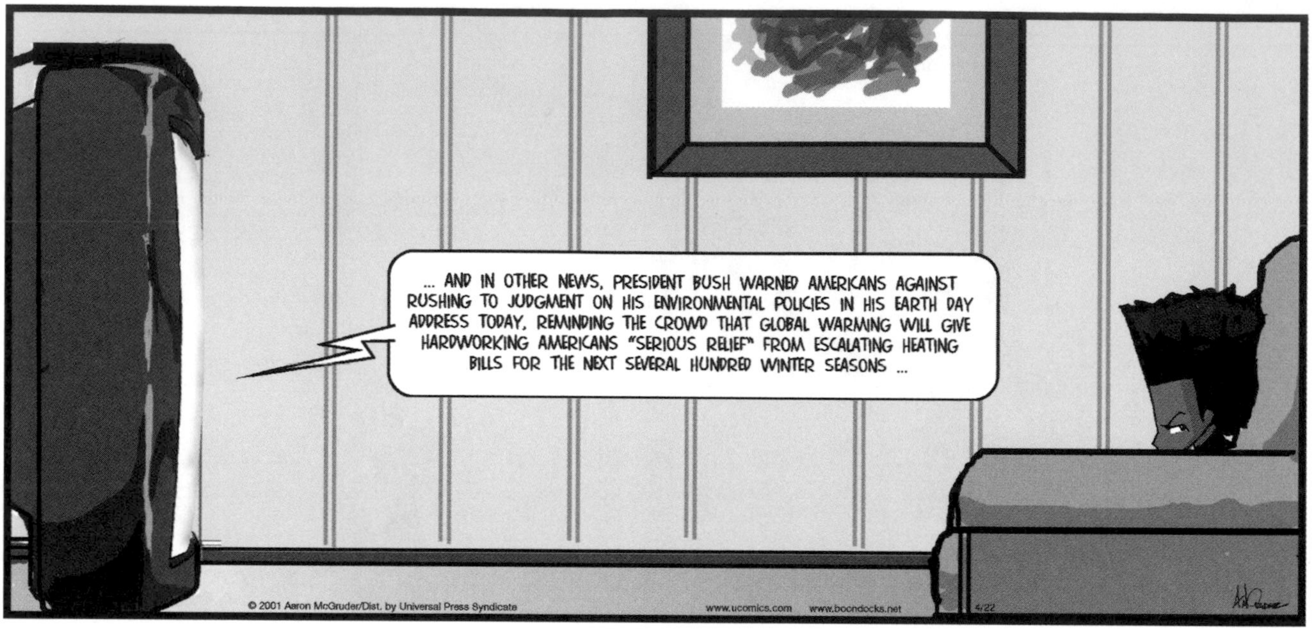
... AND IN OTHER NEWS, PRESIDENT BUSH WARNED AMERICANS AGAINST RUSHING TO JUDGMENT ON HIS ENVIRONMENTAL POLICIES IN HIS EARTH DAY ADDRESS TODAY, REMINDING THE CROWD THAT GLOBAL WARMING WILL GIVE HARDWORKING AMERICANS "SERIOUS RELIEF" FROM ESCALATING HEATING BILLS FOR THE NEXT SEVERAL HUNDRED WINTER SEASONS ...
© 2001 Aaron McGruder/Dist. by Universal Press Syndicate
www.ucomics.com www.boondocks.net
4/22

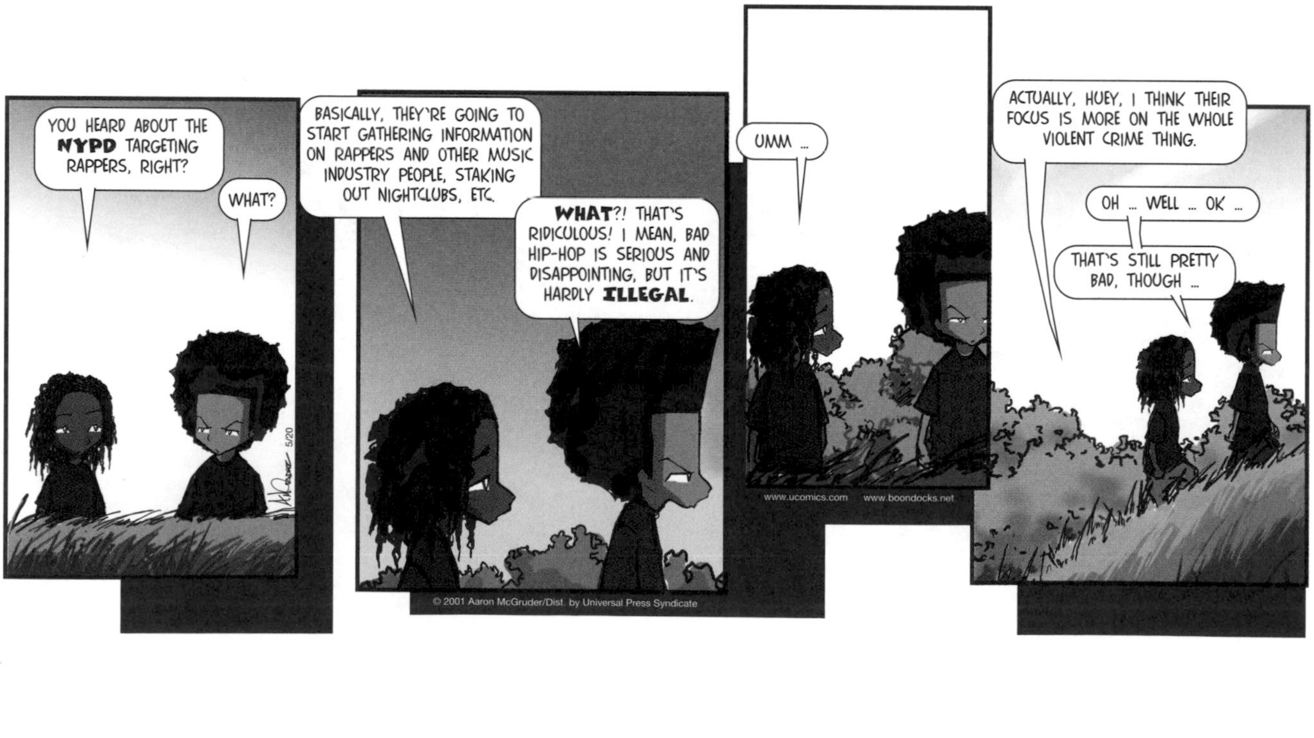
YOU HEARD ABOUT THE NYPD TARGETING RAPPERS, RIGHT?
WHAT?
5/20
BASICALLY, THEY'RE GOING TO START GATHERING INFORMATION ON RAPPERS AND OTHER MUSIC INDUSTRY PEOPLE, STAKING OUT NIGHTCLUBS, ETC.
WHAT?! THAT'S RIDICULOUS! I MEAN, BAD HIP-HOP IS SERIOUS AND DISAPPOINTING, BUT IT'S HARDLY ILLEGAL.
© 2001 Aaron McGruder/Dist. by Universal Press Syndicate
UMM ...
www.ucomics.com www.boondocks.net
ACTUALLY, HUEY, I THINK THEIR FOCUS IS MORE ON THE WHOLE VIOLENT CRIME THING.
OH ... WELL ... OK ...
THAT'S STILL PRETTY BAD, THOUGH ...

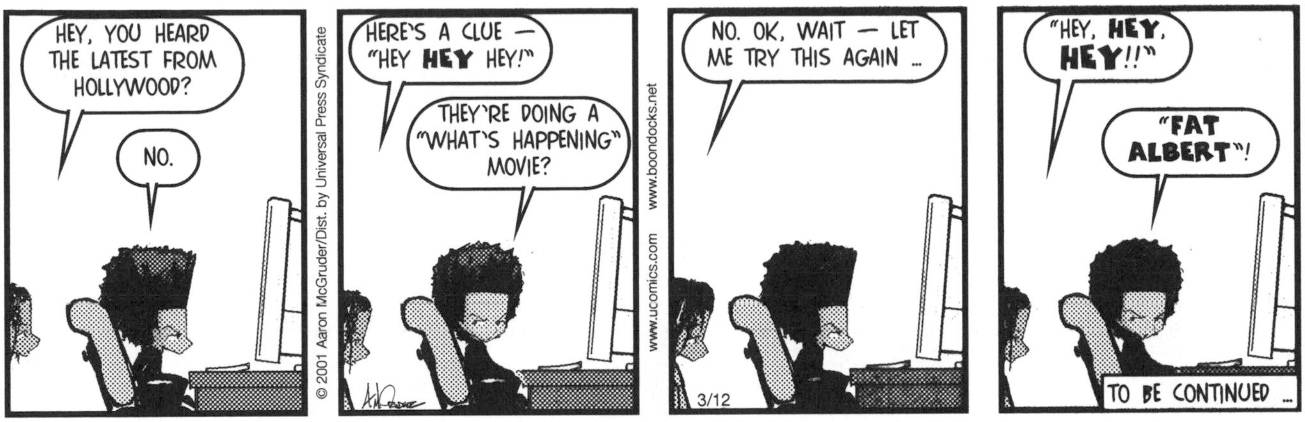
HEY, YOU HEARD THE LATEST FROM HOLLYWOOD?
NO.
HERE'S A CLUE — "HEY HEY HEY!"
THEY'RE DOING A "WHAT'S HAPPENING" MOVIE?
NO. OK, WAIT — LET ME TRY THIS AGAIN ...
"HEY, HEY, HEY!!"
"FAT ALBERT"!
TO BE CONTINUED ...
3/12
© 2001 Aaron McGruder/Dist. by Universal Press Syndicate
www.ucomics.com www.boondocks.net

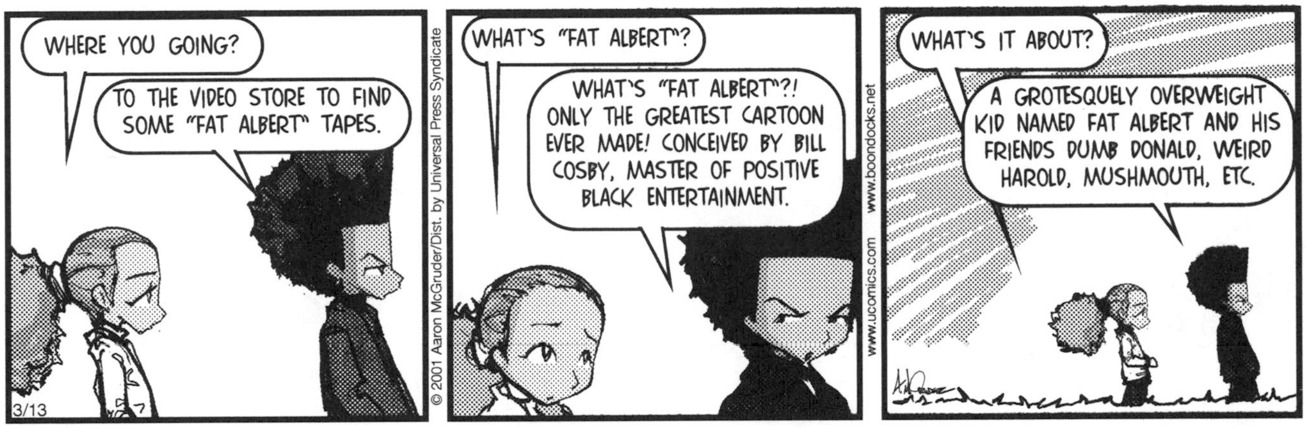
WHERE YOU GOING?
TO THE VIDEO STORE TO FIND SOME "FAT ALBERT" TAPES.
WHAT'S "FAT ALBERT"?
WHAT'S "FAT ALBERT"?! ONLY THE GREATEST CARTOON EVER MADE! CONCEIVED BY BILL COSBY, MASTER OF POSITIVE BLACK ENTERTAINMENT.
WHAT'S IT ABOUT?
A GROTESQUELY OVERWEIGHT KID NAMED FAT ALBERT AND HIS FRIENDS DUMB DONALD, WEIRD HAROLD, MUSHMOUTH, ETC.
3/13
© 2001 Aaron McGruder/Dist. by Universal Press Syndicate
www.ucomics.com www.boondocks.net

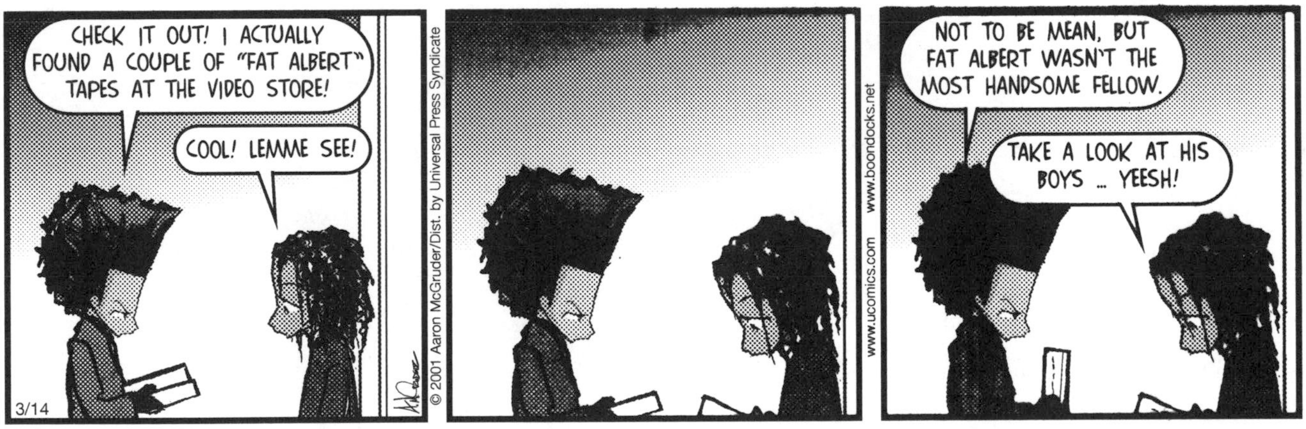
CHECK IT OUT! I ACTUALLY FOUND A COUPLE OF "FAT ALBERT" TAPES AT THE VIDEO STORE!
COOL! LEMME SEE!
NOT TO BE MEAN, BUT FAT ALBERT WASN'T THE MOST HANDSOME FELLOW.
TAKE A LOOK AT HIS BOYS ... YEESH!
3/14
© 2001 Aaron McGruder/Dist. by Universal Press Syndicate
www.ucomics.com www.boondocks.net

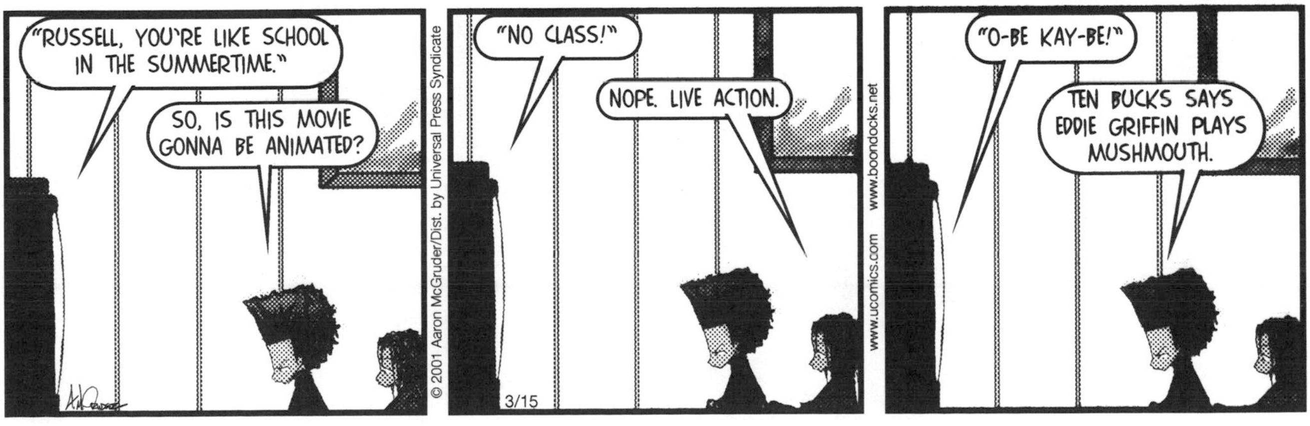
"RUSSELL, YOU'RE LIKE SCHOOL IN THE SUMMERTIME."
SO, IS THIS MOVIE GONNA BE ANIMATED?
"NO CLASS!"
NOPE. LIVE ACTION.
"O-BE KAY-BE!"
TEN BUCKS SAYS EDDIE GRIFFIN PLAYS MUSHMOUTH.
3/15
© 2001 Aaron McGruder/Dist. by Universal Press Syndicate
www.ucomics.com www.boondocks.net

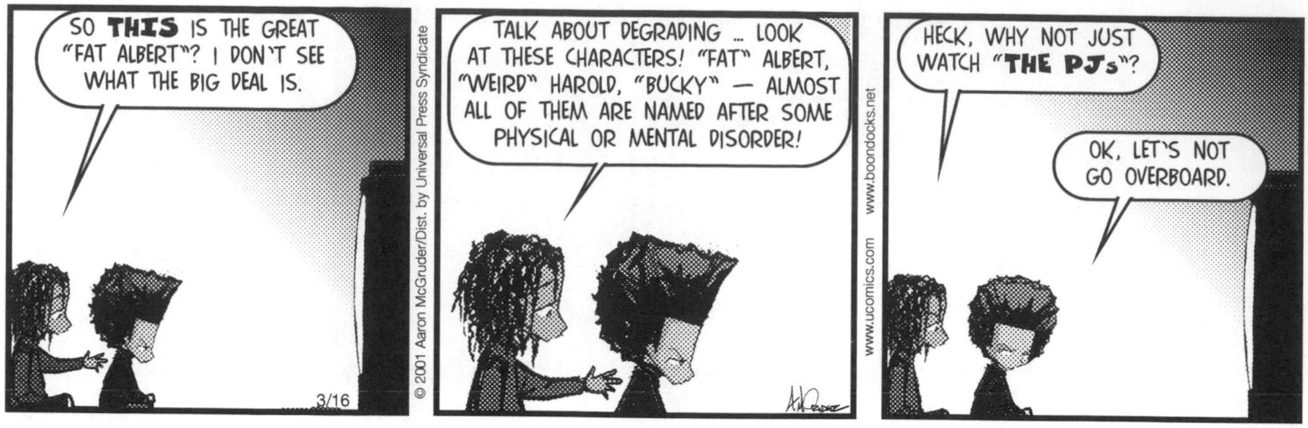
SO **THIS** IS THE GREAT "FAT ALBERT"? I DON'T SEE WHAT THE BIG DEAL IS.
3/16
© 2001 Aaron McGruder/Dist. by Universal Press Syndicate
TALK ABOUT DEGRADING ... LOOK AT THESE CHARACTERS! "FAT" ALBERT, "WEIRD" HAROLD, "BUCKY" — ALMOST ALL OF THEM ARE NAMED AFTER SOME PHYSICAL OR MENTAL DISORDER!
www.ucomics.com www.boondocks.net
HECK, WHY NOT JUST WATCH "**THE PJs**"?
OK, LET'S NOT GO OVERBOARD.

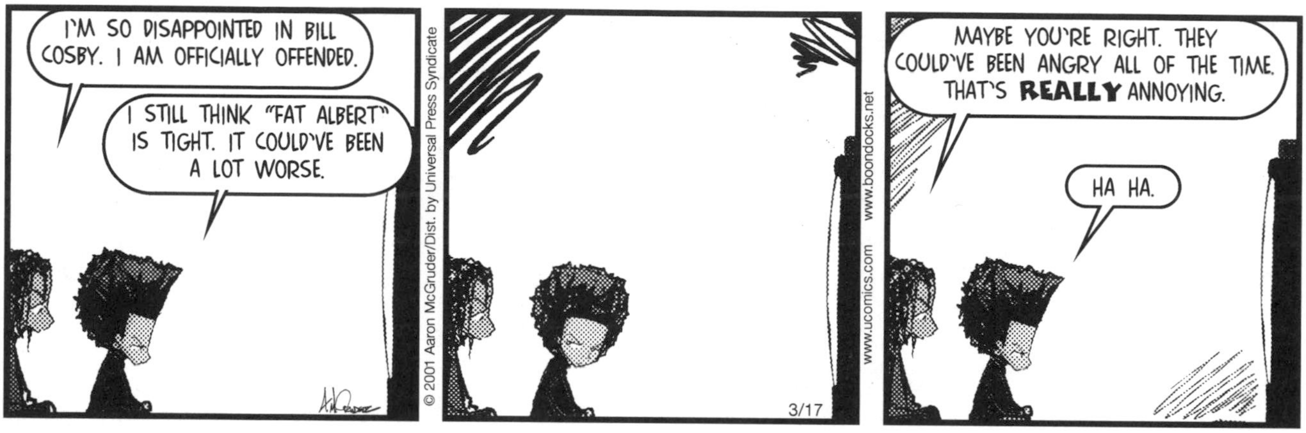
I'M SO DISAPPOINTED IN BILL COSBY. I AM OFFICIALLY OFFENDED.
I STILL THINK "FAT ALBERT" IS TIGHT. IT COULD'VE BEEN A LOT WORSE.
© 2001 Aaron McGruder/Dist. by Universal Press Syndicate
3/17
www.ucomics.com www.boondocks.net
MAYBE YOU'RE RIGHT. THEY COULD'VE BEEN ANGRY ALL OF THE TIME. THAT'S **REALLY** ANNOYING.
HA HA.

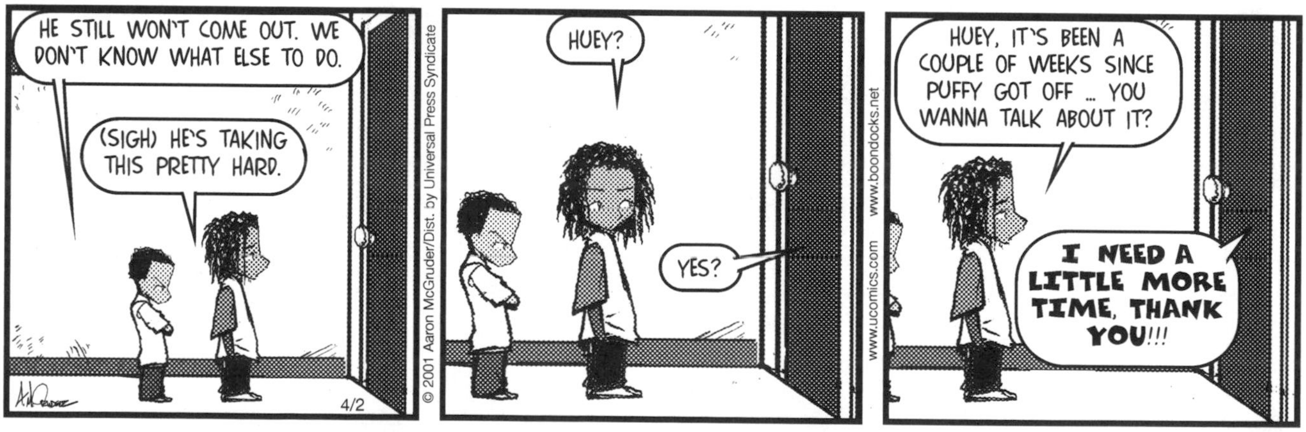
HE STILL WON'T COME OUT. WE DON'T KNOW WHAT ELSE TO DO.
(SIGH) HE'S TAKING THIS PRETTY HARD.
4/2
© 2001 Aaron McGruder/Dist. by Universal Press Syndicate
HUEY?
YES?
www.ucomics.com www.boondocks.net
HUEY, IT'S BEEN A COUPLE OF WEEKS SINCE PUFFY GOT OFF ... YOU WANNA TALK ABOUT IT?
I NEED A LITTLE MORE TIME, THANK YOU!!!

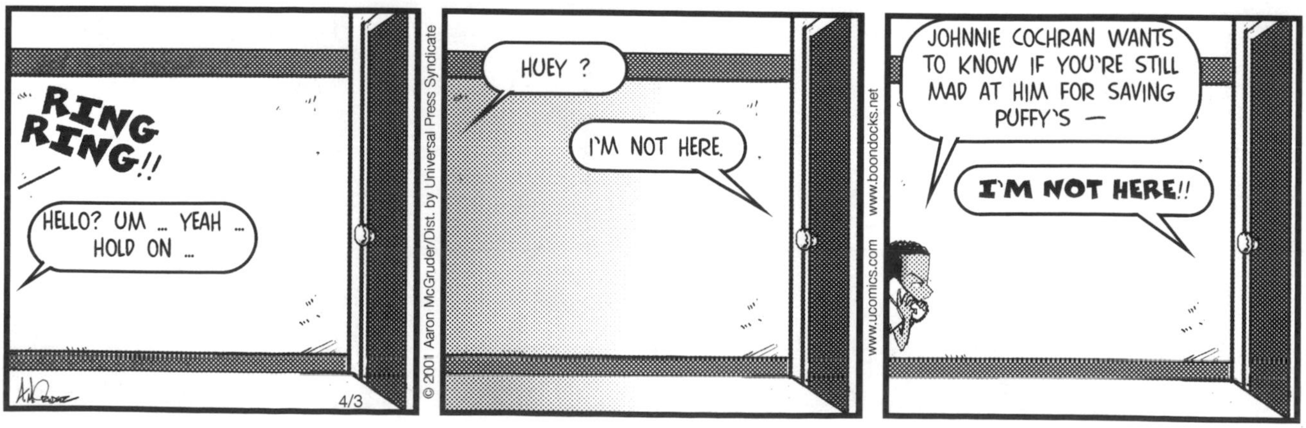
RING RING!!
HELLO? UM ... YEAH ... HOLD ON ...
4/3
© 2001 Aaron McGruder/Dist. by Universal Press Syndicate
HUEY ?
I'M NOT HERE.
www.ucomics.com www.boondocks.net
JOHNNIE COCHRAN WANTS TO KNOW IF YOU'RE STILL MAD AT HIM FOR SAVING PUFFY'S —
I'M NOT HERE!!

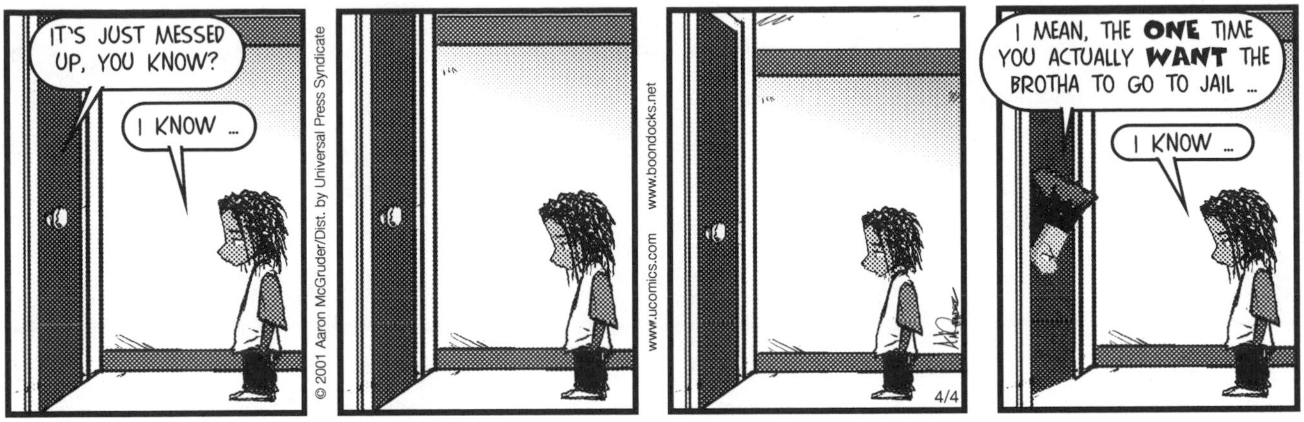
IT'S JUST MESSED UP, YOU KNOW?
I KNOW ...
I MEAN, THE **ONE** TIME YOU ACTUALLY **WANT** THE BROTHA TO GO TO JAIL ...
I KNOW ...
4/4
© 2001 Aaron McGruder/Dist. by Universal Press Syndicate
www.ucomics.com www.boondocks.net

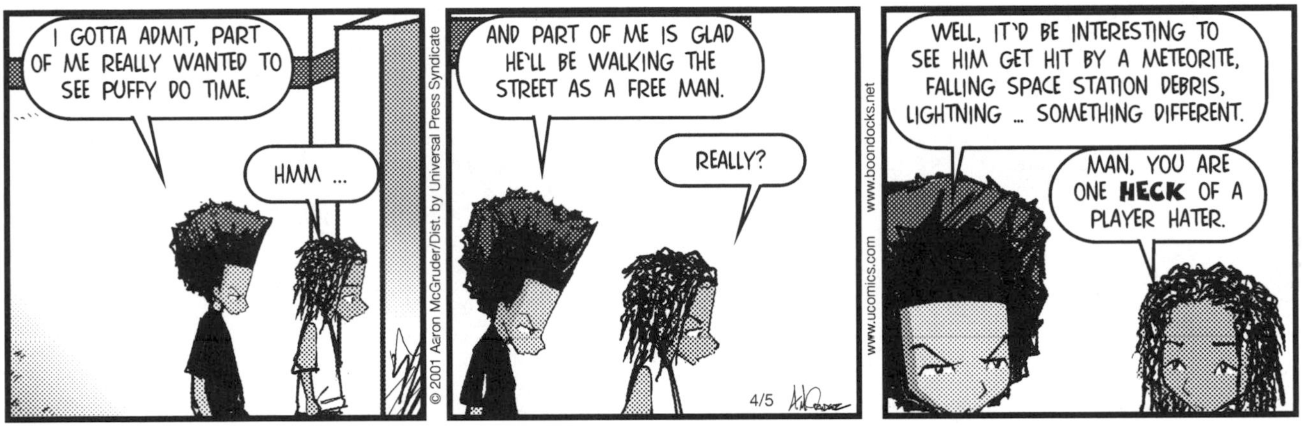
I GOTTA ADMIT, PART OF ME REALLY WANTED TO SEE PUFFY DO TIME.
HMM ...
AND PART OF ME IS GLAD HE'LL BE WALKING THE STREET AS A FREE MAN.
REALLY?
WELL, IT'D BE INTERESTING TO SEE HIM GET HIT BY A METEORITE, FALLING SPACE STATION DEBRIS, LIGHTNING ... SOMETHING DIFFERENT.
MAN, YOU ARE ONE **HECK** OF A PLAYER HATER.
4/5
© 2001 Aaron McGruder/Dist. by Universal Press Syndicate
www.ucomics.com www.boondocks.net

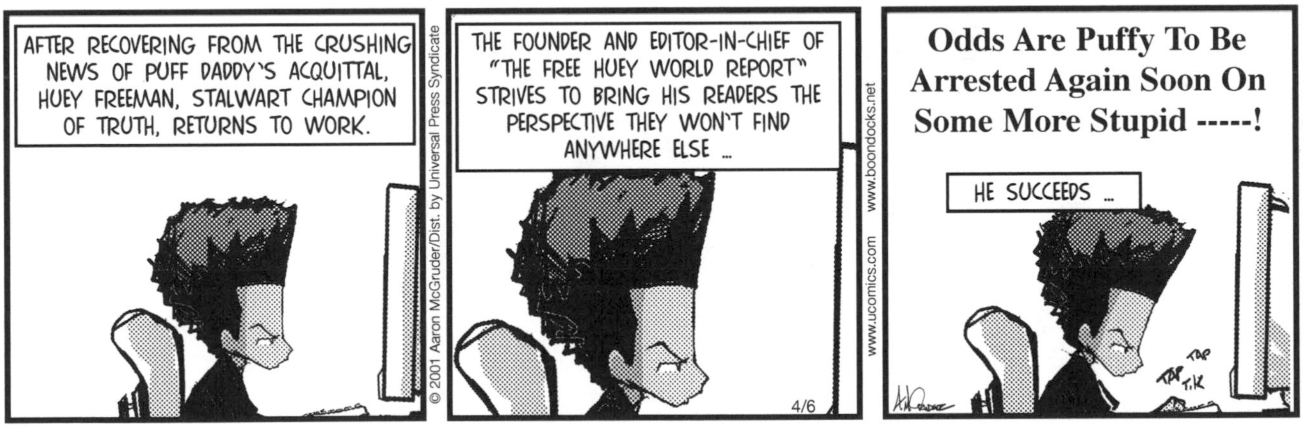
AFTER RECOVERING FROM THE CRUSHING NEWS OF PUFF DADDY'S ACQUITTAL, HUEY FREEMAN, STALWART CHAMPION OF TRUTH, RETURNS TO WORK.
THE FOUNDER AND EDITOR-IN-CHIEF OF "THE FREE HUEY WORLD REPORT" STRIVES TO BRING HIS READERS THE PERSPECTIVE THEY WON'T FIND ANYWHERE ELSE ...
Odds Are Puffy To Be Arrested Again Soon On Some More Stupid -----!
HE SUCCEEDS ...
TAP TAP TIK
4/6
© 2001 Aaron McGruder/Dist. by Universal Press Syndicate
www.ucomics.com www.boondocks.net

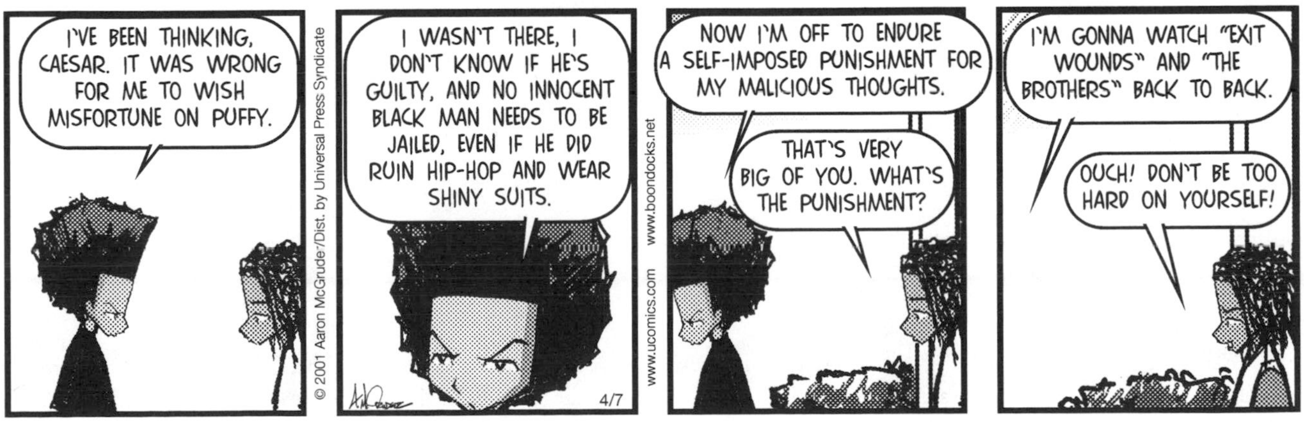
I'VE BEEN THINKING, CAESAR. IT WAS WRONG FOR ME TO WISH MISFORTUNE ON PUFFY.
I WASN'T THERE, I DON'T KNOW IF HE'S GUILTY, AND NO INNOCENT BLACK MAN NEEDS TO BE JAILED, EVEN IF HE DID RUIN HIP-HOP AND WEAR SHINY SUITS.
NOW I'M OFF TO ENDURE A SELF-IMPOSED PUNISHMENT FOR MY MALICIOUS THOUGHTS.
THAT'S VERY BIG OF YOU. WHAT'S THE PUNISHMENT?
I'M GONNA WATCH "EXIT WOUNDS" AND "THE BROTHERS" BACK TO BACK.
OUCH! DON'T BE TOO HARD ON YOURSELF!
4/7
© 2001 Aaron McGruder/Dist. by Universal Press Syndicate
www.ucomics.com www.boondocks.net

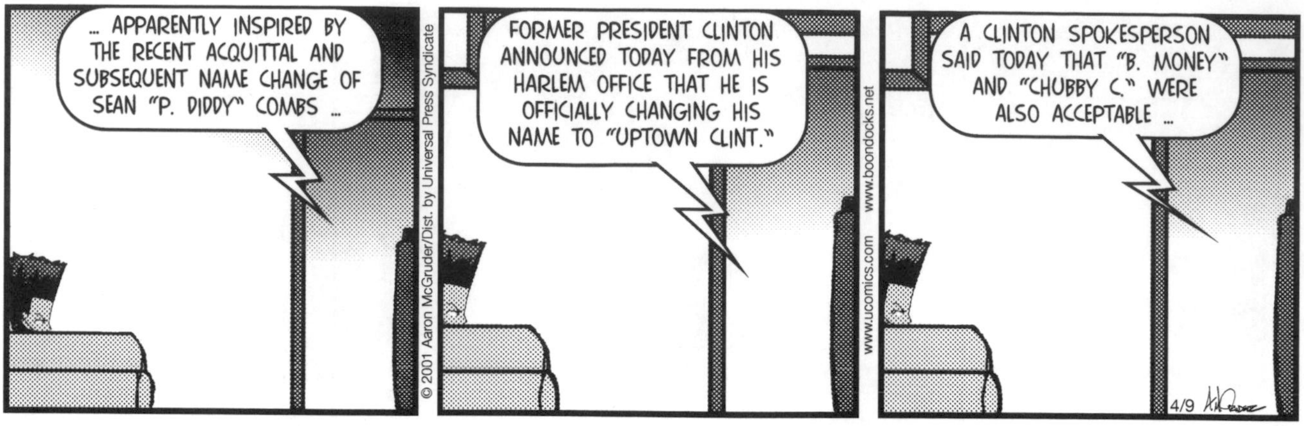
... APPARENTLY INSPIRED BY THE RECENT ACQUITTAL AND SUBSEQUENT NAME CHANGE OF SEAN "P. DIDDY" COMBS ...
© 2001 Aaron McGruder/Dist. by Universal Press Syndicate
FORMER PRESIDENT CLINTON ANNOUNCED TODAY FROM HIS HARLEM OFFICE THAT HE IS OFFICIALLY CHANGING HIS NAME TO "UPTOWN CLINT."
www.ucomics.com www.boondocks.net
A CLINTON SPOKESPERSON SAID TODAY THAT "B. MONEY" AND "CHUBBY C." WERE ALSO ACCEPTABLE ...
4/9

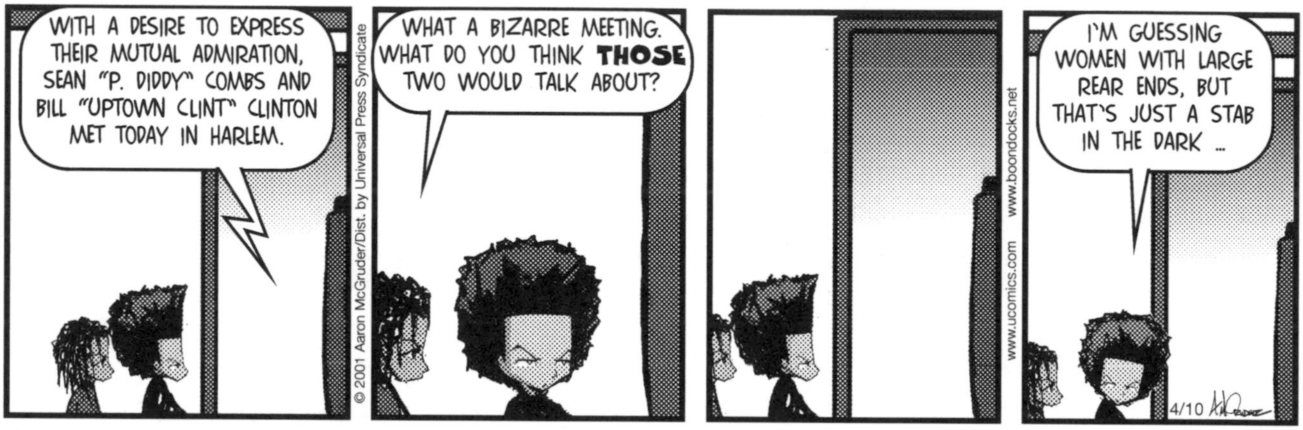
WITH A DESIRE TO EXPRESS THEIR MUTUAL ADMIRATION, SEAN "P. DIDDY" COMBS AND BILL "UPTOWN CLINT" CLINTON MET TODAY IN HARLEM.
© 2001 Aaron McGruder/Dist. by Universal Press Syndicate
WHAT A BIZARRE MEETING. WHAT DO YOU THINK **THOSE** TWO WOULD TALK ABOUT?
www.ucomics.com www.boondocks.net
I'M GUESSING WOMEN WITH LARGE REAR ENDS, BUT THAT'S JUST A STAB IN THE DARK ...
4/10

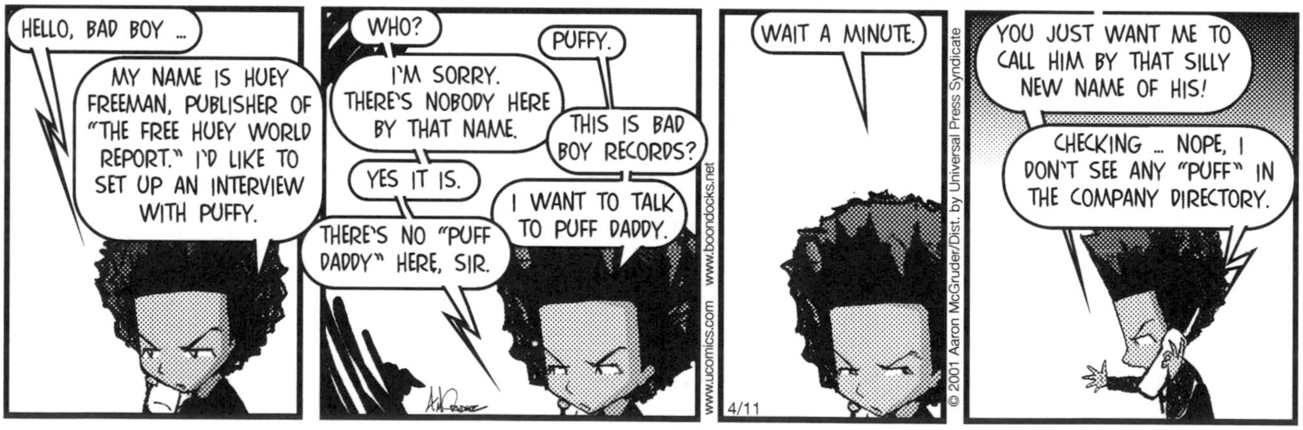
HELLO, BAD BOY ...
MY NAME IS HUEY FREEMAN, PUBLISHER OF "THE FREE HUEY WORLD REPORT." I'D LIKE TO SET UP AN INTERVIEW WITH PUFFY.
WHO?
PUFFY.
I'M SORRY. THERE'S NOBODY HERE BY THAT NAME.
THIS IS BAD BOY RECORDS?
YES IT IS.
I WANT TO TALK TO PUFF DADDY.
THERE'S NO "PUFF DADDY" HERE, SIR.
www.ucomics.com www.boondocks.net
WAIT A MINUTE.
4/11
© 2001 Aaron McGruder/Dist. by Universal Press Syndicate
YOU JUST WANT ME TO CALL HIM BY THAT SILLY NEW NAME OF HIS!
CHECKING ... NOPE, I DON'T SEE ANY "PUFF" IN THE COMPANY DIRECTORY.

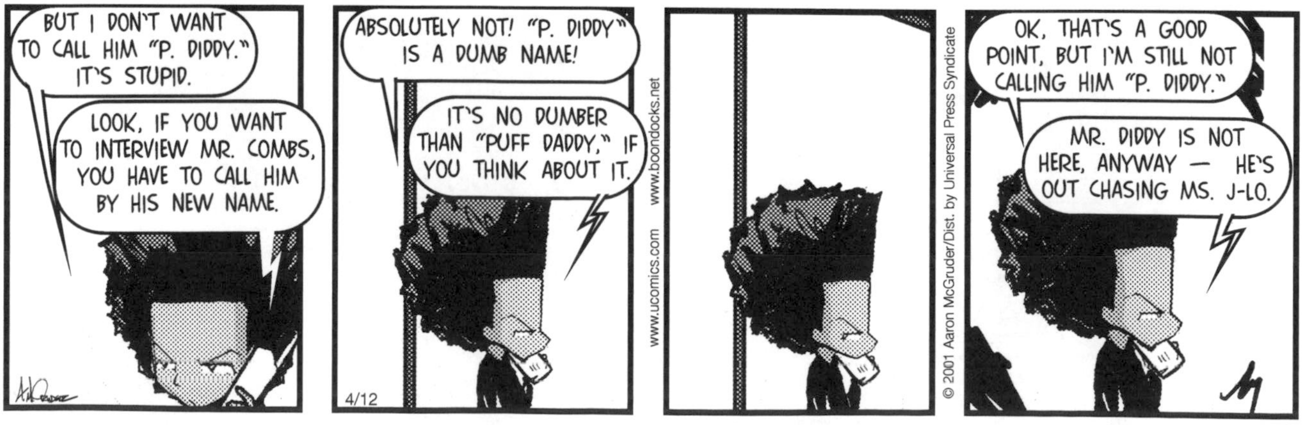
BUT I DON'T WANT TO CALL HIM "P. DIDDY." IT'S STUPID.
LOOK, IF YOU WANT TO INTERVIEW MR. COMBS, YOU HAVE TO CALL HIM BY HIS NEW NAME.
ABSOLUTELY NOT! "P. DIDDY" IS A DUMB NAME!
IT'S NO DUMBER THAN "PUFF DADDY," IF YOU THINK ABOUT IT.
4/12
www.ucomics.com www.boondocks.net
© 2001 Aaron McGruder/Dist. by Universal Press Syndicate
OK, THAT'S A GOOD POINT, BUT I'M STILL NOT CALLING HIM "P. DIDDY."
MR. DIDDY IS NOT HERE, ANYWAY — HE'S OUT CHASING MS. J-LO.

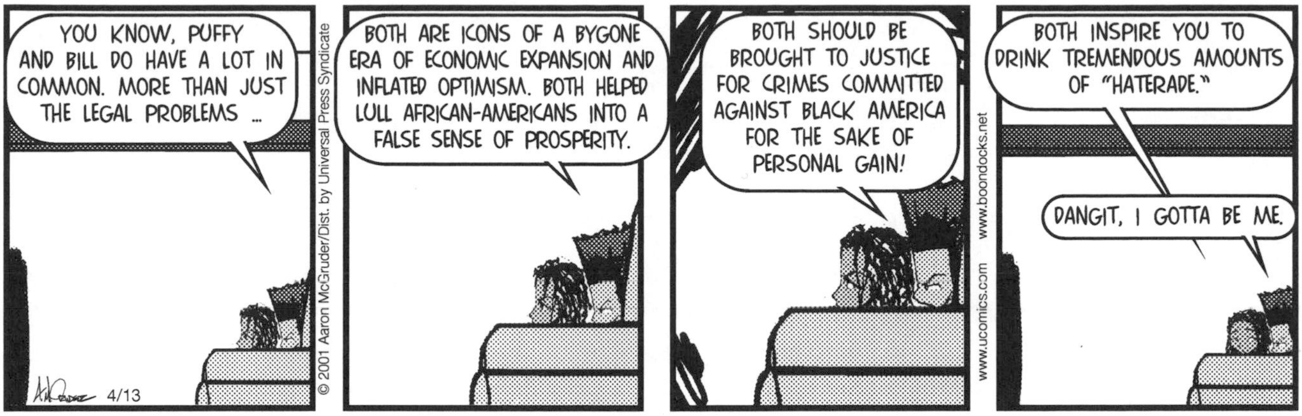
YOU KNOW, PUFFY AND BILL DO HAVE A LOT IN COMMON. MORE THAN JUST THE LEGAL PROBLEMS ...
BOTH ARE ICONS OF A BYGONE ERA OF ECONOMIC EXPANSION AND INFLATED OPTIMISM. BOTH HELPED LULL AFRICAN-AMERICANS INTO A FALSE SENSE OF PROSPERITY.
BOTH SHOULD BE BROUGHT TO JUSTICE FOR CRIMES COMMITTED AGAINST BLACK AMERICA FOR THE SAKE OF PERSONAL GAIN!
BOTH INSPIRE YOU TO DRINK TREMENDOUS AMOUNTS OF "HATERADE."
DANGIT, I GOTTA BE ME.
4/13
© 2001 Aaron McGruder/Dist. by Universal Press Syndicate
www.ucomics.com www.boondocks.net

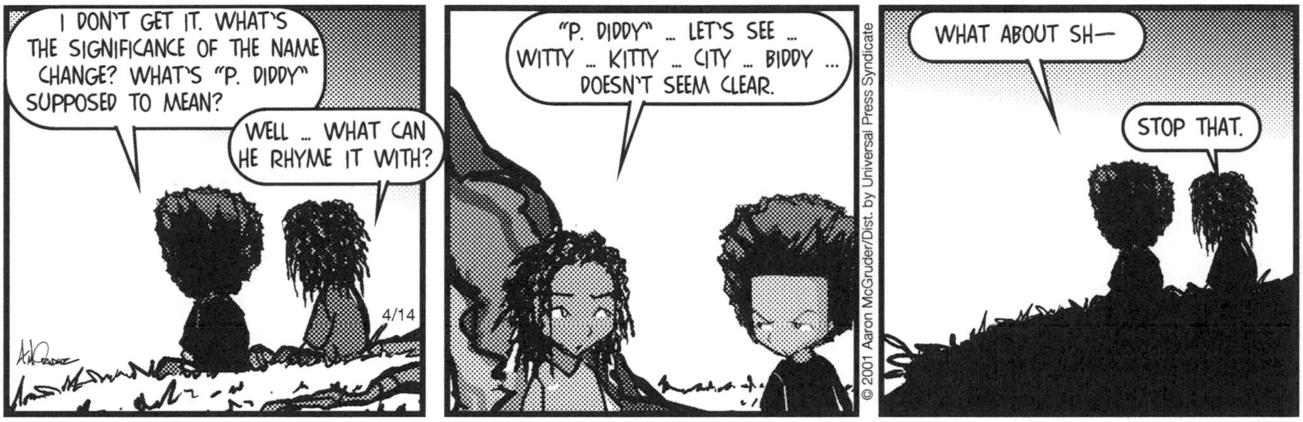
I DON'T GET IT. WHAT'S THE SIGNIFICANCE OF THE NAME CHANGE? WHAT'S "P. DIDDY" SUPPOSED TO MEAN?
WELL ... WHAT CAN HE RHYME IT WITH?
"P. DIDDY" ... LET'S SEE ... WITTY ... KITTY ... CITY ... BIDDY ... DOESN'T SEEM CLEAR.
WHAT ABOUT SH—
STOP THAT.
4/14
© 2001 Aaron McGruder/Dist. by Universal Press Syndicate

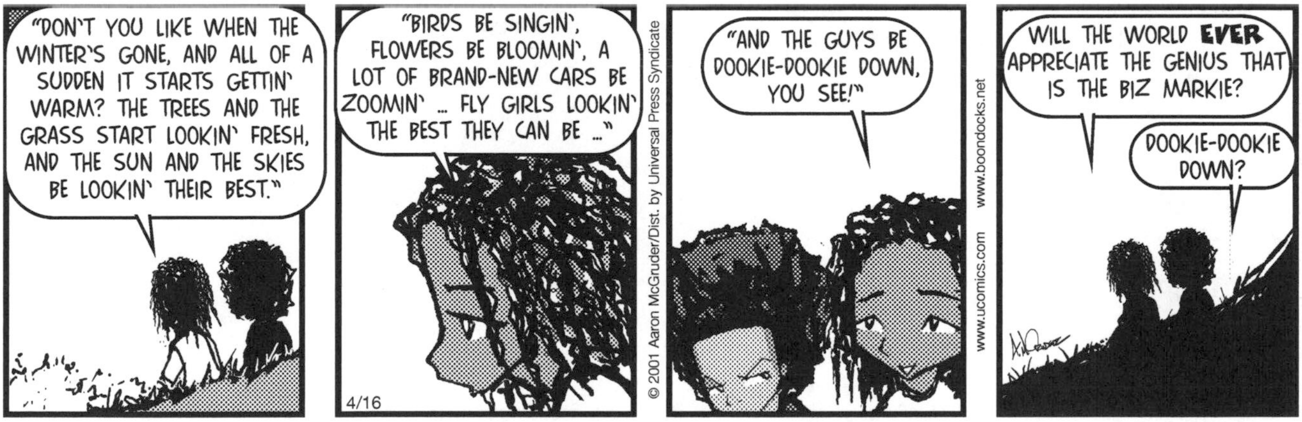
"DON'T YOU LIKE WHEN THE WINTER'S GONE, AND ALL OF A SUDDEN IT STARTS GETTIN' WARM? THE TREES AND THE GRASS START LOOKIN' FRESH, AND THE SUN AND THE SKIES BE LOOKIN' THEIR BEST."
"BIRDS BE SINGIN', FLOWERS BE BLOOMIN', A LOT OF BRAND-NEW CARS BE ZOOMIN' ... FLY GIRLS LOOKIN' THE BEST THEY CAN BE ..."
"AND THE GUYS BE DOOKIE-DOOKIE DOWN, YOU SEE!"
WILL THE WORLD EVER APPRECIATE THE GENIUS THAT IS THE BIZ MARKIE?
DOOKIE-DOOKIE DOWN?
4/16
© 2001 Aaron McGruder/Dist. by Universal Press Syndicate
www.ucomics.com www.boondocks.net

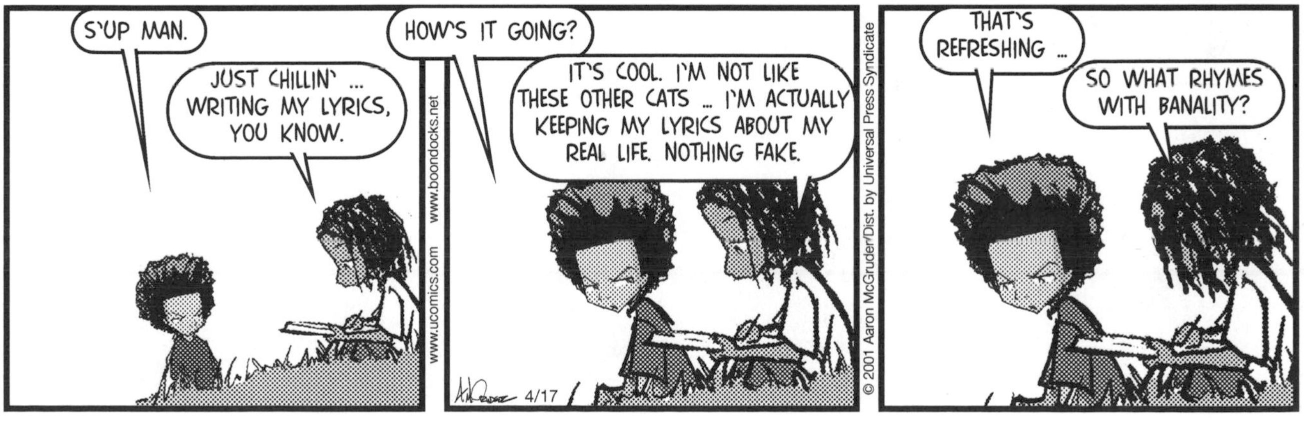
S'UP MAN.
JUST CHILLIN' ... WRITING MY LYRICS, YOU KNOW.
HOW'S IT GOING?
IT'S COOL. I'M NOT LIKE THESE OTHER CATS ... I'M ACTUALLY KEEPING MY LYRICS ABOUT MY REAL LIFE. NOTHING FAKE.
THAT'S REFRESHING ...
SO WHAT RHYMES WITH BANALITY?
4/17
www.ucomics.com www.boondocks.net
© 2001 Aaron McGruder/Dist. by Universal Press Syndicate

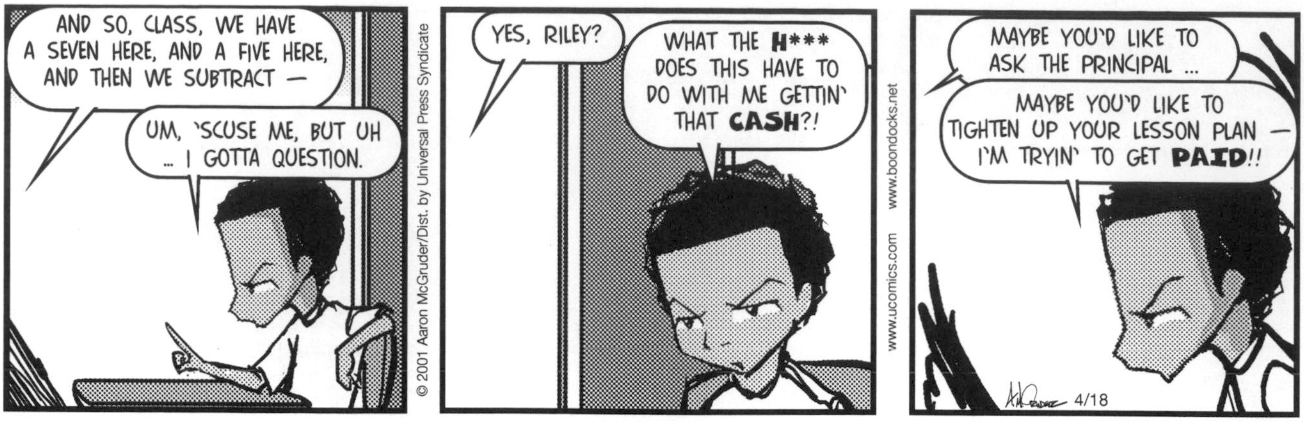
AND SO, CLASS, WE HAVE A SEVEN HERE, AND A FIVE HERE, AND THEN WE SUBTRACT —
UM, 'SCUSE ME, BUT UH ... I GOTTA QUESTION.
© 2001 Aaron McGruder/Dist. by Universal Press Syndicate
YES, RILEY?
WHAT THE H*** DOES THIS HAVE TO DO WITH ME GETTIN' THAT CASH?!
www.ucomics.com www.boondocks.net
MAYBE YOU'D LIKE TO ASK THE PRINCIPAL ...
MAYBE YOU'D LIKE TO TIGHTEN UP YOUR LESSON PLAN — I'M TRYIN' TO GET PAID!!
4/18

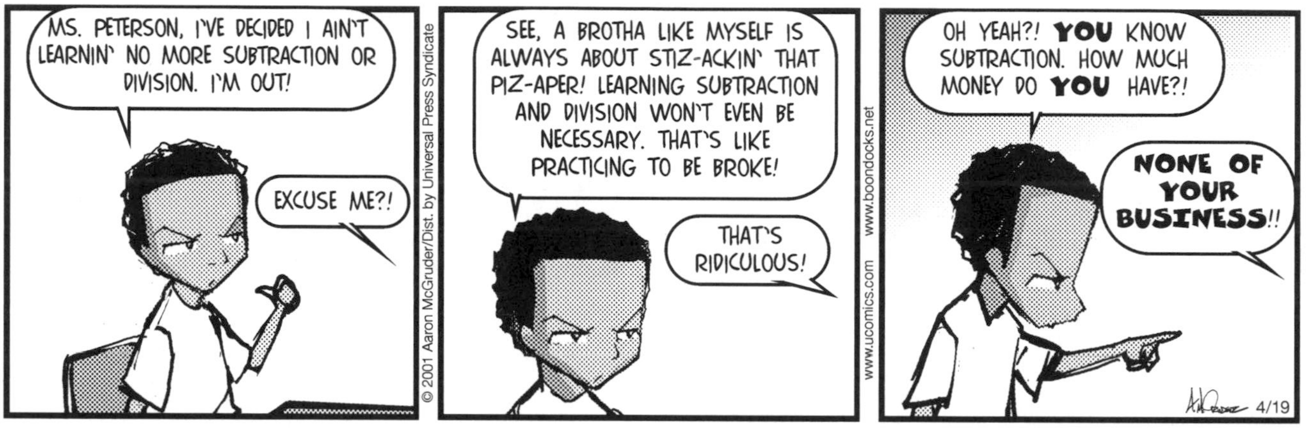
MS. PETERSON, I'VE DECIDED I AIN'T LEARNIN' NO MORE SUBTRACTION OR DIVISION. I'M OUT!
EXCUSE ME?!
© 2001 Aaron McGruder/Dist. by Universal Press Syndicate
SEE, A BROTHA LIKE MYSELF IS ALWAYS ABOUT STIZ-ACKIN' THAT PIZ-APER! LEARNING SUBTRACTION AND DIVISION WON'T EVEN BE NECESSARY. THAT'S LIKE PRACTICING TO BE BROKE!
THAT'S RIDICULOUS!
www.ucomics.com www.boondocks.net
OH YEAH?! YOU KNOW SUBTRACTION. HOW MUCH MONEY DO YOU HAVE?!
NONE OF YOUR BUSINESS!!
4/19

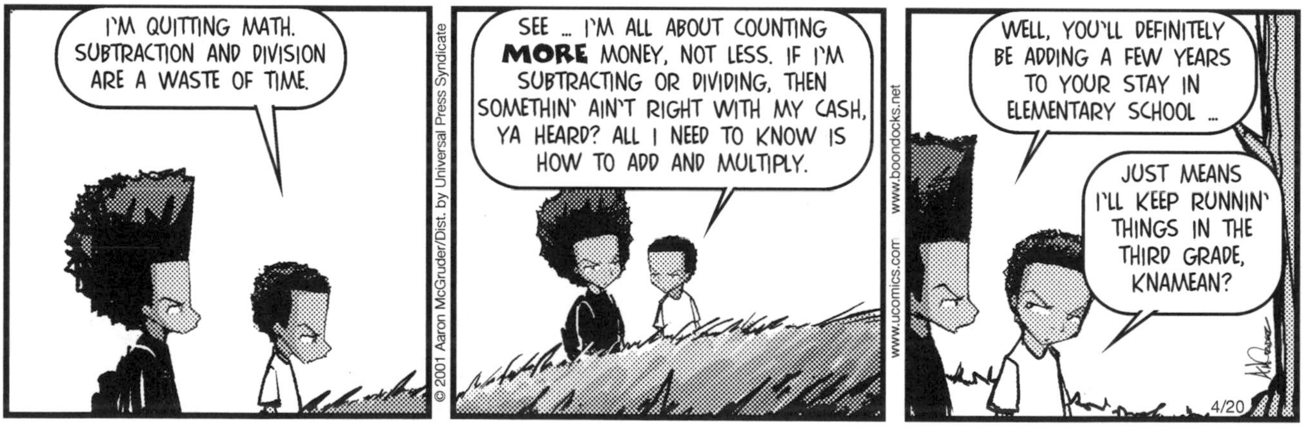
I'M QUITTING MATH. SUBTRACTION AND DIVISION ARE A WASTE OF TIME.
© 2001 Aaron McGruder/Dist. by Universal Press Syndicate
SEE ... I'M ALL ABOUT COUNTING MORE MONEY, NOT LESS. IF I'M SUBTRACTING OR DIVIDING, THEN SOMETHIN' AIN'T RIGHT WITH MY CASH, YA HEARD? ALL I NEED TO KNOW IS HOW TO ADD AND MULTIPLY.
www.ucomics.com www.boondocks.net
WELL, YOU'LL DEFINITELY BE ADDING A FEW YEARS TO YOUR STAY IN ELEMENTARY SCHOOL ...
JUST MEANS I'LL KEEP RUNNIN' THINGS IN THE THIRD GRADE, KNAMEAN?
4/20

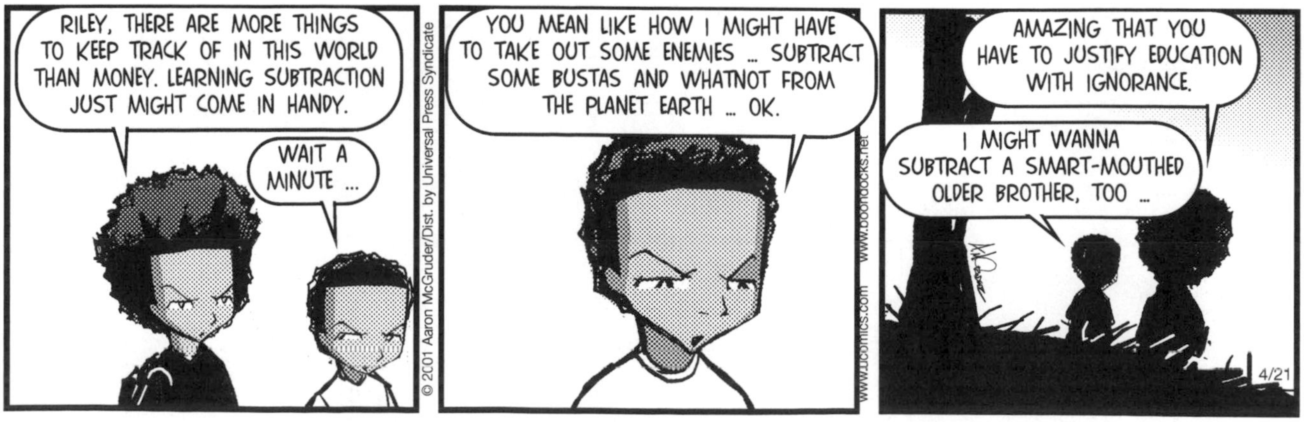
RILEY, THERE ARE MORE THINGS TO KEEP TRACK OF IN THIS WORLD THAN MONEY. LEARNING SUBTRACTION JUST MIGHT COME IN HANDY.
WAIT A MINUTE ...
© 2001 Aaron McGruder/Dist. by Universal Press Syndicate
YOU MEAN LIKE HOW I MIGHT HAVE TO TAKE OUT SOME ENEMIES ... SUBTRACT SOME BUSTAS AND WHATNOT FROM THE PLANET EARTH ... OK.
www.ucomics.com www.boondocks.net
AMAZING THAT YOU HAVE TO JUSTIFY EDUCATION WITH IGNORANCE.
I MIGHT WANNA SUBTRACT A SMART-MOUTHED OLDER BROTHER, TOO ...
4/21

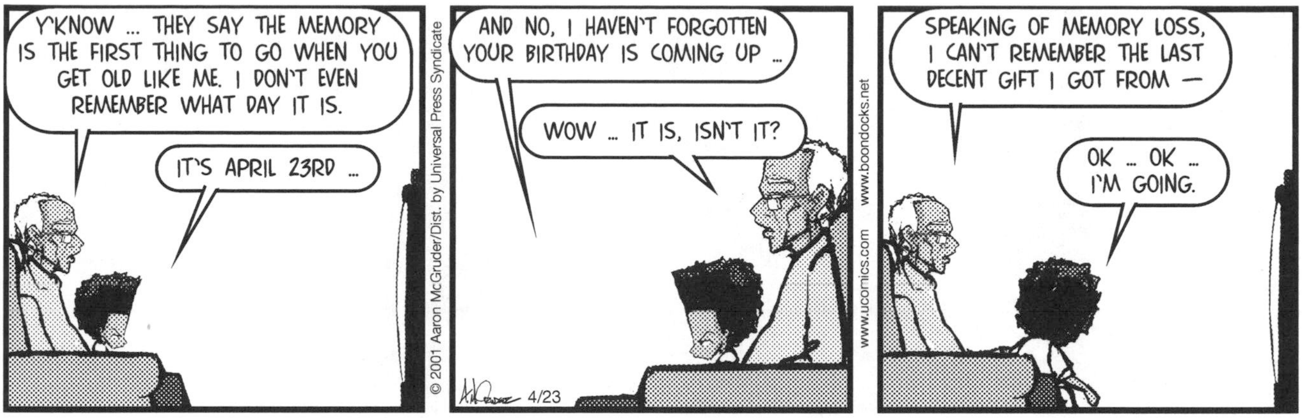
Y'KNOW ... THEY SAY THE MEMORY IS THE FIRST THING TO GO WHEN YOU GET OLD LIKE ME. I DON'T EVEN REMEMBER WHAT DAY IT IS.
IT'S APRIL 23RD ...
AND NO, I HAVEN'T FORGOTTEN YOUR BIRTHDAY IS COMING UP ...
WOW ... IT IS, ISN'T IT?
SPEAKING OF MEMORY LOSS, I CAN'T REMEMBER THE LAST DECENT GIFT I GOT FROM —
OK ... OK ... I'M GOING.
© 2001 Aaron McGruder/Dist. by Universal Press Syndicate
4/23
www.ucomics.com www.boondocks.net

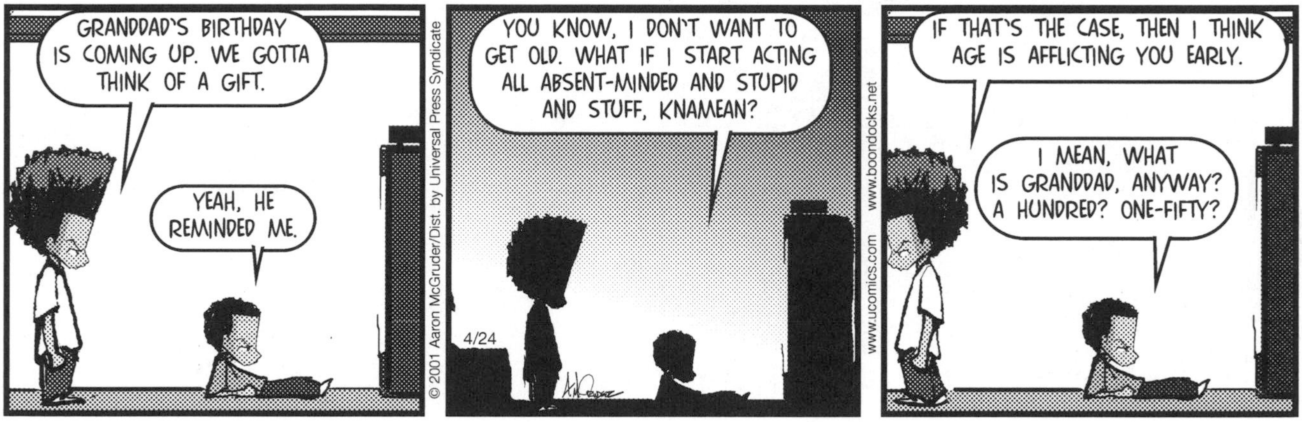
GRANDDAD'S BIRTHDAY IS COMING UP. WE GOTTA THINK OF A GIFT.
YEAH, HE REMINDED ME.
YOU KNOW, I DON'T WANT TO GET OLD. WHAT IF I START ACTING ALL ABSENT-MINDED AND STUPID AND STUFF, KNAMEAN?
IF THAT'S THE CASE, THEN I THINK AGE IS AFFLICTING YOU EARLY.
I MEAN, WHAT IS GRANDDAD, ANYWAY? A HUNDRED? ONE-FIFTY?
© 2001 Aaron McGruder/Dist. by Universal Press Syndicate
4/24
www.ucomics.com www.boondocks.net

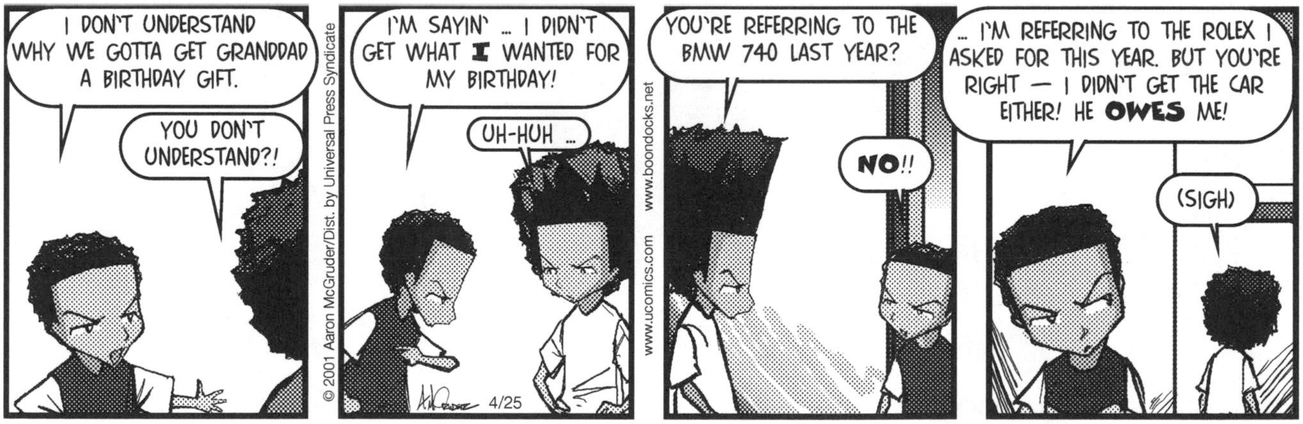
I DON'T UNDERSTAND WHY WE GOTTA GET GRANDDAD A BIRTHDAY GIFT.
YOU DON'T UNDERSTAND?!
I'M SAYIN' ... I DIDN'T GET WHAT **I** WANTED FOR MY BIRTHDAY!
UH-HUH ...
YOU'RE REFERRING TO THE BMW 740 LAST YEAR?
NO!!
... I'M REFERRING TO THE ROLEX I ASKED FOR THIS YEAR. BUT YOU'RE RIGHT — I DIDN'T GET THE CAR EITHER! HE **OWES** ME!
(SIGH)
© 2001 Aaron McGruder/Dist. by Universal Press Syndicate
4/25
www.ucomics.com www.boondocks.net

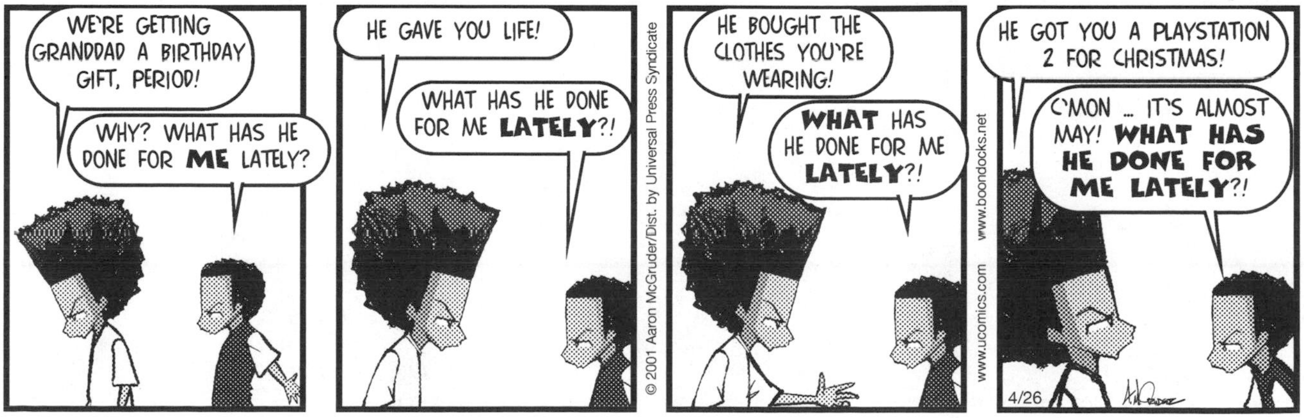
WE'RE GETTING GRANDDAD A BIRTHDAY GIFT, PERIOD!
WHY? WHAT HAS HE DONE FOR **ME** LATELY?
HE GAVE YOU LIFE!
WHAT HAS HE DONE FOR ME **LATELY**?!
HE BOUGHT THE CLOTHES YOU'RE WEARING!
WHAT HAS HE DONE FOR ME **LATELY**?!
HE GOT YOU A PLAYSTATION 2 FOR CHRISTMAS!
C'MON ... IT'S ALMOST MAY! **WHAT HAS HE DONE FOR ME LATELY**?!
© 2001 Aaron McGruder/Dist. by Universal Press Syndicate
4/26
www.ucomics.com www.boondocks.net

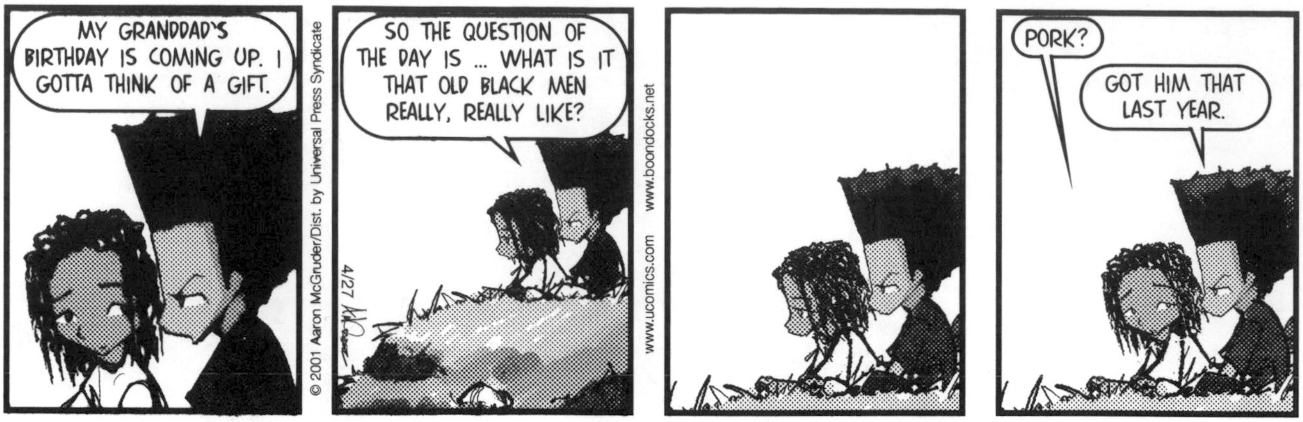
MY GRANDDAD'S BIRTHDAY IS COMING UP. I GOTTA THINK OF A GIFT.
SO THE QUESTION OF THE DAY IS ... WHAT IS IT THAT OLD BLACK MEN REALLY, REALLY LIKE?
PORK?
GOT HIM THAT LAST YEAR.
© 2001 Aaron McGruder/Dist. by Universal Press Syndicate
4/27
www.ucomics.com www.boondocks.net

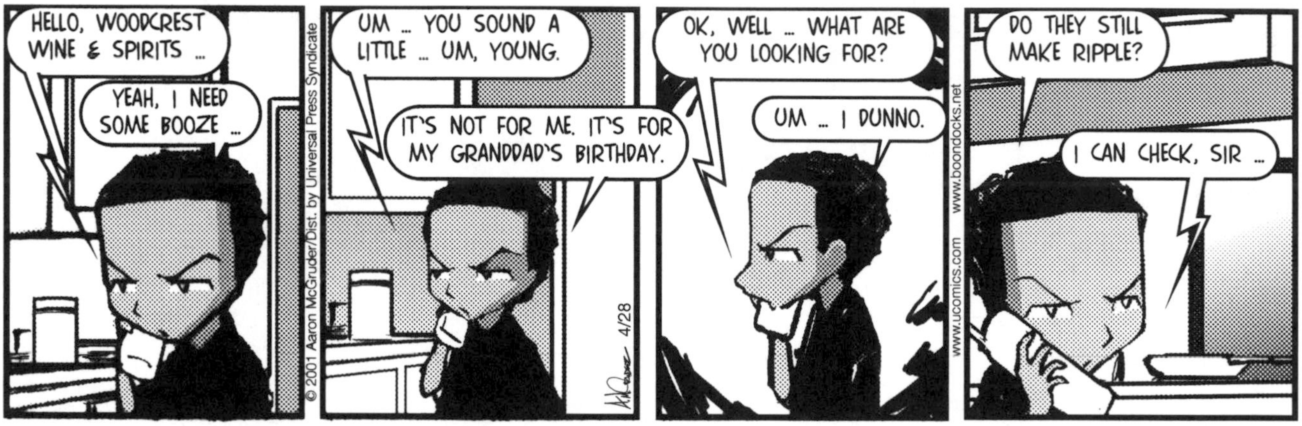
HELLO, WOODCREST WINE & SPIRITS ...
YEAH, I NEED SOME BOOZE ...
UM ... YOU SOUND A LITTLE ... UM, YOUNG.
IT'S NOT FOR ME. IT'S FOR MY GRANDDAD'S BIRTHDAY.
OK, WELL ... WHAT ARE YOU LOOKING FOR?
UM ... I DUNNO.
DO THEY STILL MAKE RIPPLE?
I CAN CHECK, SIR ...
© 2001 Aaron McGruder/Dist. by Universal Press Syndicate
4/28
www.ucomics.com www.boondocks.net

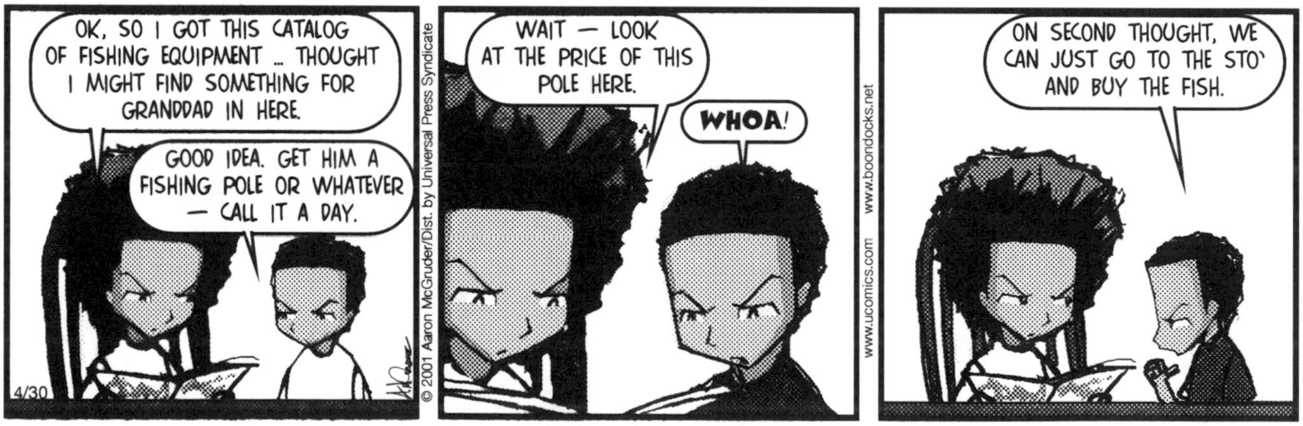
OK, SO I GOT THIS CATALOG OF FISHING EQUIPMENT ... THOUGHT I MIGHT FIND SOMETHING FOR GRANDDAD IN HERE.
GOOD IDEA. GET HIM A FISHING POLE OR WHATEVER — CALL IT A DAY.
4/30
© 2001 Aaron McGruder/Dist. by Universal Press Syndicate
WAIT — LOOK AT THE PRICE OF THIS POLE HERE.
WHOA!
www.ucomics.com www.boondocks.net
ON SECOND THOUGHT, WE CAN JUST GO TO THE STO' AND BUY THE FISH.

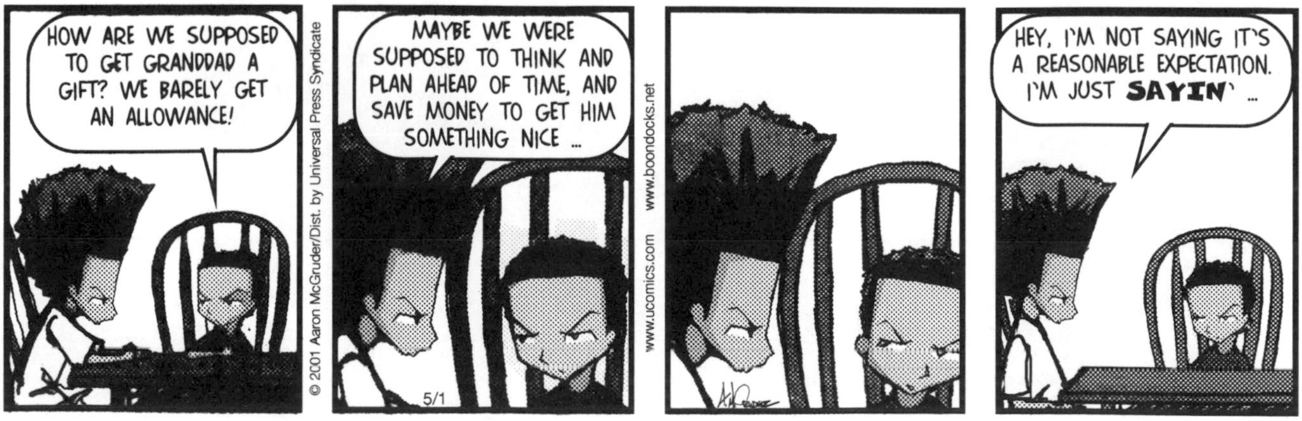
HOW ARE WE SUPPOSED TO GET GRANDDAD A GIFT? WE BARELY GET AN ALLOWANCE!
© 2001 Aaron McGruder/Dist. by Universal Press Syndicate
MAYBE WE WERE SUPPOSED TO THINK AND PLAN AHEAD OF TIME, AND SAVE MONEY TO GET HIM SOMETHING NICE ...
5/1
www.ucomics.com www.boondocks.net
HEY, I'M NOT SAYING IT'S A REASONABLE EXPECTATION. I'M JUST SAYIN' ...

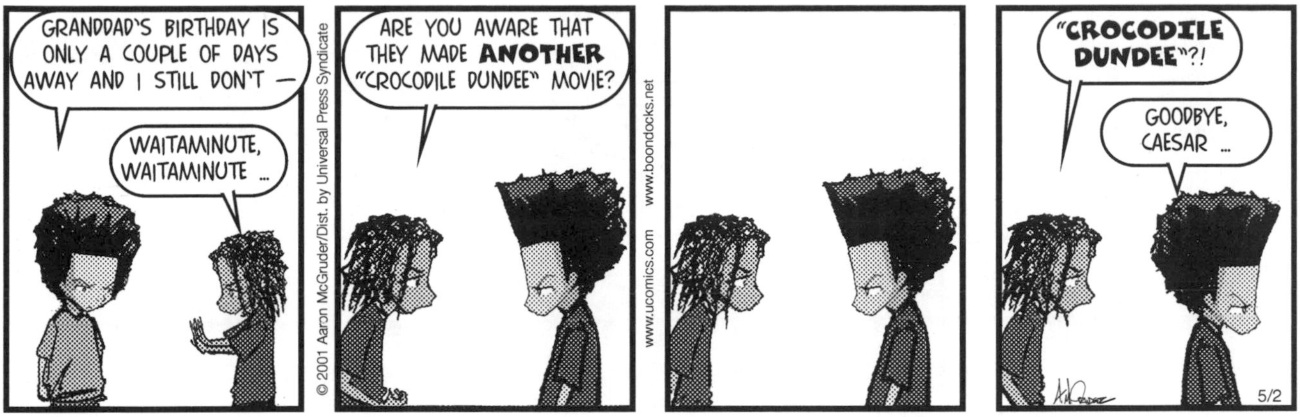
GRANDDAD'S BIRTHDAY IS ONLY A COUPLE OF DAYS AWAY AND I STILL DON'T —
WAITAMINUTE, WAITAMINUTE ...
© 2001 Aaron McGruder/Dist. by Universal Press Syndicate
ARE YOU AWARE THAT THEY MADE **ANOTHER** "CROCODILE DUNDEE" MOVIE?
www.ucomics.com www.boondocks.net
"CROCODILE DUNDEE"?!
GOODBYE, CAESAR ...
5/2

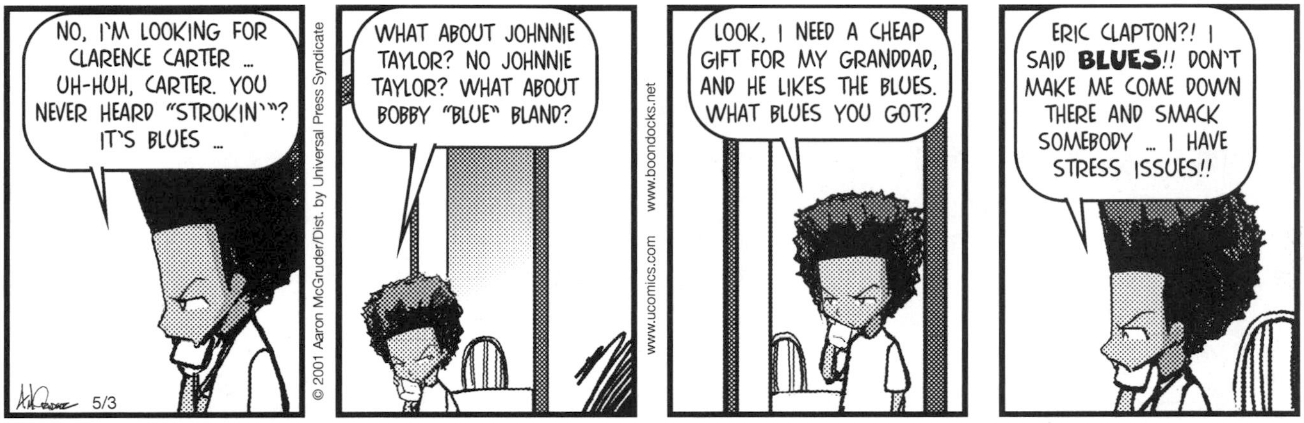
NO, I'M LOOKING FOR CLARENCE CARTER ... UH-HUH, CARTER. YOU NEVER HEARD "STROKIN'"? IT'S BLUES ...
5/3
© 2001 Aaron McGruder/Dist. by Universal Press Syndicate
WHAT ABOUT JOHNNIE TAYLOR? NO JOHNNIE TAYLOR? WHAT ABOUT BOBBY "BLUE" BLAND?
www.ucomics.com www.boondocks.net
LOOK, I NEED A CHEAP GIFT FOR MY GRANDDAD, AND HE LIKES THE BLUES. WHAT BLUES YOU GOT?
ERIC CLAPTON?! I SAID **BLUES**!! DON'T MAKE ME COME DOWN THERE AND SMACK SOMEBODY ... I HAVE STRESS ISSUES!!

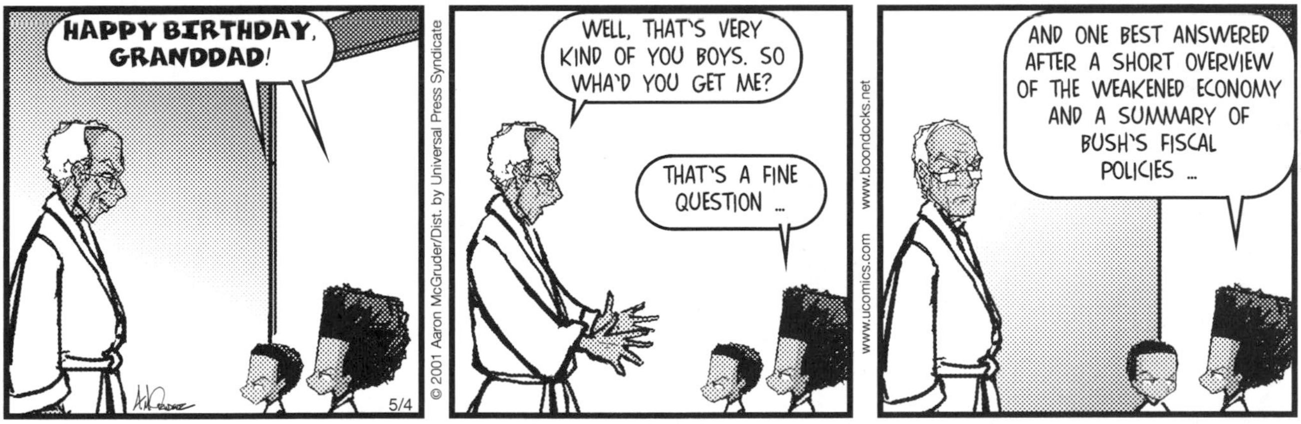
HAPPY BIRTHDAY, GRANDDAD!
5/4
© 2001 Aaron McGruder/Dist. by Universal Press Syndicate
WELL, THAT'S VERY KIND OF YOU BOYS. SO WHA'D YOU GET ME?
THAT'S A FINE QUESTION ...
www.ucomics.com www.boondocks.net
AND ONE BEST ANSWERED AFTER A SHORT OVERVIEW OF THE WEAKENED ECONOMY AND A SUMMARY OF BUSH'S FISCAL POLICIES ...

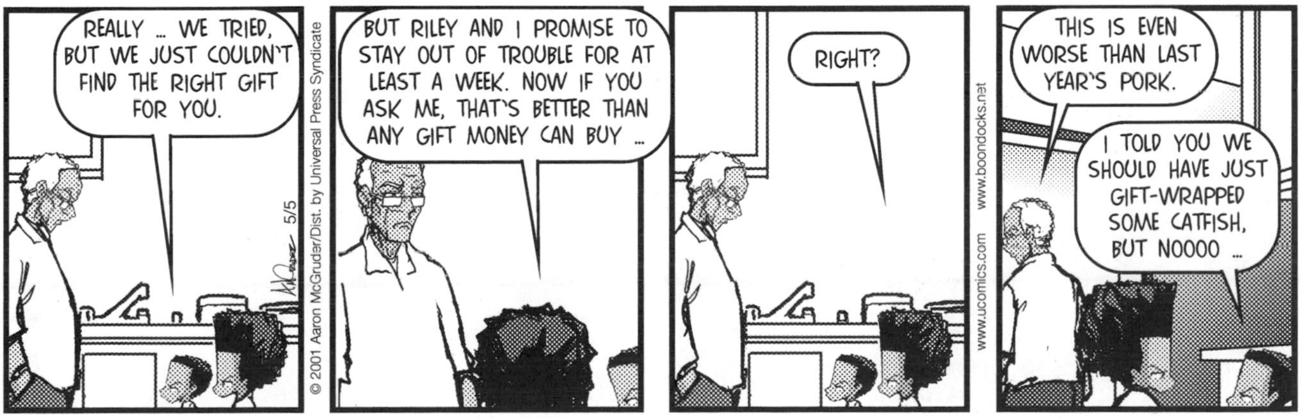
REALLY ... WE TRIED, BUT WE JUST COULDN'T FIND THE RIGHT GIFT FOR YOU.
5/5
© 2001 Aaron McGruder/Dist. by Universal Press Syndicate
BUT RILEY AND I PROMISE TO STAY OUT OF TROUBLE FOR AT LEAST A WEEK. NOW IF YOU ASK ME, THAT'S BETTER THAN ANY GIFT MONEY CAN BUY ...
RIGHT?
www.ucomics.com www.boondocks.net
THIS IS EVEN WORSE THAN LAST YEAR'S PORK.
I TOLD YOU WE SHOULD HAVE JUST GIFT-WRAPPED SOME CATFISH, BUT NOOOO ...

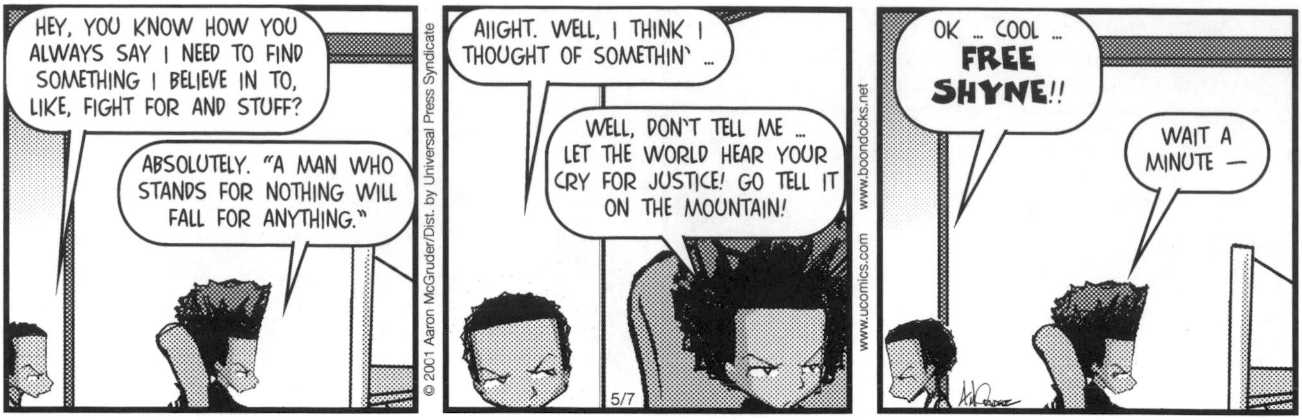
HEY, YOU KNOW HOW YOU ALWAYS SAY I NEED TO FIND SOMETHING I BELIEVE IN TO, LIKE, FIGHT FOR AND STUFF?
ABSOLUTELY. "A MAN WHO STANDS FOR NOTHING WILL FALL FOR ANYTHING."
© 2001 Aaron McGruder/Dist. by Universal Press Syndicate
AIIGHT. WELL, I THINK I THOUGHT OF SOMETHIN' ...
WELL, DON'T TELL ME ... LET THE WORLD HEAR YOUR CRY FOR JUSTICE! GO TELL IT ON THE MOUNTAIN!
5/7
www.ucomics.com www.boondocks.net
OK ... COOL ... FREE SHYNE!!
WAIT A MINUTE —

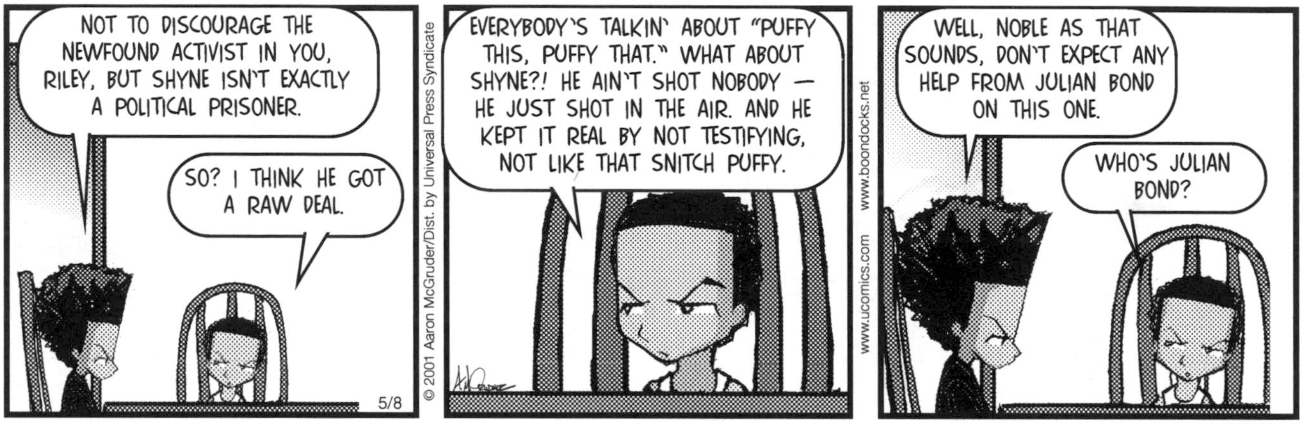
NOT TO DISCOURAGE THE NEWFOUND ACTIVIST IN YOU, RILEY, BUT SHYNE ISN'T EXACTLY A POLITICAL PRISONER.
SO? I THINK HE GOT A RAW DEAL.
5/8
© 2001 Aaron McGruder/Dist. by Universal Press Syndicate
EVERYBODY'S TALKIN' ABOUT "PUFFY THIS, PUFFY THAT." WHAT ABOUT SHYNE?! HE AIN'T SHOT NOBODY — HE JUST SHOT IN THE AIR. AND HE KEPT IT REAL BY NOT TESTIFYING, NOT LIKE THAT SNITCH PUFFY.
www.ucomics.com www.boondocks.net
WELL, NOBLE AS THAT SOUNDS, DON'T EXPECT ANY HELP FROM JULIAN BOND ON THIS ONE.
WHO'S JULIAN BOND?

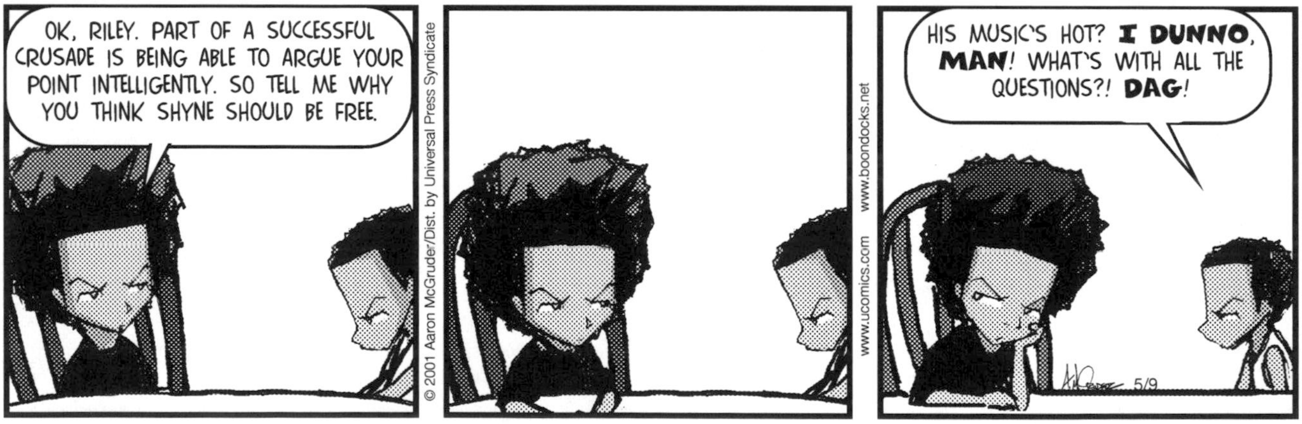
OK, RILEY. PART OF A SUCCESSFUL CRUSADE IS BEING ABLE TO ARGUE YOUR POINT INTELLIGENTLY. SO TELL ME WHY YOU THINK SHYNE SHOULD BE FREE.
© 2001 Aaron McGruder/Dist. by Universal Press Syndicate
www.ucomics.com www.boondocks.net
HIS MUSIC'S HOT? I DUNNO, MAN! WHAT'S WITH ALL THE QUESTIONS?! DAG!
5/9

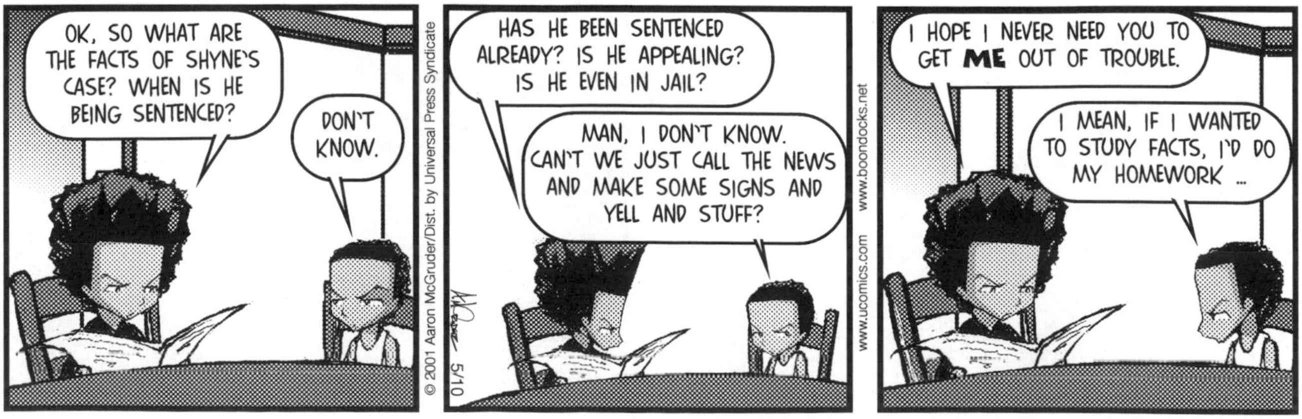
OK, SO WHAT ARE THE FACTS OF SHYNE'S CASE? WHEN IS HE BEING SENTENCED?
DON'T KNOW.
© 2001 Aaron McGruder/Dist. by Universal Press Syndicate
HAS HE BEEN SENTENCED ALREADY? IS HE APPEALING? IS HE EVEN IN JAIL?
MAN, I DON'T KNOW. CAN'T WE JUST CALL THE NEWS AND MAKE SOME SIGNS AND YELL AND STUFF?
5/10
www.ucomics.com www.boondocks.net
I HOPE I NEVER NEED YOU TO GET ME OUT OF TROUBLE.
I MEAN, IF I WANTED TO STUDY FACTS, I'D DO MY HOMEWORK ...

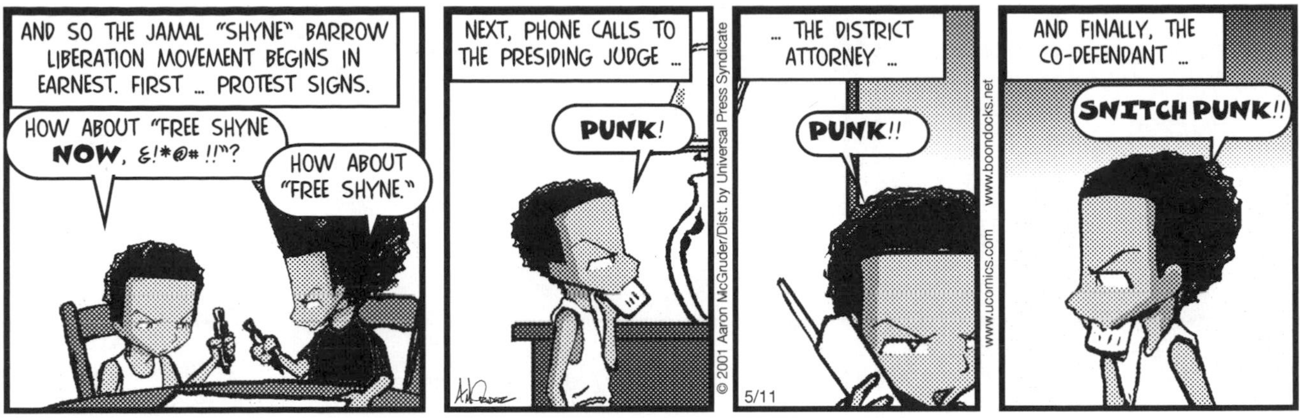
AND SO THE JAMAL "SHYNE" BARROW LIBERATION MOVEMENT BEGINS IN EARNEST. FIRST ... PROTEST SIGNS.
HOW ABOUT "FREE SHYNE NOW, &!*@# !!"?
HOW ABOUT "FREE SHYNE."
NEXT, PHONE CALLS TO THE PRESIDING JUDGE ...
PUNK!
... THE DISTRICT ATTORNEY ...
PUNK!!
AND FINALLY, THE CO-DEFENDANT ...
SNITCH PUNK!!
5/11

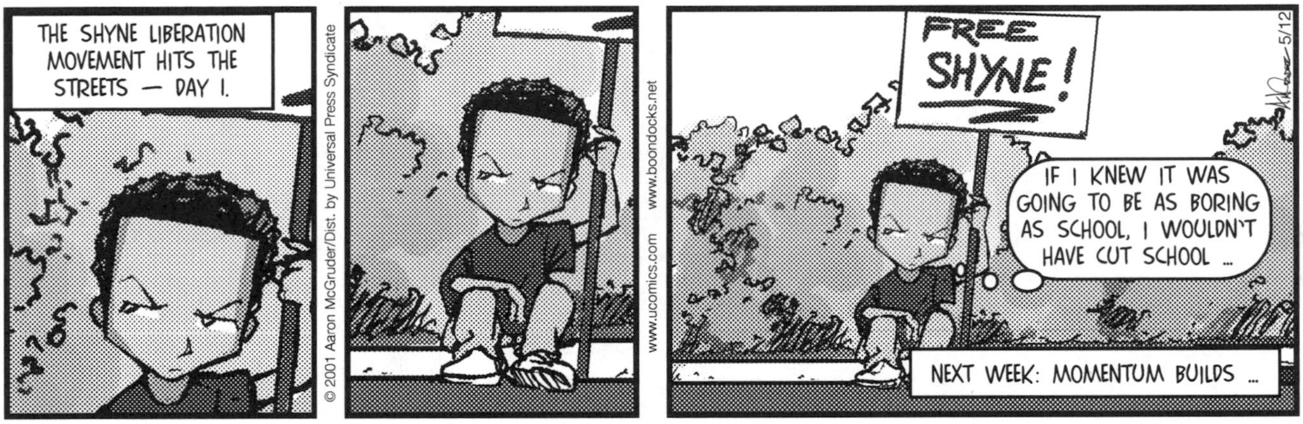
THE SHYNE LIBERATION MOVEMENT HITS THE STREETS — DAY 1.
FREE SHYNE!
IF I KNEW IT WAS GOING TO BE AS BORING AS SCHOOL, I WOULDN'T HAVE CUT SCHOOL ...
NEXT WEEK: MOMENTUM BUILDS ...
5/12

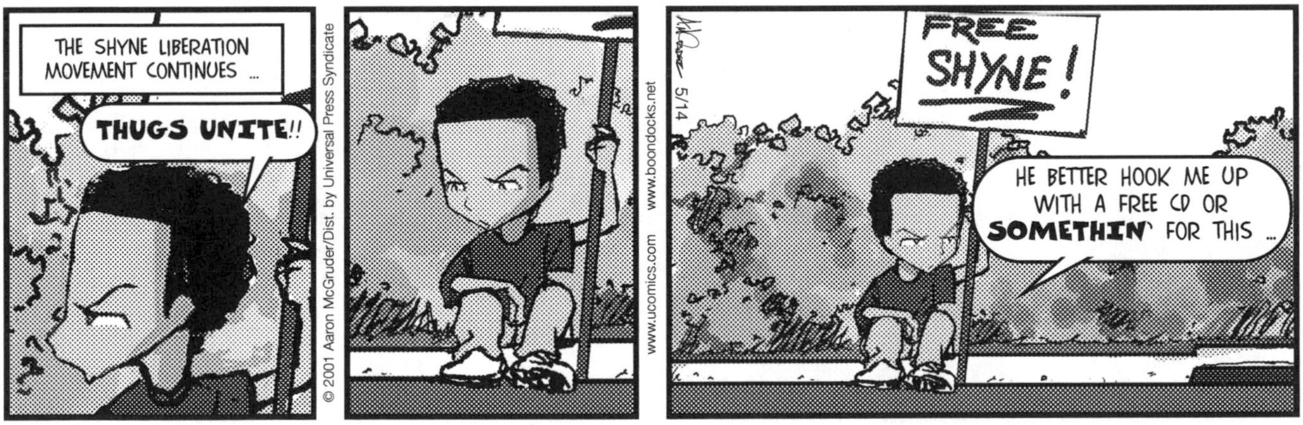
THE SHYNE LIBERATION MOVEMENT CONTINUES ...
THUGS UNITE!!
FREE SHYNE!
HE BETTER HOOK ME UP WITH A FREE CD OR SOMETHIN' FOR THIS ...
5/14

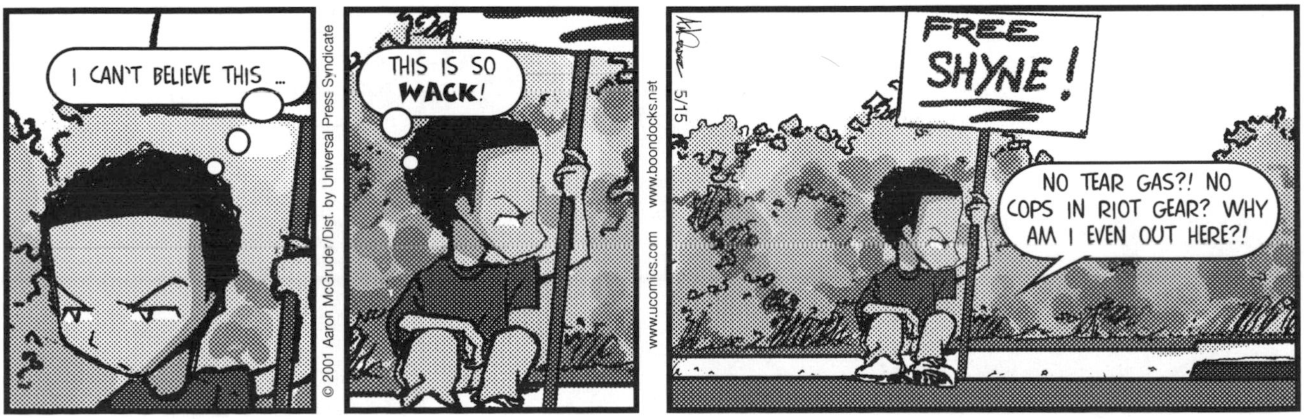
I CAN'T BELIEVE THIS ...
THIS IS SO WACK!
FREE SHYNE!
NO TEAR GAS?! NO COPS IN RIOT GEAR? WHY AM I EVEN OUT HERE?!
5/15

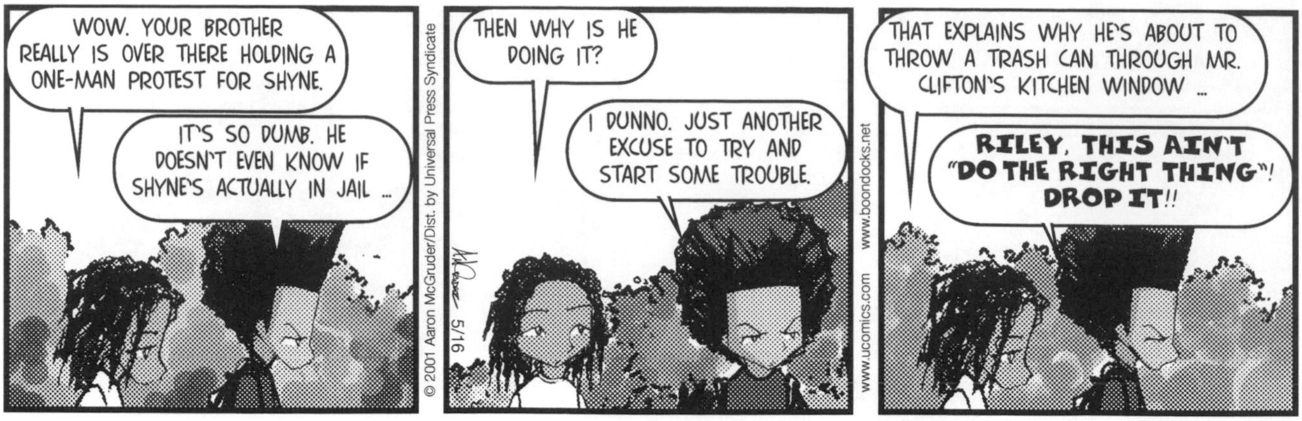
WOW. YOUR BROTHER REALLY IS OVER THERE HOLDING A ONE-MAN PROTEST FOR SHYNE.
IT'S SO DUMB. HE DOESN'T EVEN KNOW IF SHYNE'S ACTUALLY IN JAIL ...
THEN WHY IS HE DOING IT?
I DUNNO. JUST ANOTHER EXCUSE TO TRY AND START SOME TROUBLE.
THAT EXPLAINS WHY HE'S ABOUT TO THROW A TRASH CAN THROUGH MR. CLIFTON'S KITCHEN WINDOW ...
RILEY, THIS AIN'T "DO THE RIGHT THING"! DROP IT!!
© 2001 Aaron McGruder/Dist. by Universal Press Syndicate
5/16
www.ucomics.com www.boondocks.net

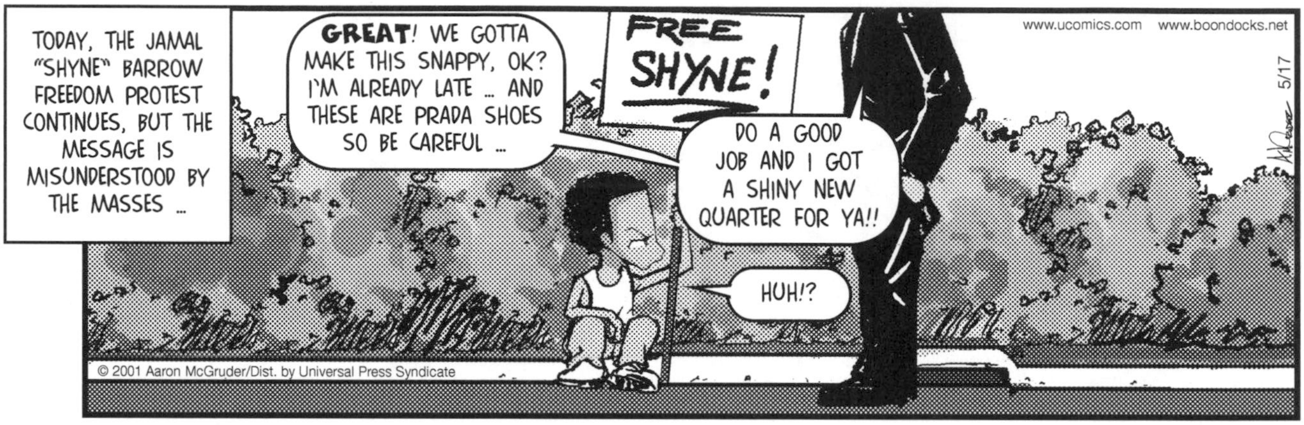
TODAY, THE JAMAL "SHYNE" BARROW FREEDOM PROTEST CONTINUES, BUT THE MESSAGE IS MISUNDERSTOOD BY THE MASSES ...
FREE SHYNE!
GREAT! WE GOTTA MAKE THIS SNAPPY, OK? I'M ALREADY LATE ... AND THESE ARE PRADA SHOES SO BE CAREFUL ...
DO A GOOD JOB AND I GOT A SHINY NEW QUARTER FOR YA!!
HUH!?
www.ucomics.com www.boondocks.net
5/17
© 2001 Aaron McGruder/Dist. by Universal Press Syndicate

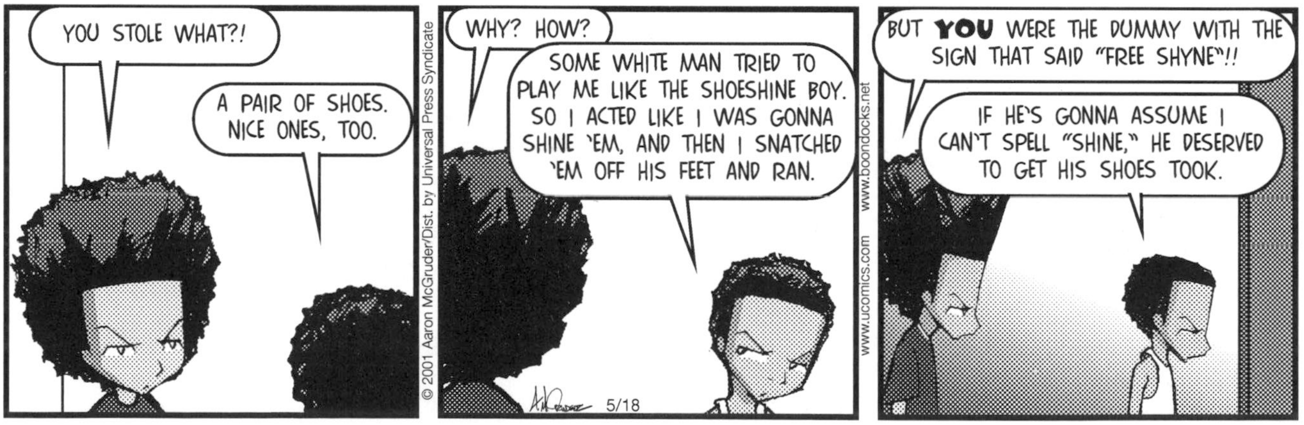
YOU STOLE WHAT?!
A PAIR OF SHOES. NICE ONES, TOO.
WHY? HOW?
SOME WHITE MAN TRIED TO PLAY ME LIKE THE SHOESHINE BOY. SO I ACTED LIKE I WAS GONNA SHINE 'EM, AND THEN I SNATCHED 'EM OFF HIS FEET AND RAN.
BUT YOU WERE THE DUMMY WITH THE SIGN THAT SAID "FREE SHYNE"!!
IF HE'S GONNA ASSUME I CAN'T SPELL "SHINE," HE DESERVED TO GET HIS SHOES TOOK.
© 2001 Aaron McGruder/Dist. by Universal Press Syndicate
5/18
www.ucomics.com www.boondocks.net

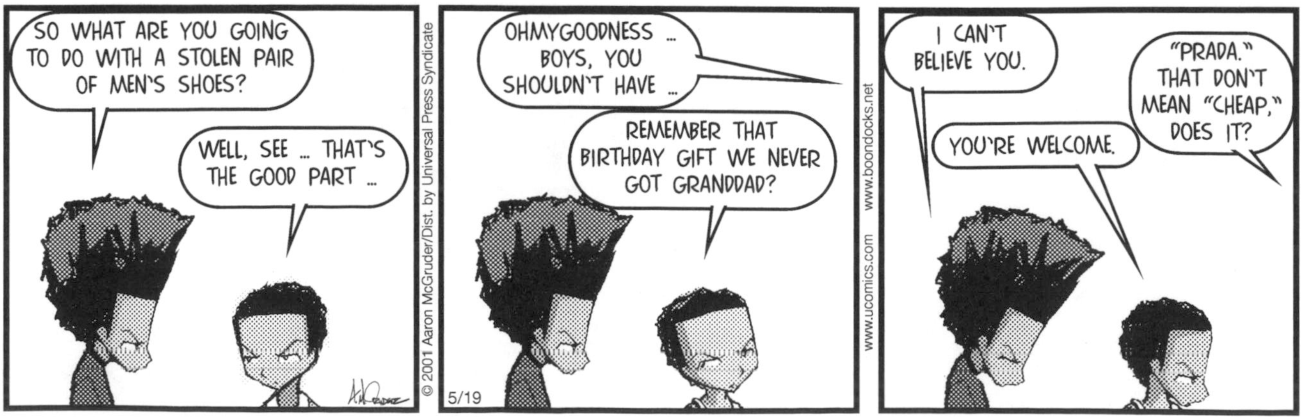
SO WHAT ARE YOU GOING TO DO WITH A STOLEN PAIR OF MEN'S SHOES?
WELL, SEE ... THAT'S THE GOOD PART ...
OHMYGOODNESS ... BOYS, YOU SHOULDN'T HAVE ...
REMEMBER THAT BIRTHDAY GIFT WE NEVER GOT GRANDDAD?
I CAN'T BELIEVE YOU.
YOU'RE WELCOME.
"PRADA." THAT DON'T MEAN "CHEAP," DOES IT?
© 2001 Aaron McGruder/Dist. by Universal Press Syndicate
5/19
www.ucomics.com www.boondocks.net

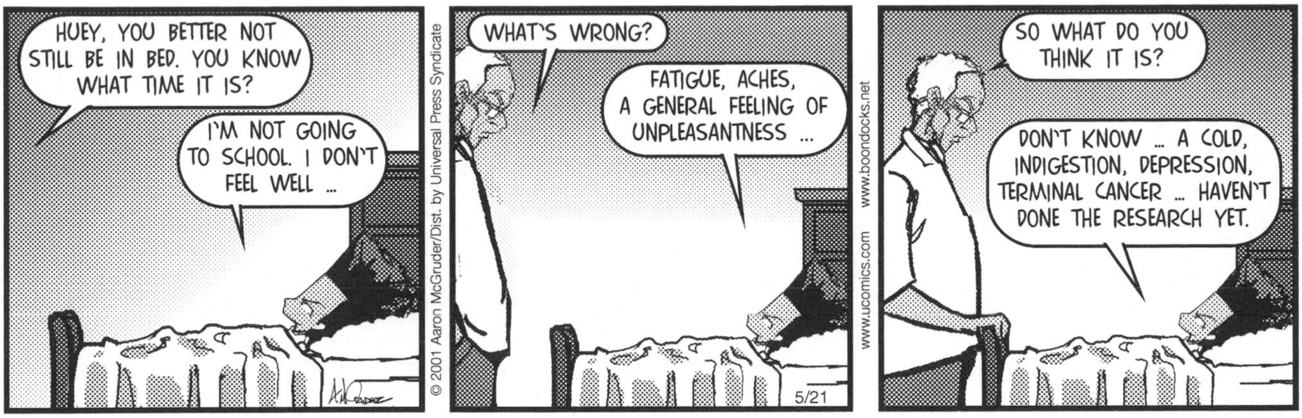
HUEY, YOU BETTER NOT STILL BE IN BED. YOU KNOW WHAT TIME IT IS?
I'M NOT GOING TO SCHOOL. I DON'T FEEL WELL ...
© 2001 Aaron McGruder/Dist. by Universal Press Syndicate
WHAT'S WRONG?
FATIGUE, ACHES, A GENERAL FEELING OF UNPLEASANTNESS ...
5/21
www.ucomics.com www.boondocks.net
SO WHAT DO YOU THINK IT IS?
DON'T KNOW ... A COLD, INDIGESTION, DEPRESSION, TERMINAL CANCER ... HAVEN'T DONE THE RESEARCH YET.

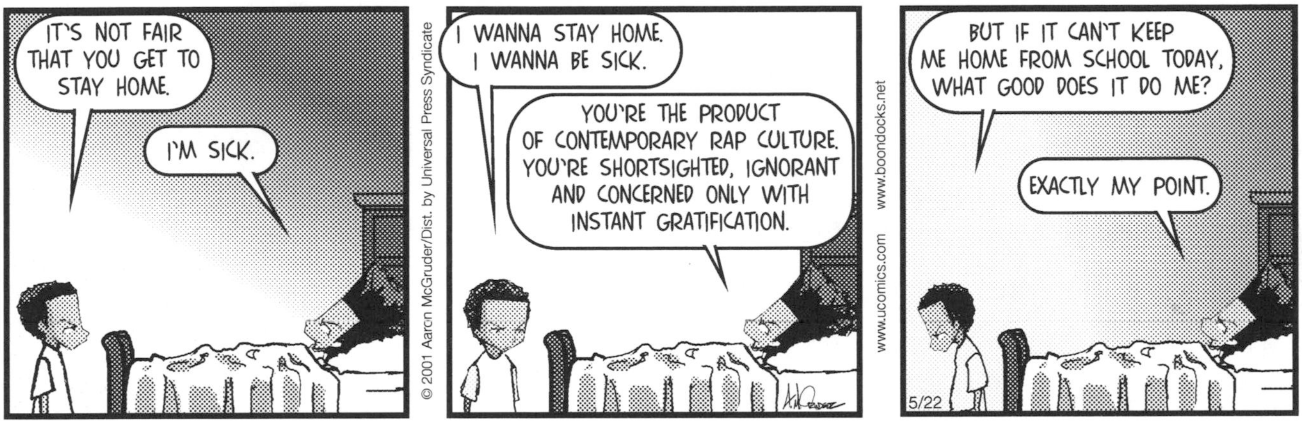
IT'S NOT FAIR THAT YOU GET TO STAY HOME.
I'M SICK.
© 2001 Aaron McGruder/Dist. by Universal Press Syndicate
I WANNA STAY HOME. I WANNA BE SICK.
YOU'RE THE PRODUCT OF CONTEMPORARY RAP CULTURE. YOU'RE SHORTSIGHTED, IGNORANT AND CONCERNED ONLY WITH INSTANT GRATIFICATION.
www.ucomics.com www.boondocks.net
BUT IF IT CAN'T KEEP ME HOME FROM SCHOOL TODAY, WHAT GOOD DOES IT DO ME?
EXACTLY MY POINT.
5/22

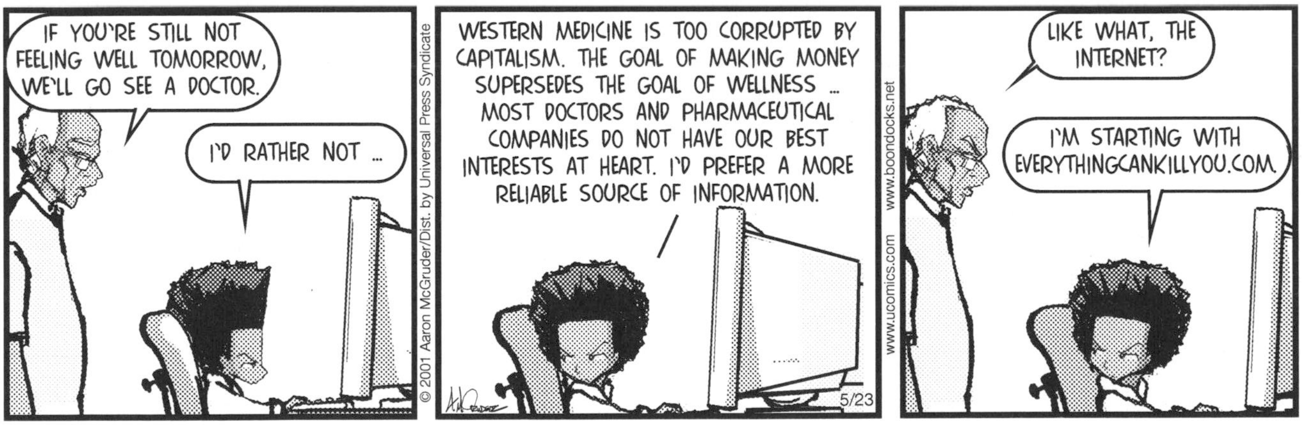
IF YOU'RE STILL NOT FEELING WELL TOMORROW, WE'LL GO SEE A DOCTOR.
I'D RATHER NOT ...
© 2001 Aaron McGruder/Dist. by Universal Press Syndicate
WESTERN MEDICINE IS TOO CORRUPTED BY CAPITALISM. THE GOAL OF MAKING MONEY SUPERSEDES THE GOAL OF WELLNESS ... MOST DOCTORS AND PHARMACEUTICAL COMPANIES DO NOT HAVE OUR BEST INTERESTS AT HEART. I'D PREFER A MORE RELIABLE SOURCE OF INFORMATION.
5/23
www.ucomics.com www.boondocks.net
LIKE WHAT, THE INTERNET?
I'M STARTING WITH EVERYTHINGCANKILLYOU.COM.

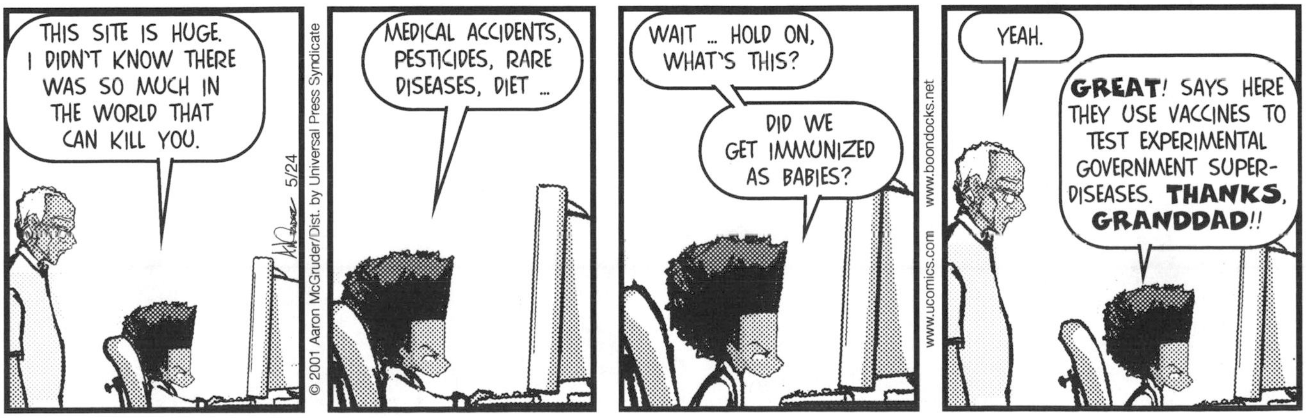
THIS SITE IS HUGE. I DIDN'T KNOW THERE WAS SO MUCH IN THE WORLD THAT CAN KILL YOU.
5/24
© 2001 Aaron McGruder/Dist. by Universal Press Syndicate
MEDICAL ACCIDENTS, PESTICIDES, RARE DISEASES, DIET ...
WAIT ... HOLD ON, WHAT'S THIS?
DID WE GET IMMUNIZED AS BABIES?
www.ucomics.com www.boondocks.net
YEAH.
GREAT! SAYS HERE THEY USE VACCINES TO TEST EXPERIMENTAL GOVERNMENT SUPER-DISEASES. THANKS, GRANDDAD!!

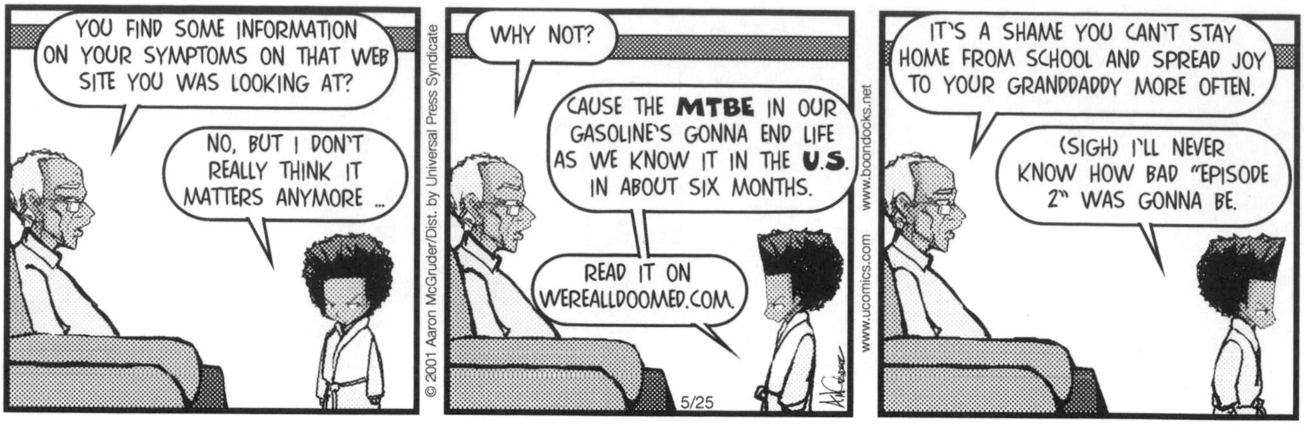
YOU FIND SOME INFORMATION ON YOUR SYMPTOMS ON THAT WEB SITE YOU WAS LOOKING AT?
NO, BUT I DON'T REALLY THINK IT MATTERS ANYMORE ...
© 2001 Aaron McGruder/Dist. by Universal Press Syndicate
WHY NOT?
CAUSE THE MTBE IN OUR GASOLINE'S GONNA END LIFE AS WE KNOW IT IN THE U.S. IN ABOUT SIX MONTHS.
READ IT ON WEREALLDOOMED.COM.
5/25
www.ucomics.com www.boondocks.net
IT'S A SHAME YOU CAN'T STAY HOME FROM SCHOOL AND SPREAD JOY TO YOUR GRANDDADDY MORE OFTEN.
(SIGH) I'LL NEVER KNOW HOW BAD "EPISODE 2" WAS GONNA BE.

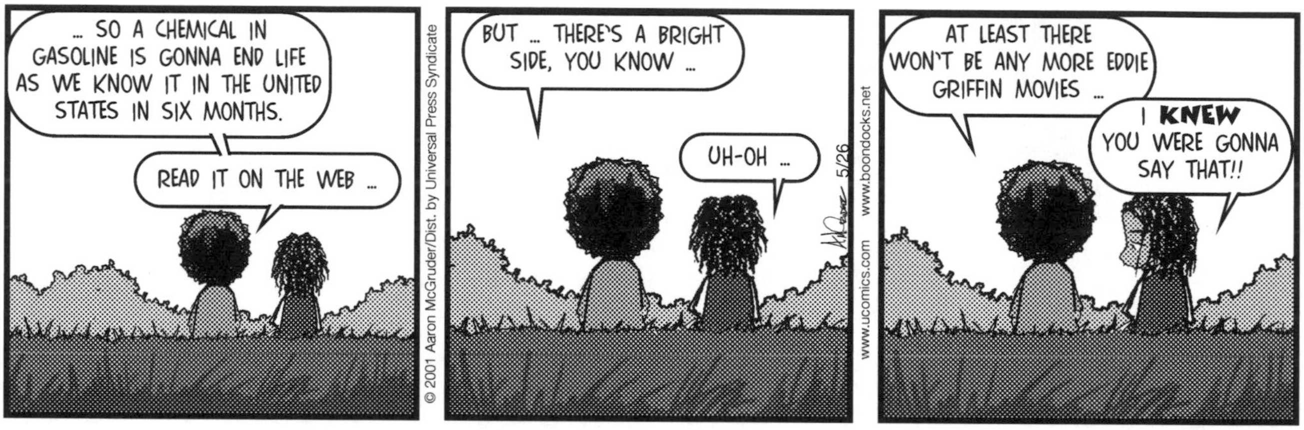
... SO A CHEMICAL IN GASOLINE IS GONNA END LIFE AS WE KNOW IT IN THE UNITED STATES IN SIX MONTHS.
READ IT ON THE WEB ...
© 2001 Aaron McGruder/Dist. by Universal Press Syndicate
BUT ... THERE'S A BRIGHT SIDE, YOU KNOW ...
UH-OH ...
5/26
www.ucomics.com www.boondocks.net
AT LEAST THERE WON'T BE ANY MORE EDDIE GRIFFIN MOVIES ...
I KNEW YOU WERE GONNA SAY THAT!!

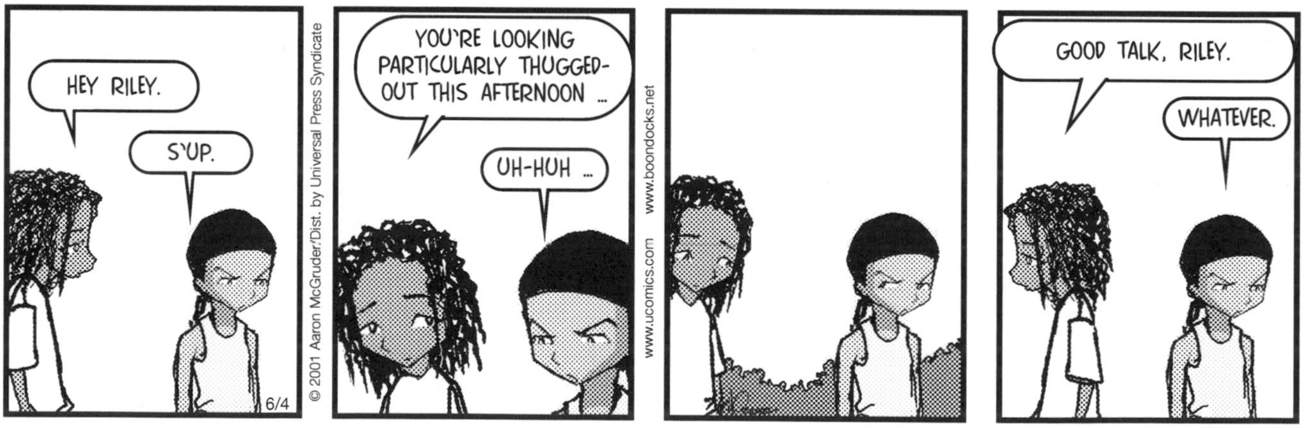
HEY RILEY.
S'UP.
6/4
© 2001 Aaron McGruder/Dist. by Universal Press Syndicate
YOU'RE LOOKING PARTICULARLY THUGGED-OUT THIS AFTERNOON ...
UH-HUH ...
www.ucomics.com www.boondocks.net
GOOD TALK, RILEY.
WHATEVER.

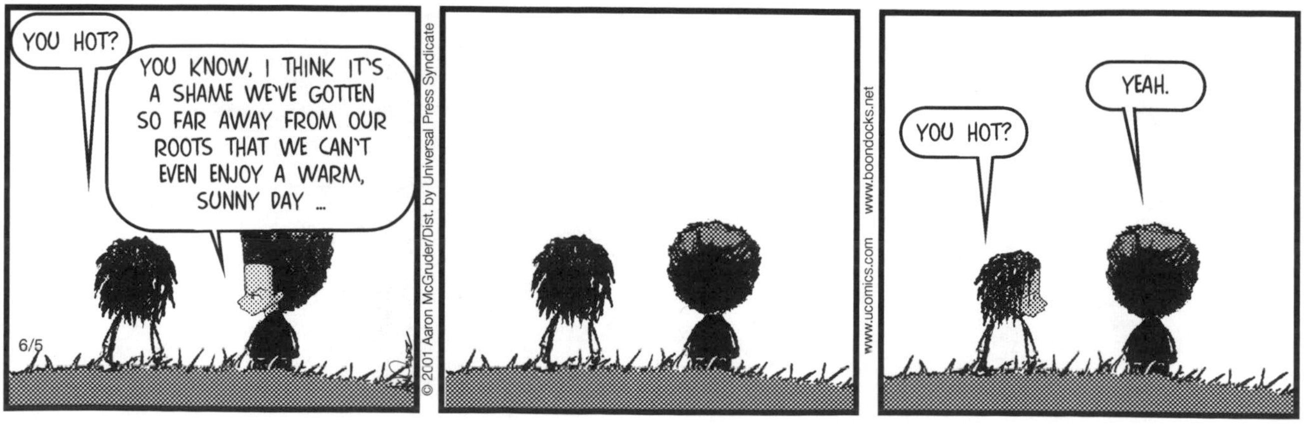
YOU HOT?
YOU KNOW, I THINK IT'S A SHAME WE'VE GOTTEN SO FAR AWAY FROM OUR ROOTS THAT WE CAN'T EVEN ENJOY A WARM, SUNNY DAY ...
6/5
© 2001 Aaron McGruder/Dist. by Universal Press Syndicate
www.ucomics.com www.boondocks.net
YOU HOT?
YEAH.

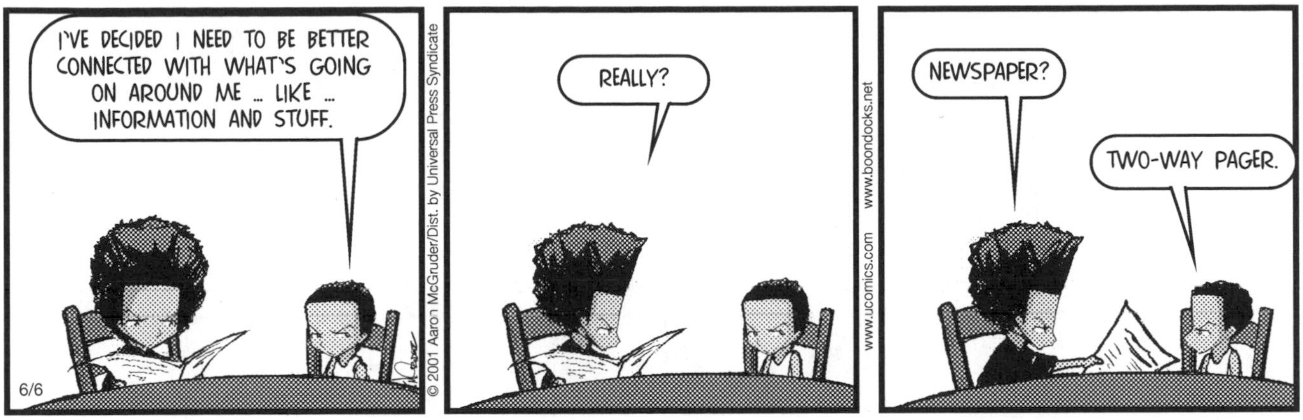
6/6
I'VE DECIDED I NEED TO BE BETTER CONNECTED WITH WHAT'S GOING ON AROUND ME ... LIKE ... INFORMATION AND STUFF.
REALLY?
NEWSPAPER?
TWO-WAY PAGER.
© 2001 Aaron McGruder/Dist. by Universal Press Syndicate
www.ucomics.com www.boondocks.net

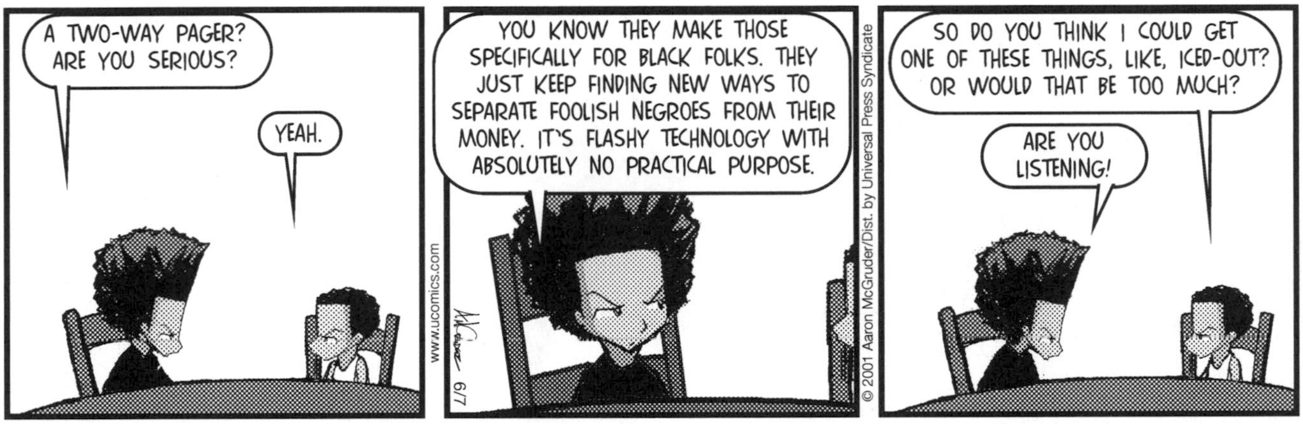
A TWO-WAY PAGER? ARE YOU SERIOUS?
YEAH.
YOU KNOW THEY MAKE THOSE SPECIFICALLY FOR BLACK FOLKS. THEY JUST KEEP FINDING NEW WAYS TO SEPARATE FOOLISH NEGROES FROM THEIR MONEY. IT'S FLASHY TECHNOLOGY WITH ABSOLUTELY NO PRACTICAL PURPOSE.
SO DO YOU THINK I COULD GET ONE OF THESE THINGS, LIKE, ICED-OUT? OR WOULD THAT BE TOO MUCH?
ARE YOU LISTENING!
6/7
www.ucomics.com
© 2001 Aaron McGruder/Dist. by Universal Press Syndicate

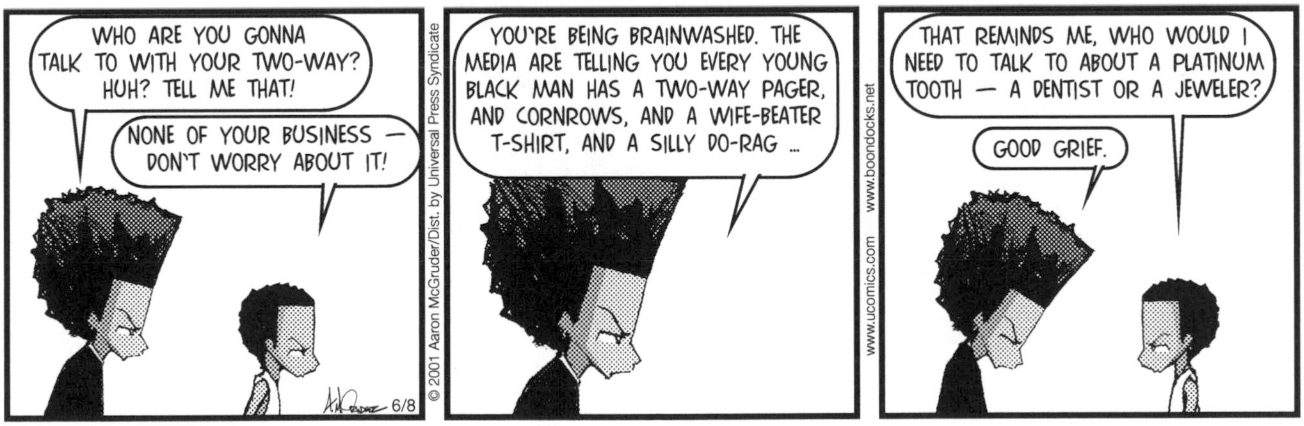
WHO ARE YOU GONNA TALK TO WITH YOUR TWO-WAY? HUH? TELL ME THAT!
NONE OF YOUR BUSINESS — DON'T WORRY ABOUT IT!
6/8
YOU'RE BEING BRAINWASHED. THE MEDIA ARE TELLING YOU EVERY YOUNG BLACK MAN HAS A TWO-WAY PAGER, AND CORNROWS, AND A WIFE-BEATER T-SHIRT, AND A SILLY DO-RAG ...
THAT REMINDS ME, WHO WOULD I NEED TO TALK TO ABOUT A PLATINUM TOOTH — A DENTIST OR A JEWELER?
GOOD GRIEF.
© 2001 Aaron McGruder/Dist. by Universal Press Syndicate
www.ucomics.com www.boondocks.net

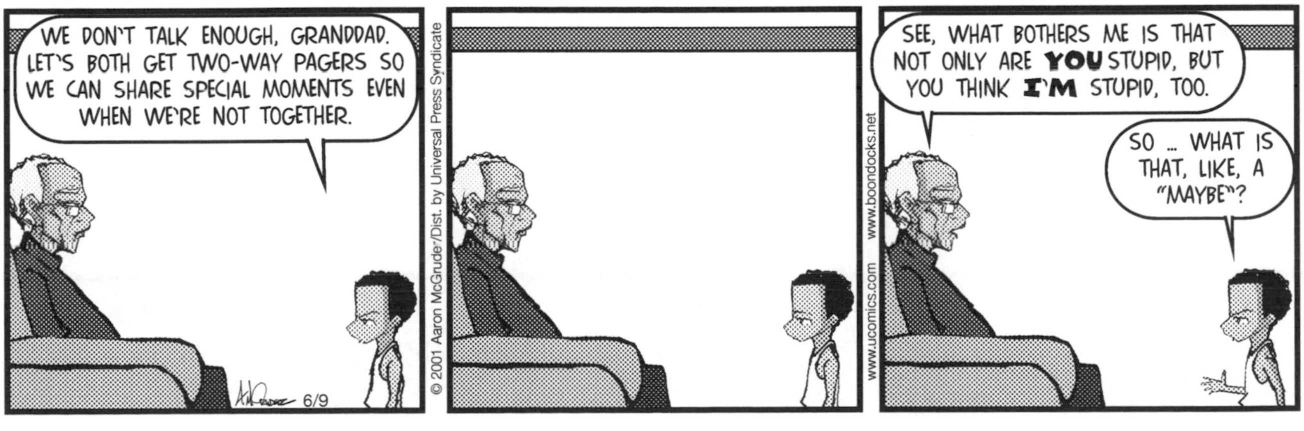
WE DON'T TALK ENOUGH, GRANDDAD. LET'S BOTH GET TWO-WAY PAGERS SO WE CAN SHARE SPECIAL MOMENTS EVEN WHEN WE'RE NOT TOGETHER.
6/9
SEE, WHAT BOTHERS ME IS THAT NOT ONLY ARE YOU STUPID, BUT YOU THINK I'M STUPID, TOO.
SO ... WHAT IS THAT, LIKE, A "MAYBE"?
© 2001 Aaron McGruder/Dist. by Universal Press Syndicate
www.ucomics.com www.boondocks.net

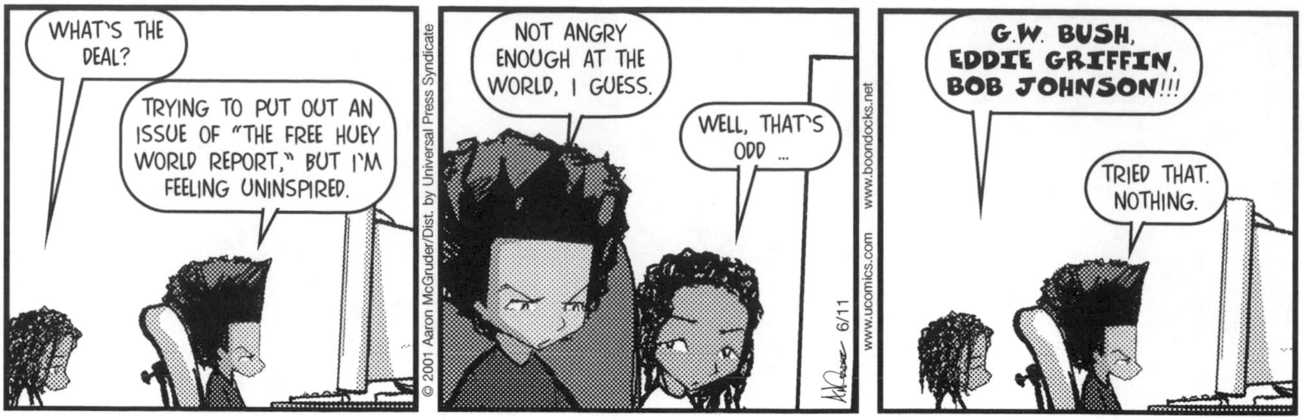
WHAT'S THE DEAL?
TRYING TO PUT OUT AN ISSUE OF "THE FREE HUEY WORLD REPORT," BUT I'M FEELING UNINSPIRED.
© 2001 Aaron McGruder/Dist. by Universal Press Syndicate
NOT ANGRY ENOUGH AT THE WORLD, I GUESS.
WELL, THAT'S ODD ...
6/11
www.ucomics.com www.boondocks.net
G.W. BUSH, EDDIE GRIFFIN, BOB JOHNSON!!!
TRIED THAT. NOTHING.

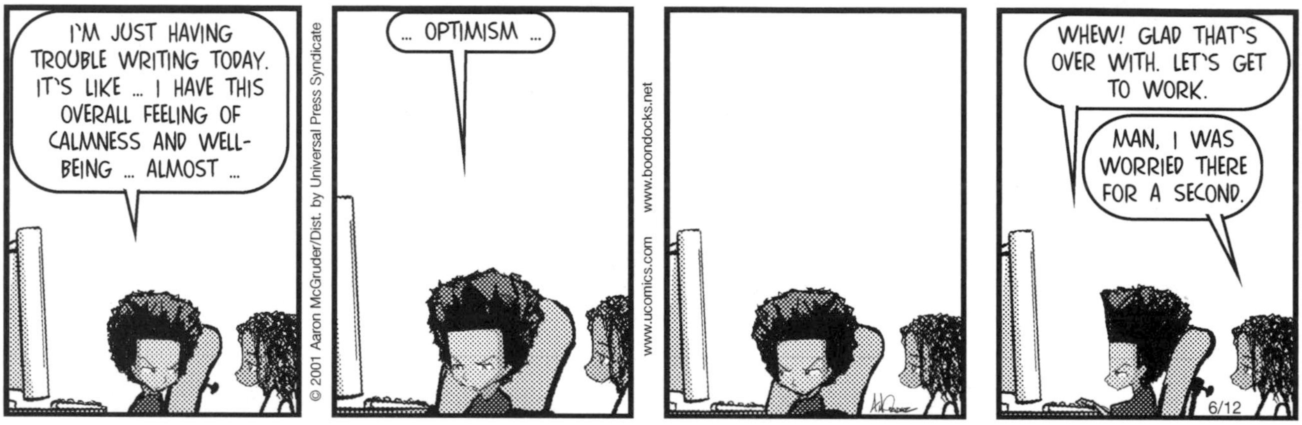
I'M JUST HAVING TROUBLE WRITING TODAY. IT'S LIKE ... I HAVE THIS OVERALL FEELING OF CALMNESS AND WELL-BEING ... ALMOST ...
© 2001 Aaron McGruder/Dist. by Universal Press Syndicate
... OPTIMISM ...
www.ucomics.com www.boondocks.net
WHEW! GLAD THAT'S OVER WITH. LET'S GET TO WORK.
MAN, I WAS WORRIED THERE FOR A SECOND.
6/12

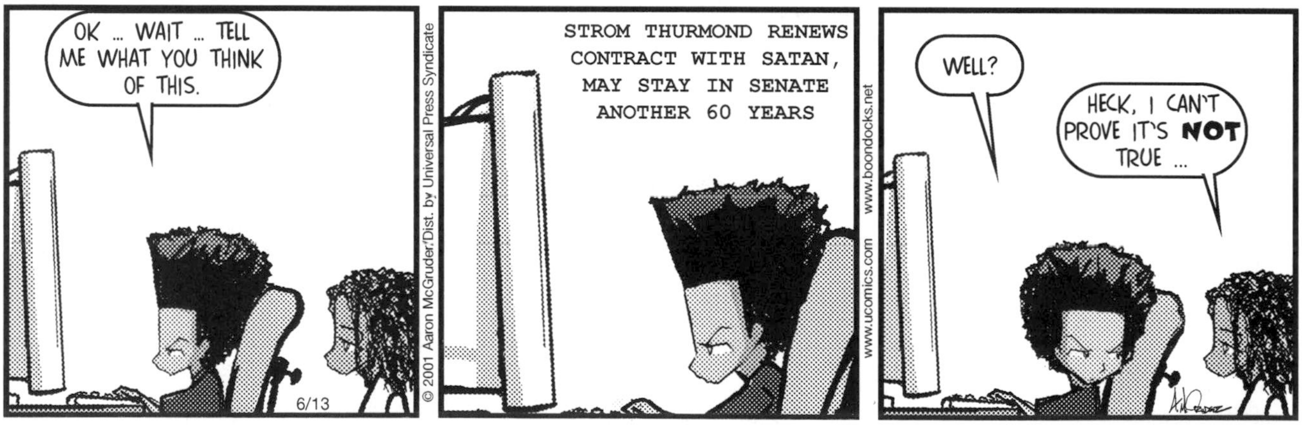
OK ... WAIT ... TELL ME WHAT YOU THINK OF THIS.
6/13
© 2001 Aaron McGruder/Dist. by Universal Press Syndicate
STROM THURMOND RENEWS CONTRACT WITH SATAN, MAY STAY IN SENATE ANOTHER 60 YEARS
www.ucomics.com www.boondocks.net
WELL?
HECK, I CAN'T PROVE IT'S NOT TRUE ...

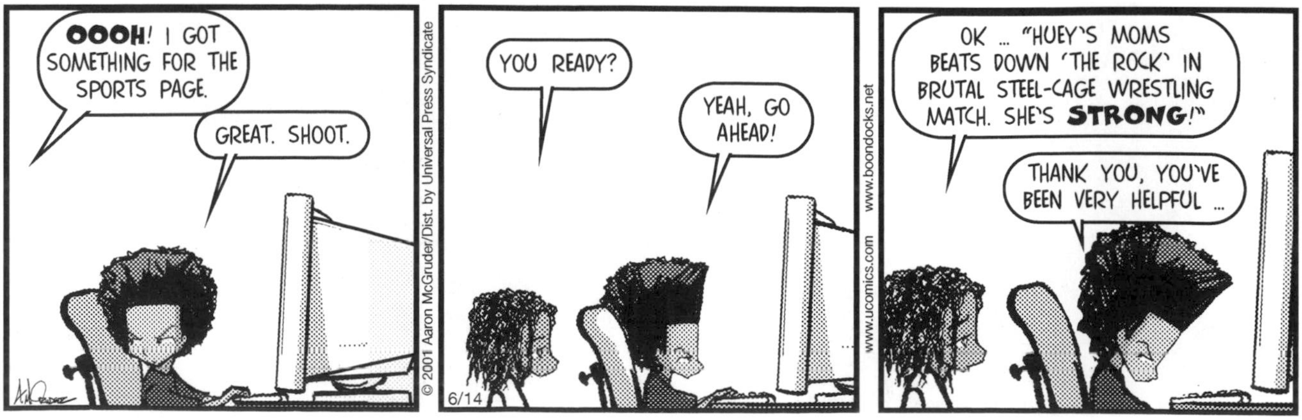
OOOH! I GOT SOMETHING FOR THE SPORTS PAGE.
GREAT. SHOOT.
© 2001 Aaron McGruder/Dist. by Universal Press Syndicate
YOU READY?
YEAH, GO AHEAD!
6/14
www.ucomics.com www.boondocks.net
OK ... "HUEY'S MOMS BEATS DOWN 'THE ROCK' IN BRUTAL STEEL-CAGE WRESTLING MATCH. SHE'S STRONG!"
THANK YOU, YOU'VE BEEN VERY HELPFUL ...

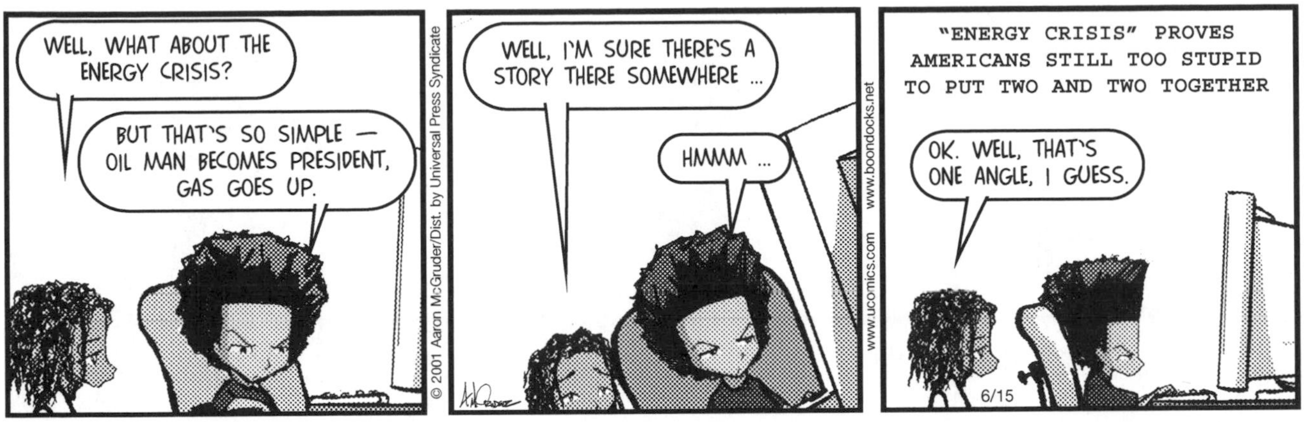
WELL, WHAT ABOUT THE ENERGY CRISIS?
BUT THAT'S SO SIMPLE — OIL MAN BECOMES PRESIDENT, GAS GOES UP.
© 2001 Aaron McGruder/Dist. by Universal Press Syndicate
WELL, I'M SURE THERE'S A STORY THERE SOMEWHERE ...
HMMM ...
www.ucomics.com www.boondocks.net
"ENERGY CRISIS" PROVES AMERICANS STILL TOO STUPID TO PUT TWO AND TWO TOGETHER
OK. WELL, THAT'S ONE ANGLE, I GUESS.
6/15

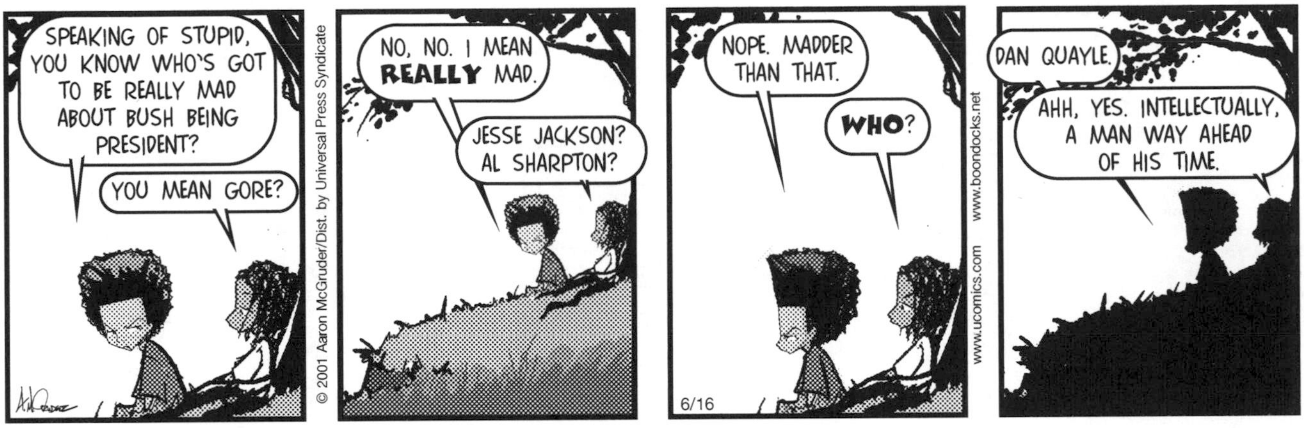
SPEAKING OF STUPID, YOU KNOW WHO'S GOT TO BE REALLY MAD ABOUT BUSH BEING PRESIDENT?
YOU MEAN GORE?
© 2001 Aaron McGruder/Dist. by Universal Press Syndicate
NO, NO. I MEAN **REALLY** MAD.
JESSE JACKSON? AL SHARPTON?
NOPE. MADDER THAN THAT.
WHO?
6/16
www.ucomics.com www.boondocks.net
DAN QUAYLE.
AHH, YES. INTELLECTUALLY, A MAN WAY AHEAD OF HIS TIME.

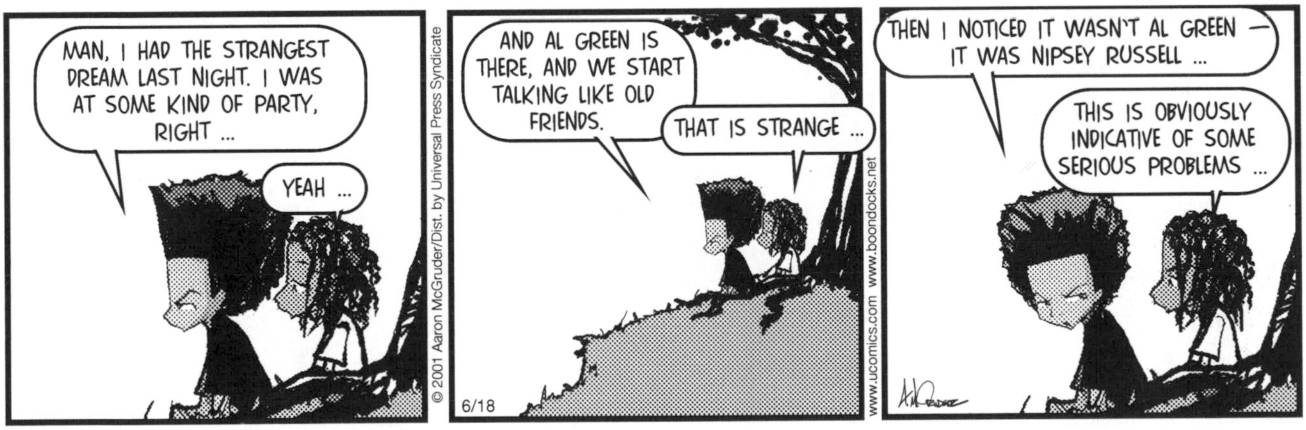
MAN, I HAD THE STRANGEST DREAM LAST NIGHT. I WAS AT SOME KIND OF PARTY, RIGHT ...
YEAH ...
© 2001 Aaron McGruder/Dist. by Universal Press Syndicate
AND AL GREEN IS THERE, AND WE START TALKING LIKE OLD FRIENDS.
THAT IS STRANGE ...
6/18
www.ucomics.com www.boondocks.net
THEN I NOTICED IT WASN'T AL GREEN — IT WAS NIPSEY RUSSELL ...
THIS IS OBVIOUSLY INDICATIVE OF SOME SERIOUS PROBLEMS ...

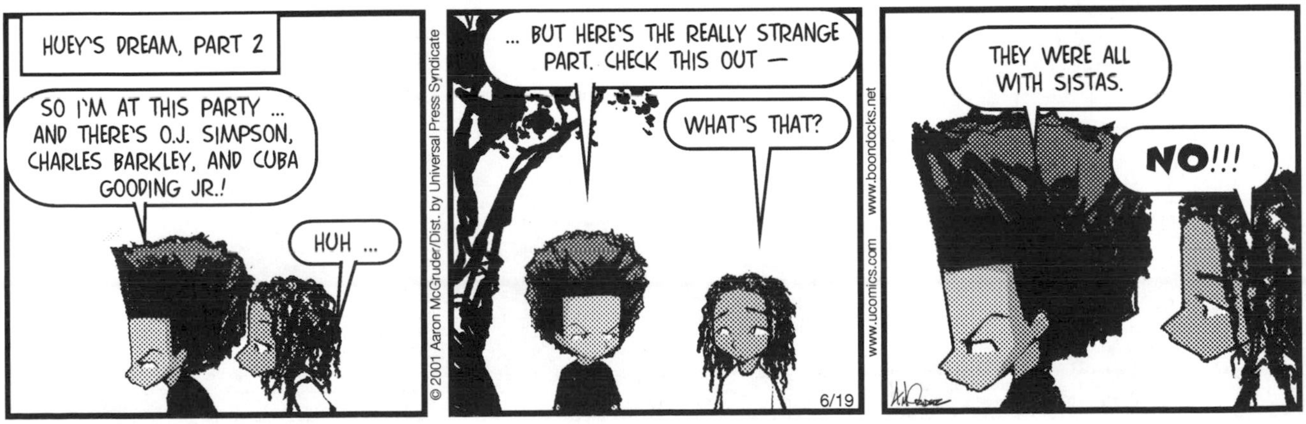
HUEY'S DREAM, PART 2
SO I'M AT THIS PARTY ... AND THERE'S O.J. SIMPSON, CHARLES BARKLEY, AND CUBA GOODING JR.!
HUH ...
© 2001 Aaron McGruder/Dist. by Universal Press Syndicate
... BUT HERE'S THE REALLY STRANGE PART. CHECK THIS OUT —
WHAT'S THAT?
6/19
www.ucomics.com www.boondocks.net
THEY WERE ALL WITH SISTAS.
NO!!!

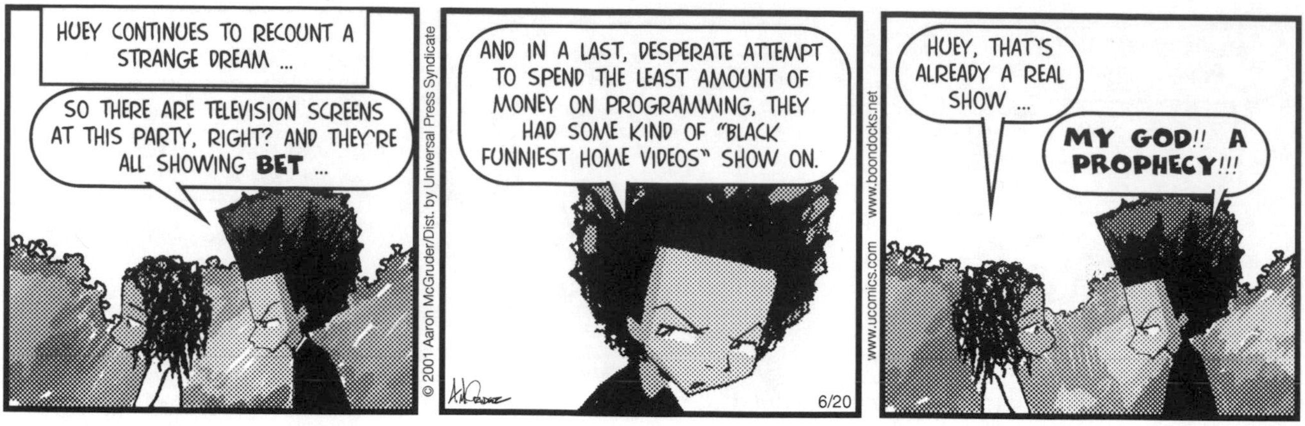
HUEY CONTINUES TO RECOUNT A STRANGE DREAM ...
SO THERE ARE TELEVISION SCREENS AT THIS PARTY, RIGHT? AND THEY'RE ALL SHOWING **BET** ...
AND IN A LAST, DESPERATE ATTEMPT TO SPEND THE LEAST AMOUNT OF MONEY ON PROGRAMMING, THEY HAD SOME KIND OF "BLACK FUNNIEST HOME VIDEOS" SHOW ON.
HUEY, THAT'S ALREADY A REAL SHOW ...
MY GOD!! A PROPHECY!!!
© 2001 Aaron McGruder/Dist. by Universal Press Syndicate
www.ucomics.com www.boondocks.net
6/20

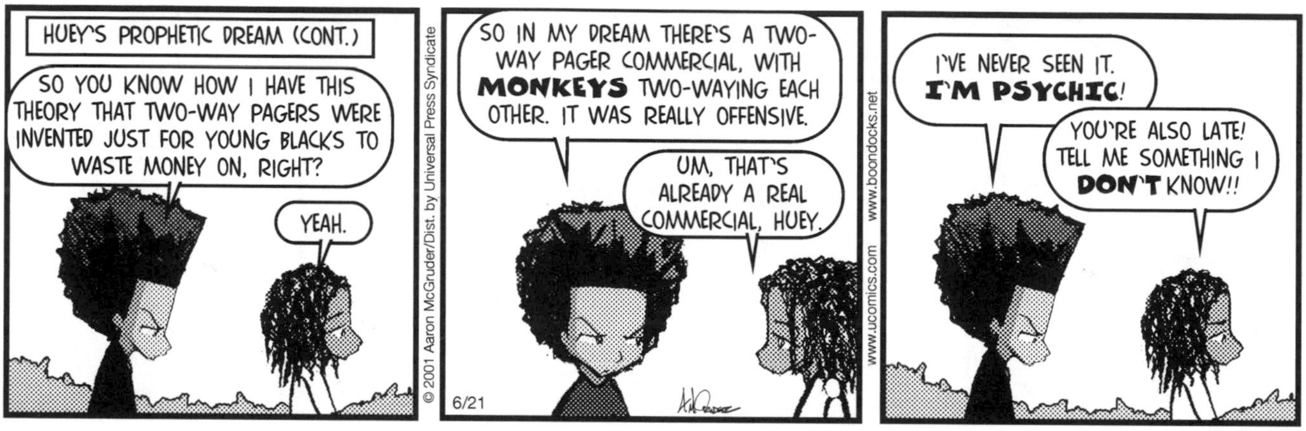
HUEY'S PROPHETIC DREAM (CONT.)
SO YOU KNOW HOW I HAVE THIS THEORY THAT TWO-WAY PAGERS WERE INVENTED JUST FOR YOUNG BLACKS TO WASTE MONEY ON, RIGHT?
YEAH.
SO IN MY DREAM THERE'S A TWO-WAY PAGER COMMERCIAL, WITH **MONKEYS** TWO-WAYING EACH OTHER. IT WAS REALLY OFFENSIVE.
UM, THAT'S ALREADY A REAL COMMERCIAL, HUEY.
I'VE NEVER SEEN IT. **I'M PSYCHIC!**
YOU'RE ALSO LATE! TELL ME SOMETHING I **DON'T** KNOW!!
© 2001 Aaron McGruder/Dist. by Universal Press Syndicate
www.ucomics.com www.boondocks.net
6/21

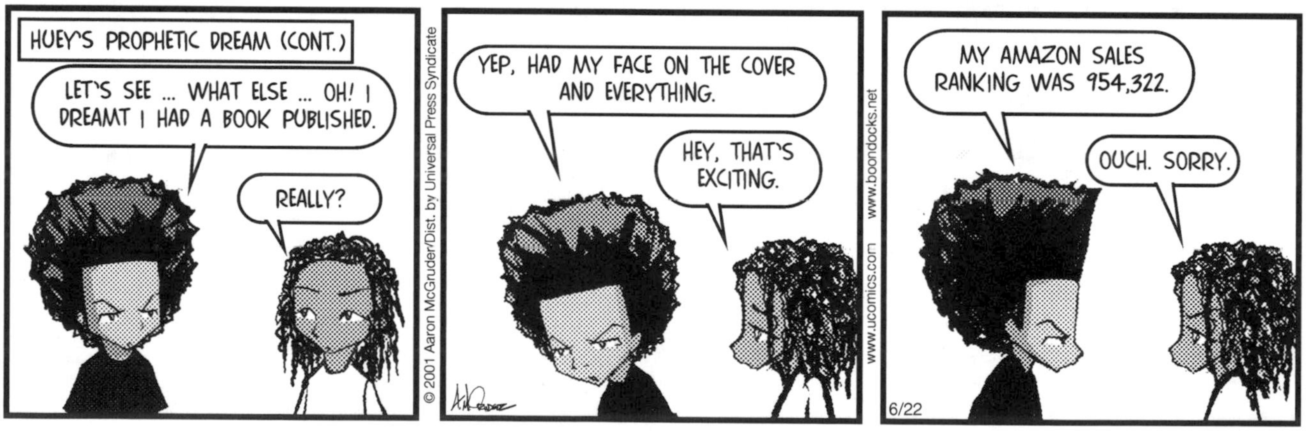
HUEY'S PROPHETIC DREAM (CONT.)
LET'S SEE ... WHAT ELSE ... OH! I DREAMT I HAD A BOOK PUBLISHED.
REALLY?
YEP, HAD MY FACE ON THE COVER AND EVERYTHING.
HEY, THAT'S EXCITING.
MY AMAZON SALES RANKING WAS 954,322.
OUCH. SORRY.
© 2001 Aaron McGruder/Dist. by Universal Press Syndicate
www.ucomics.com www.boondocks.net
6/22

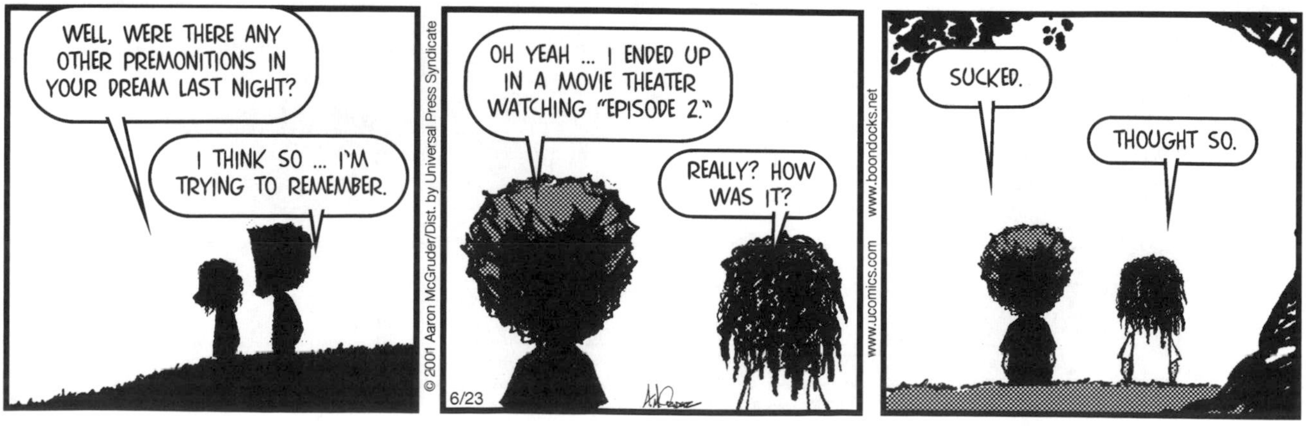
WELL, WERE THERE ANY OTHER PREMONITIONS IN YOUR DREAM LAST NIGHT?
I THINK SO ... I'M TRYING TO REMEMBER.
OH YEAH ... I ENDED UP IN A MOVIE THEATER WATCHING "EPISODE 2."
REALLY? HOW WAS IT?
SUCKED.
THOUGHT SO.
© 2001 Aaron McGruder/Dist. by Universal Press Syndicate
www.ucomics.com www.boondocks.net
6/23

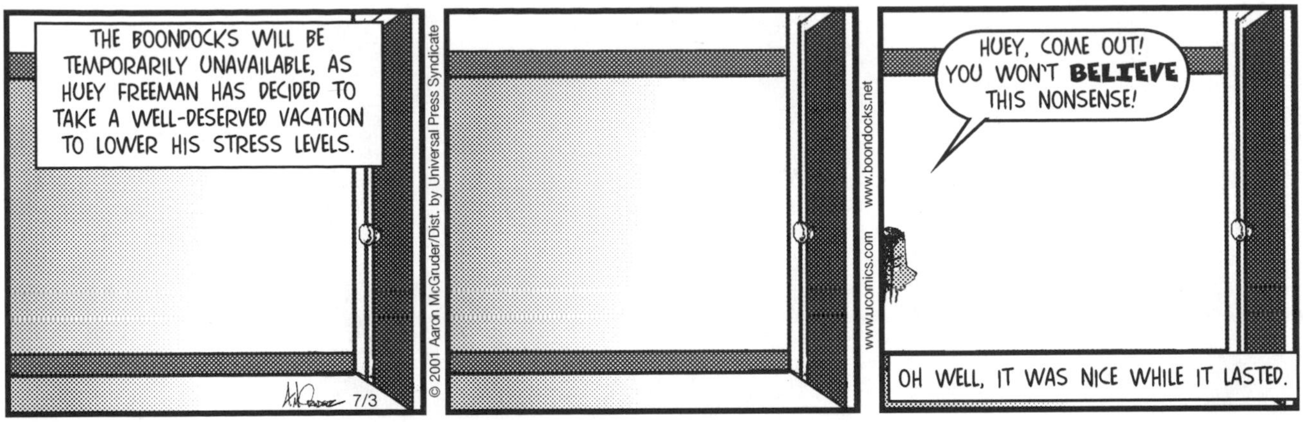
THE BOONDOCKS WILL BE TEMPORARILY UNAVAILABLE, AS HUEY FREEMAN HAS DECIDED TO TAKE A WELL-DESERVED VACATION TO LOWER HIS STRESS LEVELS.
7/3
© 2001 Aaron McGruder/Dist. by Universal Press Syndicate
HUEY, COME OUT! YOU WON'T **BELIEVE** THIS NONSENSE!
www.ucomics.com www.boondocks.net
OH WELL, IT WAS NICE WHILE IT LASTED.

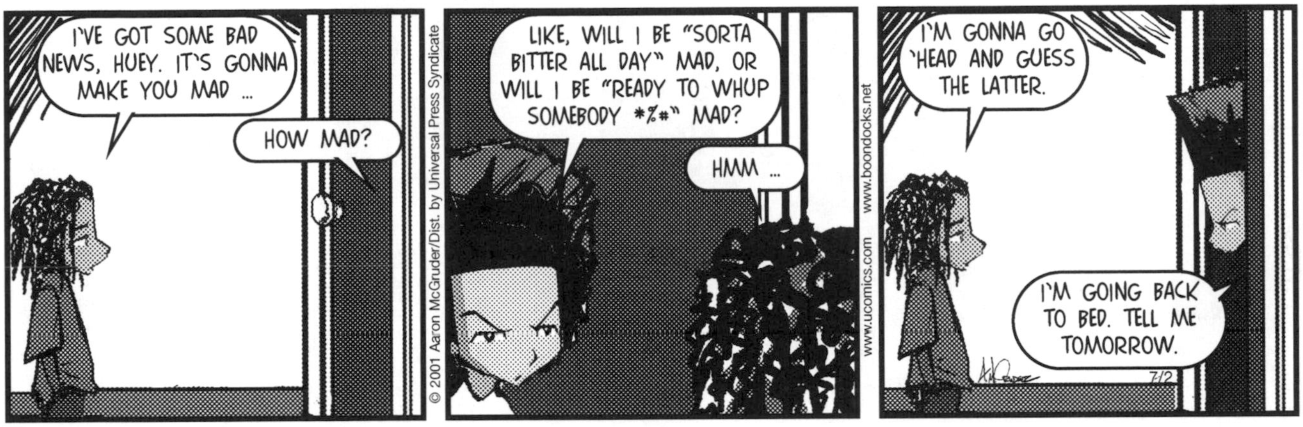
I'VE GOT SOME BAD NEWS, HUEY. IT'S GONNA MAKE YOU MAD ...
HOW MAD?
© 2001 Aaron McGruder/Dist. by Universal Press Syndicate
LIKE, WILL I BE "SORTA BITTER ALL DAY" MAD, OR WILL I BE "READY TO WHUP SOMEBODY *%#" MAD?
HMM ...
www.ucomics.com www.boondocks.net
I'M GONNA GO 'HEAD AND GUESS THE LATTER.
I'M GOING BACK TO BED. TELL ME TOMORROW.
7/2

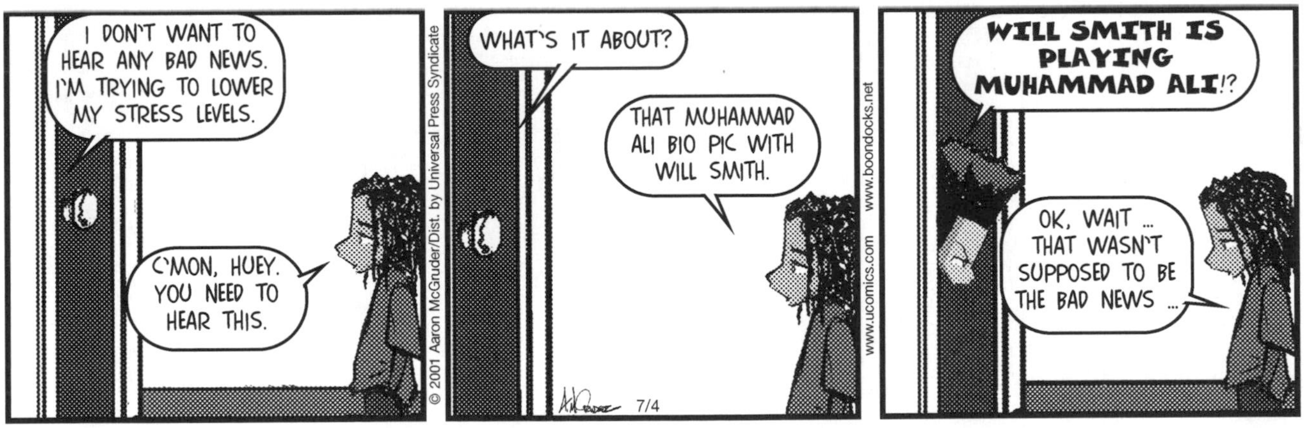
I DON'T WANT TO HEAR ANY BAD NEWS. I'M TRYING TO LOWER MY STRESS LEVELS.
C'MON, HUEY. YOU NEED TO HEAR THIS.
© 2001 Aaron McGruder/Dist. by Universal Press Syndicate
WHAT'S IT ABOUT?
THAT MUHAMMAD ALI BIO PIC WITH WILL SMITH.
7/4
www.ucomics.com www.boondocks.net
WILL SMITH IS PLAYING MUHAMMAD ALI!?
OK, WAIT ... THAT WASN'T SUPPOSED TO BE THE BAD NEWS ...

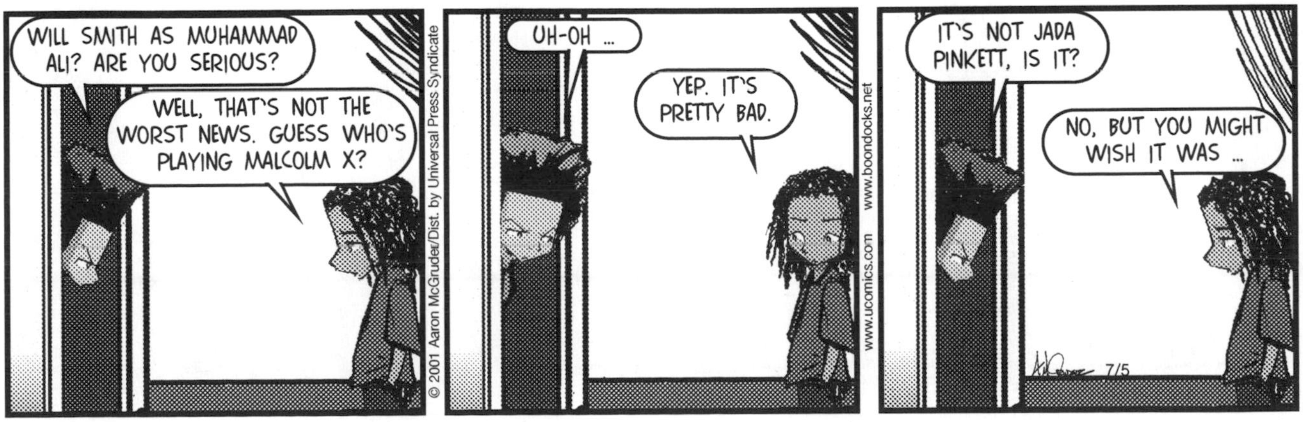
WILL SMITH AS MUHAMMAD ALI? ARE YOU SERIOUS?
WELL, THAT'S NOT THE WORST NEWS. GUESS WHO'S PLAYING MALCOLM X?
© 2001 Aaron McGruder/Dist. by Universal Press Syndicate
UH-OH ...
YEP. IT'S PRETTY BAD.
www.ucomics.com www.boondocks.net
IT'S NOT JADA PINKETT, IS IT?
NO, BUT YOU MIGHT WISH IT WAS ...
7/5

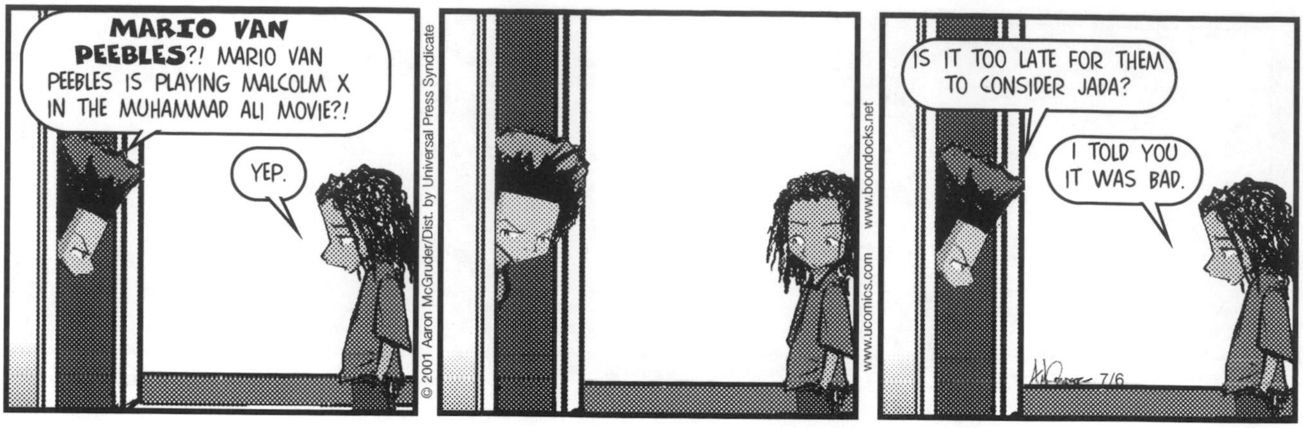
MARIO VAN PEEBLES?! MARIO VAN PEEBLES IS PLAYING MALCOLM X IN THE MUHAMMAD ALI MOVIE?!
YEP.
© 2001 Aaron McGruder/Dist. by Universal Press Syndicate
www.ucomics.com www.boondocks.net
IS IT TOO LATE FOR THEM TO CONSIDER JADA?
I TOLD YOU IT WAS BAD.
7/6

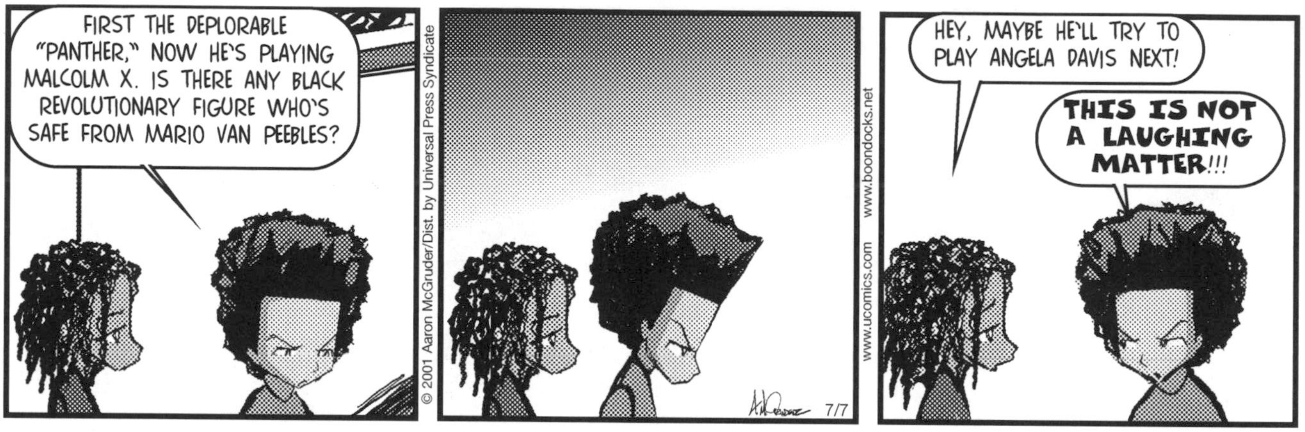
FIRST THE DEPLORABLE "PANTHER," NOW HE'S PLAYING MALCOLM X. IS THERE ANY BLACK REVOLUTIONARY FIGURE WHO'S SAFE FROM MARIO VAN PEEBLES?
© 2001 Aaron McGruder/Dist. by Universal Press Syndicate
7/7
www.ucomics.com www.boondocks.net
HEY, MAYBE HE'LL TRY TO PLAY ANGELA DAVIS NEXT!
THIS IS NOT A LAUGHING MATTER!!!

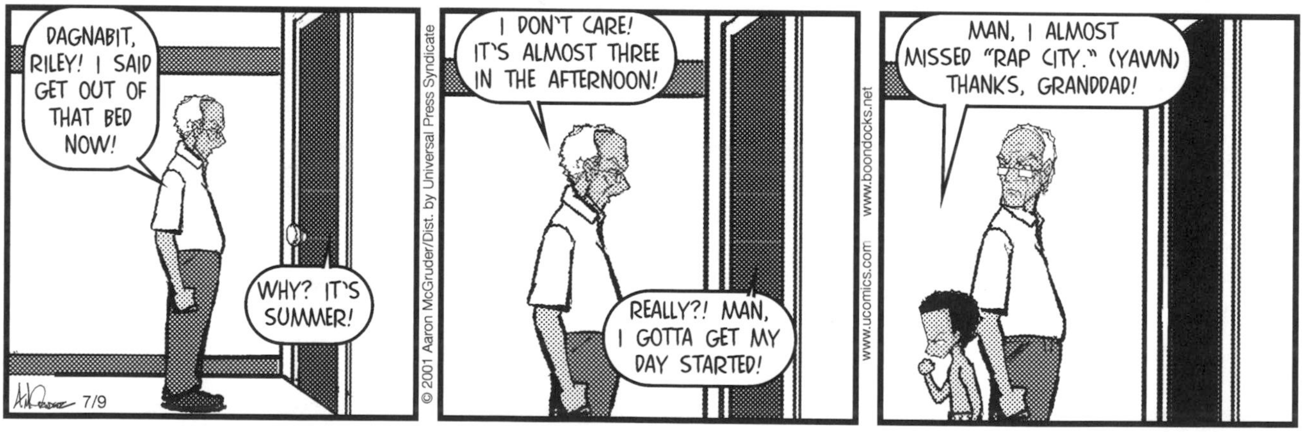
DAGNABIT, RILEY! I SAID GET OUT OF THAT BED NOW!
WHY? IT'S SUMMER!
7/9
© 2001 Aaron McGruder/Dist. by Universal Press Syndicate
I DON'T CARE! IT'S ALMOST THREE IN THE AFTERNOON!
REALLY?! MAN, I GOTTA GET MY DAY STARTED!
www.ucomics.com www.boondocks.net
MAN, I ALMOST MISSED "RAP CITY." (YAWN) THANKS, GRANDDAD!

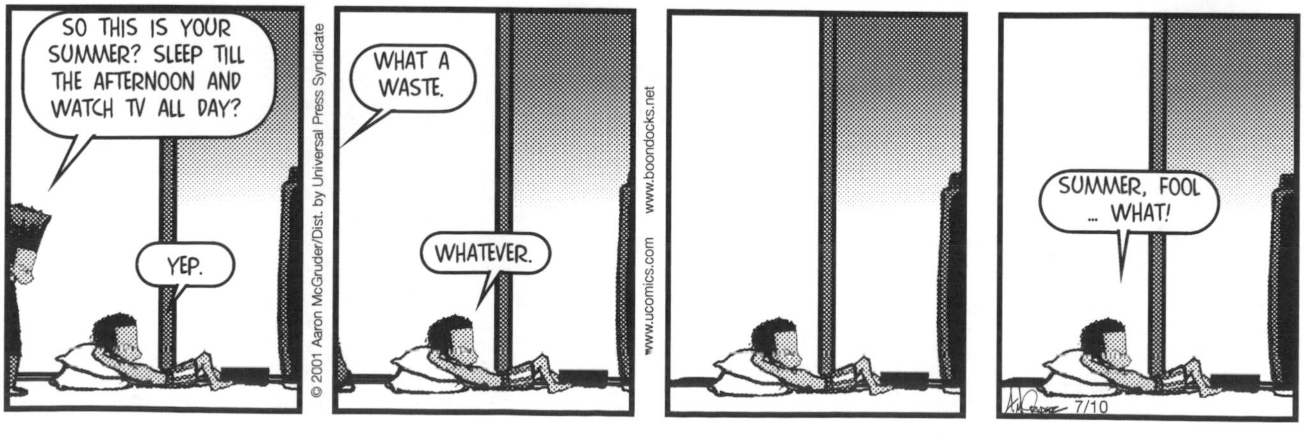
SO THIS IS YOUR SUMMER? SLEEP TILL THE AFTERNOON AND WATCH TV ALL DAY?
YEP.
© 2001 Aaron McGruder/Dist. by Universal Press Syndicate
WHAT A WASTE.
WHATEVER.
www.ucomics.com www.boondocks.net
SUMMER, FOOL ... WHAT!
7/10

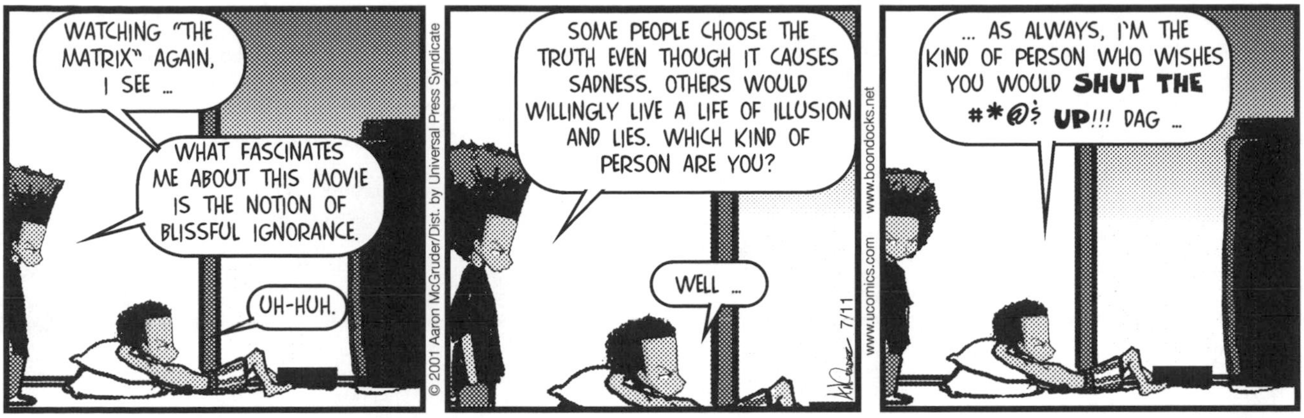
WATCHING "THE MATRIX" AGAIN, I SEE ...
WHAT FASCINATES ME ABOUT THIS MOVIE IS THE NOTION OF BLISSFUL IGNORANCE.
UH-HUH.
© 2001 Aaron McGruder/Dist. by Universal Press Syndicate
SOME PEOPLE CHOOSE THE TRUTH EVEN THOUGH IT CAUSES SADNESS. OTHERS WOULD WILLINGLY LIVE A LIFE OF ILLUSION AND LIES. WHICH KIND OF PERSON ARE YOU?
WELL ...
7/11
www.ucomics.com www.boondocks.net
... AS ALWAYS, I'M THE KIND OF PERSON WHO WISHES YOU WOULD **SHUT THE #*@$ UP**!!! DAG ...

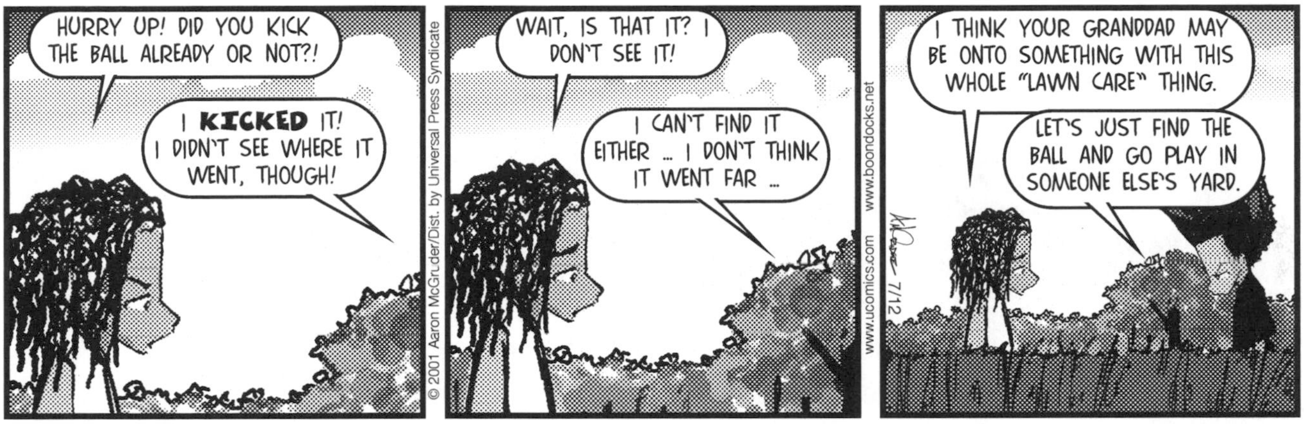
HURRY UP! DID YOU KICK THE BALL ALREADY OR NOT?!
I **KICKED** IT! I DIDN'T SEE WHERE IT WENT, THOUGH!
© 2001 Aaron McGruder/Dist. by Universal Press Syndicate
WAIT, IS THAT IT? I DON'T SEE IT!
I CAN'T FIND IT EITHER ... I DON'T THINK IT WENT FAR ...
www.ucomics.com www.boondocks.net
7/12
I THINK YOUR GRANDDAD MAY BE ONTO SOMETHING WITH THIS WHOLE "LAWN CARE" THING.
LET'S JUST FIND THE BALL AND GO PLAY IN SOMEONE ELSE'S YARD.

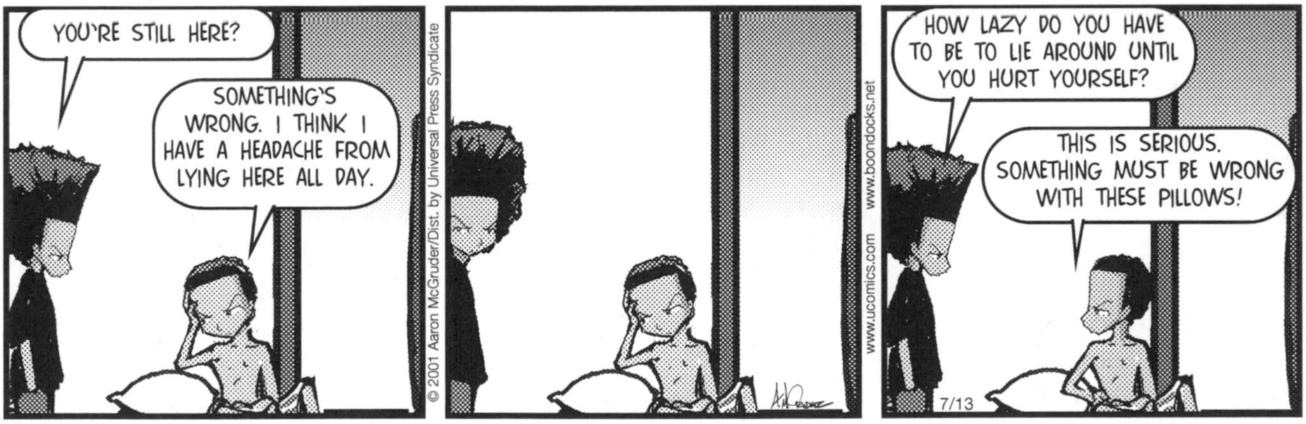
YOU'RE STILL HERE?
SOMETHING'S WRONG. I THINK I HAVE A HEADACHE FROM LYING HERE ALL DAY.
© 2001 Aaron McGruder/Dist. by Universal Press Syndicate
www.ucomics.com www.boondocks.net
HOW LAZY DO YOU HAVE TO BE TO LIE AROUND UNTIL YOU HURT YOURSELF?
THIS IS SERIOUS. SOMETHING MUST BE WRONG WITH THESE PILLOWS!
7/13

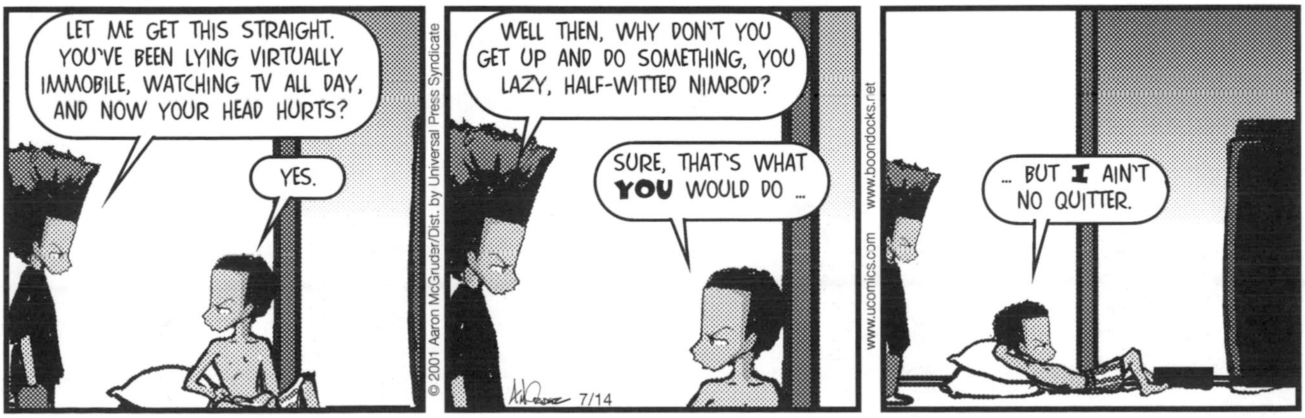
LET ME GET THIS STRAIGHT. YOU'VE BEEN LYING VIRTUALLY IMMOBILE, WATCHING TV ALL DAY, AND NOW YOUR HEAD HURTS?
YES.
7/14
© 2001 Aaron McGruder/Dist. by Universal Press Syndicate
WELL THEN, WHY DON'T YOU GET UP AND DO SOMETHING, YOU LAZY, HALF-WITTED NIMROD?
SURE, THAT'S WHAT **YOU** WOULD DO ...
www.ucomics.com www.boondocks.net
... BUT **I** AIN'T NO QUITTER.

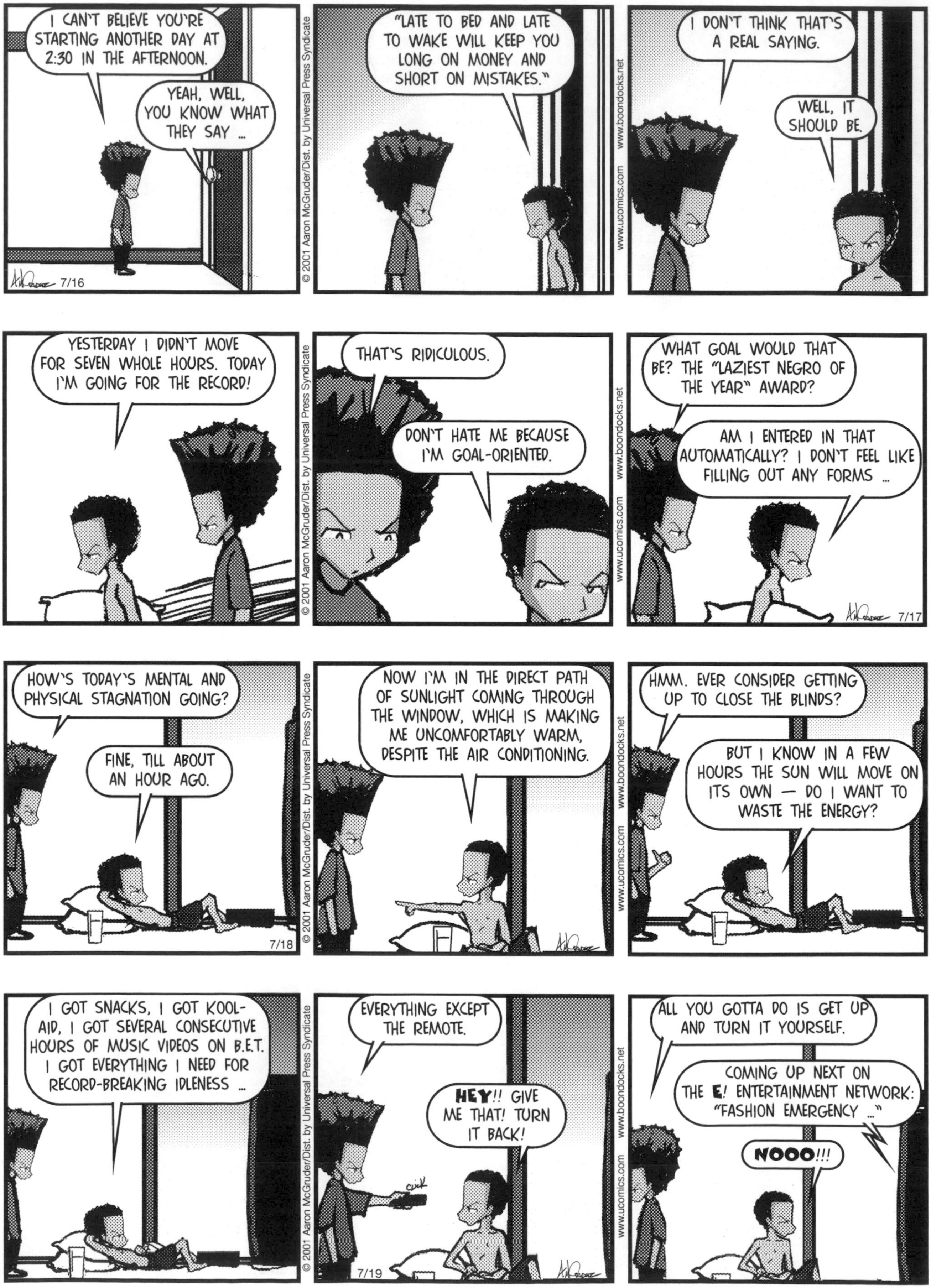
I CAN'T BELIEVE YOU'RE STARTING ANOTHER DAY AT 2:30 IN THE AFTERNOON.
YEAH, WELL, YOU KNOW WHAT THEY SAY ...
7/16
© 2001 Aaron McGruder/Dist. by Universal Press Syndicate
"LATE TO BED AND LATE TO WAKE WILL KEEP YOU LONG ON MONEY AND SHORT ON MISTAKES."
www.ucomics.com www.boondocks.net
I DON'T THINK THAT'S A REAL SAYING.
WELL, IT SHOULD BE.
YESTERDAY I DIDN'T MOVE FOR SEVEN WHOLE HOURS. TODAY I'M GOING FOR THE RECORD!
© 2001 Aaron McGruder/Dist. by Universal Press Syndicate
THAT'S RIDICULOUS.
DON'T HATE ME BECAUSE I'M GOAL-ORIENTED.
www.ucomics.com www.boondocks.net
WHAT GOAL WOULD THAT BE? THE "LAZIEST NEGRO OF THE YEAR" AWARD?
AM I ENTERED IN THAT AUTOMATICALLY? I DON'T FEEL LIKE FILLING OUT ANY FORMS ...
7/17
HOW'S TODAY'S MENTAL AND PHYSICAL STAGNATION GOING?
FINE, TILL ABOUT AN HOUR AGO.
7/18
© 2001 Aaron McGruder/Dist. by Universal Press Syndicate
NOW I'M IN THE DIRECT PATH OF SUNLIGHT COMING THROUGH THE WINDOW, WHICH IS MAKING ME UNCOMFORTABLY WARM, DESPITE THE AIR CONDITIONING.
www.ucomics.com www.boondocks.net
HMM. EVER CONSIDER GETTING UP TO CLOSE THE BLINDS?
BUT I KNOW IN A FEW HOURS THE SUN WILL MOVE ON ITS OWN — DO I WANT TO WASTE THE ENERGY?
I GOT SNACKS, I GOT KOOL-AID, I GOT SEVERAL CONSECUTIVE HOURS OF MUSIC VIDEOS ON B.E.T. I GOT EVERYTHING I NEED FOR RECORD-BREAKING IDLENESS ...
© 2001 Aaron McGruder/Dist. by Universal Press Syndicate
EVERYTHING EXCEPT THE REMOTE.
CLICK
HEY!! GIVE ME THAT! TURN IT BACK!
7/19
www.ucomics.com www.boondocks.net
ALL YOU GOTTA DO IS GET UP AND TURN IT YOURSELF.
COMING UP NEXT ON THE E! ENTERTAINMENT NETWORK: "FASHION EMERGENCY ..."
NOOO!!!

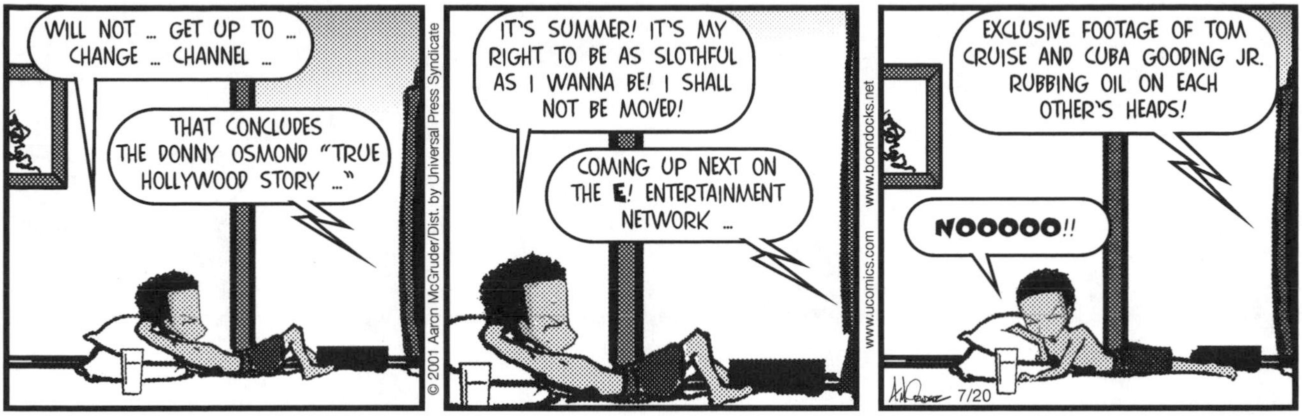
WILL NOT ... GET UP TO ... CHANGE ... CHANNEL ...
THAT CONCLUDES THE DONNY OSMOND "TRUE HOLLYWOOD STORY ..."
© 2001 Aaron McGruder/Dist. by Universal Press Syndicate
IT'S SUMMER! IT'S MY RIGHT TO BE AS SLOTHFUL AS I WANNA BE! I SHALL NOT BE MOVED!
COMING UP NEXT ON THE E! ENTERTAINMENT NETWORK ...
www.ucomics.com www.boondocks.net
EXCLUSIVE FOOTAGE OF TOM CRUISE AND CUBA GOODING JR. RUBBING OIL ON EACH OTHER'S HEADS!
NOOOOO!!
7/20

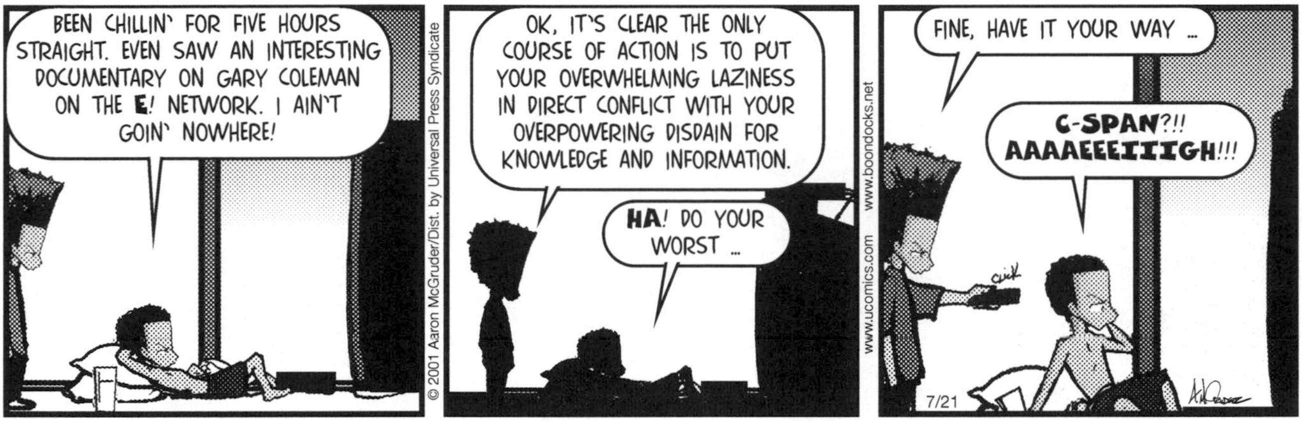
BEEN CHILLIN' FOR FIVE HOURS STRAIGHT. EVEN SAW AN INTERESTING DOCUMENTARY ON GARY COLEMAN ON THE E! NETWORK. I AIN'T GOIN' NOWHERE!
© 2001 Aaron McGruder/Dist. by Universal Press Syndicate
OK, IT'S CLEAR THE ONLY COURSE OF ACTION IS TO PUT YOUR OVERWHELMING LAZINESS IN DIRECT CONFLICT WITH YOUR OVERPOWERING DISDAIN FOR KNOWLEDGE AND INFORMATION.
HA! DO YOUR WORST ...
www.ucomics.com www.boondocks.net
FINE, HAVE IT YOUR WAY ...
C-SPAN?!! AAAAEEEIIIIGH!!!
CLICK
7/21

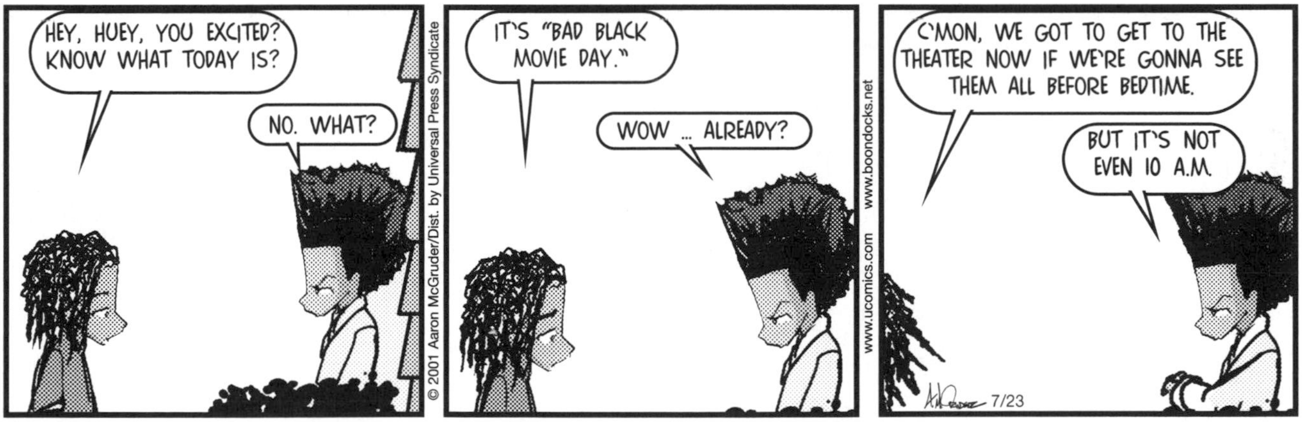
HEY, HUEY, YOU EXCITED? KNOW WHAT TODAY IS?
NO. WHAT?
© 2001 Aaron McGruder/Dist. by Universal Press Syndicate
IT'S "BAD BLACK MOVIE DAY."
WOW ... ALREADY?
www.ucomics.com www.boondocks.net
C'MON, WE GOT TO GET TO THE THEATER NOW IF WE'RE GONNA SEE THEM ALL BEFORE BEDTIME.
BUT IT'S NOT EVEN 10 A.M.
7/23

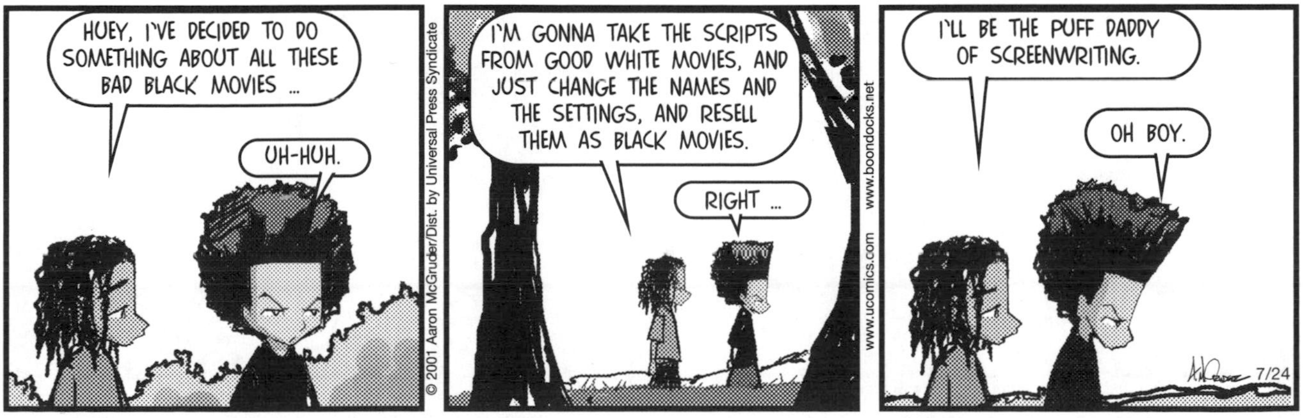
HUEY, I'VE DECIDED TO DO SOMETHING ABOUT ALL THESE BAD BLACK MOVIES ...
UH-HUH.
© 2001 Aaron McGruder/Dist. by Universal Press Syndicate
I'M GONNA TAKE THE SCRIPTS FROM GOOD WHITE MOVIES, AND JUST CHANGE THE NAMES AND THE SETTINGS, AND RESELL THEM AS BLACK MOVIES.
RIGHT ...
www.ucomics.com www.boondocks.net
I'LL BE THE PUFF DADDY OF SCREENWRITING.
OH BOY.
7/24

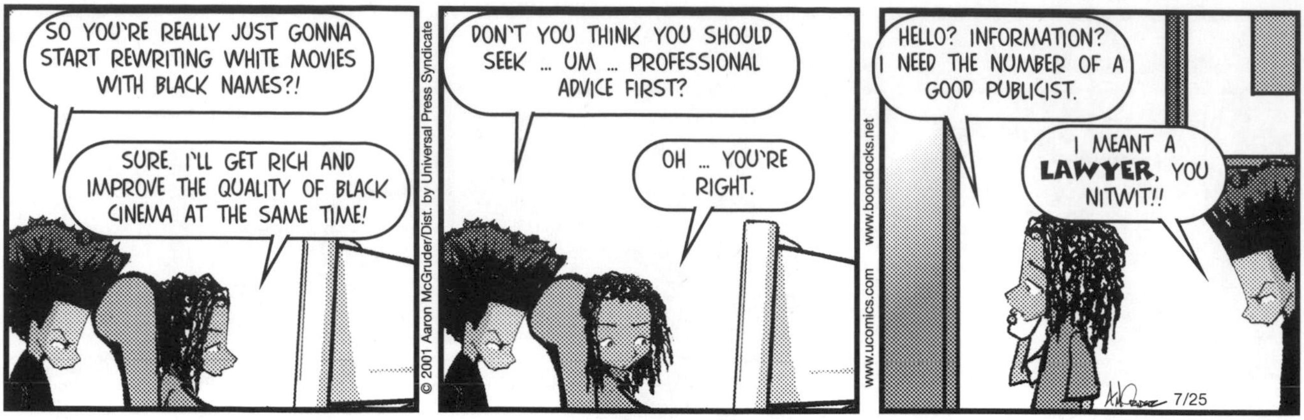
SO YOU'RE REALLY JUST GONNA START REWRITING WHITE MOVIES WITH BLACK NAMES?!
SURE. I'LL GET RICH AND IMPROVE THE QUALITY OF BLACK CINEMA AT THE SAME TIME!
© 2001 Aaron McGruder/Dist. by Universal Press Syndicate
DON'T YOU THINK YOU SHOULD SEEK ... UM ... PROFESSIONAL ADVICE FIRST?
OH ... YOU'RE RIGHT.
www.ucomics.com www.boondocks.net
HELLO? INFORMATION? I NEED THE NUMBER OF A GOOD PUBLICIST.
I MEANT A **LAWYER**, YOU NITWIT!!
7/25

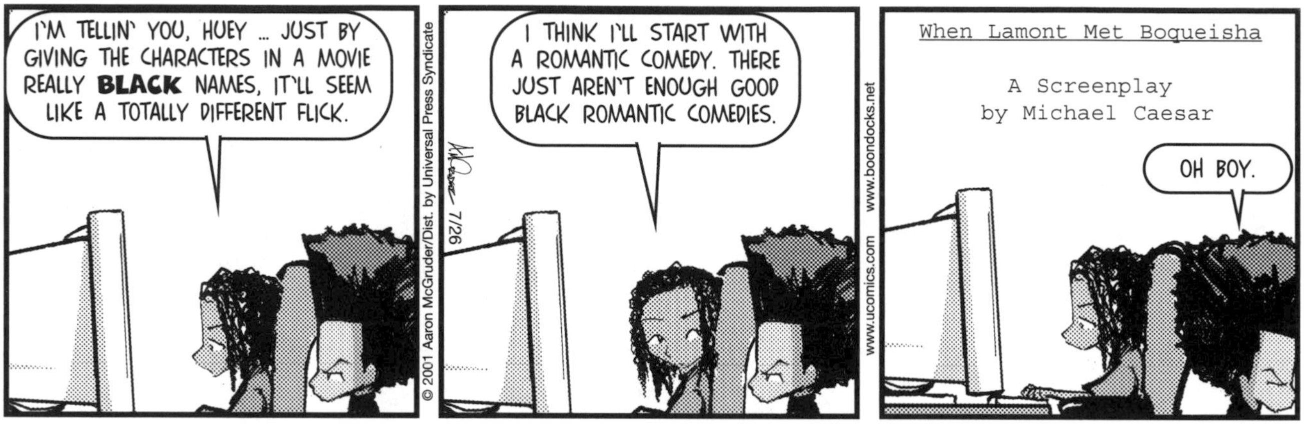
I'M TELLIN' YOU, HUEY ... JUST BY GIVING THE CHARACTERS IN A MOVIE REALLY **BLACK** NAMES, IT'LL SEEM LIKE A TOTALLY DIFFERENT FLICK.
© 2001 Aaron McGruder/Dist. by Universal Press Syndicate
7/26
I THINK I'LL START WITH A ROMANTIC COMEDY. THERE JUST AREN'T ENOUGH GOOD BLACK ROMANTIC COMEDIES.
www.ucomics.com www.boondocks.net
When Lamont Met Boqueisha
A Screenplay
by Michael Caesar
OH BOY.

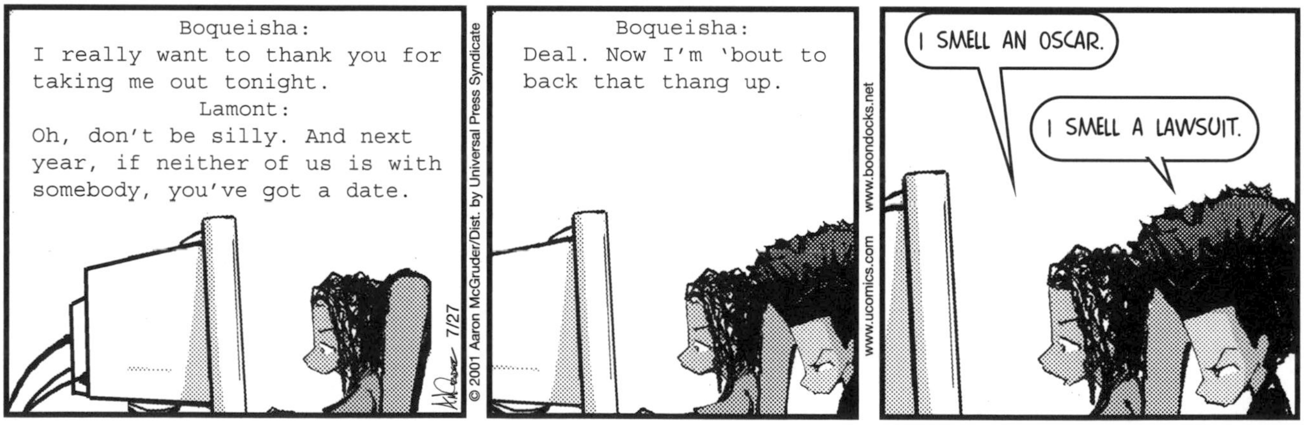
Boqueisha:
I really want to thank you for taking me out tonight.
Lamont:
Oh, don't be silly. And next year, if neither of us is with somebody, you've got a date.
7/27
© 2001 Aaron McGruder/Dist. by Universal Press Syndicate
Boqueisha:
Deal. Now I'm 'bout to back that thang up.
www.ucomics.com www.boondocks.net
I SMELL AN OSCAR.
I SMELL A LAWSUIT.

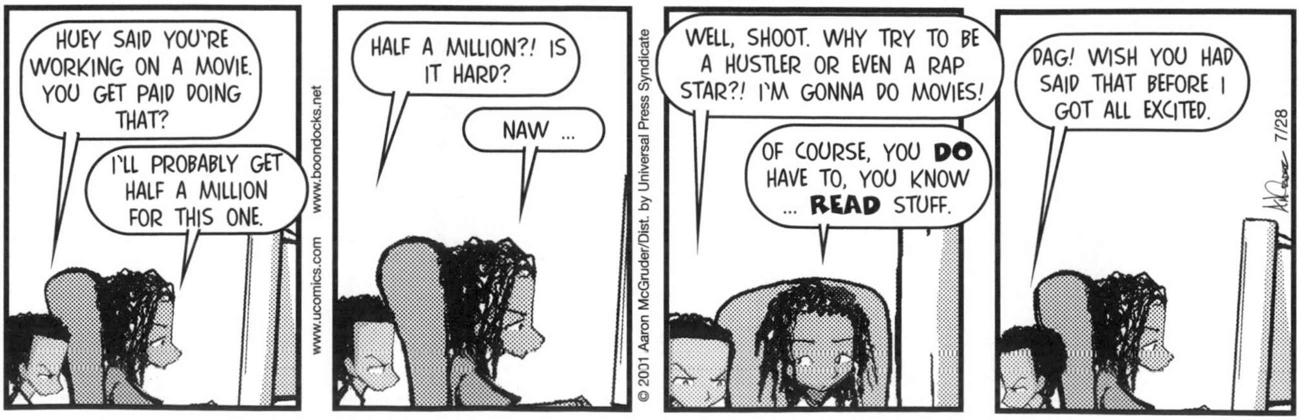
HUEY SAID YOU'RE WORKING ON A MOVIE. YOU GET PAID DOING THAT?
I'LL PROBABLY GET HALF A MILLION FOR THIS ONE.
www.ucomics.com www.boondocks.net
HALF A MILLION?! IS IT HARD?
NAW ...
© 2001 Aaron McGruder/Dist. by Universal Press Syndicate
WELL, SHOOT. WHY TRY TO BE A HUSTLER OR EVEN A RAP STAR?! I'M GONNA DO MOVIES!
OF COURSE, YOU **DO** HAVE TO, YOU KNOW ... **READ** STUFF.
DAG! WISH YOU HAD SAID THAT BEFORE I GOT ALL EXCITED.
7/28

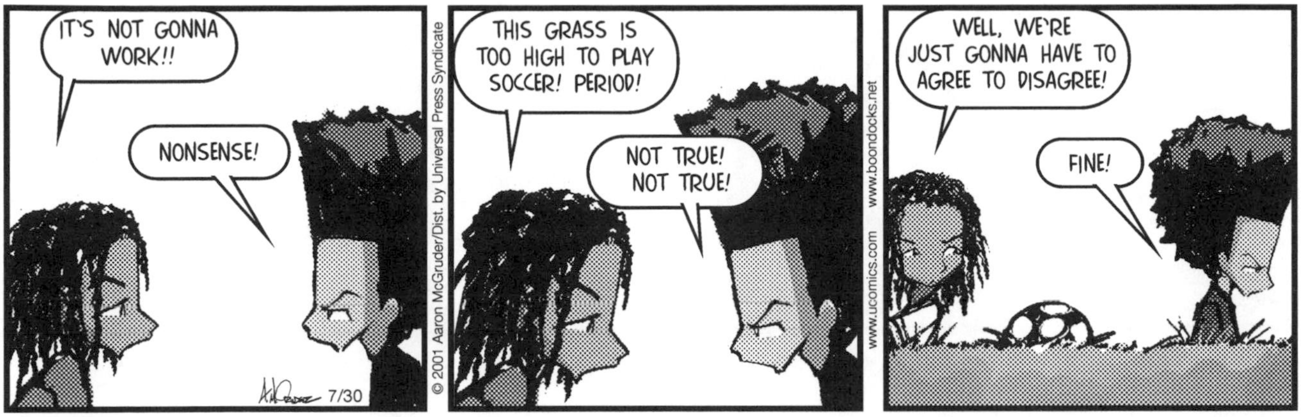
IT'S NOT GONNA WORK!!
NONSENSE!
7/30
© 2001 Aaron McGruder/Dist. by Universal Press Syndicate
THIS GRASS IS TOO HIGH TO PLAY SOCCER! PERIOD!
NOT TRUE! NOT TRUE!
www.ucomics.com www.boondocks.net
WELL, WE'RE JUST GONNA HAVE TO AGREE TO DISAGREE!
FINE!

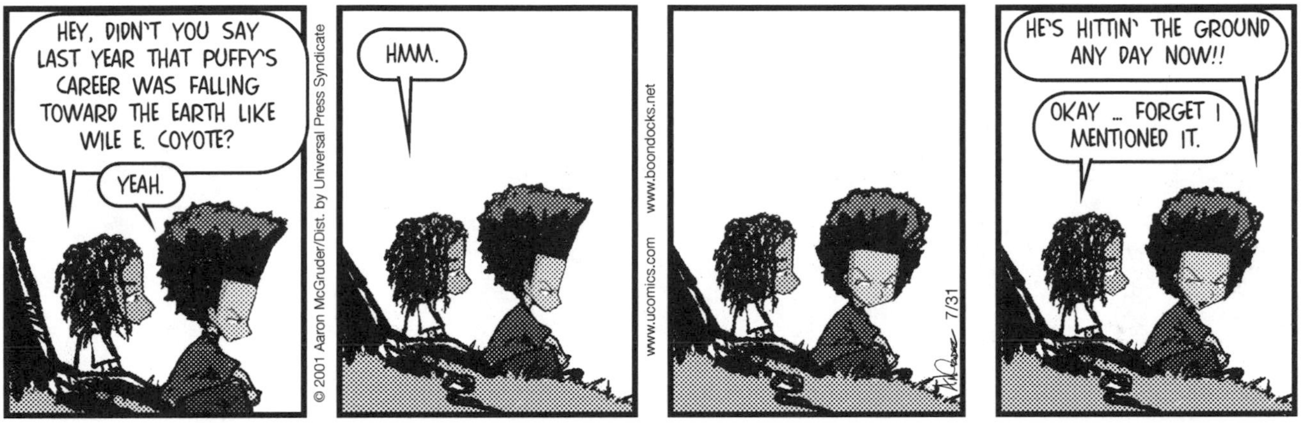
HEY, DIDN'T YOU SAY LAST YEAR THAT PUFFY'S CAREER WAS FALLING TOWARD THE EARTH LIKE WILE E. COYOTE?
YEAH.
© 2001 Aaron McGruder/Dist. by Universal Press Syndicate
HMM.
www.ucomics.com www.boondocks.net
7/31
HE'S HITTIN' THE GROUND ANY DAY NOW!!
OKAY ... FORGET I MENTIONED IT.

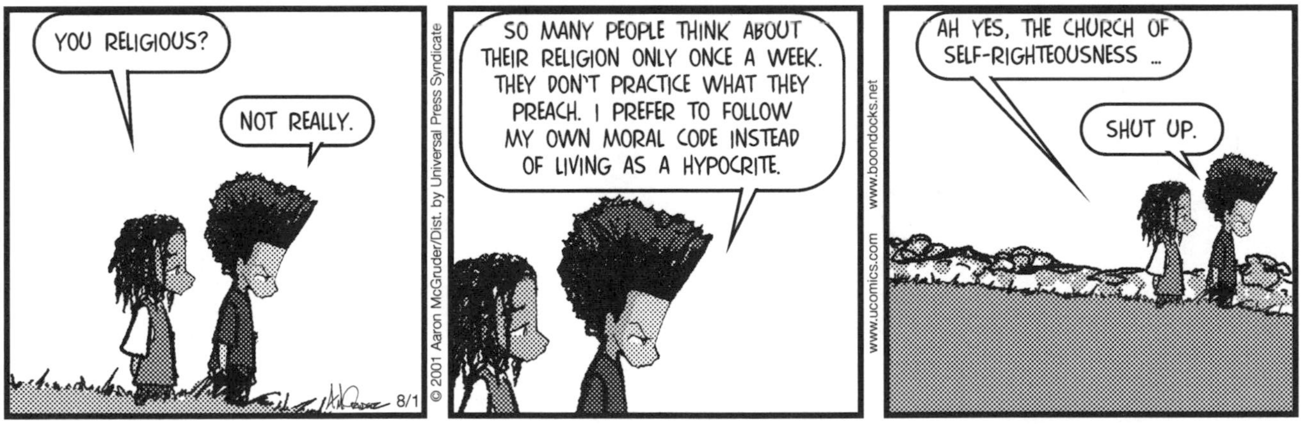
YOU RELIGIOUS?
NOT REALLY.
8/1
© 2001 Aaron McGruder/Dist. by Universal Press Syndicate
SO MANY PEOPLE THINK ABOUT THEIR RELIGION ONLY ONCE A WEEK. THEY DON'T PRACTICE WHAT THEY PREACH. I PREFER TO FOLLOW MY OWN MORAL CODE INSTEAD OF LIVING AS A HYPOCRITE.
www.ucomics.com www.boondocks.net
AH YES, THE CHURCH OF SELF-RIGHTEOUSNESS ...
SHUT UP.

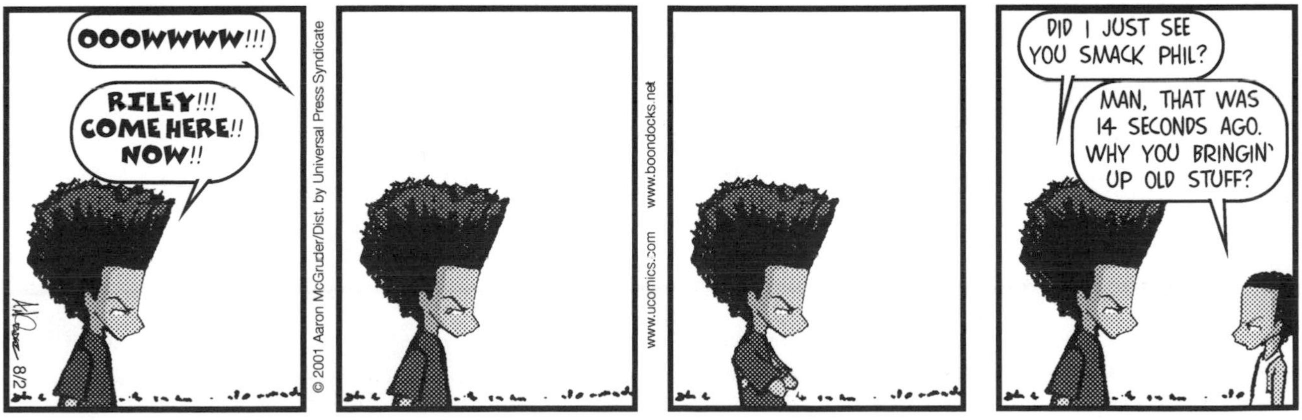
OOOWWWW!!!
RILEY!!! COME HERE!! NOW!!
8/2
© 2001 Aaron McGruder/Dist. by Universal Press Syndicate
www.ucomics.com www.boondocks.net
DID I JUST SEE YOU SMACK PHIL?
MAN, THAT WAS 14 SECONDS AGO. WHY YOU BRINGIN' UP OLD STUFF?

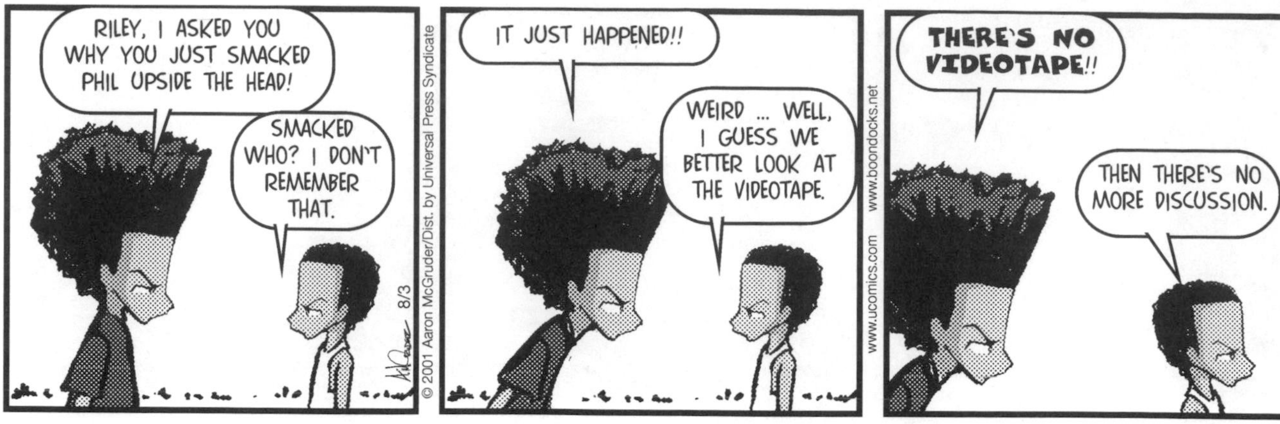
RILEY, I ASKED YOU WHY YOU JUST SMACKED PHIL UPSIDE THE HEAD!
SMACKED WHO? I DON'T REMEMBER THAT.
8/3
© 2001 Aaron McGruder/Dist. by Universal Press Syndicate
IT JUST HAPPENED!!
WEIRD ... WELL, I GUESS WE BETTER LOOK AT THE VIDEOTAPE.
www.ucomics.com www.boondocks.net
THERE'S NO VIDEOTAPE!!
THEN THERE'S NO MORE DISCUSSION.

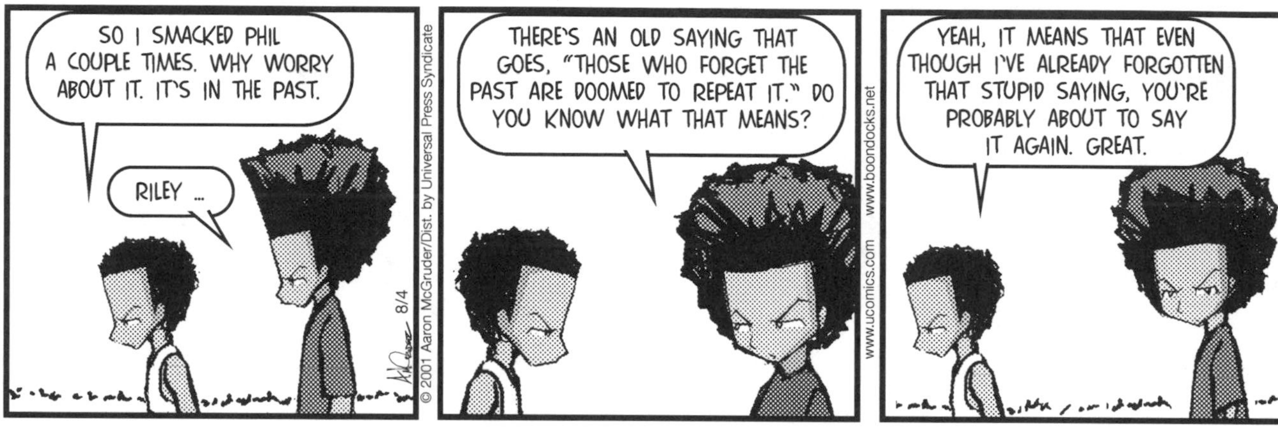
SO I SMACKED PHIL A COUPLE TIMES. WHY WORRY ABOUT IT. IT'S IN THE PAST.
RILEY ...
8/4
© 2001 Aaron McGruder/Dist. by Universal Press Syndicate
THERE'S AN OLD SAYING THAT GOES, "THOSE WHO FORGET THE PAST ARE DOOMED TO REPEAT IT." DO YOU KNOW WHAT THAT MEANS?
www.ucomics.com www.boondocks.net
YEAH, IT MEANS THAT EVEN THOUGH I'VE ALREADY FORGOTTEN THAT STUPID SAYING, YOU'RE PROBABLY ABOUT TO SAY IT AGAIN. GREAT.

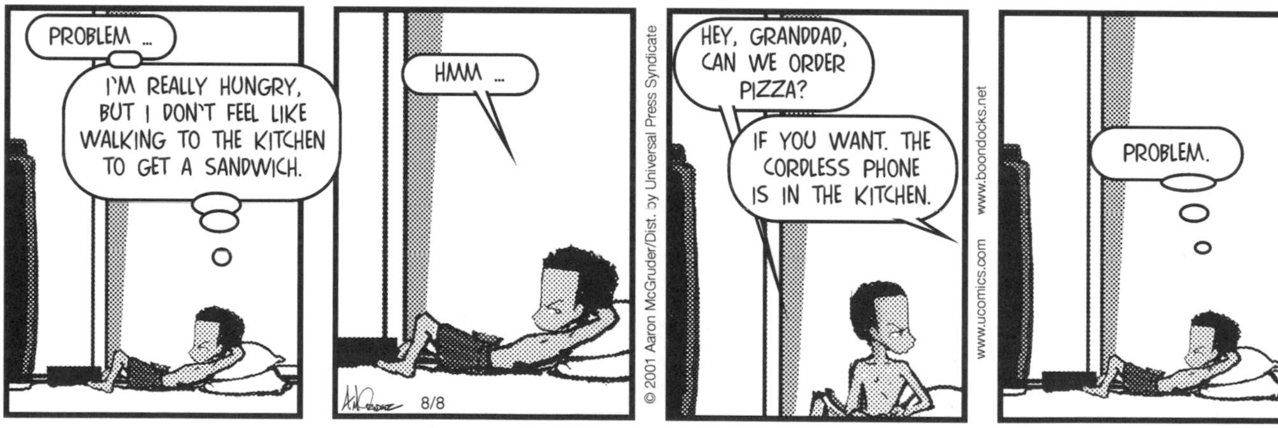
PROBLEM ...
I'M REALLY HUNGRY, BUT I DON'T FEEL LIKE WALKING TO THE KITCHEN TO GET A SANDWICH.
HMM ...
8/8
© 2001 Aaron McGruder/Dist. by Universal Press Syndicate
HEY, GRANDDAD, CAN WE ORDER PIZZA?
IF YOU WANT. THE CORDLESS PHONE IS IN THE KITCHEN.
www.ucomics.com www.boondocks.net
PROBLEM.

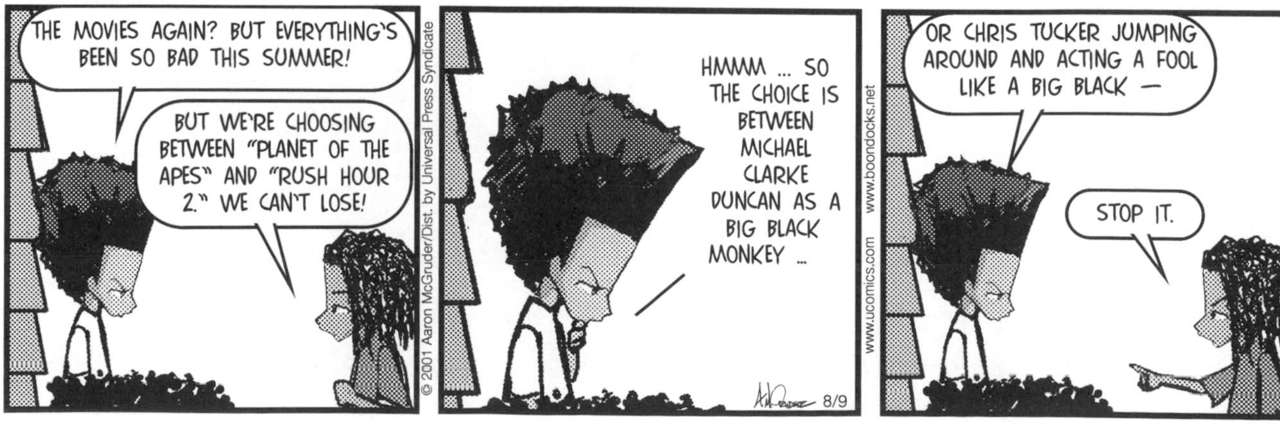
THE MOVIES AGAIN? BUT EVERYTHING'S BEEN SO BAD THIS SUMMER!
BUT WE'RE CHOOSING BETWEEN "PLANET OF THE APES" AND "RUSH HOUR 2." WE CAN'T LOSE!
© 2001 Aaron McGruder/Dist. by Universal Press Syndicate
HMMM ... SO THE CHOICE IS BETWEEN MICHAEL CLARKE DUNCAN AS A BIG BLACK MONKEY ...
8/9
www.ucomics.com www.boondocks.net
OR CHRIS TUCKER JUMPING AROUND AND ACTING A FOOL LIKE A BIG BLACK —
STOP IT.

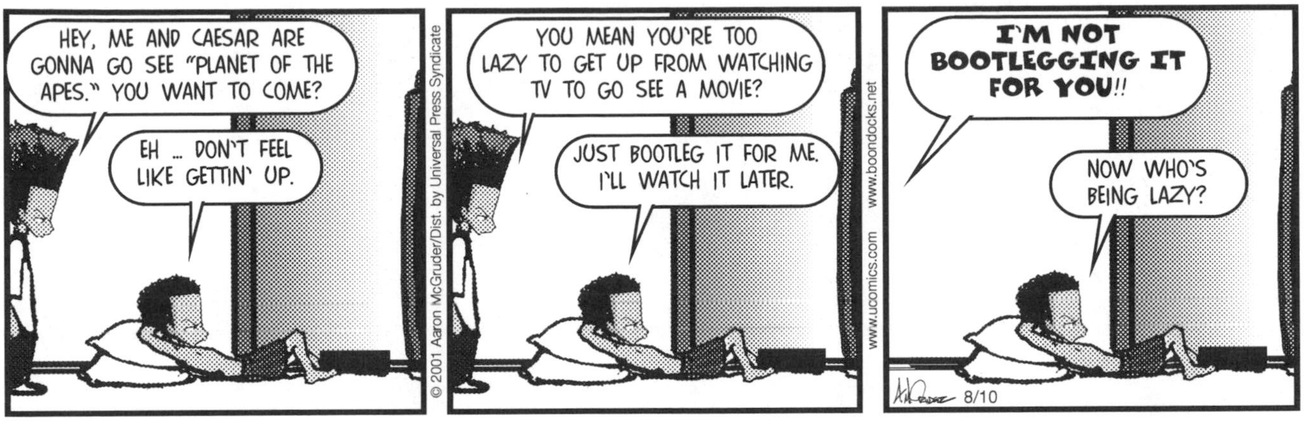
HEY, ME AND CAESAR ARE GONNA GO SEE "PLANET OF THE APES." YOU WANT TO COME?
EH ... DON'T FEEL LIKE GETTIN' UP.
© 2001 Aaron McGruder/Dist. by Universal Press Syndicate
YOU MEAN YOU'RE TOO LAZY TO GET UP FROM WATCHING TV TO GO SEE A MOVIE?
JUST BOOTLEG IT FOR ME. I'LL WATCH IT LATER.
www.ucomics.com www.boondocks.net
I'M NOT BOOTLEGGING IT FOR YOU!!
NOW WHO'S BEING LAZY?
8/10

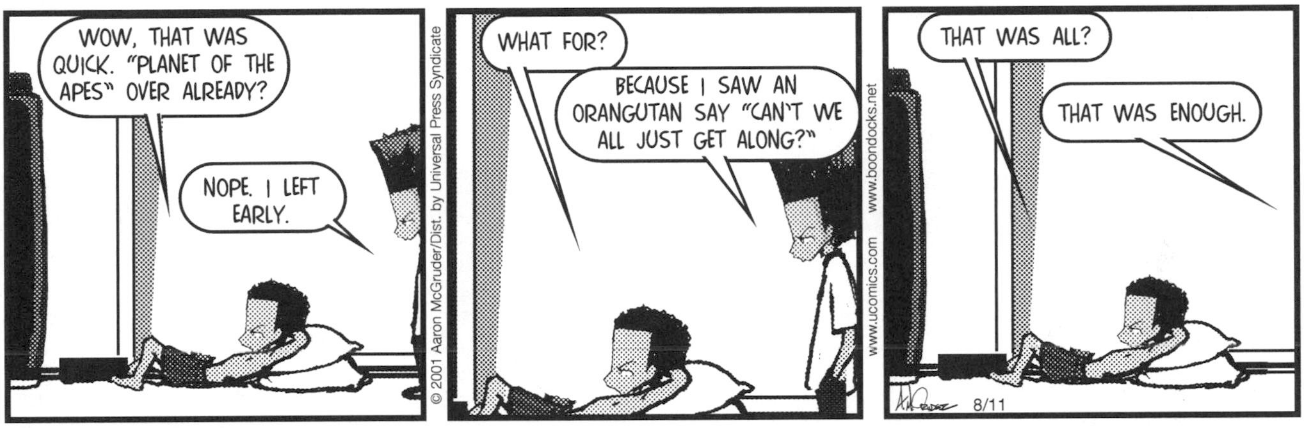
WOW, THAT WAS QUICK. "PLANET OF THE APES" OVER ALREADY?
NOPE. I LEFT EARLY.
© 2001 Aaron McGruder/Dist. by Universal Press Syndicate
WHAT FOR?
BECAUSE I SAW AN ORANGUTAN SAY "CAN'T WE ALL JUST GET ALONG?"
www.ucomics.com www.boondocks.net
THAT WAS ALL?
THAT WAS ENOUGH.
8/11

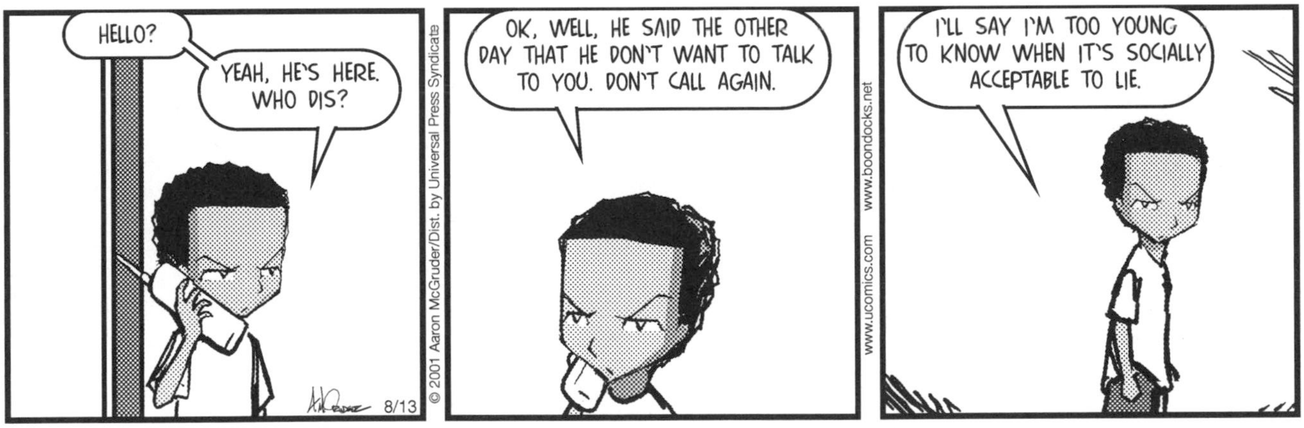
HELLO?
YEAH, HE'S HERE. WHO DIS?
8/13
© 2001 Aaron McGruder/Dist. by Universal Press Syndicate
OK, WELL, HE SAID THE OTHER DAY THAT HE DON'T WANT TO TALK TO YOU. DON'T CALL AGAIN.
www.ucomics.com www.boondocks.net
I'LL SAY I'M TOO YOUNG TO KNOW WHEN IT'S SOCIALLY ACCEPTABLE TO LIE.

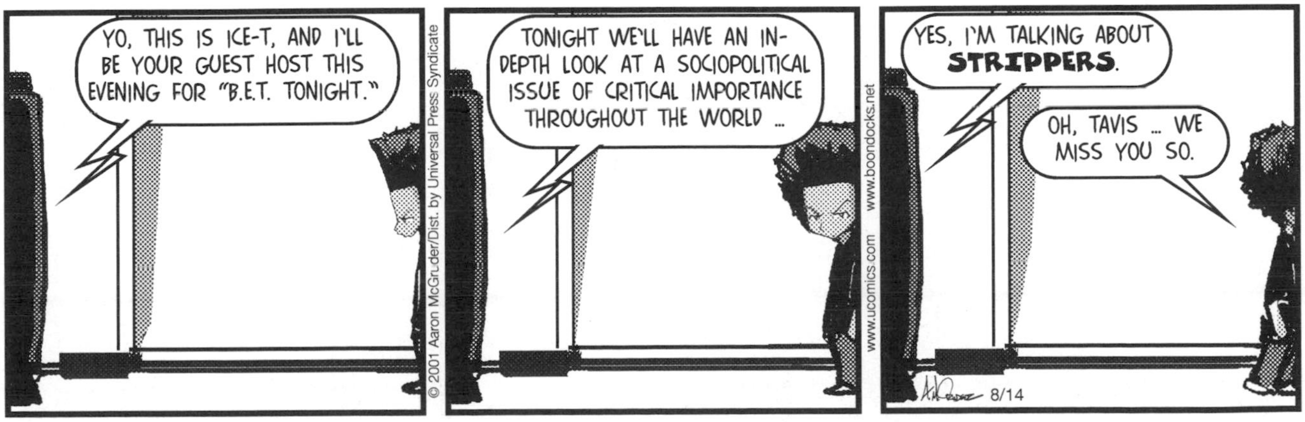
YO, THIS IS ICE-T, AND I'LL BE YOUR GUEST HOST THIS EVENING FOR "B.E.T. TONIGHT."
© 2001 Aaron McGruder/Dist. by Universal Press Syndicate
TONIGHT WE'LL HAVE AN IN-DEPTH LOOK AT A SOCIOPOLITICAL ISSUE OF CRITICAL IMPORTANCE THROUGHOUT THE WORLD ...
www.ucomics.com www.boondocks.net
YES, I'M TALKING ABOUT STRIPPERS.
OH, TAVIS ... WE MISS YOU SO.
8/14

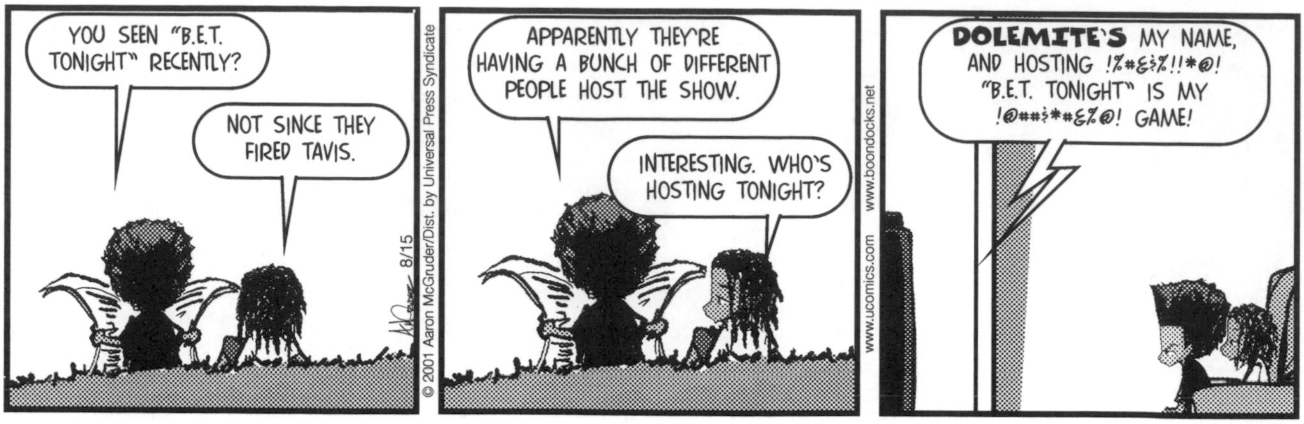
YOU SEEN "B.E.T. TONIGHT" RECENTLY?
NOT SINCE THEY FIRED TAVIS.
8/15
© 2001 Aaron McGruder/Dist. by Universal Press Syndicate
APPARENTLY THEY'RE HAVING A BUNCH OF DIFFERENT PEOPLE HOST THE SHOW.
INTERESTING. WHO'S HOSTING TONIGHT?
www.ucomics.com www.boondocks.net
DOLEMITE'S MY NAME, AND HOSTING !%*&$%!!*@! "B.E.T. TONIGHT" IS MY !@**$**&%@! GAME!

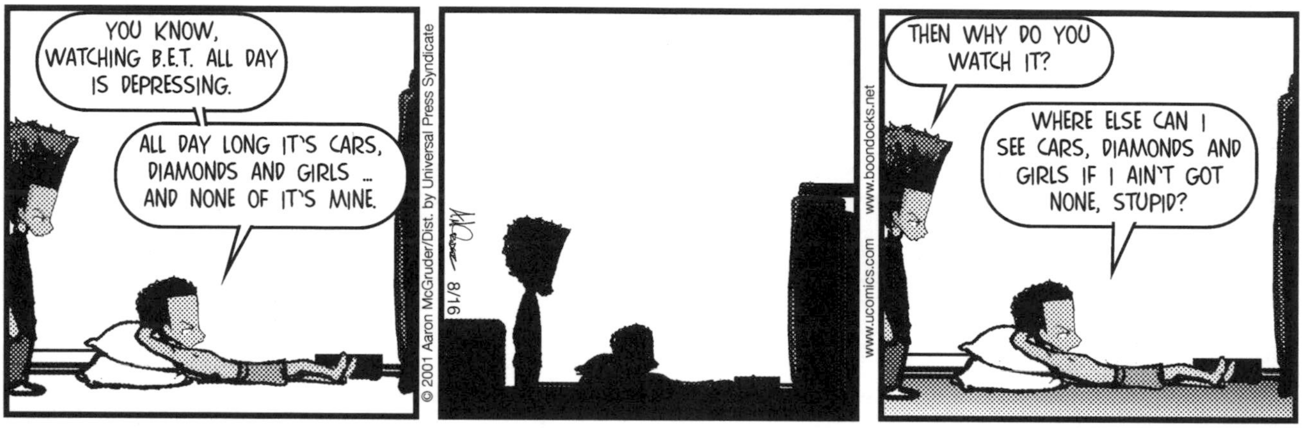
YOU KNOW, WATCHING B.E.T. ALL DAY IS DEPRESSING.
ALL DAY LONG IT'S CARS, DIAMONDS AND GIRLS ... AND NONE OF IT'S MINE.
© 2001 Aaron McGruder/Dist. by Universal Press Syndicate
8/16
www.ucomics.com www.boondocks.net
THEN WHY DO YOU WATCH IT?
WHERE ELSE CAN I SEE CARS, DIAMONDS AND GIRLS IF I AIN'T GOT NONE, STUPID?

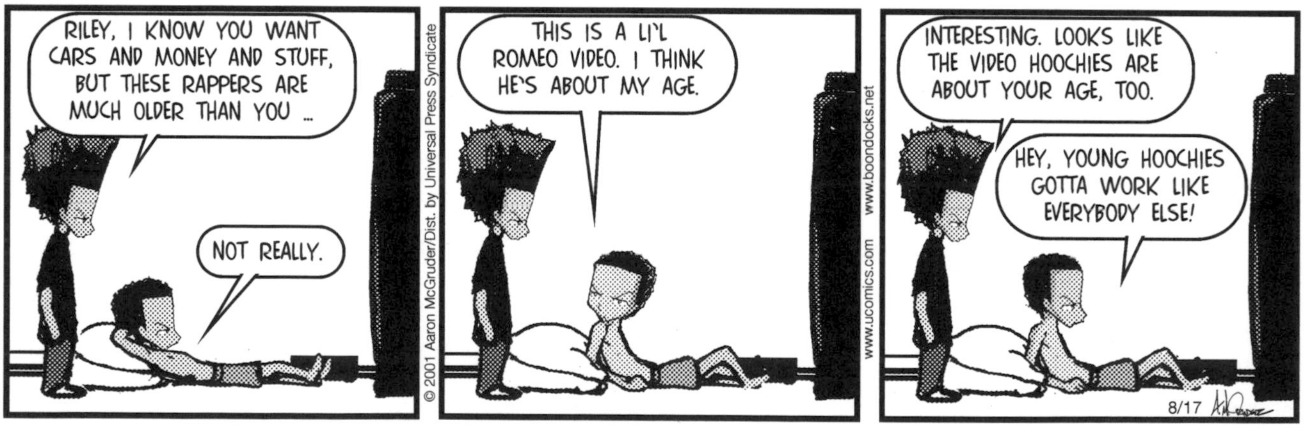
RILEY, I KNOW YOU WANT CARS AND MONEY AND STUFF, BUT THESE RAPPERS ARE MUCH OLDER THAN YOU ...
NOT REALLY.
© 2001 Aaron McGruder/Dist. by Universal Press Syndicate
THIS IS A LI'L ROMEO VIDEO. I THINK HE'S ABOUT MY AGE.
www.ucomics.com www.boondocks.net
INTERESTING. LOOKS LIKE THE VIDEO HOOCHIES ARE ABOUT YOUR AGE, TOO.
HEY, YOUNG HOOCHIES GOTTA WORK LIKE EVERYBODY ELSE!
8/17

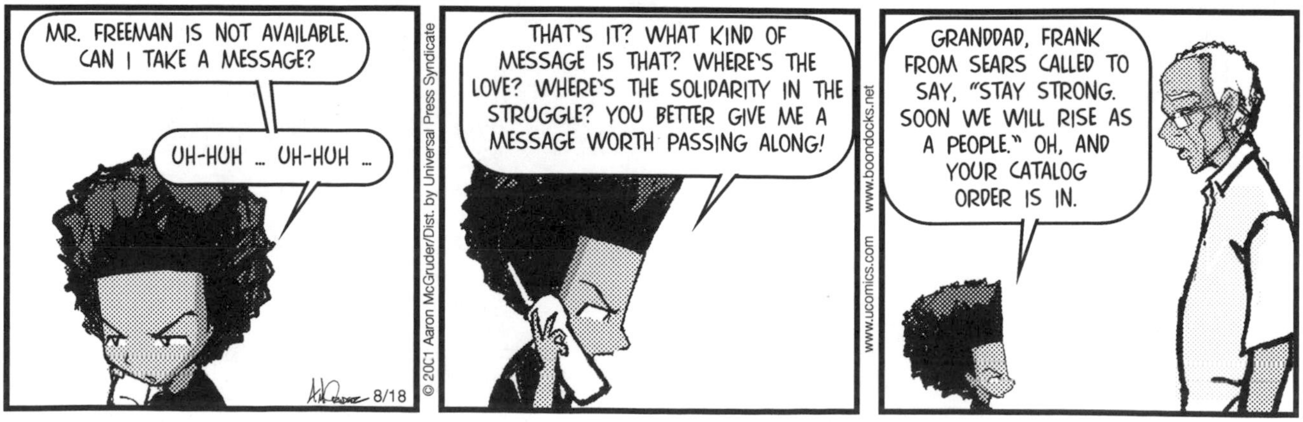
MR. FREEMAN IS NOT AVAILABLE. CAN I TAKE A MESSAGE?
UH-HUH ... UH-HUH ...
8/18
© 2001 Aaron McGruder/Dist. by Universal Press Syndicate
THAT'S IT? WHAT KIND OF MESSAGE IS THAT? WHERE'S THE LOVE? WHERE'S THE SOLIDARITY IN THE STRUGGLE? YOU BETTER GIVE ME A MESSAGE WORTH PASSING ALONG!
www.ucomics.com www.boondocks.net
GRANDDAD, FRANK FROM SEARS CALLED TO SAY, "STAY STRONG. SOON WE WILL RISE AS A PEOPLE." OH, AND YOUR CATALOG ORDER IS IN.

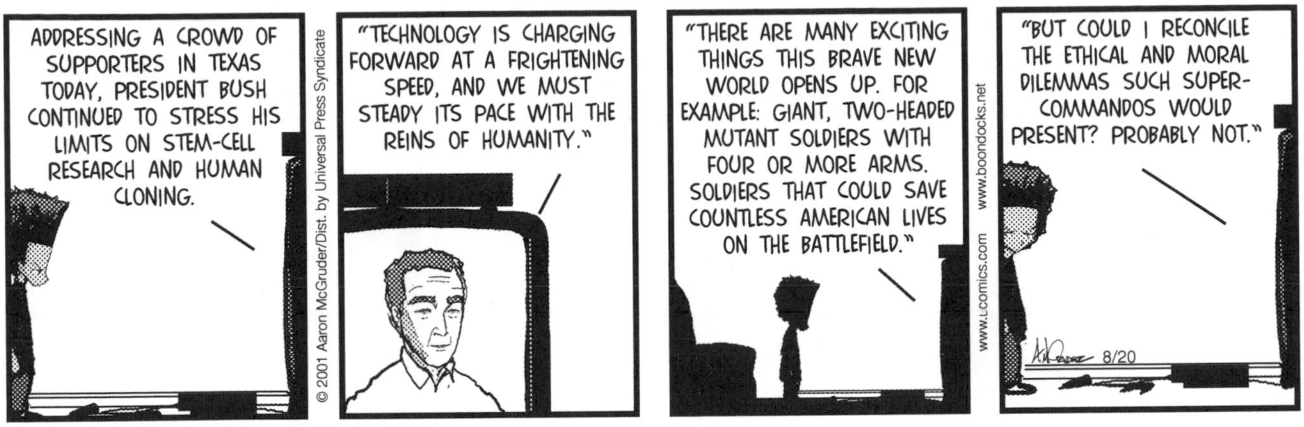
ADDRESSING A CROWD OF SUPPORTERS IN TEXAS TODAY, PRESIDENT BUSH CONTINUED TO STRESS HIS LIMITS ON STEM-CELL RESEARCH AND HUMAN CLONING.
© 2001 Aaron McGruder/Dist. by Universal Press Syndicate
"TECHNOLOGY IS CHARGING FORWARD AT A FRIGHTENING SPEED, AND WE MUST STEADY ITS PACE WITH THE REINS OF HUMANITY."
"THERE ARE MANY EXCITING THINGS THIS BRAVE NEW WORLD OPENS UP. FOR EXAMPLE: GIANT, TWO-HEADED MUTANT SOLDIERS WITH FOUR OR MORE ARMS. SOLDIERS THAT COULD SAVE COUNTLESS AMERICAN LIVES ON THE BATTLEFIELD."
www.ucomics.com www.boondocks.net
"BUT COULD I RECONCILE THE ETHICAL AND MORAL DILEMMAS SUCH SUPER-COMMANDOS WOULD PRESENT? PROBABLY NOT."
8/20

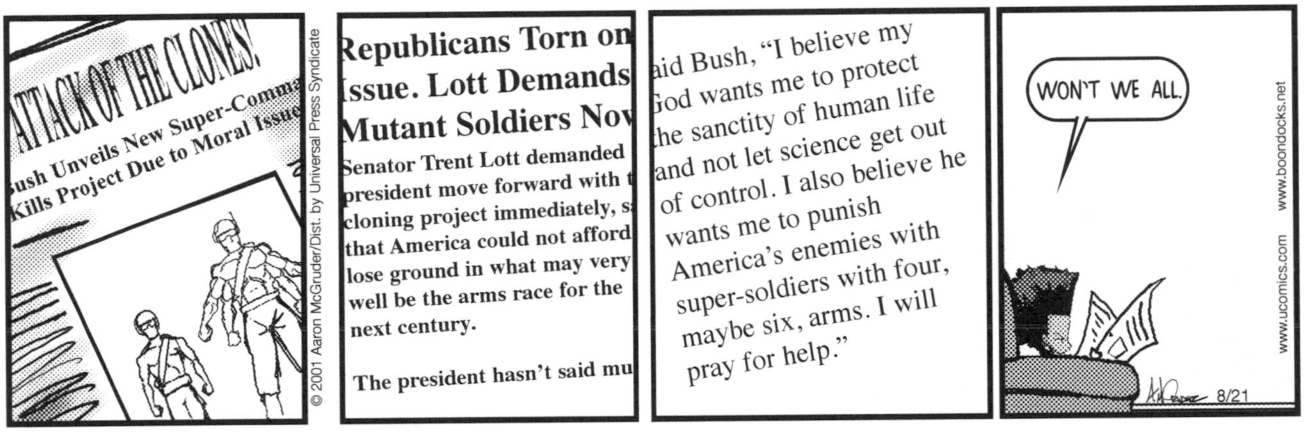
ATTACK OF THE CLONES!
ush Unveils New Super-Comma
Kills Project Due to Moral Issue
© 2001 Aaron McGruder/Dist. by Universal Press Syndicate
Republicans Torn on
Issue. Lott Demands
Mutant Soldiers Nov
Senator Trent Lott demanded
president move forward with t
cloning project immediately, s
that America could not afford
lose ground in what may very
well be the arms race for the
next century.
The president hasn't said mu
aid Bush, "I believe my God wants me to protect the sanctity of human life and not let science get out of control. I also believe he wants me to punish America's enemies with super-soldiers with four, maybe six, arms. I will pray for help."
WON'T WE ALL.
www.ucomics.com www.boondocks.net
8/21

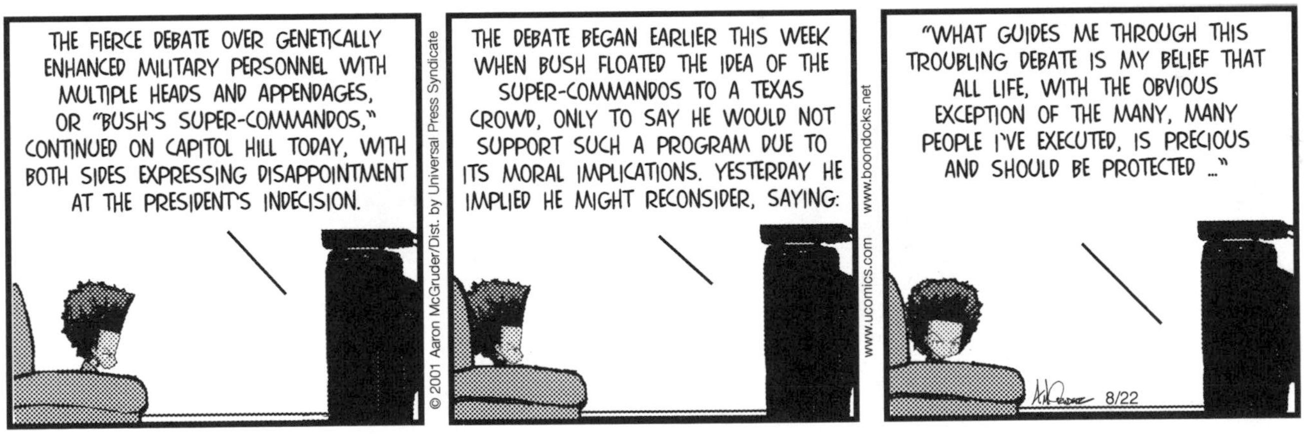
THE FIERCE DEBATE OVER GENETICALLY ENHANCED MILITARY PERSONNEL WITH MULTIPLE HEADS AND APPENDAGES, OR "BUSH'S SUPER-COMMANDOS," CONTINUED ON CAPITOL HILL TODAY, WITH BOTH SIDES EXPRESSING DISAPPOINTMENT AT THE PRESIDENT'S INDECISION.
© 2001 Aaron McGruder/Dist. by Universal Press Syndicate
THE DEBATE BEGAN EARLIER THIS WEEK WHEN BUSH FLOATED THE IDEA OF THE SUPER-COMMANDOS TO A TEXAS CROWD, ONLY TO SAY HE WOULD NOT SUPPORT SUCH A PROGRAM DUE TO ITS MORAL IMPLICATIONS. YESTERDAY HE IMPLIED HE MIGHT RECONSIDER, SAYING:
www.ucomics.com www.boondocks.net
"WHAT GUIDES ME THROUGH THIS TROUBLING DEBATE IS MY BELIEF THAT ALL LIFE, WITH THE OBVIOUS EXCEPTION OF THE MANY, MANY PEOPLE I'VE EXECUTED, IS PRECIOUS AND SHOULD BE PROTECTED ..."
8/22

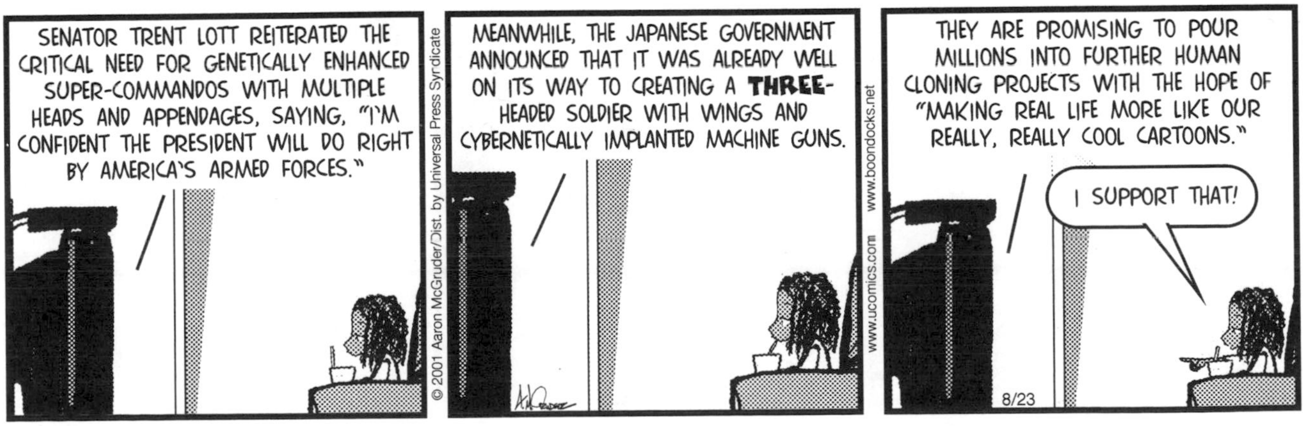
SENATOR TRENT LOTT REITERATED THE CRITICAL NEED FOR GENETICALLY ENHANCED SUPER-COMMANDOS WITH MULTIPLE HEADS AND APPENDAGES, SAYING, "I'M CONFIDENT THE PRESIDENT WILL DO RIGHT BY AMERICA'S ARMED FORCES."
© 2001 Aaron McGruder/Dist. by Universal Press Syndicate
MEANWHILE, THE JAPANESE GOVERNMENT ANNOUNCED THAT IT WAS ALREADY WELL ON ITS WAY TO CREATING A THREE-HEADED SOLDIER WITH WINGS AND CYBERNETICALLY IMPLANTED MACHINE GUNS.
www.ucomics.com www.boondocks.net
THEY ARE PROMISING TO POUR MILLIONS INTO FURTHER HUMAN CLONING PROJECTS WITH THE HOPE OF "MAKING REAL LIFE MORE LIKE OUR REALLY, REALLY COOL CARTOONS."
I SUPPORT THAT!
8/23

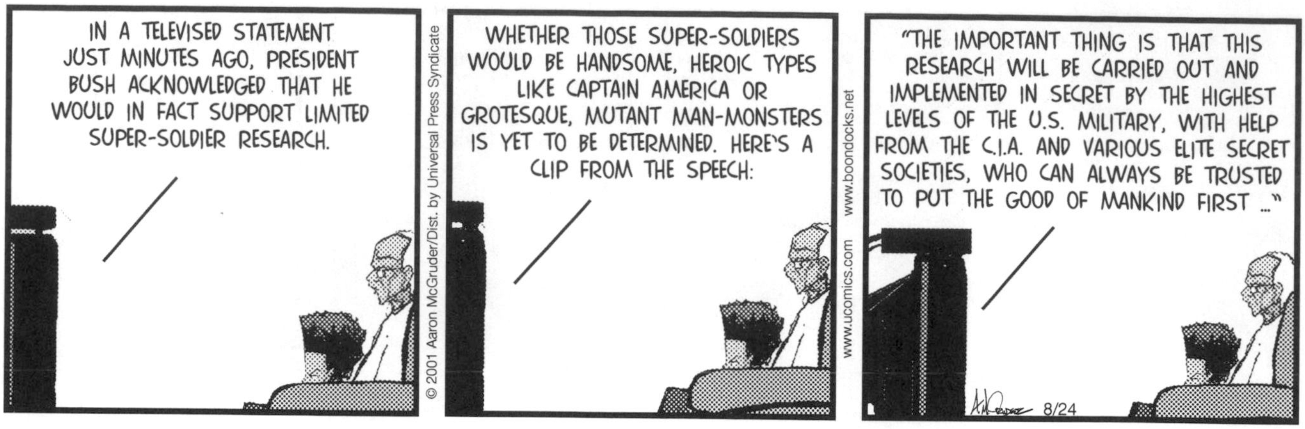
IN A TELEVISED STATEMENT JUST MINUTES AGO, PRESIDENT BUSH ACKNOWLEDGED THAT HE WOULD IN FACT SUPPORT LIMITED SUPER-SOLDIER RESEARCH.
WHETHER THOSE SUPER-SOLDIERS WOULD BE HANDSOME, HEROIC TYPES LIKE CAPTAIN AMERICA OR GROTESQUE, MUTANT MAN-MONSTERS IS YET TO BE DETERMINED. HERE'S A CLIP FROM THE SPEECH:
"THE IMPORTANT THING IS THAT THIS RESEARCH WILL BE CARRIED OUT AND IMPLEMENTED IN SECRET BY THE HIGHEST LEVELS OF THE U.S. MILITARY, WITH HELP FROM THE C.I.A. AND VARIOUS ELITE SECRET SOCIETIES, WHO CAN ALWAYS BE TRUSTED TO PUT THE GOOD OF MANKIND FIRST ..."
8/24

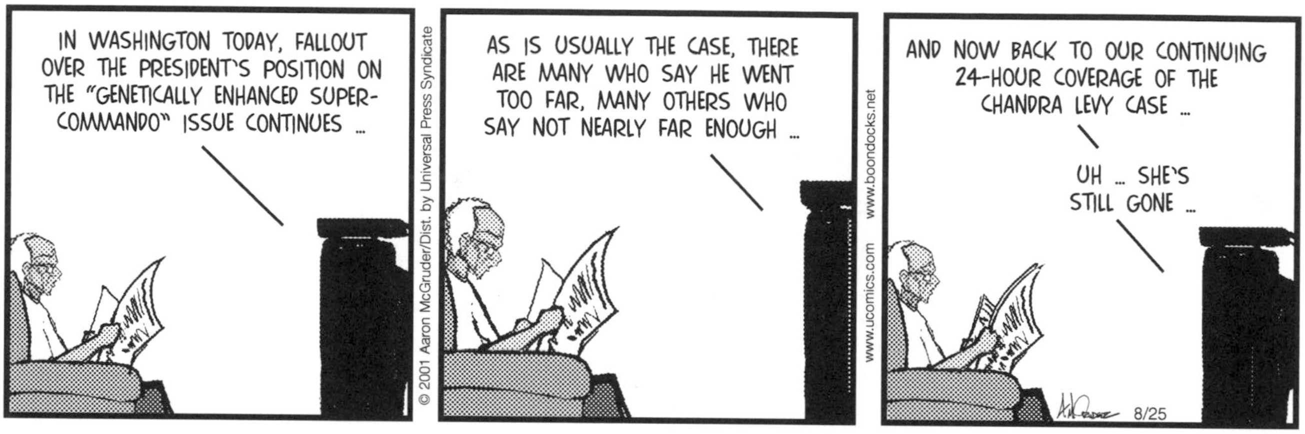
IN WASHINGTON TODAY, FALLOUT OVER THE PRESIDENT'S POSITION ON THE "GENETICALLY ENHANCED SUPER-COMMANDO" ISSUE CONTINUES ...
AS IS USUALLY THE CASE, THERE ARE MANY WHO SAY HE WENT TOO FAR, MANY OTHERS WHO SAY NOT NEARLY FAR ENOUGH ...
AND NOW BACK TO OUR CONTINUING 24-HOUR COVERAGE OF THE CHANDRA LEVY CASE ...
UH ... SHE'S STILL GONE ...
8/25

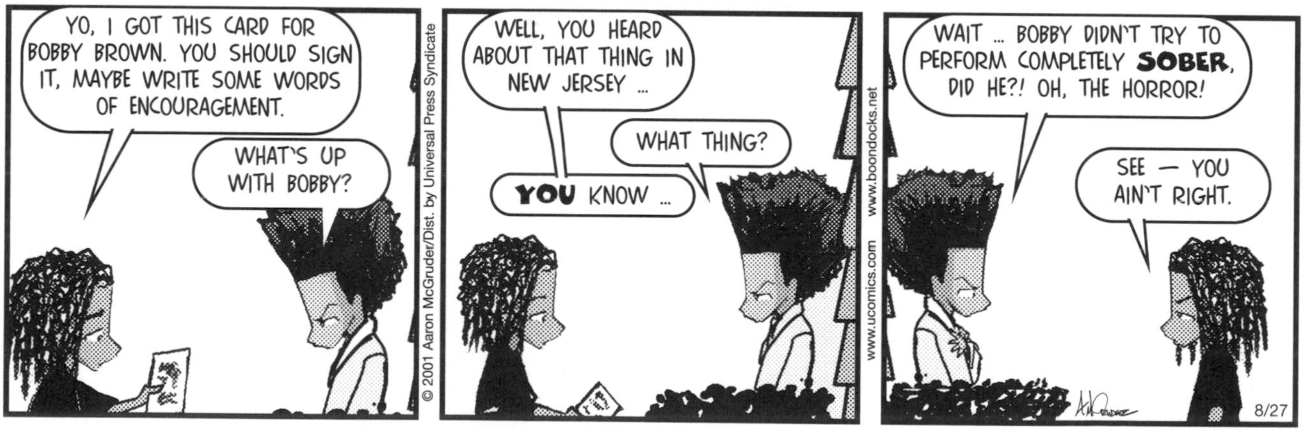
YO, I GOT THIS CARD FOR BOBBY BROWN. YOU SHOULD SIGN IT, MAYBE WRITE SOME WORDS OF ENCOURAGEMENT.
WHAT'S UP WITH BOBBY?
WELL, YOU HEARD ABOUT THAT THING IN NEW JERSEY ...
WHAT THING?
YOU KNOW ...
WAIT ... BOBBY DIDN'T TRY TO PERFORM COMPLETELY **SOBER**, DID HE?! OH, THE HORROR!
SEE — YOU AIN'T RIGHT.
8/27

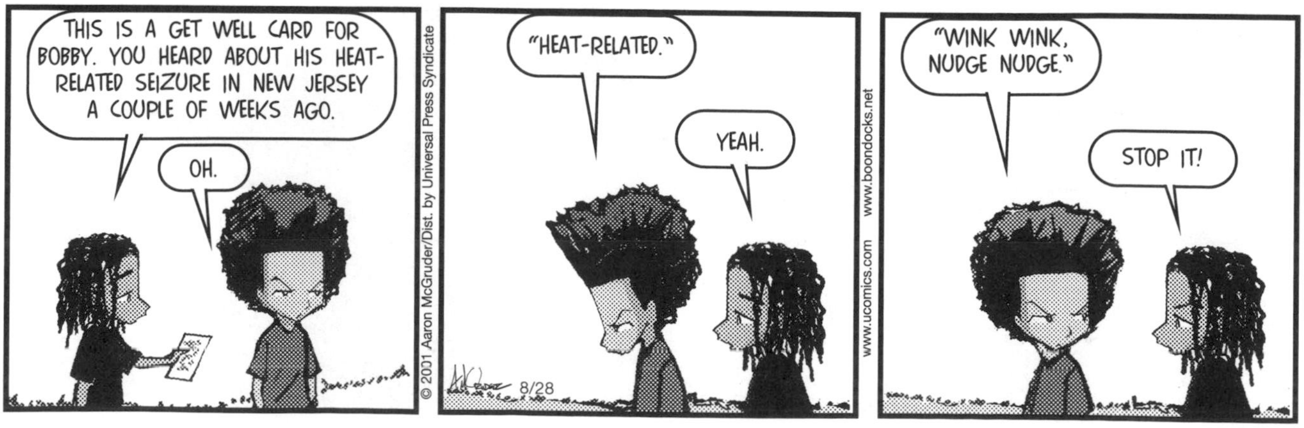
THIS IS A GET WELL CARD FOR BOBBY. YOU HEARD ABOUT HIS HEAT-RELATED SEIZURE IN NEW JERSEY A COUPLE OF WEEKS AGO.
OH.
"HEAT-RELATED."
YEAH.
"WINK WINK, NUDGE NUDGE."
STOP IT!
8/28

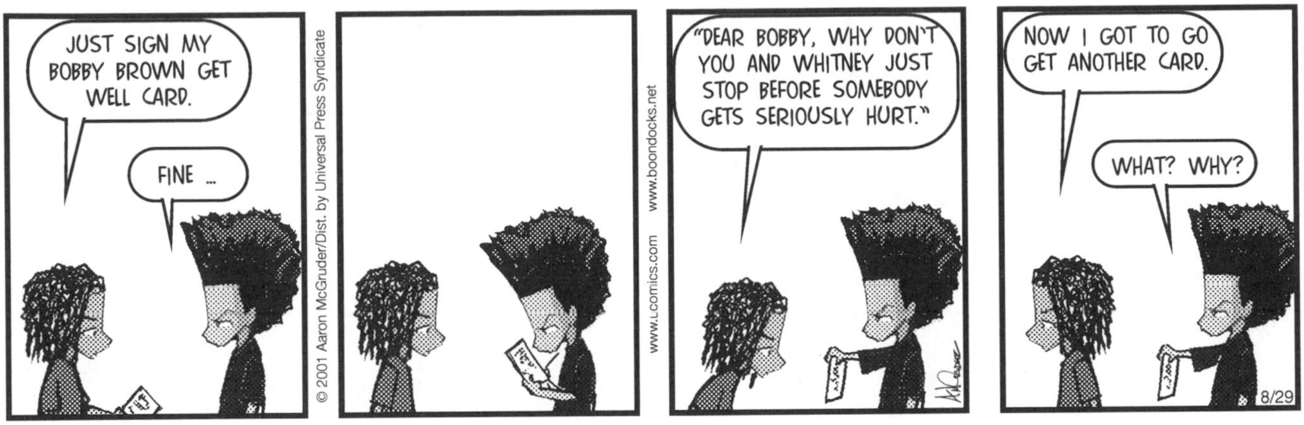
JUST SIGN MY BOBBY BROWN GET WELL CARD.
FINE ...
© 2001 Aaron McGruder/Dist. by Universal Press Syndicate
www.ucomics.com www.boondocks.net
"DEAR BOBBY, WHY DON'T YOU AND WHITNEY JUST STOP BEFORE SOMEBODY GETS SERIOUSLY HURT."
NOW I GOT TO GO GET ANOTHER CARD.
WHAT? WHY?
8/29

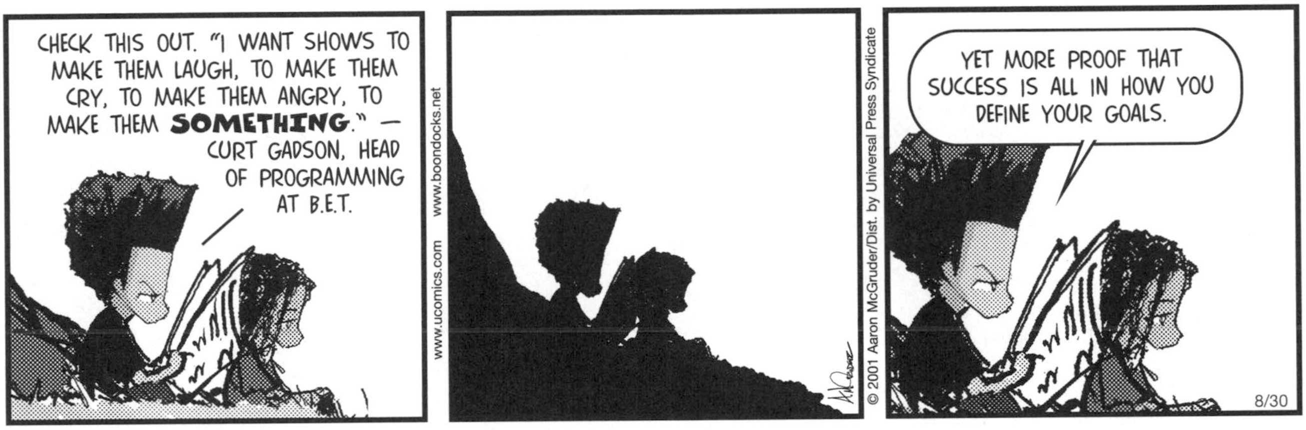
CHECK THIS OUT. "I WANT SHOWS TO MAKE THEM LAUGH, TO MAKE THEM CRY, TO MAKE THEM ANGRY, TO MAKE THEM **SOMETHING**." — CURT GADSON, HEAD OF PROGRAMMING AT B.E.T.
www.ucomics.com www.boondocks.net
© 2001 Aaron McGruder/Dist. by Universal Press Syndicate
YET MORE PROOF THAT SUCCESS IS ALL IN HOW YOU DEFINE YOUR GOALS.
8/30

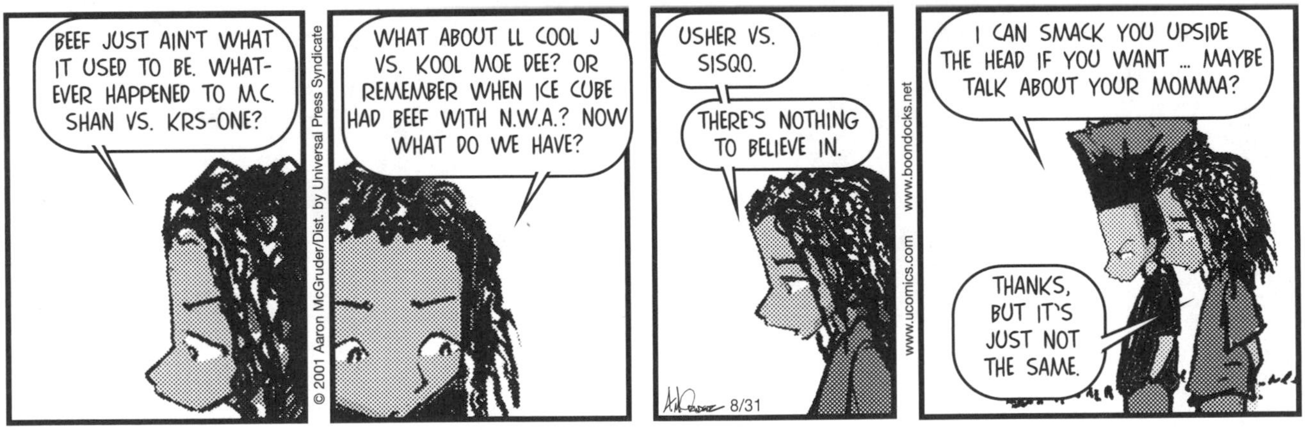
BEEF JUST AIN'T WHAT IT USED TO BE. WHATEVER HAPPENED TO M.C. SHAN VS. KRS-ONE?
© 2001 Aaron McGruder/Dist. by Universal Press Syndicate
WHAT ABOUT LL COOL J VS. KOOL MOE DEE? OR REMEMBER WHEN ICE CUBE HAD BEEF WITH N.W.A.? NOW WHAT DO WE HAVE?
USHER VS. SISQO.
THERE'S NOTHING TO BELIEVE IN.
8/31
www.ucomics.com www.boondocks.net
I CAN SMACK YOU UPSIDE THE HEAD IF YOU WANT ... MAYBE TALK ABOUT YOUR MOMMA?
THANKS, BUT IT'S JUST NOT THE SAME.

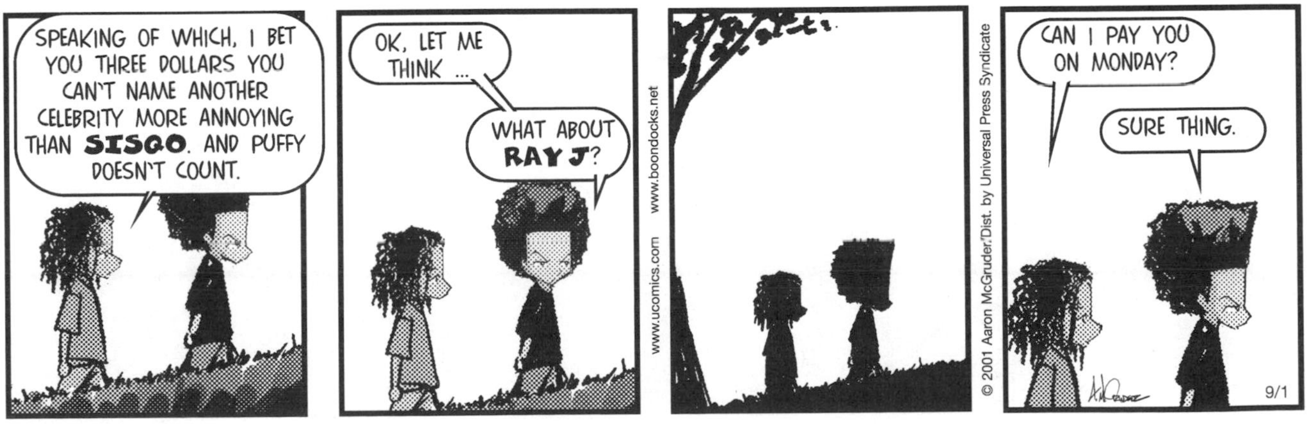
SPEAKING OF WHICH, I BET YOU THREE DOLLARS YOU CAN'T NAME ANOTHER CELEBRITY MORE ANNOYING THAN **SISQO**. AND PUFFY DOESN'T COUNT.
OK, LET ME THINK ...
WHAT ABOUT **RAY J**?
www.ucomics.com www.boondocks.net
© 2001 Aaron McGruder/Dist. by Universal Press Syndicate
CAN I PAY YOU ON MONDAY?
SURE THING.
9/1

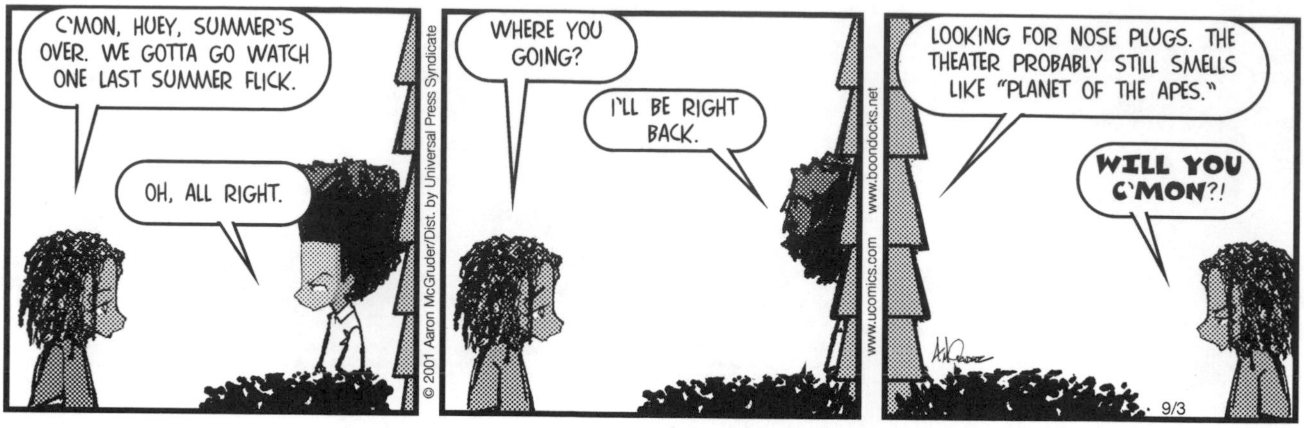
C'MON, HUEY, SUMMER'S OVER. WE GOTTA GO WATCH ONE LAST SUMMER FLICK.
OH, ALL RIGHT.
© 2001 Aaron McGruder/Dist. by Universal Press Syndicate
WHERE YOU GOING?
I'LL BE RIGHT BACK.
www.ucomics.com www.boondocks.net
LOOKING FOR NOSE PLUGS. THE THEATER PROBABLY STILL SMELLS LIKE "PLANET OF THE APES."
WILL YOU C'MON?!
9/3

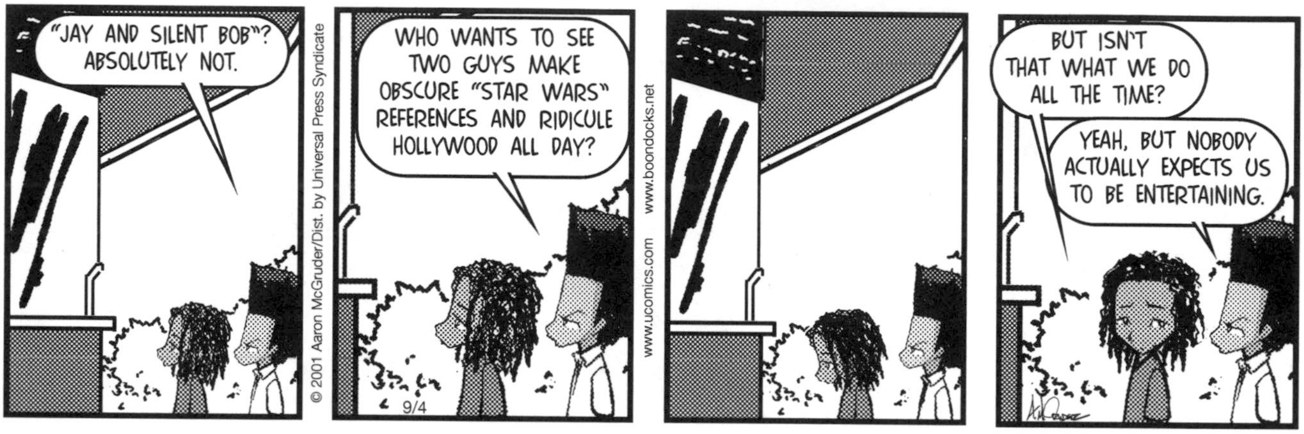
"JAY AND SILENT BOB"? ABSOLUTELY NOT.
© 2001 Aaron McGruder/Dist. by Universal Press Syndicate
WHO WANTS TO SEE TWO GUYS MAKE OBSCURE "STAR WARS" REFERENCES AND RIDICULE HOLLYWOOD ALL DAY?
9/4
www.ucomics.com www.boondocks.net
BUT ISN'T THAT WHAT WE DO ALL THE TIME?
YEAH, BUT NOBODY ACTUALLY EXPECTS US TO BE ENTERTAINING.

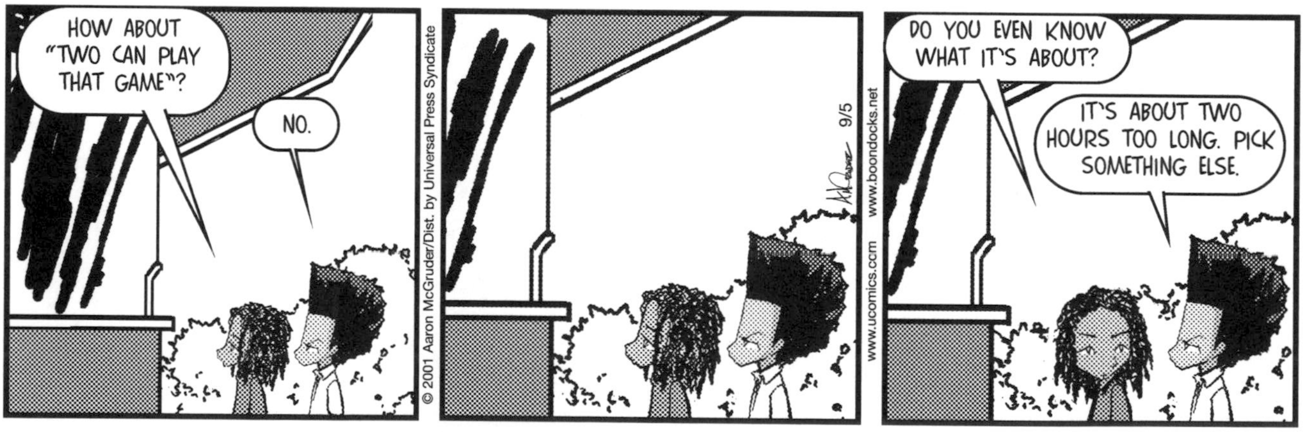
HOW ABOUT "TWO CAN PLAY THAT GAME"?
NO.
© 2001 Aaron McGruder/Dist. by Universal Press Syndicate
9/5
www.ucomics.com www.boondocks.net
DO YOU EVEN KNOW WHAT IT'S ABOUT?
IT'S ABOUT TWO HOURS TOO LONG. PICK SOMETHING ELSE.

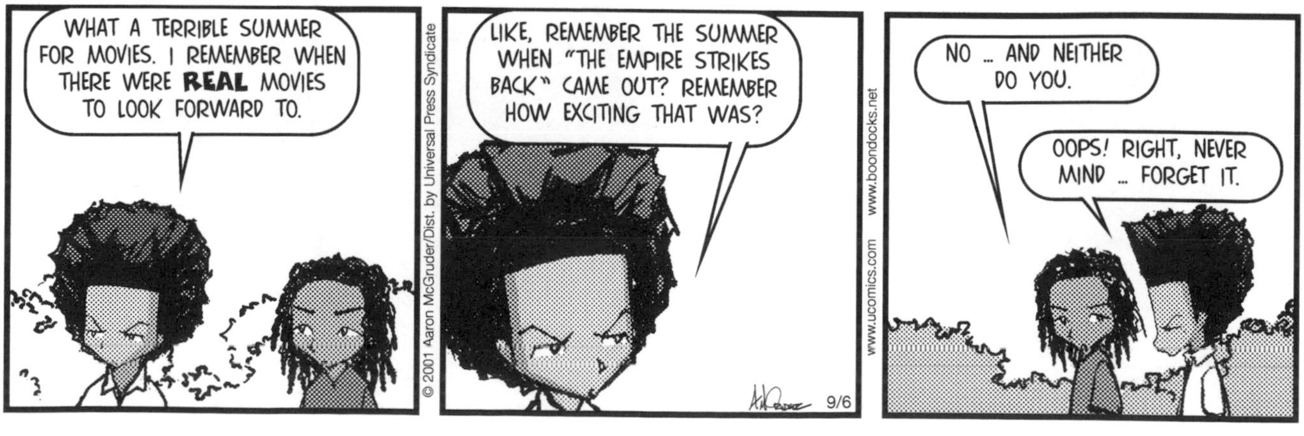
WHAT A TERRIBLE SUMMER FOR MOVIES. I REMEMBER WHEN THERE WERE REAL MOVIES TO LOOK FORWARD TO.
© 2001 Aaron McGruder/Dist. by Universal Press Syndicate
LIKE, REMEMBER THE SUMMER WHEN "THE EMPIRE STRIKES BACK" CAME OUT? REMEMBER HOW EXCITING THAT WAS?
9/6
www.ucomics.com www.boondocks.net
NO ... AND NEITHER DO YOU.
OOPS! RIGHT, NEVER MIND ... FORGET IT.

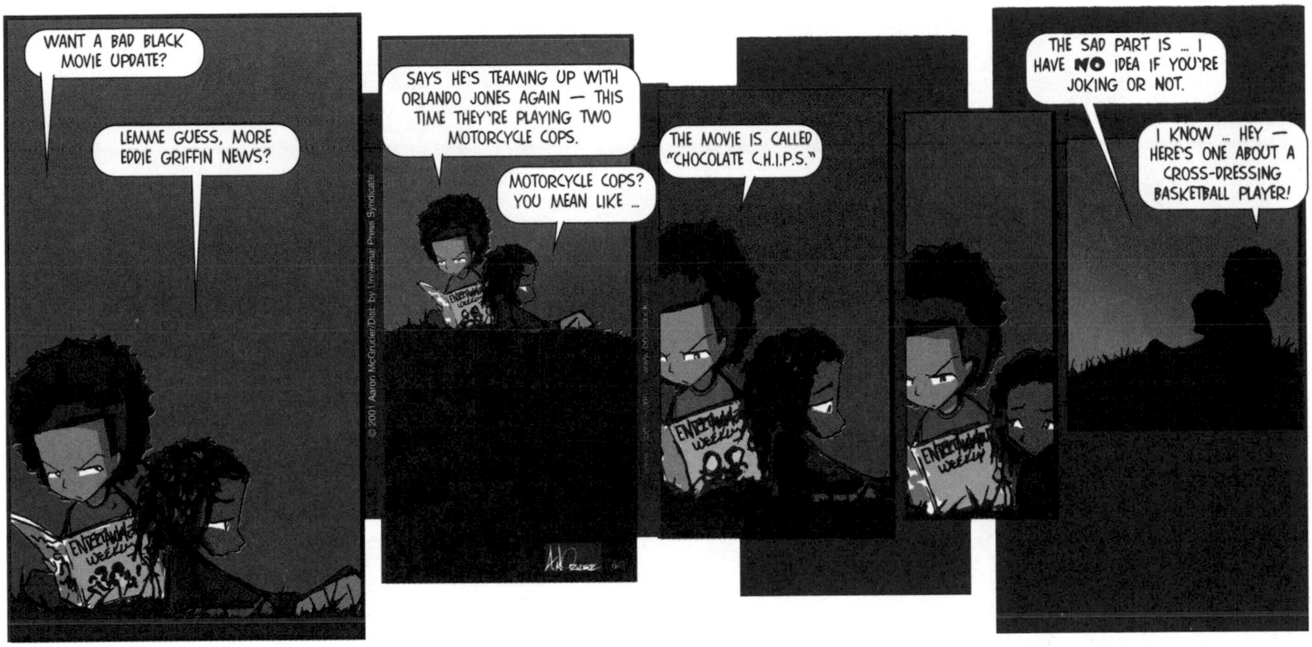
WANT A BAD BLACK MOVIE UPDATE?
LEMME GUESS, MORE EDDIE GRIFFIN NEWS?
SAYS HE'S TEAMING UP WITH ORLANDO JONES AGAIN — THIS TIME THEY'RE PLAYING TWO MOTORCYCLE COPS.
MOTORCYCLE COPS? YOU MEAN LIKE ...
THE MOVIE IS CALLED "CHOCOLATE C.H.I.P.S."
THE SAD PART IS ... I HAVE NO IDEA IF YOU'RE JOKING OR NOT.
I KNOW ... HEY — HERE'S ONE ABOUT A CROSS-DRESSING BASKETBALL PLAYER!
© 2001 Aaron McGruder/Dist. by Universal Press Syndicate

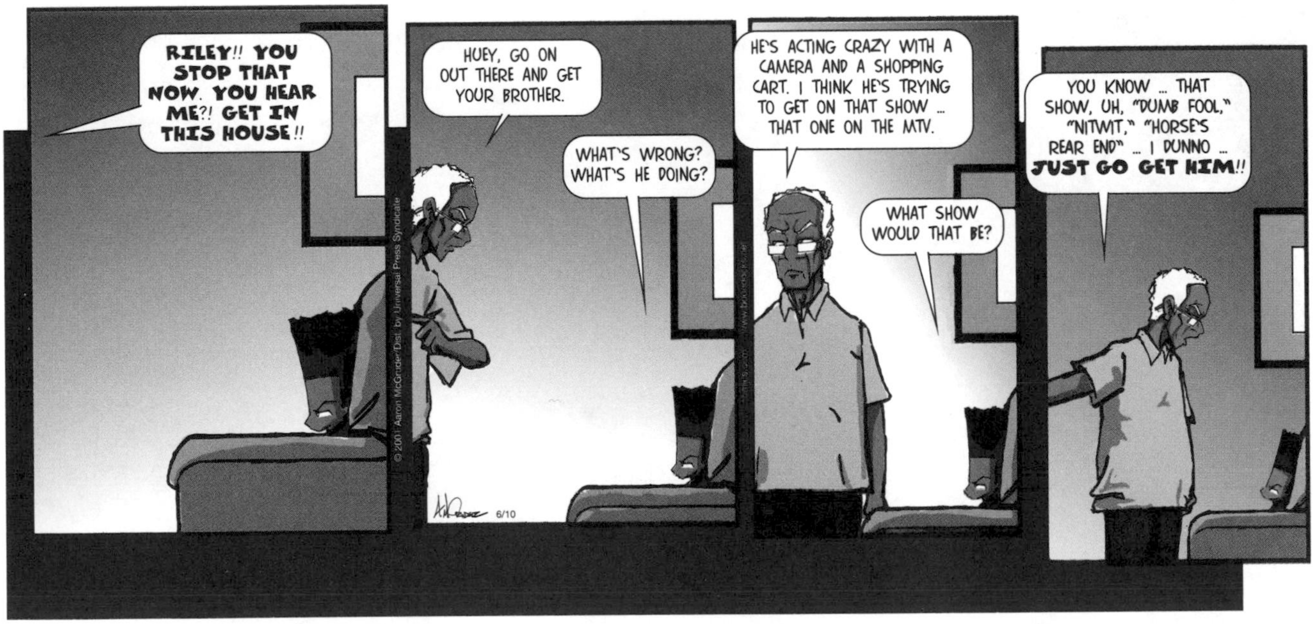
RILEY!! YOU STOP THAT NOW. YOU HEAR ME?! GET IN THIS HOUSE!!
HUEY, GO ON OUT THERE AND GET YOUR BROTHER.
WHAT'S WRONG? WHAT'S HE DOING?
HE'S ACTING CRAZY WITH A CAMERA AND A SHOPPING CART. I THINK HE'S TRYING TO GET ON THAT SHOW ... THAT ONE ON THE MTV.
WHAT SHOW WOULD THAT BE?
YOU KNOW ... THAT SHOW, UH, "DUMB FOOL," "NITWIT," "HORSE'S REAR END" ... I DUNNO ... JUST GO GET HIM!!
© 2001 Aaron McGruder/Dist. by Universal Press Syndicate
6/10

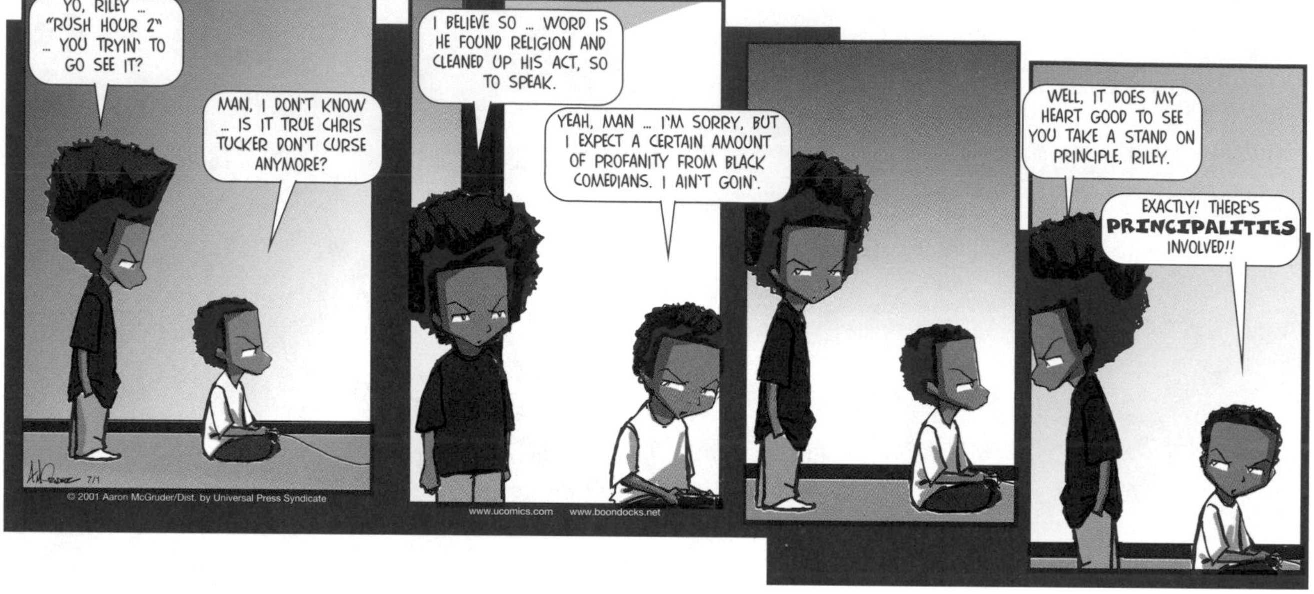
YO, RILEY ... "RUSH HOUR 2" ... YOU TRYIN' TO GO SEE IT?
MAN, I DON'T KNOW ... IS IT TRUE CHRIS TUCKER DON'T CURSE ANYMORE?
I BELIEVE SO ... WORD IS HE FOUND RELIGION AND CLEANED UP HIS ACT, SO TO SPEAK.
YEAH, MAN ... I'M SORRY, BUT I EXPECT A CERTAIN AMOUNT OF PROFANITY FROM BLACK COMEDIANS. I AIN'T GOIN'.
WELL, IT DOES MY HEART GOOD TO SEE YOU TAKE A STAND ON PRINCIPLE, RILEY.
EXACTLY! THERE'S **PRINCIPALITIES** INVOLVED!!
7/1
© 2001 Aaron McGruder/Dist. by Universal Press Syndicate
www.ucomics.com
www.boondocks.net

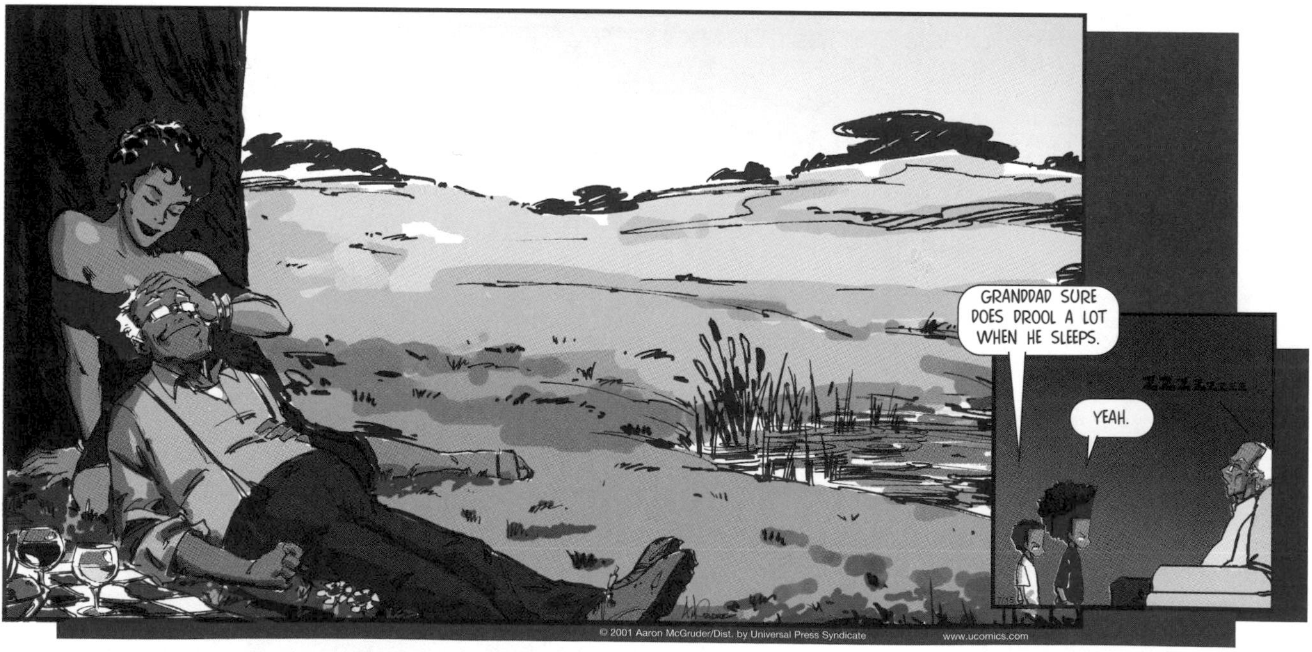
GRANDDAD SURE DOES DROOL A LOT WHEN HE SLEEPS.
YEAH.
© 2001 Aaron McGruder/Dist. by Universal Press Syndicate
www.ucomics.com

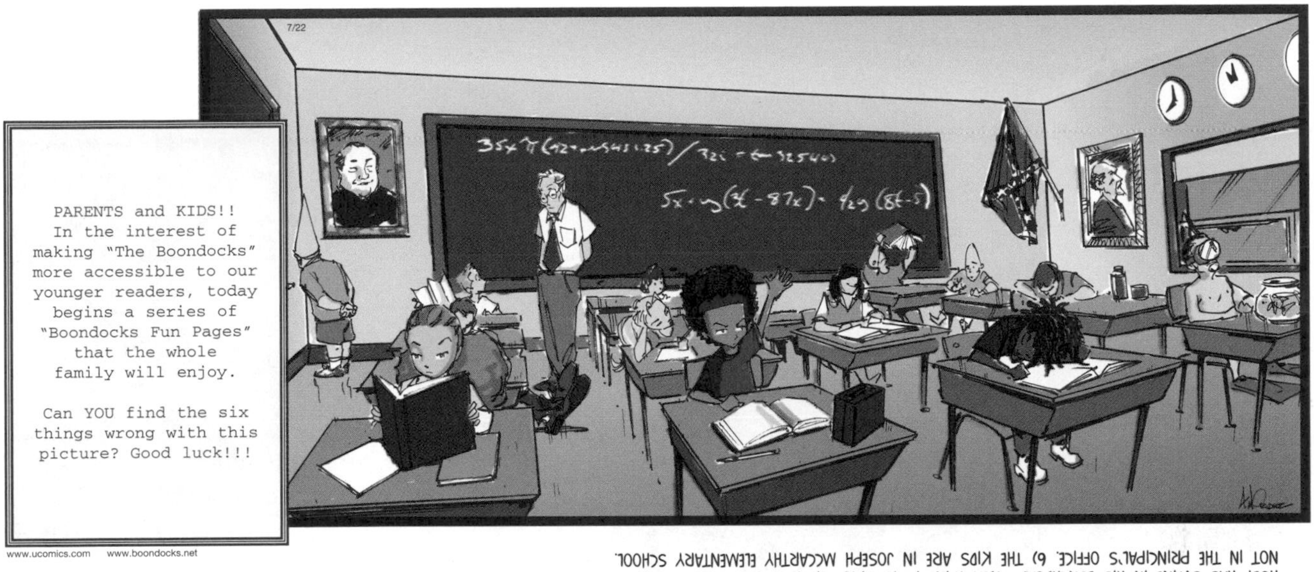

7/22
PARENTS and KIDS!! In the interest of making "The Boondocks" more accessible to our younger readers, today begins a series of "Boondocks Fun Pages" that the whole family will enjoy.
Can YOU find the six things wrong with this picture? Good luck!!!
www.ucomics.com www.boondocks.net

ANSWERS: 1) HUEY DOESN'T KNOW THE ANSWER TO THE QUESTION. 2) CAESAR IS **NOT** DREAMING ABOUT JENNIFER LOPEZ. 3) HUEY HAS SWINE IN HIS LUNCHBOX. 4) JAZMINE IS READING ELIJAH MUHAMMAD'S "MESSAGE TO THE BLACKMAN." 5) RILEY IS NOT IN THE PRINCIPAL'S OFFICE. 6) THE KIDS ARE IN JOSEPH MCCARTHY ELEMENTARY SCHOOL.

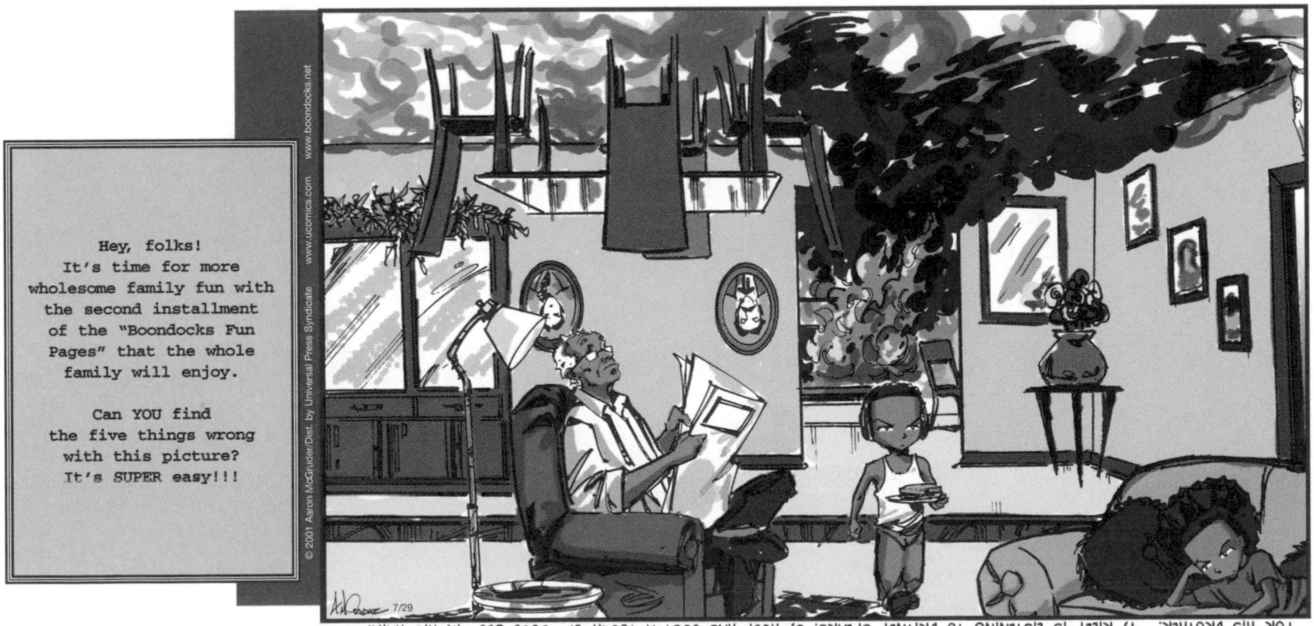

Hey, folks! It's time for more wholesome family fun with the second installment of the "Boondocks Fun Pages" that the whole family will enjoy.
Can YOU find the five things wrong with this picture? It's SUPER easy!!!
© 2001 Aaron McGruder/Dist. by Universal Press Syndicate www.ucomics.com www.boondocks.net
7/29

ANSWERS: 1) HUEY IS WEARING NIKES. 2) GRANDDAD'S GLASSES ARE THE WRONG PRESCRIPTION. 3) RILEY MADE THAT SANDWICH FOR HIS BROTHER. 4) RILEY IS LISTENING TO BRITNEY SPEARS. 5) HUEY HAS JUST A TOUCH OF "SOUL GLO" IN HIS HAIR.

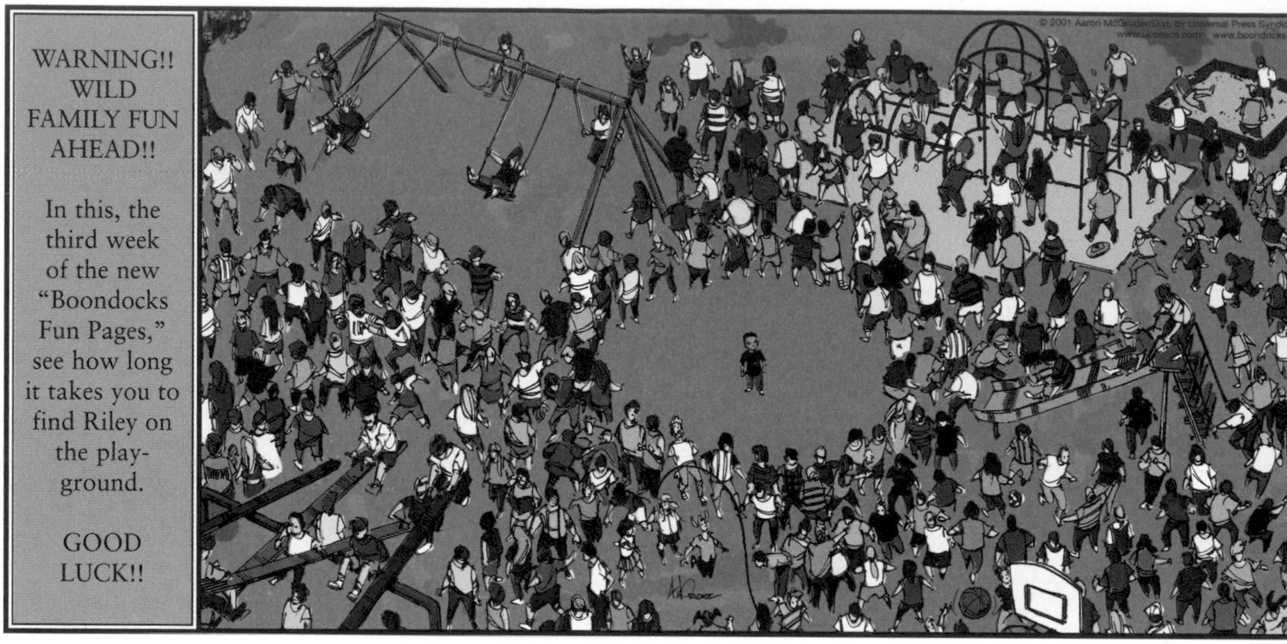
WARNING!! WILD FAMILY FUN AHEAD!!
In this, the third week of the new "Boondocks Fun Pages," see how long it takes you to find Riley on the play-ground.
GOOD LUCK!!
© 2001 Aaron McGruder/Dist. by Universal Press Syndicate
www.ucomics.com www.boondocks.net
8/5

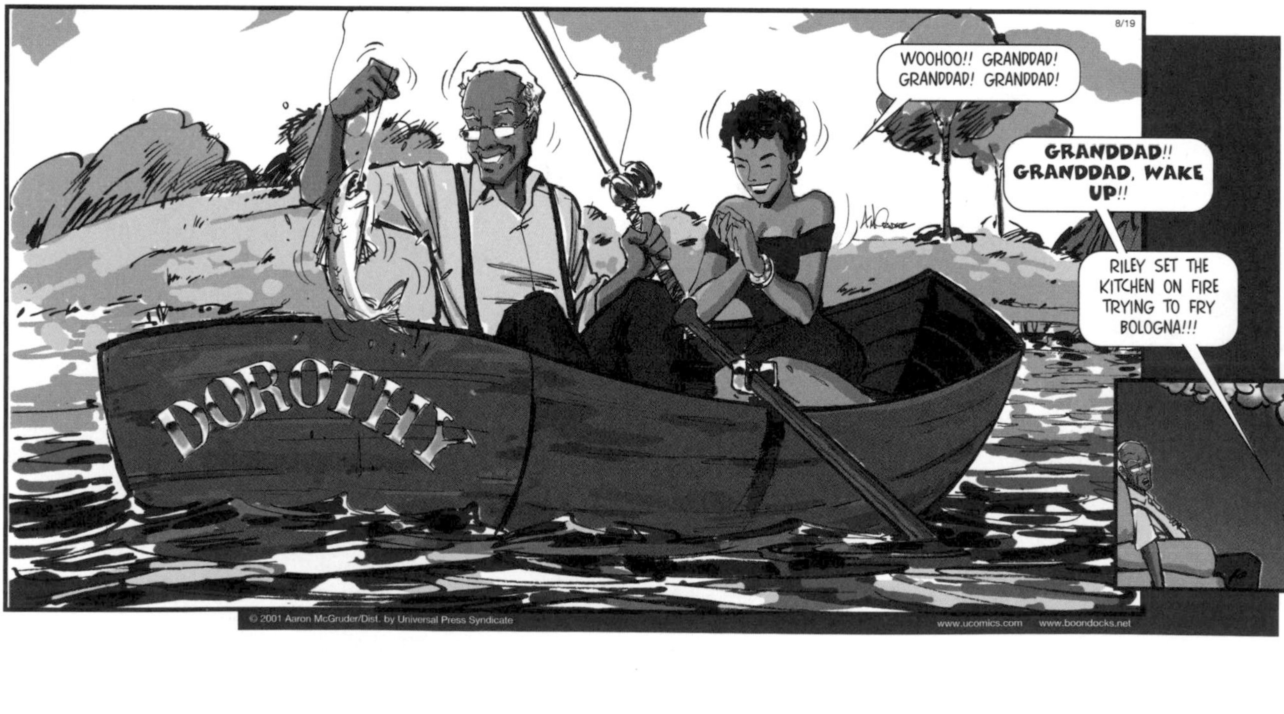
8/19
WOOHOO!! GRANDDAD! GRANDDAD! GRANDDAD!
DOROTHY
GRANDDAD!! GRANDDAD, WAKE UP!!
RILEY SET THE KITCHEN ON FIRE TRYING TO FRY BOLOGNA!!!
© 2001 Aaron McGruder/Dist. by Universal Press Syndicate
www.ucomics.com www.boondocks.net

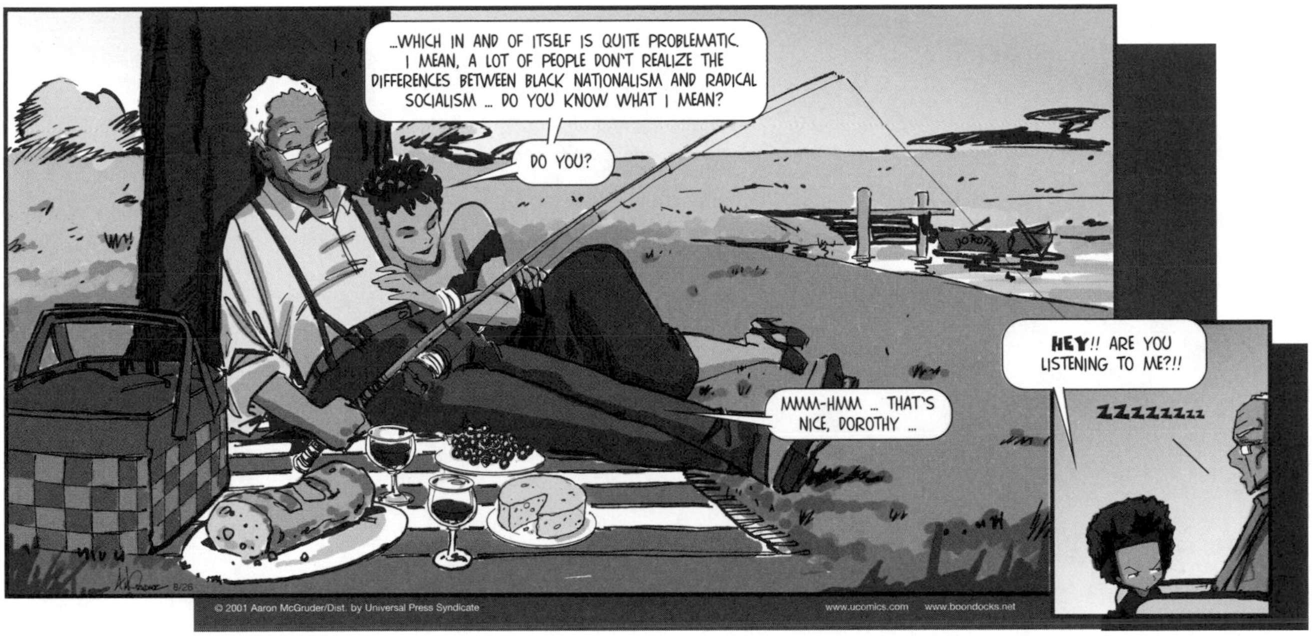
...WHICH IN AND OF ITSELF IS QUITE PROBLEMATIC. I MEAN, A LOT OF PEOPLE DON'T REALIZE THE DIFFERENCES BETWEEN BLACK NATIONALISM AND RADICAL SOCIALISM ... DO YOU KNOW WHAT I MEAN?
DO YOU?
MMM-HMM ... THAT'S NICE, DOROTHY ...
HEY!! ARE YOU LISTENING TO ME?!!
ZZZZZZZZ
© 2001 Aaron McGruder/Dist. by Universal Press Syndicate
www.ucomics.com www.boondocks.net

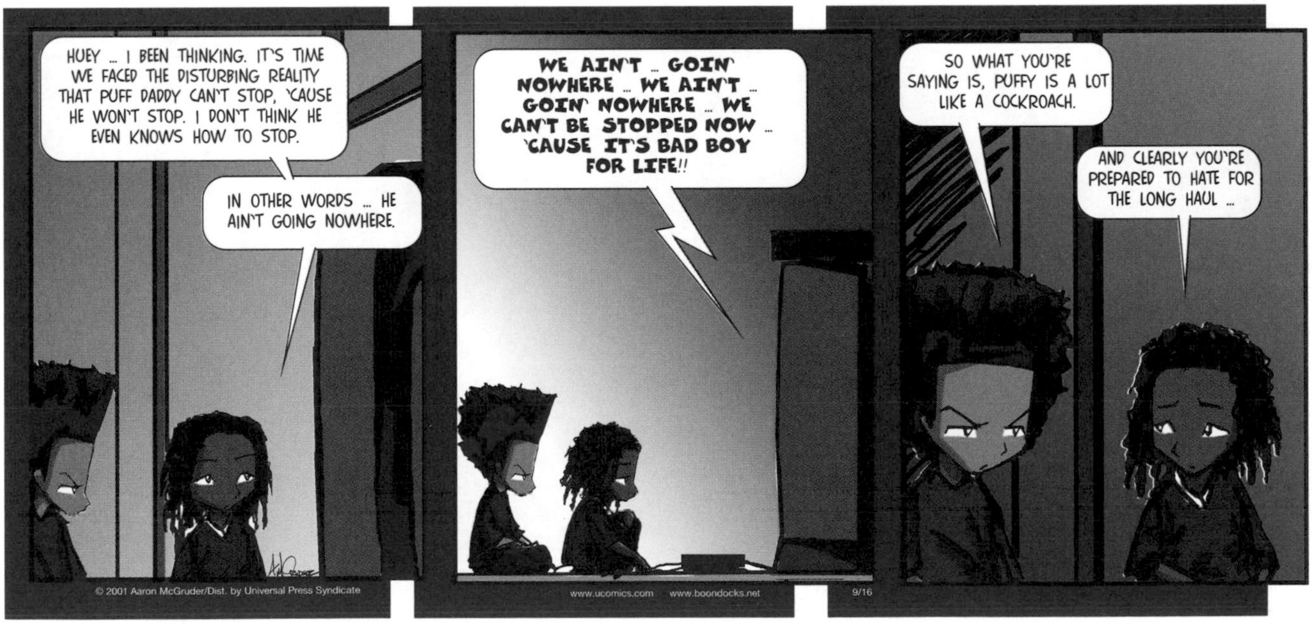
HUEY ... I BEEN THINKING. IT'S TIME WE FACED THE DISTURBING REALITY THAT PUFF DADDY CAN'T STOP, 'CAUSE HE WON'T STOP. I DON'T THINK HE EVEN KNOWS HOW TO STOP.
IN OTHER WORDS ... HE AIN'T GOING NOWHERE.
WE AIN'T ... GOIN' NOWHERE ... WE AIN'T ... GOIN' NOWHERE ... WE CAN'T BE STOPPED NOW ... 'CAUSE IT'S BAD BOY FOR LIFE!!
SO WHAT YOU'RE SAYING IS, PUFFY IS A LOT LIKE A COCKROACH.
AND CLEARLY YOU'RE PREPARED TO HATE FOR THE LONG HAUL ...
© 2001 Aaron McGruder/Dist. by Universal Press Syndicate
www.ucomics.com www.boondocks.net
9/16

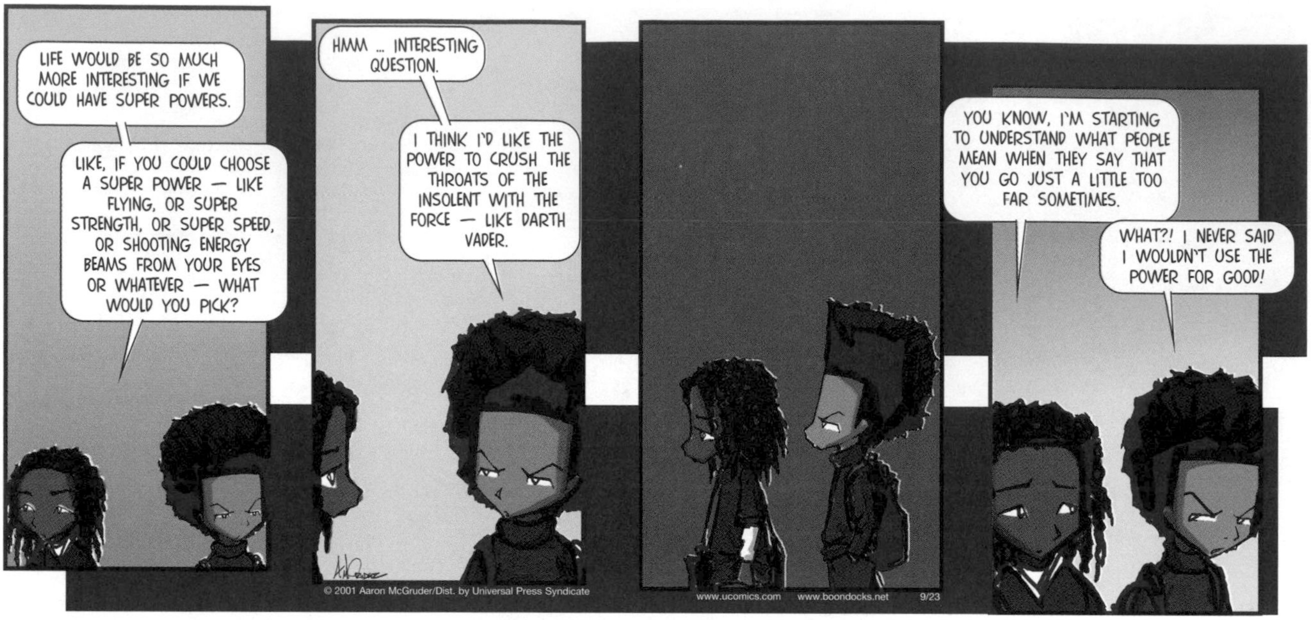
LIFE WOULD BE SO MUCH MORE INTERESTING IF WE COULD HAVE SUPER POWERS.
LIKE, IF YOU COULD CHOOSE A SUPER POWER — LIKE FLYING, OR SUPER STRENGTH, OR SUPER SPEED, OR SHOOTING ENERGY BEAMS FROM YOUR EYES OR WHATEVER — WHAT WOULD YOU PICK?
HMM ... INTERESTING QUESTION.
I THINK I'D LIKE THE POWER TO CRUSH THE THROATS OF THE INSOLENT WITH THE FORCE — LIKE DARTH VADER.
YOU KNOW, I'M STARTING TO UNDERSTAND WHAT PEOPLE MEAN WHEN THEY SAY THAT YOU GO JUST A LITTLE TOO FAR SOMETIMES.
WHAT?! I NEVER SAID I WOULDN'T USE THE POWER FOR GOOD!
© 2001 Aaron McGruder/Dist. by Universal Press Syndicate
www.ucomics.com www.boondocks.net 9/23

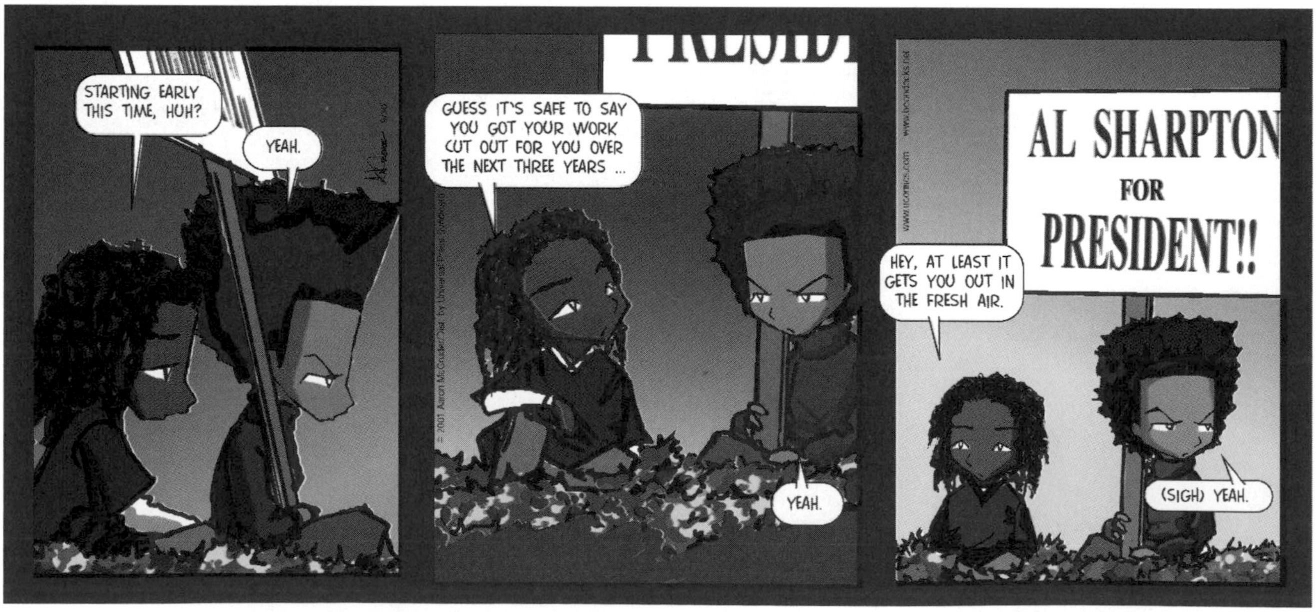
STARTING EARLY THIS TIME, HUH?
YEAH.
GUESS IT'S SAFE TO SAY YOU GOT YOUR WORK CUT OUT FOR YOU OVER THE NEXT THREE YEARS ...
YEAH.
AL SHARPTON FOR PRESIDENT!!
HEY, AT LEAST IT GETS YOU OUT IN THE FRESH AIR.
(SIGH) YEAH.

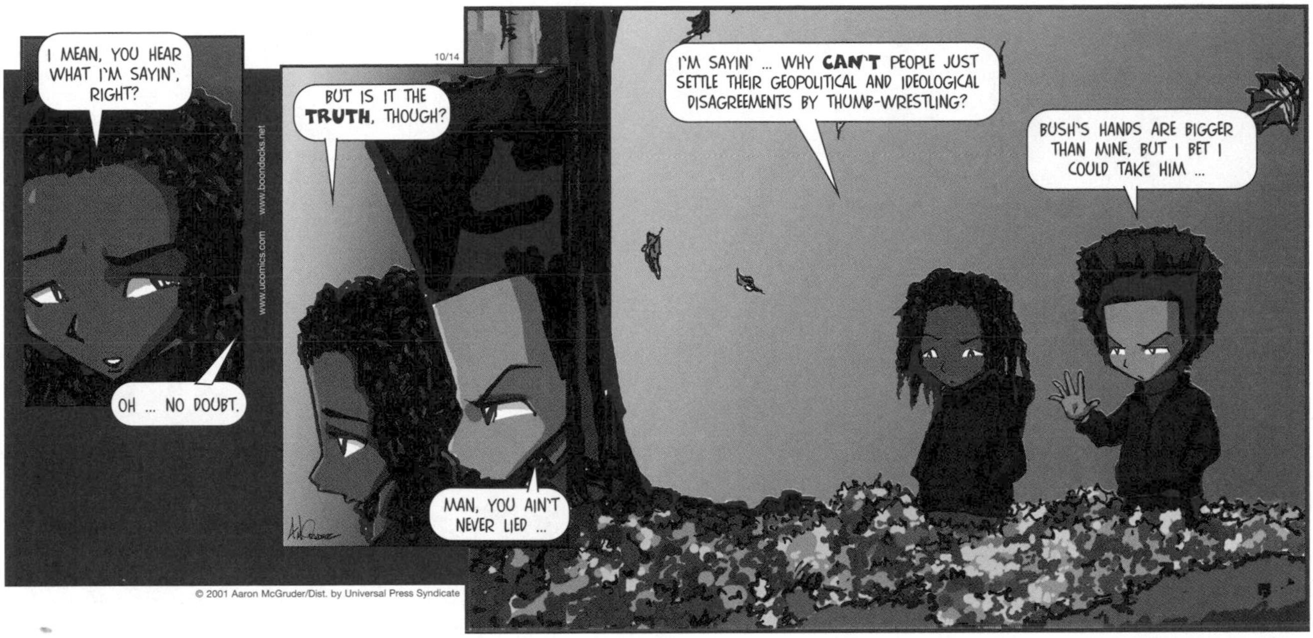
I MEAN, YOU HEAR WHAT I'M SAYIN', RIGHT?
OH ... NO DOUBT.
10/14
BUT IS IT THE TRUTH, THOUGH?
MAN, YOU AIN'T NEVER LIED ...
I'M SAYIN' ... WHY CAN'T PEOPLE JUST SETTLE THEIR GEOPOLITICAL AND IDEOLOGICAL DISAGREEMENTS BY THUMB-WRESTLING?
BUSH'S HANDS ARE BIGGER THAN MINE, BUT I BET I COULD TAKE HIM ...
www.ucomics.com www.boondocks.net
© 2001 Aaron McGruder/Dist. by Universal Press Syndicate

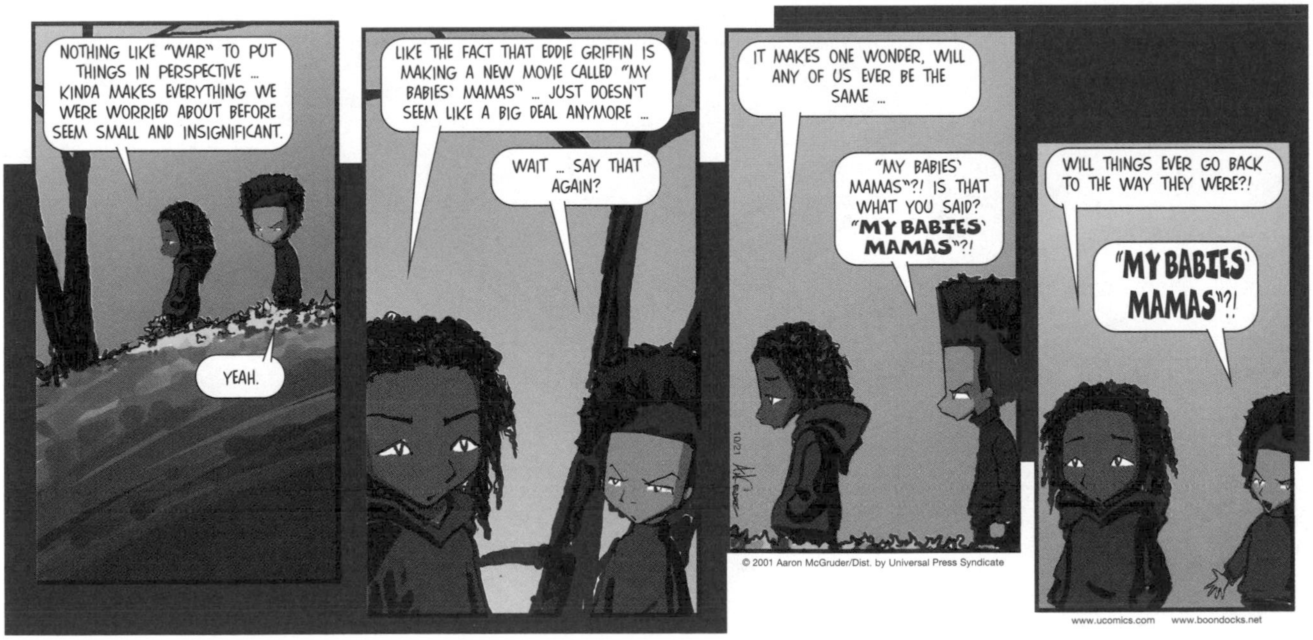
NOTHING LIKE "WAR" TO PUT THINGS IN PERSPECTIVE ... KINDA MAKES EVERYTHING WE WERE WORRIED ABOUT BEFORE SEEM SMALL AND INSIGNIFICANT.
YEAH.
LIKE THE FACT THAT EDDIE GRIFFIN IS MAKING A NEW MOVIE CALLED "MY BABIES' MAMAS" ... JUST DOESN'T SEEM LIKE A BIG DEAL ANYMORE ...
WAIT ... SAY THAT AGAIN?
IT MAKES ONE WONDER, WILL ANY OF US EVER BE THE SAME ...
"MY BABIES' MAMAS"?! IS THAT WHAT YOU SAID? "MY BABIES' MAMAS"?!
10/21
WILL THINGS EVER GO BACK TO THE WAY THEY WERE?!
"MY BABIES' MAMAS"?!
© 2001 Aaron McGruder/Dist. by Universal Press Syndicate
www.ucomics.com www.boondocks.net

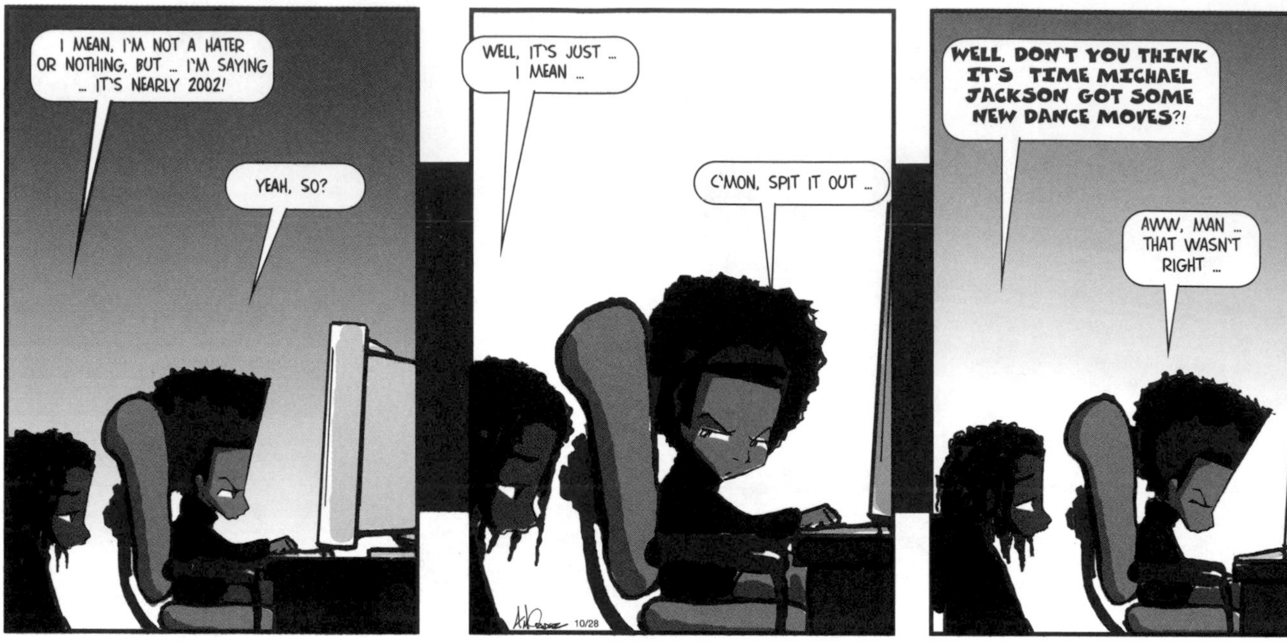
I MEAN, I'M NOT A HATER OR NOTHING, BUT ... I'M SAYING ... IT'S NEARLY 2002!
YEAH, SO?
WELL, IT'S JUST ... I MEAN ...
C'MON, SPIT IT OUT ...
WELL, DON'T YOU THINK IT'S TIME MICHAEL JACKSON GOT SOME NEW DANCE MOVES?!
AWW, MAN ... THAT WASN'T RIGHT ...
10/28

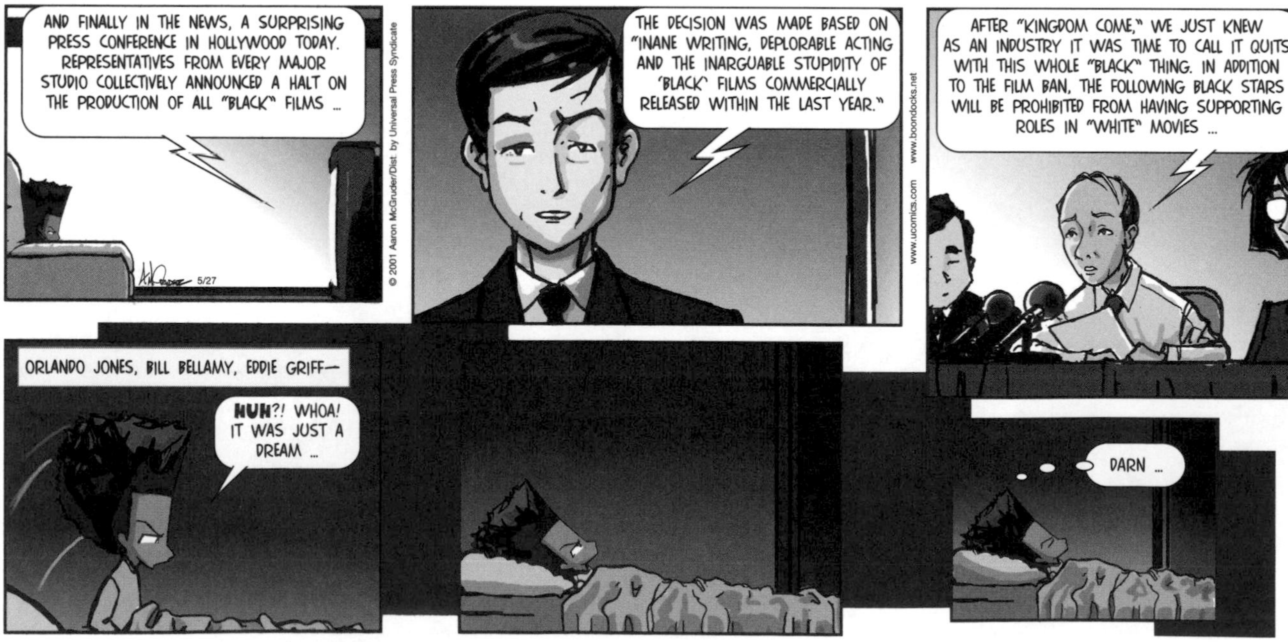
AND FINALLY IN THE NEWS, A SURPRISING PRESS CONFERENCE IN HOLLYWOOD TODAY. REPRESENTATIVES FROM EVERY MAJOR STUDIO COLLECTIVELY ANNOUNCED A HALT ON THE PRODUCTION OF ALL "BLACK" FILMS ...
5/27
© 2001 Aaron McGruder/Dist. by Universal Press Syndicate
THE DECISION WAS MADE BASED ON "INANE WRITING, DEPLORABLE ACTING AND THE INARGUABLE STUPIDITY OF 'BLACK' FILMS COMMERCIALLY RELEASED WITHIN THE LAST YEAR."
www.ucomics.com www.boondocks.net
AFTER "KINGDOM COME," WE JUST KNEW AS AN INDUSTRY IT WAS TIME TO CALL IT QUITS WITH THIS WHOLE "BLACK" THING. IN ADDITION TO THE FILM BAN, THE FOLLOWING BLACK STARS WILL BE PROHIBITED FROM HAVING SUPPORTING ROLES IN "WHITE" MOVIES ...
ORLANDO JONES, BILL BELLAMY, EDDIE GRIFF—
HUH?! WHOA! IT WAS JUST A DREAM ...
DARN ...

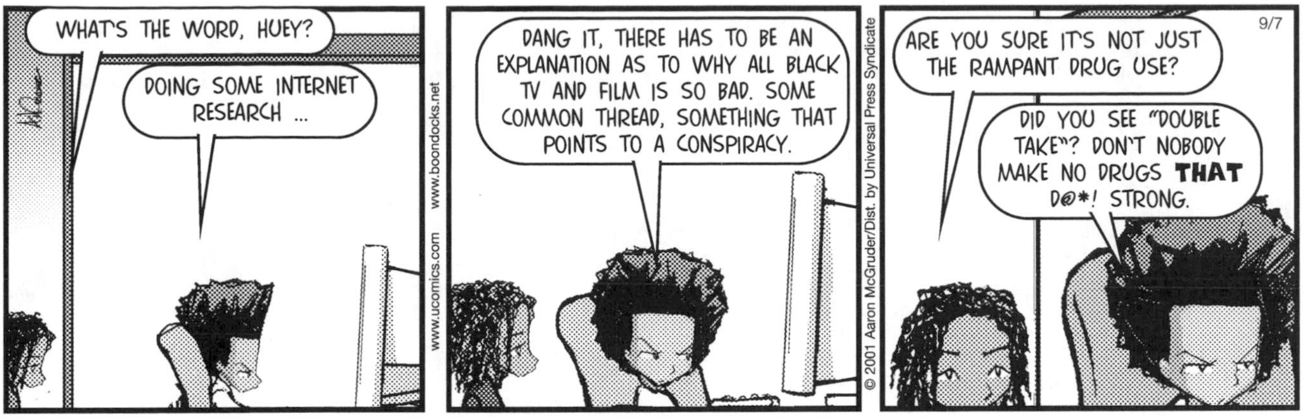
WHAT'S THE WORD, HUEY?
DOING SOME INTERNET RESEARCH ...
www.ucomics.com www.boondocks.net
DANG IT, THERE HAS TO BE AN EXPLANATION AS TO WHY ALL BLACK TV AND FILM IS SO BAD. SOME COMMON THREAD, SOMETHING THAT POINTS TO A CONSPIRACY.
© 2001 Aaron McGruder/Dist. by Universal Press Syndicate
9/7
ARE YOU SURE IT'S NOT JUST THE RAMPANT DRUG USE?
DID YOU SEE "DOUBLE TAKE"? DON'T NOBODY MAKE NO DRUGS **THAT** D@*! STRONG.

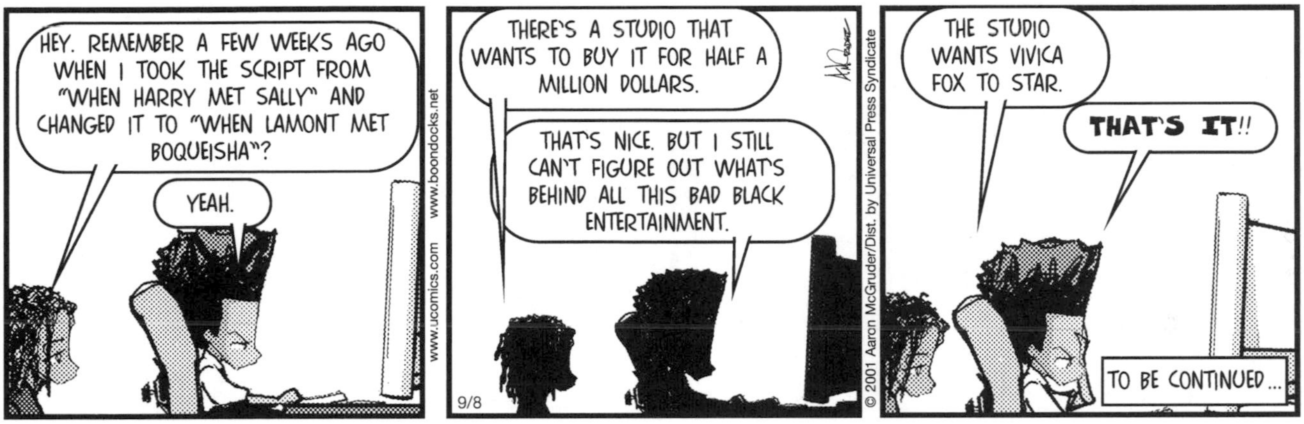
HEY. REMEMBER A FEW WEEKS AGO WHEN I TOOK THE SCRIPT FROM "WHEN HARRY MET SALLY" AND CHANGED IT TO "WHEN LAMONT MET BOQUEISHA"?
YEAH.
www.ucomics.com www.boondocks.net
THERE'S A STUDIO THAT WANTS TO BUY IT FOR HALF A MILLION DOLLARS.
THAT'S NICE. BUT I STILL CAN'T FIGURE OUT WHAT'S BEHIND ALL THIS BAD BLACK ENTERTAINMENT.
9/8
© 2001 Aaron McGruder/Dist. by Universal Press Syndicate
THE STUDIO WANTS VIVICA FOX TO STAR.
THAT'S IT!!
TO BE CONTINUED ...

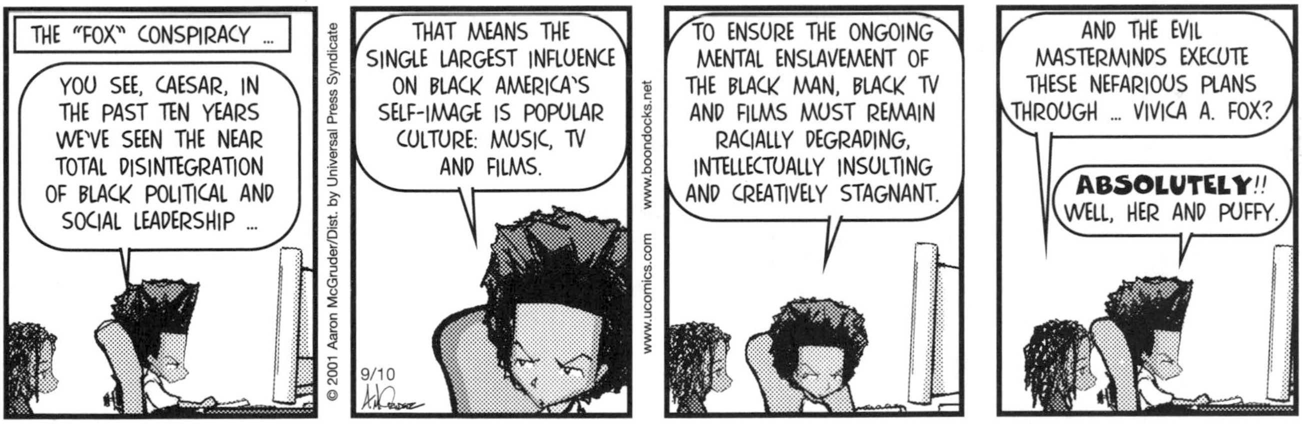
THE "FOX" CONSPIRACY ...
YOU SEE, CAESAR, IN THE PAST TEN YEARS WE'VE SEEN THE NEAR TOTAL DISINTEGRATION OF BLACK POLITICAL AND SOCIAL LEADERSHIP ...
© 2001 Aaron McGruder/Dist. by Universal Press Syndicate
9/10
THAT MEANS THE SINGLE LARGEST INFLUENCE ON BLACK AMERICA'S SELF-IMAGE IS POPULAR CULTURE: MUSIC, TV AND FILMS.
www.ucomics.com www.boondocks.net
TO ENSURE THE ONGOING MENTAL ENSLAVEMENT OF THE BLACK MAN, BLACK TV AND FILMS MUST REMAIN RACIALLY DEGRADING, INTELLECTUALLY INSULTING AND CREATIVELY STAGNANT.
AND THE EVIL MASTERMINDS EXECUTE THESE NEFARIOUS PLANS THROUGH ... VIVICA A. FOX?
ABSOLUTELY!! WELL, HER AND PUFFY.

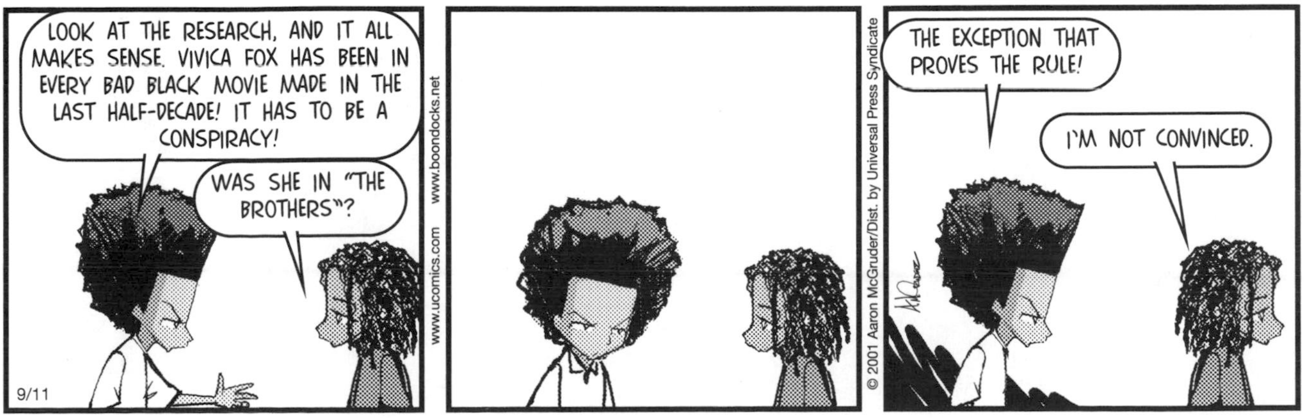
LOOK AT THE RESEARCH, AND IT ALL MAKES SENSE. VIVICA FOX HAS BEEN IN EVERY BAD BLACK MOVIE MADE IN THE LAST HALF-DECADE! IT HAS TO BE A CONSPIRACY!
WAS SHE IN "THE BROTHERS"?
9/11
www.ucomics.com www.boondocks.net
© 2001 Aaron McGruder/Dist. by Universal Press Syndicate
THE EXCEPTION THAT PROVES THE RULE!
I'M NOT CONVINCED.

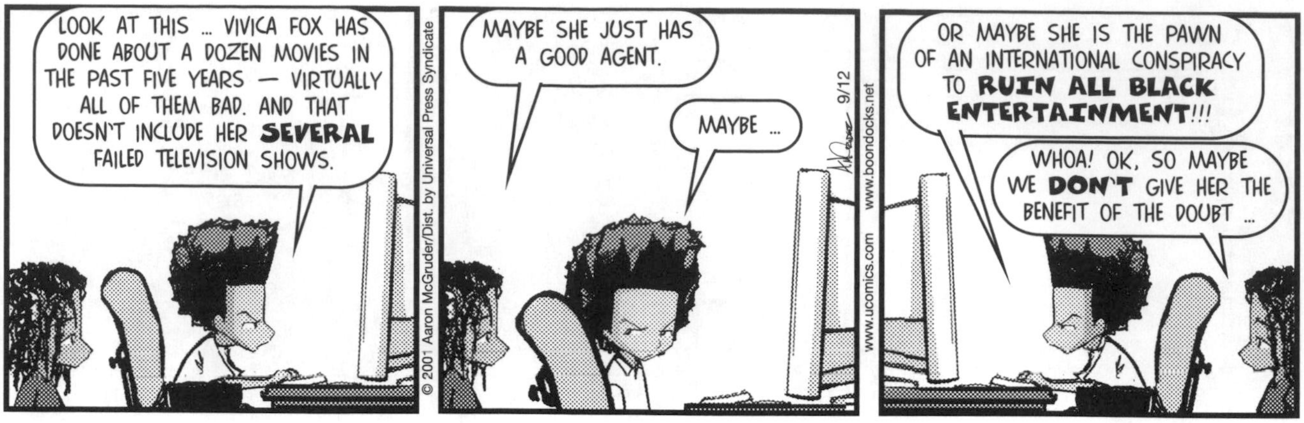
LOOK AT THIS ... VIVICA FOX HAS DONE ABOUT A DOZEN MOVIES IN THE PAST FIVE YEARS — VIRTUALLY ALL OF THEM BAD. AND THAT DOESN'T INCLUDE HER **SEVERAL** FAILED TELEVISION SHOWS.
© 2001 Aaron McGruder/Dist. by Universal Press Syndicate
MAYBE SHE JUST HAS A GOOD AGENT.
MAYBE ...
9/12
www.ucomics.com www.boondocks.net
OR MAYBE SHE IS THE PAWN OF AN INTERNATIONAL CONSPIRACY TO **RUIN ALL BLACK ENTERTAINMENT**!!!
WHOA! OK, SO MAYBE WE **DON'T** GIVE HER THE BENEFIT OF THE DOUBT ...

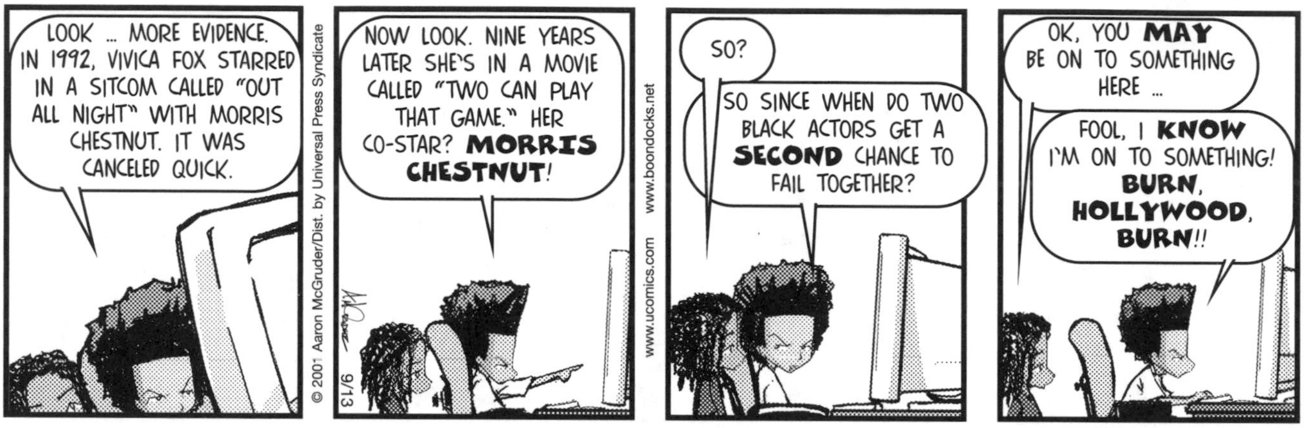
LOOK ... MORE EVIDENCE. IN 1992, VIVICA FOX STARRED IN A SITCOM CALLED "OUT ALL NIGHT" WITH MORRIS CHESTNUT. IT WAS CANCELED QUICK.
© 2001 Aaron McGruder/Dist. by Universal Press Syndicate
NOW LOOK. NINE YEARS LATER SHE'S IN A MOVIE CALLED "TWO CAN PLAY THAT GAME." HER CO-STAR? **MORRIS CHESTNUT**!
9/13
www.ucomics.com www.boondocks.net
SO?
SO SINCE WHEN DO TWO BLACK ACTORS GET A **SECOND** CHANCE TO FAIL TOGETHER?
OK, YOU **MAY** BE ON TO SOMETHING HERE ...
FOOL, I **KNOW** I'M ON TO SOMETHING! **BURN, HOLLYWOOD, BURN**!!

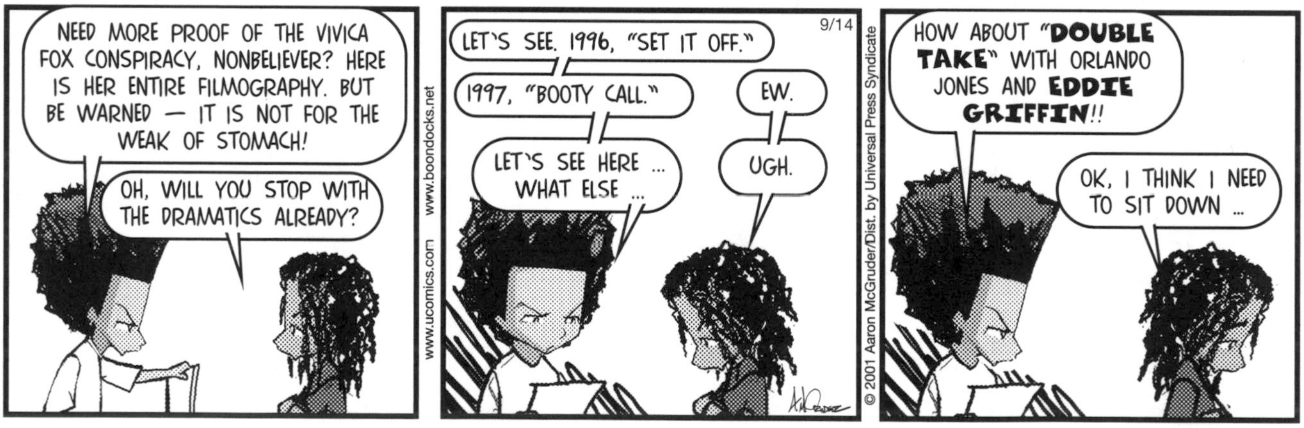
NEED MORE PROOF OF THE VIVICA FOX CONSPIRACY, NONBELIEVER? HERE IS HER ENTIRE FILMOGRAPHY. BUT BE WARNED — IT IS NOT FOR THE WEAK OF STOMACH!
OH, WILL YOU STOP WITH THE DRAMATICS ALREADY?
www.ucomics.com www.boondocks.net
LET'S SEE. 1996, "SET IT OFF."
1997, "BOOTY CALL."
EW.
LET'S SEE HERE ... WHAT ELSE ...
UGH.
9/14
© 2001 Aaron McGruder/Dist. by Universal Press Syndicate
HOW ABOUT "**DOUBLE TAKE**" WITH ORLANDO JONES AND **EDDIE GRIFFIN**!!
OK, I THINK I NEED TO SIT DOWN ...

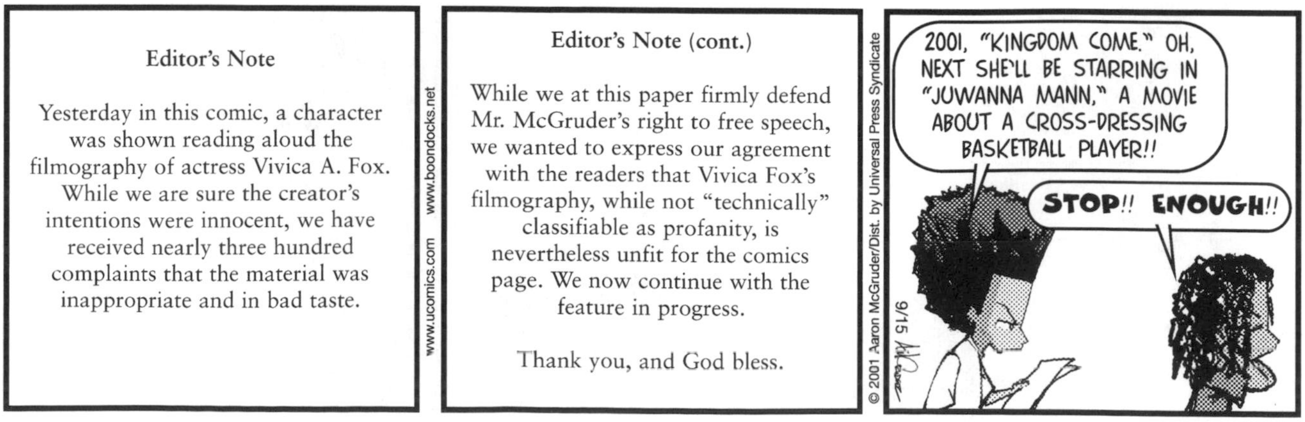
Editor's Note
Yesterday in this comic, a character was shown reading aloud the filmography of actress Vivica A. Fox. While we are sure the creator's intentions were innocent, we have received nearly three hundred complaints that the material was inappropriate and in bad taste.
www.ucomics.com www.boondocks.net
Editor's Note (cont.)
While we at this paper firmly defend Mr. McGruder's right to free speech, we wanted to express our agreement with the readers that Vivica Fox's filmography, while not "technically" classifiable as profanity, is nevertheless unfit for the comics page. We now continue with the feature in progress.
Thank you, and God bless.
© 2001 Aaron McGruder/Dist. by Universal Press Syndicate
9/15
2001, "KINGDOM COME." OH, NEXT SHE'LL BE STARRING IN "JUWANNA MANN," A MOVIE ABOUT A CROSS-DRESSING BASKETBALL PLAYER!!
STOP!! **ENOUGH**!!

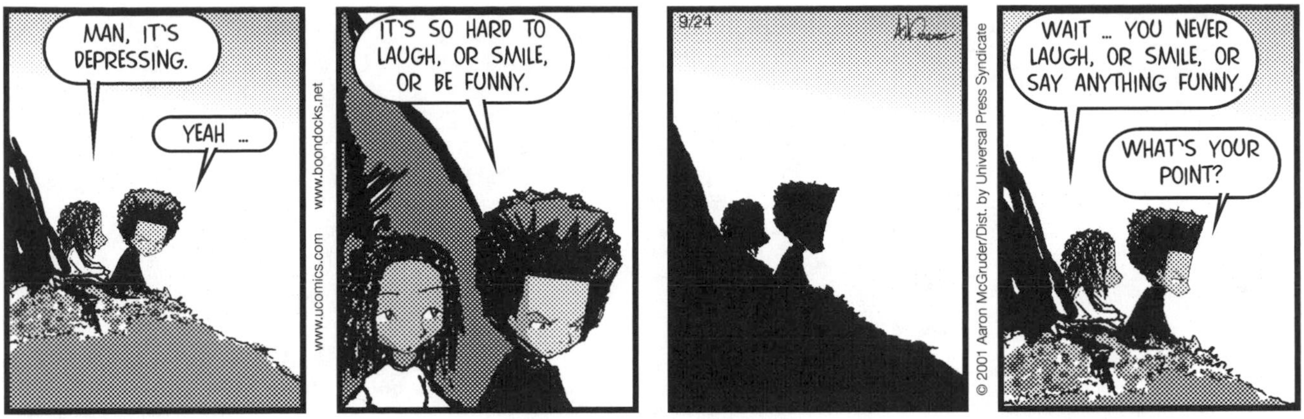
MAN, IT'S DEPRESSING.
YEAH ...
IT'S SO HARD TO LAUGH, OR SMILE, OR BE FUNNY.
9/24
WAIT ... YOU NEVER LAUGH, OR SMILE, OR SAY ANYTHING FUNNY.
WHAT'S YOUR POINT?
www.ucomics.com www.boondocks.net
© 2001 Aaron McGruder/Dist. by Universal Press Syndicate

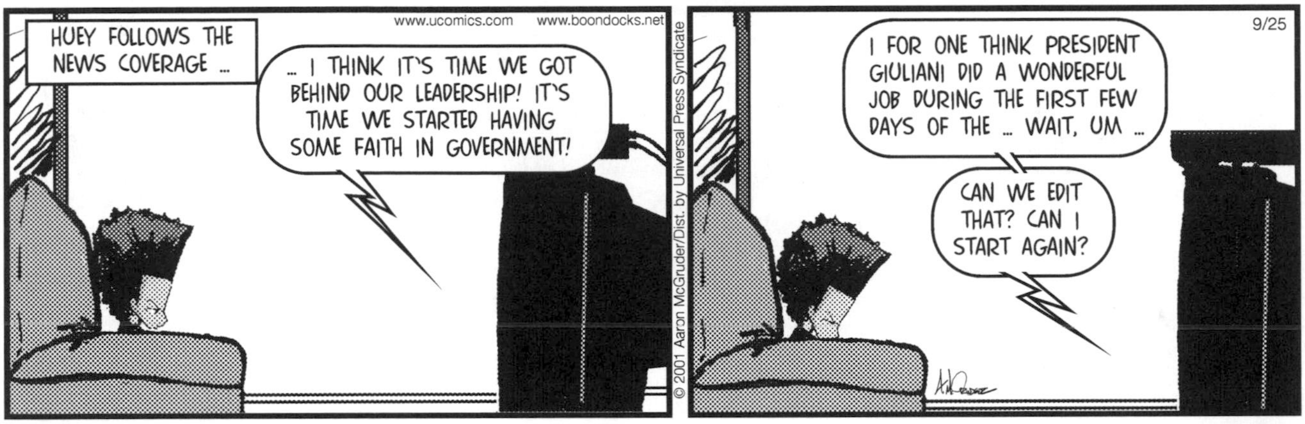
HUEY FOLLOWS THE NEWS COVERAGE ...
... I THINK IT'S TIME WE GOT BEHIND OUR LEADERSHIP! IT'S TIME WE STARTED HAVING SOME FAITH IN GOVERNMENT!
9/25
I FOR ONE THINK PRESIDENT GIULIANI DID A WONDERFUL JOB DURING THE FIRST FEW DAYS OF THE ... WAIT, UM ...
CAN WE EDIT THAT? CAN I START AGAIN?
www.ucomics.com www.boondocks.net
© 2001 Aaron McGruder/Dist. by Universal Press Syndicate

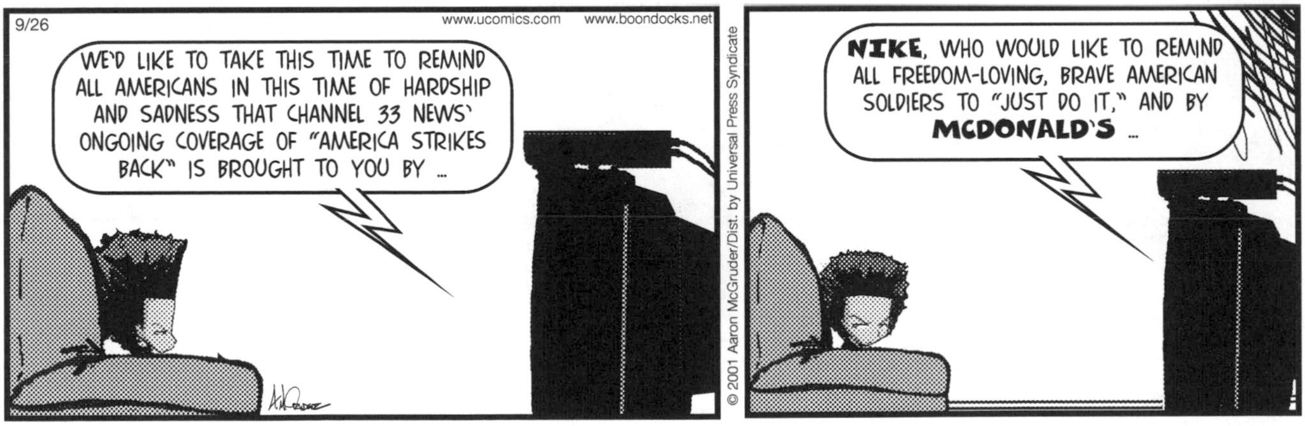
9/26
WE'D LIKE TO TAKE THIS TIME TO REMIND ALL AMERICANS IN THIS TIME OF HARDSHIP AND SADNESS THAT CHANNEL 33 NEWS' ONGOING COVERAGE OF "AMERICA STRIKES BACK" IS BROUGHT TO YOU BY ...
NIKE, WHO WOULD LIKE TO REMIND ALL FREEDOM-LOVING, BRAVE AMERICAN SOLDIERS TO "JUST DO IT," AND BY MCDONALD'S ...
www.ucomics.com www.boondocks.net
© 2001 Aaron McGruder/Dist. by Universal Press Syndicate

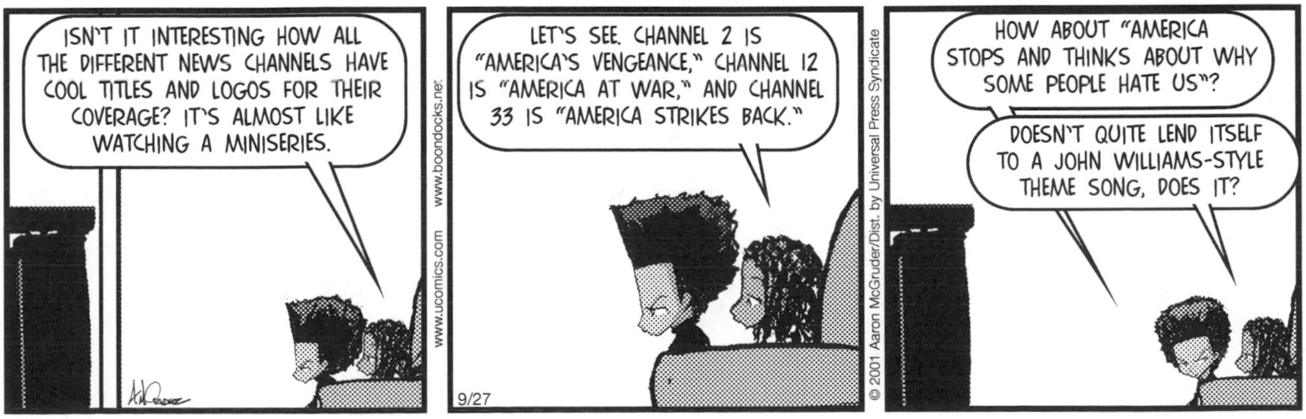
ISN'T IT INTERESTING HOW ALL THE DIFFERENT NEWS CHANNELS HAVE COOL TITLES AND LOGOS FOR THEIR COVERAGE? IT'S ALMOST LIKE WATCHING A MINISERIES.
LET'S SEE. CHANNEL 2 IS "AMERICA'S VENGEANCE," CHANNEL 12 IS "AMERICA AT WAR," AND CHANNEL 33 IS "AMERICA STRIKES BACK."
9/27
HOW ABOUT "AMERICA STOPS AND THINKS ABOUT WHY SOME PEOPLE HATE US"?
DOESN'T QUITE LEND ITSELF TO A JOHN WILLIAMS-STYLE THEME SONG, DOES IT?
www.ucomics.com www.boondocks.net
© 2001 Aaron McGruder/Dist. by Universal Press Syndicate

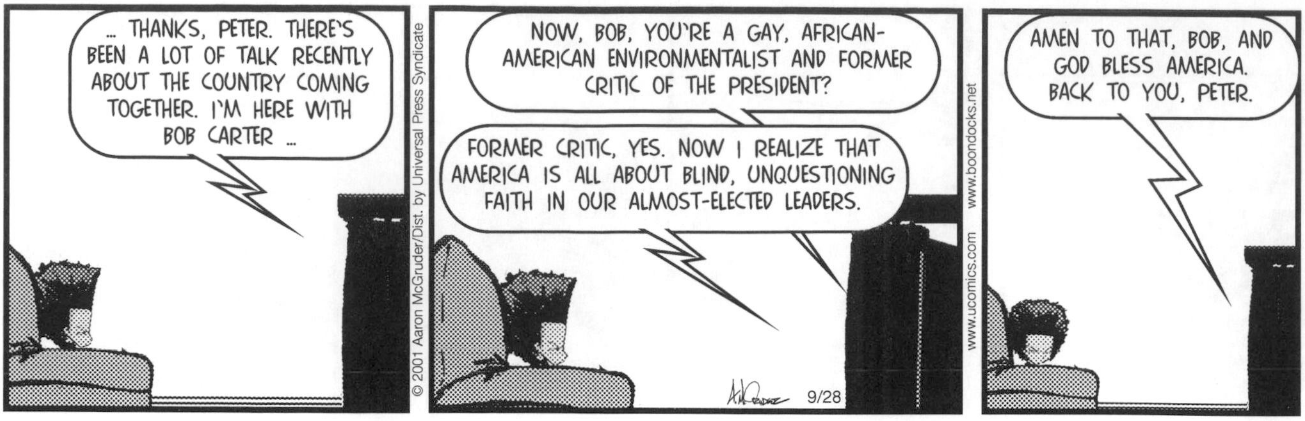
... THANKS, PETER. THERE'S BEEN A LOT OF TALK RECENTLY ABOUT THE COUNTRY COMING TOGETHER. I'M HERE WITH BOB CARTER ...
© 2001 Aaron McGruder/Dist. by Universal Press Syndicate
NOW, BOB, YOU'RE A GAY, AFRICAN-AMERICAN ENVIRONMENTALIST AND FORMER CRITIC OF THE PRESIDENT?
FORMER CRITIC, YES. NOW I REALIZE THAT AMERICA IS ALL ABOUT BLIND, UNQUESTIONING FAITH IN OUR ALMOST-ELECTED LEADERS.
9/28
www.ucomics.com www.boondocks.net
AMEN TO THAT, BOB, AND GOD BLESS AMERICA. BACK TO YOU, PETER.

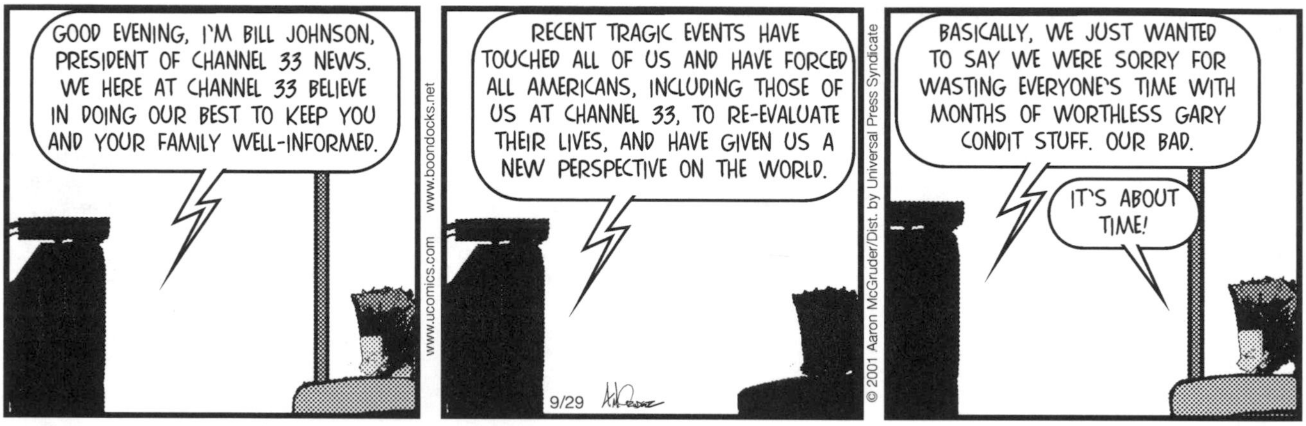
GOOD EVENING, I'M BILL JOHNSON, PRESIDENT OF CHANNEL 33 NEWS. WE HERE AT CHANNEL 33 BELIEVE IN DOING OUR BEST TO KEEP YOU AND YOUR FAMILY WELL-INFORMED.
www.ucomics.com www.boondocks.net
RECENT TRAGIC EVENTS HAVE TOUCHED ALL OF US AND HAVE FORCED ALL AMERICANS, INCLUDING THOSE OF US AT CHANNEL 33, TO RE-EVALUATE THEIR LIVES, AND HAVE GIVEN US A NEW PERSPECTIVE ON THE WORLD.
9/29
© 2001 Aaron McGruder/Dist. by Universal Press Syndicate
BASICALLY, WE JUST WANTED TO SAY WE WERE SORRY FOR WASTING EVERYONE'S TIME WITH MONTHS OF WORTHLESS GARY CONDIT STUFF. OUR BAD.
IT'S ABOUT TIME!

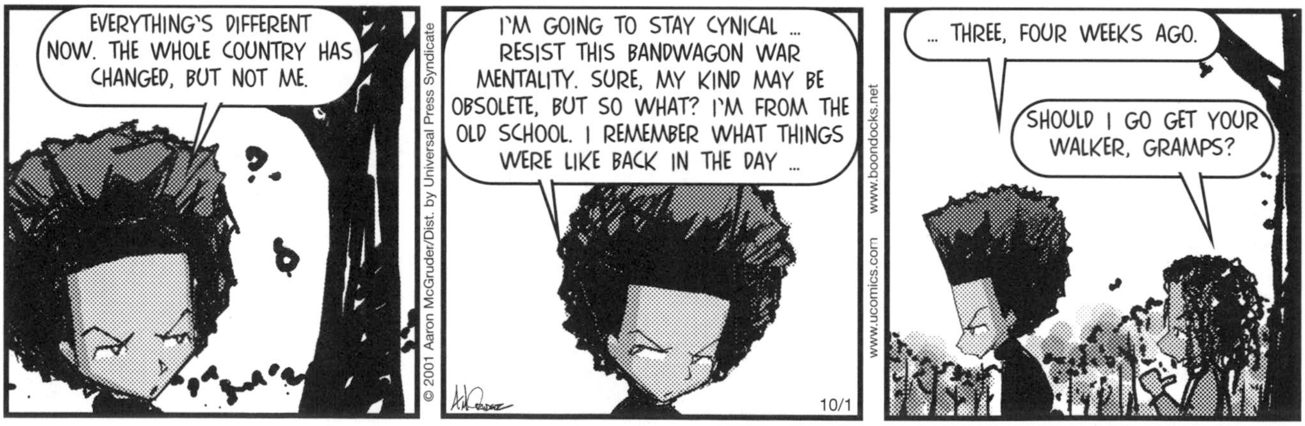
EVERYTHING'S DIFFERENT NOW. THE WHOLE COUNTRY HAS CHANGED, BUT NOT ME.
© 2001 Aaron McGruder/Dist. by Universal Press Syndicate
I'M GOING TO STAY CYNICAL ... RESIST THIS BANDWAGON WAR MENTALITY. SURE, MY KIND MAY BE OBSOLETE, BUT SO WHAT? I'M FROM THE OLD SCHOOL. I REMEMBER WHAT THINGS WERE LIKE BACK IN THE DAY ...
10/1
www.ucomics.com www.boondocks.net
... THREE, FOUR WEEKS AGO.
SHOULD I GO GET YOUR WALKER, GRAMPS?

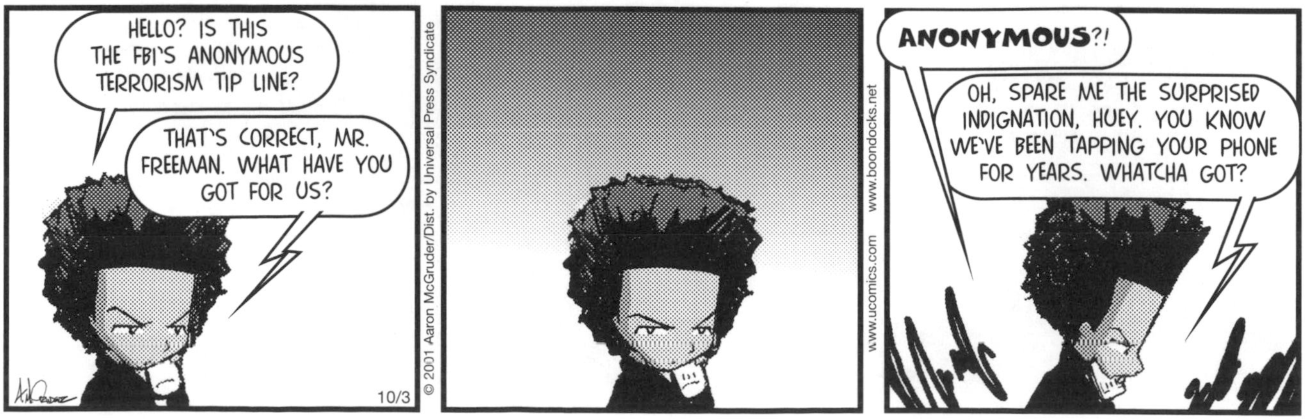
HELLO? IS THIS THE FBI'S ANONYMOUS TERRORISM TIP LINE?
THAT'S CORRECT, MR. FREEMAN. WHAT HAVE YOU GOT FOR US?
10/3
© 2001 Aaron McGruder/Dist. by Universal Press Syndicate
www.ucomics.com www.boondocks.net
ANONYMOUS?!
OH, SPARE ME THE SURPRISED INDIGNATION, HUEY. YOU KNOW WE'VE BEEN TAPPING YOUR PHONE FOR YEARS. WHATCHA GOT?

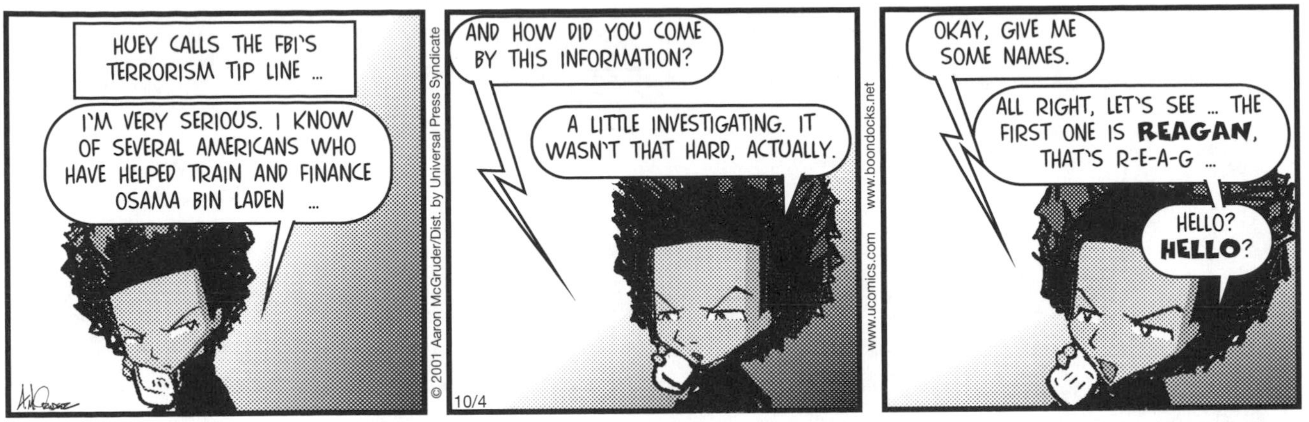
HUEY CALLS THE FBI'S TERRORISM TIP LINE ...
I'M VERY SERIOUS. I KNOW OF SEVERAL AMERICANS WHO HAVE HELPED TRAIN AND FINANCE OSAMA BIN LADEN ...
© 2001 Aaron McGruder/Dist. by Universal Press Syndicate
10/4
AND HOW DID YOU COME BY THIS INFORMATION?
A LITTLE INVESTIGATING. IT WASN'T THAT HARD, ACTUALLY.
www.ucomics.com www.boondocks.net
OKAY, GIVE ME SOME NAMES.
ALL RIGHT, LET'S SEE ... THE FIRST ONE IS **REAGAN**, THAT'S R-E-A-G ...
HELLO? **HELLO**?

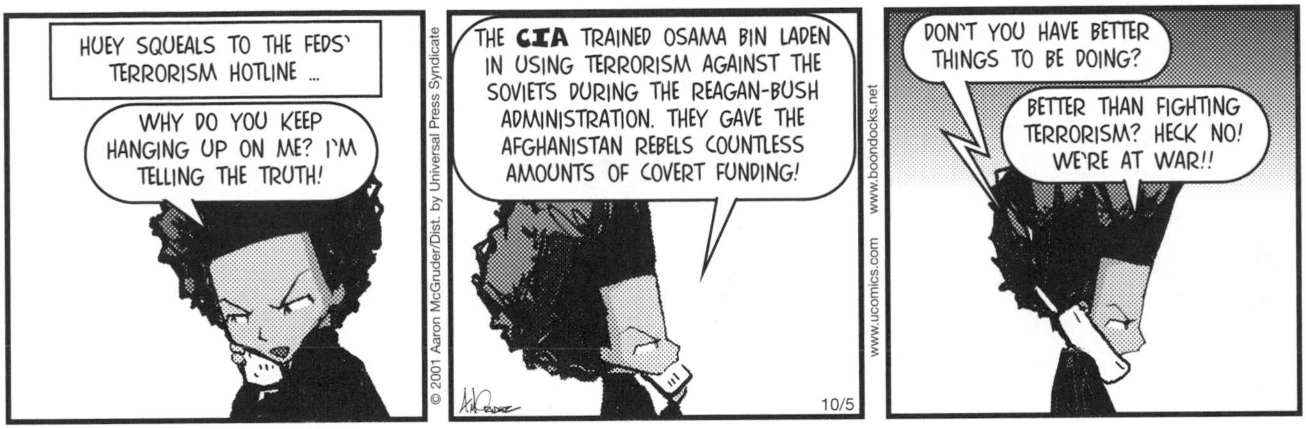
HUEY SQUEALS TO THE FEDS' TERRORISM HOTLINE ...
WHY DO YOU KEEP HANGING UP ON ME? I'M TELLING THE TRUTH!
© 2001 Aaron McGruder/Dist. by Universal Press Syndicate
THE **CIA** TRAINED OSAMA BIN LADEN IN USING TERRORISM AGAINST THE SOVIETS DURING THE REAGAN-BUSH ADMINISTRATION. THEY GAVE THE AFGHANISTAN REBELS COUNTLESS AMOUNTS OF COVERT FUNDING!
10/5
www.ucomics.com www.boondocks.net
DON'T YOU HAVE BETTER THINGS TO BE DOING?
BETTER THAN FIGHTING TERRORISM? HECK NO! WE'RE AT WAR!!

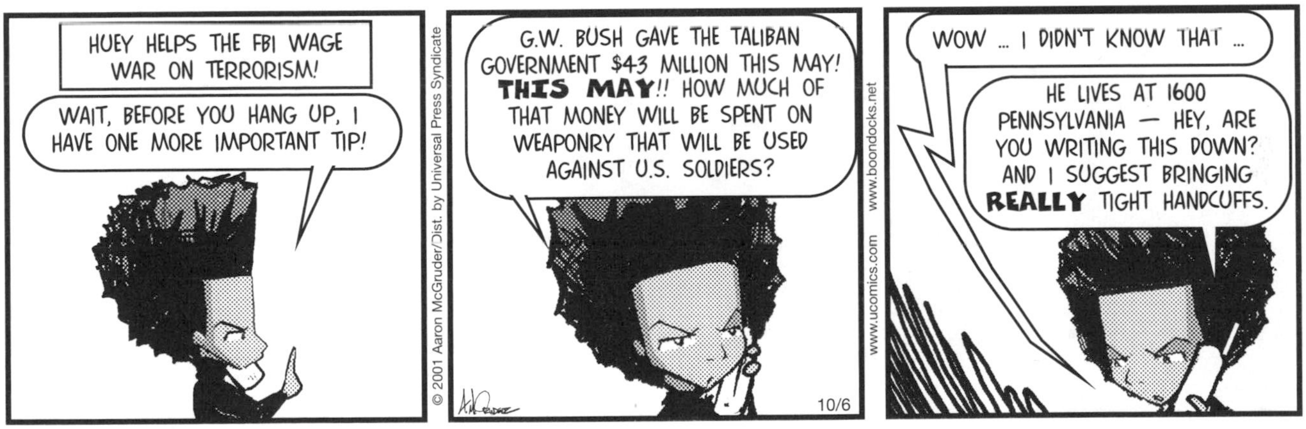
HUEY HELPS THE FBI WAGE WAR ON TERRORISM!
WAIT, BEFORE YOU HANG UP, I HAVE ONE MORE IMPORTANT TIP!
© 2001 Aaron McGruder/Dist. by Universal Press Syndicate
G.W. BUSH GAVE THE TALIBAN GOVERNMENT $43 MILLION THIS MAY! **THIS MAY**!! HOW MUCH OF THAT MONEY WILL BE SPENT ON WEAPONRY THAT WILL BE USED AGAINST U.S. SOLDIERS?
10/6
www.ucomics.com www.boondocks.net
WOW ... I DIDN'T KNOW THAT ...
HE LIVES AT 1600 PENNSYLVANIA — HEY, ARE YOU WRITING THIS DOWN? AND I SUGGEST BRINGING **REALLY** TIGHT HANDCUFFS.

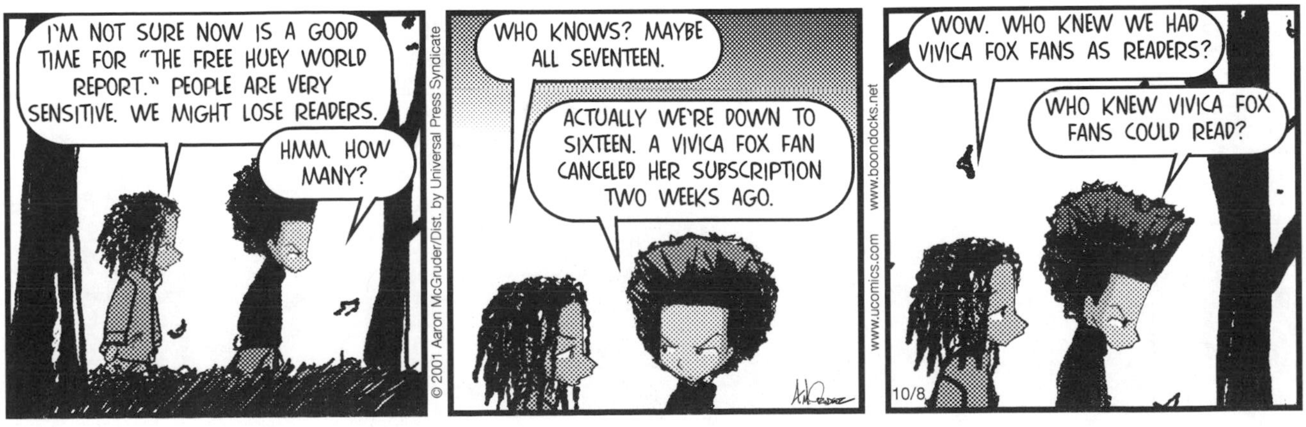
I'M NOT SURE NOW IS A GOOD TIME FOR "THE FREE HUEY WORLD REPORT." PEOPLE ARE VERY SENSITIVE. WE MIGHT LOSE READERS.
HMM. HOW MANY?
© 2001 Aaron McGruder/Dist. by Universal Press Syndicate
WHO KNOWS? MAYBE ALL SEVENTEEN.
ACTUALLY WE'RE DOWN TO SIXTEEN. A VIVICA FOX FAN CANCELED HER SUBSCRIPTION TWO WEEKS AGO.
www.ucomics.com www.boondocks.net
WOW. WHO KNEW WE HAD VIVICA FOX FANS AS READERS?
WHO KNEW VIVICA FOX FANS COULD READ?
10/8

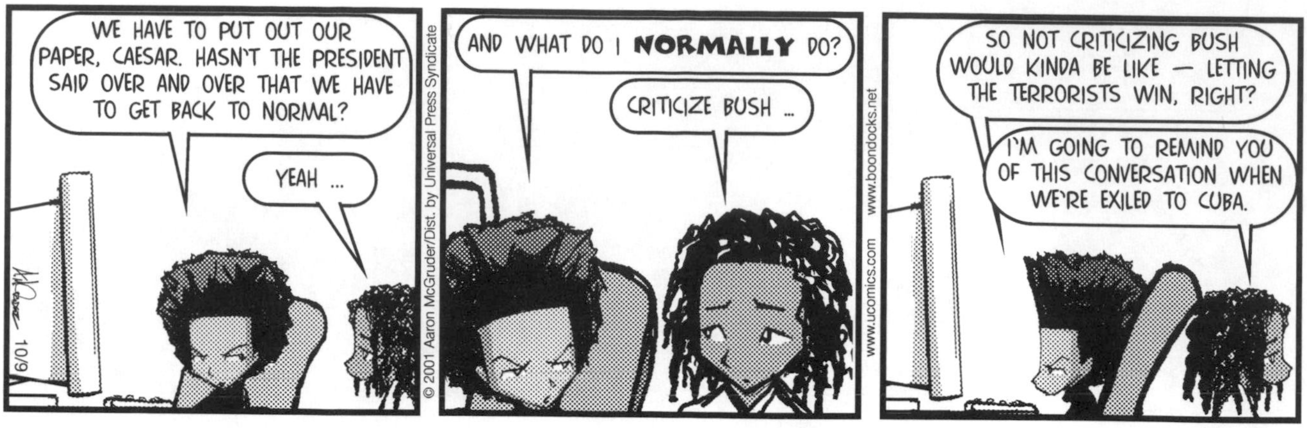
WE HAVE TO PUT OUT OUR PAPER, CAESAR. HASN'T THE PRESIDENT SAID OVER AND OVER THAT WE HAVE TO GET BACK TO NORMAL?
YEAH ...
10/9
© 2001 Aaron McGruder/Dist. by Universal Press Syndicate
AND WHAT DO I **NORMALLY** DO?
CRITICIZE BUSH ...
www.ucomics.com www.boondocks.net
SO NOT CRITICIZING BUSH WOULD KINDA BE LIKE — LETTING THE TERRORISTS WIN, RIGHT?
I'M GOING TO REMIND YOU OF THIS CONVERSATION WHEN WE'RE EXILED TO CUBA.

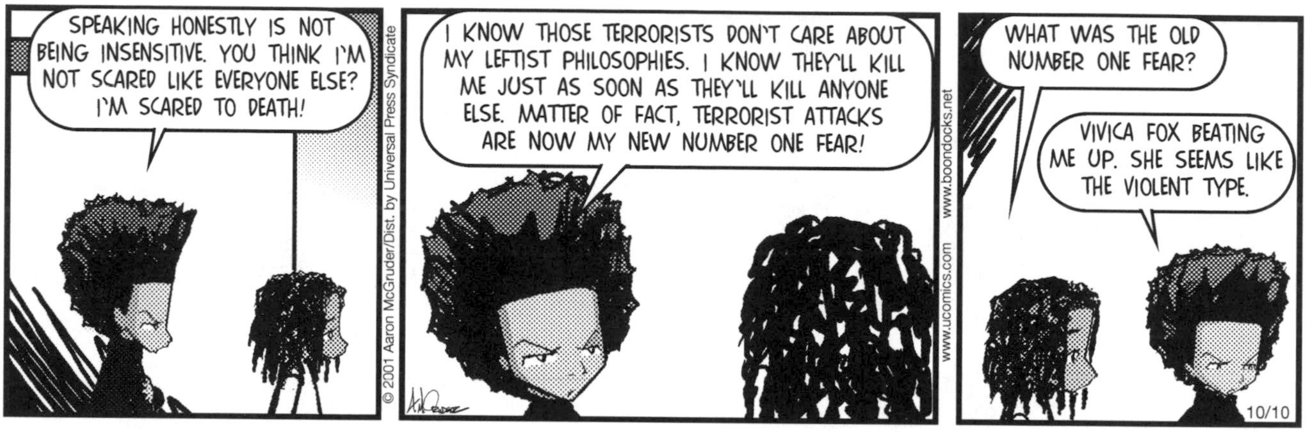
SPEAKING HONESTLY IS NOT BEING INSENSITIVE. YOU THINK I'M NOT SCARED LIKE EVERYONE ELSE? I'M SCARED TO DEATH!
© 2001 Aaron McGruder/Dist. by Universal Press Syndicate
I KNOW THOSE TERRORISTS DON'T CARE ABOUT MY LEFTIST PHILOSOPHIES. I KNOW THEY'LL KILL ME JUST AS SOON AS THEY'LL KILL ANYONE ELSE. MATTER OF FACT, TERRORIST ATTACKS ARE NOW MY NEW NUMBER ONE FEAR!
www.ucomics.com www.boondocks.net
WHAT WAS THE OLD NUMBER ONE FEAR?
VIVICA FOX BEATING ME UP. SHE SEEMS LIKE THE VIOLENT TYPE.
10/10

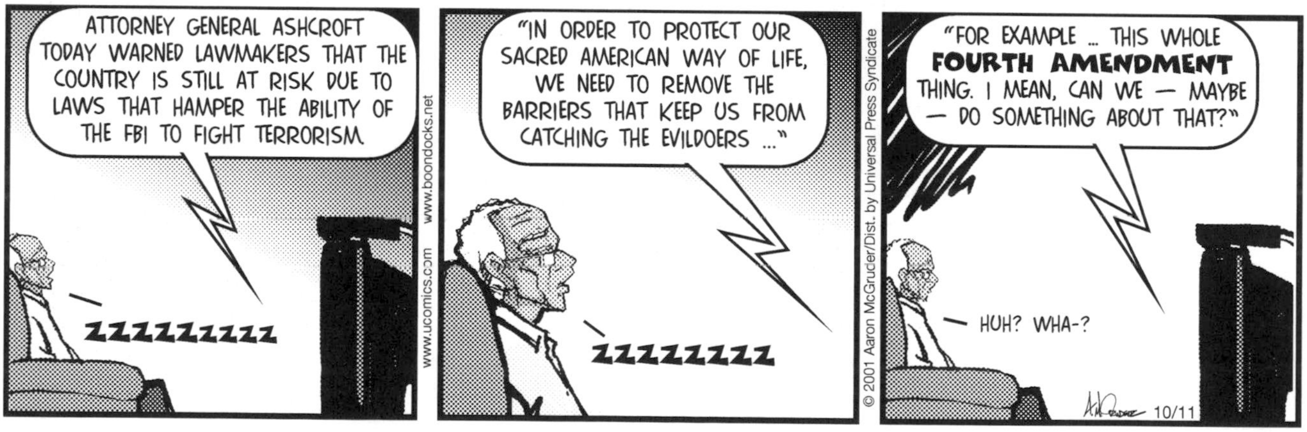
ATTORNEY GENERAL ASHCROFT TODAY WARNED LAWMAKERS THAT THE COUNTRY IS STILL AT RISK DUE TO LAWS THAT HAMPER THE ABILITY OF THE FBI TO FIGHT TERRORISM.
ZZZZZZZZZ
www.ucomics.com www.boondocks.net
"IN ORDER TO PROTECT OUR SACRED AMERICAN WAY OF LIFE, WE NEED TO REMOVE THE BARRIERS THAT KEEP US FROM CATCHING THE EVILDOERS ..."
ZZZZZZZZ
© 2001 Aaron McGruder/Dist. by Universal Press Syndicate
"FOR EXAMPLE ... THIS WHOLE **FOURTH AMENDMENT** THING. I MEAN, CAN WE — MAYBE — DO SOMETHING ABOUT THAT?"
HUH? WHA-?
10/11

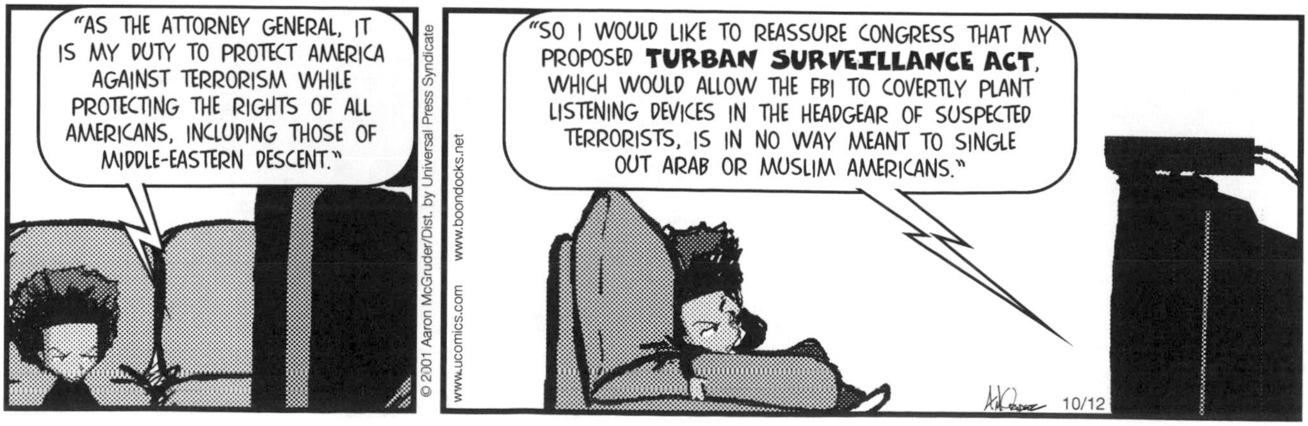
"AS THE ATTORNEY GENERAL, IT IS MY DUTY TO PROTECT AMERICA AGAINST TERRORISM WHILE PROTECTING THE RIGHTS OF ALL AMERICANS, INCLUDING THOSE OF MIDDLE-EASTERN DESCENT."
© 2001 Aaron McGruder/Dist. by Universal Press Syndicate
www.ucomics.com www.boondocks.net
"SO I WOULD LIKE TO REASSURE CONGRESS THAT MY PROPOSED **TURBAN SURVEILLANCE ACT**, WHICH WOULD ALLOW THE FBI TO COVERTLY PLANT LISTENING DEVICES IN THE HEADGEAR OF SUSPECTED TERRORISTS, IS IN NO WAY MEANT TO SINGLE OUT ARAB OR MUSLIM AMERICANS."
10/12

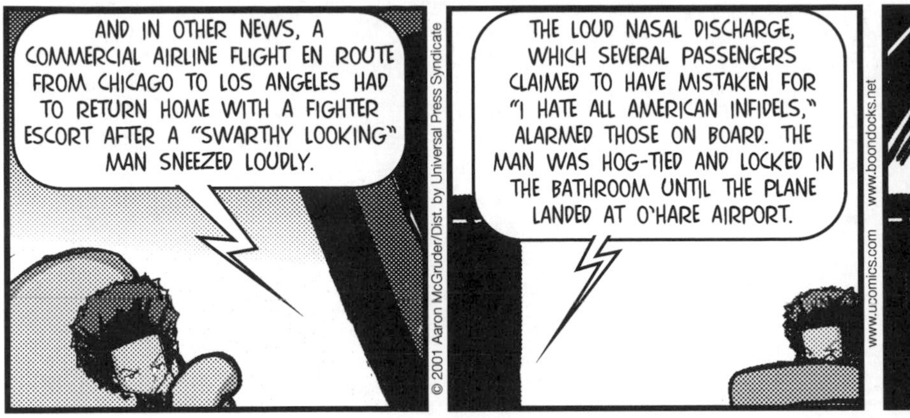
AND IN OTHER NEWS, A COMMERCIAL AIRLINE FLIGHT EN ROUTE FROM CHICAGO TO LOS ANGELES HAD TO RETURN HOME WITH A FIGHTER ESCORT AFTER A "SWARTHY LOOKING" MAN SNEEZED LOUDLY.
© 2001 Aaron McGruder/Dist. by Universal Press Syndicate
THE LOUD NASAL DISCHARGE, WHICH SEVERAL PASSENGERS CLAIMED TO HAVE MISTAKEN FOR "I HATE ALL AMERICAN INFIDELS," ALARMED THOSE ON BOARD. THE MAN WAS HOG-TIED AND LOCKED IN THE BATHROOM UNTIL THE PLANE LANDED AT O'HARE AIRPORT.
www.ucomics.com www.boondocks.net
HE WAS RELEASED SEVEN HOURS LATER AND GIVEN 1,000 BONUS MILES FOR HIS INCONVENIENCE.
10/13

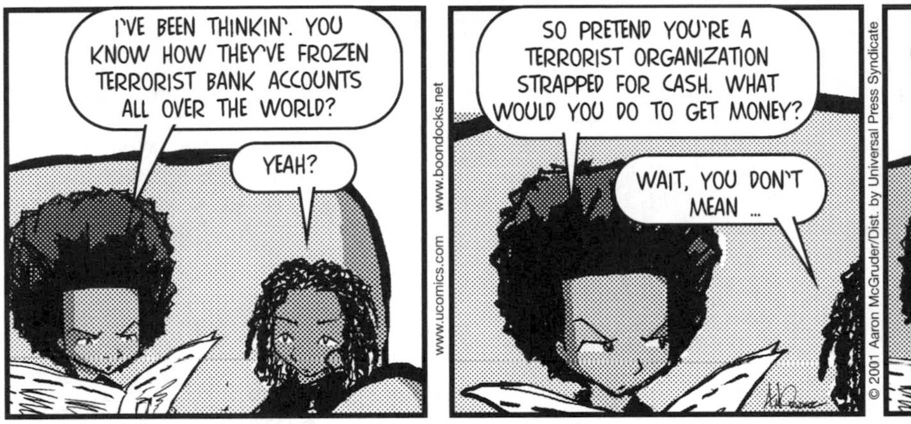
I'VE BEEN THINKIN'. YOU KNOW HOW THEY'VE FROZEN TERRORIST BANK ACCOUNTS ALL OVER THE WORLD?
YEAH?
www.ucomics.com www.boondocks.net
SO PRETEND YOU'RE A TERRORIST ORGANIZATION STRAPPED FOR CASH. WHAT WOULD YOU DO TO GET MONEY?
WAIT, YOU DON'T MEAN ...
© 2001 Aaron McGruder/Dist. by Universal Press Syndicate
YEP. JUST WHO **IS** MAKING ALL THESE AMERICAN FLAGS, HUH?
YOU KNOW, I'M ACTUALLY STARTING TO THINK IT'S DANGEROUS TO KNOW YOU.
10/15

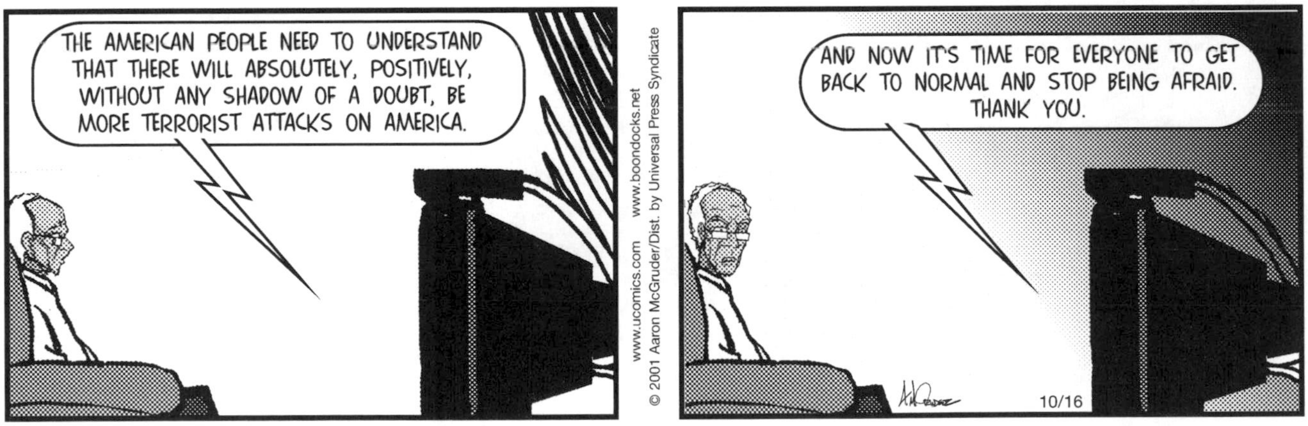
THE AMERICAN PEOPLE NEED TO UNDERSTAND THAT THERE WILL ABSOLUTELY, POSITIVELY, WITHOUT ANY SHADOW OF A DOUBT, BE MORE TERRORIST ATTACKS ON AMERICA.
© 2001 Aaron McGruder/Dist. by Universal Press Syndicate
www.ucomics.com www.boondocks.net
AND NOW IT'S TIME FOR EVERYONE TO GET BACK TO NORMAL AND STOP BEING AFRAID. THANK YOU.
10/16

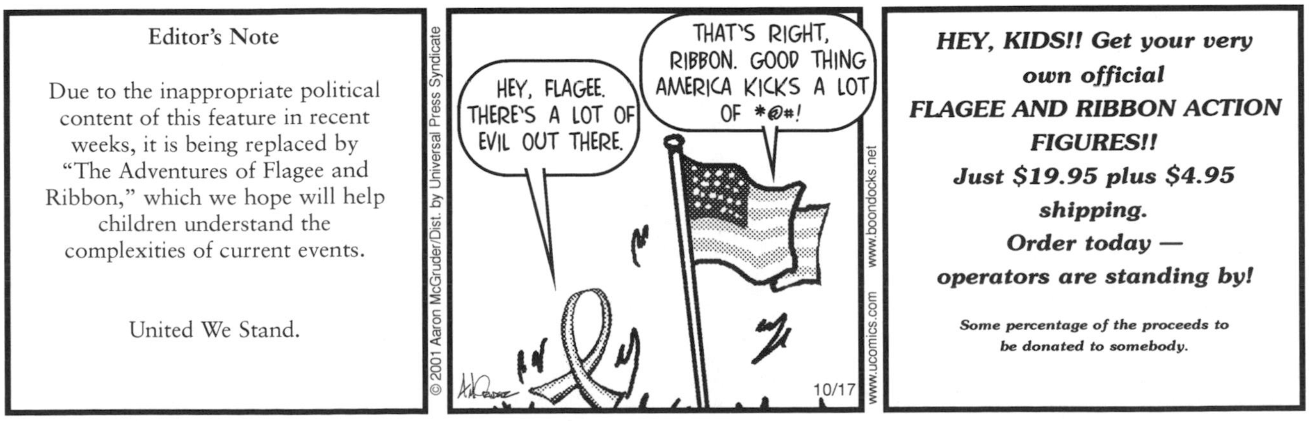
Editor's Note
Due to the inappropriate political content of this feature in recent weeks, it is being replaced by "The Adventures of Flagee and Ribbon," which we hope will help children understand the complexities of current events.
United We Stand.
© 2001 Aaron McGruder/Dist. by Universal Press Syndicate
HEY, FLAGEE. THERE'S A LOT OF EVIL OUT THERE.
THAT'S RIGHT, RIBBON. GOOD THING AMERICA KICKS A LOT OF *@#!
10/17
www.ucomics.com www.boondocks.net
HEY, KIDS!! Get your very own official FLAGEE AND RIBBON ACTION FIGURES!! Just $19.95 plus $4.95 shipping. Order today — operators are standing by!
Some percentage of the proceeds to be donated to somebody.

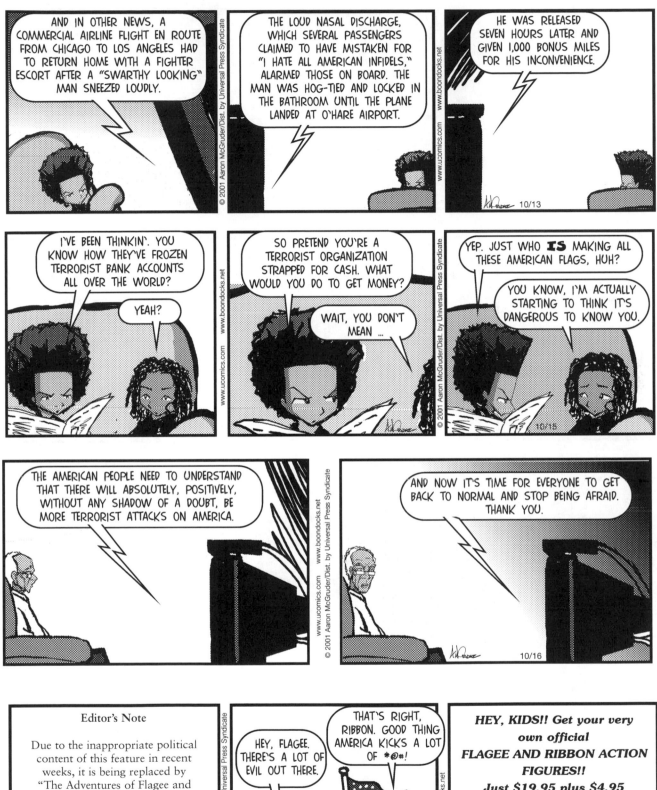

Editor's Note

"The Boondocks" is being replaced this week with "The Adventures of Flagee and Ribbon," a hilariously patriotic new offering.

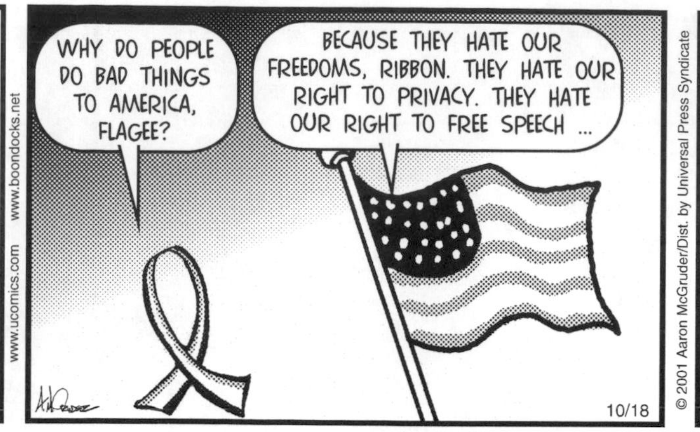

WHY DO PEOPLE DO BAD THINGS TO AMERICA, FLAGEE?
BECAUSE THEY HATE OUR FREEDOMS, RIBBON. THEY HATE OUR RIGHT TO PRIVACY. THEY HATE OUR RIGHT TO FREE SPEECH ...
10/18
www.ucomics.com www.boondocks.net
© 2001 Aaron McGruder/Dist. by Universal Press Syndicate

Editor's Note (Cont.)

Those of you who have written demanding the return of "The Boondocks," your names have been forwarded to the FBI.

Editor's Note

For the select few who are not daily readers of the comics, "The Boondocks" has been indefinitely replaced by the uproarious fun of "The Adventures of Flagee and Ribbon."

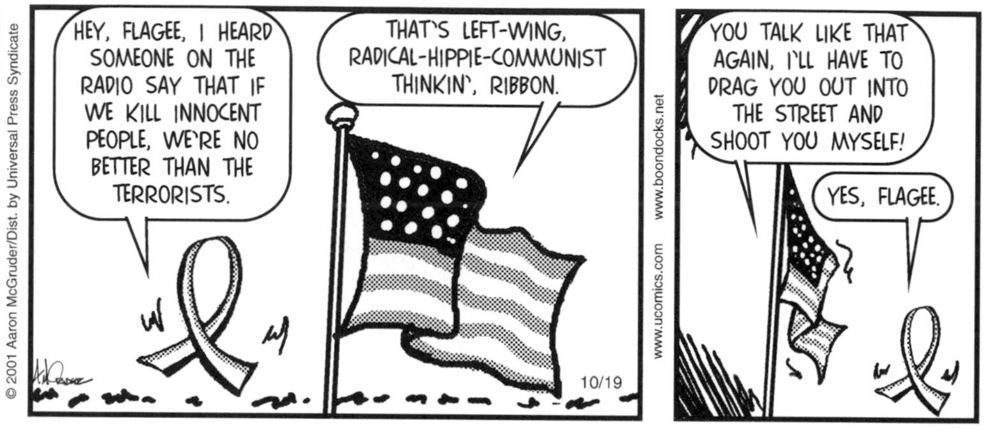

© 2001 Aaron McGruder/Dist. by Universal Press Syndicate
HEY, FLAGEE, I HEARD SOMEONE ON THE RADIO SAY THAT IF WE KILL INNOCENT PEOPLE, WE'RE NO BETTER THAN THE TERRORISTS.
THAT'S LEFT-WING, RADICAL-HIPPIE-COMMUNIST THINKIN', RIBBON.
10/19
www.ucomics.com www.boondocks.net
YOU TALK LIKE THAT AGAIN, I'LL HAVE TO DRAG YOU OUT INTO THE STREET AND SHOOT YOU MYSELF!
YES, FLAGEE.

Editor's Note

Welcome, Americans! As part of the efforts to support national unity, we are temporarily replacing "The Boondocks" with "The Adventures of Flagee and Ribbon."

Today, Flagee and his trusty sidekick, Ribbon, tackle the issue of "What can I do?"

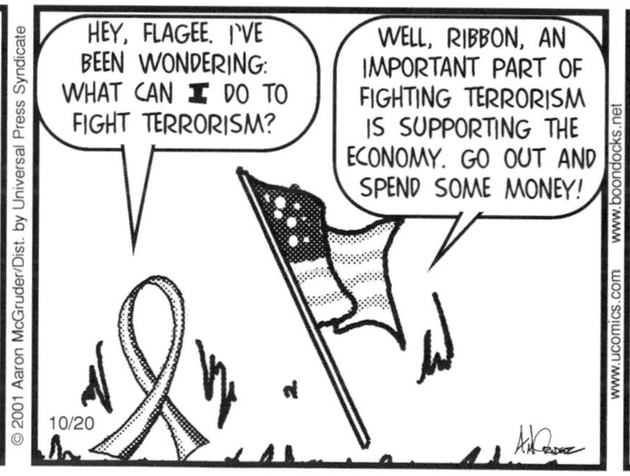

© 2001 Aaron McGruder/Dist. by Universal Press Syndicate
HEY, FLAGEE. I'VE BEEN WONDERING: WHAT CAN I DO TO FIGHT TERRORISM?
WELL, RIBBON, AN IMPORTANT PART OF FIGHTING TERRORISM IS SUPPORTING THE ECONOMY. GO OUT AND SPEND SOME MONEY!
10/20
www.ucomics.com www.boondocks.net

KIDS, what better way to spend that money than on an official Flagee and Ribbon "OSAMA BIN LADEN IS A PUNK" T-shirt. Tell bin Laden what a punk he is! Just $19.95 plus $4.95 shipping and handling. Order today — operators are standing by!

Some of the money goes to a charity or something.

Editor's Note

Despite the tremendous reader response to "The Adventures of Flagee and Ribbon," we have decided to bring back "The Boondocks" on a probationary basis. However, should the material be deemed inappropriate, we are prepared to bring back "Flagee and Ribbon" at a moment's notice.

United We Stand.

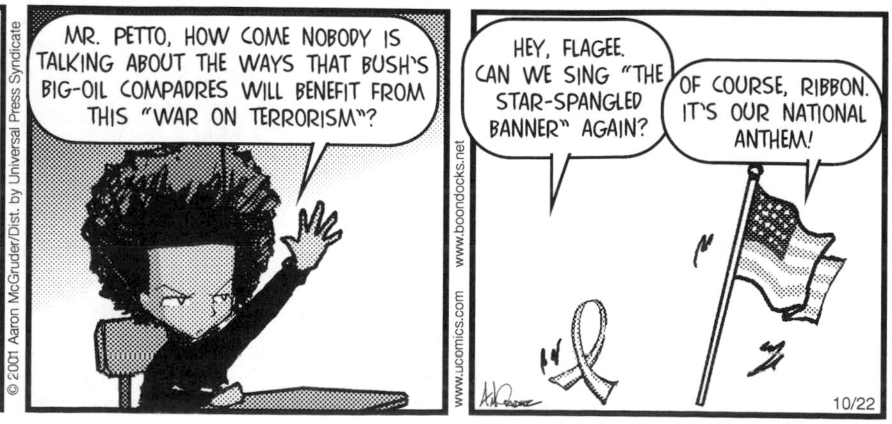

© 2001 Aaron McGruder/Dist. by Universal Press Syndicate
MR. PETTO, HOW COME NOBODY IS TALKING ABOUT THE WAYS THAT BUSH'S BIG-OIL COMPADRES WILL BENEFIT FROM THIS "WAR ON TERRORISM"?
www.ucomics.com www.boondocks.net
HEY, FLAGEE. CAN WE SING "THE STAR-SPANGLED BANNER" AGAIN?
OF COURSE, RIBBON. IT'S OUR NATIONAL ANTHEM!
10/22

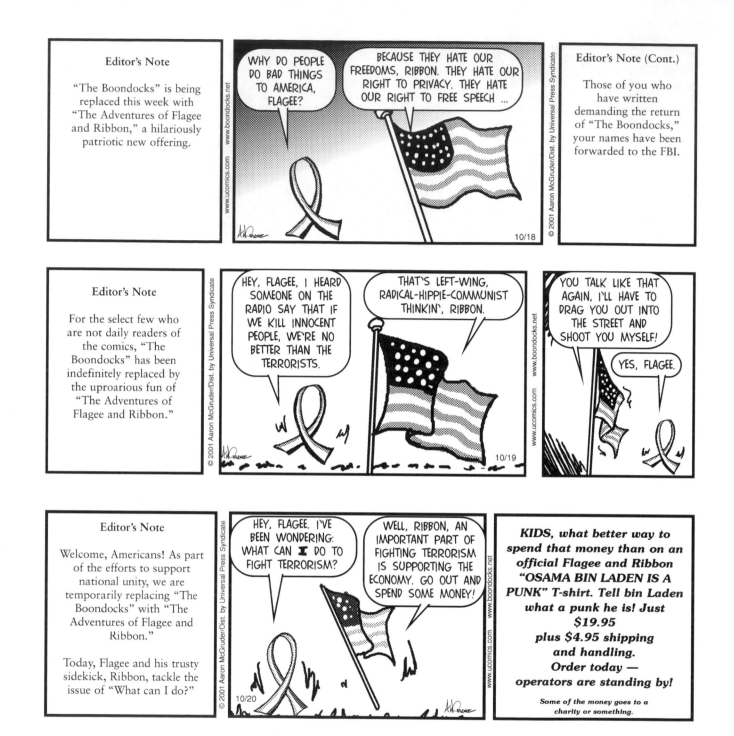

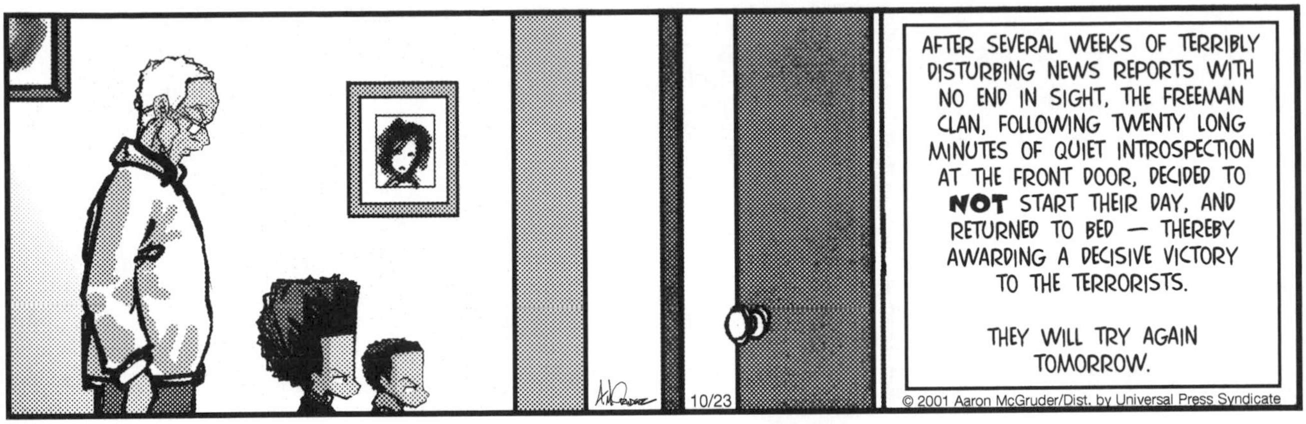
AFTER SEVERAL WEEKS OF TERRIBLY DISTURBING NEWS REPORTS WITH NO END IN SIGHT, THE FREEMAN CLAN, FOLLOWING TWENTY LONG MINUTES OF QUIET INTROSPECTION AT THE FRONT DOOR, DECIDED TO **NOT** START THEIR DAY, AND RETURNED TO BED — THEREBY AWARDING A DECISIVE VICTORY TO THE TERRORISTS.
THEY WILL TRY AGAIN TOMORROW.
10/23
© 2001 Aaron McGruder/Dist. by Universal Press Syndicate

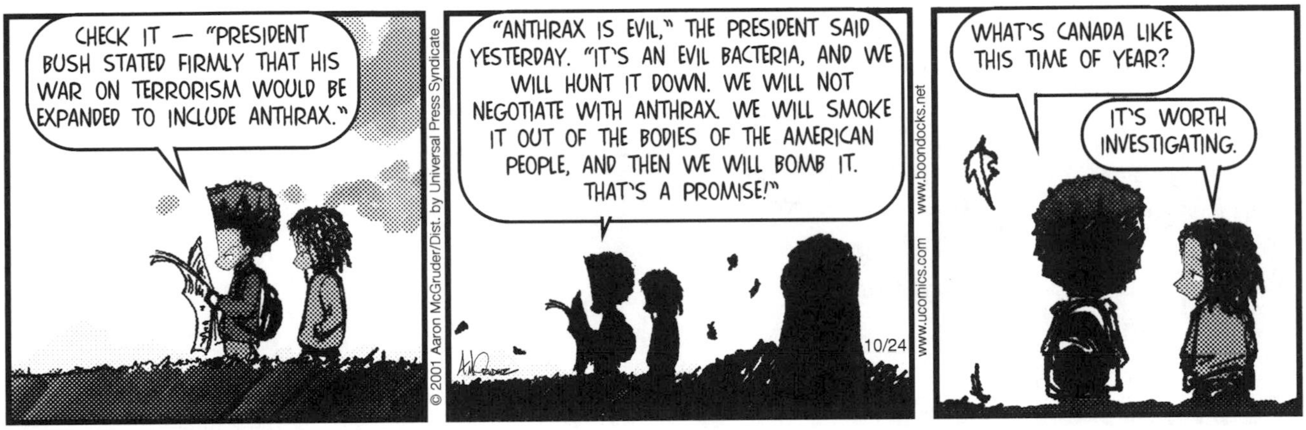
CHECK IT — "PRESIDENT BUSH STATED FIRMLY THAT HIS WAR ON TERRORISM WOULD BE EXPANDED TO INCLUDE ANTHRAX."
© 2001 Aaron McGruder/Dist. by Universal Press Syndicate
"ANTHRAX IS EVIL," THE PRESIDENT SAID YESTERDAY. "IT'S AN EVIL BACTERIA, AND WE WILL HUNT IT DOWN. WE WILL NOT NEGOTIATE WITH ANTHRAX. WE WILL SMOKE IT OUT OF THE BODIES OF THE AMERICAN PEOPLE, AND THEN WE WILL BOMB IT. THAT'S A PROMISE!"
10/24
www.ucomics.com www.boondocks.net
WHAT'S CANADA LIKE THIS TIME OF YEAR?
IT'S WORTH INVESTIGATING.

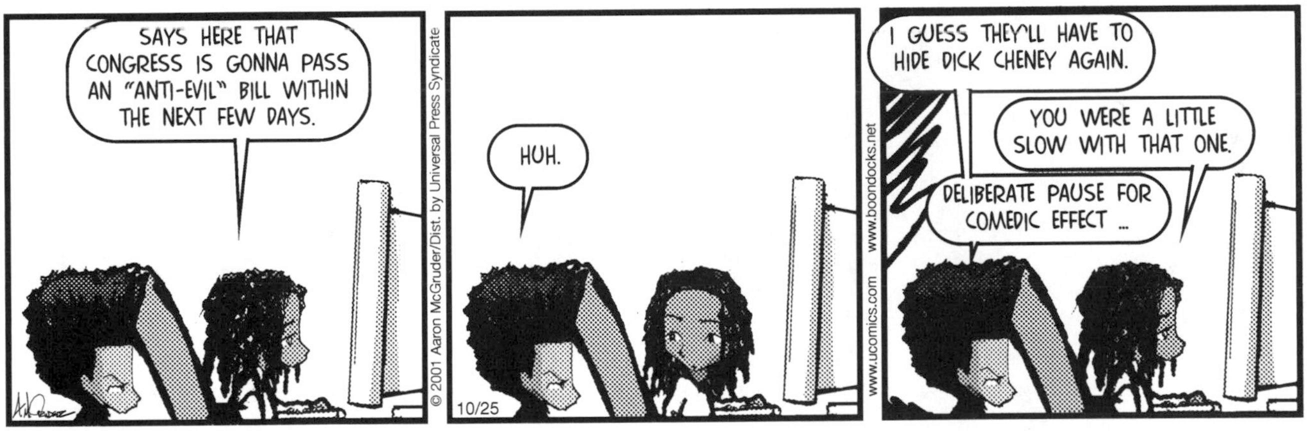
SAYS HERE THAT CONGRESS IS GONNA PASS AN "ANTI-EVIL" BILL WITHIN THE NEXT FEW DAYS.
© 2001 Aaron McGruder/Dist. by Universal Press Syndicate
HUH.
10/25
www.ucomics.com www.boondocks.net
I GUESS THEY'LL HAVE TO HIDE DICK CHENEY AGAIN.
DELIBERATE PAUSE FOR COMEDIC EFFECT ...
YOU WERE A LITTLE SLOW WITH THAT ONE.

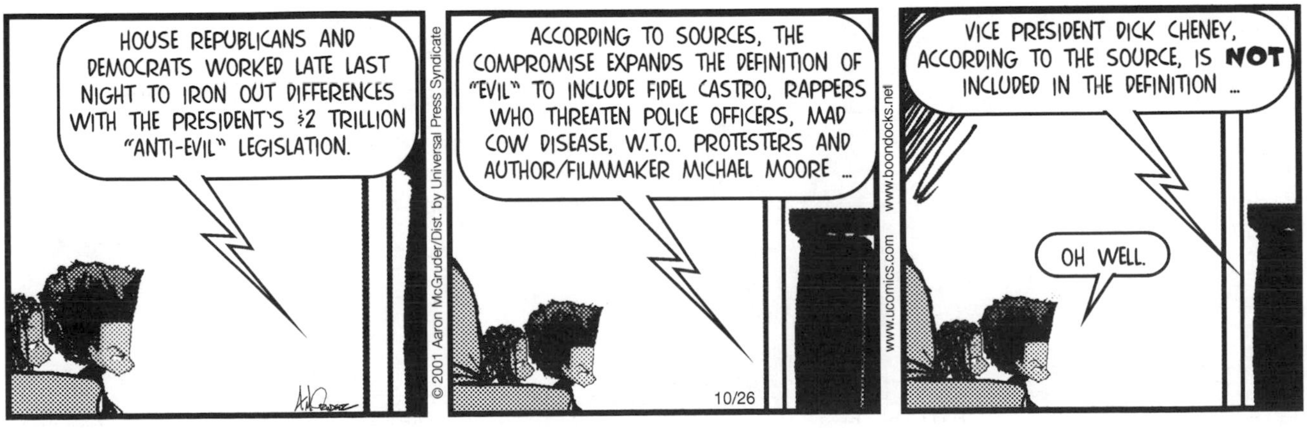
HOUSE REPUBLICANS AND DEMOCRATS WORKED LATE LAST NIGHT TO IRON OUT DIFFERENCES WITH THE PRESIDENT'S $2 TRILLION "ANTI-EVIL" LEGISLATION.
© 2001 Aaron McGruder/Dist. by Universal Press Syndicate
ACCORDING TO SOURCES, THE COMPROMISE EXPANDS THE DEFINITION OF "EVIL" TO INCLUDE FIDEL CASTRO, RAPPERS WHO THREATEN POLICE OFFICERS, MAD COW DISEASE, W.T.O. PROTESTERS AND AUTHOR/FILMMAKER MICHAEL MOORE ...
10/26
www.ucomics.com www.boondocks.net
VICE PRESIDENT DICK CHENEY, ACCORDING TO THE SOURCE, IS **NOT** INCLUDED IN THE DEFINITION ...
OH WELL.

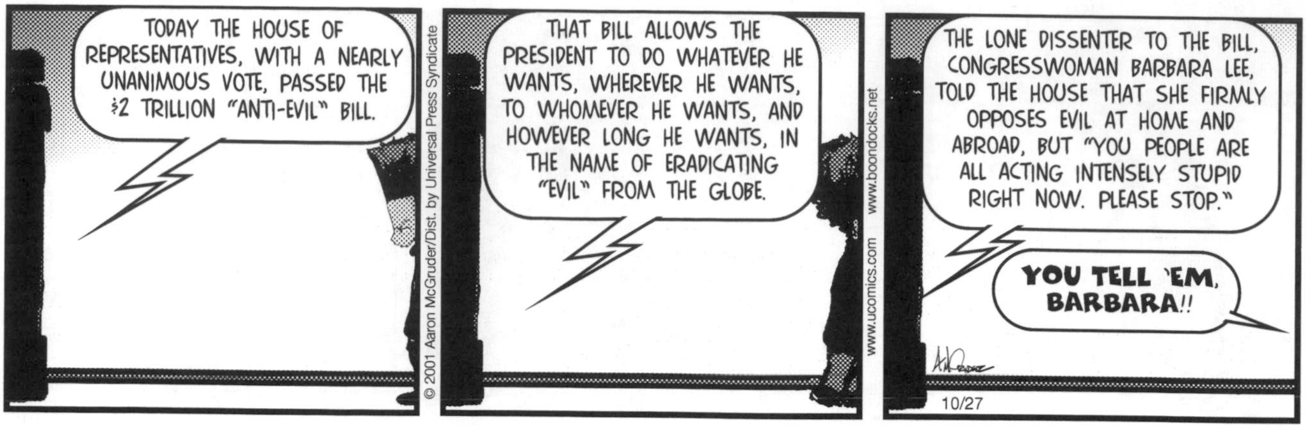
TODAY THE HOUSE OF REPRESENTATIVES, WITH A NEARLY UNANIMOUS VOTE, PASSED THE $2 TRILLION "ANTI-EVIL" BILL.
© 2001 Aaron McGruder/Dist. by Universal Press Syndicate
THAT BILL ALLOWS THE PRESIDENT TO DO WHATEVER HE WANTS, WHEREVER HE WANTS, TO WHOMEVER HE WANTS, AND HOWEVER LONG HE WANTS, IN THE NAME OF ERADICATING "EVIL" FROM THE GLOBE.
www.ucomics.com www.boondocks.net
THE LONE DISSENTER TO THE BILL, CONGRESSWOMAN BARBARA LEE, TOLD THE HOUSE THAT SHE FIRMLY OPPOSES EVIL AT HOME AND ABROAD, BUT "YOU PEOPLE ARE ALL ACTING INTENSELY STUPID RIGHT NOW. PLEASE STOP."
YOU TELL 'EM, BARBARA!!
10/27

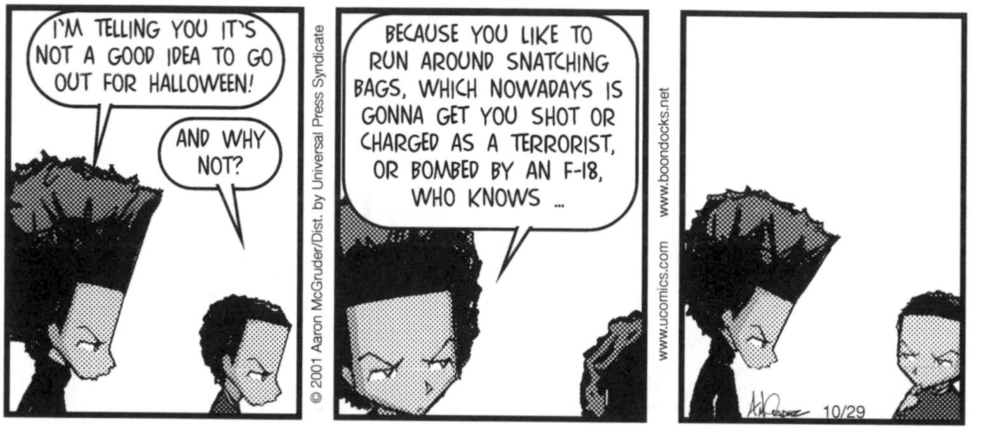
I'M TELLING YOU IT'S NOT A GOOD IDEA TO GO OUT FOR HALLOWEEN!
AND WHY NOT?
© 2001 Aaron McGruder/Dist. by Universal Press Syndicate
BECAUSE YOU LIKE TO RUN AROUND SNATCHING BAGS, WHICH NOWADAYS IS GONNA GET YOU SHOT OR CHARGED AS A TERRORIST, OR BOMBED BY AN F-18, WHO KNOWS ...
www.ucomics.com www.boondocks.net
10/29
THAT IS A HEAVY PRICE TO PAY FOR A SNICKERS.
THEY DO SATISFY, BUT YES ...

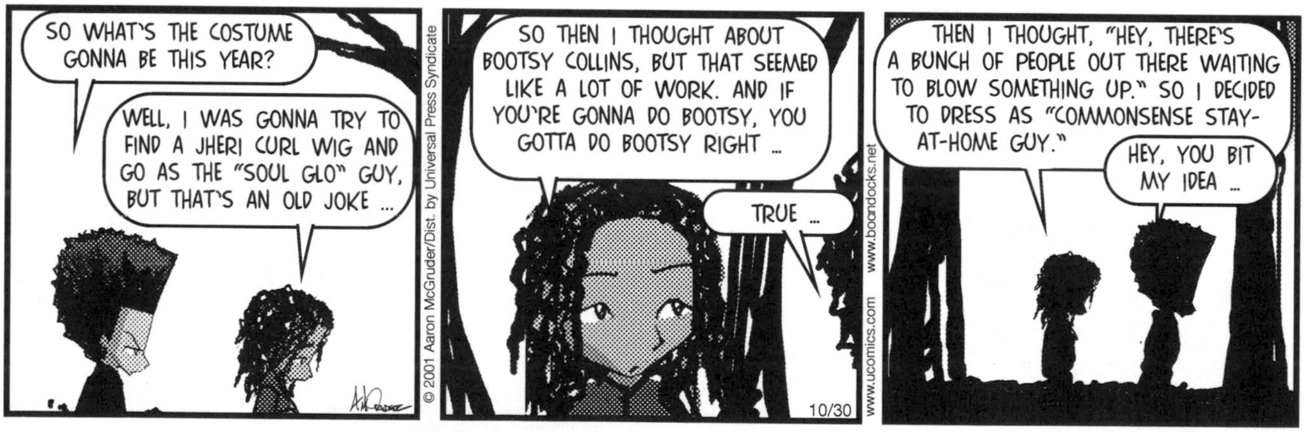
SO WHAT'S THE COSTUME GONNA BE THIS YEAR?
WELL, I WAS GONNA TRY TO FIND A JHERI CURL WIG AND GO AS THE "SOUL GLO" GUY, BUT THAT'S AN OLD JOKE ...
© 2001 Aaron McGruder/Dist. by Universal Press Syndicate
SO THEN I THOUGHT ABOUT BOOTSY COLLINS, BUT THAT SEEMED LIKE A LOT OF WORK. AND IF YOU'RE GONNA DO BOOTSY, YOU GOTTA DO BOOTSY RIGHT ...
TRUE ...
10/30
www.ucomics.com www.boondocks.net
THEN I THOUGHT, "HEY, THERE'S A BUNCH OF PEOPLE OUT THERE WAITING TO BLOW SOMETHING UP." SO I DECIDED TO DRESS AS "COMMONSENSE STAY-AT-HOME GUY."
HEY, YOU BIT MY IDEA ...

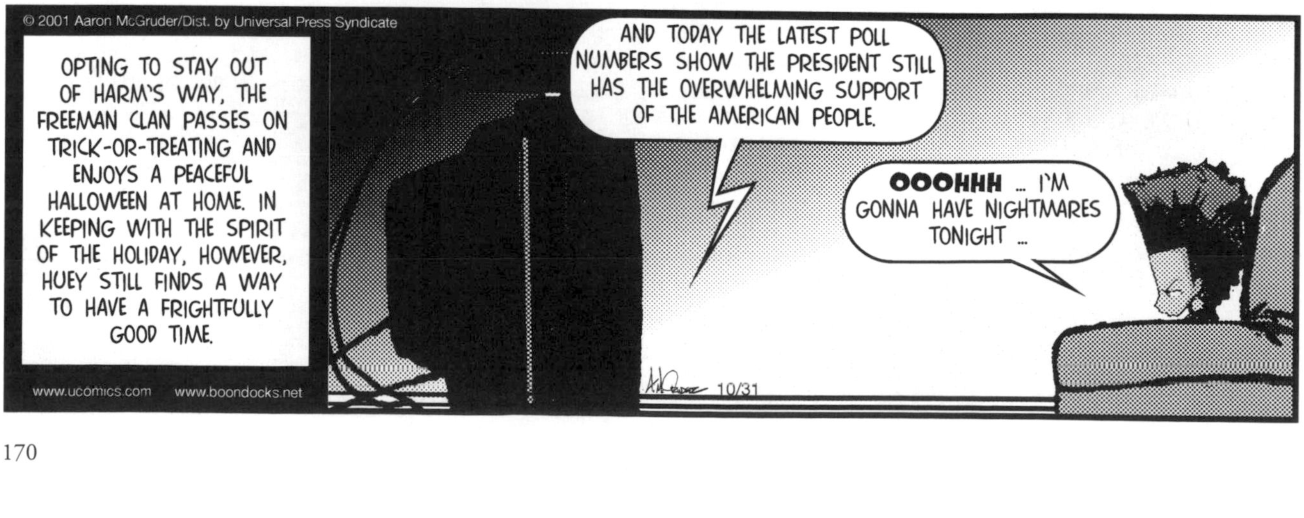
© 2001 Aaron McGruder/Dist. by Universal Press Syndicate
OPTING TO STAY OUT OF HARM'S WAY, THE FREEMAN CLAN PASSES ON TRICK-OR-TREATING AND ENJOYS A PEACEFUL HALLOWEEN AT HOME. IN KEEPING WITH THE SPIRIT OF THE HOLIDAY, HOWEVER, HUEY STILL FINDS A WAY TO HAVE A FRIGHTFULLY GOOD TIME.
www.ucomics.com www.boondocks.net
AND TODAY THE LATEST POLL NUMBERS SHOW THE PRESIDENT STILL HAS THE OVERWHELMING SUPPORT OF THE AMERICAN PEOPLE.
OOOHHH ... I'M GONNA HAVE NIGHTMARES TONIGHT ...
10/31

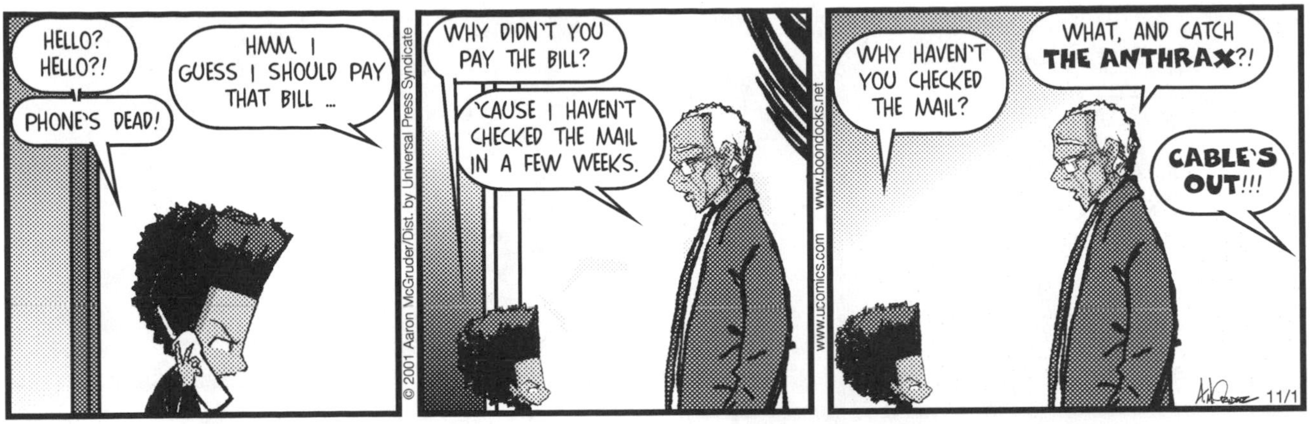
HELLO? HELLO?!
PHONE'S DEAD!
HMM. I GUESS I SHOULD PAY THAT BILL ...
© 2001 Aaron McGruder/Dist. by Universal Press Syndicate
WHY DIDN'T YOU PAY THE BILL?
'CAUSE I HAVEN'T CHECKED THE MAIL IN A FEW WEEKS.
www.ucomics.com www.boondocks.net
WHY HAVEN'T YOU CHECKED THE MAIL?
WHAT, AND CATCH THE ANTHRAX?!
CABLE'S OUT!!!
11/1

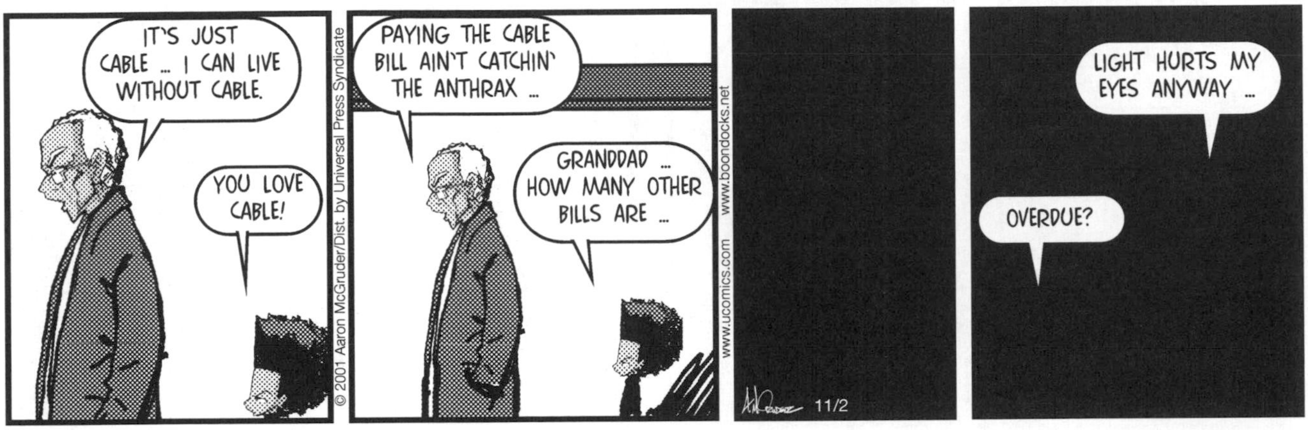
IT'S JUST CABLE ... I CAN LIVE WITHOUT CABLE.
YOU LOVE CABLE!
© 2001 Aaron McGruder/Dist. by Universal Press Syndicate
PAYING THE CABLE BILL AIN'T CATCHIN' THE ANTHRAX ...
GRANDDAD ... HOW MANY OTHER BILLS ARE ...
www.ucomics.com www.boondocks.net
11/2
LIGHT HURTS MY EYES ANYWAY ...
OVERDUE?

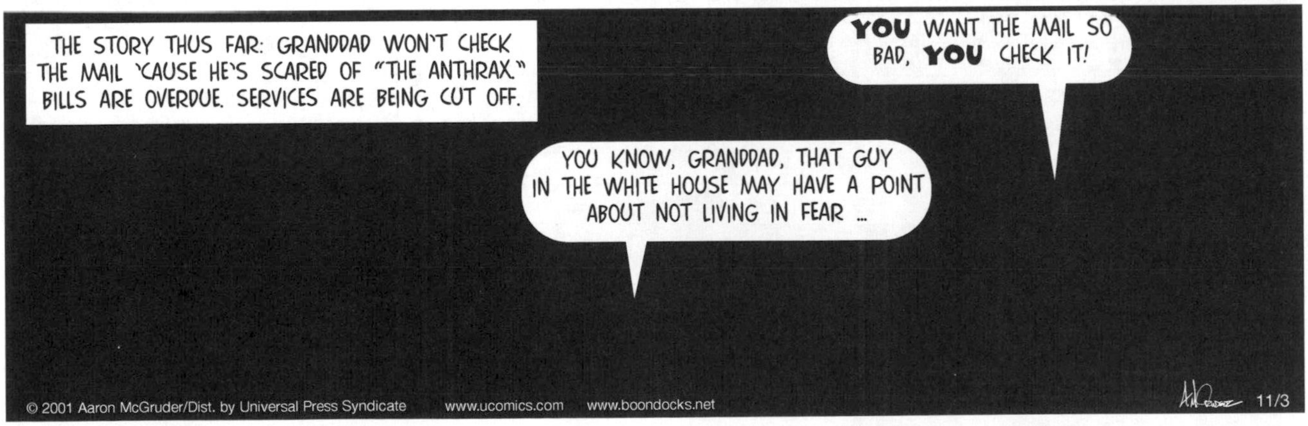
THE STORY THUS FAR: GRANDDAD WON'T CHECK THE MAIL 'CAUSE HE'S SCARED OF "THE ANTHRAX." BILLS ARE OVERDUE. SERVICES ARE BEING CUT OFF.
YOU KNOW, GRANDDAD, THAT GUY IN THE WHITE HOUSE MAY HAVE A POINT ABOUT NOT LIVING IN FEAR ...
YOU WANT THE MAIL SO BAD, YOU CHECK IT!
© 2001 Aaron McGruder/Dist. by Universal Press Syndicate www.ucomics.com www.boondocks.net
11/3

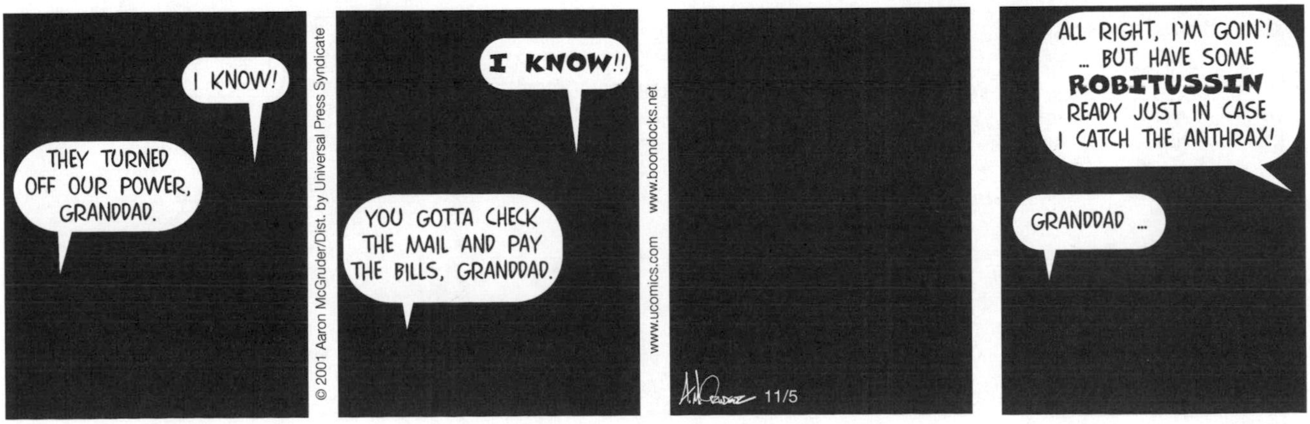
THEY TURNED OFF OUR POWER, GRANDDAD.
I KNOW!
© 2001 Aaron McGruder/Dist. by Universal Press Syndicate
YOU GOTTA CHECK THE MAIL AND PAY THE BILLS, GRANDDAD.
I KNOW!!
www.ucomics.com www.boondocks.net
11/5
GRANDDAD ...
ALL RIGHT, I'M GOIN'! ... BUT HAVE SOME ROBITUSSIN READY JUST IN CASE I CATCH THE ANTHRAX!

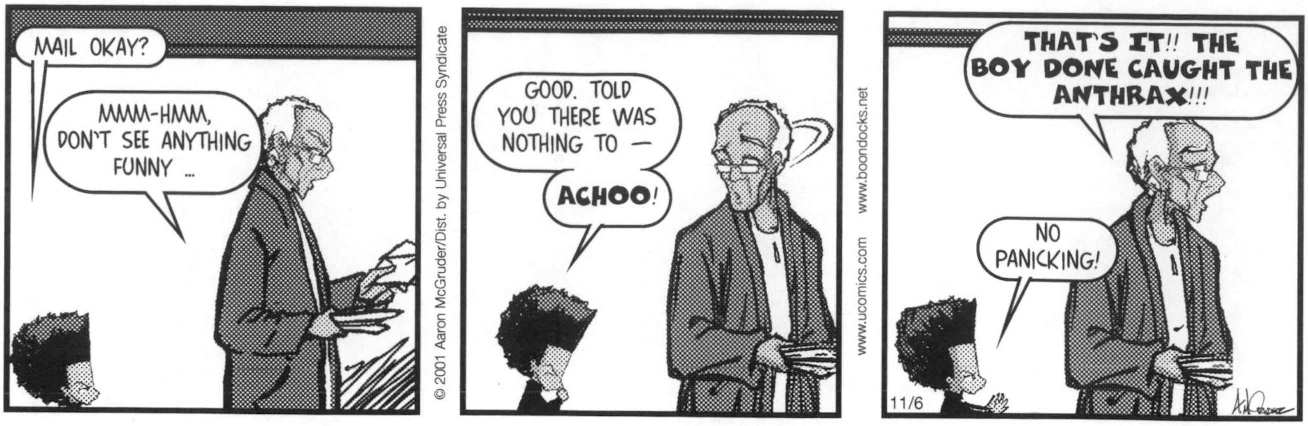
MAIL OKAY?
MMM-HMM, DON'T SEE ANYTHING FUNNY ...
© 2001 Aaron McGruder/Dist. by Universal Press Syndicate
GOOD. TOLD YOU THERE WAS NOTHING TO —
ACHOO!
www.ucomics.com www.boondocks.net
THAT'S IT!! THE BOY DONE CAUGHT THE ANTHRAX!!!
NO PANICKING!
11/6

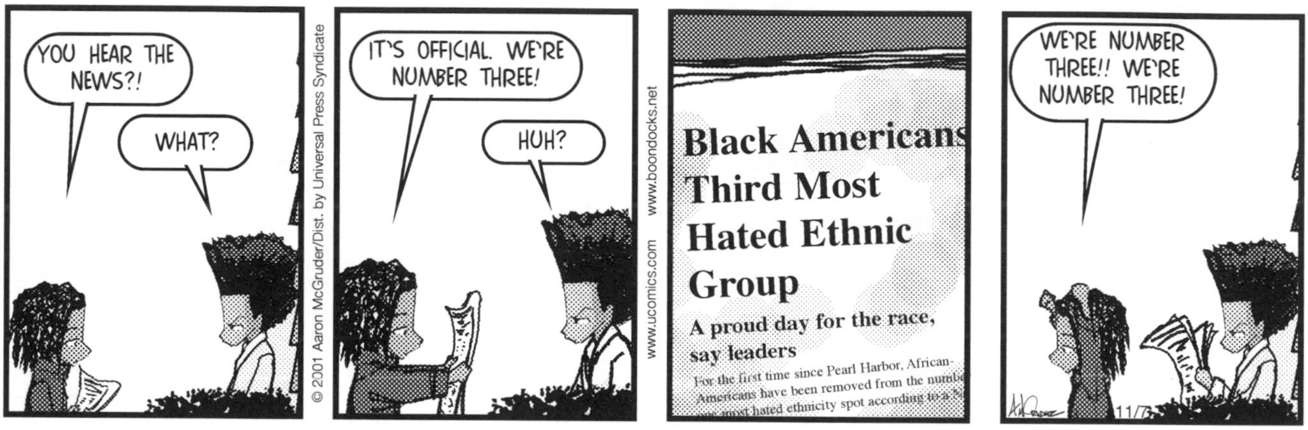
YOU HEAR THE NEWS?!
WHAT?
© 2001 Aaron McGruder/Dist. by Universal Press Syndicate
IT'S OFFICIAL. WE'RE NUMBER THREE!
HUH?
www.ucomics.com www.boondocks.net
Black Americans Third Most Hated Ethnic Group
A proud day for the race, say leaders
For the first time since Pearl Harbor, African-
Americans have been removed from the
WE'RE NUMBER THREE!! WE'RE NUMBER THREE!

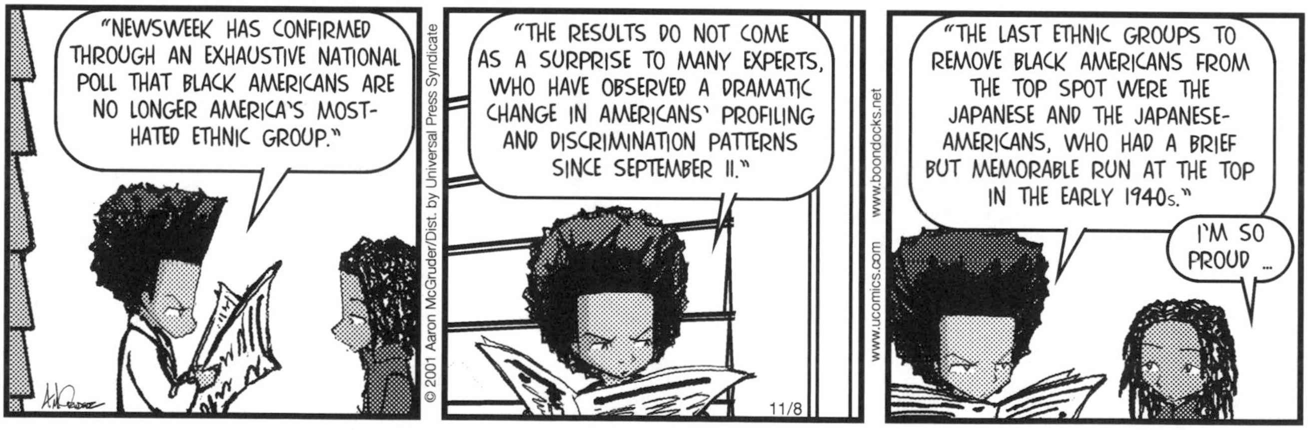
"NEWSWEEK HAS CONFIRMED THROUGH AN EXHAUSTIVE NATIONAL POLL THAT BLACK AMERICANS ARE NO LONGER AMERICA'S MOST-HATED ETHNIC GROUP."
© 2001 Aaron McGruder/Dist. by Universal Press Syndicate
"THE RESULTS DO NOT COME AS A SURPRISE TO MANY EXPERTS, WHO HAVE OBSERVED A DRAMATIC CHANGE IN AMERICANS' PROFILING AND DISCRIMINATION PATTERNS SINCE SEPTEMBER 11."
11/8
www.ucomics.com www.boondocks.net
"THE LAST ETHNIC GROUPS TO REMOVE BLACK AMERICANS FROM THE TOP SPOT WERE THE JAPANESE AND THE JAPANESE-AMERICANS, WHO HAD A BRIEF BUT MEMORABLE RUN AT THE TOP IN THE EARLY 1940s."
I'M SO PROUD ...

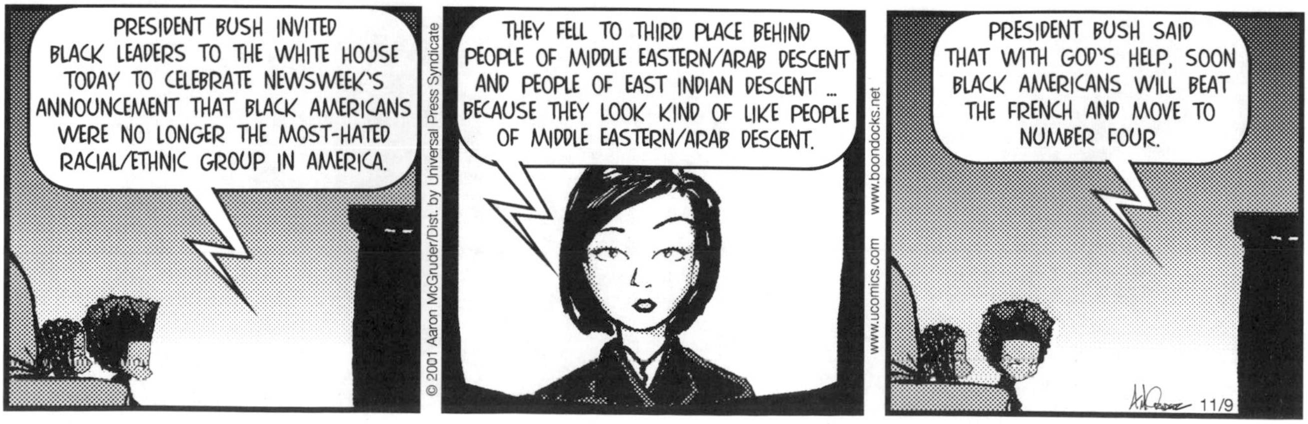
PRESIDENT BUSH INVITED BLACK LEADERS TO THE WHITE HOUSE TODAY TO CELEBRATE NEWSWEEK'S ANNOUNCEMENT THAT BLACK AMERICANS WERE NO LONGER THE MOST-HATED RACIAL/ETHNIC GROUP IN AMERICA.
© 2001 Aaron McGruder/Dist. by Universal Press Syndicate
THEY FELL TO THIRD PLACE BEHIND PEOPLE OF MIDDLE EASTERN/ARAB DESCENT AND PEOPLE OF EAST INDIAN DESCENT ... BECAUSE THEY LOOK KIND OF LIKE PEOPLE OF MIDDLE EASTERN/ARAB DESCENT.
www.ucomics.com www.boondocks.net
PRESIDENT BUSH SAID THAT WITH GOD'S HELP, SOON BLACK AMERICANS WILL BEAT THE FRENCH AND MOVE TO NUMBER FOUR.
11/9

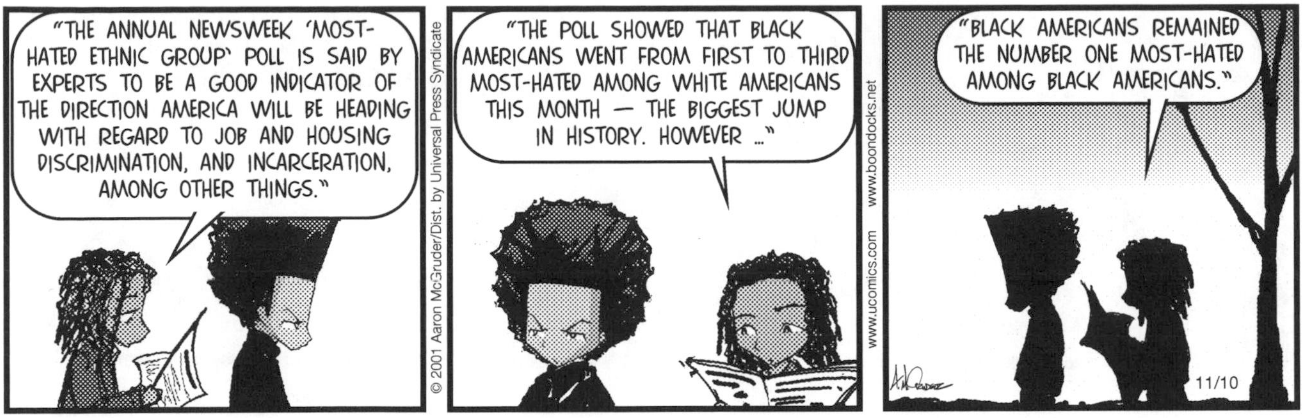
"THE ANNUAL NEWSWEEK 'MOST-HATED ETHNIC GROUP' POLL IS SAID BY EXPERTS TO BE A GOOD INDICATOR OF THE DIRECTION AMERICA WILL BE HEADING WITH REGARD TO JOB AND HOUSING DISCRIMINATION, AND INCARCERATION, AMONG OTHER THINGS."
© 2001 Aaron McGruder/Dist. by Universal Press Syndicate
"THE POLL SHOWED THAT BLACK AMERICANS WENT FROM FIRST TO THIRD MOST-HATED AMONG WHITE AMERICANS THIS MONTH — THE BIGGEST JUMP IN HISTORY. HOWEVER ..."
www.ucomics.com www.boondocks.net
"BLACK AMERICANS REMAINED THE NUMBER ONE MOST-HATED AMONG BLACK AMERICANS."
11/10

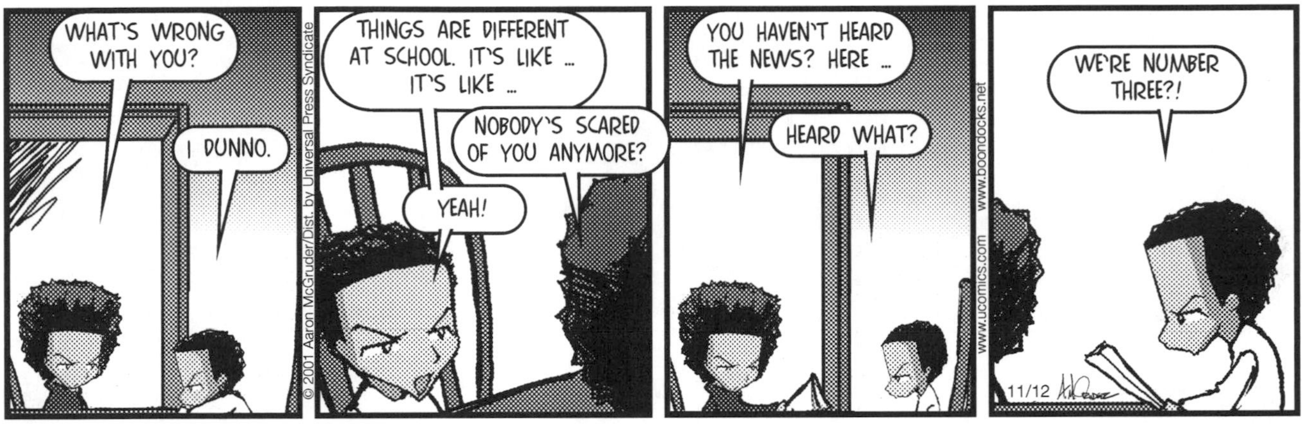
WHAT'S WRONG WITH YOU?
I DUNNO.
© 2001 Aaron McGruder/Dist. by Universal Press Syndicate
THINGS ARE DIFFERENT AT SCHOOL. IT'S LIKE ... IT'S LIKE ...
NOBODY'S SCARED OF YOU ANYMORE?
YEAH!
YOU HAVEN'T HEARD THE NEWS? HERE ...
HEARD WHAT?
www.ucomics.com www.boondocks.net
WE'RE NUMBER THREE?!
11/12

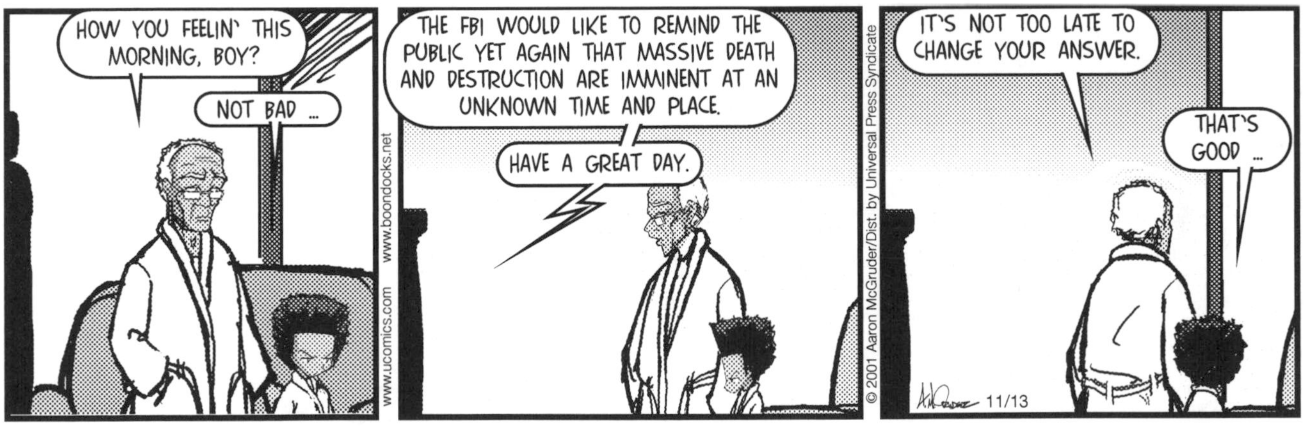
HOW YOU FEELIN' THIS MORNING, BOY?
NOT BAD ...
www.ucomics.com www.boondocks.net
THE FBI WOULD LIKE TO REMIND THE PUBLIC YET AGAIN THAT MASSIVE DEATH AND DESTRUCTION ARE IMMINENT AT AN UNKNOWN TIME AND PLACE.
HAVE A GREAT DAY.
© 2001 Aaron McGruder/Dist. by Universal Press Syndicate
IT'S NOT TOO LATE TO CHANGE YOUR ANSWER.
THAT'S GOOD ...
11/13

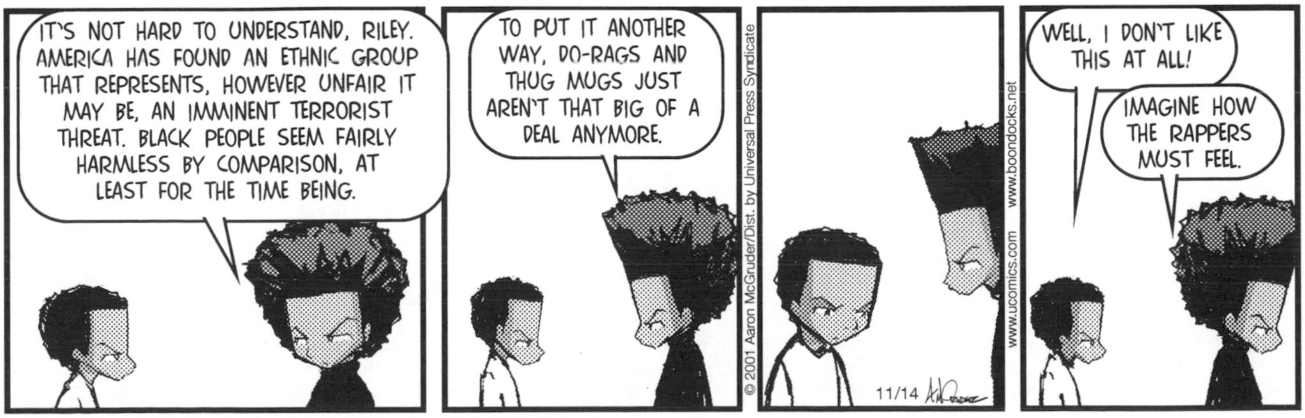
IT'S NOT HARD TO UNDERSTAND, RILEY. AMERICA HAS FOUND AN ETHNIC GROUP THAT REPRESENTS, HOWEVER UNFAIR IT MAY BE, AN IMMINENT TERRORIST THREAT. BLACK PEOPLE SEEM FAIRLY HARMLESS BY COMPARISON, AT LEAST FOR THE TIME BEING.
TO PUT IT ANOTHER WAY, DO-RAGS AND THUG MUGS JUST AREN'T THAT BIG OF A DEAL ANYMORE.
© 2001 Aaron McGruder/Dist. by Universal Press Syndicate
11/14
www.ucomics.com www.boondocks.net
WELL, I DON'T LIKE THIS AT ALL!
IMAGINE HOW THE RAPPERS MUST FEEL.

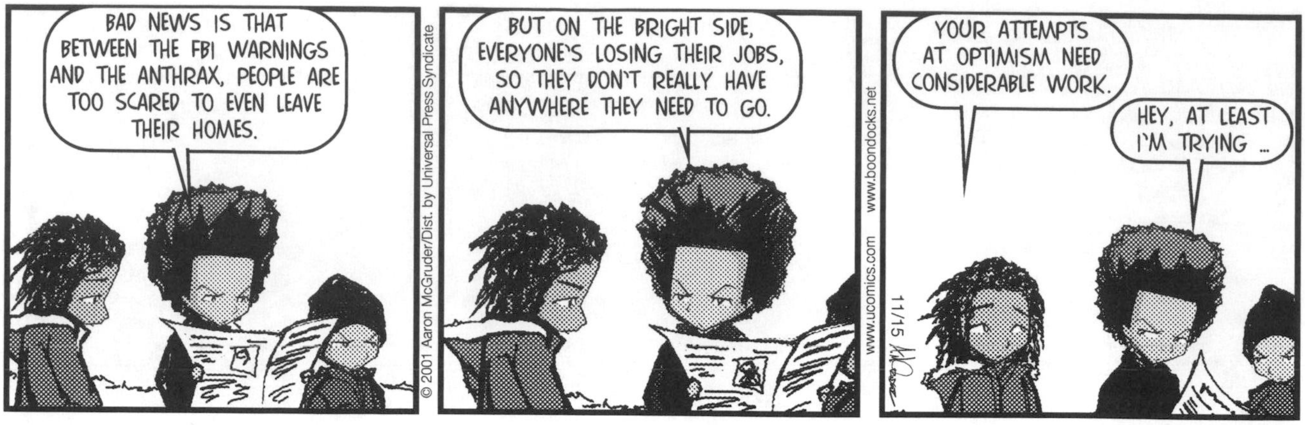
BAD NEWS IS THAT BETWEEN THE FBI WARNINGS AND THE ANTHRAX, PEOPLE ARE TOO SCARED TO EVEN LEAVE THEIR HOMES.
© 2001 Aaron McGruder/Dist. by Universal Press Syndicate
BUT ON THE BRIGHT SIDE, EVERYONE'S LOSING THEIR JOBS, SO THEY DON'T REALLY HAVE ANYWHERE THEY NEED TO GO.
www.ucomics.com www.boondocks.net
YOUR ATTEMPTS AT OPTIMISM NEED CONSIDERABLE WORK.
HEY, AT LEAST I'M TRYING ...
11/15

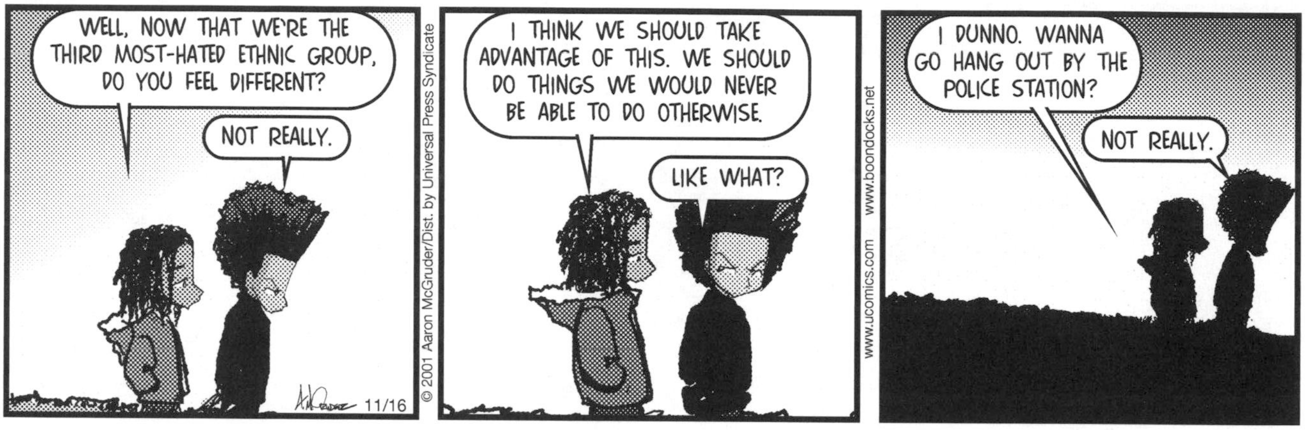
WELL, NOW THAT WE'RE THE THIRD MOST-HATED ETHNIC GROUP, DO YOU FEEL DIFFERENT?
NOT REALLY.
11/16
© 2001 Aaron McGruder/Dist. by Universal Press Syndicate
I THINK WE SHOULD TAKE ADVANTAGE OF THIS. WE SHOULD DO THINGS WE WOULD NEVER BE ABLE TO DO OTHERWISE.
LIKE WHAT?
www.ucomics.com www.boondocks.net
I DUNNO. WANNA GO HANG OUT BY THE POLICE STATION?
NOT REALLY.

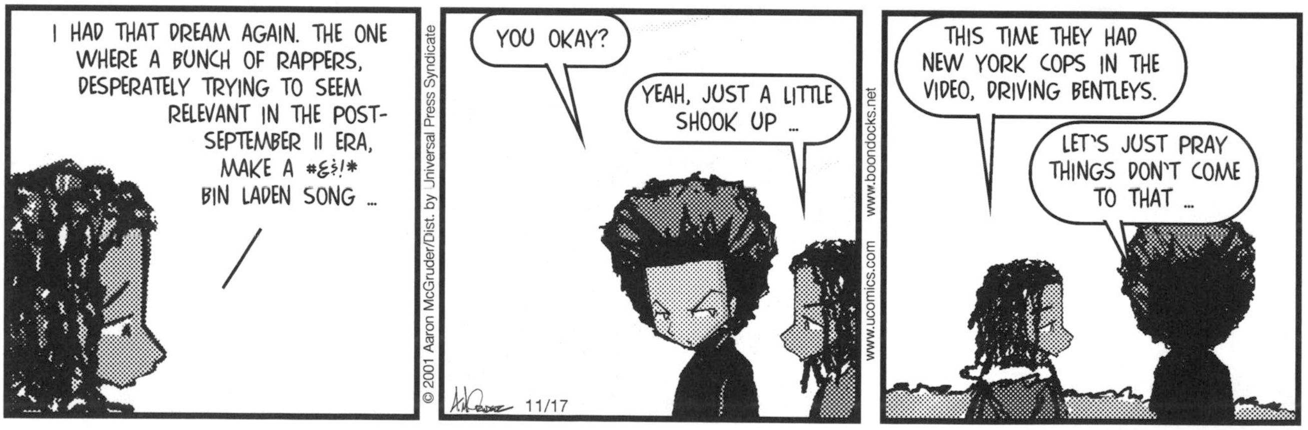
I HAD THAT DREAM AGAIN. THE ONE WHERE A BUNCH OF RAPPERS, DESPERATELY TRYING TO SEEM RELEVANT IN THE POST-SEPTEMBER 11 ERA, MAKE A #&$!* BIN LADEN SONG ...
© 2001 Aaron McGruder/Dist. by Universal Press Syndicate
YOU OKAY?
YEAH, JUST A LITTLE SHOOK UP ...
11/17
www.ucomics.com www.boondocks.net
THIS TIME THEY HAD NEW YORK COPS IN THE VIDEO, DRIVING BENTLEYS.
LET'S JUST PRAY THINGS DON'T COME TO THAT ...

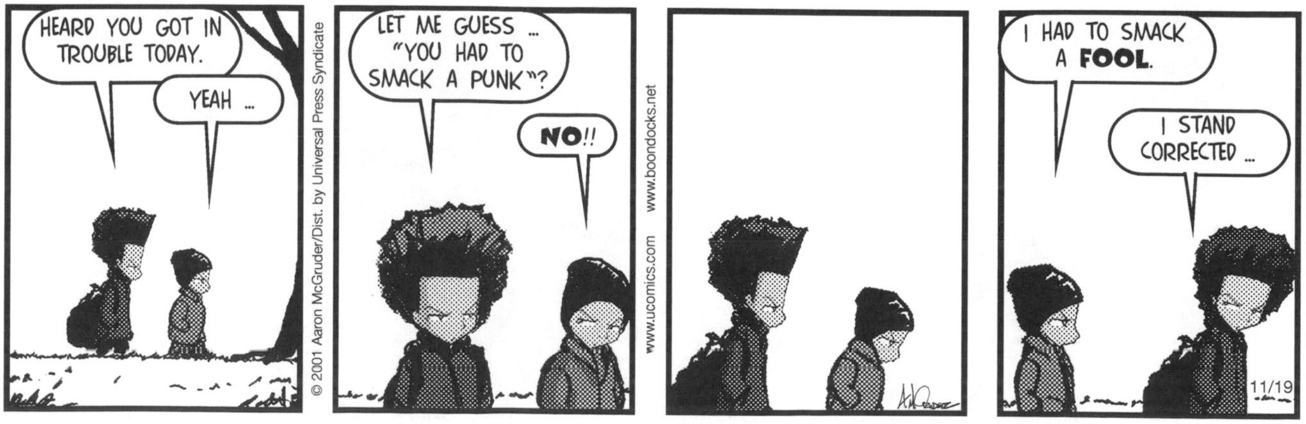
HEARD YOU GOT IN TROUBLE TODAY.
YEAH ...
© 2001 Aaron McGruder/Dist. by Universal Press Syndicate
LET ME GUESS ... "YOU HAD TO SMACK A PUNK"?
NO!!
www.ucomics.com www.boondocks.net
I HAD TO SMACK A FOOL.
I STAND CORRECTED ...
11/19

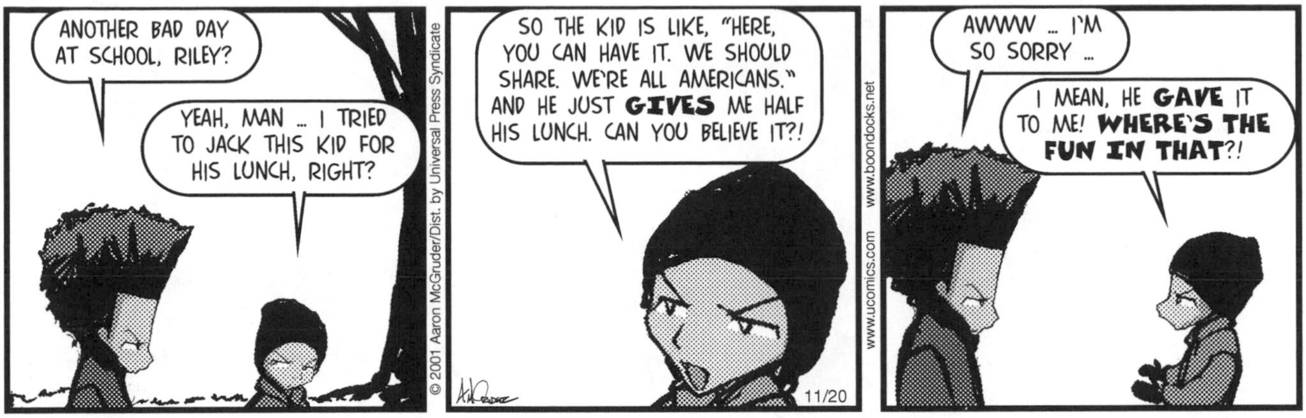
ANOTHER BAD DAY AT SCHOOL, RILEY?
YEAH, MAN ... I TRIED TO JACK THIS KID FOR HIS LUNCH, RIGHT?
© 2001 Aaron McGruder/Dist. by Universal Press Syndicate
SO THE KID IS LIKE, "HERE, YOU CAN HAVE IT. WE SHOULD SHARE. WE'RE ALL AMERICANS." AND HE JUST GIVES ME HALF HIS LUNCH. CAN YOU BELIEVE IT?!
11/20
www.ucomics.com www.boondocks.net
AWWW ... I'M SO SORRY ...
I MEAN, HE GAVE IT TO ME! WHERE'S THE FUN IN THAT?!

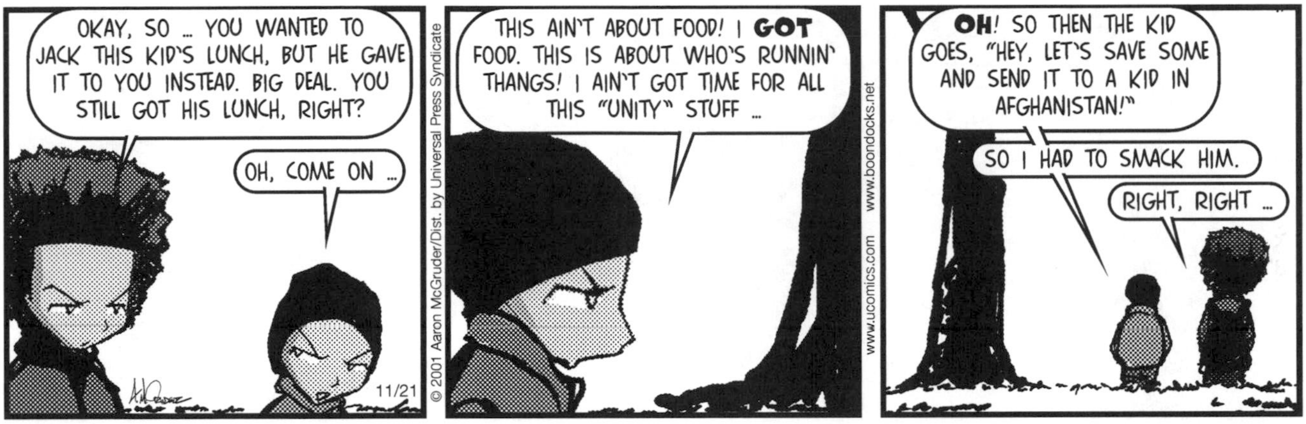
OKAY, SO ... YOU WANTED TO JACK THIS KID'S LUNCH, BUT HE GAVE IT TO YOU INSTEAD. BIG DEAL. YOU STILL GOT HIS LUNCH, RIGHT?
OH, COME ON ...
11/21
© 2001 Aaron McGruder/Dist. by Universal Press Syndicate
THIS AIN'T ABOUT FOOD! I GOT FOOD. THIS IS ABOUT WHO'S RUNNIN' THANGS! I AIN'T GOT TIME FOR ALL THIS "UNITY" STUFF ...
www.ucomics.com www.boondocks.net
OH! SO THEN THE KID GOES, "HEY, LET'S SAVE SOME AND SEND IT TO A KID IN AFGHANISTAN!"
SO I HAD TO SMACK HIM.
RIGHT, RIGHT ...

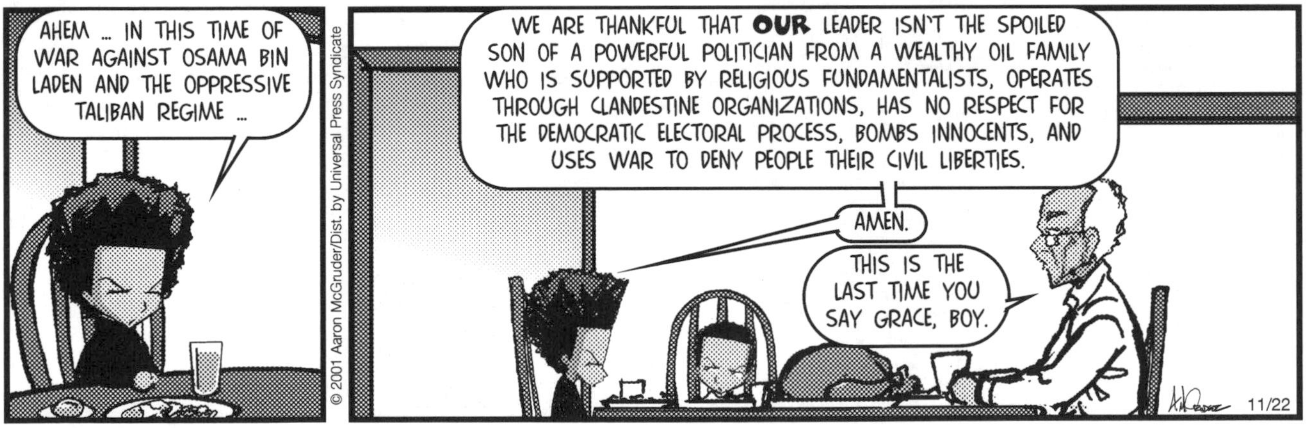
AHEM ... IN THIS TIME OF WAR AGAINST OSAMA BIN LADEN AND THE OPPRESSIVE TALIBAN REGIME ...
© 2001 Aaron McGruder/Dist. by Universal Press Syndicate
WE ARE THANKFUL THAT OUR LEADER ISN'T THE SPOILED SON OF A POWERFUL POLITICIAN FROM A WEALTHY OIL FAMILY WHO IS SUPPORTED BY RELIGIOUS FUNDAMENTALISTS, OPERATES THROUGH CLANDESTINE ORGANIZATIONS, HAS NO RESPECT FOR THE DEMOCRATIC ELECTORAL PROCESS, BOMBS INNOCENTS, AND USES WAR TO DENY PEOPLE THEIR CIVIL LIBERTIES.
AMEN.
THIS IS THE LAST TIME YOU SAY GRACE, BOY.
11/22

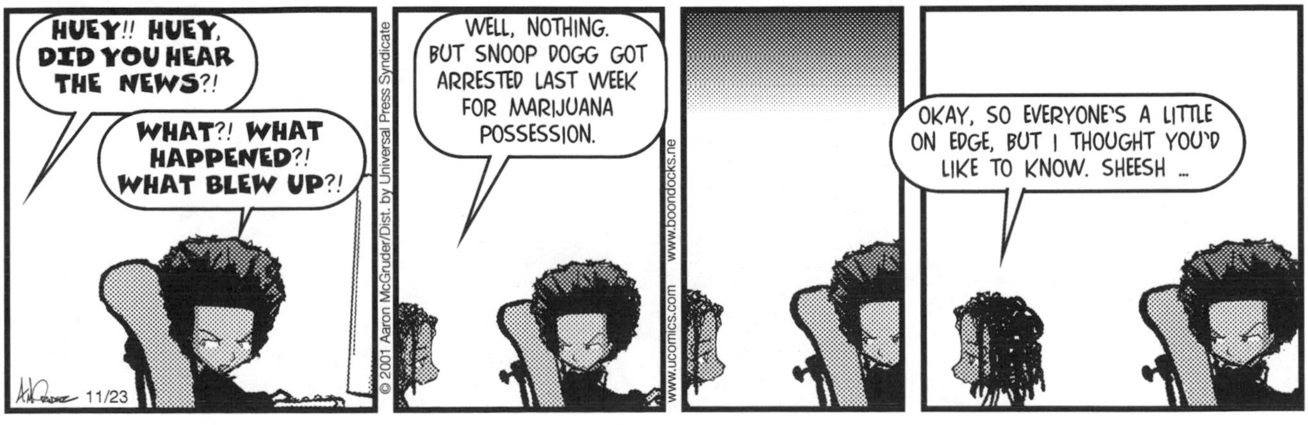
HUEY!! HUEY, DID YOU HEAR THE NEWS?!
WHAT?! WHAT HAPPENED?! WHAT BLEW UP?!
11/23
© 2001 Aaron McGruder/Dist. by Universal Press Syndicate
WELL, NOTHING. BUT SNOOP DOGG GOT ARRESTED LAST WEEK FOR MARIJUANA POSSESSION.
www.ucomics.com www.boondocks.ne
OKAY, SO EVERYONE'S A LITTLE ON EDGE, BUT I THOUGHT YOU'D LIKE TO KNOW. SHEESH ...

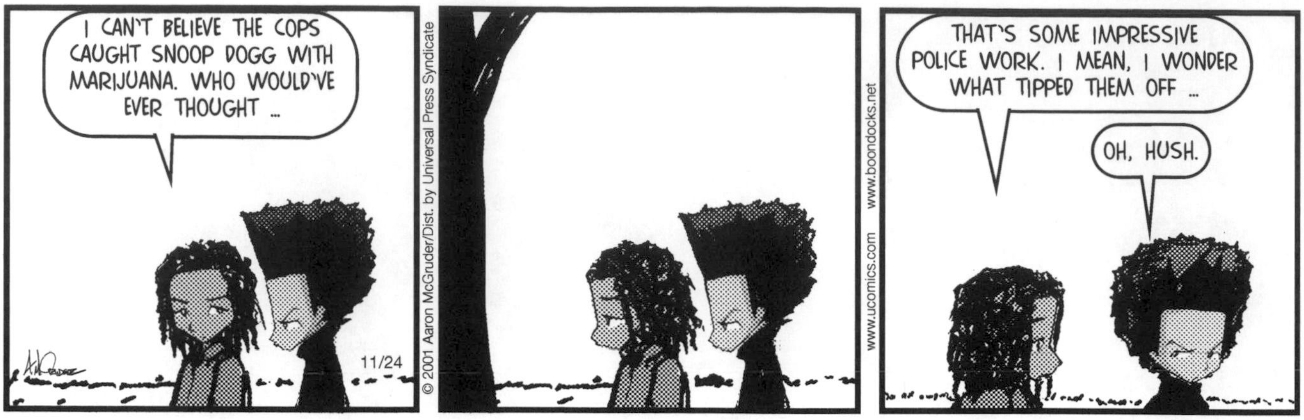
I CAN'T BELIEVE THE COPS CAUGHT SNOOP DOGG WITH MARIJUANA. WHO WOULD'VE EVER THOUGHT ...
11/24
© 2001 Aaron McGruder/Dist. by Universal Press Syndicate
THAT'S SOME IMPRESSIVE POLICE WORK. I MEAN, I WONDER WHAT TIPPED THEM OFF ...
OH, HUSH.
www.ucomics.com www.boondocks.net

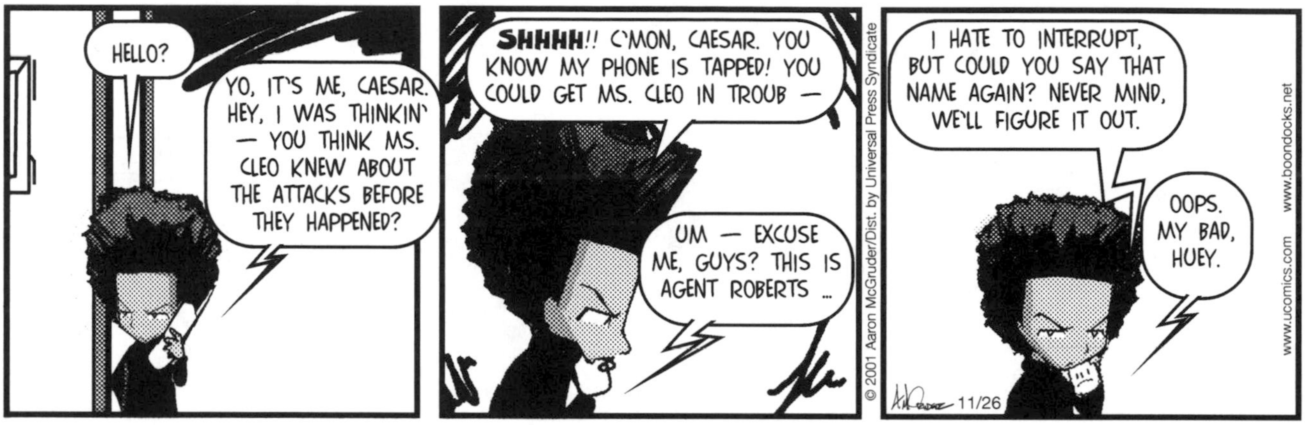
HELLO?
YO, IT'S ME, CAESAR. HEY, I WAS THINKIN' — YOU THINK MS. CLEO KNEW ABOUT THE ATTACKS BEFORE THEY HAPPENED?
SHHHH!! C'MON, CAESAR. YOU KNOW MY PHONE IS TAPPED! YOU COULD GET MS. CLEO IN TROUB —
UM — EXCUSE ME, GUYS? THIS IS AGENT ROBERTS ...
© 2001 Aaron McGruder/Dist. by Universal Press Syndicate
I HATE TO INTERRUPT, BUT COULD YOU SAY THAT NAME AGAIN? NEVER MIND, WE'LL FIGURE IT OUT.
OOPS. MY BAD, HUEY.
11/26
www.ucomics.com www.boondocks.net

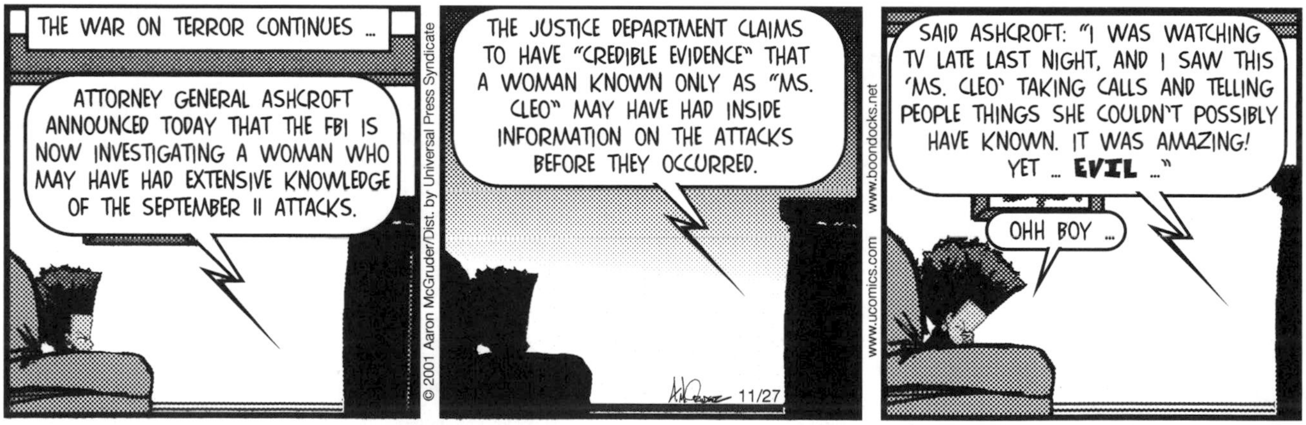
THE WAR ON TERROR CONTINUES ...
ATTORNEY GENERAL ASHCROFT ANNOUNCED TODAY THAT THE FBI IS NOW INVESTIGATING A WOMAN WHO MAY HAVE HAD EXTENSIVE KNOWLEDGE OF THE SEPTEMBER 11 ATTACKS.
© 2001 Aaron McGruder/Dist. by Universal Press Syndicate
THE JUSTICE DEPARTMENT CLAIMS TO HAVE "CREDIBLE EVIDENCE" THAT A WOMAN KNOWN ONLY AS "MS. CLEO" MAY HAVE HAD INSIDE INFORMATION ON THE ATTACKS BEFORE THEY OCCURRED.
11/27
www.ucomics.com www.boondocks.net
SAID ASHCROFT: "I WAS WATCHING TV LATE LAST NIGHT, AND I SAW THIS 'MS. CLEO' TAKING CALLS AND TELLING PEOPLE THINGS SHE COULDN'T POSSIBLY HAVE KNOWN. IT WAS AMAZING! YET ... EVIL ..."
OHH BOY ...

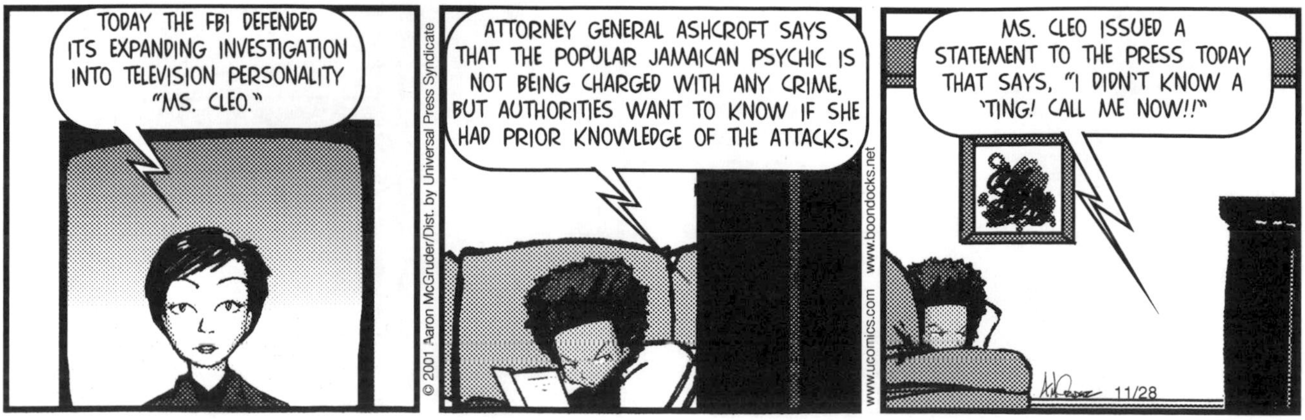
TODAY THE FBI DEFENDED ITS EXPANDING INVESTIGATION INTO TELEVISION PERSONALITY "MS. CLEO."
© 2001 Aaron McGruder/Dist. by Universal Press Syndicate
ATTORNEY GENERAL ASHCROFT SAYS THAT THE POPULAR JAMAICAN PSYCHIC IS NOT BEING CHARGED WITH ANY CRIME, BUT AUTHORITIES WANT TO KNOW IF SHE HAD PRIOR KNOWLEDGE OF THE ATTACKS.
www.ucomics.com www.boondocks.net
MS. CLEO ISSUED A STATEMENT TO THE PRESS TODAY THAT SAYS, "I DIDN'T KNOW A 'TING! CALL ME NOW!!"
11/28

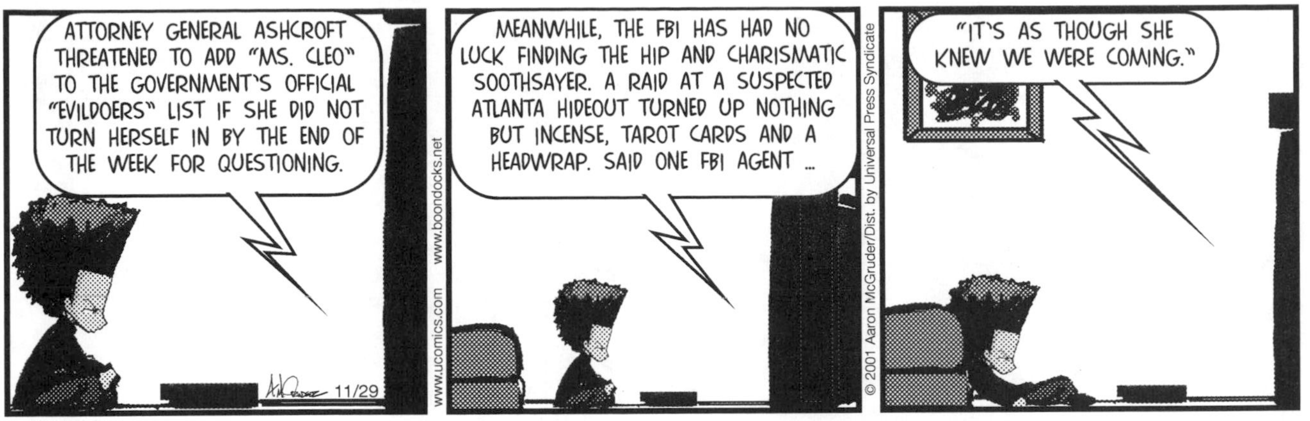
ATTORNEY GENERAL ASHCROFT THREATENED TO ADD "MS. CLEO" TO THE GOVERNMENT'S OFFICIAL "EVILDOERS" LIST IF SHE DID NOT TURN HERSELF IN BY THE END OF THE WEEK FOR QUESTIONING.
11/29
www.ucomics.com www.boondocks.net
MEANWHILE, THE FBI HAS HAD NO LUCK FINDING THE HIP AND CHARISMATIC SOOTHSAYER. A RAID AT A SUSPECTED ATLANTA HIDEOUT TURNED UP NOTHING BUT INCENSE, TAROT CARDS AND A HEADWRAP. SAID ONE FBI AGENT ...
© 2001 Aaron McGruder/Dist. by Universal Press Syndicate
"IT'S AS THOUGH SHE KNEW WE WERE COMING."

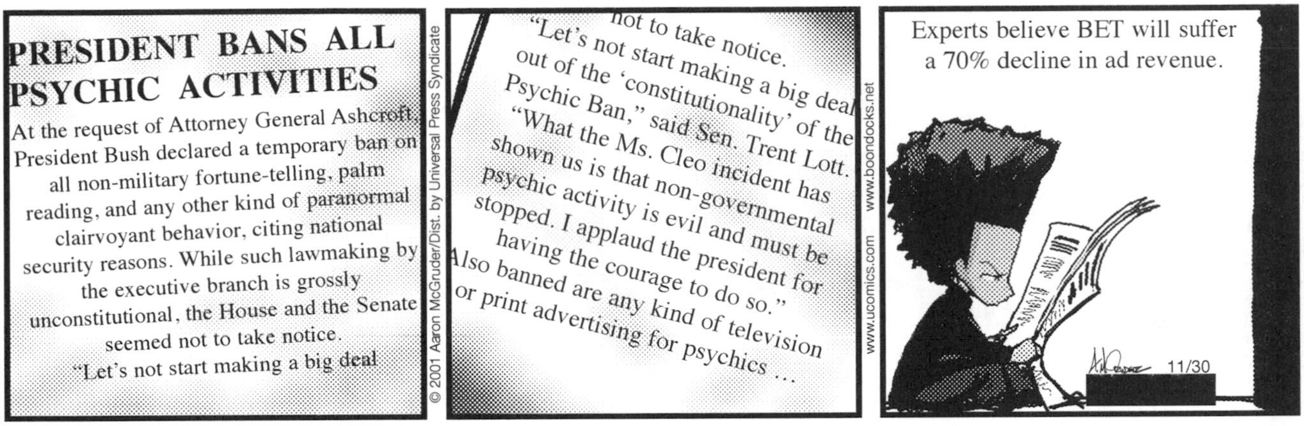
PRESIDENT BANS ALL PSYCHIC ACTIVITIES
At the request of Attorney General Ashcroft, President Bush declared a temporary ban on all non-military fortune-telling, palm reading, and any other kind of paranormal clairvoyant behavior, citing national security reasons. While such lawmaking by the executive branch is grossly unconstitutional, the House and the Senate seemed not to take notice.
"Let's not start making a big deal
© 2001 Aaron McGruder/Dist. by Universal Press Syndicate
not to take notice.
"Let's not start making a big deal out of the 'constitutionality' of the Psychic Ban," said Sen. Trent Lott. "What the Ms. Cleo incident has shown us is that non-governmental psychic activity is evil and must be stopped. I applaud the president for having the courage to do so."
Also banned are any kind of television or print advertising for psychics ...
www.ucomics.com www.boondocks.net
Experts believe BET will suffer a 70% decline in ad revenue.
11/30

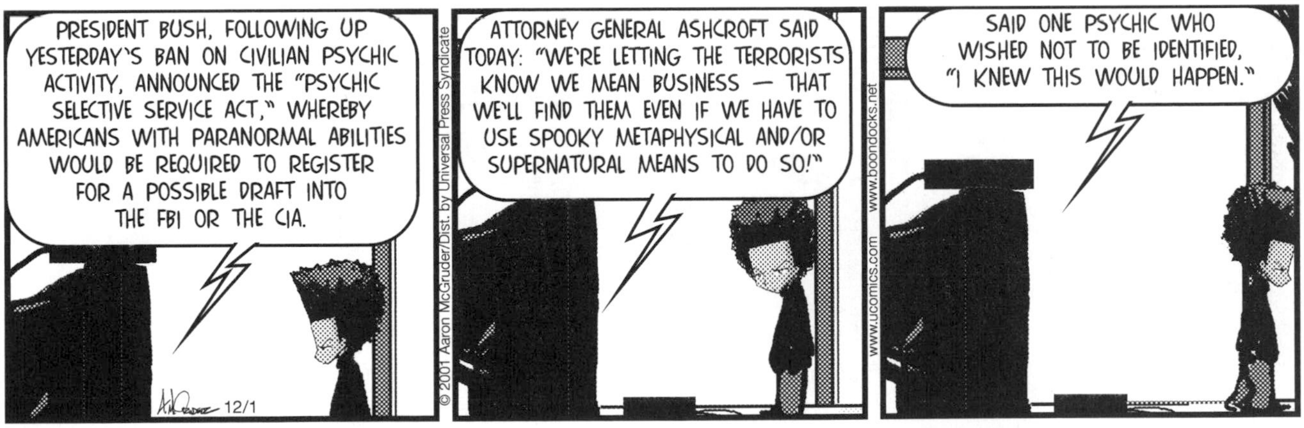
PRESIDENT BUSH, FOLLOWING UP YESTERDAY'S BAN ON CIVILIAN PSYCHIC ACTIVITY, ANNOUNCED THE "PSYCHIC SELECTIVE SERVICE ACT," WHEREBY AMERICANS WITH PARANORMAL ABILITIES WOULD BE REQUIRED TO REGISTER FOR A POSSIBLE DRAFT INTO THE FBI OR THE CIA.
12/1
© 2001 Aaron McGruder/Dist. by Universal Press Syndicate
ATTORNEY GENERAL ASHCROFT SAID TODAY: "WE'RE LETTING THE TERRORISTS KNOW WE MEAN BUSINESS — THAT WE'LL FIND THEM EVEN IF WE HAVE TO USE SPOOKY METAPHYSICAL AND/OR SUPERNATURAL MEANS TO DO SO!"
www.ucomics.com www.boondocks.net
SAID ONE PSYCHIC WHO WISHED NOT TO BE IDENTIFIED, "I KNEW THIS WOULD HAPPEN."

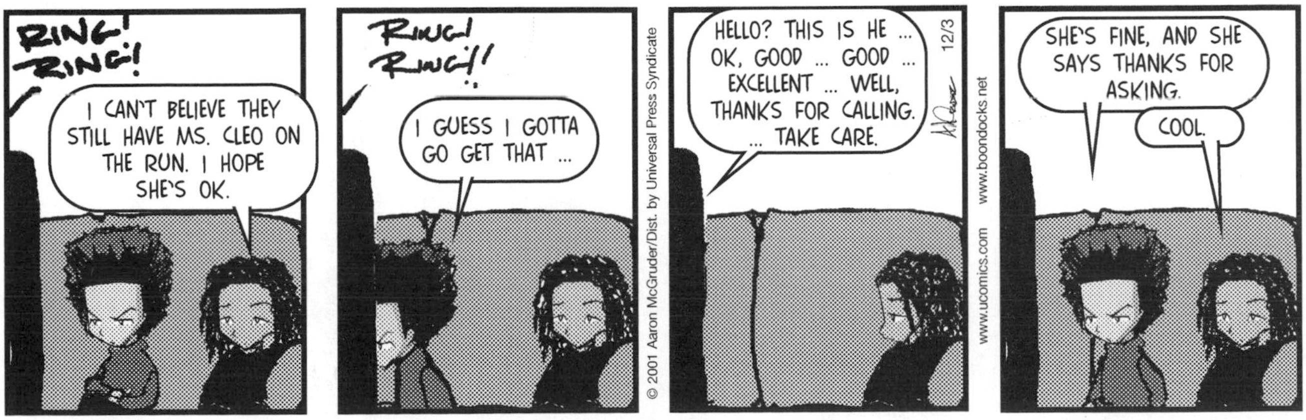
RING! RING!
I CAN'T BELIEVE THEY STILL HAVE MS. CLEO ON THE RUN. I HOPE SHE'S OK.
RING! RING!!
I GUESS I GOTTA GO GET THAT ...
© 2001 Aaron McGruder/Dist. by Universal Press Syndicate
HELLO? THIS IS HE ... OK, GOOD ... GOOD ... EXCELLENT ... WELL, THANKS FOR CALLING. ... TAKE CARE.
12/3
www.ucomics.com www.boondocks.net
SHE'S FINE, AND SHE SAYS THANKS FOR ASKING.
COOL.

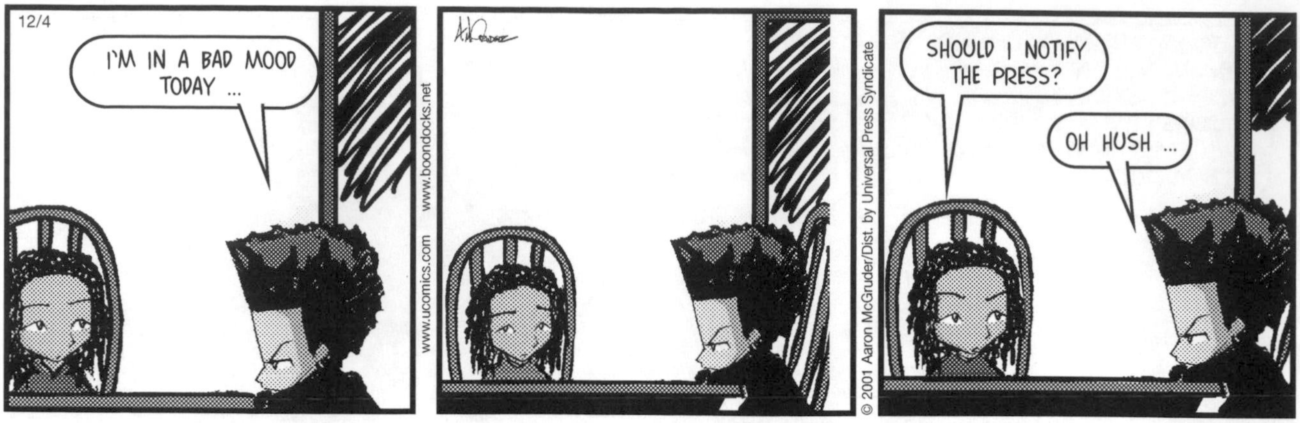
12/4
I'M IN A BAD MOOD TODAY ...
www.ucomics.com www.boondocks.net
SHOULD I NOTIFY THE PRESS?
OH HUSH ...
© 2001 Aaron McGruder/Dist. by Universal Press Syndicate

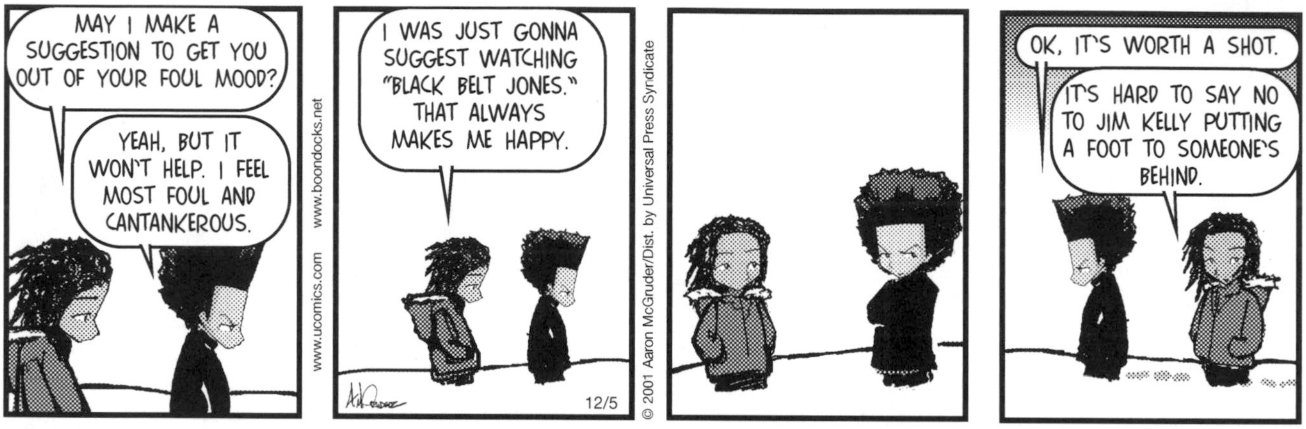
MAY I MAKE A SUGGESTION TO GET YOU OUT OF YOUR FOUL MOOD?
YEAH, BUT IT WON'T HELP. I FEEL MOST FOUL AND CANTANKEROUS.
www.ucomics.com www.boondocks.net
I WAS JUST GONNA SUGGEST WATCHING "BLACK BELT JONES." THAT ALWAYS MAKES ME HAPPY.
12/5
© 2001 Aaron McGruder/Dist. by Universal Press Syndicate
OK, IT'S WORTH A SHOT.
IT'S HARD TO SAY NO TO JIM KELLY PUTTING A FOOT TO SOMEONE'S BEHIND.

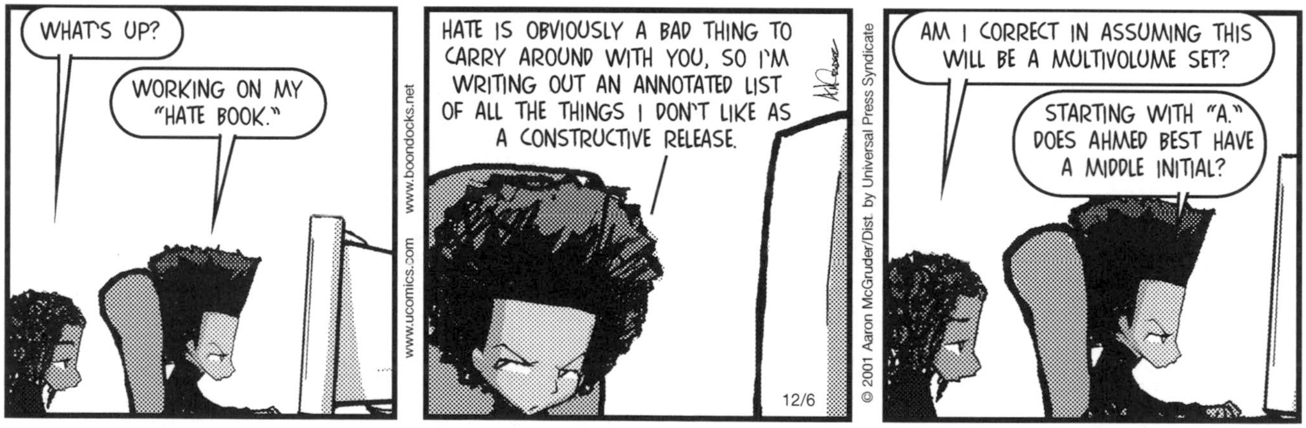
WHAT'S UP?
WORKING ON MY "HATE BOOK."
www.ucomics.com www.boondocks.net
HATE IS OBVIOUSLY A BAD THING TO CARRY AROUND WITH YOU, SO I'M WRITING OUT AN ANNOTATED LIST OF ALL THE THINGS I DON'T LIKE AS A CONSTRUCTIVE RELEASE.
12/6
© 2001 Aaron McGruder/Dist. by Universal Press Syndicate
AM I CORRECT IN ASSUMING THIS WILL BE A MULTIVOLUME SET?
STARTING WITH "A." DOES AHMED BEST HAVE A MIDDLE INITIAL?

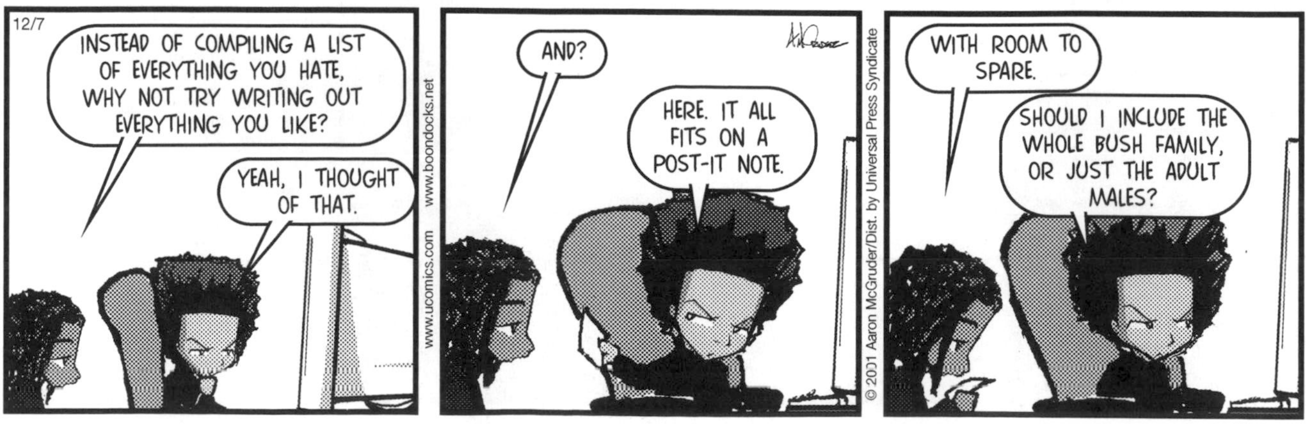
12/7
INSTEAD OF COMPILING A LIST OF EVERYTHING YOU HATE, WHY NOT TRY WRITING OUT EVERYTHING YOU LIKE?
YEAH, I THOUGHT OF THAT.
www.ucomics.com www.boondocks.net
AND?
HERE. IT ALL FITS ON A POST-IT NOTE.
© 2031 Aaron McGruder/Dist. by Universal Press Syndicate
WITH ROOM TO SPARE.
SHOULD I INCLUDE THE WHOLE BUSH FAMILY, OR JUST THE ADULT MALES?

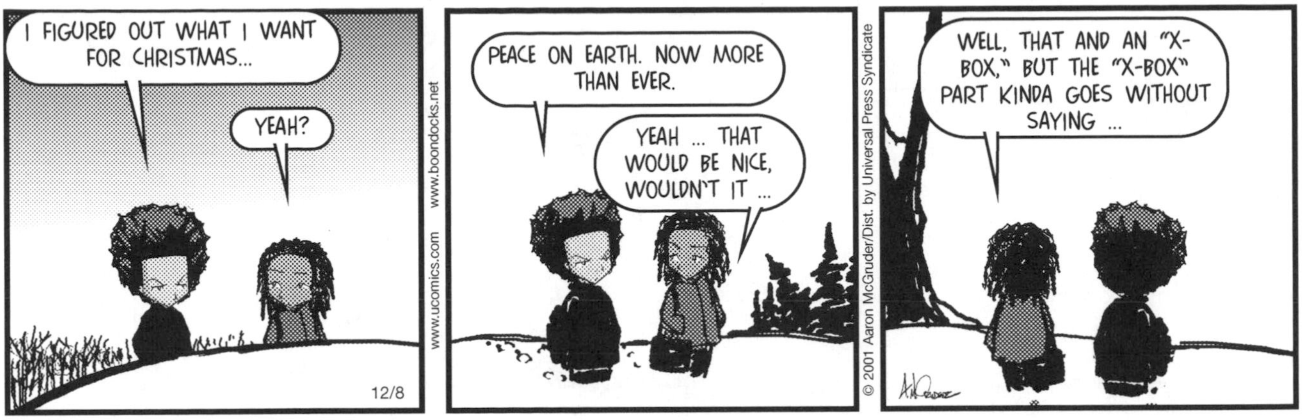
I FIGURED OUT WHAT I WANT FOR CHRISTMAS...
YEAH?
PEACE ON EARTH. NOW MORE THAN EVER.
YEAH ... THAT WOULD BE NICE, WOULDN'T IT ...
WELL, THAT AND AN "X-BOX," BUT THE "X-BOX" PART KINDA GOES WITHOUT SAYING ...
12/8
www.ucomics.com www.boondocks.net
© 2001 Aaron McGruder/Dist. by Universal Press Syndicate

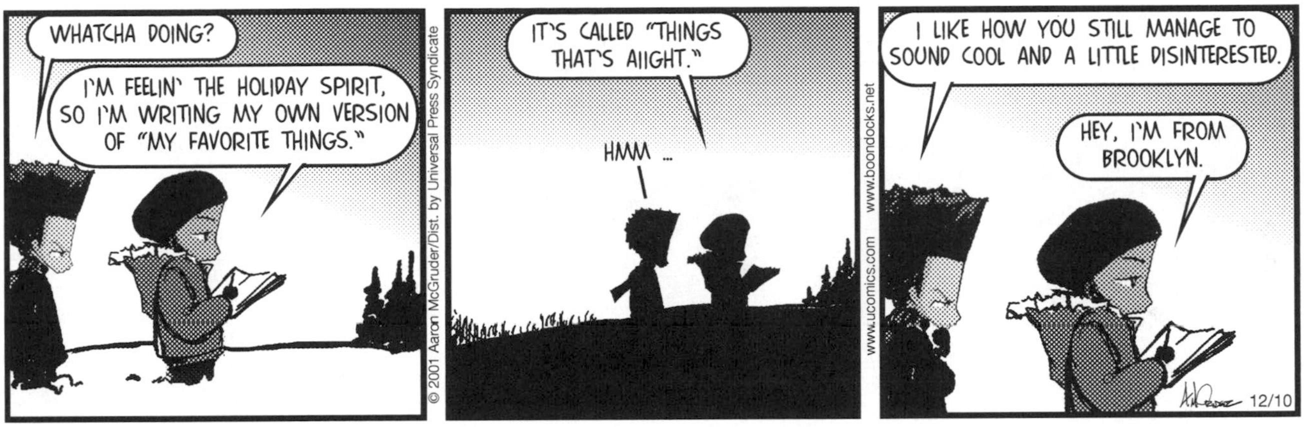
WHATCHA DOING?
I'M FEELIN' THE HOLIDAY SPIRIT, SO I'M WRITING MY OWN VERSION OF "MY FAVORITE THINGS."
IT'S CALLED "THINGS THAT'S AIIGHT."
HMM ...
I LIKE HOW YOU STILL MANAGE TO SOUND COOL AND A LITTLE DISINTERESTED.
HEY, I'M FROM BROOKLYN.
12/10
© 2001 Aaron McGruder/Dist. by Universal Press Syndicate
www.ucomics.com www.boondocks.net

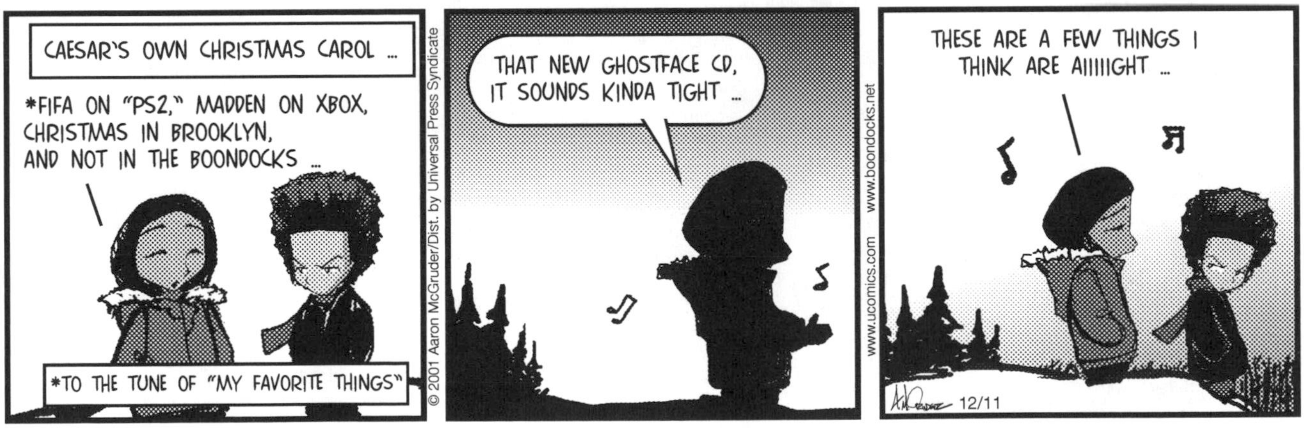
CAESAR'S OWN CHRISTMAS CAROL ...
*FIFA ON "PS2," MADDEN ON XBOX, CHRISTMAS IN BROOKLYN, AND NOT IN THE BOONDOCKS ...
*TO THE TUNE OF "MY FAVORITE THINGS"
THAT NEW GHOSTFACE CD, IT SOUNDS KINDA TIGHT ...
THESE ARE A FEW THINGS I THINK ARE AIIIIGHT ...
12/11
© 2001 Aaron McGruder/Dist. by Universal Press Syndicate
www.ucomics.com www.boondocks.net

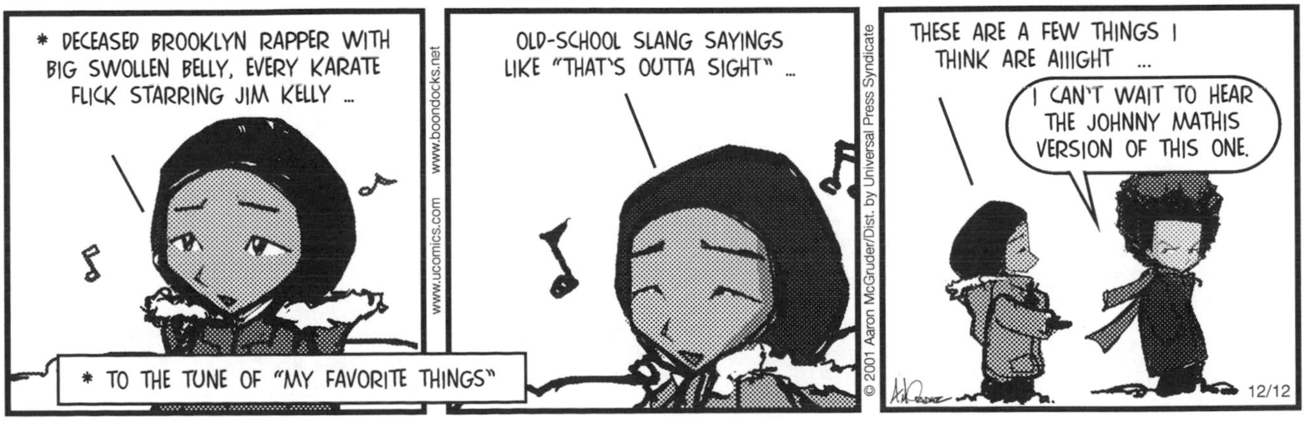
* DECEASED BROOKLYN RAPPER WITH BIG SWOLLEN BELLY, EVERY KARATE FLICK STARRING JIM KELLY ...
* TO THE TUNE OF "MY FAVORITE THINGS"
OLD-SCHOOL SLANG SAYINGS LIKE "THAT'S OUTTA SIGHT" ...
THESE ARE A FEW THINGS I THINK ARE AIIGHT ...
I CAN'T WAIT TO HEAR THE JOHNNY MATHIS VERSION OF THIS ONE.
12/12
www.ucomics.com www.boondocks.net
© 2001 Aaron McGruder/Dist. by Universal Press Syndicate

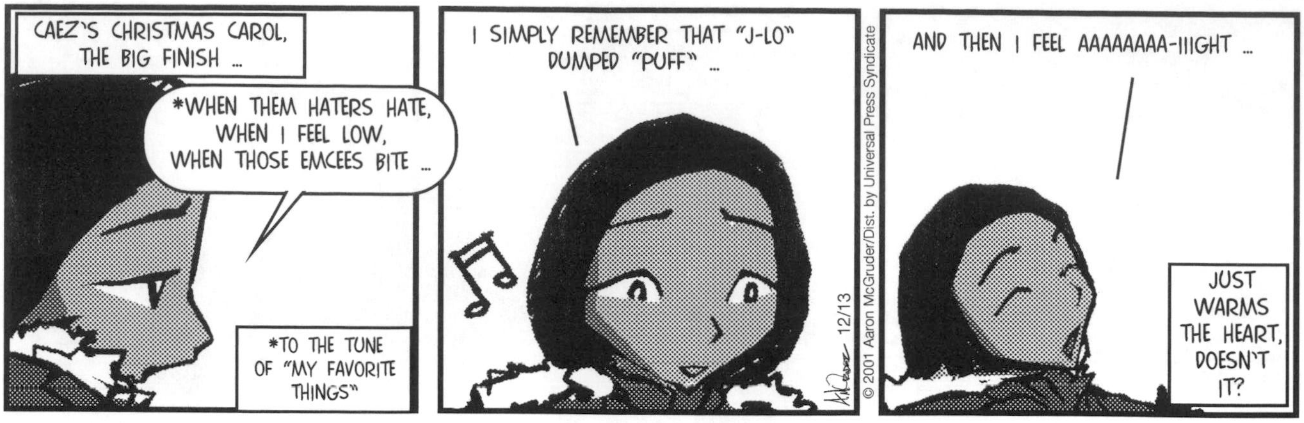
CAEZ'S CHRISTMAS CAROL, THE BIG FINISH ...
*WHEN THEM HATERS HATE, WHEN I FEEL LOW, WHEN THOSE EMCEES BITE ...
*TO THE TUNE OF "MY FAVORITE THINGS"
I SIMPLY REMEMBER THAT "J-LO" DUMPED "PUFF" ...
12/13
© 2001 Aaron McGruder/Dist. by Universal Press Syndicate
AND THEN I FEEL AAAAAAAA-IIIGHT ...
JUST WARMS THE HEART, DOESN'T IT?

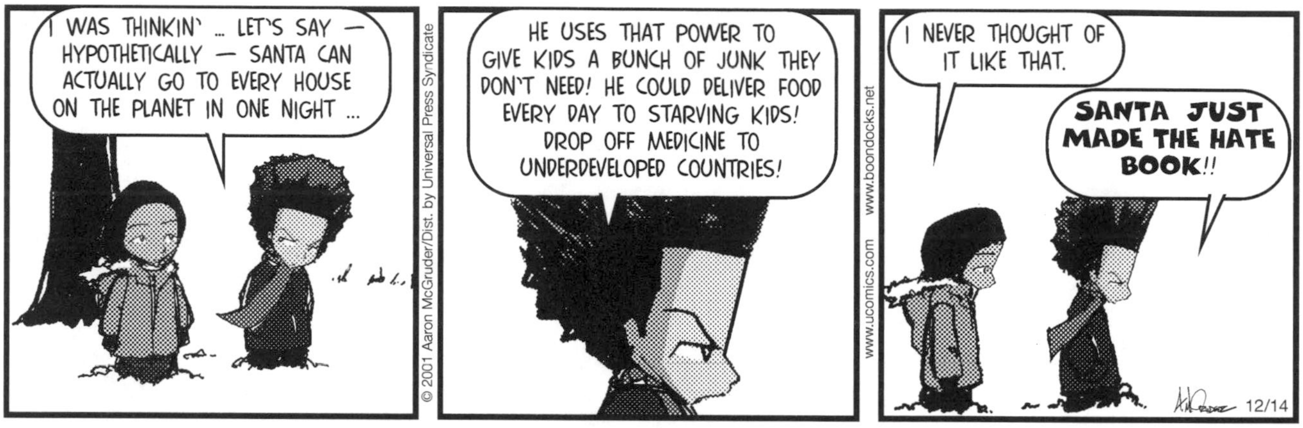
I WAS THINKIN' ... LET'S SAY — HYPOTHETICALLY — SANTA CAN ACTUALLY GO TO EVERY HOUSE ON THE PLANET IN ONE NIGHT ...
© 2001 Aaron McGruder/Dist. by Universal Press Syndicate
HE USES THAT POWER TO GIVE KIDS A BUNCH OF JUNK THEY DON'T NEED! HE COULD DELIVER FOOD EVERY DAY TO STARVING KIDS! DROP OFF MEDICINE TO UNDERDEVELOPED COUNTRIES!
www.ucomics.com www.boondocks.net
I NEVER THOUGHT OF IT LIKE THAT.
SANTA JUST MADE THE HATE BOOK!!
12/14

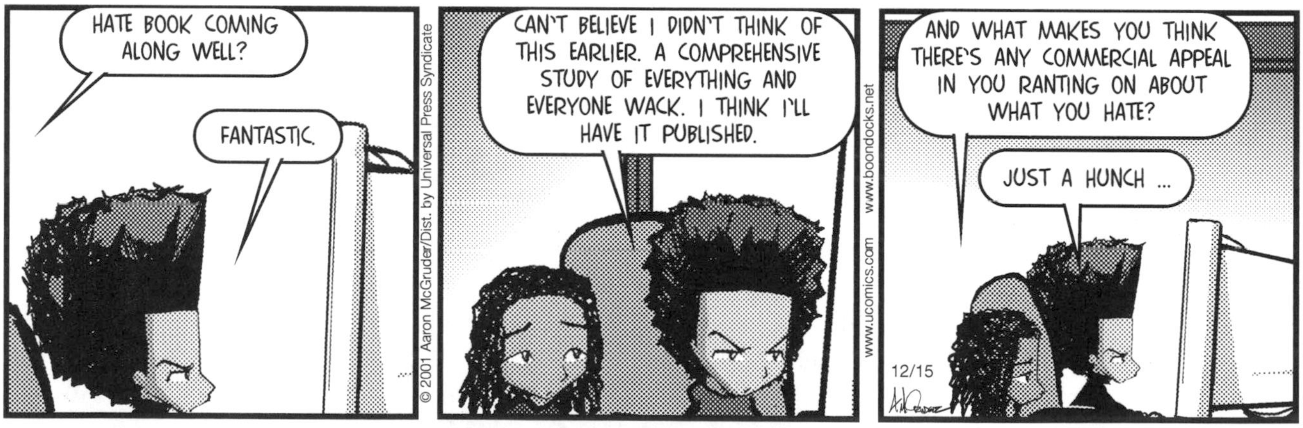
HATE BOOK COMING ALONG WELL?
FANTASTIC.
© 2001 Aaron McGruder/Dist. by Universal Press Syndicate
CAN'T BELIEVE I DIDN'T THINK OF THIS EARLIER. A COMPREHENSIVE STUDY OF EVERYTHING AND EVERYONE WACK. I THINK I'LL HAVE IT PUBLISHED.
www.ucomics.com www.boondocks.net
AND WHAT MAKES YOU THINK THERE'S ANY COMMERCIAL APPEAL IN YOU RANTING ON ABOUT WHAT YOU HATE?
JUST A HUNCH ...
12/15

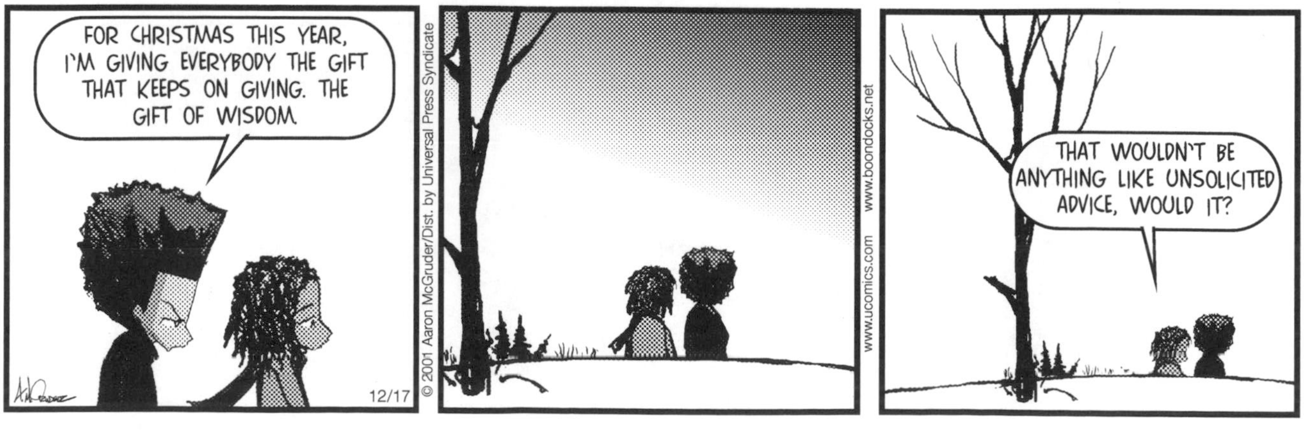
FOR CHRISTMAS THIS YEAR, I'M GIVING EVERYBODY THE GIFT THAT KEEPS ON GIVING. THE GIFT OF WISDOM.
12/17
© 2001 Aaron McGruder/Dist. by Universal Press Syndicate
www.ucomics.com www.boondocks.net
THAT WOULDN'T BE ANYTHING LIKE UNSOLICITED ADVICE, WOULD IT?

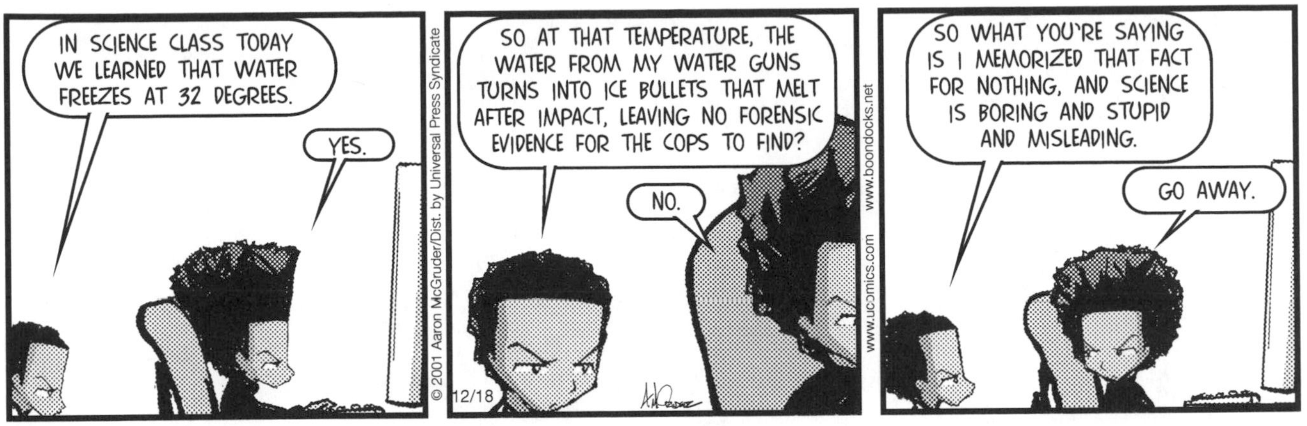
IN SCIENCE CLASS TODAY WE LEARNED THAT WATER FREEZES AT 32 DEGREES.
YES.
© 2001 Aaron McGruder/Dist. by Universal Press Syndicate
12/18
SO AT THAT TEMPERATURE, THE WATER FROM MY WATER GUNS TURNS INTO ICE BULLETS THAT MELT AFTER IMPACT, LEAVING NO FORENSIC EVIDENCE FOR THE COPS TO FIND?
NO.
www.ucomics.com www.boondocks.net
SO WHAT YOU'RE SAYING IS I MEMORIZED THAT FACT FOR NOTHING, AND SCIENCE IS BORING AND STUPID AND MISLEADING.
GO AWAY.

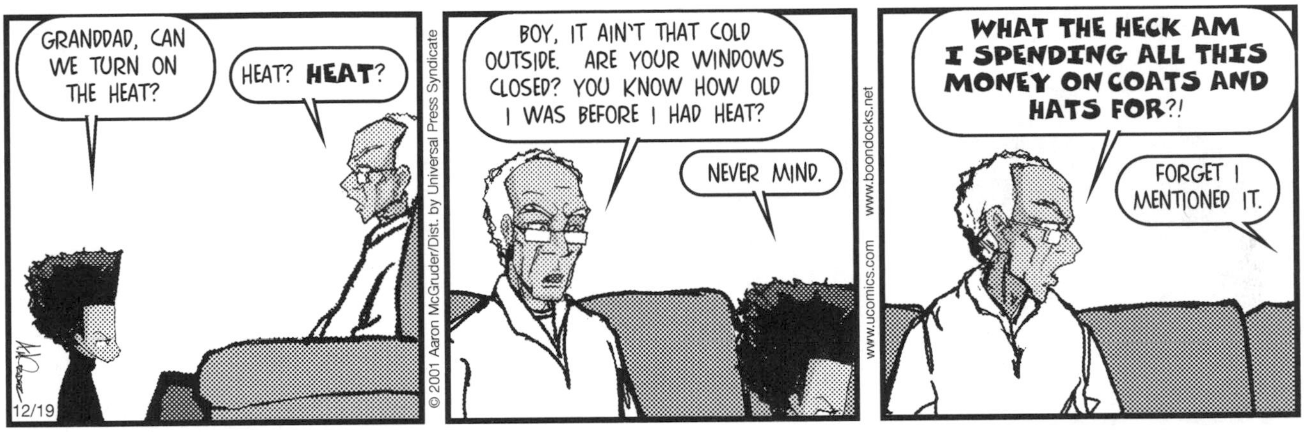
GRANDDAD, CAN WE TURN ON THE HEAT?
HEAT? **HEAT**?
12/19
© 2001 Aaron McGruder/Dist. by Universal Press Syndicate
BOY, IT AIN'T THAT COLD OUTSIDE. ARE YOUR WINDOWS CLOSED? YOU KNOW HOW OLD I WAS BEFORE I HAD HEAT?
NEVER MIND.
www.ucomics.com www.boondocks.net
WHAT THE HECK AM I SPENDING ALL THIS MONEY ON COATS AND HATS FOR?!
FORGET I MENTIONED IT.

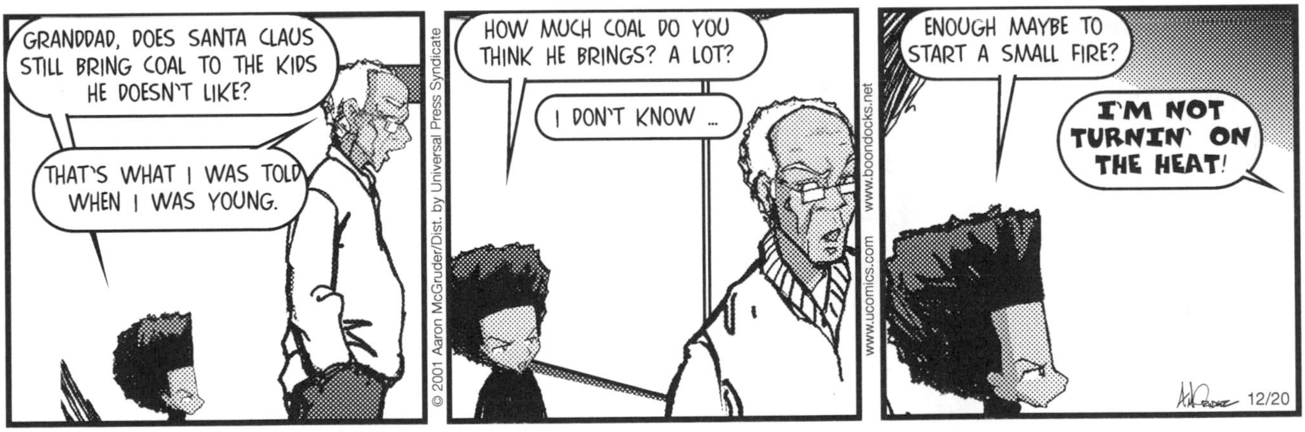
GRANDDAD, DOES SANTA CLAUS STILL BRING COAL TO THE KIDS HE DOESN'T LIKE?
THAT'S WHAT I WAS TOLD WHEN I WAS YOUNG.
© 2001 Aaron McGruder/Dist. by Universal Press Syndicate
HOW MUCH COAL DO YOU THINK HE BRINGS? A LOT?
I DON'T KNOW ...
www.ucomics.com www.boondocks.net
ENOUGH MAYBE TO START A SMALL FIRE?
I'M NOT TURNIN' ON THE HEAT!
12/20

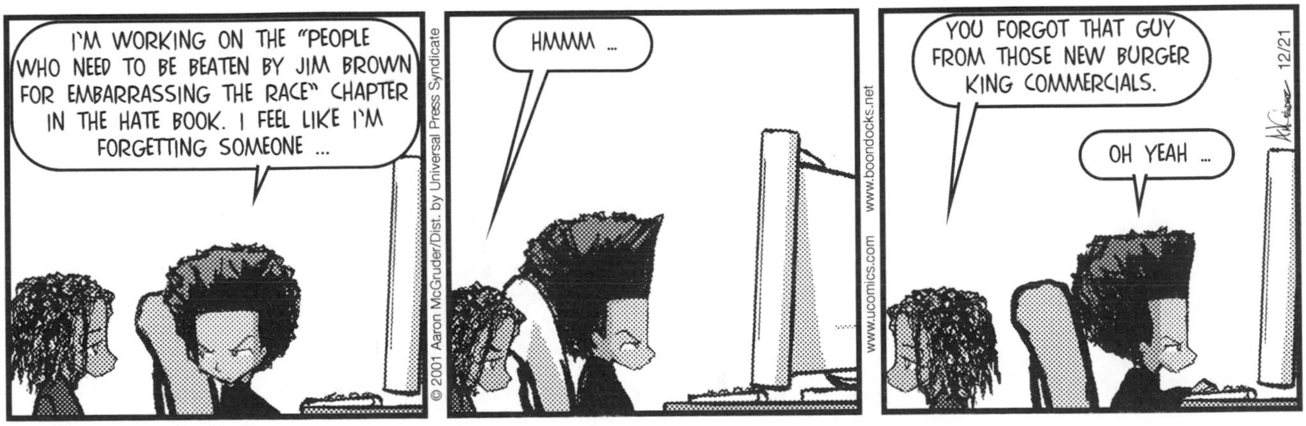
I'M WORKING ON THE "PEOPLE WHO NEED TO BE BEATEN BY JIM BROWN FOR EMBARRASSING THE RACE" CHAPTER IN THE HATE BOOK. I FEEL LIKE I'M FORGETTING SOMEONE ...
© 2001 Aaron McGruder/Dist. by Universal Press Syndicate
HMMM ...
www.ucomics.com www.boondocks.net
YOU FORGOT THAT GUY FROM THOSE NEW BURGER KING COMMERCIALS.
OH YEAH ...
12/21

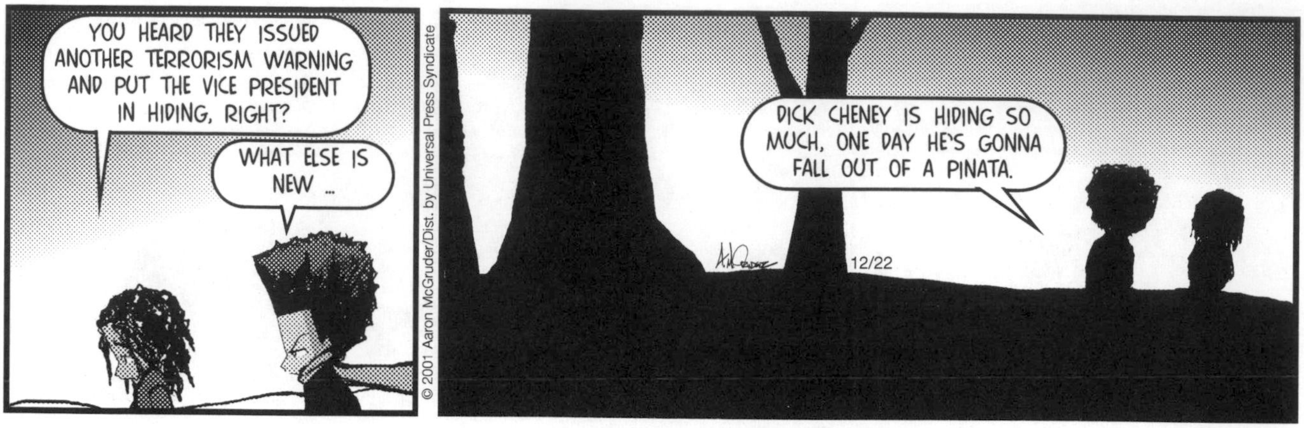
YOU HEARD THEY ISSUED ANOTHER TERRORISM WARNING AND PUT THE VICE PRESIDENT IN HIDING, RIGHT?
WHAT ELSE IS NEW ...
© 2001 Aaron McGruder/Dist. by Universal Press Syndicate
DICK CHENEY IS HIDING SO MUCH, ONE DAY HE'S GONNA FALL OUT OF A PINATA.
12/22

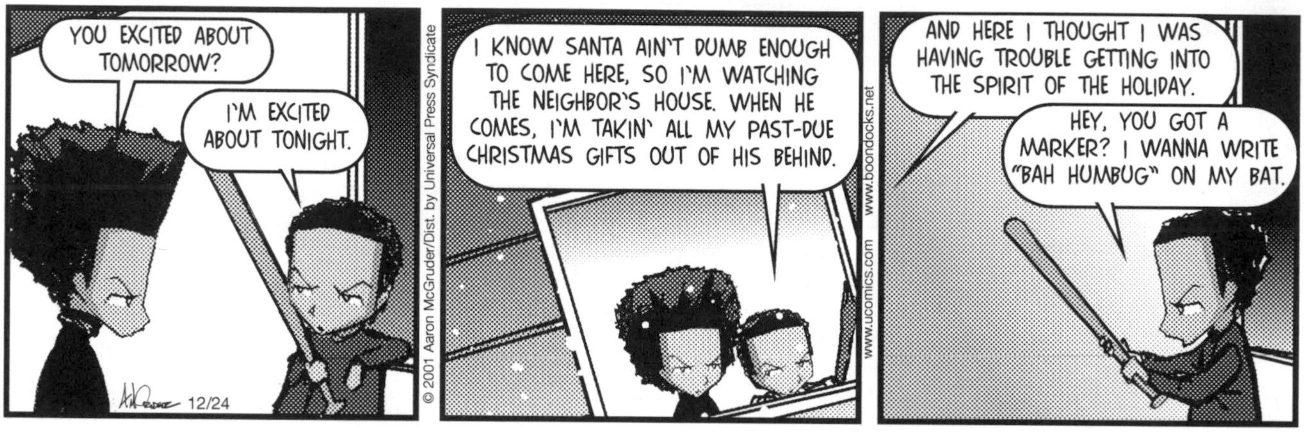
YOU EXCITED ABOUT TOMORROW?
I'M EXCITED ABOUT TONIGHT.
12/24
© 2001 Aaron McGruder/Dist. by Universal Press Syndicate
I KNOW SANTA AIN'T DUMB ENOUGH TO COME HERE, SO I'M WATCHING THE NEIGHBOR'S HOUSE. WHEN HE COMES, I'M TAKIN' ALL MY PAST-DUE CHRISTMAS GIFTS OUT OF HIS BEHIND.
www.ucomics.com www.boondocks.net
AND HERE I THOUGHT I WAS HAVING TROUBLE GETTING INTO THE SPIRIT OF THE HOLIDAY.
HEY, YOU GOT A MARKER? I WANNA WRITE "BAH HUMBUG" ON MY BAT.

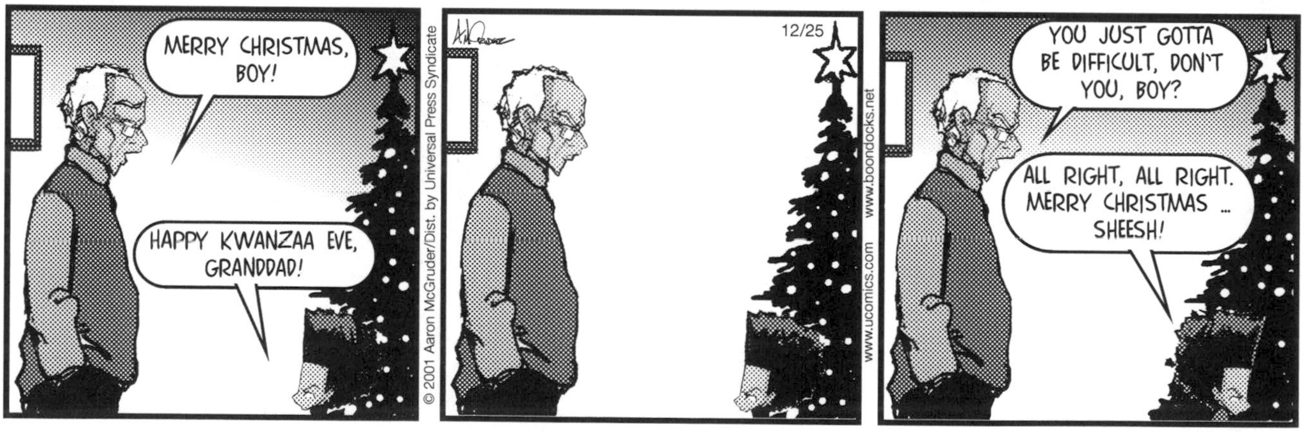
MERRY CHRISTMAS, BOY!
HAPPY KWANZAA EVE, GRANDDAD!
© 2001 Aaron McGruder/Dist. by Universal Press Syndicate
12/25
www.ucomics.com www.boondocks.net
YOU JUST GOTTA BE DIFFICULT, DON'T YOU, BOY?
ALL RIGHT, ALL RIGHT. MERRY CHRISTMAS ... SHEESH!

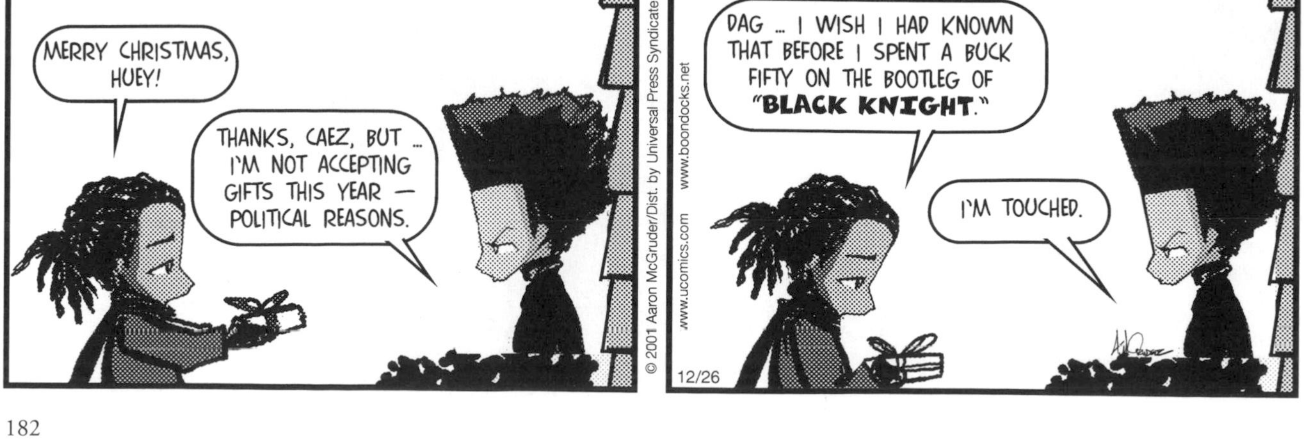
MERRY CHRISTMAS, HUEY!
THANKS, CAEZ, BUT ... I'M NOT ACCEPTING GIFTS THIS YEAR — POLITICAL REASONS.
© 2001 Aaron McGruder/Dist. by Universal Press Syndicate
www.ucomics.com www.boondocks.net
DAG ... I WISH I HAD KNOWN THAT BEFORE I SPENT A BUCK FIFTY ON THE BOOTLEG OF "BLACK KNIGHT."
I'M TOUCHED.
12/26

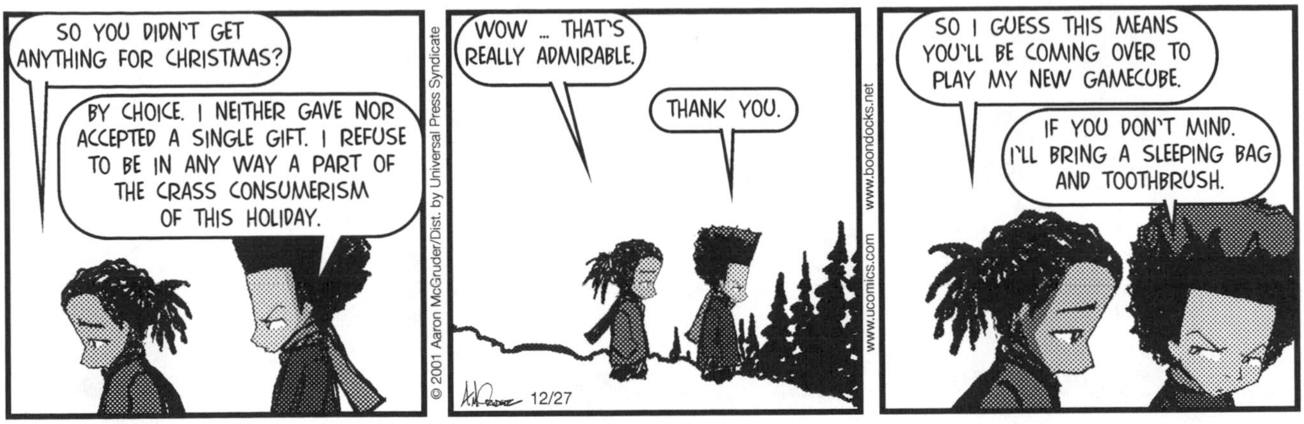
SO YOU DIDN'T GET ANYTHING FOR CHRISTMAS?
BY CHOICE. I NEITHER GAVE NOR ACCEPTED A SINGLE GIFT. I REFUSE TO BE IN ANY WAY A PART OF THE CRASS CONSUMERISM OF THIS HOLIDAY.
WOW ... THAT'S REALLY ADMIRABLE.
THANK YOU.
SO I GUESS THIS MEANS YOU'LL BE COMING OVER TO PLAY MY NEW GAMECUBE.
IF YOU DON'T MIND. I'LL BRING A SLEEPING BAG AND TOOTHBRUSH.
© 2001 Aaron McGruder/Dist. by Universal Press Syndicate
www.ucomics.com www.boondocks.net
12/27

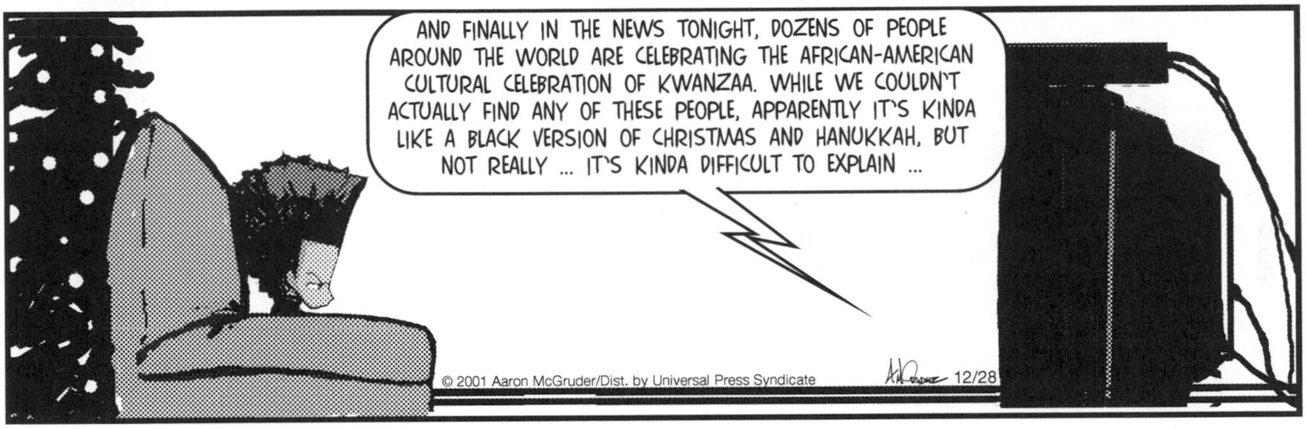
AND FINALLY IN THE NEWS TONIGHT, DOZENS OF PEOPLE AROUND THE WORLD ARE CELEBRATING THE AFRICAN-AMERICAN CULTURAL CELEBRATION OF KWANZAA. WHILE WE COULDN'T ACTUALLY FIND ANY OF THESE PEOPLE, APPARENTLY IT'S KINDA LIKE A BLACK VERSION OF CHRISTMAS AND HANUKKAH, BUT NOT REALLY ... IT'S KINDA DIFFICULT TO EXPLAIN ...
© 2001 Aaron McGruder/Dist. by Universal Press Syndicate
12/28

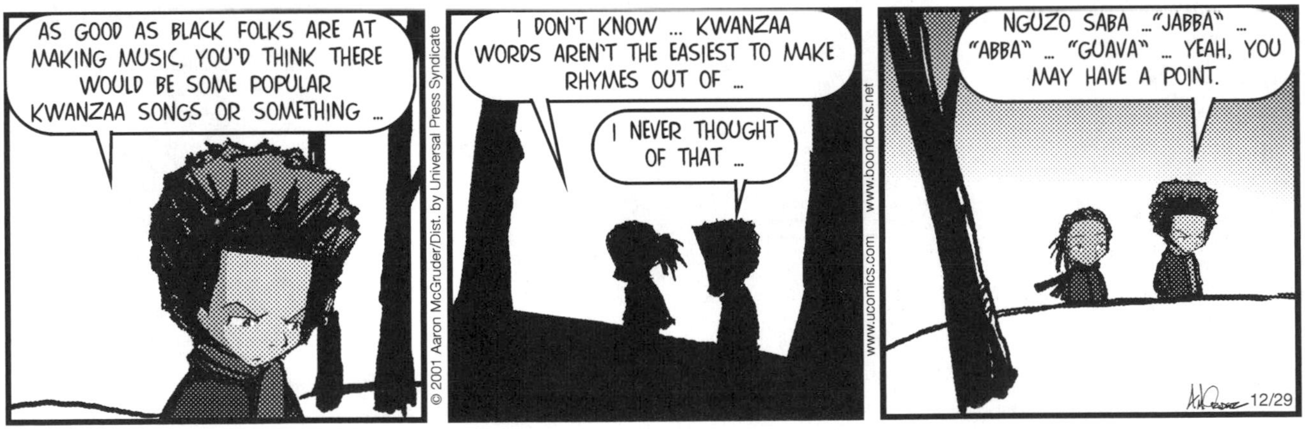
AS GOOD AS BLACK FOLKS ARE AT MAKING MUSIC, YOU'D THINK THERE WOULD BE SOME POPULAR KWANZAA SONGS OR SOMETHING ...
I DON'T KNOW ... KWANZAA WORDS AREN'T THE EASIEST TO MAKE RHYMES OUT OF ...
I NEVER THOUGHT OF THAT ...
NGUZO SABA ..."JABBA" ... "ABBA" ... "GUAVA" ... YEAH, YOU MAY HAVE A POINT.
© 2001 Aaron McGruder/Dist. by Universal Press Syndicate
www.ucomics.com www.boondocks.net
12/29

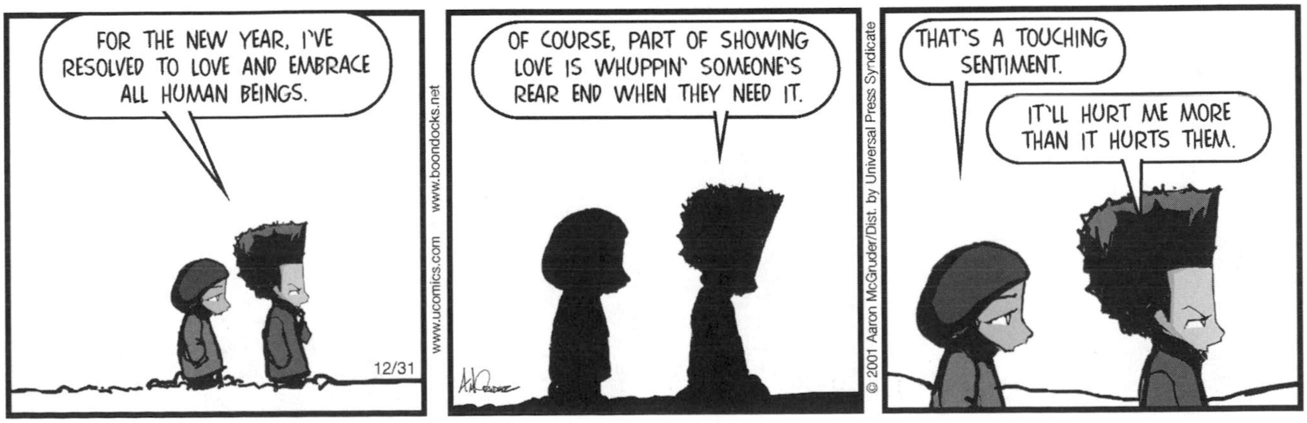
FOR THE NEW YEAR, I'VE RESOLVED TO LOVE AND EMBRACE ALL HUMAN BEINGS.
OF COURSE, PART OF SHOWING LOVE IS WHUPPIN' SOMEONE'S REAR END WHEN THEY NEED IT.
THAT'S A TOUCHING SENTIMENT.
IT'LL HURT ME MORE THAN IT HURTS THEM.
www.ucomics.com www.boondocks.net
© 2001 Aaron McGruder/Dist. by Universal Press Syndicate
12/31

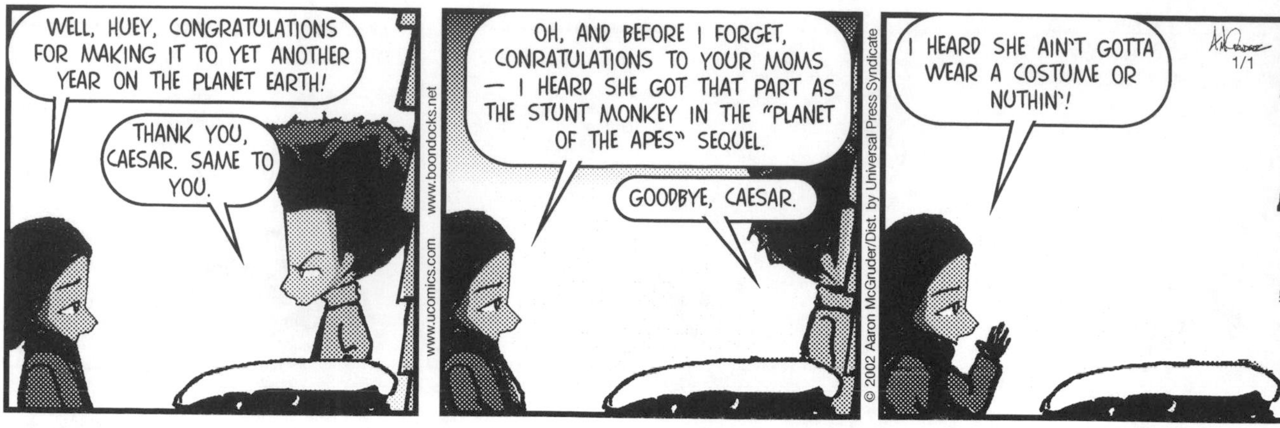
WELL, HUEY, CONGRATULATIONS FOR MAKING IT TO YET ANOTHER YEAR ON THE PLANET EARTH!
THANK YOU, CAESAR. SAME TO YOU.
OH, AND BEFORE I FORGET, CONRATULATIONS TO YOUR MOMS — I HEARD SHE GOT THAT PART AS THE STUNT MONKEY IN THE "PLANET OF THE APES" SEQUEL.
GOODBYE, CAESAR.
I HEARD SHE AIN'T GOTTA WEAR A COSTUME OR NUTHIN'!
1/1
www.ucomics.com www.boondocks.net
© 2002 Aaron McGruder/Dist. by Universal Press Syndicate

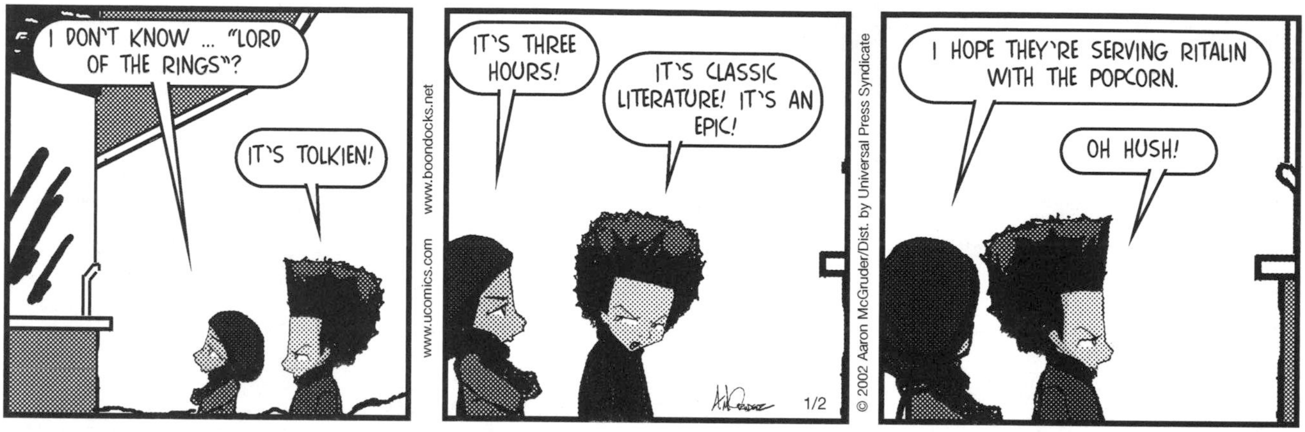
I DON'T KNOW ... "LORD OF THE RINGS"?
IT'S TOLKIEN!
IT'S THREE HOURS!
IT'S CLASSIC LITERATURE! IT'S AN EPIC!
I HOPE THEY'RE SERVING RITALIN WITH THE POPCORN.
OH HUSH!
1/2
www.ucomics.com www.boondocks.net
© 2002 Aaron McGruder/Dist. by Universal Press Syndicate

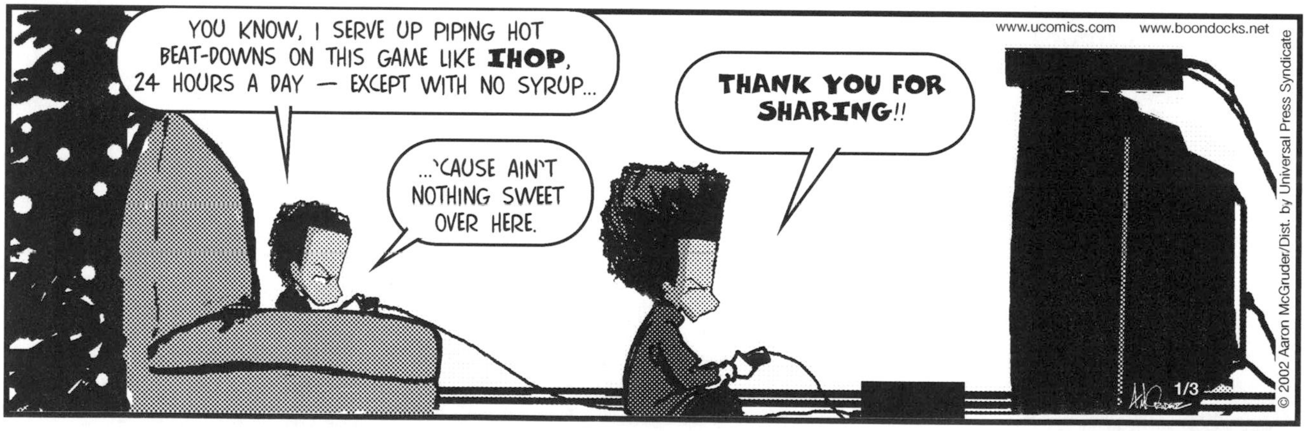
YOU KNOW, I SERVE UP PIPING HOT BEAT-DOWNS ON THIS GAME LIKE IHOP, 24 HOURS A DAY — EXCEPT WITH NO SYRUP...
...'CAUSE AIN'T NOTHING SWEET OVER HERE.
THANK YOU FOR SHARING!!
1/3
www.ucomics.com www.boondocks.net
© 2002 Aaron McGruder/Dist. by Universal Press Syndicate

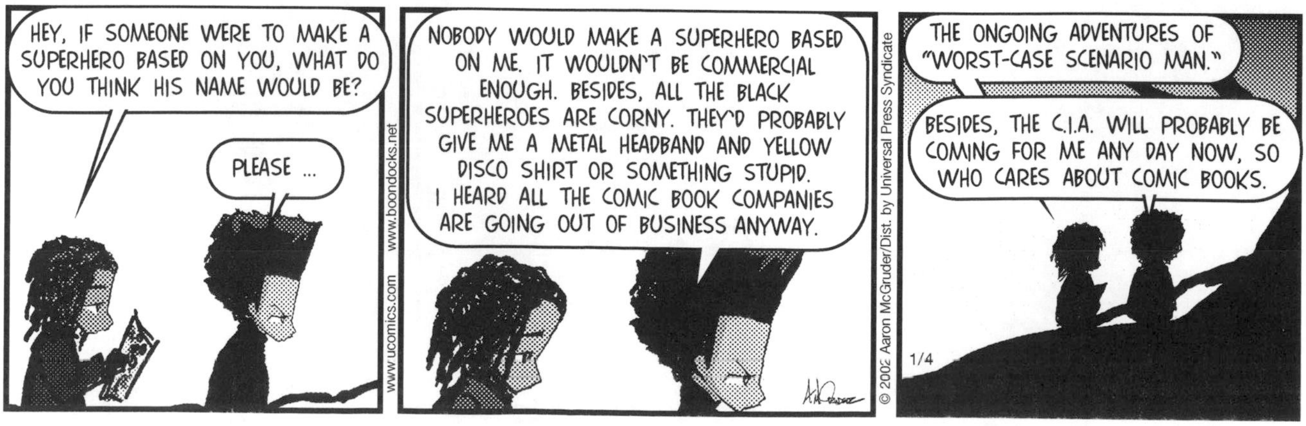
HEY, IF SOMEONE WERE TO MAKE A SUPERHERO BASED ON YOU, WHAT DO YOU THINK HIS NAME WOULD BE?
PLEASE ...
NOBODY WOULD MAKE A SUPERHERO BASED ON ME. IT WOULDN'T BE COMMERCIAL ENOUGH. BESIDES, ALL THE BLACK SUPERHEROES ARE CORNY. THEY'D PROBABLY GIVE ME A METAL HEADBAND AND YELLOW DISCO SHIRT OR SOMETHING STUPID. I HEARD ALL THE COMIC BOOK COMPANIES ARE GOING OUT OF BUSINESS ANYWAY.
THE ONGOING ADVENTURES OF "WORST-CASE SCENARIO MAN."
BESIDES, THE C.I.A. WILL PROBABLY BE COMING FOR ME ANY DAY NOW, SO WHO CARES ABOUT COMIC BOOKS.
1/4
www.ucomics.com www.boondocks.net
© 2002 Aaron McGruder/Dist. by Universal Press Syndicate

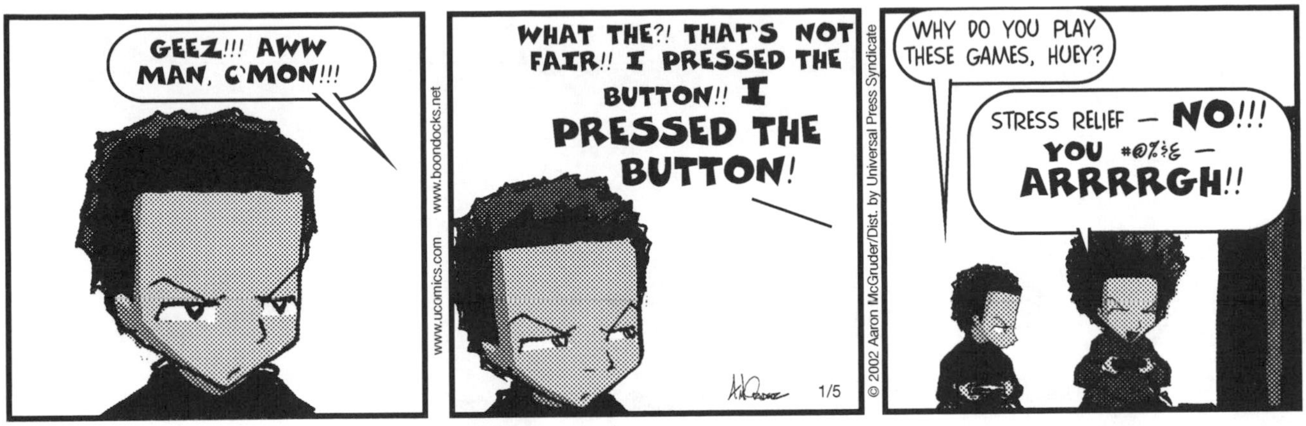
GEEZ!!! AWW MAN, C'MON!!!
www.ucomics.com www.boondocks.net
WHAT THE?! THAT'S NOT FAIR!! I PRESSED THE BUTTON!! I PRESSED THE BUTTON!
1/5
© 2002 Aaron McGruder/Dist. by Universal Press Syndicate
WHY DO YOU PLAY THESE GAMES, HUEY?
STRESS RELIEF — NO!!! YOU #@%$& — ARRRRGH!!

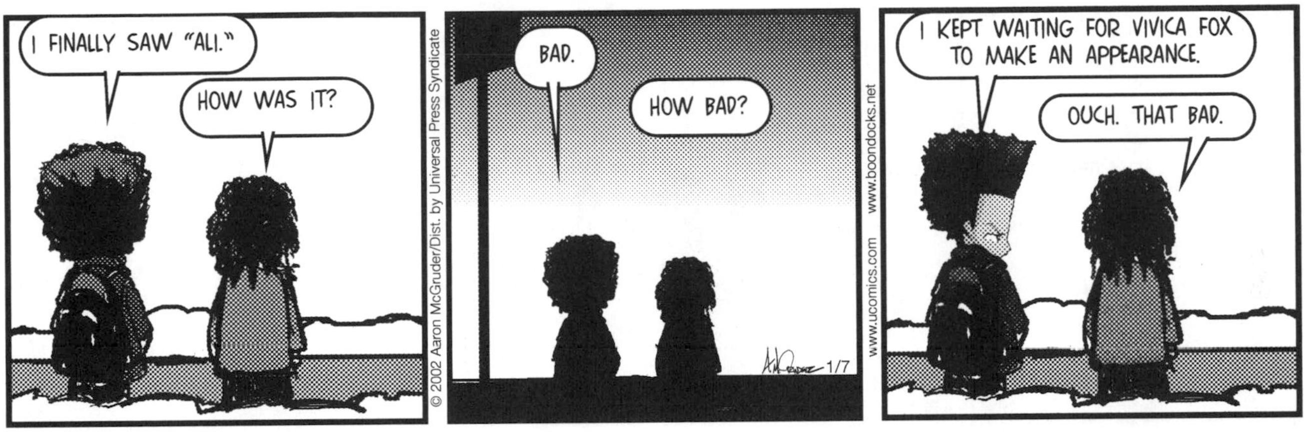
I FINALLY SAW "ALI."
HOW WAS IT?
© 2002 Aaron McGruder/Dist. by Universal Press Syndicate
BAD.
HOW BAD?
1/7
www.ucomics.com www.boondocks.net
I KEPT WAITING FOR VIVICA FOX TO MAKE AN APPEARANCE.
OUCH. THAT BAD.

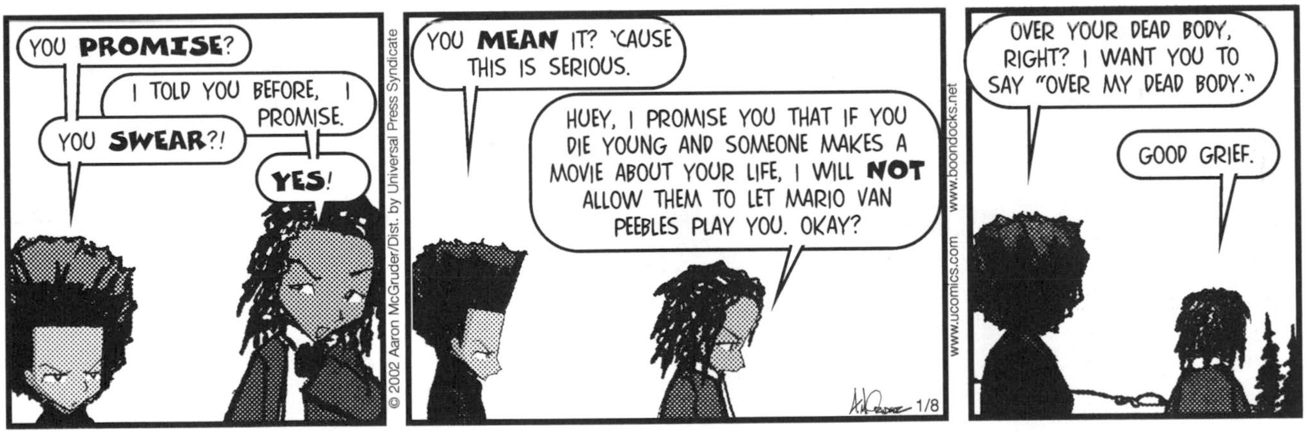
YOU PROMISE?
I TOLD YOU BEFORE, I PROMISE.
YOU SWEAR?!
YES!
© 2002 Aaron McGruder/Dist. by Universal Press Syndicate
YOU MEAN IT? 'CAUSE THIS IS SERIOUS.
HUEY, I PROMISE YOU THAT IF YOU DIE YOUNG AND SOMEONE MAKES A MOVIE ABOUT YOUR LIFE, I WILL NOT ALLOW THEM TO LET MARIO VAN PEEBLES PLAY YOU. OKAY?
1/8
www.ucomics.com www.boondocks.net
OVER YOUR DEAD BODY, RIGHT? I WANT YOU TO SAY "OVER MY DEAD BODY."
GOOD GRIEF.

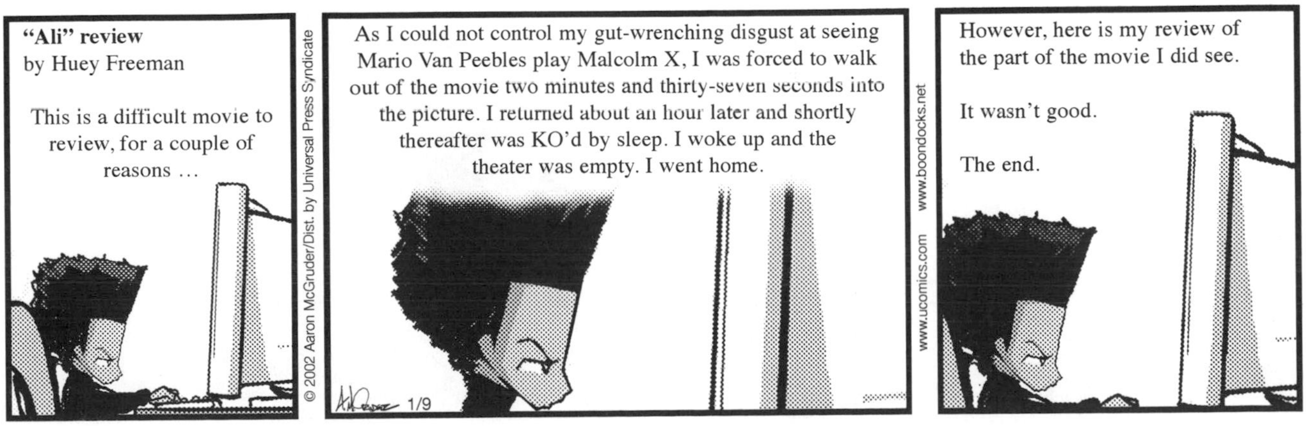
"Ali" review
by Huey Freeman
This is a difficult movie to review, for a couple of reasons …
© 2002 Aaron McGruder/Dist. by Universal Press Syndicate
As I could not control my gut-wrenching disgust at seeing Mario Van Peebles play Malcolm X, I was forced to walk out of the movie two minutes and thirty-seven seconds into the picture. I returned about an hour later and shortly thereafter was KO'd by sleep. I woke up and the theater was empty. I went home.
1/9
www.ucomics.com www.boondocks.net
However, here is my review of the part of the movie I did see.
It wasn't good.
The end.

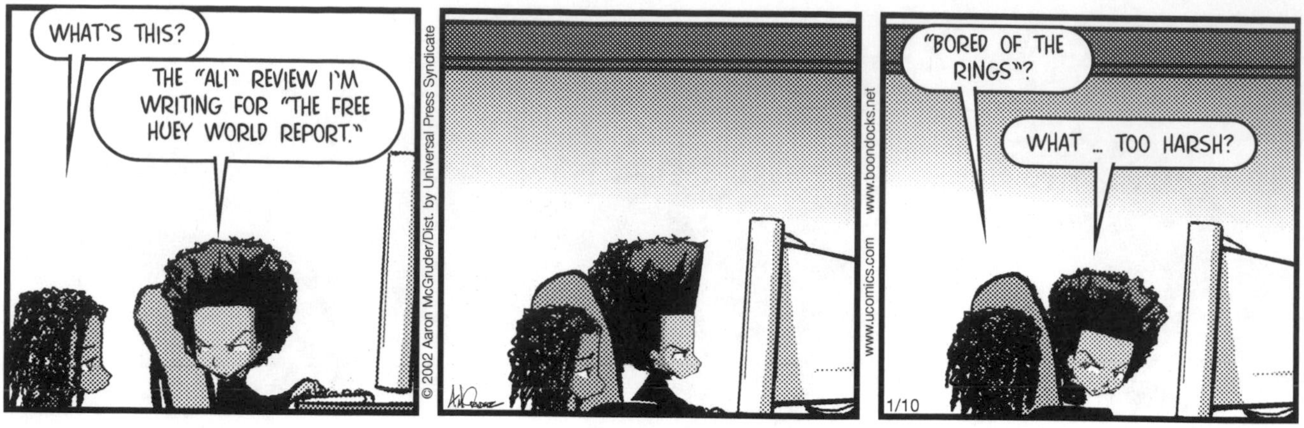
WHAT'S THIS?
THE "ALI" REVIEW I'M WRITING FOR "THE FREE HUEY WORLD REPORT."
© 2002 Aaron McGruder/Dist. by Universal Press Syndicate
"BORED OF THE RINGS"?
WHAT ... TOO HARSH?
www.ucomics.com www.boondocks.net
1/10

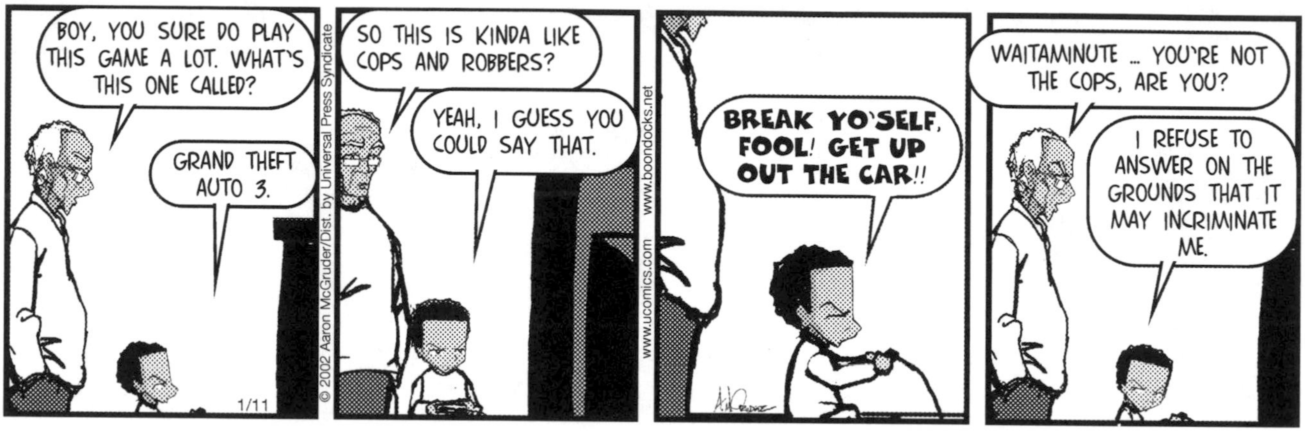
BOY, YOU SURE DO PLAY THIS GAME A LOT. WHAT'S THIS ONE CALLED?
GRAND THEFT AUTO 3.
1/11
© 2002 Aaron McGruder/Dist. by Universal Press Syndicate
SO THIS IS KINDA LIKE COPS AND ROBBERS?
YEAH, I GUESS YOU COULD SAY THAT.
www.ucomics.com www.boondocks.net
BREAK YO'SELF, FOOL! GET UP OUT THE CAR!!
WAITAMINUTE ... YOU'RE NOT THE COPS, ARE YOU?
I REFUSE TO ANSWER ON THE GROUNDS THAT IT MAY INCRIMINATE ME.

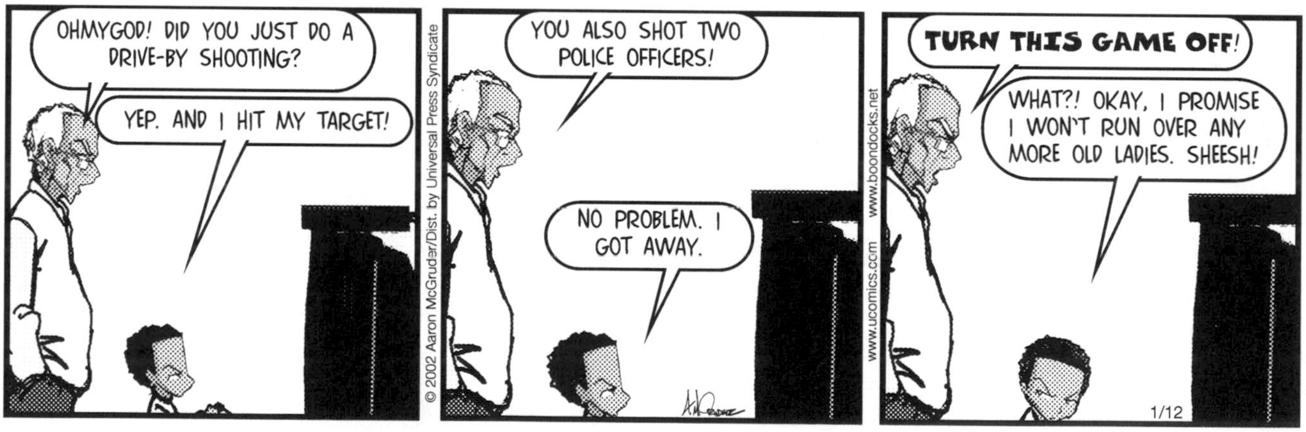
OHMYGOD! DID YOU JUST DO A DRIVE-BY SHOOTING?
YEP. AND I HIT MY TARGET!
© 2002 Aaron McGruder/Dist. by Universal Press Syndicate
YOU ALSO SHOT TWO POLICE OFFICERS!
NO PROBLEM. I GOT AWAY.
www.ucomics.com www.boondocks.net
TURN THIS GAME OFF!
WHAT?! OKAY, I PROMISE I WON'T RUN OVER ANY MORE OLD LADIES. SHEESH!
1/12

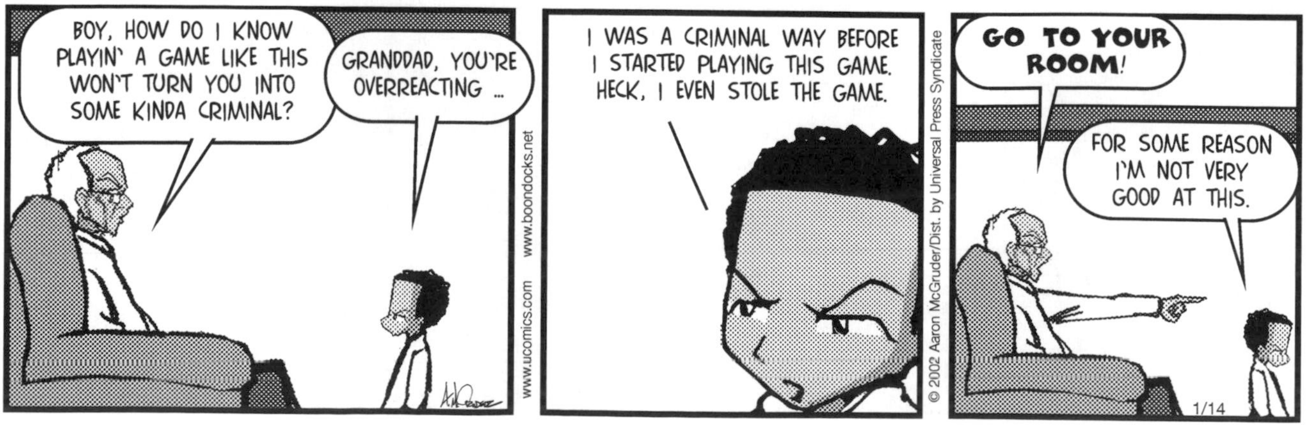
BOY, HOW DO I KNOW PLAYIN' A GAME LIKE THIS WON'T TURN YOU INTO SOME KINDA CRIMINAL?
GRANDDAD, YOU'RE OVERREACTING ...
www.ucomics.com www.boondocks.net
I WAS A CRIMINAL WAY BEFORE I STARTED PLAYING THIS GAME. HECK, I EVEN STOLE THE GAME.
© 2002 Aaron McGruder/Dist. by Universal Press Syndicate
GO TO YOUR ROOM!
FOR SOME REASON I'M NOT VERY GOOD AT THIS.
1/14

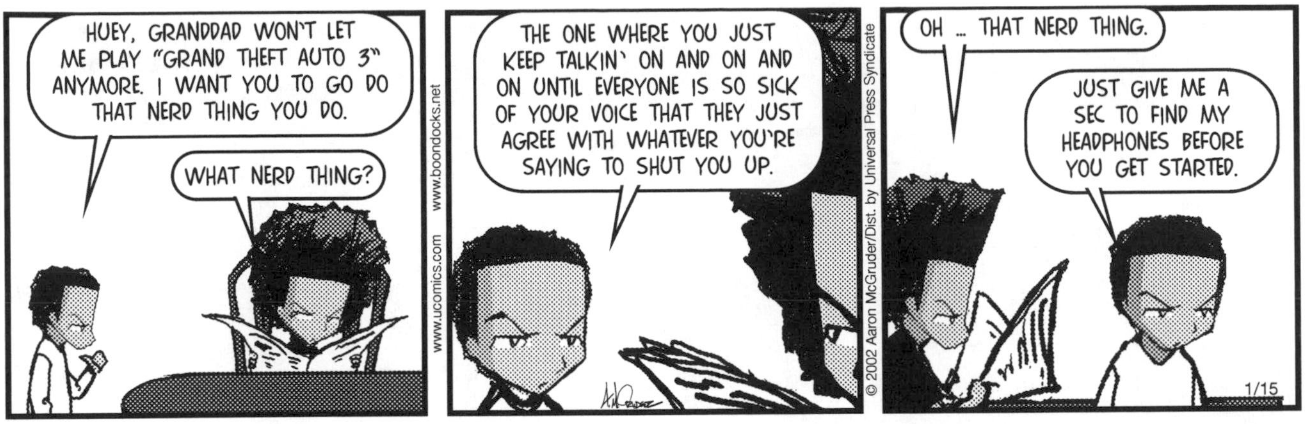
HUEY, GRANDDAD WON'T LET ME PLAY "GRAND THEFT AUTO 3" ANYMORE. I WANT YOU TO GO DO THAT NERD THING YOU DO.
WHAT NERD THING?
www.ucomics.com www.boondocks.net
THE ONE WHERE YOU JUST KEEP TALKIN' ON AND ON AND ON UNTIL EVERYONE IS SO SICK OF YOUR VOICE THAT THEY JUST AGREE WITH WHATEVER YOU'RE SAYING TO SHUT YOU UP.
© 2002 Aaron McGruder/Dist. by Universal Press Syndicate
OH ... THAT NERD THING.
JUST GIVE ME A SEC TO FIND MY HEADPHONES BEFORE YOU GET STARTED.
1/15

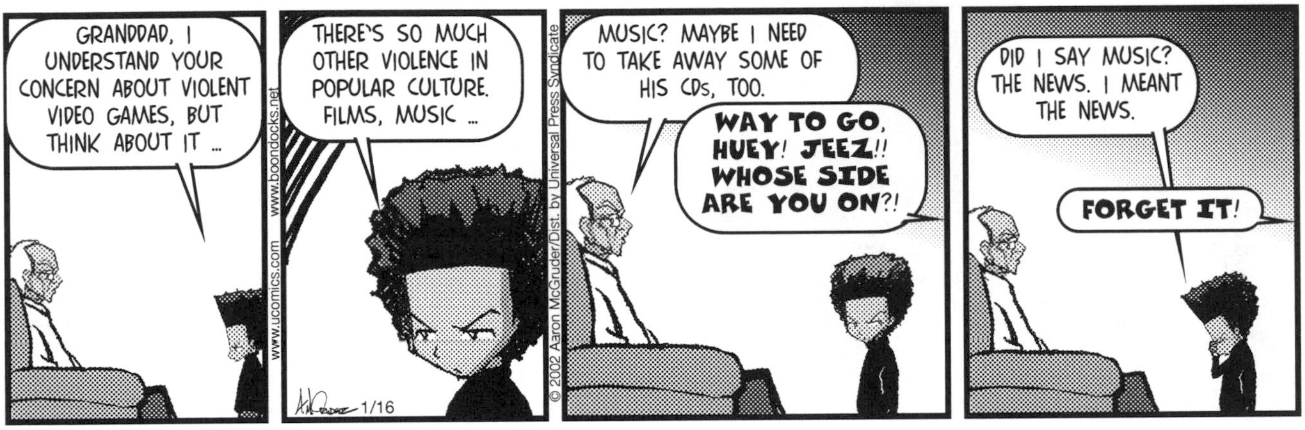
GRANDDAD, I UNDERSTAND YOUR CONCERN ABOUT VIOLENT VIDEO GAMES, BUT THINK ABOUT IT ...
www.ucomics.com www.boondocks.net
THERE'S SO MUCH OTHER VIOLENCE IN POPULAR CULTURE. FILMS, MUSIC ...
1/16
© 2002 Aaron McGruder/Dist. by Universal Press Syndicate
MUSIC? MAYBE I NEED TO TAKE AWAY SOME OF HIS CDs, TOO.
WAY TO GO, HUEY! JEEZ!! WHOSE SIDE ARE YOU ON?!
DID I SAY MUSIC? THE NEWS. I MEANT THE NEWS.
FORGET IT!

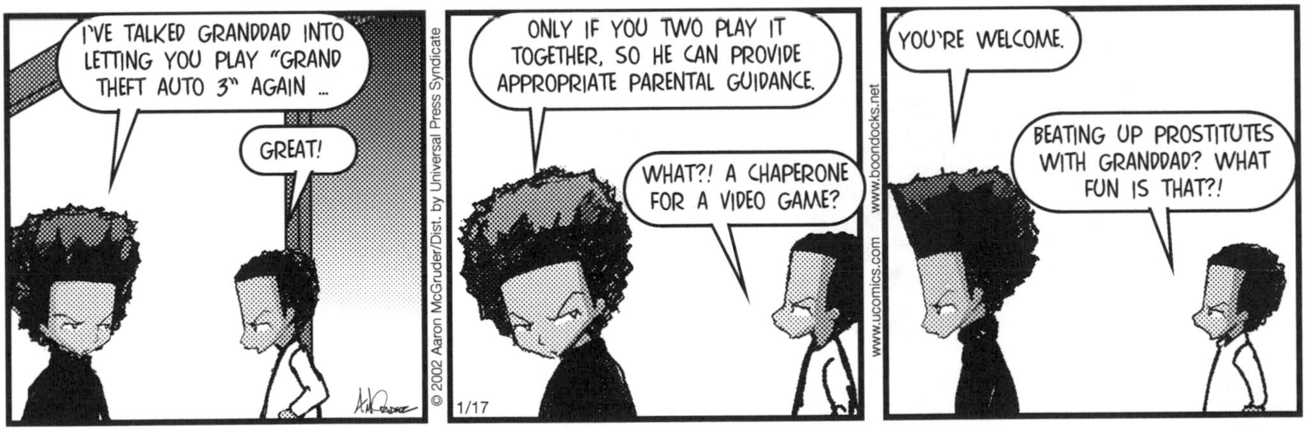
I'VE TALKED GRANDDAD INTO LETTING YOU PLAY "GRAND THEFT AUTO 3" AGAIN ...
GREAT!
© 2002 Aaron McGruder/Dist. by Universal Press Syndicate
ONLY IF YOU TWO PLAY IT TOGETHER, SO HE CAN PROVIDE APPROPRIATE PARENTAL GUIDANCE.
WHAT?! A CHAPERONE FOR A VIDEO GAME?
1/17
www.ucomics.com www.boondocks.net
YOU'RE WELCOME.
BEATING UP PROSTITUTES WITH GRANDDAD? WHAT FUN IS THAT?!

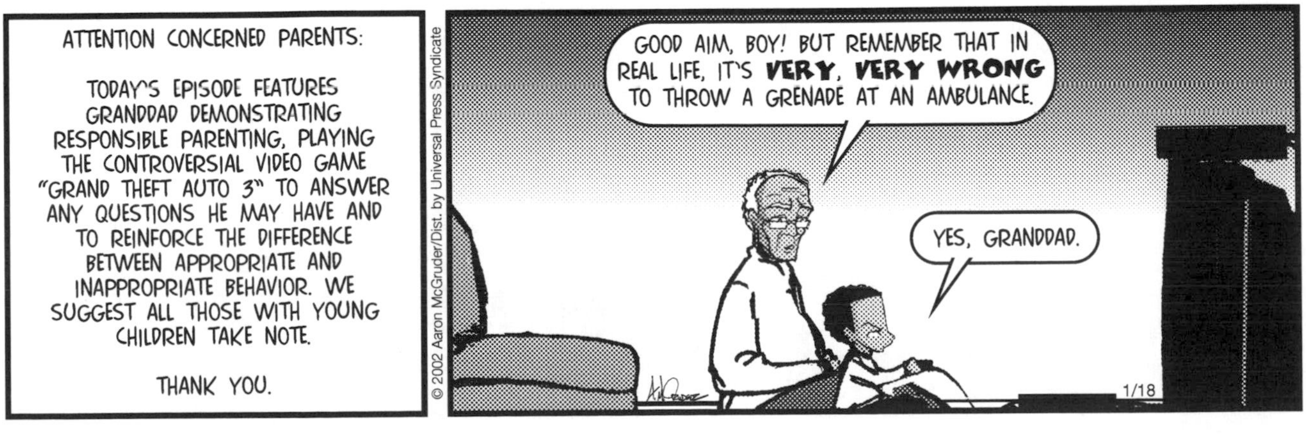
ATTENTION CONCERNED PARENTS:
TODAY'S EPISODE FEATURES GRANDDAD DEMONSTRATING RESPONSIBLE PARENTING, PLAYING THE CONTROVERSIAL VIDEO GAME "GRAND THEFT AUTO 3" TO ANSWER ANY QUESTIONS HE MAY HAVE AND TO REINFORCE THE DIFFERENCE BETWEEN APPROPRIATE AND INAPPROPRIATE BEHAVIOR. WE SUGGEST ALL THOSE WITH YOUNG CHILDREN TAKE NOTE.
THANK YOU.
© 2002 Aaron McGruder/Dist. by Universal Press Syndicate
GOOD AIM, BOY! BUT REMEMBER THAT IN REAL LIFE, IT'S VERY, VERY WRONG TO THROW A GRENADE AT AN AMBULANCE.
YES, GRANDDAD.
1/18

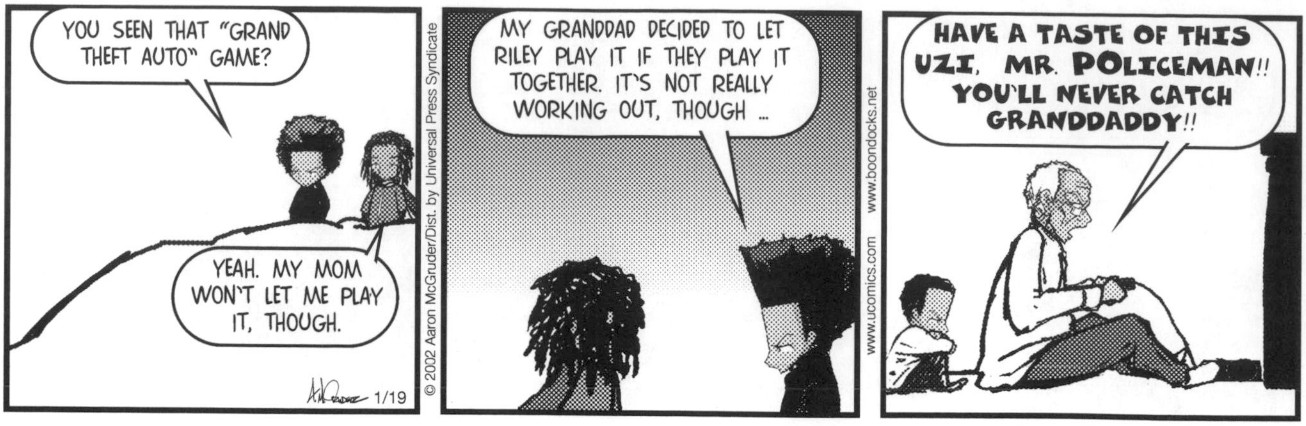
YOU SEEN THAT "GRAND THEFT AUTO" GAME?
YEAH. MY MOM WON'T LET ME PLAY IT, THOUGH.
1/19
© 2002 Aaron McGruder/Dist. by Universal Press Syndicate
MY GRANDDAD DECIDED TO LET RILEY PLAY IT IF THEY PLAY IT TOGETHER. IT'S NOT REALLY WORKING OUT, THOUGH ...
www.ucomics.com www.boondocks.net
HAVE A TASTE OF THIS UZI, MR. POLICEMAN!! YOU'LL NEVER CATCH GRANDDADDY!!

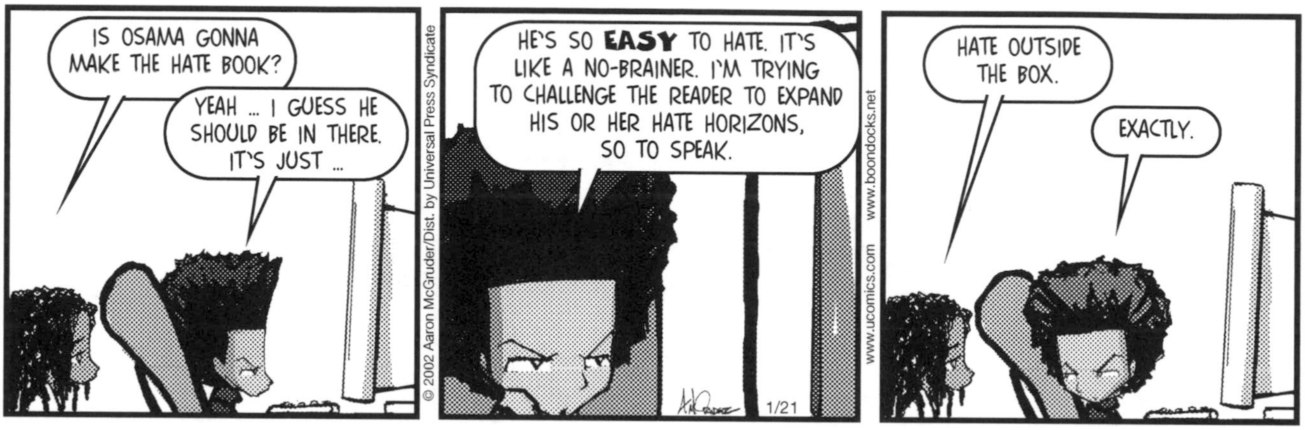
IS OSAMA GONNA MAKE THE HATE BOOK?
YEAH ... I GUESS HE SHOULD BE IN THERE. IT'S JUST ...
© 2002 Aaron McGruder/Dist. by Universal Press Syndicate
HE'S SO EASY TO HATE. IT'S LIKE A NO-BRAINER. I'M TRYING TO CHALLENGE THE READER TO EXPAND HIS OR HER HATE HORIZONS, SO TO SPEAK.
1/21
www.ucomics.com www.boondocks.net
HATE OUTSIDE THE BOX.
EXACTLY.

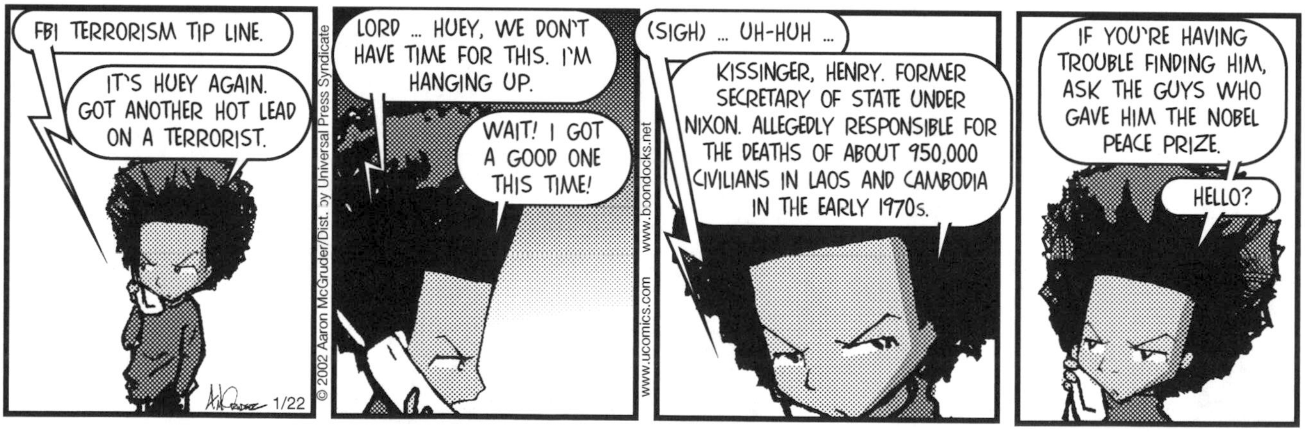
FBI TERRORISM TIP LINE.
IT'S HUEY AGAIN. GOT ANOTHER HOT LEAD ON A TERRORIST.
1/22
© 2002 Aaron McGruder/Dist. by Universal Press Syndicate
LORD ... HUEY, WE DON'T HAVE TIME FOR THIS. I'M HANGING UP.
WAIT! I GOT A GOOD ONE THIS TIME!
www.ucomics.com www.boondocks.net
(SIGH) ... UH-HUH ...
KISSINGER, HENRY. FORMER SECRETARY OF STATE UNDER NIXON. ALLEGEDLY RESPONSIBLE FOR THE DEATHS OF ABOUT 950,000 CIVILIANS IN LAOS AND CAMBODIA IN THE EARLY 1970s.
IF YOU'RE HAVING TROUBLE FINDING HIM, ASK THE GUYS WHO GAVE HIM THE NOBEL PEACE PRIZE.
HELLO?

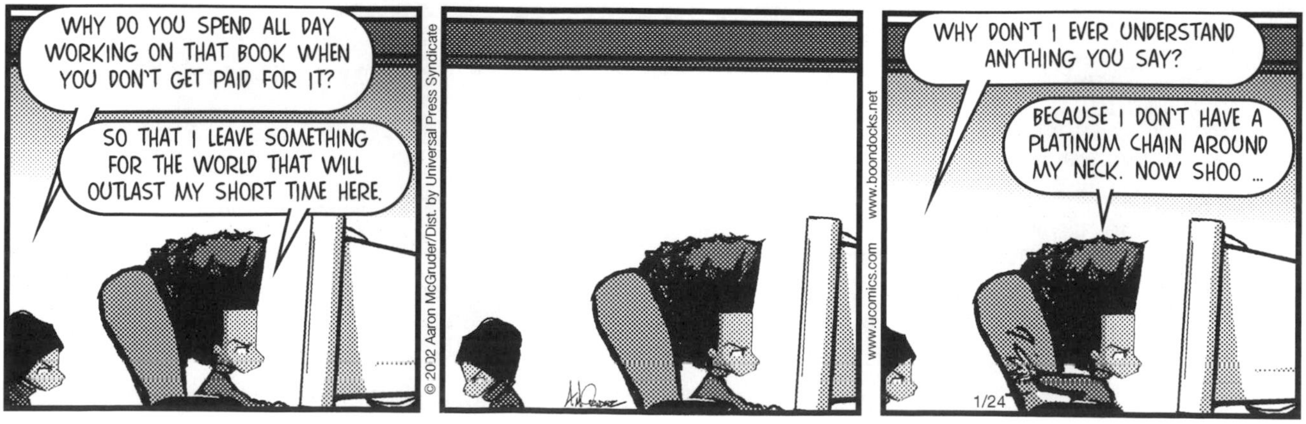
WHY DO YOU SPEND ALL DAY WORKING ON THAT BOOK WHEN YOU DON'T GET PAID FOR IT?
SO THAT I LEAVE SOMETHING FOR THE WORLD THAT WILL OUTLAST MY SHORT TIME HERE.
© 2002 Aaron McGruder/Dist. by Universal Press Syndicate
www.ucomics.com www.boondocks.net
WHY DON'T I EVER UNDERSTAND ANYTHING YOU SAY?
BECAUSE I DON'T HAVE A PLATINUM CHAIN AROUND MY NECK. NOW SHOO ...
1/24

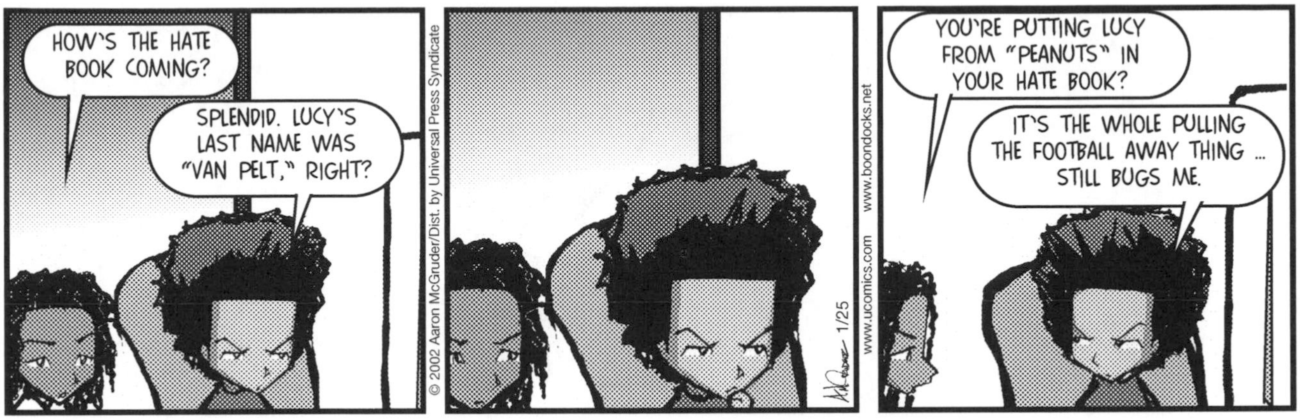
HOW'S THE HATE BOOK COMING?
SPLENDID. LUCY'S LAST NAME WAS "VAN PELT," RIGHT?
YOU'RE PUTTING LUCY FROM "PEANUTS" IN YOUR HATE BOOK?
IT'S THE WHOLE PULLING THE FOOTBALL AWAY THING ... STILL BUGS ME.
© 2002 Aaron McGruder/Dist. by Universal Press Syndicate
1/25
www.ucomics.com www.boondocks.net

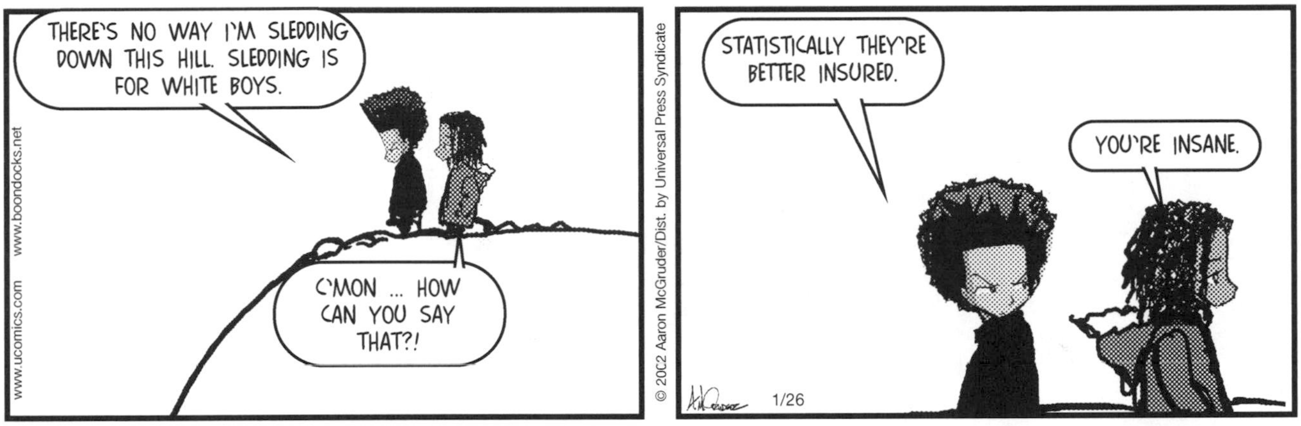
THERE'S NO WAY I'M SLEDDING DOWN THIS HILL. SLEDDING IS FOR WHITE BOYS.
C'MON ... HOW CAN YOU SAY THAT?!
STATISTICALLY THEY'RE BETTER INSURED.
YOU'RE INSANE.
www.ucomics.com www.boondocks.net
© 2002 Aaron McGruder/Dist. by Universal Press Syndicate
1/26

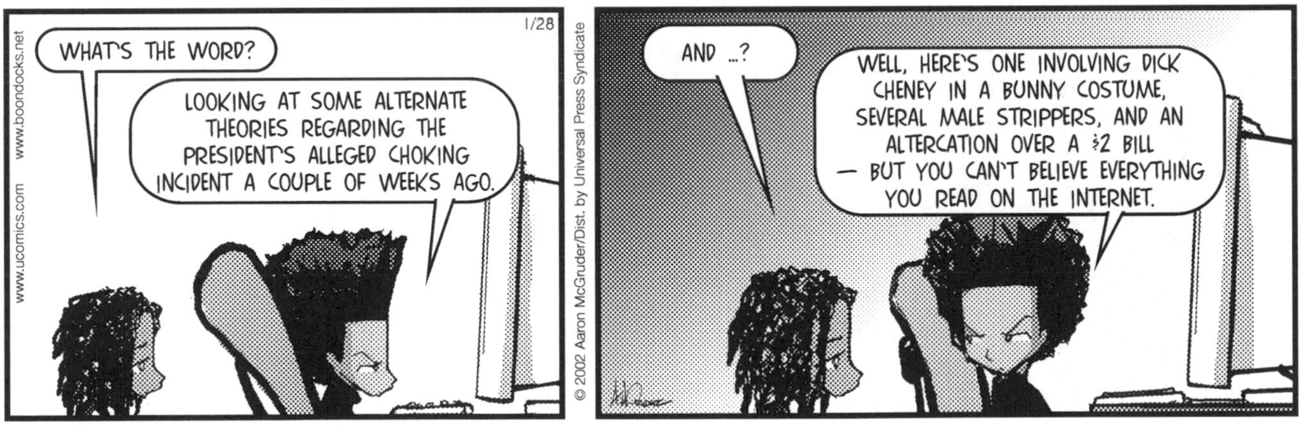
1/28
WHAT'S THE WORD?
LOOKING AT SOME ALTERNATE THEORIES REGARDING THE PRESIDENT'S ALLEGED CHOKING INCIDENT A COUPLE OF WEEKS AGO.
AND ...?
WELL, HERE'S ONE INVOLVING DICK CHENEY IN A BUNNY COSTUME, SEVERAL MALE STRIPPERS, AND AN ALTERCATION OVER A $2 BILL — BUT YOU CAN'T BELIEVE EVERYTHING YOU READ ON THE INTERNET.
www.ucomics.com www.boondocks.net
© 2002 Aaron McGruder/Dist. by Universal Press Syndicate

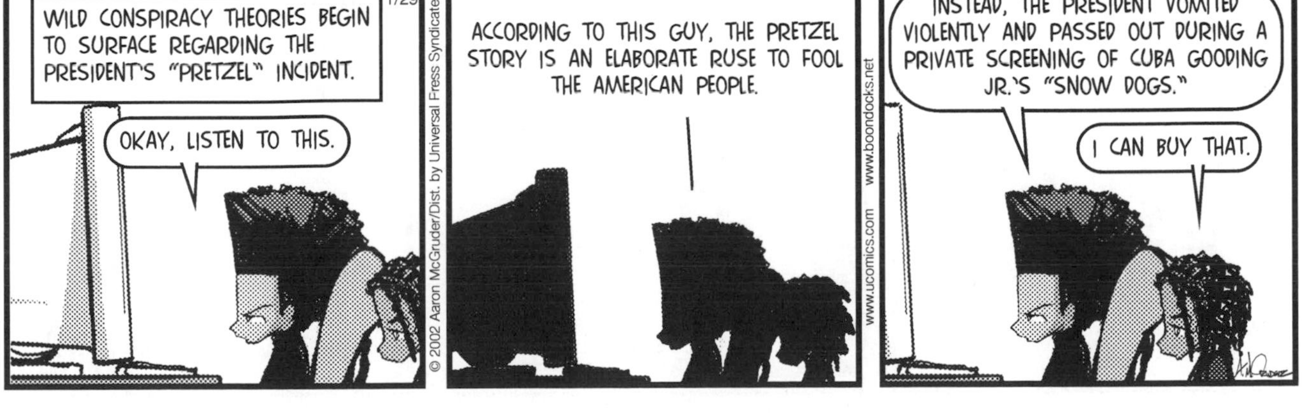
1/29
WILD CONSPIRACY THEORIES BEGIN TO SURFACE REGARDING THE PRESIDENT'S "PRETZEL" INCIDENT.
OKAY, LISTEN TO THIS.
ACCORDING TO THIS GUY, THE PRETZEL STORY IS AN ELABORATE RUSE TO FOOL THE AMERICAN PEOPLE.
INSTEAD, THE PRESIDENT VOMITED VIOLENTLY AND PASSED OUT DURING A PRIVATE SCREENING OF CUBA GOODING JR.'S "SNOW DOGS."
I CAN BUY THAT.
© 2002 Aaron McGruder/Dist. by Universal Press Syndicate
www.ucomics.com www.boondocks.net

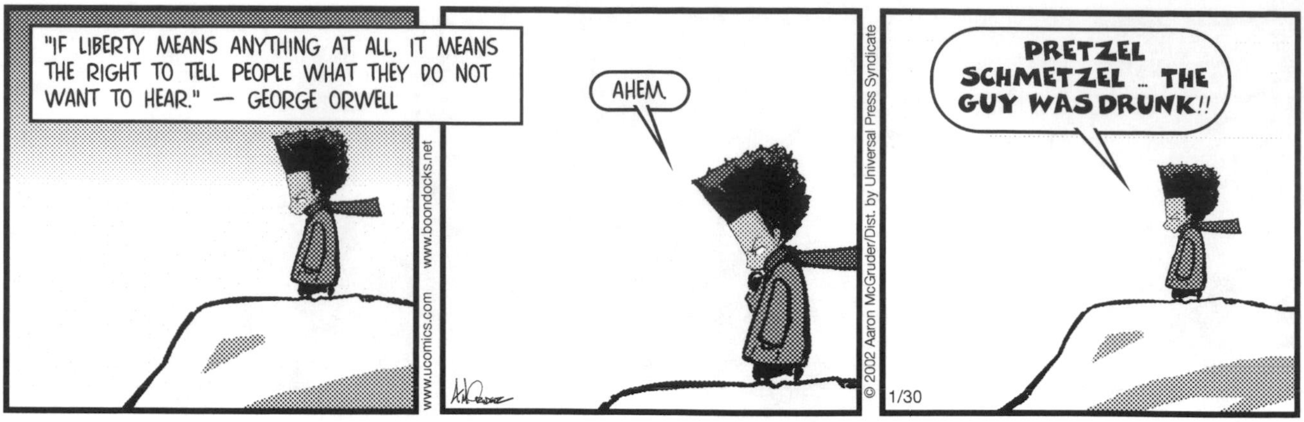
"IF LIBERTY MEANS ANYTHING AT ALL, IT MEANS THE RIGHT TO TELL PEOPLE WHAT THEY DO NOT WANT TO HEAR." — GEORGE ORWELL
www.ucomics.com www.boondocks.net
AHEM.
© 2002 Aaron McGruder/Dist. by Universal Press Syndicate
PRETZEL SCHMETZEL ... THE GUY WAS DRUNK!!
1/30

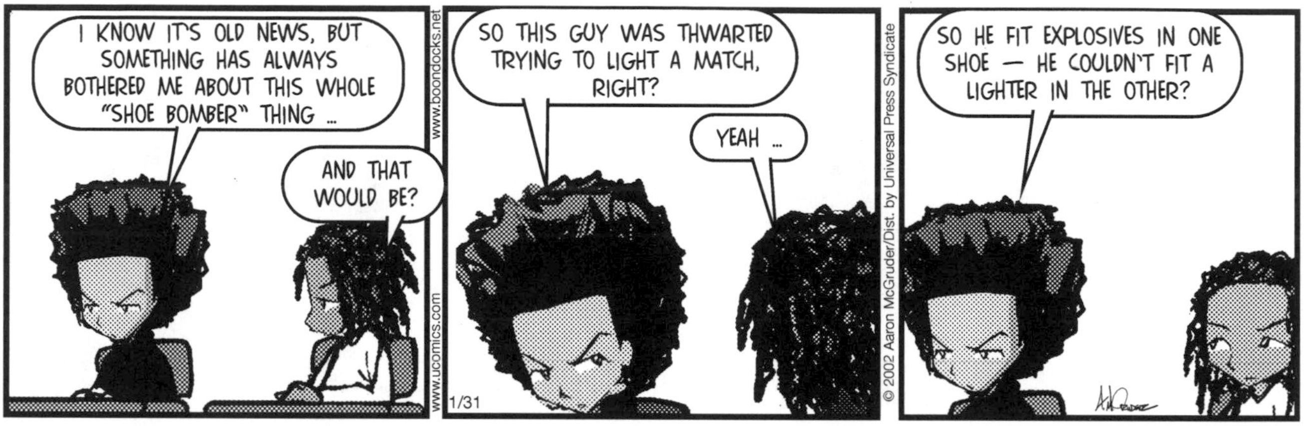
I KNOW IT'S OLD NEWS, BUT SOMETHING HAS ALWAYS BOTHERED ME ABOUT THIS WHOLE "SHOE BOMBER" THING ...
AND THAT WOULD BE?
www.ucomics.com www.boondocks.net
1/31
SO THIS GUY WAS THWARTED TRYING TO LIGHT A MATCH, RIGHT?
YEAH ...
© 2002 Aaron McGruder/Dist. by Universal Press Syndicate
SO HE FIT EXPLOSIVES IN ONE SHOE — HE COULDN'T FIT A LIGHTER IN THE OTHER?

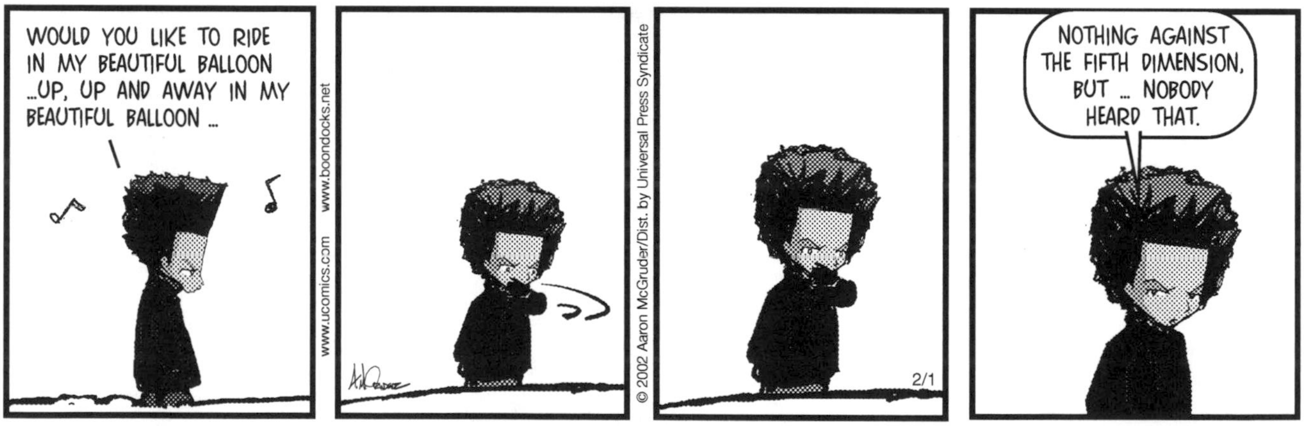
WOULD YOU LIKE TO RIDE IN MY BEAUTIFUL BALLOON ...UP, UP AND AWAY IN MY BEAUTIFUL BALLOON ...
www.ucomics.com www.boondocks.net
© 2002 Aaron McGruder/Dist. by Universal Press Syndicate
2/1
NOTHING AGAINST THE FIFTH DIMENSION, BUT ... NOBODY HEARD THAT.

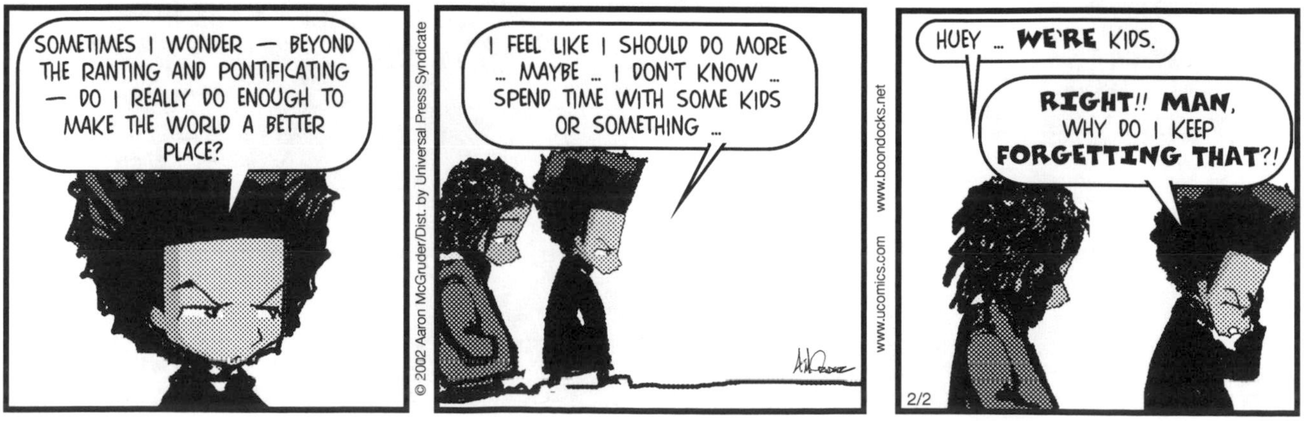
SOMETIMES I WONDER — BEYOND THE RANTING AND PONTIFICATING — DO I REALLY DO ENOUGH TO MAKE THE WORLD A BETTER PLACE?
© 2002 Aaron McGruder/Dist. by Universal Press Syndicate
I FEEL LIKE I SHOULD DO MORE ... MAYBE ... I DON'T KNOW ... SPEND TIME WITH SOME KIDS OR SOMETHING ...
www.ucomics.com www.boondocks.net
HUEY ... WE'RE KIDS.
RIGHT!! MAN, WHY DO I KEEP FORGETTING THAT?!
2/2

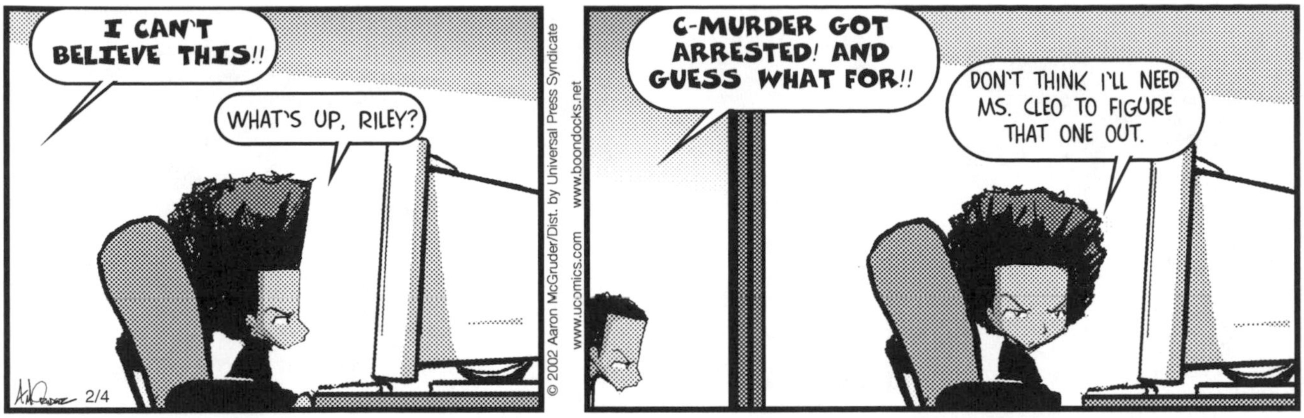
I CAN'T BELIEVE THIS!!
WHAT'S UP, RILEY?
C-MURDER GOT ARRESTED! AND GUESS WHAT FOR!!
DON'T THINK I'LL NEED MS. CLEO TO FIGURE THAT ONE OUT.
2/4
© 2002 Aaron McGruder/Dist. by Universal Press Syndicate
www.ucomics.com www.boondocks.net

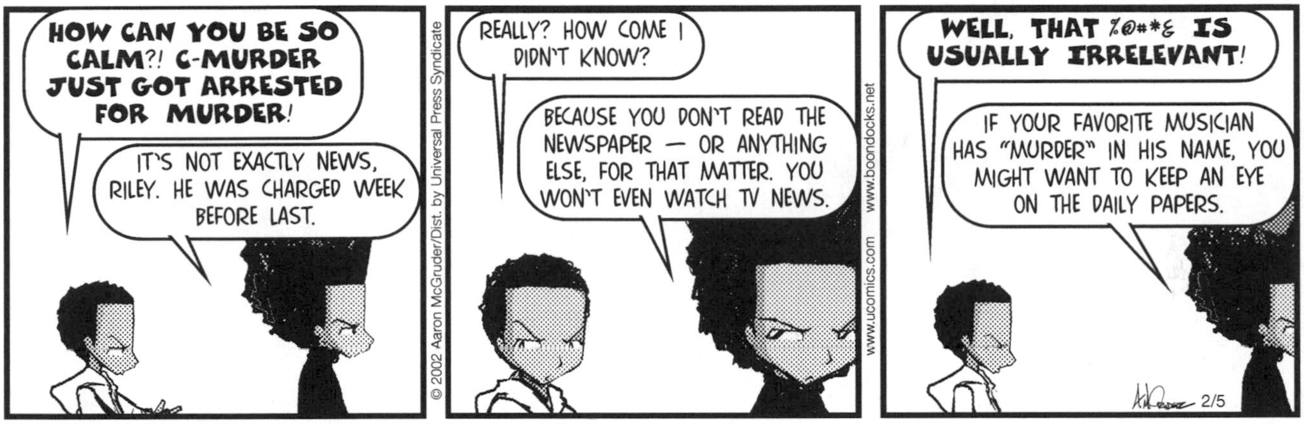
HOW CAN YOU BE SO CALM?! C-MURDER JUST GOT ARRESTED FOR MURDER!
IT'S NOT EXACTLY NEWS, RILEY. HE WAS CHARGED WEEK BEFORE LAST.
REALLY? HOW COME I DIDN'T KNOW?
BECAUSE YOU DON'T READ THE NEWSPAPER — OR ANYTHING ELSE, FOR THAT MATTER. YOU WON'T EVEN WATCH TV NEWS.
WELL, THAT %@#*& IS USUALLY IRRELEVANT!
IF YOUR FAVORITE MUSICIAN HAS "MURDER" IN HIS NAME, YOU MIGHT WANT TO KEEP AN EYE ON THE DAILY PAPERS.
2/5
© 2002 Aaron McGruder/Dist. by Universal Press Syndicate
www.ucomics.com www.boondocks.net

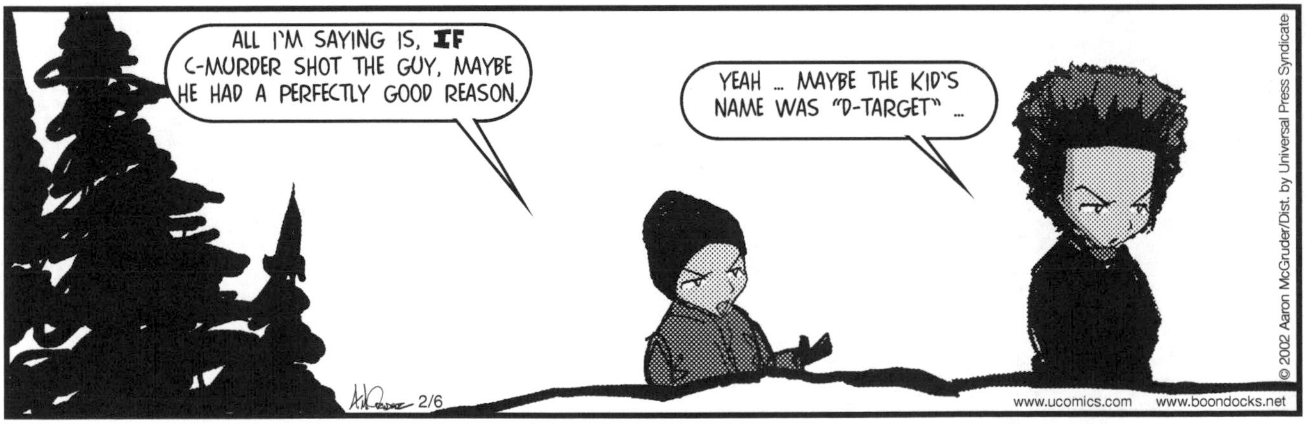
ALL I'M SAYING IS, IF C-MURDER SHOT THE GUY, MAYBE HE HAD A PERFECTLY GOOD REASON.
YEAH ... MAYBE THE KID'S NAME WAS "D-TARGET" ...
2/6
© 2002 Aaron McGruder/Dist. by Universal Press Syndicate
www.ucomics.com www.boondocks.net

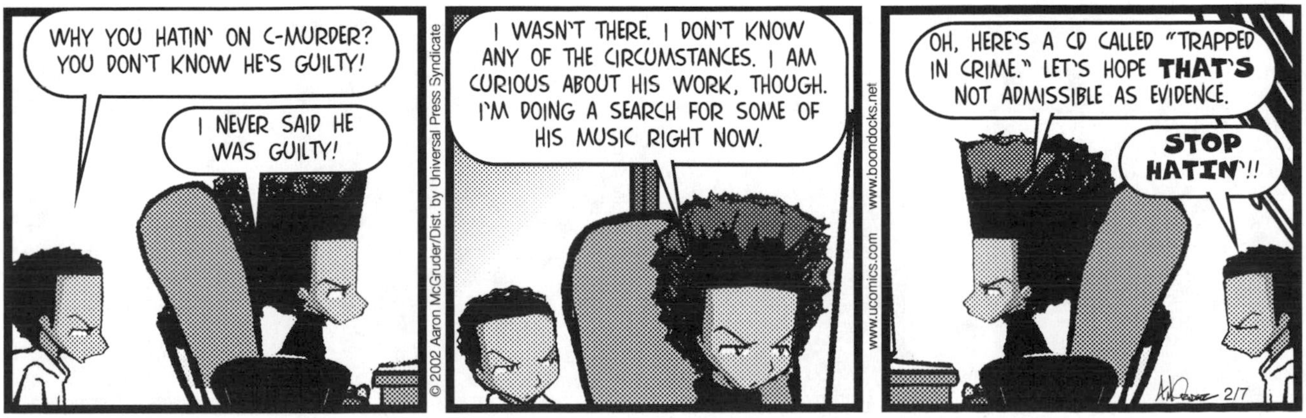
WHY YOU HATIN' ON C-MURDER? YOU DON'T KNOW HE'S GUILTY!
I NEVER SAID HE WAS GUILTY!
I WASN'T THERE. I DON'T KNOW ANY OF THE CIRCUMSTANCES. I AM CURIOUS ABOUT HIS WORK, THOUGH. I'M DOING A SEARCH FOR SOME OF HIS MUSIC RIGHT NOW.
OH, HERE'S A CD CALLED "TRAPPED IN CRIME." LET'S HOPE THAT'S NOT ADMISSIBLE AS EVIDENCE.
STOP HATIN'!!
2/7
© 2002 Aaron McGruder/Dist. by Universal Press Syndicate
www.ucomics.com www.boondocks.net

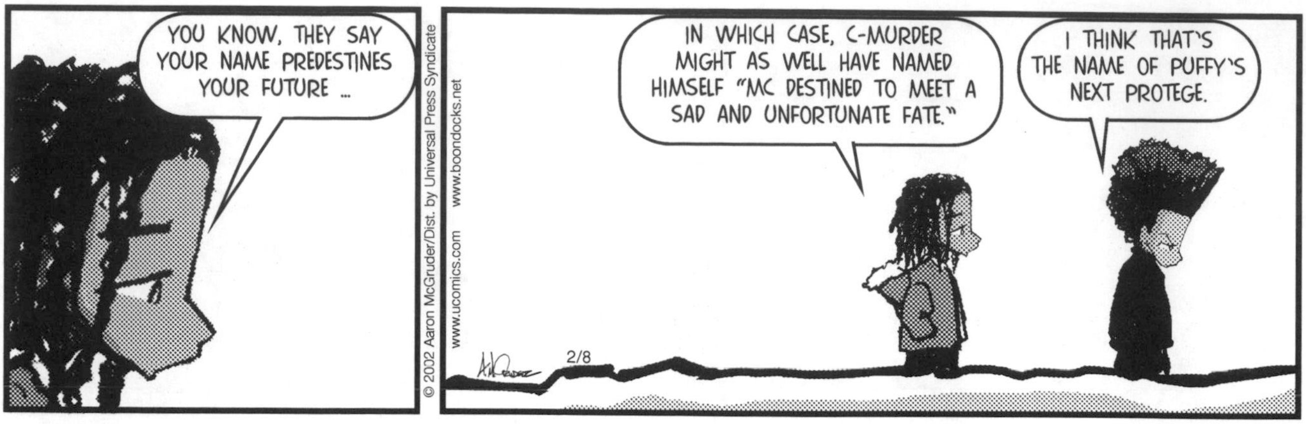
YOU KNOW, THEY SAY YOUR NAME PREDESTINES YOUR FUTURE ...
IN WHICH CASE, C-MURDER MIGHT AS WELL HAVE NAMED HIMSELF "MC DESTINED TO MEET A SAD AND UNFORTUNATE FATE."
I THINK THAT'S THE NAME OF PUFFY'S NEXT PROTEGE.
© 2002 Aaron McGruder/Dist. by Universal Press Syndicate
www.ucomics.com www.boondocks.net
2/8

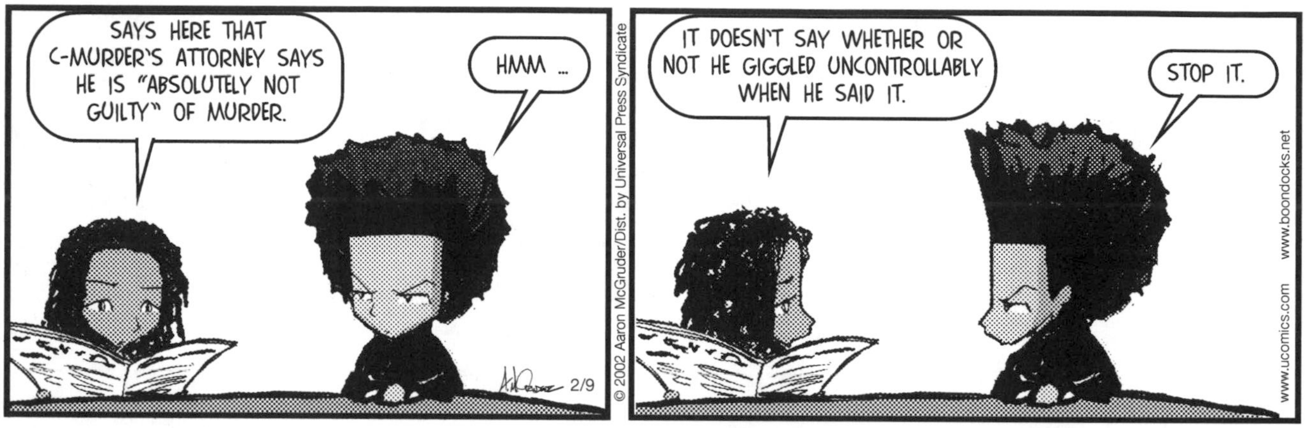
SAYS HERE THAT C-MURDER'S ATTORNEY SAYS HE IS "ABSOLUTELY NOT GUILTY" OF MURDER.
HMM ...
IT DOESN'T SAY WHETHER OR NOT HE GIGGLED UNCONTROLLABLY WHEN HE SAID IT.
STOP IT.
2/9
© 2002 Aaron McGruder/Dist. by Universal Press Syndicate
www.ucomics.com www.boondocks.net

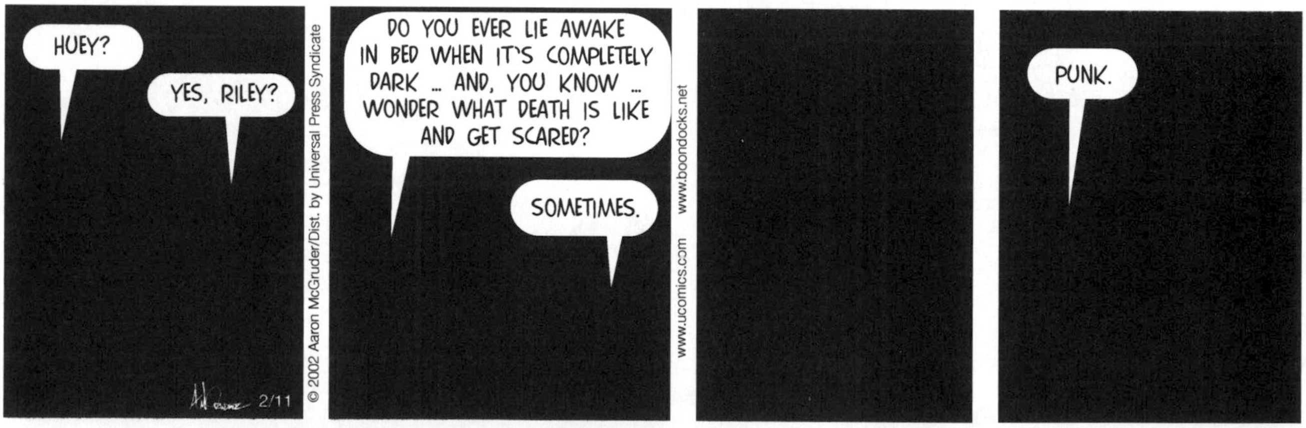
HUEY?
YES, RILEY?
DO YOU EVER LIE AWAKE IN BED WHEN IT'S COMPLETELY DARK ... AND, YOU KNOW ... WONDER WHAT DEATH IS LIKE AND GET SCARED?
SOMETIMES.
PUNK.
2/11
© 2002 Aaron McGruder/Dist. by Universal Press Syndicate
www.ucomics.com www.boondocks.net

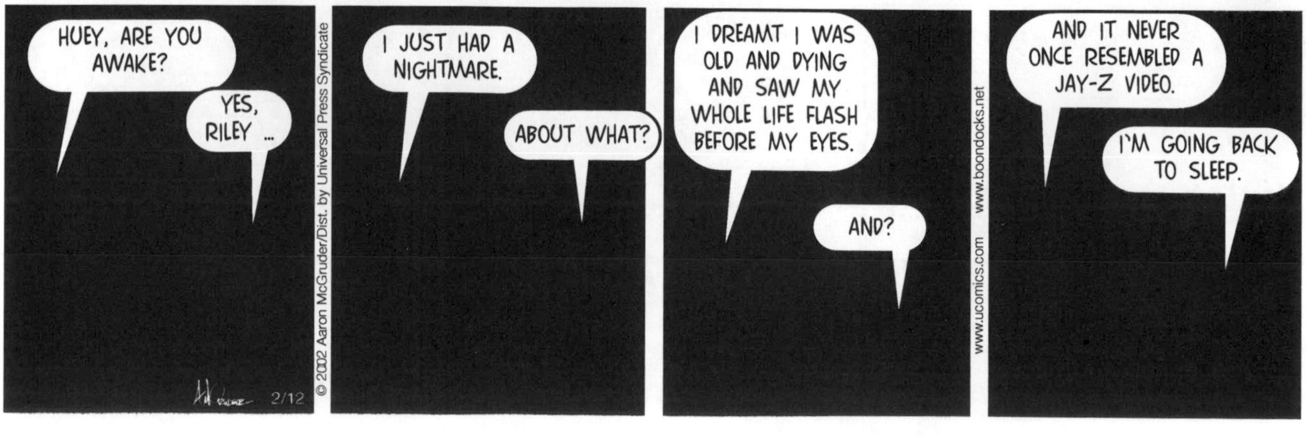
HUEY, ARE YOU AWAKE?
YES, RILEY ...
I JUST HAD A NIGHTMARE.
ABOUT WHAT?
I DREAMT I WAS OLD AND DYING AND SAW MY WHOLE LIFE FLASH BEFORE MY EYES.
AND?
AND IT NEVER ONCE RESEMBLED A JAY-Z VIDEO.
I'M GOING BACK TO SLEEP.
2/12
© 2002 Aaron McGruder/Dist. by Universal Press Syndicate
www.ucomics.com www.boondocks.net

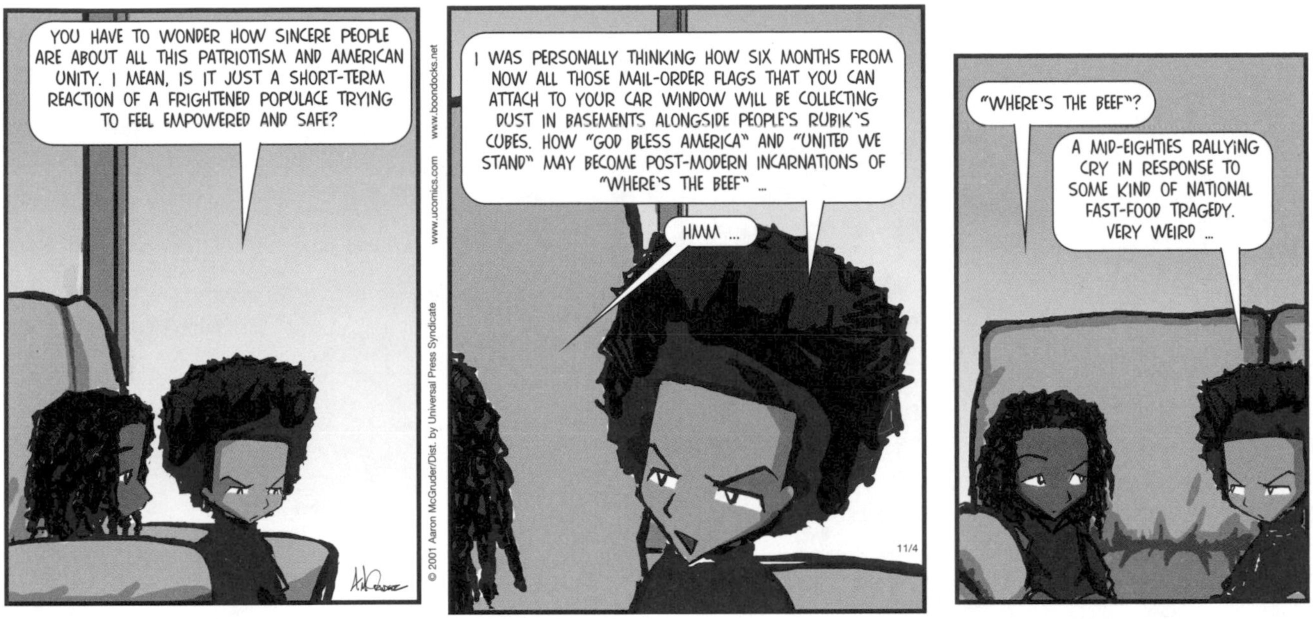
YOU HAVE TO WONDER HOW SINCERE PEOPLE ARE ABOUT ALL THIS PATRIOTISM AND AMERICAN UNITY. I MEAN, IS IT JUST A SHORT-TERM REACTION OF A FRIGHTENED POPULACE TRYING TO FEEL EMPOWERED AND SAFE?
© 2001 Aaron McGruder/Dist. by Universal Press Syndicate www.ucomics.com www.boondocks.net
I WAS PERSONALLY THINKING HOW SIX MONTHS FROM NOW ALL THOSE MAIL-ORDER FLAGS THAT YOU CAN ATTACH TO YOUR CAR WINDOW WILL BE COLLECTING DUST IN BASEMENTS ALONGSIDE PEOPLE'S RUBIK'S CUBES. HOW "GOD BLESS AMERICA" AND "UNITED WE STAND" MAY BECOME POST-MODERN INCARNATIONS OF "WHERE'S THE BEEF" ...
HMM ...
11/4
"WHERE'S THE BEEF"?
A MID-EIGHTIES RALLYING CRY IN RESPONSE TO SOME KIND OF NATIONAL FAST-FOOD TRAGEDY. VERY WEIRD ...

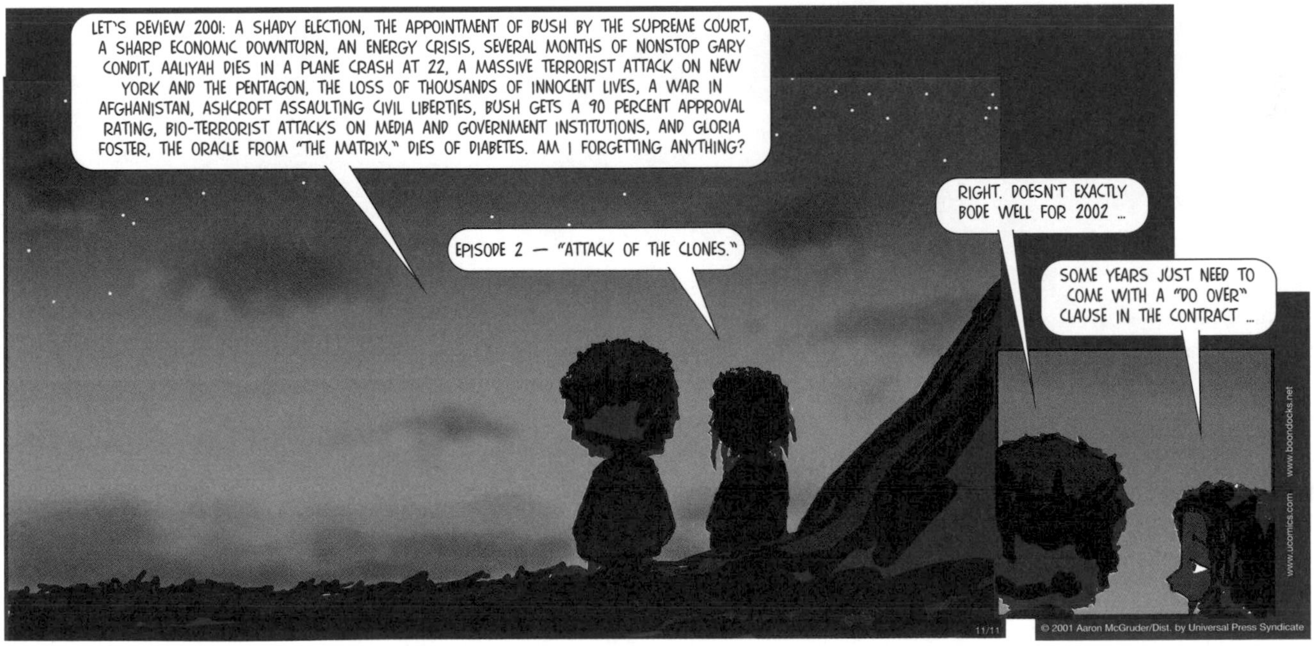
LET'S REVIEW 2001: A SHADY ELECTION, THE APPOINTMENT OF BUSH BY THE SUPREME COURT, A SHARP ECONOMIC DOWNTURN, AN ENERGY CRISIS, SEVERAL MONTHS OF NONSTOP GARY CONDIT, AALIYAH DIES IN A PLANE CRASH AT 22, A MASSIVE TERRORIST ATTACK ON NEW YORK AND THE PENTAGON, THE LOSS OF THOUSANDS OF INNOCENT LIVES, A WAR IN AFGHANISTAN, ASHCROFT ASSAULTING CIVIL LIBERTIES, BUSH GETS A 90 PERCENT APPROVAL RATING, BIO-TERRORIST ATTACKS ON MEDIA AND GOVERNMENT INSTITUTIONS, AND GLORIA FOSTER, THE ORACLE FROM "THE MATRIX," DIES OF DIABETES. AM I FORGETTING ANYTHING?
EPISODE 2 — "ATTACK OF THE CLONES."
RIGHT. DOESN'T EXACTLY BODE WELL FOR 2002 ...
SOME YEARS JUST NEED TO COME WITH A "DO OVER" CLAUSE IN THE CONTRACT ...
11/11
www.ucomics.com www.boondocks.net
© 2001 Aaron McGruder/Dist. by Universal Press Syndicate

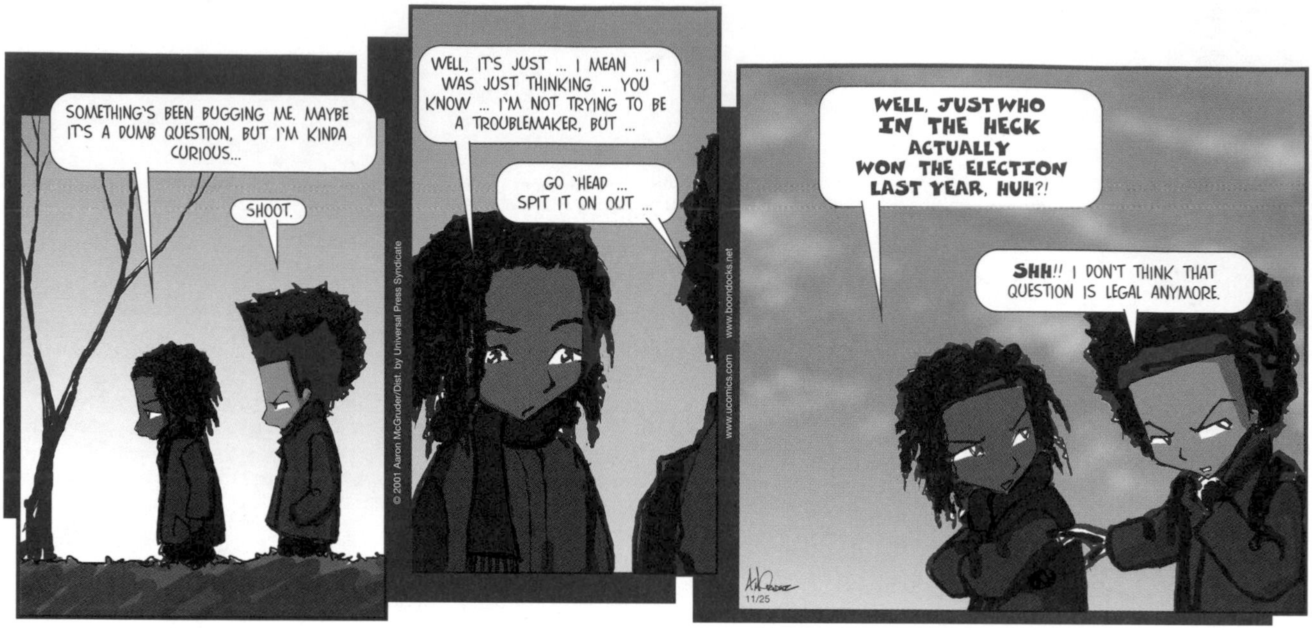
SOMETHING'S BEEN BUGGING ME. MAYBE IT'S A DUMB QUESTION, BUT I'M KINDA CURIOUS...
SHOOT.
WELL, IT'S JUST ... I MEAN ... I WAS JUST THINKING ... YOU KNOW ... I'M NOT TRYING TO BE A TROUBLEMAKER, BUT ...
GO 'HEAD ... SPIT IT ON OUT ...
WELL, JUST WHO IN THE HECK ACTUALLY WON THE ELECTION LAST YEAR, HUH?!
SHH!! I DON'T THINK THAT QUESTION IS LEGAL ANYMORE.
© 2001 Aaron McGruder/Dist. by Universal Press Syndicate
www.ucomics.com www.boondocks.net
11/25

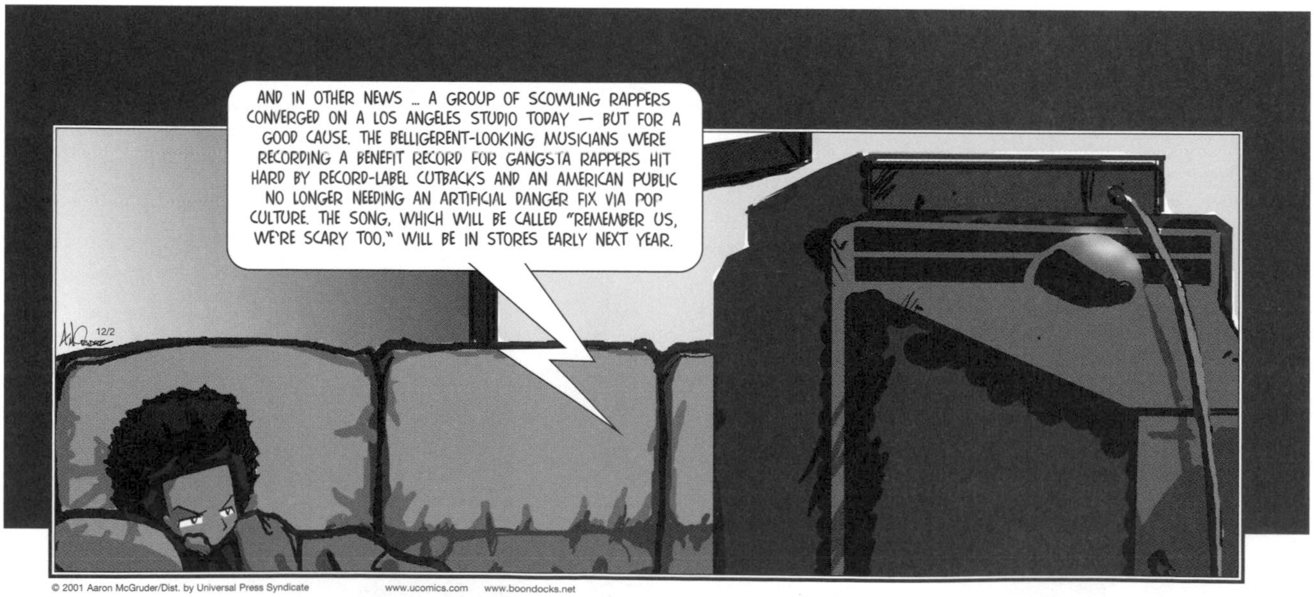
AND IN OTHER NEWS ... A GROUP OF SCOWLING RAPPERS CONVERGED ON A LOS ANGELES STUDIO TODAY — BUT FOR A GOOD CAUSE. THE BELLIGERENT-LOOKING MUSICIANS WERE RECORDING A BENEFIT RECORD FOR GANGSTA RAPPERS HIT HARD BY RECORD-LABEL CUTBACKS AND AN AMERICAN PUBLIC NO LONGER NEEDING AN ARTIFICIAL DANGER FIX VIA POP CULTURE. THE SONG, WHICH WILL BE CALLED "REMEMBER US, WE'RE SCARY TOO," WILL BE IN STORES EARLY NEXT YEAR.
12/2

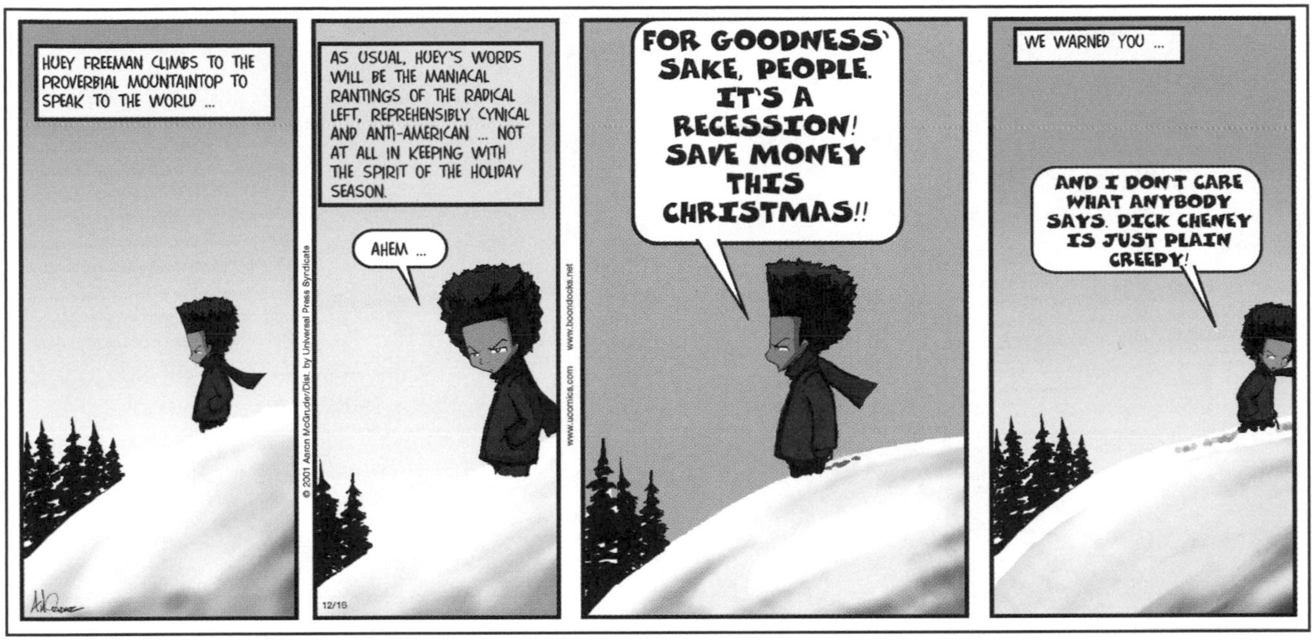
HUEY FREEMAN CLIMBS TO THE PROVERBIAL MOUNTAINTOP TO SPEAK TO THE WORLD ...
AS USUAL, HUEY'S WORDS WILL BE THE MANIACAL RANTINGS OF THE RADICAL LEFT, REPREHENSIBLY CYNICAL AND ANTI-AMERICAN ... NOT AT ALL IN KEEPING WITH THE SPIRIT OF THE HOLIDAY SEASON.
AHEM ...
FOR GOODNESS' SAKE, PEOPLE. IT'S A RECESSION! SAVE MONEY THIS CHRISTMAS!!
WE WARNED YOU ...
AND I DON'T CARE WHAT ANYBODY SAYS. DICK CHENEY IS JUST PLAIN CREEPY!
© 2001 Aaron McGruder/Dist. by Universal Press Syndicate
www.ucomics.com www.boondocks.net
12/16

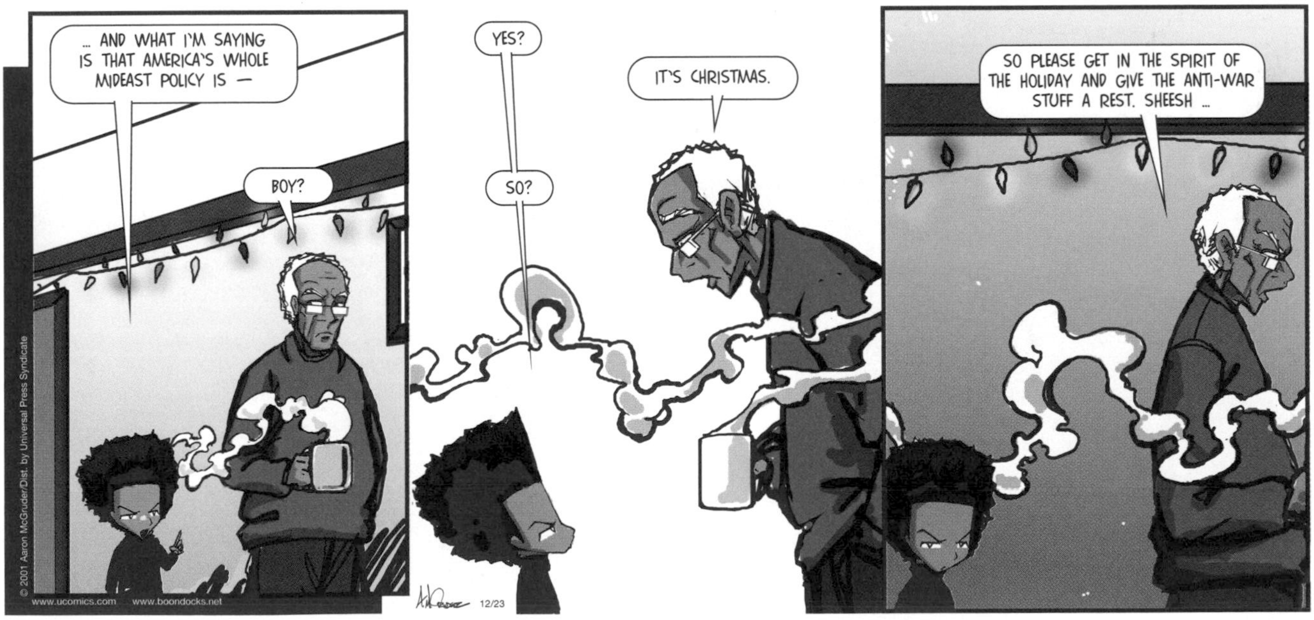
... AND WHAT I'M SAYING IS THAT AMERICA'S WHOLE MIDEAST POLICY IS —
BOY?
YES?
SO?
IT'S CHRISTMAS.
SO PLEASE GET IN THE SPIRIT OF THE HOLIDAY AND GIVE THE ANTI-WAR STUFF A REST. SHEESH ...
© 2001 Aaron McGruder/Dist. by Universal Press Syndicate
www.ucomics.com www.boondocks.net
12/23

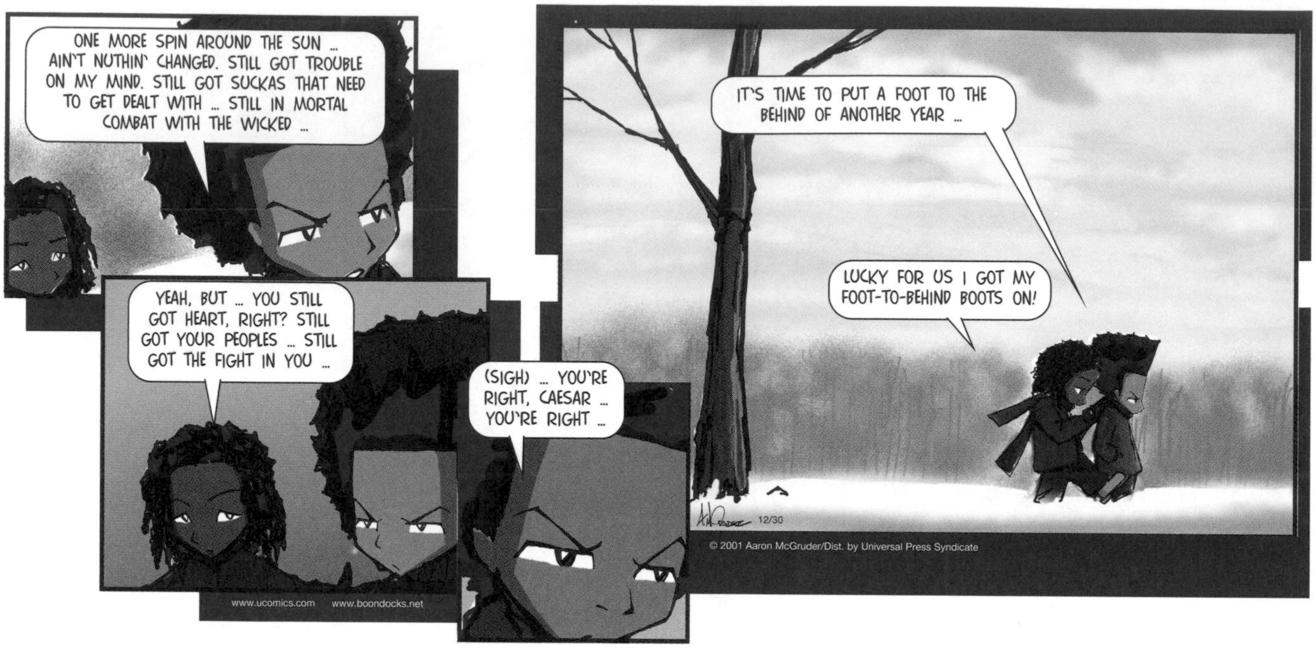
ONE MORE SPIN AROUND THE SUN ... AIN'T NUTHIN' CHANGED. STILL GOT TROUBLE ON MY MIND. STILL GOT SUCKAS THAT NEED TO GET DEALT WITH ... STILL IN MORTAL COMBAT WITH THE WICKED ...
YEAH, BUT ... YOU STILL GOT HEART, RIGHT? STILL GOT YOUR PEOPLES ... STILL GOT THE FIGHT IN YOU ...
(SIGH) ... YOU'RE RIGHT, CAESAR ... YOU'RE RIGHT ...
IT'S TIME TO PUT A FOOT TO THE BEHIND OF ANOTHER YEAR ...
LUCKY FOR US I GOT MY FOOT-TO-BEHIND BOOTS ON!
12/30
© 2001 Aaron McGruder/Dist. by Universal Press Syndicate
www.ucomics.com www.boondocks.net

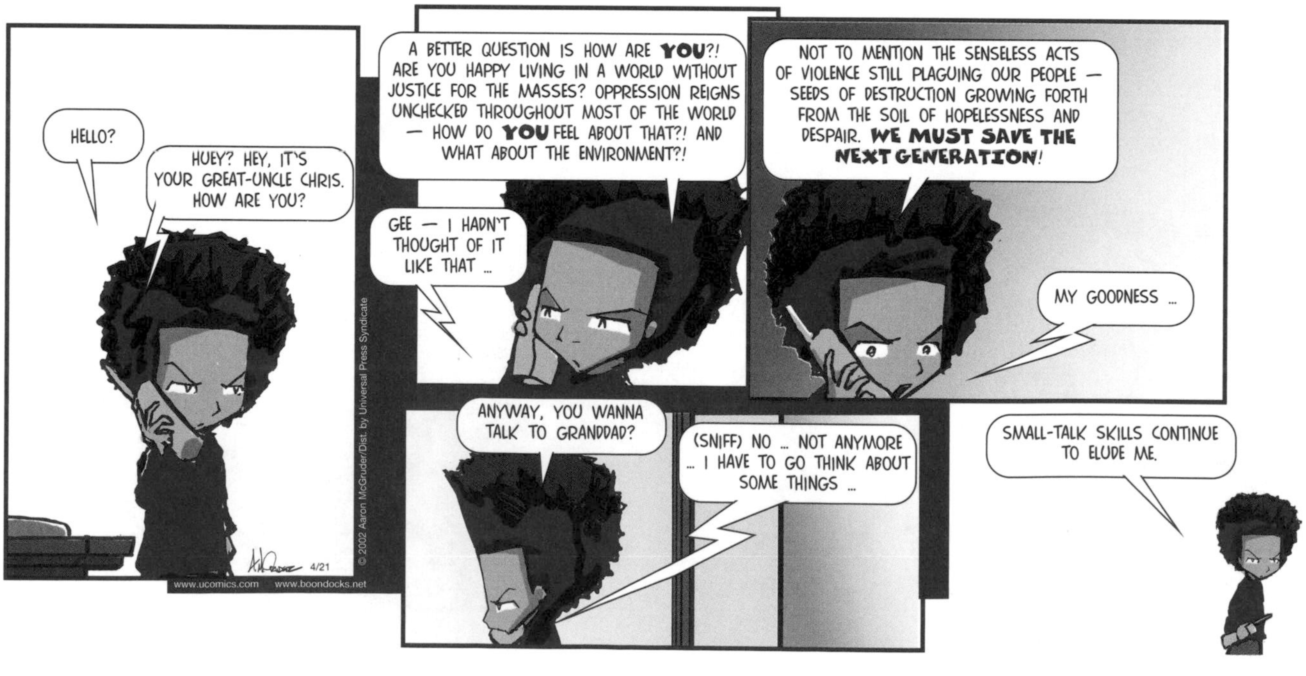
HELLO?
HUEY? HEY, IT'S YOUR GREAT-UNCLE CHRIS. HOW ARE YOU?
A BETTER QUESTION IS HOW ARE **YOU**?! ARE YOU HAPPY LIVING IN A WORLD WITHOUT JUSTICE FOR THE MASSES? OPPRESSION REIGNS UNCHECKED THROUGHOUT MOST OF THE WORLD — HOW DO **YOU** FEEL ABOUT THAT?! AND WHAT ABOUT THE ENVIRONMENT?!
GEE — I HADN'T THOUGHT OF IT LIKE THAT ...
NOT TO MENTION THE SENSELESS ACTS OF VIOLENCE STILL PLAGUING OUR PEOPLE — SEEDS OF DESTRUCTION GROWING FORTH FROM THE SOIL OF HOPELESSNESS AND DESPAIR. **WE MUST SAVE THE NEXT GENERATION**!
MY GOODNESS ...
ANYWAY, YOU WANNA TALK TO GRANDDAD?
(SNIFF) NO ... NOT ANYMORE ... I HAVE TO GO THINK ABOUT SOME THINGS ...
SMALL-TALK SKILLS CONTINUE TO ELUDE ME.
4/21
© 2002 Aaron McGruder/Dist. by Universal Press Syndicate
www.ucomics.com www.boondocks.net

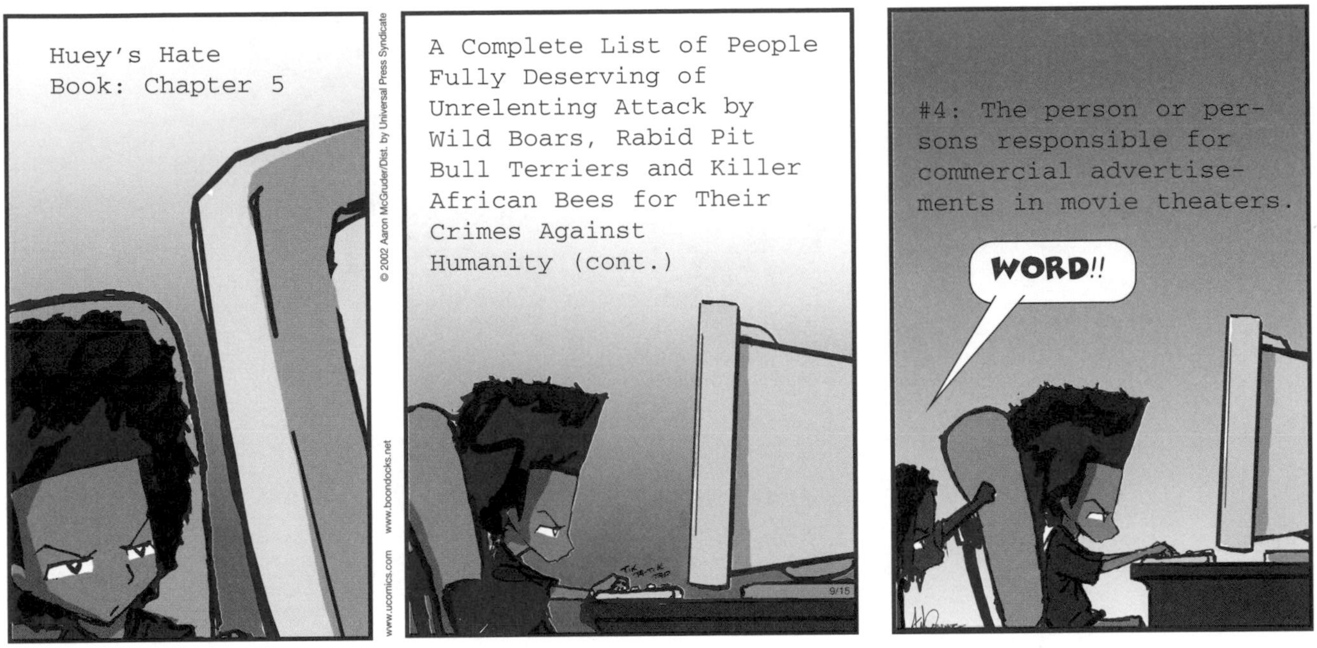
Huey's Hate Book: Chapter 5
© 2002 Aaron McGruder/Dist. by Universal Press Syndicate
www.ucomics.com www.boondocks.net
A Complete List of People Fully Deserving of Unrelenting Attack by Wild Boars, Rabid Pit Bull Terriers and Killer African Bees for Their Crimes Against Humanity (cont.)
9/15
#4: The person or persons responsible for commercial advertisements in movie theaters.
WORD!!

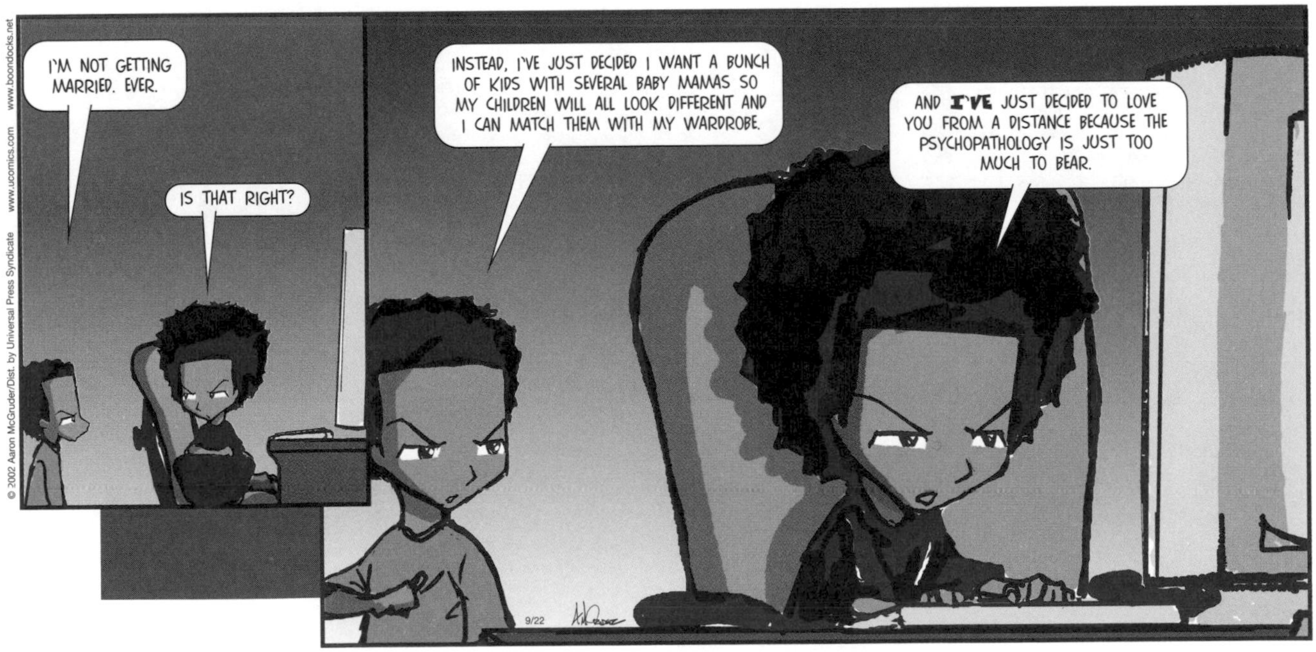
© 2002 Aaron McGruder/Dist. by Universal Press Syndicate www.ucomics.com www.boondocks.net
I'M NOT GETTING MARRIED. EVER.
IS THAT RIGHT?
INSTEAD, I'VE JUST DECIDED I WANT A BUNCH OF KIDS WITH SEVERAL BABY MAMAS SO MY CHILDREN WILL ALL LOOK DIFFERENT AND I CAN MATCH THEM WITH MY WARDROBE.
AND I'VE JUST DECIDED TO LOVE YOU FROM A DISTANCE BECAUSE THE PSYCHOPATHOLOGY IS JUST TOO MUCH TO BEAR.
9/22

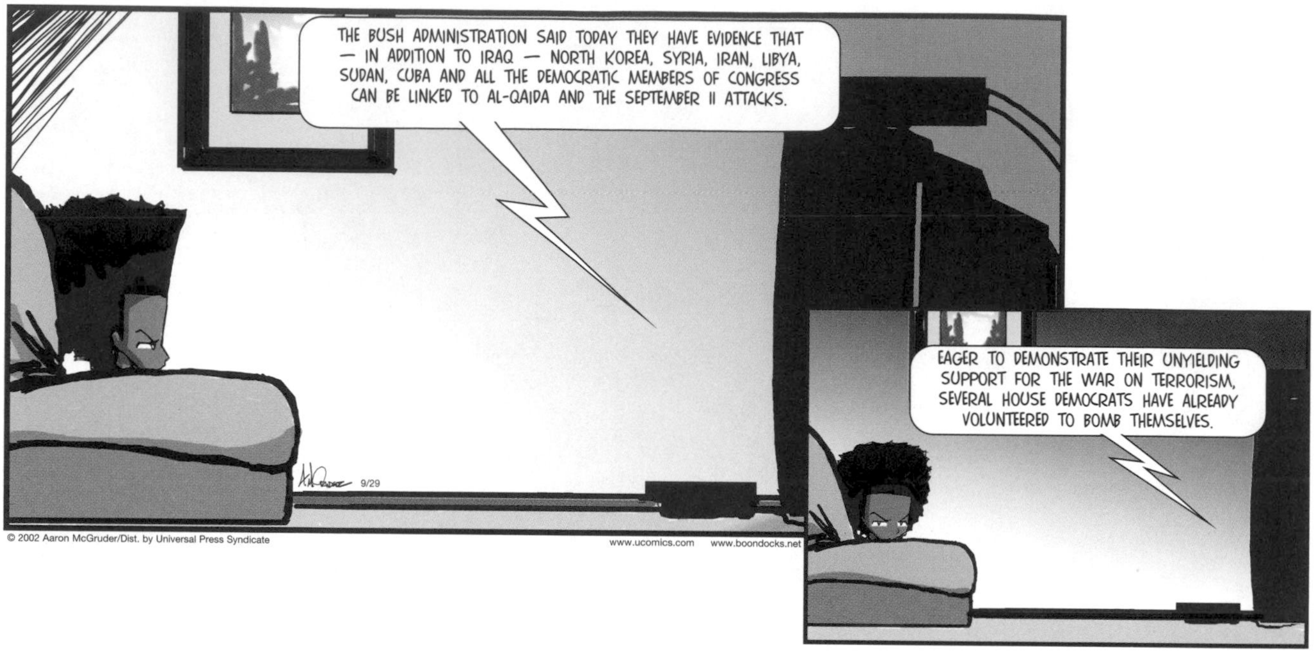
THE BUSH ADMINISTRATION SAID TODAY THEY HAVE EVIDENCE THAT — IN ADDITION TO IRAQ — NORTH KOREA, SYRIA, IRAN, LIBYA, SUDAN, CUBA AND ALL THE DEMOCRATIC MEMBERS OF CONGRESS CAN BE LINKED TO AL-QAIDA AND THE SEPTEMBER 11 ATTACKS.
EAGER TO DEMONSTRATE THEIR UNYIELDING SUPPORT FOR THE WAR ON TERRORISM, SEVERAL HOUSE DEMOCRATS HAVE ALREADY VOLUNTEERED TO BOMB THEMSELVES.
9/29
© 2002 Aaron McGruder/Dist. by Universal Press Syndicate
www.ucomics.com www.boondocks.net

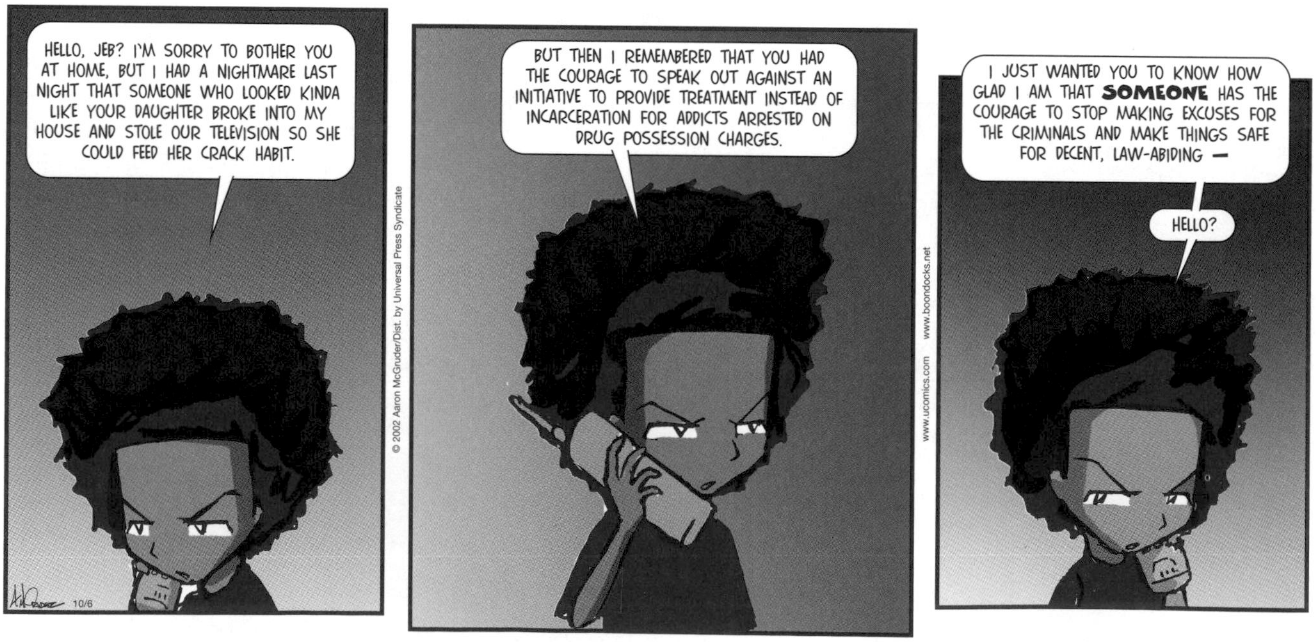
HELLO, JEB? I'M SORRY TO BOTHER YOU AT HOME, BUT I HAD A NIGHTMARE LAST NIGHT THAT SOMEONE WHO LOOKED KINDA LIKE YOUR DAUGHTER BROKE INTO MY HOUSE AND STOLE OUR TELEVISION SO SHE COULD FEED HER CRACK HABIT.
10/6
© 2002 Aaron McGruder/Dist. by Universal Press Syndicate
BUT THEN I REMEMBERED THAT YOU HAD THE COURAGE TO SPEAK OUT AGAINST AN INITIATIVE TO PROVIDE TREATMENT INSTEAD OF INCARCERATION FOR ADDICTS ARRESTED ON DRUG POSSESSION CHARGES.
www.ucomics.com www.boondocks.net
I JUST WANTED YOU TO KNOW HOW GLAD I AM THAT SOMEONE HAS THE COURAGE TO STOP MAKING EXCUSES FOR THE CRIMINALS AND MAKE THINGS SAFE FOR DECENT, LAW-ABIDING —
HELLO?

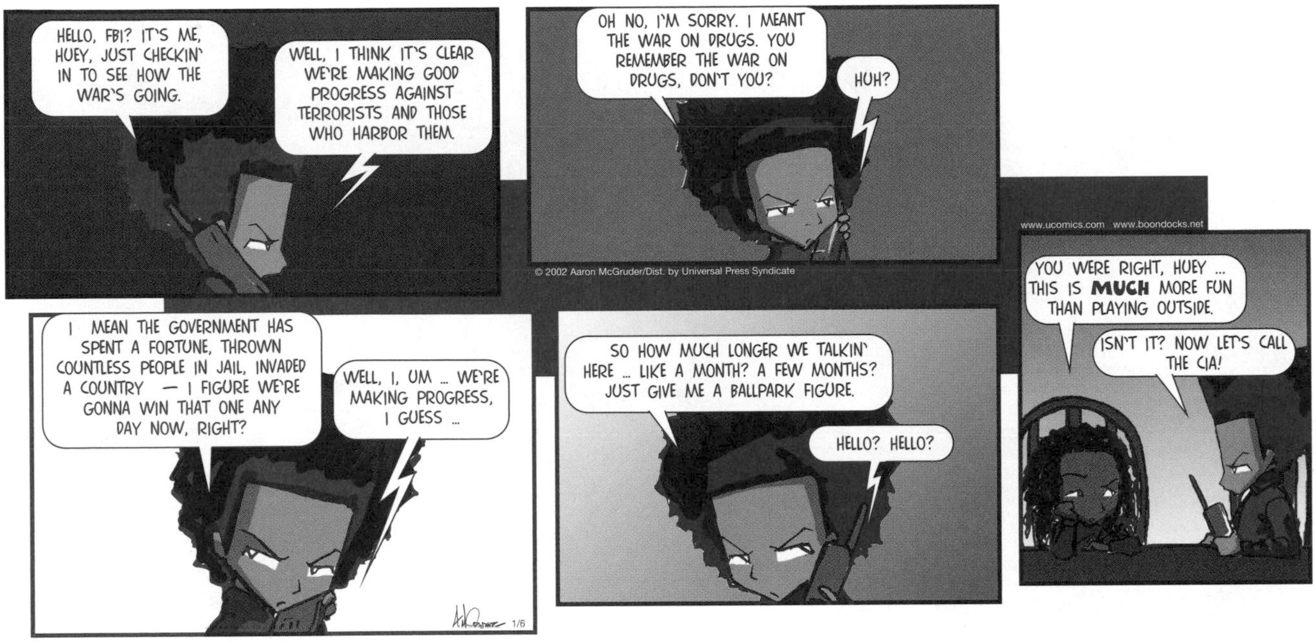
HELLO, FBI? IT'S ME, HUEY, JUST CHECKIN' IN TO SEE HOW THE WAR'S GOING.
WELL, I THINK IT'S CLEAR WE'RE MAKING GOOD PROGRESS AGAINST TERRORISTS AND THOSE WHO HARBOR THEM.
OH NO, I'M SORRY. I MEANT THE WAR ON DRUGS. YOU REMEMBER THE WAR ON DRUGS, DON'T YOU?
HUH?
© 2002 Aaron McGruder/Dist. by Universal Press Syndicate
I MEAN THE GOVERNMENT HAS SPENT A FORTUNE, THROWN COUNTLESS PEOPLE IN JAIL, INVADED A COUNTRY — I FIGURE WE'RE GONNA WIN THAT ONE ANY DAY NOW, RIGHT?
WELL, I, UM ... WE'RE MAKING PROGRESS, I GUESS ...
1/6
SO HOW MUCH LONGER WE TALKIN' HERE ... LIKE A MONTH? A FEW MONTHS? JUST GIVE ME A BALLPARK FIGURE.
HELLO? HELLO?
www.ucomics.com www.boondocks.net
YOU WERE RIGHT, HUEY ... THIS IS **MUCH** MORE FUN THAN PLAYING OUTSIDE.
ISN'T IT? NOW LET'S CALL THE CIA!

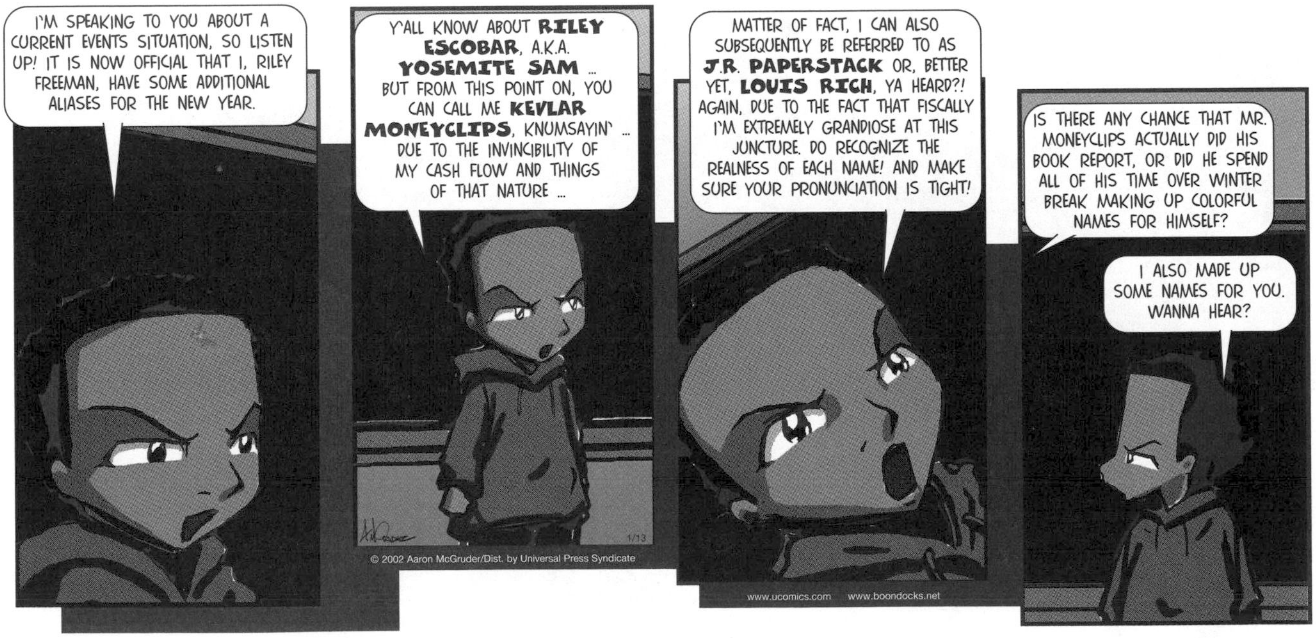
I'M SPEAKING TO YOU ABOUT A CURRENT EVENTS SITUATION, SO LISTEN UP! IT IS NOW OFFICIAL THAT I, RILEY FREEMAN, HAVE SOME ADDITIONAL ALIASES FOR THE NEW YEAR.
Y'ALL KNOW ABOUT **RILEY ESCOBAR**, A.K.A. **YOSEMITE SAM** ... BUT FROM THIS POINT ON, YOU CAN CALL ME **KEVLAR MONEYCLIPS**, KNUMSAYIN' ... DUE TO THE INVINCIBILITY OF MY CASH FLOW AND THINGS OF THAT NATURE ...
1/13
© 2002 Aaron McGruder/Dist. by Universal Press Syndicate
MATTER OF FACT, I CAN ALSO SUBSEQUENTLY BE REFERRED TO AS **J.R. PAPERSTACK** OR, BETTER YET, **LOUIS RICH**, YA HEARD?! AGAIN, DUE TO THE FACT THAT FISCALLY I'M EXTREMELY GRANDIOSE AT THIS JUNCTURE. DO RECOGNIZE THE REALNESS OF EACH NAME! AND MAKE SURE YOUR PRONUNCIATION IS TIGHT!
www.ucomics.com www.boondocks.net
IS THERE ANY CHANCE THAT MR. MONEYCLIPS ACTUALLY DID HIS BOOK REPORT, OR DID HE SPEND ALL OF HIS TIME OVER WINTER BREAK MAKING UP COLORFUL NAMES FOR HIMSELF?
I ALSO MADE UP SOME NAMES FOR YOU. WANNA HEAR?

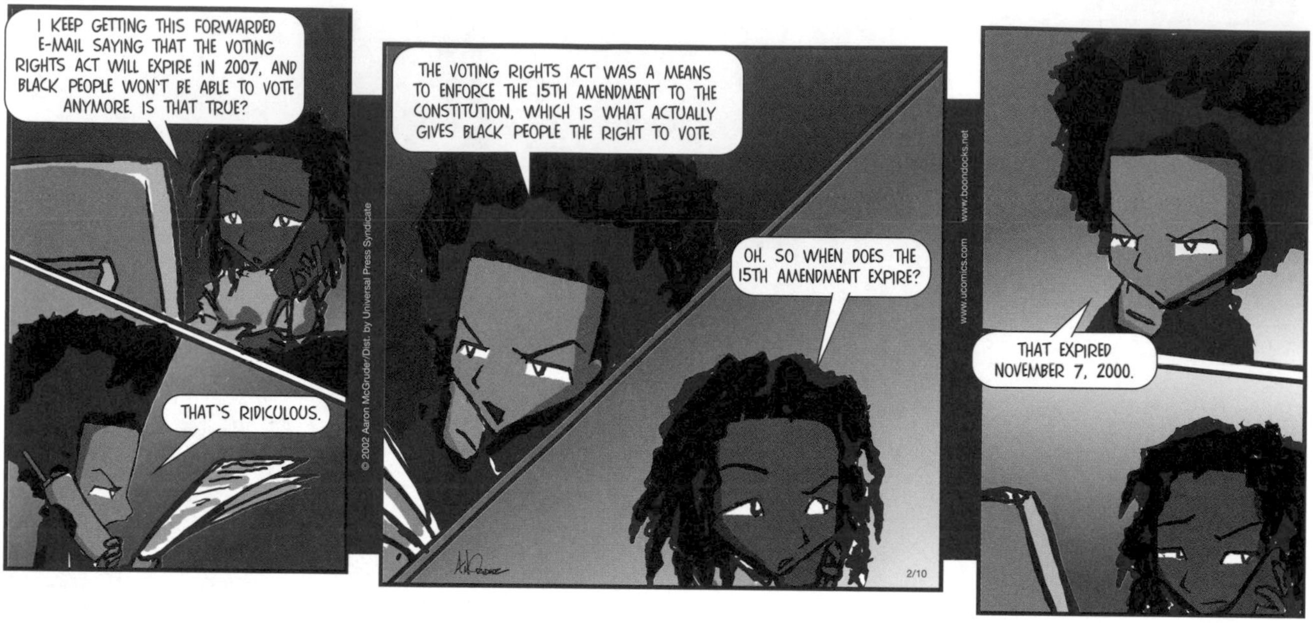
I KEEP GETTING THIS FORWARDED E-MAIL SAYING THAT THE VOTING RIGHTS ACT WILL EXPIRE IN 2007, AND BLACK PEOPLE WON'T BE ABLE TO VOTE ANYMORE. IS THAT TRUE?
THAT'S RIDICULOUS.
© 2002 Aaron McGruder/Dist. by Universal Press Syndicate
THE VOTING RIGHTS ACT WAS A MEANS TO ENFORCE THE 15TH AMENDMENT TO THE CONSTITUTION, WHICH IS WHAT ACTUALLY GIVES BLACK PEOPLE THE RIGHT TO VOTE.
OH. SO WHEN DOES THE 15TH AMENDMENT EXPIRE?
2/10
www.ucomics.com www.boondocks.net
THAT EXPIRED NOVEMBER 7, 2000.

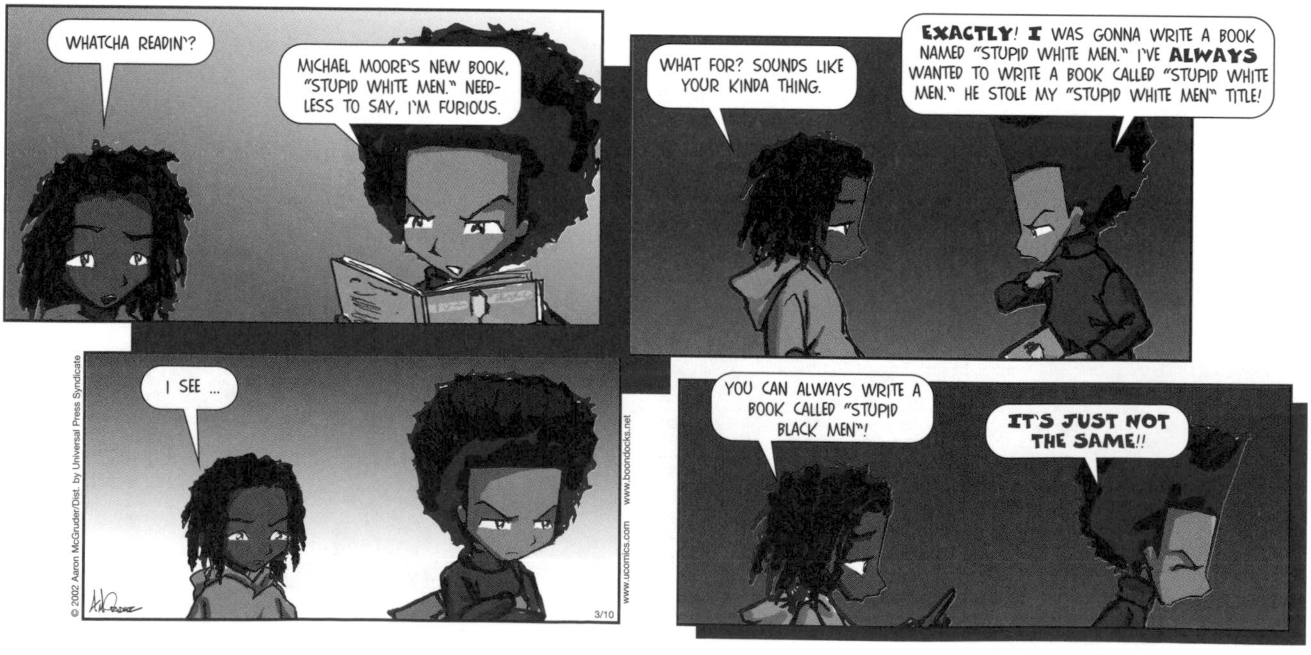
WHATCHA READIN'?
MICHAEL MOORE'S NEW BOOK, "STUPID WHITE MEN." NEEDLESS TO SAY, I'M FURIOUS.
WHAT FOR? SOUNDS LIKE YOUR KINDA THING.
EXACTLY! I WAS GONNA WRITE A BOOK NAMED "STUPID WHITE MEN." I'VE ALWAYS WANTED TO WRITE A BOOK CALLED "STUPID WHITE MEN." HE STOLE MY "STUPID WHITE MEN" TITLE!
I SEE ...
© 2002 Aaron McGruder/Dist. by Universal Press Syndicate
3/10
www.ucomics.com www.boondocks.net
YOU CAN ALWAYS WRITE A BOOK CALLED "STUPID BLACK MEN"!
IT'S JUST NOT THE SAME!!

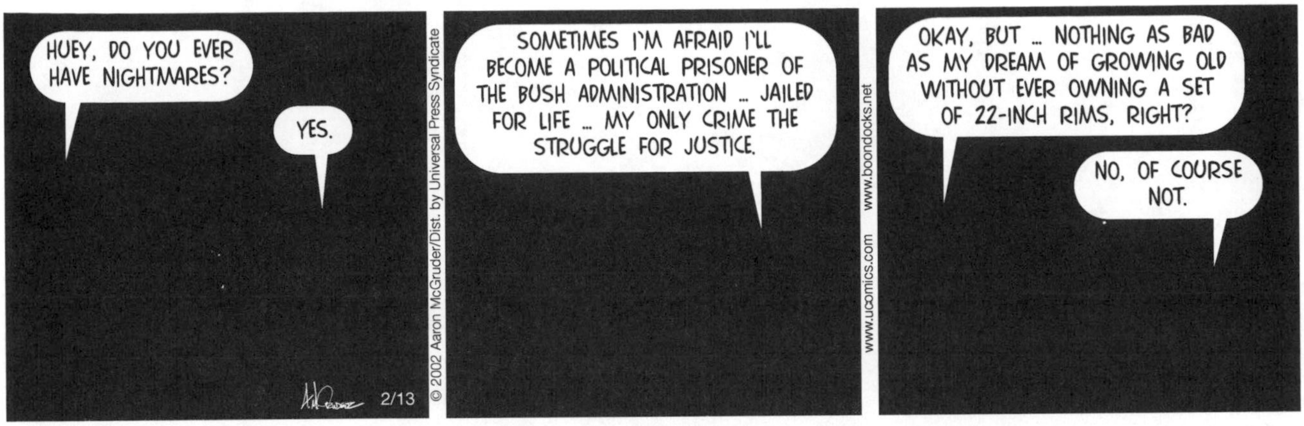
HUEY, DO YOU EVER HAVE NIGHTMARES?
YES.
2/13
© 2002 Aaron McGruder/Dist. by Universal Press Syndicate
SOMETIMES I'M AFRAID I'LL BECOME A POLITICAL PRISONER OF THE BUSH ADMINISTRATION ... JAILED FOR LIFE ... MY ONLY CRIME THE STRUGGLE FOR JUSTICE.
www.ucomics.com www.boondocks.net
OKAY, BUT ... NOTHING AS BAD AS MY DREAM OF GROWING OLD WITHOUT EVER OWNING A SET OF 22-INCH RIMS, RIGHT?
NO, OF COURSE NOT.

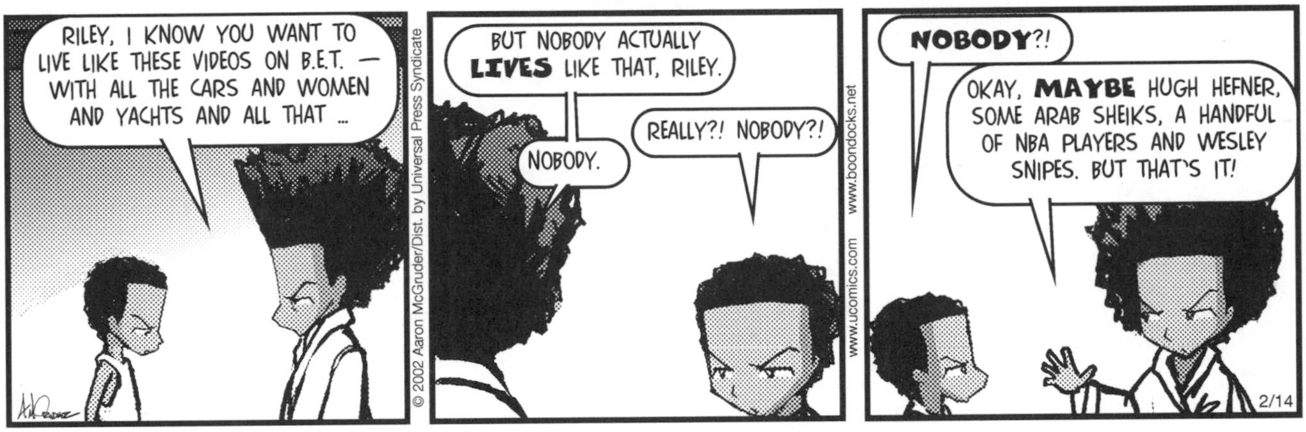
RILEY, I KNOW YOU WANT TO LIVE LIKE THESE VIDEOS ON B.E.T. — WITH ALL THE CARS AND WOMEN AND YACHTS AND ALL THAT ...
© 2002 Aaron McGruder/Dist. by Universal Press Syndicate
BUT NOBODY ACTUALLY **LIVES** LIKE THAT, RILEY.
NOBODY.
REALLY?! NOBODY?!
www.ucomics.com www.boondocks.net
NOBODY?!
OKAY, **MAYBE** HUGH HEFNER, SOME ARAB SHEIKS, A HANDFUL OF NBA PLAYERS AND WESLEY SNIPES. BUT THAT'S IT!
2/14

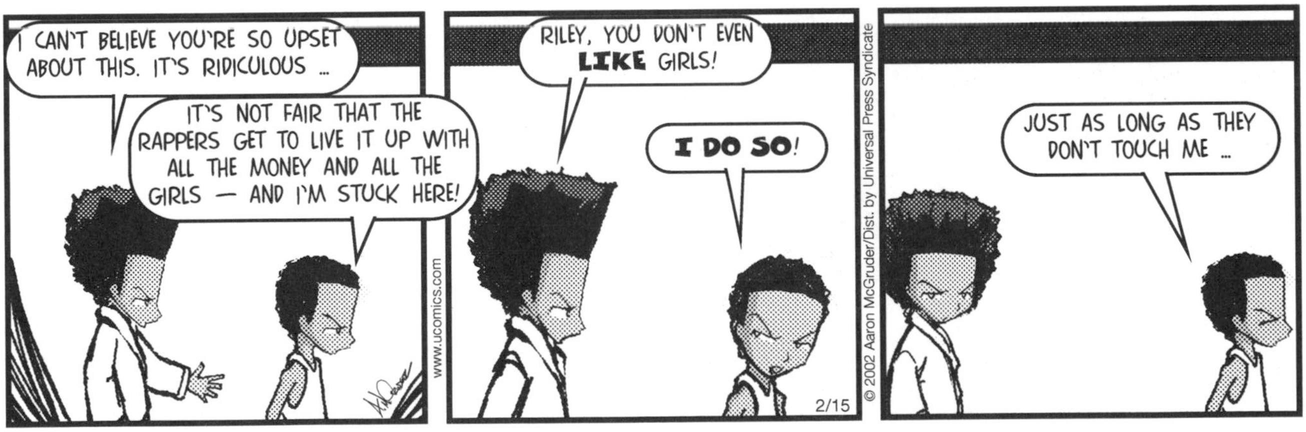
I CAN'T BELIEVE YOU'RE SO UPSET ABOUT THIS. IT'S RIDICULOUS ...
IT'S NOT FAIR THAT THE RAPPERS GET TO LIVE IT UP WITH ALL THE MONEY AND ALL THE GIRLS — AND I'M STUCK HERE!
www.ucomics.com
RILEY, YOU DON'T EVEN **LIKE** GIRLS!
I DO SO!
2/15
© 2002 Aaron McGruder/Dist. by Universal Press Syndicate
JUST AS LONG AS THEY DON'T TOUCH ME ...

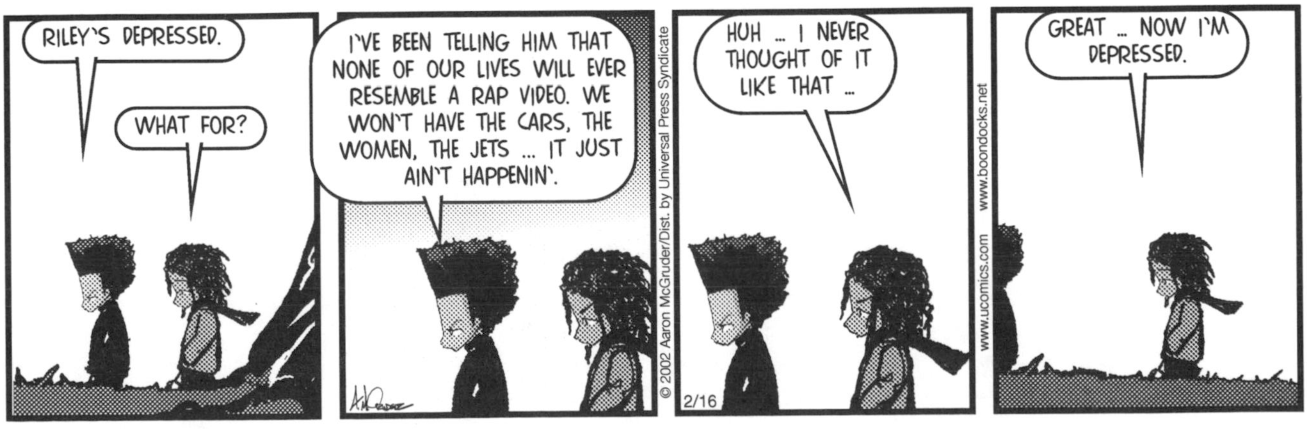
RILEY'S DEPRESSED.
WHAT FOR?
I'VE BEEN TELLING HIM THAT NONE OF OUR LIVES WILL EVER RESEMBLE A RAP VIDEO. WE WON'T HAVE THE CARS, THE WOMEN, THE JETS ... IT JUST AIN'T HAPPENIN'.
© 2002 Aaron McGruder/Dist. by Universal Press Syndicate
HUH ... I NEVER THOUGHT OF IT LIKE THAT ...
2/16
www.ucomics.com www.boondocks.net
GREAT ... NOW I'M DEPRESSED.

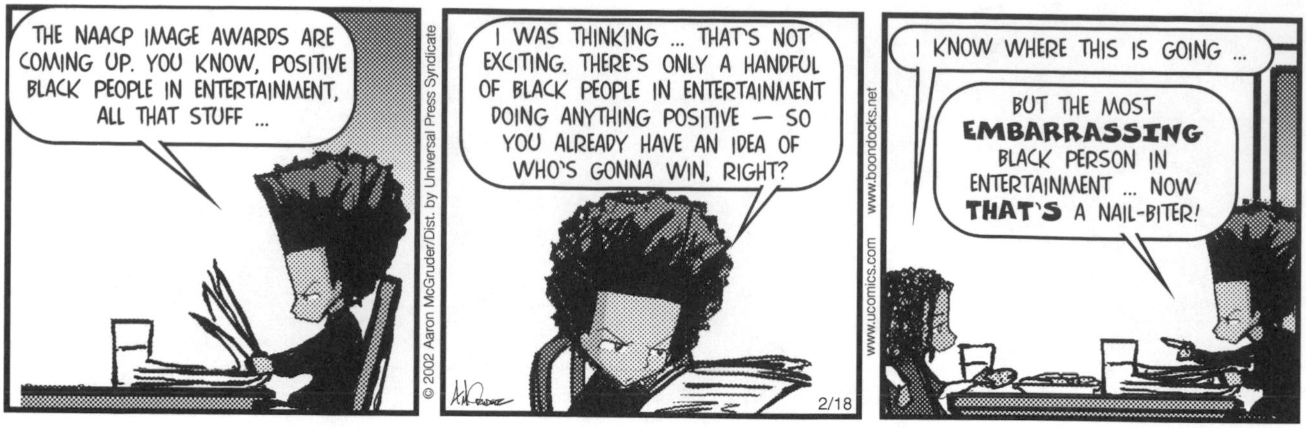
THE NAACP IMAGE AWARDS ARE COMING UP. YOU KNOW, POSITIVE BLACK PEOPLE IN ENTERTAINMENT, ALL THAT STUFF ...
I WAS THINKING ... THAT'S NOT EXCITING. THERE'S ONLY A HANDFUL OF BLACK PEOPLE IN ENTERTAINMENT DOING ANYTHING POSITIVE — SO YOU ALREADY HAVE AN IDEA OF WHO'S GONNA WIN, RIGHT?
I KNOW WHERE THIS IS GOING ...
BUT THE MOST **EMBARRASSING** BLACK PERSON IN ENTERTAINMENT ... NOW **THAT'S** A NAIL-BITER!
© 2002 Aaron McGruder/Dist. by Universal Press Syndicate
www.ucomics.com www.boondocks.net
2/18

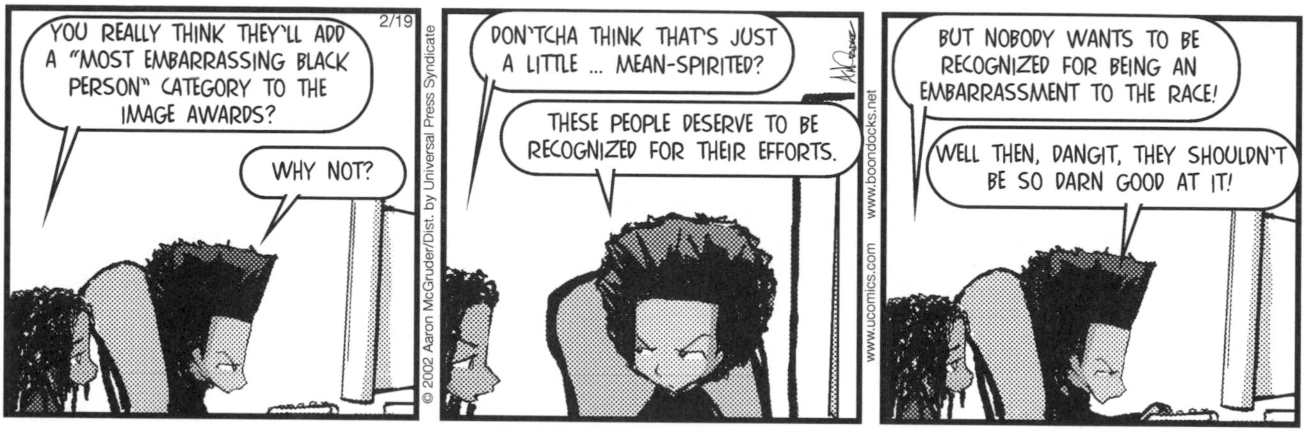
2/19
YOU REALLY THINK THEY'LL ADD A "MOST EMBARRASSING BLACK PERSON" CATEGORY TO THE IMAGE AWARDS?
WHY NOT?
DON'TCHA THINK THAT'S JUST A LITTLE ... MEAN-SPIRITED?
THESE PEOPLE DESERVE TO BE RECOGNIZED FOR THEIR EFFORTS.
BUT NOBODY WANTS TO BE RECOGNIZED FOR BEING AN EMBARRASSMENT TO THE RACE!
WELL THEN, DANGIT, THEY SHOULDN'T BE SO DARN GOOD AT IT!
© 2002 Aaron McGruder/Dist. by Universal Press Syndicate
www.ucomics.com www.boondocks.net

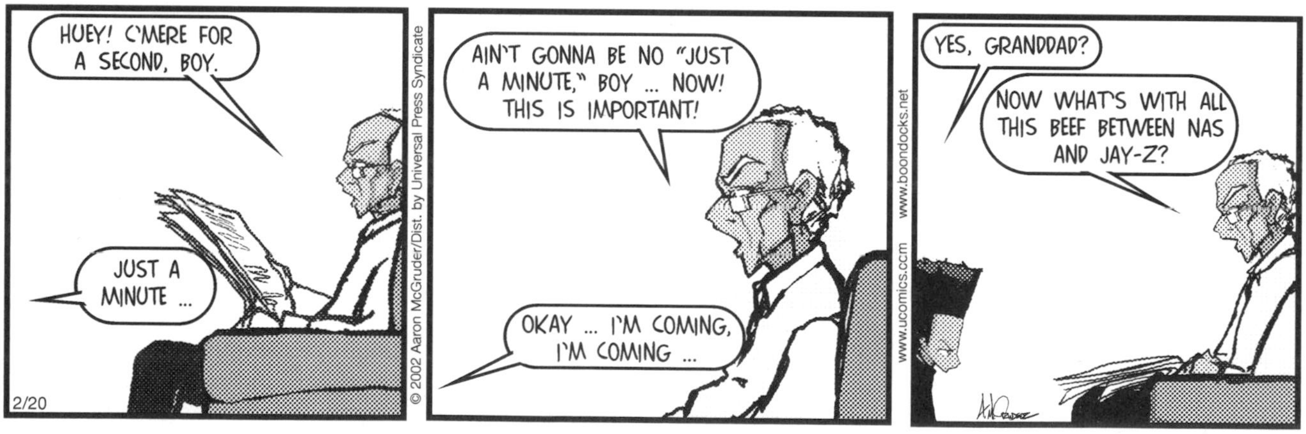
HUEY! C'MERE FOR A SECOND, BOY.
JUST A MINUTE ...
AIN'T GONNA BE NO "JUST A MINUTE," BOY ... NOW! THIS IS IMPORTANT!
OKAY ... I'M COMING, I'M COMING ...
YES, GRANDDAD?
NOW WHAT'S WITH ALL THIS BEEF BETWEEN NAS AND JAY-Z?
2/20
© 2002 Aaron McGruder/Dist. by Universal Press Syndicate
www.ucomics.com www.boondocks.net

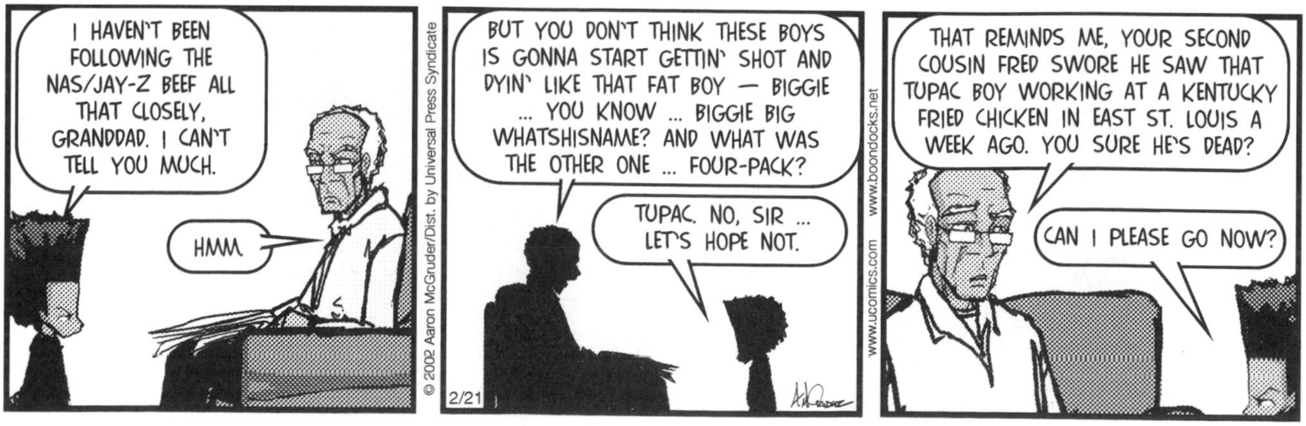
I HAVEN'T BEEN FOLLOWING THE NAS/JAY-Z BEEF ALL THAT CLOSELY, GRANDDAD. I CAN'T TELL YOU MUCH.
HMM
BUT YOU DON'T THINK THESE BOYS IS GONNA START GETTIN' SHOT AND DYIN' LIKE THAT FAT BOY — BIGGIE ... YOU KNOW ... BIGGIE BIG WHATSHISNAME? AND WHAT WAS THE OTHER ONE ... FOUR-PACK?
TUPAC. NO, SIR ... LET'S HOPE NOT.
THAT REMINDS ME, YOUR SECOND COUSIN FRED SWORE HE SAW THAT TUPAC BOY WORKING AT A KENTUCKY FRIED CHICKEN IN EAST ST. LOUIS A WEEK AGO. YOU SURE HE'S DEAD?
CAN I PLEASE GO NOW?
© 2002 Aaron McGruder/Dist. by Universal Press Syndicate
2/21
www.ucomics.com www.boondocks.net

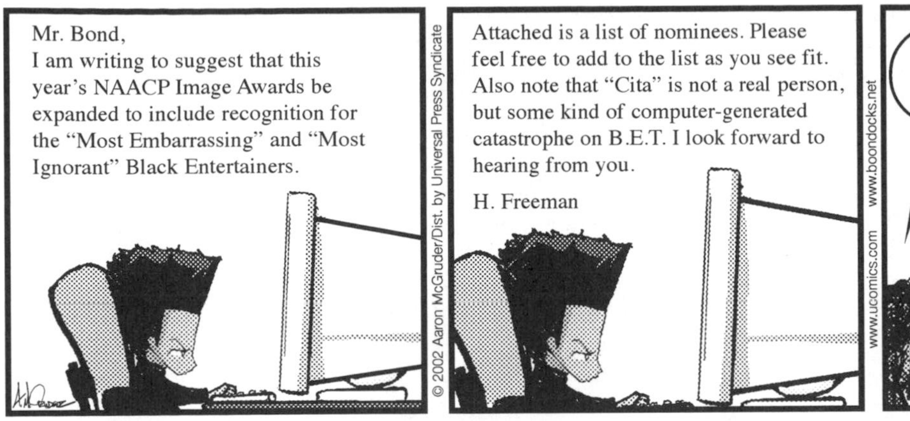
Mr. Bond,
I am writing to suggest that this year's NAACP Image Awards be expanded to include recognition for the "Most Embarrassing" and "Most Ignorant" Black Entertainers.
© 2002 Aaron McGruder/Dist. by Universal Press Syndicate
Attached is a list of nominees. Please feel free to add to the list as you see fit. Also note that "Cita" is not a real person, but some kind of computer-generated catastrophe on B.E.T. I look forward to hearing from you.
H. Freeman
www.ucomics.com www.boondocks.net
2/22
IF WE GET TO BE PRESENTERS AT THE SHOW, DO I HAVE TO RENT A TUX?
I'LL ASK ...

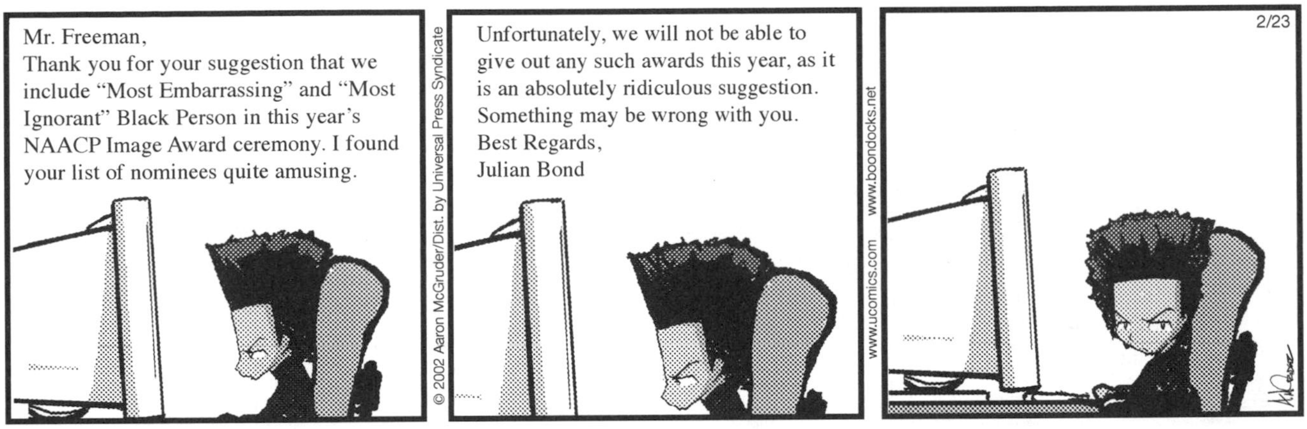
Mr. Freeman,
Thank you for your suggestion that we include "Most Embarrassing" and "Most Ignorant" Black Person in this year's NAACP Image Award ceremony. I found your list of nominees quite amusing.
© 2002 Aaron McGruder/Dist. by Universal Press Syndicate
Unfortunately, we will not be able to give out any such awards this year, as it is an absolutely ridiculous suggestion. Something may be wrong with you.
Best Regards,
Julian Bond
www.ucomics.com www.boondocks.net
2/23

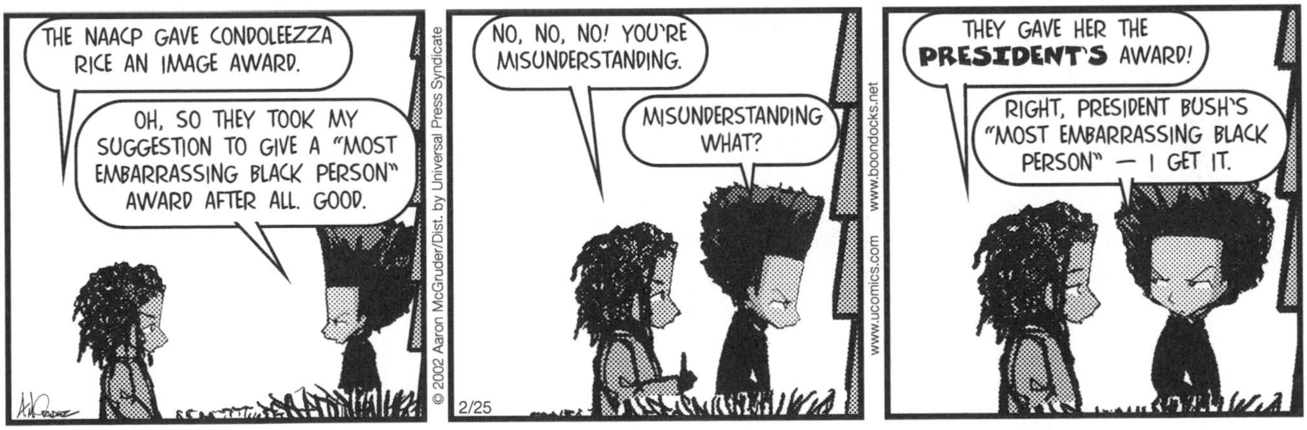
THE NAACP GAVE CONDOLEEZZA RICE AN IMAGE AWARD.
OH, SO THEY TOOK MY SUGGESTION TO GIVE A "MOST EMBARRASSING BLACK PERSON" AWARD AFTER ALL. GOOD.
© 2002 Aaron McGruder/Dist. by Universal Press Syndicate
2/25
NO, NO, NO! YOU'RE MISUNDERSTANDING.
MISUNDERSTANDING WHAT?
www.ucomics.com www.boondocks.net
THEY GAVE HER THE **PRESIDENT'S** AWARD!
RIGHT, PRESIDENT BUSH'S "MOST EMBARRASSING BLACK PERSON" — I GET IT.

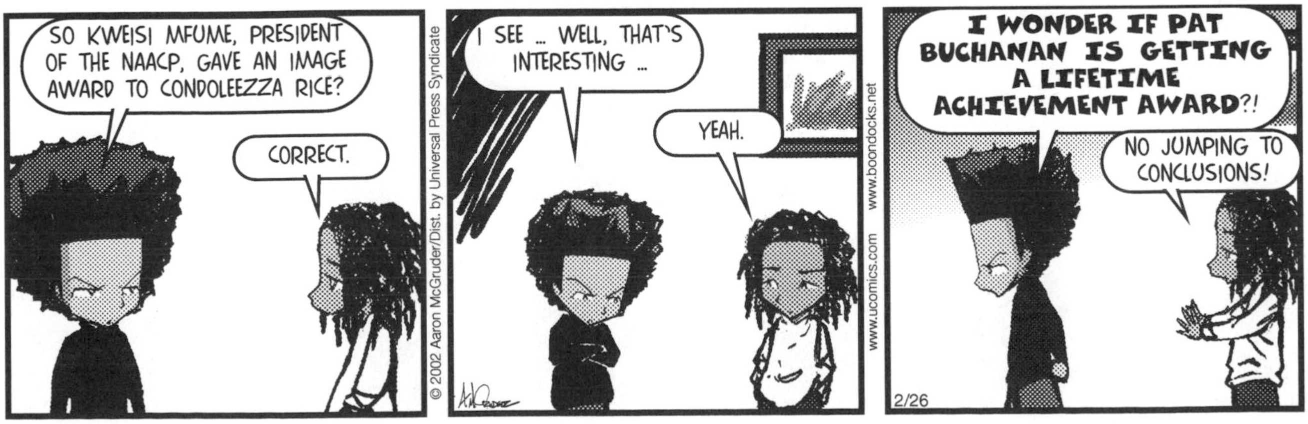
SO KWEISI MFUME, PRESIDENT OF THE NAACP, GAVE AN IMAGE AWARD TO CONDOLEEZZA RICE?
CORRECT.
© 2002 Aaron McGruder/Dist. by Universal Press Syndicate
I SEE ... WELL, THAT'S INTERESTING ...
YEAH.
www.ucomics.com www.boondocks.net
I WONDER IF PAT BUCHANAN IS GETTING A LIFETIME ACHIEVEMENT AWARD?!
NO JUMPING TO CONCLUSIONS!
2/26

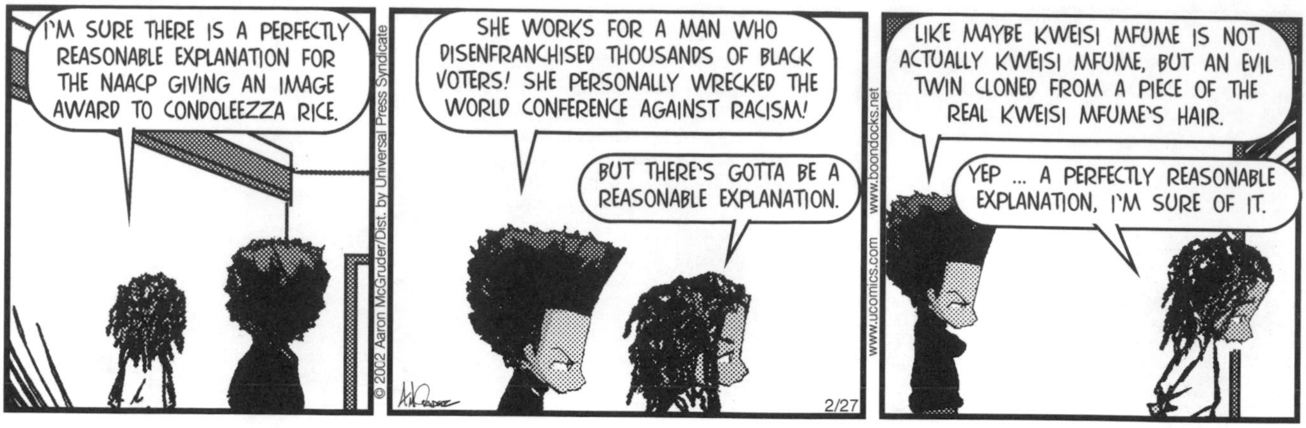
I'M SURE THERE IS A PERFECTLY REASONABLE EXPLANATION FOR THE NAACP GIVING AN IMAGE AWARD TO CONDOLEEZZA RICE.
© 2002 Aaron McGruder/Dist. by Universal Press Syndicate
SHE WORKS FOR A MAN WHO DISENFRANCHISED THOUSANDS OF BLACK VOTERS! SHE PERSONALLY WRECKED THE WORLD CONFERENCE AGAINST RACISM!
BUT THERE'S GOTTA BE A REASONABLE EXPLANATION.
2/27
www.ucomics.com www.boondocks.net
LIKE MAYBE KWEISI MFUME IS NOT ACTUALLY KWEISI MFUME, BUT AN EVIL TWIN CLONED FROM A PIECE OF THE REAL KWEISI MFUME'S HAIR.
YEP ... A PERFECTLY REASONABLE EXPLANATION, I'M SURE OF IT.

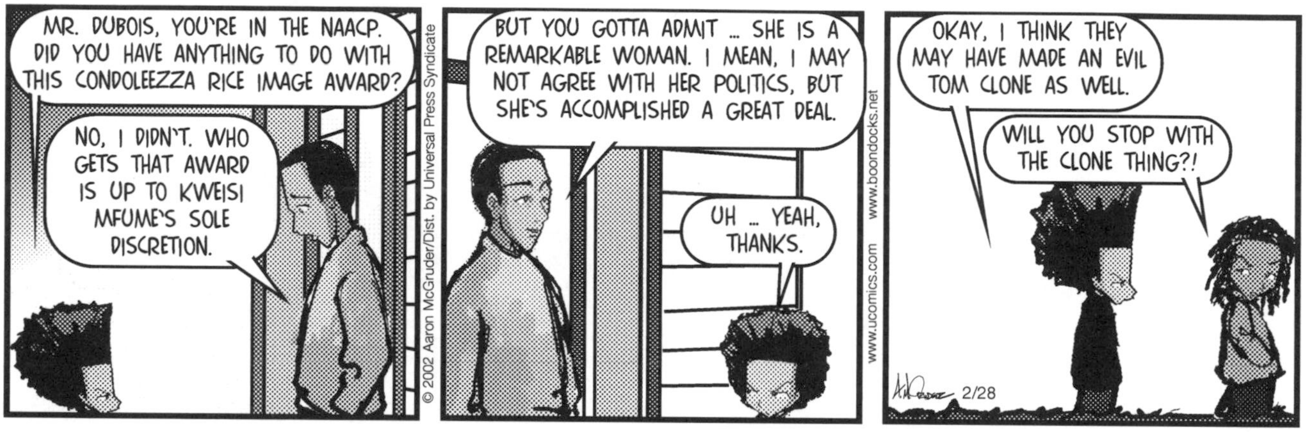
MR. DUBOIS, YOU'RE IN THE NAACP. DID YOU HAVE ANYTHING TO DO WITH THIS CONDOLEEZZA RICE IMAGE AWARD?
NO, I DIDN'T. WHO GETS THAT AWARD IS UP TO KWEISI MFUME'S SOLE DISCRETION.
© 2002 Aaron McGruder/Dist. by Universal Press Syndicate
BUT YOU GOTTA ADMIT ... SHE IS A REMARKABLE WOMAN. I MEAN, I MAY NOT AGREE WITH HER POLITICS, BUT SHE'S ACCOMPLISHED A GREAT DEAL.
UH ... YEAH, THANKS.
www.ucomics.com www.boondocks.net
OKAY, I THINK THEY MAY HAVE MADE AN EVIL TOM CLONE AS WELL.
WILL YOU STOP WITH THE CLONE THING?!
2/28

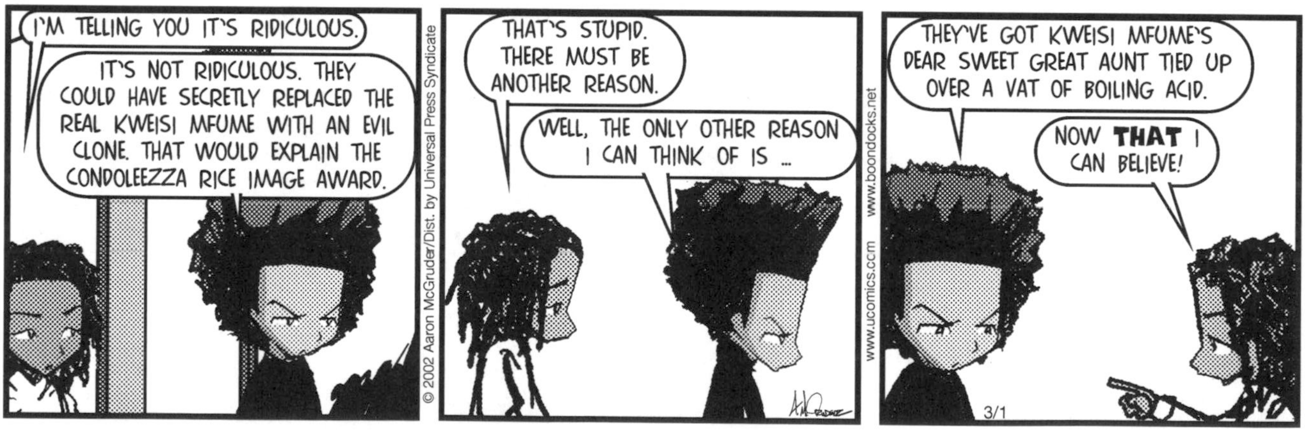
I'M TELLING YOU IT'S RIDICULOUS.
IT'S NOT RIDICULOUS. THEY COULD HAVE SECRETLY REPLACED THE REAL KWEISI MFUME WITH AN EVIL CLONE. THAT WOULD EXPLAIN THE CONDOLEEZZA RICE IMAGE AWARD.
© 2002 Aaron McGruder/Dist. by Universal Press Syndicate
THAT'S STUPID. THERE MUST BE ANOTHER REASON.
WELL, THE ONLY OTHER REASON I CAN THINK OF IS ...
www.ucomics.com www.boondocks.net
THEY'VE GOT KWEISI MFUME'S DEAR SWEET GREAT AUNT TIED UP OVER A VAT OF BOILING ACID.
NOW **THAT** I CAN BELIEVE!
3/1

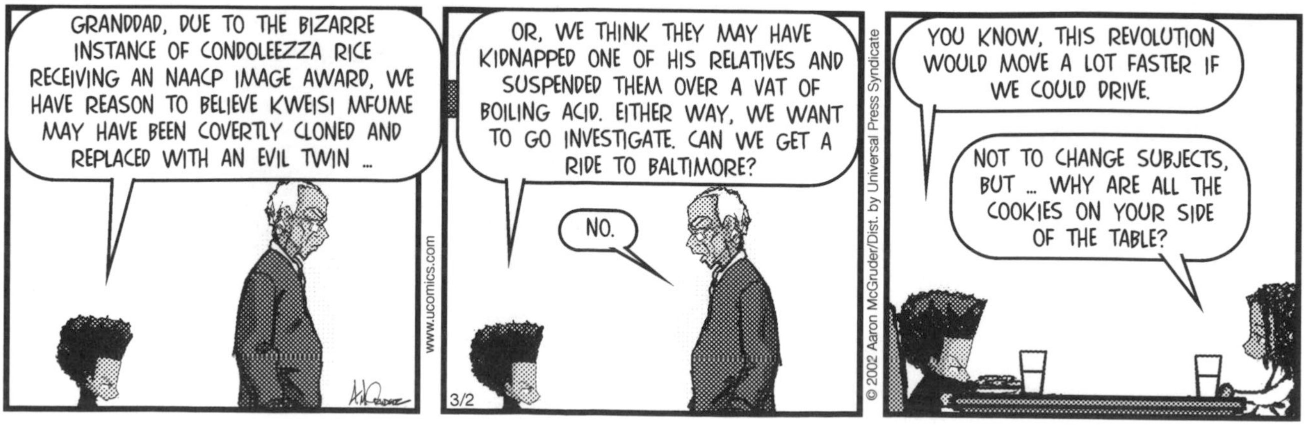
GRANDDAD, DUE TO THE BIZARRE INSTANCE OF CONDOLEEZZA RICE RECEIVING AN NAACP IMAGE AWARD, WE HAVE REASON TO BELIEVE KWEISI MFUME MAY HAVE BEEN COVERTLY CLONED AND REPLACED WITH AN EVIL TWIN ...
www.ucomics.com
OR, WE THINK THEY MAY HAVE KIDNAPPED ONE OF HIS RELATIVES AND SUSPENDED THEM OVER A VAT OF BOILING ACID. EITHER WAY, WE WANT TO GO INVESTIGATE. CAN WE GET A RIDE TO BALTIMORE?
NO.
3/2
© 2002 Aaron McGruder/Dist. by Universal Press Syndicate
YOU KNOW, THIS REVOLUTION WOULD MOVE A LOT FASTER IF WE COULD DRIVE.
NOT TO CHANGE SUBJECTS, BUT ... WHY ARE ALL THE COOKIES ON YOUR SIDE OF THE TABLE?

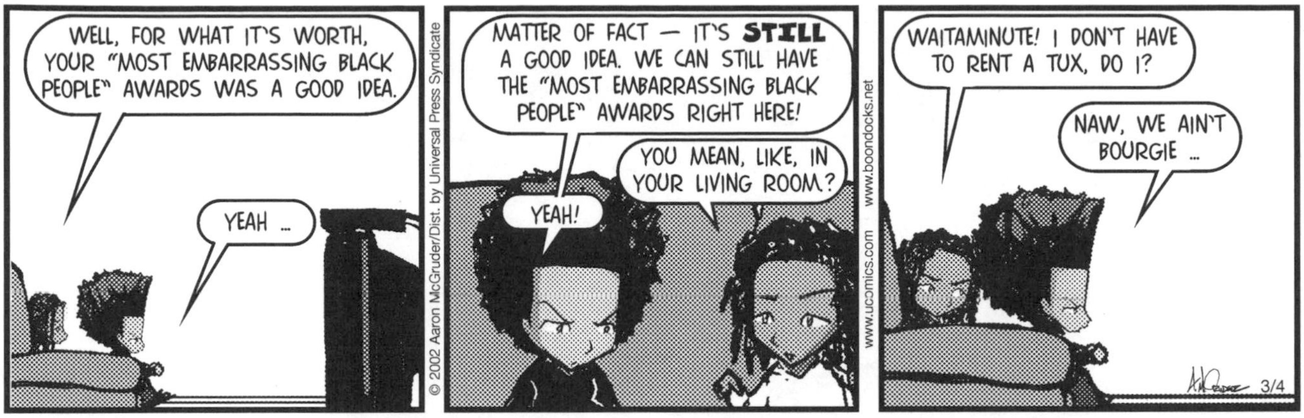
WELL, FOR WHAT IT'S WORTH, YOUR "MOST EMBARRASSING BLACK PEOPLE" AWARDS WAS A GOOD IDEA.
YEAH ...
© 2002 Aaron McGruder/Dist. by Universal Press Syndicate
MATTER OF FACT — IT'S STILL A GOOD IDEA. WE CAN STILL HAVE THE "MOST EMBARRASSING BLACK PEOPLE" AWARDS RIGHT HERE!
YEAH!
YOU MEAN, LIKE, IN YOUR LIVING ROOM?
www.ucomics.com www.boondocks.net
WAITAMINUTE! I DON'T HAVE TO RENT A TUX, DO I?
NAW, WE AIN'T BOURGIE ...
3/4

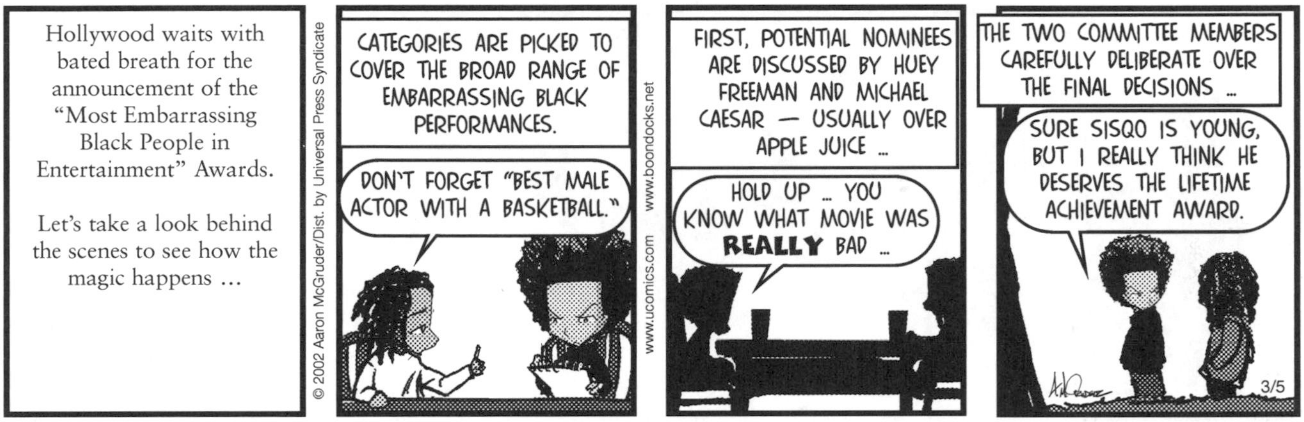
Hollywood waits with bated breath for the announcement of the "Most Embarrassing Black People in Entertainment" Awards.
Let's take a look behind the scenes to see how the magic happens …
© 2002 Aaron McGruder/Dist. by Universal Press Syndicate
CATEGORIES ARE PICKED TO COVER THE BROAD RANGE OF EMBARRASSING BLACK PERFORMANCES.
DON'T FORGET "BEST MALE ACTOR WITH A BASKETBALL."
www.ucomics.com www.boondocks.net
FIRST, POTENTIAL NOMINEES ARE DISCUSSED BY HUEY FREEMAN AND MICHAEL CAESAR — USUALLY OVER APPLE JUICE ...
HOLD UP ... YOU KNOW WHAT MOVIE WAS REALLY BAD ...
THE TWO COMMITTEE MEMBERS CAREFULLY DELIBERATE OVER THE FINAL DECISIONS ...
SURE SISQO IS YOUNG, BUT I REALLY THINK HE DESERVES THE LIFETIME ACHIEVEMENT AWARD.
3/5

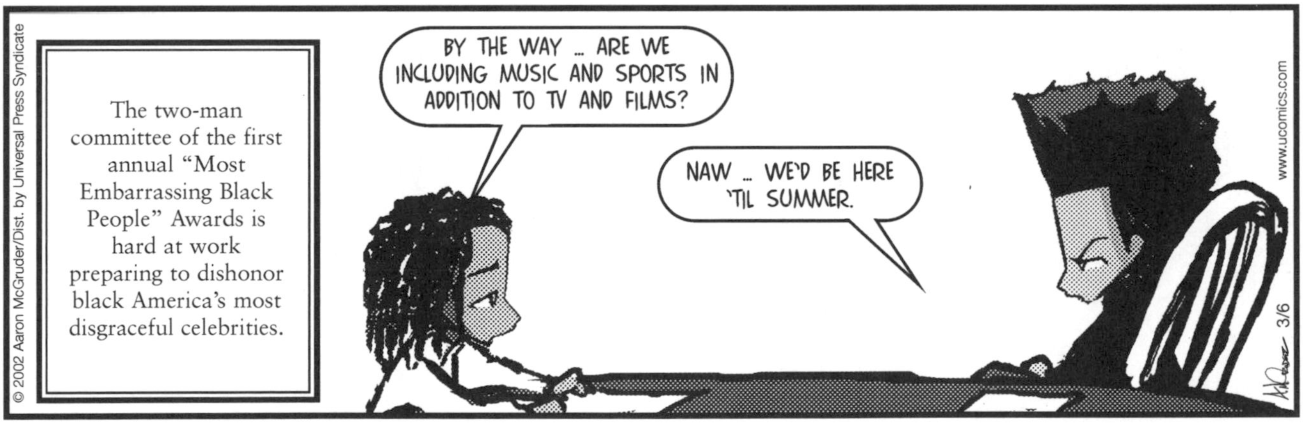
© 2002 Aaron McGruder/Dist. by Universal Press Syndicate
The two-man committee of the first annual "Most Embarrassing Black People" Awards is hard at work preparing to dishonor black America's most disgraceful celebrities.
BY THE WAY ... ARE WE INCLUDING MUSIC AND SPORTS IN ADDITION TO TV AND FILMS?
NAW ... WE'D BE HERE 'TIL SUMMER.
www.ucomics.com
3/6

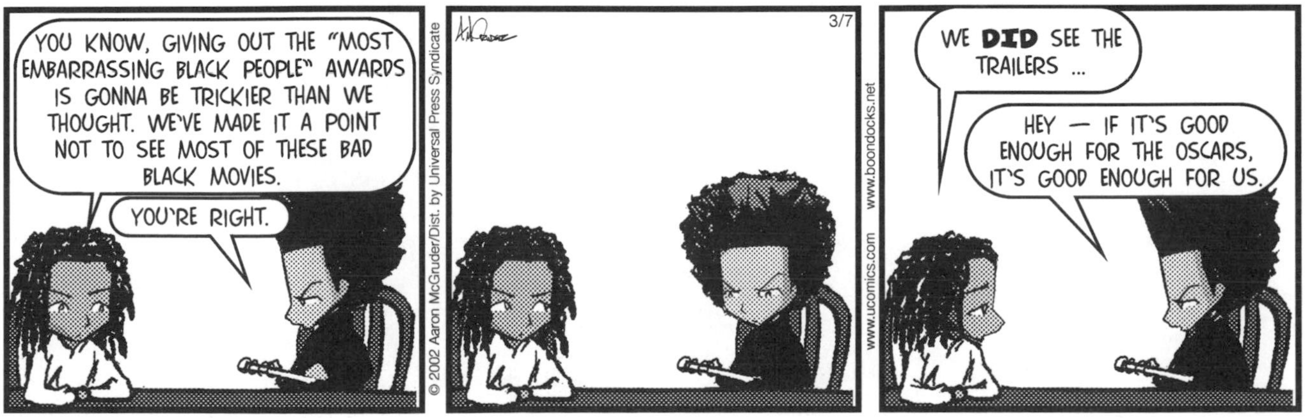
YOU KNOW, GIVING OUT THE "MOST EMBARRASSING BLACK PEOPLE" AWARDS IS GONNA BE TRICKIER THAN WE THOUGHT. WE'VE MADE IT A POINT NOT TO SEE MOST OF THESE BAD BLACK MOVIES.
YOU'RE RIGHT.
© 2002 Aaron McGruder/Dist. by Universal Press Syndicate
3/7
www.ucomics.com www.boondocks.net
WE DID SEE THE TRAILERS ...
HEY — IF IT'S GOOD ENOUGH FOR THE OSCARS, IT'S GOOD ENOUGH FOR US.

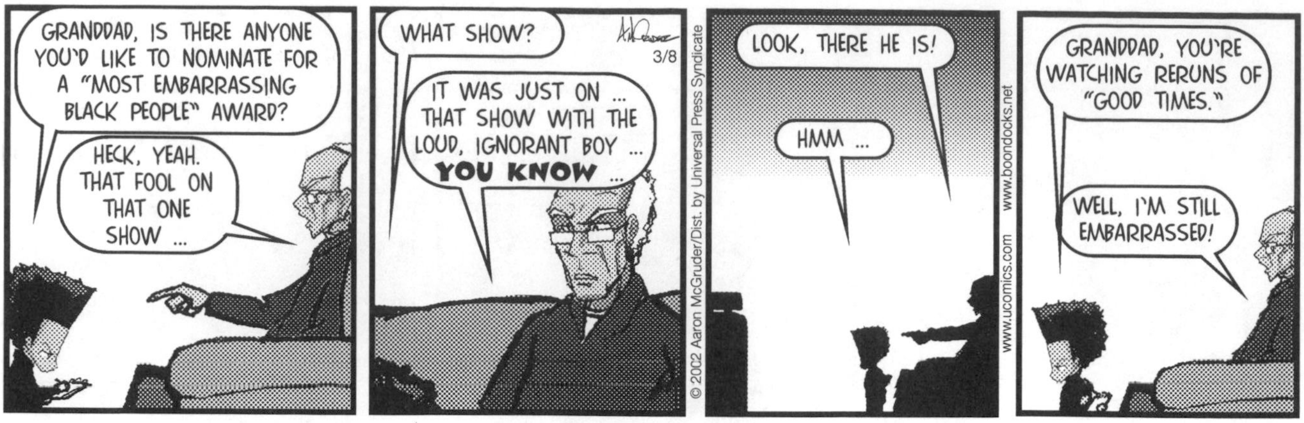
GRANDDAD, IS THERE ANYONE YOU'D LIKE TO NOMINATE FOR A "MOST EMBARRASSING BLACK PEOPLE" AWARD?
HECK, YEAH. THAT FOOL ON THAT ONE SHOW ...
WHAT SHOW?
3/8
IT WAS JUST ON ... THAT SHOW WITH THE LOUD, IGNORANT BOY ... YOU KNOW ...
© 2002 Aaron McGruder/Dist. by Universal Press Syndicate
LOOK, THERE HE IS!
HMM ...
www.ucomics.com www.boondocks.net
GRANDDAD, YOU'RE WATCHING RERUNS OF "GOOD TIMES."
WELL, I'M STILL EMBARRASSED!

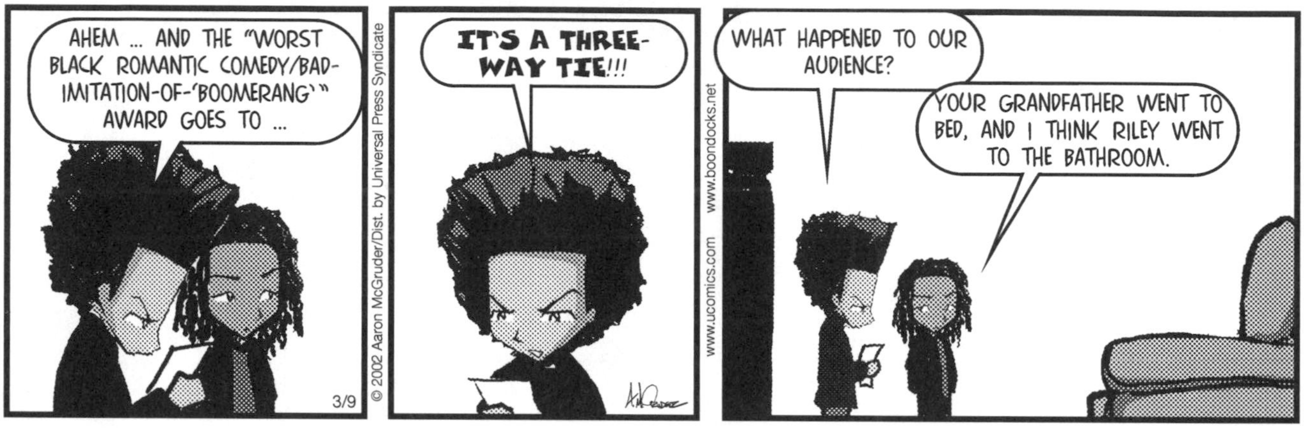
AHEM ... AND THE "WORST BLACK ROMANTIC COMEDY/BAD-IMITATION-OF-'BOOMERANG'" AWARD GOES TO ...
3/9
© 2002 Aaron McGruder/Dist. by Universal Press Syndicate
IT'S A THREE-WAY TIE!!!
www.ucomics.com www.boondocks.net
WHAT HAPPENED TO OUR AUDIENCE?
YOUR GRANDFATHER WENT TO BED, AND I THINK RILEY WENT TO THE BATHROOM.

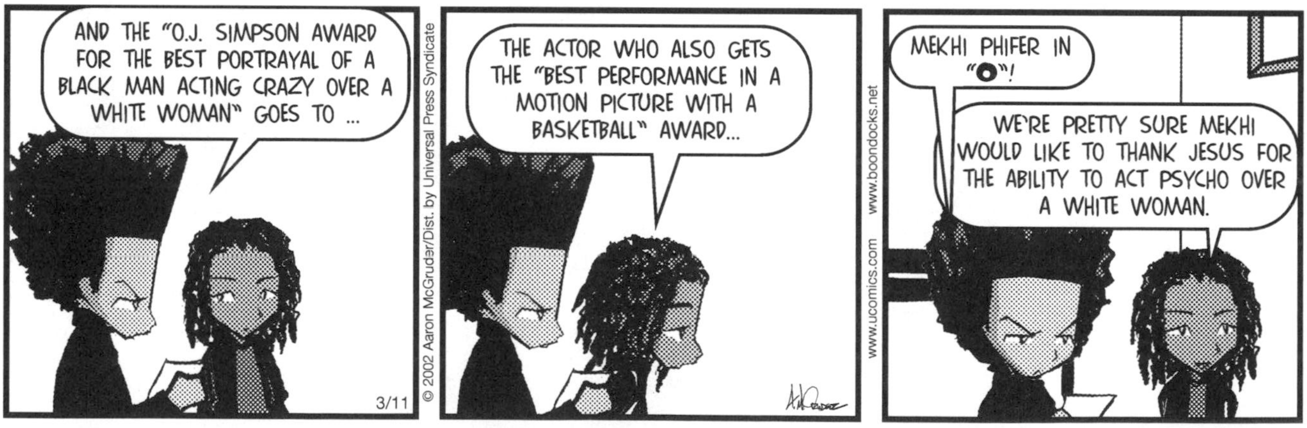
AND THE "O.J. SIMPSON AWARD FOR THE BEST PORTRAYAL OF A BLACK MAN ACTING CRAZY OVER A WHITE WOMAN" GOES TO ...
3/11
© 2002 Aaron McGruder/Dist. by Universal Press Syndicate
THE ACTOR WHO ALSO GETS THE "BEST PERFORMANCE IN A MOTION PICTURE WITH A BASKETBALL" AWARD...
www.ucomics.com www.boondocks.net
MEKHI PHIFER IN "O"!
WE'RE PRETTY SURE MEKHI WOULD LIKE TO THANK JESUS FOR THE ABILITY TO ACT PSYCHO OVER A WHITE WOMAN.

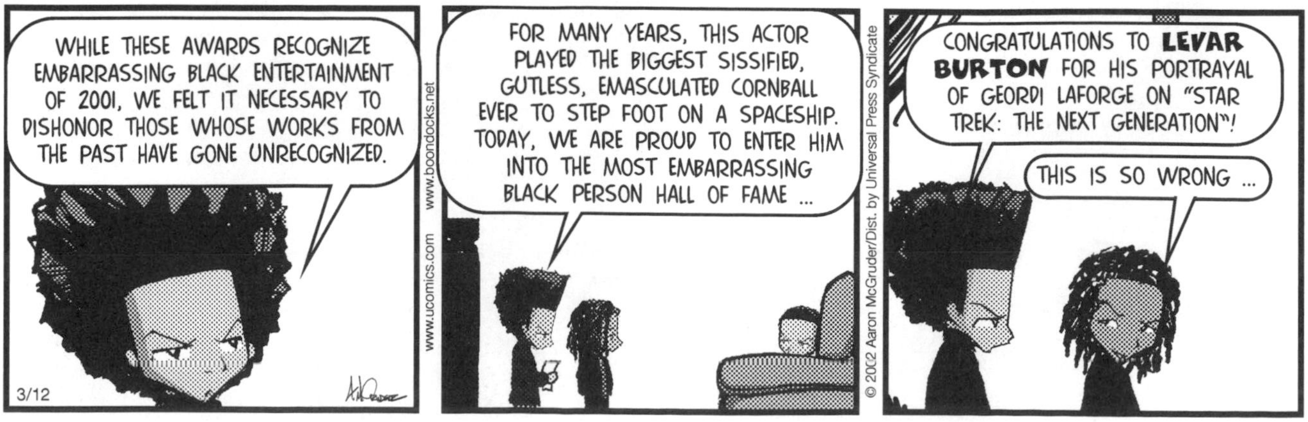
WHILE THESE AWARDS RECOGNIZE EMBARRASSING BLACK ENTERTAINMENT OF 2001, WE FELT IT NECESSARY TO DISHONOR THOSE WHOSE WORKS FROM THE PAST HAVE GONE UNRECOGNIZED.
3/12
www.ucomics.com www.boondocks.net
FOR MANY YEARS, THIS ACTOR PLAYED THE BIGGEST SISSIFIED, GUTLESS, EMASCULATED CORNBALL EVER TO STEP FOOT ON A SPACESHIP. TODAY, WE ARE PROUD TO ENTER HIM INTO THE MOST EMBARRASSING BLACK PERSON HALL OF FAME ...
© 2002 Aaron McGruder/Dist. by Universal Press Syndicate
CONGRATULATIONS TO LEVAR BURTON FOR HIS PORTRAYAL OF GEORDI LAFORGE ON "STAR TREK: THE NEXT GENERATION"!
THIS IS SO WRONG ...

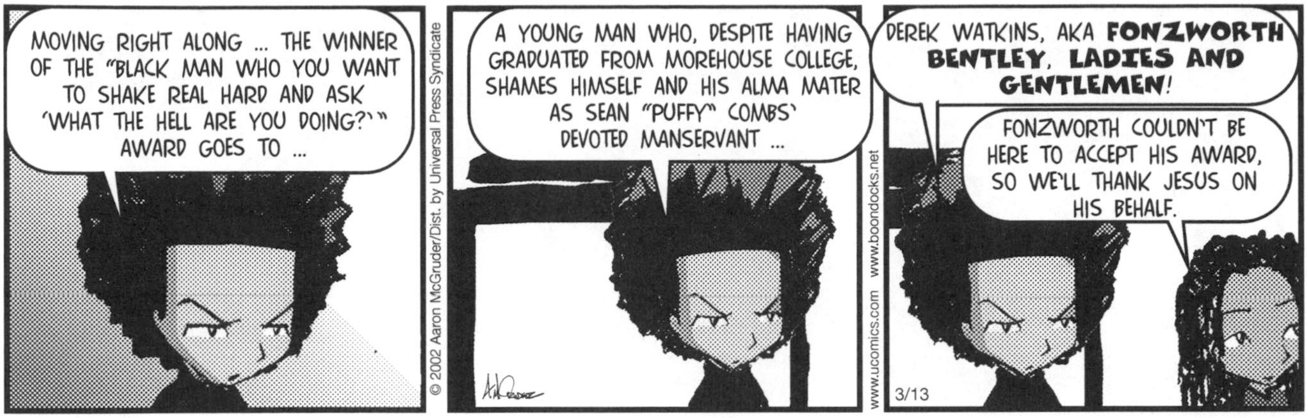
MOVING RIGHT ALONG ... THE WINNER OF THE "BLACK MAN WHO YOU WANT TO SHAKE REAL HARD AND ASK 'WHAT THE HELL ARE YOU DOING?'" AWARD GOES TO ...
A YOUNG MAN WHO, DESPITE HAVING GRADUATED FROM MOREHOUSE COLLEGE, SHAMES HIMSELF AND HIS ALMA MATER AS SEAN "PUFFY" COMBS' DEVOTED MANSERVANT ...
DEREK WATKINS, AKA **FONZWORTH BENTLEY, LADIES AND GENTLEMEN!**
FONZWORTH COULDN'T BE HERE TO ACCEPT HIS AWARD, SO WE'LL THANK JESUS ON HIS BEHALF.
© 2002 Aaron McGruder/Dist. by Universal Press Syndicate
www.ucomics.com www.boondocks.net
3/13

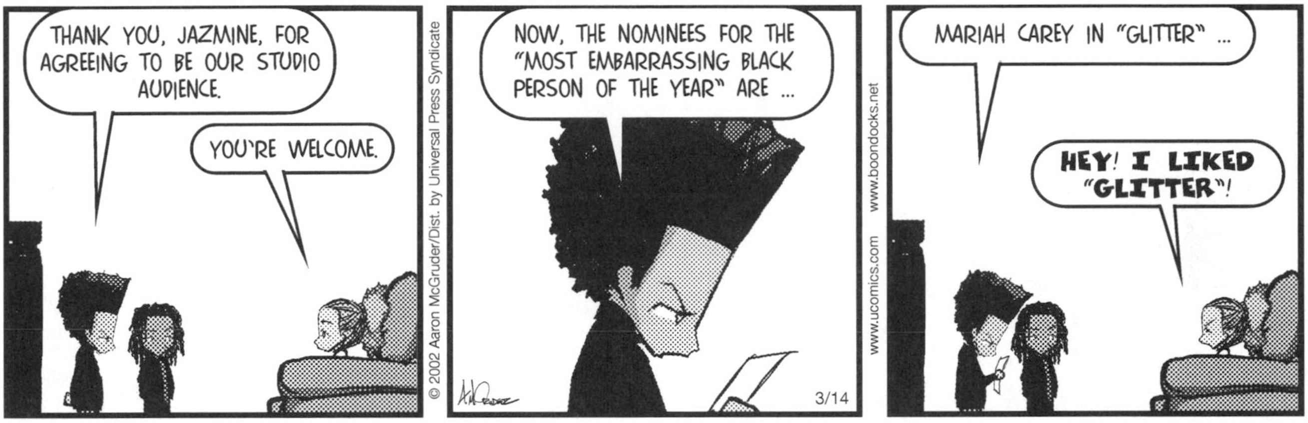
THANK YOU, JAZMINE, FOR AGREEING TO BE OUR STUDIO AUDIENCE.
YOU'RE WELCOME.
NOW, THE NOMINEES FOR THE "MOST EMBARRASSING BLACK PERSON OF THE YEAR" ARE ...
MARIAH CAREY IN "GLITTER" ...
HEY! I LIKED "GLITTER"!
© 2002 Aaron McGruder/Dist. by Universal Press Syndicate
www.ucomics.com www.boondocks.net
3/14

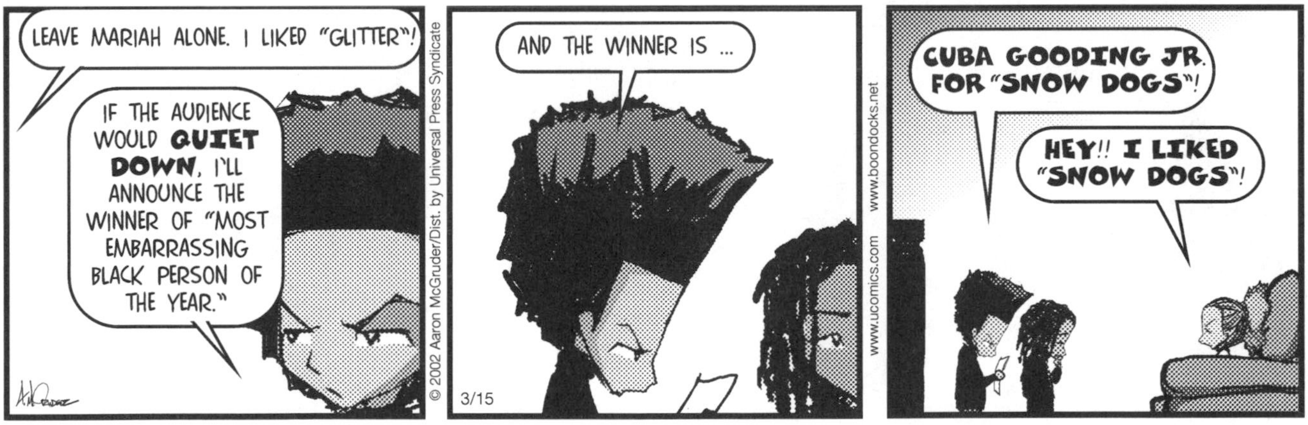
LEAVE MARIAH ALONE. I LIKED "GLITTER"!
IF THE AUDIENCE WOULD **QUIET DOWN**, I'LL ANNOUNCE THE WINNER OF "MOST EMBARRASSING BLACK PERSON OF THE YEAR."
AND THE WINNER IS ...
CUBA GOODING JR. FOR "SNOW DOGS"!
HEY!! I LIKED "SNOW DOGS"!
© 2002 Aaron McGruder/Dist. by Universal Press Syndicate
www.ucomics.com www.boondocks.net
3/15

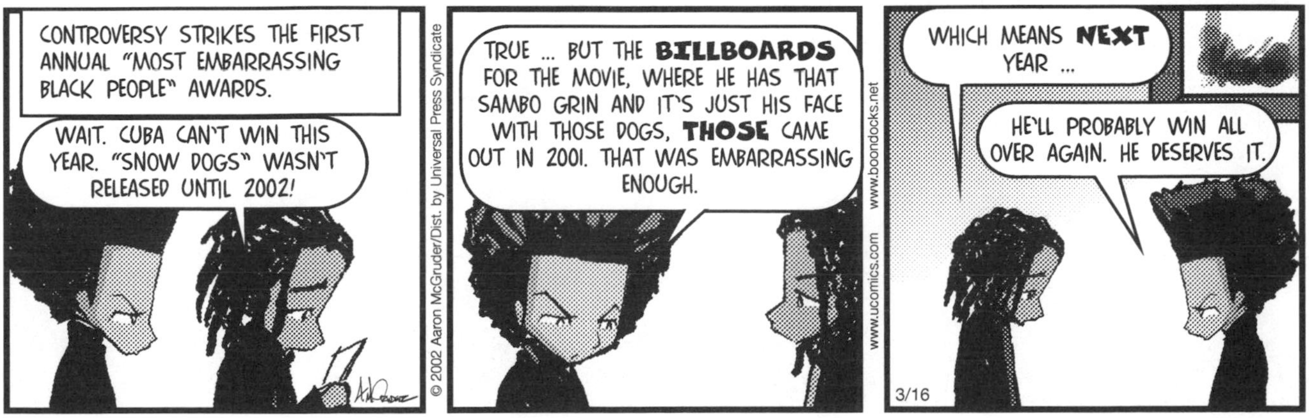
CONTROVERSY STRIKES THE FIRST ANNUAL "MOST EMBARRASSING BLACK PEOPLE" AWARDS.
WAIT. CUBA CAN'T WIN THIS YEAR. "SNOW DOGS" WASN'T RELEASED UNTIL 2002!
TRUE ... BUT THE **BILLBOARDS** FOR THE MOVIE, WHERE HE HAS THAT SAMBO GRIN AND IT'S JUST HIS FACE WITH THOSE DOGS, **THOSE** CAME OUT IN 2001. THAT WAS EMBARRASSING ENOUGH.
WHICH MEANS **NEXT** YEAR ...
HE'LL PROBABLY WIN ALL OVER AGAIN. HE DESERVES IT.
© 2002 Aaron McGruder/Dist. by Universal Press Syndicate
www.ucomics.com www.boondocks.net
3/16

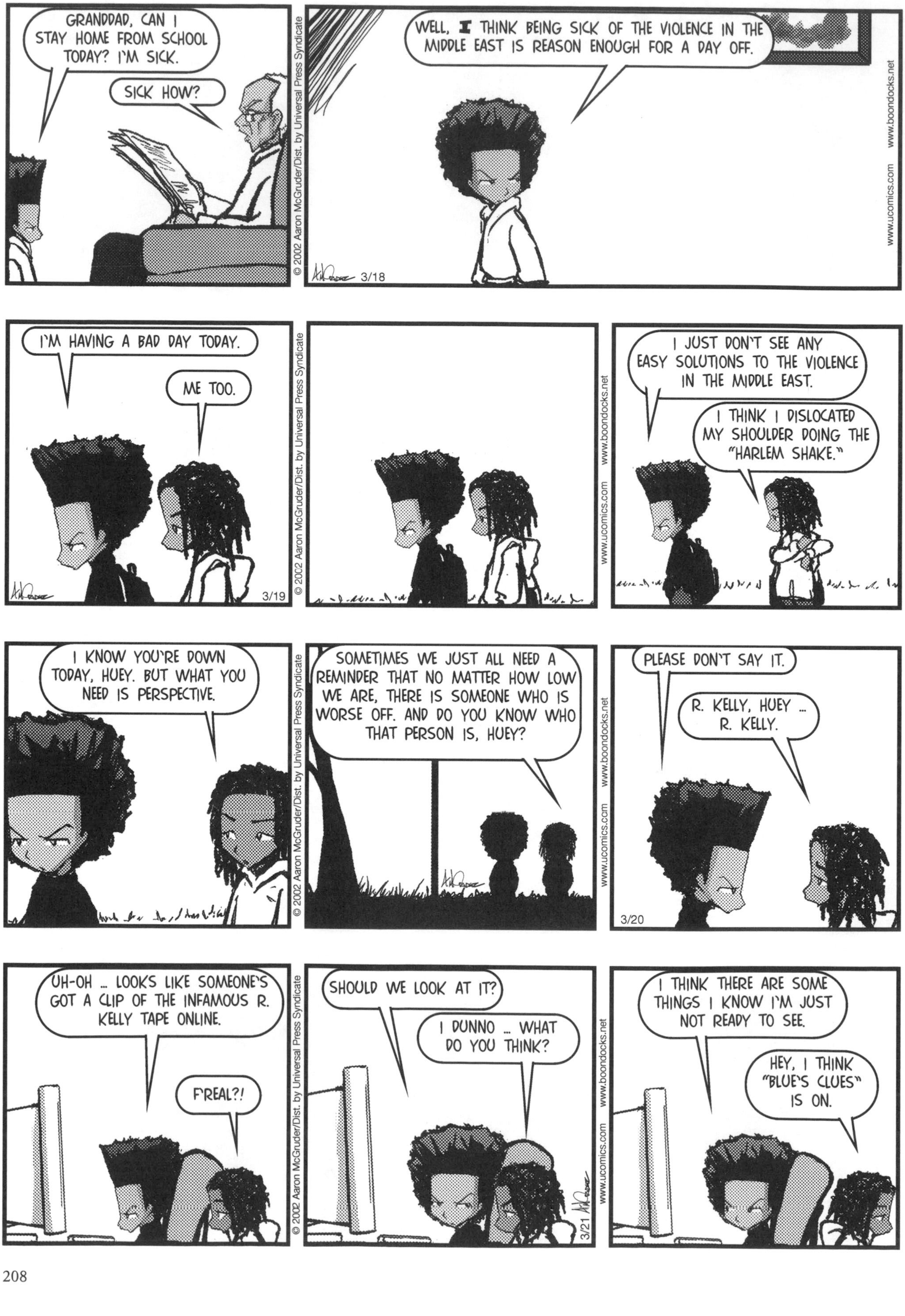
GRANDDAD, CAN I STAY HOME FROM SCHOOL TODAY? I'M SICK.
SICK HOW?
WELL, I THINK BEING SICK OF THE VIOLENCE IN THE MIDDLE EAST IS REASON ENOUGH FOR A DAY OFF.
© 2002 Aaron McGruder/Dist. by Universal Press Syndicate
3/18
www.ucomics.com www.boondocks.net
I'M HAVING A BAD DAY TODAY.
ME TOO.
I JUST DON'T SEE ANY EASY SOLUTIONS TO THE VIOLENCE IN THE MIDDLE EAST.
I THINK I DISLOCATED MY SHOULDER DOING THE "HARLEM SHAKE."
3/19
I KNOW YOU'RE DOWN TODAY, HUEY. BUT WHAT YOU NEED IS PERSPECTIVE.
SOMETIMES WE JUST ALL NEED A REMINDER THAT NO MATTER HOW LOW WE ARE, THERE IS SOMEONE WHO IS WORSE OFF. AND DO YOU KNOW WHO THAT PERSON IS, HUEY?
PLEASE DON'T SAY IT.
R. KELLY, HUEY ... R. KELLY.
3/20
UH-OH ... LOOKS LIKE SOMEONE'S GOT A CLIP OF THE INFAMOUS R. KELLY TAPE ONLINE.
F'REAL?!
SHOULD WE LOOK AT IT?
I DUNNO ... WHAT DO YOU THINK?
I THINK THERE ARE SOME THINGS I KNOW I'M JUST NOT READY TO SEE.
HEY, I THINK "BLUE'S CLUES" IS ON.
3/21

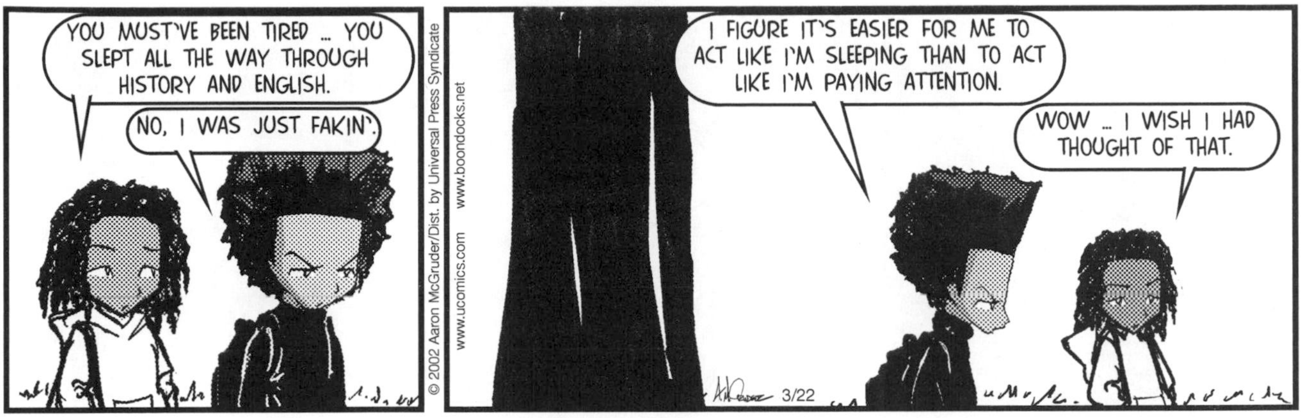
YOU MUST'VE BEEN TIRED ... YOU SLEPT ALL THE WAY THROUGH HISTORY AND ENGLISH.
NO, I WAS JUST FAKIN'.
© 2002 Aaron McGruder/Dist. by Universal Press Syndicate
www.ucomics.com www.boondocks.net
I FIGURE IT'S EASIER FOR ME TO ACT LIKE I'M SLEEPING THAN TO ACT LIKE I'M PAYING ATTENTION.
WOW ... I WISH I HAD THOUGHT OF THAT.
3/22

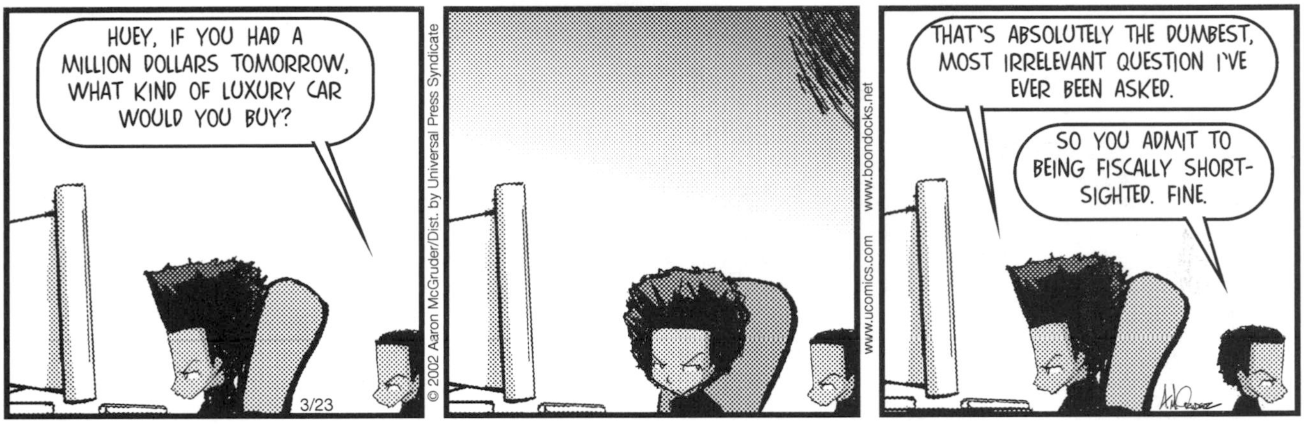
HUEY, IF YOU HAD A MILLION DOLLARS TOMORROW, WHAT KIND OF LUXURY CAR WOULD YOU BUY?
3/23
© 2002 Aaron McGruder/Dist. by Universal Press Syndicate
THAT'S ABSOLUTELY THE DUMBEST, MOST IRRELEVANT QUESTION I'VE EVER BEEN ASKED.
SO YOU ADMIT TO BEING FISCALLY SHORT-SIGHTED. FINE.
www.ucomics.com www.boondocks.net

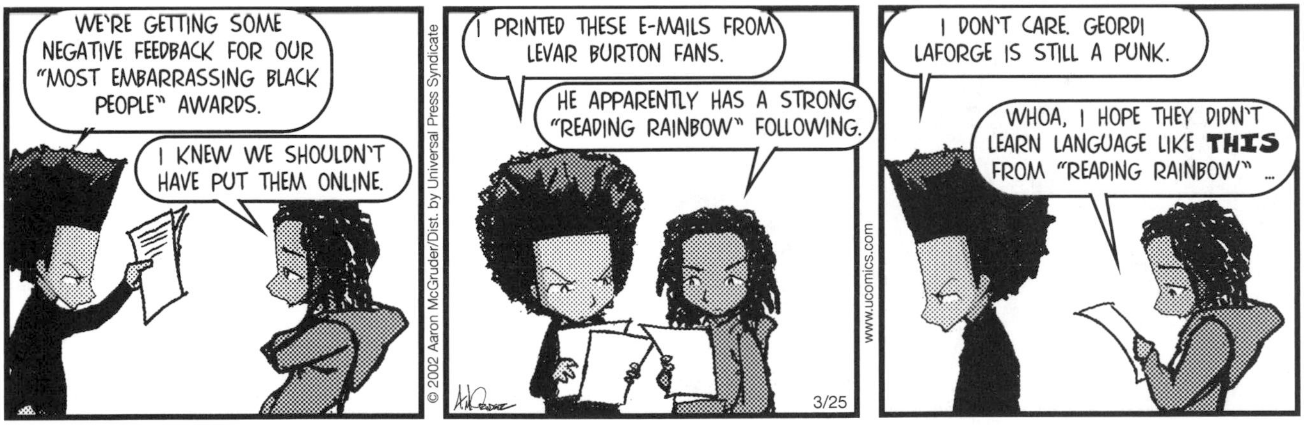
WE'RE GETTING SOME NEGATIVE FEEDBACK FOR OUR "MOST EMBARRASSING BLACK PEOPLE" AWARDS.
I KNEW WE SHOULDN'T HAVE PUT THEM ONLINE.
© 2002 Aaron McGruder/Dist. by Universal Press Syndicate
I PRINTED THESE E-MAILS FROM LEVAR BURTON FANS.
HE APPARENTLY HAS A STRONG "READING RAINBOW" FOLLOWING.
3/25
www.ucomics.com
I DON'T CARE. GEORDI LAFORGE IS STILL A PUNK.
WHOA, I HOPE THEY DIDN'T LEARN LANGUAGE LIKE **THIS** FROM "READING RAINBOW" ...

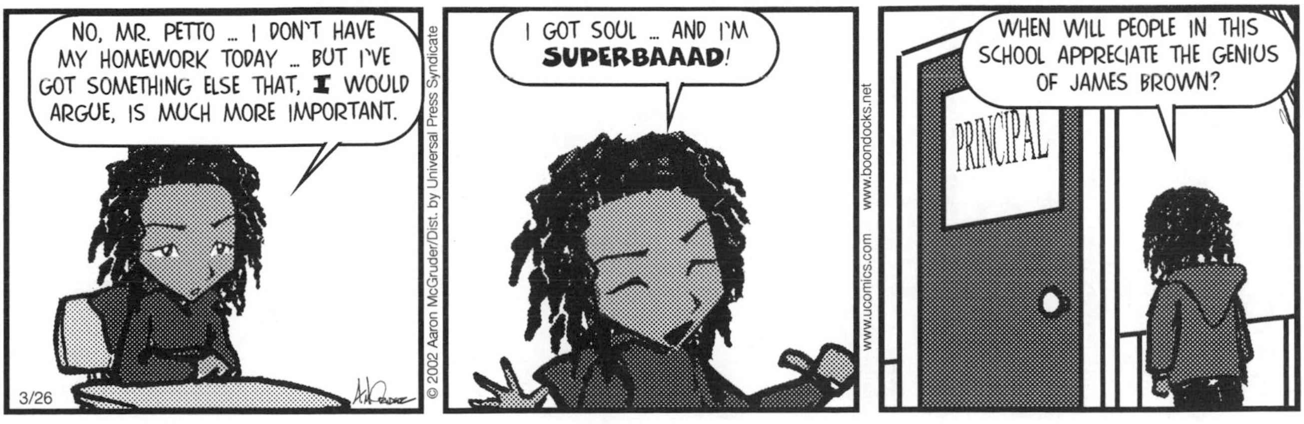
NO, MR. PETTO ... I DON'T HAVE MY HOMEWORK TODAY ... BUT I'VE GOT SOMETHING ELSE THAT, **I** WOULD ARGUE, IS MUCH MORE IMPORTANT.
3/26
© 2002 Aaron McGruder/Dist. by Universal Press Syndicate
I GOT SOUL ... AND I'M **SUPERBAAAD**!
www.ucomics.com www.boondocks.net
WHEN WILL PEOPLE IN THIS SCHOOL APPRECIATE THE GENIUS OF JAMES BROWN?
PRINCIPAL

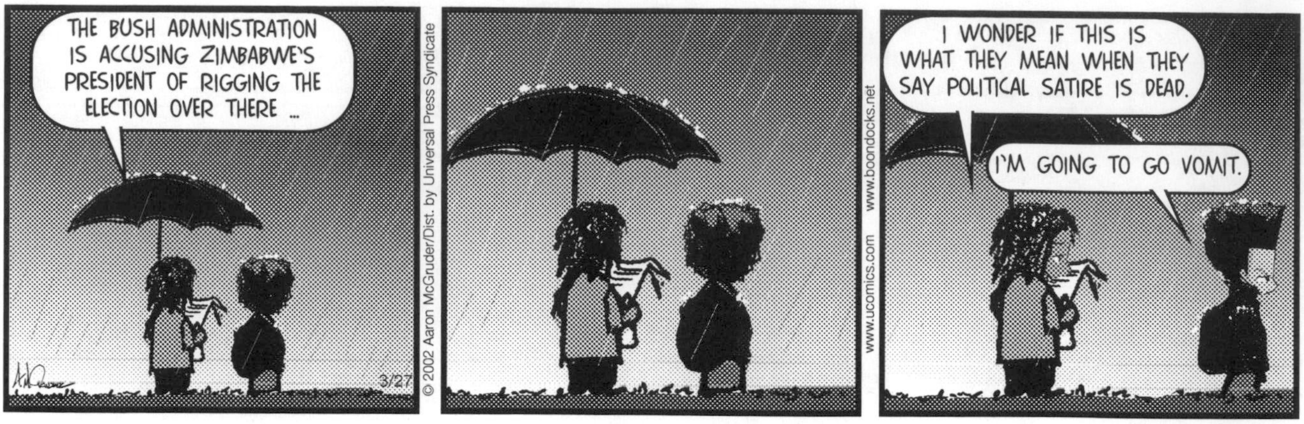
THE BUSH ADMINISTRATION IS ACCUSING ZIMBABWE'S PRESIDENT OF RIGGING THE ELECTION OVER THERE ...
3/27
© 2002 Aaron McGruder/Dist. by Universal Press Syndicate
www.ucomics.com www.boondocks.net
I WONDER IF THIS IS WHAT THEY MEAN WHEN THEY SAY POLITICAL SATIRE IS DEAD.
I'M GOING TO GO VOMIT.

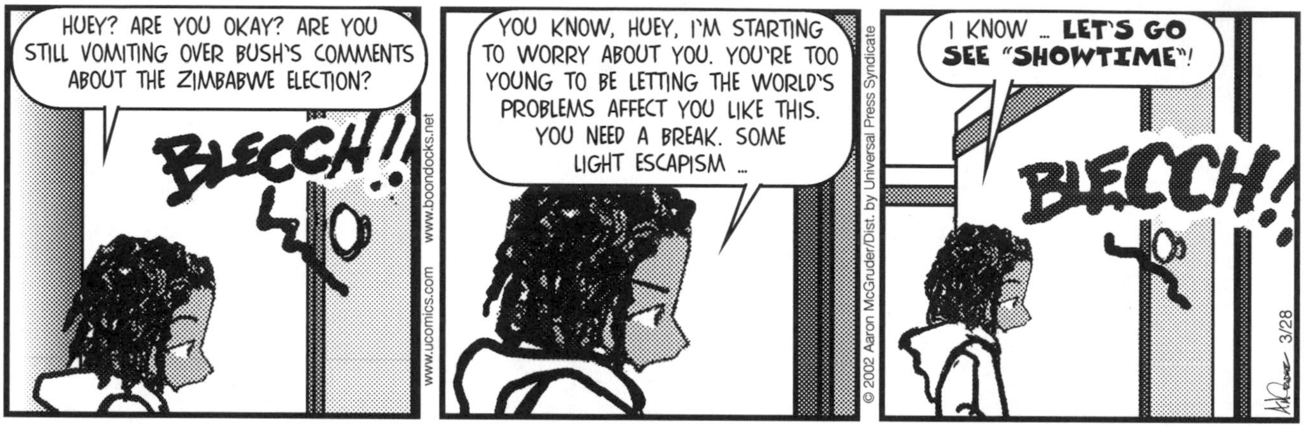
HUEY? ARE YOU OKAY? ARE YOU STILL VOMITING OVER BUSH'S COMMENTS ABOUT THE ZIMBABWE ELECTION?
BLECCH!!
www.ucomics.com www.boondocks.net
YOU KNOW, HUEY, I'M STARTING TO WORRY ABOUT YOU. YOU'RE TOO YOUNG TO BE LETTING THE WORLD'S PROBLEMS AFFECT YOU LIKE THIS. YOU NEED A BREAK. SOME LIGHT ESCAPISM ...
© 2002 Aaron McGruder/Dist. by Universal Press Syndicate
I KNOW ... **LET'S GO SEE "SHOWTIME"!**
BLECCH!!
3/28

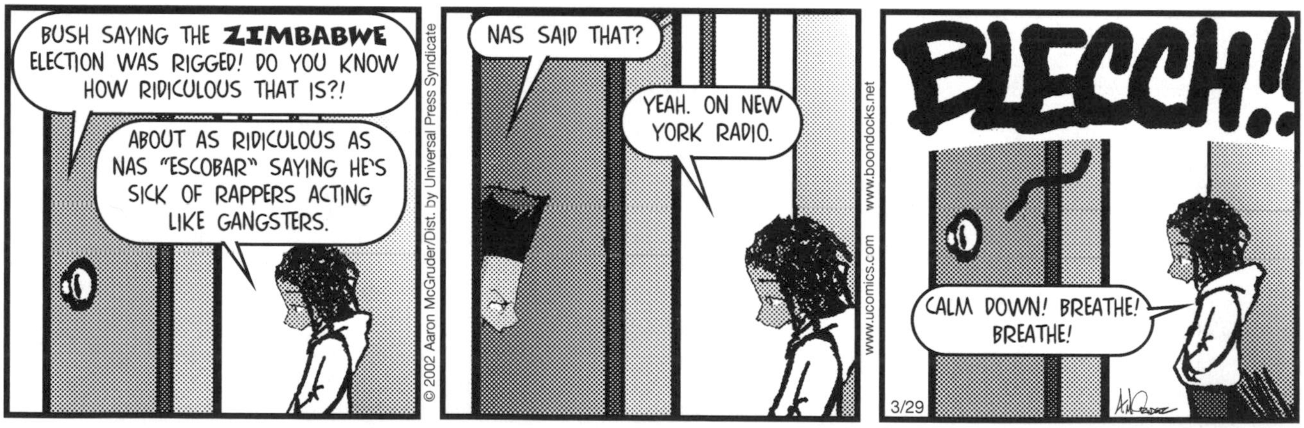
BUSH SAYING THE **ZIMBABWE** ELECTION WAS RIGGED! DO YOU KNOW HOW RIDICULOUS THAT IS?!
ABOUT AS RIDICULOUS AS NAS "ESCOBAR" SAYING HE'S SICK OF RAPPERS ACTING LIKE GANGSTERS.
© 2002 Aaron McGruder/Dist. by Universal Press Syndicate
NAS SAID THAT?
YEAH. ON NEW YORK RADIO.
www.ucomics.com www.boondocks.net
BLECCH!!
CALM DOWN! BREATHE! BREATHE!
3/29

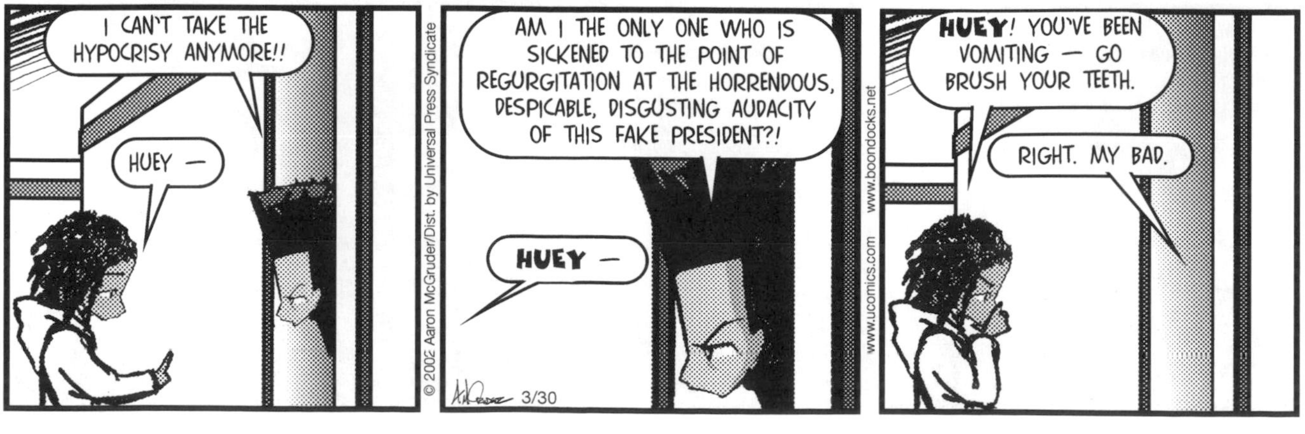
I CAN'T TAKE THE HYPOCRISY ANYMORE!!
HUEY —
© 2002 Aaron McGruder/Dist. by Universal Press Syndicate
AM I THE ONLY ONE WHO IS SICKENED TO THE POINT OF REGURGITATION AT THE HORRENDOUS, DESPICABLE, DISGUSTING AUDACITY OF THIS FAKE PRESIDENT?!
HUEY —
3/30
www.ucomics.com www.boondocks.net
HUEY! YOU'VE BEEN VOMITING — GO BRUSH YOUR TEETH.
RIGHT. MY BAD.

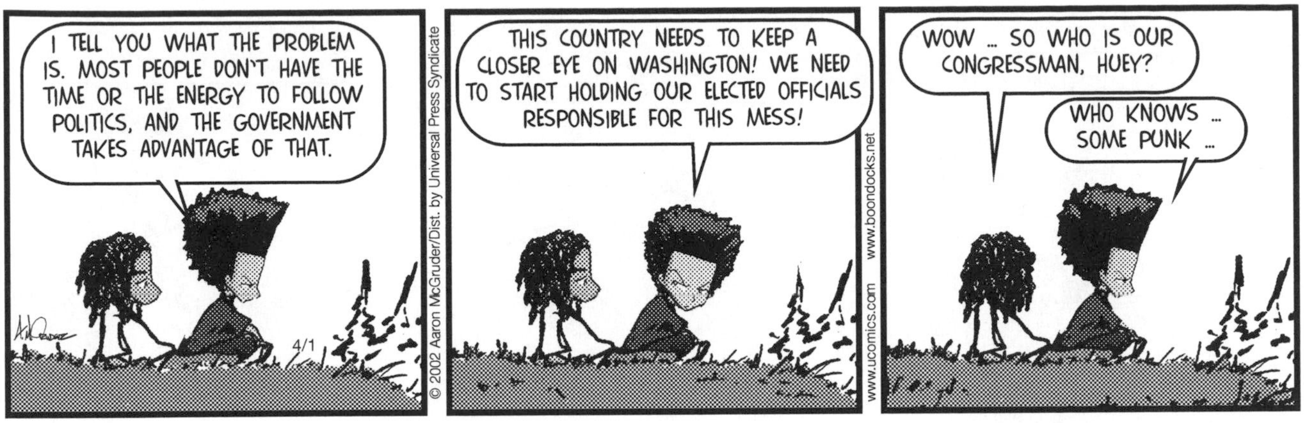
I TELL YOU WHAT THE PROBLEM IS. MOST PEOPLE DON'T HAVE THE TIME OR THE ENERGY TO FOLLOW POLITICS, AND THE GOVERNMENT TAKES ADVANTAGE OF THAT.
4/1
© 2002 Aaron McGruder/Dist. by Universal Press Syndicate
THIS COUNTRY NEEDS TO KEEP A CLOSER EYE ON WASHINGTON! WE NEED TO START HOLDING OUR ELECTED OFFICIALS RESPONSIBLE FOR THIS MESS!
www.ucomics.com www.boondocks.net
WOW ... SO WHO IS OUR CONGRESSMAN, HUEY?
WHO KNOWS ... SOME PUNK ...

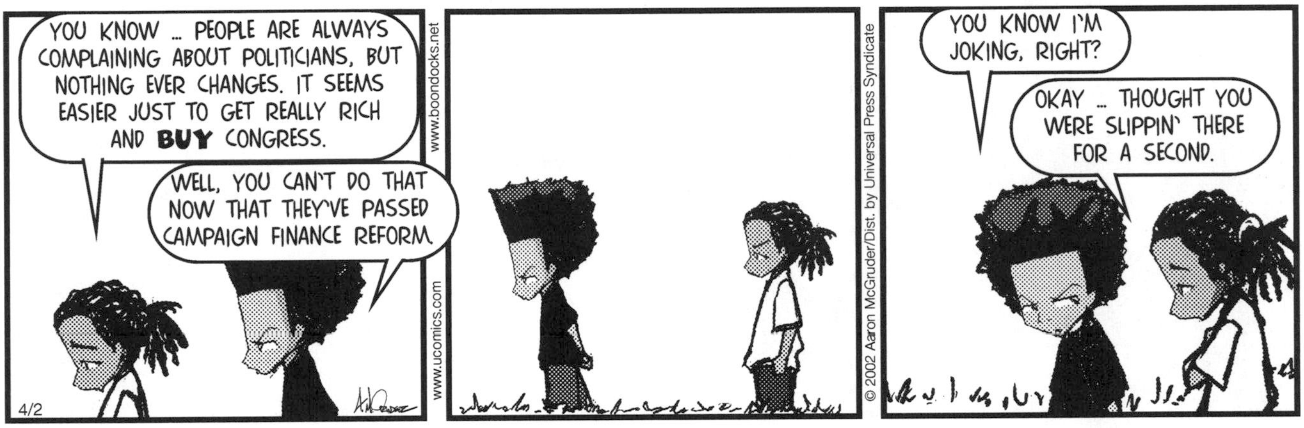
YOU KNOW ... PEOPLE ARE ALWAYS COMPLAINING ABOUT POLITICIANS, BUT NOTHING EVER CHANGES. IT SEEMS EASIER JUST TO GET REALLY RICH AND BUY CONGRESS.
WELL, YOU CAN'T DO THAT NOW THAT THEY'VE PASSED CAMPAIGN FINANCE REFORM.
4/2
www.ucomics.com www.boondocks.net
© 2002 Aaron McGruder/Dist. by Universal Press Syndicate
YOU KNOW I'M JOKING, RIGHT?
OKAY ... THOUGHT YOU WERE SLIPPIN' THERE FOR A SECOND.

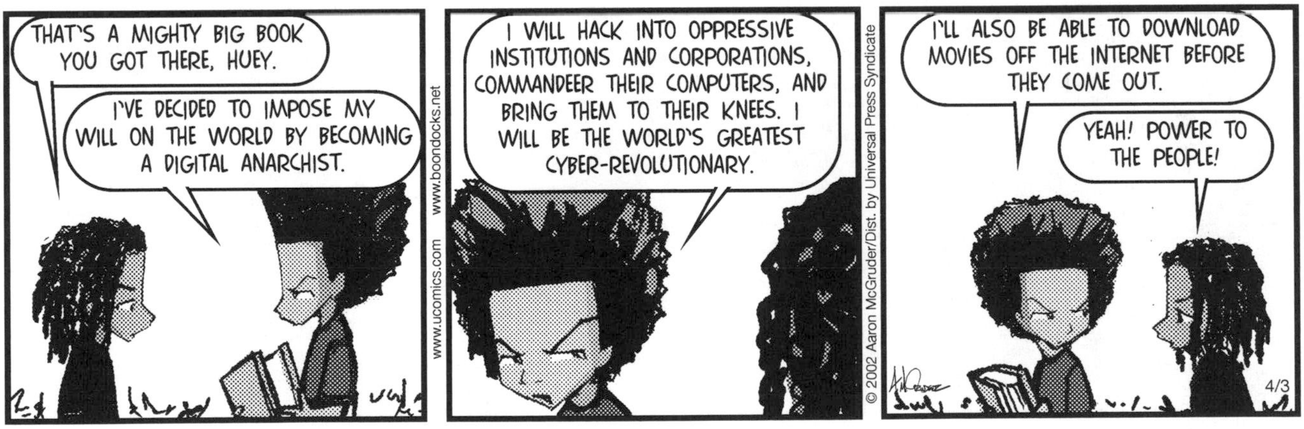
THAT'S A MIGHTY BIG BOOK YOU GOT THERE, HUEY.
I'VE DECIDED TO IMPOSE MY WILL ON THE WORLD BY BECOMING A DIGITAL ANARCHIST.
www.ucomics.com www.boondocks.net
I WILL HACK INTO OPPRESSIVE INSTITUTIONS AND CORPORATIONS, COMMANDEER THEIR COMPUTERS, AND BRING THEM TO THEIR KNEES. I WILL BE THE WORLD'S GREATEST CYBER-REVOLUTIONARY.
© 2002 Aaron McGruder/Dist. by Universal Press Syndicate
I'LL ALSO BE ABLE TO DOWNLOAD MOVIES OFF THE INTERNET BEFORE THEY COME OUT.
YEAH! POWER TO THE PEOPLE!
4/3

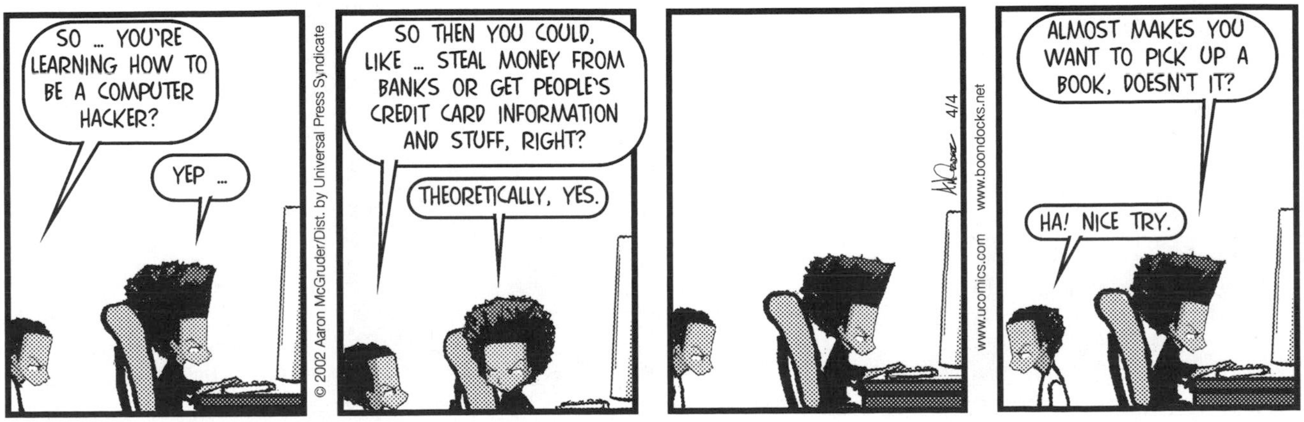
SO ... YOU'RE LEARNING HOW TO BE A COMPUTER HACKER?
YEP ...
© 2002 Aaron McGruder/Dist. by Universal Press Syndicate
SO THEN YOU COULD, LIKE ... STEAL MONEY FROM BANKS OR GET PEOPLE'S CREDIT CARD INFORMATION AND STUFF, RIGHT?
THEORETICALLY, YES.
4/4
www.ucomics.com www.boondocks.net
ALMOST MAKES YOU WANT TO PICK UP A BOOK, DOESN'T IT?
HA! NICE TRY.

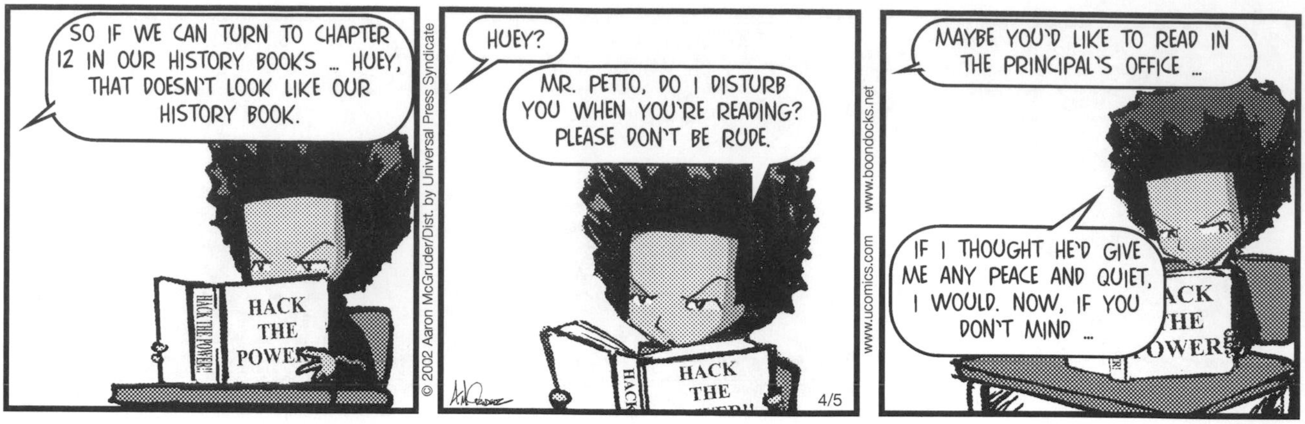
SO IF WE CAN TURN TO CHAPTER 12 IN OUR HISTORY BOOKS ... HUEY, THAT DOESN'T LOOK LIKE OUR HISTORY BOOK.
HACK THE POWER
© 2002 Aaron McGruder/Dist. by Universal Press Syndicate
HUEY?
MR. PETTO, DO I DISTURB YOU WHEN YOU'RE READING? PLEASE DON'T BE RUDE.
HACK THE
4/5
www.ucomics.com www.boondocks.net
MAYBE YOU'D LIKE TO READ IN THE PRINCIPAL'S OFFICE ...
IF I THOUGHT HE'D GIVE ME ANY PEACE AND QUIET, I WOULD. NOW, IF YOU DON'T MIND ...

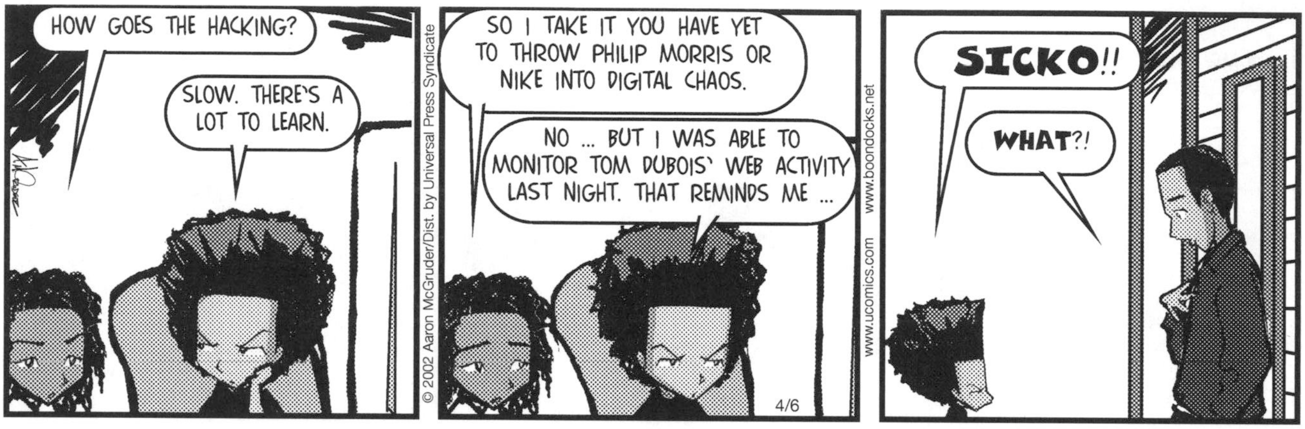
HOW GOES THE HACKING?
SLOW. THERE'S A LOT TO LEARN.
© 2002 Aaron McGruder/Dist. by Universal Press Syndicate
SO I TAKE IT YOU HAVE YET TO THROW PHILIP MORRIS OR NIKE INTO DIGITAL CHAOS.
NO ... BUT I WAS ABLE TO MONITOR TOM DUBOIS' WEB ACTIVITY LAST NIGHT. THAT REMINDS ME ...
4/6
www.ucomics.com www.boondocks.net
SICKO!!
WHAT?!

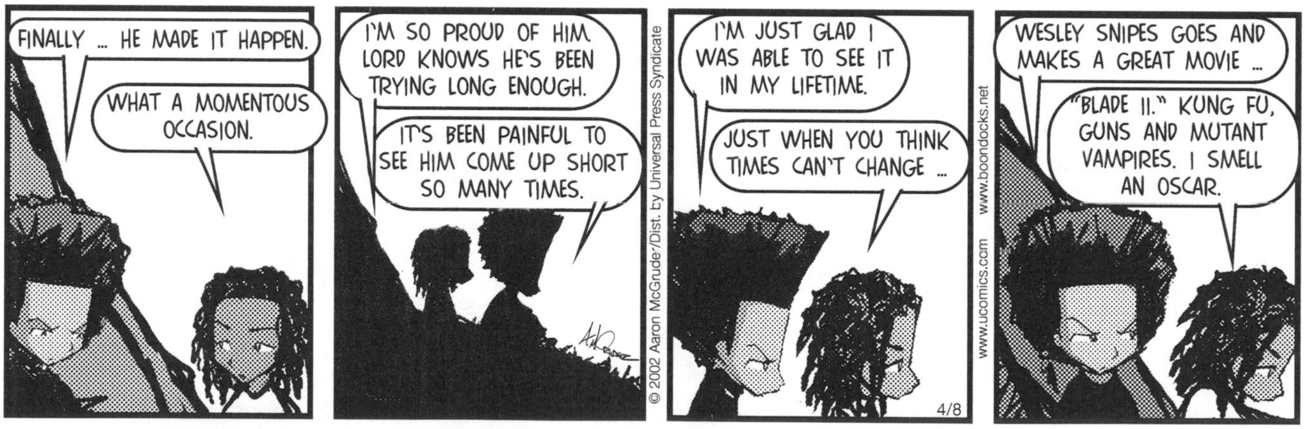
FINALLY ... HE MADE IT HAPPEN.
WHAT A MOMENTOUS OCCASION.
I'M SO PROUD OF HIM. LORD KNOWS HE'S BEEN TRYING LONG ENOUGH.
IT'S BEEN PAINFUL TO SEE HIM COME UP SHORT SO MANY TIMES.
© 2002 Aaron McGruder/Dist. by Universal Press Syndicate
I'M JUST GLAD I WAS ABLE TO SEE IT IN MY LIFETIME.
JUST WHEN YOU THINK TIMES CAN'T CHANGE ...
4/8
www.ucomics.com www.boondocks.net
WESLEY SNIPES GOES AND MAKES A GREAT MOVIE ...
"BLADE II." KUNG FU, GUNS AND MUTANT VAMPIRES. I SMELL AN OSCAR.

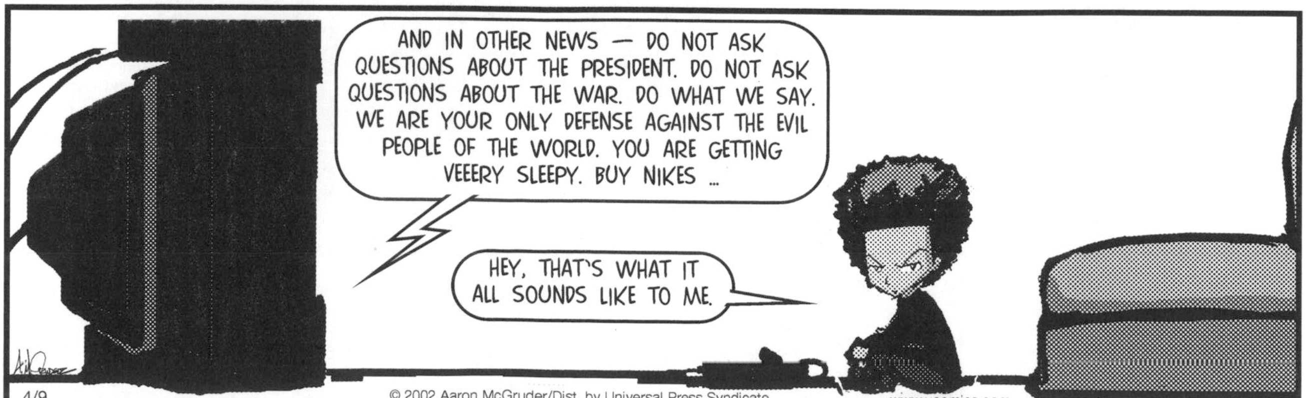
AND IN OTHER NEWS — DO NOT ASK QUESTIONS ABOUT THE PRESIDENT. DO NOT ASK QUESTIONS ABOUT THE WAR. DO WHAT WE SAY. WE ARE YOUR ONLY DEFENSE AGAINST THE EVIL PEOPLE OF THE WORLD. YOU ARE GETTING VEEERY SLEEPY. BUY NIKES ...
HEY, THAT'S WHAT IT ALL SOUNDS LIKE TO ME.
4/9
© 2002 Aaron McGruder/Dist. by Universal Press Syndicate
www.ucomics.com

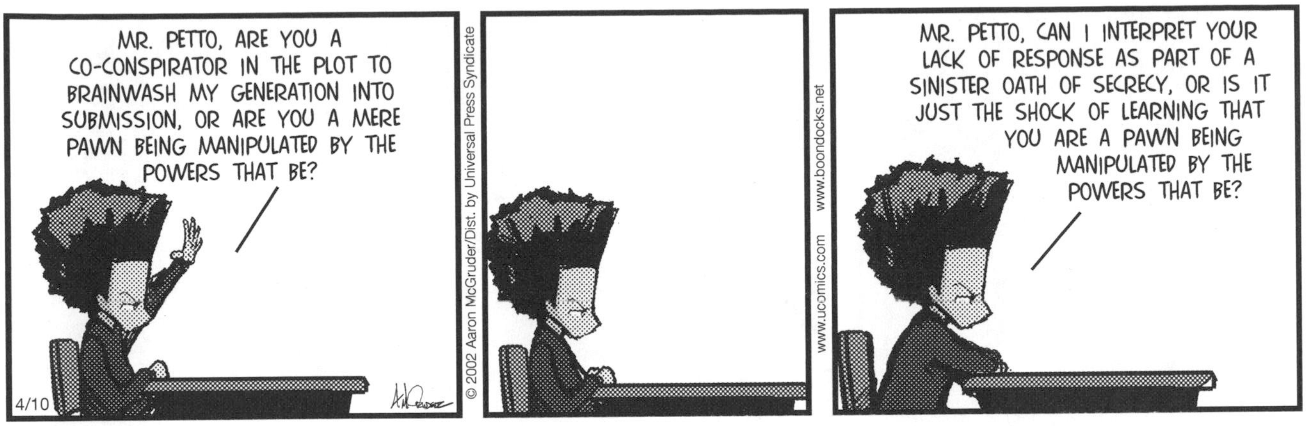
MR. PETTO, ARE YOU A CO-CONSPIRATOR IN THE PLOT TO BRAINWASH MY GENERATION INTO SUBMISSION, OR ARE YOU A MERE PAWN BEING MANIPULATED BY THE POWERS THAT BE?
MR. PETTO, CAN I INTERPRET YOUR LACK OF RESPONSE AS PART OF A SINISTER OATH OF SECRECY, OR IS IT JUST THE SHOCK OF LEARNING THAT YOU ARE A PAWN BEING MANIPULATED BY THE POWERS THAT BE?
4/10
© 2002 Aaron McGruder/Dist. by Universal Press Syndicate
www.ucomics.com www.boondocks.net

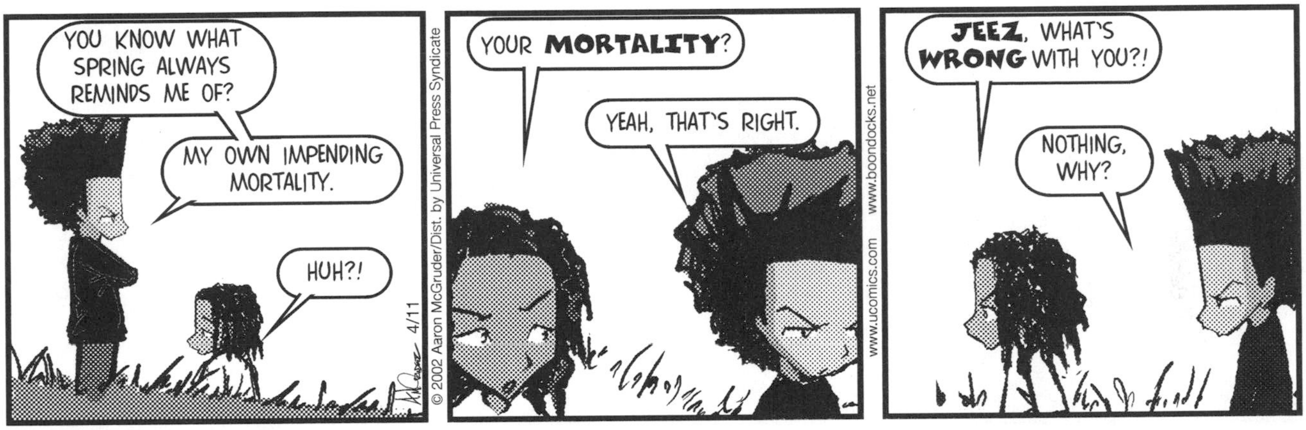
YOU KNOW WHAT SPRING ALWAYS REMINDS ME OF?
MY OWN IMPENDING MORTALITY.
HUH?!
YOUR **MORTALITY**?
YEAH, THAT'S RIGHT.
JEEZ, WHAT'S **WRONG** WITH YOU?!
NOTHING, WHY?
4/11
© 2002 Aaron McGruder/Dist. by Universal Press Syndicate
www.ucomics.com www.boondocks.net

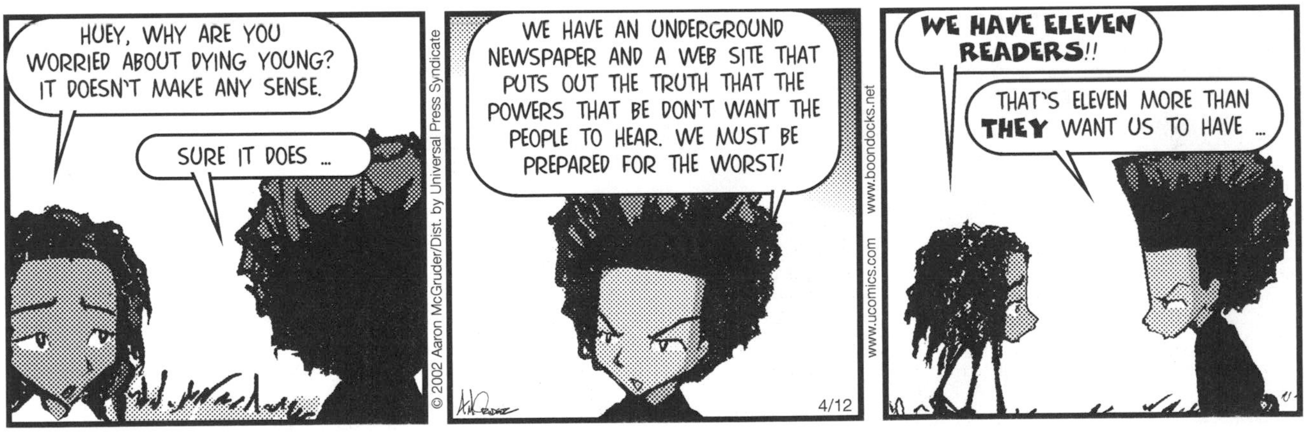
HUEY, WHY ARE YOU WORRIED ABOUT DYING YOUNG? IT DOESN'T MAKE ANY SENSE.
SURE IT DOES ...
WE HAVE AN UNDERGROUND NEWSPAPER AND A WEB SITE THAT PUTS OUT THE TRUTH THAT THE POWERS THAT BE DON'T WANT THE PEOPLE TO HEAR. WE MUST BE PREPARED FOR THE WORST!
WE HAVE ELEVEN READERS!!
THAT'S ELEVEN MORE THAN **THEY** WANT US TO HAVE ...
4/12
© 2002 Aaron McGruder/Dist. by Universal Press Syndicate
www.ucomics.com www.boondocks.net

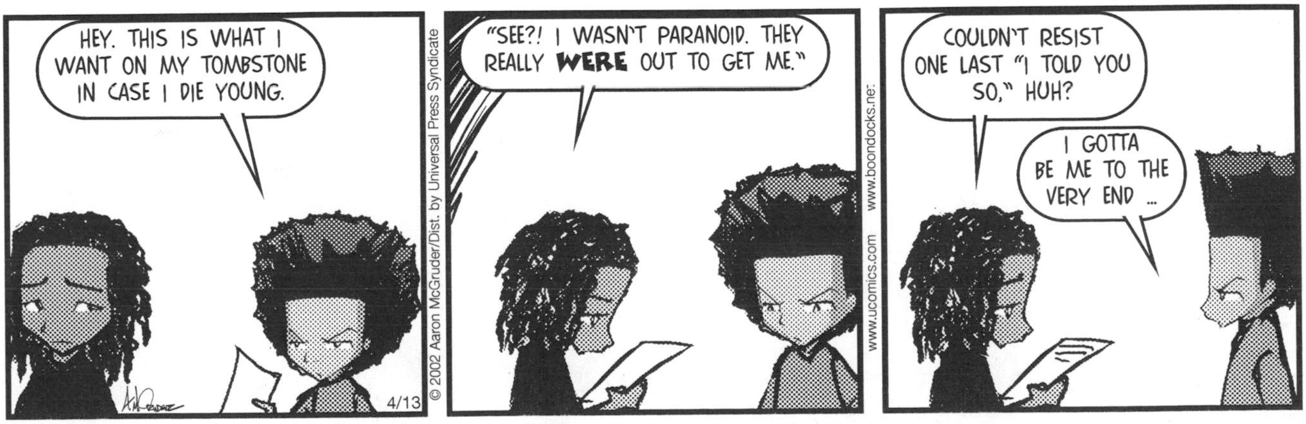
HEY. THIS IS WHAT I WANT ON MY TOMBSTONE IN CASE I DIE YOUNG.
"SEE?! I WASN'T PARANOID. THEY REALLY **WERE** OUT TO GET ME."
COULDN'T RESIST ONE LAST "I TOLD YOU SO," HUH?
I GOTTA BE ME TO THE VERY END ...
4/13
© 2002 Aaron McGruder/Dist. by Universal Press Syndicate
www.ucomics.com www.boondocks.ne

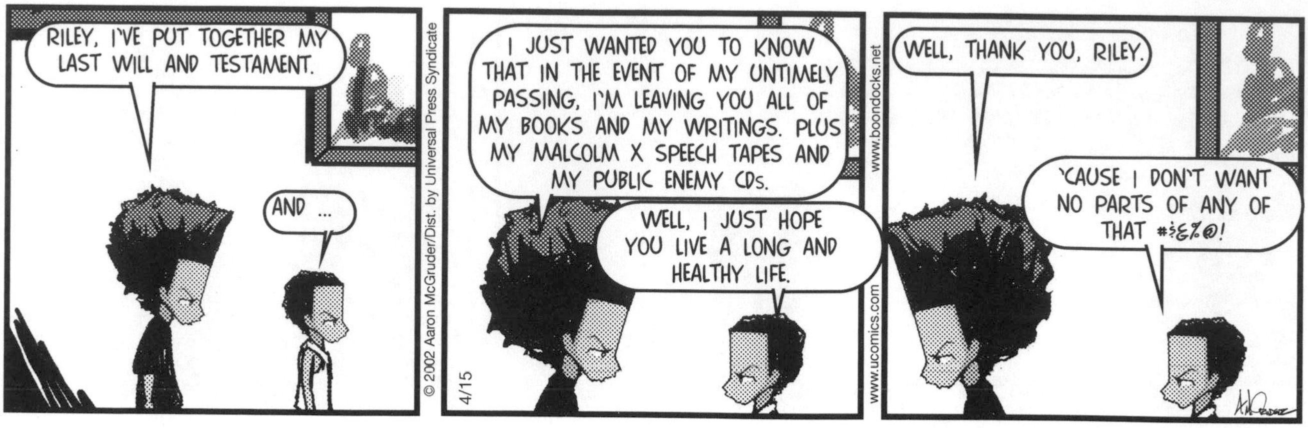

RILEY, I'VE PUT TOGETHER MY LAST WILL AND TESTAMENT.
AND ...
I JUST WANTED YOU TO KNOW THAT IN THE EVENT OF MY UNTIMELY PASSING, I'M LEAVING YOU ALL OF MY BOOKS AND MY WRITINGS. PLUS MY MALCOLM X SPEECH TAPES AND MY PUBLIC ENEMY CDs.
WELL, I JUST HOPE YOU LIVE A LONG AND HEALTHY LIFE.
WELL, THANK YOU, RILEY.
'CAUSE I DON'T WANT NO PARTS OF ANY OF THAT #$&%@!
© 2002 Aaron McGruder/Dist. by Universal Press Syndicate
www.boondocks.net
www.ucomics.com
4/15

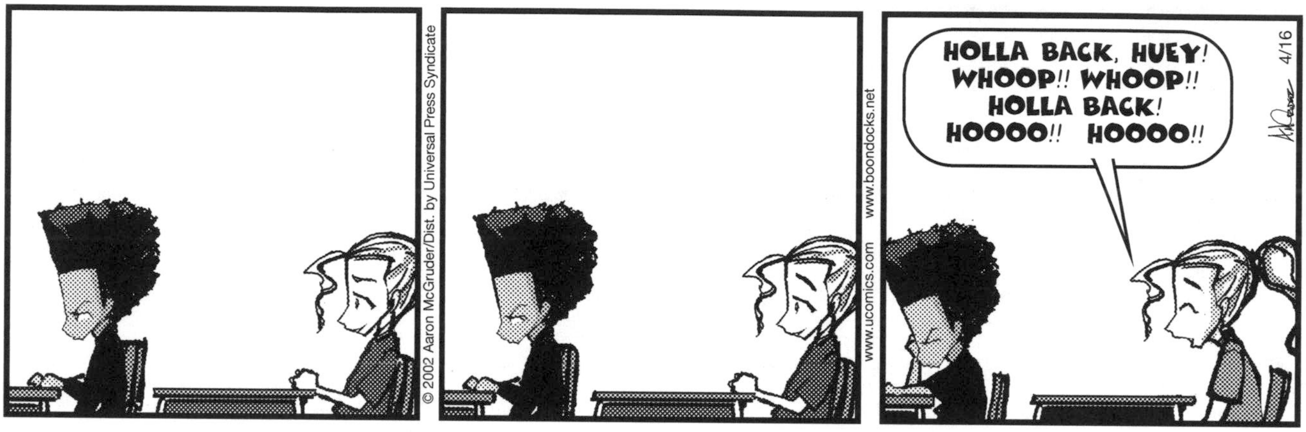

HOLLA BACK, HUEY! WHOOP!! WHOOP!! HOLLA BACK! HOOOO!! HOOOO!!
© 2002 Aaron McGruder/Dist. by Universal Press Syndicate
www.boondocks.net
www.ucomics.com
4/16

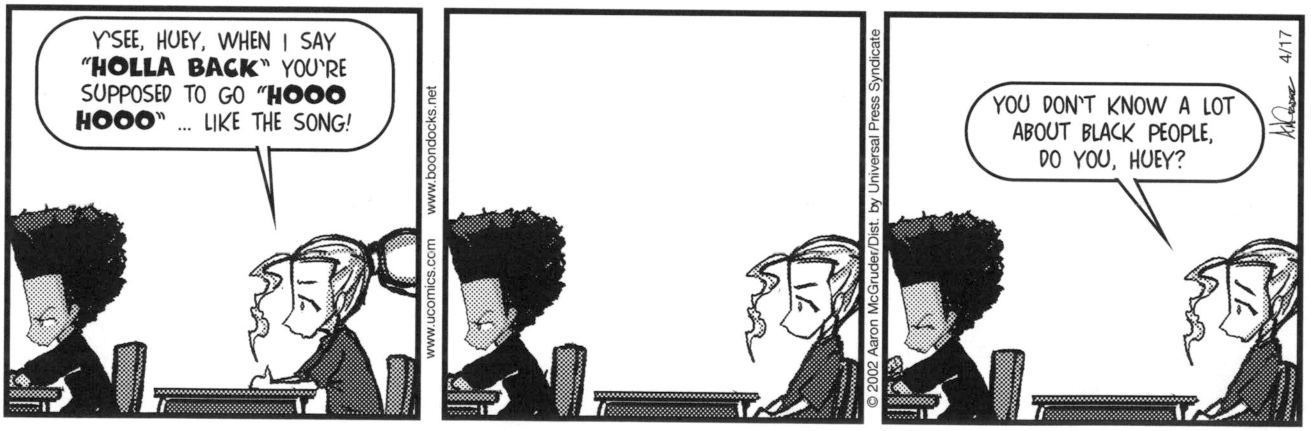

Y'SEE, HUEY, WHEN I SAY "HOLLA BACK" YOU'RE SUPPOSED TO GO "HOOO HOOO" ... LIKE THE SONG!
YOU DON'T KNOW A LOT ABOUT BLACK PEOPLE, DO YOU, HUEY?
© 2002 Aaron McGruder/Dist. by Universal Press Syndicate
www.boondocks.net
www.ucomics.com
4/17

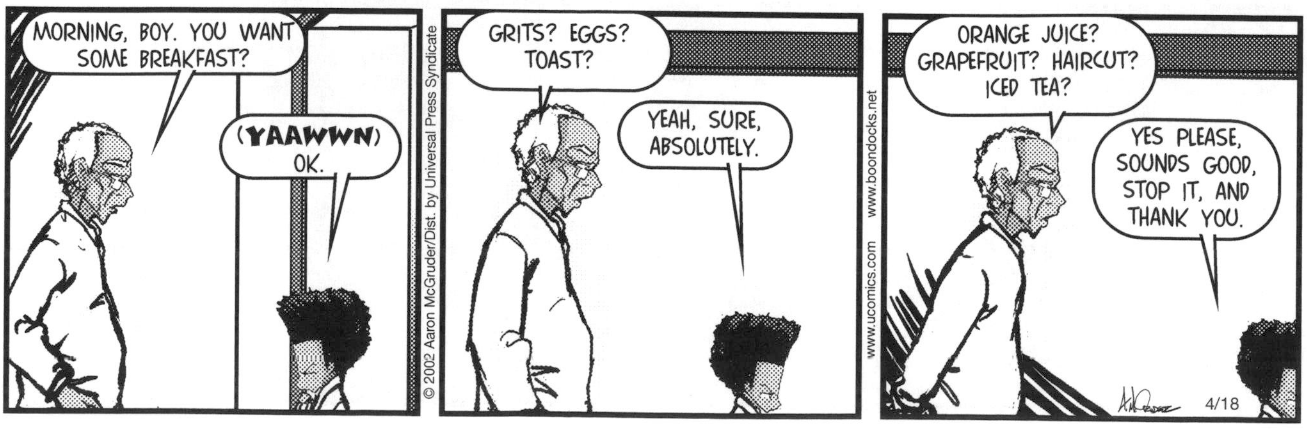

MORNING, BOY. YOU WANT SOME BREAKFAST?
(YAAWWN) OK.
GRITS? EGGS? TOAST?
YEAH, SURE, ABSOLUTELY.
ORANGE JUICE? GRAPEFRUIT? HAIRCUT? ICED TEA?
YES PLEASE, SOUNDS GOOD, STOP IT, AND THANK YOU.
© 2002 Aaron McGruder/Dist. by Universal Press Syndicate
www.boondocks.net
www.ucomics.com
4/18

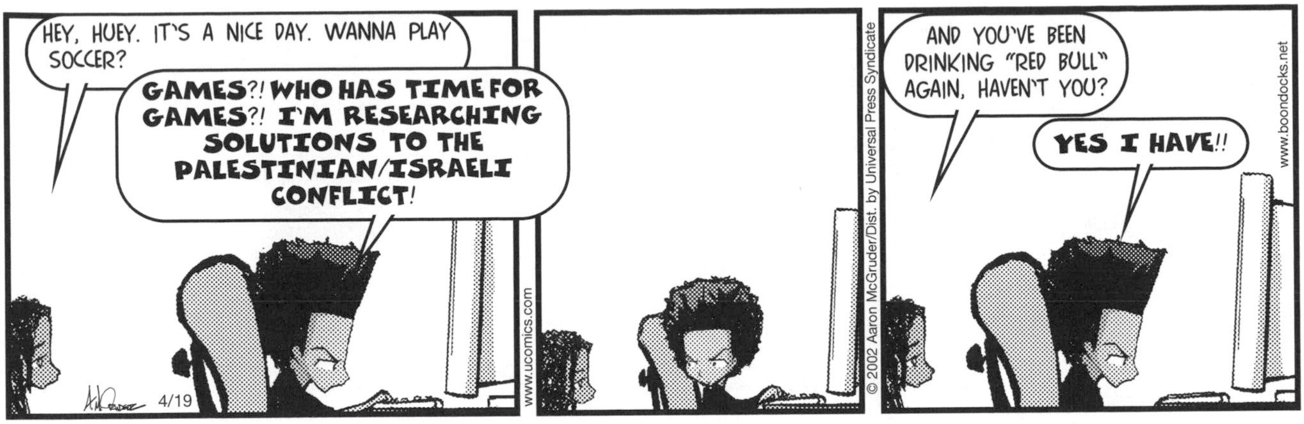
HEY, HUEY. IT'S A NICE DAY. WANNA PLAY SOCCER?
GAMES?! WHO HAS TIME FOR GAMES?! I'M RESEARCHING SOLUTIONS TO THE PALESTINIAN/ISRAELI CONFLICT!
4/19
www.ucomics.com
© 2002 Aaron McGruder/Dist. by Universal Press Syndicate
AND YOU'VE BEEN DRINKING "RED BULL" AGAIN, HAVEN'T YOU?
YES I HAVE!!
www.boondocks.net

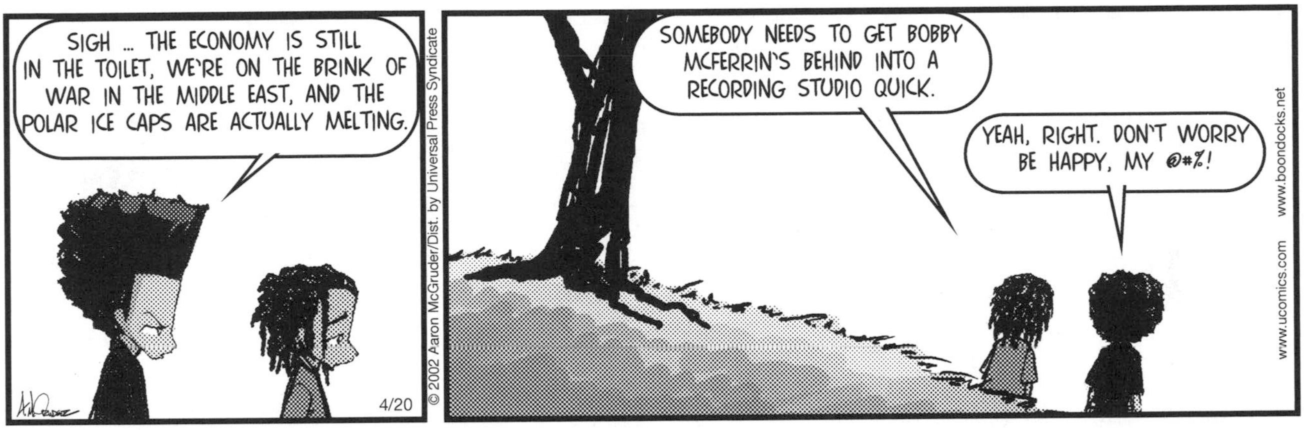
SIGH ... THE ECONOMY IS STILL IN THE TOILET, WE'RE ON THE BRINK OF WAR IN THE MIDDLE EAST, AND THE POLAR ICE CAPS ARE ACTUALLY MELTING.
4/20
© 2002 Aaron McGruder/Dist. by Universal Press Syndicate
SOMEBODY NEEDS TO GET BOBBY MCFERRIN'S BEHIND INTO A RECORDING STUDIO QUICK.
YEAH, RIGHT. DON'T WORRY BE HAPPY, MY @#%!
www.ucomics.com
www.boondocks.net

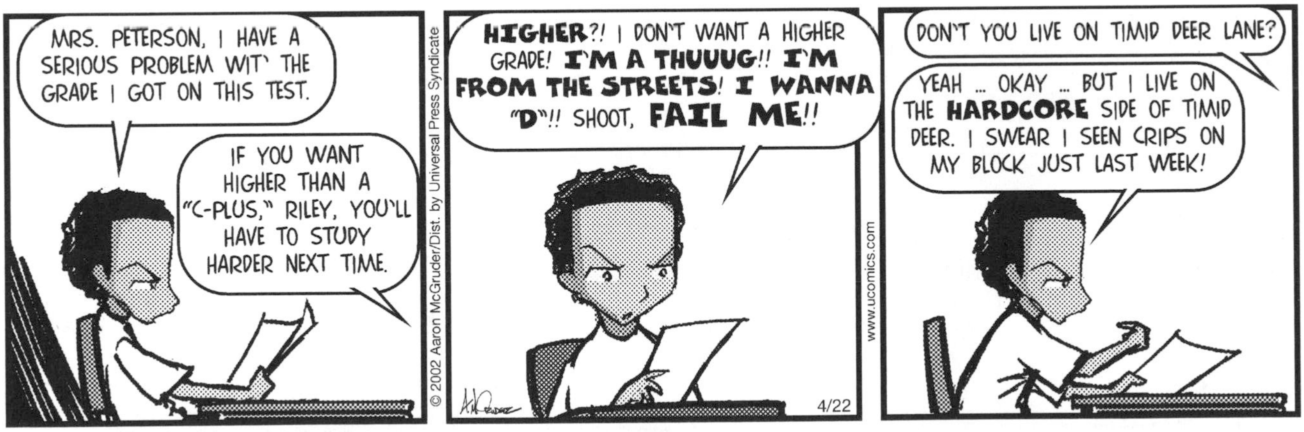
MRS. PETERSON, I HAVE A SERIOUS PROBLEM WIT' THE GRADE I GOT ON THIS TEST.
IF YOU WANT HIGHER THAN A "C-PLUS," RILEY, YOU'LL HAVE TO STUDY HARDER NEXT TIME.
© 2002 Aaron McGruder/Dist. by Universal Press Syndicate
HIGHER?! I DON'T WANT A HIGHER GRADE! I'M A THUUUG!! I'M FROM THE STREETS! I WANNA "D"!! SHOOT, FAIL ME!!
4/22
www.ucomics.com
DON'T YOU LIVE ON TIMID DEER LANE?
YEAH ... OKAY ... BUT I LIVE ON THE HARDCORE SIDE OF TIMID DEER. I SWEAR I SEEN CRIPS ON MY BLOCK JUST LAST WEEK!

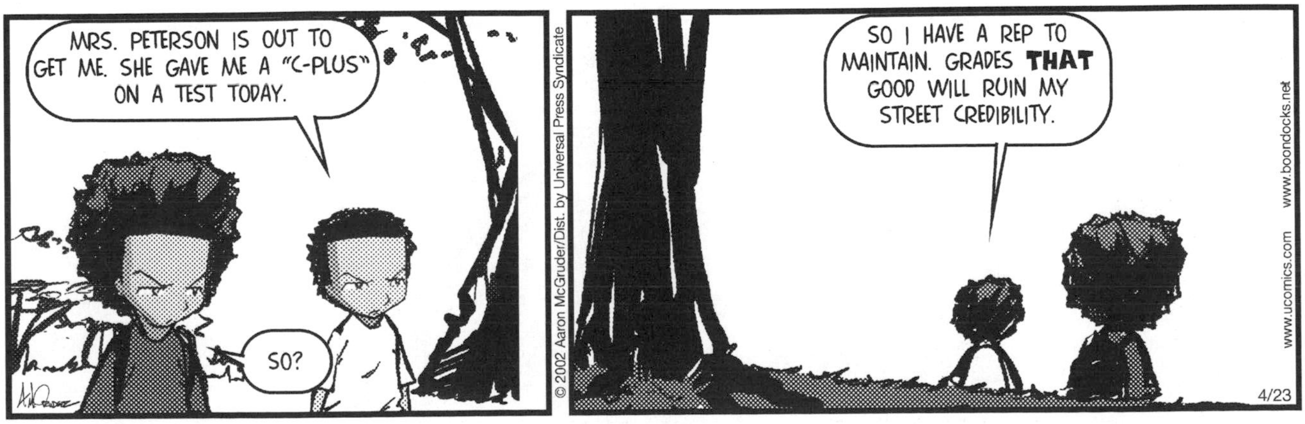
MRS. PETERSON IS OUT TO GET ME. SHE GAVE ME A "C-PLUS" ON A TEST TODAY.
SO?
© 2002 Aaron McGruder/Dist. by Universal Press Syndicate
SO I HAVE A REP TO MAINTAIN. GRADES THAT GOOD WILL RUIN MY STREET CREDIBILITY.
www.ucomics.com
www.boondocks.net
4/23

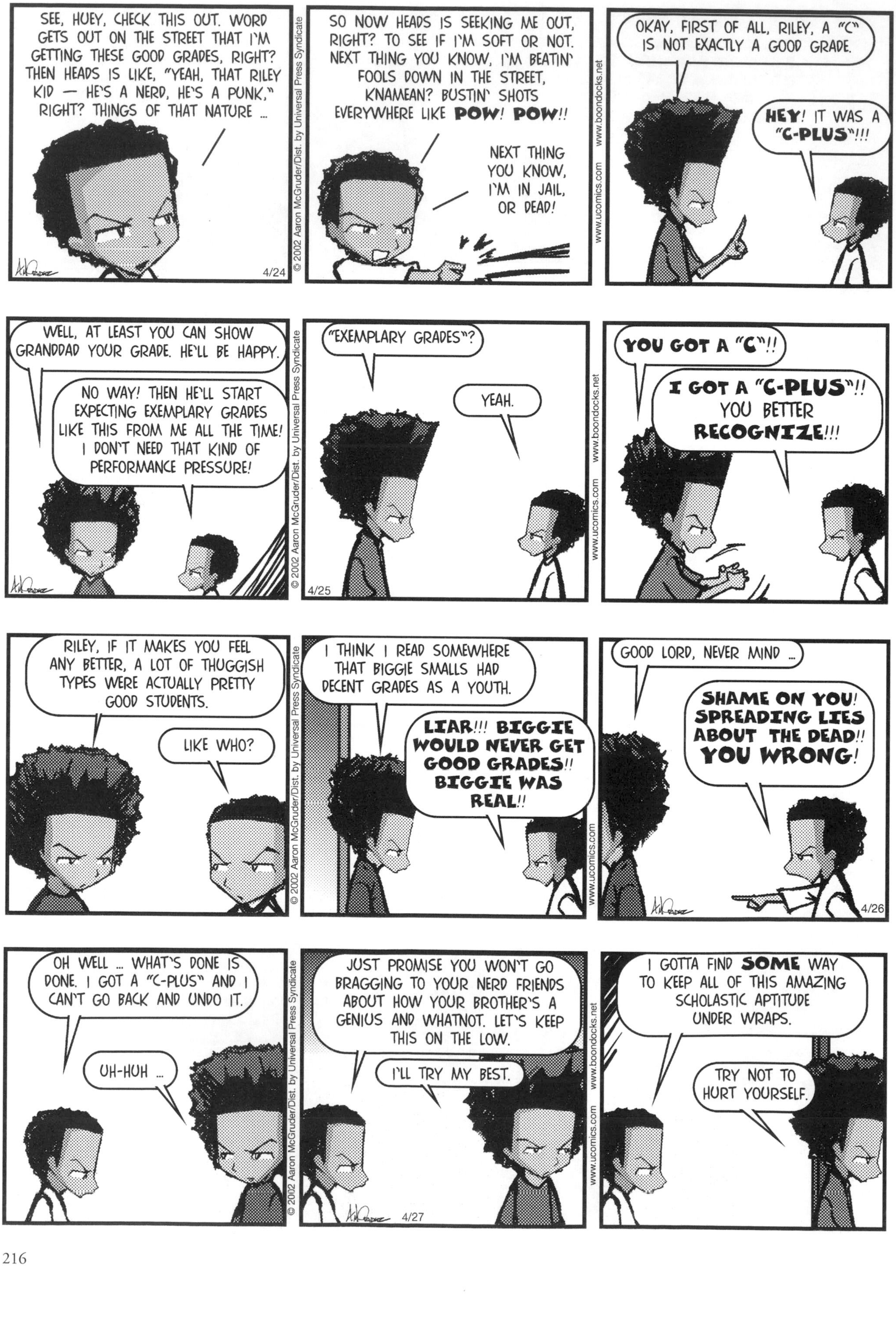

SEE, HUEY, CHECK THIS OUT. WORD GETS OUT ON THE STREET THAT I'M GETTING THESE GOOD GRADES, RIGHT? THEN HEADS IS LIKE, "YEAH, THAT RILEY KID — HE'S A NERD, HE'S A PUNK," RIGHT? THINGS OF THAT NATURE ...
4/24
SO NOW HEADS IS SEEKING ME OUT, RIGHT? TO SEE IF I'M SOFT OR NOT. NEXT THING YOU KNOW, I'M BEATIN' FOOLS DOWN IN THE STREET, KNAMEAN? BUSTIN' SHOTS EVERYWHERE LIKE POW! POW!!
NEXT THING YOU KNOW, I'M IN JAIL, OR DEAD!
OKAY, FIRST OF ALL, RILEY, A "C" IS NOT EXACTLY A GOOD GRADE.
HEY! IT WAS A "C-PLUS"!!!
WELL, AT LEAST YOU CAN SHOW GRANDDAD YOUR GRADE. HE'LL BE HAPPY.
NO WAY! THEN HE'LL START EXPECTING EXEMPLARY GRADES LIKE THIS FROM ME ALL THE TIME! I DON'T NEED THAT KIND OF PERFORMANCE PRESSURE!
"EXEMPLARY GRADES"?
YEAH.
4/25
YOU GOT A "C"!!
I GOT A "C-PLUS"!! YOU BETTER RECOGNIZE!!!
RILEY, IF IT MAKES YOU FEEL ANY BETTER, A LOT OF THUGGISH TYPES WERE ACTUALLY PRETTY GOOD STUDENTS.
LIKE WHO?
I THINK I READ SOMEWHERE THAT BIGGIE SMALLS HAD DECENT GRADES AS A YOUTH.
LIAR!!! BIGGIE WOULD NEVER GET GOOD GRADES!! BIGGIE WAS REAL!!
GOOD LORD, NEVER MIND ...
SHAME ON YOU! SPREADING LIES ABOUT THE DEAD!! YOU WRONG!
4/26
OH WELL ... WHAT'S DONE IS DONE. I GOT A "C-PLUS" AND I CAN'T GO BACK AND UNDO IT.
UH-HUH ...
JUST PROMISE YOU WON'T GO BRAGGING TO YOUR NERD FRIENDS ABOUT HOW YOUR BROTHER'S A GENIUS AND WHATNOT. LET'S KEEP THIS ON THE LOW.
I'LL TRY MY BEST.
4/27
I GOTTA FIND SOME WAY TO KEEP ALL OF THIS AMAZING SCHOLASTIC APTITUDE UNDER WRAPS.
TRY NOT TO HURT YOURSELF.
© 2002 Aaron McGruder/Dist. by Universal Press Syndicate
www.ucomics.com www.boondocks.net

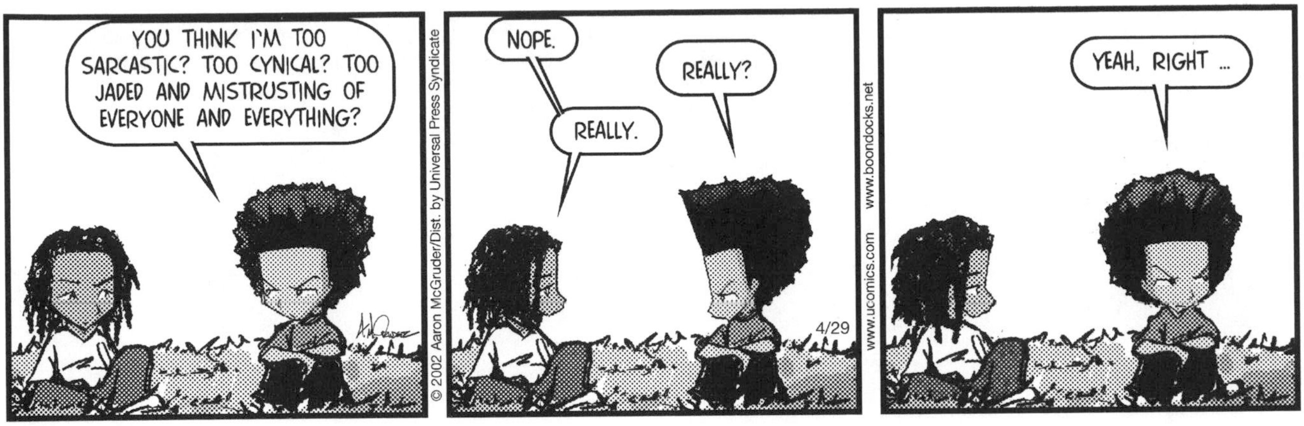
YOU THINK I'M TOO SARCASTIC? TOO CYNICAL? TOO JADED AND MISTRUSTING OF EVERYONE AND EVERYTHING?
© 2002 Aaron McGruder/Dist. by Universal Press Syndicate
NOPE.
REALLY.
REALLY?
4/29
www.ucomics.com www.boondocks.net
YEAH, RIGHT ...

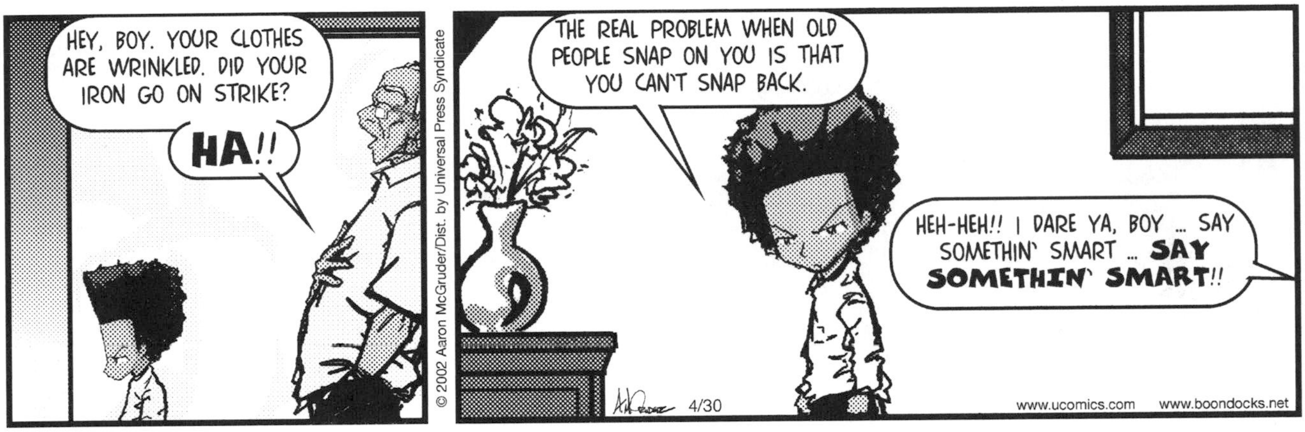
HEY, BOY. YOUR CLOTHES ARE WRINKLED. DID YOUR IRON GO ON STRIKE?
HA!!
© 2002 Aaron McGruder/Dist. by Universal Press Syndicate
THE REAL PROBLEM WHEN OLD PEOPLE SNAP ON YOU IS THAT YOU CAN'T SNAP BACK.
HEH-HEH!! I DARE YA, BOY ... SAY SOMETHIN' SMART ... SAY SOMETHIN' SMART!!
4/30
www.ucomics.com www.boondocks.net

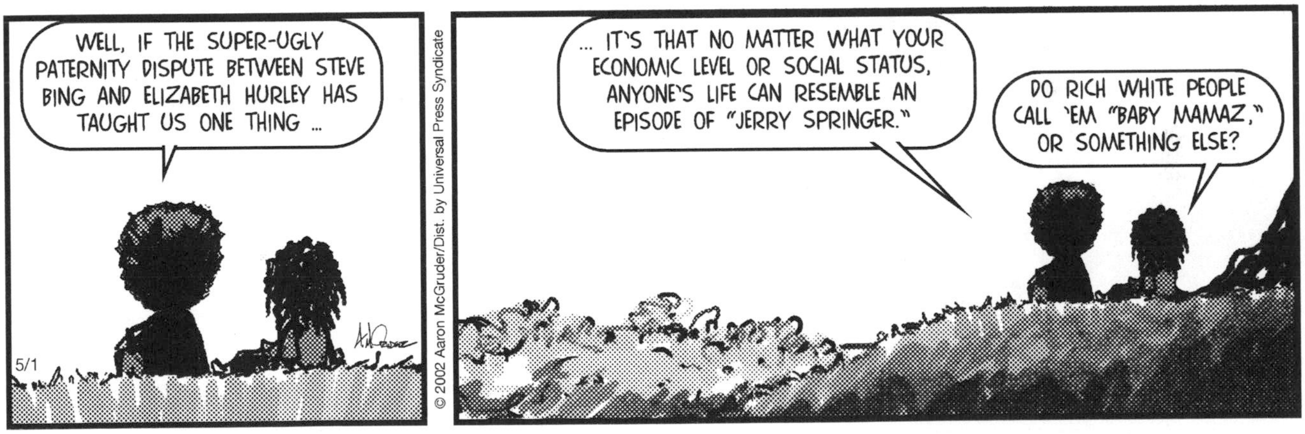
WELL, IF THE SUPER-UGLY PATERNITY DISPUTE BETWEEN STEVE BING AND ELIZABETH HURLEY HAS TAUGHT US ONE THING ...
5/1
© 2002 Aaron McGruder/Dist. by Universal Press Syndicate
... IT'S THAT NO MATTER WHAT YOUR ECONOMIC LEVEL OR SOCIAL STATUS, ANYONE'S LIFE CAN RESEMBLE AN EPISODE OF "JERRY SPRINGER."
DO RICH WHITE PEOPLE CALL 'EM "BABY MAMAZ," OR SOMETHING ELSE?

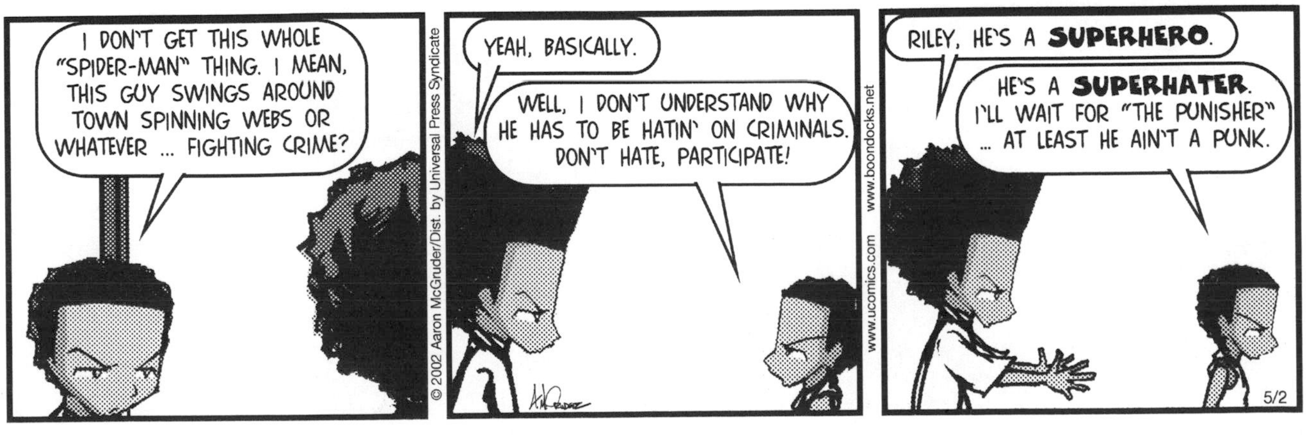
I DON'T GET THIS WHOLE "SPIDER-MAN" THING. I MEAN, THIS GUY SWINGS AROUND TOWN SPINNING WEBS OR WHATEVER ... FIGHTING CRIME?
© 2002 Aaron McGruder/Dist. by Universal Press Syndicate
YEAH, BASICALLY.
WELL, I DON'T UNDERSTAND WHY HE HAS TO BE HATIN' ON CRIMINALS. DON'T HATE, PARTICIPATE!
www.ucomics.com www.boondocks.net
RILEY, HE'S A SUPERHERO.
HE'S A SUPERHATER. I'LL WAIT FOR "THE PUNISHER" ... AT LEAST HE AIN'T A PUNK.
5/2

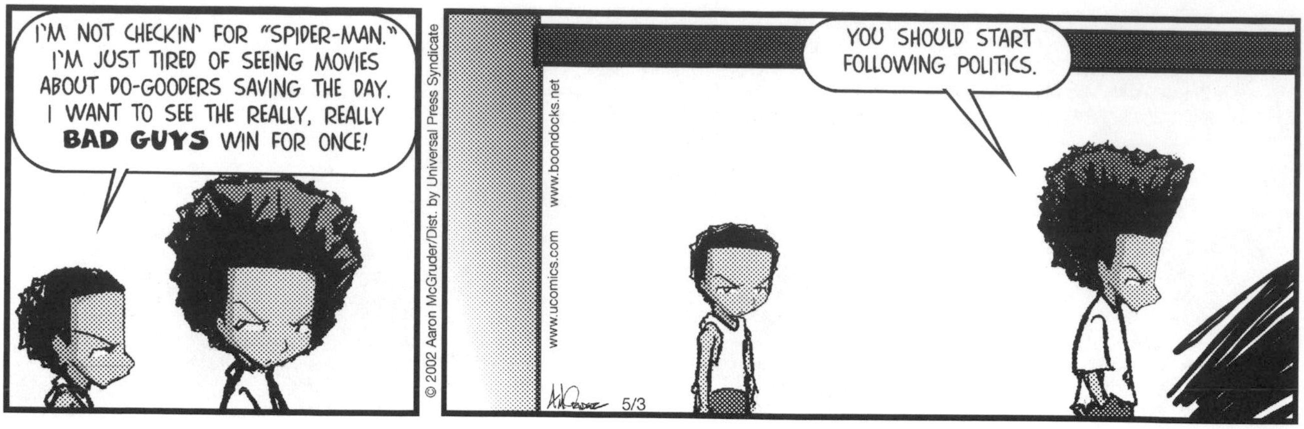
I'M NOT CHECKIN' FOR "SPIDER-MAN." I'M JUST TIRED OF SEEING MOVIES ABOUT DO-GOODERS SAVING THE DAY. I WANT TO SEE THE REALLY, REALLY **BAD GUYS** WIN FOR ONCE!
© 2002 Aaron McGruder/Dist. by Universal Press Syndicate
www.ucomics.com www.boondocks.net
YOU SHOULD START FOLLOWING POLITICS.
5/3

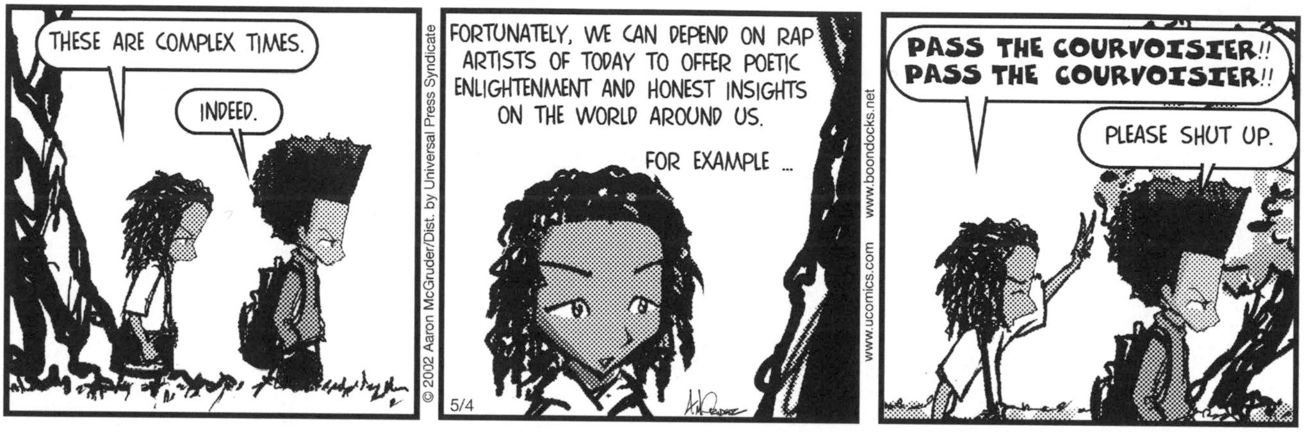
THESE ARE COMPLEX TIMES.
INDEED.
© 2002 Aaron McGruder/Dist. by Universal Press Syndicate
FORTUNATELY, WE CAN DEPEND ON RAP ARTISTS OF TODAY TO OFFER POETIC ENLIGHTENMENT AND HONEST INSIGHTS ON THE WORLD AROUND US.
FOR EXAMPLE ...
5/4
www.ucomics.com www.boondocks.net
PASS THE COURVOISIER!! PASS THE COURVOISIER!!
PLEASE SHUT UP.

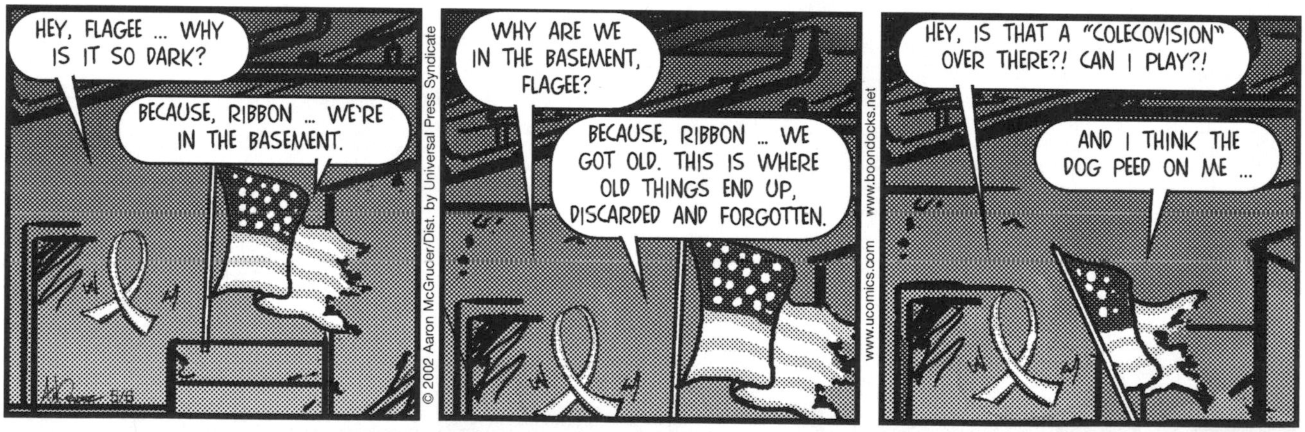
HEY, FLAGEE ... WHY IS IT SO DARK?
BECAUSE, RIBBON ... WE'RE IN THE BASEMENT.
5/6
© 2002 Aaron McGruder/Dist. by Universal Press Syndicate
WHY ARE WE IN THE BASEMENT, FLAGEE?
BECAUSE, RIBBON ... WE GOT OLD. THIS IS WHERE OLD THINGS END UP, DISCARDED AND FORGOTTEN.
www.ucomics.com www.boondocks.net
HEY, IS THAT A "COLECOVISION" OVER THERE?! CAN I PLAY?!
AND I THINK THE DOG PEED ON ME ...

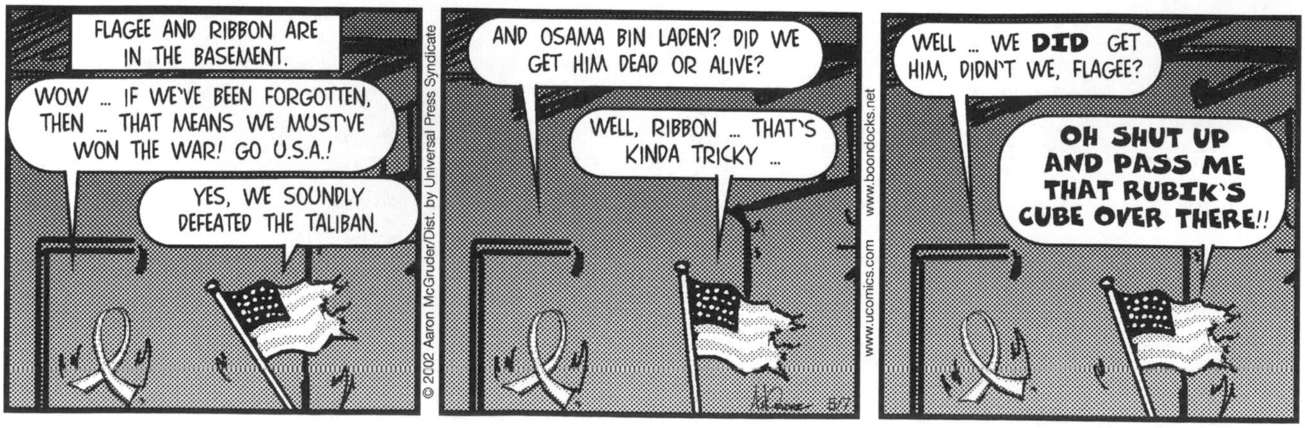
FLAGEE AND RIBBON ARE IN THE BASEMENT.
WOW ... IF WE'VE BEEN FORGOTTEN, THEN ... THAT MEANS WE MUST'VE WON THE WAR! GO U.S.A.!
YES, WE SOUNDLY DEFEATED THE TALIBAN.
© 2002 Aaron McGruder/Dist. by Universal Press Syndicate
AND OSAMA BIN LADEN? DID WE GET HIM DEAD OR ALIVE?
WELL, RIBBON ... THAT'S KINDA TRICKY ...
www.ucomics.com www.boondocks.net
WELL ... WE **DID** GET HIM, DIDN'T WE, FLAGEE?
OH SHUT UP AND PASS ME THAT RUBIK'S CUBE OVER THERE!!

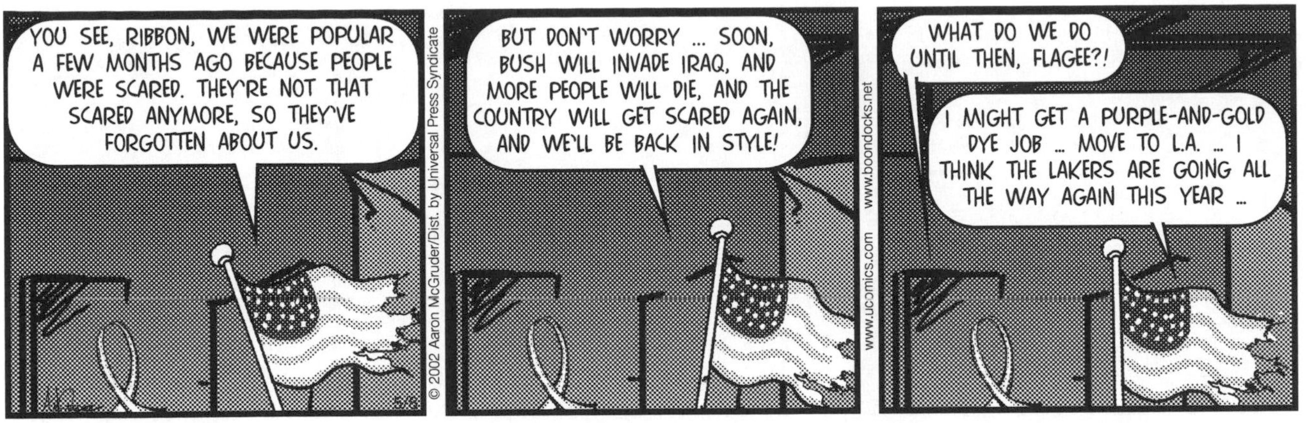
YOU SEE, RIBBON, WE WERE POPULAR A FEW MONTHS AGO BECAUSE PEOPLE WERE SCARED. THEY'RE NOT THAT SCARED ANYMORE, SO THEY'VE FORGOTTEN ABOUT US.
BUT DON'T WORRY ... SOON, BUSH WILL INVADE IRAQ, AND MORE PEOPLE WILL DIE, AND THE COUNTRY WILL GET SCARED AGAIN, AND WE'LL BE BACK IN STYLE!
WHAT DO WE DO UNTIL THEN, FLAGEE?!
I MIGHT GET A PURPLE-AND-GOLD DYE JOB ... MOVE TO L.A. ... I THINK THE LAKERS ARE GOING ALL THE WAY AGAIN THIS YEAR ...
© 2002 Aaron McGruder/Dist. by Universal Press Syndicate
www.ucomics.com www.boondocks.net

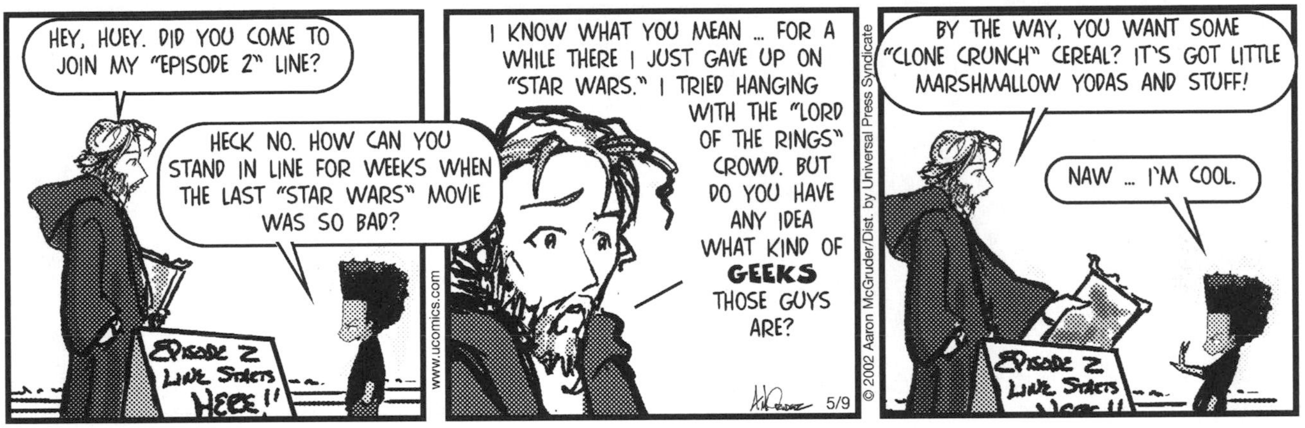
HEY, HUEY. DID YOU COME TO JOIN MY "EPISODE 2" LINE?
HECK NO. HOW CAN YOU STAND IN LINE FOR WEEKS WHEN THE LAST "STAR WARS" MOVIE WAS SO BAD?
EPISODE 2 LINE STARTS HERE!!
I KNOW WHAT YOU MEAN ... FOR A WHILE THERE I JUST GAVE UP ON "STAR WARS." I TRIED HANGING WITH THE "LORD OF THE RINGS" CROWD. BUT DO YOU HAVE ANY IDEA WHAT KIND OF **GEEKS** THOSE GUYS ARE?
BY THE WAY, YOU WANT SOME "CLONE CRUNCH" CEREAL? IT'S GOT LITTLE MARSHMALLOW YODAS AND STUFF!
NAW ... I'M COOL.
5/9
© 2002 Aaron McGruder/Dist. by Universal Press Syndicate
www.ucomics.com

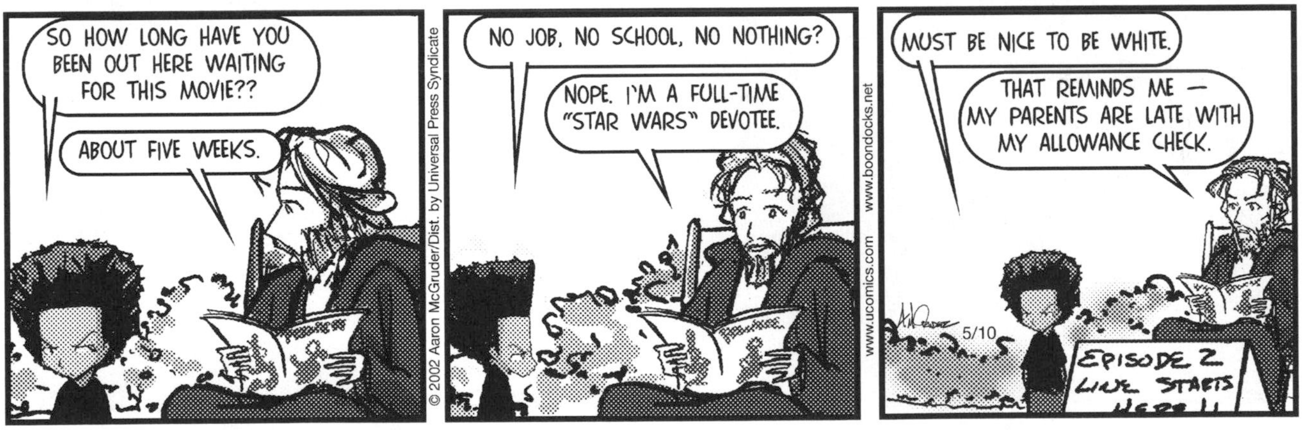
SO HOW LONG HAVE YOU BEEN OUT HERE WAITING FOR THIS MOVIE??
ABOUT FIVE WEEKS.
NO JOB, NO SCHOOL, NO NOTHING?
NOPE. I'M A FULL-TIME "STAR WARS" DEVOTEE.
MUST BE NICE TO BE WHITE.
THAT REMINDS ME — MY PARENTS ARE LATE WITH MY ALLOWANCE CHECK.
EPISODE 2 LINE STARTS
5/10
© 2002 Aaron McGruder/Dist. by Universal Press Syndicate
www.ucomics.com www.boondocks.net

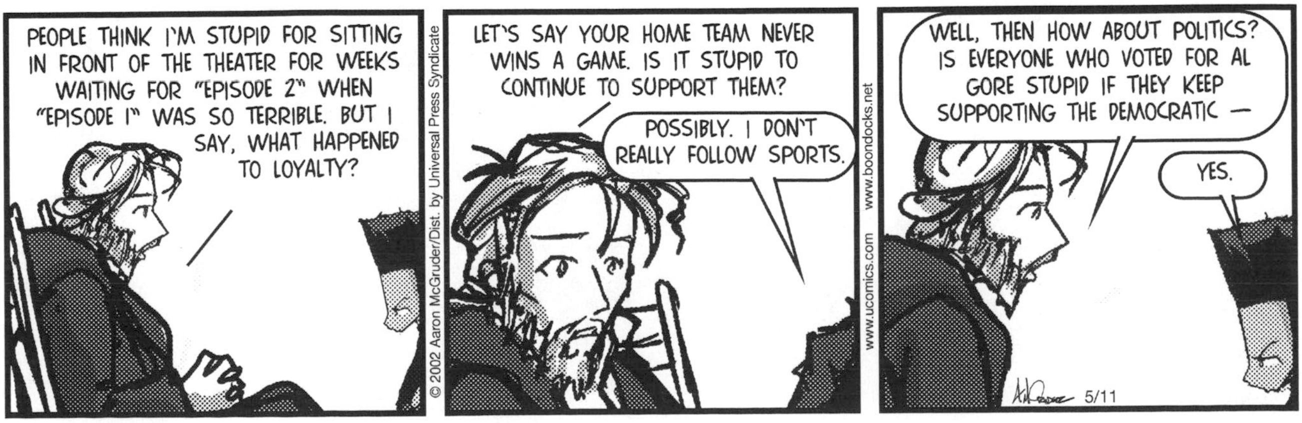
PEOPLE THINK I'M STUPID FOR SITTING IN FRONT OF THE THEATER FOR WEEKS WAITING FOR "EPISODE 2" WHEN "EPISODE I" WAS SO TERRIBLE. BUT I SAY, WHAT HAPPENED TO LOYALTY?
LET'S SAY YOUR HOME TEAM NEVER WINS A GAME. IS IT STUPID TO CONTINUE TO SUPPORT THEM?
POSSIBLY. I DON'T REALLY FOLLOW SPORTS.
WELL, THEN HOW ABOUT POLITICS? IS EVERYONE WHO VOTED FOR AL GORE STUPID IF THEY KEEP SUPPORTING THE DEMOCRATIC —
YES.
5/11
© 2002 Aaron McGruder/Dist. by Universal Press Syndicate
www.ucomics.com www.boondocks.net

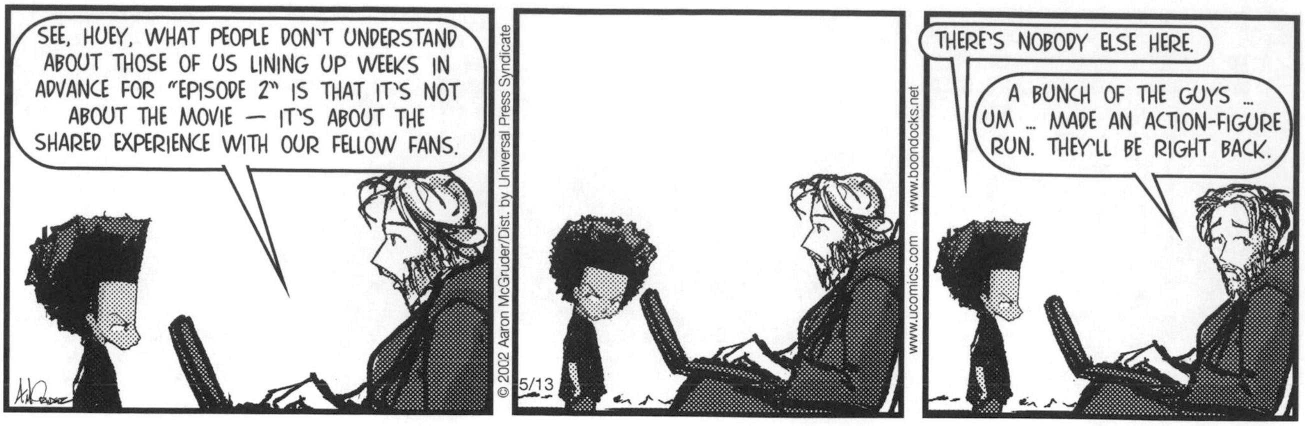
SEE, HUEY, WHAT PEOPLE DON'T UNDERSTAND ABOUT THOSE OF US LINING UP WEEKS IN ADVANCE FOR "EPISODE 2" IS THAT IT'S NOT ABOUT THE MOVIE — IT'S ABOUT THE SHARED EXPERIENCE WITH OUR FELLOW FANS.
© 2002 Aaron McGruder/Dist. by Universal Press Syndicate
5/13
www.ucomics.com www.boondocks.net
THERE'S NOBODY ELSE HERE.
A BUNCH OF THE GUYS ... UM ... MADE AN ACTION-FIGURE RUN. THEY'LL BE RIGHT BACK.

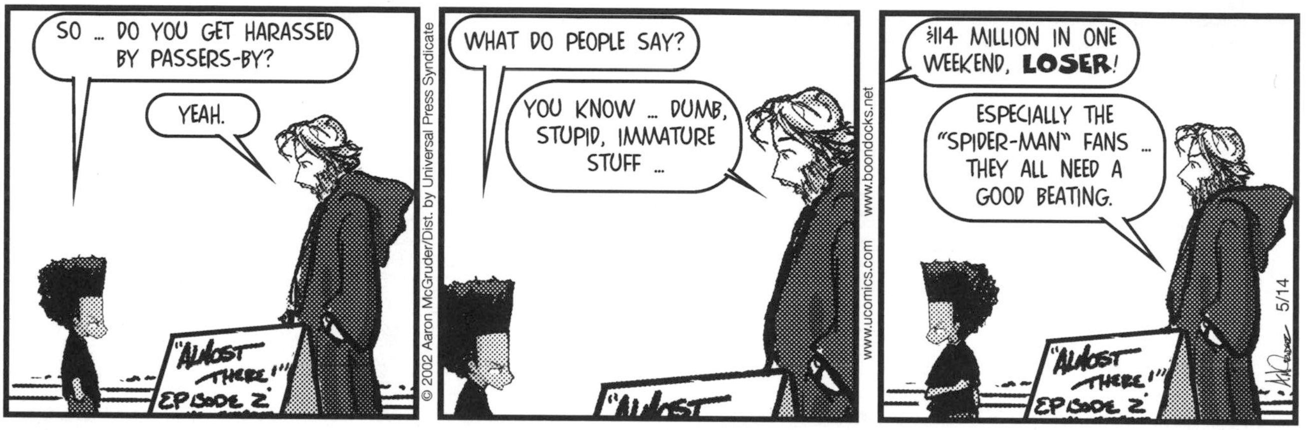
SO ... DO YOU GET HARASSED BY PASSERS-BY?
YEAH.
"ALMOST THERE!" EPISODE 2
© 2002 Aaron McGruder/Dist. by Universal Press Syndicate
WHAT DO PEOPLE SAY?
YOU KNOW ... DUMB, STUPID, IMMATURE STUFF ...
www.ucomics.com www.boondocks.net
$114 MILLION IN ONE WEEKEND, **LOSER**!
ESPECIALLY THE "SPIDER-MAN" FANS ... THEY ALL NEED A GOOD BEATING.
"ALMOST THERE!" EPISODE 2
5/14

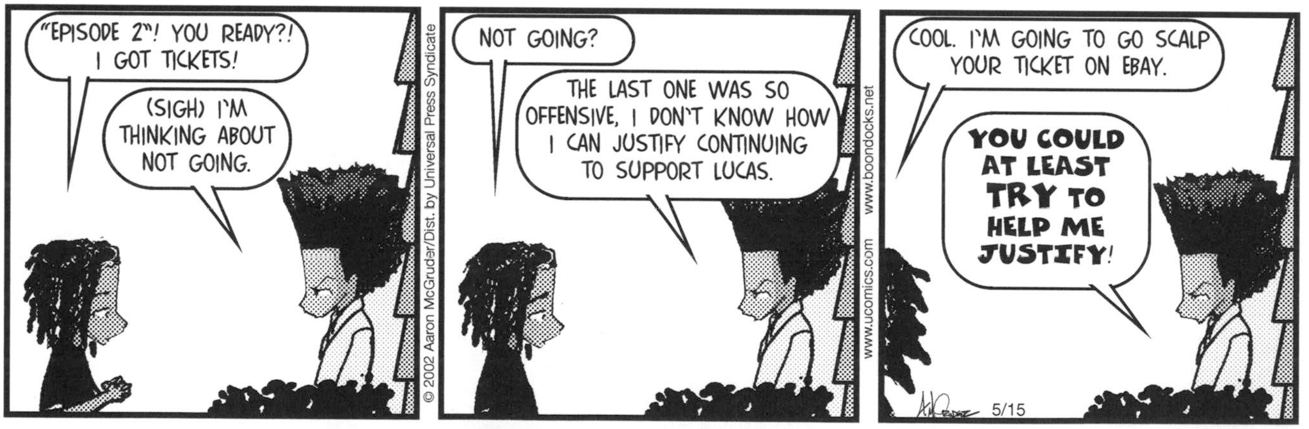
"EPISODE 2"! YOU READY?! I GOT TICKETS!
(SIGH) I'M THINKING ABOUT NOT GOING.
© 2002 Aaron McGruder/Dist. by Universal Press Syndicate
NOT GOING?
THE LAST ONE WAS SO OFFENSIVE, I DON'T KNOW HOW I CAN JUSTIFY CONTINUING TO SUPPORT LUCAS.
www.ucomics.com www.boondocks.net
COOL. I'M GOING TO GO SCALP YOUR TICKET ON EBAY.
YOU COULD AT LEAST TRY TO HELP ME JUSTIFY!
5/15

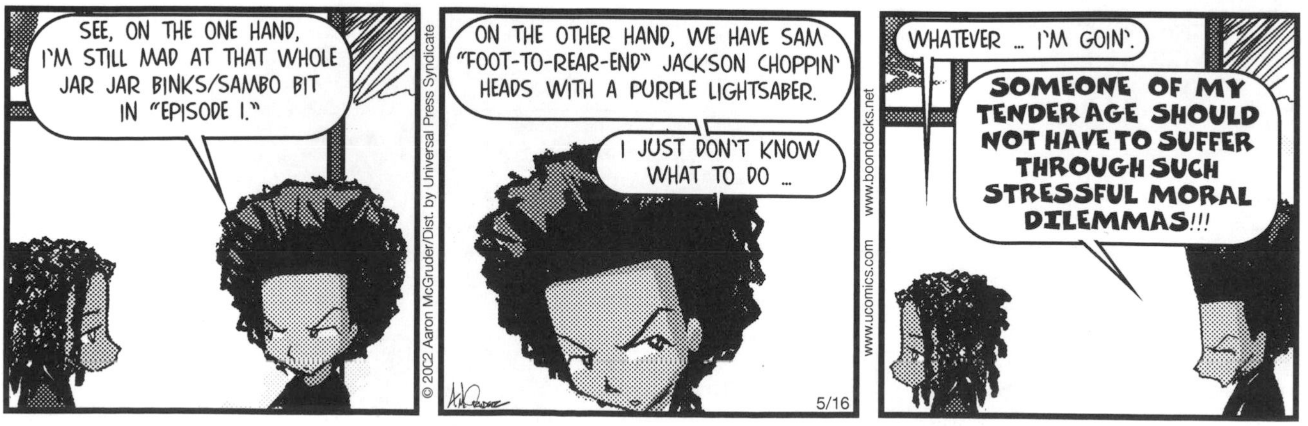
SEE, ON THE ONE HAND, I'M STILL MAD AT THAT WHOLE JAR JAR BINKS/SAMBO BIT IN "EPISODE I."
© 2002 Aaron McGruder/Dist. by Universal Press Syndicate
ON THE OTHER HAND, WE HAVE SAM "FOOT-TO-REAR-END" JACKSON CHOPPIN' HEADS WITH A PURPLE LIGHTSABER.
I JUST DON'T KNOW WHAT TO DO ...
5/16
www.ucomics.com www.boondocks.net
WHATEVER ... I'M GOIN'.
SOMEONE OF MY TENDER AGE SHOULD NOT HAVE TO SUFFER THROUGH SUCH STRESSFUL MORAL DILEMMAS!!!

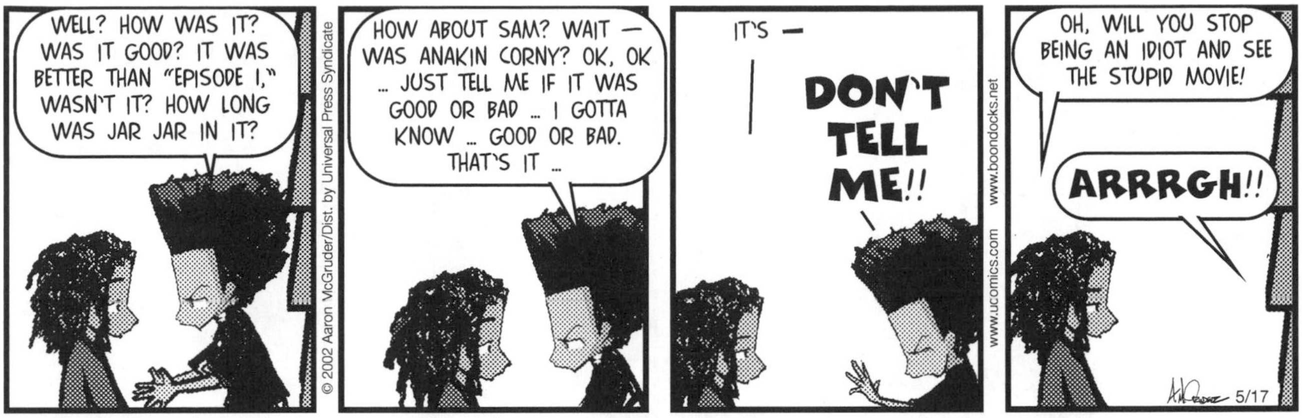
WELL? HOW WAS IT? WAS IT GOOD? IT WAS BETTER THAN "EPISODE I," WASN'T IT? HOW LONG WAS JAR JAR IN IT?
© 2002 Aaron McGruder/Dist. by Universal Press Syndicate
HOW ABOUT SAM? WAIT — WAS ANAKIN CORNY? OK, OK ... JUST TELL ME IF IT WAS GOOD OR BAD ... I GOTTA KNOW ... GOOD OR BAD. THAT'S IT ...
IT'S —
DON'T TELL ME!!
www.ucomics.com www.boondocks.net
OH, WILL YOU STOP BEING AN IDIOT AND SEE THE STUPID MOVIE!
ARRRGH!!
5/17

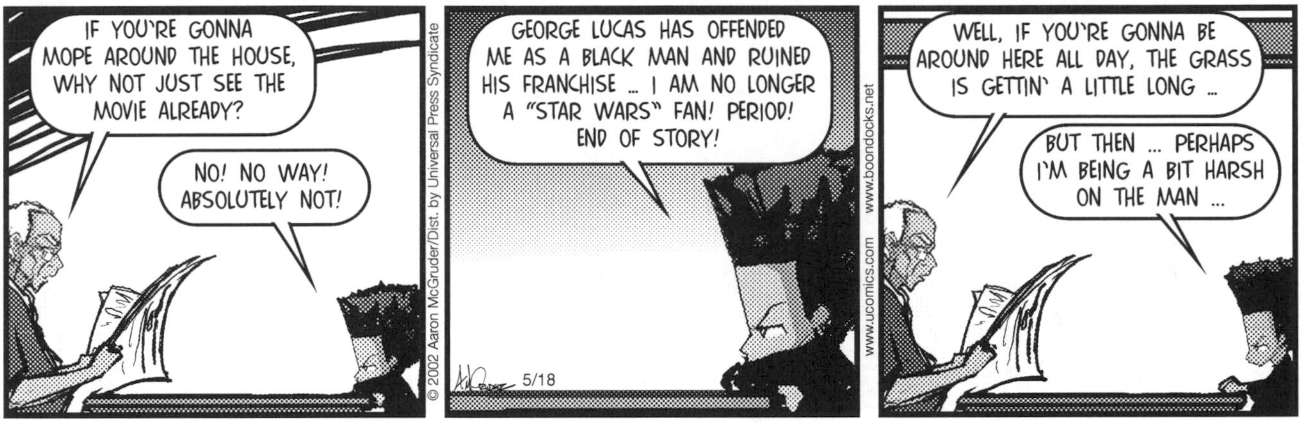
IF YOU'RE GONNA MOPE AROUND THE HOUSE, WHY NOT JUST SEE THE MOVIE ALREADY?
NO! NO WAY! ABSOLUTELY NOT!
© 2002 Aaron McGruder/Dist. by Universal Press Syndicate
GEORGE LUCAS HAS OFFENDED ME AS A BLACK MAN AND RUINED HIS FRANCHISE ... I AM NO LONGER A "STAR WARS" FAN! PERIOD! END OF STORY!
5/18
www.ucomics.com www.boondocks.net
WELL, IF YOU'RE GONNA BE AROUND HERE ALL DAY, THE GRASS IS GETTIN' A LITTLE LONG ...
BUT THEN ... PERHAPS I'M BEING A BIT HARSH ON THE MAN ...

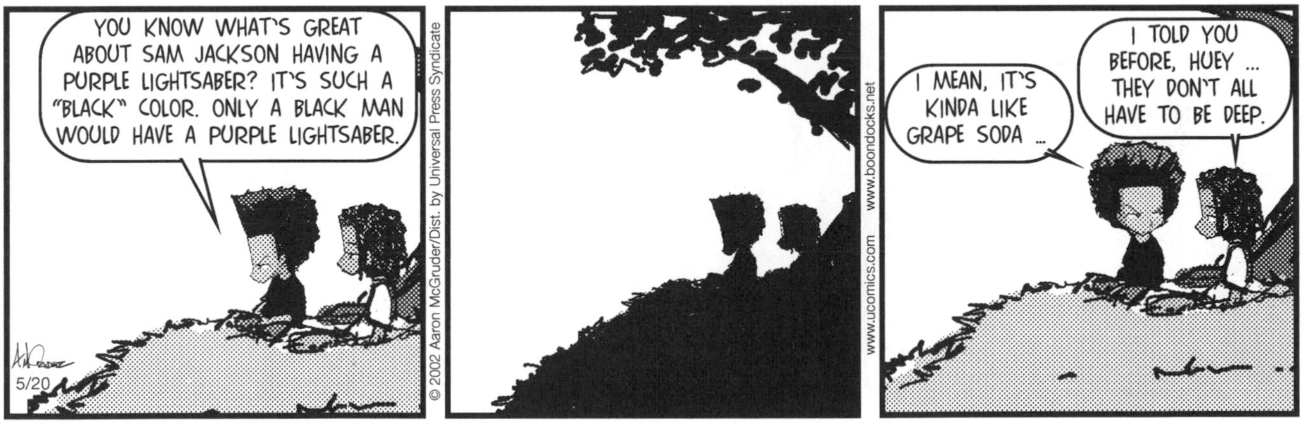
YOU KNOW WHAT'S GREAT ABOUT SAM JACKSON HAVING A PURPLE LIGHTSABER? IT'S SUCH A "BLACK" COLOR. ONLY A BLACK MAN WOULD HAVE A PURPLE LIGHTSABER.
5/20
© 2002 Aaron McGruder/Dist. by Universal Press Syndicate
www.ucomics.com www.boondocks.net
I MEAN, IT'S KINDA LIKE GRAPE SODA ...
I TOLD YOU BEFORE, HUEY ... THEY DON'T ALL HAVE TO BE DEEP.

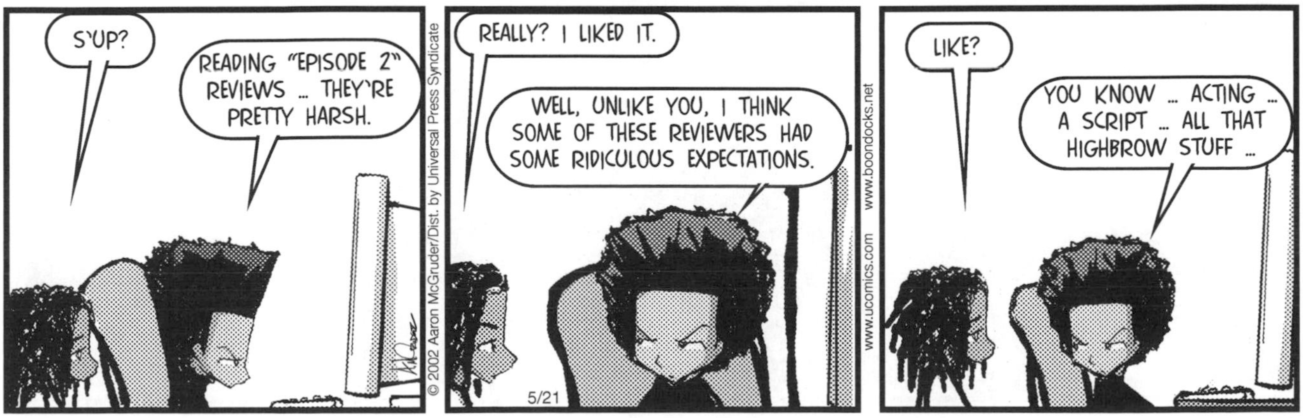
S'UP?
READING "EPISODE 2" REVIEWS ... THEY'RE PRETTY HARSH.
© 2002 Aaron McGruder/Dist. by Universal Press Syndicate
REALLY? I LIKED IT.
WELL, UNLIKE YOU, I THINK SOME OF THESE REVIEWERS HAD SOME RIDICULOUS EXPECTATIONS.
5/21
www.ucomics.com www.boondocks.net
LIKE?
YOU KNOW ... ACTING ... A SCRIPT ... ALL THAT HIGHBROW STUFF ...

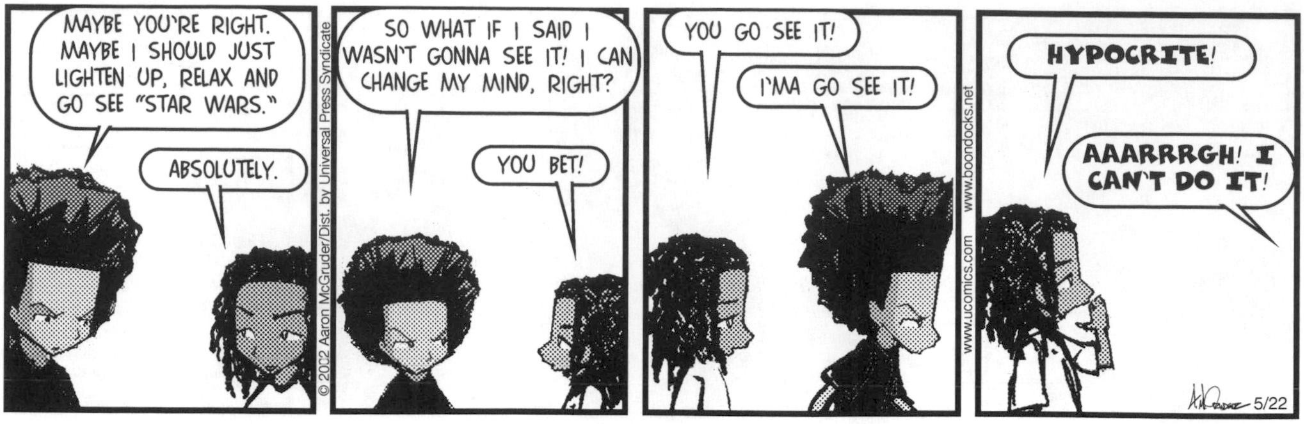
MAYBE YOU'RE RIGHT. MAYBE I SHOULD JUST LIGHTEN UP, RELAX AND GO SEE "STAR WARS."
ABSOLUTELY.
© 2002 Aaron McGruder/Dist. by Universal Press Syndicate
SO WHAT IF I SAID I WASN'T GONNA SEE IT! I CAN CHANGE MY MIND, RIGHT?
YOU BET!
YOU GO SEE IT!
I'MA GO SEE IT!
www.ucomics.com www.boondocks.net
HYPOCRITE!
AAARRRGH! I CAN'T DO IT!
5/22

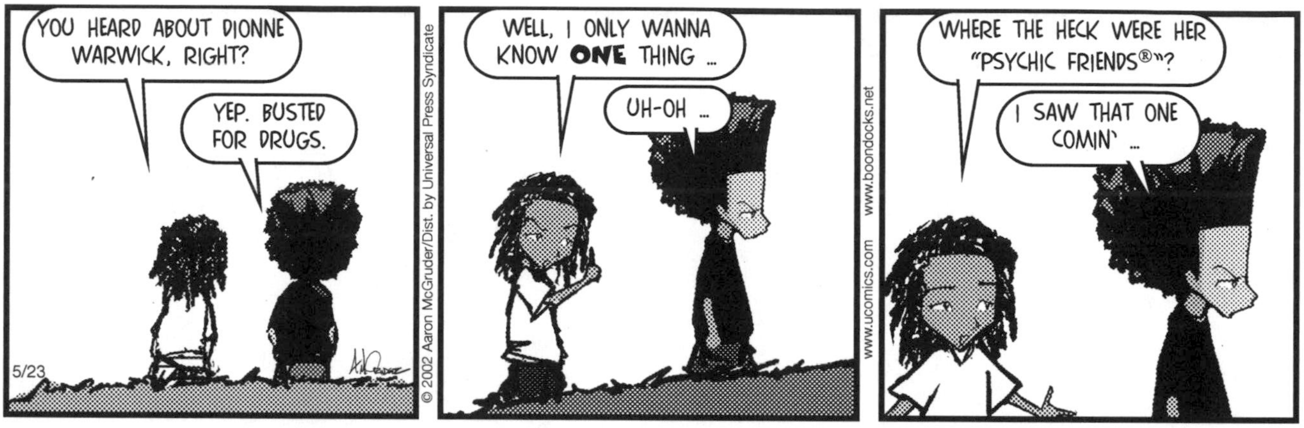
YOU HEARD ABOUT DIONNE WARWICK, RIGHT?
YEP. BUSTED FOR DRUGS.
5/23
© 2002 Aaron McGruder/Dist. by Universal Press Syndicate
WELL, I ONLY WANNA KNOW ONE THING ...
UH-OH ...
www.ucomics.com www.boondocks.net
WHERE THE HECK WERE HER "PSYCHIC FRIENDS®"?
I SAW THAT ONE COMIN' ...

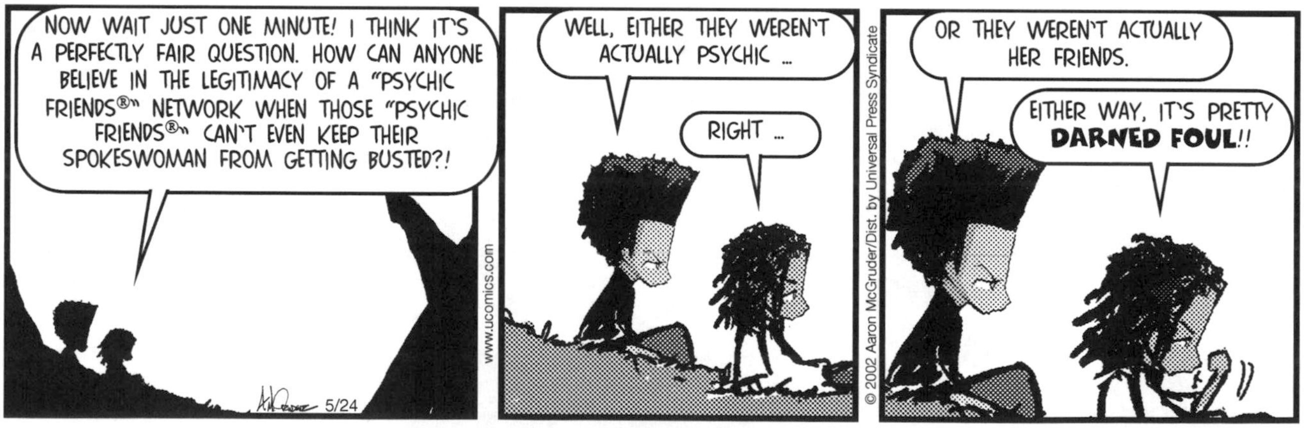
NOW WAIT JUST ONE MINUTE! I THINK IT'S A PERFECTLY FAIR QUESTION. HOW CAN ANYONE BELIEVE IN THE LEGITIMACY OF A "PSYCHIC FRIENDS®" NETWORK WHEN THOSE "PSYCHIC FRIENDS®" CAN'T EVEN KEEP THEIR SPOKESWOMAN FROM GETTING BUSTED?!
5/24
www.ucomics.com
WELL, EITHER THEY WEREN'T ACTUALLY PSYCHIC ...
RIGHT ...
© 2002 Aaron McGruder/Dist. by Universal Press Syndicate
OR THEY WEREN'T ACTUALLY HER FRIENDS.
EITHER WAY, IT'S PRETTY DARNED FOUL!!

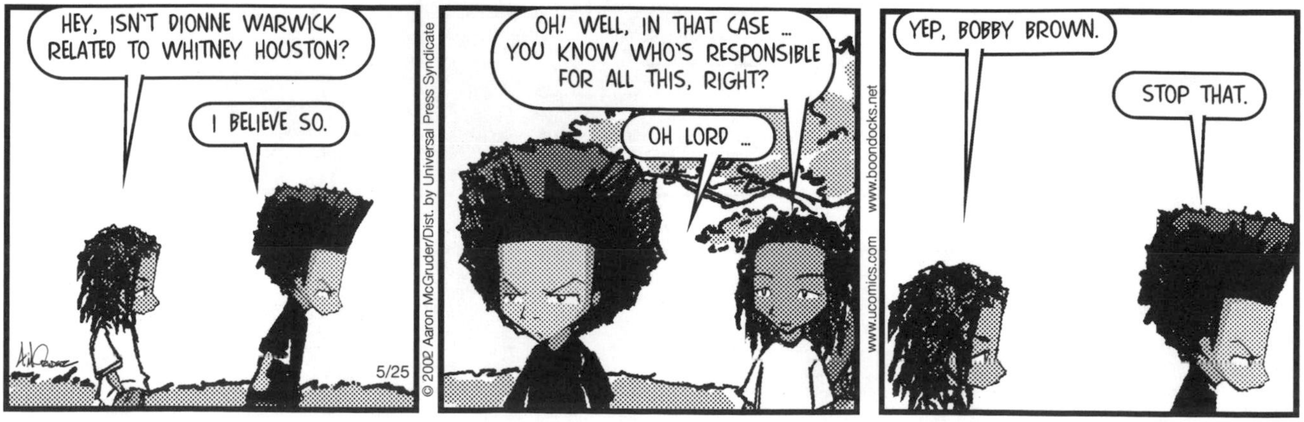
HEY, ISN'T DIONNE WARWICK RELATED TO WHITNEY HOUSTON?
I BELIEVE SO.
5/25
© 2002 Aaron McGruder/Dist. by Universal Press Syndicate
OH! WELL, IN THAT CASE ... YOU KNOW WHO'S RESPONSIBLE FOR ALL THIS, RIGHT?
OH LORD ...
www.ucomics.com www.boondocks.net
YEP, BOBBY BROWN.
STOP THAT.

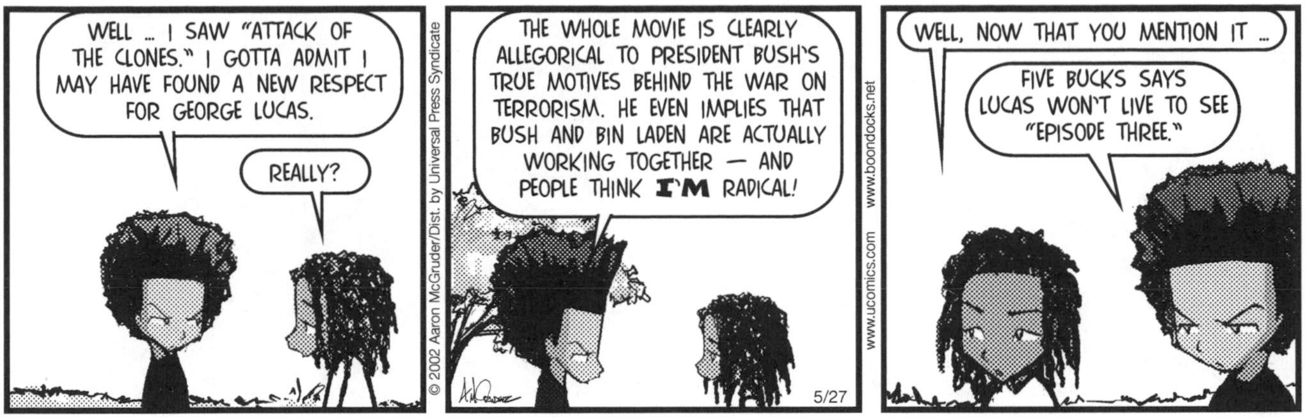
WELL ... I SAW "ATTACK OF THE CLONES." I GOTTA ADMIT I MAY HAVE FOUND A NEW RESPECT FOR GEORGE LUCAS.
REALLY?
© 2002 Aaron McGruder/Dist. by Universal Press Syndicate
THE WHOLE MOVIE IS CLEARLY ALLEGORICAL TO PRESIDENT BUSH'S TRUE MOTIVES BEHIND THE WAR ON TERRORISM. HE EVEN IMPLIES THAT BUSH AND BIN LADEN ARE ACTUALLY WORKING TOGETHER — AND PEOPLE THINK I'M RADICAL!
5/27
www.ucomics.com www.boondocks.net
WELL, NOW THAT YOU MENTION IT ...
FIVE BUCKS SAYS LUCAS WON'T LIVE TO SEE "EPISODE THREE."

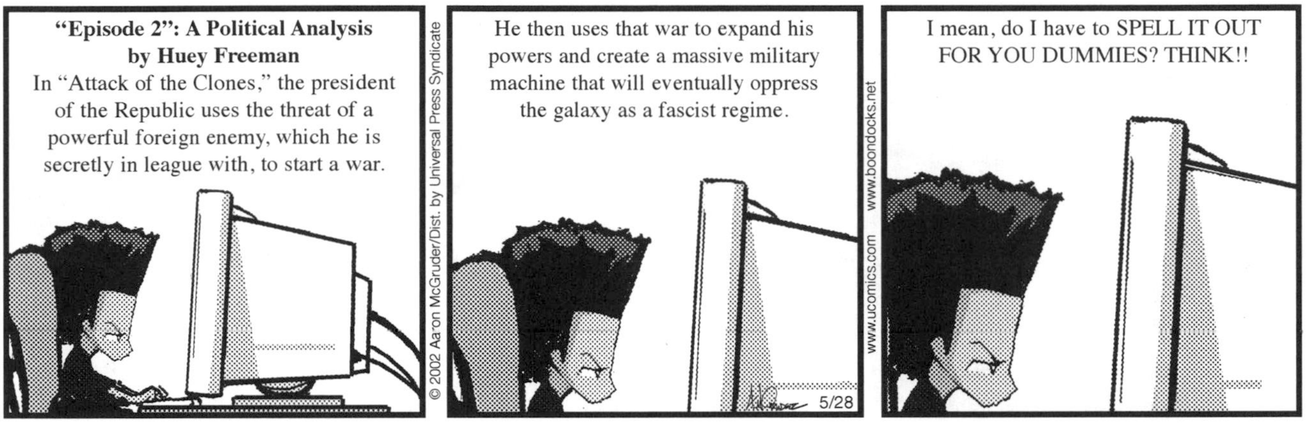
"Episode 2": A Political Analysis
by Huey Freeman
In "Attack of the Clones," the president of the Republic uses the threat of a powerful foreign enemy, which he is secretly in league with, to start a war.
© 2002 Aaron McGruder/Dist. by Universal Press Syndicate
He then uses that war to expand his powers and create a massive military machine that will eventually oppress the galaxy as a fascist regime.
5/28
www.ucomics.com www.boondocks.net
I mean, do I have to SPELL IT OUT FOR YOU DUMMIES? THINK!!

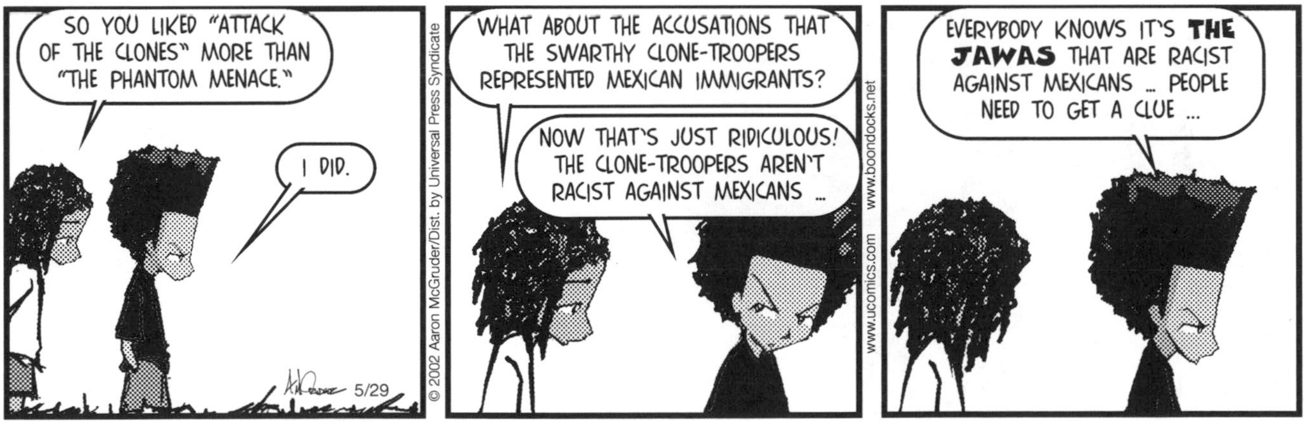
SO YOU LIKED "ATTACK OF THE CLONES" MORE THAN "THE PHANTOM MENACE."
I DID.
5/29
© 2002 Aaron McGruder/Dist. by Universal Press Syndicate
WHAT ABOUT THE ACCUSATIONS THAT THE SWARTHY CLONE-TROOPERS REPRESENTED MEXICAN IMMIGRANTS?
NOW THAT'S JUST RIDICULOUS! THE CLONE-TROOPERS AREN'T RACIST AGAINST MEXICANS ...
www.ucomics.com www.boondocks.net
EVERYBODY KNOWS IT'S THE JAWAS THAT ARE RACIST AGAINST MEXICANS ... PEOPLE NEED TO GET A CLUE ...

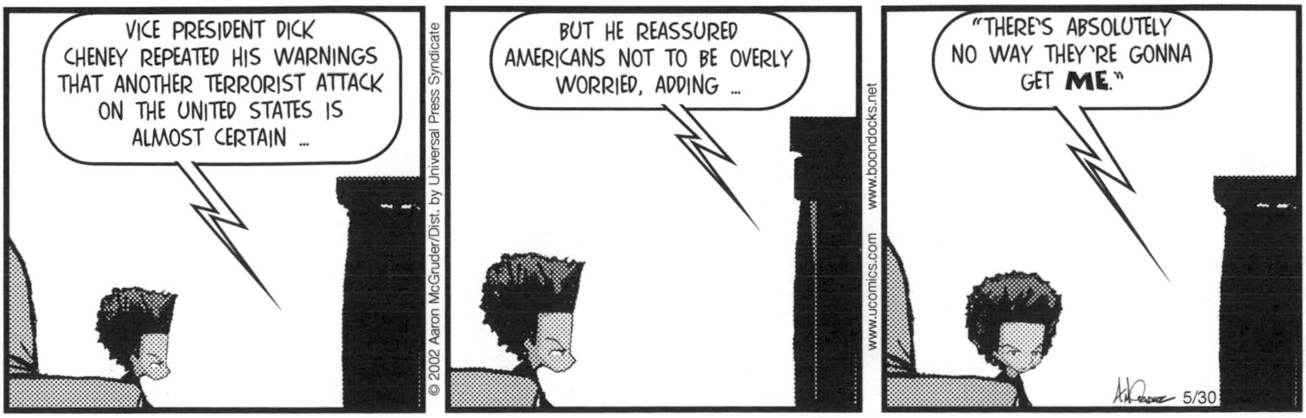
VICE PRESIDENT DICK CHENEY REPEATED HIS WARNINGS THAT ANOTHER TERRORIST ATTACK ON THE UNITED STATES IS ALMOST CERTAIN ...
© 2002 Aaron McGruder/Dist. by Universal Press Syndicate
BUT HE REASSURED AMERICANS NOT TO BE OVERLY WORRIED, ADDING ...
www.ucomics.com www.boondocks.net
"THERE'S ABSOLUTELY NO WAY THEY'RE GONNA GET ME."
5/30

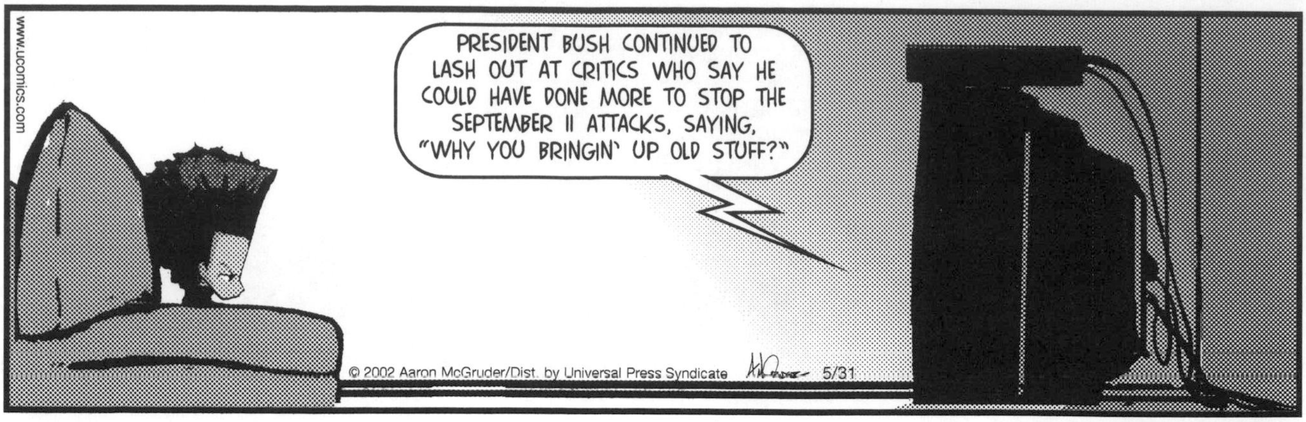
www.ucomics.com
PRESIDENT BUSH CONTINUED TO LASH OUT AT CRITICS WHO SAY HE COULD HAVE DONE MORE TO STOP THE SEPTEMBER 11 ATTACKS, SAYING, "WHY YOU BRINGIN' UP OLD STUFF?"
© 2002 Aaron McGruder/Dist. by Universal Press Syndicate
5/31

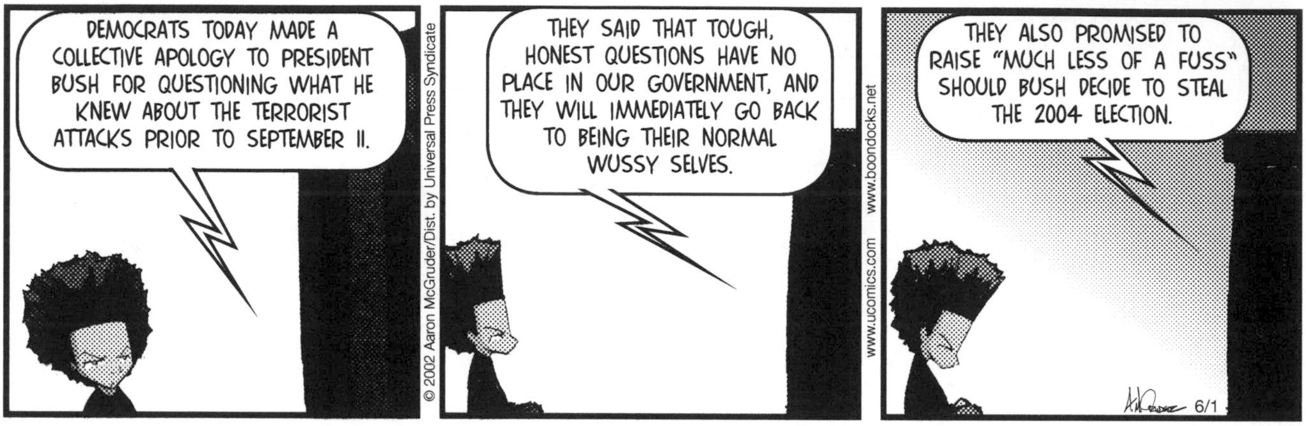
DEMOCRATS TODAY MADE A COLLECTIVE APOLOGY TO PRESIDENT BUSH FOR QUESTIONING WHAT HE KNEW ABOUT THE TERRORIST ATTACKS PRIOR TO SEPTEMBER 11.
© 2002 Aaron McGruder/Dist. by Universal Press Syndicate
THEY SAID THAT TOUGH, HONEST QUESTIONS HAVE NO PLACE IN OUR GOVERNMENT, AND THEY WILL IMMEDIATELY GO BACK TO BEING THEIR NORMAL WUSSY SELVES.
www.ucomics.com www.boondocks.net
THEY ALSO PROMISED TO RAISE "MUCH LESS OF A FUSS" SHOULD BUSH DECIDE TO STEAL THE 2004 ELECTION.
6/1

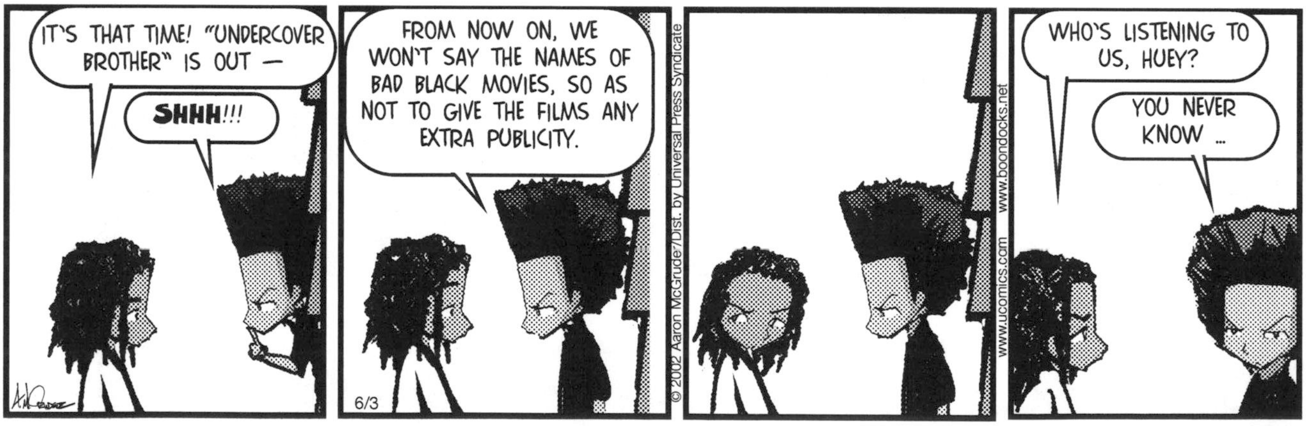
IT'S THAT TIME! "UNDERCOVER BROTHER" IS OUT —
SHHH!!!
6/3
FROM NOW ON, WE WON'T SAY THE NAMES OF BAD BLACK MOVIES, SO AS NOT TO GIVE THE FILMS ANY EXTRA PUBLICITY.
© 2002 Aaron McGruder/Dist. by Universal Press Syndicate
www.ucomics.com www.boondocks.net
WHO'S LISTENING TO US, HUEY?
YOU NEVER KNOW ...

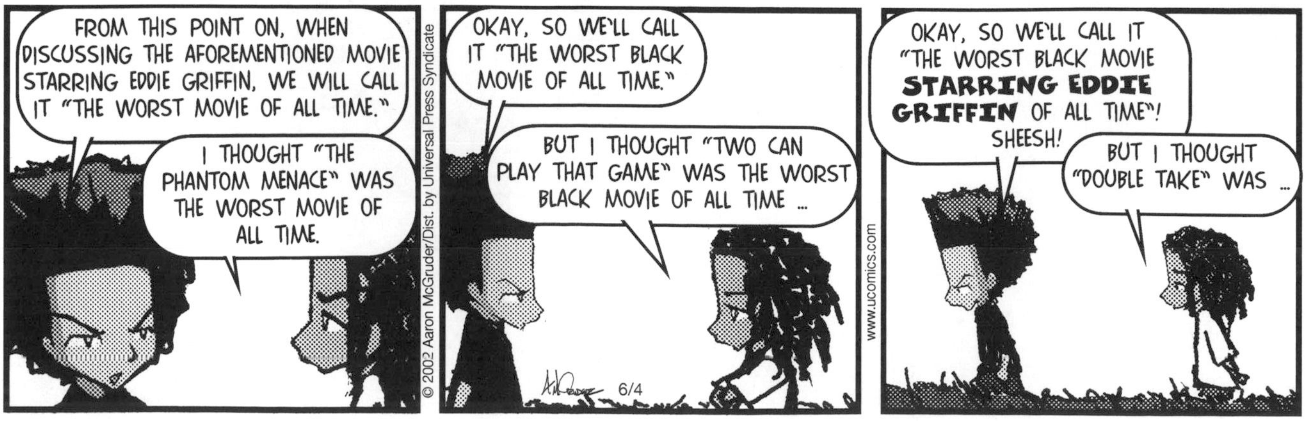
FROM THIS POINT ON, WHEN DISCUSSING THE AFOREMENTIONED MOVIE STARRING EDDIE GRIFFIN, WE WILL CALL IT "THE WORST MOVIE OF ALL TIME."
I THOUGHT "THE PHANTOM MENACE" WAS THE WORST MOVIE OF ALL TIME.
© 2002 Aaron McGruder/Dist. by Universal Press Syndicate
OKAY, SO WE'LL CALL IT "THE WORST BLACK MOVIE OF ALL TIME."
BUT I THOUGHT "TWO CAN PLAY THAT GAME" WAS THE WORST BLACK MOVIE OF ALL TIME ...
6/4
www.ucomics.com
OKAY, SO WE'LL CALL IT "THE WORST BLACK MOVIE STARRING EDDIE GRIFFIN OF ALL TIME"! SHEESH!
BUT I THOUGHT "DOUBLE TAKE" WAS ...

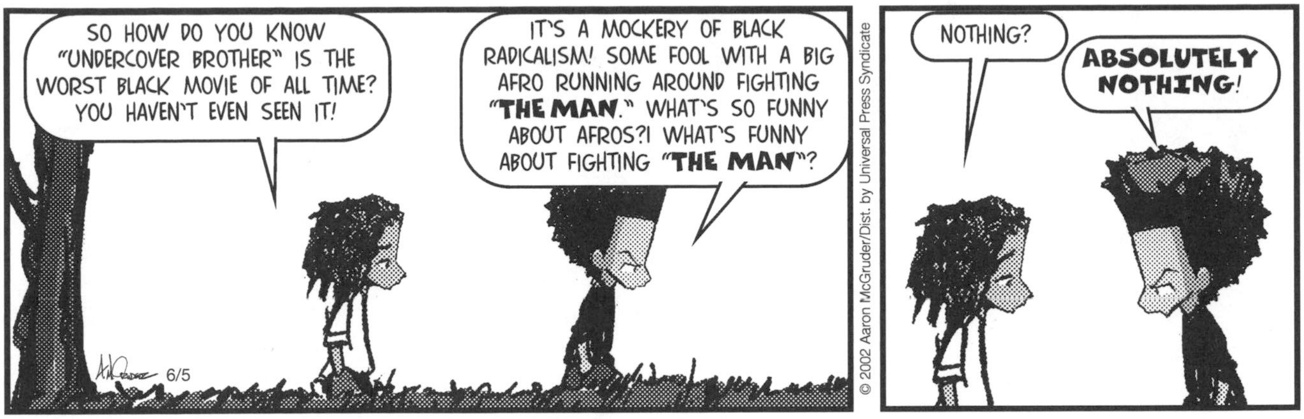
SO HOW DO YOU KNOW "UNDERCOVER BROTHER" IS THE WORST BLACK MOVIE OF ALL TIME? YOU HAVEN'T EVEN SEEN IT!
IT'S A MOCKERY OF BLACK RADICALISM! SOME FOOL WITH A BIG AFRO RUNNING AROUND FIGHTING "THE MAN." WHAT'S SO FUNNY ABOUT AFROS?! WHAT'S FUNNY ABOUT FIGHTING "THE MAN"?
6/5
© 2002 Aaron McGruder/Dist. by Universal Press Syndicate
NOTHING?
ABSOLUTELY NOTHING!

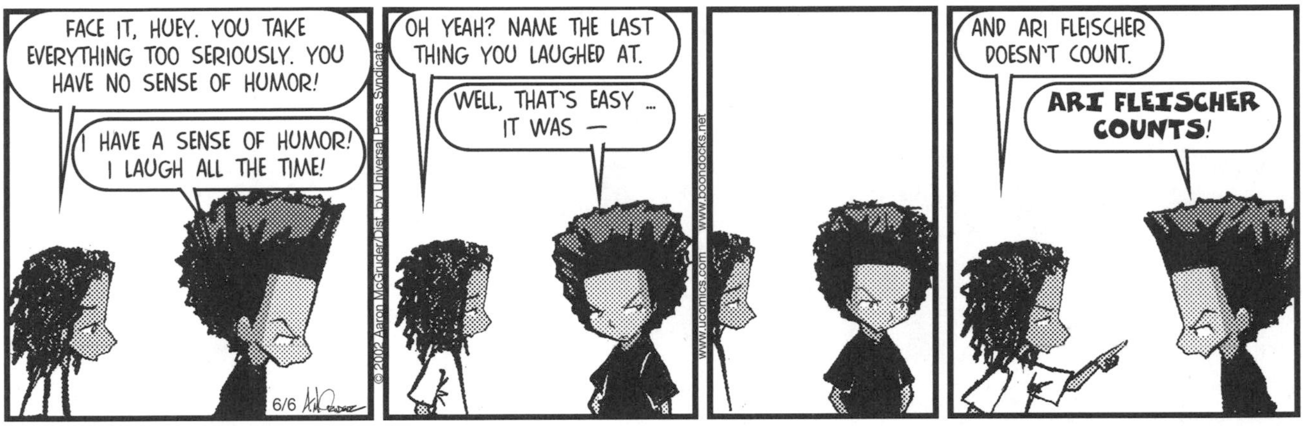
FACE IT, HUEY. YOU TAKE EVERYTHING TOO SERIOUSLY. YOU HAVE NO SENSE OF HUMOR!
I HAVE A SENSE OF HUMOR! I LAUGH ALL THE TIME!
6/6
© 2002 Aaron McGruder/Dist. by Universal Press Syndicate
OH YEAH? NAME THE LAST THING YOU LAUGHED AT.
WELL, THAT'S EASY ... IT WAS —
www.ucomics.com www.boondocks.net
AND ARI FLEISCHER DOESN'T COUNT.
ARI FLEISCHER COUNTS!

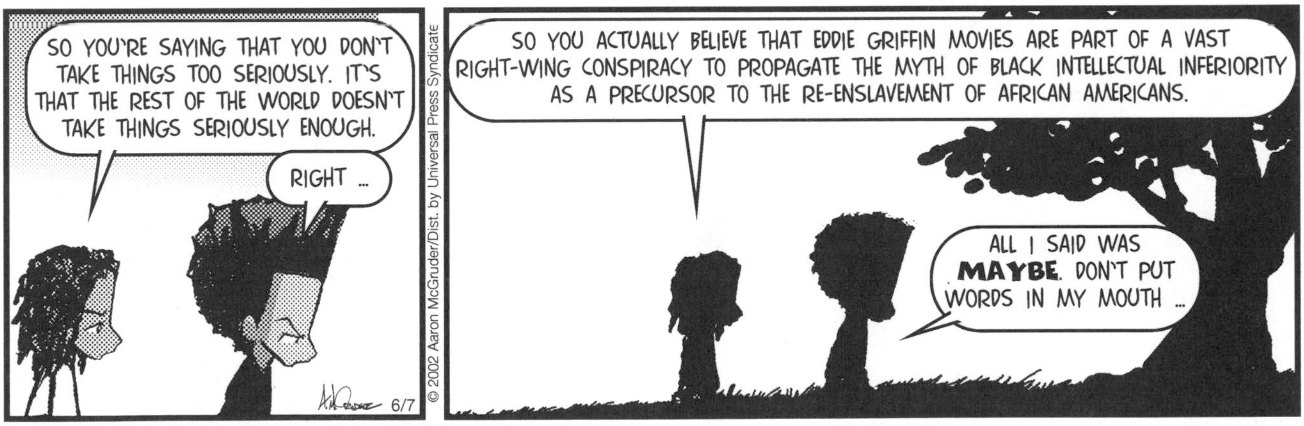
SO YOU'RE SAYING THAT YOU DON'T TAKE THINGS TOO SERIOUSLY. IT'S THAT THE REST OF THE WORLD DOESN'T TAKE THINGS SERIOUSLY ENOUGH.
RIGHT ...
6/7
© 2002 Aaron McGruder/Dist. by Universal Press Syndicate
SO YOU ACTUALLY BELIEVE THAT EDDIE GRIFFIN MOVIES ARE PART OF A VAST RIGHT-WING CONSPIRACY TO PROPAGATE THE MYTH OF BLACK INTELLECTUAL INFERIORITY AS A PRECURSOR TO THE RE-ENSLAVEMENT OF AFRICAN AMERICANS.
ALL I SAID WAS MAYBE. DON'T PUT WORDS IN MY MOUTH ...

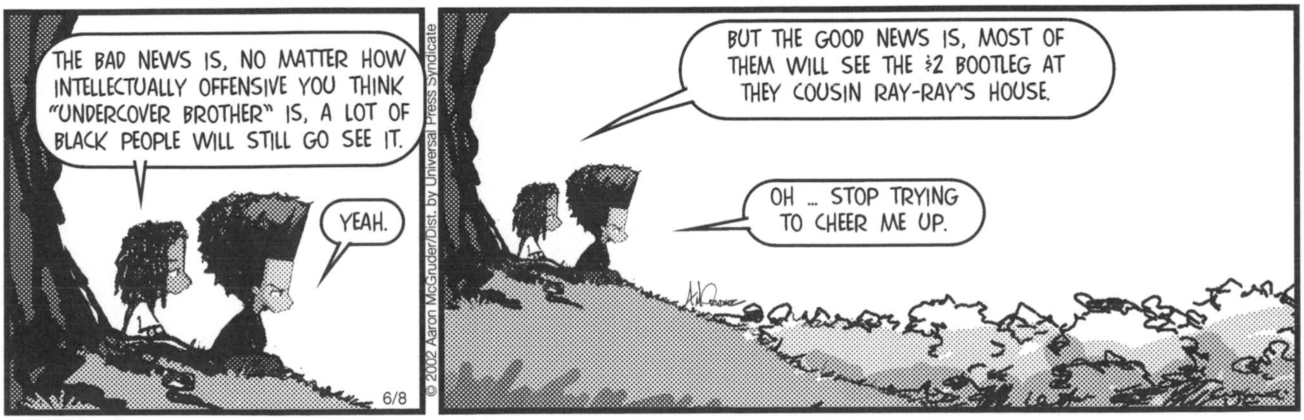
THE BAD NEWS IS, NO MATTER HOW INTELLECTUALLY OFFENSIVE YOU THINK "UNDERCOVER BROTHER" IS, A LOT OF BLACK PEOPLE WILL STILL GO SEE IT.
YEAH.
6/8
© 2002 Aaron McGruder/Dist. by Universal Press Syndicate
BUT THE GOOD NEWS IS, MOST OF THEM WILL SEE THE $2 BOOTLEG AT THEY COUSIN RAY-RAY'S HOUSE.
OH ... STOP TRYING TO CHEER ME UP.

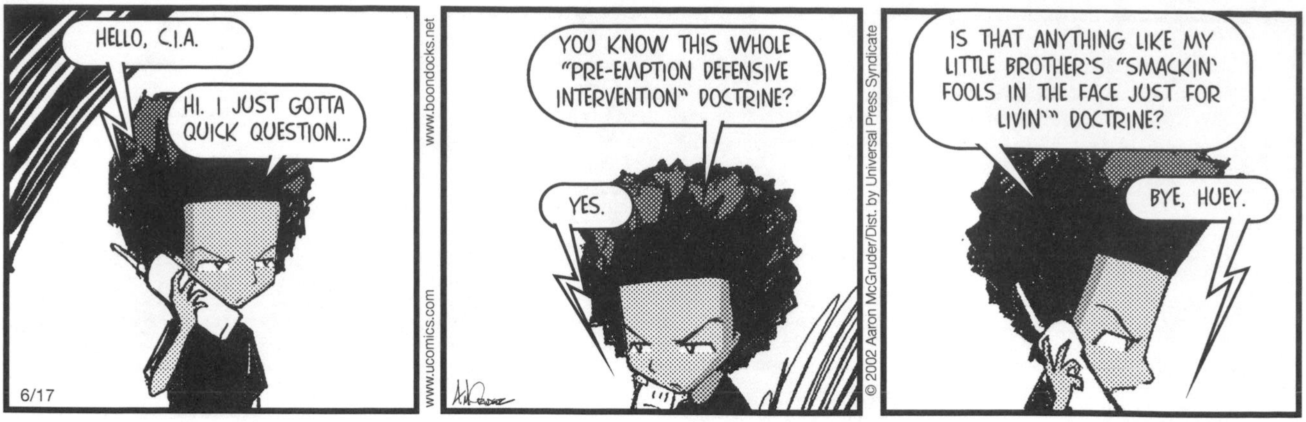
HELLO, C.I.A.
HI. I JUST GOTTA QUICK QUESTION...
6/17
www.boondocks.net
www.ucomics.com
YOU KNOW THIS WHOLE "PRE-EMPTION DEFENSIVE INTERVENTION" DOCTRINE?
YES.
© 2002 Aaron McGruder/Dist. by Universal Press Syndicate
IS THAT ANYTHING LIKE MY LITTLE BROTHER'S "SMACKIN' FOOLS IN THE FACE JUST FOR LIVIN'" DOCTRINE?
BYE, HUEY.

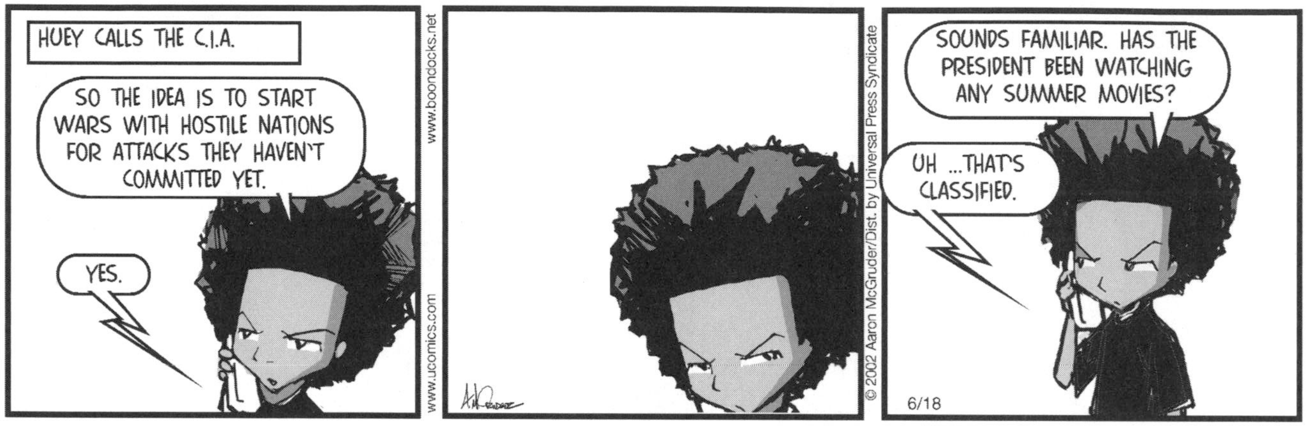
HUEY CALLS THE C.I.A.
SO THE IDEA IS TO START WARS WITH HOSTILE NATIONS FOR ATTACKS THEY HAVEN'T COMMITTED YET.
YES.
www.boondocks.net
www.ucomics.com
© 2002 Aaron McGruder/Dist. by Universal Press Syndicate
SOUNDS FAMILIAR. HAS THE PRESIDENT BEEN WATCHING ANY SUMMER MOVIES?
UH ...THAT'S CLASSIFIED.
6/18

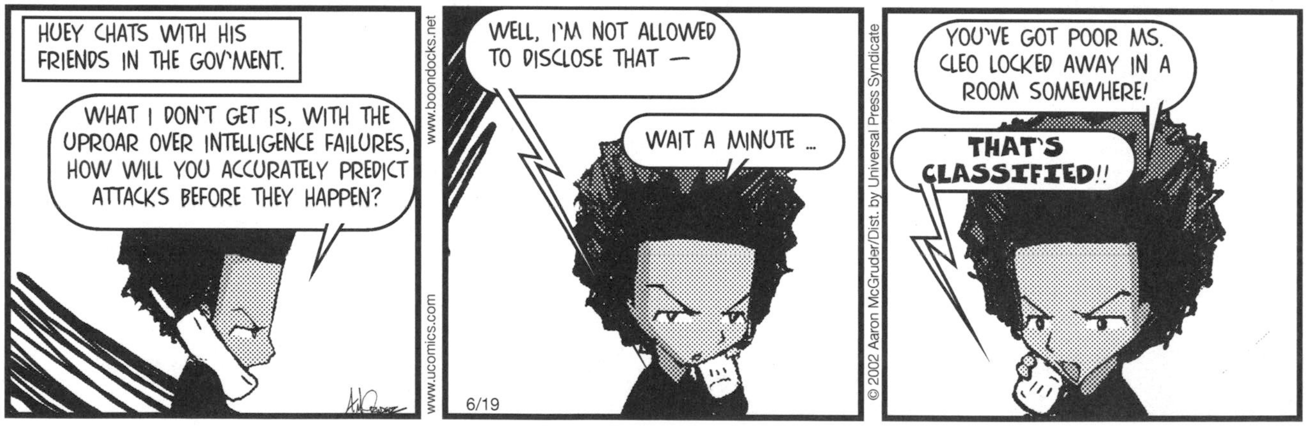
HUEY CHATS WITH HIS FRIENDS IN THE GOV'MENT.
WHAT I DON'T GET IS, WITH THE UPROAR OVER INTELLIGENCE FAILURES, HOW WILL YOU ACCURATELY PREDICT ATTACKS BEFORE THEY HAPPEN?
www.boondocks.net
www.ucomics.com
WELL, I'M NOT ALLOWED TO DISCLOSE THAT —
WAIT A MINUTE ...
6/19
© 2002 Aaron McGruder/Dist. by Universal Press Syndicate
YOU'VE GOT POOR MS. CLEO LOCKED AWAY IN A ROOM SOMEWHERE!
THAT'S CLASSIFIED!!

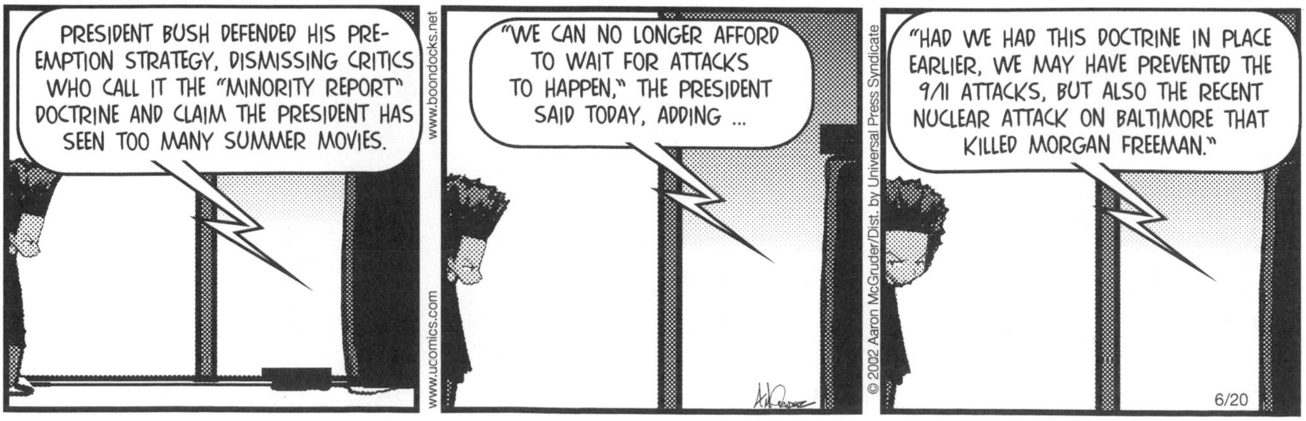
PRESIDENT BUSH DEFENDED HIS PRE-EMPTION STRATEGY, DISMISSING CRITICS WHO CALL IT THE "MINORITY REPORT" DOCTRINE AND CLAIM THE PRESIDENT HAS SEEN TOO MANY SUMMER MOVIES.
www.boondocks.net
www.ucomics.com
"WE CAN NO LONGER AFFORD TO WAIT FOR ATTACKS TO HAPPEN," THE PRESIDENT SAID TODAY, ADDING ...
© 2002 Aaron McGruder/Dist. by Universal Press Syndicate
"HAD WE HAD THIS DOCTRINE IN PLACE EARLIER, WE MAY HAVE PREVENTED THE 9/11 ATTACKS, BUT ALSO THE RECENT NUCLEAR ATTACK ON BALTIMORE THAT KILLED MORGAN FREEMAN."
6/20

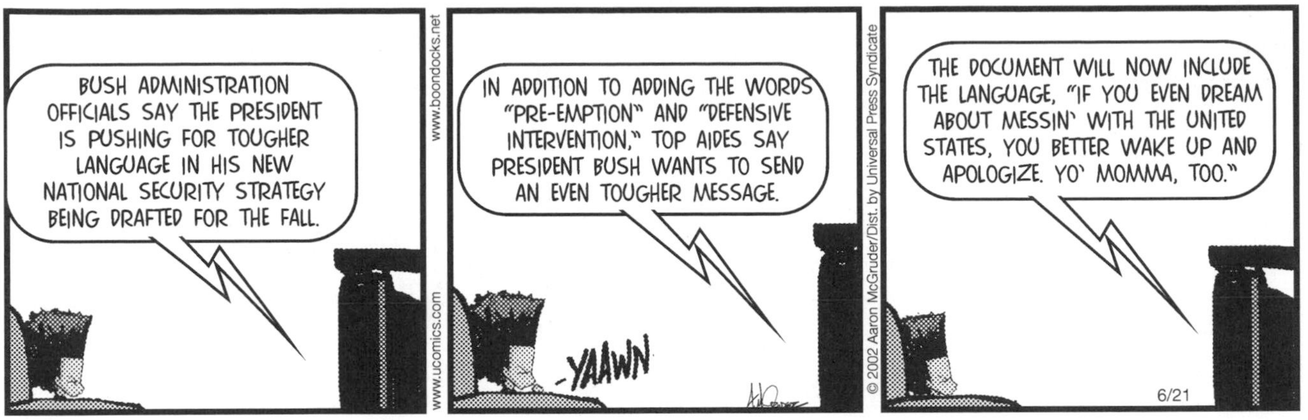
BUSH ADMINISTRATION OFFICIALS SAY THE PRESIDENT IS PUSHING FOR TOUGHER LANGUAGE IN HIS NEW NATIONAL SECURITY STRATEGY BEING DRAFTED FOR THE FALL.
www.boondocks.net
www.ucomics.com
IN ADDITION TO ADDING THE WORDS "PRE-EMPTION" AND "DEFENSIVE INTERVENTION," TOP AIDES SAY PRESIDENT BUSH WANTS TO SEND AN EVEN TOUGHER MESSAGE.
-YAAWN
© 2002 Aaron McGruder/Dist. by Universal Press Syndicate
THE DOCUMENT WILL NOW INCLUDE THE LANGUAGE, "IF YOU EVEN DREAM ABOUT MESSIN' WITH THE UNITED STATES, YOU BETTER WAKE UP AND APOLOGIZE. YO' MOMMA, TOO."
6/21

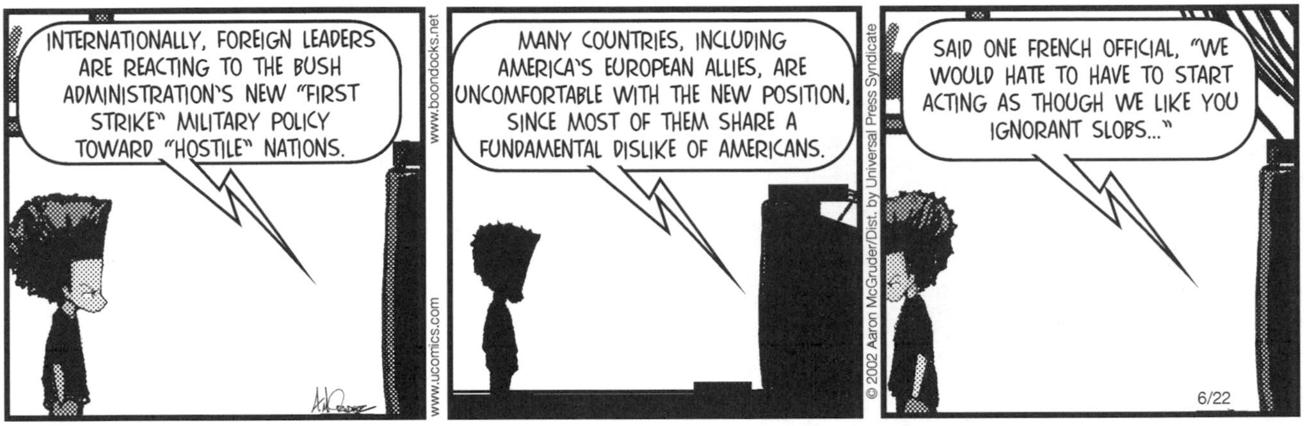
INTERNATIONALLY, FOREIGN LEADERS ARE REACTING TO THE BUSH ADMINISTRATION'S NEW "FIRST STRIKE" MILITARY POLICY TOWARD "HOSTILE" NATIONS.
www.boondocks.net
www.ucomics.com
MANY COUNTRIES, INCLUDING AMERICA'S EUROPEAN ALLIES, ARE UNCOMFORTABLE WITH THE NEW POSITION, SINCE MOST OF THEM SHARE A FUNDAMENTAL DISLIKE OF AMERICANS.
© 2002 Aaron McGruder/Dist. by Universal Press Syndicate
SAID ONE FRENCH OFFICIAL, "WE WOULD HATE TO HAVE TO START ACTING AS THOUGH WE LIKE YOU IGNORANT SLOBS..."
6/22

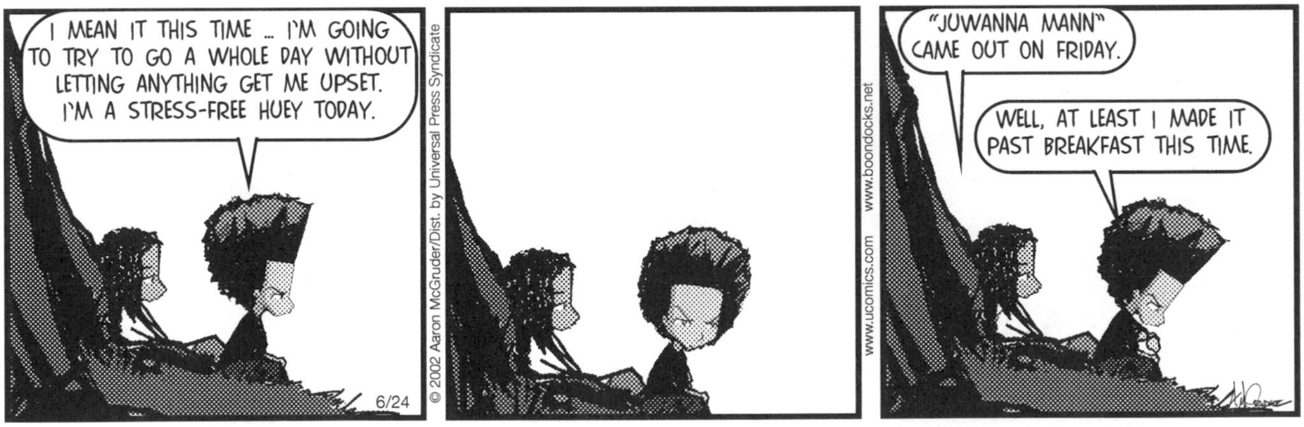
I MEAN IT THIS TIME ... I'M GOING TO TRY TO GO A WHOLE DAY WITHOUT LETTING ANYTHING GET ME UPSET. I'M A STRESS-FREE HUEY TODAY.
6/24
© 2002 Aaron McGruder/Dist. by Universal Press Syndicate
www.ucomics.com
www.boondocks.net
"JUWANNA MANN" CAME OUT ON FRIDAY.
WELL, AT LEAST I MADE IT PAST BREAKFAST THIS TIME.

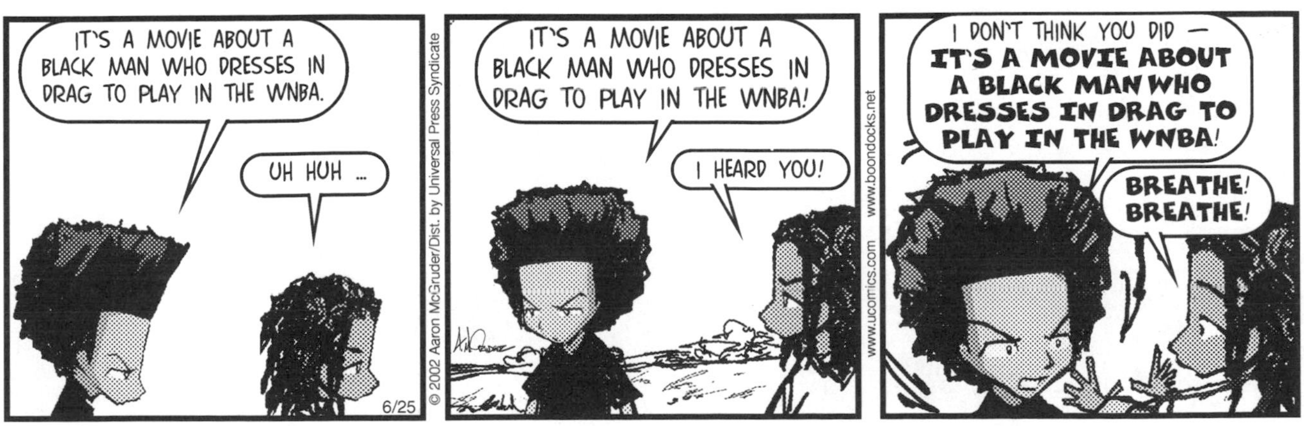
IT'S A MOVIE ABOUT A BLACK MAN WHO DRESSES IN DRAG TO PLAY IN THE WNBA.
UH HUH ...
6/25
© 2002 Aaron McGruder/Dist. by Universal Press Syndicate
IT'S A MOVIE ABOUT A BLACK MAN WHO DRESSES IN DRAG TO PLAY IN THE WNBA!
I HEARD YOU!
www.ucomics.com
www.boondocks.net
I DON'T THINK YOU DID — IT'S A MOVIE ABOUT A BLACK MAN WHO DRESSES IN DRAG TO PLAY IN THE WNBA!
BREATHE! BREATHE!

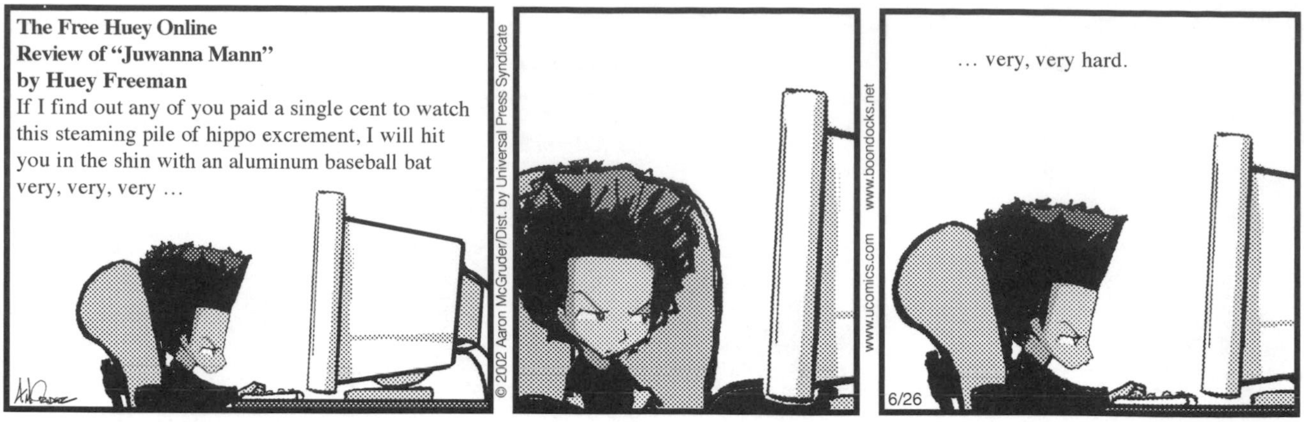
The Free Huey Online
Review of "Juwanna Mann"
by Huey Freeman
If I find out any of you paid a single cent to watch this steaming pile of hippo excrement, I will hit you in the shin with an aluminum baseball bat very, very, very …
© 2002 Aaron McGruder/Dist. by Universal Press Syndicate
… very, very hard.
www.ucomics.com www.boondocks.net
6/26

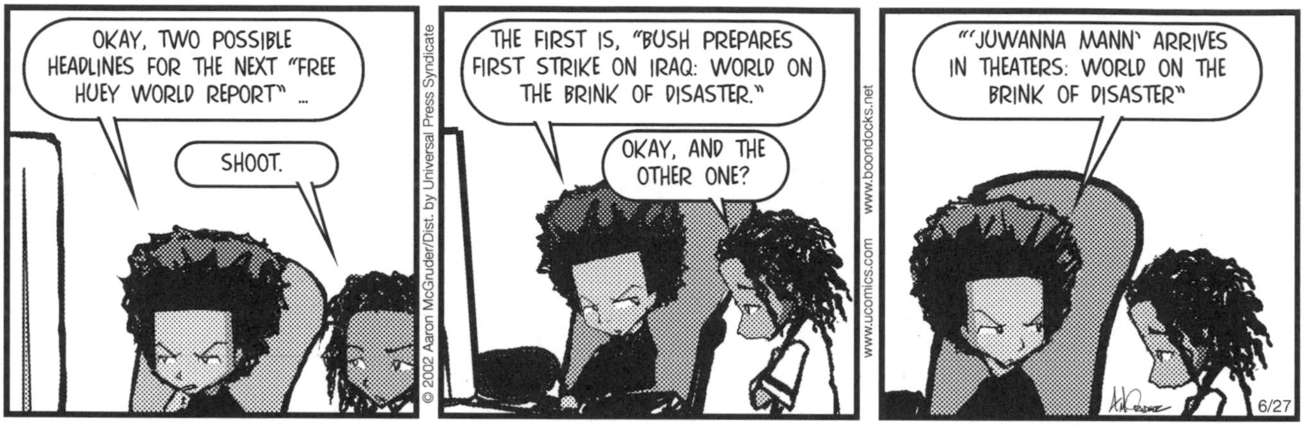
OKAY, TWO POSSIBLE HEADLINES FOR THE NEXT "FREE HUEY WORLD REPORT" …
SHOOT.
© 2002 Aaron McGruder/Dist. by Universal Press Syndicate
THE FIRST IS, "BUSH PREPARES FIRST STRIKE ON IRAQ: WORLD ON THE BRINK OF DISASTER."
OKAY, AND THE OTHER ONE?
www.ucomics.com www.boondocks.net
"'JUWANNA MANN' ARRIVES IN THEATERS: WORLD ON THE BRINK OF DISASTER"
6/27

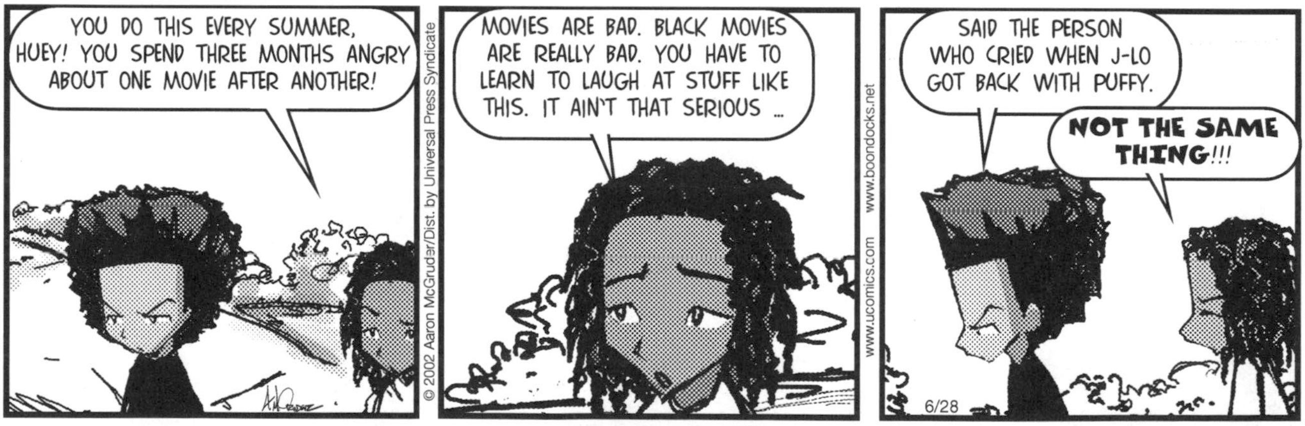
YOU DO THIS EVERY SUMMER, HUEY! YOU SPEND THREE MONTHS ANGRY ABOUT ONE MOVIE AFTER ANOTHER!
© 2002 Aaron McGruder/Dist. by Universal Press Syndicate
MOVIES ARE BAD. BLACK MOVIES ARE REALLY BAD. YOU HAVE TO LEARN TO LAUGH AT STUFF LIKE THIS. IT AIN'T THAT SERIOUS …
www.ucomics.com www.boondocks.net
SAID THE PERSON WHO CRIED WHEN J-LO GOT BACK WITH PUFFY.
NOT THE SAME THING!!!
6/28

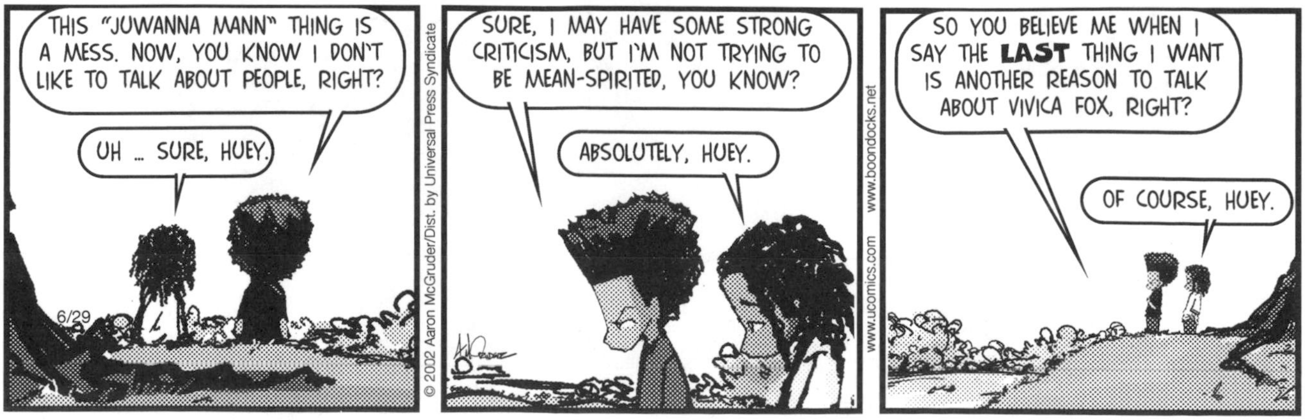
THIS "JUWANNA MANN" THING IS A MESS. NOW, YOU KNOW I DON'T LIKE TO TALK ABOUT PEOPLE, RIGHT?
UH … SURE, HUEY.
6/29
© 2002 Aaron McGruder/Dist. by Universal Press Syndicate
SURE, I MAY HAVE SOME STRONG CRITICISM, BUT I'M NOT TRYING TO BE MEAN-SPIRITED, YOU KNOW?
ABSOLUTELY, HUEY.
www.ucomics.com www.boondocks.net
SO YOU BELIEVE ME WHEN I SAY THE LAST THING I WANT IS ANOTHER REASON TO TALK ABOUT VIVICA FOX, RIGHT?
OF COURSE, HUEY.

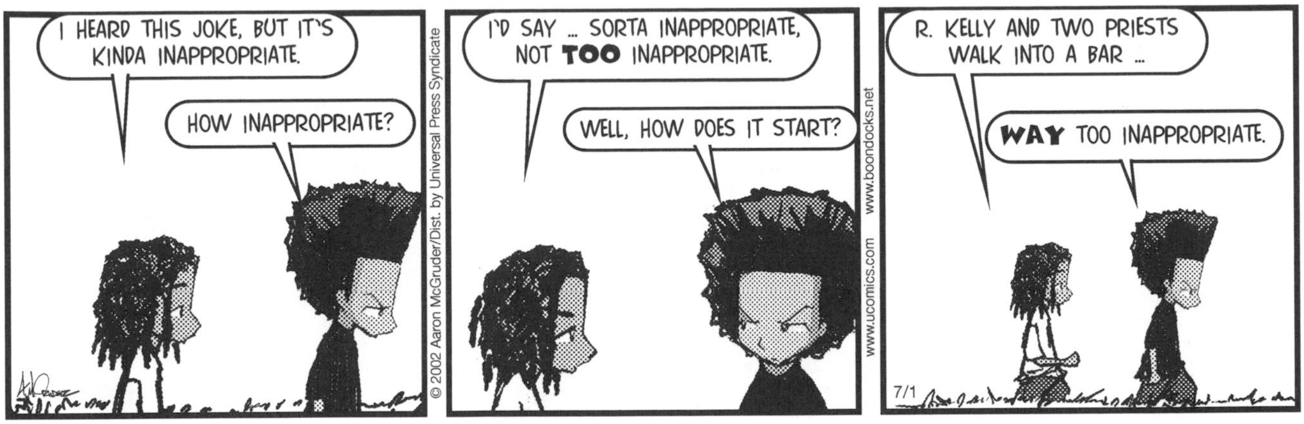
I HEARD THIS JOKE, BUT IT'S KINDA INAPPROPRIATE.
HOW INAPPROPRIATE?
I'D SAY ... SORTA INAPPROPRIATE, NOT **TOO** INAPPROPRIATE.
WELL, HOW DOES IT START?
R. KELLY AND TWO PRIESTS WALK INTO A BAR ...
WAY TOO INAPPROPRIATE.
© 2002 Aaron McGruder/Dist. by Universal Press Syndicate
www.ucomics.com
www.boondocks.net
7/1

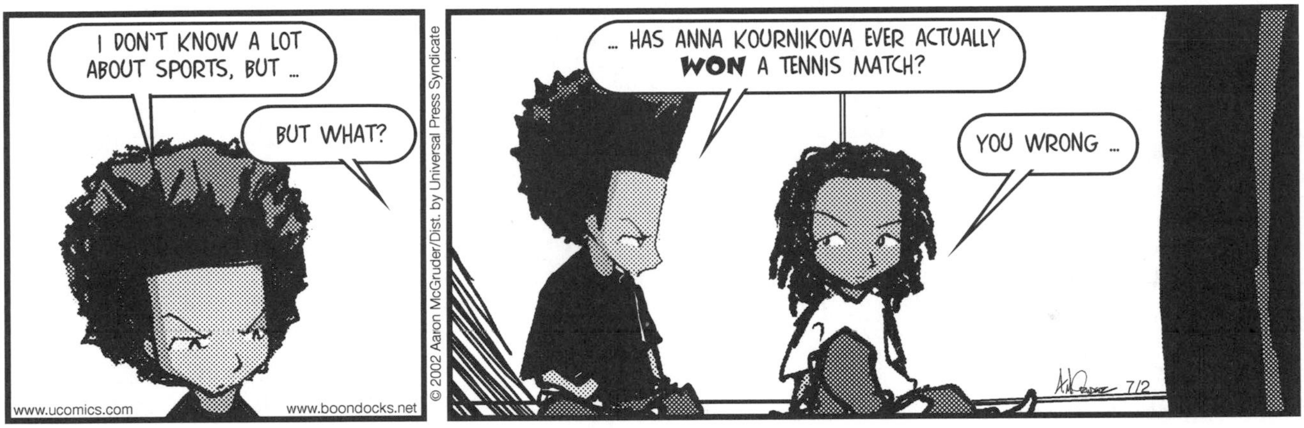
I DON'T KNOW A LOT ABOUT SPORTS, BUT ...
BUT WHAT?
... HAS ANNA KOURNIKOVA EVER ACTUALLY **WON** A TENNIS MATCH?
YOU WRONG ...
www.ucomics.com
www.boondocks.net
© 2002 Aaron McGruder/Dist. by Universal Press Syndicate
7/2

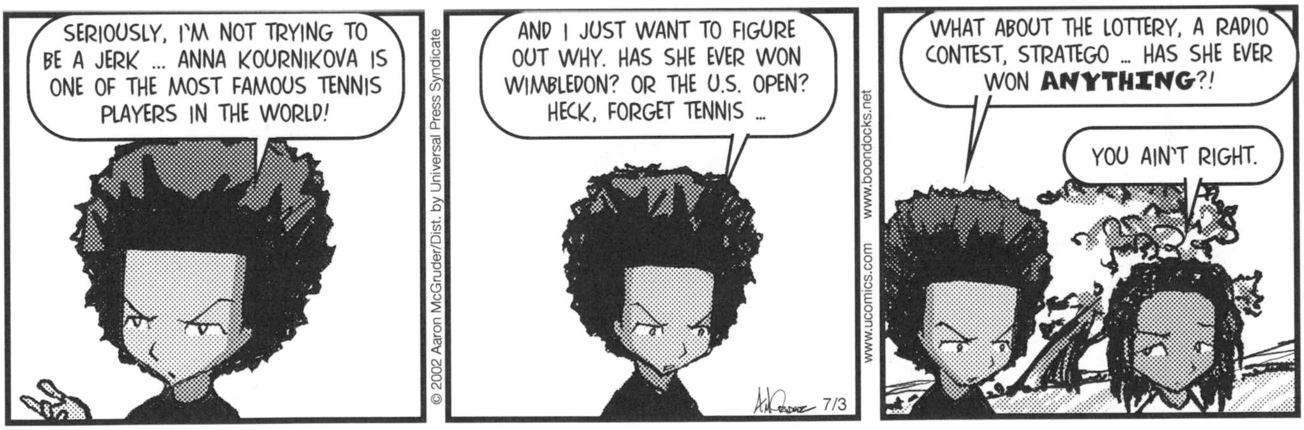
SERIOUSLY, I'M NOT TRYING TO BE A JERK ... ANNA KOURNIKOVA IS ONE OF THE MOST FAMOUS TENNIS PLAYERS IN THE WORLD!
AND I JUST WANT TO FIGURE OUT WHY. HAS SHE EVER WON WIMBLEDON? OR THE U.S. OPEN? HECK, FORGET TENNIS ...
WHAT ABOUT THE LOTTERY, A RADIO CONTEST, STRATEGO ... HAS SHE EVER WON **ANYTHING**?!
YOU AIN'T RIGHT.
© 2002 Aaron McGruder/Dist. by Universal Press Syndicate
www.ucomics.com
www.boondocks.net
7/3

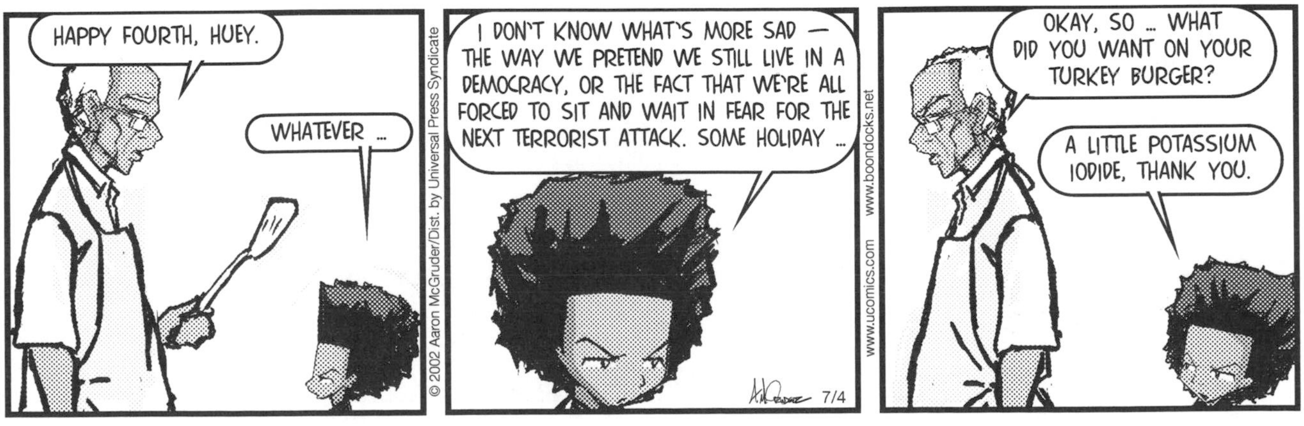
HAPPY FOURTH, HUEY.
WHATEVER ...
I DON'T KNOW WHAT'S MORE SAD — THE WAY WE PRETEND WE STILL LIVE IN A DEMOCRACY, OR THE FACT THAT WE'RE ALL FORCED TO SIT AND WAIT IN FEAR FOR THE NEXT TERRORIST ATTACK. SOME HOLIDAY ...
OKAY, SO ... WHAT DID YOU WANT ON YOUR TURKEY BURGER?
A LITTLE POTASSIUM IODIDE, THANK YOU.
© 2002 Aaron McGruder/Dist. by Universal Press Syndicate
www.ucomics.com
www.boondocks.net
7/4

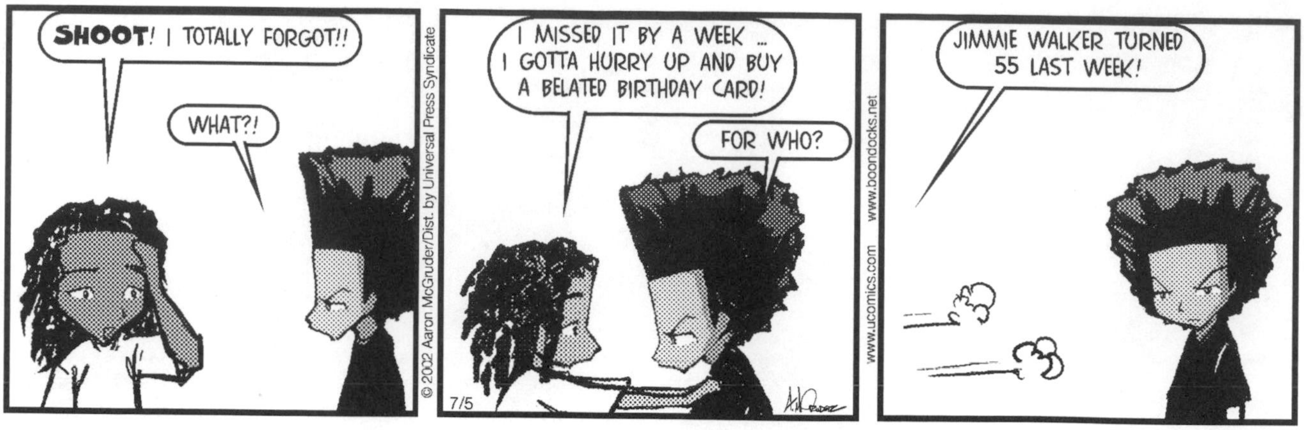
SHOOT! I TOTALLY FORGOT!!
WHAT?!
I MISSED IT BY A WEEK ... I GOTTA HURRY UP AND BUY A BELATED BIRTHDAY CARD!
FOR WHO?
JIMMIE WALKER TURNED 55 LAST WEEK!
© 2002 Aaron McGruder/Dist. by Universal Press Syndicate
7/5
www.ucomics.com www.boondocks.net

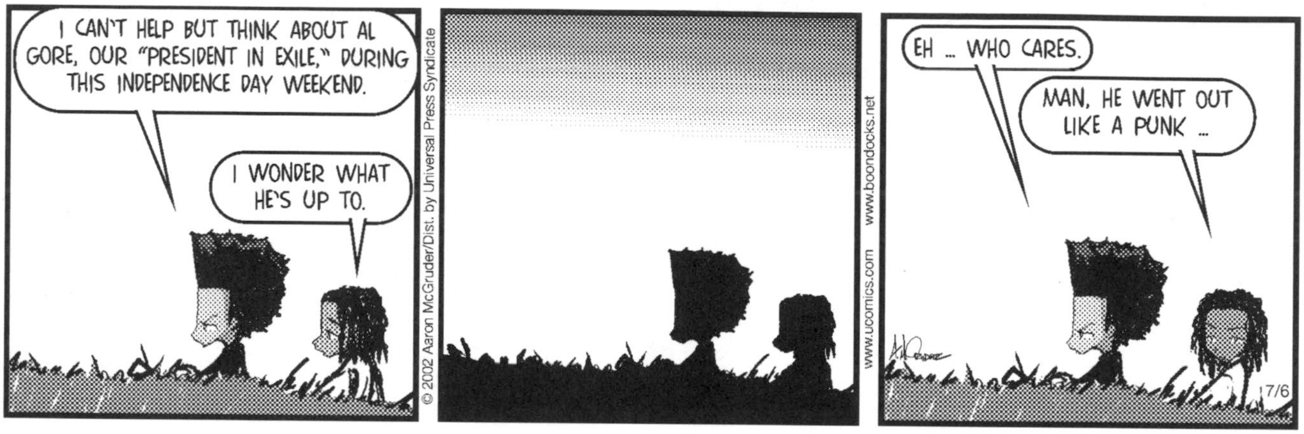
I CAN'T HELP BUT THINK ABOUT AL GORE, OUR "PRESIDENT IN EXILE," DURING THIS INDEPENDENCE DAY WEEKEND.
I WONDER WHAT HE'S UP TO.
EH ... WHO CARES.
MAN, HE WENT OUT LIKE A PUNK ...
© 2002 Aaron McGruder/Dist. by Universal Press Syndicate
www.ucomics.com www.boondocks.net
7/6

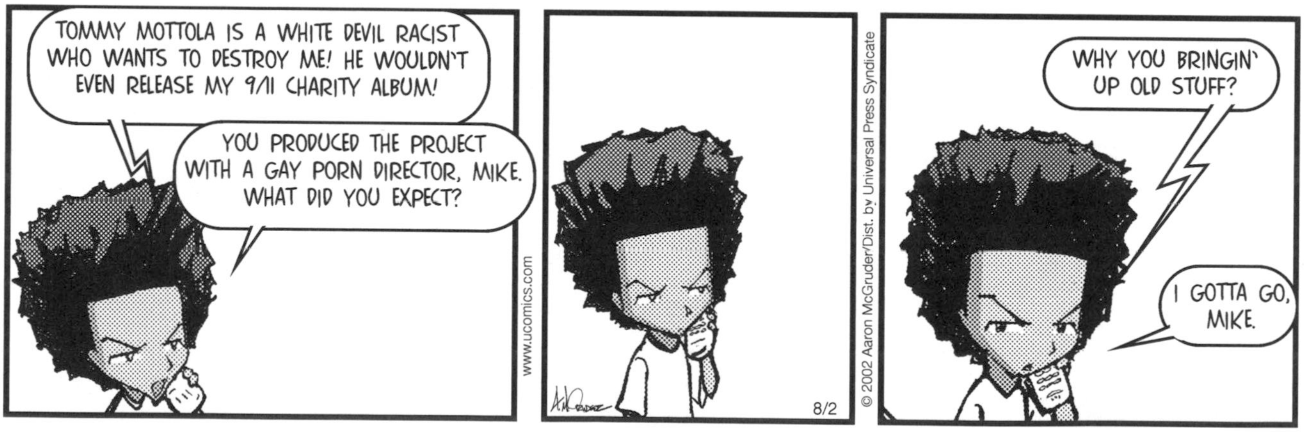
TOMMY MOTTOLA IS A WHITE DEVIL RACIST WHO WANTS TO DESTROY ME! HE WOULDN'T EVEN RELEASE MY 9/11 CHARITY ALBUM!
YOU PRODUCED THE PROJECT WITH A GAY PORN DIRECTOR, MIKE. WHAT DID YOU EXPECT?
WHY YOU BRINGIN' UP OLD STUFF?
I GOTTA GO, MIKE.
www.ucomics.com
8/2
© 2002 Aaron McGruder/Dist. by Universal Press Syndicate

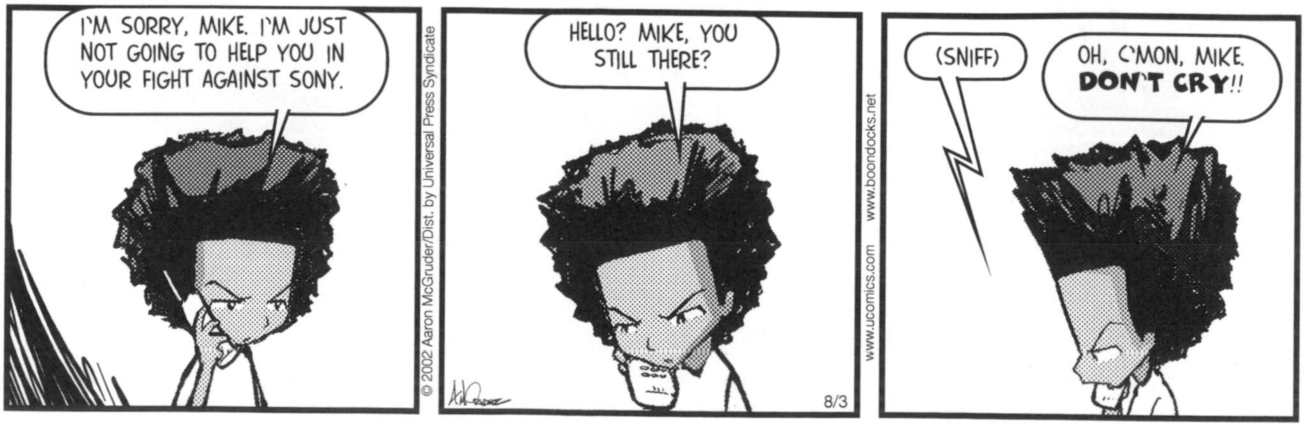
I'M SORRY, MIKE. I'M JUST NOT GOING TO HELP YOU IN YOUR FIGHT AGAINST SONY.
HELLO? MIKE, YOU STILL THERE?
(SNIFF)
OH, C'MON, MIKE. DON'T CRY!!
© 2002 Aaron McGruder/Dist. by Universal Press Syndicate
8/3
www.ucomics.com www.boondocks.net

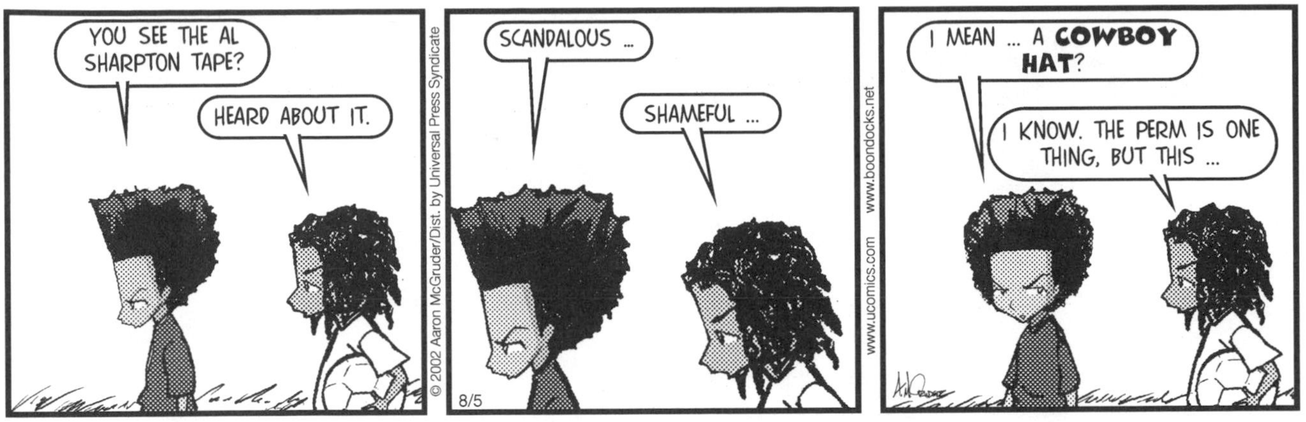
YOU SEE THE AL SHARPTON TAPE?
HEARD ABOUT IT.
© 2002 Aaron McGruder/Dist. by Universal Press Syndicate
SCANDALOUS ...
SHAMEFUL ...
8/5
I MEAN ... A COWBOY HAT?
I KNOW. THE PERM IS ONE THING, BUT THIS ...
www.ucomics.com www.boondocks.net

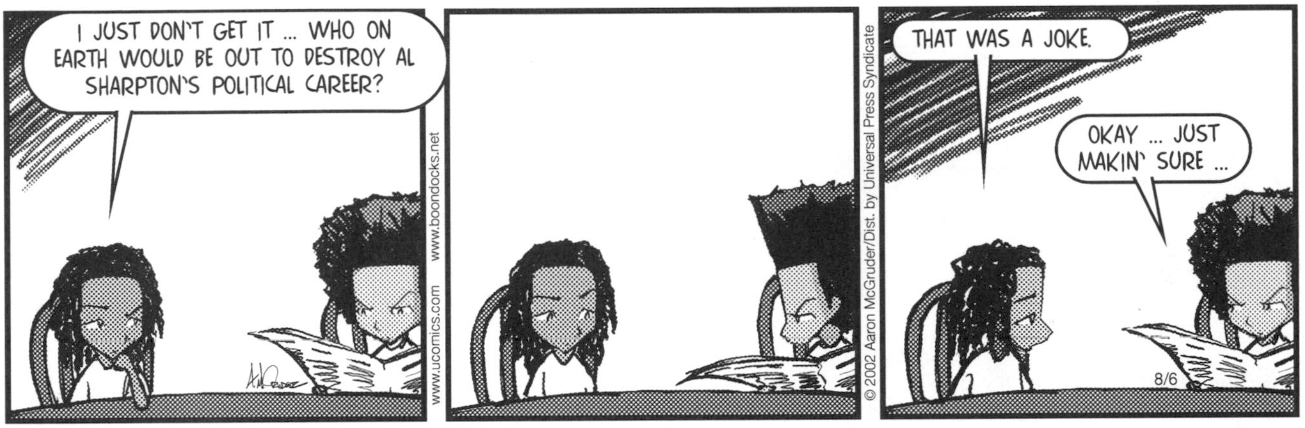
I JUST DON'T GET IT ... WHO ON EARTH WOULD BE OUT TO DESTROY AL SHARPTON'S POLITICAL CAREER?
www.ucomics.com www.boondocks.net
© 2002 Aaron McGruder/Dist. by Universal Press Syndicate
THAT WAS A JOKE.
OKAY ... JUST MAKIN' SURE ...
8/6

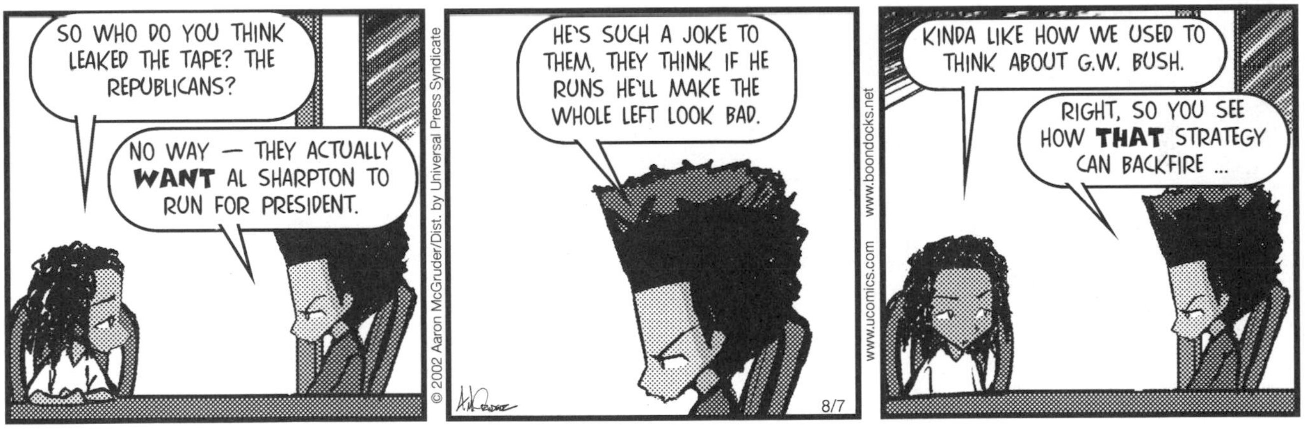
SO WHO DO YOU THINK LEAKED THE TAPE? THE REPUBLICANS?
NO WAY — THEY ACTUALLY WANT AL SHARPTON TO RUN FOR PRESIDENT.
© 2002 Aaron McGruder/Dist. by Universal Press Syndicate
HE'S SUCH A JOKE TO THEM, THEY THINK IF HE RUNS HE'LL MAKE THE WHOLE LEFT LOOK BAD.
8/7
www.ucomics.com www.boondocks.net
KINDA LIKE HOW WE USED TO THINK ABOUT G.W. BUSH.
RIGHT, SO YOU SEE HOW THAT STRATEGY CAN BACKFIRE ...

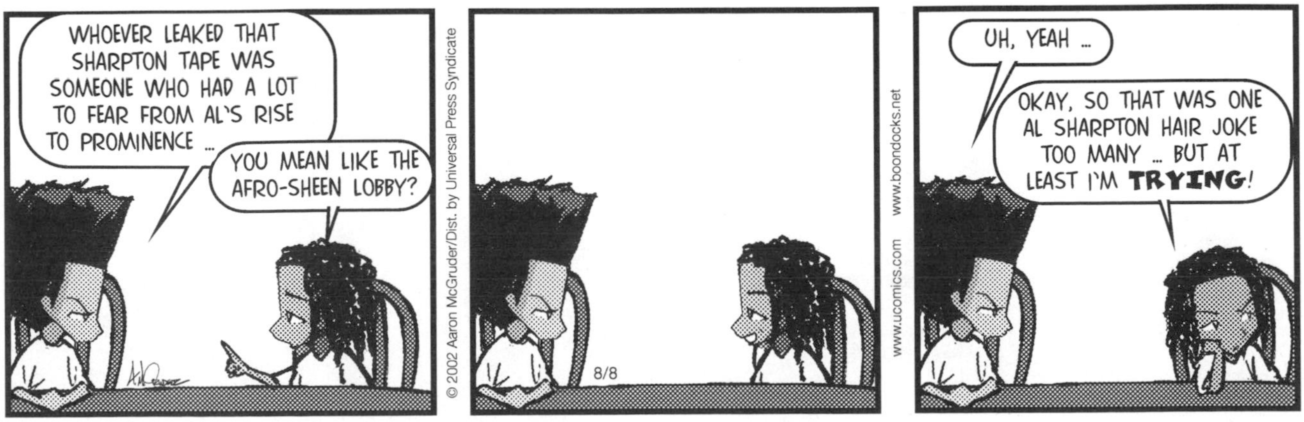
WHOEVER LEAKED THAT SHARPTON TAPE WAS SOMEONE WHO HAD A LOT TO FEAR FROM AL'S RISE TO PROMINENCE ...
YOU MEAN LIKE THE AFRO-SHEEN LOBBY?
© 2002 Aaron McGruder/Dist. by Universal Press Syndicate
8/8
www.ucomics.com www.boondocks.net
UH, YEAH ...
OKAY, SO THAT WAS ONE AL SHARPTON HAIR JOKE TOO MANY ... BUT AT LEAST I'M TRYING!

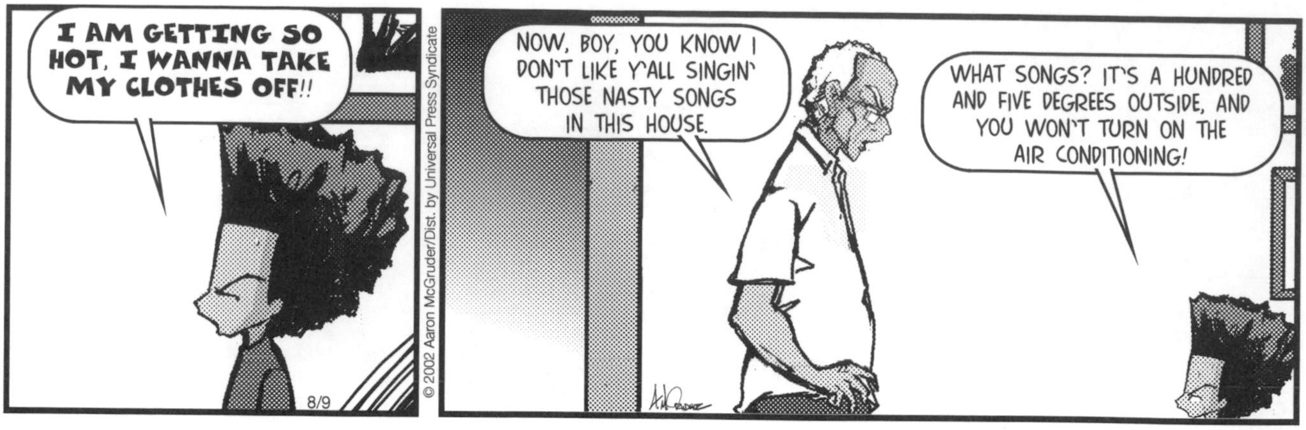
I AM GETTING SO HOT, I WANNA TAKE MY CLOTHES OFF!!
8/9
© 2002 Aaron McGruder/Dist. by Universal Press Syndicate
NOW, BOY, YOU KNOW I DON'T LIKE Y'ALL SINGIN' THOSE NASTY SONGS IN THIS HOUSE.
WHAT SONGS? IT'S A HUNDRED AND FIVE DEGREES OUTSIDE, AND YOU WON'T TURN ON THE AIR CONDITIONING!

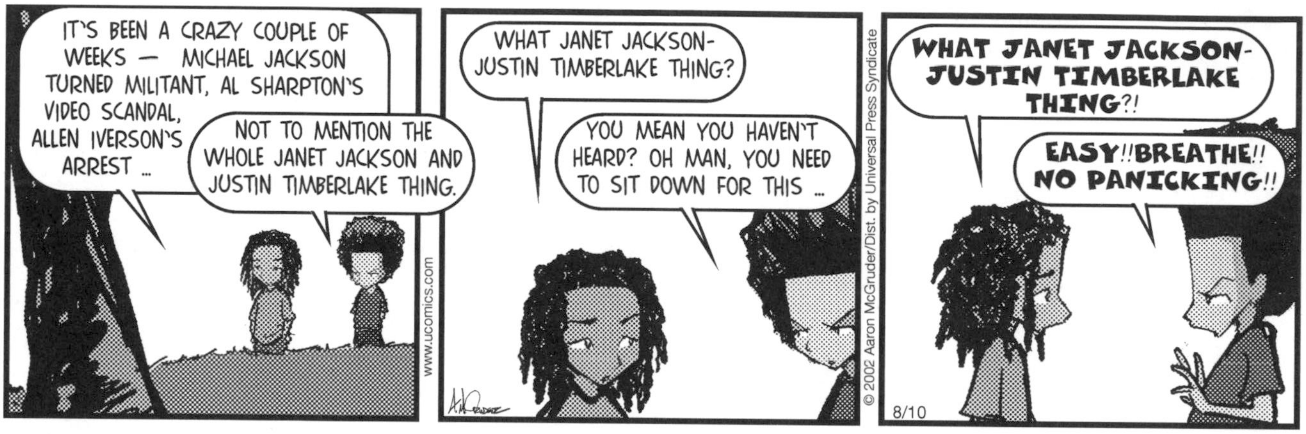
IT'S BEEN A CRAZY COUPLE OF WEEKS — MICHAEL JACKSON TURNED MILITANT, AL SHARPTON'S VIDEO SCANDAL, ALLEN IVERSON'S ARREST ...
NOT TO MENTION THE WHOLE JANET JACKSON AND JUSTIN TIMBERLAKE THING.
www.ucomics.com
WHAT JANET JACKSON-JUSTIN TIMBERLAKE THING?
YOU MEAN YOU HAVEN'T HEARD? OH MAN, YOU NEED TO SIT DOWN FOR THIS ...
© 2002 Aaron McGruder/Dist. by Universal Press Syndicate
WHAT JANET JACKSON-JUSTIN TIMBERLAKE THING?!
EASY!! BREATHE!! NO PANICKING!!
8/10

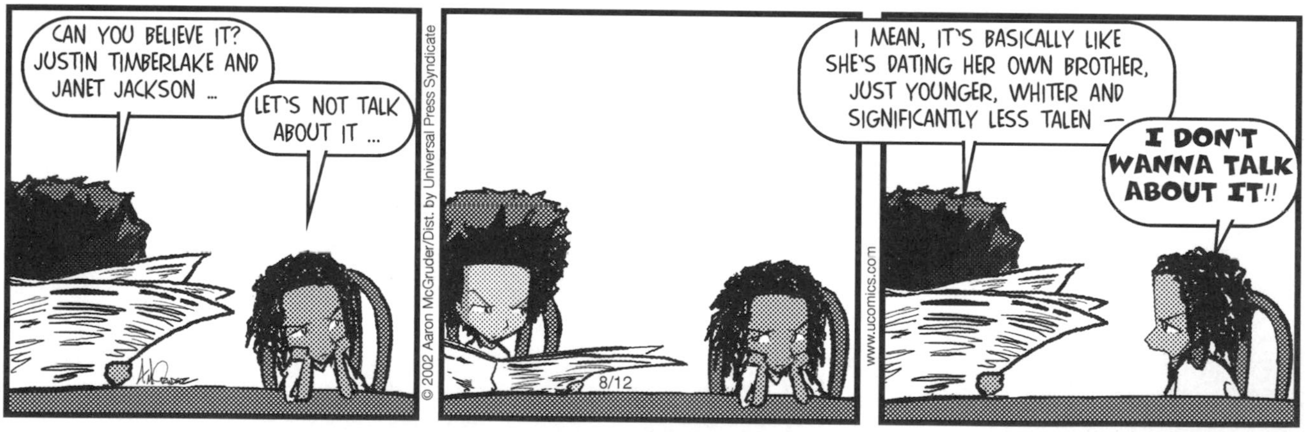
CAN YOU BELIEVE IT? JUSTIN TIMBERLAKE AND JANET JACKSON ...
LET'S NOT TALK ABOUT IT ...
© 2002 Aaron McGruder/Dist. by Universal Press Syndicate
8/12
www.ucomics.com
I MEAN, IT'S BASICALLY LIKE SHE'S DATING HER OWN BROTHER, JUST YOUNGER, WHITER AND SIGNIFICANTLY LESS TALEN —
I DON'T WANNA TALK ABOUT IT!!

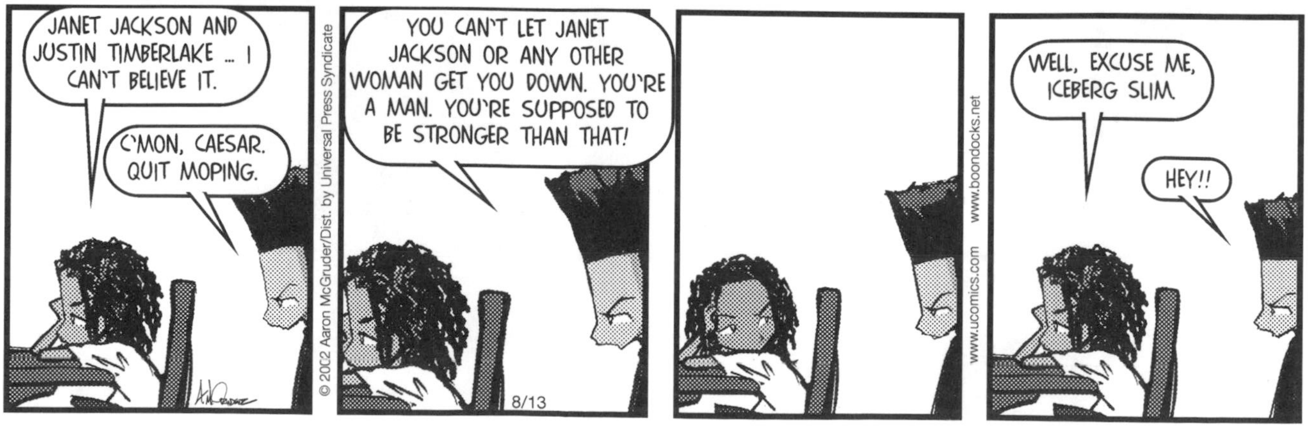
JANET JACKSON AND JUSTIN TIMBERLAKE ... I CAN'T BELIEVE IT.
C'MON, CAESAR. QUIT MOPING.
© 2002 Aaron McGruder/Dist. by Universal Press Syndicate
YOU CAN'T LET JANET JACKSON OR ANY OTHER WOMAN GET YOU DOWN. YOU'RE A MAN. YOU'RE SUPPOSED TO BE STRONGER THAN THAT!
8/13
www.ucomics.com
www.boondocks.net
WELL, EXCUSE ME, ICEBERG SLIM.
HEY!!

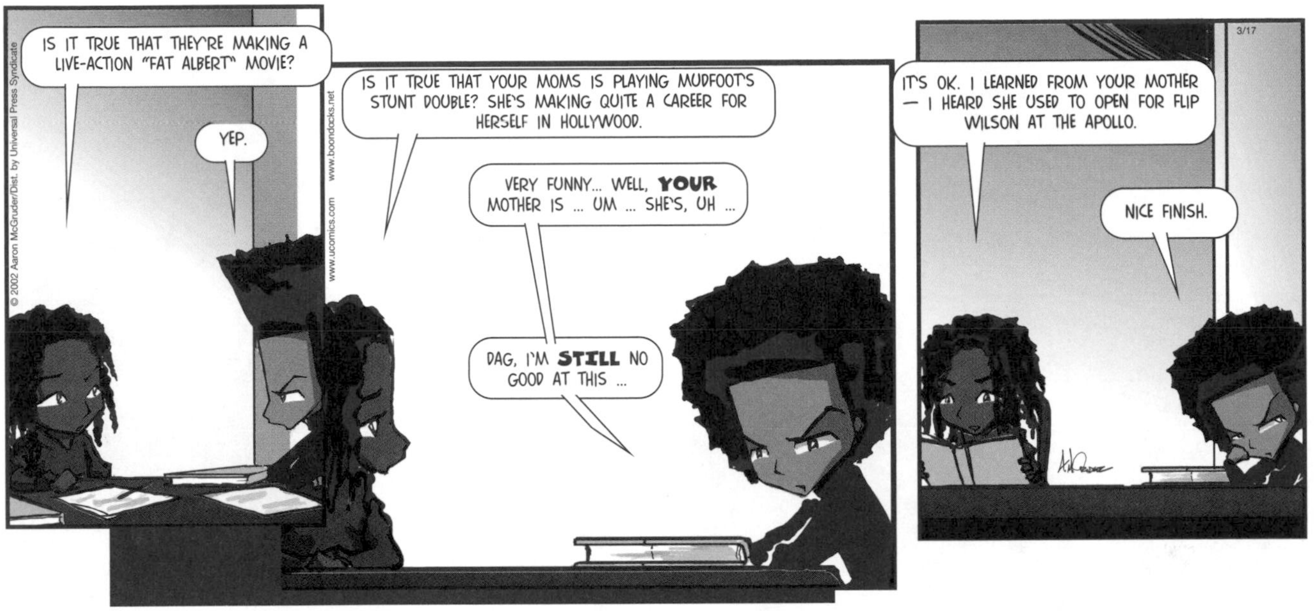

© 2002 Aaron McGruder/Dist. by Universal Press Syndicate
IS IT TRUE THAT THEY'RE MAKING A LIVE-ACTION "FAT ALBERT" MOVIE?
YEP.
www.ucomics.com www.boondocks.net
IS IT TRUE THAT YOUR MOMS IS PLAYING MUDFOOT'S STUNT DOUBLE? SHE'S MAKING QUITE A CAREER FOR HERSELF IN HOLLYWOOD.
VERY FUNNY... WELL, YOUR MOTHER IS ... UM ... SHE'S, UH ...
DAG, I'M STILL NO GOOD AT THIS ...
3/17
IT'S OK. I LEARNED FROM YOUR MOTHER — I HEARD SHE USED TO OPEN FOR FLIP WILSON AT THE APOLLO.
NICE FINISH.

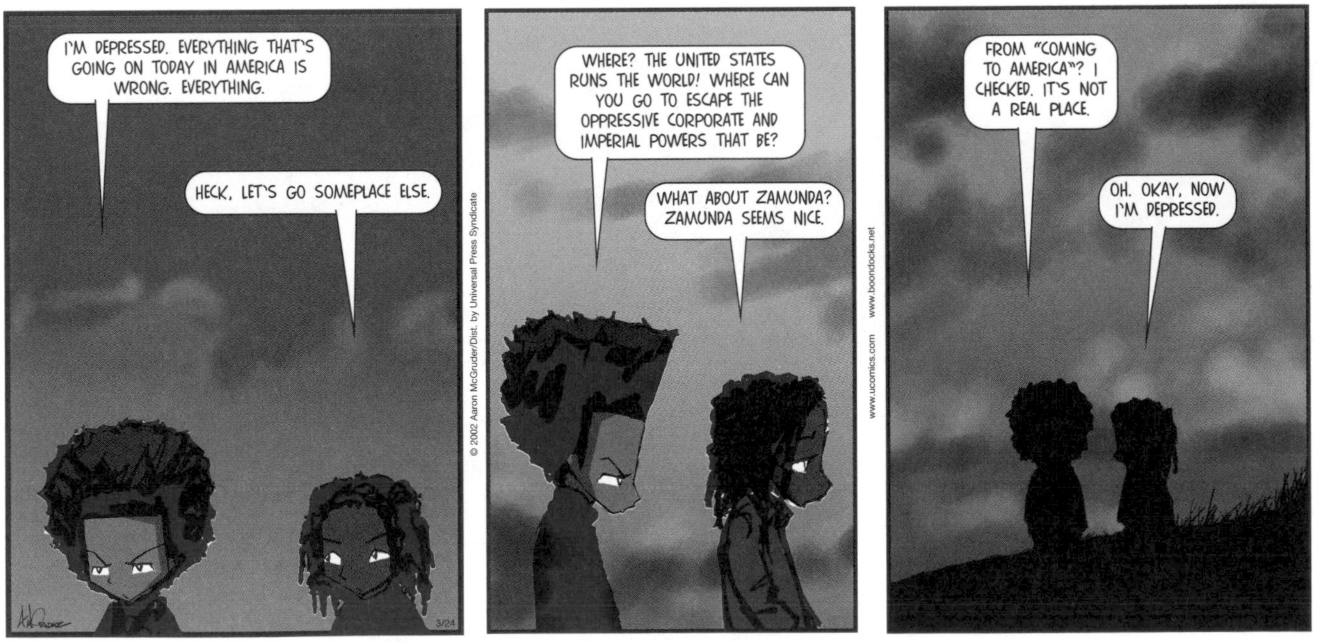

I'M DEPRESSED. EVERYTHING THAT'S GOING ON TODAY IN AMERICA IS WRONG. EVERYTHING.
HECK, LET'S GO SOMEPLACE ELSE.
3/24
© 2002 Aaron McGruder/Dist. by Universal Press Syndicate
WHERE? THE UNITED STATES RUNS THE WORLD! WHERE CAN YOU GO TO ESCAPE THE OPPRESSIVE CORPORATE AND IMPERIAL POWERS THAT BE?
WHAT ABOUT ZAMUNDA? ZAMUNDA SEEMS NICE.
www.ucomics.com www.boondocks.net
FROM "COMING TO AMERICA"? I CHECKED. IT'S NOT A REAL PLACE.
OH. OKAY, NOW I'M DEPRESSED.

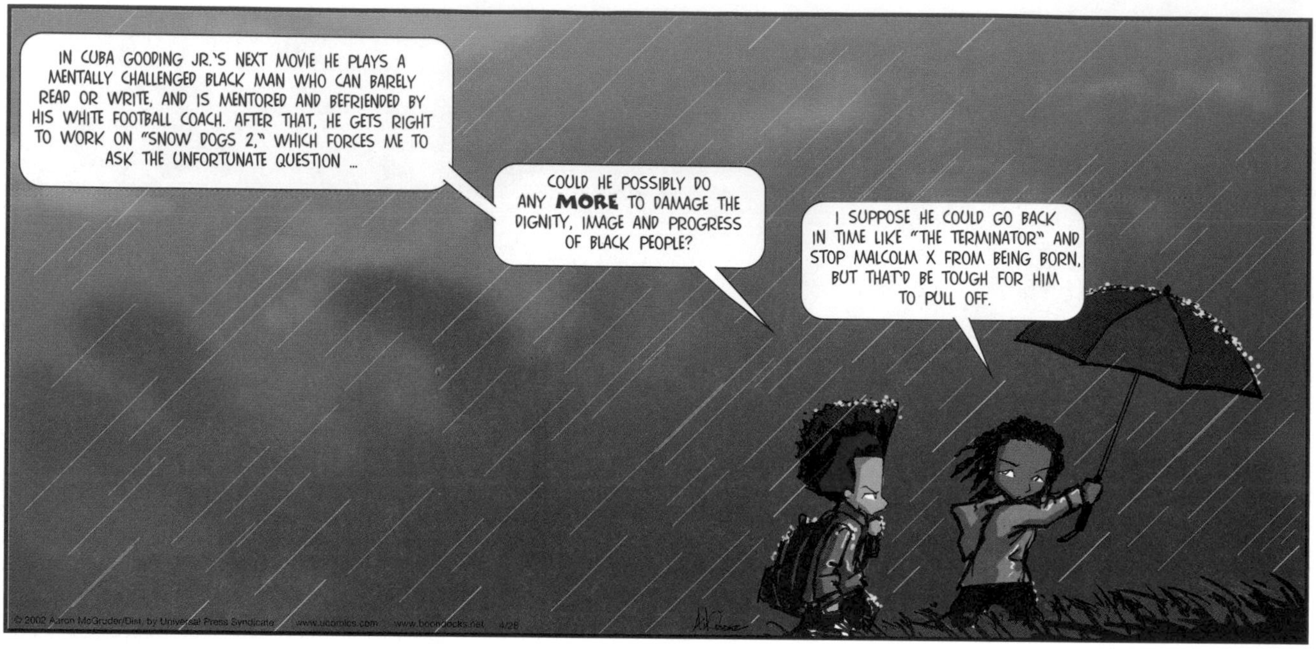
IN CUBA GOODING JR.'S NEXT MOVIE HE PLAYS A MENTALLY CHALLENGED BLACK MAN WHO CAN BARELY READ OR WRITE, AND IS MENTORED AND BEFRIENDED BY HIS WHITE FOOTBALL COACH. AFTER THAT, HE GETS RIGHT TO WORK ON "SNOW DOGS 2," WHICH FORCES ME TO ASK THE UNFORTUNATE QUESTION ...
COULD HE POSSIBLY DO ANY **MORE** TO DAMAGE THE DIGNITY, IMAGE AND PROGRESS OF BLACK PEOPLE?
I SUPPOSE HE COULD GO BACK IN TIME LIKE "THE TERMINATOR" AND STOP MALCOLM X FROM BEING BORN, BUT THAT'D BE TOUGH FOR HIM TO PULL OFF.
© 2002 Aaron McGruder/Dist. by Universal Press Syndicate www.ucomics.com www.boondocks.net 4/26

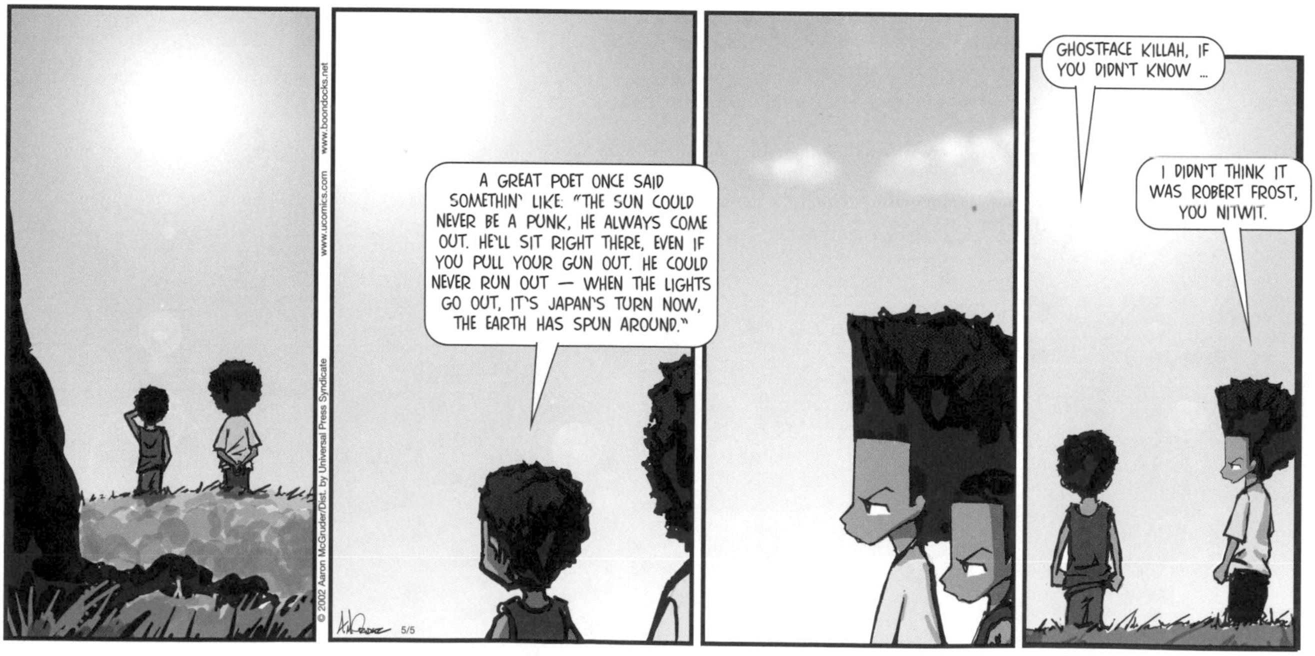
© 2002 Aaron McGruder/Dist. by Universal Press Syndicate www.ucomics.com www.boondocks.net
A GREAT POET ONCE SAID SOMETHIN' LIKE: "THE SUN COULD NEVER BE A PUNK, HE ALWAYS COME OUT. HE'LL SIT RIGHT THERE, EVEN IF YOU PULL YOUR GUN OUT. HE COULD NEVER RUN OUT — WHEN THE LIGHTS GO OUT, IT'S JAPAN'S TURN NOW, THE EARTH HAS SPUN AROUND."
5/5
GHOSTFACE KILLAH, IF YOU DIDN'T KNOW ...
I DIDN'T THINK IT WAS ROBERT FROST, YOU NITWIT.

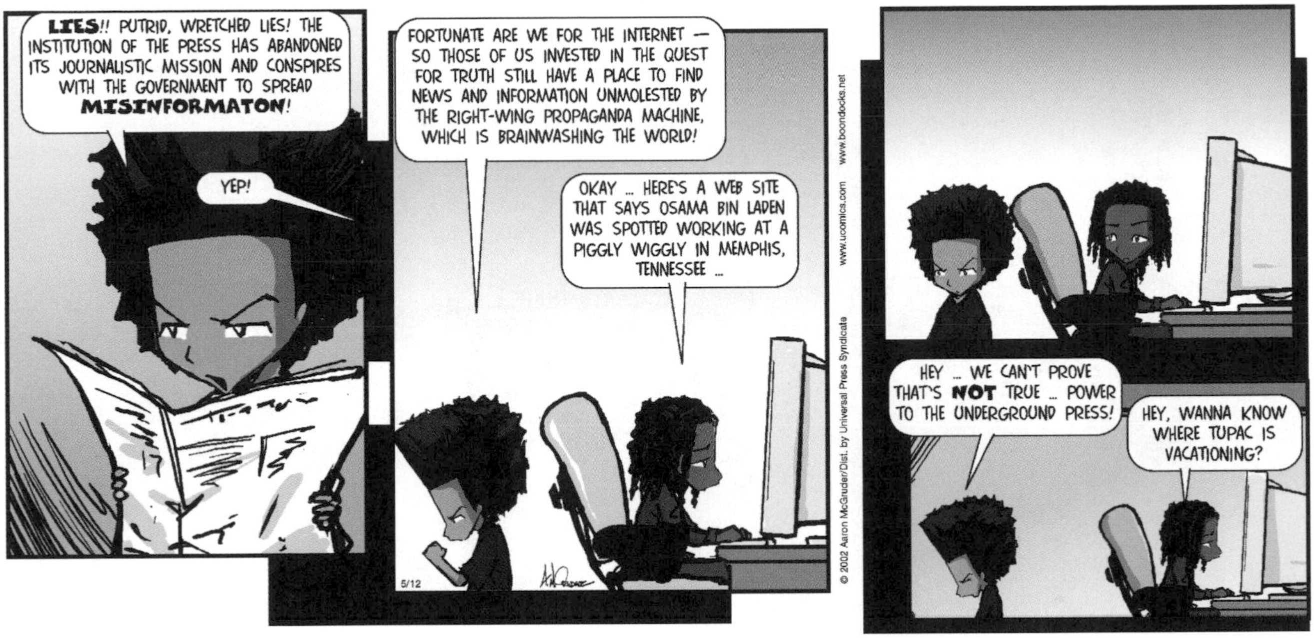
LIES!! PUTRID, WRETCHED LIES! THE INSTITUTION OF THE PRESS HAS ABANDONED ITS JOURNALISTIC MISSION AND CONSPIRES WITH THE GOVERNMENT TO SPREAD MISINFORMATON!
YEP!
FORTUNATE ARE WE FOR THE INTERNET — SO THOSE OF US INVESTED IN THE QUEST FOR TRUTH STILL HAVE A PLACE TO FIND NEWS AND INFORMATION UNMOLESTED BY THE RIGHT-WING PROPAGANDA MACHINE, WHICH IS BRAINWASHING THE WORLD!
OKAY ... HERE'S A WEB SITE THAT SAYS OSAMA BIN LADEN WAS SPOTTED WORKING AT A PIGGLY WIGGLY IN MEMPHIS, TENNESSEE ...
5/12
© 2002 Aaron McGruder/Dist. by Universal Press Syndicate www.ucomics.com www.boondocks.net
HEY ... WE CAN'T PROVE THAT'S NOT TRUE ... POWER TO THE UNDERGROUND PRESS!
HEY, WANNA KNOW WHERE TUPAC IS VACATIONING?

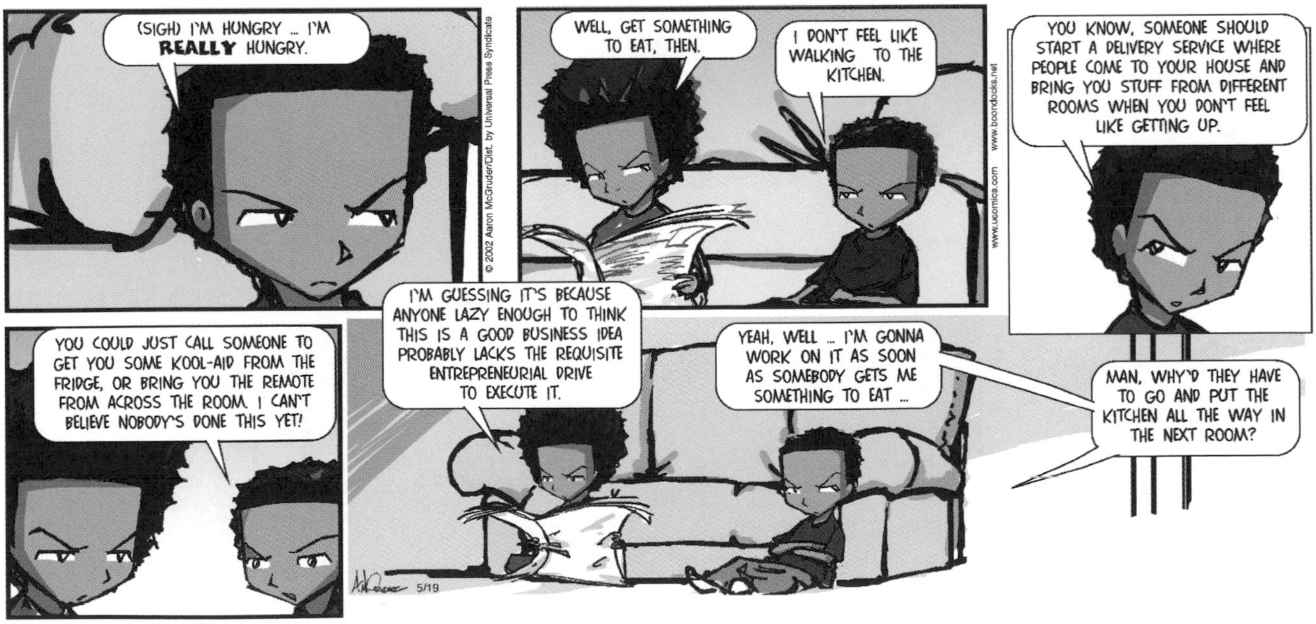
(SIGH) I'M HUNGRY ... I'M REALLY HUNGRY.
© 2002 Aaron McGruder/Dist. by Universal Press Syndicate
WELL, GET SOMETHING TO EAT, THEN.
I DON'T FEEL LIKE WALKING TO THE KITCHEN.
www.ucomics.com www.boondocks.net
YOU KNOW, SOMEONE SHOULD START A DELIVERY SERVICE WHERE PEOPLE COME TO YOUR HOUSE AND BRING YOU STUFF FROM DIFFERENT ROOMS WHEN YOU DON'T FEEL LIKE GETTING UP.
YOU COULD JUST CALL SOMEONE TO GET YOU SOME KOOL-AID FROM THE FRIDGE, OR BRING YOU THE REMOTE FROM ACROSS THE ROOM. I CAN'T BELIEVE NOBODY'S DONE THIS YET!
I'M GUESSING IT'S BECAUSE ANYONE LAZY ENOUGH TO THINK THIS IS A GOOD BUSINESS IDEA PROBABLY LACKS THE REQUISITE ENTREPRENEURIAL DRIVE TO EXECUTE IT.
YEAH, WELL ... I'M GONNA WORK ON IT AS SOON AS SOMEBODY GETS ME SOMETHING TO EAT ...
MAN, WHY'D THEY HAVE TO GO AND PUT THE KITCHEN ALL THE WAY IN THE NEXT ROOM?
5/19

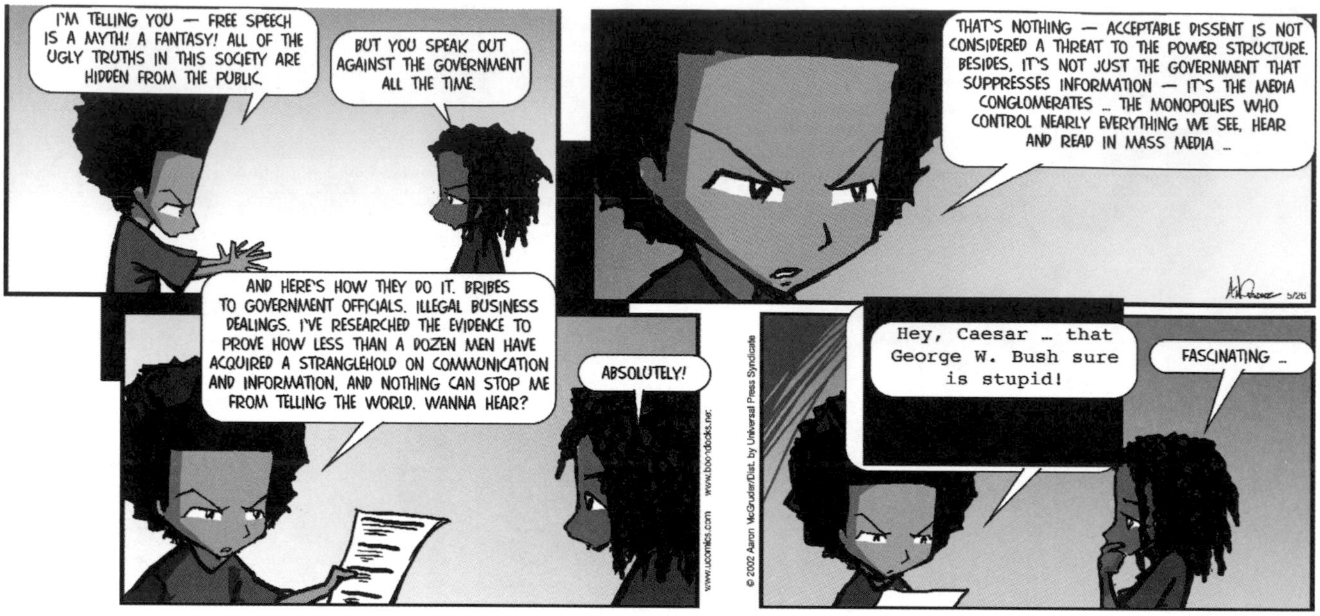
I'M TELLING YOU — FREE SPEECH IS A MYTH! A FANTASY! ALL OF THE UGLY TRUTHS IN THIS SOCIETY ARE HIDDEN FROM THE PUBLIC.
BUT YOU SPEAK OUT AGAINST THE GOVERNMENT ALL THE TIME.
THAT'S NOTHING — ACCEPTABLE DISSENT IS NOT CONSIDERED A THREAT TO THE POWER STRUCTURE. BESIDES, IT'S NOT JUST THE GOVERNMENT THAT SUPPRESSES INFORMATION — IT'S THE MEDIA CONGLOMERATES … THE MONOPOLIES WHO CONTROL NEARLY EVERYTHING WE SEE, HEAR AND READ IN MASS MEDIA …
AND HERE'S HOW THEY DO IT. BRIBES TO GOVERNMENT OFFICIALS. ILLEGAL BUSINESS DEALINGS. I'VE RESEARCHED THE EVIDENCE TO PROVE HOW LESS THAN A DOZEN MEN HAVE ACQUIRED A STRANGLEHOLD ON COMMUNICATION AND INFORMATION, AND NOTHING CAN STOP ME FROM TELLING THE WORLD. WANNA HEAR?
ABSOLUTELY!
Hey, Caesar … that George W. Bush sure is stupid!
FASCINATING …
www.ucomics.com www.boondocks.net
© 2002 Aaron McGruder/Dist. by Universal Press Syndicate

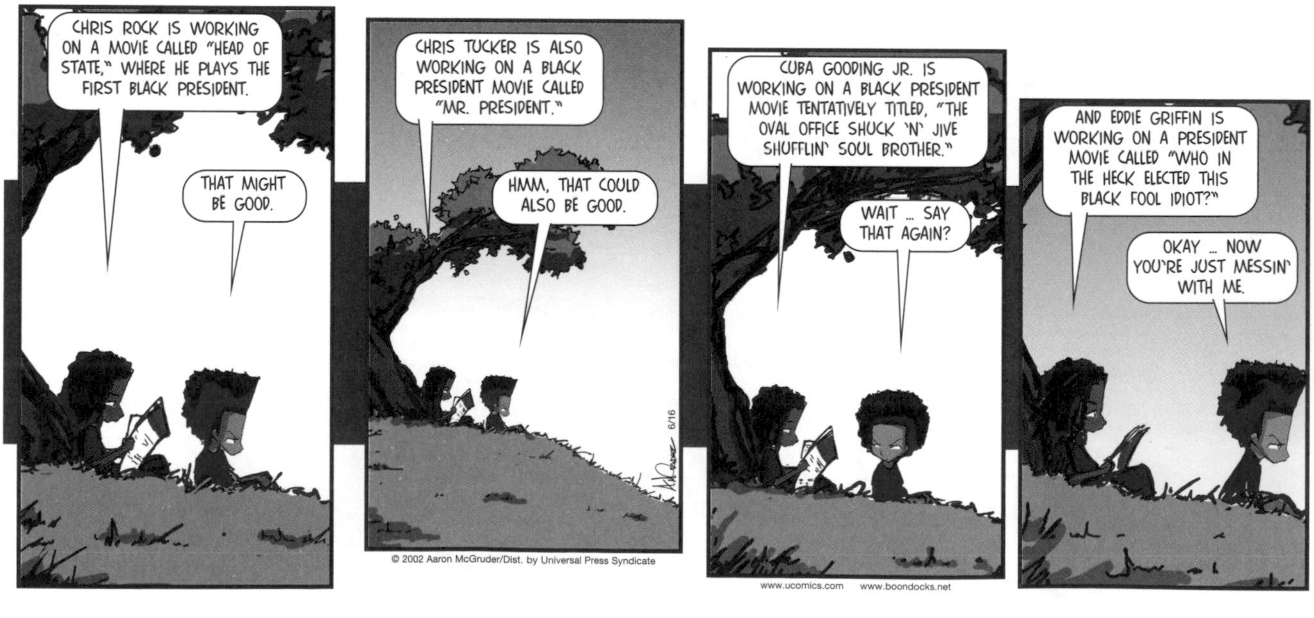
CHRIS ROCK IS WORKING ON A MOVIE CALLED "HEAD OF STATE," WHERE HE PLAYS THE FIRST BLACK PRESIDENT.
THAT MIGHT BE GOOD.
CHRIS TUCKER IS ALSO WORKING ON A BLACK PRESIDENT MOVIE CALLED "MR. PRESIDENT."
HMM, THAT COULD ALSO BE GOOD.
CUBA GOODING JR. IS WORKING ON A BLACK PRESIDENT MOVIE TENTATIVELY TITLED, "THE OVAL OFFICE SHUCK 'N' JIVE SHUFFLIN' SOUL BROTHER."
WAIT … SAY THAT AGAIN?
AND EDDIE GRIFFIN IS WORKING ON A PRESIDENT MOVIE CALLED "WHO IN THE HECK ELECTED THIS BLACK FOOL IDIOT?"
OKAY … NOW YOU'RE JUST MESSIN' WITH ME.
© 2002 Aaron McGruder/Dist. by Universal Press Syndicate
www.ucomics.com www.boondocks.net

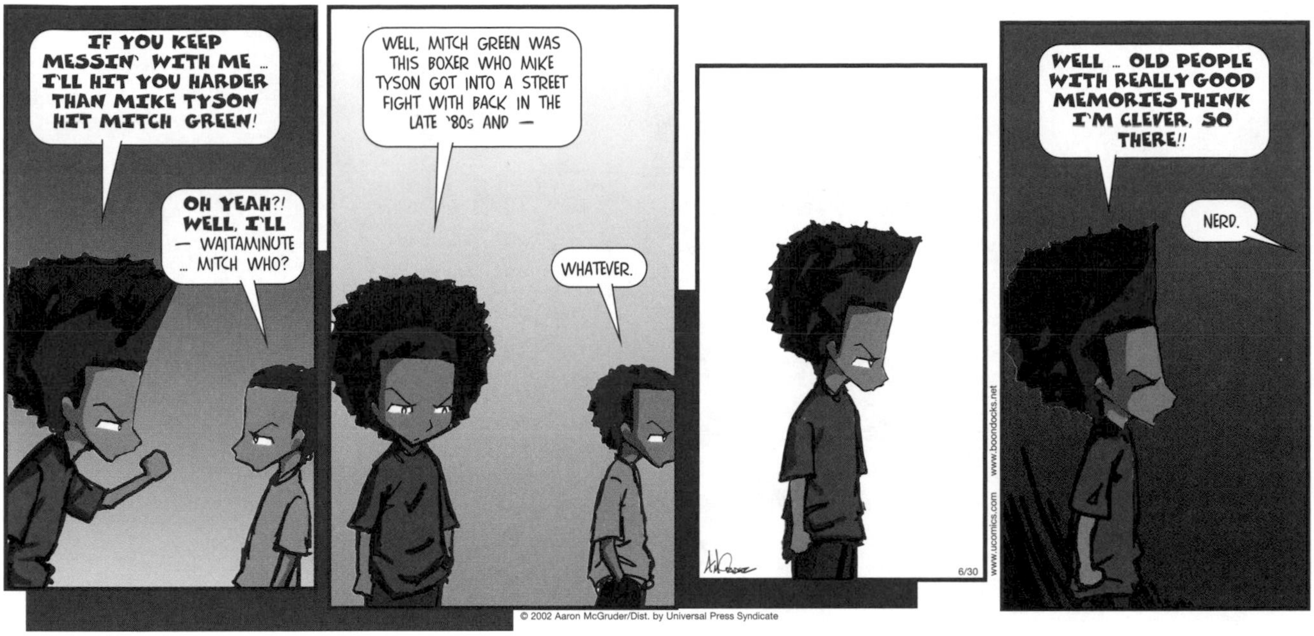
IF YOU KEEP MESSIN' WITH ME ... I'LL HIT YOU HARDER THAN MIKE TYSON HIT MITCH GREEN!
OH YEAH?! WELL, I'LL — WAITAMINUTE ... MITCH WHO?
WELL, MITCH GREEN WAS THIS BOXER WHO MIKE TYSON GOT INTO A STREET FIGHT WITH BACK IN THE LATE '80s AND —
WHATEVER.
WELL ... OLD PEOPLE WITH REALLY GOOD MEMORIES THINK I'M CLEVER, SO THERE!!
NERD.
6/30
www.ucomics.com www.boondocks.net
© 2002 Aaron McGruder/Dist. by Universal Press Syndicate

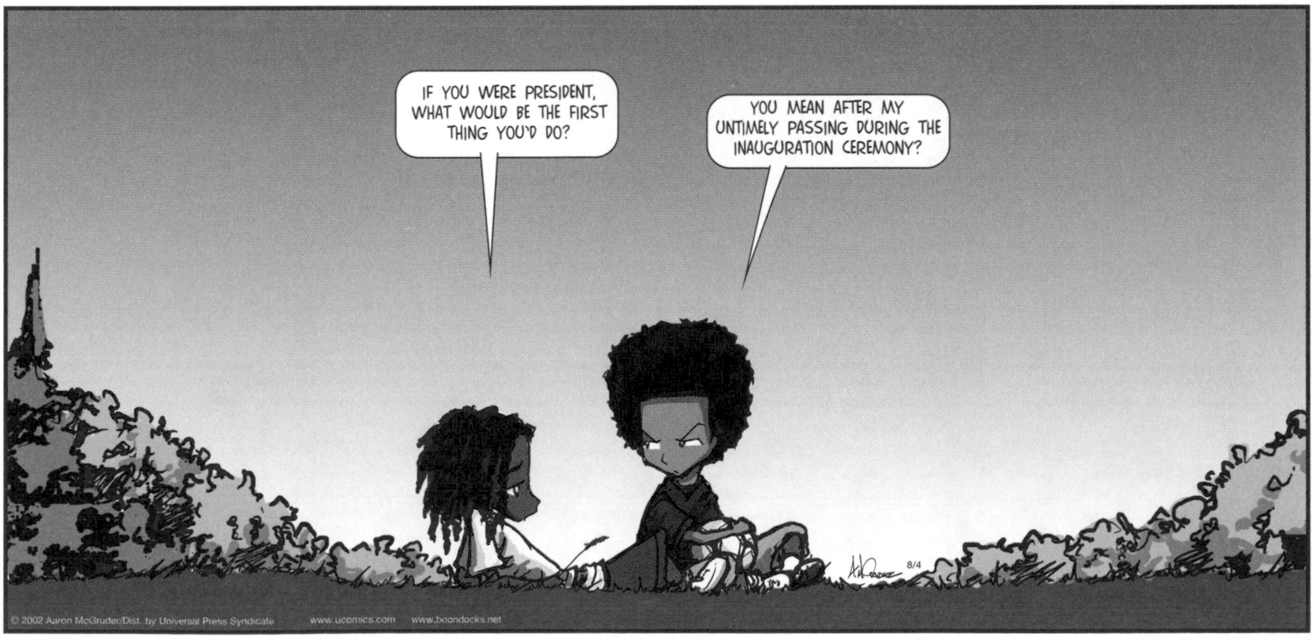
IF YOU WERE PRESIDENT, WHAT WOULD BE THE FIRST THING YOU'D DO?
YOU MEAN AFTER MY UNTIMELY PASSING DURING THE INAUGURATION CEREMONY?
8/4
© 2002 Aaron McGruder/Dist. by Universal Press Syndicate www.ucomics.com www.boondocks.net

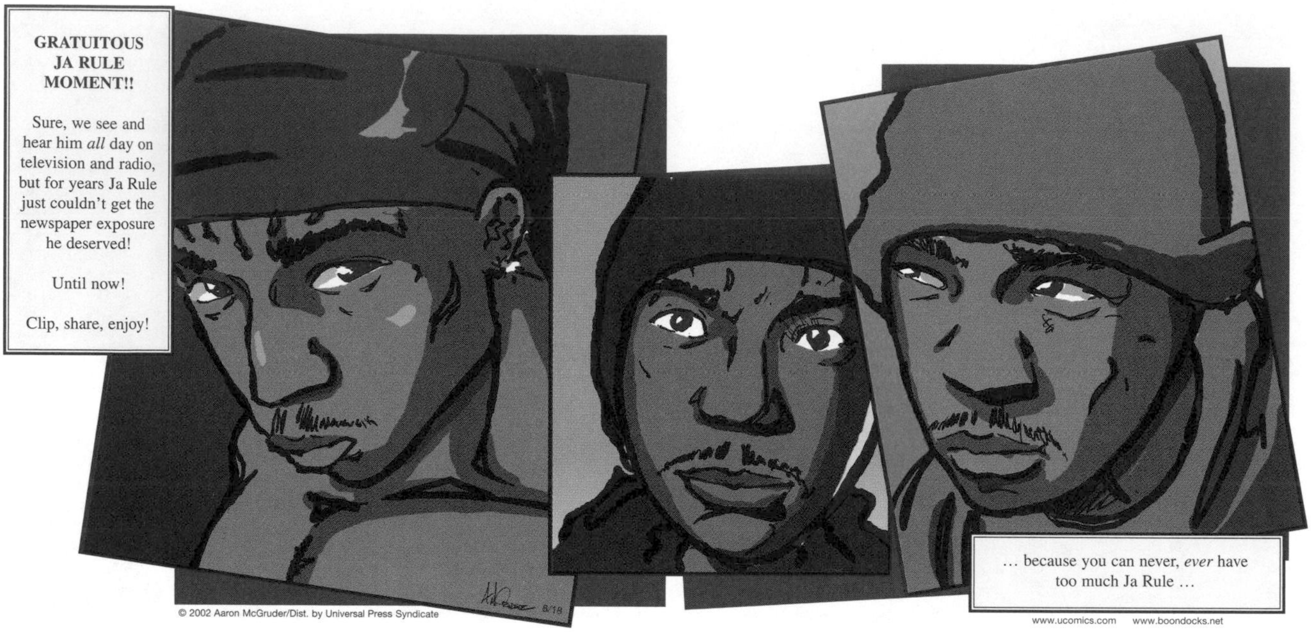
GRATUITOUS JA RULE MOMENT!!
Sure, we see and hear him *all* day on television and radio, but for years Ja Rule just couldn't get the newspaper exposure he deserved!
Until now!
Clip, share, enjoy!
… because you can never, *ever* have too much Ja Rule …
© 2002 Aaron McGruder/Dist. by Universal Press Syndicate
www.ucomics.com www.boondocks.net

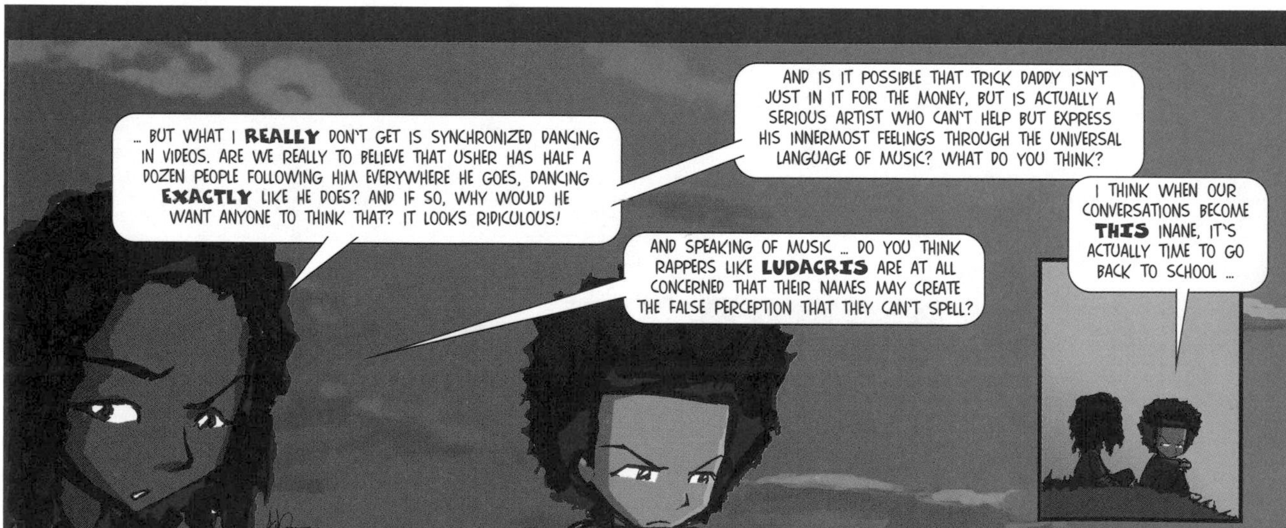
… BUT WHAT I **REALLY** DON'T GET IS SYNCHRONIZED DANCING IN VIDEOS. ARE WE REALLY TO BELIEVE THAT USHER HAS HALF A DOZEN PEOPLE FOLLOWING HIM EVERYWHERE HE GOES, DANCING **EXACTLY** LIKE HE DOES? AND IF SO, WHY WOULD HE WANT ANYONE TO THINK THAT? IT LOOKS RIDICULOUS!
AND SPEAKING OF MUSIC … DO YOU THINK RAPPERS LIKE **LUDACRIS** ARE AT ALL CONCERNED THAT THEIR NAMES MAY CREATE THE FALSE PERCEPTION THAT THEY CAN'T SPELL?
AND IS IT POSSIBLE THAT TRICK DADDY ISN'T JUST IN IT FOR THE MONEY, BUT IS ACTUALLY A SERIOUS ARTIST WHO CAN'T HELP BUT EXPRESS HIS INNERMOST FEELINGS THROUGH THE UNIVERSAL LANGUAGE OF MUSIC? WHAT DO YOU THINK?
I THINK WHEN OUR CONVERSATIONS BECOME **THIS** INANE, IT'S ACTUALLY TIME TO GO BACK TO SCHOOL …
© 2002 Aaron McGruder/Dist. by Universal Press Syndicate www.ucomics.com www.boondocks.net

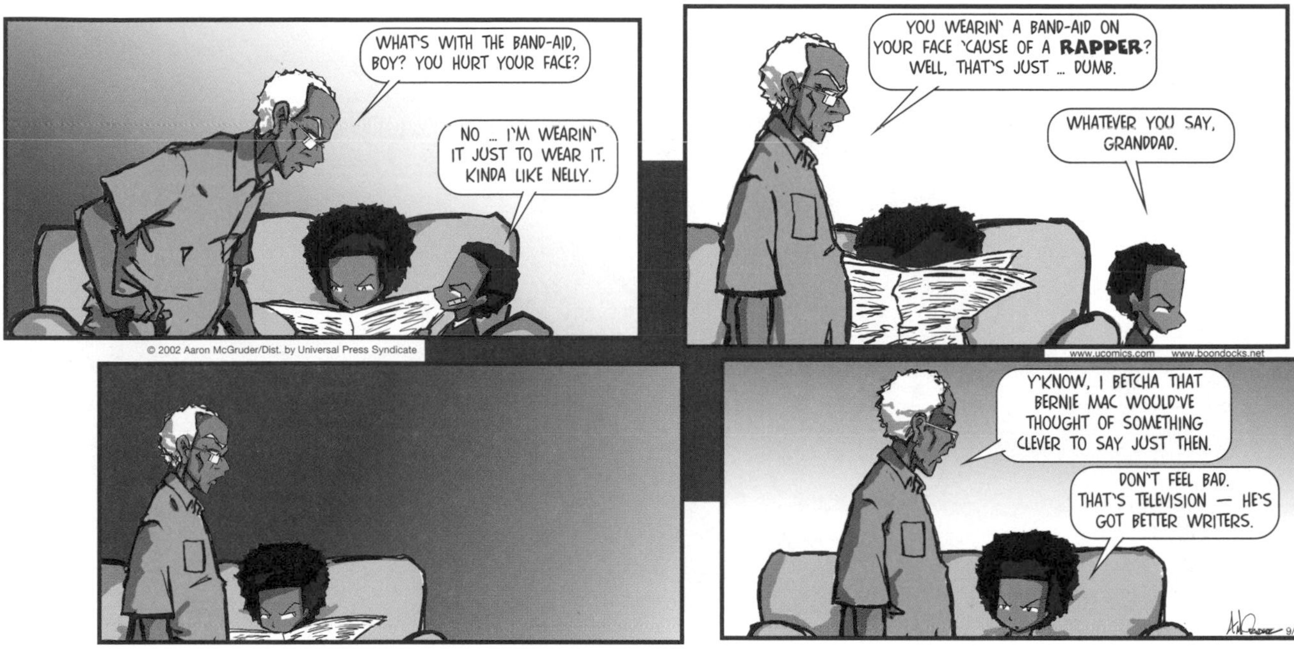
WHAT'S WITH THE BAND-AID, BOY? YOU HURT YOUR FACE?
NO ... I'M WEARIN' IT JUST TO WEAR IT. KINDA LIKE NELLY.
YOU WEARIN' A BAND-AID ON YOUR FACE 'CAUSE OF A RAPPER? WELL, THAT'S JUST ... DUMB.
WHATEVER YOU SAY, GRANDDAD.
Y'KNOW, I BETCHA THAT BERNIE MAC WOULD'VE THOUGHT OF SOMETHING CLEVER TO SAY JUST THEN.
DON'T FEEL BAD. THAT'S TELEVISION — HE'S GOT BETTER WRITERS.
© 2002 Aaron McGruder/Dist. by Universal Press Syndicate
www.ucomics.com www.boondocks.net
9/1

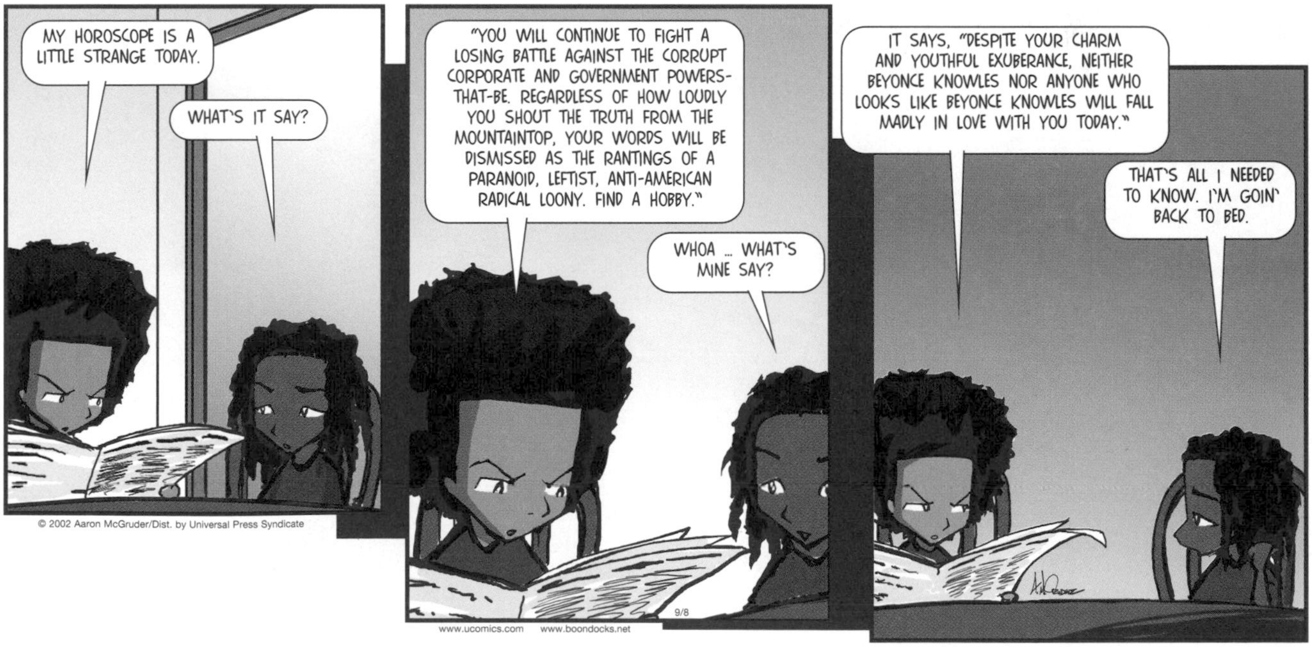
MY HOROSCOPE IS A LITTLE STRANGE TODAY.
WHAT'S IT SAY?
"YOU WILL CONTINUE TO FIGHT A LOSING BATTLE AGAINST THE CORRUPT CORPORATE AND GOVERNMENT POWERS-THAT-BE. REGARDLESS OF HOW LOUDLY YOU SHOUT THE TRUTH FROM THE MOUNTAINTOP, YOUR WORDS WILL BE DISMISSED AS THE RANTINGS OF A PARANOID, LEFTIST, ANTI-AMERICAN RADICAL LOONY. FIND A HOBBY."
WHOA ... WHAT'S MINE SAY?
IT SAYS, "DESPITE YOUR CHARM AND YOUTHFUL EXUBERANCE, NEITHER BEYONCE KNOWLES NOR ANYONE WHO LOOKS LIKE BEYONCE KNOWLES WILL FALL MADLY IN LOVE WITH YOU TODAY."
THAT'S ALL I NEEDED TO KNOW. I'M GOIN' BACK TO BED.
© 2002 Aaron McGruder/Dist. by Universal Press Syndicate
9/8
www.ucomics.com www.boondocks.net

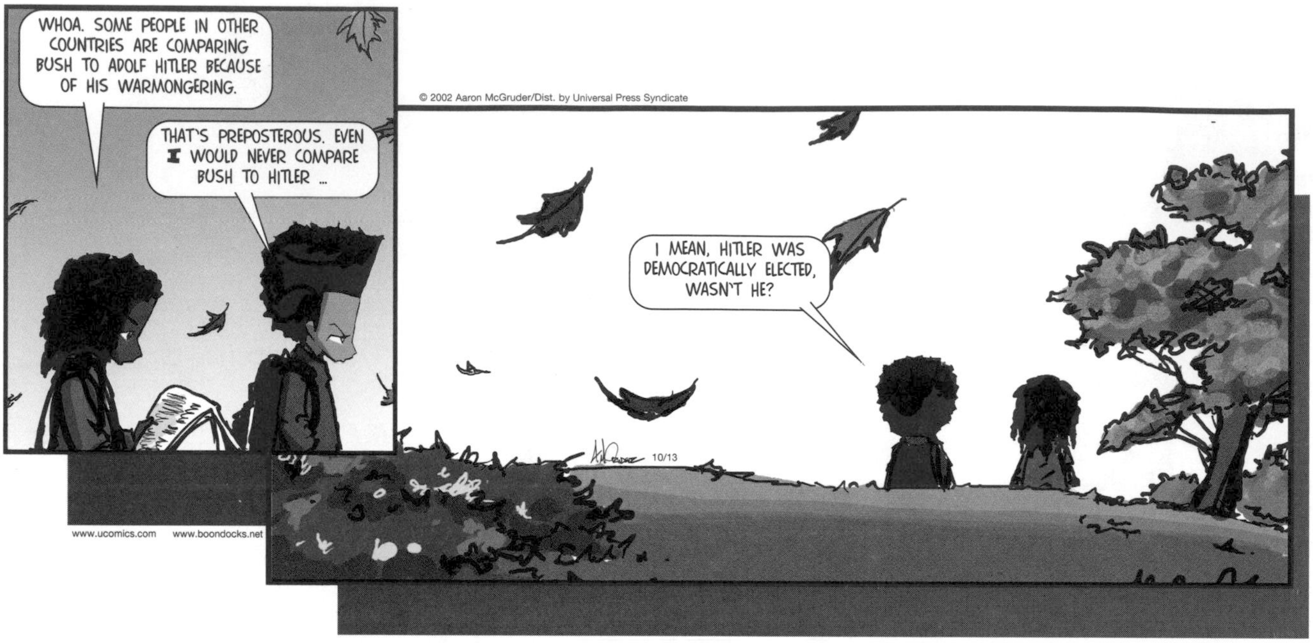
WHOA. SOME PEOPLE IN OTHER COUNTRIES ARE COMPARING BUSH TO ADOLF HITLER BECAUSE OF HIS WARMONGERING.
THAT'S PREPOSTEROUS. EVEN I WOULD NEVER COMPARE BUSH TO HITLER ...
I MEAN, HITLER WAS DEMOCRATICALLY ELECTED, WASN'T HE?
© 2002 Aaron McGruder/Dist. by Universal Press Syndicate
www.ucomics.com www.boondocks.net
10/13

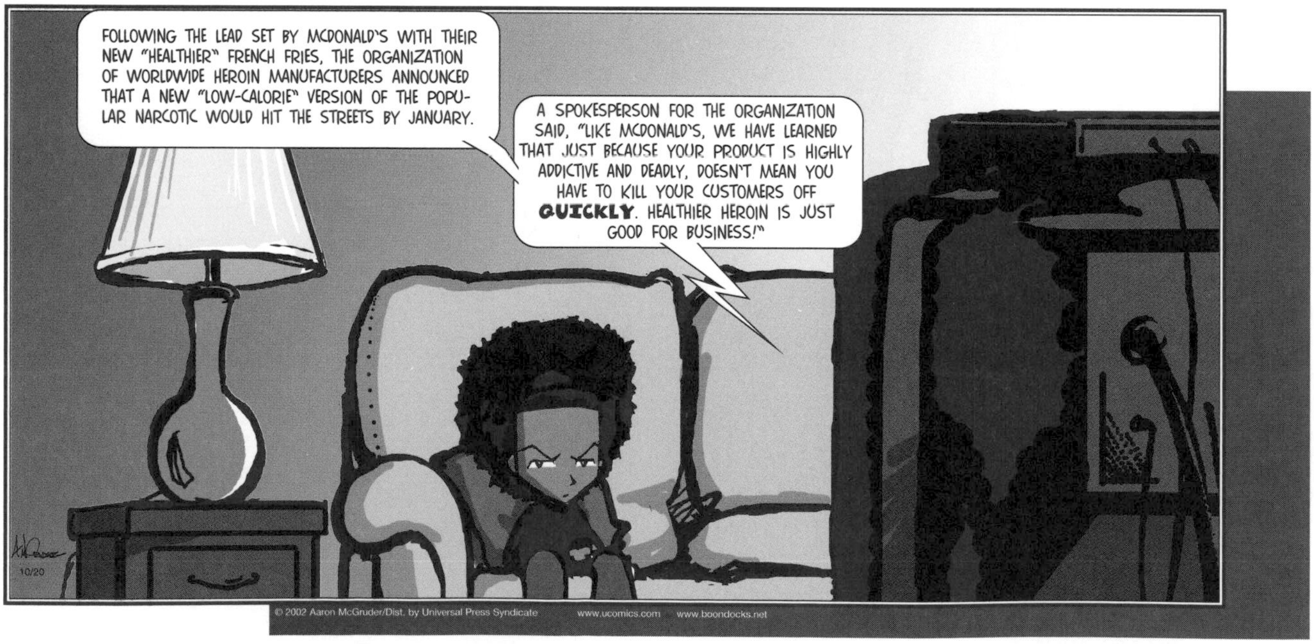
FOLLOWING THE LEAD SET BY MCDONALD'S WITH THEIR NEW "HEALTHIER" FRENCH FRIES, THE ORGANIZATION OF WORLDWIDE HEROIN MANUFACTURERS ANNOUNCED THAT A NEW "LOW-CALORIE" VERSION OF THE POPULAR NARCOTIC WOULD HIT THE STREETS BY JANUARY.
A SPOKESPERSON FOR THE ORGANIZATION SAID, "LIKE MCDONALD'S, WE HAVE LEARNED THAT JUST BECAUSE YOUR PRODUCT IS HIGHLY ADDICTIVE AND DEADLY, DOESN'T MEAN YOU HAVE TO KILL YOUR CUSTOMERS OFF QUICKLY. HEALTHIER HEROIN IS JUST GOOD FOR BUSINESS!"
10/20
© 2002 Aaron McGruder/Dist. by Universal Press Syndicate www.ucomics.com www.boondocks.net

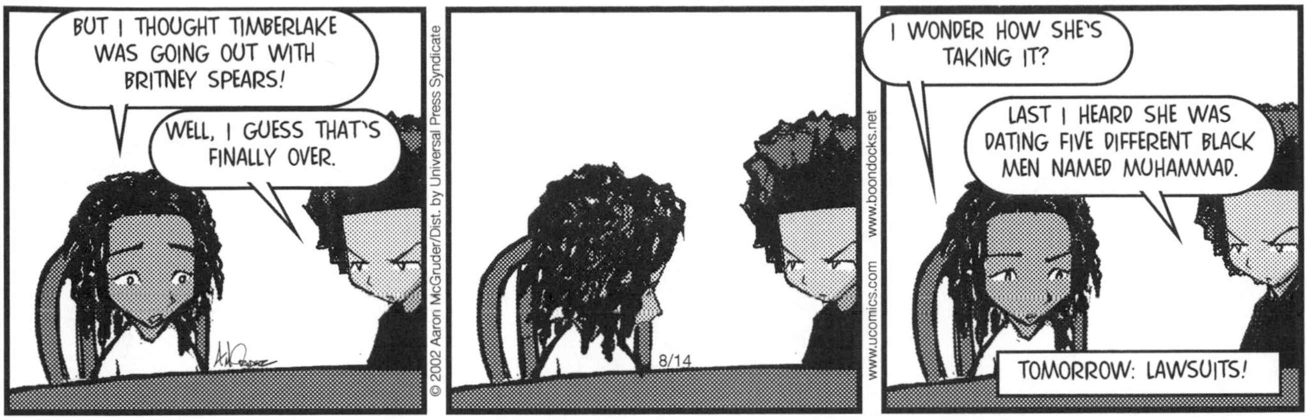
BUT I THOUGHT TIMBERLAKE WAS GOING OUT WITH BRITNEY SPEARS!
WELL, I GUESS THAT'S FINALLY OVER.
© 2002 Aaron McGruder/Dist. by Universal Press Syndicate
8/14
www.ucomics.com www.boondocks.net
I WONDER HOW SHE'S TAKING IT?
LAST I HEARD SHE WAS DATING FIVE DIFFERENT BLACK MEN NAMED MUHAMMAD.
TOMORROW: LAWSUITS!

EDITOR'S NOTE

The editorial staff of this paper would like to express regret at this feature's tasteless assertion yesterday that Britney Spears is currently dating five black men named Muhammad.

Since yesterday, we have received hundreds of calls, mostly from black men named Muhammad, asking if this is true. We assure you it is not.

We would like Ms. Spears' legal representation to accept our deepest apologies. Mr. McGruder now understands such reckless and irresponsible humor has absolutely no place in the funny pages.

And now, back to the feature.

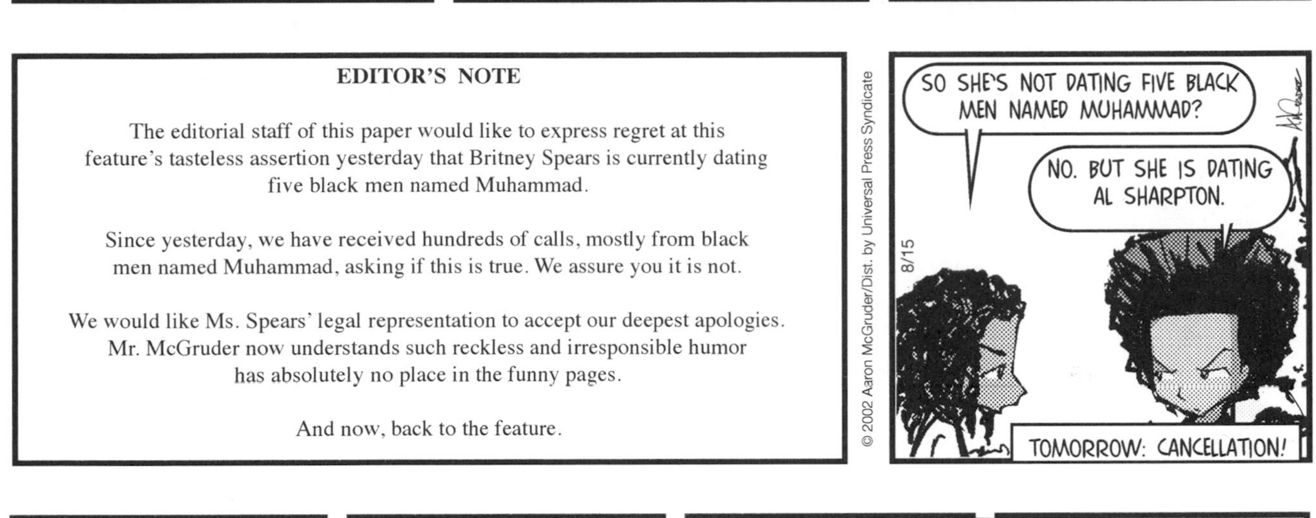
© 2002 Aaron McGruder/Dist. by Universal Press Syndicate
8/15
SO SHE'S NOT DATING FIVE BLACK MEN NAMED MUHAMMAD?
NO. BUT SHE IS DATING AL SHARPTON.
TOMORROW: CANCELLATION!

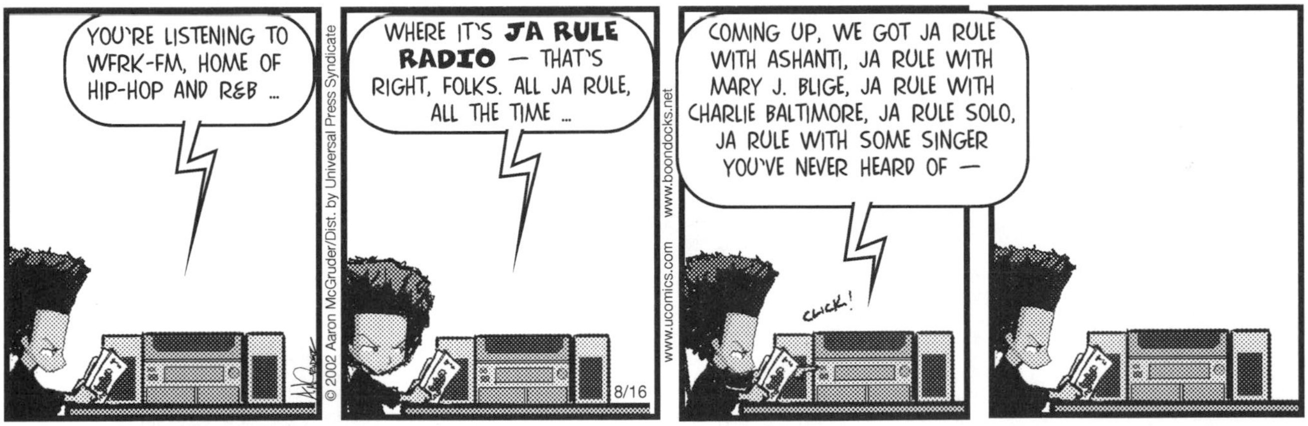
YOU'RE LISTENING TO WFRK-FM, HOME OF HIP-HOP AND R&B ...
© 2002 Aaron McGruder/Dist. by Universal Press Syndicate
WHERE IT'S **JA RULE RADIO** — THAT'S RIGHT, FOLKS. ALL JA RULE, ALL THE TIME ...
8/16
www.ucomics.com www.boondocks.net
COMING UP, WE GOT JA RULE WITH ASHANTI, JA RULE WITH MARY J. BLIGE, JA RULE WITH CHARLIE BALTIMORE, JA RULE SOLO, JA RULE WITH SOME SINGER YOU'VE NEVER HEARD OF —
CLICK!

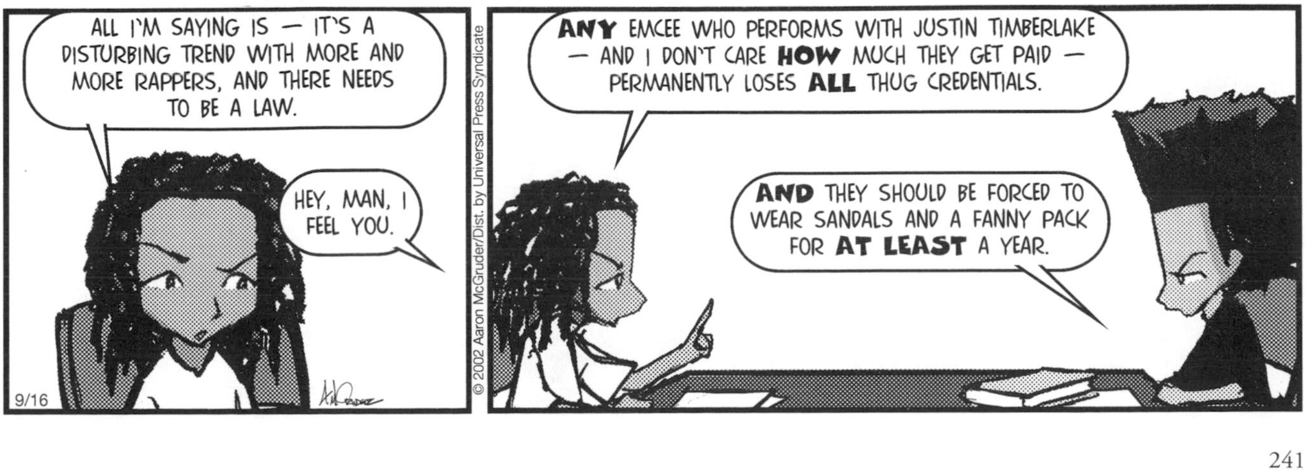
ALL I'M SAYING IS — IT'S A DISTURBING TREND WITH MORE AND MORE RAPPERS, AND THERE NEEDS TO BE A LAW.
HEY, MAN, I FEEL YOU.
9/16
© 2002 Aaron McGruder/Dist. by Universal Press Syndicate
ANY EMCEE WHO PERFORMS WITH JUSTIN TIMBERLAKE — AND I DON'T CARE **HOW** MUCH THEY GET PAID — PERMANENTLY LOSES **ALL** THUG CREDENTIALS.
AND THEY SHOULD BE FORCED TO WEAR SANDALS AND A FANNY PACK FOR **AT LEAST** A YEAR.

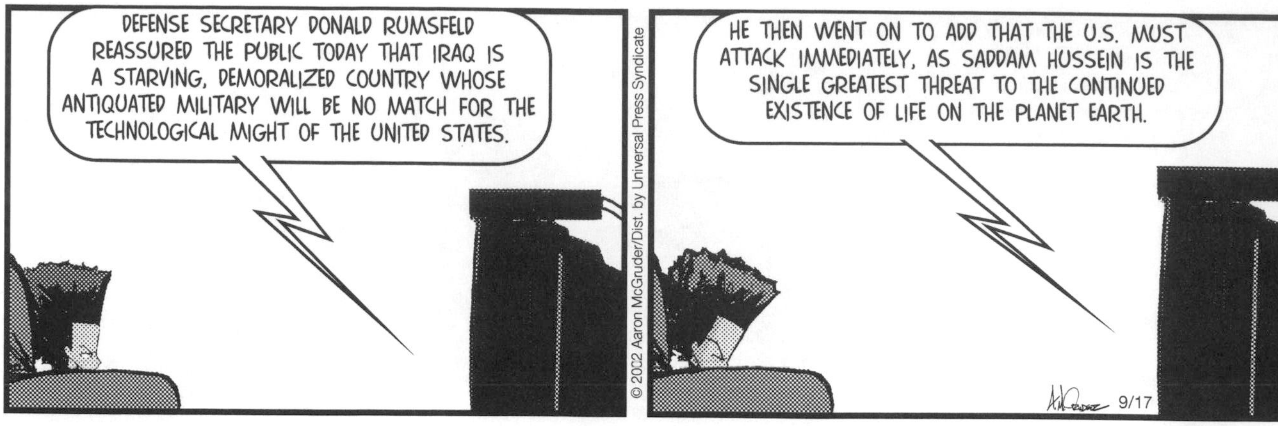
DEFENSE SECRETARY DONALD RUMSFELD REASSURED THE PUBLIC TODAY THAT IRAQ IS A STARVING, DEMORALIZED COUNTRY WHOSE ANTIQUATED MILITARY WILL BE NO MATCH FOR THE TECHNOLOGICAL MIGHT OF THE UNITED STATES.
© 2002 Aaron McGruder/Dist. by Universal Press Syndicate
HE THEN WENT ON TO ADD THAT THE U.S. MUST ATTACK IMMEDIATELY, AS SADDAM HUSSEIN IS THE SINGLE GREATEST THREAT TO THE CONTINUED EXISTENCE OF LIFE ON THE PLANET EARTH.
9/17

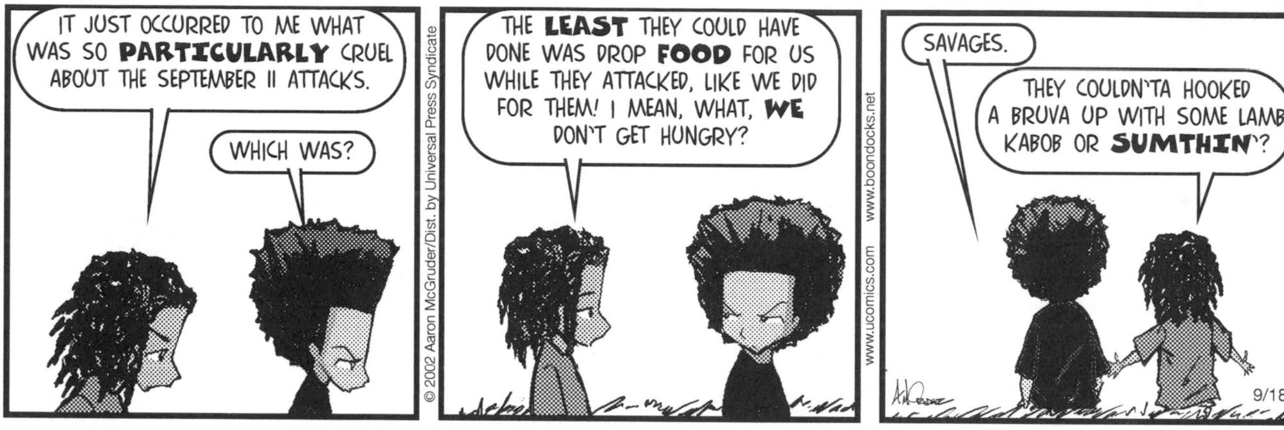
IT JUST OCCURRED TO ME WHAT WAS SO PARTICULARLY CRUEL ABOUT THE SEPTEMBER 11 ATTACKS.
WHICH WAS?
© 2002 Aaron McGruder/Dist. by Universal Press Syndicate
THE LEAST THEY COULD HAVE DONE WAS DROP FOOD FOR US WHILE THEY ATTACKED, LIKE WE DID FOR THEM! I MEAN, WHAT, WE DON'T GET HUNGRY?
www.ucomics.com www.boondocks.net
SAVAGES.
THEY COULDN'TA HOOKED A BRUVA UP WITH SOME LAMB KABOB OR SUMTHIN'?
9/18

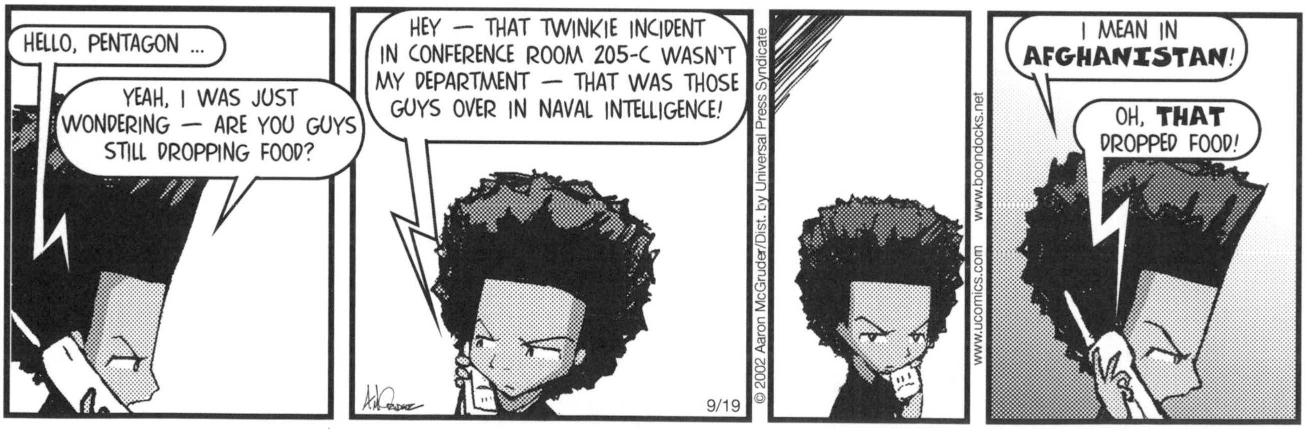
HELLO, PENTAGON ...
YEAH, I WAS JUST WONDERING — ARE YOU GUYS STILL DROPPING FOOD?
HEY — THAT TWINKIE INCIDENT IN CONFERENCE ROOM 205-C WASN'T MY DEPARTMENT — THAT WAS THOSE GUYS OVER IN NAVAL INTELLIGENCE!
9/19
© 2002 Aaron McGruder/Dist. by Universal Press Syndicate
www.ucomics.com www.boondocks.net
I MEAN IN AFGHANISTAN!
OH, THAT DROPPED FOOD!

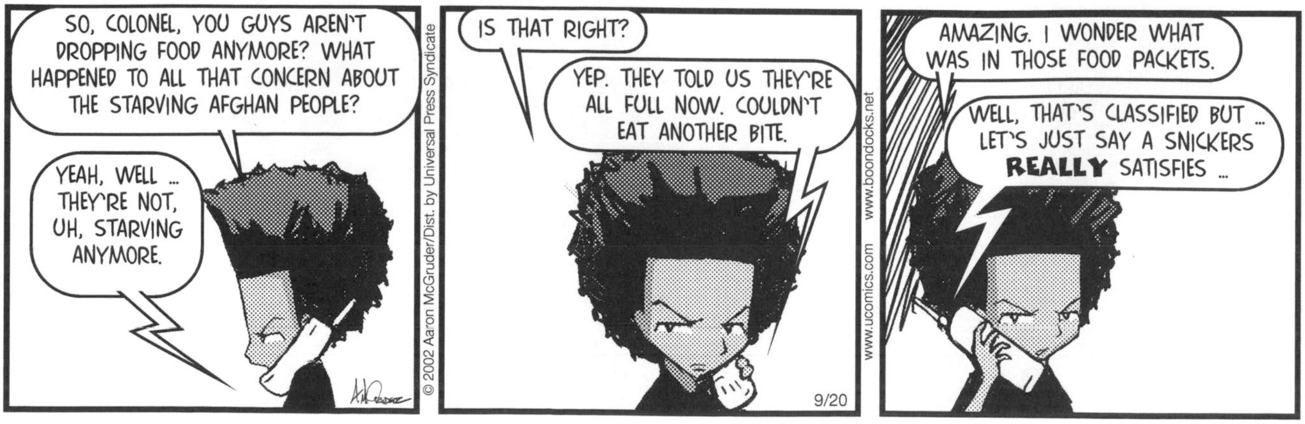
SO, COLONEL, YOU GUYS AREN'T DROPPING FOOD ANYMORE? WHAT HAPPENED TO ALL THAT CONCERN ABOUT THE STARVING AFGHAN PEOPLE?
YEAH, WELL ... THEY'RE NOT, UH, STARVING ANYMORE.
© 2002 Aaron McGruder/Dist. by Universal Press Syndicate
IS THAT RIGHT?
YEP. THEY TOLD US THEY'RE ALL FULL NOW. COULDN'T EAT ANOTHER BITE.
9/20
www.ucomics.com www.boondocks.net
AMAZING. I WONDER WHAT WAS IN THOSE FOOD PACKETS.
WELL, THAT'S CLASSIFIED BUT ... LET'S JUST SAY A SNICKERS REALLY SATISFIES ...

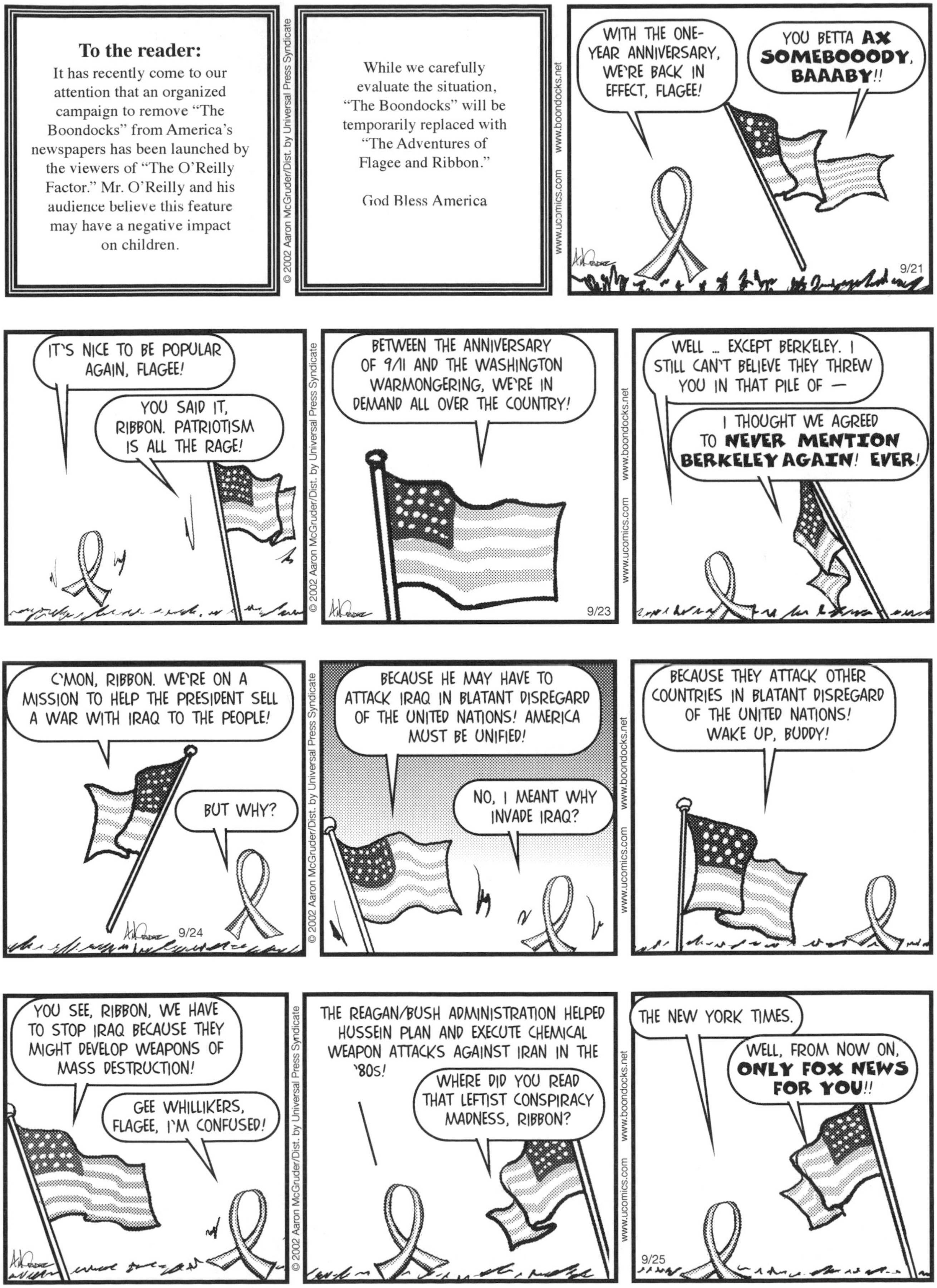
To the reader:
It has recently come to our attention that an organized campaign to remove "The Boondocks" from America's newspapers has been launched by the viewers of "The O'Reilly Factor." Mr. O'Reilly and his audience believe this feature may have a negative impact on children.
© 2002 Aaron McGruder/Dist. by Universal Press Syndicate
While we carefully evaluate the situation, "The Boondocks" will be temporarily replaced with "The Adventures of Flagee and Ribbon."
God Bless America
www.ucomics.com www.boondocks.net
WITH THE ONE-YEAR ANNIVERSARY, WE'RE BACK IN EFFECT, FLAGEE!
YOU BETTA **AX SOMEBOOODY, BAAABY**!!
9/21
IT'S NICE TO BE POPULAR AGAIN, FLAGEE!
YOU SAID IT, RIBBON. PATRIOTISM IS ALL THE RAGE!
BETWEEN THE ANNIVERSARY OF 9/11 AND THE WASHINGTON WARMONGERING, WE'RE IN DEMAND ALL OVER THE COUNTRY!
9/23
WELL ... EXCEPT BERKELEY. I STILL CAN'T BELIEVE THEY THREW YOU IN THAT PILE OF —
I THOUGHT WE AGREED TO **NEVER MENTION BERKELEY AGAIN**! **EVER**!
C'MON, RIBBON. WE'RE ON A MISSION TO HELP THE PRESIDENT SELL A WAR WITH IRAQ TO THE PEOPLE!
BUT WHY?
9/24
BECAUSE HE MAY HAVE TO ATTACK IRAQ IN BLATANT DISREGARD OF THE UNITED NATIONS! AMERICA MUST BE UNIFIED!
NO, I MEANT WHY INVADE IRAQ?
BECAUSE THEY ATTACK OTHER COUNTRIES IN BLATANT DISREGARD OF THE UNITED NATIONS! WAKE UP, BUDDY!
YOU SEE, RIBBON, WE HAVE TO STOP IRAQ BECAUSE THEY MIGHT DEVELOP WEAPONS OF MASS DESTRUCTION!
GEE WHILLIKERS, FLAGEE, I'M CONFUSED!
THE REAGAN/BUSH ADMINISTRATION HELPED HUSSEIN PLAN AND EXECUTE CHEMICAL WEAPON ATTACKS AGAINST IRAN IN THE '80S!
WHERE DID YOU READ THAT LEFTIST CONSPIRACY MADNESS, RIBBON?
THE NEW YORK TIMES.
WELL, FROM NOW ON, **ONLY FOX NEWS FOR YOU**!!
9/25

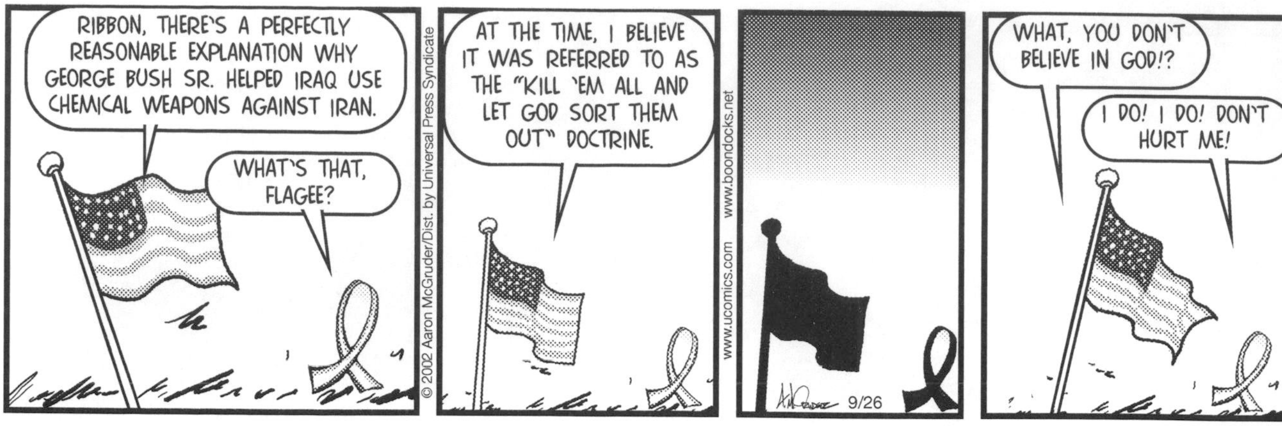
RIBBON, THERE'S A PERFECTLY REASONABLE EXPLANATION WHY GEORGE BUSH SR. HELPED IRAQ USE CHEMICAL WEAPONS AGAINST IRAN.
WHAT'S THAT, FLAGEE?
© 2002 Aaron McGruder/Dist. by Universal Press Syndicate
AT THE TIME, I BELIEVE IT WAS REFERRED TO AS THE "KILL 'EM ALL AND LET GOD SORT THEM OUT" DOCTRINE.
www.ucomics.com www.boondocks.net
9/26
WHAT, YOU DON'T BELIEVE IN GOD!?
I DO! I DO! DON'T HURT ME!

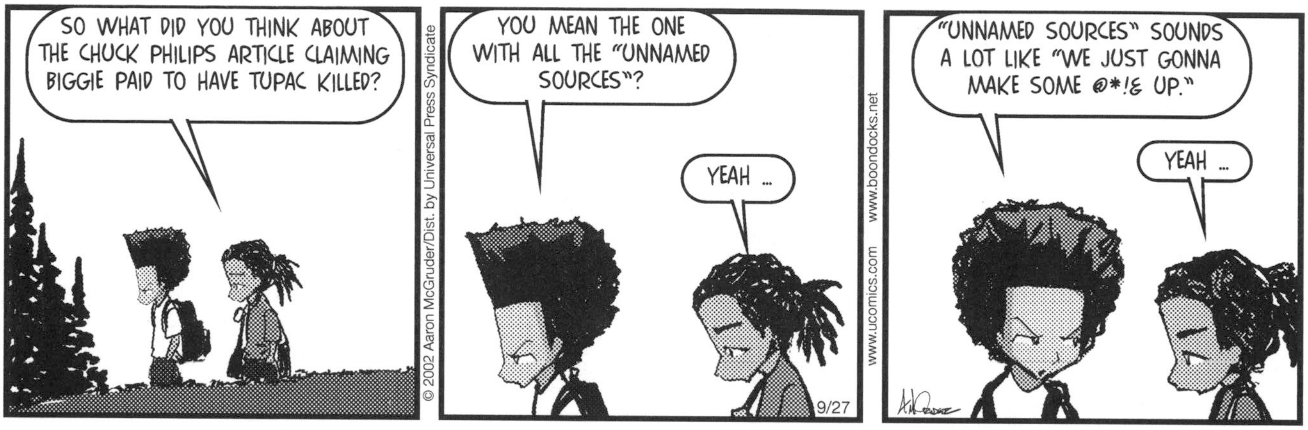
SO WHAT DID YOU THINK ABOUT THE CHUCK PHILIPS ARTICLE CLAIMING BIGGIE PAID TO HAVE TUPAC KILLED?
© 2002 Aaron McGruder/Dist. by Universal Press Syndicate
YOU MEAN THE ONE WITH ALL THE "UNNAMED SOURCES"?
YEAH ...
9/27
www.ucomics.com www.boondocks.net
"UNNAMED SOURCES" SOUNDS A LOT LIKE "WE JUST GONNA MAKE SOME @*!& UP."
YEAH ...

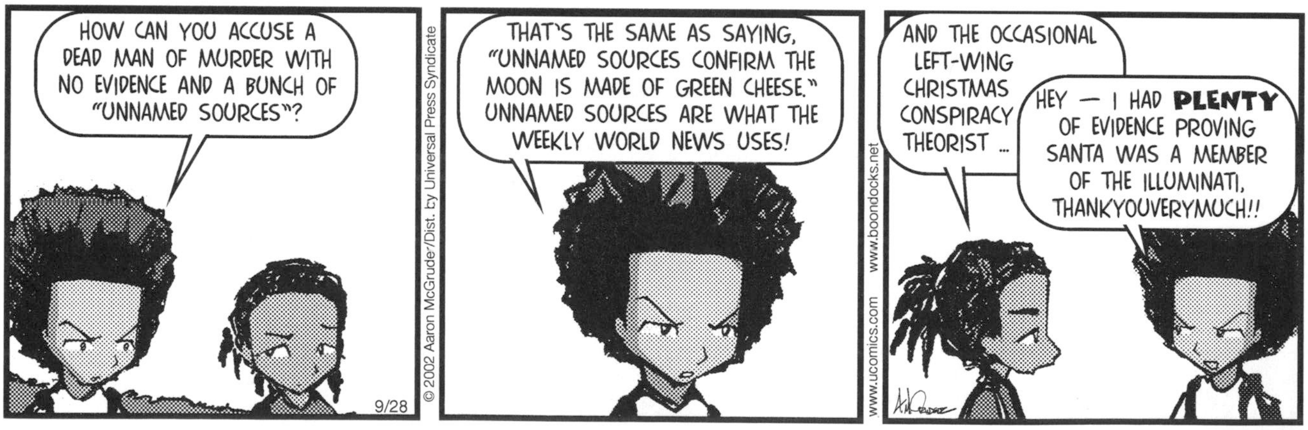
HOW CAN YOU ACCUSE A DEAD MAN OF MURDER WITH NO EVIDENCE AND A BUNCH OF "UNNAMED SOURCES"?
9/28
© 2002 Aaron McGruder/Dist. by Universal Press Syndicate
THAT'S THE SAME AS SAYING, "UNNAMED SOURCES CONFIRM THE MOON IS MADE OF GREEN CHEESE." UNNAMED SOURCES ARE WHAT THE WEEKLY WORLD NEWS USES!
www.ucomics.com www.boondocks.net
AND THE OCCASIONAL LEFT-WING CHRISTMAS CONSPIRACY THEORIST ...
HEY — I HAD PLENTY OF EVIDENCE PROVING SANTA WAS A MEMBER OF THE ILLUMINATI, THANKYOUVERYMUCH!!

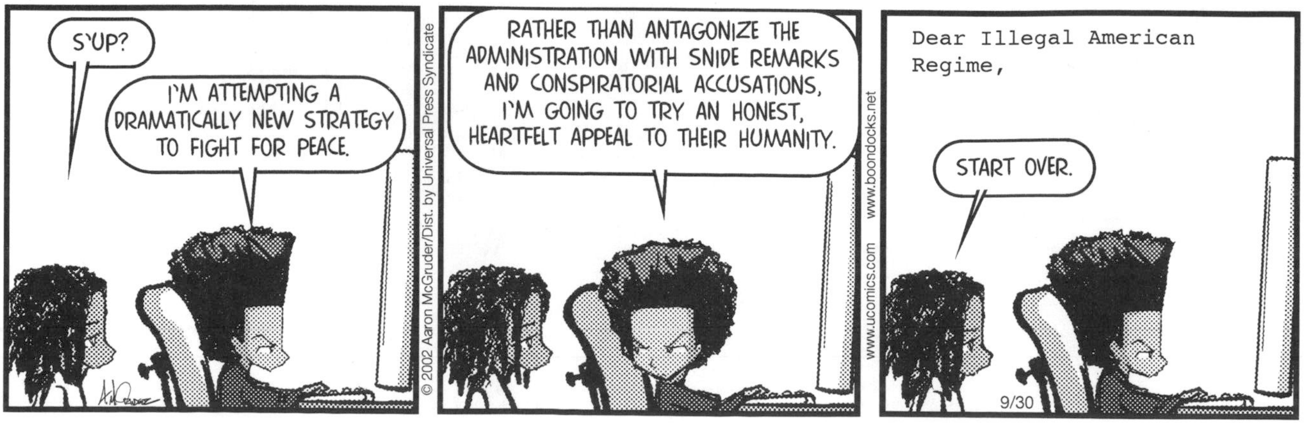
S'UP?
I'M ATTEMPTING A DRAMATICALLY NEW STRATEGY TO FIGHT FOR PEACE.
© 2002 Aaron McGruder/Dist. by Universal Press Syndicate
RATHER THAN ANTAGONIZE THE ADMINISTRATION WITH SNIDE REMARKS AND CONSPIRATORIAL ACCUSATIONS, I'M GOING TO TRY AN HONEST, HEARTFELT APPEAL TO THEIR HUMANITY.
www.ucomics.com www.boondocks.net
Dear Illegal American Regime,
START OVER.
9/30

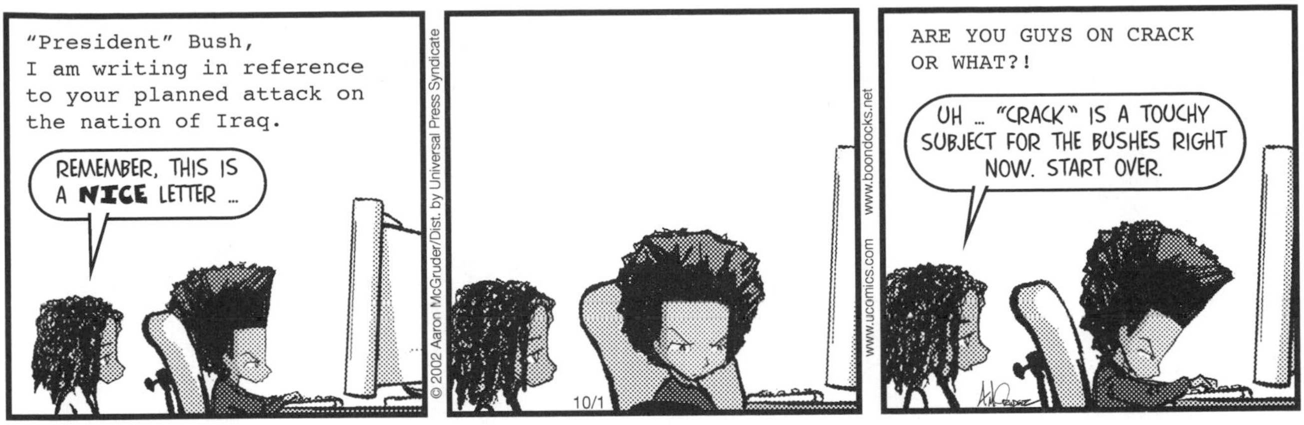
"President" Bush,
I am writing in reference to your planned attack on the nation of Iraq.
REMEMBER, THIS IS A NICE LETTER ...
© 2002 Aaron McGruder/Dist. by Universal Press Syndicate
10/1
www.ucomics.com www.boondocks.net
ARE YOU GUYS ON CRACK OR WHAT?!
UH ... "CRACK" IS A TOUCHY SUBJECT FOR THE BUSHES RIGHT NOW. START OVER.

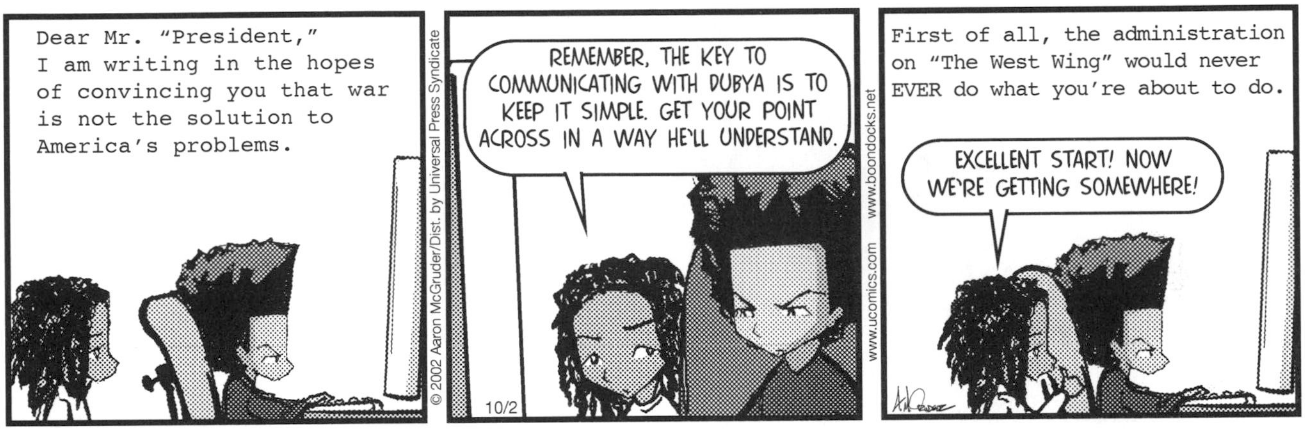
Dear Mr. "President,"
I am writing in the hopes of convincing you that war is not the solution to America's problems.
© 2002 Aaron McGruder/Dist. by Universal Press Syndicate
REMEMBER, THE KEY TO COMMUNICATING WITH DUBYA IS TO KEEP IT SIMPLE. GET YOUR POINT ACROSS IN A WAY HE'LL UNDERSTAND.
10/2
www.ucomics.com www.boondocks.net
First of all, the administration on "The West Wing" would never EVER do what you're about to do.
EXCELLENT START! NOW WE'RE GETTING SOMEWHERE!

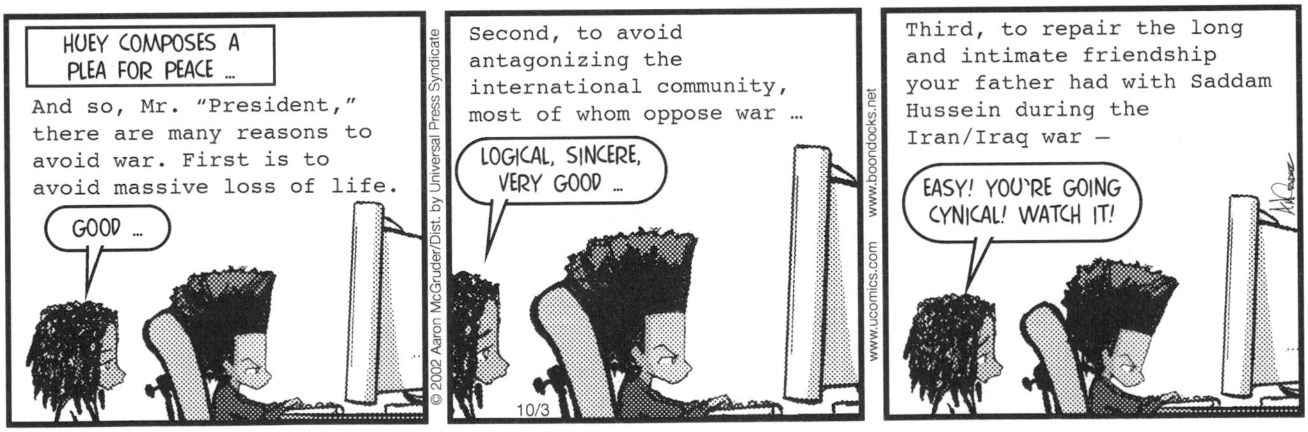
HUEY COMPOSES A PLEA FOR PEACE ...
And so, Mr. "President," there are many reasons to avoid war. First is to avoid massive loss of life.
GOOD ...
© 2002 Aaron McGruder/Dist. by Universal Press Syndicate
Second, to avoid antagonizing the international community, most of whom oppose war ...
LOGICAL, SINCERE, VERY GOOD ...
10/3
www.ucomics.com www.boondocks.net
Third, to repair the long and intimate friendship your father had with Saddam Hussein during the Iran/Iraq war –
EASY! YOU'RE GOING CYNICAL! WATCH IT!

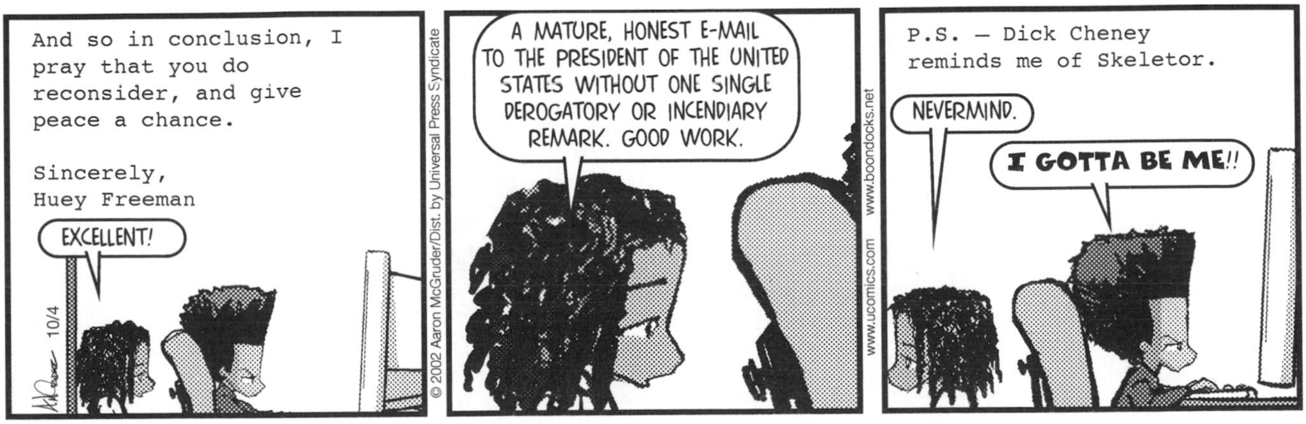
And so in conclusion, I pray that you do reconsider, and give peace a chance.
Sincerely,
Huey Freeman
EXCELLENT!
10/4
© 2002 Aaron McGruder/Dist. by Universal Press Syndicate
A MATURE, HONEST E-MAIL TO THE PRESIDENT OF THE UNITED STATES WITHOUT ONE SINGLE DEROGATORY OR INCENDIARY REMARK. GOOD WORK.
www.ucomics.com www.boondocks.net
P.S. – Dick Cheney reminds me of Skeletor.
NEVERMIND.
I GOTTA BE ME!!

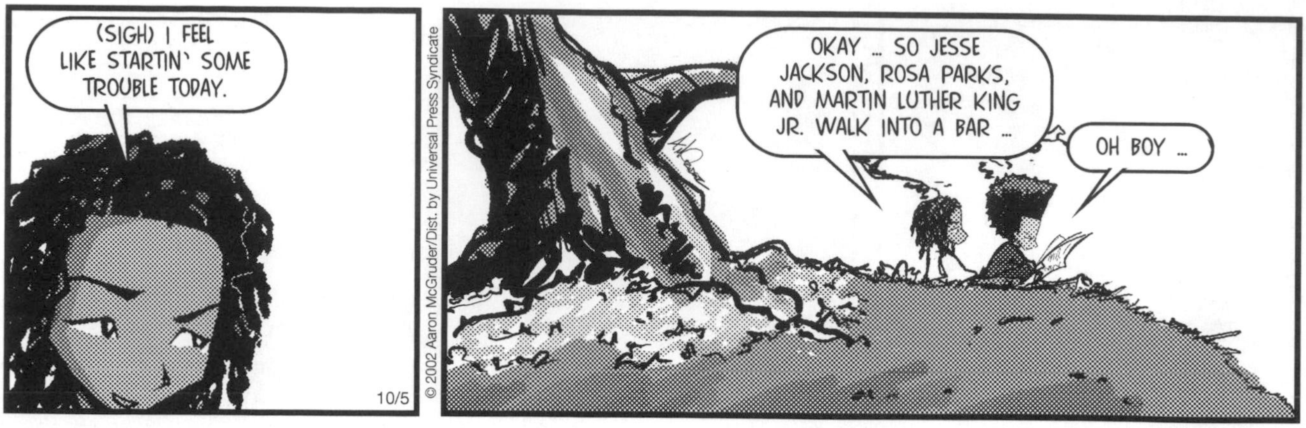
(SIGH) I FEEL LIKE STARTIN' SOME TROUBLE TODAY.
10/5
OKAY ... SO JESSE JACKSON, ROSA PARKS, AND MARTIN LUTHER KING JR. WALK INTO A BAR ...
OH BOY ...

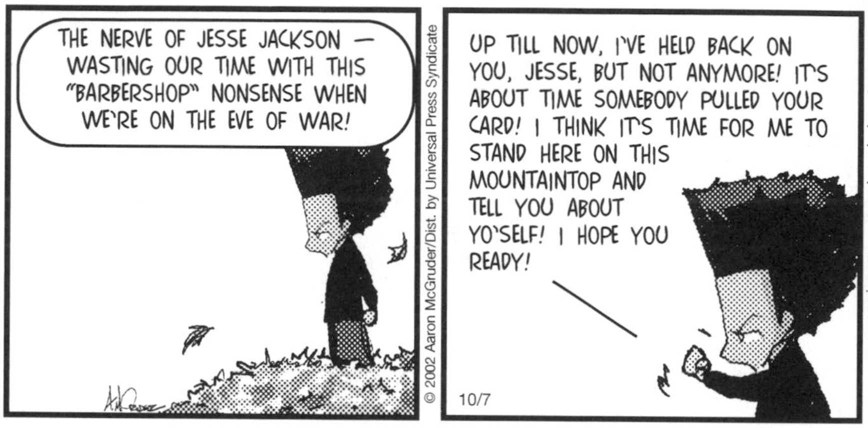
THE NERVE OF JESSE JACKSON — WASTING OUR TIME WITH THIS "BARBERSHOP" NONSENSE WHEN WE'RE ON THE EVE OF WAR!
UP TILL NOW, I'VE HELD BACK ON YOU, JESSE, BUT NOT ANYMORE! IT'S ABOUT TIME SOMEBODY PULLED YOUR CARD! I THINK IT'S TIME FOR ME TO STAND HERE ON THIS MOUNTAINTOP AND TELL YOU ABOUT YO'SELF! I HOPE YOU READY!
10/7

To The Reader

The last panel of this feature has been removed as it was deemed potentially offensive and downright nasty to Jesse Jackson, Jesse Jackson Jr., Martin Luther King the Third, Rosa Parks, Dexter King, the entire Rainbow Coalition and Nipsey Russell.

Just ... don't ask.

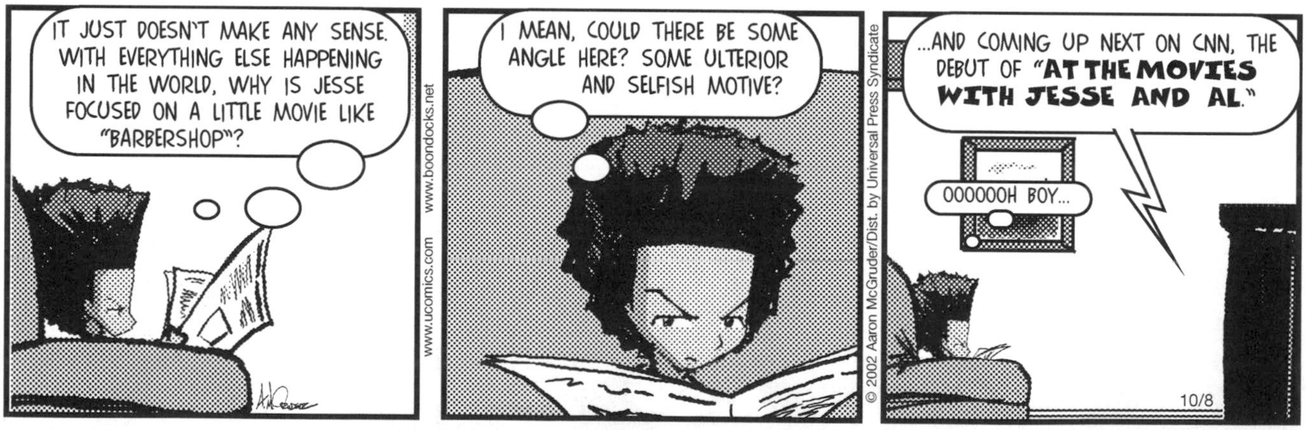
IT JUST DOESN'T MAKE ANY SENSE. WITH EVERYTHING ELSE HAPPENING IN THE WORLD, WHY IS JESSE FOCUSED ON A LITTLE MOVIE LIKE "BARBERSHOP"?
I MEAN, COULD THERE BE SOME ANGLE HERE? SOME ULTERIOR AND SELFISH MOTIVE?
...AND COMING UP NEXT ON CNN, THE DEBUT OF "AT THE MOVIES WITH JESSE AND AL."
OOOOOOH BOY...
10/8

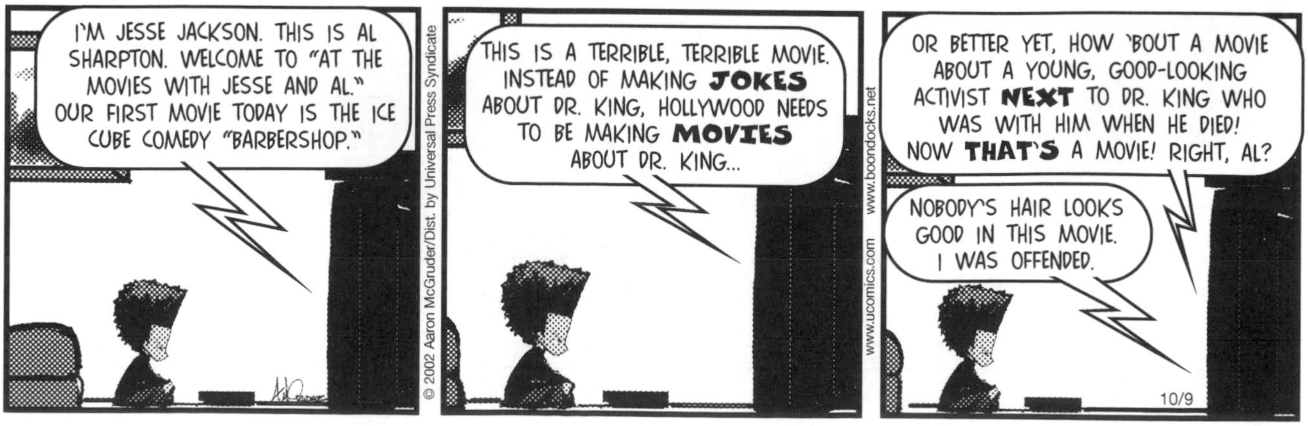
I'M JESSE JACKSON. THIS IS AL SHARPTON. WELCOME TO "AT THE MOVIES WITH JESSE AND AL." OUR FIRST MOVIE TODAY IS THE ICE CUBE COMEDY "BARBERSHOP."
THIS IS A TERRIBLE, TERRIBLE MOVIE. INSTEAD OF MAKING JOKES ABOUT DR. KING, HOLLYWOOD NEEDS TO BE MAKING MOVIES ABOUT DR. KING...
OR BETTER YET, HOW 'BOUT A MOVIE ABOUT A YOUNG, GOOD-LOOKING ACTIVIST NEXT TO DR. KING WHO WAS WITH HIM WHEN HE DIED! NOW THAT'S A MOVIE! RIGHT, AL?
NOBODY'S HAIR LOOKS GOOD IN THIS MOVIE. I WAS OFFENDED.
10/9

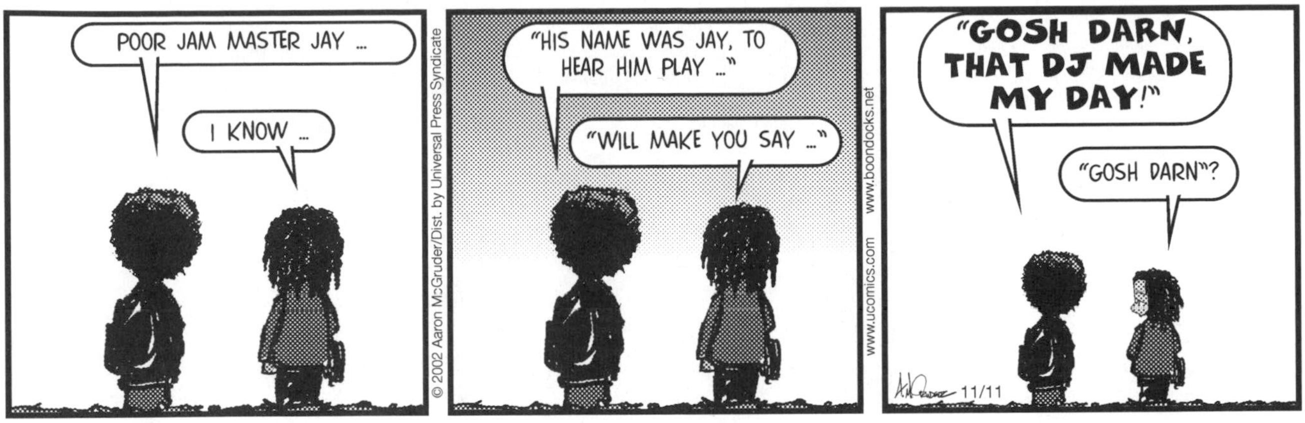
POOR JAM MASTER JAY ...
I KNOW ...
"HIS NAME WAS JAY, TO HEAR HIM PLAY ..."
"WILL MAKE YOU SAY ..."
"GOSH DARN, THAT DJ MADE MY DAY!"
"GOSH DARN"?
11/11
© 2002 Aaron McGruder/Dist. by Universal Press Syndicate
www.ucomics.com www.boondocks.net

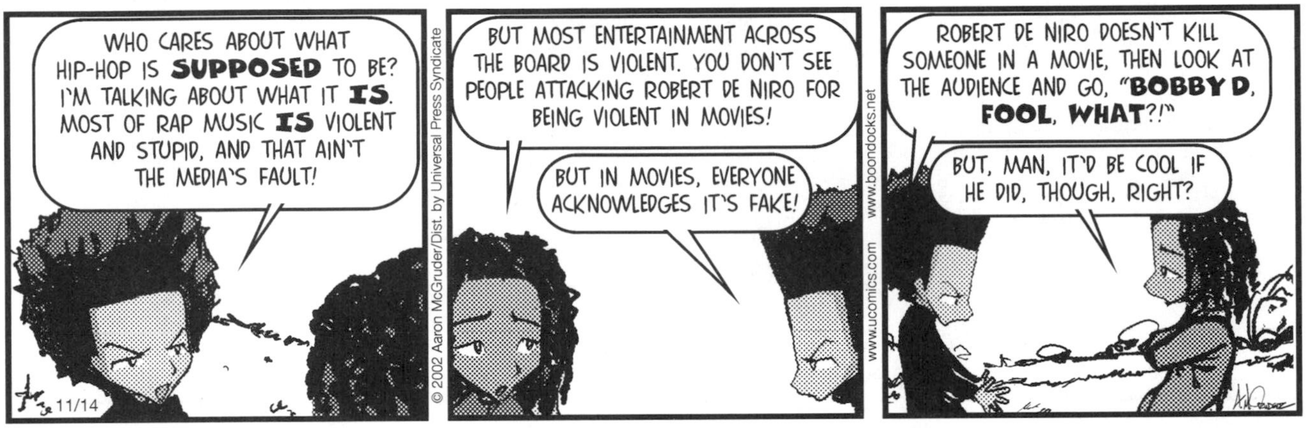
WHO CARES ABOUT WHAT HIP-HOP IS SUPPOSED TO BE? I'M TALKING ABOUT WHAT IT IS. MOST OF RAP MUSIC IS VIOLENT AND STUPID, AND THAT AIN'T THE MEDIA'S FAULT!
11/14
BUT MOST ENTERTAINMENT ACROSS THE BOARD IS VIOLENT. YOU DON'T SEE PEOPLE ATTACKING ROBERT DE NIRO FOR BEING VIOLENT IN MOVIES!
BUT IN MOVIES, EVERYONE ACKNOWLEDGES IT'S FAKE!
ROBERT DE NIRO DOESN'T KILL SOMEONE IN A MOVIE, THEN LOOK AT THE AUDIENCE AND GO, "BOBBY D, FOOL, WHAT?!"
BUT, MAN, IT'D BE COOL IF HE DID, THOUGH, RIGHT?
© 2002 Aaron McGruder/Dist. by Universal Press Syndicate
www.ucomics.com www.boondocks.net

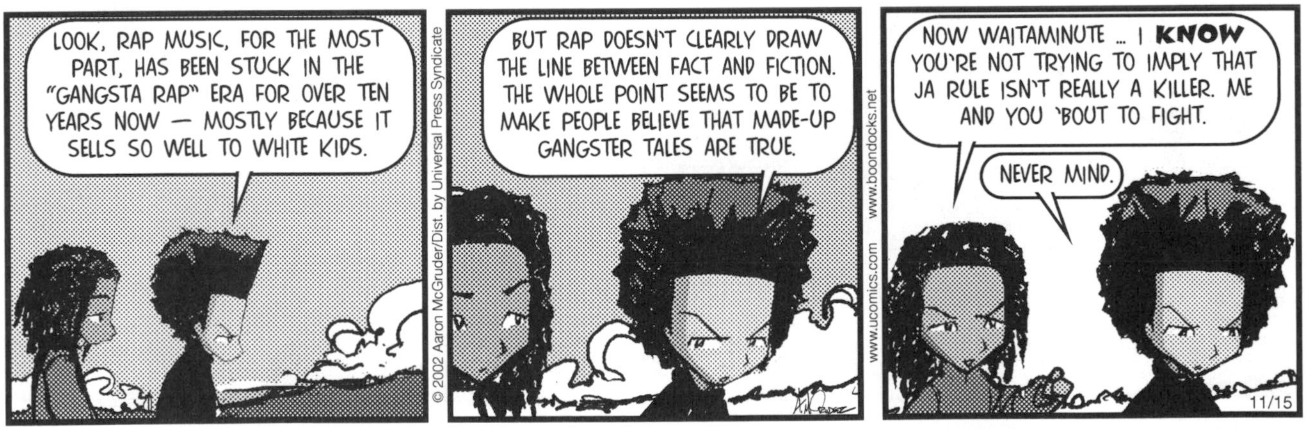
LOOK, RAP MUSIC, FOR THE MOST PART, HAS BEEN STUCK IN THE "GANGSTA RAP" ERA FOR OVER TEN YEARS NOW — MOSTLY BECAUSE IT SELLS SO WELL TO WHITE KIDS.
BUT RAP DOESN'T CLEARLY DRAW THE LINE BETWEEN FACT AND FICTION. THE WHOLE POINT SEEMS TO BE TO MAKE PEOPLE BELIEVE THAT MADE-UP GANGSTER TALES ARE TRUE.
NOW WAITAMINUTE ... I KNOW YOU'RE NOT TRYING TO IMPLY THAT JA RULE ISN'T REALLY A KILLER. ME AND YOU 'BOUT TO FIGHT.
NEVER MIND.
11/15
© 2002 Aaron McGruder/Dist. by Universal Press Syndicate
www.ucomics.com www.boondocks.net

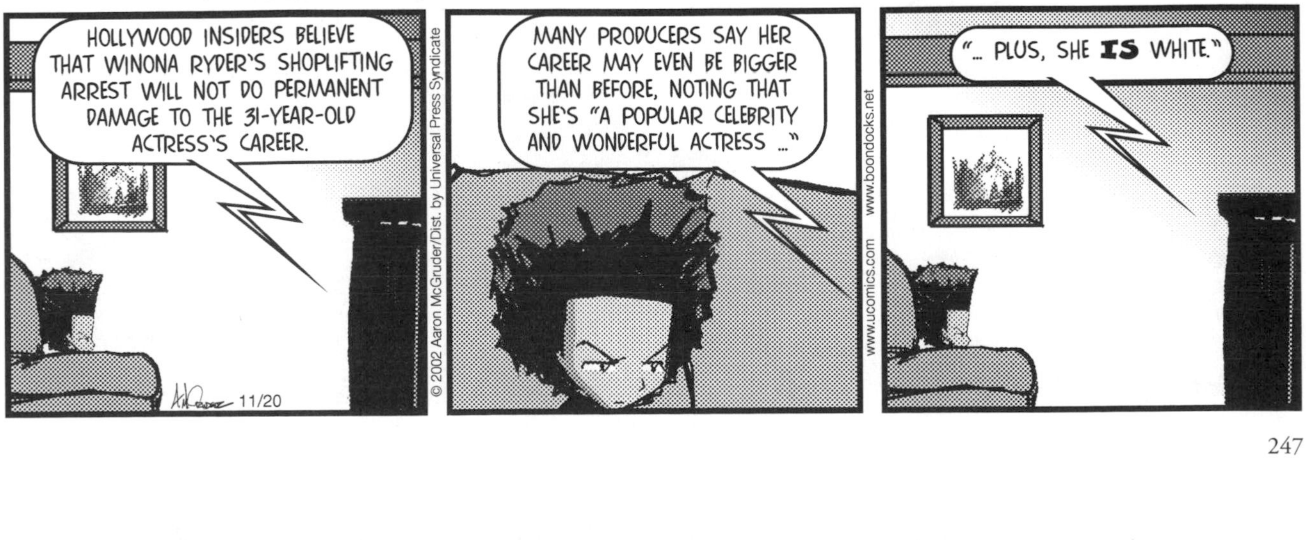
HOLLYWOOD INSIDERS BELIEVE THAT WINONA RYDER'S SHOPLIFTING ARREST WILL NOT DO PERMANENT DAMAGE TO THE 31-YEAR-OLD ACTRESS'S CAREER.
11/20
MANY PRODUCERS SAY HER CAREER MAY EVEN BE BIGGER THAN BEFORE, NOTING THAT SHE'S "A POPULAR CELEBRITY AND WONDERFUL ACTRESS ..."
"... PLUS, SHE IS WHITE."
© 2002 Aaron McGruder/Dist. by Universal Press Syndicate
www.ucomics.com www.boondocks.net

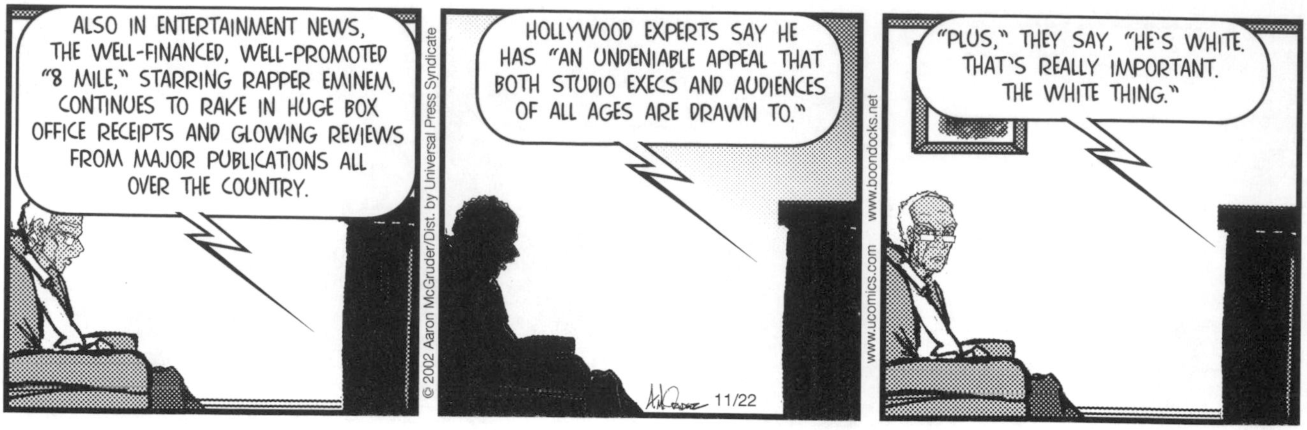
ALSO IN ENTERTAINMENT NEWS, THE WELL-FINANCED, WELL-PROMOTED "8 MILE," STARRING RAPPER EMINEM, CONTINUES TO RAKE IN HUGE BOX OFFICE RECEIPTS AND GLOWING REVIEWS FROM MAJOR PUBLICATIONS ALL OVER THE COUNTRY.
© 2002 Aaron McGruder/Dist. by Universal Press Syndicate
HOLLYWOOD EXPERTS SAY HE HAS "AN UNDENIABLE APPEAL THAT BOTH STUDIO EXECS AND AUDIENCES OF ALL AGES ARE DRAWN TO."
11/22
www.ucomics.com www.boondocks.net
"PLUS," THEY SAY, "HE'S WHITE. THAT'S REALLY IMPORTANT. THE WHITE THING."

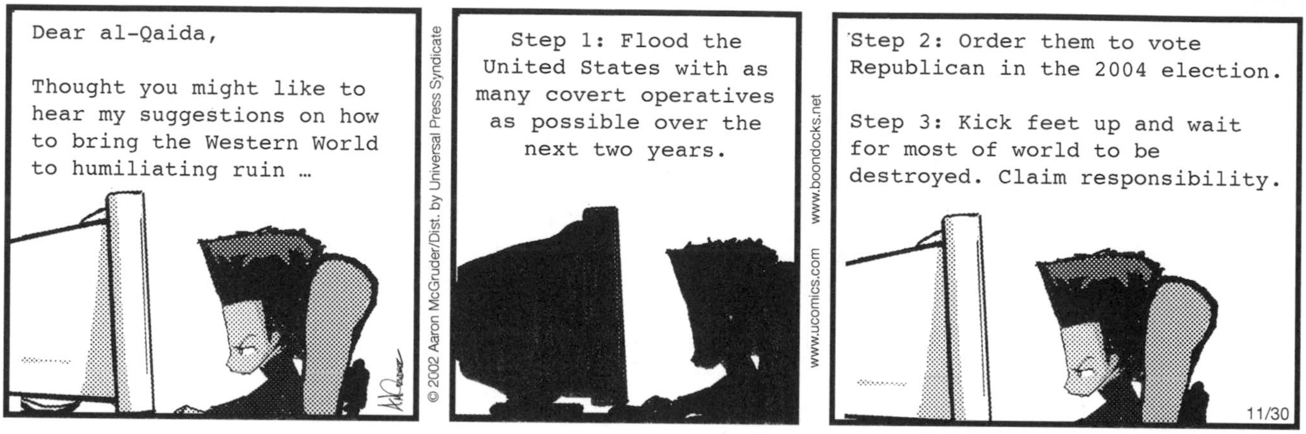
Dear al-Qaida,
Thought you might like to hear my suggestions on how to bring the Western World to humiliating ruin …
© 2002 Aaron McGruder/Dist. by Universal Press Syndicate
Step 1: Flood the United States with as many covert operatives as possible over the next two years.
www.ucomics.com www.boondocks.net
Step 2: Order them to vote Republican in the 2004 election.
Step 3: Kick feet up and wait for most of world to be destroyed. Claim responsibility.
11/30

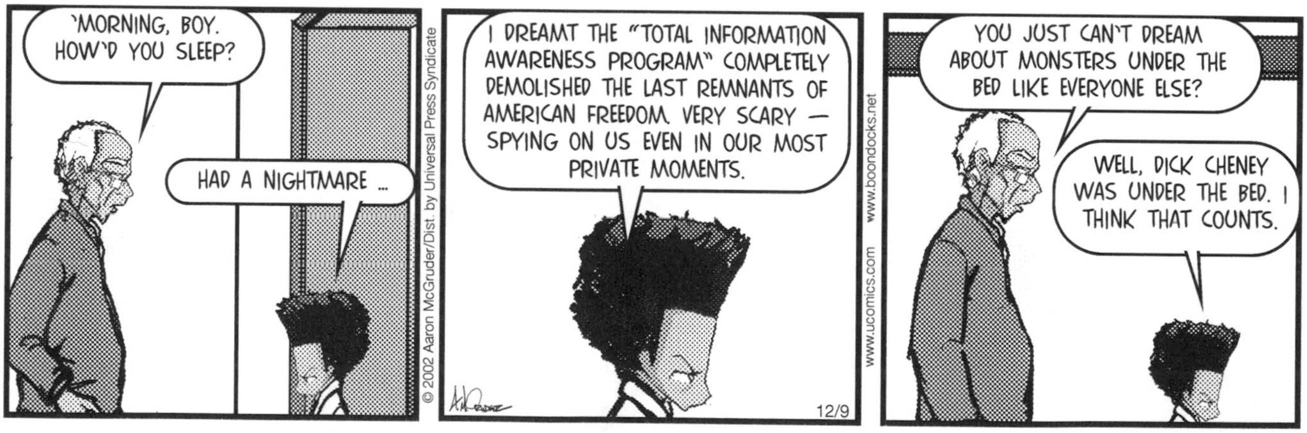
'MORNING, BOY. HOW'D YOU SLEEP?
HAD A NIGHTMARE …
© 2002 Aaron McGruder/Dist. by Universal Press Syndicate
I DREAMT THE "TOTAL INFORMATION AWARENESS PROGRAM" COMPLETELY DEMOLISHED THE LAST REMNANTS OF AMERICAN FREEDOM. VERY SCARY — SPYING ON US EVEN IN OUR MOST PRIVATE MOMENTS.
12/9
www.ucomics.com www.boondocks.net
YOU JUST CAN'T DREAM ABOUT MONSTERS UNDER THE BED LIKE EVERYONE ELSE?
WELL, DICK CHENEY WAS UNDER THE BED. I THINK THAT COUNTS.

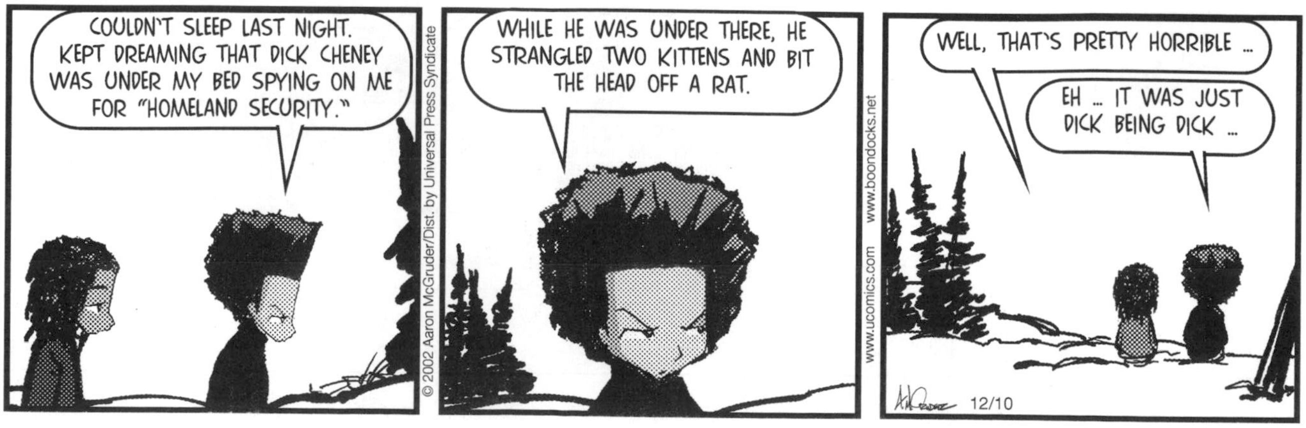
COULDN'T SLEEP LAST NIGHT. KEPT DREAMING THAT DICK CHENEY WAS UNDER MY BED SPYING ON ME FOR "HOMELAND SECURITY."
© 2002 Aaron McGruder/Dist. by Universal Press Syndicate
WHILE HE WAS UNDER THERE, HE STRANGLED TWO KITTENS AND BIT THE HEAD OFF A RAT.
www.ucomics.com www.boondocks.net
WELL, THAT'S PRETTY HORRIBLE …
EH … IT WAS JUST DICK BEING DICK …
12/10

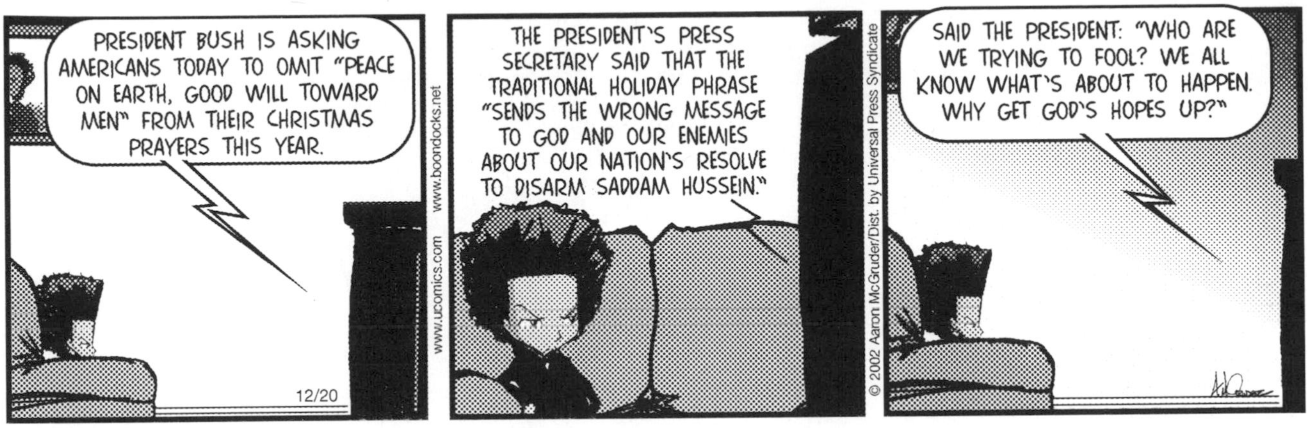
PRESIDENT BUSH IS ASKING AMERICANS TODAY TO OMIT "PEACE ON EARTH, GOOD WILL TOWARD MEN" FROM THEIR CHRISTMAS PRAYERS THIS YEAR.
12/20
www.ucomics.com www.boondocks.net
THE PRESIDENT'S PRESS SECRETARY SAID THAT THE TRADITIONAL HOLIDAY PHRASE "SENDS THE WRONG MESSAGE TO GOD AND OUR ENEMIES ABOUT OUR NATION'S RESOLVE TO DISARM SADDAM HUSSEIN."
© 2002 Aaron McGruder/Dist. by Universal Press Syndicate
SAID THE PRESIDENT: "WHO ARE WE TRYING TO FOOL? WE ALL KNOW WHAT'S ABOUT TO HAPPEN. WHY GET GOD'S HOPES UP?"

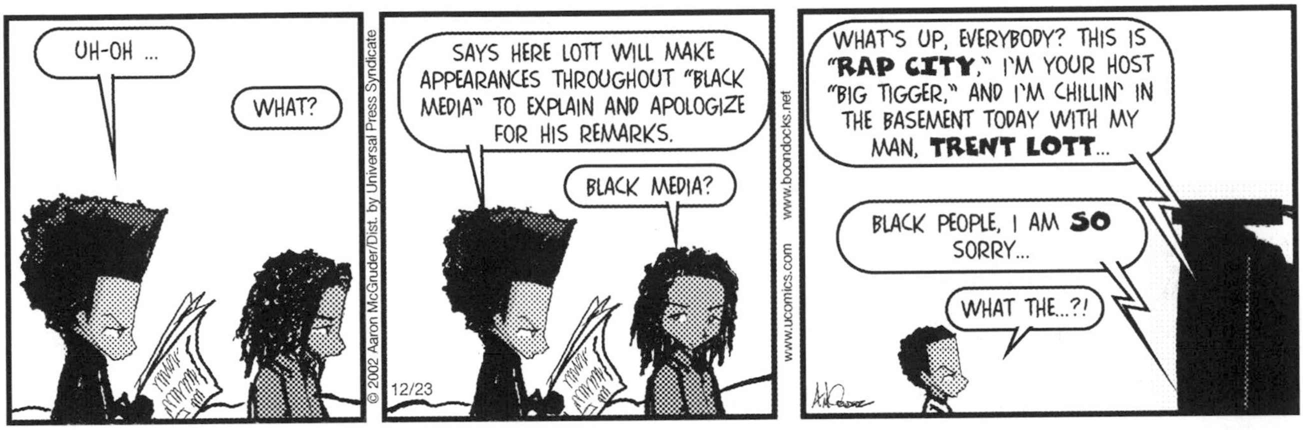
UH-OH ...
WHAT?
© 2002 Aaron McGruder/Dist. by Universal Press Syndicate
12/23
SAYS HERE LOTT WILL MAKE APPEARANCES THROUGHOUT "BLACK MEDIA" TO EXPLAIN AND APOLOGIZE FOR HIS REMARKS.
BLACK MEDIA?
www.ucomics.com www.boondocks.net
WHAT'S UP, EVERYBODY? THIS IS "RAP CITY," I'M YOUR HOST "BIG TIGGER," AND I'M CHILLIN' IN THE BASEMENT TODAY WITH MY MAN, TRENT LOTT...
BLACK PEOPLE, I AM SO SORRY...
WHAT THE...?!

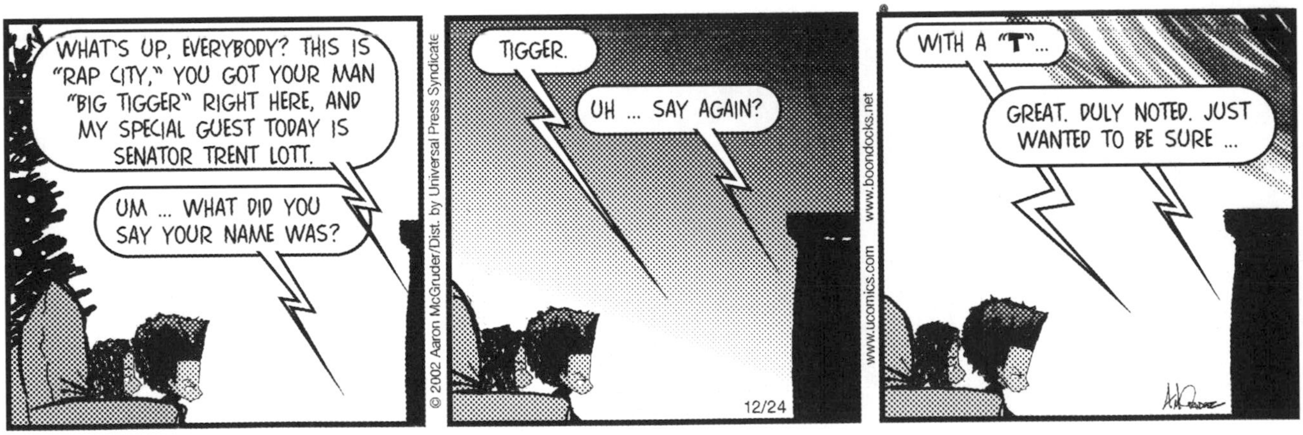
WHAT'S UP, EVERYBODY? THIS IS "RAP CITY," YOU GOT YOUR MAN "BIG TIGGER" RIGHT HERE, AND MY SPECIAL GUEST TODAY IS SENATOR TRENT LOTT.
UM ... WHAT DID YOU SAY YOUR NAME WAS?
© 2002 Aaron McGruder/Dist. by Universal Press Syndicate
TIGGER.
UH ... SAY AGAIN?
12/24
www.ucomics.com www.boondocks.net
WITH A "T"...
GREAT. DULY NOTED. JUST WANTED TO BE SURE ...

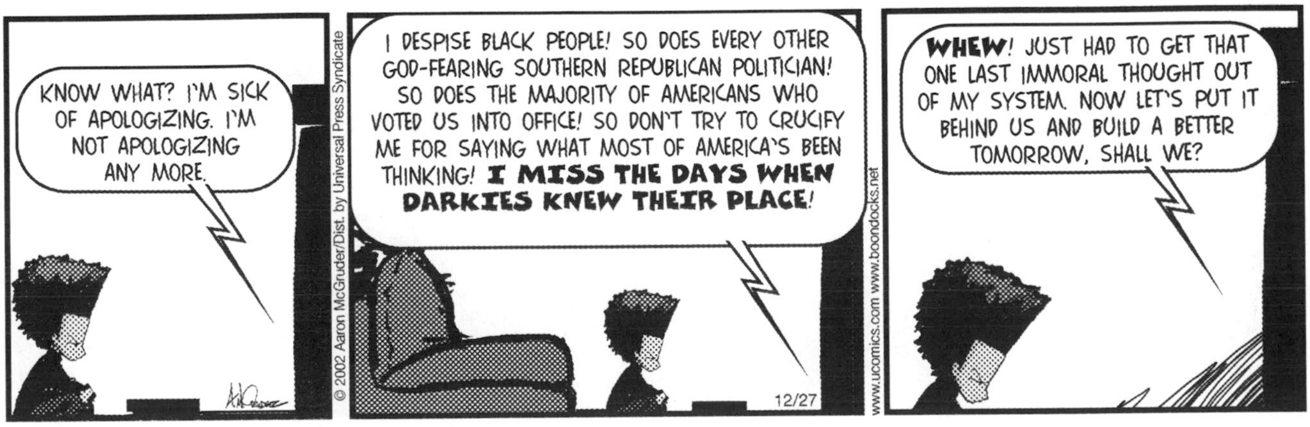
KNOW WHAT? I'M SICK OF APOLOGIZING. I'M NOT APOLOGIZING ANY MORE.
© 2002 Aaron McGruder/Dist. by Universal Press Syndicate
I DESPISE BLACK PEOPLE! SO DOES EVERY OTHER GOD-FEARING SOUTHERN REPUBLICAN POLITICIAN! SO DOES THE MAJORITY OF AMERICANS WHO VOTED US INTO OFFICE! SO DON'T TRY TO CRUCIFY ME FOR SAYING WHAT MOST OF AMERICA'S BEEN THINKING! I MISS THE DAYS WHEN DARKIES KNEW THEIR PLACE!
12/27
www.ucomics.com www.boondocks.net
WHEW! JUST HAD TO GET THAT ONE LAST IMMORAL THOUGHT OUT OF MY SYSTEM. NOW LET'S PUT IT BEHIND US AND BUILD A BETTER TOMORROW, SHALL WE?

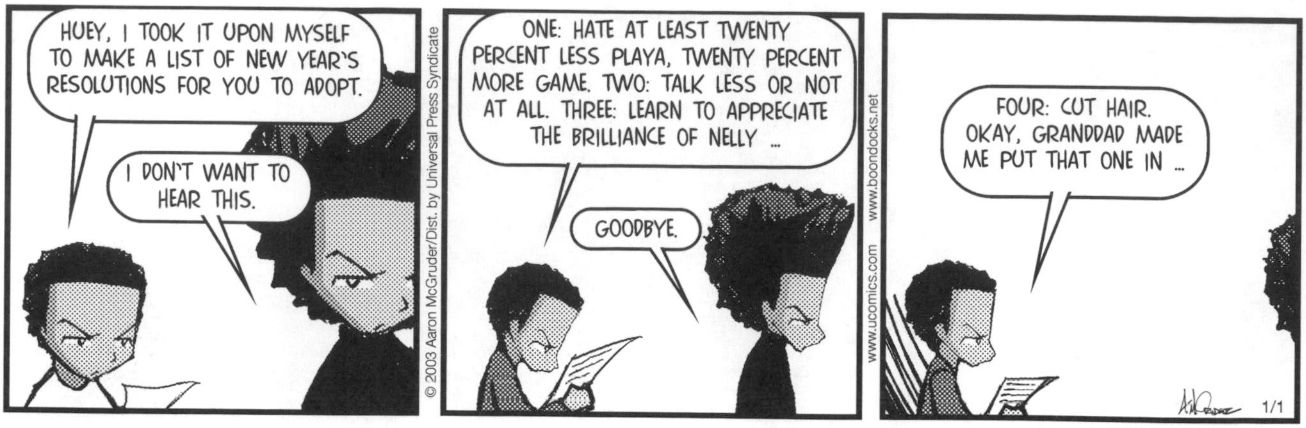
HUEY, I TOOK IT UPON MYSELF TO MAKE A LIST OF NEW YEAR'S RESOLUTIONS FOR YOU TO ADOPT.
I DON'T WANT TO HEAR THIS.
© 2003 Aaron McGruder/Dist. by Universal Press Syndicate
ONE: HATE AT LEAST TWENTY PERCENT LESS PLAYA, TWENTY PERCENT MORE GAME. TWO: TALK LESS OR NOT AT ALL. THREE: LEARN TO APPRECIATE THE BRILLIANCE OF NELLY ...
GOODBYE.
www.ucomics.com www.boondocks.net
FOUR: CUT HAIR. OKAY, GRANDDAD MADE ME PUT THAT ONE IN ...
1/1

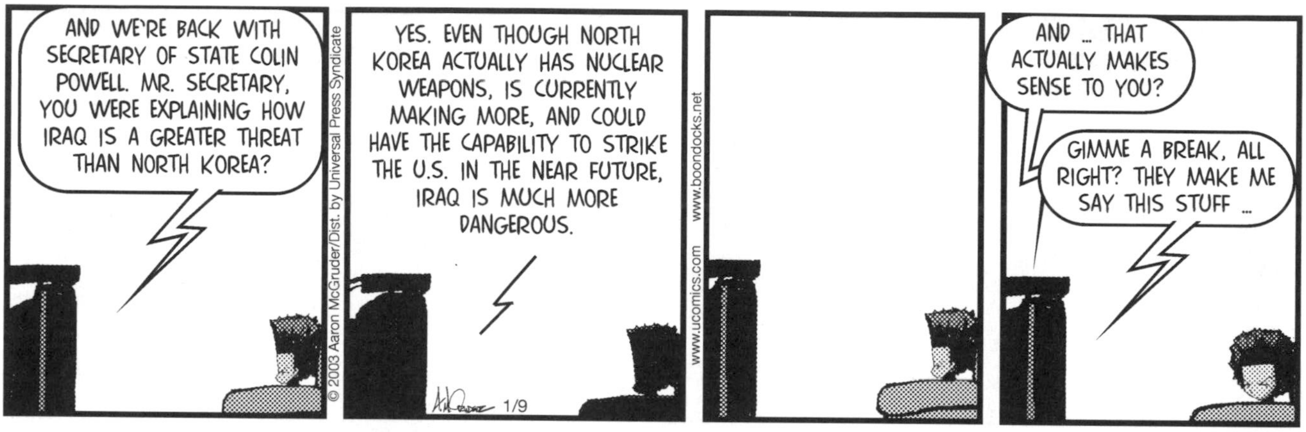
AND WE'RE BACK WITH SECRETARY OF STATE COLIN POWELL. MR. SECRETARY, YOU WERE EXPLAINING HOW IRAQ IS A GREATER THREAT THAN NORTH KOREA?
© 2003 Aaron McGruder/Dist. by Universal Press Syndicate
YES. EVEN THOUGH NORTH KOREA ACTUALLY HAS NUCLEAR WEAPONS, IS CURRENTLY MAKING MORE, AND COULD HAVE THE CAPABILITY TO STRIKE THE U.S. IN THE NEAR FUTURE, IRAQ IS MUCH MORE DANGEROUS.
1/9
www.ucomics.com www.boondocks.net
AND ... THAT ACTUALLY MAKES SENSE TO YOU?
GIMME A BREAK, ALL RIGHT? THEY MAKE ME SAY THIS STUFF ...

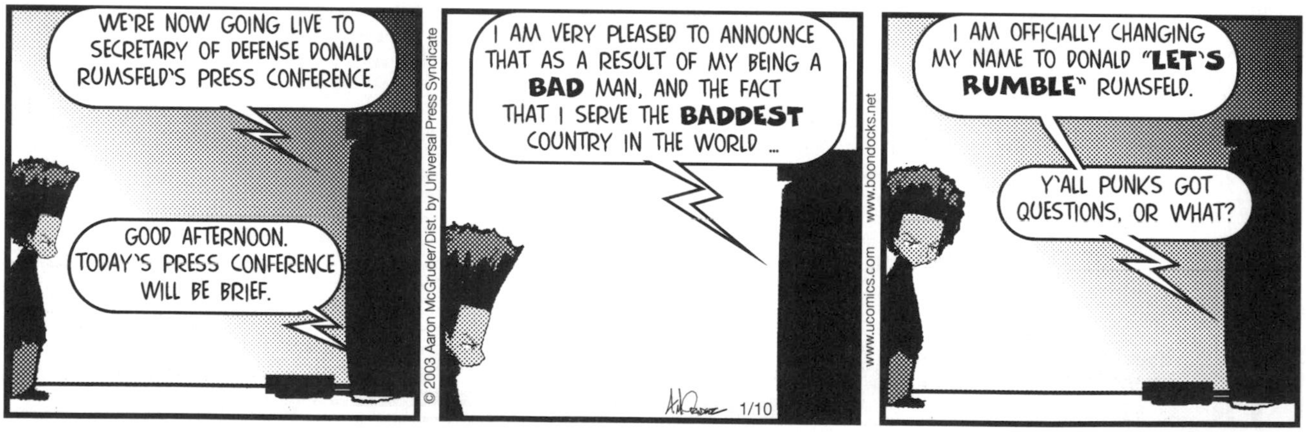
WE'RE NOW GOING LIVE TO SECRETARY OF DEFENSE DONALD RUMSFELD'S PRESS CONFERENCE.
GOOD AFTERNOON. TODAY'S PRESS CONFERENCE WILL BE BRIEF.
© 2003 Aaron McGruder/Dist. by Universal Press Syndicate
I AM VERY PLEASED TO ANNOUNCE THAT AS A RESULT OF MY BEING A BAD MAN, AND THE FACT THAT I SERVE THE BADDEST COUNTRY IN THE WORLD ...
1/10
www.ucomics.com www.boondocks.net
I AM OFFICIALLY CHANGING MY NAME TO DONALD "LET'S RUMBLE" RUMSFELD.
Y'ALL PUNKS GOT QUESTIONS, OR WHAT?

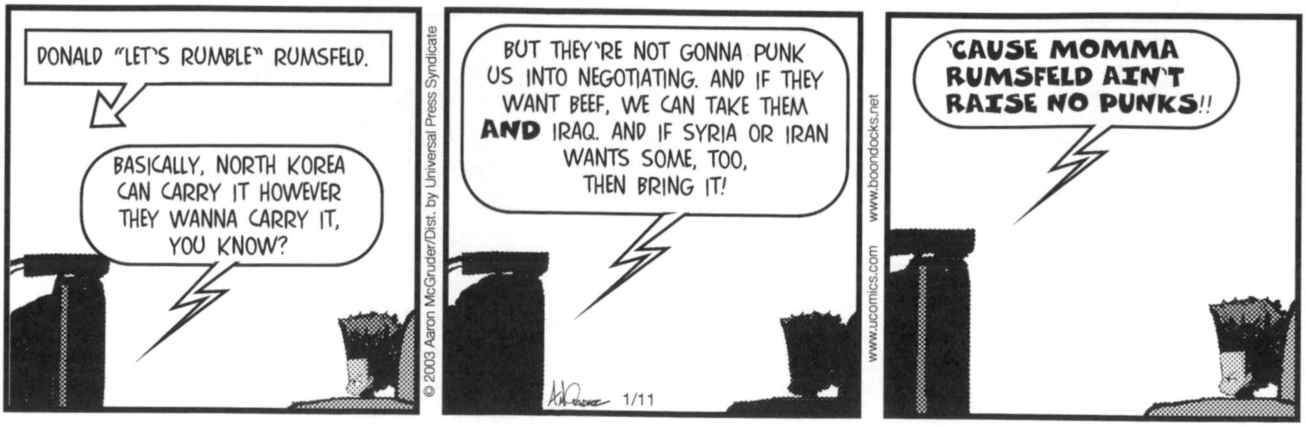
DONALD "LET'S RUMBLE" RUMSFELD.
BASICALLY, NORTH KOREA CAN CARRY IT HOWEVER THEY WANNA CARRY IT, YOU KNOW?
© 2003 Aaron McGruder/Dist. by Universal Press Syndicate
BUT THEY'RE NOT GONNA PUNK US INTO NEGOTIATING. AND IF THEY WANT BEEF, WE CAN TAKE THEM AND IRAQ. AND IF SYRIA OR IRAN WANTS SOME, TOO, THEN BRING IT!
1/11
www.ucomics.com www.boondocks.net
'CAUSE MOMMA RUMSFELD AIN'T RAISE NO PUNKS!!

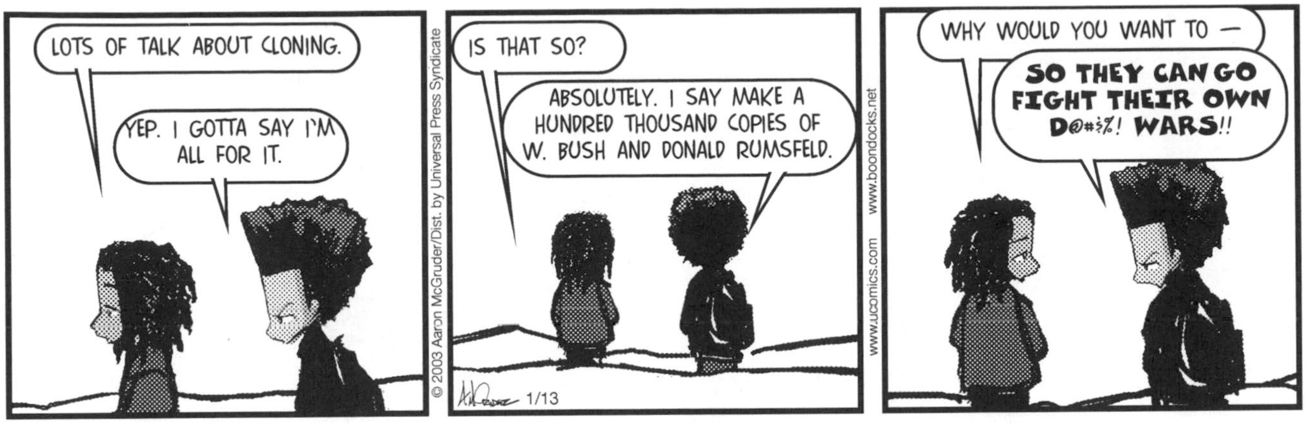
LOTS OF TALK ABOUT CLONING.
YEP. I GOTTA SAY I'M ALL FOR IT.
© 2003 Aaron McGruder/Dist. by Universal Press Syndicate
1/13
IS THAT SO?
ABSOLUTELY. I SAY MAKE A HUNDRED THOUSAND COPIES OF W. BUSH AND DONALD RUMSFELD.
www.ucomics.com www.boondocks.net
WHY WOULD YOU WANT TO —
SO THEY CAN GO FIGHT THEIR OWN D@#$%! WARS!!

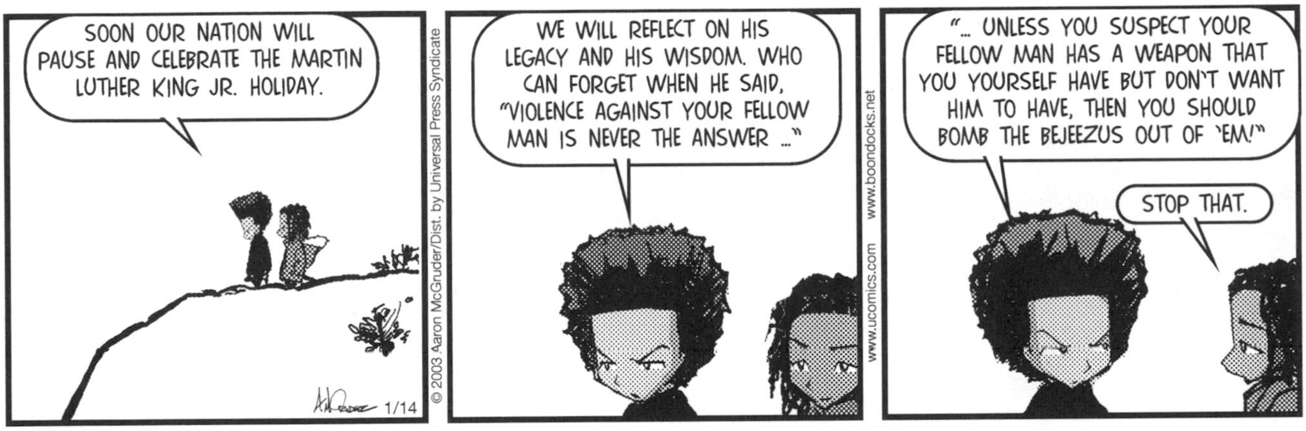
SOON OUR NATION WILL PAUSE AND CELEBRATE THE MARTIN LUTHER KING JR. HOLIDAY.
1/14
© 2003 Aaron McGruder/Dist. by Universal Press Syndicate
WE WILL REFLECT ON HIS LEGACY AND HIS WISDOM. WHO CAN FORGET WHEN HE SAID, "VIOLENCE AGAINST YOUR FELLOW MAN IS NEVER THE ANSWER ..."
www.ucomics.com www.boondocks.net
"... UNLESS YOU SUSPECT YOUR FELLOW MAN HAS A WEAPON THAT YOU YOURSELF HAVE BUT DON'T WANT HIM TO HAVE, THEN YOU SHOULD BOMB THE BEJEEZUS OUT OF 'EM!"
STOP THAT.

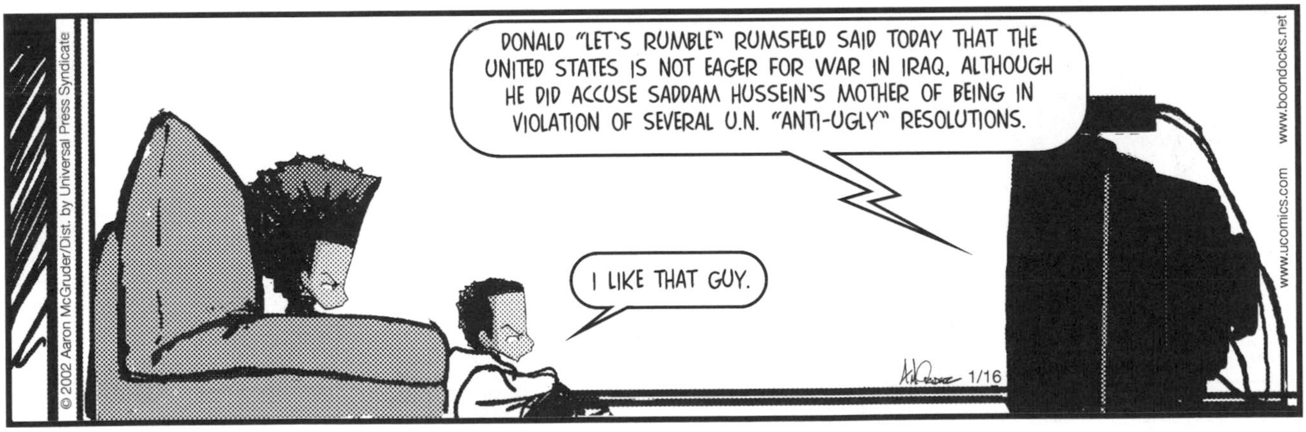
© 2002 Aaron McGruder/Dist. by Universal Press Syndicate
DONALD "LET'S RUMBLE" RUMSFELD SAID TODAY THAT THE UNITED STATES IS NOT EAGER FOR WAR IN IRAQ, ALTHOUGH HE DID ACCUSE SADDAM HUSSEIN'S MOTHER OF BEING IN VIOLATION OF SEVERAL U.N. "ANTI-UGLY" RESOLUTIONS.
I LIKE THAT GUY.
1/16
www.ucomics.com www.boondocks.net

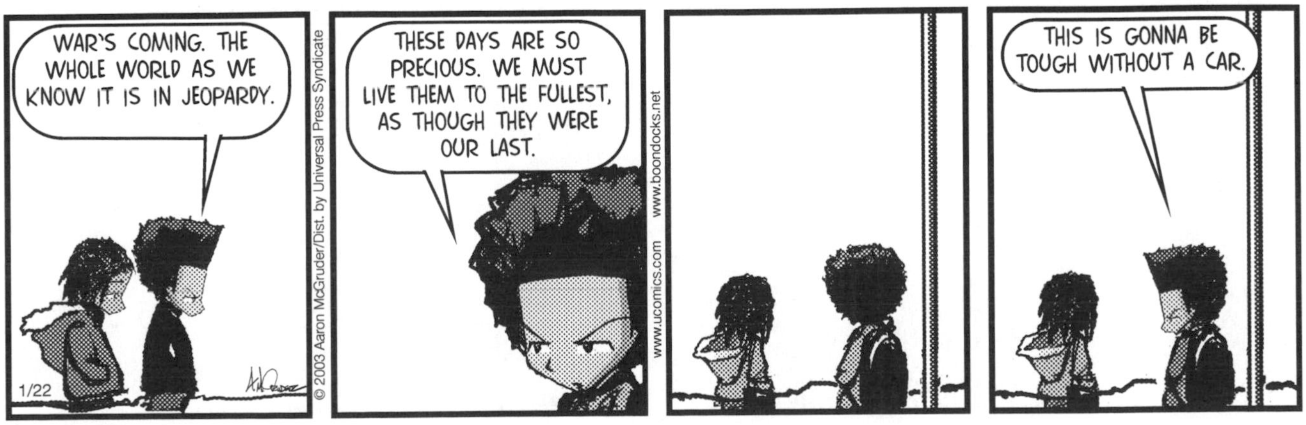
WAR'S COMING. THE WHOLE WORLD AS WE KNOW IT IS IN JEOPARDY.
1/22
© 2003 Aaron McGruder/Dist. by Universal Press Syndicate
THESE DAYS ARE SO PRECIOUS. WE MUST LIVE THEM TO THE FULLEST, AS THOUGH THEY WERE OUR LAST.
www.ucomics.com www.boondocks.net
THIS IS GONNA BE TOUGH WITHOUT A CAR.

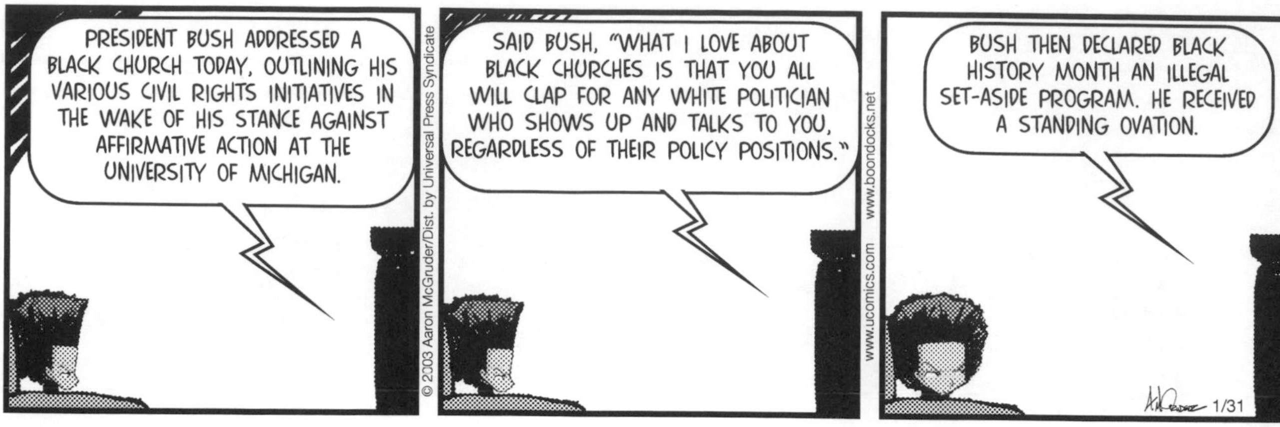
PRESIDENT BUSH ADDRESSED A BLACK CHURCH TODAY, OUTLINING HIS VARIOUS CIVIL RIGHTS INITIATIVES IN THE WAKE OF HIS STANCE AGAINST AFFIRMATIVE ACTION AT THE UNIVERSITY OF MICHIGAN.
© 2003 Aaron McGruder/Dist. by Universal Press Syndicate
SAID BUSH, "WHAT I LOVE ABOUT BLACK CHURCHES IS THAT YOU ALL WILL CLAP FOR ANY WHITE POLITICIAN WHO SHOWS UP AND TALKS TO YOU, REGARDLESS OF THEIR POLICY POSITIONS."
www.ucomics.com www.boondocks.net
BUSH THEN DECLARED BLACK HISTORY MONTH AN ILLEGAL SET-ASIDE PROGRAM. HE RECEIVED A STANDING OVATION.
1/31

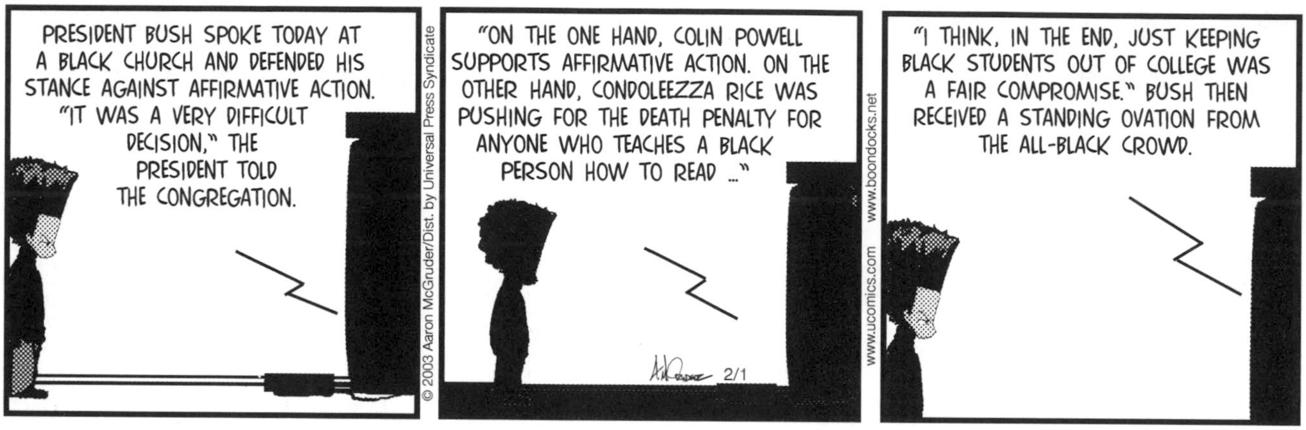
PRESIDENT BUSH SPOKE TODAY AT A BLACK CHURCH AND DEFENDED HIS STANCE AGAINST AFFIRMATIVE ACTION. "IT WAS A VERY DIFFICULT DECISION," THE PRESIDENT TOLD THE CONGREGATION.
© 2003 Aaron McGruder/Dist. by Universal Press Syndicate
"ON THE ONE HAND, COLIN POWELL SUPPORTS AFFIRMATIVE ACTION. ON THE OTHER HAND, CONDOLEEZZA RICE WAS PUSHING FOR THE DEATH PENALTY FOR ANYONE WHO TEACHES A BLACK PERSON HOW TO READ ..."
2/1
www.ucomics.com www.boondocks.net
"I THINK, IN THE END, JUST KEEPING BLACK STUDENTS OUT OF COLLEGE WAS A FAIR COMPROMISE." BUSH THEN RECEIVED A STANDING OVATION FROM THE ALL-BLACK CROWD.

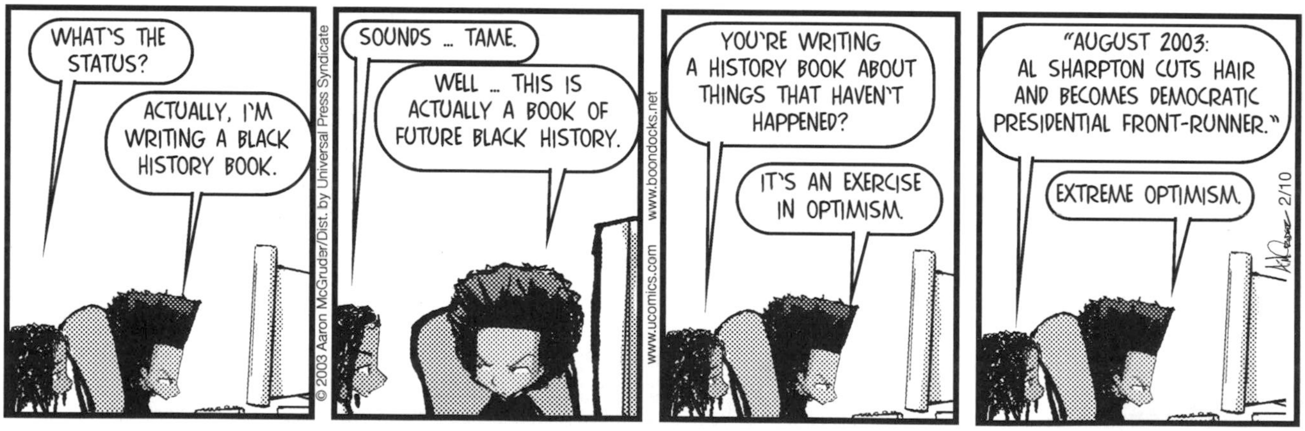
WHAT'S THE STATUS?
ACTUALLY, I'M WRITING A BLACK HISTORY BOOK.
© 2003 Aaron McGruder/Dist. by Universal Press Syndicate
SOUNDS ... TAME.
WELL ... THIS IS ACTUALLY A BOOK OF FUTURE BLACK HISTORY.
www.ucomics.com www.boondocks.net
YOU'RE WRITING A HISTORY BOOK ABOUT THINGS THAT HAVEN'T HAPPENED?
IT'S AN EXERCISE IN OPTIMISM.
"AUGUST 2003: AL SHARPTON CUTS HAIR AND BECOMES DEMOCRATIC PRESIDENTIAL FRONT-RUNNER."
EXTREME OPTIMISM.
2/10

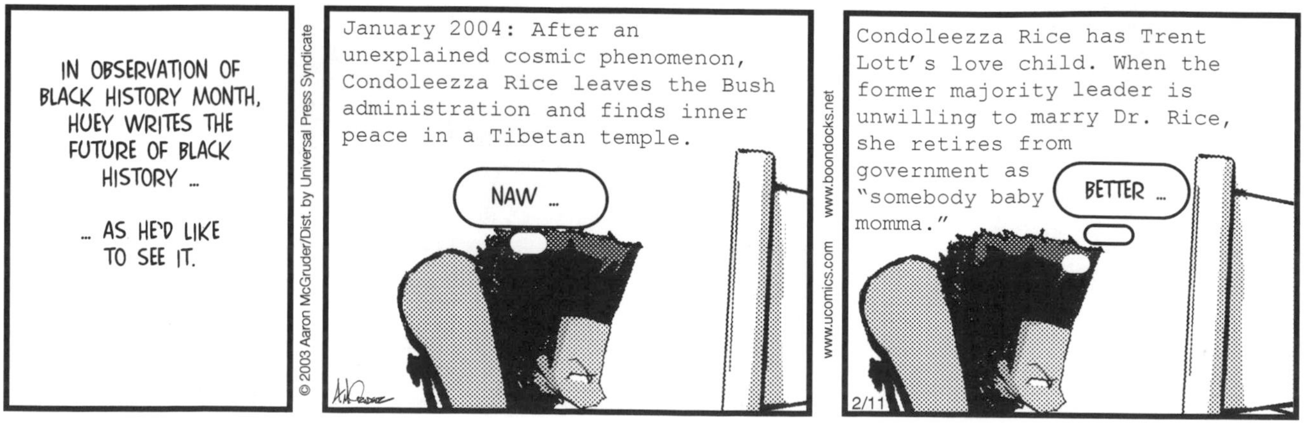
IN OBSERVATION OF BLACK HISTORY MONTH, HUEY WRITES THE FUTURE OF BLACK HISTORY ...
... AS HE'D LIKE TO SEE IT.
© 2003 Aaron McGruder/Dist. by Universal Press Syndicate
January 2004: After an unexplained cosmic phenomenon, Condoleezza Rice leaves the Bush administration and finds inner peace in a Tibetan temple.
NAW ...
www.ucomics.com www.boondocks.net
Condoleezza Rice has Trent Lott's love child. When the former majority leader is unwilling to marry Dr. Rice, she retires from government as "somebody baby momma."
BETTER ...
2/11

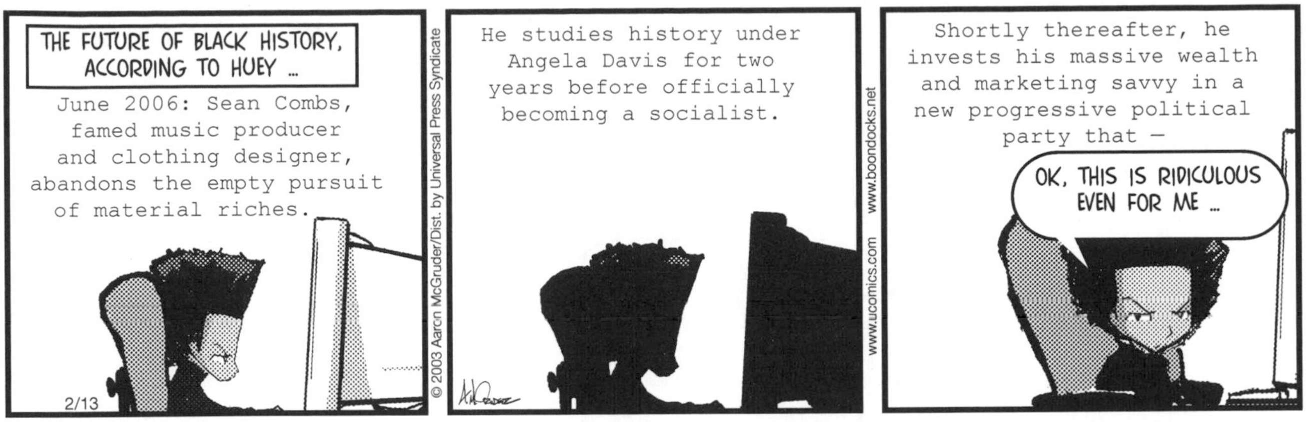
THE FUTURE OF BLACK HISTORY, ACCORDING TO HUEY ...
June 2006: Sean Combs, famed music producer and clothing designer, abandons the empty pursuit of material riches.
2/13
© 2003 Aaron McGruder/Dist. by Universal Press Syndicate
He studies history under Angela Davis for two years before officially becoming a socialist.
www.ucomics.com www.boondocks.net
Shortly thereafter, he invests his massive wealth and marketing savvy in a new progressive political party that —
OK, THIS IS RIDICULOUS EVEN FOR ME ...

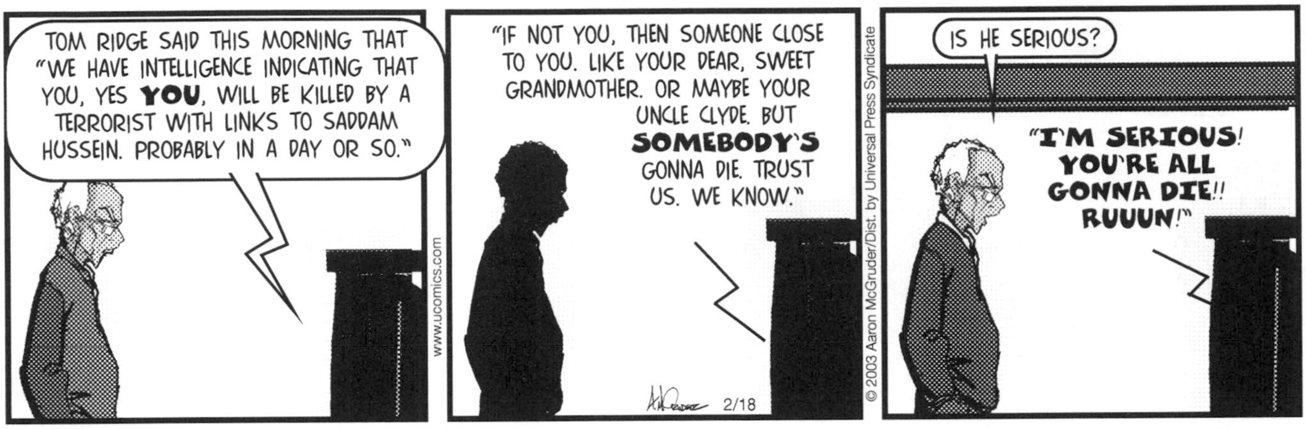
TOM RIDGE SAID THIS MORNING THAT "WE HAVE INTELLIGENCE INDICATING THAT YOU, YES **YOU**, WILL BE KILLED BY A TERRORIST WITH LINKS TO SADDAM HUSSEIN. PROBABLY IN A DAY OR SO."
www.ucomics.com
"IF NOT YOU, THEN SOMEONE CLOSE TO YOU. LIKE YOUR DEAR, SWEET GRANDMOTHER. OR MAYBE YOUR UNCLE CLYDE. BUT **SOMEBODY'S** GONNA DIE. TRUST US. WE KNOW."
2/18
© 2003 Aaron McGruder/Dist. by Universal Press Syndicate
IS HE SERIOUS?
"**I'M SERIOUS! YOU'RE ALL GONNA DIE!! RUUUN!**"

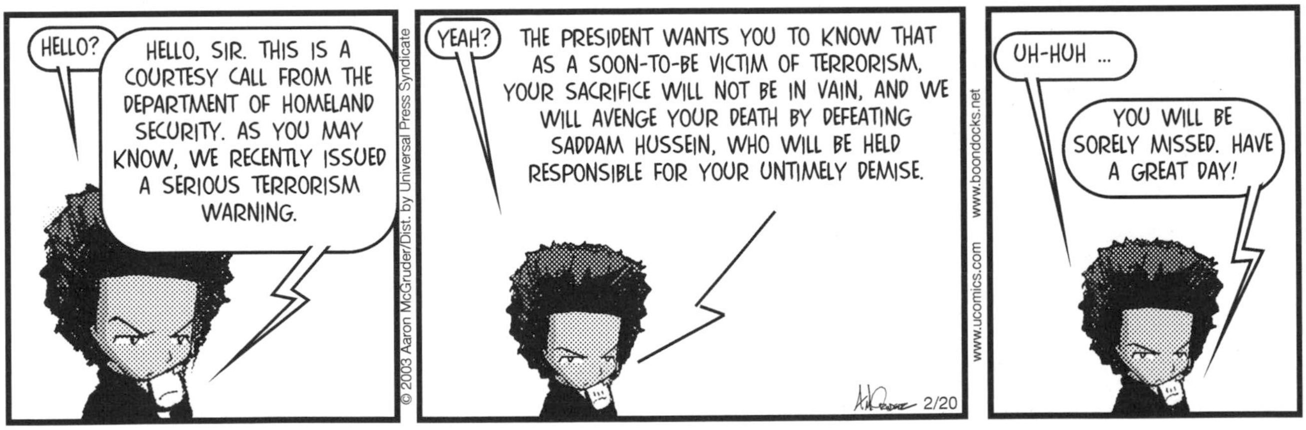
HELLO?
HELLO, SIR. THIS IS A COURTESY CALL FROM THE DEPARTMENT OF HOMELAND SECURITY. AS YOU MAY KNOW, WE RECENTLY ISSUED A SERIOUS TERRORISM WARNING.
© 2003 Aaron McGruder/Dist. by Universal Press Syndicate
YEAH?
THE PRESIDENT WANTS YOU TO KNOW THAT AS A SOON-TO-BE VICTIM OF TERRORISM, YOUR SACRIFICE WILL NOT BE IN VAIN, AND WE WILL AVENGE YOUR DEATH BY DEFEATING SADDAM HUSSEIN, WHO WILL BE HELD RESPONSIBLE FOR YOUR UNTIMELY DEMISE.
2/20
www.ucomics.com www.boondocks.net
UH-HUH ...
YOU WILL BE SORELY MISSED. HAVE A GREAT DAY!

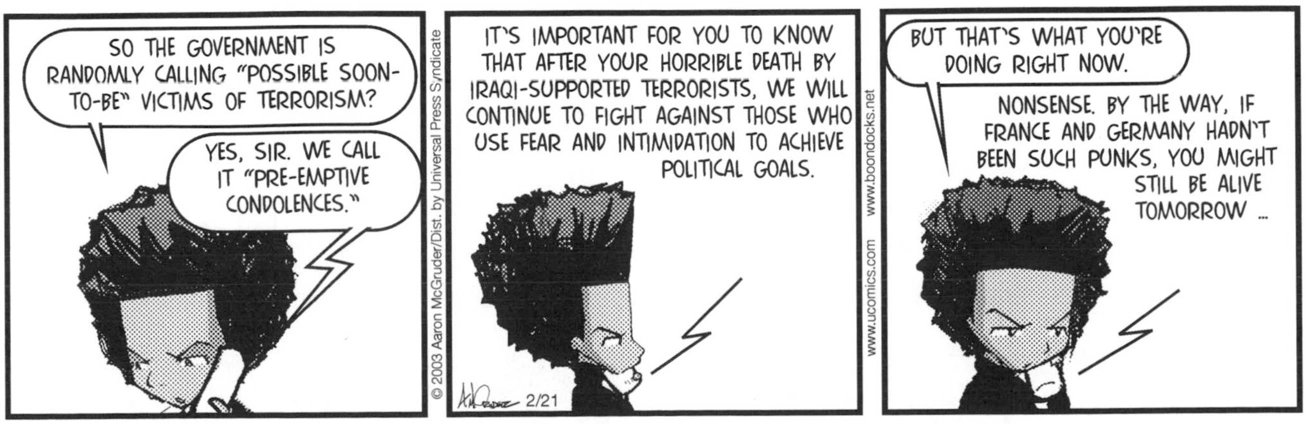
SO THE GOVERNMENT IS RANDOMLY CALLING "POSSIBLE SOON-TO-BE" VICTIMS OF TERRORISM?
YES, SIR. WE CALL IT "PRE-EMPTIVE CONDOLENCES."
© 2003 Aaron McGruder/Dist. by Universal Press Syndicate
IT'S IMPORTANT FOR YOU TO KNOW THAT AFTER YOUR HORRIBLE DEATH BY IRAQI-SUPPORTED TERRORISTS, WE WILL CONTINUE TO FIGHT AGAINST THOSE WHO USE FEAR AND INTIMIDATION TO ACHIEVE POLITICAL GOALS.
2/21
www.ucomics.com www.boondocks.net
BUT THAT'S WHAT YOU'RE DOING RIGHT NOW.
NONSENSE. BY THE WAY, IF FRANCE AND GERMANY HADN'T BEEN SUCH PUNKS, YOU MIGHT STILL BE ALIVE TOMORROW ...

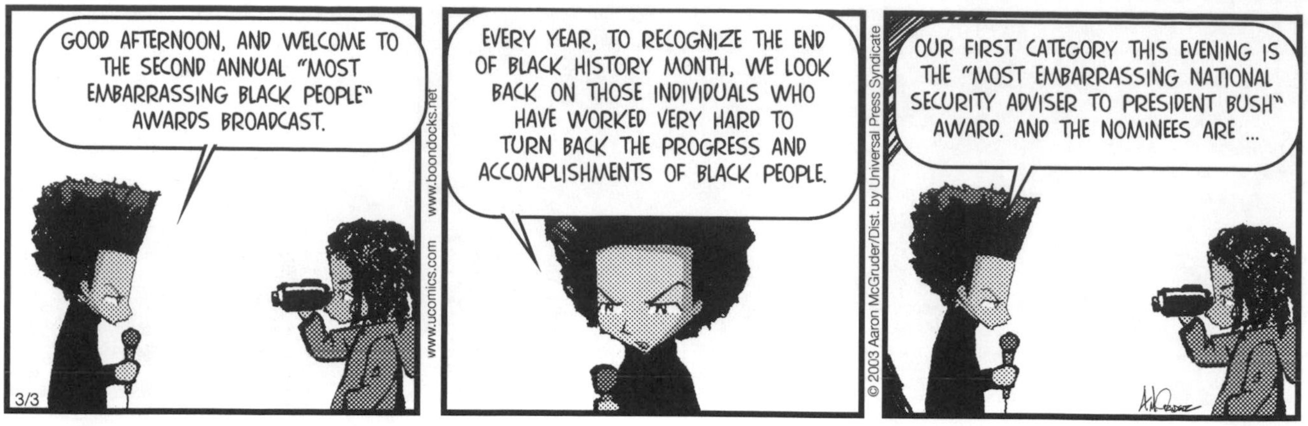
GOOD AFTERNOON, AND WELCOME TO THE SECOND ANNUAL "MOST EMBARRASSING BLACK PEOPLE" AWARDS BROADCAST.
EVERY YEAR, TO RECOGNIZE THE END OF BLACK HISTORY MONTH, WE LOOK BACK ON THOSE INDIVIDUALS WHO HAVE WORKED VERY HARD TO TURN BACK THE PROGRESS AND ACCOMPLISHMENTS OF BLACK PEOPLE.
OUR FIRST CATEGORY THIS EVENING IS THE "MOST EMBARRASSING NATIONAL SECURITY ADVISER TO PRESIDENT BUSH" AWARD. AND THE NOMINEES ARE ...
3/3
www.ucomics.com www.boondocks.net
© 2003 Aaron McGruder/Dist. by Universal Press Syndicate

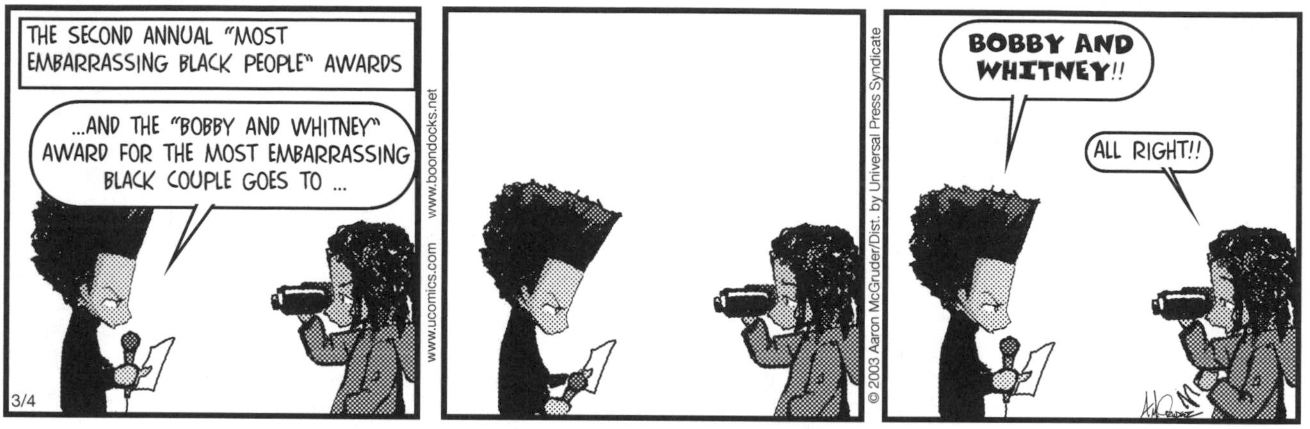
THE SECOND ANNUAL "MOST EMBARRASSING BLACK PEOPLE" AWARDS
...AND THE "BOBBY AND WHITNEY" AWARD FOR THE MOST EMBARRASSING BLACK COUPLE GOES TO ...
BOBBY AND WHITNEY!!
ALL RIGHT!!
3/4
www.ucomics.com www.boondocks.net
© 2003 Aaron McGruder/Dist. by Universal Press Syndicate

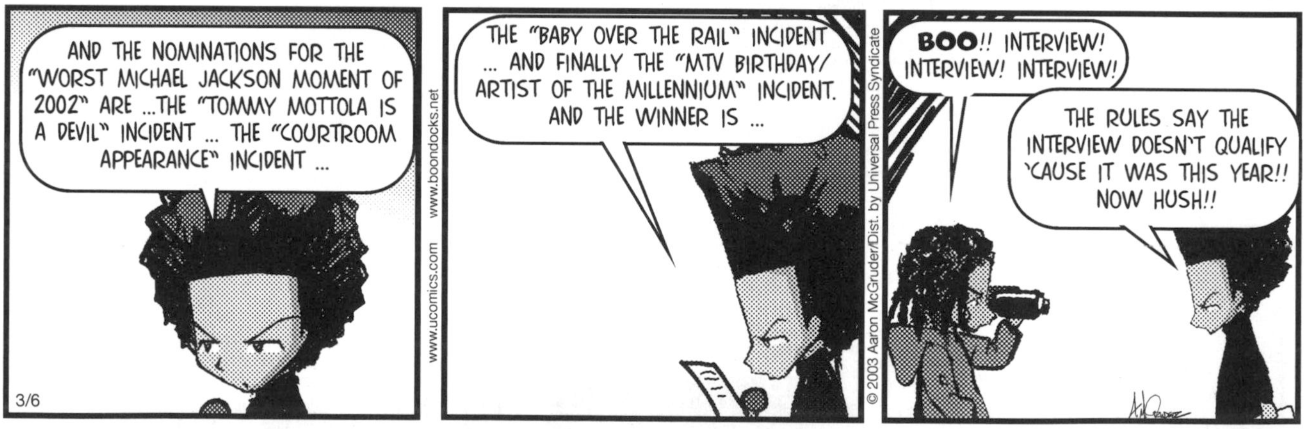
AND THE NOMINATIONS FOR THE "WORST MICHAEL JACKSON MOMENT OF 2002" ARE ...THE "TOMMY MOTTOLA IS A DEVIL" INCIDENT ... THE "COURTROOM APPEARANCE" INCIDENT ...
THE "BABY OVER THE RAIL" INCIDENT ... AND FINALLY THE "MTV BIRTHDAY/ ARTIST OF THE MILLENNIUM" INCIDENT. AND THE WINNER IS ...
BOO!! INTERVIEW! INTERVIEW! INTERVIEW!
THE RULES SAY THE INTERVIEW DOESN'T QUALIFY 'CAUSE IT WAS THIS YEAR!! NOW HUSH!!
3/6
www.ucomics.com www.boondocks.net
© 2003 Aaron McGruder/Dist. by Universal Press Syndicate

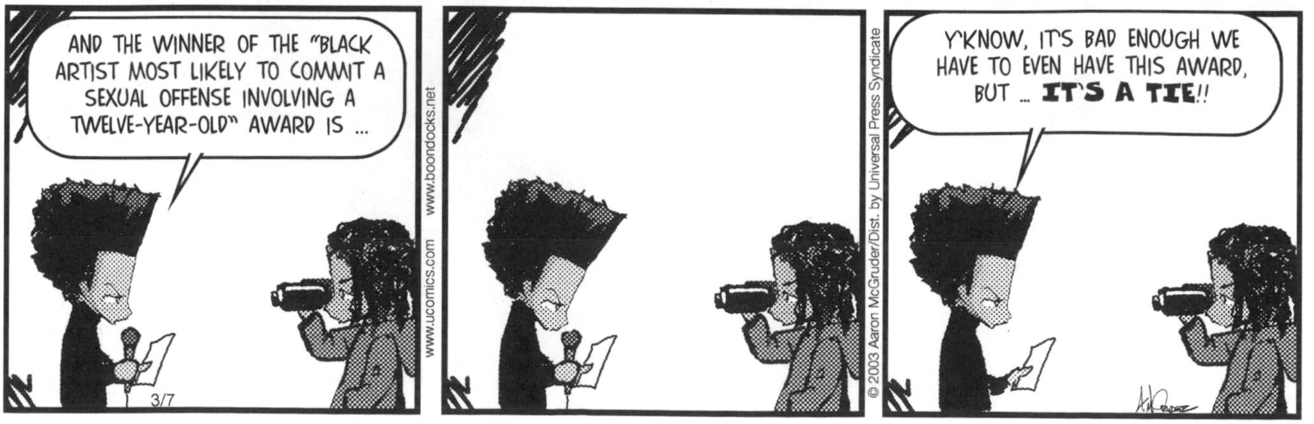
AND THE WINNER OF THE "BLACK ARTIST MOST LIKELY TO COMMIT A SEXUAL OFFENSE INVOLVING A TWELVE-YEAR-OLD" AWARD IS ...
Y'KNOW, IT'S BAD ENOUGH WE HAVE TO EVEN HAVE THIS AWARD, BUT ... IT'S A TIE!!
3/7
www.ucomics.com www.boondocks.net
© 2003 Aaron McGruder/Dist. by Universal Press Syndicate

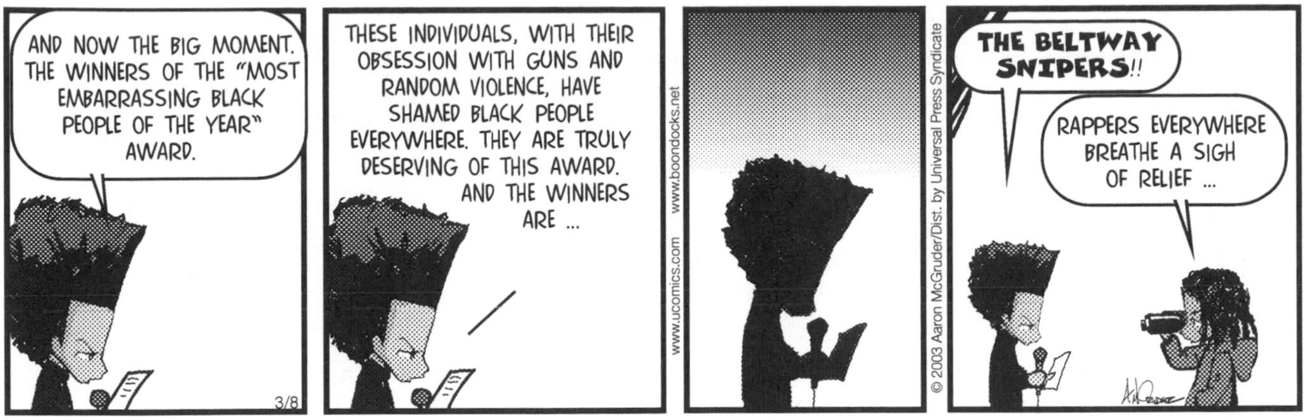
AND NOW THE BIG MOMENT. THE WINNERS OF THE "MOST EMBARRASSING BLACK PEOPLE OF THE YEAR" AWARD.
3/8
THESE INDIVIDUALS, WITH THEIR OBSESSION WITH GUNS AND RANDOM VIOLENCE, HAVE SHAMED BLACK PEOPLE EVERYWHERE. THEY ARE TRULY DESERVING OF THIS AWARD.
AND THE WINNERS ARE ...
www.ucomics.com www.boondocks.net
© 2003 Aaron McGruder/Dist. by Universal Press Syndicate
THE BELTWAY SNIPERS!!
RAPPERS EVERYWHERE BREATHE A SIGH OF RELIEF ...

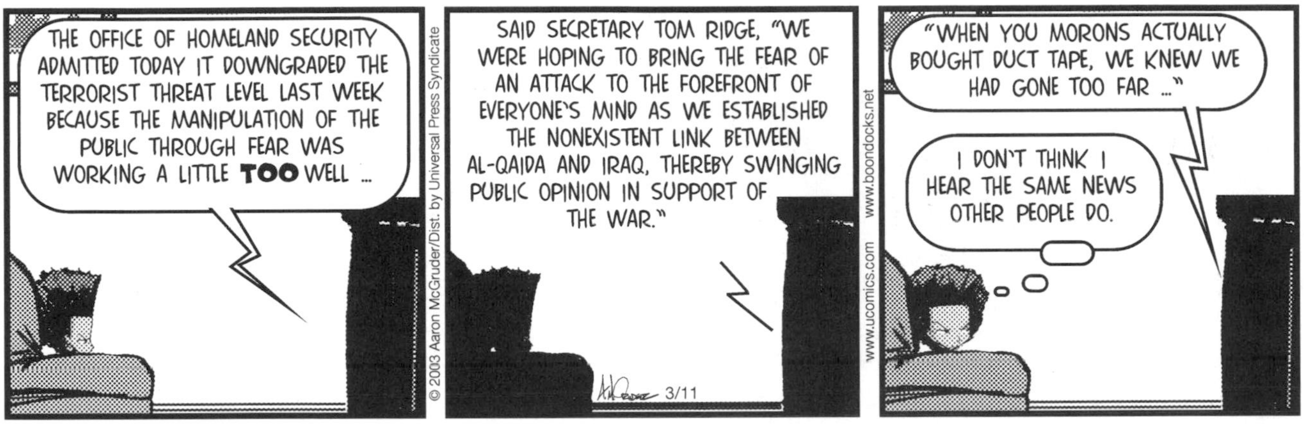
THE OFFICE OF HOMELAND SECURITY ADMITTED TODAY IT DOWNGRADED THE TERRORIST THREAT LEVEL LAST WEEK BECAUSE THE MANIPULATION OF THE PUBLIC THROUGH FEAR WAS WORKING A LITTLE TOO WELL ...
© 2003 Aaron McGruder/Dist. by Universal Press Syndicate
SAID SECRETARY TOM RIDGE, "WE WERE HOPING TO BRING THE FEAR OF AN ATTACK TO THE FOREFRONT OF EVERYONE'S MIND AS WE ESTABLISHED THE NONEXISTENT LINK BETWEEN AL-QAIDA AND IRAQ, THEREBY SWINGING PUBLIC OPINION IN SUPPORT OF THE WAR."
3/11
www.ucomics.com www.boondocks.net
"WHEN YOU MORONS ACTUALLY BOUGHT DUCT TAPE, WE KNEW WE HAD GONE TOO FAR ..."
I DON'T THINK I HEAR THE SAME NEWS OTHER PEOPLE DO.

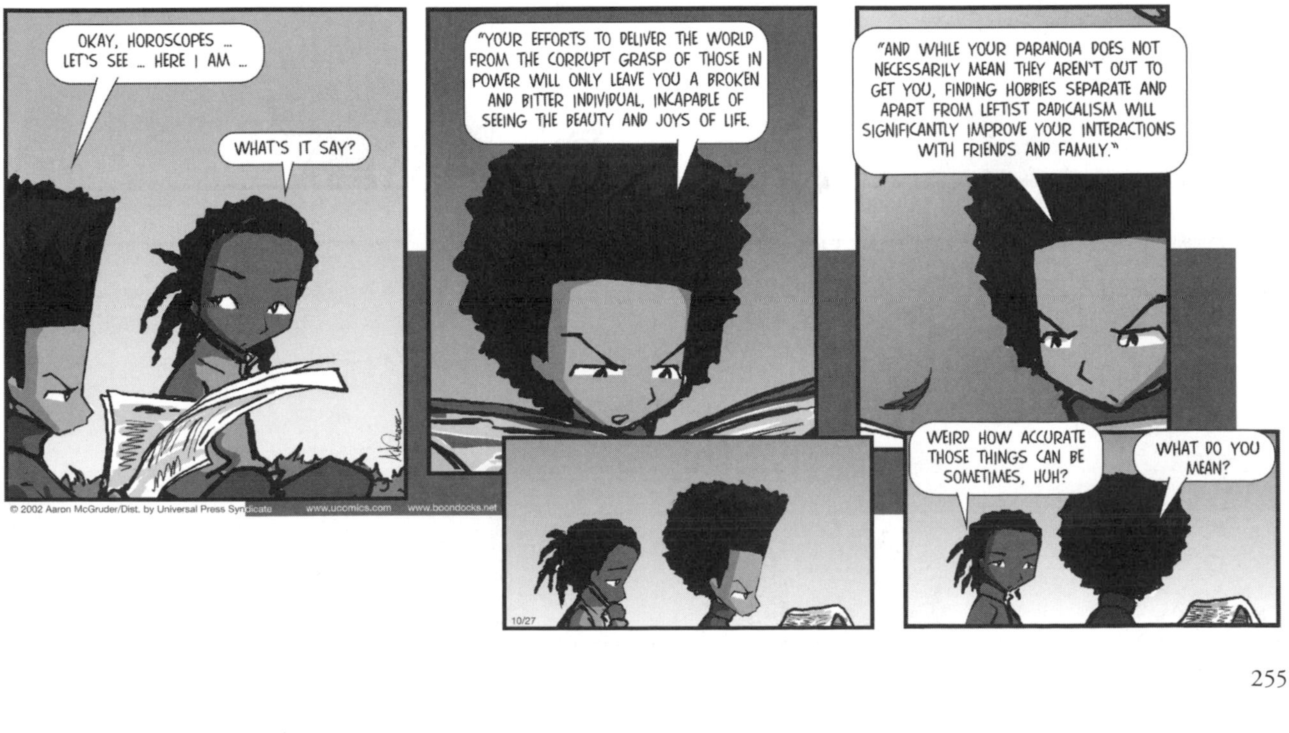
OKAY, HOROSCOPES ... LET'S SEE ... HERE I AM ...
WHAT'S IT SAY?
© 2002 Aaron McGruder/Dist. by Universal Press Syndicate www.ucomics.com www.boondocks.net
"YOUR EFFORTS TO DELIVER THE WORLD FROM THE CORRUPT GRASP OF THOSE IN POWER WILL ONLY LEAVE YOU A BROKEN AND BITTER INDIVIDUAL, INCAPABLE OF SEEING THE BEAUTY AND JOYS OF LIFE.
"AND WHILE YOUR PARANOIA DOES NOT NECESSARILY MEAN THEY AREN'T OUT TO GET YOU, FINDING HOBBIES SEPARATE AND APART FROM LEFTIST RADICALISM WILL SIGNIFICANTLY IMPROVE YOUR INTERACTIONS WITH FRIENDS AND FAMILY."
10/27
WEIRD HOW ACCURATE THOSE THINGS CAN BE SOMETIMES, HUH?
WHAT DO YOU MEAN?

ABOUT THE AUTHOR

AARON MCGRUDER graduated from the University of Maryland with a degree in Afro-American studies. Or was it African-American studies? I don't know—it was some ol' Black stuff, that much is definite. He has been a syndicated cartoonist since 1999, when *The Boondocks* first launched in newspapers around the country. He has since moved to Los Angeles, put a couple books out, been on TV a bunch of times—you know . . . the usual. "He's controversial." "He got an Image Award.". . . Blah, blah, blah. Nobody cares. When it's all said and done, his life just isn't that interesting.

Aaron is a Gemini.